ROLEX

Presents

The World of
Professional Golf
Founded by
Mark H. McCormack   **2016**

IMG

Editor: Jan Davis
Publication Coordinator: Sarah Wooldridge
Contributors: Andy Farrell, Doug Ferguson, Donald (Doc) Giffin, Marino Parascenzo
Official World Golf Ranking Statistician: Tony Greer

First published 2016
© IMG WORLDWIDE LLC 2016

Designed and produced by Davis Design

ISBN-13: 978-0-9914858-2-6

Printed and bound in the United States.

Contents

APPENDIXES

Introduction

Rolex has done so many things over the years that were and are good for golf. Sponsorship of this publication is a prime example. My friends at Rolex, recognizing the historic and research value *The World of Professional Golf* has provided to the game continuously since the middle 1960s, stepped up in 2005 with the support necessary to continue its existence and the service it extends to the world of golf.

I well remember my conversations with my close friend and business manager, the late Mark McCormack, when he outlined his concept of filling a written gap in the game's history with an annual book carrying detailed stories and statistics covering every organized national and international tournament during that particular calendar year. The idea made complete sense to me and I encouraged him to proceed. He did, recruiting a group of talented golf journalists to work with him in producing the first edition that covered the 1966 season worldwide. Its publication has continued and grown in size and scope ever since, keeping pace with the tremendous growth of the game throughout the world.

Mark McCormack passed away in 2003, but his contribution to the historical record of golf did not die. Credit for this goes to IMG executives and others within the organization who considered the book an important continuing tribute to Mark and to the executives at Rolex, whose support has kept the literary chain intact.

Arnold Palmer
Orlando, Florida

Foreword
(Written in 1968)

It has long been my feeling that a sport as compelling as professional golf is deserving of a history, and by history I do not mean an account culled years later from the adjectives and enthusiasms of on-the-spot reports that have then sat in newspaper morgues for decades waiting for some patient drudge to paste them together and call them lore. Such works can be excellent when insight and perspective are added to the research, but this rarely happens. What I am talking about is a running history, a chronology written at the time, which would serve both as a record of the sport and as a commentary upon the sport in any given year—an annual, if you will....

When I embarked on this project two years ago (the first of these annuals was published in Great Britain in 1967), I was repeatedly told that such a compendium of world golf was impossible, that it would be years out of date before it could be assembled and published, that it would be hopelessly expensive to produce and that only the golf fanatic would want a copy anyway. In the last analysis, it was that final stipulation that spurred me on. There must be a lot of golf fanatics, I decided. I can't be the only one. And then one winter day I was sitting in Arnold Palmer's den in Latrobe, Pennsylvania, going through the usual motions of spreading papers around so that Arnold and I could discuss some business project, when Arnold happened to mention that he wanted to collect a copy of each new golf book that was published from now on, in order to build a golf library of his own. "It's really too bad that there isn't a book every year on the pro tour," he said. "Ah," I thought. "Another golf fanatic. That makes two of us." So I decided to do the book. And I have. And I hope you like it. If so, you can join Arnold and me as golf fanatics.

Mark H. McCormack
Cleveland, Ohio
January 1968

Mark H. McCormack
1930 – 2003

In 1960, Mark Hume McCormack shook hands with a young golfer named Arnold Palmer. That historic handshake established a business that would evolve into today's IMG, the world's premier sports and lifestyle marketing and management company —representing hundreds of sports figures, entertainers, models, celebrities, broadcasters, television properties, and prestigious organizations and events around the world. With just a handshake Mark McCormack had invented a global industry.

Sean McManus, President of CBS News and Sports, reflects, "I don't think it's an overstatement to say that like Henry Ford and Bill Gates, Mark McCormack literally created, fostered and led an entirely new worldwide industry. There was no sports marketing before Mark McCormack. Every athlete who's ever appeared in a commercial, or every right holder who sold their rights to anyone, owes a huge debt of gratitude to Mark McCormack."

Mark McCormack's philosophy was simple. "Be the best," he said. "Learn the business and expand by applying what you already know." This philosophy served him well, not only as an entrepreneur and CEO of IMG, but also as an author, a consultant and a confidant to a host of global leaders in the world of business, politics, finance, science, sports and entertainment.

He was among the most-honored entrepreneurs of his time. *Sports Illustrated* recognized him as "The Most Powerful Man in Sports." In 1999, ESPN's Sports Century listed him as one of the century's 10 "Most Influential People in the Business of Sport."

Golf Magazine called McCormack "the most powerful man in golf" and honored him along with Arnold Palmer, Gerald Ford, Dwight D. Eisenhower, Bob Hope and Ben Hogan as one of the 100 all-time "American Heroes of Golf." *Tennis* magazine and *Racquet* magazine named him "the most powerful man in tennis." Tennis legend Billie Jean King believes, "Mark McCormack was the king of sports marketing. He shaped the way all sports are marketed around the world. He was the first in the marketplace, and his influence on the world of sports, particularly his ability to combine athlete representation, property development and television broadcasting, will forever be the standard of the industry."

The London *Sunday Times* listed him as one of the 1000 people who influenced the 20th century. Alastair Cooke on the BBC said simply that "McCormack was the Oracle; the creator of the talent industry, the maker of people famous in their profession famous to the rest of the world and making for them a fortune in the process ... He took on as clients people already famous in their profession as golfer, opera singer, author, footballer, racing car driver, violinist—and from time to time if they needed special help, a prime minister, or even the Pope."

McCormack was honored posthumously by the Golf Writers Association of America with the 2004 William D. Richardson Award, the organization's highest honor, "Given to recognize an individual who has consistently made an outstanding contribution to golf."

Among McCormack's other honors were the 2001 PGA Distinguished Service Award, given to those who have helped perpetuate the values and ideals of the PGA of America. He was also named a Commander of the Royal Order of the Polar Star by the King of Sweden (the highest honor for a person living outside of Sweden) for his contribution to the Nobel Foundation.

Journalist Frank Deford states, "There have been what we love to call dynasties in every sport. IMG has been different. What this one brilliant man, Mark McCormack, created is the only dynasty ever over all sport."

Through IMG, Mark McCormack demonstrated the value of sports and lifestyle activities as effective corporate marketing tools, but more importantly, his lifelong dedication to his vocation—begun with just a simple handshake—brought enjoyment to millions of people worldwide who watch and cheer their heroes and heroines. That is his legacy.

An exciting young guard of players came under the spotlight in professional golf in 2015, marking many memorable moments throughout the course of the season. They amply demonstrated the contribution to excellence in golf that Rolex has upheld for nearly 50 years.

Rolex Testimonee Jordan Spieth captured the attention of the golfing world already in April when, at only 21 years old, he won his first Major at the 2015 Masters. With a final score of 270, at 18 under par, Spieth succeeded in matching Rolex Testimonee Tiger Woods' record, held since 1997. The rising champion followed his Augusta breakthrough by winning another Major, the U.S. Open, as well as the Tour Championship and the FedExCup. Spieth closed his season as World No. 1 in the Official Golf Ranking.

Jason Day, 28, and Rickie Fowler, 27, also scaled new heights in 2015. Day, from Australia, won five tournaments on the PGA Tour, including his first Major at the PGA Championship, while Fowler, from the United States, won three tournaments, including The Players Championship in May. Both Day and Fowler have been part of the Rolex family of Testimonees for many years. Long-standing Rolex Testimonee Bernhard Langer also had a strong year after winning the Charles Schwab Cup and being named PGA TOUR Champions Player of the Year for a record fifth time.

In women's golf, New Zealander Lydia Ko took the sporting world by surprise, breaking records throughout the season. Just one year after going professional — the same year she joined the Rolex family — Ko became the youngest World No. 1 in men's or women's golf when she reached the top of the Rolex Women's World Golf Rankings aged just 17 years and nine months. She then became the youngest winner of a Major title at The Evian Championship in September. Ko went on to finish the year as the youngest golfer ever to be named Rolex Player of the Year.

Rolex is an integral part of the game of golf, supporting its most prestigious events, players and organizations worldwide. These talented champions open an exciting new chapter in this unique story with their blend of innovation and respect for the spirit of the ancient game. We are delighted to present the 2016 edition of *The World of Professional Golf*, a retrospective of the highlights and results of the year's golf championships and tours worldwide.

Jean-Frédéric Dufour
Rolex SA
Chief Executive Officer

Rolex and Golf

Rolex, the leading brand of the Swiss watch industry, enjoys an unrivalled reputation for quality and expertise the world over. The company's partnership in excellence with golf began with Arnold Palmer in 1967. He, along with fellow Rolex Testimonees Jack Nicklaus and Gary Player — otherwise known as The Big Three — contributed to modernizing golf and giving it a worldwide dimension. Since 1967, the relationship between Rolex and golf has continuously grown and prospered. Today, Rolex is golf's leading supporter and is associated with the most important and prestigious entities governing the game worldwide, as well as with golf's principal professional tours, competitions and players.

© Rolex/Chris Turvey

Jordan Spieth, winner of the Tour Championship and the FedExCup

© Rolex/Chris Turvey

Rickie Fowler, winner of The Players Championship

© Rolex/Chris Turvey

Lydia Ko, winner of The Evian Championship

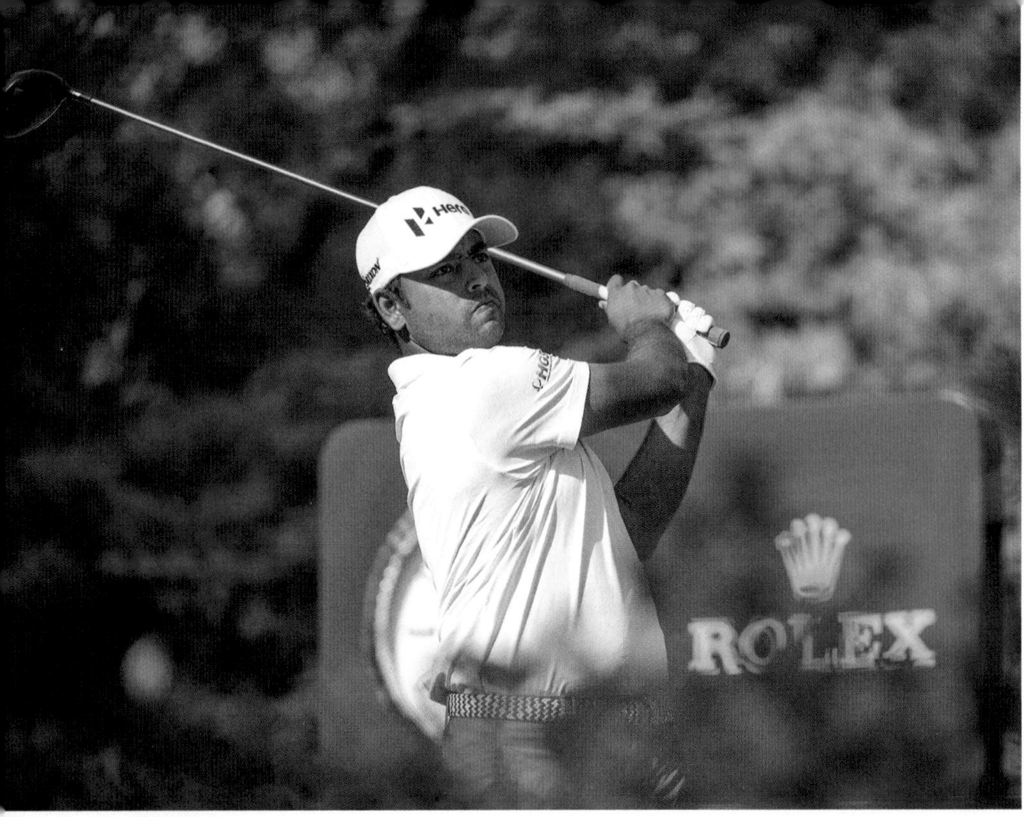

© Rolex/Chris Turvey

Anirban Lahiri

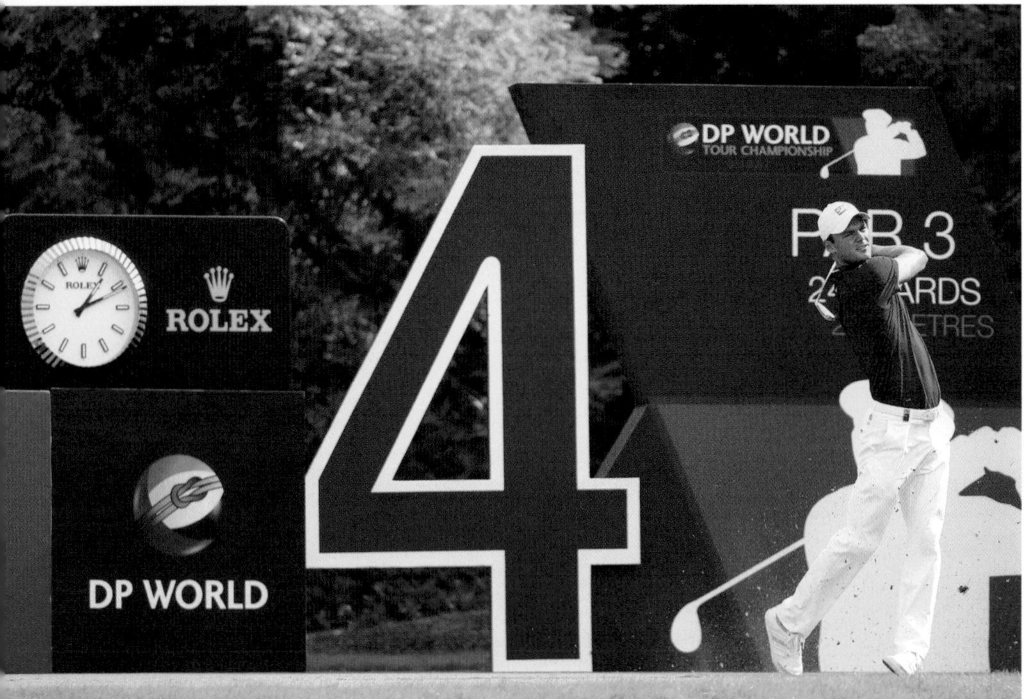

Andrew Redington/Getty Images

Martin Kaymer at the DP World Tour Championship

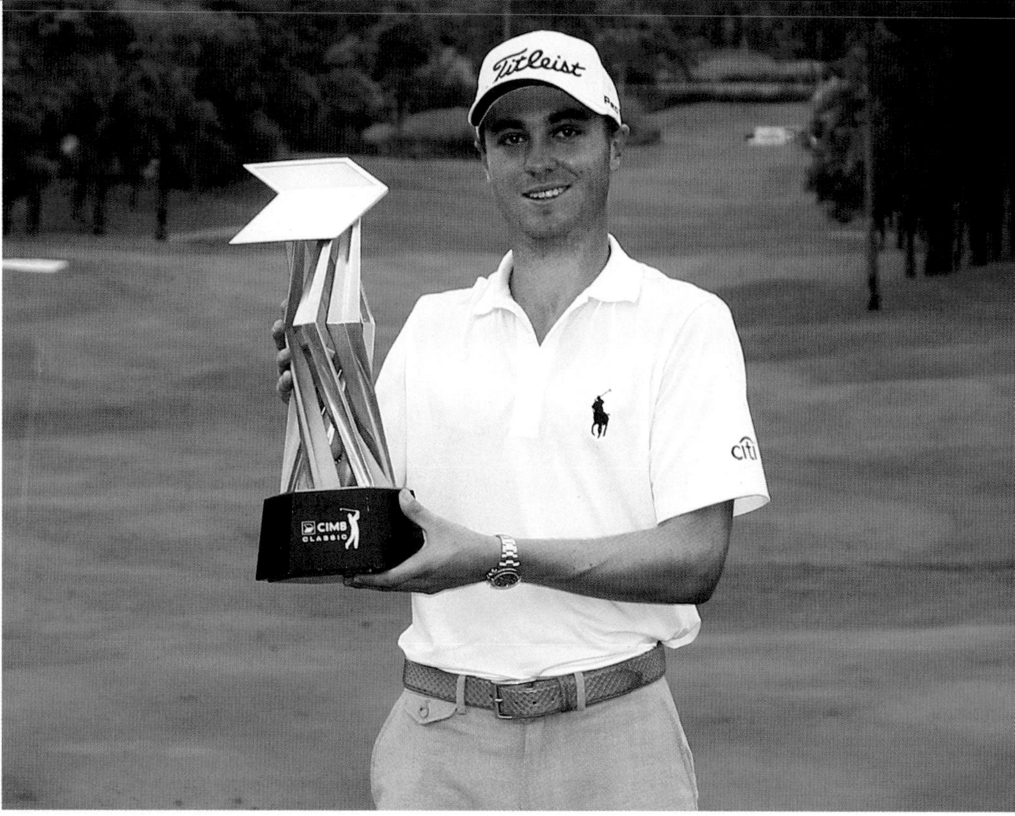

Stanley Chou/Getty Images

Justin Thomas, winner of the CIMB Classic

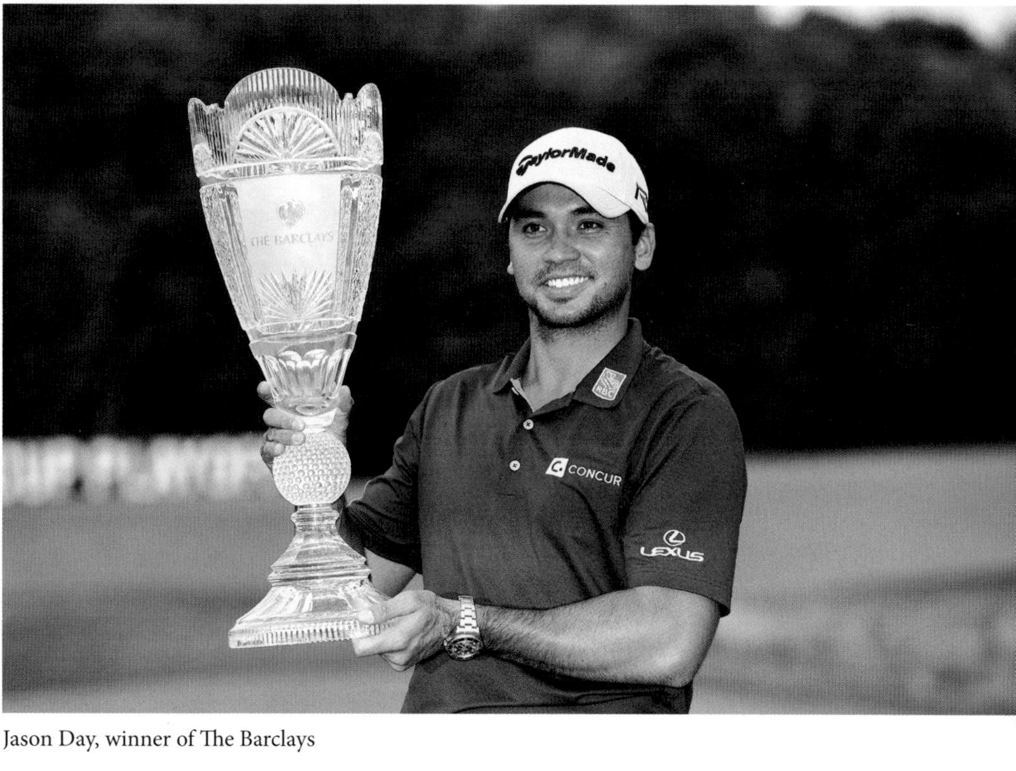

Ross Kinnaird/Getty Images

Jason Day, winner of The Barclays

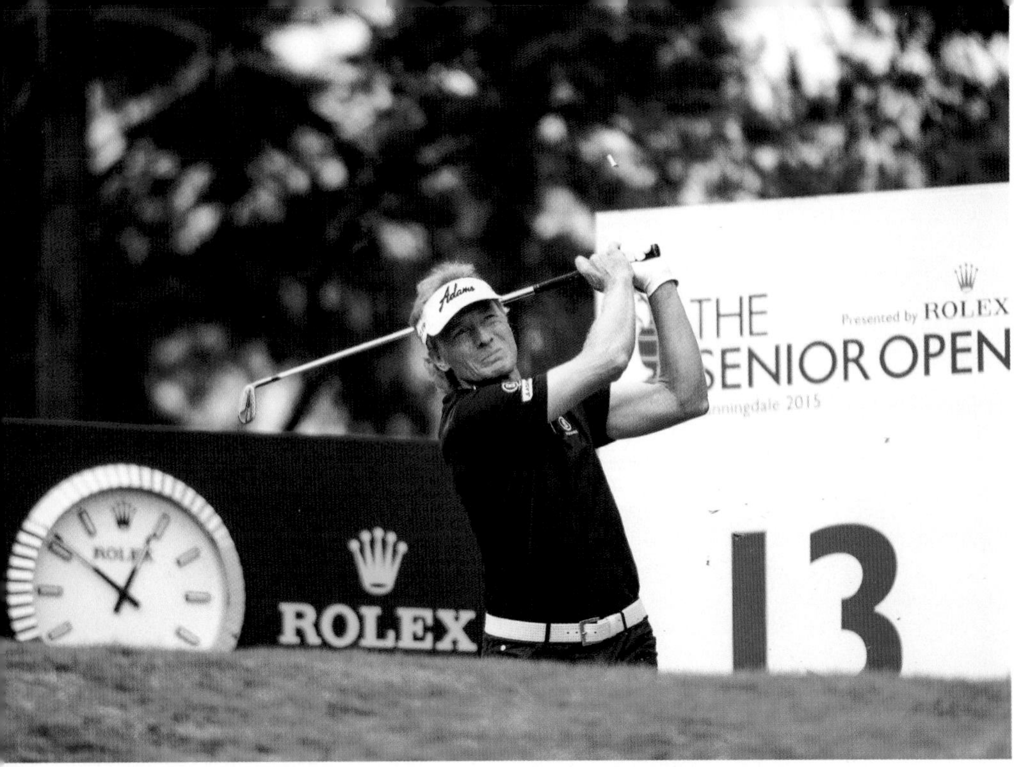

© Rolex/Chris Turvey

Bernhard Langer at The Senior Open Championship presented by Rolex

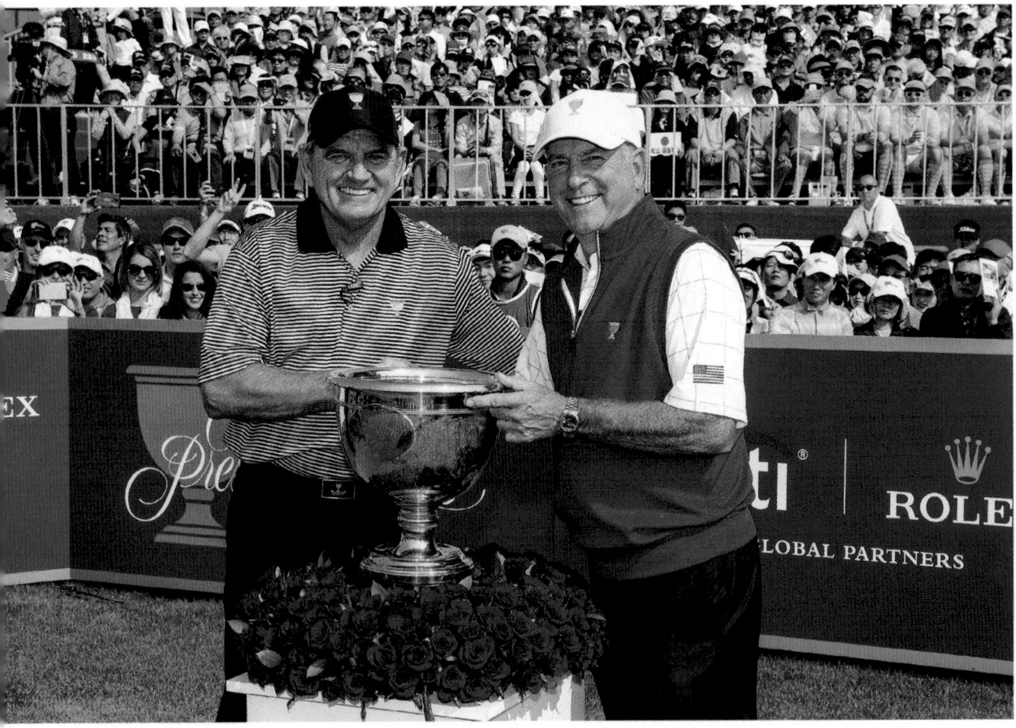

Stan Badz/PGA Tour

Nick Price and Jay Haas, captains of The Presidents Cup 2015

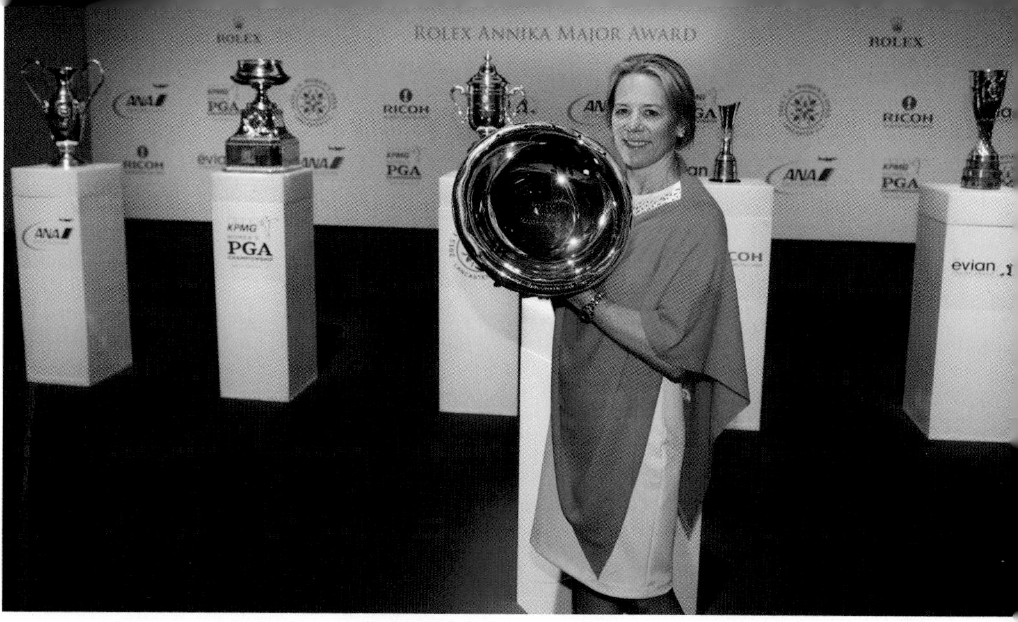

© Rolex/Chris Turvey

Annika Sorenstam with the Rolex Annika Major Award trophy

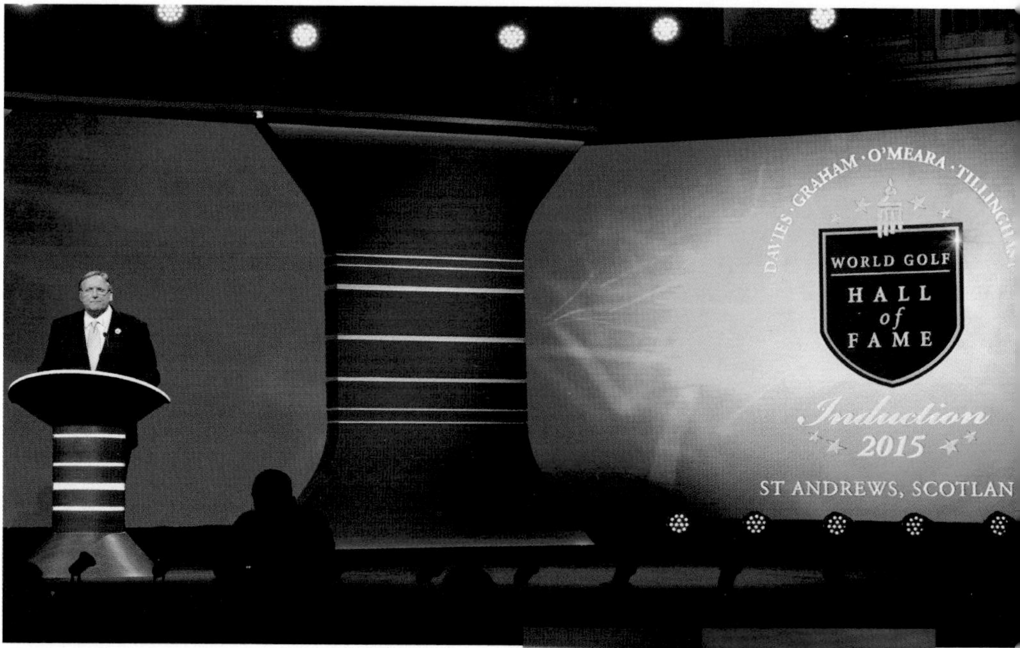

Mark Runnacles/ Getty Images

2015 World Golf Hall of Fame Induction Ceremony at St Andrews

Mark Runnacles/ Getty Images

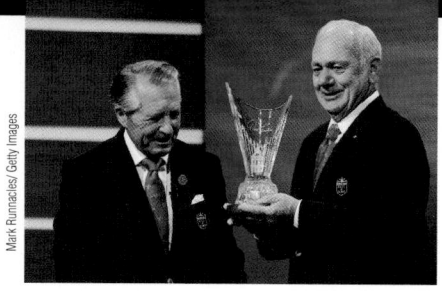

The 2015 Rolex Rankings Top Three

Sam Greenwood/Getty Images

1. Lydia Ko (New Zealand) 11.78 points

David Cannon/Getty Images

2. Inbee Park (Korea) 11.54 points

Stanley Chou/Getty Images

3. Stacy Lewis (USA) 8.04 points

Rolex Rankings

Amid the history created by Lydia Ko in 2015, the teenager from New Zealand became the youngest player in men's or women's golf to be rated as the world's best player. Ko was 17 when she overtook Inbee Park at the top of the Rolex Rankings while finishing runner-up at her first tournament of the year at the Coates Championship. Tiger Woods had been 21 when he first became the men's No. 1 in 1997.

But Park regained her crown by winning two major championships, first the KPMG Women's PGA Championship and then the Ricoh Women's British Open at Turnberry, where she was designated with an LPGA career grand slam. Yet although the Korean raised her points average over the year from 10.82 to 11.54, Ko was not to be denied, and after claiming her maiden major title at the Evian, where the then 18-year-old became the youngest ever winner, she went back into the No. 1 spot after winning for the sixth time during the year at the Taiwan Championship. By the end of the year her points average had risen from 9.80 to 11.78.

Stacy Lewis retained third place on the Rolex Rankings despite not winning a tournament in 2015, while her compatriot Lexi Thompson jumped from 10th to fourth place. Other than Shanshan Feng in sixth place, the rest of the top 10 was dominated by Korea. The country doubled its representation from three to six with Sei Young Kim, Amy Yang and U.S. Open champion In-Gee Chun joining Park, So Yeon Ryu and Hyo-Joo Kim in the top 10. Qualification for the South Korean women's Olympic golf team in 2016 was assured to be hard fought.

Suzann Pettersen remained Europe's highest ranked player but slipped from fourth to 12th place, while ANA Inspiration champion Brittany Lincicome finished the year in 16th, one place ahead of Canadian rookie Brooke Henderson.

The Rolex Rankings — which was developed at the May 2004 World Congress of Women's Golf — is sanctioned by eight women's professional golf tours: the Ladies Professional Golf Association (LPGA); Ladies European Tour (LET); Ladies Professional Golfers' Association of Japan (JLPGA); Korea Ladies Professional Golf Association (KLPGA); Australian Ladies Professional Golf (ALPG); Symetra Tour; China Ladies Professional Golf Association Tour (CLPGA) and the Ladies European Access Series (LETAS) – as well as the Ladies' Golf Union (LGU) and the United States Golf Association (USGA).

The major golf tours developed the rankings and the protocol that governs the ranking, while R2IT, an independent software development company, was retained to develop the software and to maintain the rankings on a weekly basis. The official events from all of the tours are taken into account and points are awarded according to the strength of the field, with the exception of the five major championships on the LPGA Tour and the Symetra Tour, CLPGA and LETAS events, which have a fixed points distribution. The players' points averages are determined by taking the number of points awarded over a two-year rolling period, with the points awarded in the most recent 13-week period carrying a stronger value, and then dividing that by the number of tournaments played, with a minimum divisor of 35.

The Rolex Rankings are updated and released following the completion of the previous week's tournaments around the world.

Rolex Rankings
(As of December 31, 2015)

Rank	Player	Country	No. of Events	Average Points	Total Points
1	Lydia Ko	New Zealand	53	624.16	11.78
2	Inbee Park	Korea	54	623.15	11.54
3	Stacy Lewis	USA	54	434.40	8.04
4	Lexi Thompson	USA	49	346.48	7.07
5	So Yeon Ryu	Korea	54	330.89	6.13
6	Shanshan Feng	China	59	353.25	5.99
7	Sei Young Kim	Korea	54	315.42	5.84
8	Amy Yang	Korea	45	242.29	5.38
9	Hyo-Joo Kim	Korea	58	309.78	5.34
10	In-Gee Chun	Korea	59	313.13	5.31
11	Cristie Kerr	USA	50	256.35	5.13
12	Suzann Pettersen	Norway	50	247.57	4.95
13	Anna Nordqvist	Sweden	53	242.77	4.58
14	Ha-Na Jang	Korea	57	260.47	4.57
15	Bo-Mee Lee	Korea	63	269.23	4.27
16	Brittany Lincicome	USA	52	218.85	4.21
17	Brooke M. Henderson	Canada	23	142.90	4.08
18	Minjee Lee	Australia	42	171.26	4.08
19	Na Yeon Choi	Korea	50	189.52	3.79
20	Teresa Lu	Taipei	59	221.51	3.75
21	Sun Ju Ahn	Korea	53	182.79	3.45
22	Mi Rim Lee	Korea	54	177.34	3.28
23	Alison Lee	USA	25	113.99	3.26
24	Morgan Pressel	USA	56	178.73	3.19
25	Jin-Young Ko	Korea	54	165.61	3.07
26	Jessica Korda	USA	49	150.27	3.07
27	Sung Hyun Park	Korea	53	156.13	2.95
28	Michelle Wie	USA	47	135.48	2.88
29	Gerina Piller	USA	52	147.89	2.84
30	Azahara Munoz	Spain	53	150.03	2.83
31	Karrie Webb	Australia	42	117.26	2.79
32	Jung Min Lee	Korea	50	136.52	2.73
33	Jiyai Shin	Korea	62	161.20	2.60
34	Mi Hyang Lee	Korea	61	151.47	2.48
35	Chella Choi	Korea	64	156.68	2.45
36	Shiho Oyama	Japan	56	135.51	2.42
37	Mika Miyazato	Japan	50	118.57	2.37
38	Yani Tseng	Taipei	52	123.25	2.37
39	Lizette Salas	USA	48	110.46	2.30
40	Ilhee Lee	Korea	59	135.58	2.30
41	Charley Hull	England	47	105.87	2.25
42	Jenny Shin	Korea	58	130.25	2.25
43	Pornanong Phatlum	Thailand	57	126.75	2.22
44	Brittany Lang	USA	59	130.42	2.21
45	Angela Stanford	USA	54	118.03	2.19
46	I.K. Kim	Korea	42	89.70	2.14
47	Sandra Gal	Germany	55	116.35	2.12
48	Ji-Hee Lee	Korea	58	121.16	2.09
49	Austin Ernst	USA	55	112.41	2.04
50	Candie Kung	Taipei	52	105.84	2.04

Rank	Player	Country	No. of Events	Average Points	Total Points
51	Carlota Ciganda	Spain	55	111.88	2.03
52	Q. Baek	Korea	58	117.42	2.02
53	Xi Yu Lin	China	56	112.26	2.00
54	Lee-Anne Pace	South Africa	50	99.08	1.98
55	Momoko Ueda	Japan	60	118.59	1.98
56	Mo Martin	USA	53	101.80	1.92
57	Julieta Granada	Paraguay	56	107.46	1.92
58	Ayaka Watanabe	Japan	72	138.13	1.92
59	Karine Icher	France	57	109.29	1.92
60	Eun-Hee Ji	Korea	58	110.44	1.90
61	Yoon Ji Cho	Korea	49	92.71	1.89
62	Paula Creamer	USA	49	92.58	1.89
63	Ariya Jutanugarn	Thailand	45	83.44	1.85
64	Misuzu Narita	Japan	62	113.36	1.83
65	Sakura Yokomine	Japan	58	105.11	1.81
66	Min Sun Kim$_5$	Korea	56	97.23	1.74
67	Catriona Matthew	Scotland	48	81.61	1.70
68	MinYoung Lee$_2$	Korea	50	83.09	1.66
69	Yoon-Kyung Heo	Korea	41	66.30	1.62
70	Erika Kikuchi	Japan	73	117.48	1.61
71	Ai Suzuki	Japan	61	95.19	1.56
72	Mariajo Uribe	Colombia	53	81.33	1.53
73	Nicole Larsen	Denmark	33	53.60	1.53
74	Hae Rym Kim	Korea	54	81.47	1.51
75	Hee Young Park	Korea	59	88.53	1.50
76	Seon woo Bae	Korea	52	77.62	1.49
77	Caroline Masson	Germany	62	92.54	1.49
78	Ha Neul Kim	Korea	55	81.87	1.49
79	Harukyo Nomura	Japan	56	83.00	1.48
80	Gwladys Nocera	France	42	60.83	1.45
81	Bo Kyung Kim	Korea	53	76.19	1.44
82	Christina Kim	USA	56	79.97	1.43
83	Melissa Reid	England	29	49.43	1.41
84	Jane Park	USA	42	58.78	1.40
85	Kim Kaufman	USA	53	73.71	1.39
86	Erina Hara	Japan	66	91.53	1.39
87	Pernilla Lindberg	Sweden	62	85.58	1.38
88	Sun Young Yoo	Korea	52	68.77	1.32
89	Miki Sakai	Japan	74	97.51	1.32
90	Mi Jung Hur	Korea	50	64.81	1.30
91	Kris Tamulis	USA	50	64.72	1.29
92	Holly Clyburn	England	35	45.05	1.29
93	Su Yeon Jang	Korea	56	71.70	1.28
94	Christel Boeljon	Netherlands	37	46.29	1.25
95	Jae Eun Chung	Korea	40	48.87	1.22
96	Danielle Kang	USA	53	63.69	1.20
97	Ji Hyun Kim	Korea	54	63.40	1.17
98	Jaye Marie Green	USA	49	57.29	1.17
99	Min Song Ha	Korea	55	63.76	1.16
100	Hye-Youn Kim	Korea	52	60.23	1.16

Rank	Player	Country	No. of Events	Average Points	Total Points
101	Gyeol Park	Korea	30	40.27	1.15
102	Ye Jin Kim	Korea	30	40.13	1.15
103	Sydnee Michaels	USA	49	56.05	1.14
104	Jeong Eun Lee	Korea	50	56.64	1.13
105	Jennifer Song	USA	47	52.77	1.12
106	Ritsuko Ryu	Japan	71	78.43	1.10
107	Moriya Jutanugarn	Thailand	59	64.69	1.10
108	Yumiko Yoshida	Japan	67	73.09	1.09
109	Ssu-Chia Cheng	Taipei	28	37.99	1.09
110	Beth Allen	USA	42	45.04	1.07
111	Shin Ae Ahn	Korea	44	47.10	1.07
112	Maria McBride	Sweden	35	37.10	1.06
113	Ji Hyun Kim$_2$	Korea	50	52.81	1.06
114	Lala Anai	Japan	71	74.63	1.05
115	Hee-Kyung Bae	Korea	58	59.08	1.02
116	Rikako Morita	Japan	66	66.35	1.01
117	Hye Jung Choi$_2$	Korea	27	34.84	1.00
118	Emily Kristine Pedersen	Denmark	18	34.74	0.99
119	Asako Fujimoto	Japan	69	68.17	0.99
120	Han Sol Ji	Korea	33	34.46	0.98
121	Wei-Ling Hsu	Taipei	49	48.23	0.98
122	Na-Ri Lee	Korea	67	65.92	0.98
123	Ji Young Park	Korea	28	34.15	0.98
124	Serena Aoki	Japan	41	39.74	0.97
125	Junko Omote	Japan	74	71.63	0.97
126	Seung Hyun Lee	Korea	48	46.36	0.97
127	Ji Hyun Oh	Korea	51	49.24	0.97
128	Yeun Jung Seo	Korea	55	52.98	0.96
129	Akane Iijima	Japan	69	65.79	0.95
130	Ryann O'Toole	USA	42	39.77	0.95
131	Amy Boulden	Wales	33	33.13	0.95
132	Mi Jeong Jeon	Korea	64	60.56	0.95
133	Alena Sharp	Canada	48	45.00	0.94
134	Meena Lee	Korea	51	47.40	0.93
135	Rebecca Artis	Australia	50	46.36	0.93
136	Marianne Skarpnord	Norway	36	33.16	0.92
137	Hikari Fujita	Japan	67	61.35	0.92
138	Jing Yan	China	29	31.11	0.89
139	Mayu Hattori	Japan	72	63.93	0.89
140	Song Yi Ahn	Korea	53	46.22	0.87
141	Caroline Hedwall	Sweden	42	36.43	0.87
142	Juli Inkster	USA	27	30.32	0.87
143	Beatriz Recari	Spain	52	44.21	0.85
144	Hee Won Jung	Korea	52	43.78	0.84
145	Saki Nagamine	Japan	37	30.76	0.83
146	Kotone Hori	Japan	45	36.90	0.82
147	Kotono Kozuma	Japan	53	42.62	0.80
148	So Yeon Park	Korea	54	42.67	0.79
149	Soo-Yun Kang	Korea	57	44.84	0.79
150	Marina Alex	USA	52	40.90	0.79

Rank	Player	Country	No. of Events	Average Points	Total Points
151	Kelly Shon	USA	37	29.03	0.78
152	Hannah Burke	England	43	33.48	0.78
153	Malene Jorgensen	Denmark	32	26.91	0.77
154	Yukari Nishiyama	Japan	71	54.39	0.77
155	Chae-Young Yoon	Korea	52	39.57	0.76
156	Ji Hee Kim	Korea	51	38.51	0.76
157	Maiko Wakabayashi	Japan	69	51.57	0.75
158	Yoko Maeda	Japan	73	54.44	0.75
159	Nanna Koerstz Madsen	Denmark	17	25.76	0.74
160	Thidapa Suwannapura	Thailand	56	41.10	0.73
161	Ai Miyazato	Japan	51	36.98	0.73
162	Min Lee	Taipei	50	36.23	0.72
163	Mina Harigae	USA	52	37.32	0.72
164	Hyun Soo Kim	Korea	56	39.57	0.71
165	Chae Yoon Park	Korea	29	24.40	0.70
166	Hiromi Mogi	Japan	45	31.36	0.70
167	Onnarin Sattayabanphot	Thailand	65	45.26	0.70
168	Line Vedel Hansen	Denmark	35	24.27	0.69
169	Florentyna Parker	England	38	26.26	0.69
170	Jeongmin Cho	Korea	45	31.06	0.69
171	Celine Herbin	France	35	24.05	0.69
172	Soo-Jin Yang	Korea	47	31.97	0.68
173	Ran Hong	Korea	49	33.10	0.68
174	Char Young Kim$_2$	Korea	50	33.52	0.67
175	Min Seo Kwak	Korea	38	25.24	0.66
176	Ayaka Matsumori	Japan	44	29.05	0.66
177	Saiki Fujita	Japan	61	40.27	0.66
178	Perrine Delacour	France	24	22.83	0.65
179	Rumi Yoshiba	Japan	70	45.58	0.65
180	Ka Ram Choi	Korea	53	34.41	0.65
181	Jacqui Concolino	USA	32	22.71	0.65
182	Yuki Ichinose	Japan	44	28.42	0.65
183	Pamela Pretswell	Scotland	36	22.58	0.63
184	Ayako Uehara	Japan	58	36.01	0.62
185	Yuko Mitsuka	Japan	44	27.32	0.62
186	Kaori Ohe	Japan	70	42.56	0.61
187	Cho Hui Kim	Korea	51	30.95	0.61
188	Hsuan-Yu Yao	Taipei	58	35.11	0.61
189	Megumi Kido	Japan	70	41.98	0.60
190	Jin Joo Hong	Korea	27	20.91	0.60
191	Jennifer Johnson	USA	39	23.25	0.60
192	Laura Davies	England	51	30.18	0.59
193	Shi-Hyun Ahn	Korea	47	27.70	0.59
194	Nontaya Srisawang	Thailand	34	20.60	0.59
195	Mami Fukuda	Japan	68	39.97	0.59
196	Sun Jeung Youn	Korea	29	20.45	0.58
197	Asuka Kashiwabara	Japan	29	20.42	0.58
198	Amy Anderson	USA	41	23.91	0.58
199	Joanna Klatten	France	48	27.60	0.57
200	Minami Katsu	Japan	23	20.11	0.57

Official World Golf Ranking
(As of December 31, 2015)

Ranking		Player	Country	Average Points	Total Points	No. of Events	2015 Points Lost	2015 Points Gained
1	(9)	Jordan Spieth	USA	11.509	598.49	57	-331.26	630.50
2	(8)	Jason Day	Aus	10.939	437.59	36	-247.53	452.68
3	(1)	Rory McIlroy	NIr	10.750	473.04	44	-453.66	385.60
4	(4)	Bubba Watson	USA	7.954	365.91	46	-295.97	312.72
5	(2)	Henrik Stenson	Swe	7.339	374.29	51	-361.65	312.43
6	(10)	Rickie Fowler	USA	7.127	370.65	53	-239.23	325.53
7	(6)	Justin Rose	Eng	7.022	365.16	52	-287.59	325.00
8	(19)	Dustin Johnson	USA	6.126	245.05	40	-199.77	285.87
9	(7)	Jim Furyk	USA	5.618	224.73	40	-250.86	184.18
10	(23)	Patrick Reed	USA	4.655	242.08	61	-186.04	255.76
11	(5)	Sergio Garcia	Esp	4.469	210.08	47	-276.29	151.56
12	(3)	Adam Scott	Aus	4.444	186.68	42	-269.12	131.98
13	(18)	Zach Johnson	USA	4.343	225.87	52	-211.06	237.91
14	(82)	Branden Grace	SAf	4.132	214.88	55	-105.20	228.80
15	(16)	Hideki Matsuyama	Jpn	4.019	209.01	55	-192.46	192.50
16	(34)	Brooks Koepka	USA	3.990	207.49	55	-135.79	189.63
17	(236)	Kevin Kisner	USA	3.950	205.45	56	-56.68	221.96
18	(45)	Louis Oosthuizen	SAf	3.894	186.92	48	-115.72	183.83
19	(50)	Danny Willett	Eng	3.828	199.07	53	-99.50	172.80
20	(11)	Matt Kuchar	USA	3.683	191.54	54	-247.01	172.95
21	(44)	Shane Lowry	Irl	3.538	180.46	51	-110.18	152.46
22	(75)	Paul Casey	Eng	3.472	180.57	53	-107.23	191.34
23	(25)	Kevin Na	USA	3.462	180.03	56	-117.56	162.94
24	(66)	J.B. Holmes	USA	3.407	170.35	50	-104.84	194.21
25	(21)	Jimmy Walker	USA	3.286	170.92	53	-212.18	189.03
26	(46)	Marc Leishman	Aus	3.274	163.73	50	-113.80	142.27
27	(12)	Martin Kaymer	Ger	3.240	168.51	56	-200.07	114.33
28	(37)	Thongchai Jaidee	Tha	3.227	167.83	60	-128.70	151.52
29	(179)	Byeong-Hun An	Kor	3.127	162.62	55	-56.34	169.23
30	(100)	Russell Knox	Sco	3.028	157.46	58	-77.06	159.53
31	(72)	Bernd Wiesberger	Aut	2.965	154.18	58	-113.25	168.15
32	(128)	Emiliano Grillo	Arg	2.932	152.50	56	-63.67	151.59
33	(17)	Victor Dubuisson	Fra	2.907	142.47	49	-148.87	106.29
34	(14)	Phil Mickelson	USA	2.876	117.93	41	-191.05	108.89
35	(31)	Charl Schwartzel	SAf	2.850	148.22	59	-151.58	141.74
36	(150)	Andy Sullivan	Eng	2.846	148.00	59	-71.53	162.12
37	(122)	Justin Thomas	USA	2.834	147.37	59	-53.58	149.51
38	(134)	Kiradech Aphibarnrat	Tha	2.814	146.35	60	-72.47	148.70
39	(91)	Robert Streb	USA	2.742	142.62	55	-72.01	132.29
40	(64)	Anirban Lahiri	Ind	2.726	133.61	49	-92.71	132.88
41	(13)	Billy Horschel	USA	2.721	141.50	54	-176.57	84.54
42	(39)	Bill Haas	USA	2.700	140.43	53	-150.98	144.50
43	(413)	Matthew Fitzpatrick	Eng	2.672	138.96	53	-19.72	142.23
44	(141)	Chris Wood	Eng	2.658	127.59	48	-56.24	126.51
45	(335)	Soren Kjeldsen	Den	2.656	138.13	59	-40.80	150.40
46	(24)	Jamie Donaldson	Wal	2.627	136.65	55	-153.08	111.06
47	(220)	Danny Lee	Nzl	2.607	135.60	64	-48.00	143.41
48	(184)	Scott Piercy	USA	2.595	111.59	43	-53.34	124.33
49	(58)	Brandt Snedeker	USA	2.594	134.91	56	-129.61	145.07
50	(26)	Lee Westwood	Eng	2.575	133.94	55	-140.52	103.88

( ) Ranking in brackets indicates position as of December 31, 2014.

Ranking		Player	Country	Average Points	Total Points	No. of Events	2015 Points Lost	2015 Points Gained
51	(20)	Chris Kirk	USA	2.565	133.43	52	-161.47	97.30
52	(74)	Charley Hoffman	USA	2.424	126.09	52	-97.81	126.91
53	(301)	Daniel Berger	USA	2.414	125.57	57	-43.51	145.74
54	(78)	Matt Jones	Aus	2.359	122.71	53	-98.43	127.13
55	(169)	David Lingmerth	Swe	2.297	119.45	60	-61.80	128.74
56	(27)	Ian Poulter	Eng	2.293	112.36	49	-139.88	100.33
57	(15)	Graeme McDowell	NIr	2.281	114.08	50	-158.12	72.66
58	(42)	Ryan Palmer	USA	2.245	107.80	48	-121.30	94.94
59	(79)	Shingo Katayama	Jpn	2.229	91.41	41	-58.27	70.17
60	(284)	Kyung-Tae Kim	Kor	2.223	108.96	49	-34.14	109.87
61	(137)	Jason Bohn	USA	2.162	112.42	52	-60.10	108.08
62	(30)	Ryan Moore	USA	2.151	101.13	47	-131.20	78.19
63	(48)	Gary Woodland	USA	2.141	104.91	49	-127.88	99.75
64	(60)	Russell Henley	USA	2.091	108.73	53	-107.65	99.26
65	(165)	Kristoffer Broberg	Swe	2.082	108.27	60	-42.13	97.88
66	(55)	Francesco Molinari	Ita	2.081	108.23	53	-114.98	100.23
67	(362)	Jaco Van Zyl	SAf	2.078	83.14	39	-31.25	94.81
68	(22)	Hunter Mahan	USA	2.028	105.47	54	-149.42	67.56
69	(85)	Cameron Tringale	USA	1.966	102.25	58	-80.08	93.91
70	(28)	Keegan Bradley	USA	1.960	101.95	53	-146.72	84.11
71	(69)	Marc Warren	Sco	1.946	101.23	58	-94.43	91.28
72	(89)	Steven Bowditch	Aus	1.942	101.02	70	-74.90	99.25
73	(1548)	Patton Kizzire	USA	1.895	75.82	30	-9.51	85.33
74	(43)	Webb Simpson	USA	1.894	92.85	49	-136.79	88.49
75	(1548)	Smylie Kaufman	USA	1.889	75.60	28	-5.92	81.52
76	(80)	Thorbjorn Olesen	Den	1.882	97.91	56	-70.63	73.27
77	(33)	Luke Donald	Eng	1.866	95.17	51	-127.29	75.79
78	(51)	Tommy Fleetwood	Eng	1.859	96.68	61	-101.27	73.96
79	(49)	John Senden	Aus	1.850	96.24	57	-109.01	75.82
80	(54)	Brendon Todd	USA	1.850	96.20	58	-111.57	83.72
81	(152)	Brendan Steele	USA	1.832	95.28	52	-66.12	102.58
82	(68)	Ross Fisher	Eng	1.821	94.73	54	-83.00	72.22
83	(415)	Ricardo Gouveia	Por	1.785	71.42	31	-15.98	71.00
84	(65)	Ben Martin	USA	1.781	92.62	53	-93.23	78.69
85	(29)	Joost Luiten	Ned	1.750	91.01	54	-129.88	56.94
86	(106)	Yuta Ikeda	Jpn	1.728	89.89	52	-52.80	67.69
87	(146)	Tony Finau	USA	1.692	88.01	58	-39.56	80.52
88	(240)	Thomas Pieters	Bel	1.690	87.91	53	-30.96	88.24
89	(81)	George Coetzee	SAf	1.662	83.15	50	-87.80	78.38
90	(40)	Miguel A. Jimenez	Esp	1.635	81.77	50	-116.04	68.76
91	(394)	James Morrison	Eng	1.626	84.60	56	-33.05	94.61
92	(166)	Yusaku Miyazato	Jpn	1.614	83.97	54	-42.72	74.51
93	(190)	Cameron Smith	Aus	1.597	63.90	37	-31.17	58.28
94	(721)	Patrick Rodgers	USA	1.581	63.27	40	-17.53	73.95
95	(138)	Yoshinori Fujimoto	Jpn	1.581	75.89	48	-47.05	62.40
96	(653)	Alexander Noren	Swe	1.576	63.07	19	-32.13	86.92
97	(53)	Alexander Levy	Fra	1.575	81.94	57	-90.84	45.73
98	(131)	David Howell	Eng	1.574	81.88	58	-64.17	80.19
99	(139)	Daniel Summerhays	USA	1.566	81.45	55	-65.33	82.85
100	(136)	Prayad Marksaeng	Tha	1.559	81.09	59	-53.99	73.59

( ) Ranking in brackets indicates position as of December 31, 2014.

Ranking		Player	Country	Average Points	Total Points	No. of Events	2015 Points Lost	2015 Points Gained
101	(86)	Brian Harman	USA	1.556	80.95	62	-80.33	76.41
102	(77)	Harris English	USA	1.544	80.32	57	-106.44	93.63
103	(102)	Ryo Ishikawa	Jpn	1.527	79.43	69	-69.70	73.42
104	(132)	Tyrrell Hatton	Eng	1.503	78.18	55	-53.55	70.24
105	(111)	Kevin Chappell	USA	1.490	77.52	55	-63.40	65.66
106	(363)	James Hahn	USA	1.485	77.25	54	-45.57	96.10
107	(151)	Eddie Pepperell	Eng	1.483	72.71	49	-49.46	66.60
108	(92)	Richie Ramsay	Sco	1.474	66.35	45	-56.63	55.67
109	(286)	Troy Merritt	USA	1.431	73.03	51	-34.59	78.11
110	(160)	Satoshi Kodaira	Jpn	1.418	63.82	45	-34.77	49.45
111	(67)	Hiroshi Iwata	Jpn	1.417	73.69	56	-61.48	42.09
112	(96)	Scott Hend	Aus	1.416	73.67	56	-58.55	61.69
113	(56)	Koumei Oda	Jpn	1.416	73.67	55	-89.26	45.53
114	(93)	Rafael Cabrera Bello	Esp	1.385	72.05	55	-73.40	65.11
115	(84)	Sangmoon Bae	Kor	1.384	72.01	56	-73.37	54.35
116	(88)	Hideto Tanihara	Jpn	1.344	63.17	47	-60.52	44.69
117	(124)	Morgan Hoffmann	USA	1.340	69.69	58	-61.58	63.82
118	(99)	Fabrizio Zanotti	Par	1.329	63.80	48	-54.09	41.35
119	(126)	David Hearn	Can	1.321	68.70	59	-62.67	64.81
120	(474)	Sean O'Hair	USA	1.306	67.94	54	-31.76	80.27
121	(283)	Lucas Bjerregaard	Den	1.297	67.45	59	-25.25	63.85
122	(127)	Nick Watney	USA	1.293	67.27	53	-75.40	75.45
123	(76)	Matt Every	USA	1.290	67.12	52	-101.91	72.56
124	(35)	Stephen Gallacher	Sco	1.281	66.62	55	-128.17	41.37
125	(114)	George McNeill	USA	1.280	65.31	51	-63.23	60.72
126	(669)	Dean Burmester	SAf	1.280	57.61	45	-19.41	67.74
127	(172)	Marcus Fraser	Aus	1.278	51.14	36	-35.11	46.35
128	(414)	Lee Slattery	Eng	1.271	66.10	55	-23.18	67.85
129	(149)	William McGirt	USA	1.271	66.10	58	-51.71	59.02
130	(202)	Toshinori Muto	Jpn	1.255	57.74	46	-28.93	46.39
131	(108)	Chris Stroud	USA	1.254	65.21	55	-67.85	57.16
132	(435)	Gary Stal	Fra	1.253	60.16	48	-41.65	82.58
133	(71)	Pablo Larrazabal	Esp	1.232	62.88	51	-89.98	50.92
133	(245)	Fabian Gomez	Arg	1.232	64.11	55	-33.54	58.14
135	(38)	Jason Dufner	USA	1.222	56.24	46	-124.68	45.53
136	(235)	Rikard Karlberg	Swe	1.222	56.23	46	-29.42	53.18
137	(135)	Charles Howell	USA	1.196	62.23	59	-68.43	64.24
138	(90)	Tomohiro Kondo	Jpn	1.190	55.95	47	-50.70	29.81
139	(261)	Ryan Fox	Nzl	1.182	47.31	39	-24.65	43.78
140	(94)	Geoff Ogilvy	Aus	1.172	55.09	47	-61.13	37.42
141	(83)	Brendon de Jonge	Zim	1.171	60.93	67	-82.44	50.57
142	(265)	Padraig Harrington	Irl	1.170	60.87	59	-48.20	71.93
143	(279)	Will Wilcox	USA	1.165	53.61	46	-27.86	54.61
144	(119)	Benjamin Hebert	Fra	1.164	59.39	51	-34.62	39.87
145	(423)	Davis Love	USA	1.157	46.29	38	-14.85	44.56
146	(296)	Alex Cejka	Ger	1.146	59.60	57	-38.28	67.83
147	(52)	Kevin Streelman	USA	1.143	59.45	54	-106.52	38.80
148	(215)	Kyoung-Hoon Lee	Kor	1.141	59.37	55	-35.59	52.23
149	(61)	Marcel Siem	Ger	1.127	55.22	49	-75.15	14.53
150	(263)	Jung-Gon Hwang	Kor	1.124	58.48	52	-25.52	47.50

( ) Ranking in brackets indicates position as of December 31, 2014.

Ranking		Player	Country	Average Points	Total Points	No. of Events	2015 Points Lost	2015 Points Gained
151	(62)	Tim Clark	SAf	1.119	44.76	40	-74.07	5.60
152	(115)	Shawn Stefani	USA	1.116	55.81	50	-57.73	45.48
153	(118)	Boo Weekley	USA	1.113	57.91	53	-69.10	56.06
154	(187)	Gregory Bourdy	Fra	1.113	57.91	56	-52.31	61.91
155	(155)	David Horsey	Eng	1.106	57.55	53	-43.63	49.04
156	(797)	Chez Reavie	USA	1.102	44.09	31	-8.38	47.30
157	(218)	Richard Green	Aus	1.095	52.59	48	-35.56	49.95
158	(57)	Graham DeLaet	Can	1.093	50.30	46	-114.58	45.11
159	(123)	Jerry Kelly	USA	1.092	50.24	46	-57.49	43.52
160	(129)	Prom Meesawat	Tha	1.078	53.94	50	-44.37	41.21
161	(207)	Pat Perez	USA	1.077	56.00	52	-54.25	66.45
162	(181)	Rory Sabbatini	SAf	1.075	53.76	50	-54.62	58.98
163	(153)	Thomas Aiken	SAf	1.072	55.76	57	-58.59	58.42
164	(418)	Anthony Wall	Eng	1.059	55.10	53	-22.07	60.87
165	(110)	Hyung-Sung Kim	Kor	1.052	54.73	56	-67.54	42.12
166	(1154)	Sebastien Gros	Fra	1.044	41.78	34	-5.47	45.52
167	(306)	Nathan Holman	Aus	1.033	43.41	42	-18.99	38.26
168	(186)	Ashun Wu	Chn	1.029	45.31	44	-42.47	43.00
169	(269)	Jeung-Hun Wang	Kor	1.025	48.20	47	-22.12	43.18
170	(213)	Zac Blair	USA	1.002	52.11	62	-29.28	50.69
171	(173)	Carl Pettersson	Swe	1.001	52.07	60	-45.20	46.35
172	(192)	Hao-Tong Li	Chn	0.993	51.65	54	-28.47	43.62
173	(47)	Mikko Ilonen	Fin	0.992	48.65	49	-97.29	16.12
174	(229)	Jason Gore	USA	0.990	51.51	54	-33.65	44.58
175	(175)	David Toms	USA	0.989	40.55	41	-35.02	35.96
176	(162)	Alejandro Canizares	Esp	0.988	44.47	45	-54.35	52.01
177	(189)	Brad Kennedy	Aus	0.977	45.95	47	-38.51	41.89
178	(386)	Jim Herman	USA	0.974	50.69	53	-26.97	54.04
179	(107)	Freddie Jacobson	Swe	0.973	40.88	42	-58.40	30.47
180	(501)	Peter Malnati	USA	0.971	50.51	52	-19.51	56.64
181	(154)	Katsumasa Miyamoto	Jpn	0.960	47.08	49	-32.97	27.14
182	(196)	Scott Brown	USA	0.957	49.81	60	-46.45	44.81
183	(345)	Greg Owen	Eng	0.956	43.05	45	-26.69	42.20
184	(174)	Wen-Chong Liang	Chn	0.954	40.10	42	-43.89	32.48
185	(143)	Peter Uihlein	USA	0.948	49.32	58	-59.02	46.22
186	(97)	Romain Wattel	Fra	0.946	49.23	52	-63.27	33.83
187	(145)	Camilo Villegas	Col	0.945	49.19	56	-51.33	38.95
188	(211)	Julien Quesne	Fra	0.943	47.18	50	-42.92	50.93
189	(433)	Martin Piller	USA	0.936	39.32	42	-14.38	37.86
190	(63)	Ernie Els	SAf	0.934	48.58	58	-100.13	32.24
191	(113)	Hiroyuki Fujita	Jpn	0.931	46.55	50	-47.88	22.24
192	(411)	Johnson Wagner	USA	0.918	47.77	52	-26.37	52.57
193	(133)	David Lipsky	USA	0.913	47.51	52	-38.79	28.41
194	(349)	Daisuke Kataoka	Jpn	0.911	45.55	50	-24.30	42.67
195	(399)	Kyle Reifers	USA	0.909	47.29	58	-23.92	51.37
196	(282)	Taichi Teshima	Jpn	0.904	41.62	46	-23.69	35.79
197	(289)	Graeme Storm	Eng	0.899	46.76	59	-24.45	38.84
198	(339)	Maximilian Kieffer	Ger	0.899	46.76	55	-32.70	51.20
199	(36)	Thomas Bjorn	Den	0.895	44.79	50	-130.44	26.25
200	(368)	Younghan Song	Kor	0.891	46.36	54	-19.45	43.28

( ) Ranking in brackets indicates position as of December 31, 2014.

Age Groups of Current Top 100 World Ranked Players

Under 25	25-28	29-32	33-36	37-40	Over 40
		D. Johnson			
	Day	Kisner			
	McIlroy	Na			
	Fowler	Leishman			
	Reed	Kaymer			
	Grace	Knox			
	Koepka	Wiesberger	Rose		
	Willett	Schwartzel	Garcia		
	Lowry	Horschel	Scott		
	Duibuisson	Kirk	Oosthuizen		
	Sullivan	K.T. Kim	Holmes		
Spieth	Aphibarnrat	Woodland	Walker		
Matsuyama	Streb	Broberg	B. Haas		
B-H An	Lahiri	K. Bradley	Snedeker	B. Watson	Furyk
Grillo	Wood	Bowditch	M. Jones	Stenson	Jaidee
Thomas	D. Lee	Kizzaire	McDowell	Z. Johnson	Mickelson
Fitzpatrick	Lingmerth	Simpson	Moore	Kuchar	Kjeldsen
Berger	Henley	Todd	F. Molinari	Casey	Westwood
Kaufman	Tringale	Steele	Van Zyl	Donaldson	Katayama
Fleetwood	Olesen	Luiten	Mahan	Piercy	Bohn
Gouveia	Martin	Ikeda	Warren	C. Hoffman	Senden
Pieters	Finau	G. Coetzee	R. Fisher	Poulter	Jimenez
Cam. Smith	Fujimoto	Morrison	Mayazato	Palmer	D. Howell
Rodgers	Levy	Summerhays	Noren	Donald	Marksaeng

2015 World Ranking Review

Major Movements

Upward				Downward			
Name	Net Points Gained	Position 2014	2015	Name	Net Points Lost	Position 2014	2015
Jordan Spieth	299	9	1	Adam Scott	137	3	11
Jason Day	205	8	2	Sergio Garcia	124	5	12
Kevin Kisner	165	236	17	Thomas Bjorn	104	36	199
Branden Grace	123	82	14	Billy Horschel	92	13	41
Matthew Fitzpatrick	122	413	43	Stephen Gallacher	86	35	124
Byeong-Hun An	112	179	29	Martin Kaymer	85	12	27
Soren Kjeldsen	109	335	45	Graeme McDowell	85	15	57
Daniel Berger	102	301	53	Phil Mickelson	82	14	34
Justin Thomas	95	122	37	Hunter Mahan	81	22	68
Danny Lee	95	220	47	Mikko Ilonen	81	47	173
Andy Sullivan	90	150	36	Jason Dufner	79	38	135
Emiliano Grillo	87	128	32				
Rickie Fowler	86	10	6				
Dustin Johnson	86	19	8				
Paul Casey	84	75	22				

Highest-Rated Events of 2015

	Event	No. of World Ranked Players Participating					World Rating Points
		Top 5	Top 15	Top 30	Top 50	Top 100	
1	PGA Championship	5	15	29	48	96	828
2	U.S. Open Championship	5	15	30	50	72	773
3	The Open Championship	4	14	28	48	89	771
4	Masters Tournament	5	15	30	49	69	730
5	The Players Championship	5	15	29	48	78	775
6	WGC-Cadillac Championship	5	15	30	50	65	728
7	WGC-Accenture Match Play	5	15	29	49	64	719
8	WGC-Bridgestone Invitational	4	14	28	48	63	679
9	Deutsche Bank Championship	5	13	23	37	62	638
10	The Barclays	4	12	22	37	64	623
11	BMW Championship	5	14	24	38	56	613
12	WGC-HSBC Champions	4	10	20	37	57	531
13	BMW PGA Championship	1	2	7	13	34	284
14	Arnold Palmer Invitational	4	5	13	25	47	442
15	Memorial Tournament	2	8	16	21	51	428
16	Honda Classic	1	6	18	25	49	426
17	The Tour Championship	5	12	19	25	29	425
18	Northern Trust Open	1	6	11	20	46	361
19	Waste Mgmt. Phoenix Open	1	6	13	20	46	357
20	Shell Houston Open	1	7	14	22	43	357
21	DP World Tour Championship	2	5	11	19	39	318
22	Valspar Championship	2	6	10	19	39	346
23	RBC Heritage	1	3	9	21	41	329
24	Valero Texas Open	0	6	13	18	38	318
25	Farmers Insurance Open	1	6	13	19	39	319
26	Wells Fargo Championship	3	7	10	15	36	326
27	BMW Masters	0	4	11	18	38	293
28	AAM Scottish Open	0	3	8	15	44	293
29	Omega Dubai Clasic	2	4	7	13	26	283
30	Abu Dhabi HSBC Champ.	2	5	8	11	27	271
31	Crowne Plaza Invitational	1	4	9	16	35	283
32	Duty Free Irish Open	1	3	6	13	31	268
33	CIMB Classic	0	3	8	17	35	260
34	AT&T Pebble Beach	1	5	11	14	25	246
35	Hero World Challenge	3	9	14	18	18	284
36	Frys.com Open	1	4	6	12	34	268
37	Travelers Championship	1	3	9	14	34	256
38	Sony Open	0	3	7	13	36	250
39	AT&T Byron Nelson	1	3	8	13	31	249
40	Humana Challenge	0	3	8	14	31	244

World Golf Rankings 1968-2015

Year	No. 1	No. 2	No. 3	No. 4	No. 5
1968	Nicklaus	Palmer	Casper	Player	Charles
1969	Nicklaus	Player	Casper	Palmer	Charles
1970	Nicklaus	Player	Casper	Trevino	Charles
1971	Nicklaus	Trevino	Player	Palmer	Casper
1972	Nicklaus	Player	Trevino	Crampton	Palmer
1973	Nicklaus	Weiskopf	Trevino	Player	Crampton
1974	Nicklaus	Miller	Player	Weiskopf	Trevino
1975	Nicklaus	Miller	Weiskopf	Irwin	Player
1976	Nicklaus	Irwin	Miller	Player	Green
1977	Nicklaus	Watson	Green	Irwin	Crenshaw
1978	Watson	Nicklaus	Irwin	Green	Player
1979	Watson	Nicklaus	Irwin	Trevino	Player
1980	Watson	Trevino	Aoki	Crenshaw	Nicklaus
1981	Watson	Rogers	Aoki	Pate	Trevino
1982	Watson	Floyd	Ballesteros	Kite	Stadler
1983	Ballesteros	Watson	Floyd	Norman	Kite
1984	Ballesteros	Watson	Norman	Wadkins	Langer
1985	Ballesteros	Langer	Norman	Watson	Nakajima
1986	Norman	Langer	Ballesteros	Nakajima	Bean
1987	Norman	Ballesteros	Langer	Lyle	Strange
1988	Ballesteros	Norman	Lyle	Faldo	Strange
1989	Norman	Faldo	Ballesteros	Strange	Stewart
1990	Norman	Faldo	Olazabal	Woosnam	Stewart
1991	Woosnam	Faldo	Olazabal	Ballesteros	Norman
1992	Faldo	Couples	Woosnam	Olazabal	Norman
1993	Faldo	Norman	Langer	Price	Couples
1994	Price	Norman	Faldo	Langer	Olazabal
1995	Norman	Price	Langer	Els	Montgomerie
1996	Norman	Lehman	Montgomerie	Els	Couples
1997	Norman	Woods	Price	Els	Love
1998	Woods	O'Meara	Duval	Love	Els
1999	Woods	Duval	Montgomerie	Love	Els
2000	Woods	Els	Duval	Mickelson	Westwood
2001	Woods	Mickelson	Duval	Els	Love
2002	Woods	Mickelson	Els	Garcia	Goosen
2003	Woods	Singh	Els	Love	Furyk
2004	Singh	Woods	Els	Goosen	Mickelson
2005	Woods	Singh	Mickelson	Goosen	Els
2006	Woods	Furyk	Mickelson	Scott	Els
2007	Woods	Mickelson	Furyk	Els	Stricker
2008	Woods	Garcia	Mickelson	Harrington	Singh
2009	Woods	Mickelson	Stricker	Westwood	Harrington
2010	Westwood	Woods	Kaymer	Mickelson	Furyk
2011	Donald	Westwood	McIlroy	Kaymer	Scott
2012	McIlroy	Donald	Woods	Rose	Scott
2013	Woods	Scott	Stenson	Rose	Mickelson
2014	McIlroy	Stenson	Scott	Watson	Garcia
2015	Spieth	Day	McIlroy	Watson	Stenson

(The World of Professional Golf 1968-1985; World Ranking 1986-2015)

Year	No. 6	No. 7	No. 8	No. 9	No. 10
1968	Boros	Coles	Thomson	Beard	Nagle
1969	Beard	Archer	Trevino	Barber	Sikes
1970	Devlin	Coles	Jacklin	Beard	Huggett
1971	Barber	Crampton	Charles	Devlin	Weiskopf
1972	Jacklin	Weiskopf	Oosterhuis	Heard	Devlin
1973	Miller	Oosterhuis	Wadkins	Heard	Brewer
1974	M. Ozaki	Crampton	Irwin	Green	Heard
1975	Green	Trevino	Casper	Crampton	Watson
1976	Watson	Weiskopf	Marsh	Crenshaw	Geiberger
1977	Marsh	Player	Weiskopf	Floyd	Ballesteros
1978	Crenshaw	Marsh	Ballesteros	Trevino	Aoki
1979	Aoki	Green	Crenshaw	Ballesteros	Wadkins
1980	Pate	Ballesteros	Bean	Irwin	Player
1981	Ballesteros	Graham	Crenshaw	Floyd	Lietzke
1982	Pate	Nicklaus	Rogers	Aoki	Strange
1983	Nicklaus	Nakajima	Stadler	Aoki	Wadkins
1984	Faldo	Nakajima	Stadler	Kite	Peete
1985	Wadkins	O'Meara	Strange	Pavin	Sutton
1986	Tway	Sutton	Strange	Stewart	O'Meara
1987	Woosnam	Stewart	Wadkins	McNulty	Crenshaw
1988	Crenshaw	Woosnam	Frost	Azinger	Calcavecchia
1989	Kite	Olazabal	Calcavecchia	Woosnam	Azinger
1990	Azinger	Ballesteros	Kite	McNulty	Calcavecchia
1991	Couples	Langer	Stewart	Azinger	Davis
1992	Langer	Cook	Price	Azinger	Love
1993	Azinger	Woosnam	Kite	Love	Pavin
1994	Els	Couples	Montgomerie	M. Ozaki	Pavin
1995	Pavin	Faldo	Couples	M. Ozaki	Elkington
1996	Faldo	Mickelson	M. Ozaki	Love	O'Meara
1997	Mickelson	Montgomerie	M. Ozaki	Lehman	O'Meara
1998	Price	Montgomerie	Westwood	Singh	Mickelson
1999	Westwood	Singh	Price	Mickelson	O'Meara
2000	Montgomerie	Love	Sutton	Singh	Lehman
2001	Garcia	Toms	Singh	Clarke	Goosen
2002	Toms	Harrington	Singh	Love	Montgomerie
2003	Weir	Goosen	Harrington	Toms	Perry
2004	Harrington	Garcia	Weir	Love	Cink
2005	Garcia	Furyk	Montgomerie	Scott	DiMarco
2006	Goosen	Singh	Harrington	Donald	Ogilvy
2007	Rose	Scott	Harrington	Choi	Singh
2008	Karlsson	Villegas	Stenson	Els	Westwood
2009	Furyk	Casey	Stenson	McIlroy	Perry
2010	McDowell	Stricker	Casey	Donald	McIlroy
2011	Stricker	D. Johnson	Day	Schwartzel	W. Simpson
2012	Oosthuizen	Westwood	B. Watson	Dufner	Snedeker
2013	McIlroy	Kuchar	Stricker	Z. Johnson	Garcia
2014	Rose	Furyk	Day	Spieth	Fowler
2015	Fowler	Rose	D. Johnson	Furyk	Reed

World's Winners of 2015

U.S. PGA TOUR

Hyundai Tournament of Champions	Patrick Reed
Sony Open in Hawaii	Jimmy Walker
Humana Challenge	Bill Haas
Waste Management Phoenix Open	Brooks Koepka
Farmers Insurance Open	Jason Day
AT&T Pebble Beach National Pro-Am	Brandt Snedeker
Northern Trust Open	James Hahn
Honda Classic	Padraig Harrington
WGC - Cadillac Championship	Dustin Johnson
Puerto Rico Open	Alex Cejka
Valspar Championship	Jordan Spieth
Arnold Palmer Invitational	Matt Every
Valero Texas Open	Jimmy Walker (2)
Shell Houston Open	J.B. Holmes
Masters Tournament	Jordan Spieth (2)
RBC Heritage	Jim Furyk
Zurich Classic of New Orleans	Justin Rose
WGC - Cadillac Match Play	Rory McIlroy (2)
The Players Championship	Rickie Fowler
Wells Fargo Championship	Rory McIlroy (3)
Crowne Plaza Invitational	Chris Kirk
AT&T Byron Nelson	Steven Bowditch
Memorial Tournament	David Lingmerth
FedEx St. Jude Classic	Fabian Gomez
U.S. Open Championship	Jordan Spieth (3)
Travelers Championship	Bubba Watson
Greenbrier Classic	Danny Lee
John Deere Classic	Jordan Spieth (4)
Barbasol Championship	Scott Piercy
RBC Canadian Open	Jason Day (2)
Quicken Loans National	Troy Merritt
WGC - Bridgestone Invitational	Shane Lowry
Barracuda Championship	J.J. Henry
PGA Championship	Jason Day (3)
Wyndham Championship	Davis Love

PGA TOUR PLAYOFFS FOR THE FEDEXCUP

The Barclays	Jason Day (4)
Deutsche Bank Championship	Rickie Fowler (3)
BMW Championship	Jason Day (5)
Tour Championship	Jordan Spieth (5)

START OF 2016 SEASON

Frys.com Open	Emiliano Grillo (2)
Shriners Hospitals for Children Open	Smylie Kaufman (2)
Sanderson Farms Championship	Peter Malnati (2)
OHL Classic at Mayakoba	Graeme McDowell
The RSM Classic	Kevin Kisner

SPECIAL EVENTS

CVS Health Charity Classic	Keegan Bradley/Jon Curran
The Presidents Cup	United States
TaylorMade Pebble Beach Invitational	Jeff Gove
Hero World Challenge	Bubba Watson (2)
Franklin Templeton Shootout	Jason Dufner/Brandt Snedeker (2)
PNC Father/Son Challenge	Lanny Wadkins/Tucker Wadkins

WEB.COM TOUR

Panama Claro Championship	Mathew Goggin
Colombia Championship	Patrick Rodgers
Cartagena de Indias at Karibana Championship	Andrew Landry
Brasil Champions	Peter Malnati
Chile Classic	Dawie van der Walt
Chitimacha Louisiana Open	Kelly Kraft
El Bosque Mexico Championship	Wes Roach
United Leasing Championship	Smylie Kaufman
BMW Charity Pro-Am	Rod Pampling
Rex Hospital Open	Kyle Thompson
Greater Dallas Open	Tyler Aldridge
Rush-Oleum Championship	Shane Bertsch
Air Capital Classic	Rob Oppenheim
Nova Scotia Open	Abraham Ancer
Albertsons Boise Open	Martin Piller
Stonebrae Classic	Si Woo Kim
Utah Championship	Patton Kizzire
Digital Ally Open	Martin Piller (2)
Price Cutter Charity Championship	Dawie van der Walt (2)
News Sentinel Open	Patton Kizzire (2)
WinCo Foods Portland Open	Dicky Pride

WEB.COM TOUR FINALS

Hotel Fitness Championship	Henrik Norlander
Small Business Connection Championship	Chez Reavie
Nationwide Children's Hospital Championship	Andrew Loupe
Web.com Tour Championship	Emiliano Grillo

MACKENZIE TOUR–PGA TOUR CANADA

PC Financial Open	Drew Weaver
Bayview Place Island Savings Open	Albin Choi
Syncrude Boreal Open	Kevin Spooner
SIGA Dakota Dunes Open	Michael Letzig
The Players Cup	Cheng Tsung Pan
Staal Foundation Open	J.J. Spaun
ATB Financial Classic	Daniel Miernicki
National Capital Open to Support Our Troops	Sam Ryder
Great Waterway Classic	Brad Clapp
Wildfire Invitational	Christopher Ross
Cape Breton Celtic Classic	Cheng Tsung Pan (2)
Freedom 55 Financial Championship	Jason Millard

PGA TOUR LATINOAMERICA

Avianca Colombia Open	Diego Velasquez
Mazatlan Open	Tommy Cocha
Abierto OSDE del Centro	Tommy Cocha (2)
Lexus Panama Classic	Rodolfo Cazaubon
Abierto Mexicano de Golf	Justin Hueber
Guatemala Stella Artois Open	Danny Balin
Honduras Open	Felipe Velazquez
Dominican Republic Open	Rodolfo Cazaubon (2)
All You Need is Ecuador Open	Ricardo Celia
Volvo Colombian Classic	Mitch Krywulycz
Aberto do Brasil	Alexandre Rocha
Hyundai-BBVA Abierto de Chile	Wil Bateman
Mundo Maya Open	Nicholas Lindheim
Bridgestone America's Golf Cup	Justin Hueber (2)/Matt Kuchar (2)
Roberto de Vicenzo Punta del Este Open	Lanto Griffin

VISA Open de Argentina	Kent Bulle
Personal Classic	Fabian Gomez (2)
Lexus Peru Open	Rodolfo Cazaubon (3)
Latinoamerica Tour Championship	Daniel Mazziotta

EUROPEAN TOUR

Abu Dhabi HSBC Golf Championship	Gary Stal
Commercial Bank Qatar Masters	Branden Grace
Omega Dubai Desert Classic	Rory McIlroy
Trophee Hassan II	Richie Ramsay
Shenzhen International	Kiradech Aphibarnrat
Open de Espana	James Morrison
BMW PGA Championship	Byeong-Hun An
Dubai Duty Free Irish Open	Soren Kjeldsen
Nordea Masters	Alex Noren
Lyoness Open	Chris Wood
BMW International Open	Pablo Larrazabal
Alstom Open de France	Bernd Wiesberger
Aberdeen Asset Management Scottish Open	Rickie Fowler (2)
The Open Championship	Zach Johnson
Omega European Masters	Danny Willett
Madeira Islands Open - Portugal - BPI	Roope Kakko
Saltire Energy Paul Lawrie Match Play	Kiradech Aphibarnrat (2)
Made in Denmark	David Horsey
D+D Real Czech Masters	Thomas Pieters
M2M Russian Open	Lee Slattery
KLM Open	Thomas Pieters (2)
Open D'Italia	Rikard Karlberg
Porsche European Open	Thongchai Jaidee
Alfred Dunhill Links Championship	Thorbjorn Olesen
British Masters	Matthew Fitzpatrick
Portugal Masters	Andy Sullivan (3)

THE FINAL SERIES

Turkish Airlines Open	Victor Dubuisson
BMW Masters	Kristoffer Broberg
DP World Tour Championship	Rory McIlroy (4)

CHALLENGE TOUR

Barclays Kenya Open	Haydn Porteous
Challenge de Madrid	Nacho Elvira
Turkish Airlines Challenge	Rhys Davies
Made in Denmark Challenge	Max Orrin
Karnten Golf Open	Nacho Elvira (2)
D+D Real Czech Challenge	Jens Fahrbring
Swiss Challenge	Daniel Im
KPMG Trophy	Jamie McLeary
Najeti Open	Sebastien Gros
SSE Scottish Hydro Challenge	Jack Senior
Aegean Airlines Challenge	Ricardo Gouveia
D+D Real Slovakia Challenge	Borja Virto Astudillo
Fred Olsen Challenge de Espana	Rhys Davies (2)
Le Vaudreuil Golf Challenge	Ryan Fox (2)
Northern Ireland Open	Clement Sordet
GANT Open	Dominic Foos
Rolex Trophy	Nacho Elvira (3)
Cordon Golf Open	Scott Arnold
Kazakhstan Open	Sebastien Gros (2)
EMC Challenge Open	Matteo Delpodio

Volopa Irish Challenge	Tom Murray
Foshan Open	Borja Virto Astudillo (2)
NBO Golf Classic Grand Final	Ricardo Gouveia (2)

ASIAN TOUR

Maybank Malaysian Open	Anirban Lahiri
True Thailand Classic	Andrew Dodt
Hero Indian Open	Anirban Lahiri (2)
CIMB Niaga Indonesian Masters	Lee Westwood
Bashundhara Bangladesh Open	Mardan Mamat
Queen's Cup	Prayad Marksaeng
Mercuries Taiwan Masters	Danny Chia
Yeangder Tournament Players Championship	Shaun Norris
Venetian Macau Open	Scott Hend
UBS Hong Kong Open	Justin Rose (2)
CIMB Classic	Justin Thomas
WGC - HSBC Champions	Russell Knox
Panasonic Open India	Chiragh Kumar
World Classic Championship	Danthai Boonma
Resorts World Manila Masters	Natipong Srithong
Ho Tram Open	Sergio Garcia
Thailand Golf Championship	Jamie Donaldson
Philippine Open	Miguel Tabuena

ONEASIA TOUR

Volvo China Open	Ashun Wu
GS Caltex Maekyung Open	Kyong-Jun Moon
SK Telecom Open	Jinho Choi
Singha Corporation Thailand Open	Kyung-Tae Kim
Kolon Korea Open	Kyoung-Hoon Lee
Fiji International	Matt Kuchar

PGA TOUR CHINA

Buick Open	Josh Geary
Eternal Courtyard Open	Shih-Chang Chan
United Investment Real Estate Wuhan Open	Justin Shin
Lanhai Open	Josh Geary (2)
Pingan Bank Open	Eugene Wong
Cadillac Championship	Bryden Macpherson
Yulongwan Yunnan Open	Josh Geary (3)
Lushan Open	Bryden Macpherson (2)
Chongqing Open	Xin-Jun Zhang
Nine Dragons Open	Haimeng Chao
Hainan Open	Huilin Zhang
Capital Airline - HNA Real Estate Championship	Ze-Yu He

JAPAN TOUR

Token Homemate Cup	Michael Hendry
The Crowns	I.J. Jang
Japan PGA Championship	Adam Bland
Kansai Open	Daisuke Kataoka
Gateway to the Open Mizuno Open	Taichi Teshima
Japan Golf Tour Championship	Wen-Chong Liang
ISPS Handa Global Cup	Toshinori Muto
Shigeo Nagashima Invitational	Hiroshi Iwata
Musee Platinum Open	Kyung-Tae Kim (2)
Dunlop Srixon Fukushima Open	Prayad Marksaeng (2)
RIZAP KBC Augusta	Yuta Ikeda

Fujisankei Classic	Kyung-Tae Kim (3)
ANA Open	Ryo Ishikawa
Asia-Pacific Diamond Cup	Kyung-Tae Kim (4)
Top Cup Tokai Classic	Hyung-Sung Kim
Honma TourWorld Cup at Trophia Golf	Kyoung-Hoon Lee (2)
Japan Open Championship	Satoshi Kodaira
Bridgestone Open	Michio Matsumura
Mynavi ABC Championship	Kyung-Tae Kim (5)
Heiwa PGM Championship	Hideto Tanihara
Mitsui Sumitomo VISA Taiheiyo Masters	Shingo Katayama
Dunlop Phoenix	Yusaku Miyazato
Casio World Open	Jung-Gon Hwang
Golf Nippon Series JT Cup	Ryo Ishikawa (2)

AUSTRALASIAN TOUR

Oates Victorian Open	Richard Green
Mercedes-Benz Truck & Bus Victorian PGA	Aaron Townsend
Coca-Cola Queensland PGA Championship	Ryan Fox
Holden New Zealand PGA Championship	Matthew Millar
BMW New Zealand Open	Jordan Zunic
Isuzu Queensland Open	David Bransdon
South Pacific Open Championship	James Nitties
TX Civil & Logistics WA PGA Championship	Brett Rumford
Nexus Risk TSA Group WA Open	Daniel Fox
New South Wales Open	*Ben Eccles
UNIQLO Masters	Peter Senior
Emirates Australian Open	Matt Jones
Australian PGA Championship	Nathan Holman
New South Wales PGA Championship	Jarryd Felton

AFRICAN SUNSHINE TOUR

South African Open Championship	Andy Sullivan
Dimension Data Pro-Am	Branden Grace (2)
Joburg Open	Andy Sullivan (2)
Africa Open	Trevor Fisher, Jr.
Tshwane Open	George Coetzee
Investec Cup	Jaco Ahlers
Golden Pilsener Zimbabwe Open	Dean Burmester
Mopani/Redpath Zambia Open	Ross McGowan
Zambia Sugar Open	Vaughn Groenewald
Investec Royal Swazi Open	P.H. McIntyre
AfrAsia Bank Mauritius Open	George Coetzee (2)
Lombard Insurance Classic	Dean Burmester (2)
Vodacom Origins of Golf - Langebaan	Justin Harding
Sun City Challenge	Keith Horne
Vodacom Origins of Golf - San Lameer	Jean Hugo
Sun Wild Coast Sun Challenge	Vaughn Groenewald (2)
Sun Sibaya Challenge	Michael Hollick
Vodacom Origins of Golf - Vaal de Grace	Jean Hugo (2)
Sun Windmill Challenge	Dean Burmester (3)
Vodacom Origins of Golf - St. Francis	Christiaan Basson
Sun Boardwalk Challenge	Chris Swanepoel
Sun Fish River Sun Challenge	Rourke van der Spuy
Vodacom Origins of Golf - Koro Creek	Dean Burmester (4)
Nedbank Affinity Cup	Ruan de Smidt
Vodacom Origins of Golf Final	Darren Fichardt
Lion of Africa Cape Town Open	Brandon Stone
Alfred Dunhill Championship	Charl Schwartzel
Nedbank Golf Challenge	Marc Leishman

U.S. LPGA TOUR

Coates Golf Championship	Na Yeon Choi
Pure Silk Bahamas LPGA Classic	Sei Young Kim
Honda LPGA Thailand	Amy Yang
HSBC Women's Champions	Inbee Park
JTBC Founders Cup	Hyo Joo Kim
Kia Classic	Cristie Kerr
ANA Inspiration	Brittany Lincicome
Lotte Championship	Sei Young Kim (2)
Swinging Skirts LPGA Classic	Lydia Ko (3)
Volunteers of America North Texas Shootout	Inbee Park (2)
Kingsmill Championship	Minjee Lee
ShopRite LPGA Classic	Anna Nordqvist
Manulife LPGA Classic	Suzann Pettersen
KPMG Women's PGA Championship	Inbee Park (3)
Walmart NW Arkansas Championship	Na Yeon Choi (2)
U.S. Women's Open Championship	In-Gee Chun (5)
Marathon Classic	Chella Choi
Meijer LPGA Classic	Lexi Thompson
Cambia Portland Classic	Brooke M. Henderson
Canadian Pacific Women's Open	Lydia Ko (4)
Yokohama Tire LPGA Classic	Kris Tamulis
Sime Darby LPGA Malaysia	Jessica Korda
Fubon LPGA Taiwan Championship	Lydia Ko (6)
Blue Bay LPGA	Sei Young Kim (3)
Lorena Ochoa Invitational	Inbee Park (5)
CME Group Tour Championship	Cristie Kerr (2)

LADIES EUROPEAN TOUR

World Ladies Championship	So Yeon Ryu
Lalla Meryem Cup	Gwladys Nocera
Buick Championship	Shanshan Feng
Turkish Airlines Ladies Open	Melissa Reid
Deloitte Ladies Open	Christel Boeljon
ISPS Handa Ladies European Masters	Beth Allen
Aberdeen Asset Management Scottish Open	Rebecca Artis
Ricoh Women's British Open	Inbee Park (4)
Tipsport Golf Masters	Hannah Burke
Helsingborg Open	Nicole Broch Larsen
Evian Championship	Lydia Ko (5)
The Solheim Cup	United States
Lacoste Ladies Open de France	Celine Herbin
Xiamen International Ladies Open	Hye In Yeom
Hero Women's Indian Open	Emily Kristine Pedersen
Sanya Ladies Open	Xi Yu Lin
Omega Dubai Ladies Masters	Shanshan Feng (2)

JAPAN LPGA TOUR

Daikin Orchid Ladies	Teresa Lu
Yokohama Tire PRGR Ladies Cup	Ji-Hee Lee
T-Point Ladies	Akane Iijima
AXA Ladies	Ritsuko Ryu
Yamaha Ladies Open	Ayaka Watanabe
Studio Alice Ladies Open	Misuzu Narita
Vantelin Ladies Open KKT Cup	Erika Kikuchi
Fujisankei Ladies Classic	Hikari Fujita
CyberAgent Ladies	Jiyai Shin
World Ladies Championship Salonpas Cup	In-Gee Chun (2)
Hoken no Madoguchi Ladies	Bo-Mee Lee

Chukyo TV Bridgestone Ladies Open	Yumiko Yoshida
Resort Trust Ladies	Teresa Lu (2)
Yonex Ladies	Shiho Oyama
Suntory Ladies Open	Misuzu Narita (2)
Nichirei Ladies	Jiyai Shin (2)
Earth Mondahmin Cup	Bo-Mee Lee (2)
Samantha Thavasa Girls Collection Ladies	Yoko Maeda
Century 21 Ladies	Sun-Ju Ahn
Daito Kentaku Eheyanet Ladies	Erina Hara
Meiji Cup	Yukari Nishiyama
NEC Karuizawa 72	Teresa Lu (3)
CAT Ladies	Mayu Hattori
Nitori Ladies	Bo-Mee Lee (3)
Golf 5 Ladies	Bo-Mee Lee (4)
Japan LPGA Championship Konica Minolta Cup	Teresa Lu (4)
Munsingwear Ladies Tokai Classic	Ha-Neul Kim
Miyagi TV Cup Dunlop Ladies Open	Junko Omote
Japan Women's Open Championship	In-Gee Chun (7)
Stanley Ladies	Bo-Mee Lee (5)
Fujitsu Ladies	Teresa Lu (5)
Nobuta Group Masters Golf Club Ladies	Ji-Hee Lee (2)
Hisako Higuchi Ponta Ladies	Ayaka Watanabe (2)
Toto Japan Classic	Sun-Ju Ahn (2)
Itoen Ladies	Bo-Mee Lee (6)
Daio Paper Elleair Ladies Open	Bo-Mee Lee (7)
Japan LPGA Tour Championship Ricoh Cup	Jiyai Shin (3)
The Queens	Japan

KOREA LPGA TOUR

Lotte Mart Women's Open	Bo Kyung Kim
Samchunli Together Open	In-Gee Chun
Nexen-Saint Nine Masters	Jin Young Ko
KG-Edaily Ladies Open	Min Sun Kim
Kyochon Honey Ladies Open	Jin Young Ko (2)
NH Investment & Securities Championship	Jung Min Lee
Doosan Match Play Championship	In-Gee Chun (3)
E1 Charity Open	Jung Min Lee (2)
Lotte Cantata Ladies Open	Jung Min Lee (3)
S-Oil Champions Invitational	In-Gee Chun (4)
Kia Motors Korea Women's Open Championship	Sung Hyun Park
BC Card Hankyung Ladies Open	Ha Na Jang
Kumhotire Ladies Open	Hyo Joo Kim (2)
ChoJung Sparkling Water Youngpyong Open	Jin Young Ko (3)
BMW Ladies Championship	Yoon Ji Cho
Hite Jinro Championship	In-Gee Chun (6)
Jeju Samdasu Masters	Jeong Eun Lee
Bogner MBN Ladies Open	Min Song Ha
HighOne Resort Ladies Open	So Yeon Ryu (2)
Hanhwa Finance Classic	Haru Nomura
Isugroup KLPGA Championship	Shin-Ae Ahn
KDB Daewoo Securities Classic	Sung Hyun Park (2)
YTN-Volvik Ladies Open	Ha Na Jang (2)
OKSavingsBank Se Ri Pak Invitational	Sung Hyun Park (3)
LPGA KEB HanaBank Championship	Lexi Thompson (2)
KB Financial Group Star Championship	In-Gee Chun (8)
Seokyung-Moonyoung Queens Park Classic	Hye Youn Kim
ADT CAPS Championship	Ji Hyun Oh
Chosunilbo-Posco Championship	Hye Jung Choi
Hyundai China Ladies Open	Sung Hyun Park (4)

AUSTRALIAN LADIES TOUR

Moss Vale Classic	Sarah Oh
Oates Victorian Open	Marianne Skarpnord
RACV Ladies Masters	Su-Hyun Oh
ISPS Handa Women's Australian Open	Lydia Ko
ISPS Handa New Zealand Women's Open	Lydia Ko (2)
Bing Lee Fujitsu NSW Women's Open	Holly Clyburn
Australia Classic	Yanhong Pan

CHAMPIONS TOUR

Mitsubishi Electric Championship	Miguel Angel Jimenez
Allianz Championship	Paul Goydos
ACE Group Classic	Lee Janzen
Tucson Conquistadores Classic	Marco Dawson
Mississippi Gulf Resort Classic	David Frost
Greater Gwinnett Championship	Olin Browne
Bass Pro Shops Legends of Golf	Billy Andrade/Joe Durant
Insperity Invitational	Ian Woosnam
Regions Tradition	Jeff Maggert
Senior PGA Championship	Colin Montgomerie
Principal Charity Classic	Mark Calcavecchia
Constellation Senior Players Championship	Bernhard Langer
U.S. Senior Open Championship	Jeff Maggert (2)
Encompass Championship	Jerry Smith
3M Championship	Kenny Perry
Shaw Charity Classic	Jeff Maggert (3)
Boeing Classic	Billy Andrade (2)
Dick's Sporting Goods Open	Jeff Maggert (4)
Nature Valley First Tee Open	Esteban Toledo
SAS Championship	Tom Lehman
San Antonio Championship	Bernhard Langer (2)
Toshiba Classic	Duffy Waldorf
Charles Schwab Cup Championship	Billy Andrade (3)

EUROPEAN SENIOR TOUR

SSE Enterprise Wales Senior Open	Paul Wesselingh
Acorn Jersey Open	Peter Fowler
ISPS Handa PGA Seniors Championship	Peter Fowler (2)
Swiss Seniors Open	Gordon Manson
WINSTONgolf Senior Open	Pedro Linhart
The Senior Open Championship	Marco Dawson (2)
Prostate Cancer UK Scottish Senior Open	Paul Broadhurst
Travis Perkins Masters	Colin Montgomerie (2)
French Riviera Masters	Simon P. Brown
MCB Tour Championship	Colin Montgomerie (3)

JAPAN PGA SENIOR TOUR

Kanehide Senior Okinawa Open	Katsumi Kubo
Kyoraku More Surprise Cup	Takeshi Sakiyama
Starts Senior	Kiyoshi Murota
Maruhan Cup Taiheiyo Club Senior	Takeshi Sakiyama (2)
Fancl Classic	Kiyoshi Murota (2)
Kyoshinkai Hiroshima Senior Championship	Masahiro Kuramoto
Alpha Club Cup Senior Open	Takeshi Sakiyama (3)
Komatsu Open	Takeshi Sakiyama (4)
Japan PGA Senior Championship	Kiyoshi Murota (3)
Japan Senior Open Championship	Takenori Hiraishi
Fuji Film Senior Championship	Tsukasa Watanabe
ISPS Handa Cup Philanthropy Senior	Shinichi Akiba
Iwasaki Shiratsuyu Senior	Tze-Chung Chen

Multiple Winners of 2015

PLAYER	WINS	PLAYER	WINS
In-Gee Chun	8	Ryan Fox	2
		Fabian Gomez	2
Bo-Mee Lee	7	Ricardo Gouveia	2
		Branden Grace	2
Lydia Ko	6	Emiliano Grillo	2
		Vaughn Groenewald	2
Jason Day	5	Sebastien Gros	2
Kyung-Tae Kim	5	Justin Hueber	2
Teresa Lu	5	Jean Hugo	2
Inbee Park	5	Ryo Ishikawa	2
Jordan Spieth	5	Ha Na Jang	2
		Smylie Kaufman	2
Dean Burmester	4	Cristie Kerr	2
Jeff Maggert	4	Hyo Joo Kim	2
Rory McIlroy	4	Patton Kizzire	2
Sung Hyun Park	4	Matt Kuchar	2
Takeshi Sakiyama	4	Anirban Lahiri	2
		Bernhard Langer	2
Billy Andrade	3	Ji-Hee Lee	2
Rodolfo Cazaubon	3	Kyoung-Hoon Lee	2
Nacho Elvira	3	Bryden Macpherson	2
Rickie Fowler	3	Peter Malnati	2
Josh Geary	3	Prayad Marksaeng	2
Sei Young Kim	3	Misuzu Narita	2
Jin Young Ko	3	Cheng Tsung Pan	2
Jung Min Lee	3	Thomas Pieters	2
Colin Montgomerie	3	Martin Piller	2
Kiyoshi Murota	3	Justin Rose	2
Jiyai Shin	3	So Yeon Ryu	2
Andy Sullivan	3	Brandt Snedeker	2
		Lexi Thompson	2
Sun-Ju Ahn	2	Dawie van der Walt	2
Kiradech Aphibarnrat	2	Borja Virto Astudillo	2
Na Yeon Choi	2	Jimmy Walker	2
Tommy Cocha	2	Ayaka Watanabe	2
George Coetzee	2	Bubba Watson	2
Rhys Davies	2		
Marco Dawson	2		
Shanshan Feng	2		
Peter Fowler	2		

World Money List

This list of the 350 leading money winners in the world of professional golf in 2015 was compiled from the results of men's (excluding seniors) tournaments carried in the Appendixes of this edition. This list includes tournaments with a minimum of 36 holes and four contestants and does not include such competitions as pro-ams and skins or skills contests. It does not include annual performance bonuses such as for the FedExCup (U.S.) and the Race to Dubai (Europe).

In the 50 years during which World Money Lists have been compiled, the earnings of the player in the 200th position have risen from a total of $3,326 in 1966 to $666,834 in 2015. The top 200 players in 1966 earned a total of $4,680,287. In 2015, the comparable total was $ 381,222,905.

The World Money List includes the official money lists of the U.S. PGA Tour, PGA European Tour, PGA Tour of Japan, Asian Tour, OneAsia Tour, Sunshine Tour, PGA Tour of Australasia, PGA Tour Latinoamerica and PGA Tour Canada, along with winnings in established unofficial tournaments when reliable figures could be obtained. The conversion rates used for 2015 were: Euro = US$1.11; Japanese yen = US$0.008; South African rand = US$0.08; Australian dollar = US$0.75; Canadian dollar = US$0.76.

POS.	PLAYER, COUNTRY	TOTAL MONEY
1	Jordan Spieth, USA	$12,477,758
2	Jason Day, Australia	9,403,330
3	Rory McIlroy, N. Ireland	7,351,105
4	Rickie Fowler, USA	6,648,145
5	Bubba Watson, USA	6,637,265
6	Justin Rose, England	6,469,666
7	Henrik Stenson, Sweden	6,287,540
8	Dustin Johnson, USA	5,892,967
9	Patrick Reed, USA	5,363,041
10	Kevin Kisner, USA	5,222,907
11	Zach Johnson, USA	4,998,225
12	Jimmy Walker, USA	4,428,626
13	J.B. Holmes, USA	4,214,994
14	Paul Casey, England	3,936,927
15	Brandt Snedeker, USA	3,870,196
16	Hideki Matsuyama, Japan	3,822,899
17	Brooks Koepka, USA	3,784,287
18	Branden Grace, South Africa	3,752,992
19	Jim Furyk, USA	3,732,664
20	Justin Thomas, USA	3,705,918
21	Danny Lee, New Zealand	3,691,306
22	Matt Kuchar, USA	3,686,910
23	Russell Knox, Scotland	3,686,195
24	Kevin Na, USA	3,673,333
25	Louis Oosthuizen, South Africa	3,462,622
26	Daniel Berger, USA	3,297,467
27	Shane Lowry, Ireland	3,204,114
28	Danny Willett, England	3,203,965
29	Bill Haas, USA	3,198,346
30	Charley Hoffman, USA	3,069,614

POS.	PLAYER, COUNTRY	TOTAL MONEY
31	Robert Streb, USA	3,010,179
32	Marc Leishman, Australia	2,961,597
33	Jason Bohn, USA	2,936,033
34	Scott Piercy, USA	2,879,402
35	Emiliano Grillo, Argentina	2,838,233
36	Sergio Garcia, Spain	2,824,517
37	David Lingmerth, Sweden	2,721,231
38	Andy Sullivan, England	2,679,803
39	Byeong-Hun An, Korea	2,675,643
40	Steven Bowditch, Australia	2,590,290
41	Bernd Wiesberger, Austria	2,487,555
42	Matthew Fitzpatrick, England	2,370,651
43	Victor Dubuisson, France	2,353,093
44	Cameron Tringale, USA	2,340,217
45	Adam Scott, Australia	2,337,918
46	Harris English, USA	2,326,888
47	Chris Kirk, USA	2,296,865
48	Charl Schwartzel, South Africa	2,290,864
49	Russell Henley, USA	2,288,524
50	Chris Wood, England	2,287,056
51	Thongchai Jaidee, Thailand	2,282,326
52	Soren Kjeldsen, Denmark	2,252,623
53	Kiradech Aphibarnrat, Thailand	2,251,392
54	James Hahn, USA	2,243,703
55	Graeme McDowell, N. Ireland	2,223,037
56	Gary Woodland, USA	2,218,457
57	Phil Mickelson, USA	2,191,987
58	Troy Merritt, USA	2,140,088
59	Brendan Steele, USA	2,110,903
60	Anirban Lahiri, India	2,063,631
61	Matt Jones, Australia	2,031,438
62	Keegan Bradley, USA	2,007,302
63	Ryan Palmer, USA	1,981,576
64	Billy Horschel, USA	1,967,651
65	Webb Simpson, USA	1,957,665
66	Ian Poulter, England	1,919,186
67	Kristoffer Broberg, Sweden	1,907,979
68	Francesco Molinari, Italy	1,872,018
69	Nick Watney, USA	1,821,453
70	Daniel Summerhays, USA	1,808,654
71	Brendon Todd, USA	1,806,404
72	Tony Finau, USA	1,805,015
73	Brian Harman, USA	1,793,574
74	Martin Kaymer, Germany	1,787,899
75	Patrick Rodgers, USA	1,763,629
76	Sean O'Hair, USA	1,760,685
77	Alex Cejka, Germany	1,721,791
78	David Hearn, Canada	1,684,860
79	Kevin Chappell, USA	1,674,762
80	Jaco Van Zyl, South Africa	1,664,513
81	Charles Howell, USA	1,649,575
82	Kyung-Tae Kim, Korea	1,631,687
83	Smylie Kaufman, USA	1,631,392
84	Ryan Moore, USA	1,630,345

POS.	PLAYER, COUNTRY	TOTAL MONEY
85	Ben Martin, USA	1,623,742
86	Jamie Donaldson, Wales	1,616,668
87	Fabian Gomez, Argentina	1,580,807
88	Hunter Mahan, USA	1,569,256
89	Boo Weekley, USA	1,557,007
90	Pat Perez, USA	1,552,708
91	Tommy Fleetwood, England	1,546,795
92	Luke Donald, England	1,527,765
93	Matt Every, USA	1,472,600
94	Rory Sabbatini, South Africa	1,438,590
95	Marc Warren, Scotland	1,436,403
96	Ryo Ishikawa, Japan	1,432,733
97	Padraig Harrington, Ireland	1,429,416
98	Jim Herman, USA	1,415,941
99	William McGirt, USA	1,403,615
100	Jason Dufner, USA	1,393,022
101	Will Wilcox, USA	1,375,593
102	Jon Curran, USA	1,351,052
103	James Morrison, England	1,347,347
104	David Howell, England	1,347,176
105	Johnson Wagner, USA	1,339,648
106	Chad Campbell, USA	1,332,715
107	John Senden, Australia	1,313,977
108	Lee Westwood, England	1,304,272
109	George McNeill, USA	1,301,044
110	Scott Pinckney, USA	1,278,347
111	Ross Fisher, England	1,274,338
112	Morgan Hoffmann, USA	1,267,873
113	Thorbjorn Olesen, Denmark	1,265,362
114	Kyle Reifers, USA	1,260,910
115	Sangmoon Bae, Korea	1,253,632
116	Scott Brown, USA	1,226,468
117	Zac Blair, USA	1,221,942
118	Peter Malnati, USA	1,205,601
119	Thomas Pieters, Belgium	1,202,398
120	Greg Owen, England	1,193,578
121	Jason Gore, USA	1,149,817
122	Brendon de Jonge, Zimbabwe	1,142,070
123	Chesson Hadley, USA	1,106,500
124	Shawn Stefani, USA	1,100,036
125	Tyrrell Hatton, England	1,099,597
126	Carl Pettersson, Sweden	1,094,564
127	Patton Kizzire, USA	1,091,933
128	Jerry Kelly, USA	1,083,632
129	Alex Noren, Sweden	1,078,156
130	Jason Kokrak, USA	1,068,759
131	Bryce Molder, USA	1,047,468
132	Lucas Bjerregaard, Denmark	1,047,172
133	George Coetzee, South Africa	1,042,612
134	J.J. Henry, USA	1,040,629
135	Rafa Cabrera-Bello, Spain	1,040,136
136	Joost Luiten, Netherlands	1,022,963
137	Graham DeLaet, Canada	1,017,744
138	Colt Knost, USA	1,006,095

POS.	PLAYER, COUNTRY	TOTAL MONEY
139	Gary Stal, France	991,917
140	Adam Hadwin, Canada	964,921
141	Anthony Wall, England	958,743
142	Steve Wheatcroft, USA	955,720
143	Scott Stallings, USA	951,152
144	David Toms, USA	933,603
145	Camilo Villegas, Colombia	930,626
146	Scott Hend, Australia	924,979
147	Spencer Levin, USA	921,942
148	Gregory Bourdy, France	916,005
149	Eddie Pepperell, England	899,149
150	Kevin Streelman, USA	899,034
151	Alexander Levy, France	895,717
152	Cameron Smith, Australia	892,074
153	Lee Slattery, England	873,431
154	Julien Quesne, France	865,095
155	Thomas Aiken, South Africa	858,701
156	Tom Hoge, USA	855,721
157	Martin Laird, Scotland	843,622
158	Yusaku Miyazato, Japan	831,993
159	Peter Uihlein, USA	829,636
160	Chris Stroud, USA	823,480
161	Marcus Fraser, Australia	817,068
162	Raphael Jacquelin, France	809,772
163	Richie Ramsay, Scotland	797,618
164	Yuta Ikeda, Japan	795,043
165	Yoshinori Fujimoto, Japan	789,140
166	Carlos Ortiz, Mexico	776,629
167	Michael Thompson, USA	775,482
168	Maximilian Kieffer Germany	775,198
169	Fabrizio Zanotti, Paraguay	770,752
170	Whee Kim, Korea	770,284
171	Stewart Cink, USA	769,311
172	Rikard Karlberg, Sweden	766,977
173	Chez Reavie, USA	766,142
174	Freddie Jacobson, Sweden	759,175
175	Pablo Larrazabal, Spain	757,183
176	Jhonattan Vegas, Venezuela	756,704
177	Seung-Yul Noh, Korea	750,468
178	Alejandro Canizares, Spain	748,418
179	Charlie Beljan, USA	747,106
180	Lucas Glover, USA	742,868
181	Shingo Katayama, Japan	740,321
182	Hudson Swafford, USA	738,820
183	Kyoung-Hoon Lee, Korea	737,944
184	Brice Garnett, USA	722,888
185	Benjamin Hebert, France	714,725
186	Jamie Lovemark, USA	714,431
187	Derek Fathauer, USA	714,099
188	Erik Compton, USA	711,959
189	Chad Collins, USA	711,381
190	Brian Davis, England	703,441
191	Graeme Storm, England	702,701
192	Luke Guthrie, USA	699,336

POS.	PLAYER, COUNTRY	TOTAL MONEY
193	Geoff Ogilvy, Australia	697,763
194	Hideto Tanihara, Japan	697,668
195	Ricky Barnes, USA	696,629
196	Sam Saunders, USA	693,377
197	John Huh, USA	691,191
198	Stephen Gallacher, Scotland	688,788
199	Retief Goosen, South Africa	683,678
200	Andres Romero, Argentina	666,834
201	David Horsey, England	664,493
202	Jeff Overton, USA	653,427
203	Prom Meesawat, Thailand	653,105
204	Mark Wilson, USA	650,490
205	Jung-Gon Hwang, Korea	649,276
206	Alex Prugh, USA	629,359
207	Brett Stegmaier, USA	620,284
208	Hiroshi Iwata, Japan	618,268
209	Koumei Oda, Japan	617,158
210	John Peterson, USA	613,021
211	Andrew Loupe, USA	611,932
212	Scott Langley, USA	610,231
213	Brian Stuard, USA	610,139
214	Cameron Percy, Australia	608,918
215	Trevor Fisher, Jr., South Africa	608,407
216	S.J. Park, Korea	597,103
217	Harold Varner, USA	593,712
218	Prayad Marksaeng, Thailand	593,218
219	Tom Gillis, USA	588,090
220	Dawie van der Walt, South Africa	585,420
221	Bo Van Pelt, USA	583,717
222	Richard Green, Australia	578,378
223	Tyrone van Aswegen, South Africa	577,388
224	Romain Wattel, France	576,652
225	Satoshi Kodaira, Japan	576,066
226	Michael Putnam, USA	573,870
227	Vaughn Taylor, USA	573,853
228	Andrew Dodt, Australia	558,925
229	Austin Cook, USA	554,282
230	Wen-Chong Liang, China	552,860
231	Andres Gonzales, USA	535,279
232	Roberto Castro, USA	534,240
233	Aaron Baddeley, Australia	534,037
234	Martin Flores, USA	533,542
235	Blayne Barber, USA	528,702
236	Pelle Edberg, Sweden	514,751
237	Hyung-Sung Kim, Korea	507,849
238	David Lipsky, USA	506,901
239	Jonas Blixt, Sweden	505,079
240	Jorge Campillo, Spain	502,670
241	Eduardo de la Riva, Spain	501,052
242	Michio Matsumura, Japan	500,375
243	Richard Bland, England	498,890
244	I.J. Jang, Korea	491,099
245	Y.E. Yang, Korea	489,245
246	Young-Han Song, Korea	479,777

POS.	PLAYER, COUNTRY	TOTAL MONEY
247	Adam Bland, Australia	469,292
248	Mike Lorenzo-Vera, France	469,290
249	Nathan Holman, Australia	468,494
250	K.J. Choi, Korea	467,451
251	Magnus A. Carlsson, Sweden	456,908
252	Si Woo Kim, Korea	454,861
253	Daisuke Kataoka, Japan	451,944
254	Tiger Woods, USA	448,598
255	Toshinori Muto, Japan	448,043
256	Mark Hubbard, USA	447,621
257	Ken Duke, USA	443,356
258	Morten Orum Madsen, Denmark	441,516
259	Angel Cabrera, Argentina	437,709
260	Martin Piller, USA	431,479
261	Joakim Lagergren, Sweden	430,896
262	Brad Kennedy, Australia	430,188
263	Nick Taylor, Canada	429,407
264	Robert Rock, England	426,554
265	Rod Pampling, Australia	426,347
266	Gregory Havret, France	424,000
267	Jeung-Hun Wang, Korea	419,735
268	Ernie Els, South Africa	415,709
269	Steve Stricker, USA	410,951
270	Mikko Ilonen, Finland	405,876
271	Nicholas Thompson, USA	398,956
272	S.S.P. Chawrasia, India	398,125
273	John Merrick, USA	396,988
274	Ryutaro Nagano, Japan	391,239
275	Taichi Teshima, Japan	390,802
276	Andrew Johnston, England	390,374
277	Billy Hurley, USA	390,066
278	Marcel Siem, Germany	389,775
279	Hao-Tong Li, China	384,797
280	Robert Karlsson, Sweden	381,791
281	D.H. Lee, Korea	381,250
282	Ricardo Gouveia, Portugal	380,981
283	Gonzalo Fernandez-Castano, Spain	379,176
284	Derek Ernst, USA	377,441
285	Thomas Bjorn, Denmark	374,191
286	Michael Hoey, N. Ireland	372,679
287	Kyle Stanley, USA	372,438
288	Henrik Norlander, Sweden	364,897
289	Bronson Burgoon, USA	363,894
290	Jonathan Byrd, USA	363,183
291	Shugo Imahira, Japan	362,063
292	Katsumasa Miyamoto, Japan	355,400
293	David Drysdale, Scotland	355,019
294	Tyler Aldridge, USA	353,748
295	Hyun-Woo Ryu, Korea	347,936
296	Matt Ford, England	346,801
297	Nicolas Colsaerts, Belgium	345,687
298	Mikko Korhonen, Finland	344,661
299	D.A. Points, USA	339,684

POS.	PLAYER, COUNTRY	TOTAL MONEY
300	Felipe Aguilar, Chile	338,823
301	Wade Ormsby, Australia	337,941
302	Bradley Dredge, Wales	335,839
303	John Parry, England	334,866
304	Michael Kim, USA	332,748
305	Thanyakon Khrongpha, Thailand	331,462
306	Edouard Espana, France	328,844
307	Peter Hanson, Sweden	326,576
308	Darren Fichardt, South Africa	325,578
309	Steve Marino, USA	325,300
310	Masahiro Kawamura, Japan	324,270
311	Kyong-Jun Moon, Korea	319,620
312	Tomohiro Kondo, Japan	318,189
313	Michael Hendry, New Zealand	317,972
314	Paul Peterson, USA	316,307
315	Terry Pilkadaris, Australia	315,357
316	Sebastien Gros, France	313,990
317	Max Homa, USA	310,353
318	Robert Dinwiddie, England	309,608
319	Sang-Hyun Park, Korea	308,102
320	Oliver Fisher, England	305,439
321	Paul Lawrie, Scotland	304,008
322	Yuki Inamori, Japan	298,050
323	Dicky Pride, USA	297,381
324	Ryan Fox, New Zealand	296,991
325	Richard T. Lee, Canada	292,747
326	Kelly Kraft, USA	291,135
327	Scott Jamieson, Scotland	290,812
328	Craig Lee, Scotland	289,637
329	Mikael Lundberg, Sweden	288,848
330	Jbe' Kruger, South Africa	288,446
331	Robert Garrigus, USA	288,344
332	Ben Evans, England	288,223
333	Jason Scrivener, Australia	281,559
334	Shane Bertsch, USA	281,480
335	Johan Carlsson, Sweden	280,456
336	Ben Crane, USA	278,896
337	Danny Chia, Malaysia	277,576
338	Hiroyuki Fujita, Japan	276,997
339	Rhein Gibson, Australia	274,849
340	Seve Benson, England	274,713
341	Renato Paratore, Italy	273,774
342	Ashun Wu, China	273,243
343	Daniel Brooks, England	273,034
344	Wes Roach, USA	272,494
345	Tadahiro Takayama, Japan	272,492
346	Matthew Nixon, England	270,618
347	Chris Paisley, England	270,208
348	Tom Lewis, England	266,171
349	Anders Hansen, Denmark	261,589
350	Justin Leonard, USA	260,959

World Money List Leaders

YEAR	PLAYER, COUNTRY	TOTAL MONEY
1966	Jack Nicklaus, USA	$168,088
1967	Jack Nicklaus, USA	276,166
1968	Billy Casper, USA	222,436
1969	Frank Beard, USA	186,993
1970	Jack Nicklaus, USA	222,583
1971	Jack Nicklaus, USA	285,897
1972	Jack Nicklaus, USA	341,792
1973	Tom Weiskopf, USA	349,645
1974	Johnny Miller, USA	400,255
1975	Jack Nicklaus, USA	332,610
1976	Jack Nicklaus, USA	316,086
1977	Tom Watson, USA	358,034
1978	Tom Watson, USA	384,388
1979	Tom Watson, USA	506,912
1980	Tom Watson, USA	651,921
1981	Johnny Miller, USA	704,204
1982	Raymond Floyd, USA	738,699
1983	Seve Ballesteros, Spain	686,088
1984	Seve Ballesteros, Spain	688,047
1985	Bernhard Langer, Germany	860,262
1986	Greg Norman, Australia	1,146,584
1987	Ian Woosnam, Wales	1,793,268
1988	Seve Ballesteros, Spain	1,261,275
1989	David Frost, South Africa	1,650,230
1990	Jose Maria Olazabal, Spain	1,633,640
1991	Bernhard Langer, Germany	2,186,700
1992	Nick Faldo, England	2,748,248
1993	Nick Faldo, England	2,825,280
1994	Ernie Els, South Africa	2,862,854
1995	Corey Pavin, USA	2,746,340
1996	Colin Montgomerie, Scotland	3,071,442
1997	Colin Montgomerie, Scotland	3,366,900
1998	Tiger Woods, USA	2,927,946
1999	Tiger Woods, USA	7,681,625
2000	Tiger Woods, USA	11,034,530
2001	Tiger Woods, USA	7,771,562
2002	Tiger Woods, USA	8,292,188
2003	Vijay Singh, Fiji	8,499,611
2004	Vijay Singh, Fiji	11,638,699
2005	Tiger Woods, USA	12,280,404
2006	Tiger Woods, USA	13,325,949
2007	Tiger Woods, USA	12,902,706
2008	Vijay Singh, Fiji	8,025,128
2009	Tiger Woods, USA	10,998,054
2010	Graeme McDowell, N. Ireland	7,371,586
2011	Luke Donald, England	9,730,870
2012	Rory McIlroy, N. Ireland	11,301,228
2013	Tiger Woods, USA	9,490,217
2014	Rory McIlroy, N. Ireland	10,526,012
2015	Jordan Spieth, USA	12,477,758

Career World Money List

Here is a list of the 50 leading money winners for their careers through the 2015 season. It includes players active on both the regular and senior tours of the world. The World Money List from this and the 49 previous editions of the annual and a table prepared for a companion book, *The Wonderful World of Professional Golf* (Atheneum, 1973) form the basis for this compilation. Additional figures were taken from official records of major golf associations. Conversion of foreign currency figures to U.S. dollars is based on average values during the particular years involved.

POS.	PLAYER, COUNTRY	TOTAL MONEY
1	Tiger Woods, USA	$133,766,975
2	Ernie Els, South Africa	87,684,861
3	Phil Mickelson, USA	85,218,783
4	Vijay Singh, Fiji	83,861,889
5	Jim Furyk, USA	77,405,605
6	Sergio Garcia, Spain	60,758,765
7	Lee Westwood, England	55,967,016
8	Davis Love, USA	54,041,904
9	Justin Rose, England	53,094,112
10	Adam Scott, Australia	52,752,526
11	Padraig Harrington, Ireland	52,586,382
12	Retief Goosen, South Africa	52,034,891
13	Luke Donald, England	51,993,057
14	Bernhard Langer, Germany	49,835,892
15	Rory McIlroy, N. Ireland	49,676,989
16	Colin Montgomerie, Scotland	46,712,467
17	Steve Stricker, USA	45,554,164
18	David Toms, USA	44,307,530
19	Kenny Perry, USA	43,821,323
20	Zach Johnson, USA	43,597,880
21	Fred Couples, USA	41,625,851
22	Ian Poulter, England	41,162,901
23	Matt Kuchar, USA	40,155,292
24	Graeme McDowell, N. Ireland	38,566,781
25	Nick Price, Zimbabwe	37,817,153
26	Stewart Cink, USA	37,687,462
27	Hale Irwin, USA	37,552,948
28	Justin Leonard, USA	37,245,747
29	Robert Allenby, Australia	36,773,699
30	Tom Lehman, USA	36,237,120
31	Mark Calcavecchia, USA	36,152,913
32	K.J. Choi, South Korea	35,946,390
33	Miguel Angel Jimenez, Spain	35,172,122
34	Paul Casey, England	34,866,059
35	Fred Funk, USA	34,788,584
36	Jay Haas, USA	34,203,109
37	Geoff Ogilvy, Australia	33,659,740
38	Darren Clarke, N. Ireland	33,608,163
39	Stuart Appleby, Australia	33,199,673
40	Rory Sabbatini, South Africa	32,933,257

POS.	PLAYER, COUNTRY	TOTAL MONEY
41	Dustin Johnson, USA	31,878,551
42	Tom Kite, USA	31,220,048
43	Jeff Sluman, USA	31,217,988
44	Charles Howell, USA	31,176,306
45	Bubba Watson, USA	31,063,119
46	Mike Weir, Canada	31,025,267
47	Jason Day, Australia	29,987,588
48	Jerry Kelly, USA	29,927,953
49	Mark O'Meara, USA	29,633,188
50	Tim Clark, South Africa	29,505,146

These 50 players have won $2,260,663,129 in their careers.

Women's World Money List

This list includes official earnings on the U.S. LPGA Tour, Ladies European Tour, Japan LPGA Tour, Korea LPGA Tour and Australian Ladies Tour, along with other winnings in established unofficial events when reliable figures could be obtained.

POS.	PLAYER, COUNTRY	TOTAL MONEY
1	Lydia Ko, New Zealand	$2,859,771
2	Inbee Park, Korea	2,750,367
3	In-Gee Chun, Korea	2,149,415
4	Stacy Lewis, USA	1,893,423
5	Bo-Mee Lee, Korea	1,867,976
6	Lexi Thompson, USA	1,863,904
7	Sei Young Kim, Korea	1,844,056
8	So Yeon Ryu, Korea	1,523,583
9	Amy Yang, Korea	1,438,312
10	Shanshan Feng, China	1,419,019
11	Teresa Lu, Taipei	1,303,373
12	Cristie Kerr, USA	1,294,301
13	Ha Na Jang, Korea	1,216,420
14	Hyo Joo Kim, Korea	1,214,387
15	Suzann Pettersen, Norway	1,055,687
16	Morgan Pressel, USA	1,037,794
17	Anna Nordqvist, Sweden	977,743
18	Brittany Lincicome, USA	933,521
19	Jiyai Shin, Korea	918,890
20	Sun-Ju Ahn, Korea	857,084
21	Ayaka Watanabe, Japan	846,933
22	Minjee Lee, Australia	821,121
23	Ji-Hee Lee, Korea	809,019
24	Na Yeon Choi, Korea	808,566
25	Shiho Oyama, Japan	798,209

POS.	PLAYER, COUNTRY	TOTAL MONEY
26	Jin Young Ko, Korea	797,446
27	Sung Hyun Park, Korea	774,920
28	Erika Kikuchi, Japan	769,878
29	Mi Hyang Lee, Korea	752,585
30	Momoko Ueda, Japan	749,849
31	Gerina Piller, USA	727,681
32	Mirim Lee, Korea	681,842
33	Chella Choi, Korea	663,576
34	Yani Tseng, Taipei	648,400
35	Jung-Min Lee, Korea	640,818
36	Jessica Korda, USA	633,741
37	Alison Lee, USA	628,676
38	Jenny Shin, Korea	624,834
39	Ilhee Lee, Korea	619,647
40	Brittany Lang, USA	616,097
41	Misuzu Narita, Japan	605,745
42	Yoon Ji Cho, Korea	593,034
43	Mika Miyazato, Japan	583,141
44	Candie Kung, Taipei	551,640
45	Xi Yu Lin, China	540,332
46	Haru Nomura, Japan	533,579
47	Sandra Gal, Germany	531,961
48	Lizette Salas, USA	531,096
49	Miki Sakai, Japan	530,227
50	Azahara Munoz, Spain	504,100
51	Ritsuko Ryu, Japan	503,194
52	Austin Ernst, USA	503,116
53	Erina Hara, Japan	494,403
54	Angela Stanford, USA	491,777
55	Akane Iijima, Japan	489,818
56	Karine Icher, France	483,627
57	Ariya Jutanugarn, Thailand	482,527
58	Ai Suzuki, Japan	479,786
59	Yumiko Yoshida, Japan	475,141
60	Eun-Hee Ji, Korea	474,706
61	Pornanong Phatlum, Thailand	465,729
62	Seon Woo Bae, Korea	458,207
63	Charley Hull, England	440,717
64	Sakura Yokomine, Japan	431,190
65	Min Sun Kim, Korea	430,061
66	Pernilla Lindberg, Sweden	417,225
67	I.K. Kim, Korea	409,570
68	Kris Tamulis, USA	407,086
69	Carlota Ciganda, Spain	404,849
70	Asako Fujimoto, Japan	399,379
71	Karrie Webb, Australia	394,497
72	Hikari Fujita, Japan	382,711
73	Ha-Neul Kim, Korea	381,876
74	Lala Anai, Japan	378,619
75	Kim Kaufman, USA	372,945
76	Lee-Anne Pace, South Africa	372,328
77	Bo Kyung Kim, Korea	372,181
78	Hae Rym Kim, Korea	363,548

POS.	PLAYER, COUNTRY	TOTAL MONEY
79	Paula Creamer, USA	363,485
80	Rikako Morita, Japan	351,181
81	Michelle Wie, USA	348,918
82	Jane Park, USA	348,673
83	Julieta Granada, Paraguay	348,645
84	Mayu Hattori, Japan	348,061
85	Mi-Jeong Jeon, Korea	347,805
86	Hee Young Park, Korea	347,523
87	Q. Baek, Korea	344,916
88	Jae-Eun Chung, Korea	343,478
89	Sun Young Yoo, Korea	340,324
90	Junko Omote, Japan	339,816
91	Mo Martin, USA	339,205
92	Mariajo Uribe, Colombia	333,993
93	Jaye Marie Green, USA	321,423
94	Maiko Wakabayashi, Japan	315,705
95	Catriona Matthew, Scotland	312,733
96	Yukari Nishiyama, Japan	310,187
97	Sydnee Michaels, USA	309,224
98	Min Song Ha, Korea	307,551
99	Wei-Ling Hsu, Taipei	306,364
100	Hye Youn Kim, Korea	306,230
101	Caroline Masson, Germany	301,666
102	Danielle Kang, USA	292,579
103	Ji Hyun Kim, Korea	291,644
104	Melissa Reid, England	287,574
105	Su Yeon Jang, Korea	286,533
106	Yeun Jung Seo, Korea	285,852
107	Hee-Kyung Bae, Korea	282,209
108	Moriya Jutanugarn, Thailand	281,940
109	Alena Sharp, Canada	272,757
110	MinYoung Lee$_2$, Korea	268,954
111	Serena Aoki, Japan	268,161
112	Yoko Maeda, Japan	262,709
113	Jennifer Song, USA	260,495
114	Jeong Eun Lee, Korea	257,649
115	Nicole Broch Larsen, Denmark	257,106
116	Gwladys Nocera, France	249,332
117	Na-Ri Lee, Korea	248,603
118	Song Yi Ahn, Korea	245,374
119	Hiromi Mogi, Japan	242,984
120	Min Lee, Taipei	241,634
121	Kaori Ohe, Japan	240,767
122	Ji Hyun Oh, Korea	237,950
123	Shin-Ae Ahn, Korea	236,633
124	Kotone Hori, Japan	234,441
125	Christina Kim, USA	234,153
126	Soo-Yun Kang, Korea	234,086
127	Gyeol Park, Korea	222,753
128	Ye Jin Kim, Korea	220,572
129	Megumi Kido, Japan	215,508
130	Kumiko Kaneda, Japan	213,049
131	Yuko Mitsuka, Japan	211,122

POS.	PLAYER, COUNTRY	TOTAL MONEY
132	Ryann O'Toole, USA	208,565
133	Emily Kristine Pedersen, Denmark	203,140
134	Rebecca Artis, Australia	202,254
135	Ji Hyun Kim$_2$, Korea	200,829
136	Ji Young Park, Korea	198,254
137	Saki Nagamine, Japan	198,165
138	Beth Allen, USA	197,490
139	Han Sol Ji, Korea	196,803
140	Ayaka Matsumori, Japan	191,869
141	Rumi Yoshiba, Japan	188,978
142	Mami Fukuda, Japan	188,088
143	Marina Alex, USA	187,414
144	O. Sattaya, Thailand	186,052
145	Maria McBride, Sweden	185,330
146	So Yeon Park, Korea	184,538
147	Seung Hyun Lee, Korea	183,740
148	Juli Inkster, USA	183,489
149	Hee Won Jung, Korea	177,958
150	Ah-Reum Hwang, Korea	176,204
151	Mi Jung Hur, Korea	175,764
152	Hyun Soo Kim, Korea	172,024
153	Kelly Shon, USA	170,895
154	Beatriz Recari, Spain	167,890
155	Phoebe Yao, Taipei	167,635
156	Saiki Fujita, Japan	167,483
157	Marianne Skarpnord, Norway	166,252
158	Min Seo Kwak, Korea	165,982
159	Yuki Ichinose, Japan	164,909
160	Ai Miyazato, Japan	164,446
161	Nanna Koerstz Madsen, Denmark	162,899
162	Ji Hee Kim, Korea	159,541
163	Jeongmin Cho, Korea	158,167
164	Christel Boeljon, Netherlands	157,280
165	Ayako Uehara, Japan	157,253
166	Kotono Kozuma, Japan	156,559
167	Thidapa Suwannapura, Thailand	156,342
168	Ka Ram Choi, Korea	151,542
169	Rui Kitada, Japan	149,099
170	Chae Young Yoon, Korea	144,261
171	Asuka Kashiwabara, Japan	143,328
172	Yuko Fukuda, Japan	143,143
173	Char Young Kim, Korea	141,238
174	Hikari Kawamitsu, Japan	140,623
175	Hannah Burke, England	138,075

Senior World Money List

This list includes official earnings from the U.S. Champions Tour, European Senior Tour and Japan Senior Tour, along with other winnings in established official and unofficial tournaments when reliable figures could be obtained.

POS.	PLAYER, COUNTRY	TOTAL MONEY
1	Bernhard Langer, Germany	$2,385,620
2	Jeff Maggert, USA	2,240,836
3	Colin Montgomerie, Scotland	2,225,737
4	Miguel Angel Jimenez, Spain	1,678,947
5	Billy Andrade, USA	1,589,752
6	Joe Durant, USA	1,445,956
7	Kenny Perry, USA	1,301,955
8	Kevin Sutherland, USA	1,258,015
9	Davis Love, USA	1,212,716
10	Tom Lehman, USA	1,188,128
11	Michael Allen, USA	1,152,625
12	Esteban Toledo, Mexico	1,133,612
13	Scott Dunlap, USA	1,111,250
14	Mark O'Meara, USA	1,107,834
15	Paul Goydos, USA	1,107,081
16	Marco Dawson, USA	1,073,227
17	Lee Janzen, USA	1,014,114
18	Olin Browne, USA	974,665
19	Woody Austin, USA	957,805
20	Duffy Waldorf, USA	953,140
21	Vijay Singh, Fiji	948,241
22	David Frost, South Africa	874,821
23	Bart Bryant, USA	867,779
24	Tom Pernice, Jr., USA	811,321
25	Jeff Sluman, USA	800,954
26	Kirk Triplett, USA	787,296
27	Wes Short, Jr., USA	763,637
28	Fred Couples, USA	729,991
29	Ian Woosnam, Wales	728,730
30	Fred Funk, USA	688,015
31	Jerry Smith, USA	684,702
32	Stephen Ames, Canada	680,040
33	Gene Sauers, USA	650,800
34	Russ Cochran, USA	615,207
35	Peter Senior, Australia	606,590
36	Kiyoshi Murota, Japan	588,416
37	Rod Spittle, Canada	550,908
38	Rocco Mediate, USA	506,784
39	Mark Calcavecchia, USA	491,085
40	Corey Pavin, USA	475,222
41	Jeff Hart, USA	470,902
42	Tom Watson, USA	427,072
43	Scott Hoch, USA	426,187
44	Takeshi Sakiyama, Japan	420,399
45	Tommy Armour, USA	404,271
46	Brian Henninger, USA	401,215

POS.	PLAYER, COUNTRY	TOTAL MONEY
47	John Huston, USA	373,641
48	Grant Waite, New Zealand	366,483
49	Tom Byrum, USA	360,209
50	Loren Roberts, USA	355,045
51	Sandy Lyle, England	342,444
52	Mike Goodes, USA	336,648
53	Scott McCarron, USA	333,148
54	John Cook, USA	327,772
55	Peter Fowler, Australia	326,329
56	Jesper Parnevik, Sweden	311,686
57	Barry Lane, England	307,793
58	Guy Boros, USA	303,375
59	Tsukasa Watanabe, Japan	285,151
60	Roger Chapman, England	267,812
61	Scott Verplank, USA	249,448
62	Jay Don Blake, USA	249,097
63	Steve Lowery, USA	246,373
64	Brad Bryant, USA	243,134
65	Chien-Soon Lu, Taipei	242,156
66	Mark McNulty, Zimbabwe	237,887
67	John Riegger, USA	222,712
68	Steve Jones, USA	222,094
69	Mark Brooks, USA	219,053
70	Jose Coceres, Argentina	217,588
71	Larry Mize, USA	216,825
72	Paul Wesselingh, England	209,074
73	Willie Wood, USA	207,300
74	Brad Faxon, USA	202,204
75	Joey Sindelar, USA	201,920
76	Jay Haas, USA	195,994
77	Steve Pate, USA	193,852
78	Tsuyoshi Yoneyama, Japan	191,438
79	Naoyuki Tamura, Japan	190,186
80	Mark Wiebe, USA	184,516
81	Masahiro Kuramoto, Japan	164,134
82	Gordon Manson, Austria	158,069
83	Kohki Idoki, Japan	150,844
84	Katsumi Kubo, Japan	150,689
85	Takenori Hiraishi, Japan	148,507
86	Frank Esposito, USA	147,709
87	Frankie Minoza, Philippines	143,477
88	Fran Quinn, USA	132,676
89	Nobumitsu Yuhara, Japan	132,011
90	Philip Golding, England	131,385
91	Bob Tway, USA	123,139
92	Tze-Chung Chen, Taipei	122,762
93	Miguel Angel Martin, Spain	116,222
94	Boonchu Ruangkit, Thailand	115,716
95	Skip Kendall, USA	115,062
96	Shinichi Akiba, Japan	114,827
97	Bob Gilder, USA	114,525
98	Dan Forsman, USA	106,914
99	Andre Bossert, Switzerland	104,616
100	Ikuo Shirahama, Japan	103,393

1. The Year in Retrospect

A television commercial leading into the Masters featured Rory McIlroy as a young boy in Northern Ireland. As he developed into a world-class golfer by practicing in the dark and in the rain and in his living room, video images of Tiger Woods winning championships played in the background. The boy was watching. He was mesmerized and inspired, and the spot ended with McIlroy blossoming into a star and teeing off with Woods in the final round of a World Golf Championship. The title of the commercial was "Ripple," and the concept summed up the year in professional golf because it portrayed the impact Woods had on the next generation.

Only it wasn't just McIlroy, who wound up playing a supporting role.

Consider where golf was at the end of 2014. He was coming off two straight major championships and was No. 1 with an average that was nearly three points greater than 39-year-old Henrik Stenson. Yes, this surely was the heir to Woods. The broad question going into 2015 was not who was the best in golf, it was a competition to see who would be best suited as McIlroy's chief foil. McIlroy won four times, including a World Golf Championship, and he captured the Race to Dubai on the European Tour for the second straight season. And he ended the year at No. 3 in the world.

The envy of golf turned out to be Jordan Spieth, the 22-year-old Texan whose will to win is largely derived from his hatred of losing. Spieth became only the fourth player since 1960 to win the first two legs of the Grand Slam, joining Arnold Palmer, Jack Nicklaus and Tiger Woods. He won five times and set a PGA Tour record with just over $12 million in earnings. And that doesn't include the $10 million bonus from winning the FedExCup. Spieth was the No. 1 player in the world — just barely.

Chasing him the entire summer, and catching him briefly in August and September, was Jason Day, the 28-year-old Australian who tumbled to the ground at the U.S. Open with symptoms of vertigo in a frightful scene, only to get back up and appear to be close to unbeatable over the next three months when he won four times in seven events, including his first major in the PGA Championship at Whistling Straits where he became the first player to finish 20 under par in a major.

For the first time since the Official World Golf Ranking began in 1986, the year ended with the top three players all in their 20s. There was never a time in three decades of the World Ranking where No. 1 was a game of musical chairs. It changed hands six times in six weeks from Spieth to McIlroy to Spieth to McIlroy to Day to Spieth. So close were these three young stars in points that, at one stage, McIlroy twice returned to No. 1 without playing and Spieth got back to No. 1 after missing the cut. Spieth, by virtue of his victory in the Tour Championship, held the top spot for the final two months of the year, knowing that No. 1 was up for grabs in the 2016 opener. Stay tuned.

One part of the commercial was accurate. It all evolved around Tiger Woods. His game, his future, everything about the guy who has been the face of golf for 20 years never looked more muddled. More on that later.

What became abundantly clear was the massive ripple effect he had on the world of golf. Most evident over two decades was the impact Woods had on television ratings, on prize money and on bringing more attention to the sport. No other player moved the needle since the early days of Arnold Palmer. But for the first time, at least clearly, golf began to see his effect on the competition.

"He was the inspiration for us to go out and try to be the best that we could be," McIlroy said. "You get a lot of guys that are my age and they'd say the same thing. He was a hero to us growing up, and that's why you have so many guys in their 20s that are so good right now."

And it was a long list that stretched beyond the so-called "New Big Three." Day was watching Woods in Australia. Hideki Matsuyama was watching in Japan. "Tiger was my hero growing up and still remains the man to me. When I would watch him on TV in Japan, I can remember thinking that he was so good and so cool and his swing was so pure," Matsuyama said.

Perhaps most telling was a comment from Patrick Reed, who idolized Woods so much that he wears black trousers and a red shirt on Sunday. Reed was asked how he tried to copy Woods. "Be stubborn. Focus on what you're doing and not anyone around you," Reed said. "You could see it just by looking at him in the eyes. If looks could kill you, he would literally kill you. It's not because he's not a good guy. He was just so focused and determined to play well. And that's what I'm trying to do."

The stage for 2015 was set early in the year. McIlroy was a runner-up at the Abu Dhabi HSBC Golf Championship, and then he won the Omega Dubai Desert Classic two weeks later to assert himself as the player to beat. His World Ranking average was 11.66, and Stenson was next at 7.61. Day was at No. 8 with a 5.64 average, and Spieth was another spot behind at 5.52. That same week and 11 times zones away, Woods made his 2015 debut in the Waste Management Phoenix Open by shooting a career-worst 82 to miss the cut by 12 shots. A week later, Day won for the first time of the year in a playoff at the Farmers Insurance Open at Torrey Pines, where Woods again had atrocious short-game problems and withdrew in the opening round because of what he described as his "glutes" not activating. The following week, he took an indefinite break. A month later, Spieth's slow start to the year ended with a playoff victory in the Valspar Championship when he finished with two clutch pars in regulation to get into a playoff and then won on the third extra hole at Innisbrook by pouring in a 30-foot putt.

No one was talking about a "Big Three." The first three months of the PGA Tour featured 14 tournaments and 14 different winners. On the European Tour, the only repeat winners were Andy Sullivan of England and Anirban Lahiri of India, neither of whom started the year in the top 50 in the world. In retrospect, those three months were the prelude to a drama that featured a revolving door of protagonists and ultimately defined a massive shift to a new generation.

ACT I

Even at such a young age, McIlroy already was accustomed to the spot-light from his record score in winning the 2011 U.S. Open, another major at the PGA Championship in 2012 and ending 2014 with back-to-back majors. Given his talent, and his power, it was not hyperbole to suggest he was equipped to match Woods' feat as the only players to sweep the four majors as Woods did from the 2000 U.S. Open through the 2001 Masters. This was Rory's world. As much attention as Woods commanded through-out the course of his career, even his absence didn't detract from McIlroy's road to the Masters and his quest for the career Grand Slam, and perhaps winning them all. He had either won or finished second in eight of his last 13 starts worldwide.

So during the pro-am at the Honda Classic, where McIlroy made his American debut, one television analyst mentioned what so many were think-ing: How can he not win the Masters? Who is capable of beating him? "This is the position I want to be in. And I want to be in it as long as I can," McIlroy said, clearly relishing his role as the player to beat. His opening tee shot was out of play, and two days later McIlroy had missed the cut. "I wouldn't worry and read too much into it. Rory has been by far the best player in the world for the last year or so," Luke Donald said.

Even so, frustration began to set in a week later at the WGC-Cadillac Championship at Trump Doral. Already 11 shots behind after the opening round, McIlroy pulled a three iron into the water to the left of the par-five eighth hole, took a few steps and then hurled the club into the middle of the lake. Donald Trump, no stranger to the grandiose moment, hired div-ers to retrieve the club and made a grand presentation of the three iron to McIlroy on the final day. He salvaged a top-10 at Doral, and then tied for 11th in his debut at Bay Hill for the Arnold Palmer Invitational.

Sticking to the plan, McIlroy took the next three weeks off to prepare for the Masters. It was the seventh time in the last 20 years that a player had a shot at winning three straight majors — Woods three times (at the 2007 Masters, the 2002 British Open and the 2000 PGA Championship), Padraig Harrington (2009 Masters), Phil Mickelson (2006 U.S. Open) and Nick Price (1995 Masters). And when Woods disclosed that he had solved his short-game woes and would return to competition at the Masters, Augusta National braced itself for a week of golf's two biggest stars.

Spieth went along without too much attention. After his remarkable rookie season, he went without a victory on the PGA Tour until a strong finish to 2014. He shot 63 in the final round to win the Australian Open, and then he crushed a strong field at Isleworth in the Hero World Challenge to win by 10 shots. That did more for his own psyche than to persuade anyone that he might be golf's next big thing. If anything, he became the leading contender to challenge McIlroy. The victory in the Valspar Championship was impressive, though mildly overlooked. Although the Copperhead course is regarded as among the best tournament courses in Florida, it gets the least amount of hype stacked up against a World Golf Championship, the Honda Classic and Palmer's event. But the strength of Spieth was evident. He saved par from a nasty spot in the rough above the 17th green and got up and down by making a 10-foot putt in regulation to join a three-man playoff, and then he closed it out with a 30-foot putt to beat Reed and Sean O'Hair.

Spieth also had a pre-Masters plan, though this was more about his Texas roots than preparing for a shot at history. Jimmy Walker had the Valero Texas Open seemingly wrapped up until Spieth made every putt coming down the stretch and put a scare in Walker. A week later in the Shell Houston Open, Spieth went into the final round with the lead and had to scramble to get into a playoff. He made bogey from the bunker on the 18th in the first extra hole, and J.B. Holmes went on to win over Johnson Wagner. In his three events leading to the Masters, Spieth won and was runner-up twice.

All it took was one round at Augusta National for Spieth to do the unthinkable — he managed to make the Masters about more than just the quest of McIlroy and the return of Woods. He opened with a 64 — the best opening round at Augusta National in 19 years — and no one was closer than three shots to him the rest of the week. He became the second-youngest Masters champion behind Woods (who was five months younger when he won in 1997), and a bogey on the 72nd hole forced him to share the scoring record with Woods at 18-under 270. McIlroy's bid was over quickly, thanks to Spieth. He was 12 shots behind going into the weekend and managed to finish fourth. McIlroy was still No. 1 and Spieth was a far margin behind him. But it became apparent with a 21-year-old in a green jacket that McIlroy had a clear threat.

ACT II

Spieth showed his mettle a week later when he contended in the RBC Heritage at Hilton Head while running on fumes. The day after winning the Masters for his first major, he went to New York for a media tour that featured no fewer than 12 interviews in 12 hours on television and radio. His head still dizzy when he arrived on the sleepy South Carolina beach resort, he opened with a 74 and looked certain to miss the cut. The next day, he answered with a 62, which at the time tied his career low on the PGA Tour, and contended through the weekend until fading to a 70 and a tie for 11th. And then he headed home to Dallas for a week of rest.

For McIlroy, his failure to complete the Grand Slam at Augusta National (and a shot at holding all four professional majors at the same time) was easier to take from Spieth's runaway. McIlroy knew a green jacket would have to wait over the final two rounds. The golf world was filled with talk about Spieth's first major and the palpable challenge to McIlroy's reign. Such is the sporting society of this generation. Whatever just happened today makes yesterday feel longer ago than it really was. If that's the case, the next two weeks went a long way toward reminding fans that this McIlroy kid was still pretty good.

They next met in San Francisco for the WGC - Cadillac Match Play — not on the golf course at Harding Park, but in the lunch room. Spieth was having lunch with his agent when McIlroy walked by and congratulated the Texan on his Masters victory. The conversation was easy, just as one would expect from a couple of golfers in their 20s. Spieth said he would love to support McIlroy in the Irish Open that year except that his schedule wouldn't allow, and he noted that McIlroy was about to embark on a hectic time of his own.

McIlroy let slip that he had added the Wells Fargo Championship at Quail Hollow, site of his first PGA Tour victory, which would mean five straight weeks and then a short break before the U.S. Open. That paid dividends for McIlroy in the short term.

In the previous 16 years of golf's most fickle event, the Match Play has never delivered No. 1 against No. 2, so the only way McIlroy and Spieth could face off would be to reach the final match. Under a new format this year, that was even more difficult. The 64 players were broken into 16 four-player pools over three days. McIlroy nearly didn't make it out of his group, surviving by making a 20-foot birdie putt on the 17th hole, winning the 18th hole with a birdie and then disposing of Billy Horschel in 20 holes. Spieth wasn't so fortunate. Lee Westwood make a key birdie on the 17th and held on to beat the Masters champion on the 18th hole. McIlroy had two more close calls against Paul Casey and Jim Furyk before breezing to his second WGC title by beating Gary Woodland.

The only disappointment for McIlroy was a weather delay that forced him to cancel a quick flight over to Las Vegas to watch the Manny Pacquiao-Floyd Mayweather Jr. fight. Oddly enough, the best viewing was in the press center. McIlroy and his girlfriend sat among a dozen reporters watching the fight, which would have been an anomaly with previous world No. 1s. McIlroy is comfortable in any company, and his victory seemed to be the perfect answer to Spieth winning the Masters.

"I think everyone — not just me, but everyone on tour — was inspired seeing Jordan do what he did at Augusta," McIlroy said. "This is the start of a nice little run of golf for me, and I wanted to come out and play well and increase my lead in the world rankings ... and keep going. But it's always nice to have people pushing you. And I feel like he's one of the guys doing that right now."

The tables turned a week later at The Players Championship. Instead of McIlroy being questioned about a challenge from Spieth, it was Spieth trying to downplay any rivalry. He noted that the gap between McIlroy and Spieth in the World Ranking was equal to the gap between Spieth and the eighth-ranked player. As for McIlroy, he practically yawned when asked about Spieth's challenge. "Last year it was Rickie [Fowler]. This year it's Jordan, might be someone else, could have been Tiger. There's been four or five rivalries over the past year. So it doesn't really do anything for me."

The PGA Tour put McIlroy and Spieth in the same group. Spieth opened with a 75 to match his worst score of the year, and he wound up missing the cut by three shots. McIlroy broke par all four rounds and tied for eighth, four shots out of a playoff. Spieth was upset with his game, though it was clear he could feel the attention of living up to his part in his growing rivalry. "I don't believe in this whole rivalry thing. I don't believe I'm on his level," Spieth said. "Rory McIlroy is far ahead of any younger players, including myself. I never thought there was a rivalry. He's a good player, and I have to work hard to get up to that level."

If that wasn't enough, McIlroy headed up to North Carolina the next week, shot a career-low 61 in the third round and blew away the field for a seven-shot victory. What rivalry?

Little could McIlroy know, that would be his best golf for the next six months. As the defending champion of the BMW PGA Championship at Wentworth, he missed the cut in the European Tour flagship event. The next week at Royal County Down, where he was host of his national championship, McIlroy missed another cut at the Irish Open. For all his greatness, McIlroy is prone to having spells of missed cuts. That's part of his tour DNA, different from a player like Woods. It typically is no cause of alarm, though it wasn't the best form to be taking to Chambers Bay for the U.S. Open. "I'd rather, in a six-tournament period, have three wins and three missed cuts than six top-10s," he said. "Volatility in golf is actually a good thing. If your good weeks are really good, it far outweighs the bad weeks."

Turns out the U.S. Open was an ordinary week. He flirted with a great comeback on Sunday, but ultimately tied for ninth, five shots behind Spieth. Yes, there was a rivalry. McIlroy and Spieth not only were Nos. 1 and 2 in the world, they had won the last four majors. The last time two players had split the last four was in 1971-72 by Lee Trevino and Jack Nicklaus.

ACT III

The year began to take shape at Chambers Bay in two respects. Spieth was motoring toward a Grand Slam, which not many would have predicted at the start of the year. And Woods was sinking to depths no one imagined. Just two weeks before the U.S. Open, the five-time winner of the Memorial shot a career-worst 85 in the third round. If there was any thought it was just an anomaly, he opened with an 80 at the U.S. Open. In the first 19 seasons of his PGA Tour career, Woods had only one round in the 80s — the 81 in wind and rain off Muirfield in the 2002 British Open. Halfway through his 20th season, he added three more.

The real shocker was early in the year at the Waste Management Phoenix Open. When he returned from a three-month break at the end of 2014 to let his body fully heal and to get stronger, Woods hit some curiously bad chip shots — some he duffed, some he bladed — and he tied for last. Chalk that up to rust. In what appeared to be a stock pitch, he used a four iron to bump it along the ground. He shot 82 in the second round and attributed his short-game woes to working with a new swing consultant and getting rid of old habits. But a week later at Torrey Pines, where he is an eight-time winner as a pro, nothing changed. Woods walked off the North Course after 12 holes and in a bizarre scene in the parking lot, surrounded by reporters, he said his "glutes" didn't stay "activated." A week later, Woods said he was taking time off from the game because his scores were unacceptable.

He didn't return until the Masters and, remarkably, showed few signs of any problems with his short game. It really was a stunning turnaround. After taking two months off, he tied for 17th at the Masters. Golf, however, requires a more complete game and Woods never was in contention — not at Augusta, not at The Players, not anywhere. He missed the cut in three straight majors. He went 11 straight rounds without breaking 70. And he failed to qualify for the FedExCup Playoffs.

In September, Woods announced he had another back surgery to alleviate pain. And in October, he revealed a third back surgery that would keep him out indefinitely. By the end of the year, at his Hero World Challenge in early December, he still had not started rehabilitation and said he could do little more than walk. And for the first time, Woods sounded resigned that his best golf might be behind him. Woods said he wants to play again and that anything he accomplishes the rest of his career "will be gravy."

For the players at the top — McIlroy and Spieth — their seasons suddenly were headed in different directions. The showdown in their budding rivalry figured to take place at St. Andrews in golf's oldest championship. Spieth was trying to match Ben Hogan as the only player to win the first three professional majors of the year. McIlroy was the defending champion at the Open Championship, and he tied a major championship record with a 63 the last time the Open was held on the Old Course. It just never got that far. Just two weeks before his title defense, McIlroy posted an Instagram of his feet up and a black air cast around his left ankle. He was in Northern Ireland kicking around a soccer ball with friends when he turned over his ankle, fell to the ground and began writhing in pain. He ruptured tendons in his ankle and, while he avoided surgery, he missed out on the Scottish Open, the Open Championship and another title defense at the WGC-Bridgestone Invitational a week before the final major. "It's hugely disappointing, especially with him and Jordan and everything that's going on," Graeme McDowell said.

Spieth had a lot on his plate, though he showed plenty of calm amid a torrent of talk about his bid for the Grand Slam. He had only seen St. Andrews when he was in Scotland for the Walker Cup in 2011. Instead of going over early, however, Spieth stuck to his plan. The John Deere Classic is where he won his first PGA Tour event in 2013. It gave him a sponsor's exemption and he was intent on rewarding the little tournament in Middle America by honoring his commitment to play. More than just play, he went early for a stop in Iowa to help Zach Johnson with a charity event. Spieth didn't show much charity at the TPC Deere Run. After opening with a 71, leading to speculation he would mail it in so he could get to Scotland by the weekend, Spieth responded with rounds of 64-61 to take the lead, and he wound up winning in a playoff over Tom Gillis, with Johnson finishing one shot behind.

Spieth arrived at St. Andrews on Monday and headed out to the golf course to shake off the jet lag and get ready. And he put to rest the notion that he hurt his chances at a historic Grand Slam by playing the John Deere. His fourth victory of the year gave him even more confidence. He was tied for the lead at the Open Championship with two holes to play. And he wound up one shot out of the three-man playoff. A strong effort, indeed.

Another player who missed the Open playoff by one shot didn't get nearly as much attention, although that putt Day left short on the 18th green turned into the catalyst for his remarkable push at the end of the year. For the first half of the season, Day looked like he might be having another one-and-done year. For all his ability, and his relentless work ethic, Day had never won more than one time in any year. He shot 81 at The Players and missed the cut. He missed another cut at the Memorial, where he makes his home.

The sign of life returned not long after Day was taken away from Chambers Bay in an ambulance. Playing his final hole of the second round in the U.S. Open, Day wobbled and then collapsed on the ninth tee with what turned out to be symptoms of vertigo. Spieth helped him to his feet, Day finished the round and then returned on Saturday. He felt nauseous. He had to wait for his eyes to stop dancing before he could swing. And yet he somehow managed to make three birdies on the final four holes for a 68 that gave him a share of the lead going into the final day. "That was the greatest round I've ever watched," said Colin Swatton, his caddie and longtime coach. Day couldn't keep up in the final round and tied for ninth, but he showed what was in his heart.

After a month off, he challenged every step of the way at St. Andrews and again had a share of the 54-hole lead. He looked devastated, however, when a 30-foot putt to get into the playoff came up short. What he gained that week was belief. "All those major championships I lost, it was built-up scar tissue," he said. "Scar tissue can be bad. But it can also heal and be good for you. No matter what happened that whole week, I felt calm. There was no stress. I was patient with myself. No matter what happened, I was letting it unfold and not forcing the issue."

As far as that McIlroy-Spieth rivalry, however, Day began to force himself into the conversation.

ACT IV

The first time he contended in a major, Day simply ran out of holes in the 2011 Masters. He had back-to-back runner-up finishes that year in the majors, though the U.S. Open at Congressional was simply a matter of playing as well as anyone not named Rory McIlroy, who won by eight shots. He couldn't keep up with Adam Scott and Angel Cabrera in the 2013 Masters, finishing two shots out of their playoff. A bogey on the 18th hole at Merion ended his hopes in the U.S. Open that year. And then he left a putt short at St. Andrews to get into a playoff. If there was a lingering hangover, there was an immediate answer. Six days later, the Aussie held off Bubba Watson with a birdie on the final hole to win the RBC Canadian Open, making him a multiple winner for the first time in his career.

And he was just getting started. Day has idolized Woods since he was a kid, so it was particularly meaningful when Woods sent out a tweet before the PGA Championship still had a few holes remaining, "Game over, very happy for Jason. Great dude and well deserved." The fact Woods was watching in some respects brought Day's journey full circle on the PGA Tour. As a 20-year-old rookie in 2008, he had big goals, big talent and some big talk. In an interview with Australian writers going into his rookie season, he was asked if Woods was aware of him. "I can't say for sure, but I think he is. If I was him, I would be," Day said. "I watch everyone. He watches a lot of golf. He has so much time. He played 16 events — what does he do with his time? He'd be aware of me. He'd be saying, 'Here's another kid coming up.'"

It was a slow climb, to be sure. It took three years for him to win, followed by three more years with more injuries than victories. And when he ended the drought at the WGC-Accenture Match Play Championship in Arizona, Day revealed a hand injury that slowed him the rest of the year. So consider the vertigo symptoms at Chambers Bay, and it looked like this would be yet another setback. Instead, he charged forward and brought the "Big Three" back into golf's lexicon.

The FedExCup began in 2007 and was largely misunderstood thanks to some aggressive promotion by the PGA Tour. It wasn't meant to be bigger than the majors, nor would it determine the tour's best player. It was a separate competition at the end of the year that was weighted toward players who performed the best and most consistently. Throw out the years that Woods won — 2007 and 2009 when he was in a class by himself — and this year's four-tournament "Playoffs" reflected the year. Spieth and Day were Nos. 1 and 2, and McIlroy was lagging behind from having missed two months. It was a chance for McIlroy to catch up, and barring that, it was set up as a clash between Spieth and Day.

It sure looked like a one-man show when Day won The Barclays at Plainfield by six shots, and then he blew away the field at Conway Farms north of Chicago to win by seven shots and grab the No. 1 seed going into the finale at the Tour Championship. Rickie Fowler won the other playoff event, the Deutsche Bank Championship at the TPC Boston, and so he, too, was in the mix for the $10 million bonus. As for Spieth? He missed the cut at Plainfield, and then he missed the cut at the TPC Boston. Spieth feared he was losing some of his swagger. Day's victory in the BMW Championship moved him to No. 1 in the world for the first time, making him the third Australian to reach the top behind Greg Norman and Adam Scott. And he led the PGA Tour with five victories. McIlroy, meanwhile, never got any momentum. He skipped The Barclays because he didn't want to play too much golf while coming back from ankle surgery, and he never seriously challenged in Boston or Chicago. He was No. 11 in the FedExCup going into the Tour Championship, though he still had another end to his season in Europe. For him, this was not the finish line.

The Tour Championship not only decided the FedExCup, it raised the debate over Player of the Year. With two majors, Spieth was looked upon as an easy choice (he already had won the points-based award from the PGA of America, which gives a bonus for multiple majors). He had won four times and two majors. No PGA Tour member had ever won two majors and not been voted Player of the Year by his peers. But what if Day were to win the Tour Championship? That would give him six wins, plus a major, with three victories in the FedExCup Playoffs against the strongest field? It almost was a referendum on the FedExCup, and how the players measured its value. Ultimately, however, it became a moot point. Day hit his tee shot out-of-bounds on the fifth hole of the tournament, made triple bogey, and never had any momentum the rest of the week.

Spieth, meanwhile, surged to a one-shot lead with a 68 on Saturday, and his putter was never hotter than the final round of the season. He closed with a 69 for a four-shot victory that gave him all the trimmings — a fifth PGA Tour victory, the Vardon Trophy for lowest adjusted scoring average, the Arnold Palmer Award for winning the money title with a record $12,030,465, and the Jack Nicklaus Award as Player of the Year on the PGA Tour. Throw in the $10 million bonus, and Spieth made $1 million for each of his 22 years on earth. "It's the greatest season I've ever had, obviously. But it's one where I believe we took our game on course and off course to a level that I didn't think would be possible at different times in my life," he said.

There was no denying the new Big Three because of who they are and what they had done. The five victories and two majors by Spieth. The five victories and one major by Day. The four victories and No. 1 ranking for most of the year (based on his two majors the year before) by McIlroy. Plus, they all were No. 1 at various points, and in a futuristic look at the world of golf, they all were in their 20s. Day was asked a few times toward the end of the season if he felt like an old man at 27. In some corners, however, there were suggestions that maybe this was more of a Big Four. This suggestion was based on age more than ranking. What about Rickie Fowler?

The Players Championship has been mentioned as a "fifth major" for years now, though it has been established that there are only four majors. The respect for the biggest event on the biggest tour is clear, and what Fowler did at the TPC Sawgrass was a major performance. The timing could not have been better. A golf magazine ran its annual survey — an anonymous poll of players — on a variety of topics which included, "Who is the most overrated player?" It was a tie between Fowler and Ian Poulter. Both are all about fashion, and the feeling from these anonymous players must have been they are not winning enough. The survey came out a week before The Players, and Fowler gave the best response possible. In arguably the most dynamic conclusion to any event in golf, Fowler went birdie-eagle-birdie-birdie to get into a three-man playoff. He took on the perilous flag tucked to the right of the island green on the par-three 17th for another birdie. Still tied with Kevin Kisner after the three-hole playoff, they went back to the 17th for sudden death and Fowler again took dead aim at the flag and stuffed it to five feet. Think about it. Fowler took six shots to play the 17th hole on Sunday of The Players Championship, which is not unusual — except that he played it three times. It was his first PGA Tour victory in three years, and it was just the start.

Two months later, Fowler birdied the last two holes to win the Aberdeen Asset Management Scottish Open at Gullane. And then he put himself into the hunt for the $10 million FedExCup bonus when he rolled in a 40-foot birdie putt on the 14th hole that allowed him to make up a two-shot deficit and beat Henrik Stenson in the Deutsche Bank Championship. Fowler had only two victories worldwide in his five years as a pro, and ended this year with three victories.

Oddly enough, he was lacking in the majors. So one year he was winless and yet finished in the top five at all four majors, and the next year he had a career-best three victories and never seriously challenged in any of the majors. If he finds a way to put those seasons together, look out. Still, it was premature to link him with the other three, and Fowler was aware of this. "I feel like to be in the same conversation I need to get a major to at least have some sort of credentials to be there," he said. "The ultimate goal is to be the best player in the world. I obviously have some pretty tough competition out there."

Fowler was among 25 players — men and women, young and old — who won at least three times on various tours around the world in 2015. Among men on the major tours, Kyung-Tae Kim of South Korea won five times on the Japan Golf Tour, while Fowler won three times and Andy Sullivan of England won three times on the European Tour.

Perhaps more startling about 2015 was the quality of players who didn't win at all. One could almost say that represented a "Big Three" of its own. It starts with Henrik Stenson, who was No. 2 in the world going into the year and finished at No. 5. So it wasn't a bad year, rather a frustrating one. Stenson had a two-shot lead going into the final round of the Arnold Palmer Invitational and finished second. He closed with a 65, not enough to beat Pablo Larrazabal in the BMW International Open in Germany. And then he began the FedExCup Playoffs with consecutive runner-up finishes in The Barclays and Deutsche Bank Championship. He never had a chance at The Barclays because Jason Day pulled away on the back nine and won by six. What stung was the Deutsche Bank Championship, where a tee shot into the water on the 16th hole gave Fowler the opening he needed. Either way, the runner-up finishes were starting to pile up. Stenson added yet another one at the Tour Championship in the FedExCup finale. If someone other than Spieth had won at East Lake, there's a chance Stenson could have won the FedExCup without ever having won a tournament. He closed out the year with a sixth runner-up finish at the Nedbank Challenge. For his efforts, he had to settle for $6,287,540 to finish at No. 7 on the world money list. So it wasn't a total loss. He just didn't win. "With the chances I've had this year, to be winless is a little disappointing, but all in all, it's been a solid year," he said. "I've got to look at the good results, the amount of World Ranking points and all the rest of it."

At least he was in good company. Phil Mickelson didn't come close to cracking the top 10 until he worked some of his magic at the Masters, offered a brief challenge to Spieth on the back nine Sunday and finished second. It never got much better the rest of the way. He had good results at the Wells Fargo Championship and the FedEx St. Jude Classic. He disappeared quickly at the U.S. Open, never really got into the mix at the other two majors and failed to get to East Lake for the Tour Championship for the second straight year.

His only consolation was getting on the Presidents Cup team for the Americans. Mickelson has not missed a Presidents Cup or a Ryder Cup since 1993, and he never had to rely on a captain's pick since 1994 when Presidents Cup captain Arnold Palmer chose him and Jay Haas. That was so long ago that Haas was now captain of the Presidents Cup in South Korea. He took Mickelson at No. 30 — the lowest anyone has been in the standings to get a pick — and said it was largely because all the players wanted him. Mickelson lived up to the pick by going 3-0-1. Even so, he went into 2016 have gone 49 tournaments worldwide over more than two years without winning. The last trophy he held was that silver claret jug at Muirfield in the summer of 2013.

The other member of this not-so-illustrious group was Adam Scott, who only a year ago had risen to No. 1 in the world. The former Masters champion surprised everyone when he turned up for his first event of the year at the WGC - Cadillac Championship using a conventional putter. Scott faced enormous attention in 2015 because it was the final year before the new rule that bans the anchored stroke used for the long putter. Scott tied for fourth at Doral and all was well. A week later, however, he missed the cut in the Valspar Championship when he missed four putts inside five feet and shot 75 in the second round. That ended the longest active cut streak on the PGA. He had gone 45 events on the PGA Tour — and 57 worldwide — without missing a cut, dating to the Byron Nelson Championship in May 2012. Not to worry. These things happen, Scott reasoned. But when he finished in the middle of the pack at Bay Hill the following week, and with the majors looming, Scott decided to go back to the long putter. It didn't help. He went three months without being a factor in any tournament, and only at the U.S. Open at Chambers Bay — coincidentally, the worst greens all year in America — did he find a spark, at least for one round. He closed with a 64 to tie for fourth, two shots behind Spieth.

One reason for Scott being a poster boy for the long putter was the timing. He never fared well in the majors, but the year he switched to the long putter (2011), he made a strong bid at the Masters, the next year he was runner-up at the Open Championship at Royal Lytham & St. Annes, and the following year he won the Masters. But it was in 2013 that Geoff Ogilvy once said of his friend's putting, "The long putter doesn't make Adam a great putter. It just makes his bad days less bad." What hurt Scott this year was that he putted poorly even with the long putter, and thus wasted an entire summer when he could have been making the switch. He changed back over to conventional for the Presidents Cup, and while he missed some short putts (those always make for good TV), he buried Rickie Fowler in singles.

Scott finished one shot behind Justin Thomas at the CIMB Classic in Malaysia, tied for second in the Australian Open, and put up a good fight for two days until tying for 10th in the Hero World Challenge at Albany in the Bahamas, where he lives. That was his last tournament. He went without a victory anywhere in the world for the first time since his first year as a professional in 2000.

An even bigger surprise among those who didn't win: Stacy Lewis. The LPGA Tour was slightly ahead of the curve when it came to the Big Three. Lewis and Inbee Park were the best in women's golf, and then New Zealand teenager Lydia Ko came along and captured the CME Race to the Globe as a 17-year-old in 2014. The year ended with Lewis, Park and Ko as the only LPGA Tour players to surpass $2 million in earnings. That set the stage for another battle in 2015, and it didn't disappoint.

Ko won the ISPS Handa Women's Australian Open in the third event of the year. Two weeks later, Park answered by winning the HSBC Women's Champions in Singapore. And at the first major of the season at the ANA Inspiration in Rancho Mirage, California, Lewis was primed to capture another major. Brittany Lincicome had other plans. She made an eagle on the par-five 18th at Mission Hills to pull even with Lewis, who missed a birdie putt just inside 15 feet for the win. They returned to the 18th in a playoff, and Lewis had two more chances from nearly the same line. She missed from 15 feet. She missed from 12 feet. On her fourth time playing the hole, Lewis came up short from a sand-filled divot, chipped to 12 feet and missed her par putt, and Lincicome won with two putts from 10 feet. It was Lincicome's second leap into Poppie's Pond.

"It just wasn't quite meant to be today," Lewis said. Little did she know, it wasn't meant to be the rest of the year. That was her third runner-up finish already, and it was only April. Three more would follow.

Instead, it became a show between Park and Ko for so much of the season, along with some great golf by LPGA Tour rookie Sei Young Kim, who won three times. Ko won for the second time in the year at the Swinging Skirts LPGA Classic at Lake Merced just south of San Francisco. Ko celebrated her 18th birthday on Friday, and two days later made an eight-foot birdie putt to get into a playoff with Morgan Pressel. Ko won with a birdie on the second extra hole. It was her second straight year winning the tournament. "At her age, she plays with so much poise and calmness I don't think you see from other kids her age," Pressel said, pausing before she added with a smile, "I guess she's not a kid anymore."

For a number of years, however, age was becoming a non-issue in women's golf. Michelle Wie was competing for majors at 15. Pressel won a major at 18, while Yani Tseng, Hyo Joo Kim and Lexi Thomson won majors at 19. Charley Hull of England was the youngest to play the Solheim Cup in 2013 at age 17. Even at Lake Merced, 17-year-old Brooke Henderson of Canada was on the leaderboard all week. So was it really asking too much for Ko to hurry up and win a major?

She had to hurry up and wait. Park answered Ko's victory in San Francisco by winning the following week in Texas, but where the South Korean really set herself apart was winning the KPMG Women's PGA Championship at Westchester Country Club, and then Park won at Turnberry in the Ricoh Women's British Open for her second major of the year, even if this one came two years too late. Remember, it was in 2013 when the soft-spoken Korean with the magic putting touch won the first three majors of the year, only for her bid for the Grand Slam to end in the Women's British Open at St. Andrews. She still picked up one Grand Slam, though even that required a definition. Park won her seventh major at Turnberry — the old Kraft Nabisco (now ANA Inspiration), the U.S. Women's Open twice, the LPGA Championship (now Women's PGA Championship) three times and the Women's British Open. That's the traditional career Grand Slam. But the genesis of the Grand Slam is to make it a clean sweep of the majors, and the LPGA Tour in 2013 added the Evian Championship as its fifth major. Park has yet to win that as a major, though she won the tournament (Evian Masters) the year before it became a major. The LPGA Tour called it a career Grand Slam. Park was too busy celebrating to join the debate.

Park won for the fifth time at the Lorena Ochoa Invitational. The LPGA Tour's points system for Rolex Player of the Year does not include a bonus for winning majors. That enabled Ko to end the year on top in so many ways. And most importantly, the teenage star finally picked up her first major. Ko first reached No. 1 in the Rolex Women's World Ranking even when she lost a chance to win the season-opener at the Coates Golf Championship in Ocala, Florida. But she seized the top spot with her bold finish that allowed her to capture so many big awards.

Even so, the major was, well, major. She tied for 51st in the ANA Inspiration, a finish rarely seen by the top players on the LPGA Tour. She followed that with an even poorer performance in the next major, missing the cut at the Women's PGA Championship. She tied for 12th in the U.S. Women's Open at Lancaster Country Club in Pennsylvania, and at least made progress with a tie for third in the Women's British Open. Her final chance was the

Evian Championship in France, the fifth major on the LPGA Tour docket. She won it in style. Two shots behind going into the final round, Ko closed with a 63 to win by six shots. Call it an exclamation point. "Everyone won't be asking me when I'll win my first major," she said.

She wasn't done with her year. Ko won for the fifth time at the Fubon LPGA Taiwan Championship, and her tie for seventh at the CME Group Tour Championship allowed her to win the CME Race to the Globe and its $500,000 bonus for the second straight year. Ko also won Rolex LPGA Player of the Year. "It's been a long season. Up and down," Ko said. "Mostly up."

Park, meanwhile, won the Vare Trophy for lowest adjusted scoring average, which gave her the final point needed for the LPGA Hall of Fame. All she needed to be inducted was her 10th year on the LPGA Tour, which will be 2016.

Ko and Park didn't win every week, even if it seemed that way. In-Gee Chun won the U.S. Women's Open as part of a big year that included eight victories around the world. Gerina Piller felt like the biggest winner in golf even though she still doesn't have a trophy to call her own. Her 15-foot putt was the clincher that gave the Americans a much-needed victory in the Solheim Cup in Germany, a remarkable American rally under Juli Inkster.

The other big winner was Laura Davies, who finally was inducted into the World Golf Hall of Fame — even though she missed her big moment. The World Golf Hall of Fame changed its voting method to include a panel that nominated players and another panel that voted for them. The induction is to be held every other year, and officials selected the home of golf — St. Andrews — to stage an elaborate ceremony at St. Andrews University. It was the Monday night after the U.S. Women's Open, however, and Davies had flight delays that made it look next to impossible she could make it. She had a taped acceptance that was played, and Davies actually watched it from the car that was rushing her from Edinburgh to St. Andrews. Right when it looked as though she would miss out on the entire celebration, she made it for the reception and her arrival produced one of the biggest cheers of the night. "I look in the room and see Arnold Palmer and Bernhard Langer and all these great faces," she said. "It was a bit intimidating." Also inducted were Mark O'Meara, David Graham and architect A.W. Tillinghast.

McIlroy brought a small degree of normalcy to the European Tour by winning the Race to Dubai again, though little else followed the script. The 12 players on the Ryder Cup team that beat up on the Americans at Gleneagles in 2014 combined for just 11 victories — six of those by McIlroy and Justin Rose. Two others, Sergio Garcia and Jamie Donaldson, didn't win until late in the year in Thailand and Vietnam. Stenson, Martin Kaymer, Ian Poulter didn't win at all. Much like the Americans went through with a generational shift, perhaps one is on the way in Europe. Andy Sullivan won twice at the start of the season in South Africa, and then added a third victory in Portugal. Danny Willett only won one time in at the Omega European Masters in Switzerland, though he tied for sixth in the Open Championship and reached the semi-finals of the Cadillac Match Play in San Francisco, winning the consolation match. The next Ryder Cup team could have an entirely different look.

Keith Pelley can only hope the entire European Tour has a new look. The Canadian television executive was appointed the European Tour chief when George O'Grady retired, and he didn't waste any time showing how much he would fight for his players. Because of the Olympic year in 2016, world-wide scheduling became difficult. And so when PGA Tour commissioner Tim Finchem announced that the WGC-Bridgestone Invitational would be held two weeks after the U.S. Open — and the same week as the French Open — Pelley responded with a bold move. He said the Bridgestone Invitational would not count toward prize money or Ryder Cup ranking points for European Tour members, and the French Open would have an increased prize fund and would count as two starts toward the minimum requirement for membership.

It no doubt put some players in a tough spot, particularly defending champion Shane Lowry of Ireland. Pelley, however, felt he needed to fight for the French Open and its history on the European Tour. Pelley also changed the membership requirements with a clever system that he hopes will keep more of his players from migrating to America. Instead of 13 co-sanctioned events to keep European Tour membership — for the top players, that invariably included the four majors and four World Golf Championships — he lowered the minimum to five European Tour events that did not include the majors or WGCs. That didn't change anything for a player in the top 50, though it helped players like Luke Donald and Graeme McDowell who had fallen out of the top 50 keep their European Tour membership. Still to come was Europe developing its partnership with the Asian Tour, with all signs pointing to a merger.

Asian golf on the men's side continued to make inroads. Byeong-Hun An won the BMW PGA Championship, the flagship event on the European Tour at Wentworth. Four others won on the European Tour, with two victories each by Anirban Lahiri of India and Kiradech Aphibarnrat of Thailand, Ashun Wu winning the Volvo China Open in his home country and the ageless Thongchai Jaidee of Thailand winning in Germany. Jaidee became the oldest player on the International team to make his debut in the Presidents Cup. And perhaps it was only fitting that the Presidents Cup was held in Asia for the first time. It featured players from three Asian countries, another record, with Sangmoon Bae of South Korea joining Lahiri and Jaidee.

And it was the best Presidents Cup in years, with the Americans in control all week until a surprising window of opportunity for the International team that closed quickly with two putts. The International side staged such a strong rally on the last day at the Jack Nicklaus Golf Club Korea that it looked certain to win when Lahiri had just over three feet for birdie and Chris Kirk faced a difficult 15-foot birdie putt. The match was all square. If Lahiri won, it would be enough for the International team to win. A halve would put the onus on the final match of Bae and Bill Haas, son of U.S. captain Jay Haas. Kirk holed his putt, and Lahiri missed, and all that was left was for Haas to hold on against Bae. The Americans won, 15½-14½. Lahiri starred in defeat with his grace. Bae would have had to chip in on the 18th for any reasonable chance, and he stubbed the shot and covered his face with his hands before a home crowd. A month later, Bae was off for his two-year mandatory military service.

EPILOGUE

There was the "Great Triumvirate" from more than a century ago. Harry Vardon, J.H. Taylor and James Braid won the Open Championship 16 times in a span of 21 years, and at least one of them was runner-up in the five years neither of them won. The original "Big Three" was Arnold Palmer, Jack Nicklaus and Gary Player — all three clients of IMG founder Mark McCormack — who combined to win the Masters seven straight times at the start of the 1960s and who collectively piled up 19 majors in a span of 11 years. The Big Three swept the majors in 1962. So this modern "Big Three" has a ways to go.

By the end of the year, they had won five of the last six majors (Zach Johnson's win at St. Andrews was the exception) and owned the top of the World Ranking. With technology across the board (golf equipment, teaching, launch monitors, computers), players are getting better at a younger age. Golf is getting stronger, deeper. That speaks to the performance by the best, particularly Spieth and Day. Not since 1973 had two players won at least five times on the PGA Tour (Jack Nicklaus and Lee Trevino). This is just one year. It could fizzle out. It could become a lot more than the "Big Three."

Spieth said as much toward the end of the year in Shanghai for the WGC-HSBC Champions. "In order to create an era, you almost need a decade of years like this," he said. "Sure, we have the potential to do it. But this was the first year of it. But unless we keep our heads down ... unless we're aware of it, and it drives us, and we get the right breaks, there's a lot of factors. So maybe it's a bit premature to say that. But, I believe there was step needed in the right direction, and it took place this year. If we can ride with that, it will be significant."

One thing is certain. This year deserves a sequel.

2. Masters Tournament

It isn't often that a 21-year-old can drive the statistics folks to the record books, but Justin Spieth sure did at the 2015 Masters Tournament. Kept them burrowing through the archives like a battery of CPAs at tax time.

Except for a missed five-footer for par at the final hole, Spieth would have broken even Tiger Woods' 72-hole score of 18-under-par 270. Even so, he did have a fine consolation prize — the Masters championship, his first victory in a major. And he won comfortably over two challengers who might have been quite frightening to a less-confident, less-composed, less-accomplished 21-year-old. Spieth won by four shots over Hall-of-Framer Phil Mickelson, seeking his fourth green jacket, and former U.S. Open champion Justin Rose.

"It's incredible — it's one of the best feelings I've ever felt," Spieth said. "This was arguably the greatest day of my life."

Perhaps he invoked the limiting word "arguably" because he could sense other great days ahead. Even so, it doesn't get much greater than this. He had just become the second-youngest Masters champion ever. Tiger Woods was 21 years, 3 months and 14 days old when he won the 1997 Masters. Spieth was 21 years, 9 months and 17 days old.

Spieth was born in Dallas, had an outstanding amateur golf career, and was an All-American at the University of Texas in his freshman year. He left in his sophomore year in 2012 and turned professional at age 19. In 2013, while still 19, he scored his first PGA Tour win in the John Deere Classic. He was leading the 2014 Masters heading into the final turn and finished tied for second with Jonas Blixt, behind Bubba Watson. Spieth scored his second win in the 2015 Valspar Championship, and then it was on to the Masters, to make some history.

It was perhaps as much for himself as for his play that made Spieth so admired by the fans. Noted *USA Today* columnist Christine Brennan wrote that in a time when people had become "sick of self-absorbed athletes..." Spieth won the Masters "...with a kind of unspoken class and grace that would seem to come from another era." At the 18th, when the gallery rose to applaud him, Spieth applauded them in return.

Spieth became just the fifth winner to go wire-to-wire after: Craig Wood, 1941; Arnold Palmer, 1960; Jack Nicklaus, 1972, and Raymond Floyd, 1976. He shot Augusta National's emerald reaches in 64-64-70-70, and set or tied a number of records along the way. Among them: A record 28 birdies. He failed to birdie only three holes, Nos. 7, 11 and 17.

He played 10 holes in under par, and was over par on just two: No. 7 (the only one he bogeyed more than once; he had two there and was two over) and No. 17, where he was also two over, on his only double bogey of the tournament.

As Phil Mickelson was to note, Spieth does not overpower a course, but instead has a superb all-around game and an otherworldly putter. In this Masters, he had 42 putts in the 3-to-10–foot range. He made 32 of them.

One of Spieth's strongest memories of the Masters was seeing the new champion sitting before the international media corps in his green jacket. It was his last thought leaving the room after Saturday's third round.

Said Spieth: "I walked out of this interview room saying, 'I want to walk back in there really late [Sunday] and sit there with the jacket on.'"

And Sunday evening, there he was.

FIRST ROUND

Jordan Spieth talks to his golf ball.

True, all golfers do. Hence, expressions such as "Bite!" and "Be right!"

Spieth, on the other hand, issues instructions. As he did at the par-four 14th in the first round, where he drove into the trees, then barked commands at his seven-iron escape shot and ended up with his sixth birdie in a seven-hole stretch.

Spieth shot an eight-under 64, becoming the youngest, at age 21, to lead the first round of the Masters. He'd come within a stroke of tying the record for the Masters and the other three majors — the U.S. Open, the British Open and the PGA Championship. His 64 was also the lowest Masters first round since Greg Norman's 63 start to his fateful 1996.

"It's one of the better rounds I've ever played," said the soft-spoken young Texan. And it gave him a three-stroke lead over Charley Hoffman, Ernie Els, Jason Day and Justin Rose, all at 67.

Spieth came into the Masters as the hottest player in the game, having finished 1-2-2 in his last three starts. Even so, the spotlight was on two others — Rory McIlroy, No. 1 in the world and needing the Masters to complete his career Grand Slam, and more so on the hurting Tiger Woods, four-time Masters champion, now ranked 111th, troubled by injuries in recent years and playing little. With his various health problems, Woods had played only seven times in 2014 and had made only two starts in 2015 before the Masters, missing the cut in one and withdrawing from the other with another back injury. Woods opened with a three-putt bogey at No. 1 and shot a one-over-par 73. "You know, I'm still in it," he said. "I'm only nine back."

McIlroy, after a sensational summer in 2014, resumed in 2015 by winning the Dubai Desert Classic in his second start on the European Tour. In this Masters, he was sluggish through the 11th, but perked up with birdies at the back-nine par-fives, the 13th and 15th, and shot 71. McIlroy remembered his crash in the final round of the 2011 Masters. "I know what I can accomplish," he said, "but I'm not letting myself think about it too much."

Spieth soon had the world of golf paying attention to more than McIlroy and Woods. After birdies at the easy par-five No. 2 and the tough par-three No. 4, he sped to six birdies over a seven-hole stretch from No. 8, on his way to the 64. The jewel in the streak was at the par-four, dogleg-left 14th. He drove into the trees on the right and had 179 yards remaining to the green. But a pine tree was in the way. He smacked his seven iron and barked orders. The ball obeyed. It hit the flagstick and stopped three feet away. He couldn't see it, but the gallery informed him, thunderously. The birdie put him eight under with four holes to play.

But his chances for a 63 to tie the record for majors, or a 62 to break it, flitted away with a bogey at the par-five 15th, one of the easiest holes on the course. His hybrid second shot went well over the green, and he chipped back weakly, up to the edge, and he three-putted for the bogey, slipping to seven under. He birdied the 18th on a 20-foot putt, and admitted he was thinking of a 62.

"I wasn't aware what the course record was here, let alone that it actually would have been the lowest round in major championship history," said Spieth, then grinning. "But I'm certainly OK with the day."

Meanwhile, tied for second...

Charley Hoffman, 38, playing in his second Masters, first got the autographs of the Big Three — honorary starters Arnold Palmer, Jack Nicklaus and Gary Player — then lit up Augusta's closing stretch with eagle-birdie-par-birdie (3-2-4-3) for his 67. He needed just 27 putts.

Ernie Els, a Hall-of-Famer and now 45, felt his hopes of getting a green jacket getting dimmer. So the 67, his best-ever start, was encouraging. He got to six under with an eagle at the 15th, but bogeyed the 18th. He was a kid once at the Masters, and he marveled at Spieth. "You just cannot see this kid not win many, many majors," he said. As for his own chances: "...we're running out of time."

Jason Day, 27, in his fifth Masters, a threat anytime he plays, erupted for five straight birdies from the 12th, getting to six under. Then he cooled with a three-putt bogey at the 17th. "I knew if I could just be patient, I could get something going," he said.

Justin Rose's 67 was a round that kept threatening to break loose but didn't quite — three birdies across four holes from the third, then three more from the 10th through the 15th, but with a bogey at the 11th. It was a huge relief. He'd missed three cuts in his six tournaments this year. "I knew my game was there," he said. "It just hadn't shown up yet."

Bubba Watson, defending champion and two-time champion, wasn't discouraged by his 71. He recalled finishing a nervous 50th after his first Masters win in 2012. "This time, I needed to calm down," he said, "so I started walking slower."

Three-time winner Phil Mickelson was pleased with his 70. Now: "If I could get hot with the putter a time or two," he said, "I should be able to make a run."

At day's end, it was Jordan Spieth's day, and Billy Horschel, his playing partner, summed it up best of all. Horschel said it would have been nice to have a tape recorder that just kept playing, "Nice hole, Jordan."

First-round leaders: Jordan Spieth 64, Charley Hoffman 67, Justin Rose 67, Ernie Els 67, Jason Day 67, Russell Henley 68, Sergio Garcia 68.

SECOND ROUND

There was no appreciable widening of Jordan Spieth's grin. But if it were to grow in proportion to the golf he was playing, his face wouldn't be big enough to hold it. And anyone who expected the 21-year-old to be shaky after his opening 64 would be disappointed.

Round Two: Another day, another smashing performance. Spieth shot a bogey-free, six-under 66 in the second round and expanded his lead from three to five shots over Charley Hoffman, who shot 68. The other three first-round co-leaders drifted back a bit: Justin Rose, tying for third with a 70; Ernie Els (72), solo seventh, and Jason Day (74), tying for 12th.

"This is just the halfway point," said Spieth, trying to defuse the mounting enthusiasm.

But it was difficult, considering that a young golfer playing in only his second Masters, after nearly winning his first a year earlier, had made just one bogey in two rounds at majestic Augusta National. Further, that at 14-under 130, he broke a Masters record that had stood for 39 years — Raymond Floyd's 131, set in 1976.

"It's cool," said Spieth. "Anytime you can set a record here is pretty awesome. I struck it, I thought, better than yesterday."

Someone noted that this Masters was starting to look like the one in 1997, when a certain 21-year-old named Tiger Woods, in his third visit, was running away with it.

Through the two rounds, Spieth had hit 20 of 28 driving fairways, 28 of the 36 greens in regulation, and he needed just 25 putts in each round. He hadn't had one three-putt, a remarkable performance on Augusta's fierce greens. He'd made 15 birdies and just one bogey. It was a calm 66 of six scattered birdies — all four par-fives (Nos. 2, 8, 13 and 15), plus Nos. 5 and 10. The birdie at the uphill No. 8 demonstrated what Henrik Stenson meant when he said, "He's definitely an old head on young shoulders. He's playing mature."

Spieth played it with sheer, calculated artistry. He drove into a bunker, but close to the lip. "I knew I actually couldn't get a clean strike on the ball, even with a 60-degree [wedge]," he said. So he settled for getting a club on the ball — a 52-degree wedge — even though it would go only some 20 yards. Then facing an uphill shot from 235 yards, he cut a hybrid that ended up two feet from the hole.

"The hardest thing to do is put aside wanting to win so bad," Spieth said. "This is only the halfway point."

Rory McIlroy, with the Irish gift of expression, made a pointed observation about Spieth's performance. "I think a few guys can still catch him," he said. "It will take something extraordinary from myself to get up there, but you never know. I know better than most people what can happen with the lead around here."

McIlroy was still hurting from the 2011 Masters, when he led for three rounds, was up by four, then blew to an 80 in the fourth.

This Masters was verging on harsh for McIlroy, No. 1 in the world. One birdie, three bogeys and a double bogey at the ninth had him at 40 and in danger of missing the cut. But he rallied for an inward 31 and a safe 142 total.

Tiger Woods shot a four-birdie 69 — breaking 70 for the first time since 2011 — and joined McIlroy at 142. "I'm 12 back, but anything can happen — '96 proved that," he said, summoning the ghost of Greg Norman's collapse.

Charley Hoffman clung to second place with his 68, but was two strokes further back. He birdied three straight from the 12th on putts of eight, 15 and 23 feet. "I was still aggressive where I needed to be aggressive, and took my medicine where I needed to take my medicine," he said.

Dustin Johnson rose to a tie for third on a 67 out of an electrifying historic performance. The big-hitting Johnson double-bogeyed No. 1, then became the first player ever to make three eagles in one round. He got them on the par-fives, on an 18-foot putt at No. 2, an 11-footer at No. 8 and a two-footer at the 15th. Throw in the birdie at No. 13 and he had played the par-fives in seven under. "It was pretty special and a lot of fun," Johnson said.

It was good news-bad news for the Watsons.

The one named Bubba, the defending champion, shot another 71 for a 142 to remain within shouting distance, 12 behind Spieth. "If I had those [three] three-putts back, I'd be right in the thick of this thing," said Bubba. The other Watson — Tom, age 65, a two-time champion — was encouraged by his opening 71, but shot an 81 and missed the cut, which came in at three-over 147.

History buffs pointed out that three players had five-shot leads at the halfway point and went on to win — Herman Keiser in 1946, Jack Nicklaus in 1975 and Raymond Floyd in 1976.

"It's a long, long way from being finished," cautioned Ernie Els, who had slipped nine shots behind with a 72. "A lot of work still to be done. But," he added, "he's very, very impressive."

Second-round leaders: Jordan Spieth 66–130, Charley Hoffman 68–135, Justin Rose 70–137, Dustin Johnson 67–137, Paul Casey 68–137, Phil Mickelson 68–138, Ernie Els 72–139.

THIRD ROUND

Jordan Spieth discovered the dark side of Augusta National's 17th.

Suddenly, the Masters that was a runaway train rolling toward a foregone conclusion was looking up for grabs.

How could Spieth, who had handled everything the storied course could throw at him with almost living-room ease, double-bogey the 17th? Was the kid, as everyone called him, coming undone?

That was the tale of the third round.

Not that Spieth was in desperate trouble. He led by five strokes after the second round, and was up by seven after the 16th in the third round, and by the end of the day, he was ahead by four. Overall, he had lost just one shot. But it wasn't so much losing a shot, it was how.

Augusta's 17th, even without the celebrated Eisenhower Tree — victim of an ice storm — played the toughest on the course in the third round. Spieth added his name to the list of casualties, beginning with a tee shot into the pines on the left. He punched out and was 39 yards short and left of the green. But he stubbed his chip shot and was 48 feet short. His first putt died nine feet short. Then he two-putted from there for a six, his first double bogey of the tournament. After 52 holes of golf that ranged from solid to brilliant, he had made a hash of the 17th. And maybe of the 2015 Masters.

Was the kid running scared? He answered at the 18th.

After an excellent drive, he missed the green, putting his ball above and to the right of the greenside bunker. Now he was, in golf parlance, looking at bogey, maybe double.

It had been an erratic round to now. He'd had three birdies and two bogeys on the front nine, then coming in he birdied the 12th and 13th, bogeyed the 14th, and birdied 15 and 16. And then double-bogeyed the 17th. So he was studying that chip shot at the 18th with the attention of a surgeon. What was he thinking? The answer was a rare and detailed glimpse into a golfer's mind in a time of crisis.

"I liked bumping it down the hill, and it would give myself probably 15 feet or 20 feet," Spieth said.

"It wasn't a great lie. I didn't deserve a good lie by any means, but it wasn't a great lie, a little grass behind the ball. And if it were down-grain, if it were mowed down-grain to the green, I could just kind of bump something pretty short and it would just funnel on that grass all the way down. But because it's mowed into the grain here, it still wouldn't even go all the way down that hill. I felt like the bump was just as tricky given it would be tough to judge, plus, if it took a big hop, it could go over the green. And if it hit a little short, it could be short.

"The reason I chose a flop was because if it comes out solid, it's going to fly to pin-high and then it's going to go maybe 10, 15 feet past the hole. And if it comes out the way I want it to, which is just a little heavy with that grass behind it, it's going to land halfway down that hill and it could be really good. It came out just how I expected."

Spieth took the daring flop shot and ended up nine feet from the cup, and he dropped the putt for his par. The crisis had passed. He had a 70 and a three-round total of 200, 16 under, and was leading Rose by four, Mickelson by five.

Rose had two early bogeys, then played the last 12 holes in seven under for a 67. His last birdie, on a dangerous 20-foot downhill putt at the 18th, got him into his coveted final pairing for the final round. "Given the choice," Rose said, "you'd want to be in the last group, to see what you're up against and feel the atmosphere."

Mickelson trailed Spieth by eight going into the third round and cut that deficit to five with a seven-birdie 67, the last on a 41-foot putt at the par-three 16th. The question then was how Spieth would hold up with both Rose and Mickelson bearing down on him?

"I don't think it matters who's close to him," Mickelson said, "because he's playing very good golf."

Third-round leaders: Jordan Spieth 70–200, Justin Rose 67–204, Phil Mickelson 67–205, Charley Hoffman 71–206.

FOURTH ROUND

Jordan Spieth wasn't riding the whirlwind. He was causing it.

If there still was any doubt that this was Spieth's Masters — after almost four full rounds of sharp tee shots, precise irons and uncanny putting — the fates stamped his name on it at two more holes. Spieth already had the tournament well in hand coming down the final nine. He didn't have to risk anything at the last two par-fives. He could have played them safely. But he went full-bore, like the chaser and not the leader. At the 13th, he barely cleared the stream in front of the green with his second shot. At the 15th, he knocked his second over the back of the green. He birdied both. Why aggressive, with the field in front of him? Because it might be gaining on him.

And the birdie at the 15th put him at 19 under par. Nobody in Masters history had ever gone that low. The bogey at the 18th set him back a shot.

When he tapped in his final putt on the final hole, he became — at 21 years, 9 months, 17 days — the second youngest player ever to win the Masters, just some six months older than Tiger Woods when he won in 1997.

"To join Masters history and put my name on that trophy, and to have this jacket forever," Spieth said, "it's something that I can't fathom right now."

Spieth joined an even more exclusive club-within-a-club — a wire-to-wire winner, just the fifth. With the Masters, wire-to-wire means being the sole leader after each round. Spieth followed Craig Wood, 1941; Arnold Palmer, 1960; Jack Nicklaus, 1972, and Raymond Floyd, 1976.

For the finish to such an occasion, there was the slightly awkward matter of the 72nd hole.

Masters statisticians said that Spieth had faced 42 putts in the 3-to-10–foot range and made an astounding 32 of them. But of the 10 he missed, there was one that he might like to have back more than any other. It was the five-footer for par at the final hole. The miss only dented his lead, but had he made the putt, he would have broken yet another Masters record — lowest winning total. He shot 70 for an 18-under 270 total, tying the record set, ironically, by Tiger Woods in his first Masters win, in 1997.

Spieth won by four over Justin Rose and Phil Mickelson, a pair of major winners who tried to pressure him but couldn't. Mickelson was an erratic one under through the 14th, then holed a bunker shot for an eagle at the 15th, but could only par in for a three-under 69. Rose birdied three straight from the 13th, but that wasn't nearly enough. He shot 70. They tied at 274, a significant number for them. In Mickelson's three Masters victories, 272 was his lowest score. And Rose, who had yet to win a green jacket, had lowered his Masters best by nine shots and still lost by four.

"He has no weaknesses," Mickelson said. "He doesn't overpower the golf course, but he plays the course strategically well. And he has that ability to focus and see things clearly when the pressure is on and perform at his best ... That's something that you really can't teach. Some players are able to do it, some players aren't. And he is."

Like Raymond Floyd in 1976, Spieth ruled the par-fives. He played them in 12 under par, and bogeyed only once. And he also he conquered the long and demanding par-four 10th, where Rory McIlroy blew up in 2011.

Spieth played it in three birdies and a par. "That was the key hole for me this week," Spieth said.

Spieth turned the 2015 Masters into a statistician's holiday. These were the principal records he set:

- The 36-hole record, 14-under 130.
- The 54-hole record, 16-under 200.
- Most birdies in the Masters, 28.
- Lowest first round by a winner, 64.

And no one got closer to him than three shots the entire way. Only one other winner — Craig Wood, in 1941 — held that distinction.

One other thing stamped Spieth in this Masters. When the gallery jammed at the 18th rose to salute him, he responded by applauding them.

"This," the kid said, "isn't an honor to be carried lightly."

The final leaders: Jordan Spieth 70–270, Phil Mickelson 69–274, Justin Rose 70–274, Rory McIlroy 66–276, Hideki Matsuyama 66–277.

3. U.S. Open Championship

U.S. Opens and Joneses and Texans and monsters — there seems to be a connection.

Jordan Spieth, 2015 U.S. Open, Chambers Bay. Ben Hogan, 1951 U.S. Open, Oakland Hills. Robert Trent Jones, golf course architect, and 62 years later, son Robert Trent Jones Jr., golf course architect.

This was a tale of two Texans winning U.S. Opens on monster courses authored by someone named Jones.

First, 1953: Trent, as he was known, was summoned to renovate Oakland Hills Country Club, a classic course near Detroit, that had become a bit dated in the face of advancing equipment technology. (This would be a familiar story in the game.) Trent Jones relocated fairway bunkers farther out, grew the rough and the like. The result: Only two scores under par, both in the final round. One was Clayton Heafner's one-under 69, the other Hogan's 67. It filled out Hogan's card of 76-73-71-67, for a seven-over-par 287 and a two-shot victory over Heafner. Whereupon Hogan uttered one of the most famous statements in golf history: "I'm glad I brought this course — this monster — to its knees."

Chambers Bay, which opened in 2007, did not have the time or experience to have reached full monster status by the time of the U.S. Open, the first ever held in the Pacific Northwest. But judging from some of the criticism, it was well on its way. Perhaps the harshest came from Hall-of-Famer Gary Player, 79, former U.S. Open champion, a man never timid with his opinions.

"One of the worst golf courses I've seen in my 63 years as a pro," Player said. Adding: "Basically unplayable ... the man who designed this golf course had to have one leg shorter than the other."

There would be plenty of criticism to go around. There almost always is at a U.S. Open. At Chambers Bay, much of it was directed at the greens, some at 200-foot elevations, some on rollout areas, etc. It's a treeless, windswept, seaside course that would play to as much as 7,700 yards, with a par of 70.

"Guys would say a course doesn't suit their game," said Jack Nicklaus. "It's not supposed to suit your game. You're supposed to suit your game to the golf course."

Chambers Bay, designed and built by Jones Jr. on a former sand-and-gravel quarry, is a municipal course at the southern tip of Puget Sound, near Tacoma, Washington, owned by Pierce County and the centerpiece of a county park. The Open was awarded to Chambers Bay by David Fay, then executive director of the U.S. Golf Association, who was noted for adding municipal courses — such as Bethpage Black on Long Island and Torrey Pines at San Diego, to the roll of famous country clubs and resort courses such as Pinehurst and Pebble Beach.

Criticism and the U.S. Open have gone hand-in-hand pretty much since the first one in 1895. Objections were noted, and then the gofers had the tee.

"Well, we love the fact we're in the Pacific Northwest for the first time," said Executive Director Mike Davis. "I love the fact we're at new architecture, we're at a publically municipal-owned golf course where the public can come. It's a different-looking golf course, different architecture. We're positioned to have a great championship, and honestly what we want to do at this point, the architect and then the United States Golf Association, is really hand it off to the players, and let them create the drama."

And then, 62 years after Ben Hogan, it was a Texan vs. the Joneses again.

FIRST ROUND

It is folly, of course, to begin thinking about the Grand Slam after the Masters and heading into the U.S. Open. There still are two other giant steps beyond — the Open Championship in July and the PGA Championship in August, and nobody had ever taken all four giant steps. Still, the Masters champion is the only man in the game with a chance to win the slam. So it's a brief speculation, but an irresistible one.

Jordan Spieth made it a little more irresistible this time. He had created one of the most memorable Masters, going wire-to-wire with ease and great poise, winning by four, and becoming the second-youngest winner ever, and a very convincing golfer.

"You can't win a Grand Slam unless you win the first," Spieth had said in a pre-Open interview. "So I'm the only one with that opportunity this year. So I'm going to go ahead and focus on this week and see if I can put myself in contention."

He was still only 21 coming to Chambers Bay for his fourth straight U.S. Open, after tying for 21st as an amateur in 2012, then missing the cut, then tying for 17th. This time, he opened with a two-under-par 68, three off the lead.

Chambers Bay was not a monster in its U.S. Open debut. A total of 25 golfers — a surprising number for a U.S. Open — broke the par of 70 in the first round, led by Dustin Johnson and Sweden's Henrik Stenson, tied at five-under-par 65, one ahead of Patrick Reed.

Attention was focused first on Tiger Woods, three-time U.S. Open winner, playing little because of health problems. Woods, chasing Jack Nicklaus' record of 18 majors, was stalled on No. 14, dating to the 2008 U.S. Open at Torrey Pines. He opened with his worst-ever U.S. Open score, an 80, and his second-worst in a major since the 81 in the 2002 British Open.

"Got off to a bad start," Woods said. "I stuck that six iron in the ground on the first hole, and then just couldn't quite get it turned around today." His troubles were many. At the par-four 14th, he needed three shots to get out of two different bunkers, and he missed a short putt and triple-bogeyed. On a day that found him third from the bottom, Woods still found room for a little humor. "The bright side," Woods said, "is that I kicked Rickie's butt today." Rickie Fowler shot 81.

Dustin Johnson was solving most of Chambers Bay's problems with his big driver. He averaged 336.5 yards off the tee and hit the fairway on 11 of the 14 driving holes. "The confidence is definitely there," he said, and it showed. Starting at No. 10, he birdied his first two holes, then birdied four of the first seven on his back nine. He was six under through his 16th and flirting with a 63, the record for the U.S. Open and the other three majors. But a poor chip cost him a chance at a birdie at his 17th (the par-five No. 8), and he bogeyed his last, the par-three ninth, after missing the green. The bogey didn't sour his outlook. "I definitely feel good about where I'm at, going into tomorrow," Johnson said.

And inevitably, the question of the awkward failures in majors surfaced — shooting 80 after leading going into the final round of the 2010 U.S. Open at Pebble Beach, then costing himself a chance at the PGA Championship at Whistling Straits, taking a two-stroke penalty for grounding his club in a bunker at the final hole. Those tournaments, Johnson said, "...were a long time ago."

Stenson, one under on the front nine, sprinted to four birdies over the last five holes — three straight from the 14th, then another at the 18th for his 65. He proved to be as adept at not answering a tough question as he was at golf.

He was asked whether he liked the course. "Of it's kind?" he answered. "It's one of the finest."

Eyes were on Phil Mickelson, too. Now 45 and a Hall-of-Famer, he was still looking for that first U.S. Open title after finishing second a record six times. He led much of the morning at three under before settling for a 69 — a thinking man's 69. He gave a classic example of course management at the drivable, par-four 12th. He decided the left-side pin was too risky for his game, so he played the hole with a six iron and a wedge. "I didn't want one hole to bite me," he said.

Spieth was one of seven at 68, and thanked his magical putting.

"We had some gettable pins, but all in all you have a group of holes where you just have to try and two-putt from 40 feet," he said. "And the key for me today was I had some two-putts from 95 feet, 85 feet, 75 feet, three from 65 feet."

All in all, then, was Jordan Spieth pleased with his 68?

"Yeah," he said. "I think if I did it three more times, I'd be in really good position come Sunday."

First-round leaders: Henrik Stenson 65, Dustin Johnson 65, Patrick Reed 66, Matt Kuchar 67, Ben Martin 67, amateur Brian Campbell 67.

SECOND ROUND

Golf's biggest frights are double and triple bogeys and the like. But this U.S. Open turned for-real scary in the second round.

Jason Day, the bright young Australian, was playing his final hole, No. 9, when he collapsed. Medical personnel rushed in. Day was woozy but was able to finish the hole, pitching out of a bunker and bogeying for a 70 to tie at 138, three shots behind co-leaders Jordan Spieth and Patrick Reed. Day is afflicted with benign positional vertigo, said his agent, Buddy Martin, and it has caused him to withdraw from a number of tournaments. The pressing question was, with the best start in his five U.S. Opens, would he be able to finish?

Spieth, playing with Day, notched his fourth birdie at his eighth (the par-three 17th) on an 11-foot putt. That gave him the lead at six under. Then, at his ninth (No. 18), the ground microphone caught him saying he'd just played "the dumbest hole I've ever played in my life."

He had joined the critics of Chambers Bay. The 18th played as either a par-four or a par-five, as the USGA chose each day, varying the dangers of fairway bunkers on the left and the crossbunker on the right. This time, it was a 514-yard par-four. Spieth hooked his tee shot into a fairway bunker, failed to clear the lip with his nine iron (he conceded he should have hit his sand wedge), then put his third into a bunker short of the green and double-bogeyed.

Later, he would soften his barbs. "I think 18 as a par-four doesn't make much sense," Spieth said. "Of course, at the moment when I didn't hit the right shots, it's going to make less sense."

Spieth regrouped immediately. The key, he said, was his friend and caddie, Michael Greller. At his 10th (the par-five first), Spieth, still miffed, drove into the rough. "I was really frustrated," he said, "and Michael did a great job of telling me, 'Don't let this get to you … The second something gets to you, you're in trouble in a U.S. Open.'"

He bogeyed his 16th and birdied his 18th, the par-three No. 9, putting his tee shot from the towering tee box to eight feet. He shot 67, tying Patrick Reed for the lead at five-under 135.

Reed, who tied for 35th in his only other U.S. Open, in 2014, shot an amazing 69 — six pars, five birdies, an eagle and six bogeys. A three-putt bogey from 50 feet dropped him into a tie with Spieth.

Reed, 24, part of the PGA Tour's youth movement, called it a disappointing round. "But we're in a good position," he said. With 27 players finishing within six strokes of the lead, and 34 within seven, "It's definitely going to be a tournament that anyone has a chance to win," Reed said.

The Tiger Woods Watch ended unceremoniously. After his all-time worst U.S. Open score of 80 in the first round, he added a 76 for a 16-over 156, his highest in 308 professional starts over nearly 20 years on the PGA Tour. He missed the cut for only the second time in 19 Opens. "On a golf course like this … you have to be precise and dialed in," Woods said. "I didn't have that."

Dustin Johnson's strong bid tailed off. A birdie at the 11th put him at seven under and leading by two. But he bogeyed three of the last five, shot 71, and slipped a stroke off the lead at 136. "I just didn't hole the putts like yesterday," said Johnson, who opened with a 65. "That was pretty much the only difference. I like where I'm at."

Rory McIlroy eagled the drivable par-four 12th, but double-bogeyed the par-three 17th and bogeyed the 18th for another 72.

Phil Mickelson, owner of one of the finest short games ever, was reduced to saying a strange thing: "I need to find a way to get the ball in the hole." He also had a strange round. Just one birdie, but five bogeys, and his four-over 74 had him drifting back in the field. He was at three-over 143, but eight shots off the lead, a huge deficit in a U.S. Open. It was a grinder of a round. Mickelson started at No. 10, made five bogeys, and got his only birdie at his 17th, the par-five No. 8, on a 10-foot putt. In all, he had three three-putt greens and needed 35 putts. "I need to get a hot hand," he said.

The measure of this U.S. Open could be taken by the unfamiliar leaderboard. The cut came in at 146, sweeping away, in addition to Tiger Woods, defending champion Martin Kaymer, Bubba Watson, Graeme McDowell and Rickie Fowler. And leaving, among the top 60 and ties, such lesser-knowns as Branden Grace, Joost Luiten, Tony Finau. And of the 16 amateurs in the field, Brian Campbell, 22, four off the lead, led the six who made the cut, the most in 49 years. Said Campbell, on seeing his name on the leaderboard: "I definitely want a little more of that."

Second-round leaders: Jordan Spieth 67-135, Patrick Reed 69-135, Branden Grace 67-136, Dustin Johnson 71-136, Joost Luiten 69-137, Tony Finau 68-137, Daniel Summerhays 67-137, Ben Martin 70-137.

THIRD ROUND

Now it was no longer folly to talk about the Grand Slam.

The third round of the 2015 U.S. Open was in the books, and Jordan Spieth, newly minted Masters champion, was in a four-way tie for the lead and had at least a chance to win the second leg of golf's Grand Slam.

If you win, the voice in the media said, which is going to mean more to you, the Masters or the U.S. Open? "I think that if that were to be the case," Spieth said, "then I'll be able to tell you a little bit more about it tomorrow."

Said another: The world will be focused on you. Do you think about that at all? "No, not really," Spieth said. "A little bit here and there, because I'd like to win two in a row. But ... once I get out on the golf course, I'll just be focused on the round and how to separate myself from the pack."

Yet another: "You have the chance to be the first person in over a decade to get the first two legs of the Grand Slam. How much will that contribute to your nerves tomorrow?" "None," Spieth said. "That's going to have no bearing when I tee it up. It's just going to be how can I tackle Chambers Bay."

Spieth shot a 71, South Africa's Branden Grace a 71, Dustin Johnson a 70 and Australia's Jason Day, still affected by the vertigo that hit him the day before, a heroic 68 to tie at four-under-par 206.

On a tough day at Chambers Bay, they led by a formidable three strokes over South Africa's Louis Oosthuizen, who shot a second straight 66, the day's low, Cameron Smith (69), Shane Lowry (70) and J.B. Holmes (71).

Of the 75 players left in the field, only six broke par, and the average score on the par-70 course was 73.133. This figure masked some surprising scores: Ernie Els, 76; Lee Westwood and Phil Mickelson, 77, and Zach Johnson, 78.

Spieth started with a bumpy front nine: back-to-back birdies from No. 2, followed by two straight bogeys, then a birdie-bogey, then a birdie at the ninth for an outward 36. Coming in, he bogeyed the 11th and birdied the 15th for his 71.

The irony: Spieth, the putting wizard, was up to eight three-putts through three rounds.

"Four today," said Spieth. "Two of them I couldn't do much about them. The other two were unforced. All in all, it was just a little bit off. But plenty of birdies. Just need to limit the mistakes tomorrow."

His next order of business: Sleeping on the lead in a major again.

"It's not like I'm a veteran at this by any means," Spieth said. "But by the time we tee off, if I can convince myself that I'm free-rolling — I've got one of these [majors], and the other guys are trying to chase their first. I know how hard it is to chase your first ... mentally, I think I'll be strong enough to pull it off."

Jason Day's performance was almost a rerun of Ken Venturi's victory round in the 1964 U.S. Open, when he all but collapsed, trudging through the heat and humidity at Congressional Country Club. Day was still shaky and nauseated. The admiring galleries cheered him along the way.

After two bogeys on the front nine, he staged a memorable finish: a birdie at 10, a bogey at 11, then four more birdies, at 12, 15, 17 and 18. The last seemed heaven-sent. His drive rocketed wide-right into a hospitality suite, caromed off the deck, then a glass door and back into the rough. He punched out, put his next on the green, and birdied.

Said Day, still shaky: "I think the goal was just to go through today and see how it goes."

South African Branden Grace, 27, had an awkward par 70 — two birdies on the front and a third at the 15th, but three bogeys clustered over five holes in between. "The concentration slipped a little bit around the turn," he said. "I'm still in a good position."

Next comes his best chance to win his first major. "We all dream of this, so it's a matter of if you grab it or you don't," he said. "I played really good today under the pressure. I think I'm in a good frame of mind." Some heard that as an echo of his second U.S. Open, at Merion in 2013. He shot 70-83.

Dustin Johnson was six under and leading through the 12th, then hooked his seven-iron approach at the par-four 13th into a greenside bunker. He three-putted from 40 feet for a double bogey and slipped back into a tie for the lead. He held the 54-hole lead once before, in 2010 at Pebble Beach. He closed with an 82.

"I've been in the situation a few times, so I know how to handle myself," Johnson said. "I know what it takes to get it done."

The statement would come back to haunt him.

Third-round leaders: Jordan Spieth 71–206, Jason Day 68–206, Dustin Johnson 70–206, Branden Grace 70–206, Louis Oosthuizen 66–209, Cameron Smith 69–209, Shane Lowry 70–209, J.B. Holmes 71–209.

FOURTH ROUND

Jordan Spieth had talked a good game. Spieth had said he could handle the pressure. He'd won the Masters two months earlier, the second youngest ever to lift the green jacket. Next, he stood on the threshold of winning the U.S. Open. It would be the rare back-to-back victories in the season's first two majors. More to the point, it would be the rare holding of the first two legs of golf's never-before-won Grand Slam. But going into the final round, Spieth was in a four-way tie with Dustin Johnson, Branden Grace and Jason Day. Few 21-year-olds ever get hit with that kind of pressure.

But he'd said, essentially, that he could handle it.

And the kid, as many called him, delivered again. He won the 2015 U.S. Open in as nerve-wracking a finish as the old championship has ever seen.

Pressure?

"I felt a lot," Spieth conceded. "I felt as much as I felt at Augusta. I knew that this would be the second leg and that it would be two majors in a row, and I think that that added to a little bit of the pressure."

Still, he survived the grinding finish to become the youngest champion since Bobby Jones in 1923, the youngest to win two career majors since

Gene Sarazen in 1922, and the first since Tiger Woods in 2002 to win the first two majors of the year. And he won it on the final hole.

"I'm still in shock," Spieth said. "I've never experienced a feeling like this. Just kind of total shock..."

First, Grace and Day left the chase. Grace was one under for the day, then double-bogeyed the par-four 16th and was out. "Just one bad swing cost me at the end," said Grace, who shot 71 and tied for fourth.

Jason Day had fallen to two under through the 10th, then to even with a double bogey at the par-four 13th. He shot a 74 and tied for ninth. Said Day, who suffered a vertigo attack in the second round: "Not bad considering."

Dustin Johnson seemed well on his way to his first U.S. Open win in eight tries. Birdies at the fourth and eighth put him at six under at the turn. The scramble was then on when Johnson bogeyed three of four holes from the 10th.

This was a U.S. Open that wouldn't stay put.

At the par-four 16th, Spieth's tee shot ended up on a little tuft of rough short of a bunker. He pitched weakly, to about 27 feet, and holed the big-bending putt for a birdie. Grace, after driving out of bounds, was on in four, 12 feet short of the cup. He two-putted for a double-bogey-six and trailed by three.

It was back to square one. At the par-three 17th, Spieth missed the green. "That's as far off-line as I've hit a six iron in a long time," he said. He pitched to 20 feet and three-putted for a double bogey. Johnson, next in the last group, hit his tee shot to six feet and holed the birdie putt. They were tied at four under with the 18th hole to play.

The 18th was a par-five for the finale, playing at 601 yards. Spieth drove into the fairway and hit an astounding second shot that rolled up the right side of the green, took a huge Daytona turn around the back and came back down, stopping 15 feet, 4 inches below the cup. His eagle try stopped next to the hole. He tapped in for a birdie, a 69, and a five-under 275 total.

Johnson came along and stunned him. Johnson hit a perfect drive, and fired his second to 12 feet, 4 inches.

(Said Spieth, watching from the scoring stand: "I thought, 'Shoot, I may have lost this tournament.'")

Johnson rolled his eagle putt four feet past the cup. Then he missed his birdie putt, too, hanging it on the edge. He tapped in for, as it were, a losing par and a 70. Another major had got away, like the 2010 U.S. Open and the 2010 PGA.

"Disappointed," Johnson said. "I played really well. I did everything that I could. I tried my damnedest to get in the hole. I just couldn't do it."

Spieth had the U.S. Open, his second major, and the second leg of the Grand Slam.

"You only get a few moments in your life like this," Spieth said. "And to have two in one year ... that's hard to wrap my head around."

The final leaders: Jordan Spieth 69–275, Louis Oosthuizen 67–276, Dustin Johnson 70–276, Adam Scott 64–277, Cameron Smith 68–277, Branden Grace 71–277.

4. The Open Championship

With Jordan Spieth having won the Masters and the U.S. Open, there was much talk of slams, grand or otherwise, as the young Texan and the rest of major golf's entourage moved on to St. Andrews for the 144th Open Championship. As with most things in the game, history had passed this way before at the Home of Golf.

It was Arnold Palmer who can be credited with idea of the game's modern grand slam. Crossing the Atlantic in 1960 having just won the double of the Masters and the U.S. Open, Palmer wondered what could constitute a updated version's of Bobby Jones slam from 1930. That year, uniquely, Jones won the Amateur and Open championships of Britain and America — the first of the four being the British Amateur on the Old Course.

It was only after Jones retired from competition that he created Augusta National and the Masters, a tournament that Palmer, and everyone else, became to recognize as one of the game's biggies. Put the Masters alongside the U.S. Open, the Open Championship and the PGA Championship and Palmer considered them a four-card trick for a professional that was worthy of Jones' feat.

In 1953 Ben Hogan won the Masters, the U.S. Open and the Open Championship. He was unable to play in the PGA due to health reasons and the clash of dates with his trip to Carnoustie but remains the only player to win those three titles in the same year. Tiger Woods became the only player to hold all four of them at the same time, the so-called "Tiger Slam" of 2000-2001.

Palmer made a characteristically brave charge at the Centenary Open of 1960 but came up one stroke shy of Kel Nagle, who was the oldest living Open champion at the time of his death aged 94 early in 2015. St. Andrews witnessed another slam attempt in 2013 when Inbee Park arrived having won the first three majors of the year but could not mount the sort of challenge that Palmer had, or Jack Nicklaus at Muirfield in 1972.

That year Nicklaus arrived having won the Masters and the U.S. Open and held the PGA title from 1971 which had been staged in February. Victory at Muirfield would have given him all four titles, even if non-consecutively, but he faced Lee Trevino, who had won the last two majors of 1971, the two Opens. Trevino beat Nicklaus by a stroke, though it was Tony Jacklin's late demise that lingered in most memories.

For the 2015 Open, a similar situation arose in that Spieth had won the first two majors of the year and Rory McIlroy had won the last two of the previous year. But McIlroy's dream of defending the Claret Jug at his favorite venue on the Open rota had already vanished. Little more than a week before the championship he suffered an ankle injury in a football kickabout with friends.

Spieth was to come agonizingly close to keeping his grand slam dreams alive, but it was not McIlroy who denied him. Like Palmer and Nicklaus he came up a stroke short. Jason Day came similarly close to making the three-way playoff on one of the most extraordinary final days in the Open's history.

First of all it was a Monday, the second round having been played over Friday and Saturday due first to flooding and then winds that were too strong for play. Only at Royal Lytham in 1988 had a modern Open spilled over to the start of the next working week, and that had provided a cracker of a finale with Seve Ballesteros defeating the two Nicks, Price and Faldo.

Here the net was cast even wider. As well as the three players who went to extra time, Zach Johnson, Marc Leishman and Louis Oosthuizen, others who led at some stage were Spieth, Padraig Harrington and Adam Scott. Day, Anthony Wall, Danny Willett, Sergio Garcia and amateur Ashley Chesters all got within a stroke of the top. Chesters ended up tied for 12th, as did Oliver Schniederjans, but both were denied the Silver Medal as the leading amateur by Jordan Niebrugge, who shared sixth place.

And that list of amateurs does not even include Paul Dunne, who shared the 54-hole lead with Oosthuizen and Day. It was a manic Monday all right and quite a week (and a bit). "Whoever wins, that's a hell of a major," Spieth gasped as the playoff started without him.

It was the first playoff at St. Andrews since 1995 when John Daly defeated Costantino Rocca. As if the Italian's memorable escapade at the 18th of the Old Course was enough excitement to last a while, the three subsequent Opens at St. Andrews brought processional victories for Woods (twice) and Oosthuizen in 2010.

This time the drama at the home green was relentless. First came Johnson, holing for a birdie from 28 feet, punching the air while his caddie, Damon Green, did a celebratory jig of his own. Johnson's 66 would become, by three strokes, the lowest final-round score by a champion at St. Andrews, but only after a wait and then the playoff. Leishman was next, making a par for his own 66 and matching Johnson's 15-under-par total of 273.

Spieth and Day both needed birdies at the 18th to tie, but the American always had an unlikely attempt from the Valley of Sin — he's many things but no Rocca — while Day's 20-footer, from left-to-right behind the hole, came up tantalizingly short. Oosthuizen came last, having made vital par-saves at the previous two holes and then holing from five feet for a birdie to tie.

An hour later Oosthuizen faced another putt on the same green to tie, this one from twice the distance, and it just slipped by the left lip. Johnson had put himself in command in the playoff by birdieing the first two holes. Leishman had bogeyed the first and never contended. Oosthuizen followed Johnson in on the first but not at the second. All three bogeyed the 17th and parred the last.

Johnson, at the age of 39 and in his 12th attempt at "the most fun tournament I play all year," seized the Claret Jug. He was still the "normal guy from Cedar Rapids, Iowa" who had similarly disarmed greater foes by winning the Masters in 2007. Pitching and putting are the keys to his game, and they worked just as well on the Old Course as they did at Augusta that year when, in circumspect but precise fashion, he laid up at all the par-fives every day yet played those 16 holes in 12 under par.

He become the 14th player to win the Open Championship and the Masters but only the sixth to win at both St. Andrews and Augusta. Jones is the link between the two — he put a lifetime of study of the former into the creation of the latter.

With two majors to his name, Johnson put himself into future conversations about qualification for the World Golf Hall of Fame. For the first time the Induction ceremony was held away from the Hall's home in St. Augustine, Florida. Younger Hall in St. Andrews, where Jones received the freedom of the city in an emotional ceremony in 1958, was the perfect venue for the inductions of course architect A.W. Tillinghast (posthumously), David Graham, Dame Laura Davies and Mark O'Meara, who won both the Masters and the Open Championship in 1998.

"With my passion for links golf, and that I was able to hoist the Claret Jug, the fact that the World Golf Hall of Fame is being conducted here at Younger Hall at St. Andrews the week of the Open Championship just means even that much more," O'Meara said.

FIRST ROUND

Yet it was easy to overlook Zach Johnson's challenge early in the week as he opened with a 66. He was not even the low Johnson. Dustin of that ilk led with a seven-under 65 and achieved it in a very different fashion from his namesake, blasting his familiar booming drives miles down the Old Course's double fairways. Were we still at Cambers Bay from a month earlier? Johnson was playing with Spieth, who returned a 67, as did Oosthuizen, who had finished as joint runner-up alongside Johnson in the U.S. Open. Another of the Chambers Bay cast list, Jason Day, had recovered from his bout of vertigo to post a 66 alongside Zach Johnson, Robert Streb, Retief Goosen, Danny Willett and Paul Lawrie.

"Bloody hell, they just won't go away," Day said. "It's kind of extended on from the U.S. Open with Dustin Johnson and Jordan Spieth right there." Seemingly Dustin Johnson had put behind him the disappointment of three-putting the 72nd green to lose to Spieth. "Well, you know, nothing bad happened at Chambers Bay," he said. "I couldn't control what the ball was doing on the greens there. There really are no bad feelings from that, only good."

On a still, overcast morning which retained the moisture in the ground from the Old Course's frequent recent soakings, scoring was inevitably low. Sweden's David Lingmerth, on his Open debut, equaled the St. Andrews nine-hole record with an outward 29 with eight threes and a par-five at the fifth. He could not keep it up, coming home in 40. Dustin Johnson was out in 31 thanks to birdies at the second and third, then an eagle at the fifth after a seven iron to 10 feet before he drove the green at the ninth and took his three. Another birdie came at the 10th but, as the breeze began to pick up, the key to his round was not dropping a stroke, making two fine par-saving putts at the 16th and 17th holes. His shot of the day was a three-wood approach to six feet at the 14th for his last birdie of the round.

"It's hard to argue with somebody who's splitting bunkers at 380 yards and just two-putting for par on five or six holes," marveled Spieth, who nevertheless added: "I can still trump that crazy ability he has, just with a little different route."

Spieth is happy doing things his own way and that included his route to St. Andrews. Instead of arriving early for some links preparation, Spieth honored a commitment to play in the John Deere Classic and flew on the

Sunday charter with another victory tucked under his belt. He had only once played the Old Course before, a friendly round as the U.S. Walker Cup team warmed up for the 2011 match at Royal Aberdeen. Spieth did crank up the course on his simulator at home but admitted it was more for fun than practice since nothing compares to discovering in person how the lines on each hole change with the conditions.

Still, the Spieth phenomenon appeared to just keep rolling along as he birdied the first two holes and then had three in a row from the fifth. He matched Dustin Johnson's 31 going out but stumbled with an even-par inward half, saved by a three at the 18th. Also on 67 was Niebrugge, whose score tied Joe Carr's record for an amateur at St. Andrews and gave him an early lead in what would be a highly competitive amateur race.

Zach Johnson and Willett, who matched the day's best inward score of 33, were out in the breezier afternoon for their 66s and then had the advantage of finishing their second rounds on Friday. Torrential rain flooded the course with the first group off finding the first green under water when they got there. Play was delayed for three-and-a-quarter hours, but the 27-year-old Willett produced a 69 to take the overnight clubhouse lead on nine under par, while Johnson added a 71 to be seven under. "I always feel like I'm under the radar," Johnson admitted, but he could not conceal how excited he was with his game.

First-round leaders: Dustin Johnson 65, Robert Streb 66, Retief Goosen 66, Paul Lawrie 66, Jason Day 66, Zach Johnson 66, Danny Willett 66.

SECOND ROUND

Yet this will be remembered as Farewell Friday as first Sir Nick Faldo and then five-time champion Tom Watson said their goodbyes to the Open Championship. Watson, 65, had his exemption for finishing in the top 10 at the 2009 Open — when he appeared to have claimed a sixth Claret Jug before losing a playoff to Stewart Cink — extended by a year, and so knew it was going to be his last appearance in a championship that he first won in a playoff at Carnoustie in 1975.

Faldo had first said this would be his farewell but then indicated that he might play at Royal Troon and Royal Birkdale in subsequent years. But all that changed as he battled back from an opening 83 with a 71. He might not have teed up, spending the rain delay at hospital having further treatment on an existing cut on his finger. A rare birdie at the 17th, from a long putt from the front of the green, was the highlight.

"I think I've only done it twice," Faldo said, "and that's why I looked to the St. Andrews golfing gods and thought, 'Thank you very much for that.' I felt beat up yesterday, but that was one of the great moments of my career, making a three there and walking the walk." For the walk down the 18th fairway, Faldo donned the yellow sweater from his first Open victory at Muirfield in 1987. He stopped on the Swilken Bridge, arms aloft, and savored the rainbow-capped scene. "That's the greatest view in golf," he said, adding of his future intentions: "If I'm sensible, that's it. I'll do my best to be sensible."

It was near darkness later that evening that Watson enjoyed the same walk. When the American teed off, the stands along the first fairway rose as one in acclaim. It was touch and go whether he would get finished, but playing partners Ernie Els and Brandt Snedeker agreed on the 17th tee it was the right thing to do, even if a six at the 17th cost Snedeker a chance to make the cut. It was just before 10 p.m. and cold as well as dark, but admirers rushed back from pubs and restaurants in the town to provide an emotional send off, members of the Royal and Ancient Golf Club spilling out from the clubhouse to line the first tee.

There was applause, hugs, handshakes and a final bow. But no tears from the man who was overcome with emotion when accompanying Jack Nicklaus on the Golden Bear's Open exit 10 years earlier. "My son, Michael, my caddie almost cried on the 18th tee when I said 'No tears.' But no, there weren't any tears. It's all joy. There's no reason to be sad. I played golf for a living and played it pretty well at times. It's been a heck of a ride." On the Swilken Bridge he had stopped to think of those no longer with him on the journey, former caddies Alfie Fyles and Bruce Edwards among them.

Instead of rain, Saturday brought gales that intensified just as play resumed at 7 a.m. for the 42 players still to complete their second rounds. Dustin Johnson, the overnight leader at 10 under par, immediately had a chip roll back to his feet at the 14th and he took a bogey-six. On the 13th green, Oosthuizen faced a tricky two-and-a-half–footer for par which he watched first blow to within a foot of the hole, then a further eight feet away. At the 11th green, the most exposed on the course, Brooks Koepka could not get his ball to stay still as he tried to replace it on the green.

Play was halted at 7:32 a.m. "Clearly, with the benefit of hindsight, it would have been better if play had not started," said Peter Dawson, the outgoing chief executive of The R&A. "The decision to start was taken on the evidence at the time. When play was suspended we were experiencing wind speeds of 25 mph gusting to 40 mph."

It was not until 6 p.m. that the wind dropped sufficiently for play to resume. Dustin Johnson birdied the 18th for a 69 to lead at halfway on 10 under par. Willett was one behind with Lawrie, inspired by playing with Arnold Palmer in the Champion Golfers' Challenge on Wednesday, on eight under after a 70. Oosthuizen, who made his par putt at the 13th on the resumption, scored a 70 to join the seven-unders, who included Zach Johnson, Day and Scott, after a 67 on Friday, among others. Spieth was still on five under after a 72 that contained an extraordinary five three-putts from the putting wizard.

Second-round leaders: Dustin Johnson 69-134, Danny Willett 69-135, Paul Lawrie 70-136, Marc Warren 69-137, Zach Johnson 71-137, Adam Scott 67-137, Robert Streb 71-137, Jason Day 71-137, Louis Oosthuizen 70-137.

THIRD ROUND

Sunday was the new Saturday, third-round "moving" day yet exciting enough for a final day. Except for the leaders, with none of the top four breaking par. Dustin Johnson bogeyed the last three holes for a 75 and the American would slip down the leaderboard even further with the same score on Monday.

Instead, into the lead roared Oosthuizen and Day, after both scored 67s, and Dunne with a 66. The 22-year-old from Greystones became the first amateur to lead after 54 holes of the Open since Bobby Jones at St. Andrews in 1927. Since Jones won that year and in 1930, no amateur has triumphed again. With a 12-under-par total of 204 the Irishman had smashed the previous 54-hole amateur record by six strokes and set a new record for an amateur at St. Andrews with his 66. Five under after 10 holes, Dunne did not drop a stroke all day and picked up another birdie at the 15th. Playing alongside Oosthuizen, Dunne never appeared fazed by the huge gallery and their encouraging support. He looked 12 but played with the maturity of a 32-year-old. Even Oosthuizen was impressed with his ball-striking, particularly at the 17th where Dunne hit a four iron from 220 yards to 20 feet. "That second shot into 17 was one of the best I've seen," said the South African. "He played unbelievable golf."

"It's surreal that I'm leading the Open," said the recent graduate of the University of Alabama. "If I were playing an amateur event here, I wouldn't be too surprised at my scores. It's just lucky that it happens to be in the biggest event in the world."

It was another 66, however, that had the leaderboard quaking as Spieth slipped into fourth place, one behind the leaders. Another three-putt at the ninth had frustrated the young American, but his inward nine showed how a champion can rally when a charge is required. He birdied the first three holes of the back nine and also the 15th to come home in 32. "I'm not playing for a place," said the 21-year-old hoping to keep his grand slam hopes alive, "I want to win."

Harrington returned a 65 to be two off the lead and joked: "I always wanted to shoot 65 on the Sunday of the Open, though obviously there is another round to go." The lowest score of the day, however, came from Australian Leishman with a 64. His eight birdies came from the fourth to the 15th and he missed chances at the 16th and 17th holes before finding the Valley of Sin at the last but saving par.

Leishman admitted to a new perspective on the game and life after his wife, Audrey, nearly died four months earlier from toxic-shock syndrome. A rare and often fatal bacterial infection almost meant Leishman became a single parent to his two boys, aged one and three. "It was a huge possibility that I wasn't going to be able to play golf any more," he said. "The experience changed my perspective of life. If I have a bad day, I can still go home and give Audrey a hug and cuddle my boys. For a while it didn't looked like I was going to be able to do that."

At nine under par, Leishman was in a large group that included amateur Niebrugge, Garcia, Streb, Goosen, Justin Rose, Willett, Scott and Zach Johnson, whose three-five-three finish gave him a 70 for the day. Johnson recalled playing alongside Els on the last day at Royal Lytham in 2012. "I got to witness what it takes to win from behind," he said. "It was cool to see what he was doing. You never know."

Third-round leaders: Paul Dunne 66-204, Louis Oosthuizen 67-204, Jason Day 67-204, Jordan Spieth 66-205, Padraig Harrington 65-206.

FOURTH ROUND

Johnson had clearly absorbed the lesson well. On an overcast Monday with some breeze, a little rain but with low scoring possible, and in front of a roll-up gallery of around 35,000, Johnson made the turn in 31 to take the lead. He holed an 18-footer at the second, a 35-footer at the fourth, two-putted the fifth, hit a wedge to three feet at the seventh and the same club to six feet at the ninth. "I clearly had to be somewhat aggressive early on because those outward holes are the ones you've got to take advantage of," he said.

Spieth birdied the first hole, as did Oosthuizen. Dunne was the last man to tee off, the last player announced by starter Ivor Robson, who retired after 41 years by the first tee, though he was needed again later in the afternoon for the playoff. The anticipation of an amateur champion may have weighed on the young Irishman as he left his approach at the first short of the burn. Bogeys at the first two holes were the prelude to a 78, which meant in a four-way contest for the Silver Medal it was Niebrugge with a closing 70 who took the honors. The 21-year-old Oklahoma State student set a new amateur record total of 277 in tying for sixth place.

The leaderboard was in constant flux all afternoon. Harrington birdied the first two holes and then the fifth to tie for the lead before a double bogey at the sixth when he lost a ball in a bush on the right with a wild drive. "Things were going well, why not take it on?" reasoned the two-time champion. His challenge was over and he was another Irishman who ended the day over par.

But he was not the last player to stumble on the Old Course. Garcia was five under for the day through 10 holes, one off the lead, but he played the rest of the round in three over. Scott matched Johnson's 31 out and birdied the 10th to tie before dropping five strokes on the last five holes. His horror run, that brought back sad memories of his four bogeys at Lytham to lose to Els in 2012, included a missed tap-in from a foot at the 14th. "I don't really have an explanation," Scott admitted. "I went to tap it in and it lipped out."

Leishman was also out in 31 and fared better than his compatriot. The Australian also matched Johnson's birdies at the 10th and 12th holes, and when Johnson bogeyed the 13th, Leishman went ahead. Johnson also bogeyed the 17th and was briefly two behind but made up for it with his brave putt at the last. "The emotion," Johnson said of the celebration, "was because it was the 72nd hole and I knew I had a good round going."

Moments later Leishman bogeyed the 16th after finding a bunker and missing from four feet. He had a chance of a birdie at the last but said he misread it.

In the penultimate pairing, Spieth and Day were not out of contention. Spieth had birdied three of the first six holes before inexplicably putting off the green at the eighth. "There was absolutely no reason to hit that putt off the green, but I'd left so many putts short all week that I wasn't going to leave that one short," explained the Texan. The error cost him a double-bogey-five, but he responded positively once more with birdies at the next two holes.

Pars followed until an electrifying moment at the 16th when he rolled in a 50-footer to tie for the lead. Suddenly a special feeling of imminent history hovered over the course, but Spieth missed his six-footer for par at the 17th and left his approach at the 18th, having driven well left, short in the Valley of Sin. A 69 left him one stroke short of taking his chance of a grand slam in the playoff.

Apart from birdies at the fifth and sixth holes, Day had been ultra consistent. He had not dropped a shot and his approach to the last gave him a good chance from 20 feet behind the hole. The putt broke from left-to-right but stopped tantalizingly short of the hole. "I didn't want to blast it through the break, but I thought it was a little faster," said Day, who bowed his head in his hands in disbelief. "I've been working very hard to accomplish my first major. I really want to have that shot at immortality. It'll come soon."

Oosthuizen enjoyed a triumphal march to victory in 2010 and was determined to repeat as a St. Andrews champion. He never quite got on a run of birdies, and the putts did not always drop, but they certainly did over the last three holes, for two pars and then a closing birdie. With a 69 the South African was also in the four-hole playoff.

But Johnson's pair of 15-foot birdie putts at the first two holes of the playoff put him in charge. At the last, Oosthuizen's 10-footer to extend the playoff missed.

"You never want to see a championship, specifically the Open, end on a miss," Johnson sympathized. He was congratulated by his wife Kim and Spieth, who had waited to see the end of the playoff. Johnson called the Open his "most fun tournament of the year," but now holding the Claret Jug he added: "I'm humbled right now because of what is on my lap. It's a dream realized. I am a little bit in shock."

The final leaders: Zach Johnson 66-273, Marc Leishman 66-273, Louis Oosthuizen 69-273, Jordan Spieth 69-274, Jason Day 70-274, Danny Willett 70-277, Justin Rose 70-277, Sergio Garcia 70-277, Jordan Niebrugge 70-277.

5. PGA Championship

It seems the fates took some of the steam out of the 2015 PGA Championship, the last of the year's four majors. It's as though they put up their hands at St. Andrews and said "Stop," to Jordan Spieth. "Two are enough for now." The young Texan, who was halfway to the first-ever Grand Slam with victories in the Masters and the U.S. Open, was turned aside at the Open Championship.

With the slam out of the way, the PGA settled in at Whistling Straits, on the Wisconsin shores of Lake Michigan, for as gripping a championship as any movie director could have imagined. These were the principals in the cast:

Spieth, who turned 22 in July, had four wins already this year, including the two majors, may have been stopped at the British Open, but 3-for-4 would be pretty good. He would be the first since Tiger Woods to win three majors in a calendar year. Said Spieth of the slam: "It wasn't expected, from my point of view. But it's still a whole other animal just to win a major in general."

Rory McIlroy, 26, owner of four majors, hadn't played since the U.S. Open in June, missing 53 days after hurting his ankle playing soccer. As to pre-tournament talk of a McIloy-Spieth battle for domination, McIlroy offered: "After I won this tournament [in 2014], it was the Rory Era, and then Jordan wins the Masters and it's the Jordan Era. Eras last about six months these days…"

Jason Day, blossoming on the PGA Tour, had two wins coming into the PGA and was the sympathetic favorite for the way he battled vertigo in challenging for the U.S. Open in June. "I was going to pull out three times that day [Saturday]," Day said. "I'm willing to put my body on the line just to get a taste of that greatness."

Dustin Johnson, who stumbled at the final hole at the U.S. Open in June, is forever linked to a PGA at Whistling Straits. In the 2010 PGA, he was leading going into the final hole, unknowingly grounded his club in a bunker, and the penalty knocked him out of a playoff. He was asked if he ever thought of that episode. Said Johnson: "About as many times as I've been asked the question."

Tiger Woods, a four-time PGA champion, limited by medical problems, was making just his 10th start of the bleak year. He was stuck on 14 in pursuit of Jack Nicklaus' record of 18 majors. This was Woods' 18th PGA. How had he changed? "I can't hit the ball as far as I used to, relatively speaking," he said. "I'm longer now in yardage than I was earlier in my career, but as compared to other players, no, I'm not."

Phil Mickelson, 45, the 2005 winner, would be making his 23rd start in the PGA. He also had two seconds, a third and six other top-10 finishes. One of his seconds was by a stroke to McIlroy in 2014.

The PGA being the last major of the year, it was the last chance for the golfers with the most starts in majors without winning one: Lee Westwood, 70; Miguel Angel Jimenez, 69; Sergio Garcia, 68, and Steve Stricker, 64.

With the 2015 PGA Championship about to get under way, Dustin Johnson had absolutely no fear of repeating his costly error in that bunker in 2010.

"There's a grandstand there," Johnson said. "Thank you, PGA. I appreciate that."

FIRST ROUND

An echo of Palmer-Nicklaus-Player at the 2015 PGA Championship:

Rory McIlroy, 26 and No. 1 in the world, making his first appearance since injuring his ankle in July, opened the PGA with a one-under-par 71 that put him comfortably near the lead.

Jordan Spieth, shortly after turning 22 and going for his third major since being denied at the Open Championship, also shot 71.

Jason Day, 27, showing no lingering effect from the vertigo attack that felled him at the U.S. Open in June, was only two off the lead with his 68.

The word in golf was that these were the emerging new Big Three, a concentration of talent and celebrity that echoed the triumvirate of Arnold Palmer, Jack Nicklaus and Gary Player of the 1960s and '70s. It was said that Billy Casper could have made it a foursome, but that his benign persona didn't market well. Similarly, it was widely agreed that Dustin Johnson, 31, could make it a modern Big Four except that he was known more for his close calls than his successes — grounding his club in a bunker on the final hole of the 2010 PGA at Whistling Straits, and more recently, in 2015, the three-putt par from 12 feet on the final hole that cost him a chance at the U.S. Open, and the rugged finish in the British Open, shooting 75-75 after leading through 36 holes.

"Today was pretty easy," Johnson said, opening with a six-under 66 for a one-stroke lead sparked by a strong start. Starting on the 10th, he birdied his first two holes and eagled his seventh (the par-five 16th), hitting a four iron to 30 feet. "It's only the first round," he added.

McIlroy had a four-birdie, one-bogey 71 and also answered a huge pre-tournament concern: After all that time off, would his injured left ankle hold up under the strain of walking some 7,500 yards and hitting shots after all that time off. One answer: He hit a 359-yard drive at the par-five 11th and birdied.

"It's more just being a little bit anxious, coming back and seeing how my game is going to react under pressure," McIlroy said. He started tentatively, with a bogey at No. 1, then took advantage of the par-fives, making three birdies and a great par save at the fifth, splashing his ball out of shallow water to within seven feet of the cup and holing the par putt.

McIlroy's verdict of his return: "Once I got those first couple of holes out of the way," he said "I felt like I settled into the round really nicely."

Lingmerth, the little-known Swede who won the Memorial, started on the 10th and rolled out five birdies en route to his 67, one off the lead. And he did it in the face of winds that picked up in the afternoon.

"Whatever David ate this morning," said Spieth, "I'd like to eat tomorrow." Spieth, a putting whiz, missed a number of birdie chances on the front nine and ground out 10 straight pars. He bogeyed the 11th with three putts, then birdied the 12th, chipping in, and the 16th for a one-under 71. A combination of green speed and the wind tripped him up. "I guessed wrong," he said. "If I didn't get that good break on 12," he said, when his chip shot hit the flagstick and dropped, "it could have been a different story the rest of the round."

Jason Day saw his strong round dented by a late bogey, but was happy anyway. "I feel like we've got the better side of the draw right now," Day said. "And fortunately for us, we got to attack the golf course. We only got kind of the really brute force of the wind coming in the last few holes." Starting on the back nine, Day was five under through his 14th, with an eagle and four birdies, then bogeyed his 15th (No. 6).

The lakeside course was described as "gettable," and the scores indicated as much. In the 2010 PGA, 33 golfers were under par in the first round. There were 38 under par this time.

The coincidence of the week award went to Phil Mickelson, the 2005 champion and runner-up to McIlroy in 2014. The first round fell on Thursday, August 13, National Left-Handers Day, and he cobbled together four birdies and four bogeys for a 72. Asked whether he would like to see the same weather conditions for the second round, Mickelson said, "Are you kidding?"

Tiger Woods, making his 10th start of the year, was in danger of missing the cut with a 75. "Probably one of the worst putting rounds I've had in a very long time," he said.

First-round leaders: Dustin Johnson 66, David Lingmerth 67, Jason Day 68, Harris English 68, Russell Henley 68, J.B. Holmes 68, Matt Jones 68, Matt Kuchar 68, Danny Lee 68, Scott Piercy 68.

SECOND ROUND

While the new Big Three were battling Whistling Straits and establishing their collective identity, and while Tiger Woods was in the grim process of missing yet another cut, Hiroshi Iwata, an unknown from the Japan Tour, came out of nowhere and stole the entire show in the second round.

Iwata, 34, a two-time winner in Japan, was just hoping to improve in this PGA Championship. He had opened with a top-heavy 77 and in the second round was two under par for the day and still three over for the championship through the turn, then erupted and shot 63, tying the single-round record for the majors. It was the 27th 63 in the majors, the 13th in the PGA Championship.

"When I came here," Iwata said through an interpreter, "I was thinking just to make my game better, and on Sunday, I can be in the top 10." He tore through the last eight holes, making an eagle at the par-five 11th, then getting birdies at 12, 13, 15, 16 and 17. (He made the cut easily and would go on to finish tied for 21st.)

There was more to the second round than Iwata's heroics. There was, for example, first-round leader Dustin Johnson fading, John Daly having a fit of pique, David Lingmerth making only four pars in a round of 70, two Aussies ending up atop the leaderboard and a beastly storm that forced some to complete their round on Saturday.

Daly, 49, famed for his come-from-nowhere victory in the 1991 PGA and also for his meltdowns, was only one over par coming to the lakeside par-three No. 7. There, he put three tee shots into the water, followed by his six iron. It was a mighty heave. "It shows you care," he said. He made 10, shot 82 and missed the cut.

With the field scrambling, Johnson re-took the lead with a birdie at the 10th then bogeyed the par-five 11th out of a poor lie in a bunker. He also bogeyed the 13th and 14th and shot 73, six off the lead. "I could have posted a really low one today if I could have just holed a few more putts," Johnson said.

Australian Matt Jones, a one-time winner on the PGA Tour, grabbed the halfway lead with a flawless 65 that came as no surprise to him. "You're a golfer," he said, "so you expect weeks like this." Starting at No. 10, he birdied four times on his first nine, three on his second. "I've been in the lead on a tour event, but a major's a different story," Jones said. "But I'm going to have fun with it, and I'm pretty relaxed on the golf course."

Day shot a 67 that included five birdies — and a bogey — in a nine-hole stretch from the fifth, and finished two behind his Aussie friend. "It's just — my confidence level is high," Day said, "I'm enjoying myself so much on the golf course."

New names entered the hunt. Justin Rose was third with a 67 that contained eight birdies and a double bogey and a bogey; and two newcomers reached the leaderboard — Tony Finau, with a 66, and India's Anirban Lahiri, a 67.

Though Rory McIlroy would have preferred otherwise, he shot a second and almost perfectly balanced 71 — an eagle at No. 2 and a double bogey at No. 18 for bookends, and after a birdie-bogey set, a birdie at the 16th gave him the one-stroke edge. He needed only 18 putts, but he hit only 11 greens. "I don't know if it's rust or I just didn't putt well," McIlroy said. "I don't really want to blame it to rust."

Jordan Spieth birdied five of his last 12 holes for a 67 to tie at 138, five back. At the 18th, he finessed a bunker shot that had him mopping his brow — and holed it for a birdie. He had to play the shot about 10 feet to the right of the cup with a very steep swing. "And chances of hitting that the right way are so slim, you could easily catch that thin and then you're left with a very likely double bogey," he said. "I would have taken four and walked off a very, very happy guy."

For Tiger Woods things were encouraging, but only briefly. He birdied the second and third, then double-bogeyed the fourth. He shot 73–148, missing the cut by two. It was the first time in his career that he'd missed it in three straight majors. "I putted awful," he said.

Second-round leaders: Matt Jones 65–133, Jason Day 67–135, Justin Rose 67–136, Tony Finau 66–137, Anirban Lahiri 67–137, David Lingmerth 70–137, Scott Piercy 70–138, Jordan Spieth 67–138, Brendan Steele 69–138.

THIRD ROUND

If this was the future of golf, then gentlemen, play away.

Jason Day and Jordan Spieth — two heavyweights slugging it out, two milers practically step for step. That was the third round of the 2015 PGA Championship. Two of the hottest, most imposing golfers in the game, with a third, Rory McIlroy, trying to regain his form after an injury, making up the young triumvirate who could rule the game for years to come.

Day raced to a six-under 66 to take the lead by two over Spieth, who streaked to a seven-under 65. The third of the group, McIlroy, in his first outing since being off for nearly two months, had his best round yet, a 68.

But it was far from a two-man show. Branden Grace exploded for a day's-low 64, and the ever-present Justin Rose posted a 68 to tie for third, three off the lead. Grace saw it as possibly another chance developing. That shot in the U.S. Open still hurt. He was tied for the lead with three holes to play, then hit his drive out of bounds. This time, he bunkered a shot at the 18th and holed the escape for his 64. But the scoreboard told him what was still going on out on the course. "The guys behind me, they're going to make some birdies coming in," he said. "I'm sure I won't have the lead, but it's never a bad thing coming out a little behind and heading into the final day."

Rose made a painful double bogey at the sixth and bogeyed the 18th, but posted seven birdies for his 68. What score did he have in mind for the final round? "It's never easy to close out a major championship," Rose said. "If I was to shoot 68 again, ask the question."

Day, after three birdies and two bogeys through No. 5, ran an improbable six straight threes across his card from No. 9 — two birdies, an eagle, a par, and two more birdies, going from 10 under par to 16 under, a stretch that drew the 'ahhs' from Spieth.

The crown jewel was the eagle at the par-five 11th. "That big bunker is about 305 [yards out], and we're up about 10 [yards]," Day said. "Didn't expect to hit my drive down that far on the fairway. I had a pitching wedge in my hand and hit it from 160 yards to about 15 feet and rolled in a nice putt. Once I birdied nine, and I rolled in that nice putt on 10, to be able to hit that drive down 11 and really hole that putt on 11 was nice."

Ordinarily, a double bogey might let the air out of the balloon. That might have happened to Day at the par-four 15th. He pulled his five-iron approach into a left greenside bunker. His first try came rolling back down into the bunker. He double-bogeyed the hole. Then he got one stroke back at the par-three 17th, with the green just about hanging out over the edge of Lake Michigan. He hit a four iron to 25 feet and holed the birdie putt. He parred the 18th for his 66.

Chasing Day, Spieth put on a sizzling display, birdieing three straight from the 11th, catching his breath with two pars, and closing with three more birdies in a row. "I found a lot more fairways today," Spieth explained. "I was able to be more aggressive out of the fairways. Find wedge distances, even though I hit a few that were weak, but I hit a few that were really good. And I was able to capitalize. And so once the one on 11 went, even though it was a simple up-and-down, I at least saw another birdie go. The one on 12 was nice. And we're off to the races. The holes started to look bigger. A lot of times it just takes one to go for me to really find that extra confidence, that extra little pop in my stroke."

In all, the field found an agreeable if not cooperative Whistling Straits after Friday's storm. Thirty players shot in the 60s. A mere five holes played to an average above par, and the 18th allowed nine birdies in the third round, more than in each of the first two rounds.

Third-round leaders: Jason Day 66–201, Jordan Spieth 65–203, Branden Grace 64–204, Justin Rose 68–204, Martin Kaymer 65–205, Tony Finau 69–206, Matt Jones 73–206.

FOURTH ROUND

What it came down to in the final round of the 2015 PGA was that Jason Day never gave anybody else a chance.

Jordan Spieth explained it neatly: "He played like he'd won seven or eight majors. He took it back. He whaled on it. It was a stripe show."

Spieth had won four times already in 2015, including the Masters and U.S. Open, and he played outstanding golf and still lost by three.

"I didn't expect I was going to cry," said Day, taking his first major with a 268, a 20-under-par total that was the record for all four majors. It broke Tiger Woods' record of 19 under in the 2000 Open Championship at St. Andrews.

Why the tears? Apart from the sheer joy of winning that first major, Day — playing with great power and accuracy all day — also erased harsh memories and dark doubts from missing out on a U.S. Open and a British Open after sharing the 54-hole lead.

"Not being able to finish, it would have been tough for me, mentally, to really come back from that," Day said. "Even though I feel like I'm a positive person, I think that in the back of my mind, something would have triggered, and I would have gone, 'Maybe I can't really finish it off.'"

Day led a full assault on Whistling Straits, architect Pete Dye's hand-made course laid on the shores of Lake Michigan. Spieth was second by three shots, and South Africa's Branden Grace, who blew a chance at the U.S. Open when he hit his tee shot out of bounds late in the final round, this time double-bogeyed the 10th, shot 69, and finished third, five back. Justin Rose got within two of Day at one point, but made a double bogey for the third consecutive round and shot 70, finishing fourth.

Spieth matched Day almost shot-for-shot, making six birdies to Day's seven, and both had two bogeys. Spieth couldn't close the gap and finished with a 68.

"There's nothing I could do," Spieth said, and then noted his consolation prize. His runner-up finish carried him, at age 22, over Rory McIlroy to No. 1 in the Official World Golf Ranking for the first time. "This was as easy a loss as I've ever had," he said, "because I felt that I not only couldn't do much about it, I also accomplished one of my lifelong goals in the sport of golf. That will never be taken away from me. I'll always be a No. 1 player in the world."

McIlroy moved to No. 2 and Day to No. 3. The top three in world were now under 27 and had combined to win five of the last six majors.

McIlroy, the other of the presumptive new Big Three, was making progress on his return from the ankle injury. After his 71-71 start, he finished 68-69 for a solo 17th place at 279. "I thought between 10 and 15 under would have a great chance to win," he said, "but obviously the standard is just so high these days that I didn't see close to 20 under par winning. But ... feel like I've done well to come back and shoot the scores that I have. Yeah, I'm walking away pretty happy."

Dustin Johnson, the first-round leader, saw his shrinking hopes die with a crushing eight at the par-four first hole. His approach rolled off the green and down into a bunker. It took him two shots to get back up. "But still played a pretty special round," he said. "To be five over through No. 4 and shoot three under, that's pretty damn good on Sunday in a major." He recovered, shot 69 and tied for seventh.

Day was fighting both Whistling Straits and his doubts and fears from two misses in majors. He started the last round at 15 under and was leading Spieth by two. He upped that to four with birdies at Nos. 2, 5, 6 and 7 against Spieth's three birdies and two bogeys. Neither budged in the showdown. Day birdied Nos. 11, 14 and 16 and bogeyed No. 15 in his 67. Spieth birdied Nos. 10, 13 and 16 for his 68.

At one point, rather early, Spieth realized that Day was playing with too much authority and confidence to be caught.

"The tee shot on 11," Spieth said. Day hit it 381 yards. "I actually out loud said, 'You've got to be kidding me,'" Spieth said. "I knew I was going to be playing uphill from there." Day birdied and went to 19 under, and was up by four when Spieth parred. Day birdied the par-five 16th as well, off a soaring four-iron approach and two putts from 20 feet.

A brisk rivalry was already shaping up.

"Even if I did pull off the shots at the end, it still wouldn't have been good enough," Spieth said. "Jason didn't miss enough shots. Each time he stood and took it back, I had hope. And each time after it came off the face, the hope was lost."

"To be honest, the kid just doesn't go away," Day said. "It baffles me, the stuff he can prove out there. To hold him off knowing he's going to be the best player in the world now — it felt great."

In the end it was power, accuracy, fear and guts.

"It felt like I was mentally and physically grinding it out as hard as I could," Day said. "I wasn't going to stop fighting till it was over."

The final-round leaders: Jason Day 67–268, Jordan Spieth 68–271, Branden Grace 69–273, Justin Rose 70–274, Brooks Koepka 66–275, Anirban Lahiri 68–275.

6. Women's Major Championships

ANA Inspiration

Nothing had really changed. It was still Mission Hills Country Club, and there was still Poppie's Pond, a water hazard all year round except for the few exhilarating moments it takes for a winner to make that celebratory leap. It was still the LPGA's spring frolic in sunny Southern California that began in 1972 as the Colgate-Dinah Shore Winner's Circle and went through a number of names, the latest the Kraft Nabisco Championship, which ended in 2014. It was still the first of the LPGA's five major championships.

But one thing did change: It was now the ANA (All Nippon Airways) Inspiration.

Brittany Lincicome was the first to make the leap into Poppie's Pond under the new sponsorship, and if she had the look of a veteran going in, it was because she'd done it before. She made the jump in 2009 when she won the Kraft Nabisco and also in a stunning finish. This time it was for her second major, her sixth LPGA victory.

Meanwhile, fans might be thinking it would be easier on everyone if Lincicome would just win the old-fashioned way. These thunderbolt leap-frog finishes on the very last hole can be tough on the system. She eagled it in the 2009 Kraft Nabisco. She eagled it again this time, forcing Stacy Lewis to tie her, then Lincicome beat her on the third extra hole.

"It's pretty incredible when you think about it," Lincicome said. "I mean, to make eagle on any hole is pretty incredible, and then to do it on Sunday at a major, at this major where I did it in 2009, it's really surreal."

But long before Lincicome took the leap, the focus of the inaugural ANA Inspiration was teenager Lydia Ko, Rolex world No. 1, and her pursuit of the LPGA Tour's record of consecutive rounds under par. She had 28 straight. The record was 29, set by Annika Sorenstam in 2004. The chase was magnified by the fact that Ko was 17 and approaching her 18th birthday, that on April 24, two weeks after the ANA. Could the kid make it?

Yes. But by the skin of her teeth — a one-under-par 71 in the first round, thanks to a late miracle save and a later birdie. Ko started at No. 10 and came through buffeting winds with three birdies and four bogeys to make the turn at one over. She got to even par with a birdie at her 11th (No. 2), then saved herself with a remarkable par at her 16th (No. 7), where she drove into the trees, then escaped with a hook around other trees and reached the green, 25 feet from the pin. She two-putted for her par and was even for the day. She needed one more stroke to get under par, and she got that with a birdie at her 17th, then parred the last for the 71, tying Sorenstam's record of 29. "I was so busy trying to make up-and-downs, a record was the last thing I was thinking about," said Ko. Her under-par streak ended in the second round when she took two late bogeys for a 73.

Said Ko, who would struggle from there and finish tied for 51st and was still looking for that first major: "It was pretty awesome that I was near Annika's record last week and even yesterday, and then I tied it. It was so cool that I'm tying with someone amazing and as great as her."

"The most exciting thing about Lydia Ko is she's 17 going on 18," said LPGA Tour Commissioner Mike Whan. "I've met a lot of 22-year-olds going on 40 because this job, this career, grows you up in a hurry."

There was one other thing different about this reincarnation of the Kraft Nabisco — more rough. The primary rough measured about three inches. "It definitely is playing a lot different," said Lexi Thompson, the defending champion. "The rough is up, which major championships should be." She opened with a 72, five shots off the lead, and finished solo seventh, three behind leader Morgan Pressel, the 2007 winner.

Almost unnoticed in the Lydia Ko record chase was South Korean rookie Sei Young Kim taking the second-round lead with a 65 that included six birdies and an eagle. Kim, a five-time winner in Korea who introduced herself to worldwide golf by taking the Pure Silk Bahamas Classic in February, turned up the heat with her putter.

"Yesterday I adjust a little bit my putting," she said. "Before I see the line, but now I see the line better than yesterday now." Her game plan for staying on top: "Just do it. Just do it."

Kim, at 137, led by two over Pressel, who cobbled together a par 72. "It was a little sloppy all around," Pressel said. "but I gave myself a chance for the weekend."

Lincicome, with a 68, was in a group three shots back at 140. She felt she left some shots on the course. "Yeah, for sure," she said. "I missed two five-footers and one 10-footer that could have gone in. I don't know if I'm just overthinking it or not reading them properly or what, but could have been really low today."

Stacy Lewis crept into contention with a five-birdie, two-bogey 69 for a 141 total, four off the lead. "You don't have to go out there and shoot 65 the first day," she said. "You've just got to keep hanging around, and that's the biggest key to winning majors."

"Hanging around" wasn't quite the expression for Sei Young Kim, the way the third round unfolded. She ended up with a good news-bad news situation. She closed with birdies at the 16th and 17th for a 69–206, 10 under and a three-stroke lead over Lewis, who bogeyed 15 and 17 for a 68. Pressel bogeyed 16 and 17 for 71 and a tie for third with Lincicome, who shot 70 with a birdie-birdie-bogey finish, and Ariya Jutanugarn, with a bogey-free 66.

So the good news for Kim was that she had a healthy lead. The bad news: "Those two birdies give me a wider lead, but that doesn't necessarily mean it gives me less pressure or more confidence. Back in Korea, I was known for coming from behind and winning. I don't think I ever won a tournament leading the final round."

Lewis, who birdied six of the first 12 holes before the two late bogeys, was upbeat. "Three shots on this golf course is not a lot," she said. "I've trailed by more and I've won."

Lincicome had three dazzling birdies — chip-ins at the ninth and 16th and a 20-foot putt at the 17th — before her closing bogey. Did she have a clairvoyant flash that said she would repeat her 2009 victory?

"There's no reason," she said, "why I can't be standing on 18 holding that trophy come tomorrow."

Unfortunately for Kim, her reservations bore bitter fruit. In the final round, she birdied twice on the front nine but offset them with a double bogey — a bad sign. She made three birdies coming in, but stumbled to another double bogey and four bogeys. The 75 dropped her to a tie for fourth. "Very disappointing," Kim said, through a translator. "With the wind factoring in … it really confused me."

The chase became a Brittany Lincicome-Stacy Lewis duel, all the way into a playoff.

Lewis easily made up her three-stroke deficit. She birdied the first and seventh and, after a bogey at the eighth, birdied three straight from the 10th. Lewis is not given to untimely lurches, but she suffered two coming in, bogeying the 13th and 15th. Then she missed a birdie from five feet at the 16th. The wind baffled her, too. "[It] just went crazy on us," she said. "Couldn't figure out which direction it was going."

Lincicome had a less troubled time of it. She was out in one under with two birdies and a bogey, and she had solid pars coming home until the par-five 18th. Then what an amazing parallel. In 2009, she hit a hybrid club from 210 yards to four feet and made the eagle. This time it was a five iron from 190 yards to 10 feet.

"When I got to the green I saw nine under on the board, but I was trying not to look again," said Lincicome, playing in the group ahead of Lewis. It was Lewis' nine under. "So I knew I needed to make it. And my caddie just said you have one goal, and that is to get it to the hole, and I did."

Lincicome dropped the putt for an eagle for a 69 and a nine-under 279 total. Lewis closed with a par for a 70 to tie her.

On to the playoff, at the 18th. They matched pars on the first two trips. On the third, Lewis' ball was 103 yards from home, but on a sand-filled divot hole. She was short with her approach, then weak with her chip shot, 12 feet short. Her par putt died one roll too soon. She bogeyed. Lincicome two-putted from 10 feet for a winning par. The victory hit her hard.

"I'm standing here, physically shaking like a leaf, still," Lincicome said. "It's over, and I'm still shaking."

"The initial reaction is disappointed," Lewis said. "I just played solid all day, so I have to remind myself of that and not get too frustrated. It just wasn't quite meant to be today."

While Lewis was dealing with her disappointments, Lincicome went over and jumped into Poppie's Pond. The water was cold, this first week of April. Someone wondered about the robe she wore after her first jump. In her parents' home, she said. "We had it framed, and it does not get worn."

This robe was different. "[It's] a little more expensive," Lincicome said. "I should definitely take better care of this one. But I should wear it. I'm not an expensive kind of girl, so I'd probably wear it. Wear it to the beach. Maybe," she added with a grin, "I'll wear it fishing."

KPMG Women's PGA Championship

From its start in 1955, it was the LPGA Championship, the flagship event for women professional golfers — if with a sponsor's name at times. In 2015, that all changed. The KPMG Women's PGA Championship took center stage. It was still the championship for the LPGA, but it was conducted by the PGA of America, and it bore the sponsorship name of the prominent professional services company.

Among the changes: the purse grew from the $2,250,000 of 2014 to $3,500,000, and the winner's prize from $337,500 to $525,000.

The championship was moved to Westchester Country Club, in suburban New York City, but one thing remained the same: Inbee Park.

Park became only the second golfer to win the championship three consecutive times (after Annika Sorenstam, 2003-05). The victory was her sixth win in the majors and it lifted her back to No. 1 on the Rolex Rankings, a place she had come to think of as her own. She had spent 59 weeks in it in 2013-14.

"It feels great," said Park (it was a five-shot victory). "I feel probably more happy about winning the major championship than probably being No. 1 back again. Because No. 1 spot, I had opportunity every week pretty much, and it just happened this week. I really just wanted to be No. 1 when I was really ready, and this is like the perfect tournament, perfect timing to go up there, so, really happy."

Park had more to be happy about, a carnival in the statistics. She shot the par-73 Westchester in 71-68-66-68—273, 19 under par, and in that card was the astonishing fact that she'd gone the final 56 holes without a bogey. She bogeyed three times in the first round, her last at the 16th, and she went the final two holes and three rounds without one.

"Putting really improved a lot since the first day," Park said. "Starting the second round to the final round, I had not many mistakes in either the ball-striking or putting."

Though she won by five, it was not quite the lark it might have seemed. It was a head-to-head battle over the last three rounds with countrywoman Sei Young Kim, 22, the rookie who beat her for her second win this season. Kim won the Pure Silk Bahamas in February, holing a four-foot birdie putt on the first playoff hole. Then in the Lotte Championship in April, Kim chipped in to tie Park at the final hole, then holed out an eight-iron approach for an eagle on the first playoff hole.

"I have to say my history with her is not great," Park said, with a chuckle. "I lost in a playoff to her in the Lotte, and she won in Bahamas when I played with her. So she probably feels like, you know, I win when I play with Inbee … There is always a first time. Like I said, I never won in front of Sei Young yet, so you never know — hopefully tomorrow."

Kim started the final round two strokes behind and got within one at mid-round, but no closer.

"Everything fell apart at the ninth hole," Kim said. She four-putted for a double-bogey-seven, and with Park's birdie, it turned into a three-shot swing. Park came out of it leading by four and added two more birdies in her bogey-free frolic for a 68 and the five-shot win. It was the easiest of her three victories in the event (by whichever name). The other two came in playoffs. In 2013, she beat Catriona Matthew on the third extra hole and in 2014 she beat Brittany Lincicome on the first. Her other three majors were the U.S. Women's Open in 2008 and 2013, and the 2013 Kraft Nabisco Championship (now the ANA Inspiration).

Although it was the Park-Kim show, there were some interesting sidelights of various kinds. Among them:

• South Korea's Jenny Shin, a 22-year-old rookie, approached the tournament as a nervous wreck. "I was freaking out for this round," she said. "So I tried not to think of it as a major, and it turned out great." It turned out, in fact, to be a seven-under 66 and a one-stroke lead. (Shin apparently could not sustain that frame of mind. She shot 75 in the second round and was out of the running.)

• Hall-of-Famer Karrie Webb, 40, seeking her eighth major and second Women's PGA, opened with a 68. Someone asked her about the talented youth cropping up everywhere. "You were a Brooke Henderson at one time...," someone said. Said Webb, in tribute: "I was in high school when I was Brooke Henderson."

• Canadian whiz Brooke Henderson, 17, shot 67, missed a share of the lead by a three-putt bogey at the last hole. She finished tied for fifth, nine behind. What would she take from the tournament? "I think just the experience," she said. "It was awesome."

• It wasn't as nice for all youth. Lydia Ko, now 18 and No. 1 in the Rolex Rankings, shot 72-76–148 and missed the cut for the first time in her 53 events. Said Ko: "You just never know what's going to happen. Even if you think it might never happen, some things do."

The real Park-Kim battle began in the third round when Park, who trailed by a stroke at the start, inched ahead of Kim by two. This two-stroke margin was deceptive. "Inched" is the word. It was the measure of their struggle that they battled for 17 holes and Park could never get the lead until the final hole of the round.

Kim birdied the first two and went ahead by three. Park cut her deficit back to one with birdies at the third and sixth. Both birdied the ninth, and Park finally drew even on Kim's bogey at the 10th. Both birdied the 12th, then Kim moved ahead with a birdie at the 13th, and they matched birdies at the 15th. It came down to the last two holes. Park tied the match — that's pretty much what it was — with a birdie at the 17th. Park then notched her seventh birdie of the day at No. 18 while Kim bogeyed, missing a four-footer for par. Park shot 66, Kim 69.

"Everything was great, up until the last hole," Kim said. "I left something out on the last hole today."

Park was up by two going into the final round. It would be the veteran vs. the upstart.

"It feels like the first time is always hard, and it puts extra pressure on yourself," Park said. "But when you're trying to do the second, third time in a row, it just feels like you've done your homework. So you feel a little bit more relaxed and you know how I feels like and how it's going to play like."

Someone offered that Kim, going after that first major, could draw on that spectacular hole-out win over Park in the Lotte Championship. Kim dismissed the notion. "That's a past story," she said, speaking through an interpreter. "I want to write a new story tomorrow."

The tournament turned, oddly enough, on the old debate of which is superior — accuracy or length? There's no answer, of course. It just depends on a lot of things. But it was the defining question for her at Westchester and its five par-fives.

"It's just a matter of playing the par-fives here," Park said. "Just make pars on the tough holes and go for the middle of the green, and try to make birdies on the par-fives."

Park wasn't conceding them to Kim, but she gave her the big edge on them. "She's a long hitter and this golf course really suits her because a lot of the par-fives are reachable," Park said. "A couple of the par-fives that I can't get to, she can get to. It's a matter of keeping up with her on the par-fives."

Park did far better than keep up. She dominated. Kim had nine birdies and an eagle on the par-fives, but also two bogeys and a double bogey. Park had 12 birdies and one bogey. The score: Park played them in 11 under, Kim in seven under.

Park, continuing her bogey-free run, spread out five birdies in her final-round 68 and only two were on par-fives — No. 9 and No. 18.

Kim went through a choppy 71. She had seven birdies and got four in succession from No. 5 just when Park seemed ready to run completely away with it. Kim birdied two of the par-fives, Nos. 5 and 12, and the latter pulled her to within one of Park. Then came the disaster, Kim's four-putt for a double bogey at the ninth. Park walked off that green with a four-stroke lead. Kim's birdie-bogey exchange from the 12th nudged the lead down, then back up, and Park came to the 18th, the final par-five, with a four-stroke lead. She birdied it for the last time for a 68, a 273 and the five-shot win.

The supporting cast had changed dramatically. Lexi Thompson birdied eight of her first 13 holes in a 66 and finished a distant third, two behind Kim and seven behind Park. Brittany Lincicome closed with a 68 and was fourth, eight behind, and tied at nine back were Morgan Pressel (70) and Brooke Henderson (71).

"I wanted to have a very aggressive game today and I shook off a few holes in the beginning," Kim said. "I settled down and played well. [But] I couldn't pull it out, so I still left something out there today."

Park was hit by the history of it all.

"It feels amazing — it feels amazing to win three times in a row," Park said. "I always dreamed myself being a part of history, leaving my name — even before I die, there is my name on this trophy. There's a name on the U.S. Open trophy. There's my name on great championships."

U.S. Women's Open Championship

Golf came to the little South Korean girl in the form of a challenge from her dad.

In-Gee Chun was a fourth-grader when her dad thought she could take a break from math — at which she excelled — and go to a driving range and hit a few balls.

"I tried to swing the club, but the results weren't that good," said Chun, now 20. "My father and his friend teased me a little bit."

Whereupon he discovered that his problem-solving kid was a fighter who wasn't about to be confounded by a club and a ball.

"And I got fired up and felt I could do it," she said. "Then I decided to spend some time in golf, and I fell in love with it."

For those who wonder how the South Koreans have come to dominate women's golf, Chun stands as a object lesson.

The young girl who could solve intricate math problems also went hard to work on the intricacies of the golf swing and solved them — or at least tamed them, truth of the game be told. Chun had seven victories on the Korean LPGA Tour — three this year — and one on the Japan LPGA. But she was a stranger at her first U.S. Women's Open Championship, and even then, she had barely surfaced by the third round. Then she stormed to the finish, three straight birdies late in the final round for a one-stroke victory over Amy Yang, who might be feeling star-crossed.

This 70th U.S. Women's Open Championship came to Lancaster Country Club, a par-70 course across some 6,400 yards of rolling hills at Lancaster, in southeastern Pennsylvania, to the accompaniment of a number of tournament records: 1,873 entries, attendance of 135,000 for the week and a purse of $4.5 million.

This one was shaping up as Amy Yang's time, a reward for all the close calls. But this one would hurt worst of all. She would, after all, see her bid fail at the very last hole.

Chun was just a face in the field for the first two rounds. The tournament opened with a three-way tie for the lead a four-under-par 66 — Hall-of-Famer Karrie Webb, the veteran Jane Park and Marina Alex, a second-year LPGA Tour player who missed five straight cuts. "I'm not a front-runner for this tournament, really," Alex said. "So I'm just going to go out there and have fun tomorrow." Webb, 40, a two-time Open champion, notched four birdies on her back nine and noted that a third Open and an eighth major title were not on her mind. "I'm just happy to get off to a good start," she said.

Yang got in before bad weather halted play and forced it over to Friday morning. She had three birdies and a bogey over the first five holes, birdied four of five from the 12th, but closed with two bogeys for her 67. All told, she was pleased. "I drove really well today," she said. "I missed a couple of drives to the left into the rough, but most all day I hit it really well. And I also putted fairly well today."

Defending champion Michelle Wie, hobbled by a sore hip and thigh, shot 72. "I definitely get moments, but it's definitely getting better," Wie said.

Stacy Lewis, runner-up in 2014, had a 69, and Lydia Ko, the sensational youngster, shot 70.

Chun's opening two-under 68 was the next thing to a stroll in the park. She birdied the 10th, then the 13th and parred all the others, and sat two off the lead. All things considered, it was a strong start for a young golfer in her first U.S. Women's Open.

Chun posted another impressive rookie accomplishment in the second round: She made the halfway cut. Noted veterans such as Yani Tseng, Shanshan Feng, Suzann Pettersen, Cristie Kerr, and 2009 champion Eun-Hee Ji were swept away when the cut came in at four-over 144. Chun went largely unnoticed with her workaday par 70 — bogey-birdie at the sixth and seventh, and bogey-birdie at the 15th and 16th for a two-under 138, five shots behind rising Yang.

Yang, a two-time winner on the tour since joining in 2006, had sparkled in the Women's Open, posting four top-10 finishes in her last five. This time, she birdied four straight from the 11th and shot 66 for a seven-under 133, the second-lowest score ever over the first two rounds. This put her three ahead of Stacy Lewis (67) and Shiho Oyama (66). What is it about the Women's Open, someone wondered to Yang, that brings out your best golf?

"I just enjoy it out here," Yang said. "And I know the golf courses are very tough. And make sure I be patient on the course."

Lewis finessed the course for her five-birdie 67, hitting fades off most tees. "Just to keep it in play," she said, "because I think being 10 yards closer [but] in the rough doesn't help you." Japan's Oyama made six birdies in a 12-hole stretch for her 66, and plotted her strategy for the third round: Don't think about winning.

Amy Yang got one step closer to that coveted first major in the third round, keeping a determined Stacy Lewis at arm's length in a combination of golf and heavyweight slugfest. They were the last pairing, and the action couldn't have been scripted more dramatically. Yang led by three at the start of the round and immediately went up by five with a birdie at No. 1 to Lewis' bogey. Then Lewis reversed it back to three with a birdie at No. 2 to Yang's bogey. In lockstep, they birdied the fourth and sixth, and bogeyed the eighth. Yang gained a stroke, birdieing the 13th, then Lewis closed to within two with a birdie-bogey two-shot swing at the 14th. The final margin was set when Lewis three-putted the 17th for bogey. Both shot 69, and they ended up where they started, with Yang again leading by three. Lewis' putter was hurting her. She'd averaged 32 putts for the three rounds. And Yang was now one round closer to that major.

In-Gee Chun finally was no longer just a name. She put a face to that good golf. It was a choppy 68 she shot, but it brought her up to a solo third on the leaderboard at four-under 206. It was an encouraging showing but, to the golf cognoscenti, not much else. A rookie, after all, does not figure to make up four strokes in the final round of a major.

"Today my shots were not as good as the first two days, but I tried to manage it," Chun said. "I tried to be thinking always. Golf is a percentage game, so I tried to be on the more safer side and tried to survive. She didn't play like a nervous rookie. She bogeyed No. 2, then birdied the fifth and seventh. She followed a bogey at the 10th with birdies at the 13th and 15th. She bogeyed the 16th, but snapped back for a birdie at the 17th for her 68.

"Everything I experience here, it is new, completely new," said Chun. "So this is an adventure to me. So tomorrow it's going to be the same thing. I just want to be enjoying every bit of the time."

In the final round, Stacy Lewis' bid for that first U.S. Women's Open sank under the weight of two double bogeys. The second hurt the most. Lewis, playing in the last grouping with Yang, had just tied her for the lead. But at the 15th, she drove into the rough, hit her second into more rough and her third into a greenside bunker. "Probably hit the worst drive of the week," she said. "That's the one I wish I could have over again." Lewis shot 70 and tied for third with Inbee Park, Rolex World No. 1 and a two-time Open champion, who had a six-birdie 67. Canadian teen whiz Brooke Henderson tied for fifth on a five-birdie 66. "It's exciting to know that I do have a chance to get my card for next year and doing something that a lot of people didn't believe was possible," Henderson said.

Unfortunately for Amy Yang, history repeated itself all too soon. In 2014, she'd started the final round tied with Michelle Wie for the lead and stumbled coming out of the gate, taking two bogeys and a double through the first four holes. She shot 74 and finished a solo fourth behind Wie. This time, trouble hit in the middle of her round. From No. 9, she bogeyed four of seven holes. Lewis was struggling and Inbee Park was stirring. Against this backdrop, Chun, playing in the next-to-last group ahead of Yang and Lewis, was still not a figure. On the front nine, three birdies and a bogey put her two under through the turn. A bogey at the 10th slowed her. Then her finish was explosive — a four-birdie blitz over six holes. She birdied the 12th to get within a stroke of the lead, then birdied three in succession: the 15th from nine feet, the 16th from 10 — this one gave her the lead — and the par-three 17th from four feet.

Behind her, Yang was one under through the eighth. Then her game came unraveled. She bogeyed Nos. 9, 11, 14 and 15. Time was running out when she came to the shortened 16th. "I already had practiced going to the green," Yang said. "It was very important to me that I had to make that putt and just happy that I did." She drove the green to 11 feet and dropped the putt for an eagle, then birdied the par-three 17th from seven feet. The championship would be decided at the par-four 18th.

Chun, playing just ahead, drove into the rough, then two-putted from 12 feet for a bogey. It dropped her into a tie with Yang behind her. Yang had to par the 18th to tie. But she also drove into the rough, then two-putted from 10 feet for a bogey, a 71 and a seven-under 273 to fall short again, this time by a stroke. Would she ever win a U.S. Women's Open?

"Yes," Yang said. "It was another good experience. And it's going to make me a better player."

Chun finished with a card of 68-70-68-66–272, eight under, and someone had an academic thought: Did mathematics help her game?

"As far as I experience," Chun said, "I play better when I respond to my instinct rather than thinking logically. So the more I think about playing golf, the more I get in trouble. So I try to stay with my instinct."

Ricoh Women's British Open

In keeping with the understated nature of Inbee Park, it was a modest moment of history. Her putt for birdie on the final green had just missed and she tapped in for a par. Warm applause rang out under the overcast skies at Trump Turnberry Resort but there were no histrionics. At the time Park thought her 12-under-par total of 276 would be only good enough for a playoff.

It was only after she got back to the recorder's hut that she learned Jin Young Ko, her young protégé who appeared to be running away with the title in true Park fashion by holing everything on the front nine, had just found the burn at the 16th for a double bogey and then achieved no better than a par-five at the 17th. Then she realized what everyone else knew, that her brilliant closing 65, in which she was seven under par for the last 12 holes, had sealed victory in the Ricoh Women's British Open.

It was brilliant and historic, even if finding a simple description of what Park had achieved was overly complicated. Was it was a career grand slam or not? There was no easy answer. The designation of major championships can get tricky. In the men's game four obvious majors that everyone accepts as such have evolved over the last half century. In the women's game, there tends to be a top-down approach. This became controversial when the Evian Masters became the Evian Championship in 2013 and was deemed a major by the LPGA, making five for the year.

The LPGA went further. A career grand slam would be achieved by winning four of the five, despite the origins of the term in card games referring to winning all available tricks. Instead a "super" grand slam would be achieved by winning five out of five. This has it origins from Turnberry in 2002. The previous year Karrie Webb won the LPGA Championship to earn a grand slam. But it was also the year that the du Maurier Classic, which Webb had won in 1999, disappeared and was replaced as a major by the Women's British Open. When Webb won the British Open she became the first player to win five different majors.

Here Park became the seventh player to win at least four different majors and, at 27, the second youngest after Webb. Park's story gets complicated because she won the Evian Masters in 2012 before it was a major. At the time the significance to Park was that it was her first victory since claiming the 2008 U.S. Women's Open and started the run that has made her the most dominant player in the game. This was her second major of the year, after the Women's PGA title, and her sixth in the last 14.

What really marked out Park's achievement was that she had clearly stated winning this title was her sole priority. She had been runner-up in 2012 at Hoylake, albeit nine strokes behind Jiyai Shin, and at Royal Birkdale in 2014 she was ahead at the turn in the final round but ended fourth. "I was so disappointed because it was something I really wanted," she said, "but the experience helped me this year."

Park started the final round three off the lead. She was still that far back with five holes to play before she ended up three ahead of Ko and four in front of fellow Korean So Yeon Ryu and Korean-born New Zealander Lydia

Ko, with Suzann Pettersen a further shot back. "Greatest day of my life yet for sure," was Park's immediate reaction. "It was a great day of golf today. I played great golf out there. The golfing God was on my side for sure."

Park added: "Being the only goal I set, it feels great to finally put my name on this British Open trophy. I gave it a few cracks and it's just been so hard. Every time I come to the British Open, everything seems so hard: the wind, the rain, the tee times. This is obviously the birth place of golf and this feels like real golf. This is definitely the golfer's most wanted trophy."

That the week ended with such a noble achievement, aside from the semantics of whatever labels applied, was fortunate given the way the championship was almost overshadowed by the new owner of Turnberry, Donald Trump, who bought the scenic Ayrshire resort in 2014 and arrived by helicopter during the first round.

There was a press conference to discuss the changes to the Ailsa course that had already been announced and will provide a significant upgrade — turning the ninth into a par-three with the green under the famous lighthouse among the improvements — once work began shortly after this championship. But the occasion was inevitably hijacked by his Presidential aspirations and his controversies, while out on the course, in the best weather of the week, some fine golf was being produced.

Leading the way was another of the brigade of young Koreans in Hyo Joo Kim who matched the best score from the 2002 championship with a seven-under 65. Kim, who won the Evian in 2014 on her major debut with a record 61 in the opening round, came home in 32 including an eagle at the 449-yard 14th when her approach finished 10 inches away. Only one shot at the hole was better, a five wood from Morgan Pressel which found the cup for an albatross.

Lydia Ko, with four birdies in the first five holes, shared second place with Cristie Kerr on 66, one ahead of Ryu and Q. Baek. Jin Young Ko and Pettersen were among those on 68 with Park and Anna Nordqvist on 69, Stacy Lewis on 70, Lexi Thompson on 71, and Pressel having to settle for a 74 despite her dramatic blow on the 14th.

There were 52 scores under par on Thursday but only five on Friday when it turned wet and windy. Pettersen's 69 appeared to be the best of the day, and it took the Norwegian, recently a new student of coach Butch Harmon, to the top of the leaderboard on seven under.

But late in the day, not that the weather had eased up at all, Maria McBride (Hjorth that was) produced something special with a 66 that was three better than anyone else. McBride had been nine over par after 12 holes of her first round but managed to improve on her opening 79 by 13 strokes. She did not drop a stroke and produced four birdies in the last seven holes.

Jin Young Ko finished as darkness began to fall, her 71 taking her two behind Pettersen, sharing second place with her unrelated namesake Lydia Ko, Ryu and Teresa Lu. Park's 73 kept her five back but much worse befell plenty of others. Kim plummeted down the standings with a 78, while among those missing the cut were Pressel (after a 76), Dame Laura Davies (78), Paula Creamer (79), Juli Inkster and defending champion Mo Martin (both 80s) and Webb (a 75 after an opening 80). One amateur made the cut, Spain's Luna Sobron, to take the Smyth Salver, but Michelle Wie, who began the week with hip and leg issues, had to retire after twisting her ankle on a bank walking off the 13th tee.

Park had skipped Tuesday's pro-am after suffering a sore back on the transatlantic airplane journey. But there were no ill effects on her swing by the weekend, and a 69 on Saturday, one more than Amy Boulden's best-of-the-day 68, left the world No. 1 tucked in at five under par, sharing fifth place with Lydia Ko. Mika Miyazato was on six under after a 70, and Pettersen on seven under after a 72 in which she could not capitalize with the putter, an annoyance which would plague the Norwegian on Sunday as well.

Sharing the lead on eight under were Lu, the Japan-based player from Taipei, and Jin Young Ko, who both returned 69s. The 20-year-old Ko was playing in her first major championship and on a links course for the first time. Rather like Tony Lema being guided around St. Andrews by caddie Tip Anderson to win the 1964 Open, Ko simply went where directed by her guide, Jeff Brighton, a local caddie from Girvan.

Lu dropped out of contention early in the final round with a double bogey at the first and a bogey at the second. Pettersen briefly tied for the lead before ending up with a 72. Lydia Ko's 69 was eventful in the extreme, including a double bogey at the 12th when she left a bunker shot in the trap and also an eagle at the 14th. Her third place was her best finish in a major as a professional, having been runner-up at the 2013 Evian as an amateur, while Ryu joined her on eight under par with a 68.

Jin Young Ko, donning a red puff jacket between shots, parred the first six holes and then her putter came to life. She holed putts of between 20 and 30 feet to eagle the seventh and birdie the eighth and 10th holes to get to 12 under par and ahead by three. The first sign that the nerves might finally be getting to her came with a three-putt at the 13th, while she failed to do better than a par at the 14th. But it was her second into the burn at the 16th that sunk her chances. "I was a little over-thinking, and then I was a little bit nervous," she said. "I made a mistake. But overall, second place is not bad for the first time."

Ko closed with a 71 to claim second place on her own, but by then Park had screamed past her. She birdied the second and third and then bogeyed the next two. Then it all started coming together with four birdies in a row from the seventh. She got lucky at the 13th when a poor drive found an awful lie in the rough only for a drain cover affecting her stance to gain her a free drop.

Fortune also smiled on her when she holed from 30 feet for an eagle at the 14th, but no luck was required at the 16th, the hardest hole on the course, when Park hit a six iron to three feet for her third birdie of the week at the hole. "I played that hole really fantastic. That's probably the shot of the day," she said. "It's the toughest hole and I thought about that hole in my dreams."

It was another moment of precise brilliance from the 27-year-old Korean. How many more are there to come?

Evian Championship

"Winning a major at any age," Lydia Ko reflected on the eve of the final round of the Evian Championship, "is pretty hard." Never a truer word, but the most gifted at any activity make it look easy and so, ultimately, Ko's six-stroke victory may appear. Easy it was not, for the game's latest much-heralded prodigy was forced to produce a new level of brilliance to claim her maiden major championship.

Ever since Ko finished runner-up as an amateur in Evian's inaugural year as a major in 2013, one of many career highlights before she had even turned professional, most thought this moment would be an inevitability. Yet it still had to be achieved and there was little inevitable about a Ko victory when she started the final round two off the top of the leaderboard, where Mi Hyang Lee had sat throughout the first three days. Nor when after seven holes she was still three adrift of new leader Lexi Thompson, another of the game's young stars who started strongly.

Ko, however, was not daunted. The New Zealander did what she does best, she kept her head, let others make the mistakes and remained patient, believing the birdies would come. There were eight in all, seven in the last 12 holes. She came home in 31 for a 63, the lowest final round ever to win a women's major, bettering the 64 of Karen Stupples at Sunningdale in the 2004 Women's British Open.

As if that were not a significant enough record, Ko also became the youngest woman ever to win a major championship. Only Young Tom Morris, who was 17 at the 1868 Open Championship, has won what are currently considered majors at a younger age. Ko was 18 years, four months and 20 days old, while Morgan Pressel was 18 years, 10 months and nine days old when she won what was then termed the Kraft Nabisco Championship in 2007. Her timing was perfect as this was her last opportunity to claim the record — by the time of the 2016 ANA Inspiration it would have been too late.

Ko claimed on the Saturday night that the record was not on her mind — "No, not at all," she said — but she was fully aware of it, aware that everyone else was aware of it and sick of answering questions about it. "To say that I'm the youngest in history for now, it's so cool," Ko said after her victory. "But the big thing for me is I won't be asked that question. And even if I didn't win today, I think I would have been really relieved because I'd be too old for it by the time of ANA. But it's amazing that I can leave my name a little bit in the history books."

Make that a lot. The age record was fitting because it completed a unique set. Aged 14, at an ALPG event, she become the youngest winner of a professional tournament. Aged 15 she became the youngest winner of both LPGA and LET events. Early in 2015, while still 17, Ko became the youngest — male or female — to be ranked world No. 1 in the relatively short history of such rankings.

Being designated the best player in the world brought even more focus to when Ko would win a major championship. At the ANA Inspiration she broke Annika Sorenstam's record for consecutive rounds under par but trailed in joint 51st place. At the KMPG Women's PGA she missed the cut for the first time on the LPGA circuit. With Inbee Park regaining her crown at the top of the Rolex Rankings, Ko regrouped by tying for 12th at the U.S. Women's Open and third at the Ricoh Women's British Open.

At the scenic Evian Resort overlooking Lake Geneva, Ko opened with a two-under-par 69. But it was Thompson who made the early running. Starting at the 10th in the morning, the American birdied the 12th, eagled the 13th and then had two more birdies in the next two holes. After playing the back nine in 31 she parred the front side for a five-under 66.

Later in the day she was joined by Mi Hyang Lee, who had seven birdies and two bogeys. The pair were one ahead of Eun-Hee Ji, Gerina Piller and Pornanong Phatlum. It was Lee who kept making progress on Friday, going to the turn in 31 and reaching nine under par thanks to a 67. The Korean, whose debut victory on the LPGA circuit came at the Mizuno Open in Japan in 2014, had a chance to reach 11 under at the final green but ended up with a bogey. "That's not a big deal, that's okay, just one miss," she said.

Thompson fell five behind after struggling with her putting in a 72. Ko was on the same mark after a second consecutive 69, as was Amy Yang after a 66. Pressel produced the best round of the day with a 65 which included eight birdies, two bogeys and only two pars on the back nine. At 134, Pressel was one behind Lee and one ahead of Nicole Broch Larsen, who scored 67, with Shanshan Feng moving to 136 thanks to a second 68.

In Saturday's third round, in contrast to her start the previous day, Mi Hyang Lee bogeyed the first two holes. "I didn't worry, no," said Lee. "Just first two holes. I have another 16 holes today, so that's fine." Lee got back to even par for the day but the leaderboard suddenly got congested. Lee-Anne Pace had one of the few really low rounds with a 65 to move into the top 10, but it was Thompson who made a dramatic resurgence with a 66 which featured six birdies in 10 holes from the sixth. Instead of the 36 putts that frustrated the 20-year-old on Friday, she needed only 25 hits with the flat stick this time around. "I figured out a little something with my putting that worked and that helped me out today," Thompson said. "I didn't hit it that great off the tee today. I hit it a lot better off the tee yesterday, but I just got more putts today."

After her solitary bogey at the 16th, there were five players tied for the lead at nine under par. Thompson was the only player to finish on that mark. In the final group, Lee and Pressel both birdied the 15th to move to 10 under, while further ahead Ilhee Lee dropped three strokes over the last two holes to fall back. Ko, after serenely collecting five birdies during the day, then three-putted the 18th for her third successive bogey at the finishing hole. She signed for a 67 but, importantly, that was to be her only dropped shot of the weekend.

While Mi Hyang Lee holed a 10-footer at the last for a par and a 70 to set the 54-hole lead at 10 under par, in the heavy late-afternoon rain Pressel found the greenside creek for a double bogey to fall into a tie for third with Ko at eight under, one behind Thompson and one ahead of Yang, Feng and Broch Larsen. "It's stupid now, but I felt in that moment I could hit the shot," admitted the American. "I'm still only two back going into tomorrow, so I can't dwell too much on it."

When Ko said winning a major at any age is pretty hard, Pressel can only agree. Despite consistent play in 2015, she had not added to her sole major title. With tee times brought forward to escape a possible storm on Sunday, Pressel had a fraught opening 38 that included five bogeys and only two pars. A closing 75 dropped her into a tie for 11th place. Park, who had already claimed the Rolex Annika Major award for the year, posted an early 68 to tie for eighth and so retained her Rolex Rankings No. 1 spot even with a Ko victory. Setting out as the 54-hole leader for the first time, Mi Hyang Lee struggled, making a double bogey at the third and dropping two other strokes in an outward 38. She ended up with a 74 to tie for fourth with Ilhee Lee, one behind Feng, and left her two playing partners to it, Thompson and Ko.

It looked like being quite a duel. Thompson birdied the second, Ko the third, then the American had three birdies in a row from the fifth. She was three ahead as both birdied the par-five seventh, but Thompson missed a short putt to bogey the eighth and there her challenge stalled. Ko birdied the ninth from 10 feet to get within one, then used the contours on the 11th green to get her approach to eight feet and holed the putt to tie. At the next her approach hit the flagstick and stuck two feet away. She had the lead.

How quickly the gap opened up. Thompson overshot the green at the short 14th, failed to make the green with her chip and made a double bogey while Ko holed a good par-saver. The New Zealander then birdied three of the last four holes, including the last two with putts of 20 and 15 feet. "My goal was to par the 18th today and that's still not accomplished yet," Ko said. "I'll be back next year to do that." After the putt went in on the final green she admitted to tears welling up and feeling a "little overwhelmed."

Her bogey-free eight-under-par 63 was not only a new record for a major champion in a final round but was the lowest score of the week and seven better than anyone else who teed off in the last six three-balls. Thompson, who ended with a 70 for 10 under par, said: "It's hard to beat somebody that shoots 63. She played amazing. She deserves it, she ball-struck the heck out of this golf course and putted it really well. You can't get much better than that."

Ko had doubled her 54-hole tally to finish at 16 under par with a total of 268. "It was like a whole three days' worth of work today," she said. "Not to make any bogeys, I think that's a bigger thing because it meant that when I was in trouble I got myself out of it, and when I had the opportunities, I was able to grab it."

One major title grabbed. How many more to come?

The Solheim Cup

Prior to the 2015 match at St. Leon-Rot, near Heidelberg in Germany, the talk was of the Solheim Cup coming of age following Europe's back-to-back victories in Ireland and, for the first time on American soil, in Colorado; the sort of moment the Ryder Cup had in the 1980s. Yet few could have expected the 14th transatlantic match would be such a heady cocktail of brilliant golf, fierce match-play encounters, drama and controversy.

It led to the narrowest of victories for America, 14½-13½, the first time the match had been settled by a single point. They did so with a record comeback from 10-6 behind — they had not rallied from more than two points down going into the singles previously — which puts St. Leon-Rot into the same breath as Brookline and Medinah from the Ryder Cup. It was a stunning achievement, propelled by some outstanding golf and fuelled by a burning sense of injustice.

International team matches can turn on a single moment but never quite as it happened here, early on Sunday morning as fourball matches were completed from the previous day. The last of them would prove the key to Europe having a two-, three- or four-point lead going into the singles. Rookie Alison Lee had birdied the 15th to give her and Brittany Lincicome a 1-up lead overnight. Charley Hull responded with a birdie at the 16th the next morning to square the match. At the 17th, the hole rested on whether Lee could hole from 12 feet for a win. Her putt missed, running on no more than 18 inches.

As Hull marched towards the front of the green, her playing partner Suzann Pettersen and, seemingly, the next tee, Lee scooped up her ball, believing she had heard a concession. Yet Pettersen, albeit from distance, argued to the referee that there had been no concession and, after interviewing participants, he concurred. Lee received a one-stroke penalty rather than being allowed to replace the ball had it been accepted she had acted mistakenly. Europe won the hole in four. Europe 1 up.

Confusion over the sequence of events only delayed the shock at what had taken place. However, from the reaction on Juli Inkster's face, the American captain knew instantly. "It's just B.S. as far as I'm concerned," she said. "You don't do that to your peers. It puts a damper on the whole thing."

Europe's captain, Carin Koch, appeared not to get involved until she approached the referee as the match went down the 18th hole. Her only option at that point, she was told, was to concede the 18th and leave the match all-square. Instead, the hole played out with Hull conceded two putts on the green for a two-hole victory. It was certainly in contrast to the pair's thrilling win in the Saturday foursomes against Morgan Pressel and Paula Creamer when they had rallied from 4 down with seven to play and 2 down after 14 by birdieing the last four holes.

Europe led by four points amid unique scenes. There was the sad sight of Lee and Hull bursting into tears and being comforted by teammates. Meanwhile, Pettersen was forthright in her self-justification to her captain. "We're just playing by the books," she repeated, expletives deleted.

For all the debate that raged about sportsmanship and the spirit of the game, Pettersen's action was simply bad strategy, favoring short-term gain over long-term pain. That was not in hindsight, but an instinctive reaction of many, including Dame Laura Davies, a guest analyst for Sky Sports who said: "We've got the point, but they've got the moral high ground. If America go on to win, there is only one person to blame, and that's Suzann."

Above playing for pride and honor and the flag, the American players now had a tangible, personal focus for the singles. Lee, 20, was the baby of the team, a college student the year before, the only newcomer to the match on either side. She had suffered food poisoning earlier in the week, missing the gala dinner and the Friday morning session. "I think the motivation, it honestly came from the fact that happened to Alison this morning," said Stacy Lewis. "When it happened to her, we all jumped in there and said we've got to change this, we've got to right a wrong."

Yet not the least remarkable aspect of the day was that there was not a torrent of USA points from the start to set the tone, as had been the case with Ryder Cup comebacks in 1999 and 2012. The Europeans were playing fine golf and had thoroughly deserved their lead. That did not change. Karine Icher produced the first point of the day with a 3-and-2 win over Lincicome.

Carlota Ciganda and the unbeaten Lexi Thompson had an almighty tussle in the top match, sharing 14 birdies in a halved match of good spirit that ended slightly unfortunately with two bogeys at the last. Both had makeable par putts, Ciganda missing hers for the match which only later would turn out to be crucial. Pressel claimed America's first point with a 2-and-1 win over Catriona Matthew but had to play superbly do so, Matthew having won her three previous matches in the week and not having lost a singles since her debut in 1998.

Melissa Reid then beat Brittany Lang 2 and 1 to claim three and a half points out of four on an emotional return to Germany, where her mother died in a car crash in 2012. Grief-stricken, her career had been in doubt as late as November 2014, but with the help of a new coach and the support of her family she not only regained her Solheim place but proved the engine room of the team with Hull and Ciganda. One of the moments of the week came in the Friday fourballs when Reid and Ciganda were 2 down to Cristie Kerr and Thompson. Reid holed from 25 feet to win the 16th and then Ciganda holed out with a nine iron for an eagle at the 17th in near darkness. Returning the next morning, Reid on her 28th birthday hit a three iron to 15 feet and holed the putt, only for Thompson to make a 12-footer for the half.

But now points were thin on the ground for Europe. Anna Nordqvist was again impressive in beating Lewis 3 and 1, but with only a half point needed for a retention, elsewhere America ruled. Lee beat Gwladys Nocera 3 and 1 in a match that was level-pegging in the early stages, but at the bottom of the order the away players were in command. In match 11, Michelle Wie had six birdies in the first eight holes and beat Caroline Hedwall 6 and 4. In match 9, Kerr, 3 down to Hull after four holes, playing brilliant golf with a controlled fury, rallied with eight birdies in nine holes. In the anchor match, Creamer won three holes in a row from the sixth.

Confidence flowed up the order, not down it. Lisette Salas had four birdies in six holes to go from 1 down to Azahara Munoz to a 3-and-1 victory. America could not afford a single error if they wanted to get to 14½ points. Gerina Piller was dormie-up against Caroline Masson but bogeyed the 17th, and the German came to the last green with two chances to be the hero on home soil. When her 12-footer to halve the match missed, Piller still had to hole from nine feet to win. With her husband, Web.com Tour player Martin, watching on, she buried it.

"I looked up and saw they were 13½, and if I missed it, that was it," Piller said. "I just can't believe I made that putt." Pressel called it "the most clutch putt I've ever seen in my life."

Kerr defeated Hull 3 and 2, the scoreline a mark of how well the Englishwoman played given her four wins out of four up to that point. Europe's last hope was, ironically and inevitably, Pettersen.

Yet despite an eagle at the second and three birdies on the back nine, she trailed Angela Stanford, who had not won any of her previous nine matches dating back to 2009. Three down after six, Pettersen leveled the match at the 14th only to see Stanford hole a monster on the short 15th and then birdie the 16th before securing a 2-and-1 win. The celebrations could begin in earnest then because Creamer, a wild-card selection whose form had been poor in recent months, was on the verge of taking America across the line with a 4-and-3 win over Sandra Gal.

"I can't describe the difference in my emotions of this morning to this afternoon," Inkster said. "My team played so damned good out there. They just never gave up. I saw a real team out there today. It didn't look good early, but they hung in there.

"I think they were ready to go," Inkster added of the morning's flashpoint, "but I also think that incident maybe just lit the fire a little bit more. I think in their bellies they wanted to just maybe do a little bit more. That little bit more got us the Solheim."

"Both teams played their hearts out," said Koch. "It could have gone either way today. We had a couple of chances to finish it off and win, and in the end it was their putts that won this. It's just so exciting. It's great for women's golf. And we really showcased how good these players are."

Late that evening, Inkster was prepared to forget the unsavory incident of the morning. "I'm over it," she said. "We got the cup." The following morning, having been trenchantly unapologetic at Sunday night's press conference, Pettersen had a clear-the-air meeting with Inkster and issued a statement on social media.

It read in part: "I've never felt more gutted and truly sad about what went down Sunday on the 17th at the Solheim Cup. I am so sorry for not thinking about the bigger picture in the heat of the battle and competition. I was trying my hardest for my team and put the single match and the point that could be earned ahead of sportsmanship and the game of golf itself! I feel like I let my team down and I am sorry. I hope in time the U.S. team will forgive me and know that I have learned a valuable lesson about what is truly important in this great game of golf which has given me so much in my life."

7. American Tours

When 2015 was closing out, three compelling questions were hanging over golf like towering wedge shots:
- Was Tiger Woods through?
- Was this the dawn of the Jordan Spieth Era?
- Was this the long-predicted youth movement?

The answers were: Maybe, maybe, and it sure looks like it.

Not to put Rory McIlroy aside, but Spieth, still 21, certainly took over the world of golf with his extraordinary year. He won five times, but made his greatest impact with a gripping run at the never-attained Grand Slam. He won the Masters and the U.S. Open, becoming only the sixth player ever to win them back-to-back, but his run ended in the Open Championship, where he tied for fourth one stroke back. He was a solo second in the PGA Championship. He was the youngest U.S. Open winner since Bobby Jones in 1923. He ended by winning the Tour Championship, totaling a season-record $12 million in winnings, was Player of the Year and swept all the major performance awards, including the Vardon Trophy for the lowest stroke average, 68.911.

But even the glare of Spieth's performance couldn't obscure the fact that there were really fine talents that were, if not right alongside him, then close behind.

Thus history may one day mark 2015 as the dawn of a new age in golf.

This might have been the rise of a new Big Three — Spieth, 22; Jason Day, 27, and Rory McIlroy, 26, standing 1-2-3 in the Official World Golf Rankings at the end of the year and raising memories of the Big Three of decades earlier: Arnold Palmer, Jack Nicklaus and Gary Player.

Day was a late-blooming member of the youth movement. He arrived on the tour in 2008 amid high expectations, scored his first win in 2010, his second in 2014, then had a sensational five-win 2015. The last four came in a six-start stretch. These included the PGA Championship, his first major.

McIlroy won twice in June, then sat out part of the season after injuring his ankle playing soccer. He returned to play four more times in the U.S., and a tie for fourth was his best finish. He was named European Tour Golfer of the Year for the third time in four years.

Rickie Fowler, 26, fulfilled a lot of predictions with an excellent 2015, capped by wins at The Players Championship in May and the Deutsche Bank Championship in September. His win in The Players was electrifying. He played the last six holes in six-under-par, including an eagle at the 16th, tied Kevin Kisner and Sergio Garcia, and beat them in a playoff.

Justin Thomas, 22, capped an outstanding 2015 with his first victory in the co-sanctioned (with the Asian Tour) CIMB Classic in Malaysia. It included a 61 in the second round. (This was the attitude Thomas would bring to the tour. When asked whether he had expected to win so soon, he said, "I expected to win a lot sooner than this, honestly.")

Patrick Reed, 25, won the 2015 Hyundai Tournament of Champions in January for his fourth tour win in some 15 months.

Japan's Hideki Matsuyama, 23, best known for his play in two Presidents Cups, marked his first year on the PGA Tour, 2014, with a win in the Memorial Tournament. In 2015, he had a second and two thirds in his nine top-10 finishes.

High on the watch list were Brooks Koepka, 25, who won the Waste Management Phoenix Open; big-hitting Tony Finau, 26, who had five top-10 finishes in his first full year on the tour, and Daniel Berger, 22, whose two seconds and four other top-10s won him the Rookie of the Year award.

"A lot of great young players, and none of us are afraid," Fowler said.

By late October, the last six winners were all in their 20s — Smylie Kaufman (23), Emiliano Grillo (23), Spieth (22), Day (27), Fowler (26) and Day again.

Meanwhile, Tiger Woods labored on, troubled by three more surgeries and lengthy attempts at regaining his game. He made only 11 starts, missed four cuts, withdrew once, and a tie for 10th was his best finish. By December, when he would turn 40, Woods had nothing bright to say about his future. "The hardest part for me," he said, "is there's really nothing I can look forward to, nothing I can build toward."

Hence the question that golf was asking: Is Tiger Woods through?

Tids and Bits from 2015:

• Phil Mickelson, who turned 45 in June and whose last victory was in the 2013 British Open, parted ways with coach Butch Harmon. Mickelson wanted "to hear new ideas from a different perspective."

• Rickie Fowler birdied the TPC Sawgrass' intimidating island par-three 17th three times in the same day to win The Players Championship — once in regulation and twice in the tournament's first three-hole aggregate playoff against Sergio Garcia and Kevin Kisner.

• Rickie Fowler, on winning the Deutsche Bank Championship after being branded "overrated" in a magazine poll: "Being called overrated, I won three times. So thanks for the poll — I guess."

• Bill Haas, on the secret to the miraculous recovery shots like the one that helped him win the Humana Challenge: "You got to come up with something."

• Jordan Spieth, after scoring his fifth and final victory in the Tour Championship, on what he would do for an encore: "Hopefully, improve."

• Steven Bowditch, on a scary shot he feared might cost him the AT&T Byron Nelson Championship: "It was eyes closed and stomach to the floor for a little bit."

• Jason Day, after closing with 63-62 to win The Barclays by six shots: "I feel like Jordan Spieth with how I'm putting."

• Justin Thomas, at the CIMB, on staggering across the finish line for his first win: "I don't care how I got it done. It just feels awesome."

• Jim Furyk, on winning the RBC Heritage after going 0-for-9 when leading going into the final round: "The losing hurts a lot more than the winning feels good."

• Scott Piercy, Barbasol Championship winner, on birdieing No. 2 in the final round on a 57-foot putt: "When that goes in, you're thinking, hmmm — maybe it's my day."

U.S. PGA Tour

Hyundai Tournament of Champions
Maui, Hawaii
Winner: Patrick Reed

If first place is already taken, then second wouldn't be all that bad. With Jimmy Walker looking like a sure winner, that's the reality Patrick Reed was left to contemplate in the final round of the Hyundai Tournament of Champions, the winners-only opener for 2015.

"I thought my chances were slim," Reed said. "So I was thinking, 'Let's try to birdie three of the last four and get ourselves a chance to secure second alone.'" (And under his breath, he added, "And give ourselves a chance — just maybe.")

The "just maybe" came to pass, but in an odd way. Most times, when a comfortable front-runner gets caught, he's hit a bad patch. But what doomed Walker was simply falling calm in the water. The par-73 Kapalua Plantation course was a shooting gallery for the 34-man field. But with Walker managing only pars over the last four holes, Reed caught him with two birdies, an eagle and even a bogey over that stretch to tie him at 21-under-par 271. Then Reed birdied the first playoff hole for his fourth win.

Someone reminded Reed that he trailed by four heading for the 15th tee. "I thought it was a lot," Reed said. "I didn't know how many it was. When I didn't make birdie on 13 or 14, I thought my chances were slim."

Slim and none, actually. For one thing, the scoreboards showed Chris Kirk, then Jason Day, burning up the course with 62s, and Walker making five birdies in an eight-hole stretch from No. 3 and reaching 22 under. Then came Reed's opening.

Walker missed the green at the 14th for his only bogey of the round and only the second of the entire tournament. Moments later, up ahead, Reed began his sizzling charge. He two-putted the par-five 15th for a birdie, holed out an 80-yard wedge shot for an eagle at the par-four 16th, and after a three-putt bogey at the 17th, he two-putted for a birdie at the par-five 18th for his 67–271. Coming in, Walker missed two birdie chances from inside 10 feet, and missed an 18-footer for birdie and the win at the 18th. The playoff started at the 18th, and ended there. Reed holed an 18-footer for birdie while Walker missed the green, chipped over, and never got to his six-footer for par. "It was there for me to win," Walker said. "It was a bummer. I didn't close the door on it."

Reed, just 24, became the fifth player in the past 25 years to win four or more times on the PGA Tour before turning 25. His play was more than solid, and it was blistering on the four par-fives. He played them in 13 under, with 13 birdies and three pars. He devoured No. 9 and No. 18, birdieing them all four times. But there was one other thing...

Said Reed: "I kept on saying to myself, be patient. You don't know what can happen."

Sony Open in Hawaii
Honolulu, Hawaii
Winner: Jimmy Walker

That was a sobering thought that hit Jimmy Walker that Sunday, the final day of the Sony Open in Hawaii, when he went down for his morning coffee. TV was showing that Martin Kaymer had led the Abu Dhabi HSBC Championship by 10 shots with 13 holes to play — and lost. He got back to the room and told his wife, "Winning is hard. It just really is."

On the other hand, sometimes it's easy. Or at least it looks easy, as Walker made it look in the Sony Open. Walker, the defending champion and leading by two going into the final round, finished his coffee and went out and blew away the field by a tournament-record nine shots. It was not only his fourth win over 32 starts, it was also a bit of redemption for letting the Hyundai Tournament of Champions get away the week before.

"I'm not saying I was hanging on or anything, or trying to hang on last week or today," Walker said. "I still was hitting the shots. But made some putts to really kind of distance us today — made that putt on 12 — I just kept making putts. That's the difference, I think."

It was a classic blow-away. Walker trailed through the first two rounds on 66-66 at the par-70 Waialae Country Club, took the lead with a 62 in the third, and raced away with a 63 for a 23-under 257, leaving Scott Piercy the runner-up with 66–266.

The agreeable Waialae took a beating from the start, with Webb Simpson and Paul Casey sharing the lead at 62. The second round was the stage for rookie Justin Thomas, 21, making his sixth start, who "zoned" his way to a 61 with a birdie-birdie-eagle finish. "It was probably the best zone I've ever been in," Thomas said. "I didn't know how many under I was ... I just kept playing. It's really fun." He finished 70-70 and tied for sixth.

Walker flirted with the course record in the third round. He bogeyed No. 2, then from No. 3 birdied nine of the next 14, bogeyed the 17th and birdied the 18th for a 62 and the two-shot lead. He had nine one-putts in his birdie romp. "It's nice to get back ... having a chance to win, especially after last week," he said. Walker was leading the year-opening Hyundai by three with five holes to play, got caught by Patrick Reed and lost to him in a playoff.

Walker left no doubt this time. He parred the first seven holes, if grudgingly. "I felt like ... everything was kind of stale and playing hard," he said. Then at the eighth, he lofted a wedge to three feet and birdied against Kuchar's bogey for a four-stroke lead, and was on his way. He birdied six of the last nine holes, taking all the spark out of the tournament.

Humana Challenge
La Quinta, California
Winner: Bill Haas

As Bill Haas was saying, after plucking off the Humana Challenge, "I think of myself as more of a painter than a mechanic." That being the case, he'd just created another masterpiece, this time with his eight iron.

This wasn't as dramatic as that uphill splash out of water to three feet that set up his playoff win in the 2011 Tour Championship. But it sat just as comfortably in his trophy case.

Nursing a one-shot lead with five guys hot on his heels, Haas was wide right with his tee shot at the final hole, the par-five 18th at the Palmer course. He ended up on the front lip of a fairway bunker in deep grass 250 yards from home. His escape options were few and scary. He could hit left-handed, but that brought water and out-of-bounds into play. Then maybe the backwards, one-handed shot. Forget that one.

If that eight iron at the 18th was the masterpiece, a few other shots in the final round certainly had their uses. Haas eagled the par-five sixth with a spectacular five wood from 260 yards to 15 feet. It tied him for the lead. "Just fortunate that five wood came out like it did," Haas said, "because out of that Bermuda rough, anything can happen." He kept pace with birdies at Nos. 8 and 11 and made an outstanding save at the par-three 15th, blasting out of a bunker on the dangerous short side to six feet.

With that close call behind him, Haas broke out of a six-way tie for the lead with a birdie at the par-four 16th on a 20-foot putt. Then came the stray tee shot at the 18th.

How to escape the nearly waist-high grass from an awkward stance? It didn't help that this was Haas' first start since hurting his wrist in November. Haas studied the situation, then made his decision. He'd have to stand in the sand, choke down on the eight iron and hack.

"I easily could have whiffed it, could have chunked it and moved it five yards," Haas said. Instead, he knocked it 80 yards down the fairway, then covered the remaining 170 yards with another eight iron, this to the middle of the green, an easy two-putt for a par and the one-stroke win. Haas shot 67-63-69-67–266, 22 under par, leaving a five-way tie for second at 267 — Charley Hoffman (64), Brendon Steele (64), S.J. Park (65), Steve Wheatcroft (67) and Matt Kuchar (67).

Haas might not have had a chance if Ryan Palmer hadn't cooled off. Palmer shot a blistering 61 at La Quinta in the second round, going 10 under in an eight-hole stretch with two eagles and six birdies. He finished three behind. And Phil Mickelson, making his first start since the Ryder Cup in September, tied for 24th.

Haas, by the way, revealed the secret to his great recovery shot. Said Haas: "You got to come up with something."

Waste Management Phoenix Open
Scottsdale, Arizona
Winner: Brooks Koepka

The announcer at the first tee at the Waste Management Phoenix Open introduced him as Brooks Cupcake. Brooks Koepka (KEPP-kuh) just chuckled. Wasn't the first time, won't be the last. When the tournament was over, nobody had any trouble pronouncing the word "winner."

But who was this fellow and where did he come from?

The thumbnail resume: Koepka, 24, is out of Wellington, Florida; played college golf at Florida State University, made his name overseas and wasted no time doing it.

Koepka turned professional in 2012. He joined the European Tour's Challenge Tour, and three wins there in 2013 put him on the European Tour itself, where he won the 2014 Turkish Airlines Open. He tied for fourth in the 2014 U.S. Open, and then in the fall, on the PGA Tour, tied for eighth in the Frys.com Open and tied for fourth in the Shriners Hospital for Children Open. It shouldn't be long, observers said, before this big hitter wins on the PGA Tour.

And that came at the Waste Management Phoenix Open early in February. But, ironically, Koepka's breakthrough had to share top billing with Tiger Woods' breakdown.

In his charity event, the Hero World Challenge in December, Woods' game was in disarray. He suffered the "chip yips" along with wild tee shots. This time, in his disastrous first outing of 2015, he had a whole catalogue of loose golf. He shot 73-82 and missed the cut by 12 shots. His plans? "Just practice each and every day," Woods said.

Koepka was just another name in the pack with his 71-68 start. A streaking seven-under 64 in the third round moved him up the leaderboard in a hurry. Martin Laird was leading at 13 under, and Koepka, Hideki Matsuyama (63) and Zach Johnson (67) were tied for second, three back. Koepka had one birdie on the front nine, at No. 5, and torched the back, with birdies at Nos. 10, 11, 13, 15, 16 and 17 for a three-round total of 10-under 203.

"Drove the ball a lot better today," Koepka explained. "The first few days, I was all over the map." He also corrected a problem with his putting under pressure. "I was going left," he said.

Koepka, who went the last 47 holes without a bogey, resumed his tear in the final round, notching birdies at Nos. 6, 7 and 13, which left him two strokes off the lead. Then came the heart-stopping, par-five 15th. Koepka had reached in two, but sat 50 feet from the cup. "I left every long putt short today," Koepka said. "I said to my caddie, 'I'm finally going to get this one there.'" And so he did, rapping his ball from the fringe, up a ridge and into the cup for a 66 and a 15-under 269, leaving himself — after the challengers fell short — with a one-stroke win.

"It's unbelievable," Koepka said. "Especially the failure I've had. I can't tell you how much I learned from that."

Farmers Insurance Open
San Diego, California
Winner: Jason Day

Jason Day didn't merely go against the book at the Farmers Insurance Open. He went so far that he could come out with a book of his own. He could title it: "Forget the Other Books."

That was pretty much his strategy in taking the Farmers at Torrey Pines in February. All he did was turn much of honored golf lore on its head. For one thing, instead of fighting to control his fears, he met them head-on. Then take golf's classic truths — stay in the moment, play 'em one at a time and, most of all, don't compose your victory speech until you're sure you'll need one.

Day tore that one to shreds. He was already winning the Farmers two weeks earlier. Where most golfers visualize the next shot, Day was focusing on the presentation ceremonies, much as he did in winning the World Match Play almost a year ago.

"I really wanted this win," said Day, posting his third on the PGA Tour. "I visualized myself winning and holding the trophy ... over and over, in my head ... kind of what I did at the Match Play."

Fortunately, Day didn't try to visualize a winning score. Who would dare picture a four-way tie and playoff? Day came from nine strokes behind in the first round and tagged along the rest of the way. The field alternated for the first two rounds at Torrey's par-72 courses, the South and the easier North, then played the last two on the South. Day opened with a 73 on the South, nine behind Nicholas Thompson's 64, then came back with a 65 on the North to get within four of Harris English (66–134) at the halfway point. He closed with 71-70 and tied at nine-under 279 with English, J.B. Holmes and Scott Stallings.

Day was sure he was done for at the final hole, the South's par-five 18th, when his chip from behind the green rolled off the front toward the water. But he found the ball had stopped just short of it. Relieved, he chipped on and joined the tie with a par.

English and Stallings went out on the first extra hole, the 18th. Day's excellent pitch set up a birdie that matched Holmes. At the second extra hole, the par-three 16th, Holmes hit over the green with a six iron and bogeyed, and Day put his five iron to 15 feet and won with a par.

Day's victory was upstaged in advance when the long-troubled Tiger Woods, making only his second start of the year, withdrew after 11 holes in the first round with back pain. "It's just [that] my glutes ... never stayed activated," he explained.

Day didn't only win a tournament, he beat an old enemy.

"I just said — enough," Day said. "Instead of feeling the fear and running away from it, I got to run towards it and try and face it. And did I that this week and I'm happy with the win."

AT&T Pebble Beach National Pro-Am
Pebble Beach, California
Winner: Brandt Snedeker

Brandt Snedeker's record-setting success in the AT&T Pebble Beach National Pro-Am was due principally to his rapport with his putter. They were on speaking terms — in a manner of speaking.

"Sometimes," explained Snedeker, having returned his old favorite to his bag the previous November, "you got to use some harsh words. If it's not paying attention, bench them. Let them know they can be replaced. And luckily, she understood and got back into working form."

Actually, Snedeker's performance in the February classic on the Northern California coast bordered on the supernatural. In 72 holes over three courses, and on greens trampled by 156 starters and their partners, he had no three-putts and made only one bogey. It came in the third round, out of a bunker at Pebble Beach's par-four No. 3, which was playing as his 12th. True to the golfer's code, that one slip irked him.

"[It was] from the middle of the fairway, from a hundred yards," he said. "I'll probably look back and kick myself." But reason prevailed after he'd wrapped up the win. "For me to play one bogey in 72 holes, I've never thought that that was possible," he said. "To do that over four days … lets me know that I'm thinking and doing the right stuff."

Snedeker could enjoy the thought in the glow of his seventh career victory and his first in a year and a half. He shot a tournament-record 22-under-par 265, breaking the record he set when he won his first AT&T in 2013. Snedeker opened with a 64 at the par-71 Monterey Peninsula, a stroke off the lead, then shot 67 at Spyglass Hill, a par-72, and closed with 67-67 at the par-72 Pebble Beach.

He could also enjoy the thought that it was a tough come-from-behind win. Snedeker shared the lead with Matt Jones after 36 holes, and in the third, fell a stroke behind Jim Furyk, who birdied seven of his last 10 holes for a 63. And then Nick Watney opened the final round with four straight birdies, sprinting into a two-stroke lead. But at the par-three No. 5, Watney flinched at the click of a camera, hit short into a bunker and bogeyed. Snedeker tied him with a birdie from 15 feet, then took the lead for good on Watney's bogey at the par-five No. 6. After three more birdies, the erratic Watney bogeyed 13 and 14, and got to within three with two closing birdies for a 69–268. Snedeker's birdies, at Nos. 3, 5, 7, 11 and 15, made for smooth sailing while Watney and others had their problems.

Snedeker had said that his 18 months of doldrums made him feel irrelevant. "Not fun," he said. "I don't like playing golf and not feeling like I can compete and win." The victory lifted him to No. 31 in the world and put him into three majors and four World Golf Championships.

"I think I'm relevant again," Snedeker said.

Northern Trust Open
Pacific Palisades, California
Winner: James Hahn

James Hahn might look like the guy next door. Or he might look like the clerk who just sold you a nice pair of shoes. Which is exactly what he was back in a desperate time.

Hahn, 33, once was on the verge of quitting golf, broke and discouraged. But times improved, and then he finally set his future with a remarkable win in the Northern Trust Open in February.

"I never would have thought I would win this tournament," Hahn said. And truth be told, he was not alone in that belief. The field that descended on Riviera Country Club in February did not lack for stars, and so a player still seeking his first win did not figure to break through at this time. But Hahn did, beating both Dustin Johnson and Paul Casey in a playoff. The win brought him a berth in the coming Masters and also brightened the future for his first child, due in a few days.

If the finish was wild, the beginning was surreal. Hahn was in a six-way tie for the first-round lead at five-under-par 66, along with Retief Goosen, 46, and Vijay Singh, 51. "It was nice to see the two old boys play pretty well," said Goosen, offering that his disc replacement surgery had given him "a second life." Goosen held the solo lead through the second and third rounds, then blew to a ragged 75 in the fourth.

The final nine got frantic. Seven players had at least a share of the lead. Then things sorted themselves out. Four players missed the playoff by a shot, tying for fourth.

Sergio Garcia, leading by one coming to the 17th, finished with two bogeys. He three-putted the 17th from 50 feet, then chipped weakly at the 18th for a 71. "I didn't deserve to win this week," he said. Keegan Bradley (68) bogeyed No. 10 and double-bogeyed 12, then birdied 15 and eagled 17. Hideki Matsuyama (67) finished birdie-birdie, and Jordan Spieth (70) bogeyed the 18th, leaving three guys in a playoff.

All three parred the first extra hole, the 18th. At the second, the 303-yard 10th, a vexing risk-reward hole, Casey drove just left of the green. He chipped to 15 feet. Hahn and Johnson were both in the rough behind the green. Both hit excellent flop shots over the back bunker. Casey missed his 15-footer and was knocked out when Hahn dropped his 10-footer for a birdie. Johnson followed him in from three feet. Next, at the par-three 14th, Hahn faced a 25-footer, left-to-right, for birdie. He rolled it in. Johnson missed from 12 feet. Hahn had his first win.

Then something more important came up in his media interview: The coming birth of his daughter. Had he and his wife picked a name yet? Hahn grinned. "I'm going to have to talk to my wife about Riviera," he said.

P.S. James and Stephanie Hahn's new daughter arrived a week after the Northern. They named her Kailee.

Honda Classic
Palm Beach Gardens, Florida
Winner: Padraig Harrington

The world of golf was doubly surprised when an Irishman had won the Honda Classic. First, because it wasn't Rory McIlroy. And second, because it was Padraig Harrington.

McIlroy, No. 1 in the world, who had won the Dubai Desert Classic just a month earlier, was having his troubles at PGA National, his first PGA Tour outing of the year. In fact, he missed the cut.

Harrington, on the other hand, now 43, had been off his game for years and lost his tour playing card in 2014 and was in the Honda on a sponsor's exemption. It was quite a drop for the man who won three majors in two years — the 2007 British Open and, back-to-back, the 2008 British Open and PGA Championship. His next win came six years later, in the 2014 Indonesia Open on the Asian Tour. He was still laboring in 2015. In eight starts before the Honda, he made three cuts and his best finish was a tie for 56th in the Northern Trust Open the week before. Little wonder that nothing was expected of Harrington.

A lot, of course, was expected of McIlroy, but that began to evaporate immediately. On his opening hole, he opted for his two iron against the heavy wind, knocked it out of play and double-bogeyed. He also double-bogeyed the par-three fifth, and shot a three-over 73. Things got worse in the second round. He had only one birdie against a scattering of bogeys and shot 74. Because of a long rain delay, the cut wouldn't be made until Saturday, but McIlroy could read the numbers. "I'm not going to be playing this weekend," he said, "which is not nice."

Harrington, who shot 67-66-71-70, wasn't a real force until the final nine. He was five behind through the 10th. Then he ran off four straight birdies from the 11th and took the lead. A watered five iron and a double bogey at the par-three 17th complicated things, and then he birdied the 18th, dropping a clutch 15-foot birdie putt to tie rookie Daniel Berger (68-71-71-64) at six-under 274. Harrington won it with a par on the second playoff hole, the par-three 17th, after Berger hit his tee shot into the water.

"It's not about what it means to my career, or what it means going forward," said Harrington, in an existential frame of mind. "You don't win that often. When you win, make sure you enjoy it."

If Harrington was a surprise, what can be made of Ian Poulter? Poulter seemed headed for his third PGA Tour victory when a weird spell of loose golf broke out in the final round, which began Sunday afternoon because of rain delays. He hit five shots into the water. One wiped out a three-stroke lead, the next erased a two-stroke lead, and then he was finished when he watered two at the par-four 14th and triple-bogeyed.

"It's a shame to hand tournaments away," Poulter said. "I've handed one away this week."

WGC - Cadillac Championship
Miami, Florida
Winner: Dustin Johnson

Dustin Johnson wasn't exactly tiptoeing with his one-shot lead.

Johnson was facing one of the scariest shots in the game — the tee shot at the 18th at Trump National at Doral. It's a dangerous par-four of 467 yards, a slight dogleg-left with water down the left side, requiring a tee shot challenged by water.

Johnson had fought his way from behind for three rounds — shooting 68-73-69 — in the World Golf Championships-Cadillac Championship, and was leading by a stroke standing on the 18th tee. Noted for his power and his guts — and maybe his disdain — Johnson never gave the tee shot a second thought. He went right at it.

"I absolutely smashed it," Johnson said. "I wasn't worried about getting it over the lake. I played the hole the best I've played it all week." (For sure: He had bogeyed it three days running.)

Johnson reached safely, two-putted for his only par at the hole for a three-under-par 69, a nine-under 279 and a one-stroke win over J.B. Holmes.

Holmes led from the start and was five ahead of both Johnson and Bubba Watson going into the final round, then stumbled.

The tournament didn't lack for a few oddities: Rory McIlroy, miffed at a shot, hurled his three iron into the water at No. 8 in the second round, and in the third, Johnson aced the par-four No. 4, and a few minutes later, Holmes aced it as well.

Holmes looked like a sure winner for a while. He opened with a dazzling 10-under-par 62 that had others wondering, as did Shane Lowry, who labored for a 71: "Ten under? You're joking."

"I was able to hit the shots where I envisioned, and today the putter was on," Holmes said. His round included, for example, a 362-yard drive and an iron to the green at the 616-yard 10th. Middle rounds of 73-70 put him five up on Johnson and Watson going into the final round. Then his lead evaporated in a hurry. He bogeyed three of the first six holes, and Watson birdied four of the first seven. Watson then fell short with three bogeys and no birdies on the back nine and finished third.

Holmes bogeyed the 14th, but drew within one of Johnson with a birdie at the 16th, with a huge three-wood tee shot from 293 yards. He parred home for a 75–280, eight under.

"I just didn't make any putts today," Holmes said. "Used all mine up on Thursday."

Johnson took the lead on a par at the 14th, then went ahead by two with a 15-foot birdie putt at the 15th. He parred in to beat Holmes by one, posting his ninth tour win and the first since returning a month ago from his mysterious self-imposed six-month leave of absence.

"I knew I was really good," Johnson said. "I knew there was something I was missing that could make me great ... and I think it's showing right now."

Puerto Rico Open
Rio Grande, Puerto Rico
Winner: Alex Cejka

Time was, in the early 1990s, when Alex Cejka, with his amiable personality and long hair, was known as the guy who would challenge Bernhard Langer as the best golfer out of Germany. But while Langer chewed up all the golf he met, Cejka, 44, the long hair long gone, was still winless coming to his 287th start at the Puerto Rico Open in March, playing opposite the WGC-Cadillac Championship. He would finally break through, but barely.

Cejka flirted with the lead from the start, slumped in the third round and so was resigned to another so-so finish at best. But he burst into the final round at windy Trump National with birdies at Nos. 1, 2, 5 and 6 and was back in the running. Then came the discouraging finish — a bogey at the 11th and pars the rest of the way for a three-under-par 69 and seven-under 281. Cejka figured it would never hold up against the host of challengers coming. He was done for. And so he got ready to leave.

"I changed," he said. "I had everything ready to go to the airport and almost was very satisfied with a third [place] finish. And suddenly it changed..."

"We had a couple of minutes," Cejka said. "I had shorts on and a T-shirt and I had everything packed. Luckily, there was one more group, the final group coming, so I changed. But I didn't hit balls. Some of the guys were hitting balls in the rain or putting. But I literally just put some fresh clothes on me and some dry clothes and I was ready to go."

He found himself in a five-way tie for the lead that developed like a suspense tale. Tim Petrovic had a fierce start, birdie-birdie-eagle over the first three holes, but he trailed by one coming to the 18th. He birdied for a 67 and his 281. Argentina's Emiliano Grillo birdied the 13th and carried a one-stroke lead the rest of the way, but missed a short par putt at the 18th, and the bogey cost him an outright win. He shot 70 and tied. John Curran also ran afoul of the 18th. He grabbed the lead with a birdie at the 17th, then bogeyed the last and shot 70, and he was tied. And Sam Saunders, Arnold Palmer's grandson — it seems he will forever be introduced that way — got to seven under with a birdie at the 17th, but with victory beckoning, a par at the 18th was the best he could do. He shot 68 and joined the tie.

Blessed with the reprieve, Cejka came back out. The playoff was at the par-five 18th, which Cejka had battled, playing it 5-4-7-5. He birdied it again, this time on a 15-foot putt. His long wait was over.

"I won in Europe. I won on the Web.com, and finally now," Cejka said. "At least I can say I played the PGA Tour for a long time and I won."

Valspar Championship
Palm Harbor, Florida
Winner: Jordan Spieth

True enough, the kid had all the makings of a genuine prodigy — skill, guts, flair and the like. But the jury was still out. Then came the Valspar Championship, and he had them reaching for the "Real McCoy" stamp. Not only because he won, but the way he won — hitting impossible shots and standing up under crushing pressure.

"A crazy back nine," said Jordan Spieth, now all of 21, after beating Patrick Reed and Sean O'Hair in a playoff. It was the second win of a PGA Tour career that began when he left the University of Texas midway through his sophomore year and turned professional at age 19.

Spieth chased the ever-changing leaders across Innisbrook Copperhead from the start. In the first round Brian Davis shot 65 for a one-stroke lead with a chip-in birdie at his last hole. Spieth was five back with his 70. In the second, Spieth holed a birdie putt from the fringe at the 18th for a 67 to pull to within one of Brendon de Jonge (69–136). Next came Ryan Moore. After a run of 12 pars, he birdied four of the last six for a 67 and a one-stroke lead over Spieth. It was close, though. Spieth saved par from six feet at the 18th and was tied for the lead until Moore birdied. "I expect him to shoot a few under tomorrow," Spieth said, "and I'm going to have to have a really good round to win."

Spieth was only partly right. What a surprise he was in for in the final round.

Spieth fell three behind when Moore birdied the 11th and 12th, and then the situation was abruptly reversed. Moore began to wobble and fell away with bogeys on three of the last six holes. Spieth pulled ahead with birdies at the 13th and 14th, but now two new faces were in hot pursuit — Reed and O'Hair.

Reed started the round four off Moore's lead, and after a birdie at the first and nine straight pars he birdied four of the last eight holes, the last on a 30-foot putt at the 18th for a bogey-free 66, making him the first to get in with a 10-under 274. O'Hair was next, birdieing four of six holes from No. 11 for a 67.

Spieth had used up his birdies. He had to make some breathtaking par saves to stay afloat. At the 16th, he had to reach down to blast out of a bunker, with his left foot up on the grass. At the 17th, he hit a high flop shot from deep rough on a hill to six feet. And at the 18th, he dropped a 12-foot putt for a 69.

They parred the first two holes in the playoff, Nos. 18 and 16, and then Spieth ended it at the par-three 17th with a flourish, a 30-foot birdie. Was this a legend in the making? His first victory also came in a three-way playoff, the 2013 John Deere Classic. But on the fifth extra hole.

Arnold Palmer Invitational
Orlando, Florida
Winner: Matt Every

Was Matt Every hearing things, or was that man in the gallery trying to coach him on that putt? Or worse, trying to steer him wrong?

Every had crept up the leaderboard from the first round, and now he'd come to the final hole of the Arnold Palmer Invitational looking at an 18-foot putt for a birdie he was sure he'd need before it was over. Every was in the third-from-last pairing, chasing Henrik Stenson and Morgan Hoffmann.

Every, the defending champion, could trust his own read, but here came some outside information that no one could shake off.

"I walked up to the green and this guy in the crowd kept coughing, 'Straight putt, straight putt,'" Every said. "This guy is a real [expletive] if he's lying to me because it's a pretty important moment. I looked over it pretty hard and I didn't see anything."

Both the mystery man and Every's read were correct. Every made the birdie. After a bogey at No. 1, he made seven birdies over his last 16 holes, completing a card of 68-66-69-66–269, 19 under par. He'd have a short wait to see whether it was good.

It was little-known Hoffmann's stage for a while. Hoffmann, 25, looking for his first win in three years on the tour, held his first-ever tour lead in the first round and led by three through the second before slipping a bit. He started the fourth round on fire, with five birdies through the eighth to lead by two. Then three bogeys plus a double bogey at the 18th dropped him to fourth place.

Stenson, 38, the powerful Swede, regained the lead with birdies at the 11th and 12th, and was at least in view of his fourth tour title until he ran afoul of the timer. "Problems started on 15," he said. "We got on the clock again, which when you're coming down the stretch, you want to be able to have five extra seconds." Upset with the timer, he three-putted the 15th from 45 feet for a bogey, and after reaching the par-five 16th in two, he three-putted from 40 feet for a par. Then he needed a birdie at the 18th. He was looking at a 20-footer.

Every was looking at it, too, and wishing it ill, knowing that a victory would put him in the Masters in a few weeks. "That was the No. 1 thing on my mind — 'You're already in. Miss it. I need to get in,'" Every said.

Stenson did miss, made par for a 70 and finished second by a stroke.

Every earned his win and his Masters berth by shaking off that opening bogey, then birdieing Nos. 3, 4, 6, 8, 10, 11 and 18. Then he recalled twitting Tiger Woods, who had won eight times at Bay Hill but sat this one out. Said Every: "Actually told him, 'Don't worry, man, I'll hold it down for you until you get back.'"

Valero Texas Open
San Antonio, Texas
Winner: Jimmy Walker

It was tough at the Valero Texas Open for the fans to root for the native son. Which one? Jimmy Walker or Jordan Spieth?

In truth, Walker probably got the nod, coming from just half an hour away from the TPC San Antonio. Spieth is from Dallas, nearly 300 miles to the north. It also didn't hurt that Walker took a four-shot lead over Spieth into the final round. Spieth trailed by seven with eight holes to play, but rallied and closed the final margin to four.

"Jordan — wow — he kept firing right at me," Walker said. "And it was actually really fun and it really showed what he was made of, what I was made of. He was grinding all the way to the end, and so did I."

Walker, who took the lead in the second round, shot 71-67-69-70—277, 11 under par. Spieth, who won the Valspar Championship two weeks earlier, closed with a rush, running off four straight birdies from the 14th. The streak triggered a memory in Walker, not that he is likely to have forgotten. He remembered the 2014 AT&T Pebble Beach, when he led by six going into the final round and had to scratch to win by one.

"No lead is safe," Walker said. "Because … a little bit of doubt creeps in and it can start to snowball on you. You have to execute and don't rush."

The tournament opened with stiff late March winds, stiff enough that of the 69 players with morning tee times, 23 didn't break 80, nobody broke the par of 72, and only two, Matt Kuchar and Cameron Percy, matched it. Charley Hoffman took advantage of a calmer afternoon, shooting 67 for a one-stroke lead over Aaron Baddeley, who logged a birdie that surely should take its place in golf lore. At the 336-yard, par-four 17th, Baddeley lost his tee shot on a snap hook into the woods and had to go back and hit another. "I hit it, started walking, and the crowd starts going crazy," Baddeley said. "It rolls up and goes in. That was crazy. Man, why didn't I do that the first time?"

Friday opened with temperatures in the 40s. "But it wasn't windy," Walker said. He made 40 feet of putts for birdies at Nos. 15, 16 and 17 for a six-under 138 total and a one-stroke lead. Spieth, with a 69, was two back at 140. The big jump came in the third round, when Walker birdied 14, 17 and 18 for a 69, and Spieth posted an erratic 71, including a double bogey at the par-three 16th. Walker was leading by four.

Walker closed strong in the final round, with four birdies and a bogey over the last 11 holes for a 70. But he felt the pressure from Spieth's four straight birdies from the 14th. "It looked like I had a chance," said Spieth, despite the seven-shot deficit with eight to play. "But Jimmy shut that down pretty quickly."

Shell Houston Open
Humble, Texas
Winner: J.B. Holmes

When it comes to J.B. Holmes, who can resist making that obvious play on words, courtesy of Arthur Conan Doyle. In the Shell Houston Open, it was anything but elementary for Holmes. When you start the final round of any tournament tied for 18th and six shots off the lead and you end up winning in a three-way playoff, things had to be rather involved.

Holmes wrote his story in the last round, starting with five straight birdies, seven going out for a course-record 29 and nine through the first 12 holes. The birdie at the seventh tied him for the lead with young whiz Jordan Spieth, and another at the eighth, combined with Spieth's bogey at the sixth, put Holmes into the lead. Two more birdies coming in, and a clumsy bogey at the 16th left him with the clubhouse lead and some heavy work to do — sweating out a long wait.

The five straight birdies triggered it.

"When you got it going, you keep doing what you're doing," Holmes said. "So really I didn't look at the scoreboard all day, tried to do the best I could on each hole..."

After a 65-70-73 start, Holmes rolled on to an eight-under 64 finish and a 16-under 272 total at the Golf Club of Houston. He had the clubhouse lead. Now came the interminable wait. He had teed off about an hour and a half before Spieth and Johnson Wagner.

Wagner birdied the 13th and the 18th for a 69. Spieth birdied the 13th and 14th, then slugged it out in pars the rest of the way for a 70, both tying Holmes at 272.

Wagner, who played on a sponsor's exemption, narrowly missed a trip to the Masters. He had to win at Houston for the berth and he had at least a chance when he holed a 25-foot putt at the final hole for a 69 to get into the playoff. "Birdieing 18 to even get into the playoff was pretty incredible," he said.

A win would have made Spieth No. 2 in the world heading into the Masters, but even so, he remained the hottest player in golf. His record to date: A win and two seconds in his last three starts.

The playoff was held at the par-four 18th, which all three had played in a birdie and three pars.

Spieth was eliminated by a bogey out of a bunker on the first trip, and Holmes won on the second with a par against Wagner's two-putt bogey.

Spieth was the only one of the three to lead the tournament, that by a shot in the third round. Holmes' four-bogey 73 in the third round left him laboring six shots off the lead for the fourth.

"I didn't tee off expecting to win today," Holmes said, "but, you know, it's a nice surprise."

Masters Tournament
Winner: Jordan Spieth

See Chapter 2.

RBC Heritage
Hilton Head Island, South Carolina
Winner: Jim Furyk

Jim Furyk's plaintive comment slipped by with little notice. Too bad. Coming from a guy who had known such pain and frustration for years, it was the stuff of philosophers and psychologists.

Said Furyk: "The losing hurts a lot more than the winning feels good."

There was a world of hurt in those words. Furyk, nearing 45, knew what he was talking about. The pain had been all his.

This was Furyk in his mass interview after winning the RBC Heritage in April. Sweet as the win was, he couldn't forget — not yet — the very recent and bitter past. It had been 100 starts since his last win in the 2010 Tour Championship, but more to the point, in that stretch he went 0-for-9 when leading going into the final round. There was a difference this time: Furyk wasn't leading going into the final round. He entered trailing by four shots, then proceeded to burn up the front nine, shoot Harbour Town in eight-under 63, then beat Kevin Kisner in a playoff.

"I was starting to feel," said Furyk, the man with the loopy swing, "like this game was beating me up."

Furyk shot 71-64-68-63 for an 18-under 266 and was tied by Kisner (68-67-67-64).

Jordan Spieth, just the week after winning the Masters, his first major, opened the Heritage with a three-over 74 and a sweeping analysis of his game: "I didn't drive the ball well, didn't particularly strike my irons well. My chipping and putting weren't there. It was just an off day."

Harbour Town was taking a beating. As Furyk noted: "I've never seen scoring this low [here]. But without the wind, some of the defense was gone." The second round was a bookkeeper's holiday. Spieth rebounded from his 74 with a 62, and a few hours later, Troy Merritt, 29, a four-year man looking for his first victory, tied the course record with a 61, taking the halfway lead. Furyk was five behind on his 64.

Merritt cooled to a 69 but kept the lead through the third round, three up on Matt Kuchar, Brendon Todd and Kisner. Furyk, with a 68, was four behind and giving no sign of being a threat. That came in the final round, when he took the lead with a birdie at the eighth, rolling in a 48-foot putt for the fifth of his six front-nine birdies. A bogey at the 11th dropped him back into a tie, but he birdied three of the next four for the clubhouse lead. Kisner, seeking his first tour win, caught him with birdies at 14, 15 and 18, the last on a gutsy approach to seven feet.

In the playoff, both birdied the 18th, then Furyk dropped a 12-footer on the second hole, the par-three 17th, for his 17th tour win. Then he dropped his putter and punched the sky. What a relief.

"It's zero percent relief," Furyk said, "and 100 percent joy."

Zurich Classic of New Orleans
Avondale, Louisiana
Winner: Justin Rose

Justin Rose, starting the tournament on the back nine, doubled-bogeyed his fifth hole and bogeyed his sixth (Nos. 14 and 15), then ran through the rest of the tournament without a flaw. That's 66 holes. But no shot was more crucial than his tee shot at the TPC Louisiana's 17th in the final round. The golfer's-eye view shows why.

Rose was looking at a 210-yard par-three with the pin cut well toward the left side, which drops sharply down into the water — a dangerous risk-reward proposition.

"It would have been easy to hit it 20, 30 feet right of the pin," Rose said. "But I knew that, because I was three or four holes ahead of some of the other guys in contention, I knew they had birdie opportunities."

In short, Rose had to make hay. He wanted birdies at the last two holes.

First he would go right at that scary pin at the 17th. He smacked his five iron to 10 feet beyond the hole and dropped the putt for the first birdie. At the 18th, a 588-yard par-five, Rose hit a 295-yard drive, then a three wood 243 yards just left of the green. He chipped on over a bunker and got that birdie. He'd made his hay. He was four under par coming to the 17th and left the 18th with a six-under 66, completing a card of 69-66-65-66–266, a tournament-record 22 under par.

His threats failed to materialize. Cameron Tringale came the closest. Tringale, seeking his first win, bogeyed the 13th, shot 65 and finished a solo second by a stroke. Boo Weekley needed a bit more, but tripped at the 12th, also shot 65 and finished third, two behind. Jason Day (69) and Jim Herman (65) chased their best but tied for fourth.

Day, in particular, was a threat that ran down in the steamy weather. Day and Rose began the final round tied for the lead at 16 under. But the rains that had interrupted play left Day to finish most of his third round Sunday morning. At the par-five No. 2, which he had birdied in the first and third rounds, he hooked his tee shot into the trees on the left. Then his ball hit a tree and came back to him. He bogeyed. At the 13th, he left a mere 70-yard approach short. He said the dense heat and humidity had sapped him over the course of 32 holes.

"The early days and the hot days, and just the long days in general finally caught up to me," Day said. "This final round just had a lot of mental errors."

Even so, it was a duel. Rose birdied Nos. 7 and 8 on putts of over 10 feet, taking the lead at 19 under. Playing behind him, Tringale went birdie-eagle-birdie from No. 6 and got to 20 under. Ultimately, Rose knew he needed to birdie the last two holes — and he did.

WGC - Cadillac Match Play Championship
San Francisco, California
Winner: Rory McIlroy

Rory McIlroy, grinding through the World Golf Championships - Cadillac Match Play Championship, perhaps would be best viewed through the eyes of an opponent.

"My putt drops on 13 and it's a different ball game," Gary Woodland was saying. "But I missed that one. And he was like a shark. Smelled blood. And it was game over, quickly."

That was in the championship match, and Woodland was speaking about what six others had observed before him, in one form or another. And so McIlroy swept through the field like only one other before him in the Match Play's 17 years — unbeaten as the No. 1 seed. The other: Tiger Woods, who did it three times. The troubled Woods wasn't in this field of 64 at Harding Park.

This was McIlroy's 10th tour title, and it came just in time. Only two other players in the past 75 years had won 10 tour events before turning 26 — Tiger Woods and Jack Nicklaus. And McIlroy would turn 26 on May 4, the day after he won.

McIlroy's toughest match was against Paul Casey, the easiest against Hideki Matsuyama. McIlroy's wins: Jason Dufner 5 and 4; Brandt Snedeker 2 up; Billy Horschel 20 holes; Matsuyama 6 and 5; Casey 22 holes; Jim Furyk 1 up, and Woodland for the championship, 4 and 2.

Woodland started by ousting Jimmy Walker in 19 holes, and from there beat Ian Poulter 3 and 2; Webb Simpson 1 up; Marc Leishman 2 and 1; John Senden 5 and 3, and Danny Willet, 3 and 2.

In three matches, McIlroy trailed coming to the 17th, and if Woodland remembers the clutch putt that didn't drop, McIlroy remembered the one that did — a 30-foot birdie putt on the 17th against Horschel in the third round Friday. "Basically, I don't hole that and I'm going home," McIlroy said. He made it and went on to beat Horschel on the 20th hole.

It was self-imposed pressure that inspired him in the quarter-finals against Casey. Their match had been suspended because of darkness Saturday evening, and the prospect of being eliminated early Sunday did not appeal to him. "I'd say the toughest thing," McIlroy said, "was standing on the first tee this morning at 6:45 and thinking, 'If I've just got up to come all this way to play one hole...' So I was putting a lot of pressure on myself. I don't want to have to do this just for one hole. I want to be here all day." He won the hole and the match, and kept on winning. Against Furyk in the semi-finals, he made two late birdies and then won on a 45-foot eagle putt. And in the final against Woodland, he won four straight holes and, after a few slips, wrapped it up soon after Woodland missed his four-footer at the 13th for his first WGC match play title.

"No matter what the format is," McIlroy said, "it's always nice to get a trophy."

The Players Championship
Ponte Vedra Beach, Florida
Winner: Rickie Fowler

Rickie Fowler arrived at The Players Championship as an angry young man. A *Sports Illustrated* magazine poll of tour golfers — anonymous — voted Fowler and Ian Poulter the most overrated players in the game. Many observers had been saying as much about Fowler, noting that for all of the acclaim, he had won just twice — the 2011 Kolon Korea Open on the OneAsia Tour, then the 2012 Wells Fargo Championship, his only win on the PGA Tour.

The poll would be the nagging theme of the week at TPC Sawgrass while Fowler was playing catch-up. He finally did in a burst of fireworks, going six under par over the last six holes, and then beating Sergio Garcia and Kevin Kisner in a playoff.

Fowler opened with a three-under-par 69, trailing a quartet at 67 — David Hearn, Hideki Matsuyama, Kevin Na and Charley Hoffman. (Hoffman had eight birdies and a triple bogey, which he addressed by saying, "Pardon my French.") Fowler started at No. 10, birdied six of his first 11 holes but had a double bogey and a bogey in the last seven.

Jerry Kelly, 48, jumped atop the leaderboard with an eight-birdie 65, tying Na (69) for the lead at 136. Fowler remained two behind with another 69. He was asked whether the poll would be any motivation the rest of the way. "Definitely — if I need any extra," he answered, civilly.

The tournament turned wild in the third round, with a gridlock jam of 24 players separated by four strokes, headed by Chris Kirk (68) at 10 under. Rookie Justin Thomas, with a course-record 10 birdies, joined the group with his 65. Fowler slipped to three behind on a patchy 71 that included three bogeys and a double bogey.

Fowler opened the final round with a pedestrian one over through the 10th. Then he wrote an explosive dissenting opinion to the poll. He went six under for the last six holes — a birdie at the 13th, then a birdie-eagle-birdie-birdie finish from the 15th for a 67 to tie Garcia (68) and Kisner (69) at 12-under 276. They went into the first three-hole aggregate playoff in the tournament's history, at Nos. 16, 17 and 18 (par 5-3-4). Garcia was eliminated with his par-par-bogey for 13 points. Fowler and Kisner both went par-birdie-par for 11. Then the playoff became sudden death at the island 17th. Kisner's tee shot finished 15 feet from the flag, but Fowler stuck his to four feet. Kisner missed his birdie try, but Fowler didn't.

Fowler had tamed the dragon again. He had just birdied Sawgrass' scary 137-yard island 17th for the third time that day and fifth time in six trips. The other was a par.

One last mention of the poll: Did it motivate you?

"No," Fowler said. "No, I laughed at the poll."

Wells Fargo Championship
Charlotte, North Carolina
Winner: Rory McIlroy

They were left talking to themselves, or thinking awfully hard, at the Wells Fargo Championship.

Former U.S. Open champion Webb Simpson, for example, on the futility of playing against a such a big lead: "For us guys, when you relax you seem to play worse," Simpson said. "I felt like we play better if we need to make something happen. [Even so] … early, I had to do a lot of self-talking, try to get myself back into it mentally."

At the other end of the spectrum was Web.com Tour player Patrick Rodgers, in the Wells Fargo on a sponsor's exemption, who thought he was getting close. But…

"He kept playing awesome so I tried to finish it off the best I could and post a number but — that didn't happen," he said.

The cause of their consternation was Rory McIlroy, No. 1 in the world, racing away with the Wells Fargo by seven shots with a 21-under-par 267 at Quail Hollow, his second win of the year. It wasn't just inspired golf but cold, calculated golf.

"It's out there," McIlroy said. "You take advantage of the holes. For someone with my length off the tee, you should be making six birdies — the four par-fives and the two drivable par-fours. That's 24 under. Then throw in a few mistakes here and there. It is possible."

After trailing by three on his 70-67 at the halfway point, McIlroy took over the tournament with a record 11-under 61 in the third round. He started with two pars, then off he went. He birdied the third and fifth, four straight from the seventh, then five straight from the 12th. When he dropped an eight-footer at the 13th, he admitted that he started thinking about shooting 59. He got another birdie at the par-four 14th, driving the green again. "If I could take any shot back today, it was that seven iron on 17," he said. "I just bailed out right." So he parred the last two for the 61. "A little disappointed," McIlroy said, "but still a great round."

Simpson said he thought he'd tied for the lead with his birdie at the 13th. Then he saw McIlroy's round on the scoreboard. "Oh, really? — on this golf course?" he said. He found he was three behind.

Rodgers got a similar shock in the final round. He thought he could catch McIlroy. He'd got to 17 under and saw that McIlroy was at 19 under. "So I felt like I was within two, three," Rodgers said. "And walking down 16, I saw he had it to 21 [under]." That must have been an empty feeling. He finished double bogey-bogey for a 68 and a tie for second with Simpson (72) at 274.

McIlroy, who scored his first tour win in the 2010 Wells Fargo, turned in a methodical 69 for the seven-shot cushion. How was he different now?

"Mentally," he said. "Mentally I'm so much better. I'm at staying patient, not being afraid to go low."

Crowne Plaza Invitational
Fort Worth, Texas
Winner: Chris Kirk

The way things were going in the Crowne Plaza Invitational, the wild start deserved a wild finish. There were, for example, Kevin Na breaking out his Big Bird Dance, Ian Poulter winning (or was it losing) an election, then Poulter four-putting from 16 feet, and phenom Jordan Spieth making a triple bogey. And so it went, ending with nervous Chris Kirk, about to blow it on the final hole, but chopping his way to a gutsy par to win by one for his fourth PGA Tour victory.

"Kind of surprised that I'm sitting here," Kirk said in his media interview. "To be able to do it when I didn't really feel like I quite had it ... is a huge step for me."

Kirk didn't have his "A" game and it really showed at the near-fatal final hole. He came to the 18th tee leading by a stroke. He didn't trust the driver. "I just didn't think I was going to hit it anywhere on the planet," Kirk said. "So I tried to hit a little hook three wood around there." It turned into a big hook well into the left rough. Kirk, unsettled, hit a nine iron from 155 yards over the green, but chipped on to seven feet and made the clutch par to win.

"Something I'll never forget," Kirk said. And thus ended four days of free-wheeling golf at the par-70, rain-soaked Colonial Country Club. With 68-69-65 through the first three rounds, Kirk trailed by four, then seven, then three strokes. He closed with a 66 for a 12-under 268, winning by one over playing partner Brandt Snedeker (67), Masters champion Jordan Spieth (65) and Jason Bohn (63). Snedeker had a chance to tie at the final hole, but he missed a birdie try from 12 feet. "Right in my wheelhouse," Snedeker. "I should make it. It's where my strength is."

Kevin Na, in a four-way tie for the lead in the first round, dropped a 22-footer at the 13th and a 30-footer at the 14th for birdies, and shot 66 for a two-stroke lead in the second. And then broke into a spontaneous dance. "I want to call it the Big Bird dance," he said. "It just came out." A closing 72 left him tied for 10th.

Poulter knew they were coming: Questions about him and Rickie Fowler tying for first in a magazine poll to name the most overrated players. "Do you think I pay a lot of attention to what people think?" said Poulter. His big damage came at the 10th in the third round, a four-putt from 16 feet for a double bogey. He tied for fifth.

Spieth tripped to a triple bogey at No. 5 in the second round. "That's kind of unlike me," Spieth said. He fell short with a 65 in the final round, and Bohn birdied seven of the first 12 holes to finish tied, a stroke short of Kirk. Said Bohn: "I just started holing some putts."

AT&T Byron Nelson
Irving, Texas
Winner: Steven Bowditch

The AT&T Byron Nelson turned into an all-Texas affair — a tournament honoring a great Texan, played on a Texas course and finally becoming a Tale of Two Texans: native son Jordan Spieth, 21, the PGA Tour's bright young star, who won the Masters only a month earlier, and the adopted son, transplanted Australian Steven Bowditch.

They drew most of the spotlight — Spieth because the fans wanted to see him keep on rolling, and Bowditch because he did keep rolling, from a dazzling start to an almost uncontested finish, a wire-to-wire victory.

Once, that is, the tournament survived the tremendous rainstorms. First, a storm early in tournament week poured five inches of rain on TPC Four Seasons, washing out bunkers. Then another five-incher hit overnight Thursday, after the first round, water-logging the 14th fairway so badly that the hole had to be shortened from the 406-yard par-four of the first round to a 100-yard par-three the rest of the way, thus dropping par from 70 in the first round to 69 for the last three.

Bowditch jumped on the softened course for an eight-under-par 62 and the first-round lead by two over Jimmy Walker, noting, "I got off to a pretty good start, made a couple putts early and had some momentum." The "pretty good start" amounted to five birdies over his first nine holes. He rolled from there to rounds of 68-65-64 for an 18-under 259 total, a four-stroke win and his second tour victory. Dustin Johnson sparked a moment of drama, catching Bowditch early in the final round, but then he crashed to a quadruple-bogey-eight at the sixth. He tied for eighth, seven behind.

Not that the tournament lacked entirely for suspense. The gallery couldn't take their eyes off Bowditch in the second round. There was no telling what he might do. On the now-saturated par-69 course, Bowditch shot a wild 68 — seven birdies, six bogeys. "I missed a lot of putts today, made a lot of soft bogeys," Bowditch offered.

Spieth shot four rounds in the 60s — 69-64-68-69 — but was never in the hunt. He tied for 30th, 11 off the lead. "I just didn't have it," said Spieth, frustrated by the greens. "I needed to make a lot of putts in order to play well this week and I didn't do so. I haven't done so since I was an amateur, really, on this course. Just can't really quite figure them out."

There was, finally, a little tension at the shortened and easy 14th. Bowditch ended up facing a 12-foot putt to save his par. Well, he got it. Then he got a scare at the par-three 17th. He'd aimed safely left, but his tee shot seemed headed for the water.

"Yeah," Bowditch said, "it was eyes closed and stomach to the floor for a little bit."

But his ball ended up on the back of the green. He coolly holed the putt for a birdie, then wrapped up his 64 and the win.

Memorial Tournament
Dublin, Ohio
Winner: David Lingmerth

The Memorial Tournament could be summed up as the tale of two quotes. This was at Muirfield Village's amphitheater 18th green, with England's Justin Rose facing a bending 20-foot putt for a par, and Sweden's David Lingmerth just 10 feet away, also for par. This was on the first hole of a playoff.

But moments earlier, in regulation, Lingmerth was amazed that Rose found a way to tie him after a shank out of a fairway bunker and off a fan's head. And Rose got up and down from 55 yards.

Now Rose, who had blown the three-stroke lead he started the round with, didn't think he could make that 20-footer on that quick, sloping green. But in it went.

"When I made that putt," Rose admitted, "I thought, 'Wow, I'm going to steal this one.'"

Lingmerth had brightened when he first saw he had only a 10-footer. "I was thinking to myself," Lingmerth said, "that I'd probably have a putt to win the tournament right there." But then Rose holed his. Now Lingmerth was in a do-or-die situation. "I didn't feel it was my turn to lose this time," he said. "I was telling myself that I was going to make that putt."

And then he did, matching Rose.

They parred the 18th again, and then at the third extra hole, the par-four 10th, Lingmerth holed a par putt from just inside five feet for his first win in three years on the PGA Tour.

"It's one thing to be a PGA Tour player, and it's a whole other thing to be a winner out here," said Lingmerth, making his 68th tour start.

The affable Rose looked back to praise Lingmerth. "He needs to look at that putt that kept it going on the first extra hole," Rose said. "He did everything he needed to."

Lingmerth had missed the cut in four of his last five starts and was looking shaky in this one, going two over par on the first four holes. But he rebounded with seven birdies in his last 12 holes, and made seven more in the second round. "I started giving myself some opportunities," he said, "and the putts started dropping in."

Lingmerth shot the par-72 Muirfield Village in 67-65-72-69 to tie at 15-under 273 with Rose (68-67-66-72).

Rose seized what seemed a substantial edge with a seven-birdie, one-bogey 66 to take the third-round lead by three over a faltering Lingmerth (72) and Francesco Molinari (69). Then Rose turned wildly erratic in the fourth round, posting a six-birdie, six-bogey 72 to get tied by Lingmerth's 69.

Both were overshadowed for a while by Tiger Woods' performance — a career-worst 85 in the third round. The struggling Woods, a five-time winner of the Memorial, making only his sixth start of the year, finished 71st and last on a 14-over 302. "Hopefully, in two weeks' time," he said, "things will be a lot better and I'll be ready to try to win a U.S. Open."

FedEx St. Jude Classic
Memphis, Tennessee
Winner: Fabian Gomez

Ryan Palmer was burning up the course with his putter — only 24 putts in his first-round 64, and the closest from six feet. Brooks Koepka admitted his expectations were too high, but added, unrepentant at the halfway point, "I haven't blitzed the course yet." Phil Mickelson, in his final tune-up before the U.S. Open, was saying "...these last five days, I've had the biggest strides in my game." And going into the final round, there was that huge jam atop the leaderboard — 23 players within four shots of the lead.

The FedEx St. Jude Classic had turned into a free-for-all, and hardly anyone was paying any real attention to the diminutive Argentine, Fabian Gomez, a 36-year-old journeyman still hunting for his first PGA Tour title and hoping to be mentioned in the same discussion with such countrymen as Roberto de Vicenzo, Angel Cabrera, Jose Coceres and Andres Romero.

"That list for me is an honor," Gomez was saying, racing off with a four-stroke win and becoming the fifth Argentine to win on the PGA Tour. He not only won, he proved himself first by breaking out of a third-round tie, and then out-dueling Australian veteran Greg Owen down the stretch for his first tour victory in 70 starts. The frustrated Owen had been turned away in his 214th.

The breakthrough puts an exclamation point to Gomez's record. He'd won four times on the Tour de las Americas (the old Latin American tour), twice on the PGA Tour Latinoamerica and once on the Web.com Tour (then the Nationwide Tour).

Gomez was trying to keep up through the first two rounds. His opening four-under-par 66 left him two behind co-leaders Palmer, Koepka and Owen. A 68 in the second round put him three behind Koepka. Then he and Owen, both with 67s, tied for the third-round lead at nine-under 201.

Owen was encouraged, going into the final round. "I'm hitting the fairways ... and taking advantage of my opportunities," he said. "I just have to keep doing the same stuff."

Gomez was not nearly so reassured. "This course ... many holes you need to play a fade," he said, "and I cannot play that. For me, really tough to hit a fade."

Gomez fell behind Owen early in the final round, tied him when he bogeyed the ninth, and took the lead for good on an eight-foot birdie putt at the par-three 11th. He all but locked up the win with a sharp play at the par-five 16th, when he blasted out of a bunker to within two feet and birdied for a three-stroke lead.

"After that, I knew that the chance to win was close," said Gomez. He finished grandly, dropping a 30-foot putt at the 18th for a 66 and a 13-under 267 total, a luxurious four shots up on Owen, who closed with a par 70.

"Even if I won many tournaments," Gomez said, "winning here on the PGA Tour is something amazing."

U.S. Open Championship
Winner: Jordan Spieth

See Chapter 3.

Travelers Championship
Cromwell, Connecticut
Winner: Bubba Watson

Bubba Watson never laid claim to being a down-home psychologist, but it seems he'd figured out the dynamics of the playoff, golf's cruel "him-or-me" moment.

"It's just about staying calm," Watson said. "That's what you have to do. You just breathe and walk slower, take some deep breaths and," he said, coming to the crucial point, "focus on the fact that no matter what, you still come in second place."

Watson had a point. Somehow, being the runner-up in regulation seems easier on the psyche than being the loser in a playoff. His view, 180 degrees away from the conventional, apparently paid off for him. But not in finishing second. He dropped an eight-foot birdie putt on the second extra hole to beat Paul Casey and win his second Travelers Championship. Ironically, the first, in 2010, was his first tour victory and it also came in a playoff. This was his eighth tour victory and it gave him a 5-1 record in playoffs.

The way Watson started out, it didn't seem things would ever come to a playoff. He scorched the par-70 TPC Highlands for a nine-birdie, one-bogey 62 for a two-stroke lead over a bunch at 64. The field had battered the vulnerable course — 93 players broke par in the first round. Watson, playing late, birdied four of his last five holes and missed an eagle at the par-four 18th by a tad. His 139-yard approach bounced off the flagstick and stopped a tap-in away. "I just kept grinding it out," Watson said. "Whatever shot was called for, I tried to hit it, and somehow today, I hit it good."

He wasn't nearly as efficient in the second round, but kept a two-stroke lead with a 67 for an 11-under 129. Brian Harman, like Watson a former University of Georgia player, took the lead from him in the third round with a 65. Watson (68) was a stroke behind, but the signs were most favorable for him. At the par-four 15th, his errant drive caromed off a tree and back into a fairway bunker. He saved par and shot 68.

England's Paul Casey, 37, a one-time winner in his 15 years on the tour, trailed by three starting the round, then erased the deficit quickly. He eagled the par-four third, birdied the eighth, went birdie-bogey-birdie-birdie from the 14th for a 65 for the clubhouse lead. Watson birdied the first two holes, eagled the par-five 13th, but bogeyed the 17th. He needed a par at the 18th to force a playoff, and got it on a three-and-a-half–foot putt for a 67 to tie the waiting Casey.

In the second try at the playoff hole, the 18th, Casey's chances sputtered out when his blast out of a greenside bunker ended up on a cart path. Watson set up his winning eight-footer with an approach from 160 yards.

"I hung on," a relieved Watson said, "and that's what you have to do sometimes to win."

Greenbrier Classic
White Sulphur Springs, West Virginia
Winner: Danny Lee

As victory speeches go, it wasn't much. But it came from the heart. And Danny Lee said it all in 10 words: "All I can say is, wow! I finally did it."

Lee, age 24 — a South Korean-born New Zealander, winner of the 2008 U.S. Amateur at 18, professional since 2009 — finally had his first victory on the PGA Tour. Lee came through a flurry of low scores in the West Virginia hills to win the Greenbrier Classic in a four-man playoff.

Lee, David Hearn, Kevin Kisner and Robert Streb tied at 267, 13 under par at the par-70 Old White TPC. Streb and Kisner were knocked out when Lee and Hearn birdied the first extra hole, the par-three 18th, and Lee won with a par at the par-five 17th after Hearn put his tee shot behind a tree and bogeyed.

"That was probably the only bad tee shot I hit all day," said Hearn, still winless after 164 starts.

Lee was surprised to learn that Hearn had hit into trouble.

"Yeah, I thought when I walked up there, I thought it was my ball, and I was thinking, that's going to be a tough one," Lee said. "Unfortunately, it was David's ball, and I don't know how my ball got [to the] left side of that tree ... and I just had an easy seven iron, hit it over the tree and put it in the fairway. But David looked like he had to hit a low, strong draw that just caught the top of the lip of the bunker and just stayed there, unfortunately."

Lee two-putted and had his first victory.

The tournament ended the way it began, with a traffic jam. Scott Langley, also seeking his first tour win, opened with a bogey-free, eight-under 62 and was being crowded. Lee and Jonathan Byrd were at 63, and Brian Davis and Ryo Ishikawa at 64. Langley, with a 69, and Jhonattan Vegas, a 65, tied for the halfway lead at nine-under 131, and 23 golfers were within three strokes, and Lee (69) and six others were just a stroke behind. And the third round ended up in gridlock traffic, with 27 players within four shots of the lead. And the lead itself was a four-way tie at 11-under 199 — Jason Bohn, who birdied six of his first 10 holes and shot 61, and Sean O'Hair (66), S.J. Park (66) and Bryce Molder (67). Lee was a shot behind.

As badly as Lee wanted that first win, he was shocked when the opportunity finally arrived. "After I finished at 13 under, I was just trying to calm down," he said. "I was so nervous. My head was blank, and I was just trying to breathe."

But he pulled himself together. "As soon as I stand on the 18th tee box, first playoff, I felt ready," Lee said. "I felt like I could really win this thing."

John Deere Classic
Silvis, Illinois
Winner: Jordan Spieth

Jordan Spieth was faced with a tough choice. He had long since committed to play in the John Deere Classic. But then he won the Masters, and then the U.S. Open, the first two legs of golf's unattained Grand Slam. The third leg, the Open Championship, was coming up in two weeks. Should he play the John Deere, or should he skip it and head for St. Andrews early, to get over the jet lag and to immerse himself in links golf? The debate raged throughout golf.

There was no debate for Spieth. The brilliant 21-year-old had given his word.

"I committed to this event well ahead of time," Spieth said. "It never really crossed my mind to drop out." The Deere people had given him a sponsor's exemption in 2012, when he was 18 and still an amateur. He hadn't forgotten that. And he scored his first professional win there the following year. So Spieth headed for TPC Deere Run, not St. Andrews. At first, it seemed an iffy choice.

Justin Thomas and Nicholas Thompson shot eight-under 63s, leaving Spieth in danger of missing the cut after his patchy par 71. Worse, he'd made three bogeys in a four-hole stretch. "Just a rusty round," Spieth said. And so it seemed the next day when a 64 brought him within five of Thomas' lead at 130.

Spieth exploded in the third round, starting at the par-five No. 2 with a 260-yard approach to within three feet. He got the eagle and added three birdies on the front. Coming in, he birdied the 13th and made a dynamite finish — birdie-eagle-birdie from the 16th. Maybe the eagle at the par-five 17th was a sign. He drove into the trees, escaped into the fairway, then hit a wedge that scared him. "I thought it was going past the hole," he said. But it spun back into the cup. At the 18th, he birdied off a stray tee shot for a 61 and a two-stroke lead at 196.

Spieth saved himself with a charge in the final round. He'd thrown open the race with a pedestrian two-birdie, two-bogey front nine and found himself two behind at the final turn, trailing Tom Gillis, who had six birdies and a bogey through the ninth. Gillis, 46, was trying to become the tour's oldest first-time winner in 20 years. In 11 previous starts, he'd missed six cuts and his best finish was a tie for 26th. He kept rolling this time, completing a nine-birdie, two-bogey 64 for a 20-under 264.

Spieth, still oddly erratic, bogeyed the 11th. Then he sprinted home with birdies at 13, 14, 16 and 17 to tie Gillis, and won the playoff with a par on the second extra hole. Did the victory, someone wondered, end the debate over his choice?

Spieth laughed. "I really didn't care anyway," he said. "I came here for a reason, and we accomplished that reason, and certainly have some momentum going into next week."

The Open Championship

Winner: Zach Johnson

See Chapter 4.

Barbasol Championship
Auburn, Alabama
Winner: Scott Piercy

If Scott Piercy had any lingering questions about his surgically repaired right elbow, it seems they were clearly answered in the inaugural Barbasol Championship.

Across 72 holes in the July heat in Alabama, he averaged 306.7 yards on his drives, with a longest of 348, and across the four rounds he hit, in order, 16, 15, 15 and 17 greens in regulation. That about sums up his profile on strength and accuracy.

Then add the victory. Piercy won the tournament comfortably — his third win on the PGA Tour, his first since 2012, and one he wondered might ever be possible again.

"I was scared at first," Piercy said. "I just knew it was a matter of time coming back, and it's been a long road. My whole goal after coming back from surgery was to come back better. The way I played [Sunday] compared to my last two victories was a lot better. I struck the ball so well, so I'd say I'm kind of right where I imagined I would be."

After warming up with 69-66 in the first two rounds, Piercy leaped to the top of the leaderboard with a pair of 65s, tying Ricky Barnes through the third round, then cruising to a three-stroke win over Will Wilcox, 29, a one-time winner on the Web.com Tour in his second full year on the PGA Tour.

Piercy, who finished at 19-under-par 265, arrived at the Grand National Lake course on Wednesday and didn't have a practice round. It showed in the first round, when he bogeyed the first and double-bogeyed the fourth. Then he settled down and birdied five of 10 holes from the fifth.

The Barbasol, played opposite the Open Championship, began with promise for Sam Saunders, 27, Arnold Palmer's grandson. He took the first-round lead with a bogey-free, seven-under 64, but cooled off and finished tied for 32nd. Australia's Mark Hensby, with a 64, and South Korea's Whee Kim (66) tied for a one-stroke lead at 133 in the second round, and Piercy moved to within two with his 66.

Barnes, 34, was taunted again. He was in his 202nd tour start and still seeking his first win, and things looked at least promising when he matched Piercy's 65 and tied him for the third-round lead. It was only the second time he was in the 54-hole lead. But a closing 70, featuring a bogey-bogey finish, dropped him to joint third.

Wilcox, who once made dough in a pizza shop, closed birdie-birdie — that was a 60-footer he dropped at the 18th — for a 67 to lock up second, his best finish on the tour. "That's something," Wilcox said, "I never thought in a million years I would have done."

Piercy had an inkling that the Barbasol was his: He opened the last round with two birdies, the second on a 57-foot putt after having trouble on the grainy greens. "When that goes in," he said, on his way to another 65, "you're thinking, hmmm — maybe it's my day."

RBC Canadian Open
Oakville, Ontario, Canada
Winner: Jason Day

The situation was tense: Jason Day was on the final green, Glen Abbey's par-five 18th, leading by a stroke with Bubba Watson just behind, breathing down his neck. He was facing a birdie putt that he had to make, to hold off Watson. But this was a 22-footer — makeable, true, but far more missable.

"I knew that when I hit my wedge in there, I knew, okay, I need to hole this," Day was to explain. "Because I looked back and saw Bubba's ball down there [in the fairway], and he's only got like a flick in there ... he was going to give himself a good shot at making a birdie. I knew that I needed to hole that putt. It was crucial."

A moment later, Day was roaring. "I felt like I nearly threw my throat out," he said. "I was yelling before it went in. Then I just can't even remember what I did. I don't know what I did. I was so pumped that it went in the hole..."

Day dropped the improbable putt, closing with three straight birdies, for a come-from-behind, one-stroke victory over Watson, his fourth win since his first full year on the PGA Tour, 2008. Chasing from the start, Day shot 68-66-69-68–271, 17 under par. Watson shot a ragged three-under 69 and a 272 total.

With the Farmers Insurance Open in February, this became Day's first multi-win year. Then there were other strong performances — challenging in the U.S. Open before tying for ninth and, just a week before, finishing a stroke out of the playoff at the Open Championship. From the time he arrived from Australia, a bright future was seen for Day. Was he starting to fulfill the predictions?

Day and Watson opened with 68s, four strokes behind 22-year-old Argentine Emiliano Grillo, who birdied three of the four par-fives in a 64. Chad Campbell's bogey-free 63–130 left Day still four behind with a 66 in the second round.

Canadian fans, starved for the first Canadian winner of their national championship in 61 years, got up steam over David Hearn taking the third-round lead with a 68, two ahead of Day (69) and Watson (68).

Hearn's chances died in a scattering of bogeys after he'd birdied the first two holes starting the final round. It became a Day-Watson shootout. Day got off to a hot start, with birdies at Nos. 2, 5 and 7, but got cooled by two bogeys heading into the turn. But Watson didn't take advantage of the opportunity. He birdied No. 2, then bogeyed three straight and was two behind at the turn. Day came home with three birdies, including the clincher at the 18th. Watson fell short dramatically. He bogeyed the 10th, then birdied five of the last six holes for a 69, a stroke behind.

"This must feel like what Tiger did for so many times," Day said, "and it feels good."

Quicken Loans National
Gainesville, Virginia
Winner: Troy Merritt

On the subject of winning on the PGA Tour, Troy Merritt — who finally did at the Quicken Loans National — put it best himself. "You have to go out," he said, "and have a great game plan, pure it all week, make some putts, get some good breaks and luck and," he added, prudently, "maybe have a guy or two stumble at the end."

That, in effect, was the anatomy of his breakthrough victory after five years and 96 starts. It also took faith. He made only eight cuts in 23 events in 2011, and it cost him his tour playing card. He didn't get it back until 2014. And this time, he'd missed five straight cuts coming into this steamy weekend turning July into August. It was hardly a good sign.

Merritt started with 70-68 at the par-71 Robert Trent Jones Golf Club, trailing Ryo Ishikawa and a rejuvenated Retief Goosen by seven in the first round, and Ishikawa by seven in the second. Then came the dynamite 10-under 61 in the third. He birdied the first five holes and the seventh, bogeyed the eighth, and got five more birdies on the back nine for a share of the lead with Kevin Chappell. Merritt closed with a 67 and an 18-under 266 and a three-stroke victory that wasn't as comfortable as it looked. He didn't get a good grip on the tournament until the final stretch.

Tiger Woods, tournament host and beneficiary (for his Tiger Woods Foundation), was making his 10th start and showed signs of finding his lost game. A third-round 74 hurt and sent him to a tie for 18th, 10 off the lead.

The magic in Merritt's 61? "The biggest difference was, the first two days I missed 11 putts inside of 12 feet," he said. "Today they all went right in the hole. Found a little something on the putting green. Squared my shoulders up just slightly. As a result, I was picking the ball up out of the hole versus tapping it in."

But Merritt got even more help from his challengers. Chappell, his co-leader going into the final round, disappeared with a 77. Bill Haas birdied six of the first 10 holes and tied him at a three-stroke lead, then took four bogeys and a double bogey over the last seven holes. David Lingmerth, who also had tied for the lead, stalled out with three bogeys over the last 11 holes. Players champion Rickie Fowler started the day one off the lead, had a choppy seven-birdie, five-bogey 69, and finished second by three.

Merritt was slapping hands with the fans as he walked to the final green, and then as if to say "Thanks," he rolled in a 34-foot putt for his 22nd and final birdie. Was there a lesson in his win?

"You don't give up," Merritt said. "You keep grinding. We found that one little thing. It's always close. Just need to find it."

WCG - Bridgestone Invitational
Akron, Ohio
Winner: Shane Lowry

In a field of 77 starters from around the globe in the no-cut World Golf Championships - Bridgestone Invitational, was anybody less expected to win than Shane Lowry? Consider that Lowry — a burly, bearded Irishman, age 28 — was known for winning the 2009 Irish Open as an amateur, then turning pro and winning the 2012 Portugal Masters on the European Tour. He had, at best, indifferent results in a handful of PGA Tour events. These were not exactly the credentials that recommended him against an international field on long, demanding Firestone Country Club.

Yet who was the golfer stepping forward in the presentation ceremonies? In one of the more unlikely tales of the season, Lowry was just a name in the background for three rounds, and then Firestone couldn't hold him and Firestone's trees couldn't contain him, and he walked away with his third career victory and his first outside the European Tour.

"To beat those guys down the stretch on a golf course like this," Lowry said, "it just shows a lot about my game. That it's good enough to compete at any level."

Lowry proved it with that finish, a bogey-free 66 consisting of four birdies and a number of breathtaking saves that held off three winners of major championships — Bubba Watson by two, and Justin Rose and Jim Furyk, each by four. Lowry scattered seven bogeys through the first three rounds (none in the fourth) in shooting the par-70 Firestone in 70-66-67-66–269, 11 under par.

"I can't believe it," Lowry said. "I've been playing good most of the year, and things just haven't been going my way. And I was getting very down on myself. I played as good a golf as I've ever played the last four days. Managed to hole a few putts and get a bit of luck."

Lowry couldn't have been more of a surprise. He trailed Danny Lee by five in the first round, then Furyk by four, and Furyk and Rose by two, and he didn't start to catch real attention until he birdied the second and eighth. A stunning birdie at the 10th brought a roar from the crowd. He'd hit a wild hook off the tee and seemed dead behind a 50-foot tall tree. But he lifted a powerful wedge over the tree stiff to the pin. At the 14th, he came out of a deep fairway bunker to 18 feet and holed the par putt to keep his two-stroke lead. Watson, playing ahead, put the pressure on with a birdie at 17. Lowry had to get up and down, dropping a six-foot putt, for another crucial par. Then at the tough 18th, he hooked his drive behind the trees and this time wedged through them to 10 feet and birdied for his two-stroke win.

Then Lowry admitted he'd been daydreaming about his first win. "And I'd give myself a little slap in the face and say, right, you need to get back to work," he said.

Barracuda Championship
Reno, Nevada
Winner: J.J. Henry

"A lot of math this week," J.J. Henry was saying. "Adding, subtracting, elevation change and such."

And with that, Henry pretty well characterized the Barracuda Championship, played in the thin high desert air of Reno, Nevada, in early August, and under a modified-Stableford scoring system.

Henry, having won the 2012 edition of the tournament (when it was the Reno-Tahoe Open), knew the oddities of playing for points, and he was also familiar with Montreux Golf and Country Club, a 7,400-yard course in the high altitude.

It all served him well. Henry posted his third tour victory and his second in the Stableford event. He took the lead in the third round and got caught in the fourth by Kyle Riefers' tremendous three-eagle outburst down the stretch, then beat him in a playoff with an eagle of his own.

"I think," said Henry, 40, "I figured out how to play out here in the altitude."

Under the scoring system, birdies were worth 2 points, eagles 5 and double eagles 8. On the downside, bogeys cost 1, double bogey or worse, 3.

Henry scored 13-11-17-6 and Riefers 9-14-2-22 to tie at 47 points.

"I think it's the format I needed with the year I've had," said Zach Sucher, a tour rookie who made only four cuts in his 16 starts, the first-round leader with 18 points — nine birdies and no bogeys. "Like, 'All right, let's go out and don't try to post a number, just make a bunch of birdies.'"

Henry took the lead in the third round at 41 points after a robust 17 points on nine birdies and a bogey and noted: "A fun format. When you make a lot of birdies like I did today, it makes it even more fun."

That seemed to sum up the prevailing sentiments.

Henry might have had an easier time of it if Riefers hadn't caught fire down the final stretch. Henry wobbled with three early bogeys in the fourth round, but birdied four of the last seven. Riefers trailed Henry by 16 points — roughly eight shots. Then after three mid-round birdies, he eagled the par-five 13th on a 12-foot putt, the par-four 14th on a 90-yard hole-out and the par-five 18th on a 15-footer to tie. On the second playoff hole, No. 18, Henry rolled in a 15-footer for eagle, and Riefers missed his eagle try from 10 feet and remained winless in 90 tour starts.

There was another victim. Argentina's Andres Romero, in the third round, furious over two bogeys, punched a sign at the 15th. Unable to grip a club, he putted his ball off the tee and picked up the rest of the way, taking double bogeys — the most allowed — and then withdrew. He would be out of action for some time.

"All I can say [is] to have broken the hand is not important," Romero said, apologizing, "because I have more broken heart for doing what I did."

PGA Championship
Winner: Jason Day

See Chapter 5.

Wyndham Championship
Greensboro, North Carolina
Winner: Davis Love

Tiger Woods thrilled them at the Wyndham Championship, and Davis Love confounded them.

Woods left disappointed, and Love left as the third oldest ever to win on the PGA Tour.

Love arrived at Sedgefield Country Club as a throwback. He had won two previous incarnations of the tournament — the 1992 KMart Greater Greensboro Open and the 2006 Chrysler Classic of Greensboro, both at Forest Oaks. He was 51 now, reluctant to join the Champions Tour, and beset by various physical problems that, most notably, had required neck and foot surgery.

Woods, wrestling with his game, was playing the Wyndham for the first time, seeking both his first win since 2013 and the victory that would get him into the coming FedExCup Playoffs. He was, of course, the star attraction, and got the fans and the media almost feverish when he tied for the halfway lead. But he would tail off enough to drop out of the hunt.

Love was at best a nostalgic memory. It was warming to fans that he could stay close to the lead for the first three rounds. He started the final round four shots off the lead and was five back with a bogey at No. 1. Then came the shock wave. From No. 2 he went birdie-birdie-birdie-eagle-birdie — six under in five holes. He bogeyed the seventh but got another eagle at the 15th and parred in for a 64, capping a 64-66-69 start for the clubhouse lead at 17-under 263. Next came the wait.

Woods started the final round two off and was at even par through the 10th but then three behind the co-leaders, Jason Gore and Scott Brown. Then the chip-yips struck again. At the par-four 11tth, he ran his chip all the way off the green, chipped off coming back and three-putted for a triple bogey. He notched four birdies coming in, but they only got him a 70 and a tie for 10th. "I had my chances to get it going," Woods said. "I just never did."

When Love finished, he had a two-shot lead on Brown and Gore. Brown got within one with a birdie at the 15th, and Gore eagled it. Both needed a birdie at the par-four 18th to tie Love. But Brown three-putted from 60 feet for a bogey and a 68 and tied for third, and Gore two-putted from 50 for a par and a 69, and finished second by a stroke.

Love, who hadn't won since 2008, now had his 21st career victory and became the third oldest winner in PGA Tour history. Sam Snead was the oldest, at 52 years, 10 months, 8 days when he won the 1965 Greater Greensboro Open (ironically, forerunner of the Wyndham, and at Sedgefield). Art Wall was 51 years, 7 months, 10 days old when he won the 1975 Greater Milwaukee Open, and Love was 51 years, 4 months, 10 days of age.

Said Love: "Any victory now is going to be really sweet."

PGA Tour Playoffs for the FedExCup

The Barclays
Edison, New Jersey
Winner: Jason Day

Uneasy lies the head ... etc.

Jordan Spieth rose to No. 1 in the World Ranking on his runner-up finish in the PGA Championship on August 16, and two weeks later he slipped, missing the cut in The Barclays, the first stop in the FedExCup Playoffs. Being No. 1 was great, said Spieth, after his 74-73 start, "...but not something that I'm going to live or die on each week."

Spieth's fall lifted Rory McIlroy, who skipped the tournament, back to No. 1. The cut, at two-over-par 142, simplified life for Jason Day, taking away such challengers as Rickie Fowler and Adam Scott.

Day opened with 68-68, then scorched Plainfield Country Club for a 15-under 63-62 finish for a 19-under 261 total and a six-stroke win over Henrik Stenson, who kept hearing the roars three groups behind him.

"I think there was only one player out there today," said Stenson, who shot 68-66-67-66.

South Korea's Sangmoon Bae, paired with Day in the final grouping, came away with an even loftier assessment: "He's the best in the world."

Bae, a two-time winner, matched Day with a 63 in the third round and shared a one-stroke lead over Bubba Watson going into the final round. Bae slipped behind Day on a bogey at No. 3, finished with a two-over 72 and tied for sixth. Watson's thin hopes were dashed in the fourth round with a bogey at No. 1 and a double bogey at No. 8. He closed with a 69 and finished third, eight back. Stenson bogeyed the second and the 16th, but from No. 5 he birdied six of the next 10 holes for a 66 and the runner-up spot.

Day had his uncertain moments off the tee on the final nine, though. "I didn't really have the control over the drives," he said. "I'm sitting there going, 'Why is this going to the right?'" He was two ahead at the 13th, but in the trees. He hit a gap wedge over and saved par. But Stenson surged to within two strokes with birdies at the 13th and 14th. Day made up for his driving with a hot putter. He birdied the 10th from 30 feet, got the par-three 14th from 30 and added the 15th from 35. He got his eighth and final birdie at the 18th for a bogey-free 62.

The victory put Day atop the FedExCup ranking and established him among the top five who had a clear chance at the $10 million bonus at the Tour Championship, the fourth and final Playoff leg.

It was the second straight victory and fourth of the year for Day, ranked No. 3 in the world. The Spieth-McIlroy chase for No. 1 suddenly became a three-man affair.

"It's been a special summer for me, and it's not over," Day said. "To be able to play the way I did over the weekend is fantastic."

Deutsche Bank Championship
Norton, Massachusetts
Winner: Rickie Fowler

Someone wondered about Rickie Fowler's hat size.

"I don't know if I should give away my hat size," Fowler cracked.

The question was pressed. Fowler relented.

"I have a small noggin, up here," he said, noting his hat. "I wear a size seven. I know — I'm a little kid."

Not any more. He's playing with the big boys now, notwithstanding the *Sports Illustrated* magazine poll in May, in which tour players said he and Ian Poulter were overrated. Fowler leaped at his chance and took the Deutsche Bank Championship, the second leg of the FedExCup Playoffs, when Henrik Stenson finally tripped late in the final round. It was Fowler's second win of the year, after The Players Championship, and the third of his career.

"It's pretty special to fight it out like that," Fowler said. Something of a heavyweight bout across the TPC Boston. Stenson had taken the lead in the third round and was up by three in the fourth, dropping a 15-foot birdie putt at No. 10. It went back to one up at No. 11 on Fowler's birdie to his bogey. And then Stenson birdied the 12th from 35 feet and was up by two. The frustrated Fowler got a shot back with a 40-foot birdie putt at the par-four 14th, and things stayed that way until Stenson's fatal error at the par-three 16th.

"I obviously pulled the wrong club," Stenson said, "and was trying to get the most out of a seven iron into the wind. Ballooned that one a little bit..."

Said Fowler: "It definitely was a shock to me when I saw it land and come back in the water."

Stenson double-bogeyed, and Fowler parred and leapfrogged into a one-stroke lead and parred in, completing a card of 67-67-67-68–269, 15 under par, one ahead of Stenson, four ahead of Charley Hoffman. Stenson, closing with a one-under 70, was also the runner-up in the Playoffs opener a week earlier, the Barclays.

"A little disappointing," said Stenson. "But you have to take the positives."

Jordan Spieth had a worse two-week disappointment. Shooting 75-73–148, he missed consecutive cuts for the first time in his career. "Normally, my mental game is a strength of mine," said Spieth. "These past two weeks, it was a weakness."

One would think Stenson's crash at the 16th would have Fowler champing at the bit. Not so, he said.

"No, I wasn't thinking about winning at that point," Fowler said. "There was still a lot of golf to be played. The 17th and 18th are both birdie holes with the right shots. And I was able to give myself looks and same with Henrik. And I was fortunate that he didn't make one of those, if not both. So, no, I never got ahead of myself out there."

And the question of the "overrated" poll came up again. Did it put the spurs to him?

"Being called overrated, I won three times," Fowler said. "So thanks for the poll — I guess."

BMW Championship
Lake Forest, Illinois
Winner: Jason Day

For collectors of great golf questions, an absolute masterpiece was to be had at the BMW Championship at Conway Farms Golf Club. It came in the first round as Jason Day and Jordan Spieth were walking across a bridge.

"How are you doing, Jason?" someone asked.

Spieth jumped in: "Really? You're asking him that?" (Translation: "You gotta be kidding.")

The reason for Spieth's little joke: Day was in the process of blowing the BMW away. Spieth felt the futility. He had a hole-in-one at the par-three second, and Day birdied from 20 feet. Spieth chipped in from 80 feet at No. 3 and Day matched his birdie from five feet. "He's still the clinic," Spieth said. "I've barely got the [honors on the] tee."

Day was nine under par and playing his last hole, the par-four ninth. A wind-aided tee shot of 346 yards left him just 44 yards from the green, then thunderstorms halted play. He returned Friday morning. If he makes that short wedge shot, he has a 59. But he merely birdied it for a 10-under-par 61 and a four-stroke lead over Spieth in a crowd of six at 65. Then he needled the media corps.

"I came in this morning and didn't shoot 59," Day said, "and felt like everyone was disappointed in me."

Day dealt the course a 61-63-69-69 battering for a 22-under 262 total and a six-shot victory. It was his fifth tour win of the season, his second in these FedExCup Playoffs, and it lifted him to the No. 1 World Ranking over Spieth and Rory McIlroy.

Day kept going in the second round. He birdied five of the first 12 holes, bogeyed the 13th, and after birdies at the 14th and 15th, rolled in a 43-foot putt for eagle at the par-five 18th. The 63 gave him a record-tying 18-under 124 and upped his lead to five over rookie Daniel Berger (64) and Brendon Todd (63). Day was outrunning the tour's powerful new youth movement. Spieth (66), who had missed two consecutive cuts, was seven back, McIlroy (65) nine, and Rickie Fowler (66) 11.

"I feel," said Spieth, "like I should be paying to come watch some of this."

An overnight storm left Saturday cool and windy and the course unfriendly. It put a crimp in Day's high-flying game. "The most difficult round of the week by far," said Day, after bumping around for a six-birdie, four-bogey 69. But he actually increased his lead to six.

Said Fowler: "It's almost like there's a secondary tournament going on."

The fourth round was pretty much a pro forma finale to Jason Day's frolic. He birdied No. 8, bogeyed No. 9, and birdied twice coming in for another 69 and the six-shot win over Berger.

"I don't know how to explain the way I've been playing," the new World No. 1 said. "I feel very free, like there's no stress. There's obviously stress, but I'm enjoying it."

Tour Championship
Atlanta, Georgia
Winner: Jordan Spieth

Just yesterday Jordan Spieth was the latest in that parade of young whizzes who so often flash then flame out. Now, in September 2015, Spieth, at age 22 — with stroke after stroke of his other-worldly putter — wrote an electrifying Finis to a signature season in only his third full year on the PGA Tour.

Spieth trailed Sweden's Henrik Stenson by five strokes in the first round, by three in the second, then led from there with relentless golf marked by demoralizing putting to take the rich Tour Championship. The tournament first prize of $1.485 million raised his season winnings to a record $12 million. Add the $10 million FedExCup bonus and Spieth became golf's first $22 million man. And Jason Day was king for only a week. The win vaulted Spieth back to No. 1 in the world.

"This is incredible," said Spieth, who remains boyish, warm and engaging.

Spieth, who won the Masters and U.S. Open and two other tournaments in the season, surprisingly missed back-to-back cuts in the first two FedEx-Cup Playoffs. Had his game slipped a gear? He answered the speculation on a late September week at historic East Lake Golf Club, shooting the home course of the legendary Bobby Jones in 68-66-68-69–271, nine under par, for a four-stroke win over Stenson, his chief threat, and Danny Lee and Justin Rose. Of the others in the youth movement: Day tied for 10th, Rickie Fowler for 12th and Rory McIlroy for 16th.

A tight stretch in the fourth round typified Spieth's performance. Dueling the tenacious Stenson, the 2013 winner, Spieth made three birdies in that four-hole stretch, and they had to be spirit-sappers for Stenson. At the par-four No. 8, Spieth holed a 20-foot putt for birdie — a two-stroke swing when Stenson bogeyed it. At the par-five No. 9, the expectant Stenson had a tap-in for birdie, but Spieth got down first from 18 feet for his own birdie. And then came the crusher at the par-three 11th. Stenson had stuck his tee shot about three feet away. Spieth hit the green, but was 45 feet from the cup.

"You can't expect him to make it," Stenson said. "You're feeling like you got a good chance to make up some ground."

But Spieth quickly did his mental calculations and sent his cross-country putt on its way.

"He just poured that one in the middle," a stung but admiring Stenson said. "It's fun to watch and just say, 'Well done.'"

Actually, Stenson gave Spieth a fist bump, a little grin and a sideways glance that said, "You've got to be kidding me."

"Eleven was a dagger," Spieth said.

Said Stenson: "Well done. The best player this week won the FedExCup."

Spieth ended the tournament the way he played it. At the final hole, he faced a face-saving eight-footer for par. He drilled it.

Now, after this year, what would Spieth do for an encore?

"Hopefully," Spieth said, "improve."

Start of 2016 Season

Frys.com Open
Napa, California
Winner: Emiliano Grillo

The golf gods must have stamped Emiliano Grillo's name all over the Frys.com Open. Anyone who reached for it was getting his hand slapped away from the cookie jar. How else to explain all those fatal misses at just the right time?

Grillo, a 23-year-old Argentine rookie just up from winning the Web.com Tour Championship, was playing his eighth PGA Tour event but first as a member. He would do some agonizing missing of his own, but that was just the gods setting the stage for a playoff in which he would score his first PGA Tour win. He won on the second extra hole, leaving the frustrated Kevin Na, a one-time winner, runner-up for the seventh time in his career.

The victory gave Grillo precious status on the tour and a check for $1.08 million, and one other thing equally sweet — a berth in the 2016 Masters.

"You see this?" Grillo said, flashing a grin. "That is what I'm going to do every single time you say Masters."

But before Grillo could lift the trophy and the riches that went with it, fortune had to clear the way for him.

The unkindest cut fell on Brendan Steele. He led all the way from the first round, then on the final nine crashed to five bogeys over the last six holes.

Seasoned veteran Justin Rose was tied for the lead till he two-putted from three feet for a bogey at the 12th.

Jason Bohn was the solo leader till the par-five 16th, where he chunked a wedge from only 46 yards, put his next to eight feet and two-putted for a bogey. He missed making the playoff by that stroke.

Grillo and Na were hardly immune in this outbreak of errors.

Grillo had a miss that made headlines. At the risk-reward 296-yard 17th in the third round, he'd been told the green was open. He fired away. Then he learned that his tee shot had zipped right past Rory McIlroy. And if it hadn't missed? Said McIlroy, who was to finish tied for 26th: "Would have put me out of my misery."

Grillo and Na went practically arm-in-arm down Silverado. Both started 68-71. Grillo finished 65-69, Na 64-70, tying at 15-under 273, a stroke ahead of Tyrone van Aswegen, Justin Thomas and Bohn. Grillo went from hero to goat, back-to-back at the par-five 18th. He holed a 25-foot birdie putt in regulation that forced the playoff with Na. Then he missed a three-footer for a winning birdie on the first playoff hole. Next it was Na's turn to miss. He tried to reach the green in two with a driver from the fairway. He hooked it and bogeyed. Grillo only had to two-putt from 25 feet for a par to win — and he made the first for birdie. The win meant two things to him.

"The greatest moment in my life," Grillo said. The other? "I didn't want to be the guy who almost hit Rory McIlroy."

Shriners Hospitals for Children Open
Las Vegas, Nevada
Winner: Smylie Kaufman

The finish of the Shriners Hospitals for Children Open was something for the mathematicians to contemplate.

The problem might be stated this way: Player A finishes the final round with the clubhouse lead. Six other players, who led him by from one to six shots at the start, are strung out behind him, still on the course. What are the odds that all six, one by one, would fall short of him, and by one shot. To sweeten the problem, there's this: There were no collapses. All six shot under-par rounds, ranging from two to eight under.

"I dodged a lot of bullets coming down the stretch with guys coming in," marveled Smylie Kaufman — Player A — who streaked to the clubhouse lead with a 10-under-par 61 in the final round. "And," he said, "really just thankful to get the 'W.'"

The little-known Kaufman, 23, from Birmingham, Alabama, a one-time winner on the Web.com Tour earlier in the year, was a rookie on the PGA Tour making only his fifth start in late October. He was well back in the pack in the first round, trailing Mark Hubbard, Tyler Aldridge, David Hearn and Michael Thompson, who opened with 64s then lost their way.

Kaufman had to be on the unlikely-to-succeed list at the TPC Summerlin. He had opened the Web.com schedule by missing three straight cuts, but ended it by graduating off the money list to the PGA Tour. In the Shriners, he struggled to keep up through the first three rounds, shooting 67-72-68, and was seven behind middle-rounds leader Brett Stegmaier going into the fourth. Kaufman started off modestly enough, one under over the first seven holes. Then he went on a tear, playing the last 12 holes in nine under. He birdied four straight from No. 8, and his back-nine 29 included an eagle at the drivable par-four 15th, off a three wood to 15 feet, and a birdie from 20 feet at the 18th.

Then Kaufman settled in for the longest two and a half hours of his life, waiting to see who would beat him. "So much more stressful than on the course," he said. "So much worse." But hope mounted as the challengers fell, one at a time: Patton Kizzire (63), Cameron Tringale (66), Jason Bohn (66), Alex Cejka (66) and, the two most disappointed, Kevin Na and Stegmaier.

Na, a frustrated playoff loser to Emiliano Grillo in the Frys.com Open the week before, birdied the 16th to tie for the lead, but bogeyed the 17th on a flubbed chip and shot 67. "I just went under it," he said. And Stegmaier's chance to tie Kaufman evaporated when his 20-foot birdie try at the 18th pulled up short and left him with a 69.

A relieved Kaufman, having come from seven shots behind, had just beaten almost impossible odds. "I just wanted to give myself a chance," he said.

A 61 will often do that for a golfer.

CIMB Classic
Winner: Justin Thomas

See Asia/Japan Tours chapter.

WGC - HSBC Champions
Winner: Russell Knox

See Asia/Japan Tours chapter.

Sanderson Farms Championship
Jackson, Mississippi
Winner: Peter Malnati

To borrow from a famous old adage: There is more than one way to skin a golf course.

In this day of the power game, when golfers routinely bite off huge chunks of the course at a time, Peter Malnati turned to the sweet strains of finesse to tame the Country Club of Jackson and made off with the Sanderson Farms Championship. He thus became the fifth consecutive first-time winner in five PGA Tour events. It came on his 22nd start, at age 28, in his second visit to the tour. He had lost his playing card in 2014, then regained it on his ninth-place finish on the Web.com Tour money list last season.

"I'm not a big stats guy," said Malnati, "but I'll enjoy looking at my stats because I bet I hit a lot of greens, particularly over the last two rounds."

True, but he forgot putting. Overall, Malnati, who averaged only about 266 yards per drive, hit 83 percent of the greens in regulation, including a superb 16 of the 18 — nearly 90 percent — in each of the last two rounds. And once on the green, he cashed in on his accuracy, averaging 1.6 putts per hole. If that average isn't impressive enough, consider this: All told, he made 496 feet of putts, with 110 in the first round, then 127, 133 and 126, and had only one three-putt all week.

Most of this was not readily apparent as Malnati battled his way up the leaderboard in the weather-beaten tournament. It was delayed five times and had to finish on Monday, when some golfers had to play 30 holes. Malnati, who played 27 holes on Monday, posted an 18-under-par 270 on card of 69-66-68-67, and won by one.

Robert Castro opened with a 10-under 62 and led through the first two rounds. A 75 in the third derailed him.

William McGirt, seeking his first tour win, needed three days to complete his second-round 66 and two more for his third-round 66. A closing 68 tied him for second at 17-under 271 with David Toms, who closed with 66-69.

Malnati had to play 27 holes on Monday, and trailed by one heading into the final round. He birdied the third and fourth, bogeyed the next two, then birdied five of his last 12 holes — Nos. 7, 9, 11, 12 and 15. Came the 18th and he faced the last three of his 496 feet of putts. True, he had promised not to look at the leaderboard, but now his curiosity was killing him. He turned to his caddie, Shane Joel, and asked where he stood. Joel ignored the request and dragged Malnati's attention back to the task at hand.

"How about we just hit a good putt," said Joel.

Thus chastened, Malnati holed the par putt that, he would find out after a wait, gave him a one-stroke win.

"It was kind of all surreal," Malnati said. "I don't really know what all I was feeling."

OHL Classic at Mayakoba
Playa del Carmen, Mexico
Winner: Graeme McDowell

Graeme McDowell was beginning to wonder. "You go through a year like this," he was saying. "You think — 'Am I finished? Am I not good enough?' You ask yourself all the questions."

And then he answered all his questions with a superlative five iron that burned the cup and stopped three feet away, setting up the birdie putt that ended the three-way playoff on the first extra hole and delivered the OHL Classic at Mayakoba. It not only was his first win in two years but his first top-10 finish in nine months.

"It's been a rough year for all the right reasons," McDowell said. "I've been enjoying life off the golf course with my beautiful family. Golf hasn't been the priority it should be." McDowell, the 2010 U.S. Open champion, worked some of his old magic just to get into the playoff. He'd entered the final round three strokes off the lead, and he had to hole an eight-foot putt for par at the 18th to wrap up a card of 67-63-70-66 on the par-71 El Camaleon, tying Russell Knox and Jason Bohn at 18-under 266.

McDowell got a reprieve when Knox bogeyed the 18th after driving into a bunker, shot 66 and slipped back to the 266 total. Bohn was gritty coming down the stretch, holing clutch par putts on four of his last five holes for a 68.

The tournament ended on Monday morning, after a rain delay on Sunday.

McDowell used his three wood off the tee at the 18th in the playoff, then hit the brilliant five-iron second. Knox missed the green with his approach, and Bohn reached but missed his 18-foot birdie putt. McDowell, with that three-footer, didn't give either of them another chance.

"I gave it my best shot and got beat by a great birdie there," said Knox, who scored his first win the week before in the HSBC in Shanghai.

Bohn was going for his third win, his first since 2013. "I worked hard to get into that playoff," he said. "So I gave myself a chance. That's all I can do."

For McDowell, it looked like the same old story starting out. He double-bogeyed No. 1 and shook it off and birdied five straight from No. 4 en route to a 67, two off the lead. He caught fire in the second round, shrugging off a bogey and posting nine birdies for the 63, a 12-under 130 and only his third 36-hole lead in a tour event. The keys, he said, were "the driver and the putter, the two things that haven't been performing this season." Another double bogey at the first hole in the third round sent him to a 70, three back and tied with Knox and others. In the fourth round, McDowell notched six birdies over a nine-hole stretch from No. 5 for a 66 and the tie and then the playoff.

"I'm going to appreciate this one," McDowell said, "because this year has been a grind."

The RSM Classic
Sea Island, Georgia
Winner: Kevin Kisner

Kevin Kisner, winless in four different cracks at the PGA Tour, had the remarkable record in 2015 of finishing second four times and three of those in playoffs. Who could blame him if he felt like the favorite whipping boy of the gods of golf.

"No," said Kisner. "Never crossed my mind. Because in my previous four years on tour, I never felt like I had the game to win. I wasn't playing well enough to win."

Kisner did this time at The RSM Classic in mid-November, the final PGA Tour event of 2015. His 65-67-64-64–260, 22 under par, gave him his first win by a luxurious six strokes.

It all began to change in the first round, at his 17th hole, the par-five No. 8 at Sea Island's Plantation Course. He hit a three-wood second to 25 feet and made the eagle, finishing with a bogey-free, seven-under-par 65 and a one-stroke lead on three others, based on par. Host Davis Love and son Davis both shot par-70s at the Seaside course.

A 67 at Seaside tied Kisner for second behind Kevin Chappell's 65–131 at the halfway point, and he took off from there. He raced to a three-stroke lead in the third round with a one-bogey 64 for a 16-under 196, a record at Sea Island. It was his first 54-hole lead on the tour.

"What I've learned is you just can't hold back on this tour," Kisner said. "Any time you think you're doing great, somebody else is, too."

A three-stroke lead was huge, he said, but it was also uncomfortable.

"That was the hardest thing I had to deal with all day," Kisner was to say. "I was as jumpy — or ready to go — as I recall."

But Kisner didn't play jumpy in the final round. After the six-footer he dropped for birdie at No. 2, he led by at least four the rest of the way. He was out in 30 and raced home for a 64.

The only tight moment came at the par-five No. 7, where he knocked his second shot into a bush short of the green. Instead of taking a penalty drop, he opted to hack it out, and moved it only about five feet. Then he complicated his problem by chipping eight feet past the flag. And after Graeme McDowell missed a birdie from 10 feet, Kisner calmly holed his eight-footer for par. Birdies at No. 8, from eight feet, and No. 9, from 30 "pretty much calmed me down for the back nine," Kisner said. Indeed, he was six ahead.

Soon enough, he was haunted by thoughts of success. "It's hard to keep your mind from thinking, 'What if it doesn't work out,'" he said.

He finally had the luxury of lagging an ultra-cautious three-foot par putt at the final hole. "I told my caddie, if this one gets near the hole, it's a mistake," Kisner said.

(P.S.: He holed it.)

Special Events

CVS Health Charity Classic
Barrington, Rhode Island
Winners: Keegan Bradley and Jon Curran

Keegan Bradley and Jon Curran not only had the tie that binds, but also the one that wins — the old school tie, that is.

The twosome, former stars at Hopkinton High School in Massachusetts, paired up for a 60-61–121 total, 21 under par, for a two-shot victory in the CVS Health Charity Classic at Rhode Island Country Club. Bradley locked it up with a birdie at the uphill, 392-yard, par-four 18th to close two strokes ahead of Harris English and LPGA Tour star Lexi Thompson (60-63–123).

"We're attached at the hip," Curran said. "We don't go anywhere without each other. It's kind of embarrassing sometimes."

Said Bradley: "The thing that was most important was playing with Jon. Once we got the go-ahead to do that, it was automatic."

Thompson and English fell behind with five straight pars from the 13th. English holed a long birdie putt at the 18th to break a tie for second with Billy Horschel and Jimmy Walker.

Bradley and Curran made seven of their 10 birdies in the second round from the par-four fourth to the par-five 11th. "The last four or five holes were playing tough," Bradley said. "We were lucky to have a little bit of a lead going in."

The Presidents Cup
Incheon, South Korea
Winners: United States

The 2015 Presidents Cup opened like just another ho-hum U.S. runaway. Then the Internationals, weary of being knocked around, rebelled and turned it into one of the most gripping of the 11 playings of the biennial event. Just what Internationals captain Nick Price said was needed for a competition so one-sided it had become boring. Price had asked for — and got — the matches reduced from 34 to 30, to offset the U.S. advantage in depth.

It was a thriller, coming down to the final hole of the final singles match between two captain's picks — the Americans' Bill Haas, a controversial choice because the captain who picked him was his dad, Jay, and Korea's Sangmoon Bae, playing heroically before his countrymen on the eve of his departure for nearly two years of mandatory military service.

The par-five 18th at the Jack Nicklaus Golf Club Korea became the decisive hole. Bae, one down to Haas, had to win the 18th to halve their match and throw the Presidents Cup into a tie. But Bae chunked a simple uphill chip shot, sank almost to his knees and buried his face in his hands. He eventually conceded to Haas, who was facing a six-foot birdie putt after a bunker splash. Hass won, 2 up, and the Americans had taken the cup by a single point, 15½-14½, in the tightest match since a tie in 2003, extending their domination to 9-1-1.

The U.S. opened with a 4-1 foursomes (alternate shot) runaway, led by Rickie Fowler and Jimmy Walker's 5-and-4 thumping of India's Anirban Lahiri and Thailand's Thongchai Jaidee, the first players from their countries to play in the Presidents Cup.

In the Friday fourball (better-ball), South Africa's Branden Grace and Louis Oosthuizen whipped Dustin Johnson and Jordan Spieth, 4 and 3, leading the Internationals' bounce-back to a 3½-1½ win and cutting the Americans' lead to a point, 5½-4½. From there, the U.S. couldn't pull away and the Internationals couldn't pull ahead.

Johnson and Spieth beat Jason Day and Charl Schwartzel 1 up in the final Saturday morning foursomes to salvage a 2-2 tie. In the afternoon fourball, Bae and Hideki Matsuyama crushed Walker and Chris Kirk, 6 and 5, in another 2-2 tie.   ·

That left the Presidents Cup up to the dramatic singles. As the script-writer would have it, the singles also ended in a tie, 6-6.

Phil Mickelson played in his 11th Presidents Cup, thanks to a captain's pick for which Haas was criticized. Mickelson had had a lackluster year. He repaid Haas' faith with an outstanding showing, teaming with Zach Johnson to lead the U.S. with 3-0-1 performances. Grace, 0-4-0 in 2013, this time went 5-0.

"I don't think it could have got a whole lot more exciting than that," said Price. "We put on a show of golf this week."

Said Jay Haas, whose son won the cup: "There were no individuals. Everybody came together as a team — a moment I'll never forget."

TaylorMade Pebble Beach Invitational
Pebble Beach, California
Winner: Jeff Gove

"When I birdied 17, I said 'Oh my gosh, I've got a one-shot lead going to 18 at Pebble Beach, which is what I've thought about all my life,'" Jeff Gove was saying.

The TaylorMade Pebble Beach Invitational was at his fingertips. A one-shot lead at the famed par-five finishing hole, with the Pacific Ocean on the left and no picnic on the right: Smart money says this is the time to lay up.

"No," said Gove, who hadn't won since a domestic event in Washington state in 2012. "We're going for this."

Gove then hit his approach to the back fringe, chipped to eight feet and holed the putt for a birdie-birdie finish, wrapping up a card of 69-69-69-66–273, a cumulative 15 under for Pebble Beach, Del Monte and Spyglass Hill, the rotation of courses for the mixed field from the PGA, Champions, Web.com and LPGA tours.

Gove, a Web.com player, won by two over Kevin Sutherland (67) and Duffy Waldorf (67) of the Champions Tour. Gove took the lead at the celebrated par-three 17th, firing his tee shot to three feet and making the birdie. Gove had seven birdies and a bogey for the final round.

"I felt in the moment all day," Gove said. "I love this. I love the pressure of having a chance to win. I haven't had a good past couple of years, so when you're coming down the last hole against all those players, it just gives you great confidence."

Hero World Challenge
New Providence, Bahamas
Winner: Bubba Watson

Bubba Watson was thanking the people who made it possible for him to win the Hero World Challenge, an odd and diverse group of two — Jason Day and the U.S. Passport services.

The happy drama began when Watson turned down his invitation to play in the 18-man Tiger Woods-hosted event in the Bahamas early in December because he had no passport for his newly adopted daughter, Dakota. Then Day withdrew to remain at home with his newborn daughter. There was a vacancy for Watson — if he could get a passport. And the passport people scrambled.

Watson did the rest, shooting the par-72 Albany Golf Club in 67-67-63-66, 25-under 263, picking up the $1 million first prize with a three-stroke win over Patrick Reed.

It was the first time for the tournament in the Bahamas. It was held in Florida in 2014, and in California for 14 years.

Watson trailed by one through the first two rounds, then crashed into the lead at 19-under 197 in the third with a hole-out eagle and seven birdies to tie the course-record 63 just set by Paul Casey. Watson stayed in command in the fourth. He birdied four of the first seven holes and he was on his way to his closing 66 and the three-shot win — and a kind of early New Year's resolution.

Said Watson: "I want my name to be close to that leaderboard every tournament, every year."

Franklin Templeton Shootout
Naples, Florida
Winners: Jason Dufner and Brandt Snedeker

Ham-and-egged it. Hand-in-gloved it. Arm-in-armed it.

However one describes the ideal pairing, Jason Dufner and Brandt Snedeker were it at Tiburon Golf Club to close out the 2015 competitions in mid-December in the 27th Franklin Templeton Shootout, the unofficial but lucrative fixture on the PGA Tour. They combined for a 30-under-par 186 in the three-round event, birdieing the last two holes for a two-stroke victory over Harris English and Matt Kuchar.

Dufner summed up the partnership. "I'm pretty consistent," he said. "I'm in the fairway, I'm on the greens. That gives him a lot of confidence. He putts really well, so that gives me more confidence."

They combined for an 11-under 61 in the scramble format in the first round, then shot 64 in the modified alternate-shot in the second, and finally another 61 in the better-ball in the third and won $385,000 each.

Dufner and Snedeker, one shot behind starting the final round, erupted for six birdies on the front nine, and two of them were on chip-ins — Snedeker from 30 feet at No. 3, and Dufner from 40 at No. 7. They were tied for the lead at 28 under heading to the par-five 17th. There, Dufner holed a four-footer for birdie and the outright lead. Then at the 18th, Snedeker just needed two putts for the win, and instead holed his 25-footer for one last birdie and the two-stroke margin.

"I think we're a great partnership," Snedeker said. "It worked out great. Kind of one of those perfect weeks."

PNC Father/Son Challenge
Orlando, Florida
Winners: Lanny and Tucker Wadkins

"Dad's still got a little bit left," Tucker Wadkins said. "That's one I'll remember."

It was the understatement of the week in the PNC Father/Son Challenge. Tucker Wadkins, 23, was talking about his dad, Lanny, former PGA Tour star, who at 66 showed he could still perform under pressure. Lanny rolled in a 12-foot birdie on the final hole of regulation to give him and Tucker a 61-63–124, 20 under par and put them into a four-way playoff. Then it was dad's turn to praise.

On the first extra hole, the par-five 18th at the Ritz-Carlton Golf Club, Tucker blasted a drive 304 yards, hit a four iron from 225 yards to the green, 40 feet from the flag, and knocked in the putt for an eagle to beat Fred and Taylor Funk (62-62), Davis and Dru Love (61-63), and Larry and Drew Nelson (62-62). They tied at 20-under-par 124 in regulation in the two-round scramble event two weeks before Christmas.

Vijay and Qass Singh took the first-round lead with a 59, but came back with a 66 and tied for fifth in the 20-team field.

This was the first win in nine appearances for the Wadkinses, and Lanny credited his son.

"Tucker hit a spectacular tee shot, one of the best he's hit all week," said Lanny. "He made a 40-footer. I'll remember what he did in making that putt.

"He played spectacular. Dad was along for the ride."

Web.com Tour

Who was the happiest man on the 2015 Web.com Tour?

Patton Kizzire would be the most logical choice. Topping the Web.com money list and winning the PGA Tour playing card that went with it would tend to brighten one's day.

Much the same could be said for Chez Reavie. He was the leading money winner on the four-tournament Web.com Tour Finals, and also won his PGA Tour playing card.

But the happiest man might well have come not from the top of the magical top 25 who won their PGA Tour cards, but the bottom.

This would be Rob Oppenheim, 35, stamped the Hard-Luck Guy of the Year in the season finale, the Web.com Tour Championship. He closed with two 67s and tied for 12th, but dropped from 24th to 26th on the final money list. He'd missed his PGA Tour card by one spot. Dejected, he was in his car and a half hour down the road, wearily making his way home. Then he got the call: Lucas Glover had bogeyed the final hole, and that lifted Oppenheim to the precious 25th and final spot. He'd won his card by $101.

"The golfing gods, they owe me," Oppenheim had said earlier.

A short while later: "We're all square now," he said.

One man's joy was another man's sorrow: Eric Axley, who took the final card in 2014 by $31.66, was the player knocked out by Glover's bogey. This time, Axley missed by $101.

Kizzire, a 6-foot-5 Alabaman, was voted the Player of the Year by his peers after one of the most consistent seasons ever on the Web.com Tour. Kizzire, 29, won a total of $567,866 in 23 starts, the second most in tour history. He won two tournaments three weeks apart in August, and he also was second twice (once in a playoff), and had four other top-six finishes. Overall, he had 12 top-10s, the most since Stewart Cink's 14 in 1996.

Through 81 rounds, he was a cumulative 212 under par. He led in scoring (averaging 68.68 per round), putting (1.694) and birdies (4.81).

As the combined Regular Season/Finals' leading money winner, Kizzire became fully exempt on the PGA Tour and earned a spot in The Players Championship.

"It's hard to believe," Kizzire said. "I've always believed in myself ... I don't like to think about what I've done, I just like to keep going and try to do better."

In the Utah Championship, Kizzire tied a tour record with 12 birdies in his second-round 62 and beat South Korea's Sung Kang with a three-foot birdie on the second playoff hole after they tied at 19-under 269.

In the News Sentinel Open, Kizzire made only three bogeys but 23 birdies in a 20-under 264 and won by four.

Chez Reavie also earned fully exempt status as the top money winner — $323,067 — in the four-tournament Tour Finals.

"It's everything," Reavie said. "A couple of years ago I was hurt and didn't know where I was going to end up, and here I am playing the best golf of my life and I've got a spot back on tour."

It was one of the more vigorous Web.com Tour seasons, with success spread out from top to bottom. In addition to Kizzire, there were only two other multiple winners, both winning twice. Martin Piller took the Albertsons Boise Open and the Digital Ally Open, and South Africa's Dawie van der Walt the Chile Classic and the Price Cutter Charity Championship.

There were 16 first-time winners. Among them:

Andrew Landry took the wind-battered Cartagena de Indias at Karibana Championship, shooting a remarkable 11-under-par 277 and winning by five. He closed on an especially tough Sunday with a day's-low 69. "It was one of those days when you're going to struggle," he said, "but you do what you can to get the ball in the hole and let everyone else make the mistakes."

Rob Oppenheim, who would end the season with a burst of relief, won the Air Capital Classic with a burst of scoring in the final round. Oppenheim, who started six shots behind the leader, eagled the par-five 14th from 25 feet and parred in for a 64 and a one stroke win. "It's a lot less pressure and definitely easier playing from where I was than being in the lead," Oppenheim said. "The leaders don't want to make mistakes and I'm just firing at pins and trying to go as low as I can."

Among other highlights from the 2015 Web.com Tour:

• There were 22 different winners, 15 of them American, seven born outside the United States. And there were five first-time winners.

• Rookie Patrick Rodgers, 22, ex-Stanford University standout, put his name up in a hurry. Rodgers took the Colombia Championship, the second stop on the tour, beating Steve Marino on the second hole of a playoff. "This is huge," Rodgers said.

• The tour opened with five tournaments in Latin America: Panama Claro Championship (won by Mathew Goggin), Colombia Championship (Patrick Rodgers), Karibana Championship (Andrew Landry), Brasil Champions (Peter Malnati) and Chile Classic (Dawie van der Walt).

• Dicky Pride finally revealed the contents of that note he'd been carrying all season long. It was after he won the WinCo Foods Portland Open late in August. Said the note: "I will win on the Web.com Tour in 2015 and be exempt on the PGA Tour in 2016."

• Robert Garrigus, on pressure in the season-ending Web.com Tour Championship: "It's like playing the first hole of the Masters for four days."

• Australia's Matthew Goggin, on winning the Panama Claro Championship at age 40: "It just reminds you that you can still play a bit."

• Dawie van der Walt, after winning the Chile Classic: "I wasn't thinking I wasn't going to make the cut but ... I certainly wasn't expecting to win."

Mackenzie Tour–PGA Tour Canada

The Mackenzie Tour-PGA Tour Canada celebrated a riotous 2015, with nine first-time winners in the 12 events; a player who cracked the coveted "The Five" without winning; a rookie who scored not only his first win but went on to become the only multiple winner, and a winner who made up nine shots in the final round. Among other things.

First came the name change. The PGA Tour Canada, in its third year, took on the Mackenzie name when the investment firm became the umbrella sponsor this year.

"The Five" is the Holy Grail of the tour, the top five on the money list who win berths on the Web.com Tour: 1. J.J. Spaun, U.S., $91,193; 2. Cheng Tsung "C.T." Pan, Taiwan, $79,896; 3. Taylor Pendrith, Canada, $60,736; 4. Sam Ryder, U.S., $57,168, and 5. Jason Millard, U.S., $57,040.

Spaun, 24, a first-time winner, took the Staal Foundation Open and had six other top-10 finishes to top the money list.

"I'm so glad all the hard work paid off," said Spaun, who came from a stroke behind and shot 67 in the final round of the Staal to win by one. "There was always a feeling of envy to see The Five at the end of my first two years, and to be here finally, after three years, it's a great feeling."

This was a first-timers year. The only one of the 12 tournaments not won by first-time winners was the Cape Breton Celtic Classic, which was taken by Cheng Tsung Pan, who had won his first just a few weeks earlier, in the Players Cup.

Pan, 23, making only his fourth start as a pro in the Players, started the final round three strokes behind and shot 31 on the back nine for a five-under 66 to win by two. "I didn't expect it so soon," Pan said. "But I guess it happened, and it's awesome."

A few weeks later, Pan was saying, "I can't find words to describe how I feel right now." In Cape Breton, he was four behind through the 13th, then birdied the last five holes for a 66 to tie Taylor Pendrith and make him a playoff loser for, amazingly, the third time this season.

Even so, with two other top-10 finishes, Pendrith piled up enough money to finish third in The Five. "While I wasn't able to win," he said, "I gave myself a lot of confidence."

Sam Ryder, No. 4 on The Five, and Pendrith were tied for the lead starting the final round of the National Capital Open to Support Our Troops, and they battled all the way, bogey-free and trading birdies until they ended up with 66s, still tied. Back to the 18th for the playoff: Pendrith had a 10-foot putt for a winning birdie, but he knocked it past the cup and missed the short return and bogeyed. Ryder had a four-footer for a par. He nailed it for the win. "Honestly, I wasn't expecting him to miss that second one," Ryder said. "I didn't really want it to end like that, but I'll take it."

Jason Millard, having a blah year, saved his best for last and ended up as the star success story of the season. In his first 10 starts, his best finish was a tie for second and he missed four cuts, two of them just before heading into the tour's season finale, the Freedom 55 Financial Championship. Then he shot four rounds in the 60s, tied Ryan Williams and beat him on the second playoff hole. The victory, worth the tour's season-high $36,000, lifted him from 30th on the money list to the magical fifth spot, the last of The Five.

"I was 30th coming into the week, so I felt like I had no pressure compared to the guys in the top five or 10," Millard said. "I was just trying to have a good week. Earning Web.com Tour status is what we play for all year long, and the fact I'll be able to play on that tour next year feels great."

That left some other winners not feeling so great. Among them:

• Michael Letzig, 35, had made 114 starts on the PGA Tour, 80 others on the Web.com Tour and won over $3.3 million overall, but the SIGA Dakota Dunes Open was his first-ever victory as a pro. "I think the more experience you get, the more comfortable you are under pressure," said Letzig, who won on the second playoff hole after coming from six behind in the fourth round to tie Spaun and Clark Klaasen.

• In what started as a five-man playoff for the season-opening PC Financial Open, Drew Weaver tapped in for a winning birdie at the third playoff hole when Adam Svensson chipped long and lipped out his try. "All I know," said Weaver, "is I'm glad that last putt was about four inches."

• If it wasn't a record, it was a start: Kevin Spooner started the final round of the Syncrude Boreal Open nine off the lead, shot 63, and after a wait of almost two hours, he found himself in a playoff with Talor Gooch and Ben Silverman. Spooner won with a par on the fifth extra hole. "Teeing up this morning, I thought I had absolutely no chance, being nine shots back," Spooner said. "It was quite the grind."

• Albin Choi seemed poised to win the Bayview Place Island Savings Open, but his five-shot lead evaporated in the third round. Then he birdied four of the first five holes in the fourth round and went on to win by three. "I feel," said Choi, "like I just won a battle."

Elsewhere in the bookkeeping: Svensson, who didn't win, led the tour in scoring with a 67.67 stroke average; Curtis Reed shot the low round, a 60, tying for fifth in the Freedom Financial; Reed and Pendrith also tied for the most eagles, 11; and Pan led in birdies, averaging 5.07 per round.

PGA Tour Latinoamerica

The PGA Tour Latinoamerica completed its fourth season in 2015 and produced possibly the most interesting Los Cinco (The Five) yet. One went a hefty 3-for-16 in victories, another went 0-for-17. Another had to go through a seven-hole playoff for one win, another missed five straight cuts, then turned into "Mr. October."

When the numbers were added up, these were the five who won the coveted tickets to the 2016 Web.com Tour: Mexico's Rodolfo Cazaubon, Kent Bulle of the United States, Puerto Rico's Rafael Campos, Brazil's Alexandre Rocha, and Argentina's Tommy Cocha.

No. 1: Rodolfo Cazaubon, 26, was the leading money winner with $129,203, and also was the first to win three times in one season. He started with his first Latinoamerica win in the Lexus Panama Classic in May. Thanks to experience, he said.

"Last year, my first year on tour, helped me mature and adjust to competing at this level," said Cazaubon, who turned professional in 2013 after graduating from the University of North Texas.

He solved Buenaventura Golf Club for a closing 69, a 12-under-par 276 and a two-shot victory.

"I think it was a matter of time," he said, "and here we are."

It was time again a month later in the Dominican Republic Open at the Teeth of the Dog course. Cazaubon went par-par-birdie from the 15th to up his lead to four. A watery bogey at the 18th left him with a 72, a 10-under 278 and a three-shot win.

For his landmark third win, Cazaubon beat Bulle in a playoff in the Lexus Peru Open. Bulle closed with a 64 for the clubhouse lead and Cazaubon shot 70 to tie him at 20-under-par 268 at Los Inkas Golf Club. Cazaubon then won with a 12-foot birdie putt on the first extra hole.

No. 2: Kent Bulle, No. 2 on the money list with $112,874, had the oddest of seasons. He missed five consecutive cuts (three before the summer break, two afterward in September), then made hay in an eight-tournament stretch that included his first tour victory in the Argentina Open, three seconds (twice in playoffs) and a tie for ninth.

In the Argentina Open at the Jockey Club, Bulle ended a duel with Uruguayan amateur Juan Alvarez on a short birdie putt at the final hole. "Probably the longest two-footer I've ever seen in my life," Bulle said.

No. 3: Puerto Rico's Rafael Campos, 27, who piled up his $74,666 without the benefit of a win, was the tour's "Mr. October." He had five top-10s, beginning with a tie for fourth in the Honduras Open in May. He posted the other four after the summer hiatus: A second in the Chile Open, a sixth in the Mundo Maya Open, second in the Roberto de Vicenzo Open, and then a tie for seventh in the season-ending Latinoamerica Tour Championship.

Campos had one other distinction. He scored a rare hole-in-one on a par-four hole. He used a hybrid club on El Rancho's 295-yard ninth in the final round of the Volvo Colombian Open, where he tied for 36th. "The tee shot on that hole," Campos noted, "had been giving me trouble all week."

No. 4: Brazil's Alexandre Rocha, 37, with $71,930, won the Brazil Open in a tour-record seven-hole playoff. It was the ninth win of his career, but his first on the tour. Rocha and Americans Kent Bulle and Keith Mitchell all closed with 67s and tied at 17-under 267 at Itanhanga Golf Club. Bulle dropped out with a bogey on the second extra hole. Rocha and Mitchell parred the first six holes, then Rocha parred the seventh against Mitchell's bogey. Said Rocha, who had four other top-10s: "It's been a while since my last win in a tournament this important. I have lifted a huge weight off my shoulders."

No. 5: Argentina's Tommy Cocha took the fifth and final Web.com card with his $70,342 in a season of good news-bad news. The good was that Cocha became the first to win back-to-back tournaments when he took the Mazatlan Open in March and the Centro Open in April. The bad news was that he had missed nine cuts and withdrawn once.

The Centro win was storybook material. He started the final round with a four-putt double bogey and ended it with three birdies down the last four holes for a four-shot win over Argentine hero Angel Cabrera, former winner of the U.S. Open and the Masters. "I didn't come here seeking a win," Cocha said. "My only goal was to have another solid week. And I ended up winning."

Elsewhere on the tour:

• The PGA Tour Latinoamerica Tour Championship, new on the tour schedule, was swept up by American Daniel Mazziotta, 27. He charged to five birdies across eight holes in the final round to a 68 and a four-stroke win at 11-under 273. The $36,000 first prize lifted him to sixth on the money list, some $7,700 short of the magical No. 5.

• Cazaubon was the tour scoring leader with an average of 69.76 in 55 rounds.

• Most Interesting Twist Department: Justin Hueber, 28, from Fort Wayne, Indiana, won the Mexico Open (his career-first) in May. In October, Tiger Woods had to scratch from the unofficial Bridgestone Americas Golf Cup because of back surgery, and partner Matt Kuchar then picked Hueber as his partner. They won.

• Angel Cabrera, former U.S. Open and Masters champion, played in two events and won a total of $26,950.

• Three players tied in most rounds in the 60s — 26, by Kent Bulle, Rafael Echenique and Rafael Campos.

• Campos, the man who didn't win, led in consecutive cuts made with 15.

• Bulle led in top-10 finishes, with eight, playing all 18 events.

• Fabian Gomez posted the lowest round of the year, a 61, in the Personal Classic, which he won. There were also 13 scores of 63.

8. European Tours

Rory McIlroy achieved one of his goals for the 2015 season by retaining his Race to Dubai title. But the Northern Irishman was unable to put a tick in the column for adding more major titles to his CV and that sense of it being a "not quite" season mirrored the European Tour as a whole. For the first time since 2006 no member of the circuit won a major championship.

In McIlroy's case, after two start-slow-finish-fast top-10s in the first couple of majors, his year was rudely interrupted by an ankle injury suffered during a "kick-about" football game with friends just before the tournament he was looking forward to most of all. He lost the chance to defend the Claret Jug on his favorite Open venue at St. Andrews, and his game was still rusty when he returned at the PGA Championship a month later. As a result, McIlroy slipped from being the world No. 1 to No. 3 behind the two players who dominated the year, Jordan Spieth and Jason Day.

For all that, four victories worldwide made it a fine campaign. He opened and closed with victories in Dubai, at the traditional Desert Classic and the DP World Tour Championship. He also won the WGC-Cadillac Match Play for the first time, as well as the Wells Fargo Championship for a second time on the PGA Tour.

"To be European No. 1 for the third time in four years, that was a goal of mine at the start of the year," McIlroy said. "It was a goal of mine in the middle of the year and it was definitely a goal coming into these last few weeks. Obviously I wanted to win majors. I wanted to improve in certain areas of my game, and didn't quite do that, but these things happen. You have to set yourself these lofty goals to try and get better."

But the biggest lesson learned was not to endure any more self-inflicted mishaps, on the course or off it. "This is my time to capitalize on my career. The next 10, 15 years is my time. I really can't be doing silly things like playing football in the middle of the season to jeopardize even six months of my career. It's a big chunk where I could make some hay and win a major or two. I won't be making those mistakes again next year."

Only Andy Sullivan could match his three wins on the European Tour in 2015. The pair fought a thrilling duel at the season-ending event in Dubai with McIlroy pushed to his finest golf of the year on the final day to secure a one-stroke victory. Sullivan's game and confidence grew visibly throughout the year. He won twice in South Africa early in the season and then added the Portugal Masters in October before going toe-to-toe with McIlroy in Dubai.

It is safe to say that the European No. 1 had noted the improvement. "Any time I've played with Andy, I have been very impressed," McIlroy said. "To battle the way I had to out there today is testament to how good he is and how much he has improved. I know one of his big goals next year is to make the Ryder Cup team and he would be a great asset for Europe to have in the team."

Another player with Ryder Cup ambitions was the one McIlroy pushed into second place on the Race to Dubai. Danny Willett was never out of the top two on the table after he won the Nedbank Challenge at Sun City in the first week of the 2014-15 season. The Yorkshireman also claimed the European Masters a week after finishing sixth at the Open Championship.

Others pushing to be on Darren Clarke's team at Hazeltine in 2016 will be Ireland's Shane Lowry, who won the WGC-Bridgestone Invitational; Bernd Wiesberger, whose consistency was rewarded with victory at the Open de France; Thorbjorn Olesen, who recovered from injury to win the Alfred Dunhill Links Championship, and Thomas Pieters, who won twice in three weeks in the Czech Republic and the Netherlands. Matthew Fitzpatrick, the former U.S. Amateur champion, won his maiden title at the age of 21 at the restored British Masters at Woburn and could also challenge for a Ryder Cup berth. He was pipped for the Sir Henry Cotton Rookie of the Year award by Korean Byeong-Hun An, who finished seventh on the Race to Dubai after winning the BMW PGA Championship on his debut at Wentworth.

It may well be that the 2015 season is remembered as a season of transition with only three members of the 2014 Ryder Cup team winning on the circuit the following season. As well as McIlroy, Justin Rose won the Hong Kong Open to go with his Zurich Classic title and a strong run at the majors that saw him finish three times in the top six. Victor Dubuisson rallied after a poor stretch in America at the start of the year to win the Turkish Airlines Open for a second time.

Yet, extraordinarily, there were no wins at all for the likes of Henrik Stenson, despite six runner-up finishes worldwide, Martin Kaymer, Sergio Garcia, Lee Westwood, Ian Poulter, Luke Donald or Graeme McDowell. However, there were wins on the Asian Tour for Westwood at the Indonesian Masters, Garcia at the Ho Tram Open, and Jamie Donaldson at the Thailand Championship, while McDowell won the OHL Classic at the start of the 2016 PGA Tour season.

A sense of transition was also apparent in the administration of the European Tour as Keith Pelley, a Canadian broadcasting executive, succeeded George O'Grady at the helm. Pelley made a number of noteworthy decisions including forming an alliance with the Asian Tour, which may lead to a merging of the two organizations, and refusing to sanction the WGC -Bridgestone Invitational for 2016 after a shuffling of the schedule due to the Olympics led to the PGA Tour slating the event opposite the Open de France. Controversially, he also allowed McIlroy to play only 12 events in 2015, instead of 13, due to his mid-season injury that prevented him playing in the Scottish Open, the Open Championship and the Bridgestone. Without the dispensation, McIlroy would not have remained in the Race to Dubai standings.

At the end of the season, Pelley announced that the minimum criteria for retaining membership on the tour would change from 13 events to five, but excluding the four majors and the four WGC events. The move was designed to help those outside, or on the cusp of, the world's top 50 and mainly based in America, to plan their schedules. In a bizarre scenario preceding the Final Series, Poulter fell out of the world top 50 on the cut-off week for the HSBC Champions, and to play enough events to retain his membership he had to fly to the Hong Kong Open at the last minute. He could only play on an invitation returned by former PGA champion-turned-commentator Rich Beem on hearing of Poulter's plight.

The new regulation was not enough to persuade Paul Casey to take up membership in order to be eligible for the 2016 Ryder Cup. Casey's return to form in 2015 was due, he felt, to basing his family in America and concentrating on the PGA Tour, and he wanted to follow the same formula in 2016. It was a mark of the problem facing the new chief executive. Pelley's vowed intent over the coming years was to make his circuit a "viable alternative to the PGA Tour" by raising prize money substantially. As an example, the event billed for decades as the tour's "flagship" event, the BMW PGA Championship, offers less prize money than the same week's event in America at Colonial.

European Tour

South African Open Championship
Winner: Andy Sullivan

See African Sunshine Tour chapter.

Abu Dhabi HSBC Golf Championship
Abu Dhabi, United Arab Emirates
Winner: Gary Stal

When even the world No. 1 Rory McIlroy is reduced to playing for second place, then a dominant, runaway victory is on the cards. So it was for Martin Kaymer, six strokes ahead after rounds of 64, 67 and 65, who was looking to win the Abu Dhabi HSBC Golf Championship for the fourth time and repeat his wire-to-wire win from the 2014 U.S. Open. While McIlroy succeeded in his quest, Kaymer failed in his, a turnaround even more stunning considering the German birdied three of the first four holes in the final round to lead the field by 10 strokes.

Kaymer's collapse was due to some loose play, a couple of unfortunate bounces and a brilliant rally by 22-year-old Frenchman Gary Stal, who claimed his maiden title in his 41st event on the European Tour. Stal, who won twice on the Challenge Tour in 2012, started the last round eight strokes behind, tied with McIlroy in fifth place. Stal made four birdies in an outward 32, then three more coming home. When he holed from 20 feet at the 16th he suddenly led by two and, although feeling the nerves, Stal made two solid pars to clinch the victory.

His previous best finish had been a tie for fifth recorded the previous week at the South African Open, while the win lifted him from 357th in the World Ranking to 103rd. His closing 65, added to scores of 68, 69 and 67, gave Stal a 19-under-par total of 269. He won by one over McIlroy and by two over Kaymer. "It was a crazy day but obviously I'm very happy to win,"

Stal said. "It's unbelievable, because I saw the leaderboard on the fifth and I thought it's not possible to win. When I saw my name on the leaderboard on the 16th green, I saw everything had changed."

Kaymer suffered his first bogey for three days at the sixth hole, then drove into a bush at the ninth and had to take a penalty drop. He ended up with a double bogey, and then at the 13th he did exactly the same. With a duffed chip thrown in as well, the German had a triple bogey there that handed the lead to Stal. "I'm surprised and a little shocked," Kaymer said.

McIlroy almost holed a bunker shot at the last for an eagle but finished with a 66, though he had missed a plethora of putts throughout the week, especially in a third-round 71. On Friday he dispensed with the putter as he made his first hole-in-one as a professional, with a nine iron from 177 yards at the 15th hole.

Commercial Bank Qatar Masters
Doha, Qatar
Winner: Branden Grace

A superb eagle at the 16th hole helped Branden Grace to victory in the Commercial Bank Qatar Masters, but it was not the South African's only brilliant shot at Doha Golf Club. In the third round, off the back of consecutive bogeys, Grace drove into the trees on the fifth hole. With a blind approach, he snap-hooked a wedge through a gap in the leaves, and after hearing the applause from the gallery discovered his ball had not only finished on the green but within five feet of the hole. He made the putt for a birdie on the way to joining a four-way tie for the 54-hole lead on 13 under alongside Marc Warren, Bernd Wiesberger and Emiliano Grillo.

Grace, who maintained his 100 percent record of converting a lead or share thereof with a round to go, started with a birdie in the final round, but Warren birdied the first two holes. But the Scot dropped a shot at the fifth and then had a double bogey at the short eighth where he hit into the water. For a time Wiesberger made the running, but on the back nine no less than six players were tied for the lead. Warren made four birdies in six holes after his double, but Grace finally got going again when he birdied the 12th and 14th holes.

At the short par-four 16th the players drive over a rock that blocks their view of the green. Grace produced the perfect drive to five feet and holed for an eagle to go two ahead. "It's not actually my favorite tee shot, especially with the wind off the left," Grace said. "It's one you have to really commit to and it's one of those where it's a good driver, but it's not a smash. I managed to hit a great shot and got it up in the air, which allowed for the soft bounce."

Warren birdied the 16th and 17th holes to tie, but Grace then pitched close at the par-five 18th and made a birdie while Warren could only find a par. Grace had rounds of 67, 68, 68 and 66 for a 19-under-par total of 269, while Warren finished one back after a 67. Wiesberger took third place and Eddie Pepperell fourth, with Grillo, Gregory Bourdy and Byeung-Hun An tying for fifth place. It was Grace's sixth victory on the European Tour and his second in four events after claiming the Alfred Dunhill Championship at the end of 2014 (but part of the 2015 schedule).

Omega Dubai Desert Classic
Dubai, United Arab Emirates
Winner: Rory McIlroy

At the Abu Dhabi HSBC Championship Rory McIlroy set a new European Tour record for consecutive top-two finishes. His run starting at the Open Championship in 2014 was: win, win, win, second, second, second. Entering the Omega Dubai Desert Classic the 25-year-old world No. 1 was determined not to come second again — and he did not mean by finishing third or fourth. The Northern Irishman duly extended his own record to seven straight top-twos but got back in the winner's circle for the first time since the PGA Championship at Valhalla with a comfortable three-stroke victory at Emirates. It was his 10th European Tour victory and came at the scene of his first in 2009.

Chances to win the title again had come and gone, notably in 2014, but this time there was no hint of a collapse from McIlroy. After opening with a 66, two behind Bernd Wiesberger's 64, it was his play in the middle of the tournament that separated him from the rest. He had his own 64 on Friday, coming home in five-under-par 32 with three birdies in a row to finish and go one ahead of the field. He then went out in 30 on Saturday with five birdies in the first eight holes and posted a 66 to lead by four strokes. In a final round of 70 there were few dramas as he birdied the first three par-fives and dropped a shot at the seventh but otherwise calmly went on his way, a long par-putt on the 12th leaving little hope for the rest. On 22 under par, McIlroy equaled the tournament record total of 266 held by Thomas Bjorn and Stephen Gallacher.

"It's nice to be able to put my name on that trophy again," said McIlroy. "It felt like I was coming second every time I was teeing it up, so it was time for a change and obviously the only way I wanted to go was one better. Thankfully, I was able to do that today."

Sweden's Alex Noren took second place on 19 under after a closing 65 for his best result since the third of his three wins in 2011. It was his third event of the year after a fraught 2014 season in which he played only twice due to tendonitis in his wrists. Gallacher took third place to add to his run of second-first-first in the previous three years.

Maybank Malaysian Open
Winner: Bernd Wiesberger
See Asia/Japan Tours chapter.

True Thailand Classic
Winner: Andrew Dodt
See Asia/Japan Tours chapter.

Hero Indian Hero Open
Winner: Anirban Lahiri

See Asia/Japan Tours chapter.

Joburg Open
Winner: Andy Sullivan

See African Sunshine Tour chapter.

Africa Open
Winner: Trevor Fisher, Jr.

See African Sunshine Tour chapter.

Tshwane Open
Winner: George Coetzee

See African Sunshine Tour chapter.

Trophee Hassan II
Agadir, Morocco
Winner: Richie Ramsay

A back injury while training at home at Christmas had a lasting effect for Richie Ramsay on the start of his 2015 campaign. He missed four of his first five cuts and had to withdraw the only time he had qualified for the weekend. But the 31-year-old former U.S. Amateur champion took advantage of better form at the Trophee Hassan II to claim his third title on the European Tour. On a rollercoaster of an afternoon at the Golf du Palais Royal in Agadir, Ramsay won by one stroke over Romain Wattel and by two over a group of six players.

Ramsay and fellow Scot Andrew McArthur started the final day tied for the lead with Wattel. Four birdies in a row from the third put Ramsay in front by three strokes, but then he gave back those four shots gained. After a bogey at the seventh, where Wattel birdied, Ramsay duffed two chips at the par-three eighth and took a triple bogey. He steadied the round by making two par saves at the next two holes and then hit close at the 12th to spark another run of birdies, this time three in a row. When Wattel bogeyed the 14th, Ramsay was two ahead. The Frenchman chipped in to save par on the 15th before picking up a shot at the 17th, but had to chip-in again at the last to tie. A fine effort ran just past.

Ramsay closed with a round of 69, to Wattel's 70, after earlier scores of 72, 66 and 71, and finished on a 10-under-par total of 278. Among those sharing third place was George Coetzee, who needed to win to get into the world's top 50 and earn a place in the Masters. He finished alongside Chris Wood, Pablo Larrazabal, Mikael Lundberg, Jaco Van Zyl and Kevin Phelan. Former Masters champion Jose Maria Olazabal closed with a 66 to finish tied for ninth place.

"It is a great honor to win this dagger," Ramsay said of the winner's trophy.

"It is a tournament unlike any other and it is a piece of history. It will be great when we have children to say this is where I went to Morocco and won a dagger."

At the presentation ceremony there was a minute's silence in tribute to the late Billy Casper, a double winner of the tournament in the 1970s before it was an official event and a friend of the late King Hassan II, the pair playing more than 150 rounds together.

Shenzhen International
Shenzhen, China
Winner: Kiradech Aphibarnrat

In winning the inaugural Shenzhen International, Kiradech Aphibarnrat rallied late in the final round to deny a home victory for local favorite Hao-Tong Li. Aphibarnrat eagled the 17th hole to tie and then won with a birdie at the first extra hole at Genzon Golf Club in Shenzhen, China.

The 25-year-old Thai had a commanding lead in the third round before dropping three strokes on the last two holes. He was two ahead of Peter Uihlein after 54 holes but struggled on the final day with four bogeys and only two birdies in the first 16 holes. By then Li, the 19-year-old who won the PGA Tour China Order of Merit in 2014, had posted the clubhouse target at 12 under par after weekend rounds of 65 and 67 which included only one bogey.

As Li watched on television from the clubhouse, Aphibarnrat hit his approach at the par-five 17th to 20 feet and holed the putt. After driving into a fairway bunker at the last, the Thai hit a fine approach but missed his putt for victory. A closing 72, after earlier rounds of 67, 69 and 68, matched Li's total of 276. At the 18th again for the first playoff hole, Aphibarnrat had a similar putt to the one he missed in regulation, but this time holed from 12 feet for the win as Li had already two-putted for his par.

It was Aphibarnrat's second victory on the European Tour, following his win at the Malaysia Open in 2013. Since then he had been affected by the death of his coach, Natpasit Chokthanasart, in December of 2013, and later on adapting to an equipment change that took longer than he hoped. "There have been lots of changes since I won, so I'm so happy to get my hands on another trophy," he said. "I've been struggling for a year.

"But today special thanks goes to my caddie, he was always pushing me. When we were two behind on the last two holes he said, you have not lost, we have not signed the scorecard yet. He was completely right, and I just got the job done. I had a chance to win in 72 holes, but the putt in the playoff is the best putt I have ever made in my life."

Volvo China Open
Winner: Ashun Wu
See Asia/Japan Tours chapter.

AfrAsia Bank Mauritius Open
Winner: George Coetzee
See African Sunshine Tour chapter.

Open de Espana
Barcelona, Spain
Winner: James Morrison

On a breezy final day of the Open de Espana at El Prat, in Barcelona, only three of the 72 players managed to keep any dropped shots off their cards. Two of them were Scott Jamieson, with a 64 to finish 31st, and Wade Ormsby, with a 65 to finish ninth, but both were playing relatively early in the day. James Morrison, on the other hand, was out in the last pairing as the co-leader with David Howell. A closing 69 from the 30-year-old Englishman ensured a four-stroke victory over a quartet that included Howell, defending champion Miguel Angel Jimenez, France's Edouard Espana and Francesco Molinari.

Morrison had won at the Madeira Islands Open in 2010, his rookie season, but in 2013 he had to regain his card at the qualifying school. Yet his relative inexperience compared to most of his challengers mattered for little as Morrison produced a commanding performance. He chipped in for a birdie at the fifth and holed from 12 feet for another at the ninth to go out in 34, while Howell played the first 11 holes in four over par.

A string of eight pars in a row secured the victory, while his pursuers had an up-and-down time. There was no more important moment than his lag putt from 60 feet at the 16th which allowed merely a tap-in for his four. A 10-footer at the 18th for a closing birdie gave Morrison a 10-under-par total of 278.

"It feels amazing, five years since my first win, a lot of chances in between," he said. "Today I just drew on my experience and got over the line. In years past when I haven't done it, it's been too much looking at leaderboards and outside influences. Today, I stuck to my process all day long and executed it. I was desperate to make a birdie on the last, and I did it."

Howell recovered with three birdies in the last five holes for a 73, while the appropriately named Espana, the halfway leader, birdied the last two. Jimenez, 51, had provided some excitement, as well as showing off his trademark celebratory jig, when he holed his approach at the fifth for an eagle and almost holed his tee shot at the eighth, where he had holed-in-one on Friday.

BMW PGA Championship
Virginia Water, Surrey, England
Winner: Byeong-Hun An

Winning the BMW PGA Championship on debut is a rare feat. In six decades of the tournament, in recent times the flagship event of the European Tour, Byeong-Hun An became only the sixth player to achieve a victory on his first appearance. And what a win it was. The 23-year-old from South Korea finished six strokes clear of two tour veterans, 51-year-old Miguel Angel Jimenez and 45-year-old Thongchai Jaidee, with a record tournament total of 267, 21 under par.

An posted a best-of-the-week 64 around the West course at Wentworth in the second round and a best-of-the-day 65 in the final round. He was one behind at the halfway stage and it was a 67 in the third round that took him into a share of the lead with Francesco Molinari, who had led on his own for the first two days.

While the Italian fell back to fifth place on the final day, An had two birdies in the first four holes to stay one ahead of Jaidee, who had three birdies in a row from the fourth. But on the inward half, An was unstoppable. He had tap-in birdies at the 11th and 15th, and was only two inches away from an albatross at the 12th as his superb five-iron approach set up the easiest of eagles. He also got up and down for a four at the 17th as he came home in 32.

Only Scott Drummond in 2004 had won on debut since Arnold Palmer did so in 1975. "I didn't know that a win was this close," said An, a former U.S. Amateur champion. "It came all of a sudden. I've been playing well all year, but not at this event. I never thought I would win this event, it's like a fifth major to me. I love that I'm the first Asian to win this event."

Although world No. 1 and defending champion Rory McIlroy missed the cut after two wins in the last three weeks in America, record galleries attended all week at Wentworth and were rewarded with some fine golf. On Saturday England's Tommy Fleetwood had an albatross at the fourth hole, holing from 198 yards with a seven iron, and then played the remaining par-fives in eagle, birdie and par. He went on to finish tied for sixth place. The same day Miguel Angel Jimenez holed in one with a nine iron at the second hole for his 10th ace on the European Tour, a week after his ninth and 25 years after his first, to pass Colin Montgomerie for the most holes-in-one on the circuit. On Sunday, Chris Wood, on the way to finishing fourth, had a hole-in-one at the 14th with a seven iron, the first at the hole in the championship since 1999. It was also the fifth ace of the week, which equaled the record for a European Tour event.

Dubai Duty Free Irish Open
Newcastle, Co. Down, Northern Ireland
Winner: Soren Kjeldsen

In terms of being a sell-out, with 107,000 braving all conditions throughout the week at Royal County Down, and raising hundreds of thousands more for the event's charity, the Rory Foundation, the Dubai Duty Free Irish Open was a success even before it started. And though the host and driving force behind the event's return to Northern Ireland, world No. 1 Rory McIlroy, was at Sunday's prize-giving ceremony, he was only there to present the trophy to Denmark's Soren Kjeldsen. McIlroy, after opening with a nine-over 80, missed the cut for the second week running and for the third Irish Open in a row.

It was at County Down, just 40 miles from where he grew up in Holy-wood, that McIlroy spent hours preparing prior to his Open Championship victory at Hoylake in 2014. But his course knowledge counted for little as he failed to birdie a single hole on the first day. He was not the only one to struggle in this reunion from the 2007 Walker Cup. Rickie Fowler did make the weekend but finished his third round with consecutive eights, while Jonathan Moore, whose eagle at the 18th sealed America's victory eight years earlier, had a 13 at the par-four 13th.

With wind and rain turning the classic links into a brutal test, Kjeldsen did use his knowledge gained from playing the course during social rounds with friends who live nearby to good effect. A 67 on the third day, after a 69 and a 70, gave the 40-year Swede a two-stroke lead over Maximilian Kieffer, whose 65 on Saturday beat Jimmy Bruen's course record from 1939.

But with the wind howling again on Sunday, Kieffer dropped back with a 77, while Kjeldsen's 76 became the highest final-round score to win the tournament. He had gone out in four over but still led until three-putting the 17th. He tied Eddie Pepperell, who had the only bogey-free round of the weekend with a 69, and Bernd Wiesberger, who closed with a 73, on two under par.

After his stumbles, Kjeldsen won the tournament with a superb three wood onto the final green. With his two opponents unable to get up and down for a birdie, the Dane two-putted for victory. "My last breath was at the 14th," he admitted after his fourth victory, six years after his last. "Three weeks ago I was 112th on the Order of Merit and my game was not in good shape. Then I turned 40 and you think, 'is that it?' To stand here now is pretty remarkable."

Nordea Masters
Malmo, Sweden
Winner: Alex Noren

Friday (June 5) at the Nordea Masters celebrated Denmark's national day with the flagsticks at each hole on Malmo's PGA Sweden National course featuring the flag of the neighboring country connected to Sweden by the bridge over the Oresund. Saturday (June 6) was Sweden's national day and the flags changed accordingly.

Home advantage proved crucial as six of the top-eight places after 54 holes were held by Swedes, and Alex Noren, the overnight leader by two, going on to a four-stroke victory. Soren Kjeldsen, winner of the Irish Open the previous week, kept up the honor of the Danes by finishing second after matching Noren's closing 71. Alexander Levy of France and Germany's Maximilian Kieffer shared third place with two other home players, Jens Dantorp and Sebastian Soderbergh.

Noren missed eight months in 2014 with tendonitis in each wrist, return-ing at the start of 2015 on a medical exemption. This was his 12th event and the 12th time he had made the cut. But it was his first victory since claiming the same title in 2011. His scores of 70, 68, 67 and 71 gave him a 12-under-par total of 276 on a weekend of particularly blustery conditions.

After a birdie-bogey start to his final round, the 32-year-old posted 15 pars in a row to extend his lead as others fell away. A birdie at the last provided a suitably crowning moment.

"Now I can relax a bit, because it was probably the toughest weekend in terms of wind I've ever felt," Noren said. "The win in the 2011 Nordea Masters was very thrilling; this one is very pleasing. I wasn't too confident coming into this week because I've had a tough time in the wind lately and here you really have to hit the right shots to get around. I got better as the week went on."

Marcus Kinhult, an 18-year-old Swedish amateur who had won the Lytham Trophy a few weeks earlier, shared the lead after each of the first two rounds with scores of 67 and 68. He was only the second amateur to lead after 36 holes of a European Tour event since Aaron Pike did so in the MasterCard Masters in 2007. Kinhult ultimately finished tied for 33rd place after weekend scores of 77 and 75.

Lyoness Open
Atzenbrugg, Austria
Winner: Chris Wood

Six times Andrey Pavlov found the water at the opening hole in the second round of the Lyoness Open. The Russian played the par-five in 17 strokes, with Phillipe Porquier's 20 at the French Open in 1978 being the only worse score recorded on the modern European Tour. Pavlov was only five over for the other 35 holes he played before departing Austria, but it was a reminder that danger lurks everywhere on the Diamond course in Atzenbrugg.

Gregory Bourdy hardly imagined so for the first three days. He opened with a flawless 65 and led by four at halfway and by two with a round to play. But after a birdie at the first on Sunday, Bourdy found the water at the short second and took a double bogey. The Frenchman's form evaporated and he closed with a 78 to fall into a tie for sixth place. Cabrera-Bello, who won the event with a stunning closing 60 at Fontana in 2009, inherited the lead, but three bogeys in a row from the ninth proved a fatal hiccup.

Instead it was Chris Wood who claimed victory. The 27-year-old Englishman had been around the lead all week, only two behind after an opening 67 but finding himself seven back as he teed off on Friday afternoon. A 69 kept him within four of Bourdy, but a 70 on Saturday dropped him five behind.

With a closing 67, for a 15-under-par total of 273, he timed his challenge to perfection. Birdies at the first, third and sixth put the willowy man from Bristol out in 33, but he only found himself in the lead as Bourdy and Cabrera-Bello came back to him. Immediately Wood powered away with birdies at the back-to-back par-fives, the 15th and 16th holes. He won by two over Cabrera-Bello and by five over Robert Rock, Robert Dinwiddie and Matthew Fitzpatrick.

This was Wood's second victory, after winning the 2013 Qatar Masters, and came after a winter in which he sat out for five months after injuring his wrist playing tennis. "It was a long winter sitting at home with a cast on my wrist getting frustrated and just wanting to be out here playing and competing," he said. "It has been a while since the win in Qatar, but let me tell you it feels a lot better to say I am a two-time winner on tour."

BMW International Open
Munich, Germany
Winner: Pablo Larrazabal

Reading is believing, possibly not always, but it was the case for Pablo Larrazabal at the BMW International Open. "There was an article that said I was a giant killer," he said. When the 32-year-old Spaniard won for the first time at the French Open, Colin Montgomerie was the runner-up. When he won the BMW International for the first time in 2011, he beat Sergio Garcia in a playoff. And when he triumphed at the 2014 HSBC Abu Dhabi Championship, he overcame Rory McIlroy and Phil Mickelson.

In winning a second title at Munchen Eichenried, Larrazabal emerged from a congested leaderboard to pip former European No. 1 Henrik Stenson by one stroke. Stenson closed with a 65 that included an eagle at the 11th where he holed from 30 feet.

After rounds of 70, 66 and 69, Larrazabal was five strokes off the lead but sprinted to the turn in 31 with five birdies. He then holed from 15 feet for a birdie at the 16th to move ahead of Stenson and then parred in for a bogey-free 66 and a 17-under-par total of 271. England's Chris Paisley, lying second overnight, closed with a 71 to take third place, ahead of a group that included Retief Goosen. James Morrison, whose scores of 67, 66 and 67 gave him a two-stroke lead after 54 holes, finished just outside the top 10 after a 77.

Larrazabal, looking forward to getting married later in the summer, became the third player after Paul Azinger and Thomas Bjorn to win the title twice. "Every title is very special, but this place, from the first time I arrived to this golf course, it's something that suits my eye," Larrazabal said. "I knew that I was in a good position, and I knew that I had to start very fast. I had to start with a few birdies in the first few holes and was hitting the ball as good as I've hit it all year, and my putting was awesome. Coming in, it was tough. You have a lot of holes with a lot of trouble."

Stenson, who followed his eagle with a tee shot to six feet at the next hole, said: "I guess those two holes were worth coming and watching. It was not free today. You had to pay admission to come in, so I guess I gave them something to watch there."

Alstom Open de France
Paris, France
Winner: Bernd Wiesberger

Since he won twice in 2012, including his home tournament at the Lyoness Open, Bernd Wiesberger was due a victory. Five top-six finishes in 2015, including two runner-up finishes, in one of which he lost a playoff to Soren

Kjeldsen at the Irish Open, suggested his third European Tour title might not be far away. A weekend return of 66 and 65 at the Alstom Open de France duly gave the 29-year-old Austrian a three-stroke victory over James Morrison at Le Golf National.

Wiesberger shared the first-day lead on 68 but fell back with a 72 on Friday and was three strokes behind Jaco Van Zyl starting the final round. A brief interruption for lightning seemed to spark him into action as he returned to the course to post four birdies in a row from the fourth, a run that included a chip-in at the fifth. His short-iron approach to the ninth finished an inch from the hole to put him out in 31 and four ahead of the field.

Eight pars followed on the back nine with playing partner Morrison, who lost the 54-hole lead in Munich the previous week, putting the pressure on with three birdies, including at the dangerous par-three 16th. But Wiesberger held firm to keep a bogey off his card and then holed from 15 feet for a birdie at the last to finish on 271, 13 under par. Morrison, who dropped only one stroke over the last three rounds, closed with a 67, while Van Zyl was third after a 73. Martin Kaymer had a double bogey at the last after finding the water to place fourth, while his playing partner, home favorite Victor Dubuisson, went out of bounds at the seventh for a triple bogey.

"This tournament is very special to me," Wiesberger said. "It's one of the biggest events we have on tour and the oldest one on Continental Europe. I'm very proud to be on the winners' list on this trophy, dating back to 1906."

Morrison, Van Zyl and Rafa Cabrera-Bello, who came home in 29, earned qualifications to the Open Championship at St. Andrews. On Friday, Renato Paratore created history as the first person on the modern European Tour, since 1972 so far as it is known, to play all 18 holes with fours, birdieing all the par-fives and bogeying all the par-threes.

Aberdeen Asset Management Scottish Open
Gullane, East Lothian, Scotland
Winner: Rickie Fowler

Four rounds in the 60s on a classic links was just the sort of warm-up Rickie Fowler would have settled for heading to the Open Championship at St. Andrews. But in what is rapidly becoming the 26-year-old Californian's trademark, a late charge brought Fowler victory at the Aberdeen Asset Management Scottish Open.

At Sawgrass in May, Fowler was five under par for the last four holes before winning the biggest title of his career at The Players Championship in a playoff. Extra holes was on the cards all day at Gullane, a near neighbor of Muirfield, where a composite course was used to stage the Scottish Open for the first time. With overnight leader Daniel Brooks falling back into a packed leaderboard, many players had a chance, including Marc Warren, who finished early with a 64 to post the clubhouse lead at 10 under par.

Raphael Jacquelin took the top spot until a bogey at the 14th, when Matt Kuchar, who birdied the 13th and 16th, took over. He also posted four rounds under 70, closing with a 68 for 11 under par. When Fowler, who had recorded scores of 66, 68 and 66 for the first three days, bogeyed the 14th himself, he was two off the lead. Then he birdied three of the last four holes.

At the 15th he holed from nine feet. At the short par-four 16th, he two-putted from distance after driving the green, and then hit a big drive down the 18th and a wedge to two feet. Jacquelin needed to hole his approach to the last to tie and saw his ball spin back to two inches. The Frenchman's consolation was qualifying for the Open Championship along with Brooks and Rikard Karlberg.

Fowler, who had missed the cut at the U.S. Open following his Players victory, joined Michael Allen, Tom Lehman and Phil Mickelson, in 2013, as an American winner at the Scottish Open. "Phil mentioned to me win this and there's a good chance you win next week, so I had to take care of business," said Fowler.

"I don't know what's so special about links golf, but it's my favorite. It was a good test this week at Gullane. I felt really good coming down the stretch. It was nice to be back in contention again, and I'm excited about where the game is at. I'm very excited about next week now."

The Open Championship
Winner: Zach Johnson
See Chapter 4.

Omega European Masters
Crans Montana, Switzerland
Winner: Danny Willett

After his impressive sixth-place tie at the Open Championship, which finished a day late, Danny Willett drove home from St. Andrews on the Monday night and travelled to Switzerland the next morning, finally reaching his destination "up the mountain" at Crans-sur-Sierre. It was well worth the trip as Willett won the Omega European Masters for his third European Tour victory. His previous one had been at the Nedbank Challenge at the end of 2014 but counted on the 2015 season, so combined with a strong showing at the WGC-Cadillac Championship and the Open Championship, the 27-year-old Englishman jumped into second place on the Race to Dubai and into the world's top 25 for the first time.

The traditional Swiss event, moved from its usual September date to the week after the Open, turned into something of a local affair for two men from Sheffield. While Willett moved into the halfway lead with rounds of 65 and 62, a windy Saturday brought him a 71 which meant he shared the lead with Matthew Fitzpatrick, who posted a 64 earlier in the day.

Although Tyrell Hatton romped to a 62, having gone out in 29 with four birdies and an eagle, to take third place, Pelle Edberg scored a 63 to be fourth and Sergio Garcia a weekend 66-64 to move up from the cut-line to sixth place, it was a battle of the Yorkshiremen.

Fitzpatrick, the former U.S. Amateur champion, bogeyed the first hole but then had four birdies in the next eight holes to lead by one. The 20-year-old dropped a shot at the 11th and could only match Willett's birdies at the 14th and 15th. Willett had gone out in two under, getting away with a par at the seventh despite finishing a foot from going out of bounds when trying to drive the green.

Willett would not drop a shot all day and his three birdies in a row from the 13th proved decisive. But the one-shot lead stayed all the way to the last, where Willett got his long approach putt close to secure the win. "Matt was snapping at my heels all day, so I'm delighted to get the job done," Willett said. "He played some great golf and really kept the pressure on me. Winning is always tough, and the heart rate on 18 was pretty high. Having a lag putt is almost trickier than trying to hole one sometimes, so I was very relieved to see it stop a foot or two from the hole."

Madeira Islands Open - Portugal - BPI
Madeira, Portugal
Winner: Roope Kakko

After weather forced the Madeira Islands Open - Portugal - BPI to be cancelled with only one round completed earlier in the year, the rescheduled event at Santo da Serra saw Roope Kakko become the second Finnish winner on the European Tour after Mikko Ilonen. Kakko produced a magnificent weekend with rounds of 64 and 63 to win by three strokes over Scott Henry, the runner-up for the second year in a row.

After rounds of 66 and 71, the 33-year-old was four off the halfway lead, and even after his eight-under effort on Saturday he was a shot adrift of Pontus Widegreen. But while Widegreen returned a 72 to share fourth place with Sebastian Soderburg, Andrew McArthur had a 63 to take third place and Henry a 66.

But Kakko, finishing with a record 24-under-par total of 264, ran away from the rest with an outward 32, including three birdies in a row from the fifth and then chipped in for an eagle at the 10th before collecting three more birdies coming home. Kakko won as an amateur on the Challenge Tour but then had to wait nine years before his second victory on that circuit in 2013. "I came here to try and win this event and change my career, so I'm over the moon to have done it," he said. "There was a lot of pressure but I had some pretty good thoughts in me, so I was able to handle it today. Sometimes it doesn't go the way you plan it, but it all went my way today.

"I told myself to just stick to my game plan and eventually I'm going to make a few birdies. I actually targeted a 67 today and I went a bit lower than that, so that was great. On Saturday I had a plan to just get into contention on Sunday and it worked. Scott and I played incredible golf today. This is definitely the best moment of my career, but I have to say that it really helped me to have won two years ago on the Challenge Tour in Oman. I was at a stage where I really needed to win and I did it, and that really helped me today, calmed me down when the pressure was on."

Saltire Energy Paul Lawrie Match Play
Aberdeen, Scotland
Winner: Kiradech Aphibarnrat

Host Paul Lawrie had to invite himself to the Satire Energy Paul Lawrie Match Play at Murcar Links, where the former Open champion began his career as an assistant professional. Although Lawrie departed after the second round, the first regular tour match-play event in decades was a huge success. It was a 64-man straight knockout tournament, and after beating Romain Wattel on day one, Lawrie lost to fellow Scot Chris Doak the next — this after Doak had rallied in the first round from 4 down after five to beat Anthony Wall at the last.

The other high-profile invitee, John Daly, lost to Jorge Campillo on the first day, but it was fitting that "Asia's Daly," the big-hitting Kiradech Aphibarnrat went on to triumph. The 26-year-old Thai defeated Wade Ormsby, Graeme Storm, Thomas Aiken, Michael Hoey and another local favorite, Marc Warren, in the semi-final before beating Robert Karlsson at the 18th in the final.

Warren won his place in the semis by beating Tyrell Hatton after the Englishman had chipped in on the 18th to force extra holes. Warren then holed out with his approach for an eagle-two at the 19th for the most sudden of wins. David Howell, who took Karlsson to the 20th in the semi-finals, beat Warren at the 18th in the third-fourth playoff.

Aphibarnrat never trailed to Karlsson in the final, going ahead at the second and moving to 3 up after six holes. He was pegged back to one ahead at the turn but produced a superb drive at the downhill 11th to find the green and go 2 up. Karlsson then bogeyed the 14th to go 3 down with four to play before rallying to win the next three holes with two birdies and a par. When the Thai drove into the rough at the last and Karlsson put his approach to 10 feet, the veteran Swede looked in command.

But Aphibarnrat responded with a brilliant second shot to inside four feet and, after Karlsson missed for his three, made no mistake with the putt. It was his third European Tour title and his second of the season after winning the Shenzhen International. "This is a very important win for me because it is the first time I have won outside Asia," he said. "I sank a lot of important putts — especially the putt to win which was very short but it was great to see it hit the middle of the hole."

Made in Denmark
Farso, Denmark
Winner: David Horsey

Little over a year after winning the 2014 Russian Open wire-to-wire, David Horsey achieved the feat again for his fourth European Tour at the Made in Denmark event at Himmerland. The 30-year-old Englishman hit the front with an eight-under 63 on the opening day but led by only one over Australian Terry Pilkadaris after 54 holes.

Sunday afternoon's windy conditions meant that it was a matter of survival for Horsey after Sweden's Kristoffer Broberg, with a 62, and Daniel Gaunt, with a 66, had posted totals of 11 under par. A bogey at the seventh meant Horsey was knocked off the top spot for the first time in 41 holes. But Pilkadaris bogeyed the eighth and ninth, as well as the 14th, before a double bogey at the 15th for a 74 and 11 under.

Home favorite Soren Kjeldsen, making his 501st European Tour appearance, went out in 33 and birdied the 13th but had two short birdie tries lip out and bogeyed the last for a 68 to share second place.

Horsey bogeyed the 14th and 16th holes so still had work to do at the last after he pulled his drive into rough on a bank. But a fine seven iron onto the green secured his par, a 73 and a 13-under-par total of 271 for a two-stroke victory. "It was a bit of a strange week," Horsey admitted. "I've been focusing on myself and not trying to get caught up in the tournament and I managed to do that so well it's nearly a bit of surprise."

Horsey added: "The crowds were unbelievable. We have good fans in the UK, but the fans here are just fantastic. They are so loud. To get clapped in on all the greens like we did was amazing." There were 24,000 spectators for the final round and over 86,000 for the week, many thousands on the amphitheater banking around the host 16th.

Denmark's Andreas Harto birdied the hole on Friday from five feet and then, to the delight of the gallery, went down on one knee to propose to his girlfriend Louise. She said yes. "I don't know how I hit that shot or made that putt," Harto said after missing the cut. "I was almost crying when I hit the putt because I knew what was about to happen. I know she might think I'm a bit silly, but it's going to be a great memory for us as we grow older."

D+D Real Czech Masters
Prague, Czech Republic
Winner: Thomas Pieters

Thomas Pieters may be one of the young long-drivers on the European Tour, but it was the nine-hour through-the-night drive of his parents which was rewarded when they were able to watch their son win for the first time in the D+D Real Czech Masters at the Albatross course near Prague. Pieters became the third Belgian player to win on the European Tour after Philippe Toussaint and Niclas Colsaerts and, at the age of 23, the youngest.

His victory came in his 48th appearance of a promising career which saw him lose a playoff to Miguel Angel Jimenez at the Spanish Open in 2014. With scores of 66, 68, 65 and 69, Pieters finished on a 20-under-par total of 268 and three clear of Pelle Edberg, with Matthew Fitzpatrick a further stroke behind in third. In his last tournament before turning 21, Fitzpatrick opened the final round with four straight birdies but could not overcome a five-stroke deficit. He finished two ahead of Robert Dinwiddie, with 18-year-old Italian Renato Paratore, who shared the lead after an opening 65, tying for fifth place.

Pieters, one off the lead after the first two rounds, was particularly impressive on the weekend when he played only two holes over par. After starting the third round with an eagle and a birdie, the Belgian's only blip came at the 11th when he was penalized two strokes for playing a wrong ball from the rough. It dropped him out of the lead, but three birdies in the next five holes helped him regain the advantage, but a double bogey at the third hole on Sunday again stalled his progress.

Yet he rallied once more by birdieing the fourth and came home in 33 while Edberg bogeyed the 11th. "To be a European Tour winner is an amazing feeling right now," Pieters said. "I'm happy to have my family with me and I'm very proud of the way I played today, especially after that early double. It was mentally tough those last 14 holes.

"It was special having my family here with me. I called them yesterday and they were in Belgium. For them to be here right now is pretty cool that they can experience this with me. They drove through the night to get here. It is a nine-hour journey, but it is great to have them here."

M2M Russian Open
Moscow, Russia
Winner: Lee Slattery

Since Lee Slattery won the Madrid Masters in 2011, a second victory had proved elusive. In 2014 he got married and a first child arrived, but he finished 111th on the Race to Dubai to lose his exempt status by one place. A recent illness for his father-in-law added to the emotion when the 37-year-old Englishman won the M2M Russian Open at the new Moscow venue of Skolkovo.

"My wife's dad is very ill so this is for him," Slattery said. "It's just nice to be able to finish the year off like this with a win, knowing that I can plan next year now and hopefully get myself going again to where I belong, I feel."

Rounds of 66, 67 and 67 put Slattery two ahead after 54 holes, and after the final round was delayed by fog for two hours, he holed a long putt on the first green for the perfect start. But two bogeys followed on the front nine, and by the time Estanislao Goya made his fourth birdie of the day at the 12th, the Argentine was two ahead. But two bogeys in the next three holes along with a long birdie putt by Slattery at the 14th swung the advantage back to the Englishman.

Slattery came home in three under with a chip-in birdie at the 17th giving him a cushion for the last where Goya birdied for a 68. Slattery made his three-footer for a par, and a closing 69 left him on 15-under-par 269 and the victor by one stroke. Defending champion David Horsey took third place, one behind Goya and one ahead of Michael Hoey, James Heath, Oskar Henningsson and Pablo Martin Benavides.

"Holing the long putt on 14 was very important and the chip-in was massive," Slattery said. "It's funny, the thing that's been letting me down most has probably been my short game in the last few months, so I've worked so hard at that. To chip one in at such an important time meant so much and it shows that practice pays off eventually."

KLM Open
Zandvoort, The Netherlands
Winner: Thomas Pieters

Thomas Pieters, and his family, had a slightly shorter journey for his second successive victory as the 23-year-old Belgian popped over the boarder to win the KLM Open at Kennemer. After a week off to celebrate his maiden success at the Czech Masters, Pieters won by a single stroke over Lee Slattery, himself looking for back-to-back wins after his triumph at the Russian Open the previous week.

After opening with rounds of 68 and 66, Pieters got motoring over the weekend with scores of 62 and 65 for a 19-under-par total of 261. He made four birdies in the first seven holes, holed a good par-saver at the ninth, hit close at the 10th and dropped his only shot of the day at the 11th. But another birdie at the 13th got him back to 19 under and even with Slattery.

The Englishman had moved into contention with a 63 in the third round to share the overnight lead with Rafa Cabrera-Bello, who closed with a 71. Slattery had three birdies and dropped only one stroke, but it came at the last where, after a first putt, he missed a five-footer to force a playoff and fell back into a tie for second place with Eduardo de la Riva, who closed with a 63.

"I feel bad for Lee as he played great," Pieters said. "It wasn't comfortable watching him play the last couple of holes. I was wishing I'd made one more birdie. It's special winning here, just down the road from home. It was great hearing all the Dutch fans cheering my name. Our two countries kind of stick together."

Scoring was spectacular all week, not least from the 66-year-old Tom Watson. On his first visit to a Dutch tournament and attracted by the quality of the Kennemer links, Watson was under the par of 70 each day with rounds of 69, 68, 68 and 68. Meanwhile Paul Lawrie, in his 1,917th round on the European Tour, posted his lowest ever round of 61 on Thursday, matched later in the day by Wade Ormsby.

Then on Friday Matthew Fitzpatrick went one better, just missing out on the first 59 on the European Tour (although preferred lies were in operation) when a 20-footer at his last hole came up short. And on Saturday Magnus A. Carlsson, with a three iron at the 227-yard eighth hole, and Ormsby, with a seven iron at the 169-yard 11th, recorded the 40th and 41st aces of the European Tour season, beating the previous record of 39 set in 2006.

Open D'Italia
Parco Reale di Monza, Italy
Winner: Rikard Karlberg

Having failed to qualify for the FedExCup Playoffs on the PGA Tour, Martin Kaymer had returned to the European Tour and appeared to be heading for his first victory since the 2014 U.S. Open when he led by three strokes at the turn of the final round of the 72nd Open D'Italiai. A 65 in the third round put the German into a share of the lead after 54 holes, and then an outward 32 at Golf Club Milano, with birdies on the first, second, eighth and ninth holes, put him at 21 under par.

But three bogeys in the next five holes changed the tournament completely. Kaymer fell back to 18 under par, joining a host of players who sat in the clubhouse on that mark, including Joakim Lagergren after a 63, Matthew Fitzpatrick after a 65 and Danny Willett after a 66. At one point nine players shared the lead, but Rikard Karlberg got to 19 under after a bogey-free round which saw him make five birdies, including at the 14th, 16th and 17th. His total of 269 came from scores of 67, 67, 68 and 67.

Kaymer almost chipped in for an eagle at the 16th and missed chances for birdies at the last two but joined Karlberg on 19 under with a 70. Jens Fahrbring, completing a 72-hole event on the European Tour for the first time, also got to 19 under with a birdie at the 17th but then bogeyed the last to share third place with Lucas Bjerregaard, Fabrizio Zanotti, David Lipsky and the earlier finishers on 18 under.

Kaymer missed a chance to win on the first extra hole at the 18th, but the second time around, again at the 18th, Karlberg hit his approach to 15 feet and holed the putt for a winning birdie. The 28-year-old Swede from Gothenburg had won twice on the Asian Tour but only earned exempt status on the European Tour from the 2014 qualifying school.

"To win against a player as good as Martin Kaymer in sudden-death makes it very special," Karlberg said. "It feels amazing to get my first win and it has been a pretty crazy year for me. I got married and now my wife is expecting twins in December."

Kaymer said: "It was a disappointing finish to be honest. There were two or three tactical and clubbing mistakes. That happens sometimes, but it shouldn't have happened in that situation today."

Porsche European Open
Bad Griesbach, Germany
Winner: Thongchai Jaidee

Bernhard Langer co-designed the Beckenbauer course at Golf Resort Bad Griesbach in Bavaria and at the age of 58 finished as the leading home player at the Porsche European Open. Langer finished in a tie for 24th place at a tournament that he won in both 1985 and 1995 and which returned to the schedule for the first time since 2009 under a new sponsor. The German star had played in the first ever European Open in 1978, while in that time there had only been one Asian winner, Isao Aoki in 1983 at Sunningdale.

Thongchai Jaidee joined his name to that of the famous Japanese player with a one-stroke victory here over Graeme Storm. It was a seventh European Tour victory for the former paratrooper who only turned professional aged 30 and a third on European soil since 2012.

After opening with two rounds of 68, the Thai powered to the top of the leaderboard with an eight-birdie 64 on Saturday and then closed with a bogey-free 67 for a 17-under-par total of 267. Storm was the only rival to stay with Jaidee. Both went out in two under, and then the Englishman birdied the 10th to share the lead.

Playing in successive groups, both birdied the 12th and then the 15th, but Storm found water at the 17th to drop one behind. He holed a brave 12-footer for a par at the last and his own 67, but Jaidee, despite clattering into a hospitality unit beside the final green with his approach, also got up and down, holing from eight feet for the victory.

"It is the third time I have won outside of Asia, so I'm very excited about that and I'm happy to win this tournament," Jaidee said. "I didn't make many mistakes this week — only one bogey all week. I liked the golf course. It's not very long and you have to keep it in play. Graeme Storm played very well too. It was very exciting on the last three holes. The 18th is tough and you can't miss the fairway. I had to go left and then it was a good chip and a good putt at the last to win."

Storm, having started the week in 127th place on the Race to Dubai, secured his card for 2016 by finishing two ahead of Pelle Edberg, whose monster putt at the 17th gave him third place over Scott Hend.

Alfred Dunhill Links Championship
St. Andrews & Fife, Scotland
Winner: Thorbjorn Olesen

A frustrating season in 2015 for Thorbjorn Olesen included three months on the sidelines after hand surgery and a string of missed cuts. But some things do not change for the 25-year-old Dane. Put him three shots clear with a round to play and he wins on the European Tour. It was the case at the Sicilian Open in 2012 and again at the 2014 Perth International. Olesen put himself in the same position with rounds of 68, 66 and 65 around the links of St. Andrews, Kingsbarns and Carnoustie, before closing with a 71 on the Old Course for a two-stroke victory in the Alfred Dunhill Links Championship over Americans Brooks Koepka and Chris Stroud.

It was far from plain sailing for Olesen after he birdied the first hole on the final day. He had a double-bogey-six at the second and bogeyed the third before birdieing the next two. Then a string of pars followed, only broken by a stunning putt for birdie from 50 feet at the 15th hole which extended his lead to two strokes. With his nearest challengers falling back, it was the American Koepka with a 67 and Stroud with a 68 who set the clubhouse target on 16 under. Olesen closed with a 71 for an 18-under total of 270.

"On these three golf courses and finishing off especially on St. Andrews is a great feeling," he said. "It's been a very tough season for me, so standing here with the trophy is unbelievable. I got too aggressive on the second hole and got punished, but I just kept myself together and stayed very patient."

There were memorable debuts in the professional game for Jimmy Mullen and Paul Dunne, members of the victorious Great Britain & Ireland Walker Cup team. They shared the first-round lead, along with Kristoffer Broberg, after eight-under-par 64s at Kingsbarns, with Dunne making a hole-in-one on the 15th hole with a five iron. Mullen still shared the lead after day two, with Dunne, returning to St. Andrews where he was a joint third-round leader at the Open Championship, one behind. The pair fell away over the weekend with Dunne finishing 19th and Mullen 30th.

Florian Fritsch, a rookie who does not fly and only plays events he can get to by car and ferry, fell back after lying second individually after 54 holes but claimed victory in the pro-am event with former German international footballer Michael Ballack.

British Masters
Woburn, England
Winner: Matthew Fitzpatrick

In 2002 at Woburn's Ian Poulter just lost the British Masters on his home course to 21-year-old Justin Rose. In 2015 Poulter returned as the "host" of the prestigious event, now supported by Sky Sports and being resurrected for the first time since 2008. Part of Poulter's role was to help hand over the trophy to the new champion, Matthew Fitzpatrick, who having only just turned 21 beat Rose's record in a tournament that has also been won by the likes of Tony Jacklin, Lee Trevino, Nick Faldo, Greg Norman, Seve Ballesteros, Bernhard Langer and Colin Montgomerie.

Fitzpatrick, the 2013 U.S. Amateur champion, turned professional in 2014 and earned his card for 2015 at the qualifying school. His goal of retaining his card was easily met with the victory, but with a season's best five top-three finishes, it was already a successful campaign. This was just his 34th appearance on the European Tour.

His slight frame belies a good distance off the tee, but his relentless finding of the tree-lined Marquess fairways proved invaluable during a wire-to-wire two-stroke victory. He led with an opening 64, seven under par, and then shared the lead with Soren Kjeldsen after a second round of 69, and with Kiradech Aphibarnrat after a 68 in the third round. The Thai faltered early in the final round, but Fitzpatrick recovered his dropped shot at the third with a birdie at the next. With Shane Lowry, with 67, Kjeldsen and Fabrizio Zanotti all in contention and ending up sharing second place, Fitzpatrick made a stunning charge on the back nine. He birdied the 11th and 12th holes, then the 15th to go ahead by one. Zanotti birdied the 16th and hit close at the short 17th before Fitzpatrick replied with his own two at the 17th. Both bogeyed the 18th from a bunker behind the green to give Fitzpatrick a winning score of 269, 15 under par, after a closing 68.

"It's not going to sink in for a long time, I know that," said the young man from Sheffield. "It was a long day and I didn't really know what I had to do to win, but I just sort of ground it out."

Poulter said: "Being able to bring this tournament back the way we have, has been a huge honor. To have the fans come out like they have come out the last four days has been incredible. We had 15,000 fans on Thursday and we have had similar from every day on in."

Portugal Masters
Vilamoura, Portugal
Winner: Andy Sullivan

Arriving at the Portugal Masters, England's Andy Sullivan was one of nine players to have won twice during the 2014-15 season on the European Tour. The 28-year-old departed the Oceanic Victoria Golf Club as the first to claim three victories as he coasted to a tournament-record nine-stroke victory.

The wire-to-wire success was Sullivan's third in 23 events dating back to his wins at the South African and Joburg Opens earlier in the year. The difference this time, in addition to his commanding performance in which he made only three bogeys and none during a closing 66, was that family and friends from Nuneaton were able to witness the victory, spraying him in champagne after his birdie at the 18th hole.

"Those two wins in South Africa were unbelievable, but to show your peers that you can do it in Europe as well is unbelievable, and to do it in front of so many people from my home golf club. My mum and dad are here and it's been incredible," Sullivan said.

Sullivan shared the lead in the first round by matching Nicolas Colsaerts' seven-under 64. He repeated the score the next day to go ahead by three and then extended his lead to five with a 67 on the third day. It was a round in which Sullivan coped better than most with the strong winds after play got underway early with a shotgun start to avoid a storm later in the day.

Unusual but far from unique at tour level, a shotgun start was again employed for the final round and, although there was a two-hour delay due to areas of the course being waterlogged overnight, it allowed the tournament to be completed on time. Sullivan hardly put a foot wrong, extending his lead with birdies at the fourth and fifth before adding three more in the last five holes.

Chris Wood overcame an early bogey to take second place with a 68, finishing one ahead of Anthony Wall, who closed with a 66, Trevor Fisher and Eduardo de la Riva, who dropped out of a tie with Wood after a bogey at the last. Sullivan finished on a 23-under-par total of 261.

"To lead from day one right through the final day, it's nothing I've ever experienced before, so I wasn't sure how I'd cope, but I think I did alright," Sullivan said. "It was a lot harder than I made it look."

UBS Hong Kong Open
Winner: Justin Rose

See Asia/Japan Tours chapter.

The Final Series

Turkish Airlines Open
Antalya, Turkey
Winner: Victor Dubuisson

Two years after his maiden victory at the Turkish Airlines Open, Victor Dubuisson claimed the title for a second time in an emotional finale at Montgomerie Maxx Royal. His first victory in 2013 propelled the 25-year-old Frenchman to a Ryder Cup debut in 2014. But after a starring role at Gleneagles, Dubuisson endured an unsuccessful, and lonely, spell on the PGA Tour early in 2015 which prompted a crisis of confidence.

All that disappeared as he claimed the opening event of the Final Series by birdieing three of the last four holes to beat longtime leader Jaco Van Zyl by one stroke. Having tied for the lead at the 17th, Dubuisson hit an eight iron to 10 feet at the last and two-putted for the winning birdie before dissolving into tears on his caddie's shoulder.

"It's so hard because there were so many personal reasons why I didn't play that much this year," Dubuisson said. "It's not because I didn't want to play. I was really counting on this Final Series to give me some confidence back, because I completely lost it a few months ago. Sometimes you feel like your game is never going to come back, and this week I realized that my whole game was here."

A lack of practice led to a dip in his putting during the season, but it was back to its best as he posted rounds of 69, 64, 67 and 66 for a 22-under-par total of 266. Van Zyl had led from an opening 61, 11 under par, which was not a new course record as preferred lies were in operation after heavy rain the previous week. He followed up with scores of 69 and 70 to be caught by Dubuisson after 54 holes with Rory McIlroy and Kiradech Aphibarnrat a shot back.

McIlroy had returned three successive 67s to that point but slipped back to tie for sixth with an untidy 71. Aphibarnrat opened with four successive birdies and got to 20 under at the 10th before parring the last eight holes. He finished with a 67, matching Van Zyl, to hold off Byeong-Hun An for third place, while Chris Wood was fifth.

Dubuisson birdied three of the first four holes, then had a double bogey at the fifth and dropped another shot at the seventh. But he went six under for the last 10 holes, saving par at the 10th thanks to a brilliant chip out of the trees and eagling the 11th by chipping in from just off the green.

WGC - HSBC Champions
Winner: Russell Knox

See Asia/Japan Tours chapter.

BMW Masters
Shanghai, China
Winner: Kristoffer Broberg

Having won four times on the Challenge Tour in 2012, it was seemingly only a matter of time before Kristoffer Broberg won on the main European Tour. The wait ended for the 29-year-old Swede when he claimed not just his maiden title but one of the Final Series events in the BMW Masters at Lake Malaren. Broberg defeated American Patrick Reed at the first playoff hole after hitting a nine iron to 15 feet and holing the putt for a winning birdie.

The pair tied at 17 under par on a total of 271 after a 68 from the Swede and a 67 from the American. Starting the final round two and three strokes respectively behind leader Thongchai Jaidee, Broberg made four birdies in the first eight holes while Reed left his challenge late. After a birdie at 13, Reed holed out from 97 yards from a bunker for an eagle at the 15th and birdied the 16th to take the lead on his own. But he missed a four-foot par putt at the 17th and had little chance of a birdie at the 18th in extra time after finding a greenside bunker.

Jaidee, after a 71, finished in a tie for third place one stroke behind with Lucas Bjerregaard, who had led at halfway following twin 66s, Byeong-Hun An and Henrik Stenson, who made five birdies in six holes from the 11th but fell one short. Justin Rose tied for seventh place, and Sergio Garcia, the first-round leader, for 11th.

This was the 100th win by the 30th different Swedish player on the European Tour dating back to Ove Sellberg at the 1986 Epson Grand Prix. "I worked so hard all my life for this," Broberg said. "I'm just so happy to win on the main tour, because I won four times on the Challenge Tour. The players out there are really, really good and this is just a really good field. So I'm just happy to beat all of them. This means a lot to me. A few weeks ago, I could never win here. I was just so down, and I'm so happy right now. I have no words."

DP World Tour Championship
Dubai, United Arab Emirates
Winner: Rory McIlroy

A mark of how well Andy Sullivan played at the DP World Tour Championship, the season-ending tournament, was that he pushed Rory McIlroy to play some of his best golf of the year. Sullivan, with two rounds of 66 followed by a pair of 68s, led for virtually the whole tournament until McIlroy made four birdies in five holes from the 11th on the final day.

McIlroy had scores of 68, 68, 65 and 66 on the Earth course at Jumeirah Estates for a 21-under-par total of 267 to win by one stroke. Branden Grace took third place, five adrift of the runner-up after the final day came down to a duel between the top two. Sullivan, leading by one after 54 holes, did not appear to be concerned with playing alongside the former world No. 1 as he birdied four of the first six holes. He dropped a shot at the eighth but remained one ahead with a birdie at the 11th.

Then McIlroy took over. He was two ahead with two to play before a wild tee shot at the short 17th found the water. However, McIlroy mitigated the error by holing a putt from 30 for a bogey to stay one ahead going to the last.

It was McIlroy's second victory in the tournament, and it brought him a third Race to Dubai title in four years. His nearest challenger, Danny Willett, kept up the pressure by finishing in a tie for fourth place alongside Francesco Molinari, Charl Schwartzel, Matthew Fitzpatrick, Emiliano Grillo and Byeong-Hun An.

McIlroy, whose season was interrupted by an ankle injury which meant he missed the Open Championship, started the year with a victory at the Dubai Desert Classic and also won the WGC-Cadillac Match Play, as well as the Wells Fargo Championship on the PGA Tour.

"I'm happy that this was my last event of the year," he said. "I'm happy to put the clubs away for a while. I've played really good golf this week, 13-under-par weekend, I couldn't think of a better way to finish the season.

"I knew today wasn't going to be easy. Andy was playing phenomenal golf over the first three days. The birdie on 12 was huge to tie the lead, and then the two birdies on 14 and 15, when he didn't make them, that gave me a nice little cushion going into the last three holes. Thankfully I rolled that putt in on 17, as giving myself that one-shot cushion made a huge difference."

Alfred Dunhill Championship
Winner: Charl Schwartzel

See African Sunshine Tour chapter.

Australian PGA Championship
Winner: Nathan Holman

See Australasian Tour chapter.

Nedbank Golf Challenge
Winner: Marc Leishman

See African Sunshine Tour chapter.

Challenge Tour

Ricardo Gouveia finished in style as the 24-year-old Portuguese player set a new record for earnings on the Challenge Tour with €251,592. Gouveia beat Edoardo Molinari's record from 2009 by claiming his second win of the season at the NBO Golf Classic Grand Final to seal his place at the top of the Race to Oman standings.

Gouveia made five birdies in a row from the 12th hole at Almouj Golf, The Wave in Muscat, to post the low round of the week with a 65. He had earlier won the Aegean Airlines Challenge in Germany, but it was his consistency that was the key to his fine season as he recorded 11 top-10 finishes in 17 appearances.

While his European Tour card for 2016 was already secured going into the final event, Gouveia said: "I just wanted to get that number one spot. I knew most of the players were coming out this week, so I didn't want to just take the week off and leave ranking points out there for the other guys."

With a fine college career in America behind him and now a record-breaking season on the Challenge Tour, Gouveia was not short of confidence. "My goal is to be one of the top players in the world," he said. "My goals are global and if I keep playing like this I will reach my long-term goals."

Sebastien Gros and Borja Virto Astudillo also won twice to finish second and third respectively on the ranking, while Nacho Elvira finished fourth but had an early promotion to the European Tour after winning three times. Elvira regained the card he had lost in 2014 with victories at the Challenge de Madrid, the Karnten Golf Open and the Rolex Trophy. Curiously, he was the third player in recent years to gain his third win of the season at that event following Benjamin Hebert and Kristopher Broberg.

"It is a dream to be back on the European Tour so soon," said the 28-year-old Spaniard. "After I got my second win, I got a bit too worked up trying to get the third win, but I then started to relax and it went better. My aim for the season had been to get in the top 15 in the Rankings, so this is beyond my expectations but so much better."

Elvira returned to the circuit for the Grand Final and finished tied for third place, but all around him were players who did not know their fate until the last putt dropped. Joachim B. Hansen birdied the last three holes to finish second and jump from 17th to fifth on the final ranking. Sharing third place with Elvira were Jeff Winther, who moved from 18th to 11th to get his card, and Callum Shinkwin, who leapt from 23rd to 13th. South African Brandon Stone finished sixth at the Grand Final to move from 19th to 14th on the ranking.

The others to finish in the top 15 and gain their cards were: Bjorn Akesson, Gary Boyd, Rhys Davies, Thomas Linard, Jens Fahbring, Andrew McArthur and Jamie McLeary. New Zealander Ryan Fox got bumped to 16th place in the last week, so went to the qualifying school at PGA Catalunya but missed out there by two strokes.

The six-round qualifying school was won by Ulrich van den Berg, Daniel

Im and Adrian Otaegui, with cards earned by amateur sensations Marcus Kinhult and Paul Dunne, while Edoardo Molinari, after a long series of injuries, regained his card on the cut-off by coming home in four under par on the last day. Matthew Southgate also claimed a card by going through all three stages after missing two months in the summer undergoing treatment for testicular cancer.

9. Asia/Japan Tours

As 2015 was coming down the back nine, the Asian Tour was about a lot more than just birdies and bogeys. The geopolitics of golf had worked their spell once again, this time to everyone's surprise.

The European Tour and the Asian Tour had begun talking about a merger. Or, as some said, a European takeover. The situation reached a crisis of sorts when the Asian Tour announced early in December that CEO Mike Kerr, after three and a half years in the post, abruptly resigned. This after Kerr had earlier said the merger would mean one tour with a single membership coming from both tours. Speculation was that Kerr had lost the confidence of the members.

"What I can say very confidently is that no Asian professional is going to lose any opportunity," Kerr had said, seeking to calm the tour players' fears that they would become secondary figures in the proposed organization.

As Thai star Thongchai Jaidee put it: "The main thing for me is that Asian players have a chance to improve in the future. We are waiting still for our concerns to be addressed."

A merger would be the biggest development in Asian golf since the tour began play in 1994. Details of the proposed arrangement were not announced as the end of the year approached.

Meantime, shrinkage hit the other Asian body, the OneAsia Tour, which formed in 2009 as a challenge to the Asian Tour. The OneAsia had announced a 2015 schedule of 11 tournaments but played seven.

"We've struggled — it's been a difficult year," said David Parkin, OneAsia's director of tour operations. "But we're still offering our members the chance to earn good money and play in big tournaments and that's what it's about at the end of the day."

That's where things stood as 2015 signed off. Meanwhile, back at the golf course...

India's Anirban Lahiri, 28, had a smashing year. He was the only multiple winner on the Asian Tour, winning twice in nine starts, the Maybank Malaysian Open and the Hero Indian Open, and topped the money list with $1,139,084, more than double second-place Scott Hend's $491,631.

Lahiri, who joined the Asian Tour in 2008, quickly gained international stature. Overall, he has 18 victories, seven of them on the Asian Tour and two on the European. In 2015, he played in all four majors. He tied for 49th in his first Masters, missed the cut in the U.S. Open, tied for 30th in the British Open, tied for fifth in the PGA Championship. He joined a number of tour golfers on the Official World Golf Rankings: Thongchai Jaidee 29th, Kiradech Aphibarnrat 37th and Lahiri 41st.

"Now when I go and play with the best in the field, I am not intimidated, I am not overwhelmed, I am not scared," Lahiri said.

On the OneAsia Tour, Korea's Kyong-Jun Moon took the money title with $224,953, just $7,506 over Jinho Choi. And Moon also topped the tour in wild finishes.

Moon scored his career-first victory in a trainwreck finish at the GS Caltex

Maekyung Open. The top of the leaderboard — Moon and four others — all collapsed. Moon led by four coming to the last hole, made a triple bogey, and still won by two.

Choi, recently returned from his mandatory 20 months of military service, made the SK Telecom Open his first victory by holing an 18-foot birdie putt at the final hole. "I'm so relieved," he said.

Kyung-Tae Kim took the Singha Corporation Thailand Open by a very tight three shots. He came to the last hole leading by one, holed a 12-footer for birdie, and Jeung-Hun Wang, a mere 19, three-putted from seven feet for a bogey.

On the Japan Tour, South Korea's Kyung-Tae Kim emerged from a dry spell with a spurt of five victories that made a runaway of the money race. Kim, who had done little after winning the No. 1 spot in 2010 and playing well in 2011 in the Presidents Cup, finished more than ¥60 million ahead of runner-up Yusaku Miyazato and his ¥165,981,625.

In a strange development in the 25-tournament season, the only other player to win more than once was the highly popular Ryo Ishikawa, who played primarily in America, yet in his seven starts won the ANA tournament and the season-ending Nippon Series, and finished sixth on the money list.

Another oddity was the absence of new winners after an early splurge. Four of the first five tournaments went to players without previous victories in Japan and that was it for the season. And, until Ishikawa landed the Nippon Series, the year's major titles were taken by lesser-lights — Australian Adam Bland (PGA), China's Wen-Chong Liang (Tour) and Satoshi Kodaira (Open).

Koumei Oda, the leading money winner in 2014, went winless in 2015, finishing 10th.

When the year was said and done, Asian golf had its share of pithy observations. Among them:

Anirban Lahiri, on staggering home to win the Malaysian Open: "I've got a bad habit of making it hard for myself. But I'm happy I got over the line, as ugly as it was towards the end."

Korea's Kyong-Jun Moon, on scoring his first win after four others folded and he himself triple-bogeyed the final hole at the Maekyung Open: "I really don't know what happened, but thankfully I had a good lead."

England's David Howell, on missing a short putt at the final hole that left native son Ashun Wu the winner in the Volvo China Open in Shanghai: "There's I don't know how many billion people who are rather pleased I made six on the last."

Taiwan's Chien-Yao Hung, on a costly closing 73 in the Resorts World Manila Masters that included four early bogeys, a hole-in-one and a closing double bogey: "I wasn't stressed but I thought I was too uptight."

Asian Tour

Maybank Malaysian Open
Kuala Lumpur, Malaysia
Winner: Anirban Lahiri

Golf is a hard enough game, but India's Anirban Lahiri was wondering why he makes it even tougher.

"I've got a bad habit of making it hard for myself," said Lahiri, 27, at the Maybank Malaysian Open, the Asian Tour's season-opener, co-sanctioned by the European Tour. That being said, he was pleased to add, "But I'm happy I got over the line, as ugly as it was towards the end."

Lahiri trailed by nine at the halfway point, and a scorching 10-under-par 62 in the third still left him five behind going into the fourth. But a quick burst of birdies and some errors from Austria's Bernd Wiesberger carried Lahiri over the line to his sixth Asian title and his first on the European Tour. He shot Kuala Lumpur Golf Club in 70-72-62-68–272.

"I don't think it's sunk in just yet," said Lahiri. "But I'm pretty sure when it hits home it's going to be a really happy moment for me."

Wiesberger took a two-stroke lead with his third-round 63 and was comfortably five ahead of Lahiri, who tied the course record with a flawless 62 built on six birdies on the front nine, four coming in.

In the final round, Lahiri made up ground in a hurry, with Wiesberger stumbling. Lahiri birdied four of the first five holes, bogeyed No. 9, and came home with a bogey and two birdies, the second on a 50-foot putt at the 17th — which proved the winner — for a 68. Wiesberger opened with two birdies, then slid to a 74, and Lahiri came along behind to win by one.

"I finally won a big event … not just in prize money, but in terms of the field," Lahiri said. "That's something I've been wanting to do for a long time."

True Thailand Classic
Hua Hin, Thailand
Winner: Andrew Dodt

Allowing for a little hedging, it was something of a case of back-to-back victories for Australia's Andrew Dodt — first regaining his European Tour card late in 2014, then winning the inaugural True Thailand Classic in mid-February (the second event on the 2015 Asian Tour schedule, after he warmed up with a tie for 36th in the season-opening Maybank Malaysian Open). The co-sanctioned event also marked his first European Tour win in five years, since the 2010 Avantha Masters, and Dodt was dumbstruck.

"There are no thoughts at the moment — I'm speechless," said the 29-year-old Australian, who trailed through the tournament and was still four behind at the start of the final round.

He shot 71-67-67-67–272, 16 under on Black Mountain for a one-shot win over two veterans, fellow Aussie Scott Hend, the third-round leader, and Thai legend Thongchai Jaidee. Jaidee's bid effectively ended with a double bogey at the par-five 13th. He still could have won, but he missed an eagle for the win at the 18th, then missed the 10-foot birdie for a tie and shot 71. Hend's chances sputtered out with bogeys at Nos. 7, 14 and 17. "I pressed for the win on 17 and got a bit aggressive with my bunker shot," said Hend (72).

Dodt trailed Michael Hoey by seven in the first round and Miguel Angel Jimenez by five in the second. In the third round, another 67 got him to within four of Hend. He made his move in the fourth, birdieing the first three holes, and after eight steady pars, he birdied the 12th and 15th, then cautiously parred in as the wind picked up.

"I tried to play as sensibly as I could," said Dodt, who made only three bogeys in the tournament. "I'm glad I did it."

Hero Indian Open
New Delhi, India
Winner: Anirban Lahiri

For a golfer making up a seven-shot deficit in the final round, one wonders why a chip-in for par would be his shot of the day.

Simple, said native son Anirban Lahiri, who at the time was deep in the process of trying to make the Hero Indian Open his second victory in three weeks, after the season-opening Maybank Malaysian Open. He'd started the final round a near-hopeless seven behind, so it was only when his game clicked and leader S.S.P. Chawrasia's crumbled in blustery winds that the chip shot became so vital.

Playing just in front of Chawrasia, Lahiri had got to seven under par and faced a 25-foot chip shot for par at Delhi Golf Club's par-three 17th.

"That chip was crucial," Lahiri said. "I didn't want to come down 18 needing to eagle it. Even in regulation, I thought I needed to birdie it. That chip-in was easily the shot of the day. It was magical when it went in."

Lahiri played the front nine in four under with five birdies and a bogey and came home with a bogey and birdie. Behind him, Chawrasia squandered his lead early — a bogey at the third, a double bogey at the fourth, a bogey at the seventh. Then three bogeys and a birdie over five holes from the 12th, and he was tied with Lahiri, who shot 73-65-70-69–277, matching Chowrasia's 65-67-69-76.

"I had some bad shots in the final round," Chowrasia said. "The problem today was the wind — very difficult."

In the playoff, at the par-five 18th, Chowrasia was done when his tee shot ended up under some branches, and Lahiri, taking no chances, birdied for his seventh Asian Tour and second European Tour title.

"The new Hero Indian Open winner?" Lahiri said. "That has a nice ring to it."

CIMB Niaga Indonesian Masters
Jakarta, Indonesia
Winner: Lee Westwood

It's probably impossible to quantify, but that was an interesting thesis advanced by England's Lee Westwood on winning the CIMB Niaga Indonesian Masters for the third time: "There are a lot of good players on the Asian Tour now, and the standard is getting higher," Westwood said, "and it's getting harder to come over here and win."

His own record suggested as much. He won the inaugural event in 2011, beating Thailand's Thongchai Jaidee by three strokes. He won again in 2012, by two over another Thai, Thaworn Wiratchant. And this time it was over yet another Thai, Chapchai Nirat, with a birdie on the first hole of a playoff. And this after Westwood seemed on his way to a runaway win.

Westwood stayed close with rounds of 69-74, one-under-par 143 on wind-swept Royale Jakarta, then raced ahead with a seven-under 65 in the third round. Westwood shot a quiet 36 going out but exploded coming home — an eagle at the par-five 12th on a 25-foot putt, then five straight birdies for a 29 and a 65. The parallel to 2012 was almost spooky. Back then, he led by eight going into the final round. This time, he led by five and, more to the point, by seven over Nirat.

But the touch deserted Westwood in the final round — two early bogeys, three birdies out of the turn, then bogeys at the 16th and 17th for a 73. Nirat, 31, a four-time Asian Tour winner, made five birdies over his last 11 holes for a 66, tying Westwood at seven-under 281. Nirat bunkered his approach at the playoff hole, the 18th, while Westwood birdied with a five-foot putt for the win.

"I've never been beaten around this golf course," Westwood said. But in his own words, the Asian golfers are getting closer.

AfrAsia Bank Mauritius Open
Winner: George Coetzee

See African Sunshine Tour chapter.

Bashundhara Bangladesh Open
Dhaka, Bangladesh
Winner: Mardan Mamat

They were coming at him from all directions, all of them kids by his standards. There was American Casey O'Toole, 24, a regular on the Asian Development Tour, birdieing all the par-fives in a bogey-free 66 to tie him for the lead in the first round. Spain's Carlos Pigem, 24, got within one with a 67 in the second round, posting six birdies over the last 12 holes. "I look forward to challenging for the title," he said. Two shot 65s in the third round — South Korea's Soomin Lee, 21, who had six birdies and an eagle, and India's Khalim Joshi, 22, with seven birdies and an eagle.

But Singapore's Mardan Mamat, 47, made his way serenely from wire to wire to make the inaugural Bashundhara Bangladesh Open his fifth Asian Tour victory.

O'Toole's tie in the first round was the closest anyone got. Mamat shot the par-71 Kurmitola Golf Club in 66-67-68-69, and led by one through the second round and three through the third, and he won by two over Lee and Joshi with a 14-under-par 270.

Mamat had caught a spark since missing the cut in the Indonesian Masters in April. Since then he had a run of 26 under par in his last two tournaments. In Bangladesh, he had six birdies in 11 holes from No. 6 in the first round and five birdies in 14 holes from No. 1 in the second. And there was this remarkable performance: He played Nos. 5, 6 and 7 in eight under — eight birdies and four pars.

The secret to his surge: Domestic intervention.

"My wife and I have been talking," Mardan said. "She sent me a message saying, 'You are the champion, you are the winner and you are the man.' That really inspired me."

Queen's Cup
Koh Samui, Thailand
Winner: Prayad Marksaeng

Prayad Marksaeng was in the role of selfless native son in the seventh playing of the Queen's Cup, the tournament honoring Queen Sirikit of Thailand. He didn't mind who was leading, he said, as long as it was a Thai. As poetic justice would have it, it was Marksaeng himself, the tough veteran, who assured the trophy remained in Thailand.

It was his ninth Asian Tour win, and he took it under the pressure of challengers about half his age. It was another Week of the Veteran. First Singapore's Mardan Mamat in the previous stop, winning the Bangladesh Open at 47, and now Marksaeng.

"To be able to win at 49 years old is just incredible for me," said Marksaeng. "I am very proud of myself." Marksaeng led the second round, then entered the final round trailing Japan's Akinori Tani by three strokes and had to hold off some restless young Asian Tour talent led by two fellow Thais. Thanyakon Khrongpha, 24, closed with a 65 that included five birdies and an eagle at the par-five No. 6 and finished second by two strokes. Jazz Janewattananond, 19, tied for third with two eagles coming home, the par-four 16th and the par-five 18th, for a 66.

Marksaeng, who won the tournament in 2013, took this one with a card of 69-65-71-65, a 14-under-par 270 total at Santiburi Samui. He did it in a set of sprints, getting five birdies in eight holes from the second, then four in the closing five holes.

"I started with a bogey, but I wasn't worried," Marksaeng said. "I knew Thanyakon was making a fast charge, but I didn't feel the pressure ... I thought it doesn't matter if I lose because I was already sure the trophy will remain in Thailand."

Omega European Masters
Winner: Danny Willett

See European Tours chapter.

Asia-Pacific Diamond Cup
Winner: Kyung-Tae Kim

See Japan PGA Tour section.

Mercuries Taiwan Masters
Chinese Taipei
Winner: Danny Chia

Danny Chia was 42 now and the top-ranked Malaysian but 342nd in the world, and his one victory came 13 years ago. Altogether, this didn't exactly spell victory at the Asian Tour's Mercuries Taiwan Masters.

But there were signs that his fortunes were brightening.

Such as eagles at Nos. 7 and 13, both par-fives, in the first round, booting him to a five-under-par 67 and a one-stroke lead.

Dimmer in the second round. He bogeyed three of the first five holes. A 72 left him a shot off the lead, behind India's Rashid Khan.

Then it seemed he was headed for more of the same-old, same-old when he bogeyed twice early in the third round, then bogeyed three straight from No. 9. "It was quite a struggle for me out there," Chia said. "I missed quite a few short putts, from four to five feet." But he did produce a big bright spot. He regained his footing and birdied the two remaining par-fives, the 13th on a chip to two feet and the 15th on a 10-foot putt. It was another 73. He was still a shot off the lead, this time behind China's Wen-Chong Liang, who came from five behind with four birdies for a 68–211.

Chia had a tough finish. "I couldn't sleep last night," he said. "I thought of my win 13 years ago."

Then things got worse in the final round. "I was really nervous heading into the last five holes," he said. "I thought my hands were shaking, but I am actually shaking inside my heart." He had three birdies on the front, then four bogeys coming in for a 73–285, three under, and won by two. He had help: Liang and Kahn each stumbled to 76s.

Said Chia: "It's been only 13 years."

Yeangder Tournament Players Championship
Chinese Taipei
Winner: Shaun Norris

There's nothing like a spot of nasty weather to warm a guy's heart, Sean Norris was saying. "I always joke that I play better in the worst conditions," said the 33-year-old South African, an Asian Tour rookie. "I think it makes me concentrate more. I probably focus more."

Well, that was some properly lousy October weather that hit the Yeangder Tournament Players Championship at Linkou International in Chinese Taipei. Lousy enough to force officials to reduce the tournament to 54 holes. Norris, posting three 68s, trailed through the first two rounds, but his 12-under-par 204 held up for a two-stroke win for his first tour victory as the Philippines' Miguel Tabuena stumbled into second place with a closing 73.

"The [Asian Tour] players are so good, for me to accomplish what I have just done is great," said Norris. "Words can't describe how I feel with this win."

The opposite, of course, was true of Tabuena. He had come to the Yeangder with a chip on his shoulder. "I want vengeance," he said. On the gods of golf, of course. He was 19 when the veteran Prom Meesawat beat him in a playoff in the 2014 Yeangder. A year older, now 20, and a year wiser. "If I stick to my game plan and focus on myself and the course, then I can get it done," he said.

But he didn't factor in the quirks of golf. Meaning, in this case, three bogeys and a birdie over the last seven holes for a 73. Norris made five birdies over the first seven holes and bogeyed the 18th for the two-stroke victory.

Said Tabuena: "How many times do I have to finish second?"

Venetian Macau Open
Macau
Winner: Scott Hend

Big-hitting Aussie Scott Hend had this fundamental hate-love relationship with Macau Golf and Country Club. "The first few times I came here, I just didn't want to come back as it killed me," Hend said. "But we've seem to found a way to play the course — where to hit it, what to do, and when to be aggressive."

This time, in the 2015 Venetian Macau Open, he went the first 27 holes and the last 29 without a bogey, and had just four in between in taking his second title in three years and his seventh on the Asian Tour. As for the course he loved to hate: He shot the par-71 venue in 66-68-64-66–264, 20 under, and won by three in this installment of the shootout with India's Anirban Lahiri. Hend beat Lahiri by one to win the 2013 Macau, and Lahiri beat Hend by one to take the 2014 Macau. Now it was Hend by three over Lahari, along with India's Chiragh Kumar.

Hend hung close through the first two rounds, and then, as the poet might say, he soared into the lead on the wings of eagles. In the third round, he eagled the par-five second, and after five birdies and two bogeys, he eagled the par-five 18th, holing a 30-foot putt from the edge for a 64 and a three-stroke lead.

Hend stayed three ahead in the final round with a bogey-free 66 that kept Lahiri at arm's-length.

"All credit to Hendy," said Lahiri, who closed with a 66 of his own. "He's earned this win."

"I just tried to make the right choices ... and not let Anirban have a sniff," Hend said. "Once he gets a sniff, it's pretty hard to get in front of him."

UBS Hong Kong Open
Hong Kong
Winner: Justin Rose

Every tournament has its sympathetic favorite, but the UBS Hong Kong Open, with the season running out, was brimming over with them.

The No. 1 Peoples' Choice in the Asian-European Tours co-sanctioned event had to be Taiwan's Wei-Chih Lu, 36, still struggling to come back from surgery for a non-malignant brain tumor three years earlier. He opened the Hong Kong with an inspiring six-under-par 64 to share the first-round lead with Italy's Andrea Pavan. (Lu would finish tied for 42nd.)

Next came India's Anirban Lahiri, hurting from some embarrassing failures in the recent Presidents Cup. He contended for three rounds, then tied for seventh. "I just felt like I ran out of gas," Lahiri said.

Then there was Ian Poulter, trying to play his mandated 13th event in order to keep his European Tour card for 2016. He only got into the Hong Kong Open when American Rich Beem gave him his spot. "I don't play to take part, I play to win," Poulter said. But a third-round 73 tripped him and he finished tied for 29th.

The tournament came down to a running battle between England's Justin Rose and Denmark's little known Lucas Bjerregaard, 24. They dueled from the second round on. Rose (65-66-64) and Bjerregaard (66-66-63) shared a four-shot lead going into the final round. Bjerregaard stumbled over a double bogey at the 14th. "But I'm happy," he offered, noting that the last time he was in the hunt at the end, he shot 89. "So I'm 20 shots better today," he said of his 69–264 finish, one behind Rose.

Said Rose: "I had a chance to win last week [at the PGA Tour's Frys.com Open], and let that one flitter away. So I wanted to hang on to this one." Which he did, with a 68–263.

CIMB Classic
Kuala Lumpur, Malaysia
Winner: Justin Thomas

Justin Thomas, yet another entry in the PGA Tour's youth parade, was only 22 but wise enough to understand a fundamental truth: "It's not how — it's how much."

Case in point: Thomas led from the second round, but staggered across the finish line for his first PGA Tour victory in the CIMB Classic (co-sanctioned with the Asian Tour). Said Thomas: "I don't care how I got it done. It just feels awesome."

In an odd finish, one wondered whether Thomas was inspired or cracking under the pressure. There was the double bogey at the 14th, then three straight birdies, then the chopped-up par at the 18th. Whichever, Thomas blossomed under the strain. He opened with a 68, in a crowd with Adam Scott and Padraig Harrington, six behind Scott Piercy's 10-under 62, then shot 61-67-66 for a tournament-record 26-under 262 at Kuala Lumpur Golf and Country Club and a one-stroke win over Adam Scott in the punishing heat.

The 61 in the second round was a dazzling, flawless piece of work — nine birdies and an eagle at the par-five No. 3. "Being five under through the first five holes ... got me in that attack frame of mind," Thomas said.

The attack frame of mind saved him in the final round. Adam Scott gave him something to shoot at. Playing two groups ahead, Scott posted an eagle and seven birdies for a 63. Thomas birdied the 13th, then double-bogeyed the 14th off a watered shot. He birdied the next three and lurched to a par at the 18th — missing the fairway, catching a greenside bunker, blasting out, running his 20-footer six feet past, then having to make that for the 66 and the one-stroke win.

"I still can't believe what happened," Thomas said.

WGC - HSBC Champions
Shanghai, China
Winner: Russell Knox

A search of the golf lexicon reveals no listing for "Cinderella," but if there were one, this Cinderella would be a 5-foot-10, 155-pound male, age 30, with a Scottish accent.

This would be Russell Knox, and much to his surprise, a late withdrawal got him into the exclusive field for the World Golf Championships - HSBC Champions. Much to everyone's surprise, he soon had his first PGA Tour victory — the first player to win a WGC in his debut and the first Scot to win one.

"I always thought I was going to win a big one for my first one," Knox said. "This is going to take a long time to sink in."

Knox, a veteran of the Hooters Tour and with a win on the Web.com Tour (then the Nationwide), opened the HSBC with a 67 and was one of 15 players within four shots of Branden Grace and his leading 63. Sore-backed Kevin Kisner, also in as an alternate, led the second round with 66–130 and had the solo clubhouse lead with 70–200 until Sunday morning, when Knox returned from a darkness suspension and birdied his last hole to tie him, with 67-65-68.

Kisner had a quiet two-under 70, with a bogey and three birdies in the final round. By comparison, Knox had a wild 68 — six birdies and two bogeys. He took the lead for good with a birdie at the 10th, and pretty well locked up his win with a fighting birdie at the reachable 16th. He opted for an iron off the tee to play it safe, then wedged to 12 feet behind the cup, then holed the birdie putt and was the picture of confidence heading for his first win.

"I was terrified," Knox said.

Major Champions

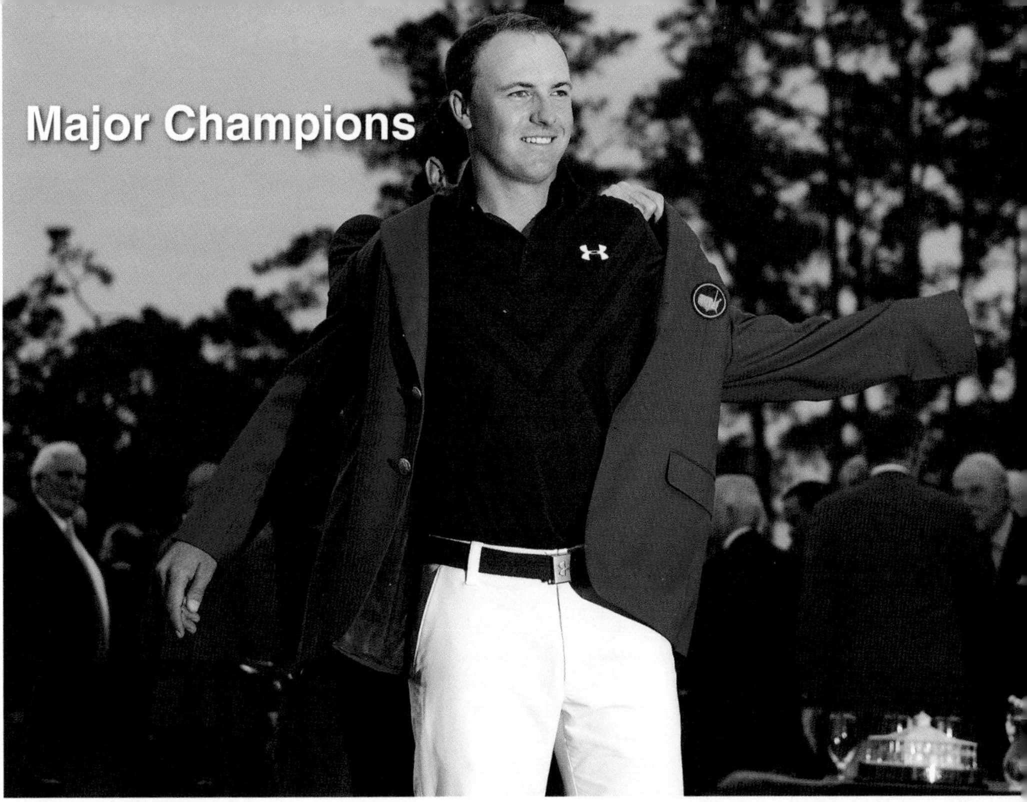

Ross Kinnaird/Getty Images

Masters and U.S. Open champion Jordan Spieth contended at all four majors.

Ross Kinnaird/R&A

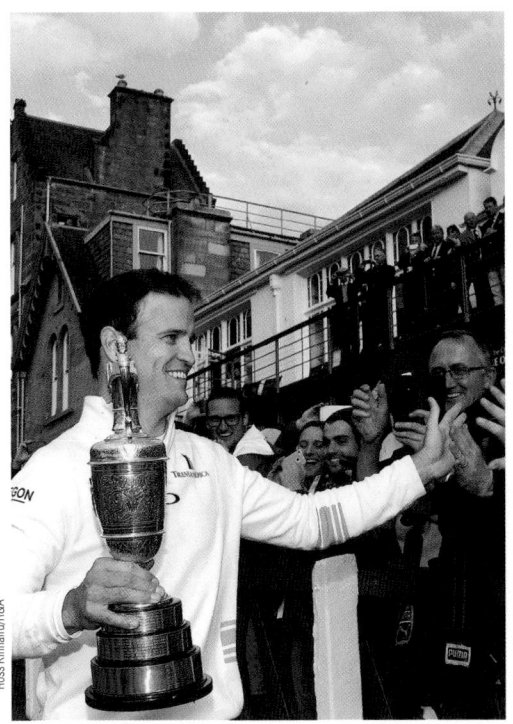

The Open champion Zach Johnson

Andrew Redington/Getty Images

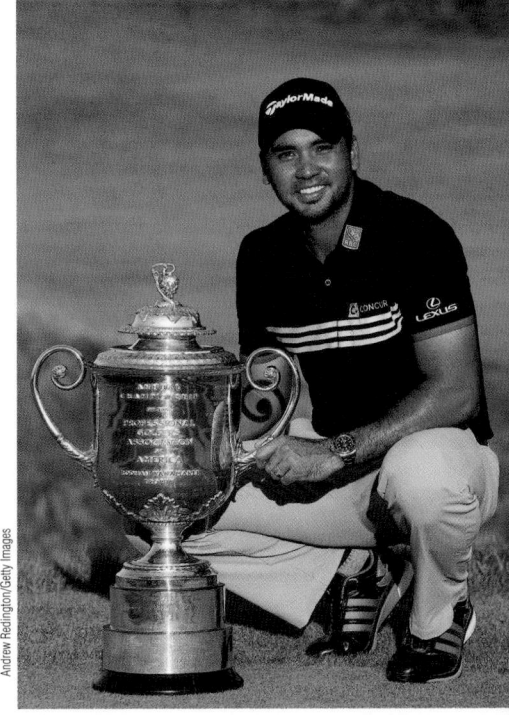

PGA champion Jason Day.

Masters Tournament

Jordan Spieth celebrates a four-stroke victory. Aged 21, he was the second youngest winner.

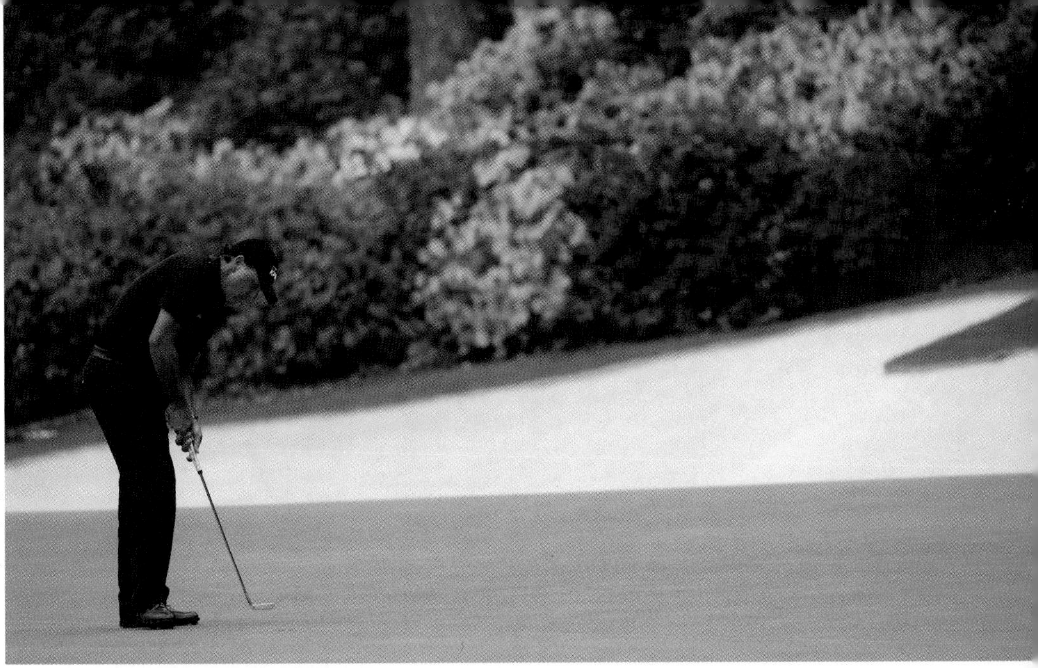

Andrew Redington/Getty Images

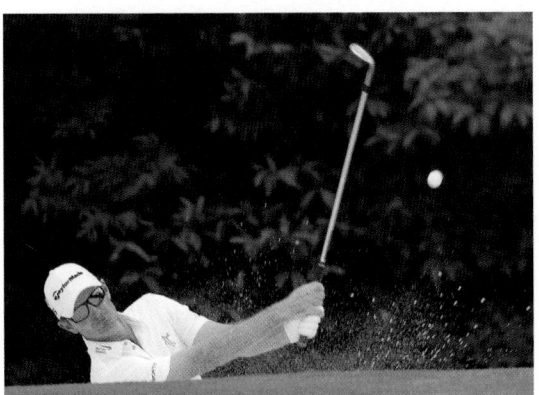

Three-time champion Phil Mickelson came home in 33 to share second place.

Ross Kinnaird/Getty Images

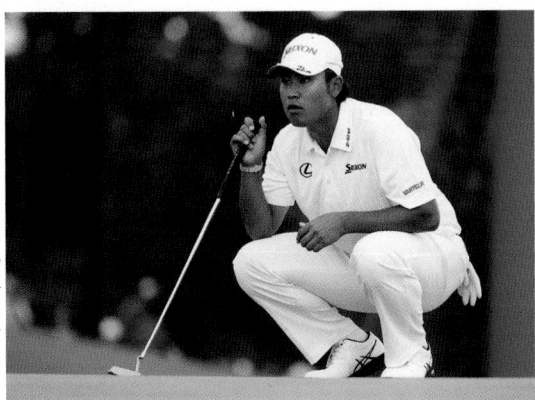

Justin Rose was the other runner-up.

Jamie Squire/Getty Images

David Cannon/Getty Images

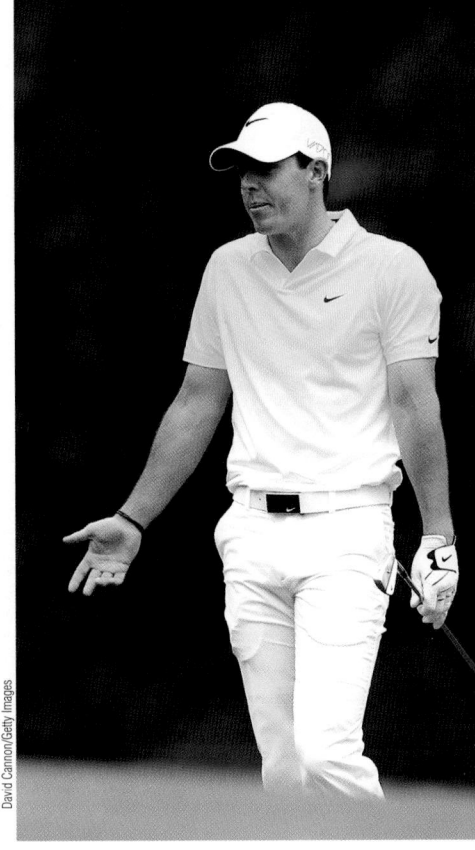

Hideki Matsuyama closed with a 66, as did Rory McIlroy, who was fourth after a slow start.

U.S. Open

Jordan Spieth won his second major in a row after a thrilling finale at Chambers Bay.

Louis Oosthuizen finished one back.

Adam Scott was two back after a closing 64.

Big-hitting Dustin Johnson came unstuck on the final green.

Vertigo-sufferer Jason Day still tied ninth.

The Open Championship

Zach Johnson lifted the Claret Jug after a three-way playoff at St. Andrews.

Marc Leishman was one of the runners-up.

Louis Oosthuizen finished second again.

Jason Day and Jordan Spieth both finished one stroke outside the playoff on a remarkable final day.

PGA Championship

Jason Day claimed his first major at Whistling Straits in record-setting fashion.

Richard Heathcote/Getty Images

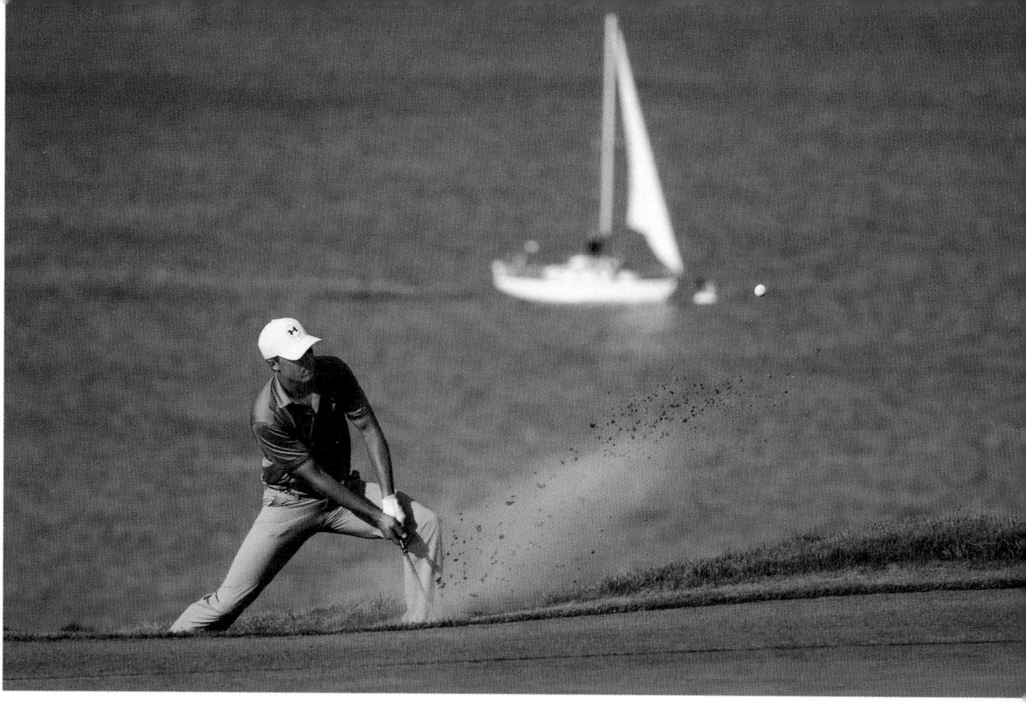

Jordan Spieth chased Day home but finished three adrift to end his amazing major season.

Andrew Redington/Getty Images

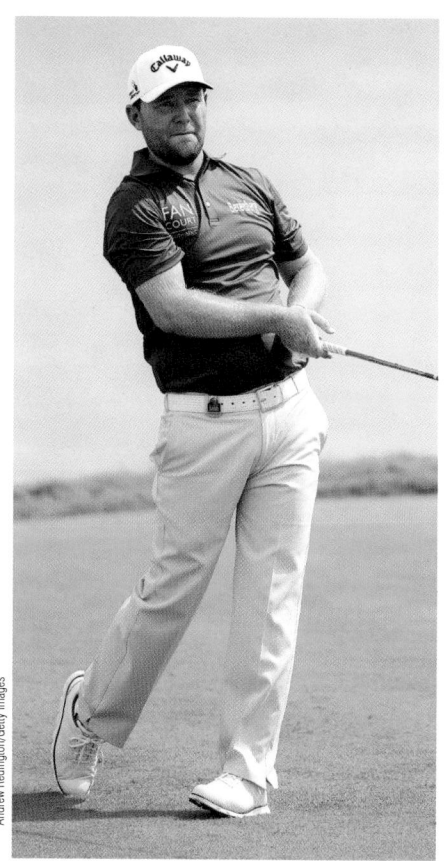

South African Branden Grace was third.

Tom Pennington/Getty Images

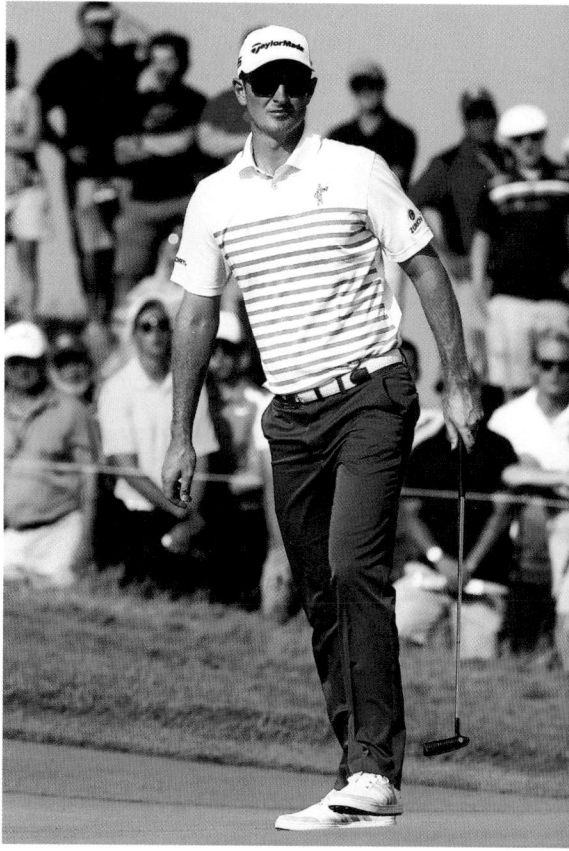

Justin Rose was fourth, his third top-six in the majors.

Presidents Cup

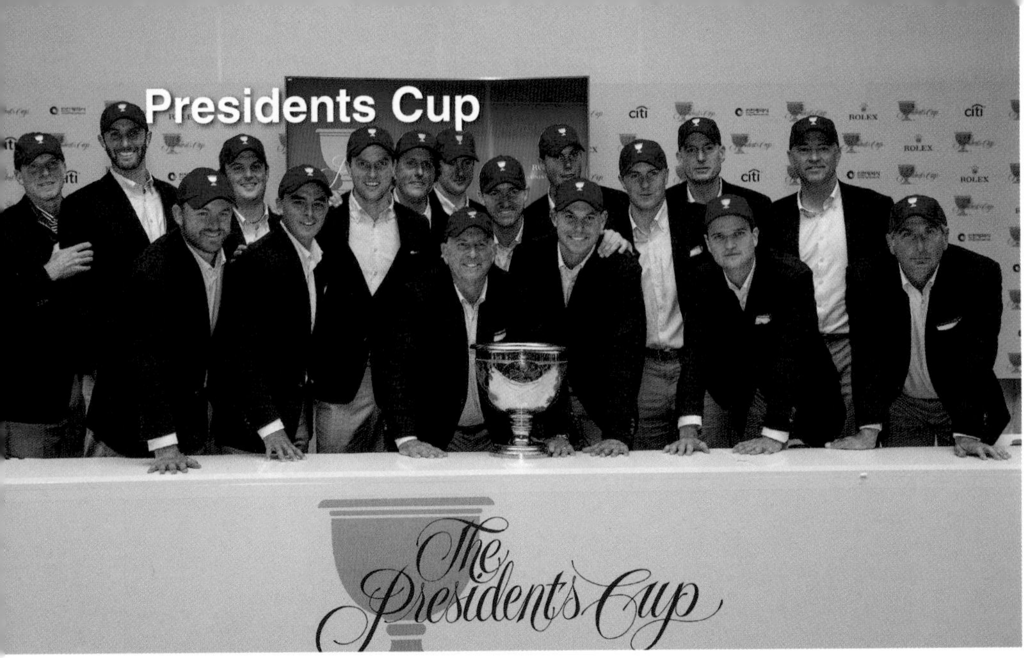

Rolex/Chris Turvey

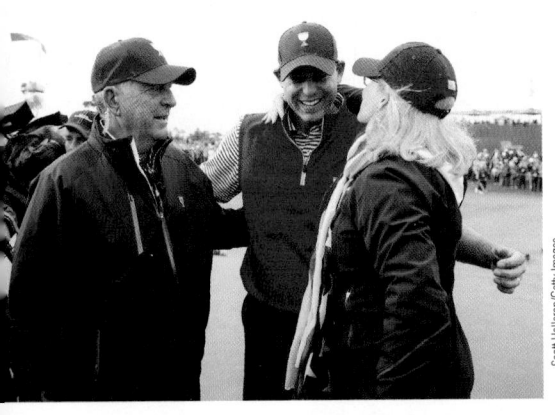

In the most exciting Presidents Cup for years, America won by one point in South Korea.

Scott Halleran/Getty Images

Captain Jay Haas with son Bill and wife Jan.

Scott Halleran/Getty Images

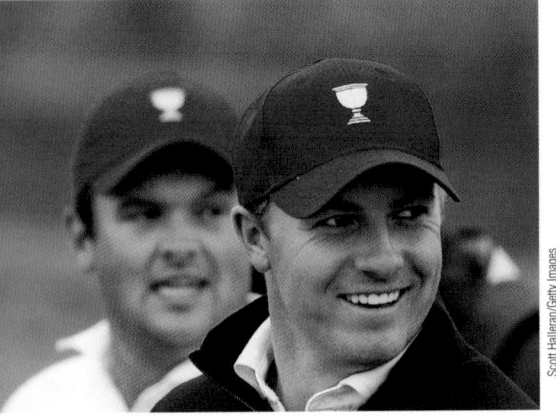

Patrick Reed and Jordan Spieth teamed well again.

Chung Sung-Jun/Getty Images

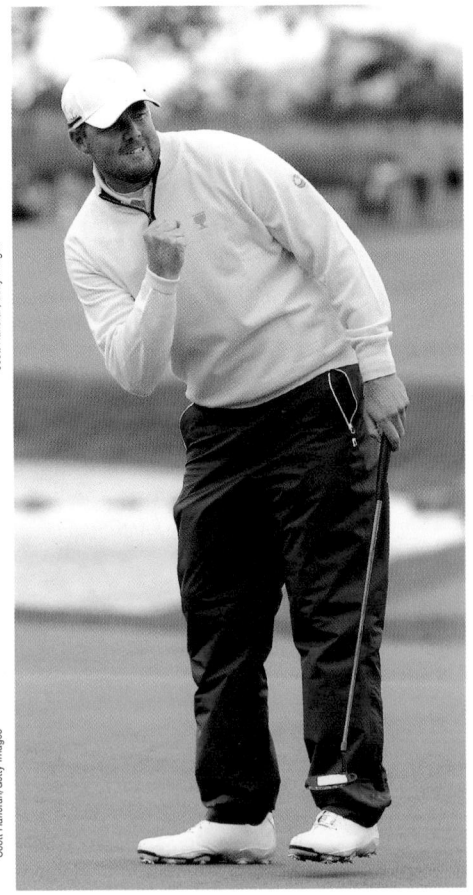

Marc Leishman defeated Spieth for a vital point.

David Cannon/Getty Images

Scott Halleran/Getty Images

Phil Mickelson beat Charl Schwartzel 5 and 4…

Harry How/Getty Images

Branden Grace won all five of his matches.

…while Zach Johnson won 3 and 2 over Jason Day.

Chung Sung-Jun/Getty Images

Bill Haas commiserates with Sangmoon Bae after clinching the winning point at the final hole.

Around The World

Jason Spieth shows off his trophies for winning the Tour Championship and the FedExCup.

Rory McIlroy took the Race to Dubai honors.

Jason Day's five wins included two FedExCup events.

Rickie Fowler won three times at The Players, Scottish Open and Deutsche Bank Championship.

Henrik Stenson was a runner-up five times.

Bubba Watson at the Travelers Championship.

Danny Willett won the Omega European Masters.

David Cannon/Getty Images

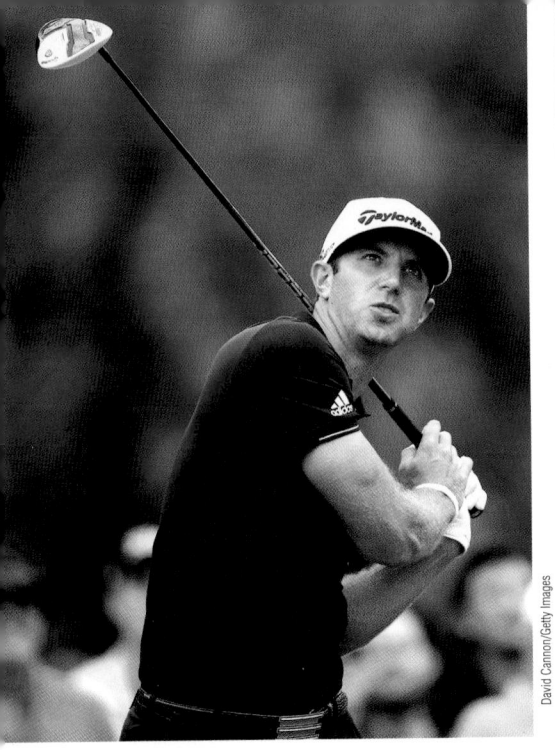

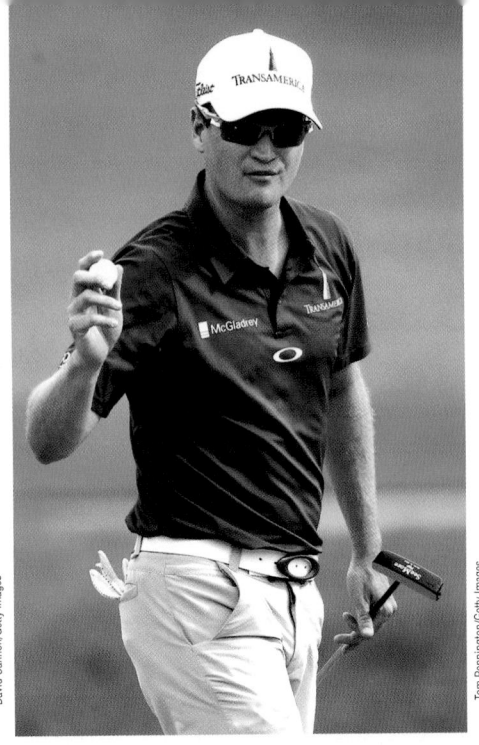

Dustin Johnson won the Cadillac Championship.

Tom Pennington/Getty Images

Zach Johnson finished sixth in FedExCup points.

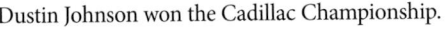

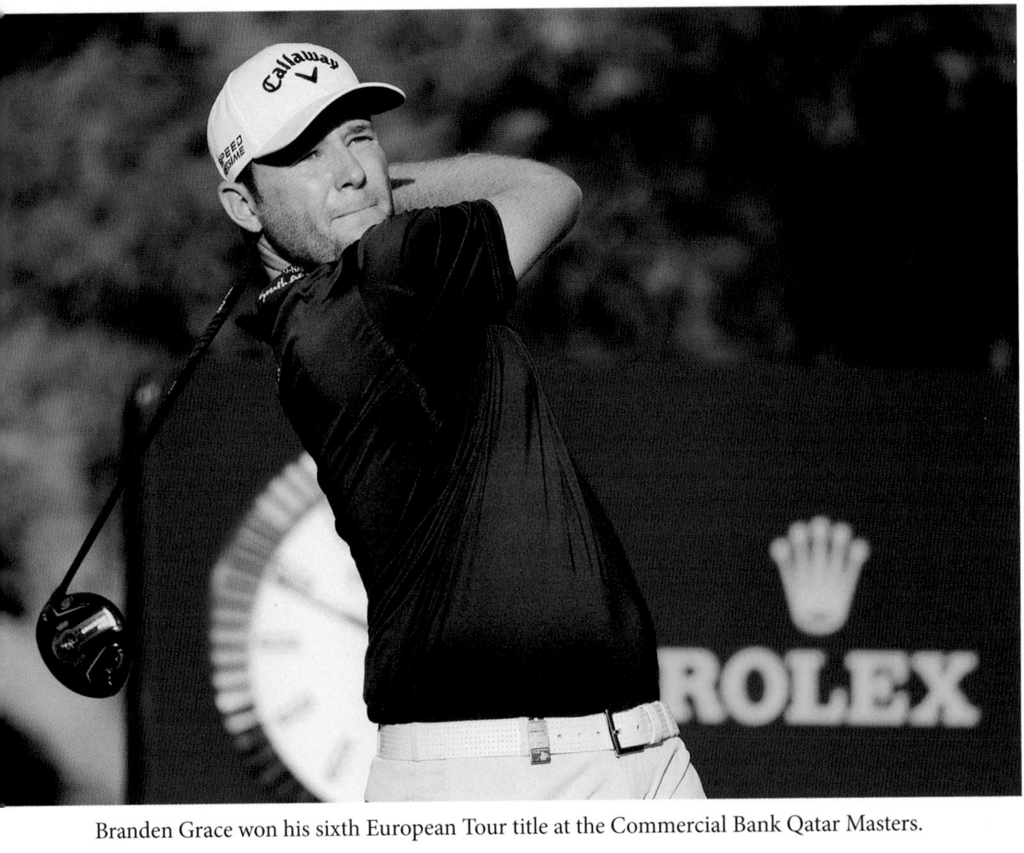

Ross Kinnaird/Getty Images

Branden Grace won his sixth European Tour title at the Commercial Bank Qatar Masters.

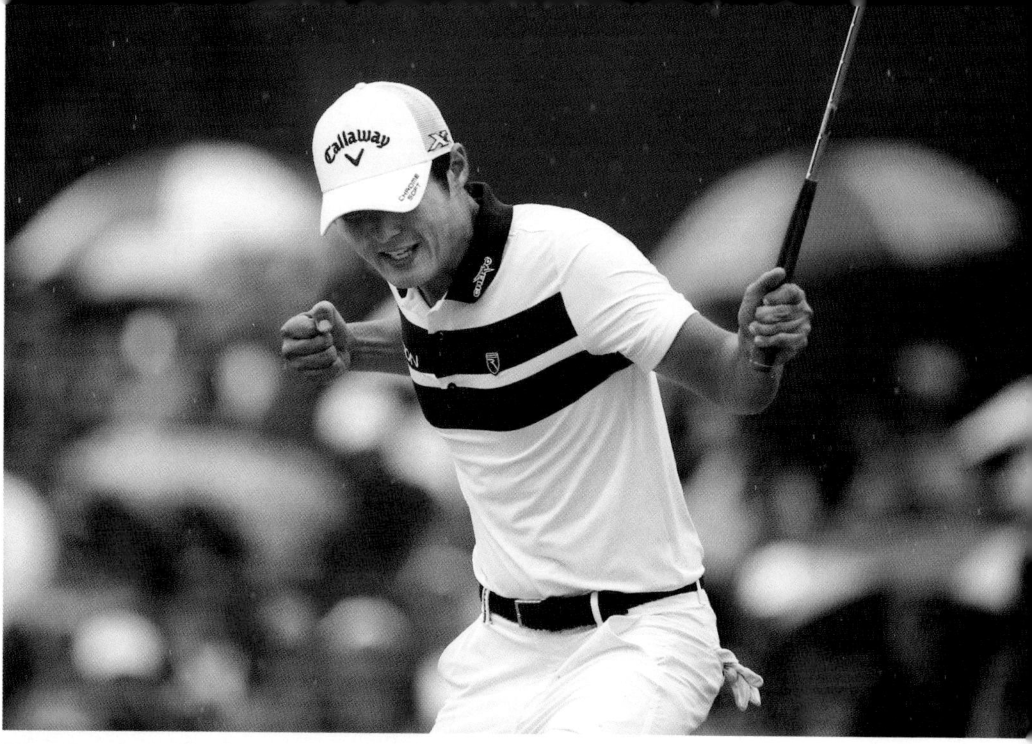

Darren Carroll/Getty Images

Danny Lee claimed his first victory on the PGA Tour at the Greenbrier Classic.

Christian Petersen/Getty Images

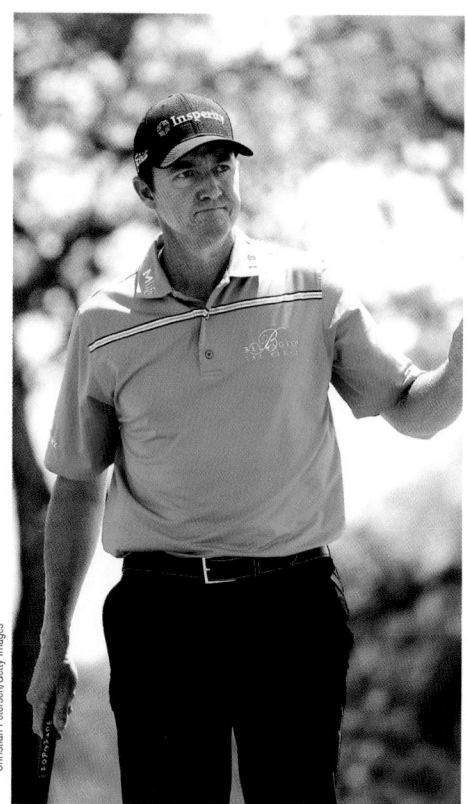

Jimmy Walker won in Hawaii and Texas.

Victor Fraile/Getty Images

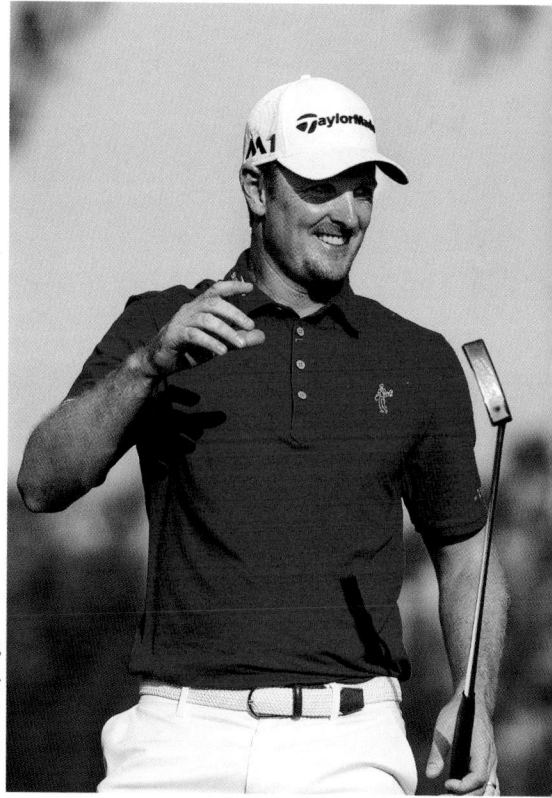

Justin Rose won in New Orleans and Hong Kong.

Andy Sullivan had three European Tour wins.

Shane Lowry won the Bridgestone Invitational.

Louis Oosthuizen was sixth in the Race to Dubai.

Byeong-Hun An was the BMW PGA champion.

Kyung-Tae Kim won five times in Asia and Japan.

Panasonic Open India
New Delhi, India
Winner: Chiragh Kumar

The spark was a sure birdie blown. "I missed a short birdie putt on the 14th hole, and I kept telling myself to move on," Chiragh Kumar said. "Everything fell into place after that, so I'm glad I missed that putt."

That was in second round, and Kumar, 31, surviving some squeaks along the way, rolled on to his first Asian Tour victory in the Panasonic Open India at Delhi Golf Club. He trailed by one after his opening five-under-par 67, then shot 66-72-70 for a 13-under 275 total, outlasting Bangladesh's sore-backed Siddikur Rahman and Thailand's Thaworn Wiratchant for a three-stroke win that was tighter than it looked.

Kumar started that pivotal second round on the back nine and was two over after four holes, then missed the short birdie at the 14th, his fifth hole. It was an inspired sprint from there. He birdied nine of the next 11 holes — including six straight — then bogeyed his last for the 66 and a three-stroke lead.

From there, it was a duel with Siddikur. Kumar, whose previous best finishes were a second and a tie for second, started the third round with a double bogey, but recovered and shot 72 to lead Siddikur (68) by one. In the final round, Siddikur's bad back kicked up, and it took a quick physiotherapy treatment at No. 4 tee to keep him from withdrawing. He caught up at the turn, but Kumar pulled away with birdies at the 11th and 13th — the latter from 25 feet. Siddikur birdied the 15th but bogeyed the last two for a 72. Kumar parred in for a 70 that included a flash of déjà vu — another blown short birdie at the 14th.

"But I told myself not to let it get to me," Kumar said.

World Classic Championship
Singapore
Winner: Danthai Boonma

Next up in golf's worldwide youth movement is Thailand's Danthai Boonma, a mere 19, an Asian Tour rookie previously best known for winning some honors at the 2012 South East Asia Games. That changed in mid-November 2015 when Danthai survived possibly the tour's toughest test of the season to score his breakthrough in the inaugural World Classic Championship.

Boonma prevailed when most rookies crack — under the pressure of the final round. Or in this case, the final nine. He hung close for the first three rounds and entered the fourth two strokes behind Malaysia's Nicholas Fung and Bangladesh's Siddikur Rahman. It became a Boonma-Fung duel when Siddikur blew to an 82 on Laguna National's tough par-71 World Classic course.

Boonma opened with 72-69-72, Fung with 74-67-70. Things looked bad early for Boonma when he bogeyed No. 8. "I didn't want to think too much about winning, especially after dropping a shot there," he said. Then there was a quick change. "But after making three birdies in four holes after the turn," he said, "I started to believe this could be my week." And so it proved to be, thanks to a little help from Fung.

"The hole that cost me the title was the 16th," said Fung, 25. Fung bogeyed the par-four in the first round, then again in the fourth, missing a two-foot second putt for par.

Boonma birdied the 10th, 12th and 13th, closing with a 69 for a two-under 282 total. Fung shot 72 for a 283. They were the only players to finish under par. Boonma did it with accuracy, hitting 49 of 56 fairways and 52 of 72 greens in regulation.

"I haven't played well since earning my Asian Tour card earlier this year," Boonma said, "so this is a great boost of confidence."

Resorts World Manila Masters
Manila, Philippines
Winner: Natipong Srithong

Thailand's Natipong Srithong had little to recommend him coming into the Resorts World Manila Masters. He was too young, only 22; he was a mere rookie who turned professional just two months earlier; and having no status on the Asian Tour, he was in the event on a sponsor's invitation, and he was making only his fourth start.

He did have two powerful inducements, however. First, the thought of countryman Danthai Boonma, age 19, winning the World Classic just the week before, had him thinking, "Why not me?" And then there was the sobering though of having to go through the tour's qualifying school.

Shooting the par-72 Southwoods course in 71-69-66, he trailed by five, six and four strokes, respectively, and even stumbled early in the fourth round, bogeying No. 2. Then a depressing reality hit him. "I thought, if I didn't win, I [will have to] go to qualifying school to get my card," Srithong said. Thus inspired, he birdied six of the last 13 holes for a 67, a 15-under 273 and a one-stroke win over South Africa's frustrated Jbe' Kruger, stuck at second when his chip shot for a tying eagle at the 18th rimmed out. "If it's not meant to be," said Kruger, "it's not meant to be."

Taiwan's Chien-Yao Hung was even more frustrated. He led by one entering the final round but tied for third on a shaky 73 that included four quick bogeys, an ace at the 13th, two more birdies and a double bogey at 18. He had a puzzling explanation. "I wasn't stressed," he said, "but I thought I was too uptight."

Srithong thanked Boonma, his roommate for the past two weeks. "He said it would be my turn soon," Srithong said. "I didn't expect it to be so soon."

Ho Tram Open
Ho Tram, Vietnam
Winner: Sergio Garcia

The Ho Tram Open, brand new on the Asian Tour, was a tournament the battle-tested Sergio Garcia thought he had won a couple of times. And also lost. But he finally pinned it down in a four-man playoff that had him mopping his brow and thanking his lucky stars at the Bluffs Ho Tram Strip.

"I was fortunate to get a second chance after I pretty much gave it away," said Garcia, 35, posting his first win since January 2014, his fifth win on the Asian Tour, and his career 23rd. "It was a strange day," Garcia said. "It felt like I was so much under control, the way I played the front nine."

Garcia trailed by two entering the final round and led by three at the turn after blitzing the front nine for a 29.

"Then," Garcia added, "I hit a bad tee shot on 10 [he bogeyed] and ... I hit a poor shot on 17 [he double-bogeyed]. I gave it away, and they gave me another chance."

Garcia stuck tight for the first three rounds, shooting 66-68-68, then scrambled to a closing 68 to tie at 14-under-par 270 with India's Himmat Rai (67), Thailand's Thaworn Wiratchant (67) and Taiwan's Wen-Tang Lin (70). It was a great escape for Garcia.

Wiratchant and Lin were eliminated on the first extra hole when Garcia holed a 35-foot putt for birdie and Rai followed him in from five feet. Rai then drove into the bushes on the second extra hole and Garcia won with a par. It was a liberating win.

"After you've been up there and you don't win, a lot of things go through your mind," Garcia said. "I was fortunate — and you have to be lucky to win."

Thailand Golf Championship
Chonburi, Thailand
Winner: Jamie Donaldson

The Thailand Golf Championship, a jewel on the Asian Tour, didn't lack for marquee glitter — American Bubba Watson, Spain's Sergio Garcia, England's Lee Westwood and Germany's Martin Kaymer. But it was Welshman Jamie Donaldson, best known for starring in Europe's 2014 Ryder Cup victory, who stole the show.

Donaldson, who trailed only in the third round, gave himself a scare coming down Amata Spring's final stretch.

"I had a great birdie on 15 after hitting two very good shots before sinking a 20-foot putt," Donaldson said. He was seven under for the round and leading by three at that point. Then came trouble, a bogey at the 16th off a stray tee shot, while his playing partners — Westwood, the defending champion, and France's Clement Sordet, a professional for just six months — both birdied. "My comfortable three-shot lead was reduced to one," Donaldson said. "I just had to remain calm and keep hitting good shots." He finished birdie-par, wrapping up a card of 63-68-71-65–267, 21 under, and scored his first win of the year by three over Westwood (67) and Sordet (70).

"There are a lot of good players in the tournament this week, and to beat these guys is great," Donaldson said.

Sordet, a spring graduate of Texas Tech University, where he starred, was a surprise. "I didn't expect such a result this week," said Sordet. "I was lucky to get an invitation."

The tournament also served as a qualifier for the 2016 British Open. Donaldson, Westwood and Sordet took three of the four available berths. With Garcia and Byeong-Hun An already qualified, the fourth berth went to Thai whiz Phachara Khongwatmai, 16, who finished sixth. "I didn't think so much and I surprised even myself," he said. "I played without much expectations and I guess that was the key."

Philippine Open
Tarlac, Philippines
Winner: Miguel Tabuena

The Philippines' Miguel Tabuena was only 21 but he felt twice as old, given the frustrations he'd known. Actually, impatience was probably his biggest problem. Winning is a noble ambition for a teenager, but when it doesn't happen, letdown follows.

Tabuena was singing another song when he finally broke through in the Philippine Open, giving himself a week-early Christmas gift in the Asian Tour's 2015 finale. He was the first Filipino to win his country's national championship since 2008.

"I'm glad the Philippine Open is my first Asian Tour title," said Tabuena. "I'm really happy that my name will be on this prestigious trophy alongside some of the legends in golf in Asia's oldest national open."

Bad weather cut the tournament to 54 holes, leaving Tabuena the winner by a stroke on a card of 67-69-66–202, 14 under par at the Luisita Golf and Country Club. Tabuena came from behind, trailing Canada's Lindsay Renolds by one in the first round and two in the second. At that point, the outlook was iffy for Tabuena, given his past. In the 2012 Philippine Open, Tabuena was one shot out of the lead, then shot 81. That shouldn't be a surprise for an 18-year-old. In the 2014 Yeangder Tournament Players Championship, he lost on the second playoff hole to veteran Prom Meesawat.

Tabuena seemed a totally mature player this time. He was a shot behind entering the final round, and after two birdies and a bogey from No. 4, he was in control, posting birdies at 10, 12, 13, 14 and 16 for his 66. It eased a lot of pain.

"You have to take your defeats as a positive," Tabuena said. "It definitely made me a stronger golfer mentally. I knew I was playing for the win."

OneAsia Tour

Volvo China Open
Shanghai, China
Winner: Ashun Wu

As the saying famously goes, "Youth will be served." It's not generally known, but it comes with a postscript: "But not necessarily right this minute."

That enduring truth was underlined at the season-opening Volvo China Open, the OneAsia-European Tour co-sanctioned tournament at Tomson Shanghai Pudong in April. The final round began with four players tied for the lead. All eyes and the smart money were on Hao-Tong Li, the 19-year-old kid often called the "future" of Chinese golf. He won the China Masters in 2014, and just the previous week was the playoff runner-up in the European Tour's Shenzhen International. Two were veteran European Tour pros — France's Alexander Levy, the defending champion, and England's David Howell, a six-time winner. China's Ashun Wu was the tag-along of the group. He'd won twice on the Japan Tour, and nearing 30, he'd taken six months off to rebuild his swing.

In this case, the chase went to the steady. Wu, trailing through the first two rounds, shot 73-66-69 to join the tie. Then in a steady final round, he birdied the fifth, bogeyed the eighth and birdied the 10th for a one-under 71 and a nine-under 279 total. The others were erratic: Howell finished second on a four-birdie, four-bogey 72; Levy tied for third on a 73 with three birdies, three bogeys and a double bogey, and Li was sixth with a 74 that included an eagle, one birdie and five bogeys.

"I tried my best to play every shot well," Wu said. "I played very well today — not down, not up. Just simple golf today."

Howell would have forced a playoff with Wu but missed a five-foot par putt at the 18th. "There's I don't know how many billion people," he cracked, "who are rather pleased I made six on the last."

GS Caltex Maekyung Open
Seoul, South Korea
Winner: Kyong-Jun Moon

It was what golfers often term a "train wreck," but in this case, the entire top of the leaderboard crashed at Namseoul Country Club, and the last man standing was Korea's Kyong-Jun Moon, taking the OneAsia Tour's GS Caltex Maekyung Open for the first victory of his career.

"Unbelievable," said Moon, 32. "I have waited a long time for this."

Start with the end of the third round, when Australia's Jason Norris finally took the lead with a superb bump-and-run shot, saving par off the cart path at the 18th. "That was my shot of the year," Norris said. He led by two going into the final round. Then the fun started, though five golfers didn't think it was fun.

Do-Hoon Kim rushed into the chase with a burst of six birdies on the back nine, but a double bogey-bogey at Nos. 7 and 8 and a bogey at the 18th sidetracked him. Norris stumbled to three bogeys on the front, then two double bogeys coming in for a 77. Ryan Fox bogeyed the first two holes, then the 18th for a 72. Gareth Paddison had a fireworks 74, with clusters of birdies offset by a double bogey at the 11th and three straight bogeys at the end.

By comparison, Moon had a serene time of it. He was even par through the 11th with two birdies and two bogeys, then went two under with birdies at the 13th and 14th. He was leading by four coming to the 18th, and then the crash — four to get on and three putts for a triple-bogey-seven. After a 71-66-74 start, he finished with a 73 and a four-under 284 for a two-stroke win over the other four.

"I really don't know what happened," Moon said. "But thankfully I had a good lead."

SK Telecom Open
Incheon, South Korea
Winner: Jinho Choi

Jinho Choi didn't need to see any scores. "I didn't watch the leaderboard," Choi was saying, "and it was probably just as well, looking at the scores."

This was after the third round at the SK Telecom Open, and Choi was doing pretty well chasing his first win on the OneAsia Tour. But the scores at the Sky 72 Ocean course were dropping, and his two-under-par 70 wasn't looking too robust, especially not against that pair of course-record 63s posted by those kids, Soomin Lee, 21, and Jeung-Hun Wang, 19. And Choi, nearing 31, was just back from 20 months of mandatory South Korean military service, and in just his third event since returning. Wang was one shot behind and Lee two, going into the final round.

Choi won, but in a tight finish. He led for the first three rounds, tied at 68 in the first, and alone with 68-70 in the middle. He was up by one going into the fourth round but by two over Lee. Choi and Lee were tied at the turn, courtesy of some interesting golf. Choi eagled the par-five fifth but bogeyed the ninth. Lee birdied the fifth, and after a bogey at the sixth he eagled No. 7 and birdied No. 9 to tie Choi at 11 under.

Then came a classic twist of golf. Choi opened the door with bogeys at the 12th and 15th, but Lee, after double-bogeying No. 11, couldn't step through, and they were tied at nine under at the 18th. Lee, playing in the group ahead, could only manage seven pars. Choi then faced an 18-foot birdie putt at the 18th — makeable but missable. But he made it for a 72 and a one-stroke win at 10-under 278.

"Amazing," Choi said, with his first OneAsia win. "I'm so relieved."

Singha Corporation Thailand Open
Pattaya, Thailand
Winner: Kyung-Tae Kim

Korea's Kyung-Tae Kim finally found the secret to golf. Or the secret to his own game, at least. And that was — be yourself.

And it paid off handsomely in the Singha Corporation Thailand Open, where Kim, 28, ended three frustrating years of trying to become someone else and picked up his first win since 2012. Previously, he'd won once on the Asian Tour, once on the OneAsia and five times on the Japan Tour.

This time, Kim won the OneAsia-Japan Golf Tour co-sanctioned event by the tightest three-stroke margin imaginable.

Kim trailed the talented Korean Jeung-Hun Wang, 19, by a stroke at the final turn. Wang, who won on the PGA Tour China in 2014, was out in six-under 30, on six birdies, and Kim in 32, on two birdies and an eagle at the par-five second hole. Kim made up ground coming in. After a birdie-bogey exchange, he birdied the 13th and 17th, setting the stage for a dramatic finish. Wang bogeyed the 14th and birdied the 16th. Both hit the green at the par-four 18th. Kim, leading by one, holed his 12-foot putt for a birdie. Wang then three-putted from seven feet for a bogey for a 67 and lost by three.

"I have no regrets," Wang said. "I did my best."

Kim shot 71-64-67-65–267, 21 under par at Siam Country Club's Plantation course, and explained the change in his game.

"The last three years, I did not do well because I wanted to go to America, and I thought if I had 20 more yards, I would have a chance to win over there," he said. "I changed my swing and my rhythm, and it changed my results.

"From there, I tried changing back to my usual swing, but it took quite a while."

Kolon Korea Open
Cheonan, South Korea
Winner: Kyung-Hoon Lee

The trophy for the Kolon Korea Open, the country's national championship, bears some impressive names — Rickie Fowler, Sergio Garcia, K.J. Choi and John Daly, among others. Native son Kyung-Hoon Lee, 24, with one victory on the Japan Tour, was working hard to join them. But he was playing steady if unspectacular golf and was going to need some help. He got it in the third round: The door was thrown wide open.

Australia's Scott Jeffress, solo leader in the first round, and Korea's Young-Han Song were co-leaders by a stroke at the halfway point. Then they started to slide in the third round. Jeffress bogeyed the eighth and ninth and had a 73 at the par-71 Woo Jeung Hills. Song's fold was abrupt. He was two under for the day and leading the tournament at nine under coming to the par-five 18th. Then he drove out of bounds, triple-bogeyed, and fell to a tie for second with a 72.

"I drove poorly over the closing holes and was punished," said Song, 24, still looking for his first win as a professional. "I guess it is better to do that today as opposed to tomorrow."

"I don't think anyone expected Song to finish like that," said Lee. "I am surprised to be in the lead." He closed with birdies at 15, 17 and 18. With rounds of 68-69-68, he was eight under and leading by two going into the final round of the OneAsia Tour classic.

By now, he had his head. After a bogey at No. 2 and an eagle at No. 5, he played the last 12 holes in five birdies and a bogey for a 66, and a 13-under 271 to win by four.

"It was all much closer than that," Lee said.

Fiji International
Sigatoka, Fiji
Winner: Matt Kuchar

It's an academic exercise to think of where Matt Kuchar rates the shot: Best of the tournament? Of the year? Of his career? He didn't rate it, but it's etched in his mind.

"It was one of the scariest shots to try and pull off," Kuchar said. "Sitting in a fairway bunker and had to get up over a lip, over the rocks and underneath a tree limb. There was just enough of a window between the two."

Kuchar was making his first visit to Fiji, playing the OneAsia Tour's Fiji International after helping the U.S. win the Presidents Cup in South Korea. It was a profitable visit.

Kuchar's scary shot came at the par-four 16th in the third round. He'd led since the second round, and was now in a fix — his ball in a hazard and a shot that had to thread the needle. "It looked like a perfect five iron," Kuchar said. "Fortunately, I pulled it off."

Kuchar finished the round with a two-stroke lead over Aron Price, who holed his approach at the par-five 17th for an eagle.

Kuchar opened with a two-over-par 74, two behind New Zealander Josh Geary. Kuchar took the lead in the second round and stayed there, finishing with 72-69-69 for a four-under 284 and a four-stroke win over Price. While Kuchar had to invent his miracle shot, the wind created one for him in the first round. His ball sat two feet from the hole at the par-four No. 2, and the wind blew it in. That held his damage to a bogey.

"It was so challenging on Thursday and Friday," Kuchar said. "I ... played some really steady golf and that was a real difference — I got off to a start where most people got beat up."

PGA Tour China

It seems to have been just a matter of geography for Bryden Macpherson. Macpherson, 25, a third-year pro out of Canada, lost his Web.com Tour playing card in the United States earlier in 2015, and came to the PGA Tour China, in its second year, and played in eight of the 12 events. He swept to the top of the class, and once again heard that magical expression.

On the Mackenzie Tour-PGA Tour Canada, the list is called "The Five." On the PGA Tour Latinoamerica, it's "Los Cinco." And on PGA Tour China, it's "Zhe Ge Wu." Whatever the language, the top five money winners from each of these developmental tours won the coveted playing cards for 2016 on the Web.com Tour, which is the final stepping stone to the ultimate level, the PGA Tour.

"What a success story Bryden was this season," said Greg Carlson, executive director of the PGA Tour China. "But beyond what Bryden did, we also have four other talented players who have gained great experience ... It will be enjoyable watching them [on] ... the Web.com Tour."

Macpherson shook off his disappointing Web.com season and won twice in China and had six straight top-five finishes, topping the money list with $118,862. He was followed by New Zealand's Josh Geary, $115,359; China's Xin-Jun Zhang, $84,144; China's Ze-Cheng Dou, $74,690, and Canada's Eugene Wong, $70,204.

Geary, who also had lost his Web.com card, won three times but was edged out by Macpherson's other high finishes.

Macpherson won the Cadillac Championship late in September and the Lushan Open two weeks later. In the Cadillac, he started the final round trailing by two and finally broke through in a showdown of, oddly enough, two poor bunker shots. At the 327-yard, par-four 15th, he and Korea's Byungmin Cho drove into the same greenside bunker. Macpherson, leading by one, came out 25 feet short. Cho was 25 feet long. Cho missed his birdie try, but Macpherson rolled his in — "I read it nicely, and it went straight in the center" — and led by two. Macpherson shot Topwin in 72-63-69-68–272, 16 under, and won by three.

In the Lushan Open, he rang up four straight 68s, an eight-under 272 total at Lushan International, and he got enough help from his challengers that, although he double-bogeyed the final hole, he still won by two. He never let up, however. "I wanted to keep attacking," he said. "If you play to make pars, you can make bogeys. But if you play to make birdies, you probably can make birdies."

Josh Geary, the second three-time winner in the tour's two years, won his three by a stroke. He launched his 2015 campaign in the season-opening Buick Open, shooting Sandbelt Trails in 73-70-69-68–280, eight under. He started the final round trailing by four, made five birdies on the front nine, then took the lead on a 30-foot birdie putt at the 11th. He bogeyed two of the last four, but was spared when Yi Cao finished bogey-triple bogey. Geary also survived a tight battle in the Lanhai Open, bogeying the final hole to shoot Lan Hai International in 67-72-68-69–276, 12 under. Geary took the lead with four birdies on the final nine and was dueling Korea's Jeung-Hun Wang, a talented 19-year-old. Geary, leading by one, missed the green at the 18th and was on in three. Wang, needing a birdie to tie, was on in two. But Wang three-putted from 26 feet for a bogey. Geary missed his nine-foot par putt and also bogeyed, and won by a stroke. "It feels pretty surreal," Geary said. "It wasn't the best way to win." Geary's third and final win, in the Yulongwan Yunnan Open, was just as rewarding but artistically more pleasing to him. Geary was locked in a hole-by-hole battle with Thailand's Gunn Charoenkul and Geary finally broke loose at the par-five 16th, dropping a nine-foot putt for an eagle. He shot Yulongwan Golf Club in 66-65-64-71, 22-under 266, to win by one. "It's just one of those things where someone has to win," Geary said. "It happened to be me this time."

Xin-Jun Zhang became the first Chinese winner of 2015 in the Chongqing Open. He shot King Run Nanshan in 69-74-65-65–273, 15 under, for a four-stroke victory over Macpherson that wasn't nearly as comfortable as it looked. Zhang lost the lead in the final round, then regained it, then outran Macpherson with birdies at the 13th, 14th and 16th. "I felt some pressure on the front nine, especially when Bryden made his four-birdie streak," Zhang said. "We were neck-and-neck. But on the back nine, I felt relaxed in my putting."

Ze-Cheng Dou, 18, took the fourth spot and Rookie of the Year honors with $74,690 and without a win. He piled up the total with a playoff second and six other finishes from third to seventh. A kid's error may have cost him his best chance at a victory. He tied Haimeng Chao in the Nine Dragons Open, but while waiting for regulation play to finish, he went to the practice green rather than hit balls to stay loose in the cool, damp weather. Then he hooked his tee shot on the first playoff hole, hit his second into a hazard and was done. "My back did feel a little tight," Dou said. "I learned a lot."

Canada's Eugene Wong, former University of Oregon standout, had the easiest win of the year in the Pingan Bank Open at Qinghe Bay. After starting 70-67, he raced to a nine-under 63 in the third that had his caddie muttering. "[He] kept telling me, 'You're OK, you're doing fine,'" Wong said. He led by eight through the third round and was nine ahead with a birdie at No. 1 in the fourth. "I didn't need to feel nervous out there," Wong said. "I could make a few mistakes and not worry about it."

Japan Tour

Token Homemate Cup
Nagoya, Mie
Winner: Michael Hendry

Michael Hendry "streamlined" his practice sessions toward the end of 2014 to spend more time with his newborn daughter and he credited that decision for the improved play that brought him victory in the Token Homemate Cup, the opening event on the 2015 Japan Tour.

The 35-year-old New Zealander had barely held on to his Japan playing privileges after a mediocre 2014 season, but now guaranteed a spot in circuit tournaments through 2017, "having that security is great," he said. "It's a perfect start to the season."

Hendry secured his first win in Japan with a closing, seven-under-par 64 that brought him from three shots behind leader Hyun-Woo Ryu to a one-stroke victory margin at 15-under-par 269 over Kazuhiro Yamashita, who shot a final-round 66 and, like Hendry, a back-nine 31.

The Kiwi golfer contended all week at Token Tado Country Club at Nagoya, sitting in a second-place tie with 67-69–136, a shot behind South Korea's I.J. Jang (66-69) after first-round leader Kodai Ichihara evaporated from 64 to 77 en route to a 64th-place finish. Ryu moved ahead with 65–202 Saturday, with Yamashita (68-70-66) and Daisuke Kataoka (67-69-68) two back and Hendry, with a 69, and three others three off the lead.

Hendry was just two under on the front side Sunday. "All of a sudden on the back nine the ball started going in from all over the place," he enthused after the five-birdie 31 that produced the most important international win for a New Zealand male since Danny Lee won on the European Tour in 2009.

The Crowns
Togo, Aichi
Winner: I.J. Jang

I.J. Jang surely will forever harbor fond thoughts about Nagoya Golf Club and its Wago course. The 42-year-old South Korean veteran has notched three victories on the Japan Tour and the last two of them came there, the annual site of the Crowns tournament, one of the circuit's oldest non-major events. Three years after winning it for the first time and four years after finishing second, Jang finished the week with a three-under-par 67 for 270 and a four-stroke victory.

Jang was solid all week, piecing out four rounds in the 60s, beginning with a 66 the first day and resting in a tie for second with 2011 champion Brendan Jones of Australia. They were a shot behind leader Kyoung-Hoon

Lee, who followed with a 67 for 132 to open a two-shot margin over Taichi Teshima (68-66) and three ahead of Jang (69) and Kazuhiro Yamashita (67-68).

When Lee faltered with a 73 in the third round, Jang (68) and Shingo Katayama (72-65-66) climbed into joint first place at 203, two strokes ahead of Lee, Yamashita, Teshima and Tomohiro Kondo.

Jang left all the contenders in the dust with his 67 Sunday. Hideto Tanihara, with 68, joined Yamashita and Kondo (69s) in the runner-up slot. Defending champion Hyung-Sung Kim missed the cut by a stroke.

Japan PGA Championship
Saitama
Winner: Adam Bland

World traveler Adam Bland, who had success in the past in Canada and his native Australia but little in recent years, came up blazing in the Japan Tour's first major of 2015, virtually running away with the title in the Japan PGA Championship. The win by the 32-year-old Aussie came pretty much out of the blue, since he had only a missed cut and a tie for 56th place in the two previous tournaments that opened the season, his second in Japan. He finished 38th in Japan in 2014 and had only two wins on the Canadian Tour and a runner-up finish on the U.S. Web.com Tour in his more recent forays to the Western Hemisphere.

Bland missed a wire-to-wire performance in the PGA Championship only because his opening seven-under-par 64 was surpassed by K.T. Kwon's 63 that day on the Kohnan course of the Taiheiyo Club in Saitama. Bland jumped two strokes in front of Kwon Friday with his 68–132 to the South Korean's 71–134 and widened the gap to six strokes with his second 64 in the third round for an impressive 196 total. Kwon fell seven back at 203 as Japan's Hiroshi Iwata (64) and Masahiro Kawamura (67) took over second place.

The issue was never in doubt Sunday as the left-hander won easily with a one-over 71, finishing with a three-stroke margin at 268 despite bogeys on the last two holes. South Korea's Sang-Hee Lee, who started the day seven strokes back, claimed second place with his 68–271.

Bland joined New Zealand's Michael Hendry as a first-time winner in Japan, as overseas players took the first three titles of the season.

Kansai Open
Shiga
Winner: Daisuke Kataoka

The Japan Tour spawned first-time winners in the early stages of the 2015 season. Daisuke Kataoka became the third one in the year's fourth tournament when he scored a three-stroke victory in the Kansai Open in late May at Meishin Yokaichi Country Club.

A shot off the pace after 54 holes, Kataoka, without a victory in his eight seasons on the Japan Tour, came out firing Sunday. He birdied five of the first seven holes to swish past Kazuhiro Yamashita and rode the lead home for 67–267 and a three-stroke victory. Kataoka had shared the lead the first two days. He matched opening 66s with Jung-Gon Hwang, the 2011 Mizuno Open winner, then with 67 on Friday remained in a first-place tie, then with Won-Joon Lee, who had rounds of 68 and 65.

Yamashita, who opened with 70, paired up middle rounds of 64 and 65 for a 14-under-par 199 to grab a one-stroke advantage over Kataoka (67) and Hiroshi Iwata (65) heading into Sunday's finale. Brad Kennedy, a two-time winner on the Japan Tour with a particularly impressive record in the Kansai Open, was Kataoka's strongest challenger the last day though, as Yamashita shot 74 and slipped down to ninth place. Kennedy, with a win and a third in his two previous appearances in the tournament, duplicated Kataoka's fast start, eagling the first hole and going five under on the first seven holes. However, he couldn't make up his beginning three-shot deficit behind Kataoka, particularly when he double-bogeyed the 12th hole. Kennedy's 67–270 earned him the runner-up spot, a shot ahead of Lee and Yosuke Tsukada.

"The Japanese players have to do something," smiled the long-suffering Kataoka, the first native son to win on the 2015 circuit after the first three titles went to players from Australia, New Zealand and South Korea.

Gateway to the Open Mizuno Open
Kasaoka, Okayama
Winner: Taichi Teshima

Taichi Teshima picked a good tournament in which to acquire his eighth victory on the Japan Tour. Not only did the 46-year-old veteran and former Japan Open and PGA Champion grab the Mizuno Open title but, along with three others, earned an invitation to the Open Championship at revered St. Andrews.

A third-round, six-under-par 66 carried Teshima into a share of the lead at JFE Setonaikai Golf Club with Scott Strange, and he outdueled the Australian the last day and won by two strokes with his final 273. He shot 69 to Strange's 71.

New Zealander Michael Hendry, who won the season-opening Token Homemate Cup, made an early run at another 2015 title. He blazed an opening 63 for a two-stroke lead over Yoshinori Fujimoto and remained in first place Friday even though following with a 73. He wound up in a four-way tie at 136 with Shugo Imahira (67-69), Shinichi Yokota (70-66), and Strange (69-67).

As the others fell away and Teshima charged, Strange held on to his share of the lead with 68 for his 214, setting up the Sunday battle. Shinji Tomimura (67) and Tadahiro Takayama (70) tied for third at 277 and nailed the other two Open invitations. Only Tomimura was Open-bound for the first time.

Japan Golf Tour Championship
Kasama, Ibaraki
Winner: Wen-Chong Liang

A 12-year quest for victory on the Japan Tour ended in a blaze of glory for Wen-Chong Liang when the 36-year-old Chinese pro rolled to a solid, wire-to-wire win in the Japan Golf Tour Championship, the season's second major.

Liang had made passes at victory in those earlier seasons, notably a year earlier when he lost to Hiroyuki Fujita in a playoff in the KBC Augusta tournament, and had played well through his previous four starts in 2015 with finishes no higher than 21st. Then, on Shishido Hills Country Club's West course, his opening 67 in the Tour Championship gave him a one-stroke lead over six other players and he rode it home from there.

Liang shot a three-under-par 68 Friday to maintain the one-shot margin, then over South Korea's Young-Han Song (68-68), with Australia's Brad Kennedy, a multiple winner on the tour, another stroke back. Church was out when Liang jumped five strokes ahead of Kennedy with a five-birdie 67–200 on the par-71 course Saturday. Kennedy shot 68. Liang expanded the lead early in the final round before settling for his closing 70 and 14-under-par 270 winning score. Kennedy shot 70 and shared the runner-up spot with Young-Han Song and Ryutaro Nagano, who closed with 69s.

The ¥30 million first prize boosted Liang from 23rd place to the top of the circuit's money list.

Singha Corporation Thailand Open
Winner: Kyung-Tae Kim

See OneAsia Tour section.

ISPS Handa Global Cup
Hokuto, Yamanashi
Winner: Toshinori Muto

Toshinori Muto hadn't won on the Japan Tour in three years, and things weren't particularly promising for the 37-year-old veteran when he teed it up in the new ISPS Handa Global Cup tournament. He had missed cuts the two previous weeks and finished better than 37th only once all season.

Yet, he led the way after 54 holes at the Vintage Golf Club, but faced a serious challenge when he reached the 16th tee in the final round. Already in the clubhouse was Angelo Que of the Philippines after firing a bogey-free, seven-under-par 64 and recording a 14-under-par 270. This meant Muto had to birdie all three remaining holes to snag his sixth Japan Tour victory and first since taking the Kansai Open in 2012. He didn't accomplish that feat but did birdie the 16th and 18th, forcing the season's first playoff, which he won with another birdie on the second extra hole. That deprived the 36-year-old Que, an Asian Tour regular with three victories on that circuit, of his first win in Japan and initial victory anywhere since 2010.

"Over the past three years, I got injured and thought I could not play golf anymore," an elated Muto exclaimed. "I had much support from a lot of people, so I am glad to win for them, too."

Hyung-Sung Kim, who eventually finished third, a shot out of the playoff, shared the first-round lead at 66 with Azuma Yano, Taichi Teshima, Satoru Hirota and Kyung-Tae Kim, fresh from his Sunday victory in the Thailand Open. Yano, whose only Japan Tour victory came in 2005, repeated his 66 Friday, moving three strokes in front of visiting European Tour stars Ian Poulter and Thomas Aiken.

Muto (68-68) and Hyun-Woo Ryu (69-67) produced 66s Saturday to overtake Yano, who shot 70 for his 202. Muto took it from there Sunday to his rewarding finish. Poulter, closing with 68-69, wound up in a fourth-place tie with David Smail, Ippei Koike and Ryu. Aiken faded to a 30th-place finish.

Shigeo Nagashima Invitational
Chitose, Hokkaido
Winner: Hiroshi Iwata

Things certainly blossomed for Hiroshi Iwata after he finally won his first Japan Tour tournament in 2014 following nearly a decade of winless play in his professional career. Iwata landed the Fujisankei Classic title in September and two months later picked up a big check when he finished third in the World Golf Championships - HSBC Champions tournament in China. Eight months after that, the 34-year-old won again in Japan and vaulted to the top of the money list.

As he did in his Fujisankei victory, Iwata came from behind in the final round to capture the Shigeo Nagashima Invitational Sega Sammy Cup crown in early July. Sitting in a third-place tie with 22-year-old rookie Shugo Imahira after 54 holes, Iwata shot a flawless, six-under-par 66 to notch a one-stroke victory with his 272 total. The ¥30 million prize jumped him from 29th place as he supplanted Wen-Chong Liang atop the money list.

J.B. Park, whose only previous win came in the 2011 Japan Tour Championship, made a strong run at No. 2. Leading off with a 65, a shot better than the rounds of Hyung-Sung Kim and Kyung-Tae Kim, Park retained sole possession of the lead with his second-round 68, then two shots ahead of Koumei Oda, 2014's leading money winner. Hyung-Sung Kim, with a 67, joined Park (71) in first place at 204. Iwata and Imahira were at 206.

In the course of shooting his bogey-free 66 Sunday, Iwata missed only one green, barely edging playing partner Imahira, who birdied two of the last three holes for 67–273. Park and Hyung-Sung Kim closed with 71s for 275.

Musee Platinum Open
Miki, Hyogo
Winner: Kyung-Tae Kim

The first half on the 2015 season saw a revival of sorts for Kyung-Tae Kim.

The 28-year-old South Korean, who won three times and captured the Japan

Tour's money title in 2010 and played successfully on the International team in the 2011 Presidents Cup, had gone into a decline since then, finishing 35th on the money list in 2014 and going winless since 2012 until his victory in June in the Thailand Open. A month later, Kim won again, becoming the first multiple victor of the season with his come-from-behind triumph in the inaugural Musee Platinum Open. The win, his seventh, boosted him into a substantial lead in the money race.

While Kim was just keeping himself in contention during the early going with 68-67 rounds, fireworks were exploding elsewhere. J.B. Park started things with a first-round 63 and South Korean compatriot Min-Gyu Cho unloaded an 11-under-par 60, the season's lowest round, on the Japan Memorial Golf Club at Miki, Hyogo Prefecture, the next day to tie Park (66) for the lead at 129.

It was Kim's turn to go low Saturday. His 63–198 moved him within four strokes of leader Park, who maintained his fast pace with a bogey-free 65–194, with Australians Brad Kennedy (65) and Michael Hendry (64) two and three shots back. Kim sailed past all three of them Sunday as he shot a bogeyless 66 for 264 and a one-shot victory over Park (71), Kennedy (69), and up-and-down Cho, who bounced back from a third-round 72 with 64 for his 265.

Dunlop Srixon Fukushima Open
Nishigo, Fukushima
Winner: Prayad Marksaeng

Advancing age hasn't slowed down Prayad Marksaeng. Only months away from senior golf eligibility, the 49-year-old Thailand pro generated a brilliant finish and snatched the Dunlop Srixon Fukushima Open title from South Korea's winless Young-Han Song. It was his fifth victory on the Japan Tour and 15th as a professional worldwide.

Marksaeng was brilliant the final three rounds at Grandee Nasushirakawa Golf Club after starting the tournament three strokes off the lead with a three-under-par 69. He didn't make a bogey the last three days and polished off Song Sunday with a dazzling 63 for his winning 264 total. Song, who had another runner-up finish earlier in the season in the Japan Tour Championship, did his best that day. He was the only challenger to the veteran Marksaeng, also managing a bogey-free round and shooting 66 to finish second by a stroke with his 265.

Another South Korean, S.K. Ho, commanded the first two rounds with his 66-67–133 start. He shared the lead with senior star Kiyoshi Murota, Hidemasa Hoshino and Ryuji Masaoka the first day and with Satoshi Kodaira and Song on Friday. With 66 in the third round, Song moved a stroke in front of Ho (67) and two ahead of Marksaeng (67), Dong-Kyu Jang (65) and Hiroyuki Fujita (64), the 2012 leading money winner and 2014 runner-up.

Marksaeng took charge early Sunday with birdies on three of the first four holes, and secured the victory, his second of the year following the Queens Cup in Thailand, with two more birdies on the final three holes. Kyung-Tae Kim, the money leader coming off his victory earlier in July in the Musee

Platinum Open, posted his third straight top-10 finish, tying for ninth with Hideki Matsuyama (64), home for a week from the U.S. PGA Tour.

RIZAP KBC Augusta
Shima, Fukuoka
Winner: Yuta Ikeda

So consistent has Yuta Ikeda been since his smashing debut on the Japan Tour in 2009 that his 13th circuit victory in August's RIZAP KBC Augusta tournament was close to being a foregone conclusion. Since his four victories and runner-up finish on the 2009 money list behind Ryo Ishikawa, Ikeda has won at least one tournament every season, including the Japan PGA that first year and the Japan Open in 2014, and has never finished worse than 11th on the year-end standings.

The KBC Augusta was another of his rookie-season victories — in a playoff after shooting a 63. His second win in that tournament at Keya Golf Club six years later was much more decisive. Holding at least a share of first place all week, the 29-year-old Ikeda broke from a one-stroke lead after 54 holes and strolled to a five-shot victory with his 20-under-par 268.

His opening 66 was matched by little-known K.T. Kwon, but Ikeda raced in front to stay in Friday's round, shooting 65 for 131 and a three-stroke lead over Koumei Oda, the tour's No. 1 in 2014, and 41-year-old Australian Brad Kennedy. A mediocre 71 the third day left Ikeda at 202, a stroke in front of Keichiro Fukabori and Tomoyo Ikemura, but he bounced back with another 66 Sunday for the victory. Fukabori and Ikemura faltered in that last round and Oda took over second place with 69–273. Kennedy tied for third at 274 with Atomu Shigenaga. Both men closed with 68s.

Fujisankei Classic
Yamanashi
Winner: Kyung-Tae Kim

Things brightened in early September for Kyung-Tae Kim in his bid for a second money title on the Japan Tour. For one, Kim eked out his third victory on the season in the Fujisankei Classic. For another, Hiroshi Iwata, sitting in the runner-up position, went to America after his fourth-place finish to play in the four-tournament Web.com Tour qualifying series for PGA Tour cards. Australian Brad Kennedy, in third position, trailed Kim by nearly ¥40 million.

The 29-year-old Kim, who was the leading money winner in Japan in 2010, took command of the Fujisankei in the second round with a seven-under-par 64. His 134 gave him a three-stroke lead over Masahiro Kawamura as Kyoung-Hoon Lee, whose 64 led the first day, slipped into a third-place tie with Kodai Ichihara (70-68) after shooting 74.

Kim extended his lead to four strokes Saturday with 68–202 as Kennedy shot 67–206 and moved into second place, a stroke ahead of Kawamura and two in front of Lee. Both carded 70s. The win, Kim's eighth in Japan and second in the Fujisankei Classic (2012), did not come easily. He struggled to a two-over-par 73, and countryman Lee, with birdies on three of the last five holes, produced a 68, falling just one stroke short of Kim's total with his 276. Kawamura, with 70, finished at 277. Kennedy (73) tied for sixth.

ANA Open
Kitahiroshima, Hokkaido
Winner: Ryo Ishikawa

Home is where the heart is — and the victories as well. Back in Japan after a mediocre season on the PGA Tour in America, Ryo Ishikawa quickly revived his game in a familiar setting and picked off his 12th Japan Tour win. It was his first start after being eliminated after the first round of the FedExCup Playoffs in the United States. He pulled away to a two-stroke victory in the ANA Open in Hokkaido three days after his 24th birthday and nine years after his astonishing first win on the Japan Tour at age 15.

Ishikawa lingered just off the lead as Thailand's Prayad Marksaeng, the Dunlop Open winner in July, commanded first place during the opening rounds on Sapporo Golf Club's Wattsu course with a pair of six-under-par 66s. At that point, Ishikawa was four back, tied for second with veteran star Toru Taniguchi. Both shot two 68s. A third-round 67 moved Ishikawa into a first-place tie with 2014's leading money winner, Koumei Oda, who came out of nowhere (tied 31st) with a dazzling 61 after starting with a pair of 71s. They had a three-shot margin over defending champion Katsumasa Miyamoto, Daisuke Kataoka and Satoshi Tomiyama. Marksaeng fell from contention with a 75.

The competition remained close, but without Oda, in Sunday's final round until Ishikawa birdied the 13th hole and chipped in for another at the 14th. He parred in for 69–272 and the two-shot win over Yusaka Miyazato, who birdied two of the last three holes for 67–274. It was the fourth top-five finish of the season for the two-time tour winner. Oda bogeyed twice on the front nine, shot 75 and finished in a four-way tie for sixth.

Asia-Pacific Diamond Cup
Ibaraki
Winner: Kyung-Tae Kim

Kyung-Tae Kim's comeback express roared on in a familiar setting. The 29-year-old South Korean, targeting his second money title on the Japan Tour, chalked up his fourth triumph of the season with a three-stroke victory in the Asia-Pacific Diamond Cup. It was there he posted one of his earlier wins in 2010, the year he became the circuit's first top money winner from his country.

His successes in 2015 had surprised Kim. "I didn't expect to win so many titles this year. I hadn't won in three years, so I was hoping to win at least one tournament."

With runner-up Hiroshi Iwata in America successfully winning playing privileges on the PGA Tour, the ¥30 million first prize widened Kim's lead on him to more than ¥50 million. No other player had multiple victories to that point in the season.

Kim took the lead on Otone Country Club's West course in the third round after Australian Scott Strange led the first day with 64 and Thailand's Prayad Marksaeng, the Dunlop winner in July, was in front with 67-68–135 after 36 holes. With rounds of 67-69-67, Kim's 203 staked him to a two-stroke margin over Yuta Ikeda, third on the money list, and Satoshi Kodaira after three rounds. As happened the previous week, Marksaeng fell back on "moving day."

Although starting the day four shots back, Toshinori Muto gave Kim his biggest scare Sunday. The six-time winner, his latest the ISPS Handa Global Cup in June, rang up four birdies over the first 13 holes and was tied for the lead when Kim bogeyed the 11th hole behind him. But an errant drive on No. 14 cost Muto a shot and the winner established his three-stroke margin and final 68 for his nine-under-par 271 with two birdies coming home.

Muto, with 67, and Ikeda, with 69, finished second at 274.

Top Cup Tokai Classic
Miyoshi, Aichi
Winner: Hyung-Sung Kim

As far as Shingo Katayama was concerned, Hyung-Sung Kim picked the wrong time to right a poor stretch of golf and snag his annual victory on the Japan Tour. After a fast start to the 2015 season, Kim came to the Top Cup Tokai Classic in a short-term slump. At the same time, Katayama, who had scored just two of his 28 tour victories since 2008, had been getting closer to No. 29 with improving showings in his last three tournaments.

The long-time star, now 42, whose 27th victory came in the 2013 Tokai Classic, got away in front again on Miyoshi Country Club's West course with a seven-under-par 65. He dropped three behind Sang-Hyun Park (67-69–136) when he slipped to 74 Friday, but trailed co-leaders Seuk-Hyun Baek and Yuta Ikeda, the KBC Augusta winner, by only a shot going into the final round after his 70–209. Katayama was tied with Park (73) and Ryo Ishikawa, back home after a so-so season on the PGA Tour in America, and a stroke in front of Kim (69-72-69), who had missed cuts in three of his previous four starts.

A wild scramble ensued Sunday with five different players holding the lead at one time or another. Katayama seized the top spot with four birdies in the middle of the round and had four shots on Kim when the South Korean reached the 14th tee. Katayama made no mistakes, but also no birdies, in the stretch, and Kim blazed home with birdies on four of the last five holes with 66–276, forcing a playoff as Katayama posted 67–276.

Kim birdied the second extra hole for the victory, his fourth on the Japan Tour, one in each of the last four years. Both Ikeda and Park, who finished two back, had their chances but bogeyed the final hole.

Honma TourWorld Cup at Trophia Golf
Ibaraki
Winner: Kyoung-Hoon Lee

Kyoung-Hoon Lee made a big splash when he arrived on the Japan Tour in 2012 as a 21-year-old rookie, reeling off four top-10s in his first eight starts and bagging the Sega Sammy tournament in July. He finished 10th on the money list. Two routine seasons followed, but things perked up for the 24-year-old South Korean in 2015. After four top-10s and a win in Korea, he squeezed out a one-stroke victory in the inaugural Honma TourWorld Cup at Trophia Golf in Ibaraki.

Scoring the third straight victory and seventh of the season by a South Korean player, Lee blazed home with a final-nine 31 — five birdies in a six-hole stretch — for the winning 67–268 on the Ishioka Golf Club course in early October. He edged four players — Ryuichi Oda, Ashun Wu, Taichi Teshima and Tomohiro Kondo, all former tour winners.

Kondo, a six-time winner in Japan who suffered through mid-season doldrums that included eight straight missed cuts, had taken the lead with a 62–132 the second day and led by two strokes after 54 holes. His 67–199 gave him that margin over Lee, who had followed a 71 with a pair of 65s, and Yusaku Miyazato (69-68-64). Kondo managed only a 70 Sunday as he finished in the runners-up tie at 269 with Oda, who shot 63; Wu, with 65, and Teshima, who scored 67.

Japan Open Championship
Kobe, Hyogo
Winner: Satoshi Kodaira

Things had not gone well for Satoshi Kodaira in his last two starts prior to the Japan Open Championship — two missed cuts — and they weren't looking up when he finished his first round on the Rokko Kokusai Golf Club's East course. He had just shot a one-under-par 71 and rested in a tie for 35th place.

He turned it all around the next day with a dazzling 62 that rocketed the 26-year-old Kodaira into first place and a lead he never lost in battling to a one-stroke victory with a 13-under-par 275. The win, his second major and career third, boosted him into third place on the money list. He won the Japan Tour Championship in 2013.

Kodaira's toughest opponent at Rokko Kokusai was Yuta Ikeda, the defending champion, who was riding a remarkable run of five straight top-10 finishes since winning the KBC Augusta in August. With steady rounds of 68-68-69, Ikeda, No. 2 on the money list, moved into second place, just two strokes off the pace. Kodaira, whose 62 had given him a two-shot lead over amateur Takumi Kanaya, added a 70 Saturday for the leading 203.

At the end, it came down to Kodaira and Ikeda. Ikeda caught Kodaira with a birdie on the 71st hole, but he bogeyed the 72nd for 71–276 and lost by a stroke as Kodaira finished with a 72 for his 275. Young-Han Song, winless in Japan, took third place with 71–278. Australian star Adam Scott, fresh from the Presidents Cup in nearby South Korea, tied for seventh with leading money winner Kyung-Tae Kim and Japanese veteran Hideto Tanihara.

Bridgestone Open
Chiba
Winner: Michio Matsumura

Back in mid-September, Michio Matsumura, a four-time winner of the Japan Tour, was floundering so badly that he wasn't even among the leading 100 players on the money list. His season had gone so wrong that he had missed seven cuts and finished no better than 30th in his other six starts. Abruptly, Matsumura regained his touch, finished fifth and fourth in his next four tournaments and then carved out a two-stroke victory in the Bridgestone Open.

Much of the credit for the win went to his putter. In his final-round surge from four strokes off the pace, Matsumura needed only 23 putts, at one point running off nine straight one-putts, in fashioning a 67 and his winning, nine-under-par 275.

Mikumu Horikawa, a 22-year-old tour rookie, drew most of the attention the first three days at Sodegaura Country Club. He led Tomohiro Kondo by a shot after his first-round 64, slipped a stroke behind 21-year-old Yuki Inamori (68-66) and Kondo (65-69) with his 71 Friday, and regained the top spot with a 69–204 Saturday. He was one in front of Inamori (71) and two ahead of major winners Shingo Katayama (69), Hideto Tanihara (69) and David Smail (70). With rounds of 69-68-71, Matsumura sat in a five-way tie for seventh place.

As the front-runners struggled Sunday, and after an early bogey, Matsumura jumped into a tie for the lead with his third birdie of the day at the 13th hole. He took charge when he holed from off the green for an eagle at the 16th, then bogeyed the 17th and nailed his final birdie at the last hole for the win. Money leader Kyung-Tae Kim climbed into a four-way tie for second with a closing 66, joining Australian Adam Bland (69), Inamori (72) and Horikawa (73) at 277.

Besides the ¥30 million first-place check, Matsumura earned an invitation to the 2016 Bridgestone Invitational, a World Golf Championship event in America.

Mynavi ABC Championship
Kato, Hyogo
Winner: Kyung-Tae Kim

Talk about dominance. In the course of his previous five starts leading up to his fifth victory of the season in the Mynavi ABC Championship, South Korea's Kyung-Tae Kim won twice, finished in a second-place tie and placed in the top 10 in the other two events. Furthermore, with the season in its final rich stretch, Kim was the only player with more than a single victory and without a missed cut. After a two-year slump that saw him drop to

352nd on the Official World Golf Ranking, the Mynavi ABC win elevated him to 61st place.

The 28-year-old widened his lead in his quest for his second money-winning title in Japan to nearly ¥76 million with nearly a wire-to-wire run at ABC Golf Club in the late October tournament in Kato, Hyogo. His 12-under-par 272 gave him a two-stroke victory over Katsumasa Miyamoto, Daisuke Kataoka and Won-Joon Lee.

Kim's sequence the first three days:

First round: 66 and a one-stroke lead over Dong-Kyu Jang, Hyun-Woo Ryu, Jung-Gon Hwang and Yuki Inamori.

Second round: 69–135 and a two-stroke lead over Kataoka (70-67), Ryu (67-70) and Yoshinori Fujimoto.

Third round: 68–203, tied for the lead with Ryu, who shot 66.

Yuta Ikeda, the distant money list runner-up, was never under the 70s and finished in a 44th place tie, just ahead of No. 3 Satoshi Kodaira, who tied for 46th.

Heiwa PGM Championship
Sohbu, Chiba
Winner: Hideto Tanihara

The hopeful signs were there. Winless for two years, Hideto Tanihara came to the Heiwa PGM Championship off two top-10 finishes and a runner-up showing in the tournament in 2014. The result was his first victory in two years and the 11th of his solid career.

The first round of the tournament at Sohbu Country Club near Tokyo belonged to Ho-Sung Choi with a seven-under-par 63 and Ryutaro Nagano with a 64. Choi held onto the lead Friday with 70–163, but Tanihara moved into the picture, his second straight 67 lifting him into a tie one stroke back with Nagano (64-70) and Satoshi Tomiyama (68-66).

The weekend belonged to the 36-year-old Tanihara. A third-round 66 moved him into a two-stroke lead over Choi (69), Kodai Ichihara (67) and Yoshinori Fujimoto, another past winner without a victory in two years, who matched Tanihara's 66.

Tanihara strengthened his grip on first place with a front-nine 32 Sunday, extending his margin to four shots. He was a bit ragged on the back nine, but his 37–69 gave him an 11-under-par 269 and a two-shot win over the 26-year-old Fujimoto, who was a top-10 finisher for the seventh time. The victory elevated Tanihara into third place on the money list. No. 2 Yuta Ikeda, who tied for sixth, picked up a little ground on runaway leader Kyung-Tae Kim, who played in the World Golf Championship event in Shanghai that week.

Mitsui Sumitomo VISA Taiheiyo Masters
Gotemba, Shizuoka
Winner: Shingo Katayama

The victories don't come as frequently as they did in his younger days, but Shingo Katayama still has the winning touch. Japan's brightest star in the early years of the 21st century picked off victories one at a time in 2013, 2014 and his 29th in the 2015 edition of the venerable Mitsui Sumitomo VISA Taiheiyo Masters in mid-November.

The 42-year-old Katayama got a bit of a break in winning the Taiheiyo Masters for a second time (2008). The leader by a stroke after 54 holes, he was awarded the victory when heavy fog encompassed and lingered over the Taiheiyo Club's Gotemba course Sunday.

He, American ace Bubba Watson and Thailand's Thanyakon Khrongpha dominated the tournament from the start. Watson, needing only 23 putts, opened with 63, Katayama with 64 and Khrongpha with 65. Then, the trio wound up in a tie at 12-under-par 132 Friday with 69, 68 and 67 respectively before Katayama gained that opportune one-shot edge Saturday. He shot a 70 for what turned out to be the winning, 14-under-par 202 total as the 25-year-old Thailand pro, who plays an international schedule and is winless, came up with 71 and Watson, the two-time Masters champion, settled for third place with his 72.

The win moved Katayama, already the second leading player on the all-time Japan Tour money list behind Jumbo Ozaki, into sixth place on the career wins list. Traditionally a stronger player in the latter part of the season, Katayama had shaken off a slow start to the 2015 campaign and had four top-10 finishes in his six starts prior to Gotemba. The ¥22.5 million Taiheiyo Masters purse moved him into fourth place on the current money list. No. 1 Kyung-Tae Kim was not in the field.

Dunlop Phoenix
Miyazaki
Winner: Yusaku Miyazato

Perhaps it would be fair to say that the shoe is now on the other foot in the Miyazato family. For years, Yusaku Miyazato was usually referred to as the older brother of Ai Miyazato as she shone brightly in women's golf in Japan and on the international scene. Ai's star has dimmed a bit the last few seasons, but brother Yusaku's fortunes have blossomed since he first broke the victory ice in the Nippon Series in the final week of the 2013 Japan Tour season after 12 years of trying.

Wins followed in 2014 (Token Homemate Cup) and in November 2015's rich Dunlop Phoenix Open. The latter victory capped a fine season in which the 35-year-old Okinawa native had a runner-up finish, five top-fives and nine top-10s and advanced to second place on the tour's money list behind runaway No. 1 Kyung-Tae Kim.

The Dunlop Phoenix lead bounced around in the visitor-studded field the first two days at Phoenix Country Club before Miyazato seized it in the third round with a 64, the week's best score. Unheralded Yoshitaka Takeya went in front Thursday with a 65, two better than runner-up Miyazato's starting round. Yoshinori Fujimoto and Thailand's Thanyakon Khrongpha, the second-place finisher the previous Sunday in the Taiheiyo Masters, took over the lead the second day with matching 69-66s as Miyazato shot 70–137.

The 64 Saturday gave Miyazato a two-shot margin over Fujimoto, three over Tatsunori Nukaga, but the advantage dwindled early when he bogeyed two of the first four holes the final day. Miyazato was solid the rest of the way, though, three back-nine birdies giving him a two-under-par 69, a 14-under-par 270 and a two-stroke victory over Fujimoto (69) and Hideki Matsuyama (67), the defending champion who was back in Japan from his season in America.

Casio World Open
Geisei, Kochi
Winner: Jung-Gon Hwang

Struggling early in the 2015 Japan Tour season in a morass of missed cuts, young South Korean Jung-Gon Hwang later regained the form, he exhibited when he won as a 19-year-old rookie in 2011 and again the following season. In fact, as Hwang, now 23, teed off in the Casio World Open, the tournament he captured in 2012, he was coming off a once-interrupted run of six finishes of 11th or better. That led to another victory in a breathtaking finish against Japanese idol Ryo Ishikawa at the Casio World's home at Koichi Kuroshio Country Club.

Ishikawa, a PGA Tour regular in America who was playing just his sixth tournament in his native country, seemed well on his way to his second win of the season and 13th overall on the Japan Tour until the closing stretch. The extremely popular 24-year-old had grabbed a four-stroke lead over Hwang (70-67) with 68-65–133 after two rounds, and remained a shot ahead of Hwang (70) and 40-year-old Australian Brendan Jones (68), after slipping to 73 Saturday.

Ishikawa came out blazing Sunday with a front-nine 32, but he misfired with a double bogey at the 12th hole and fell a shot behind the Korean when he bogeyed and Hwang birdied at the 14th. Ishikawa tied things up with a birdie at the 17th and birdied again at the last hole, but it wasn't enough. Although outdriven by 30 yards on the par-five hole, Hwang rifled his second shot 10 feet from the cup and dropped the eagle putt for 66, 15-under-par 273 and the victory

Shingo Katayama, the defending champion and winner of the Taiheiyo Masters two weeks earlier, finished third, four back. His second money title already secure, Kyung-Tae Kim had a rare bad week, finishing tied for 31st, his worst finish since the end of August.

Golf Nippon Series JT Cup
Inagi, Tokyo
Winner: Ryo Ishikawa

Ryo Ishikawa's second victory after returning to Japan from his winless season in America makes one wonder what his record might be had he not decided to embark on an international career on the PGA Tour years earlier. Although he played in only seven tournaments in Japan during the season, he had four top-six showings and finished sixth on the money list.

As he observed after landing his 13th title on the Japan Tour at the season-ending Golf Nippon Series JT Cup, "When I play in America, I feel like I'm all alone. However, I can think back on this wonderful view here. I'm extremely happy."

Ishikawa's third-round 63 at Tokyo Yomiuri Country Club set the stage for the victory that complemented his September win in the ANA Open and made him the only player besides Kyung-Tae Kim, the clear-cut No. 1 on the money list, with more than a single triumph all season. Kim had five.

Veteran star Shingo Katayama, with his 29th victory (Taiheiyo Masters) in his pocket, went after No. 30 with an opening 64, but a following 74 blighted his hopes. Ishikawa, with a pair of 68s shared first place with Koumei Oda and Jung-Gon Hwang, who had nipped him for the Casio Open title the previous Sunday. Both had 66-70 rounds.

The 24-year-old Ishikawa wasn't about to let this one get away. The seven-under-par 63 boosted him into a three-stroke lead over Oda (66) and, with six birdies and three bogeys Sunday, he put up a 67 for the winning 266. He finished five strokes in front of runners-up Oda (69) and Yoshinori Fujimoto, who closed with a 65 and placed fourth on the money list behind Kim, Yusaku Miyazato and Yuta Ikeda.

10. Australasian Tour

For the inaugural presentation of the PGA of Australia's Greg Norman Medal, the judging panel, led by the former world No. 1 after whom the award was named, could not have had an easier task. Jason Day was the unanimous winner as the best performing touring professional after the Queenslander's momentous year. "Jason has stood out head and shoulders above all other players, both male and female," Norman said, "and he's a great representative of Australian golf."

Day briefly matched Norman's feat in being ranked the world's best player and ended the year in the No. 2 spot behind only Jordan Spieth. He won five times, including the Farmers Insurance Open, the Canadian Open and two FedEx Playoff events, the Barclays and the BMW Championship. At the U.S. Open he defied a recurrent bout of vertigo — at one point collapsing on a fairway during the second round — to share the lead after 54 holes and finished tied for ninth with a courageous performance that won many admirers.

Only a few weeks later he was back on top form at St. Andrews and only missed out on the playoff won by Zach Johnson when his putt on the final green stopped agonizingly inches short of the hole. "I've been working very hard to accomplish my first major," he said through his disappointment. "I really want that shot at immortality. It'll come soon."

It came immediately at the PGA Championship as Day defeated Spieth by three strokes at Whistling Straits in a virtuoso performance. At the age of 27 he had achieved his dream, and there was an emotional embrace on the 18th green with his caddie Colin Swatton, his coach and mentor since Day was a troubled 12-year-old finding sanctuary in golf from a life that threatened to go off the rails even at so early an age.

Following the birth of his daughter Lucy in November, Day was unable to travel to the Gold Coast to receive the award in person, but his mother Dening did the honors and he said via video link: "It's an honor and a privilege to win the Greg Norman Medal, it caps off an amazing year. I'd like to thank the PGA of Australia for launching this medal with Greg Norman and their support over the past 10 years."

Day also received Australia's top sporting honor, the Don Medal, named after Don Bradman, as Adam Scott had in 2013. Scott was also on the short list for the 2015 Norman Medal, along with Australian Open champion Matt Jones, Marc Leishman, Steven Bowditch, Karrie Webb, Minjee Lee and Rebecca Artis.

Leishman experienced an emotional year after he flew home from the Masters to be with his wife Audrey, who was close to death after suffering from toxic shock syndrome. Leishman was contemplating life as a single father to his two boys before Audrey recovered sufficiently for him to return to the tour. At St. Andrews, a third round of 64 and a closing effort of 66 saw the Australian into the playoff in which he always trailed Johnson and Louis Oosthuizen.

A new, but hard-earned, perspective on life helped him deal with the disappointment. Yet he subsequently struggled with his game until a brilliant week at the Nedbank Golf Challenge at Sun City at the end of the year, which he won by six strokes. "I'm pretty happy to have this year over, to be honest," he admitted. "Audrey got very sick and I lost an uncle who I was very close to. This tops off what was otherwise not a great year. Three weeks ago we moved into a new house, so this will help pay for that."

Another notable performance in the majors came from Cam Smith, who tied for fourth place with Scott at the U.S. Open at Chambers Bay. On the PGA Tour, Bowditch won for the second time at the Byron Nelson Classic, and New Zealander Danny Lee, once the youngest-ever winner on the European Tour and still only 24, achieved his first win in America at the Greenbrier Classic and finished ninth in the FedExCup.

On the domestic scene, Matthew Millar was voted the PGA Tour of Australasia Player of the Year at the Norman Medal awards. Millar had a highly consistent season which included his first win, at the New Zealand PGA Championship, after 16 years on the circuit. Nathan Holman claimed the Order of Merit prize after winning his maiden title at the Australian PGA in a playoff at Royal Pines. Jones, a former Houston Open winner, won for the first time in Australia, appropriately at his home club of The Australian in Sydney, by holding off Scott and defending champion Spieth.

Peter Senior achieved the incredible feat of winning the UNIQLO Masters at the age of 56, wrapping up a second sweep of the Triple Crown events, but this time all in his 50s. He won the PGA in 2010 and the Open two years later, while he had previously won the Masters twice at Huntingdale in 1991 and 1995. At the other end of the age spectrum, 20-year-old Ben Eccles won the NSW Open as an amateur and Jarryd Felton, also 20, won the NSW PGA in his fifth start as a professional.

The most romantic tale of the year came right at the start, however, as engaged couple Richard Green and Marianne Skarpnord won twin Victoria Opens on the same day at Thirteenth Beach Golf Links.

Oates Victorian Open
Barwon Heads, Victoria
Winner: Richard Green

Richard Green rounded off the perfect week by beating Nick Cullen at the second extra hole to win the Oates Victorian Open. Moments before, as Green was on the practice range preparing for a playoff, his fiancée Marianne Skarpnord won the women's version of the tournament that is played alongside the men's event. The couple had gotten engaged the previous week and on the Monday had moved into their new home at the Thirteenth Beach Golf Links, venue for the Vic Open. As if that was not all, in the pro-am on Wednesday Green holed in one for an albatross at the 310-yard 15th hole after his drive bounded through a greenside bunker and ricocheted onto the green.

In the tournament proper, Green shared the first-round lead with a 66 but was three behind the leader after further rounds of 72 and 67. But the 43-year-old left-hander closed with another 67, including a birdie at the last, to post a total of 272, 16 under par, which Australian Masters champion Cullen equaled with his own birdie at the 18th for a 69. Amateurs Ben Eccles and Ryan Ruffels shared third place with Scott Arnold, two shots behind.

It was a second win in Australia for Green, who has also won three times on the European Tour. "It's been a long time coming. I have wanted to come back to win and support the tournament and finally, after 23 years of trying, I have got it finally," said Green.

Mercedes-Benz Truck & Bus Victorian PGA Championship
Oakleigh South, Victoria
Winner: Aaron Townsend

A holed bunker shot at the 18th green helped Aaron Townsend win the Mercedes-Benz Truck & Bus Victorian PGA Championship at Huntingdale. Townsend claimed his third title by one stroke over Scott Strange after coming from four shots adrift with a closing 66. The 33-year-old had previously won his state Open and PGA titles in New South Wales, but this was a first visit to the winner's circle for six years.

New Zealand's Ryan Fox had led after the second and third rounds and claimed the team title in the 54-hole pro-am event but slipped to a closing 73 to tie for fifth place. Townsend, after scores of 67, 73 and 69, opened with six birdies in the first 10 holes before a bogey at the 16th. But his grandstand finish on a course that was once the traditional home of the Australian Masters left him on a 13-under-par total of 275. Strange matched Townsend's birdie at the last to finish one back, having included an eagle at the 10th hole in a closing 67. Kris Mueck and Ryan Haller shared third place a shot further back.

"I played great today, I couldn't have asked for a better start," said Townsend. "I've always liked the golf course, but now I love the golf course, I've just enjoyed every round here this week. It's nice to get a win so early in the season, hopefully I can build on it and maybe play better in some events coming up."

Coca-Cola Queensland PGA Championship
Toowoomba, Queensland
Winner: Ryan Fox

A week after failing to convert a 54-hole lead into victory at the Victorian PGA, Ryan Fox produced a stunning finish to steal the Coca-Cola Queensland PGA Championship at City Golf Club in Toowoomba. Fox made back-to-back eagles at the par-four 16th and par-five 17th holes to win by one over long-time leader Matthew Millar and Cameron Smith.

Fox, a 28-year-old New Zealander who is the son of former All Black rugby legend Grant, had been the runner-up at Toowoomba the previous year before securing his maiden victory at the Western Australia Open at the start of the Australian summer of 2014-15. A closing 62, after scores of 72, 64 and 65, included four birdies and no dropped shots before his dramatic finale. At the 16th he drove the green and converted from eight feet for a two, while two big blows at the 17th set up a more conventional eagle. Smith closed with a 63, making three birdies in the last four holes, while Millar came up just short with a 65.

"To do what I did on 16 and 17, it was a bit surreal," Fox said. "The 16th is certainly not one, standing on the tee, that you think you are going to hit on the green. But I just figured I needed to do something. I aimed at the green and hit driver as hard as I could. I thought maybe at best I would get it 10 meters short of the green, but a little bit of adrenaline helped."

Holden New Zealand PGA Championship
Auckland, New Zealand
Winner: Matthew Millar

"Why has it taken me so long? I wish I had the answer to that." Better why than why not? After 16 years as a professional, Matthew Millar, a 38-year-old from Canberra, won for the first time on the Australasian Tour at the Holden New Zealand PGA Championship. The Australian's long-awaited win had been getting closer after three top-10 finishes in his previous three starts, including a runner-up finish to New Zealander Ryan Fox at the Queensland PGA two weeks earlier. "I am so relieved, gee, it was tough out there today," said Millar. "Remuera certainly showed its teeth. The wind was strong, blowing in different directions."

Millar led by two strokes after 54 holes and held on with a closing 71 in the tricky conditions in Auckland to win by three shots. With earlier rounds of 68, 67 and 64, he finished on an 18-under-par total of 270. Out in one under par, Millar twice bogeyed on the back nine but birdied the very next hole on each occasion. Kristopher Mueck, the leader for the first two days, got within one stroke at the turn before following into a tie for second with Geoff Drakeford and Josh Geary, who claimed the inaugural Sir Bob Charles Cup for the leading home player. Drakeford's dramatic finish included an eagle, four birdies, a bogey and a double bogey in the last seven holes. He drove to four feet at the 387-yard 12th for the eagle but lost a ball up a tree at the 14th.

BMW New Zealand Open
Arrowtown, New Zealand
Winner: Jordan Zunic

In August 2013 Jordan Zunic was a passenger in a car accident in America that left him with a triple-fracture of his left elbow. He lost a significant amount of blood and was hospitalized for a week and bed-ridden for months. "When I started playing again, I just felt so grateful to be breathing and out there playing golf. I could have easily died, and that actually helped me play better," said the 23-year-old from New South Wales. Zunic turned professional at the start of 2015 despite not gaining his card on the Australasian Tour and was only playing in the BMW New Zealand Open because he Monday-qualified for the Holden NZ PGA the previous week and finished tied for eighth.

After an opening three-under 68 at Millbrook, Zunic returned three straight 66s at The Hills for a 21-under-par total of 266 and a one-stroke victory over David Bransdon. His 41-year-old opponent had a remarkable eight birdies in his last 10 holes for a closing 64, though a par at the 12th and, crucially, a bogey at the last would cost him dearly. Zunic had four birdies in a row from the 12th but bogeyed the 16th, so needed a birdie at the last to win. His nine-iron approach hit the flagstick and finished two feet away.

"I picked my target, and when I hit it, it felt perfect," he said. "I'm still in disbelief. I'm trying to pinch myself to say that this happened. I can't wait to start the journey. This is only the beginning." Zunic also won the pro-am team event with Hills member Maryanne Marlow.

Isuzu Queensland Open
Brisbane, Queensland
Winner: David Bransdon

Five months after finishing runner-up at the New Zealand Open, David Bransdon went one better at the Isuzu Queensland Open for his third career victory. The 41-year-old defeated Rohan Blizard in a three-hole playoff after holing a lengthy birdie putt at the 18th hole with Blizard missing from closer range to extend the action.

Bransdon recorded scores of 69, 71, 67 and 69 for a 12-under-par total of 276. He led by two over Blizard overnight but parred the first 11 holes before birdieing three of the next four holes. Blizard's 67 was built around back-to-back eagles at the end of the front nine. At the par-five eighth he hit a three wood to eight feet and made the putt, while at the next he holed out with a full lob wedge shot. "I kind of had the feeling it was going to be my day after those two eagles," he said. He went on to birdie the 18th to tie Bransdon but could not repeat the birdie in the playoff. Mark Brown finished third, four behind, with amateur Jake McLeod among those in fourth.

"I am shaking like a leaf, it's unbelievable. It's been a couple of years since my last win, but I am pretty proud of the way I played today and the way I hung in there," Bransdon said. "I was trying to stay patient because that's what's my new mantra, stay patient, because it's not exactly been my forte."

South Pacific Open Championship
Winner: James Nitties

What had been a tight contest between James Nitties and Matthew Millar for the South Pacific Open Championship suddenly became a convincing win for Nitties by six strokes over the closing holes. It was a second victory for the 32-year-old and came after a poor season on the Web.com Tour in America. He led after the second and third rounds, but a bogey-birdie exchange over the first three holes brought Millar level. Nitties went ahead again at the sixth only for Millar to birdie the 11th and 12th holes to go ahead himself.

Nitties birdied the 14th, but then a double bogey from Millar changed everything. Having driven through the green, Millar attempted to play over a palm tree but the ball never emerged. "I've had it twice now on that hole," he said. Millar dropped five strokes on the last four holes as Nitties birdied the 16th. His scores of 65, 67, 67 and 69 gave Nitties a 16-under-par total of 268.

"It was a great tussle between me and Matty," Nitties said. "He got a really bad break on the 15th hole when his ball got caught up a tree. You never want to see that, but I was able to play well the last couple of holes and get the victory, so I am very happy. I have to thank my coach, Jason Laws. I came home from playing really badly in the U.S. and got some great stuff to work on right before this tournament."

Fiji International
Winner: Matt Kuchar

See Asia/Japan Tours chapter.

TX Civil & Logistics Western Australian PGA Championship
Kalgoorlie, Western Australia
Winner: Brett Rumford

After winning in successive weeks in South Korea and China in 2013 for his fourth and fifth European Tour victories, Brett Rumford suffered a loss of form in 2014 and two health scares in 2015. In March, during the Tshwane Open in South Africa, the Western Australian had surgery to remove over 10 inches of his small intestine to relieve a blockage caused by eating an apple. He did not touch a club for 11 weeks as he recovered, while in September he suffered from shingles and was off the game for another six weeks.

Yet at the TX Civil & Logistics Western Australian PGA Championship Rumford completed a two-stroke victory over Daniel Fox, with Ed Stedman and Daniel Nisbet a further stroke behind. After three rounds of 67 at Kalgoorlie which gave him a four-stroke lead, Rumford closed with a 71 for a 16-under-par total of 272. Though Fox closed with a 66 and Stedman a 65, Rumford was always ahead on the final day. It was the 38-year-old's second win on the PGA Tour of Australasia, the first having come at the ANZ Players as an amateur in 1999.

"What I have been through has been pretty horrendous all year," Rumford said. "Seven weeks ago I had shingles, so I have had very large periods of the year where I haven't picked up a golf club. Certainly the preparation hasn't been anywhere near where what I would have expected to go out and win a championship. I have just been preaching patience all week."

Nexus Risk TSA Group Western Australian Open
Fremantle, Western Australia
Winner: Daniel Fox

For the second week running an amateur was leading on day one. While Min Woo Lee, Minjee Lee's younger brother, slipped out of contention at the WA PGA, Chris Luck kept his challenge going late into the last day at Royal Fremantle. Six birdies in nine holes from the fourth put Luck in command before he fell to earth with four bogeys in the last five holes.

Instead, another local player, albeit at a different stage of his career, claimed the Nexus Risk TSA Group Western Australian Open. Daniel Fox, a 39-year-old journeyman, won his maiden title by three strokes over Luck after both men closed with 70s. Luck comfortably took second place, three ahead of the next contenders.

Fox, with rounds of 70, 68 and 69, had led by one overnight, but two early bogeys dropped him out of the lead. He got a shot back at the ninth and then birdied the 11th and 12th holes. He recovered from a bogey at 14 with a birdie at 15 and finished in style by holing a 25-footer at the last.

"Emotions are everywhere at the minute, very pleased, of course, but it was a tough day," Fox said. "It hit me in a rush late in the round that the scoreboard had changed dramatically. I thought I was a couple behind, then all of a sudden I was in front."

New South Wales Open
Sydney, New South Wales
Winner: Ben Eccles

Ben Eccles became the third amateur in a row to be a first-round leader on the PGA Tour of Australasia, but the 20-year-old British-born golfer, now based at the Victorian Institute of Golf, stayed in the lead every day to win the New South Wales Open at Stonecutters Ridge. He became the first amateur to win on tour since Jake Higginbottom and Oliver Goss both achieved the feat in 2012.

After equaling the course record of 64 at the Greg Norman-designed layout on the opening day, as did Darren Beck and Hayden Beard, Eccles added a 67 on Saturday morning after much of Friday's play was wiped out by a storm. He shared the halfway lead with Aaron Wilkin and Rohan Blizard, but a third-round 66 put him four ahead.

A closing 72, for a 19-under-par total of 269, was enough to give Eccles a three-shot victory over Blizard and Matthew Millar. Eccles had a couple of birdies going out and bogeys at the back-to-back par-threes, the 16th and 17th holes, proved no hindrance. "I'm absolutely over the moon," Eccles said. "I've never led from start to finish — it's a pretty amazing feeling to be honest."

Eccles, who was third at the Vic Open earlier in the year, added: "I'm 21 in two weeks. It's a nice early birthday present." But this day was also about his mother. "It's her birthday today. I'm actually flying straight home to celebrate."

UNIQLO Masters
South Oakleigh, Victoria
Winner: Peter Senior

Peter Senior was already one of the few players to claim the Triple Crown of Australian golf but has now lived up to his name by repeating the feat as a golfing senior. Senior won the 2010 Australian PGA Championship aged 51, the Australian Open two years later as a 53-year-old, and at the age of 56 won the UNIQLO Masters at Huntingdale. He collected a third gold jacket, having formerly won the Australian Masters in 1991 and 1995.

Two off the lead going into the final round, Senior closed with a 68 to win by two strokes over Andrew Evans, John Senden and American amateur Bryson DeChambeau. Adam Scott was fifth, while overnight leader Matthew Millar tied for sixth place after a 75. Senior had earlier rounds of 70, 70 and 68 to finish on an eight-under-par total of 276.

Out in two under par, birdies at the 10th and 13th holes gave Senior a three-shot lead. But Evans birdied the 15th and 16th holes and Senior bogeyed the 17th before saving par from a bunker at the last. He then had to wait while Evans bogeyed the last two holes.

"To win this tournament, the Aussie Open a few years ago and the PGA a couple of years before that, all of them over 50 years of age, I think that's a big thing for me," Senior said. "Nearly every hole on the back nine everyone was cheering me, even my poor shots. It was just great. I have not had that sort of following for a very, very long time."

Emirates Australian Open
Sydney, New South Wales
Winner: Matt Jones

Playing on his home course of The Australian was an advantage, but Matt Jones still had to win the hard way at the 100th Emirates Australian Open. He won by just one stroke over Adam Scott and defending champion, and world No. 1, Jordan Spieth.

Jones began the last day three ahead of Spieth, and while a bogey-double bogey start kept him two ahead of the American, the field concertinaed with Rod Pampling setting a new course record of 61 to finish at six under par. Pampling bogeyed the first but was out in 31 and came home in 30 after a birdie-eagle finish capped by holing a monster putt on the final green.

Scott, who at two over after 36 holes was again struggling to adapt to a short putter, sprung into contention by adding a 65 to his Saturday 68 to post seven under. Jones' struggles continued with a triple-bogey-seven at the ninth when his second shot found the water. But he holed a bunker shot for a par at the 12th and birdied the 14th and 16th holes to keep his nose in front. Rounds of 67, 68, 68 and 72 left him at 276, eight under par. Spieth had a 20-footer for eagle at the last but had to settle for a birdie and a 71.

Jones, who qualified for the 2016 Open at Royal Troon along with Pampling and Nick Cullen, is a member at The Australian and idolized Greg Norman while growing up. "To have my name on this trophy with Nicklaus,

Newton, Norman, all those guys, it's a dream come true for me," said the 35-year-old.

Australian PGA Championship
Gold Coast, Queensland
Winner: Nathan Holman

With the Australian PGA Championship part of the 2016 European Tour, Nathan Holman received a double bonus for claiming his maiden professional title at RACV Royal Pines on the Gold Coast. After winning a three-way playoff at the first extra hole, the 24-year-old received A$315,000 to secure the PGA Tour of Australasia Order of Merit and earned an invitation to the 2016 Open at Royal Troon. He also gained membership of the European Tour until the end of the 2017 season.

I didn't realize what was on the line really, which is probably a good thing to be honest," Holman said. "To be a full member of the European Tour is huge. I did think I'd get to those events in the future, but didn't think it was going to be this quickly. For a young Australian guy to be able to go and play those events, play British Opens, it's stuff you dream of playing golf when you're a kid, to get into those events, just to play them. It's going to be an amazing feeling and to do it off the back of a victory."

Holman started the final round two strokes off the lead and fell further behind with a double bogey at the first hole. But with the baked Graham Marsh-redesigned layout playing extremely hard all week, everyone struggled. Of the overnight leaders, Zander Lombard had three bogeys in the first four holes, Dylan Frittelli had three bogeys and a double in the first seven, and American Harold Varner had only one birdie in a 75. Frittelli also had a 75, but fellow South African Lombard missed the playoff by a stroke with a 76.

Holman parred seven holes in a row before the first of three birdies at the ninth. Further gains came at the 12th and 15th, and he took a two-shot lead to the 17th before bogeying the last two. Having opening with a 77, 10 shots off the lead, Holman had fought back with rounds of 68, 70 and 73 to post the clubhouse lead at even-par 288. Frittelli and Varner matched him, the American missing chances for birdie at the last two.

In the playoff at the 18th, both Frittelli and Varner missed the fairway on the left and could not reach the green. Bogeys followed, while Holman two-putted for his par.

New South Wales PGA Championship
Cattai, New South Wales
Winner: Jarryd Felton

Jarryd Felton belied his youth and inexperience to claim a maiden victory at the New South Wales PGA Championship. The 20-year-old from Western Australian was playing in only his fifth tournament as a professional and had to pre-qualify for the event. An opening 65 gave him a share of the first-round lead before he slumped to a 74 the following day. But twin rounds of 68 gave Felton a 13-under-par total of 275 on the Bungool course at Riverside Oaks and a two-stroke victory. Five players shared runner-up honors — James Nitties, Anthony Summers, Matthew Millar, Geoff Drakeford and Rhein Gibson — but none could better the winner's final-round score. Gibson closed with a 72 after sharing the 54-hole lead with Lucas Herbert, who finished with a 76 to drop into a tie for 13th place.

Felton was two behind starting the final day and followed a birdie at the first with two more at the fifth and ninth holes. The key to his impressive performance was not dropping a stroke all day, and when he holed from 20 feet for a birdie at the 17th, he went two ahead. Not that he knew at the time.

"Walking down the last I didn't really know what the situation was, but I saw the leaderboard and it was quite overwhelming," Felton said. "I started with a birdie and normally I would get a little ahead of myself. But it was definitely too early to think about winning, and I just kept going along making some birdies and some nice par saves."

11. African Sunshine Tour

When Louis Oosthuizen played his first practice round ahead of the 2015 Open Championship at St. Andrews he experienced a tingle of excitement as memories came flooding back from his victory five years earlier. Little did he know a week later, on that extra Monday afternoon, he would again be battling for the Claret Jug, though in very different circumstances to his processional triumph of 2010. This time he had to hole a string of putts, including for a birdie at the Home hole, to make it into a playoff. When he could not repeat the feat at the end of the four-hole playoff, he was one short of new champion Zach Johnson and had to settle for second place alongside Marc Leishman.

"I was really motivated to win this Championship," Oosthuizen said. "It's never nice to lose a playoff, but I love this place. I can't wait to come back again." Oosthuizen is not the first, nor will he be the last, to fall in love with the Home of Golf. He will have to wait another five or six years to regain his tag as a St. Andrews Open Champion, but it was a mighty fine "defense."

Just the previous month Oosthuizen had missed out on a playoff at the U.S. Open when he finished one stroke shy of Jordan Spieth at Chambers Bay. Having opened with a 77, he improved steadily over the week on the controversial new course near Seattle, closing with a round of 67. His twin runner-up finishes at the two Opens, a feat also achieved by Rickie Fowler in 2014, proved the highlight of his season and yet were tinged with the disappointment of being so close and yet so far.

Branden Grace was South Africa's other main contender at the majors in 2015. He shared the lead with a round to play at Chambers Bay and finished tied for fourth place just two behind Spieth after an agonizing double bogey at the 16th hole. Two months later Grace finished third at the PGA Championship at Whistling Straits, the best of the rest as Spieth lost out on his duel with Australian Jason Day.

Grace won twice in 2016, at the Dimension Data Pro-Am at home and at the Qatar Masters on the European Tour, in whose Race to Dubai he finished third behind Rory McIlroy and Danny Willett. He produced fine, consistent golf all year. Oosthuizen finished sixth on the Race to Dubai and Jaco Van Zyl a career best 21st. In America, Oosthuizen's 30th was the best finish of any South African in the FedExCup.

Dean Burmester dominated the season on the Sunshine Tour with four victories. Everything seemed to click in his life both on and off the course. "It's been a special year," he said. "I got married last November, settled down with the wife, and we had our first child." He won at the Zimbabwe Open on the Royal Harare course where he spent much of his youth playing and where his mother has been club champion. He followed up with victories at the Lombard Insurance Classic, the Sun Windmill Challenge and the Vodacom Origins of Golf event at Koro Creek Bushveld.

Burmester was only fourth on the Order of Merit at the end of the year, behind George Coetzee, Charl Schwartzel and Jacques Blaauw. Coetzee won two co-sanctioned tournaments, including the Tshwane Open at his home course of Pretoria Country Club where he won the first golf tournament he entered as a 10-year-old. His other win came in the inaugural AfrAsia Bank Mauritius Open, an event tri-sanctioned with the Asian Tour as well as the European Tour.

Other two-time winners included Jean Hugo and Vaughn Groenewald, who had waited nine years for his third win and added a fourth only a few months later. Schwartzel won the Alfred Dunhill Championship at Leopard Creek for the fourth time, his first win since claiming the title two years ago and after struggling with his form in-between times.

Burmester did hold pole position in the Race to the 2016 Investec Cup at the turn of the year, an event won in 2015 by Jaco Ahlers which gave him the biggest prize from the sponsor's bonus pool. Rookie of the year honors went to Rourke van der Spuy after his win at the Sun Fish River Sun Challenge, while Brandon Stone won the Lion of Africa Cape Town Open just days after securing his card on the European Tour by finishing 14th on the Challenge Tour. In America Dawie van der Walt's successful season on the Web.com Tour brought two wins, second place on the money list and a card for the PGA Tour in 2016.

After 32 years as an unofficial event and three as a co-sanctioned event with the European Tour, the Nedbank Golf Challenge at Sun City, often referred to as "Africa's major" and won by Leishman in 2015, will undergo another change in 2016. It will expand to a 72-player field, move to early November and feature as part of the European Tour's Final Series.

South African Open Championship
Gauteng, Johannesburg, South Africa
Winner: Andy Sullivan

Having won a trip into space for a hole-in-one during the 2014 season, Andy Sullivan was "over the moon" in the delighted sense when his first event of 2015, the South African Open Championship, became his maiden professional victory. Sullivan beat home favorite Charl Schwartzel in a playoff with a super approach from the left rough on the 18th hole. Sullivan put his approach to 12 feet and then saw Schwartzel, who had laid up after pushing his drive well right, pitch to two feet, but still holed the putt for the victory. The 27-year-old became only the second English winner of the 104-year-old tournament after Tommy Horton in 1970.

A member of the winning Great Britain and Ireland Walker Cup team in 2011, Sullivan was in his third full year on tour and shared the first-round lead with Jbe' Kruger after a 66 and then went one ahead of Schwartzel at eight under at halfway. He started the third round with four straight bogeys, while Schwartzel had four consecutive birdies. Sullivan was out in 40 but rallied for a 74, though he still trailed Schwartzel by seven strokes. The South African had a 66 and was five ahead of David Drysdale and former U.S. Amateur champion Matthew Fitzpatrick.

Schwartzel was the third-round leader in the previous South African Open but had collapsed and history would repeat itself. Out in even par, he holed a long par putt at the 10th, then birdied the 12th and 13th holes to be four ahead with five to play. A plugged lie in a bunker at the 14th meant a bogey, but he was still three ahead when Sullivan returned a 67 that included a chip-in eagle at the 12th. His long putt at the 18th was just short and he stood at 11 under par. Schwartzel was wayward at the 16th and then three-putted for a double-bogey-six, and missed the 17th green by 40 yards, meaning another dropped shot. He did well to par the last, but Sullivan's birdie at the 18th in the playoff sunk his hopes of a first South African Open title.

"After Saturday I didn't think I stood much of a chance with Charl getting ahead that far," Sullivan said. "I was delighted just to hit the green in the playoff and have a chance to win, and I'm just glad I took it."

Dimension Data Pro-Am
George, South Africa
Winner: Branden Grace

Branden Grace claimed a third victory in as many months with his win at the Dimension Data Pro-Am at Fancourt, the resort the 26-year-old South African represents and where he has a base. A windy final day on the Montagu course proved a stern test, but Grace compiled a 70, after earlier scores of 71, 68 and 69, for an 11-under-par total of 278 and a two-stroke victory over Keith Horne. It was a fifth Sunshine Tour victory for Grace and the ninth of his career, including the Alfred Dunhill Championship and the Qatar Masters most recently.

Starting the day two behind Darren Fichardt, Grace opened with a double bogey and looked an unlikely winner. But he rallied with birdies at the sixth and ninth holes and, after a bogey at the 11th, closed with three more birdies at the 12th, 14th and 16th. Fichardt had also opened with a double bogey but only fell out of the lead with a back nine that included bogeys at the 10th and 14th holes and another double bogey at the 16th. He finished tied for third place, while Horne closed with a 69 to take second place on his own.

"The wind really blew out there today, sometimes it was up to three clubs," Grace said. "I knew it was going to be a grind and you needed to keep calm. I love it down here. Fancourt has been a great supporter of myself and I think it's one of the best resorts in the world. It really helped being a local, because you know where to hit the ball."

Joburg Open
Johannesburg, South Africa
Winner: Andy Sullivan

After returning to the same city where he won little more than a month earlier, Andy Sullivan repeated the feat by claiming the Joburg Open at Royal Johannesburg and Kensington. At the start of the year Sullivan had won the South African Open at Glendower for his first career victory and now has two victories in events co-sanctioned by the Sunshine and European Tours. While he needed a playoff for the first victory, this time Sullivan won by two strokes over Wallie Coetsee, David Howell, Anthony Wall, Jaco Van Zyl and Kevin Phelan.

Sullivan started the last day three behind overnight leader Coetsee and set a stunning pace with five birdies in an outward 32. Only Howell, who was out in 33, could keep up, and Sullivan found the water at the 11th to drop one behind. However, while Howell found water at the 14th and came home in one over, and Wall splashed into trouble at the 15th, Sullivan not only kept his composure but thoroughly enjoyed himself over the closing holes. Birdies at the 15th and 18th gave the 28-year-old the cushion he needed, although he rated his bogey putt from 25 feet at the 11th as the most important. "That putt was crucial in the context of the win," he said.

Sullivan started the week as the highest ranked player in the field and jumped from 73rd to 58th with his victory. Rounds of 71, 65, 68 and 66 gave him a 17-under-par total of 270. Phelan and Van Zyl also closed with 66s, while Wall had a 68, Howell a 69 and Coetsee a 71. A three-putt bogey at the second disrupted Coetsee's rhythm, but he birdied the last to join the tie for second place.

"It's unbelievable," Sullivan said. "I never imagined it would happen again so quickly. Coming down the stretch me and my caddie were loving life again and enjoying it. It seems to be a theme, enjoying my golf and getting the right results at the moment. I've been working hard but enjoying myself along the way. It just seems to be that every time I get into contention down that stretch lately — I wish I could bottle up the emotions I go through. It's like a drug. And having done it once in the SA Open, I was maybe even more relaxed down the stretch today."

In addition, Sullivan earned a place in the Open Championship at St. Andrews, along with Howell and Wall due to their superior world rankings.

Africa Open
East London, Eastern Cape, South Africa
Winner: Trevor Fisher, Jr.

Perseverance paid off for England's Matt Ford when he earned his European Tour card at his 10th attempt at the qualifying school late in 2014. It meant his winter plan to work as a postman was replaced with a chance to play golf at a higher level than ever before. Rounds of 67 and 68 had the 36-year-old sharing the first-round lead at the Africa Open and then taking a one-stroke advantage into the weekend at East London. A maiden victory was within his grasp but for a tour de force from Trevor Fisher, Jr., whose 17-under-par weekend propelled the South African to a five-stroke victory.

Fisher returned scores of 63 and 64 to finish on a 24-under-par total of 264, while Ford's 69 and 67 left him comfortably in second place, three ahead of Eduardo de la Riva, Jorge Campillo and Morten Orum Madsen. Fisher did most of his damage on the back nine, where he did not drop a shot all week, with inward halves of 30 on Saturday and 31 on Sunday.

Two ahead of Ford at the start of the final round, the pair both birdied the first, third, sixth and seventh holes. But Fisher had dropped a shot at the fifth, so his lead was down to one. That all changed around the turn.

At the ninth Ford bogeyed while Fisher's fine four-iron shot set up a birdie. With another birdie at the 10th, Fisher was four ahead, and he finished with three birdies in the last four holes.

"He is a little British bulldog. He sank putts and I thought 'jeez, I'm not going to get away from this guy!'" Fisher said of Ford. "It is always nerve-racking leading, not to think about the result, but it's quite hard and I think I did a good job today. I was nervous the last few holes, I think that is natural."

It was Fisher's eighth Sunshine Tour victory but his first on the European Tour, where he claimed his card after seven failed attempts at the qualifying school. "I've tried so hard to get that European Tour card, for so many years — obviously it's a massive step for my career because that's where all South African golfers want to be."

Tshwane Open
Waterkloof, South Africa
Winner: George Coetzee

On his 10th birthday George Coetzee won the first golf tournament he ever played in. It came at Pretoria Country Club, where he has been a member ever since he started to play the game. More victories on home turf followed, but none meant more to the 28-year-old South African than winning the Tshwane Open, his sixth Sunshine Tour victory and a second on the European Tour following his win at the Joburg Open in 2014.

"I've won so many times on this course, and now I've won in the biggest tournament that will ever be played here, so I'm really pleased about that," Coetzee said. "To win at your own club in front of all your friends and family — the crowds were amazing, I could just feel the momentum building. It's a great experience and a very special day for me."

Coetzee was one of six players who shared the 54-hole lead but the only one to contend on the final day. Yet this was not a lap of honor for the home favorite as Jacques Blaauw equaled the course record with a nine-under-par 61 to set the clubhouse target at 13 under par. Blaauw, whose round included six birdies in seven holes around the turn, finished two hours before the leaders and could only await a possible playoff.

Coetzee started with five pars and then almost drove the sixth green, getting up and down for a birdie. Three more followed in a row from the eighth, which tied him with Blaauw. His fifth birdie of the day did not come until the short par-four 17th. His drive finished right of the green, but a delicate chip between two bunkers finished five feet away and he holed the putt to go one ahead.

"I think I've got this course down after 18 years and knowing when to be aggressive and when not to," Coetzee said. "I was waiting for the 17th. I threw one club championship away here by playing conservative on 17, so today it was quite an easy decision to hit driver. I knew if my drive went right, I'd have a way to the flag through the bunkers."

Coetzee finished with a 65, after scores of 67, 66 and 68, for a 14-under-par total of 266. He had only one bogey in his last 51 holes. Of his co-leaders overnight, Craig Lee closed with a 70 to be third with Dean Burmester and Tjaart van der Walt, five behind, while Adrian Otegui had a 71, David Horsey a 73, Trevor Fisher, Jr. a 75 and Wallie Coetsee a 76.

Investec Cup
Sun City, South Africa
Winner: Jaco Ahlers

Jaco Ahlers collected the biggest win of his career when victory at the Investec Cup also brought him the top spot on the Chase to the Investec Cup bonus pool. The 32-year-old South African won R163,400 for beating Jaco Van Zyl at the third extra hole of a playoff and then added R3.5 million at the culmination of the summer season on the Sunshine Tour. It was a summer that started well for Ahlers as he won a four-hole playoff to claim the Lion of Africa Cape Town Open, a second career victory that spurred him on to add a third title four months later.

Ahlers opened with rounds of 72 and 73 on the Millvale course and then added scores of 68 and 66 at Lost City to close on a nine-under-par total of 279. Van Zyl also finished with a 66 as the pair came from four behind overnight leader George Coetzee, who tied for third place with Justin Harding after a double bogey at the 17th hole.

At the par-five 18th in the playoff, Van Zyl found the water off the tee on the second hole but escaped with a par to stay alive, but could not repeat the trick again when he again found water on the third extra hole. "That win in Cape Town gave me a lot of confidence," said Ahlers. "I've just bought a new house in George and this means I'll be able to pay cash for it. But I'm going to rest for two weeks and let it all sink in."

Golden Pilsener Zimbabwe Open
Harare, Zimbabwe
Winner: Dean Burmester

Dean Burmester grew up playing Royal Harare, but if he needs any more local knowledge, he can always call on his mother, who holds the women's course record. So it was a fitting place for the 25-year-old to claim the biggest of his three Sunshine Tour wins to date as he birdied the 18th hole to win the Golden Pilsner Zimbabwe Open. Burmester won by one stroke over overnight leader Adilson Da Silva and by five over Eric van Rooyen and J.C. Ritchie.

Four birdies in the last seven holes enabled Burmester to overtake Da Silva, who led by three strokes until a bogey at the 15th, combined with birdies by Burmester at the 14th and 16th holes, meant the pair were tied coming down the last. In front of a large gallery, Burmester hit his approach with a wedge to two feet to take the title, calling the shot the best of his life.

"I had to go for the flag and that was the moment that did it for me, that shot," said Burmester, who closed with a 67 after scores of 67, 66 and 72 for a total of 16-under-par 272. "I knew I had that putt to win and the hole looked very small. There was a lot of pressure in the air and I told myself to commit as much as I could. The locals always come out to support me, and to pull off a win in front of them is probably the most emotional thing I've done in my life."

Mopani/Redpath Zambia Open
Kitwe, Zambia
Winner: Ross McGowan

Just as 18-year-old Lydia Ko did on the same weekend in San Francisco, Ross McGowan celebrated his birthday during the Mopani/Redpath Zambia Open by winning the title. The Englishman turned 33 on the first day when a 68 put him two strokes off the lead. Rounds of 69 and 71 kept him a similar distance adrift, but a closing 67 gave McGowan a 13-under-par total of 275 to win by two strokes over Danie van Tonder and by three over Rhys West. While West was the overnight leader who closed with a 72, van Tonder took the lead with a brilliant inward half of 31, including eagles at the 12th and 17th holes, for a 66.

McGowan was two under par for the day when he birdied the last three holes to take victory. He two-putted from the fringe on the 17th and then holed from six feet at the last. "I said to my caddie after I had made pars at 14 and 15 that I thought I needed to get to 12 under if I was to have a chance of winning," McGowan said. "I just fired at the flags on those final holes."

McGowan won the Madrid Masters in 2009 but suffered a persistent wrist injury the following year and lost his European Tour card in 2011. He won in Morocco on the Middle East and North African Tour a month before claiming his maiden Sunshine Tour victory.

Zambia Sugar Open
Lusaka, Zambia
Winner: Vaughn Groenewald

Vaughn Groenewald won twice on the Sunshine Tour in 2006 and since then the wait for a third title was proving a lengthy one. But if life begins at 40 then Groenewald, who reached that mark at the end of 2014, certainly gave his golfing life a new lease of life with victory at the Zambia Sugar Open at Lusaka.

"I really didn't know if I would ever win again over the last few years," said Groenewald, "so I'm almost in tears thinking about it." He won by four strokes over Jean Hugo and by five over Dean Burmester after finishing at a 20-under-par total of 272. Rounds of 68 and 65, coming home in six-under 32 on the second day, put Groenewald in a share of the lead, and a 71 on day three kept him there. But his closest rivals on the final day dropped away as Andrew Georgiou returned a 76 and Rhys Enoch, of Wales, a 74.

Instead, Hugo made a challenge sparked by an eagle at the second, but a double bogey at the 17th gave Groenewald all the breathing room he needed. A bogey at the second was quickly repaired with birdies at the next two holes, and four more on the way home meant Groenewald closed with a 68. A fine form with the putter helped him get up and down from a bunker at the 17th and sign off with a fourth four at the 18th. An excited champion stated: "Watch me — I'm 40 years old and I'm coming!"

Investec Royal Swazi Open
Mbabane, Swaziland
Winner: P.H. McIntyre

Winning for the second time on the Sunshine Tour was a special moment for P.H. McIntyre as it came at the Investec Royal Swazi Open. The 28-year-old claimed the modified-Stableford points event by two over Morne Buys and three over Grant Veenstra at the Royal Swazi Sun Resort. "This has always been one that I've wanted to win, it's been on my calendar for a long time," said McIntyre, whose victory fell on the day before Mother's Day in South Africa. "My mother was born here and I have family here in Swaziland, so it's a special place."

With eight points for an albatross, five for an eagle, two for a birdie, minus-one for a bogey and minus-two for anything worse, McIntyre had scores of 11, 7, 15 and 12 for a total of 45. He started the final day one behind Tyrone Mordt, who fell back to fourth place, and collected five birdies, three bogeys, including at the 17th, and an eagle at the 12th, helped by a huge drive.

McIntyre said: "Standing on the 12th tee my caddie told me I needed a good drive, and I hit one. I had 96 meters to the flag and I knew it was going to be close, which it was. That eagle made the day for me, it was the key point. This format gives you a chance to go for it when you normally wouldn't. This game is about big points, which makes it a nice change in how you approach the week."

AfrAsia Bank Mauritius Open
Domaine de Bel Ombre, Mauritius
Winner: George Coetzee

George Coetzee birdied the 18th hole at Heritage three times in a row to win the inaugural AfrAsia Bank Mauritius Open. The 28-year-old South African beat Thorbjorn Olesen at the second extra hole after the pair tied on 13 under par. With the event the first to be tri-sanctioned by the European, Sunshine and Asian Tours, Coetzee claimed his second victory of the year after claiming the Tshwane Open in March, with all three of his European Tour wins coming in events also on his home tour.

Olesen was playing for the first time in three months following surgery on a tendon injury in his left hand. But the Dane led for the first two days and fell only one behind Coetzee after 54 holes. Coetzee had rounds of 70, 67 and 65 before closing with a 69 for a total of 271, matching the mark set by Olesen after a 68. Coetzee went clear of the field early on with three birdies in the first five holes, but Olesen, who bogeyed the first, responded with four birdies in five holes to close out the front nine and tie for the lead. A bogey at the next dropped him one behind, but Coetzee bogeyed the 16th just as Olesen got a two at the 17th with a five iron to six feet.

Coetzee now needed a birdie at the last to tie and almost made an eagle to win when his putt from 30 feet stopped inches short. At the 18th again in the playoff, his 40-footer lipped out for eagle as the pair halved in fours, with another birdie at 18 claiming the win for the South African. Singapore's Mardan Mamat, 47, was third a stroke behind, with Thomas Aiken in fourth.

"I'm happy the job is done and it doesn't matter how many holes it took," Coetzee said. "Thorbjorn did unbelievably well to put pressure on me the whole day. I actually had to work to catch him in the end."

Javier Colomo came to his final hole on Friday evening requiring a birdie to make the cut, but the Spaniard fared even better than that when he holed his drive from 322 yards. This was the first ever albatross at a par-four hole recorded on any of the Asian, Sunshine or European Tours. "I hit a very high driver, straight to the flag, and I thought the ball was close, possibly for eagle, but I couldn't believe it went in," he said. "My next goal is to make a hole-in-one at a par-five!"

Lombard Insurance Classic
Mbabane, Swaziland
Winner: Dean Burmester

Dean Burmester claimed his second victory in just over a month at the Lombard Insurance Classic. The 25-year-old finished five strokes ahead of the field with a record tournament score of 193, 23 under par. "Red 23 is my grandfather's lucky number," he observed, "and I managed to pull it off."

After an opening bogey-free 63, which left him one off the lead, Burmester added twin scores of 65 over the weekend. A one-stroke overnight lead was extended with a two-under outward half, but it was coming home that Burmester really turned on the magic with five birdies for an inward 31. Keith Horne, after a 62, shared second place with Peter Karmis, one ahead of Thanda Mavundla.

As well as winning the Zimbabwe Open, Burmester had finished in the top 20 of each of his 10 tournaments to date in the 2015 season. "A week like this is massive and long may this good form continue. The putter has been hot all season, so hopefully they keeps going in for me," he said. "Every time you have a victory it secures your place on tour. In world golf people notice when you win tournaments, and it helps you get overseas and move to bigger things."

Vodacom Origins of Golf - Langebaan
Western Cape, South Africa
Winner: Justin Harding

With Vaughn Groenewald setting the clubhouse target at eight under par after a fine closing 66, Justin Harding knew what he needed to do. In testing, windy conditions, he had to play the back nine at Langebaan in 32 to force a playoff and managed just that. He hit a four iron to 12 feet at the 12th for an eagle and also birdied the 15th and 18th holes for a 68, which after earlier scores of 72 and 68 gave him a total of 208. Harding then claimed the Vodacom Origins of Golf title with another birdie at the 18th in the playoff. Groenewald found water off the tee and faced a 35-footer for a birdie. It came up short, and Harding, who had faced a 40-footer for his eagle, just had to tap in for a winning birdie.

It was Harding's fourth victory on the Sunshine Tour but a first for the 29-year-old since the 2012 Zambia Open. "It's easier when you know what needs to be done, because it's win or go home," Harding said of his back-nine charge. "I was quite focused on getting the job done. Vaughn set a good target and fortunately I matched him. My family was watching, my mom saw me win for the first time, and it was great to have their support in such trying conditions."

Sun City Challenge
Sun City, South Africa
Winner: Keith Horne

After a two-month break over the winter, the Sunshine Tour resumed with Keith Horne collecting his eighth career title at the Sun City Challenge. The 44-year-old, who was two strokes behind after rounds of 68 and 71 on the Lost City course, closed with a 64 to finish on a 13-under-par total of 203 and win by five strokes over Andrew Curlewis, with Breyten Meyer two further back in third place.

Horne birdied the first two holes and was five under for the day after eight holes before his only bogey at the ninth. Further birdies at the 11th, 14th, 15th and 17th holes kept him well clear of his rivals. Curlewis, who shared the overnight lead, closed with a one-under 71.

"I tried to keep things simple and I'm very happy to win," Horne said. "It's a nice kickstart and this is a good momentum shift to move into the remainder of the year. I'm very proud of the round I played today, I hit the ball fantastically in all departments and really never put myself under pressure. I just kept going forward the whole time."

Vodacom Origins of Golf - San Lameer
Southbroom, South Africa
Winner: Jean Hugo

Jean Hugo's record 10th victory in the Vodacom Origins of Golf Series at San Lameer came nine years after his first. It was also his 16th Sunshine Tour victory dating back to 1999. A four-stroke overnight lead suggested it might be straightforward, yet it was anything but. After rounds of 67 and 69, he added a 74 for a six-under-par total of 210 for a one-stroke win over Derick Petersen and Peter Karmis.

After an even-par front nine, Hugo had bogeys at the 12th, 14th and 16th holes before finding the birdie he required at the 17th. Petersen closed with a 68 and Karmis a 69 to finish one ahead of Jacques Blaauw.

"A huge thank you to Vodacom, because they have been supporting us for a long, long time," said the 39-year-old Hugo. "The events that I won eight or 10 years ago felt like they just happened naturally. Now I have to make it happen. It doesn't get easier as time goes by. It was a struggle out there today and the guys didn't let up. We're getting older and it's one of those things. It's a different ball game for me these days, but more consistent."

Sun Wild Coast Sun Challenge
KwaZulu-Natal, South Africa
Winner: Vaughn Groenewald

After waiting nine years for his third victory on the Sunshine Tour when he won the Zambia Sugar Open, Vaughn Groenewald only had to wait a few months for his fourth as he claimed the Sun Wild Coast Sun Challenge.

In an unusually calm week at the Sun Wild Coast Country Club, the 40-year-old beat Mark Williams by a stroke after rounds of 64, 67 and 67 for a 12-under-par total of 198. Williams had blitzed the final round with a 62 to post an early clubhouse target, but Groenewald came home in 33 to claim his second win of the season. After three birdies in a row to start the back nine, he found himself under the lip of a bunker at the 15th and dropped a shot but birdied the par-five next when he found the green with his long approach and two-putted. Jaco Van Zyl took third place after a closing 66, but the second-round leader Ulrich van den Berg crashed out of contention with a 74 following a triple-bogey-seven at the second hole.

"I only saw that guys were 11 under par when I got to the ninth," Groenewald said. "At least I knew what I had to shoot and it got me going on the back nine. I felt good all the way, but when I birdied 10, 11 and 12 it made the difference."

Sun Sibaya Challenge
Mount Edgecombe, South Africa
Winner: Michael Hollick

Michael Hollick grew up in a house behind the first tee at Mount Edgecombe, where he started playing the game at the age of four. Fast forward to the Sun Sibaya Challenge and the 28-year-old from Durban won his first professional title by making a birdie on the 18th green of his home club. Hollick beat Jean Hugo and Zambia's Madalitso Muthiya by a stroke aided by the support of family and friends.

Hugo, looking for his second victory in a three weeks, led with an opening 64 and was still ahead after a 71 in blustery conditions in the second round. Hollick had scores of 67 and 70 and went out in two under in the final round to challenge for the lead as Hugo opened with two bogeys in the first three holes on the way to a closing 70.

Muthiya came home in 32 for a 65 to set the clubhouse target, and Hollick was two back after a bogey at the 13th before he launched a three wood at the 14th to four feet and holed for eagle.

"Everyone on tour thinks about that moment," Hollick said after birdieing the last for a 67 and a winning total of 204, nine under par. "You never really know if you'll win as a professional, so it's quite a relief to actually do it. I hit two perfect shots on the 18th and managed to sink the putt, which just ended a special day at my home club."

Vodacom Origins of Golf - Vaal de Grace
Parys, South Africa
Winner: Jean Hugo

After just missing out the previous week at Mount Edgecombe, Jean Hugo made no mistake in collecting his second victory within a month at the Vodacom Origins of Golf series at Vaal de Grace. Hugo could not afford a mistake as he overcame a two-stroke deficit with a closing 64 to beat Jacques Kruyswijk by one shot.

Building on his previous scores of 65 and 66, Hugo made five birdies in the first seven holes in the final round to be out in 31. He was tied with Kruyswijk who made three early birdies then bogeyed the eighth — the only dropped shot by the leading two all day — before regaining it immediately at the ninth. Kruyswijk regained the solo lead with a birdie at the 10th, but Hugo responded with birdies at the 11th and 14th holes, while both birdied the 17th. Hugo finished on a 21-under-par total of 195, while Kruyswijk, who closed with a 67, was two ahead of Zander Lombard, with Mount Edgecombe winner Michael Hollick taking fourth place after a 63.

"I'm lucky to have pulled this off," Hugo said. "It took 64. It was one of the best rounds that I've ever played. Seeing Jacques play as well as he did made it tough. He didn't let up. I didn't really make mistakes, but he didn't make mistakes either. It was a great battle."

Sun Windmill Challenge
Bloemfontein, South Africa
Winner: Dean Burmester

Dean Burmester produced the most stunning late charge to win the Sun Windmill Challenge. A third victory of the season looked unlikely when his third bogey of the day at the 11th hole left him two behind Callum Mowat. Then the 26-year-old clicked into action with a chip-in birdie at the 12th. It was the first of five birdies in a row and, after a par at the 17th, he eagled the 18th for good measure — a run of seven under par for the last seven holes.

It gave him a four-stroke victory over Mowat, who had little choice but to settle for second place. Mowat opened with a 10-under 62 at Bloemfontein for a four-shot lead but closed with rounds of 71 and 69 to finish two ahead of Makhetha Mazibuko, with Rourke van der Spuy taking fourth place. But Burmester topped the leaderboard with scores of 69, 64 and 65 for an 18-under-par total of 198.

"I was under the gun, and that stretch has got to rank right up there with the best golf I've ever played," said Burmester. After a huge drive at the last, he was blocked out by overhanging tree branches but hit a low three iron which ran up to 15 feet and then holed the putt. "That was pretty good," he said. "We decided if I pitch it with 100 left, it should run up somewhere close. It just kept going and going, and ended up on the right level of the green."

Vodacom Origins of Golf - St. Francis
Eastern Cape, South Africa
Winner: Christiaan Basson

Christiaan Basson conquered his nerves to win for the fourth time in his Sunshine Tour career at the Vodacom Origins of Golf event at St. Francis Links. The 33-year-old took the two putts he could spare on the final green from 10 feet to win by one over Mark Williams and two over Zander Lombard and Bryce Bibby.

Basson had scores of 70, 66 and 69 for an 11-under-par total of 205. Bibby had led by three strokes after a second round of 64 but struggled to recapture the magic and closed with a 74 despite two birdies in his first six holes. Basson, playing alongside Bibby, had three birdies in his first eight holes and then parred his way home, not having dropped a shot all day.

"I was glad to have two putts in hand to give me the win," Basson said. "I wasn't at all relaxed going down the stretch. I started the day very nervous on the first three holes, and then I kind of got into the groove. But for the last three holes, the nerves came back. I could see Bryce was also nervous, so I think my experience came into play."

Sun Boardwalk Challenge
Port Elizabeth, South Africa
Winner: Chris Swanepoel

In what turned into a match-play duel between the pair, Chris Swanepoel needed an extra hole to finally defeat Ulrich van den Berg to win the Sun Boardwalk Challenge at Humewood. The 30-year-old from Pretoria started the last day one ahead but had a double bogey at the second and bogeyed the fourth. Van den Berg also dropped three shots in the first seven holes before both players picked up four birdies — van den Berg doing that at consecutive holes from the 13th to the 16th, where he just missed an eagle chance.

At the same hole Swanepoel found his ball in the rough only just in time and parred to stay one ahead but bogeyed the last. After earlier scores of 67 and 69, he closed with a 72 to van den Berg's 71 as the pair tied on eight-under 208, three clear of Andrew Georgiou, Lindani Ndwandwe and Mark Frensham. In the playoff at the 18th, Swanepoel hit his approach with a wedge to five feet and, after van den Berg made his par, holed the putt for victory.

"This was my third playoff and my second time winning from one," Swanepoel said after his fourth Sunshine Tour victory, and first for three years. "It's not ideal to be in a playoff, but I think I'm a good match-play player, so I tried to play match-play against Ulrich."

Sun Fish River Sun Challenge
Port Alfred, South Africa
Winner: Rourke van der Spuy

With the second day's play of the Sun Fish River Sun Challenge cancelled due to strong winds and the event reduced to 36 holes, the leaders were not playing together in what turned into the final round. Rourke van der Spuy, after his 65 on the opening day, consolidated his lead with a morning 67 that put him at 12 under par on a total of 132. The 25-year-old rookie made seven birdies in his first 12 holes but dropped two shots, including at the 18th hole, and then had a long wait to see if his score would be good enough for a maiden victory.

Merrick Bremner was the man to make a charge at the leader with eight birdies in a 65. With three holes to play he needed to birdie each of them to tie and only slipped up at the last with a par.

"You always dream of these moments and never really know when they will come — winning is a bit of a surreal feeling right now," said van der Spuy, a member at Durban Country Club. "Merrick had it going and you can never count him out, so I wanted to stay warmed up just in case. I saw he turned on four under and he was playing well, but luckily it didn't go to extra holes."

Vodacom Origins of Golf - Koro Creek
Modimolle, South Africa
Winner: Dean Burmester

Dean Burmester gave himself the perfect boost ahead of the co-sanctioned events at home at the end of the year by winning for the fourth time this season on the Sunshine Tour. His wire-to-wire victory at the Vodacom Origins of Golf at Koro Creek Bushveld was completed by five strokes over Vaughn Groenewald after scores of 64, 66 and 67 for a 19-under-par total of 197.

It was a second consecutive victory in South Africa for Burmester following his win at the Sun Windmill Challenge and contained only one hole out of 54 when he was over par. That was a double bogey on the seventh the final day which followed an eagle and three birdies in the previous six holes. Ahead by two at the turn, birdies at the 13th and 14th put the 26-year-old clear of the field as Groenewald came home in one over for a 70. Toto Thimba finished a shot out of second place, with Anthony Michael in fourth.

"It's been a special year," Burmester said. "I got married last November, settled down with the wife, and we had our first child. My family moved back to South Africa a couple of years ago, so they're a phone call away, and I had my dad on the bag this week, so the support has been endless."

Nedbank Affinity Cup
Sun City, South Africa
Winner: Ruan de Smidt

Ruan de Smidt made swift work of the playoff to decide the winner of the Nedbank Affinity Cup when he eagled the 18th hole at Lost City. De Smidt had earlier set the clubhouse target at 207, nine under par, after rounds of 70, 70 and 67. Andrew Curlewis parred the last for a 69 to tie, and then Jean Hugo, the overnight leader, birdied the last for a 71 to make it a three-way playoff.

But the other two men did not get a look in once they returned to the 18th for the first extra hole. "I got lucky with my tee shot and had a nice gap to play through to the green," de Smidt explained. "I couldn't see the flag, but knew that a little draw would be good. My approach pitched perfect and finished perfect, so I can't complain about that. With my first putt I was trying to lag the ball up to hole, but luckily it dropped."

This was de Smidt's second win on the Sunshine Tour and he celebrated with his brother who is also his caddie. The 26-year-old from Krugersdorp had waited three years since his maiden triumph. "This win means a lot," he said. "I feel like I've proved something to myself, especially because it's been a few years since my breakthrough win."

Vodacom Origins of Golf Final
Limpopo, South Africa
Winner: Darren Fichardt

Darren Fichardt showed his experience and patience in winning the Vodacom Origins of Golf Final for the second time in his career. The 40-year-old had opened with a 61 at Zebula for a four-shot lead but eventually won by a single stroke over Jake Redman, Callum Mowat and Tyrone Mordt. It was his 15th win on the Sunshine Tour but his first since the Africa Open in 2013.

A 71 in the second round allowed Redman to tie for the lead on 12 under and then the pair started in extraordinary fashion in the final round. Both birdied the second and eagled the short par-four third. Redman, however, then had a hole-in-one at the 243-yard, par-three fourth with a four iron. "I got off to a flying start," Fichardt said. "I was three under after three and I found myself two back."

Redman struggled to keep his composure after that, dropping shots at three of the next four holes. He ended with a 71, while Mowat and Mordt both had 68s. Fichardt also failed to recapture the brilliance of his start, making three bogeys and only two birdies the rest of the way, but a 70 gave him a winning total of 202, 14 under par.

"I was lucky that no one made a charge," he said. "I was very happy to see I needed three putts for the win, and then I used them all."

Lion of Africa Cape Town Open
Cape Town, South Africa
Winner: Brandon Stone

Having made the cut in the Lion of Africa Cape Town Open himself, Kevin Stone was on hand to congratulate his son Brandon on winning his maiden title. Kevin was the first to meet Brandon off the 18th green after the latter had recorded a five-stroke victory at Royal Cape in the first 72-hole tournament of the summer. "I couldn't ask for anything more. To not only play in the event with him, but to win it and share a hug with him after walking off the 18th is story book. It's definitely something I'll remember for the rest of my life," Brandon said.

After opening with a 73, Stone recovered with a 66 and then added a 63 to take the 54-hole lead by three strokes. A closing 70, with four birdies and two bogeys in the middle of the back nine, gave him a 16-under-par total of 272. Ockie Strydom and Steve Surry both finished with 67s to tie for second place, with Scott Vincent taking fourth place.

Stone, 22, turned professional in 2013 and had just secured his European Tour card by graduating from the Challenge Tour.

"It's tough when you've got to close it out," he said. "That middle portion of the back nine is tricky at Royal Cape and I hit a few snags along the way, so it's nice to come through like I did and to sign that score card."

Alfred Dunhill Championship
Malelane, South Africa
Winner: Charl Schwartzel

After a two-year drought Charl Schwartzel returned to the winner's circle at the venue he likes better than anywhere else. The 31-year-old South African won the Alfred Dunhill Championship for the fourth time, previously having done so in 2004, 2012 and 2013, having not been victorious since his last triumph on the island green at Leopard Creek. "I love this place, it's definitely one of my favorites," he said. "I wish we could play some majors here."

Schwartzel has collected four wins and four runner-up finishes in 11 appearances at the venue on the edge of Kruger National Park. He seemed perfectly at home with opening rounds of 66 and 67 to take a five-stroke lead at halfway. While he stayed three ahead with a round to play, Schwartzel struggled with his game and battled a loss of confidence on Sunday.

Yet twin 70s gave him a 15-under-par total of 273 and a four-stroke victory over Gregory Havret, who led a trio of Frenchmen filling places two, three and four, with Benjamin Hebert one further back and Sebastian Gros another shot adrift. Though Schwartzel was out in one over par and the Frenchmen were pressing hard, birdies at the 11th, 13th and 14th holes gave the South African the breathing room he needed.

Schwartzel said: "The way I've played the last few years, I've been down in quite a slump, I didn't really see myself coming out and winning. But we've put in so much hard work in the last 18 months and it's frustrating when week-in, week-out you're playing and it feels like it's never going to turn.

"I was battling a lot of demons out there. I felt more comfortable today. I didn't play much better, but I chipped and putted well and that's where scoring lies."

Schwartzel became the first South African to win a European Tour event four times and the third after Ernie Els and Retief Goosen to win at least 10 times on the European circuit. "I guess there's no better fit than for it to turn around here," he said. "This place has treated me really well. I got my first win here and now my 10th, so I think it's pretty fitting."

Nedbank Golf Challenge
Sun City, South Africa
Winner: Marc Leishman

Marc Leishman brought his golfing year to a happy conclusion with a six-stroke victory over Henrik Stenson at the 35th (and last of its type) Nedbank Golf Challenge. Leishman pulled away from 2008 winner Stenson with six birdies in the last 12 holes to become the second Australian champion after Robert Allenby in 2009.

Leishman, whose only win on the PGA Tour came at the 2012 Travelers Championship, lost in the playoff for the Open Championship at St. Andrews in July but suffered far more off the course in 2015. He left the Masters in April to be with his wife Audrey after she was placed in an induced coma after contracting toxic shock syndrome. Audrey survived against the odds, but then Leishman lost a close uncle. "I was going to be pretty happy to have this year to be over with, to be honest," the 32-year-old said. "It wasn't easy, but this just tops off what was not a great year. I hope it's a springboard for big things next year."

Stenson opened with rounds of 66 and 67 and looked to be on the way to a repeat victory. The Swede had spent three days in bed before the tournament suffering from a virus and did not quite have the stamina to keep his form going over the sweltering weekend. He lost the lead on Saturday evening after a bogey at the 18th, while Leishman had birdied the last two holes.

Leishman had rounds of 68, 68, 66 and 67 for a 19-under-par total of 269. He dropped only three strokes all week, the last of them at the third hole on Sunday. His first birdie did not come until the seventh, but it was his approach to three inches at the 13th that broke Stenson's resolve. The Swede had to settle for a sixth runner-up finish of the year, while Leishman added two more birdies at the 15th and 16th holes.

Chris Wood, who was also unwell before the event and was put on a drip for 13 hours, closed with a 68 to take third place, four behind Stenson. Defending champion Danny Willett shared fourth place with Branden Grace, Victor Dubuisson and Robert Streb.

The tournament, for much of its history an unofficial invitational known as the Million Dollar Challenge, will expand to 72 players in 2016 as part of the Final Series of the European Tour.

12. Women's Tours

Not that Inbee Park had intended to, but upon wrapping up a smashing 2015 — five victories, two of them majors — she pretty much summed up young Lydia Ko's impact on the LPGA Tour.

The occasion was the tour's rich, season-ending CME Tour Championship. Neither one won it — Cristie Kerr did — but Park edged out Ko for the Vare Trophy, the scoring title, with an average of 69.415 to 69.441 per round. This gave her the points she needed to qualify for the LPGA Hall of Fame. There was one other requirement: A player has to be an LPGA member for 10 years. Park was expected to reach that point after her 10th start in 2016, sometime before turning 28 in July, at which time she would be the youngest inductee in history.

Said Park, at 27: "I thought the youngest 'everything' was Lydia. It feels great to hear that I'm still young."

Lydia Ko was making everybody in women's golf feel old. She's been stacking up "youngests" since she won the 2012 Women's NSW Open in Australia as a 14-year-old amateur.

Said Ko: "Earlier in the week, I said if I could choose one of the awards, I would love it to be the Player of the Year."

That made her only the fourth player in LPGA history to win the Rookie of the Year award and follow it up the next year with the Player of the Year award. That put her with Nancy Lopez, Beth Daniel and Annika Sorenstam.

"Awesome," Ko said. "They are legendary players. I'm still thinking — hey, am I deserving to be along those names?"

Ko spread five victories across the 2015 LPGA schedule (plus a sixth victory in the New Zealand Open) becoming — in her second year — the youngest player to win 10 events on a major tour. She was age 18 years, 6 months, 2 days, surpassing Horton Smith, who was 21 when he won his 10th in 1929.

Ko won the ISPS Handa Women's Australian Open by two strokes, beat Morgan Pressel in a playoff in the Swinging Skirts Classic, then beat Stacy Lewis in a playoff in the Canadian Pacific Women's Open, and in September, at the Evian Championship, she closed with a 63, record low final round of an LPGA major, and at 18 years, 4 months, 20 days, not only won her first major but also became the youngest ever to win one. Finally, she ran away with the Fubon LPGA Taiwan Championship by nine shots.

How to explain her success? She wasn't impressively long, ranking 60th on the tour with an average of 250.39 yards, and she was pretty accurate, ranking 43rd with 75 percent of fairways hit. Her strength was in her sharp short game — second in hitting greens in regulation at 77 percent, and second in putting, averaging 1.74 per green.

Park's five victories gave her a career-total of 17 wins, and seven majors. She won the HSBC Women's Champions by two strokes in March (beating Ko), the North Texas Shootout in May by three, the inaugural KPMG Women's PGA Championship in June by five (her sixth major), the Ricoh Women's British Open in August by three (her seventh major), and the Lorena Ochoa

Invitational in November by three — the win and the points from the Vare Trophy that would get her into the Hall of Fame.

"The trophy — that sounds really good," Park said. "Being the last putt to achieve all the points for the Hall of Fame, it's even more special. I'm not going back with nothing in my hands, so that's great."

Ko topped the money list with $2,800,802. Park was second at $2,630,011, and Stacy Lewis third with $1,893,423. Korea's Sei Young Kim was fourth in a sizzling first year, taking the Rolex Rookie of the Year award with $1,820,056. She won three tournaments in clutch finishes in the wind on seaside courses. "I like the windy weather," Kim explained, "because I'm using a lot of skills and low cut shots."

Among other developments:

• The next Korean to star on the LPGA Tour could well be In-Gee Chun, 20, who crowned a sensational eight-win 2015 by winning the U.S. Women's Open at Lancaster Country Club. Chun, only the fourth to win it on her first try, shot a closing 66 to beat Amy Lang by one. Inbee Park and Stacy Lewis finished two strokes further back. Chun also had four other majors in her eight wins — the Salonpas Cup and the Japan Woman's Open on the Japan Tour, and the Hite Jinro Championship and the KB Financial Group Star Championship in Korea. Chun will play on the LPGA Tour in 2016.

• The LPGA Championship, one of the tour's five majors, established in 1955, came to an end in 2014 and was replaced in 2015 by the KMPG Women's PGA Championship, run by the PGA of America and played at Westchester Country Club outside New York City. Inbee Park won it for the third straight time.

• There were five first-time winners: Kris Tamulis, Yokohama Tire LPGA Classic; Chella Choi, Marathon Classic; Sei Young Kim, Pure Silk Bahamas LPGA Classic; Hyo Joo Kim, JTBC Founders Cup, and Minjee Lee, Kingsmill Championship.

• The U.S. beat Europe in a contentious Solheim Cup by the closest score yet, 14½-13½.

• Next up in the young phenomenon department: Canada's Brooke Henderson won the Cambia Portland Classic at age 17 — and by eight shots.

The LPGA Tour season ended spectacularly in the CME Tour Championship. Cristie Kerr finished eagle-par for a 17-under 271 total and her second victory of the year. Park (276) parred the 18th and won the scoring title by .026 of a stroke, getting to within a step of the Hall of Fame. And Ko (277) tied for seventh and won the $1 million bonus but missed the scoring title when she bogeyed the 18th.

Said Ko: "For it to come down to the last hole, last group, last putt — it's been a great season on the LPGA."

Elsewhere, Shanshan Feng made history in 2015 by becoming the first Chinese player to win the Ladies European Tour's Order of Merit. Having won the Buick Championship in Shanghai and with two other top-three finishes, including at the Evian Championship, Feng was assured of topping the list even before winning the Omega Dubai Ladies Masters for a third time in four years. "Overall I think I did well this year on the European Tour," said Feng. "I always love this tour and it is getting better and better."

The 26-year-old from Guangzhou finished with earnings of €399,213, with

Melissa Reid taking second place. Reid's resurgence in form, including victory at the Turkish Airlines Open, was one of the stories of the year. The Englishwoman starred on her return to the European Solheim Cup team, but the home side at St. Leon Rot could not make it three wins in a row after being unable to resist a thrilling American comeback in the Sunday singles.

Emily Kristine Pedersen, 19, was the Rookie of the Year after a tight duel with fellow Dane Nanna Koertz Madsen, while their compatriot, Nicole Broch Larsen, 22, was voted the Players' Player of the Year.

On the Japan LPGA Tour, South Korea's Bo-Mee Lee won more money there — ¥230,497,057 — than any male or female professional. Her outstanding record included seven wins, seven second-place finishes and three thirds. Taiwan's Teresa Lu, with five wins, claimed second place, a distant ¥84 million behind Lee, a season that in a way overshadowed the underwhelming year compatriot Yani Tseng endured on the LPGA Tour. Five other South Koreans were multiple winners and collected 16 titles. Only four players picked up maiden victories during the year.

U.S. LPGA Tour

Coates Golf Championship
Ocala, Florida
Winner: Na Yeon Choi

If you can lose and still become No. 1 in the world, then losing can't be all that bad.

This little nugget of logic comforted whiz kid Lydia Ko when she stumbled badly at the 71st hole and Na Yeon Choi slipped past her to pluck off the inaugural Coates Golf Championship, the LPGA's season opener. Ko tied for second, and the high finish lifted her to No. 1 on the Rolex Rankings. This, at age 17, made her the youngest of either sex to become world No. 1, breaking Tiger Woods' record by almost four years.

Ko acknowledged the bitter and the sweet of this outcome. "This was a loss," Ko granted, "but there was a huge positive. That's pretty awesome."

The tournament, with an ever-changing leaderboard, ended the way it had started — frantically. Ko took her first lead in the third round, running off five straight birdies from the 12th for a 65. Was she on her way? "It's never over," Ko said, "until you pull the glove out of your pocket and put it in your bag."

How fittingly cautious of her. She led by as many a four on the front nine in the final round, and the back nine was a shootout. Ko was trailing Choi by one at the par-three 15th. Ko rolled in a 60-footer for birdie, and Choi three-putted from six feet for bogey. Ko led again, with the two-stroke swing. Choi parred in, and Ko crashed to a double bogey at the par-four 17th, driving into a bunker and hitting out into some trees to fall one behind. Choi was one ahead, and it stayed that way.

Choi was six behind after 36 holes and shot 68-70-66-68–272, 16 under, to win by one over Ko (71), Ha Na Jang (70) and Jessica Korda (66). It was her eighth tour win but the first since late 2012, and it left her in tears.

"I was so nervous," Choi said. "I was waiting so long for this moment."

Pure Silk Bahamas LPGA Classic
Paradise Island, Nassau, Bahamas
Winner: Sei Young Kim

South Korea's Sei Young Kim had a definite goal in mind coming into the Pure Silk Bahamas LPGA Classic — a top-10 finish. The rookie probably wasn't bold enough to think of "1," but when it arrived, she was ready for it.

"Since 10 years ago," said Kim, 22, "it's what I've dreamed of."

The last putt was a four-footer for a birdie at the first playoff hole, the par-five 18th, against Sun Young Yoo and Ariya Jutanugarn after they tied at 14-under-par 278 at the par-73 Ocean Club. Kim found a home at the water-guarded 18th. She birdied it all five times she played it — four times in regulation, once in the playoff in a card of 70-68-72-68. She finished the weather-delayed third round on Sunday and found herself two shots off the lead. Yoo (69) and Inbee Park (70) were tied at 11-under 208, and Jutanugarn (70) was a stroke behind.

Two back-nine bogeys took Park out of the chase in the last round. Yoo led by two with three holes to play, but took her only three-putt bogey of the week from 60 feet at the 16th and was tied at 14 under with Jutanugarn, who birdied the 18th from six feet.

Kim climbed the leaderboard in a hurry, birdieing three of the first five holes, then bogeyed No. 8. With Yoo and Jutanugarn already in at 14 under, Kim needed a birdie at the 18th to tie. She missed the green but chipped to three feet and dropped the putt for her 68 and the tie. The playoff held no mysteries for her. She went 4-1 on the Korean LPGA.

Then power paid off in the playoff. Kim reached the 18th in two while Yoo and Jutanugarn needed three to get on. Both missed birdie tries — Yoo from 17 feet and Jutanugarn from eight. Kim, anxious, had left her 20-foot eagle try four feet short, then stepped up and holed the birdie putt for her first win.

"Just before the last putt I was super-nervous," Kim said, "but I'm fine now."

ISPS Handa Women's Australian Open
Winner: Lydia Ko

See Australian Ladies Tour section.

Honda LPGA Thailand
Chonburi, Thailand
Winner: Amy Yang

The big bump in the Honda LPGA Thailand came at Siam Country Club's 15th. Stacy Lewis, No. 3 in the world, had tied for the lead in the first round and had the solo lead through the next two, but she began having problems in the fourth. Came the crucial moment. She was two under for the round, then stumbled to a double bogey at the par-four 15th while Amy Yang birdied it for the third time and was on her way to her second LPGA Tour victory.

"I don't know what just happened," said a breathless Yang, whose first win came in the 2013 HanaBank Championship. "I still can't believe I did it today." But she did, battling down the homestretch to wrap up a card of 67-66-71-69–273, 15 under par at Siam Country Club. She won by two strokes over Lewis (72), Yani Tseng (67) and Mirim Lee (69).

Spain's Beatriz Recari tied the course record with a nine-under 63, tying Sei Young Kim (65) for fifth.

The tournament turned into something between a shootout and match play in the final round. Yang tied Lewis with a birdie at the first, but the resilient Lewis slipped away with a birdie at the third. Then Yang took the lead with a birdie at the sixth after Lewis' bogey at the fifth. Yang birdied the 10th and went two ahead. At the 14th, Yang bogeyed and Lewis birdied, and the two-shot swing left them tied at 15 under. Then came what proved to be the pivotal 15th. Lewis tripped to a double bogey and Yang leaped to a three-stroke lead with a birdie. It was an important cushion. Yang bogeyed No. 16, three-putting from the fringe to lose a shot of her lead. But she steadied herself and parred the last two holes for her two-shot victory.

"Oh, my gosh, it feels great," Yang said. "I don't know what just happened today. I was actually so nervous out there, but I tried to focus, do my best one shot at a time. It feels sweet."

HSBC Women's Champions
Singapore
Winner: Inbee Park

It wasn't exactly a dad promising his little daughter some ice cream if she'd eat her broccoli.

Inbee Park's dad listened patiently as his daughter talked about how mean the Serapong course would be for the HSBC Women's Champions, then made her a bet. He would pay her $500 for each birdie she made, but she would pay him $1,000 for each bogey. Bad move.

"He ran out of money since yesterday," Park was saying after the tournament, with a winner's grin. "I think it ended up really nicely."

One could just imagine dad, watching in pride and dismay as the meter was running. Park posted 15 birdies and went all 72 holes without a bogey. That comes to $7,500. But he was already tapped out.

"I'm lending him the money," Park said.

And as an aside, Park also won the tournament — her 13th on the LPGA

Tour — and in the process won the Battle of the Rolex Rankings. Park, world No. 2, went wire-to-wire, shooting the par-72 Serapong in 66-69-68-70–273, 15 under, beating No. 1 Lydia Ko, the 17-year-old prodigy, by two, and No. 3 Stacy Lewis by four.

"No bogeys around here and on a course where you can hit a good shot and you can get bad luck," Ko said. "That's pretty phenomenal."

"It was fun out being in the final group," said Lewis, whose closing par 72 was the highest of the group all week. "That's where you want to be. But even par usually doesn't cut it."

Park's dad should have been looking at the form sheet. Park last made a bogey at the 16th in the third round of the Honda LPGA Thailand the week before. This gave her a run of 92 holes without a bogey. "I don't think I can even believe myself that I didn't make any bogeys," Park said.

Playing with Ko, the teen sensation, was another revelation. "I thought she doesn't make any mistakes," Park said. "But I definitely saw her making a couple of mistakes today and thought she is actually human."

JTBC Founders Cup
Phoenix, Arizona
Winner: Hyo Joo Kim

Hyo Joo Kim, 19, was discussing the bristling 2015 LPGA Tour rookie corps. "I'm a rookie, too," Kim was saying after the JTBC Founders Cup, "so I don't have time to think too much about it. I'm just trying to find my place."

Kim's place was looking very much like the winner's circle. That was an impressive performance she put on under pressure, birdieing five of the last eight holes to outrun Stacy Lewis, now a tough veteran, for a three-stroke victory. And it was Kim's second victory already. Her first was in the 2014 Evian Championship, the previous September, when she held off Karrie Webb, World Golf Hall of Fame member, dropping a 12-foot birdie putt on the final hole. And that was in the first major she had ever entered. The chief characteristic to her game thus far? Her ability to stand up under pressure.

"She's just really solid," said Lewis, no slouch herself under pressure. "On the front, I didn't put much pressure on her, but even when I did make some putts, she made putts to follow, and she put a lot of pressure on and was just really solid all day."

In a tournament fragmented by a number of delays, Kim thumped the par-72 Wildfire Golf Club in 65-69-66-67–267, a robust 21 under par. She played 30 holes Friday, completing a 65 for the first round and shooting 69 for the second. She went on to beat Lewis by three strokes for her career 17th runner-up finish.

Kim had her game well under control, with bursts of birdies. In the first round, she birdied five straight from No. 6. In the third, she birdied four of the first 10 and three straight from the 14th. And in the clinching fourth, she birdied five of the last eight holes and, after a disappointing ruling and bogey at No. 10, three straight birdies from No. 11.

"If anything," she said, "I think the situation on No. 10 helped, because after … I just realized … I've just got to go out there and play."

Kia Classic
Carlsbad, California
Winner: Cristie Kerr

What with Mirim Lee putting like a magician, young Lydia Ko rolling along in the 60s, and the field having a field day at Aviara Golf Club (one-under-par 143 made the cut), it's a wonder that Cristie Kerr could see any encouragement in the Kia Classic late in March.

"It's just a matter of putting four solid rounds together," Kerr was saying after the second round, but with how much conviction, under the circumstances? "Just have to be consistent with my rounds the next couple days, and I'll have a shot."

The blueprint seemed simple enough. Execution, however, was another matter. Except to Kerr, a savvy veteran of 37.

Kerr was soundly consistent, starting 67-68-68. But she was still three off the lead entering the final round. Then she raced off to five birdies in six holes from No. 5 and, after a bogey at the 12th, four straight birdies from the 13th. A bogey at the 18th gave her a 65 and a 20-under 268 total that broke the tournament record by four strokes. She beat Mirim Lee, the leader for the first three rounds, by two strokes and Rolex No. 1 Lydia Ko by three for her 17th tour win and her first in nearly two years.

Lee, a tenacious competitor, needed just 25 putts in her first-round 65, two of them 40-footers for birdies. She shared the second-round lead and was the solo leader through the third. Kerr streaked by in the fourth, but Lee closed to within a stroke at the 16th, driving the green and holing the four-foot putt for an eagle. But at the 17th, a tee shot into the woods cost her a double bogey and a three-stroke deficit.

Ko tied for the lead with a birdie at No. 14, but it was her last birdie — while Kerr was streaking away — and a three-putt bogey at the 18th gave her a 67 and dropped her to third.

Then there was a bonus for Kerr. Her young son Mason was waiting for her behind the 18th green, in his stroller.

ANA Inspiration
Winner: Brittany Lincicome

See Chapter 6.

Lotte Championship
Kapolei, Hawaii
Winner: Sei Young Kim

It was the Lotte Championship, and Sei Young Kim, a 22-year-old rookie, had come to a bad time: She had the third-round lead. The memory was still raw. At the ANA Inspiration two weeks earlier, Kim, making just her 13th LPGA Tour start, led by three entering the final round. She shot 75 and tied for fourth.

"Believe it or not," Kim said at the Lotte, through a translator, "every tournament I won, I was the chaser and coming from behind." That was the case in the Pure Silk Bahamas Classic, the second tournament of the season. Kim caught the leaders, then scored her first tour win in a playoff. "Being able to be in the lead and close out the tournament is probably something that I need to overcome," Kim said.

If it was nerves, as circumstances suggested, they twitched again, but not fatally this time. Kim entered the final round leading I.M. Kim by one and Inbee Park by two. I.M. Kim fell back with a closing 74. Sei Young Kim started shakily. She birdied the first, then went bogey-double bogey. Then came a wild finish. At the 18th, Park chipped stiff and tapped in for a par. Sei Young needed a miracle — like the hole-in-one that won for her in Korea — and got it. She'd watered her tee shot and put her third into the fringe, 18 feet from the cup. And she chipped in for her par, finishing a card of 67-67-70-73 to tie Park at 277, 11 under at Ko Olina.

In a sense, Sei Young would be chasing in the playoff, back at the 18th. Though they were tied, she was a rookie against the mighty Park, No. 3 in the world. But Park never had a chance. Kim's eight-iron approach bounced twice and dropped for an eagle. She raised both hands and grinned wide.

"I don't know what I've done to deserve this," Kim said, "but I feel like every time I win a tournament I have to do something crazy. I don't know why it keeps happening, but it feels good."

Swinging Skirts LPGA Classic
Daly City, California
Winner: Lydia Ko

Lydia Ko, who started winning professional tournaments as a 14-year-old amateur, came of age at the 2015 Swinging Skirts LPGA Classic. That is, she turned 18. And she celebrated by winning the tournament — her second win of the year and seventh on the LPGA Tour.

"It's been a great birthday week again," said Ko, who turned 17 while winning the 2014 Skirts. She rallied to beat Stacy Lewis in that one, and this time beat Morgan Pressel in a playoff.

But first Ko had to share the spotlight with the new kid on the fairway. And ironically, this was the first time that Ko was not the kid chasing but the pro being chased by a kid. Ko turned 18 on April 24, Friday of tournament week, and this made Canada's Brooke Henderson, 17, the new young threat. She had turned pro in December and was trying for an age waiver that would get her on the LPGA Tour, as Ko had done.

Henderson, who led through the middle rounds, set a tournament record at the par-72 Lake Merced with her 70-65–135 at the halfway point. She was leading by two and was four up on Ko. But she would close with 72-74–281, finishing third by a stroke.

Ko, who shot 67-72-71-70, led by one in the first round and came from behind in the fourth to tie Pressel at eight-under 280. Pressel led by two with four holes to play, but bogeyed the 15th and 16th and shot 72. "I just couldn't convert the putts," Pressel said.

Ko bogeyed the first two holes, but recovered and played the rest of the way in two more bogeys and six birdies, including her only birdie at the par-five 18th in regulation, that on an eight-foot putt for the 70 that caught Pressel. Ko got a second birdie at the 18th at the second playoff hole. It was a five-foot putt that wrapped up her birthday present.

"It's really cool, now that I'm an adult," Ko said. "It won't change how people will look at me, but — Big 18."

Volunteers of America North Texas Shootout
Irving, Texas
Winner: Inbee Park

It's not known whether Inbee Park could belt out a stirring rendition of "The Eyes of Texas," but the record shows she was feeling mighty at home in the Lone Star State. It was a strong test, but Park, world No. 2, battled through veterans and talented youth to win her second Volunteers of America North Texas Shootout in three years.

"I don't know how I did it, but I did it twice," Park said.

Actually, in a way, she did know. Her putting had soured so she changed putters, and she also found that some of Las Colinas' fairways sloped down left-to-right, which made them receptive to her controlled draw. Park, who won the inaugural Shootout in 2013, tied for the lead in the third round and pulled away in the fourth, shooting 69-66-69-65–269, 15 under par, to win by three over Cristie Kerr (66) and Hee Young Park (66). It was her 14th tour win.

The veterans had their say. Kerr, who made the recent Kia Classic her 17th win, and Hall-of-Famer Juli Inkster were in the first-round lead at five-under 65, three ahead of Park. Karrie Webb, another Hall of Fame member, got within one with her third-round 64. Kerr challenged at the end, but her three closing birdies for a 66 just got her within three.

Youth was also in the mix. Canadian whiz Brooke Henderson, 17, who had to Monday-qualify, took the halfway lead with a 65. "I stayed patient," she said. But she blew up early in the final round and tied for 13th. Lexi Thompson, now 20, tied Park in the third round and was about to tie her again at No. 9 in the fourth. But before she could knock in her five-footer for birdie, Park rolled in a long one of her own. "That gave me a lot of confidence," she said. She added birdies at the 12th, 15th and 18th for her 65. Thompson tied for fourth.

Park was then waving goodbye. "I love to come here to Texas," she said, to no one's surprise.

Kingsmill Championship
Williamsburg, Virginia
Winner: Minjee Lee

Minjee Lee, 18, already eight months a pro and in her 11th start on the LPGA Tour, had the distinction of cutting her way through the entire spectrum of the tour to make the Kingsmill Championship her first victory. That's veteran, youth and all stops in between.

"I didn't think this moment would come this year," said Lee, the seventh player to get her first win before her 19th birthday, "so I'm so stoked to have won."

What did it was an amazing burst in the final round. Lee had trailed all the way, then in the fourth round she torched a nine-hole stretch in seven under par. Darkness, following an earlier storm delay, forced play over into Monday. She finished bogey-par-par for a six-under-par 65 at the Kingsmill River course. With her 68-67-69 start, she finished with a 15-under total of 269 and a two-stroke win over So Yeon Ryu. Among others in her wake: Inbee Park, Lydia Ko, Suzann Pettersen, Lexi Thompson and Stacy Lewis. And among the more interesting in the field was France's Perrine Delacour, 21, ranked No. 311 in the world, who took her first lead ever through the third round. Her strategy for the fourth? "Just breathe and not think about leading and everything," she said. (Delacour would finish fourth, the best of her three-year career.)

Lee started the final round two shots off the lead and was at even par through the sixth. Then came the rampage — birdies at Nos. 7, 9, 11, 12 and 14 and an eagle at the par-five 15th. She led by four over Alison Lee and was on the 16th green when darkness stopped play. The next morning, she three-putted for bogey, and her lead was cut in half when Alison Lee birdied the 15th behind her. Minjee Lee then parred the last two for her first win, and she left Kingsmill with a full load of confidence.

"Just because I won in my rookie season," Lee said, "I feel like I could probably do it again."

ShopRite LPGA Classic
Galloway, New Jersey
Winner: Anna Nordqvist

Anna Nordqvist was becoming a little uneasy. She had lost track of her mother in the gallery. She'd seen her just after making her second straight birdie at the 17th. Then as she looked down the line of her winning putt at the 18th, there she was, standing at greenside.

"It's the first time I've won on the LPGA Tour [that] one of my family members were there with me," Nordqvist said. "It's Mother's Day in Sweden, so I couldn't have given her a better present than to spend the day with her."

It was a present some time in coming. First, there was Morgan Pressel, leading through the first two rounds. Pressel faltered, and there was the Netherlands' Christel Boeljon, winless in five years on the tour, to be reckoned with, and then rookie Kelly Shon. The tournament would be decided over the last few holes.

The hopeful Boeljon was four under through the 10th, but bogeyed the 13th. She missed an 18-inch birdie putt at the 18th, shot 68, and was a career-best second by a stroke to Nordqvist. Shon got to within one with a birdie at the 14th, then double-bogeyed the 15th and tied for third with

Pressel, three behind. Pressel, a two-time winner who last won in 2008, birdied the third but got knocked out of the lead after a bogey at No. 6 on a bad chip shot and double bogey at the par-three No. 7 after missing the green short.

Nordqvist was a discouraged golfer. She won both the LPGA Championship and the LPGA Tour Championship in her rookie year, 2009, then fell into a five-year drought and considered quitting. But she came back strong, winning twice in 2014. In the ShopRite, she birdied the 16th on a 12-foot putt and the 17th from eight feet for a two-stroke lead. A bogey at the 18th merely cut her margin to a stroke. Nordqvist shot the Seaview Bay course in 67-69-69, eight-under 205. And when she lined up that final putt, she had both the win and her mom in her sights.

Manulife LPGA Classic
Cambridge, Ontario, Canada
Winner: Suzann Pettersen

Suzann Pettersen's pain, it would seem, is behind her. It looked that way at the Manulife LPGA Classic in June, when she tied for the lead in the second round and rolled from there to her 15th tour victory. And she was perhaps more relieved about knowing the peace of not being in pain.

"I've been pain-free for almost two weeks," said Pettersen, who battled a bad back through much of 2014 and then had a shoulder injury early this season. "No painkillers, nothing, and doing all my rehab."

Subtract the pain and add Butch Harmon as her coach, and she had a winning combination. Pettersen, shooting Whistle Bear in 22-under-par 266, survived threats from Mariajo Uribe and Brittany Lang for a one-stroke victory — her first win since October 2013, the year she won four times on the tour.

Pettersen, shooting 66-65-66-69, went the first 55 holes without a bogey and got under way in the second round with a seven-under 65 to tie Uribe (66) at 13-under 131. She took a one-stroke lead through the third round at 19-under 197, and then things got a little dicey, courtesy of Lang.

Lang, five behind Pettersen starting the final round, roared down a 13-hole stretch in seven under from No. 5, shooting 65 and posting the clubhouse lead at 21-under 267.

Pettersen started the final round with a one-shot lead, then fell behind with two early bogeys and had to fight her way from there. She eagled the 12th, bogeyed the 13th, then tied Lang at the par-five 16th when she blasted out of a greenside bunker to two feet and birdied. Then she birdied the par-three 17th from eight feet and parred the par-four 18th for a 69 and the one-stroke win.

And she praised her new coach. "I have only good things to say about Butch," Pettersen said. As to how she came to sign him on: They speak the same language, she said. "I have a sailor's mouth," she offered, "and Butch has a sailor's mouth, too."

KPMG Women's PGA Championship
Winner: Inbee Park

See Chapter 6.

Walmart NW Arkansas Championship
Rogers, Arkansas
Winner: Na Yeon Choi

No matter how full Na Yeon Choi's trophy case gets, she'll always find room for her trusty eight iron. It was vital in her first eight LPGA Tour victories. In win No. 9, the Walmart NW Arkansas Championship, it was the hammer.

"I like the eight iron forever," Choi said, after two brilliant shots set up her win. "If someone asks me what's your favorite club, I always answer the eight iron. So I like that club, and when I pull the eight iron, I always feel good."

In the final round, Choi was running out of holes, and the pursuit, especially defending champion Stacy Lewis, was closing in. In fact, Lewis had come from behind and had taken a one-stroke lead at the 10th and was still one ahead after just missing a birdie try at the par-three 17th. Then she heard a huge roar back at the par-four 16th — the roar greeting Choi's eight iron from 142 yards that one-hopped into the hole for an eagle. Choi had leapfrogged back into the lead, and for good.

"I thought it's going to be good, but I didn't expect [it to] go in," Choi said. "I couldn't see the ball going in. I just heard a lot of screaming around the green."

There was more screaming at the 17th. Choi hit the eight iron again, from about the same distance, 142 yards, and nearly holed it. She tapped in from a foot for another birdie and a two-stroke lead. A par at the 18th gave her a card of 66-63-69–198, 15 under at the Pinnacle Country Club, and a two-stroke win over Japan's Mika Miyazato.

Lewis made one last stab at catching Choi, but bogeyed the par-five 18th for a 68 and slipped to a tie for third. "You can't be too upset," Lewis said. "When somebody holes out and makes birdie on 16 and 17, it's one of those things that it's kind of meant to be for her."

Said Choi: "That two shot, I think I have to remember for my future ... then try to [have the] same feeling."

U.S. Women's Open Championship
Winner: In-Gee Chun

See Chapter 6.

Marathon Classic
Sylvania, Ohio
Winner: Chella Choi

If there was anyone happier than Chella Choi over her first LPGA Tour victory, it would be her caddie. Now he could quit.

He had agreed to caddie for her until she won, but he wasn't bargaining for 157 starts and some seven years. So now, at last, he could put down the bag. But it might not be that easy. It's a rare father who can say no to his little girl.

"My father wants to retire because we promise," said Chella Choi. "But I don't know," she added. And Ji Yeon Choi knows what that means. Chella was 24 now, but she was still his daughter.

Chella Choi's happiness was all sorrow for rookie Ha Na Jang, 23, a fellow Korean. Winless in her 23 starts, Jang led from the first round until Choi tied her in the last, then beat her on the first playoff hole. "You know, first time win is hard," Choi said. "Hopefully, this is a turning point for me."

Choi trailed by seven, then six shots after shooting 73-66 at the par-71 Highland Meadows. She started to show some muscle on the back nine of the second round, birdieing five of the last six holes and the last four in a row. She resumed her sprint in the third round. She bogeyed No. 1 for the third straight day, then birdied seven times the rest of the way for a 65, moving within two of Jang, who had made only two bogeys in 54 holes. And while Jang cooled off in the final round, making a bogey and double bogey in her 68, Choi kept rolling for a no-bogey 66, meaning she'd gone the last 35 holes in 12 birdies and no bogeys.

Jang bogeyed in the playoff off an aggressive chip that ended up in heavy rough beyond the 18th green. Choi was weak with her chip, but two-putted from 25 feet for a par-five and her first victory.

A proud dad cried. And then, his work done, he could quit. Said his daughter: "We will talk later."

Meijer LPGA Classic
Grand Rapids, Michigan
Winner: Lexi Thompson

Food. That's what won for Lexi Thompson in the Meijer LPGA Classic. Not any particular kind of food. Just the word "food."

Thompson faced a crisis on the final hole. "I called my caddie over and I told him to give me something to think about to get my mind off it," said Thompson. "He just said something so random. Like, food. But it ... got me laughing, and it helped me go into that putt confident."

That, plus an abundance of birdies, saw Thompson through a running battle down the final round against Lizette Salas and Gerina Piller and into her fifth tour win, her first since the then-Kraft Nabisco Championship early in 2014. Thompson won by a stroke with a clutch par on the final hole, completing a card of 69-64-68-65–266, 18 under at the par-71 Blythefield Country Club.

Salas seemed on target for her second tour win, sharing the first-round lead on a 64 and then leading by four going into the final round.

But Salas was quickly caught, parring the first six holes while Thompson birdied three of the first five, and Piller, starting from six behind, went on a seven-under tear through the 12th. Salas was trading birdies and bogeys and finally birdied the 17th for a one-under 70. Piller bogeyed the 16th, then birdied the 18th for a 64. Thompson bogeyed the sixth, then birdied Nos. 7, 8, 10, 11 and 15, the last putting her 19 under and three ahead. With Salas birdieing the 17th and Piller the 18th, a bogey at the 17th put Thompson in a bind at the par-four 18th. Leading by one, she got a scare, hitting a drive that bounced off a tree.

"I got pretty lucky with having a shot in the rough, and hit a good shot to about 20 feet," she said. Then she summoned her caddie to break the tension. "Food," he said.

Still, she missed her first putt about two feet left and needed that for the win. "I didn't really want that putt," she said. "But it's all good."

Ricoh Women's British Open
Winner: Inbee Park

See Chapter 6.

Cambia Portland Classic
Portland, Oregon
Winner: Brooke M. Henderson

It might make an outstanding trivia question someday: Who finished second in the 2015 Cambia Portland Classic? The answer is Pornanong Phatlum, Ha Na Jang and Candie Kung.

The reason for the question was that Canadian Brooke Henderson won it by eight shots — at the age of 17 years, 11 months and 6 days.

"It's such an unbelievable thing," Henderson said, "and I can't really — it's not even real-life yet. I was just trying to play my own game and I kept trying to get it to minus-24 all day today, and I came up a little bit short, but I got the win and I'm extremely excited."

Henderson became the third youngest ever to win an LPGA Tour event, after Lydia Ko, 15, and Lexi Thompson, 16. She was a youngster on a mission. The LPGA wouldn't admit her to the 2014 qualifying school because she was under 18, so she turned professional in December and was playing tournaments on sponsor invitations and Monday-qualifying, and won nearly $466,900 in nine events.

Henderson Monday-qualified for the Portland Classic and started with a bogey-free, six-under-par 66 and trailed by one. She took a one-stroke lead with a second-round 67, went ahead by five with a 65, then ran away by eight with a 69 for a 267, 21 under at Columbia Edgewater Country Club.

As a teenager, she had the poise of a veteran. In the final round, she took advantage of the par-fives, birdieing three of the four, got to eight under on a 20-foot putt at the ninth. She bogeyed the 13th, got her 24th and last birdie at the 17th, and at the 18th, it was as though she finally realized what she was about to accomplish.

"Today, the first time I really felt nerves was on 18," she said. She drove into a bunker and took only her third bogey of the tournament. And she got a winner's champagne shower. Did she get to taste it? "No, not really," Henderson said. "I can just smell it, though."

P.S.: Henderson was granted full LPGA membership two days after winning at Portland.

Canadian Pacific Women's Open
Vancouver, British Columbia, Canada
Winner: Lydia Ko

This was getting to be positively old hat for Lydia Ko — if winning can ever get old. All grown up now, at age 18, she won her third Canadian Pacific Women's Open, tying Pat Bradley, of the 1980s, and Meg Mallon, of the early 2000s, for the most wins.

But this was Ko's first as a professional. The previous two times, she was a kid amateur. In 2012, she became the youngest ever to win on the LPGA Tour, at age 15 years, 4 months, and she repeated in 2013. It was after that that the LPGA waived the age-18 requirement and granted her membership.

"I had an amazing week," Ko said. "I didn't know in 2012 that I might be coming back here in a couple years, then winning here again."

Ko won her first by three strokes, her second by five, but she had to go to a playoff for this one, beating fast-closing Stacy Lewis on the first extra hole. Lewis wasn't a real contender until her closing 67. "If you would have told me at the beginning of the day I was going to be in a playoff, I would have been pretty happy," Lewis said. And so she added to her remarkable record. She won 11 times and she's been the runner-up 19 times, and six of those came since her last win in the 2014 NW Arkansas Championship.

Ko, shooting 67-68-69, had her foot in the door until she cooled to a one birdie, one-bogey par 72 in the final round and tied Lewis, who was already in at 12-under 276. Lewis drove into the rough in the playoff and missed the green with her approach and bogeyed. Ko was on in two and two-putted from 50 feet, the second from 30 inches, for the win.

This win was different in another way. This time, she could cash a check, this one for $337,500. "The check is the last thing I'm thinking about," Ko said. "It's great to be back in the winner's circle."

Yokohama Tire LPGA Classic
Prattville, Alabama
Winner: Kris Tamulis

Kris Tamulis, 34, long a veteran on the tour, had entered the Yokohama LPGA Tire Classic with just a couple simple goals — have a good week (meaning a nice payday) and lock up her playing spots for the coming Asian swing.

Satisfied that she'd accomplished these goals, Tamulis left the final green with the clubhouse lead but hardly with a confident thought. Still, it would be about 45 minutes before the field would finish. She would wait it out and hope. She didn't go to the practice range to stay loose in case of a playoff because, thanks to weather delays, she had to play 29 holes on Sunday. "It was a long day," she said. She was edgy enough that she wouldn't watch TV, but concerned enough to have a friend bring her updates. Imagine her surprise, then, when the final update told her she had the first win of her career — after 11 years and 186 starts.

"It was amazing," Tamulis said. "I was definitely not expecting this today."

Her last two threats were Austin Ernst, seeking her second career win, and Yani Tseng, 26, whose game mysteriously disappeared after she spent 109 weeks as the Rolex No. 1 in the world. Both had makeable birdie putts at the final hole to tie her.

"When they both missed, I was just shocked," Tamulis said.

Tamulis put on quite a show at the par-72 Senator course. After a rocky three-bogey 71 in the first round, she bogeyed No. 1 in the second round then went five under for the last 15 holes for a 68, and had a bogey-free 67 in the third. And in the final round, she birdied four of the first six holes, and when she bogeyed No. 7, that was the end of a string of 41 holes without one. She added four more birdies for a 65, a 17-under 271 and a one-stroke win over Ernst and Tseng.

But she didn't see it arrive. "I didn't really want to watch," she said. "I had done what I could do."

Evian Championship
Winner: Lydia Ko
See Chapter 6.

The Solheim Cup
Winners: United States
See Chapter 6.

Sime Darby LPGA Malaysia
Kuala Lumpur, Malaysia
Winner: Jessica Korda

The first thing Jessica Korda did was grab her cell phone. Dad would want to be the first to know. But Malaysia was halfway around the world from him.

"I didn't actually get to talk to my dad," Korda said. "It went straight to voice mail. But I did get a series of text messages."

The good news to former tennis star Petr Korda was that his daughter had broken out of her eight-month slump and won the Sime Darby LPGA Malaysia. She had her best raw start of the year, a 69-67 opening. And then with the pursuit including the top of the Rolex World Rankings — Inbee

Park, Lydia Ko and Stacy Lewis in 1-2-3 order — Korda led the rest of the way with 65-65 in the intense October heat and humidity at the par-71 Kuala Lumpur Golf and Country Club. She won by four shots at 18-under 266.

"When you have a two-shot lead and shoot six under, it's pretty hard to beat," said Lewis, who tied for second with Ko and defending champion Shanshan Feng.

Korda's secret: Patience. "I knew I was getting really close," Korda said, "and just needed to stay patient."

What was one day more? Korda, 22, joined the tour in 2011, scored her first win in 2012, won twice in 2014, and after tying for second (her only top-10) in the 2015 season opener, the Coates Championship in January, slipped into the slump.

Her two-round start was her most promising of the year. She had five birdies and three bogeys in her opening 69, then five birdies against only one bogey in her 67 for a 136. She trailed by four in each round — behind Alison Lee in the first and Ha Na Jang in the second. She took a two-shot lead with a bogey-free 65 in the third, and doubled it with a seven-birdie, one-bogey 65 in the fourth. And then noticed something odd.

"I was weirdly calm today," Korda said. "I knew what I needed to do."

After that, there was only one thing left to do: Call home.

LPGA KEB HanaBank Championship
Incheon, South Korea
Winner: Lexi Thompson

There aren't many who can hit it as long as Lexi Thompson can. There aren't many who can hit it as short, either.

Enter Lexi Thompson and the Tale of the Elegant Flop Shot at the LPGA KEB HanaBank Championship.

The tournament had reached a crucial point. Thompson was leading by a stroke coming to the risk-reward par-four 15th in the final round. Opportunity wasn't merely knocking, it was yelling out loud. She couldn't resist, even knowing that risk-reward holes don't carry that tag for nothing.

"When I went for that green and I saw my ball bounce over, I'm like, 'Probably not going to be the best chip shot, or the easiest,'" Thompson said. "But I love hitting flop shots out of the rough. I just opened the blade wide open and just took a big swing at it. I figured, at worst, it would run through the fringe but have a straight uphill putt."

Thompson put it eight feet from the flag. She left the 15th with a two-stroke lead.

Next came the par-five 18th. She bashed a drive 290 yards and had 190 left. Her second ended up in deep rough to the left, and she left that final green with her second win of the year, after the Meijer Classic in July, and the sixth of her young career.

Thompson lofted a flop shot out of the rough to 12 feet and two-putted for her par, completing a card of 68-67-69-69–273, 15 under par for a one-stroke victory over Yani Tseng and Sung Hyun Park. And she did this with golfers streaking by. Park opened with a 10-under 62, leaving Thompson six behind. And in the last round, Amy Yang, playing earlier, gave her something to think about with another 62, becoming the first ever to close with nine straight birdies.

"I'm overall a very aggressive player," Thompson said. "So, if I have 190 [to the] front, I'm not laying up. But it's good to play aggressive and know that I can get up-and-down."

Fubon LPGA Taiwan Championship
Chinese Taipei
Winner: Lydia Ko

Lydia Ko ran off with the tournament by nine shots. Amazing stuff.

For really amazing, try this: She did it over the last 27 holes.

Ko, the whiz kid now 18, trailed through the first two and a half rounds of the Fubon LPGA Taiwan Championship. Then things started falling into place on the back nine of the third round. When it all ended, Ko had her third win in five starts, fifth of 2015 and 10th of her young career. She also was the Rolex Rankings No. 1 again.

"The winning part is probably the most memorable," Ko said. "If you get the extra bonus with it, it's even better."

And at age 18 years, six months and one day, Ko became the youngest to post 10 wins on any major tour.

Shooting the par-72 Miramar Golf Club in 69-67-67-65, Ko trailed through the first two rounds, and in the third, in the wind on the rain-soaked course, Ko stumbled going out, erasing her three-birdie surge with a double bogey and a bogey. Then things started falling into place on the back. Eun-Hee Ji bogeyed the 12th and missed a short birdie putt on the 13th. Charley Hull triple-bogeyed the 10th off a stray tee shot. Ko was off and running for five birdies, starting with a chip-in at the 11th and ending with an eight-foot putt at the 18th for a 67 and a four-stroke lead.

"It's always good to finish with a birdie," Ko said. "Especially with the weather conditions."

But it was sunny and breezy for the final round, and Ko finished the job with mature authority. She birdied four of the first six holes, bogeyed the seventh, then closed with a pitch-in eagle at the par-five 12th and birdied 14 and 18 for a 65 and the nine-stroke win on a 20-under 268 total. She boosted her season winnings to over $2.7 million. For the record, Ji and So Yeon Ryu tied for second.

"It's never easy," Ko said. "It's a little easier when you have a couple shots leeway."

"Nine," someone reminded her.

Ko laughed. "Nine," she conceded.

Blue Bay LPGA
Hainan Island, China
Winner: Sei Young Kim

For fans who don't know the players yet, that young Korean woman who breaks into big smiles when the wind kicks up is Sei Young Kim.

It was happy days again in the Blue Bay LPGA, on the shores of the South China Sea, and if Kim keeps this up, she'll be the stuff of legend.

This was her third victory of the season, and she won all three on windy seaside courses. And more compelling, she took all three with stunning clutch finishes. This time, in the final round — with the blustery weather moderating to breezes and rain — she dropped into a tie, and then at the 18th, Stacy Lewis missed her birdie from 20 feet, Candie Kung from 10, and Kim holed from six for the win.

"I was really nervous," Kim said. "I just focus, and when I hit the putt, I couldn't believe it."

Kim, leading or tied through the middle rounds, shot Jian Lake Blue Bay in 70-72-74-70 to win by one at two-under 286.

One would think she'd be used to this stuff by now. Her first two were real pressure cookers. In February, Kim birdied the 18th in the final round of the Pure Silk Classic in the Bahamas (for the fourth straight time) to tie Ariya Jutanugarn and Sun Young Yoo, then birdied it for the fifth consecutive time in the playoff to win. She was even more dazzling in the Lotte Championship in Hawaii in April. She chipped in for par at the final hole to tie Inbee Park, then beat her with a hole-out eagle at the first playoff hole, the 18th.

Surviving the wind at China's Hainan Island was the story of the week. The numbers were punishing: In the first round, only 10 of the 80 starters broke the par of 72, and after two withdrawals, only five of 78 broke par in the second round. But Kim, as ever, felt quite at home. Her secret?

"I like the windy weather," Kim said, "because I'm using a lot of skills and low cut shots."

Toto Japan Classic
Winner: Sun-Ju Ahn

See Japan LPGA Tour section.

Lorena Ochoa Invitational
Mexico City, Mexico
Winner: Inbee Park

First, said Inbee Park, you have to control the air, and then the greens. Her strategy was simple enough. Making it work was another matter. Could she? Well, the Korean star was not a force on the LPGA Tour by accident.

Park did both with authority and cruised to her fifth victory of the year and her career 17th, taking the Lorena Ochoa Invitational by three strokes.

Once she got the hang of the elevation, she cruised the Club de Golf Mexico in 68-71-67-64–270, 18 under par.

The tournament, next-to-last of the year, is staged in honor of Lorena Ochoa, the brilliant Mexican star who was such a power on the tour for seven years, till she retired in 2010 and got married.

It didn't take Park long to warm up after her two-week layoff with a cyst problem on her finger. She took the first-round lead with that four-under 68 on seven birdies and three bogeys. She trailed Minjee Lee in the second round, then took command on a cool day in the third.

"It's not so much about the weather as it is about the altitude," Park said. "It's about distance control. Whenever I hit it on line, it's over, and whenever I get the distance right, it's right or left. It's tough with the altitude, and I've been really struggling. I'm just trying to get used to it."

Two late birdies in the third round put her three ahead of the dynamic rookie Sei Young Kim, who tied Park, then beat her in a playoff at the Lotte Championship.

"She's a fighter," Park said. "And she makes those shots where she needs them." But it was Spain's Carlota Ciganda who was the bigger threat in the final round. Kim managed a 66 to finish third, but Ciganda put on the pressure with an eagle and eight birdies in a one-bogey 63. Park kept her at bay with birdies at the 17th and 18th for a bogey-free 64. She had tamed the greens, as well.

"It was definitely the putter," Park said. "It was really good all week."

CME Group Tour Championship
Naples, Florida
Winner: Cristie Kerr

The CME Group Tour Championship, ringing down the curtain on the LPGA's 2015 season, was a four-round tournament that had three winners, all of them decided on the final hole.

That takes some sorting out.

Said a tour official: "Rolex Player of the Year, the Vare Trophy, tournament title, the Race all came down to the 72nd hole. Pretty unbelievable."

And so it was. The CME, a no-cut finale at Tiburon Golf Club, was expected to be a shootout between the brilliant 18-year-old Lydia Ko, Rolex No. 1 in the world, and Inbee Park, 27, No. 2. Cristie Kerr, a tough veteran of 38, didn't read the script.

Herewith the Tale of Tiburon's 18th:

• Ko tied for seventh, getting the points for her second straight $1 million Race to the CME Globe bonus. She topped the money list with $2,800,202, won the Player of the Year Award and kept her Rolex No. 1 ranking. She bogeyed the 18th and missed the scoring title by .026 of a stroke.

• Park, finishing sixth, parred the 18th and posted a season average of 69.415 for the microscopic Vare victory over Ko. It left her needing only to complete her 10th year on the tour in 2016 to enter the LPGA Hall of Fame.

• Kerr surged down the final stretch, posting 68-69-66-68–271, 17 under, to take the CME tournament and the $500,000 first prize. It was her second win of the season, her career 18th. Kerr made her move brilliantly. She tied for the lead with a 35-foot birdie putt at the 15th, then took it with an eagle at the par-five 17th on a 224-yard five wood to 15 feet. At the 18th, Gerina Piller birdied and Ha Na Jang parred and they tied for second. Kerr parred it to preserve her one-shot edge for the win.

Said Kerr: "All of a sudden at the end, I was there when I needed to be."

Said Ko: "For it to come down to the last hole, last group, last putt — it's been a great season on the LPGA."

Ladies European Tour

RACV Ladies Masters
Winner: Su-Hyun Oh
See Australian Ladies Tour section.

ISPS Handa Women's Australian Open
Winner: Lydia Ko
See Australian Ladies Tour section.

ISPS Handa New Zealand Women's Open
Winner: Lydia Ko
See Australian Ladies Tour section.

World Ladies Championship
Haikou, Hainan, China
Winner: So Yeon Ryu

For the second year running the South Korean pairing of Inbee Park and So Yeon Ryu won the team event at the World Ladies Championship at Mission Hills Haikou. Their winning margin of 28 strokes from 2014 was, however, cut to a mere 15 strokes over Norway's Suzann Pettersen and Marianne Skarpnord, and the individual champion was not Park but Ryu. Park shared the lead or held it outright for the first three days, but Ryu, following a 65 in the third round after opening with a 72 and a 73, came from one behind to win by one on the final day.

Ryu, the 2011 U.S. Open champion, was two behind after three-putting the first green and three behind after a double bogey at the seventh where she took a penalty drop after finding black lava rocks off the tee. But three birdies in four holes from the 10th put her into the lead, and although Park birdied the 16th, Ryu went ahead again one hole later. A closing 69 gave her a 13-under-par total of 279 on the Blackstone course, while Park closed with her second 71 of the weekend. Pettersen tied for third place with China's Xi Yu Lin, two behind Park.

"I didn't expect that I had a chance to win this tournament, because on the first two days, I didn't play really well," Ryu said. "It was good to play with Inbee, my best friend on the tour. She is not number one right now, but I believe she is the true number one, so it was great to compete with her."

Lalla Meryem Cup
Agadir, Morocco
Winner: Gwladys Nocera

Despite a late wobble, Gwladys Nocera, who had led from the second round, hung on to win the Lalla Meryem Cup at Golf de l'Ocean in Agadir, an event held alongside the Trophee Hassan II on the men's European Tour. Nocera had won the tournament in 2007 before it was an official LET event, but in 2014 had bogeyed the 18th and lost in a playoff to Charley Hull.

Three birdies going out and another at the 11th put Nocera four clear of the field, but when Felicity Johnson claimed her sixth birdie of the day at the 13th and then Nocera had a double bogey at the 14th, the lead was down to one. It was the only fairway the 39-year-old Frenchwoman missed all day, but she compounded the error by three-putting for a six. But with Johnson bogeying two of the last three holes, Nocera could afford another three-putt at the 17th and still win by two strokes.

Rounds of 68, 65, 68 and 70 gave Nocera a 13-under-par total of 271, with Johnson, who closed with a 67, sharing second place with Melissa Reid, after a 66, and South African Nicole Garcia, who closed with a 70. It was the 14th win of Nocera's LET career and on 19 points leaves her one point short of Life Membership of the tour.

"I took a really stupid double bogey which put me in trouble, but I wanted to win this tournament again. I've always said it, and I'm really happy I did it."

Buick Championship
Shanghai, China
Winner: Shanshan Feng

Shanshan Feng dominated the Buick Championship, featuring for the first time on the Ladies European Tour, to win on home soil for the third time and in a tournament hosted by her own sponsor. Feng won by six strokes over Hyeon Seo Kang despite starting her final round with a double bogey. It was a tremendous piece of front-running by the 25-year-old, who won the LPGA Championship in 2012. Her opening 65 was only bettered by Stacy Keating's course record of 63, but after that the Chinese player was in command. She added a 67 on day two to go seven clear, a 69 in the third round to lead by seven strokes, and closed with a 70 to finish on a 17-under-par total of 271.

Kang got within three of the lead by birdieing the first two holes on the final day but finished with a 69 to end up three clear of Denmark's Nicole Broch Larsen. Feng recovered from her poor start with birdies at the fourth and fifth holes, and despite three more dropped shots on her card, never looked in trouble. She closed out the win with birdies at the last two holes. It was a fourth victory on the LET for Feng, who has twice won the Omega Dubai Ladies Masters and became the first Chinese player to win on the circuit at the 2012 World Ladies Championship.

Turkish Airlines Ladies Open
Belek, Antalya, Turkey
Winner: Melissa Reid

Melissa Reid scored her career low round of eight-under-par 65 on Sunday at the Turkish Airlines Ladies Open at Carya. Usually that might propel a player to victory, but this year's event started on the Sunday and finished on Wednesday in order to allow television coverage and attention away from weekends crowded with other golf tournaments and sports events. For Reid, it still worked out perfectly as the 27-year-old from Derby led from start to finish for her fifth LET title and a second Turkish Open victory after her win at National in 2010.

A second-round 69 put Reid three ahead of the field and even a 74 in breezy conditions on the third day kept her in front by one. With Pamela Pretswell, her nearest challenger, falling away with four dropped shots in the first five holes, Reid held a comfortable lead following a birdie at the first. Other than a bogey at the sixth, Reid parred her way to victory with a 73 for an 11-under total of 281. She won by four strokes over Gwladys Nocera, who got within two with three birdies in four holes around the turn but dropped two shots in the last four holes. The Frenchwoman had almost not teed up after an ankle injury a month earlier. Dame Laura Davies finished tied for third with Scots Sally Watson and Kylie Walker.

"When you win, you want to win properly and to lead every single day has been nice. I've not been in that position before, so to win in that way does make it extra special," said Reid. This was Reid's first win since the Prague Masters in 2012, a month after the death of her mother in a car accident in Germany.

Deloitte Ladies Open
Amsterdam, The Netherlands
Winner: Christel Boeljon

It took 21 years but Christel Boeljon delivered a second home victory for the Dutch fans at the Deloitte Ladies Open at The International in Amsterdam. Boeljon led from start to finish to repeat the feat first achieved by Liz Weima in 1994. The 27-year-old opened with two rounds of four-under 69 to lead by three strokes and then closed with a 71 for a 10-under-par total of 209. That gave her a four-stroke victory over Finland's Ursula Wikstrom and Denmark's Emily Kristine Pedersen.

Boeljon was out in even par, with a birdie and a bogey, but with Wikstrom getting within one after 10 holes, the Dutchwoman pulled away with birdies at the 11th and 12th. "This is a big one," said Boeljon, the former Solheim Cup player whose fourth win came three years after her last. "To be able to do it, leading from the start in front of a home crowd in my home country means a lot and it's something that I will never forget."

Both Wikstrom and Pedersen scored 70s to finish one ahead of Christine Wolf, Lucie Andre and Stacy Lee Bregman, who had been lying second overnight but closed with a 73. Pedersen, a rookie, found the tournament a welcome distraction from her final high school examinations, of which she had only one remaining.

ISPS Handa Ladies European Masters
Denham, England
Winner: Beth Allen

Four years after donating a kidney to her brother Dan, and three years after finishing runner-up at The Buckinghamshire, Beth Allen won her maiden Ladies European Tour title at the ISPS Handa Ladies European Masters. The 33-year-old from San Diego joined the tour in 2008, and if possibly one of the best players never to have won, she was certainly one of the most popular. Perhaps the difference this week was a new association with caddie Sophie Gustafson, the former tour winner and Solheim Cup vice captain in the first week of her new role as bag carrier and mentor.

"Sophie kept me grounded and I ended up getting it done, so I'm really happy," Allen said. "I wasn't sure if it was ever going to happen. I've waited a long time for this and I wanted it so, so bad, I'm ecstatic."

Allen started the final round five behind Caroline Masson and went to the turn in 31 on the last day before adding a birdie and a bogey coming home. She finished on a 12-under-par total of 276 after rounds of 71, 70, 68 and 67. Her victory was not confirmed until Leona Maguire, the world No. 1 ranked amateur who had birdied the short par-four 17th to tie for the lead, found a bunker behind the green at the 18th and took a bogey. The 20-year-old Irishwoman finished with a 69 to pip Nontaya Srisawang for second place, with Masson, after a 75, tying for fourth with Rebecca Artis and Nicole Broch Larsen.

Aberdeen Asset Management Ladies Scottish Open
Troon, Scotland
Winner: Rebecca Artis

Do not count out Rebecca Artis when it gets cool, drizzly and blustery, even if she is trailing by as many as half a dozen strokes. At the Helsingborg Open in 2013 the 26-year-old Australian rallied from five behind Caroline

Hedwall to win her maiden LET title. Two years later at Dundonald Links in North Ayrshire, Artis collected her second victory after recovering from a six-stroke deficit.

Her best-of-the week 66 in tricky conditions was all the more impressive for overtaking the likes of world No. 2 Lydia Ko and seven-time Solheim Cup player Suzann Pettersen. The pair appeared to be getting the ideal preparation for the Ricoh Women's British Open the following week when they shared the first-round lead, with Pettersen taking a two-shot advantage over Holly Clyburn after day two of the pro-am format event.

Artis, after opening with a 75, had a bogey-free 69 in the second round and then overcame a double bogey at the short par-four fourth. Having already birdied the third, she fought back with birdies at the fifth and sixth, then the eighth, had three in a row from the 12th and chipped in from 30 feet at the 16th.

Artis, with a six-under-par total of 210, won by two over Pettersen, four over Clyburn and five over Ko and Klara Spilkova. The first three of those all scored 74s. "Sometimes you fight all your life to try and get that first win and sometimes the second win is maybe even harder," Artis said. The win came a day after husband-caddie Geoff's 31st birthday.

Ricoh Women's British Open
Winner: Inbee Park

See Chapter 6.

Tipsport Golf Masters
Czech Republic
Winner: Hannah Burke

With Golf Park Pilsen next door to the Pilsner Urquell brewery in the Czech Republic, the champion at the Tipsport Golf Masters got drenched in beer rather than merely water. It tasted sweet to England's Hannah Burke, who won for the first time in her fourth year on tour. The 27-year-old from Welwyn Garden City came from four strokes behind to beat Denmark's Nicole Broch Larsen by two on a 13-under-par total of 200, with Lina Boqvist and Becky Morgan sharing third place a further shot back.

Burke opened with two 68s, her only dropped shots on the second day coming with a double bogey at the 18th hole. She dropped none at all in a closing 64 which featured seven birdies, four going out and then at the 12th, 14th and 17th holes. Broch Larsen, in her second year on tour, held the lead for much of the day until a triple bogey at the 16th where she drove into a bunker, found thick rough by the green and took five to get down.

"I didn't really focus too much on winning but setting little goals," Burke said. "I missed my goal yesterday, because I doubled the last, but it was to have no bogeys in 18 holes. Today I had seven birdies and no bogeys, so I managed my goal."

Melissa Reid's share of fifth place pushed her into an automatic qualifying spot for the Solheim Cup, just squeezing out Anna Nordqvist. Suzann Pettersen, Gwladys Nocera and Charley Hull also qualified.

Helsingborg Open
Helsingborg, Skane, Sweden
Winner: Nicole Broch Larsen

Three weeks after her triple bogey on the 52nd hole to lose the Tipsport Golf Masters to Hannah Burke, Nicole Broch Larsen bounced bark in fine style to win the Helsingborg Open wire-to-wire at Vasatorps. The 22-year-old Dane from Hillerod hit the front with a 68 on the first day and moved four clear with further rounds of 69 and 68. With three birdies in the first six holes on Sunday she was seven ahead, but with wind gusting up to 35 mph there was still drama to come.

After dropping shots at the eighth and 10th holes, she birdied the 11th but then drove into water at the 13th for a double bogey. South Africa's Ashleigh Simon birdied the 10th and 12th holes before a bogey at the 13th to draw within three but then parred in for a 72. She lipped out for a birdie on the 17th and almost holed a bunker shot at the last. Broch Larsen felt the pressure and bogeyed the last two holes, but a 75 for a 12-under-par total of 280 gave her a one-stroke victory. Fellow Danes Malene Jorgensen, with 71, finished in third place, while Nanna Koerstz Madsen shared fourth place with France's Joanna Klatten.

"It was close and I got very nervous in the end," Broch Larsen said. "I didn't get into the flow today but this win couldn't come at a better place, here in Sweden with a lot of guys from home. After my second place in the Czech Republic, it's just amazing."

Evian Championship
Winner: Lydia Ko
See Chapter 6.

The Solheim Cup
Winners: United States
See Chapter 6.

Lacoste Ladies Open de France
Saint-Jean-de-Luz, France
Winner: Celine Herbin

It took until the 75th hole but Celine Herbin fought all the way to record an unlikely victory at the Lacoste Ladies Open de France, her maiden professional title and the first home triumph for 11 years. The 32-year-old from Avranches now resides in Santander, in Spain, and had Vicente Ballesteros,

Seve's brother, as her caddie at Chantaco. Three over par for the front nine, Herbin had fallen five behind Emily Kristine Pedersen, whose 64 on the second day was the best round of the week.

Herbin got two shots back with birdies at the 10th and 14th holes but only ended up in a playoff after Danish rookie Pedersen bogeyed the 16th and had a double bogey at the 17th. Both finished on 269, 11 under par, with Herbin posting rounds of 66, 68, 65 before closing with a 70 as Pedersen did. Malene Jorgensen took third place, two behind after a 67, with Charley Hull in fourth ahead of a field which also included two-time winner Azahara Munoz and Solheim Cup winner Cristie Kerr.

After pars each at the first two extra holes, Pedersen three-putted the 18th for a bogey to give Herbin victory. "Emily was playing very well, so I knew I had to fight until the last hole — or until hole 75," she said. "To win my first tournament in my home country with so many people cheering for me, it's like a dream."

Xiamen International Ladies Open
Xiamen, China
Winner: Hye In Yeom

In her fifth season on the China LPGA Tour, South Korea's Hye In Yeom won the Xiamen International Ladies Open, a co-sanctioned event with the Ladies European Tour, by a comfortable margin of five strokes. The 23-year-old had started the final round tied for the lead with Thailand's Kusuma Meechai, who shared second place with defending champion Ssu-Chia Cheng.

Cheng, who scored a 64 in the third round, won the inaugural event in 2014 as a 17-year-old amateur and this was a best result in her first year as a member of the Ladies European Tour. Yeom now also has the opportunity to take up membership of the LET. "I feel like I'm still dreaming because I didn't expect to win," Yeom said. "I didn't see the scoreboard, so I just focused on my own game and didn't know I'd won until the last hole."

Yeom was four strokes behind after rounds of 71 and 68, but weekend scores of 65 and 68 left her clear of the field with a 16-under-par total of 272. She had only one bogey on the final day and collected a hat-trick of birdies from the 12th, while Meechai closed with a 73 and Cheng a 68. China's Jing Yan was disqualified for signing for a wrong score at the 14th hole, a three instead of a four, otherwise she would have tied for fourth place with Gwladys Nocera, who led for the first two days, Nanna Koerstz Madsen and Tzu-Chi Lin.

Hero Women's Indian Open
Gurgaon, India
Winner: Emily Kristine Pedersen

After losing a playoff for a maiden victory in France a month earlier, Emily Kristine Pedersen could not be denied at the Hero Women's Indian Open. On the challenging new Gary Player-designed course, the "Black Knight" at DLF Golf and Country Club in Gurgaon, Pedersen led from start to finish, an opening 70 followed by a pair of 73s to finish as the only player to match the par of 216. The 19-year-old Danish rookie finished one ahead of Cheyenne Woods, Malene Jorgensen and Becky Morgan.

Woods, the niece of Tiger, challenged with four birdies in the first 11 holes, but after a bogey at the 14th, the American missed a six-footer for birdie at the 17th and double-bogeyed the last after finding a bush from a fairway bunker. Pedersen also bogeyed the 14th to be even par for the day, but then birdied the next and, although she dropped shots at the last two holes, she kept her nose just in front.

"It's amazing and I'm so happy. The course has been a big challenge for us. My game has been very good, very steady. I didn't make any huge mistakes. I kept focused all day," said Pedersen.

Sanya Ladies Open
Sanya, China
Winner: Xi Yu Lin

Xi Yu Lin's love affair with the Sanya Ladies Open and the Yalong Bay course in Hainan continued as she successfully defended her title by rallying from four strokes behind with a round to play. After opening with rounds of 70 and 68, Lin charged to victory with a closing 65 with seven birdies, including three in a row from the 12th, to finish at 13 under par on a total of 203.

Lin won by two strokes over compatriot Jing Yan, who closed with a 68 following the disappointment of her disqualification from the Xiamen Open after signing for a wrong score on the final day. China's leading player Shanshan Feng made it a 1-2-3 for the home nation.

After first playing in the Sanya Open as a 14-year-old amateur, Lin has never been outside the top 10 in six appearances. "I just love this course so much and every hole, every fairway, every green," Lin said. "I need to find out why I always play well in Sanya."

Lin credits Feng's father for starting her playing the game and calls Feng a friend and "still my idol." Of the Chinese taking the top three spots, Feng said: "I think that's the first time ever. First and second place, they are both under 20, so I'm really happy to see that. I feel like the pressure is off now, because they are good enough to be on the leaderboard. It's not just me, I'm not lonely anymore."

Omega Dubai Ladies Masters
Dubai, United Arab Emirates
Winner: Shanshan Feng

Shanshan Feng calls the Emirates Club a "lucky place" for her, but the 26-year-old Chinese player performed brilliantly to win the Omega Dubai Ladies Masters for the second time in a row and the third year out of four. In those four appearance Feng is 64 under par on the Majlis course as she equaled her own record of 21 under par for the week to win by a runaway

12 strokes over Thidapa Suwannapura. It was a fine way for Feng to cap a season in which she became the first Chinese player to win the Ladies European Tour Order of Merit.

Although Feng was a shot off the lead on the opening day, she then went on to lead by two and then five strokes after days two and three. She had only two bogeys all week, both on the back nine in the third round following an outward 30. She scored successive 67s on the first three days and closed with a 66 with three birdies on each nine. On a day when the wind made scoring tricky, Suwannapura scored a 73 and Melissa Reid a 69 to take solo third place. Dame Laura Davies had been Feng's closest pursuer after two days but finished with scores of 77 and 73 to tie for 17th.

"Dubai has been really good to me, a lucky place, indeed," said Feng. "It wasn't easy out there in the windy conditions, but I kept my composure and got the job done in the end."

Japan LPGA Tour

Daikin Orchid Ladies
Nanjo, Okinawa
Winner: Teresa Lu

Most of the stars on the 2014 Japan LPGA Tour made their presences felt in Okinawa's season-opening Daikin Orchid Ladies tournament. Teresa Lu made the most of it, racing from a one-stroke deficit to a four-stroke victory. The 27-year-old Taiwanese ace, who had scored the third of her 2014 triumphs in the Japan LPGA Tour Championship finale, again victimized Lala Anai as she picked off her fifth career title with her closing 65 and 14-under-par 202.

Winless Anai, 28, who lost a playoff against Lu in the Tour Championship, held a one-shot lead over Lu entering the final round at Ryukyu Golf Club with her 69-67–136 after No. 1 Sun-Ju Ahn opened the week on top with her 68.

Things started brightly for Lala Sunday when she eagled the fourth hole, but, as she admitted later, "After that I played it overly safe," winding up in third place at 207 with a 71. From the seventh hole on, it was all Lu. She birdied Nos. 7, 9, 11 and 12 to surge in front and added three more on her way home. Rikako Morita, the 2013 Daikin Orchid victor, shot 66 and took second place with her 206. Multiple 2014 winners Bo-Mee Lee, Jiyai Shin and Momoko Ueda all finished in the top 10, but Ahn dropped to 14th after a second-round 74.

Yokohama Tire PRGR Ladies Cup
Konan, Kochi
Winner: Ji-Hee Lee

A surprising dry spell ended for South Korea's Ji-Hee Lee in the Yokohama Tire PRGR Ladies Cup tournament. Although remaining a strong contender during the ensuing years, Lee had not won since scoring her 17th victory on the Japan LPGA Tour in early 2012. It took a playoff, though, to snap the drought.

Lee seized the lead in Saturday's windy second round at Tosa Country Club in Koichi Prefecture, shooting 69 for 136 to move two in front of Soo-Yun Kang, Erina Hara and Mi-Jeong Jeon, the 2013 Yokohama Tire champion who had 22 victories on her tour record. Jeon had opened with a blazing, eight-under-par 64, but managed just 74 the second day.

Ai Suzuki, the 21-year-old 2014 Japan LPGA champion, who trailed by three shots entering the Sunday round, generated a 68 that carried her into a tie at 207 with Lee, who shot a final 71, but Suzuki lost in the subsequent playoff.

T-Point Ladies
Takeo, Saga
Winner: Akane Iijima

It hadn't been quite as long as it had been for compatriot South Korean star Ji-Hee Lee to end an absence from the winner's circle, but Mi-Jeong Jeon was on the verge of her 23rd victory and first in two years on the Japan LPGA Tour in the T-Point Ladies a week after Lee's win in the Yokohama Tire tournament. Then Akane Iijima intervened in a lengthy playoff.

With rounds of 74-72, Jeon languished eight strokes off the 36-hole lead of Thailand's O. Sattaya (Onnarin Sattayabanphot), whose 67-71–138 gave her a three-shot edge on Ritsuko Ryu, Yuki Ichinose and 31-year-old Iijima, who herself had gone five years unable to add to her six-win record.

Sattaya's game inexplicably fell apart Sunday at Wakagi Golf Club, her 81 opening the door to a flock of contenders. Iijima and Jeon jumped on the opportunity. Jeon put together a five-under-par 67 for 213, which would have been enough had Iijima not staged a strong finish after a double bogey at the 13th dropped her to even par for the tournament. She birdied three of the last five holes for 72 and her 213, forcing the young season's second playoff.

This one lasted an hour and 47 minutes and six holes before Iijima ended it with a birdie.

AXA Ladies
Miyazaki
Winner: Ritsuko Ryu

Ritsuko Ryu had good reason to be apprehensive about going overtime in her bid for the AXA Ladies tournament title, even if she didn't know everything about her opponent at the time. Not only did Bo-Mee Lee have eight Japan LPGA victories on her record and a third-place finish on the previous year's final money list, but she had won all of her previous four playoffs.

Fearful or not, Ryu matched Lee with birdies the first two times they played the par-five 18th hole in the playoff, then won the tournament with a third birdie there after Lee managed only a par. "After doing it, it was fun," Ryu conceded afterwards.

Lee and Onnarin Sattaya broke in front with five-under-par 67s Friday at UMK Country Club, Sattaya an early leader for the second week in a row. And once again, she faltered, as Lee followed with 73–140, winding up in a four-way tie for the 36-hole lead with Hiromi Mogi (69-71), Yun-Jye Wei (71-69) and Ryu (70-70). Ryu and Lee both shot 69s in the final round, one better than the other two leaders, to bring about the playoff. The victory was the third on tour for the 27-year-old Japanese player and her first in three years.

Yamaha Ladies Open
Fukuroi, Shizuoka
Winner: Ayaka Watanabe

The season's first 72-hole tournament came at the right time for Ayaka Watanabe and the wrong time for Asako Fujimoto.

Fujimoto, 25, whose only victory on tour came at the end of the 2011 season, led the way for three rounds, the usual duration of the ladies events, only to falter over the concluding 18 holes of the Yamaha Ladies Open and yield the title to Watanabe, who came from five shots off the pace to win her second career title.

Fujimoto jumped off in front on Katsuragi Golf Club's Yamana course with a five-under-par 67, a bare stroke ahead of Hikari Fujita. But with 68–135 Fujimoto ballooned her lead Friday to seven shots over Fujita (74), Watanabe (72-70), Sun-Ju Ahn (74-68), Airi Saitoh (73-69) and Ritsuko Ryu (69-73), the AXA Ladies winner in March.

Even when she slipped to 74–209 Saturday, Fujimoto retained a four-stroke lead over Bo-Mee Lee (68) and Yuko Mitsuka (70). On Sunday, though, she slumped to 76 and fell to fourth place as the 21-year-old Watanabe, with seven birdies and two bogeys, raced by to 67–281, two shots better than Yoko Maeda (69) and Lee (70), a runner-up for the second week in a row.

Studio Alice Ladies Open
Miki, Hyogo
Winner: Misuzu Narita

Talk about clutch performers. In a period of less than three full seasons from her first win, 22-year-old Misuzu Narita captured six tournaments on the Japan LPGA Tour without ever taking a lead into a final round and nailing four of them in playoffs.

The Studio Alice Ladies Open was her sixth and latest conquest. Narita produced a brilliant, eight-under-par 64 over the final 18 holes to snatch a first victory away from Hikari Fujita by two strokes with her nine-under-par 207.

It was a second straight week of disappointment for Fujita, who was an early contender in the Yamaha Ladies before crashing with a third-round 83.

Fujita came back on Hanayashiki Golf Club's Yokawa course in the Studio Alice with a pair of two-under-par 70s, sharing the first-round lead with Ritsuko Ryu. Then on Saturday she moved three strokes ahead of Narita (73-70) and three others — Erika Kikuchi (72-71), Saki Okamura (76-67) and Ayaka Watanabe (73-70), fresh from her Yamaha victory six days earlier.

Fujita did not falter this time, shooting a 69 Sunday, but it was no match for Narita's blazing finish. Kikuchi also shot 69 to finish third at 212, a stroke ahead of Teresa Lu (67), the leading money winner.

Vantelin Ladies Open KKT Cup
Kikuyo, Kumamoto
Winner: Erika Kikuchi

"Firsts" abounded for Erika Kikuchi at the Vantelin Open KKT Cup.

In an impressive breakthrough in her eighth season on tour, Kikuchi won her first tournament, was the year's first winner to lead from start to finish and, when her ¥18 million paycheck was added, she wound up in first place on the season's money list.

Kikuchi, entering the tournament off her second third-place finish of the year in the Studio Alice tournament and placements of seventh or better in four of the season's six previous events, squeezed out a one-stroke lead over four others with her four-under-par 68. Maiko Wakabayashi, Hikari Kawamitsu, Kotono Kozuma and Ayaka Watanabe, the Yamaha winner two weeks earlier, shot 69s.

Kikuchi doubled her margin Saturday with 70–138, two in front of Wakabayashi, establishing the edge with an eagle on the 18th hole. A closing 69 for a final, nine-under-par 207 gave her a five-stroke victory over Wakabayashi (72) and Bo-Mee Lee, a second-place finisher in her last three starts.

Fujisankei Ladies Classic
Ito, Shizuoka
Winner: Hikari Fujita

The 18th green of the Kawana Hotel Golf Club's Fuji course definitely was the place to be at the conclusion of the Fujisankei Ladies Classic on a late Sunday afternoon toward the end of May.

Six players came to the 54th hole of the tournament each at six under par, but none of the others could match the 17-foot birdie putt Hikari Fujita dropped to score her first win on the Japan LPGA Tour. "I can't believe it," exclaimed the 20-year-old, who was in her second full season on the circuit. "I was determined not to hesitate on that final putt, even if it missed the hole."

Fujita began the last round in a five-way tie for third place with her

71-69–140, three strokes behind leader Yuki Ichinose (70-67–137). Na-Ri Kim (73-66) occupied second place after 36 holes. In the end Sunday, though, the result turned on Fujita's putt as, all with a winner's chance at the 18th, Ichinose, Kim, Junko Omote, Bo-Mee Lee and Ayaka Matsumori, the first-round leader with 67, came up one shot short.

It was particularly disappointing for Lee, who had a fine 2014 season with three wins and a third-place finish on the money list. It was her fourth consecutive second-place finish, a tour record.

CyberAgent Ladies
Ichihara, Chiba
Winner: Jiyai Shin

In this case, familiarity bred contentment, not contempt, for Jiyai Shin. Playing on the course where she won the CyberAgent Ladies tournament in 2010, the South Korean star rolled, not without some anxiety, to a wire-to-wire victory in the 2015 edition on the West course of Tsurumai Country Club. It was her 10th win on the Japan LPGA Tour and fifth since returning full-time to the circuit and winning four times in 2014 after several successful seasons on the U.S. LPGA Tour.

Although she never trailed, Shin had to overcome a final-round charge by Erika Kikuchi, the leading money winner who picked up her first tour victory two weeks earlier in the Vantelin Open.

Shin opened with a four-under-par 68 and a one-stroke lead over amateur Mao Nozawa and remained a shot in front with her second-round 71–139, then with Megumi Kido (71-69) in the runner-up slot. Kikuchi, four back going into the last day, stirred up a 66 to make the strongest challenge against Shin, but the South Korean showed why she was once No. 1 in the Rolex Rankings by scoring four birdies on her last six holes for a 69–208 for a one-shot triumph. Kido shot 70 and finished third. Sadly, amateur Nozawa tumbled all the way from that first-round No. 2 position to dead last when she followed with 80-81.

World Ladies Championship Salonpas Cup
Tsukubamirai, Ibaraki
Winner: In-Gee Chun

They keep coming out of South Korea.

The latest young player from that nation to make a big early splash on the international scene was 20-year-old In-Gee Chun and it was quite a splash. Starting her first tournament on the Japan LPGA Tour in the season's first major — the World Ladies Championship Salonpas Cup — Chun romped to a four-stroke victory.

In the process, she became the youngest winner of that championship and the first player in tour history to win any of its major titles in her initial start. She supplanted Misuzu Narita, the 2014 victor at age 21, as the youngest World Ladies winner.

Although a newcomer in Japan, Chun didn't come out of the blue at Ibaraki Golf Club. She had won five times in Korea, the first in the 2013 Korea Women's Open, and lost in a three-way playoff in the LPGA/KLPGA co-sanctioned KEB HanaBank Championship in 2014.

Chun moved in front in the second round after opening with a six-under-par 66, one behind Bo-Mee Lee, once again a solid contender in her thus-far-futile bid for a 2015 victory. Chun's 70–136 put her a shot ahead of Lee (65-72) and two in front of Momoko Ueda (69-69), the eventual runner-up.

A six-birdie 67 Saturday fattened Chun's lead to five strokes over Ueda (70) and six ahead of Lee (72). Her 73–276 and Ueda's 72–280 Sunday settled the issue. Despite her 75–284, Lee held third place and took over the money lead from Erika Kikuchi, who finished 11th at 287.

Hoken No Madoguchi Ladies
Asakura, Fukuoka
Winner: Bo-Mee Lee

Finally! After nine starts replete with four second-place finishes, including a playoff loss, a third, a fifth, a sixth and no placing higher than 18th, a series of performances that elevated her to the top of the Japan LPGA Tour money list, Bo-Mee Lee picked off her first 2015 victory in the Hoken No Madoguchi Ladies tournament in mid-May.

It came appropriately as the 27-year-old South Korean defended one of her three 2014 victories. A strong presence on the circuit since her arrival off the Korean Tour in mid-2011, Lee scored her overdue ninth victory with a closing, bogey-free 66 that overcame the one-shot deficit that she had behind Jae-Eun Chung going in the final round. It spurted her to a four-shot victory margin over Shiho Oyama (68) with 206, 10 under par on Fukuoka Country Club's Wajiro course.

Chung led for two days, tied for first on Friday with Teresa Lu at 67, then a stroke ahead of Lee Saturday with her 72 follow-up. Lee had rounds of 68 and 72, a shot better than Lu and two ahead of Oyama in the fourth-place position. As Lee and Oyama finished one-two, Chung managed only a 74 Sunday and dropped back to a fifth-place finish at 213.

The first-place prize expanded Lee's lead on the money list to more than ¥24 million.

Chukyo TV Bridgestone Ladies Open
Toyota, Aichi
Winner: Yumiko Yoshida

Yumiko Yoshida had posted four victories during the previous three seasons on the Japan LPGA Tour, but was showing no sign that No. 5 was in the works when she teed off in the Chukyo TV Bridgestone Ladies Open. In her performances in her previous two starts, Yoshida finished 13 and 11 over par.

At Chukyo Golf Club, though, par was no problem for the 28-year-old. She carved out two rounds of 68 to go with the 65 on the par-72 Ishino course that gave her the 36-hole lead that she didn't relinquish in Sunday's final round. She went on to a one-stroke victory at 201 over Jae-Eun Chung, the tournament runner-up for a second straight week.

Mayu Hattori and Lala Anai shared the first-round lead with 67s, a stroke ahead of Yoshida, Chung and Yoko Ishikawa, who eventually tied for last place with following rounds of 77 and 75. Yoshida's second-day 65 jumped her two shots into the lead over Chung (67) and she clung to first place with the five-birdie, one-bogey 68 Sunday. Five strokes behind Chung were Anai and Momoko Ueda, who had not finished worse than fourth in her previous four starts and then had eight top-10s in her nine 2015 appearances on the circuit.

Resort Trust Ladies
Yamanashi
Winner: Teresa Lu

Teresa Lu put an end to the string of successive different winners from the start of the season when she scored a come-from-behind victory in the Resort Trust Ladies. At the same time, the 27-year-old Lu became the second player in three weeks to stage a successful title defense, matching Bo-Mee Lee's feat in the Hoken No Madoguchi tournament.

Lu, who won the season-opening Daikin Orchid tournament, shot a final-round 67 for her 14-under-par 202, as she picked up her sixth Japan LPGA Tour win at Maple Point Golf Club in Yamanashi.

She was in contention all week, opening with a 68, sitting in a massive third-place tie a shot off the lead of Jae-Eun Chung and Yeon-Ju Jung, a pair of non-winners. Lu's Saturday 67 moved her into solo second place behind Kaori Ohe, who fired a 65–134.

When Ohe fell back, the final round became a duel between Lu and Jiyai Shin, the one-time Rolex world No. 1, who had trailed by two after 36 holes having posted a pair of 68s. They were tied for the lead after nine holes, then the Taiwanese star nailed birdies on the 10th and 11th to move ahead. Lu clinched her triumph when she birdied the 17th and zeroed in her approach to two feet at the home hole for the winning birdie.

Yonex Ladies
Nagaoka, Niigata
Winner: Shiho Oyama

Shiho Oyama continued her rebirth play on the Japan LPGA Tour with her one-stroke victory in the Yonex Ladies, a tournament that climaxed her run to the tour money title when it was her fifth and final win of the 2006 season. After her ninth and 10th victories a year later, Oyama, plagued by a nagging elbow injury, went into a five-year mini-slump before getting back on the winning track in the final event of the 2013 season. She won twice more in 2014 before making the Yonex her 16th circuit victory.

Although she started solidly with a four-under-par 68, the 38-year-old veteran's first day was overshadowed by Teresa Lu, who came off her Resort Trust victory the previous Sunday with a leading 66, one better than Junko Omote. Oyama, with 67–135, joined Omote (67-68) at the top Saturday as they edged two strokes in front of Lu, who managed only a 71 for her 137.

Oyama outplayed Omote Sunday to grab her second Yonex title, shooting 71–206 to Omote's 73. Lu slipped into second place with 70–207, solidifying her hold on second place on the money list, but well behind leader Bo-Mee Lee, who had a rare off-her-game week with a tie-for-41st finish.

Suntory Ladies Open
Kobe, Hyogo
Winner: Misuzu Narita

Victory came in a much easier fashion when Misuzu Narita won her seventh tournament on the Japan LPGA Tour in the Suntory Ladies Open. In acquiring her six earlier victories, all since late 2012, Narita never led going into the final round and needed to win playoffs for four of them. Not this time at Rokko Kokusai Golf Club.

The 22-year-old Narita blistered the course with an opening-round, nine-under-par 63, led runner-up Sun-Ju Ahn by three shots and never trailed the rest of the way as she posted a two-stroke triumph with her 16-under 272. The only serious challenge came in the second round, when Hikari Fujita, the Fujisankei winner in April, shot 66–134 to match her 71–134.

However, Fujita struggled to a 76 the third day, much as Ahn did Friday with a 77, and Narita spurted four strokes in front of money leader Bo-Mee Lee and Ritsuko Ryu, the AXA Ladies victor in March, with 68–202. Lee cut that lead in half with four front-nine birdies Sunday and moved within one before Misuzu cushioned her margin with a birdie at the par-three 16th.

"I had goose bumps at that moment," she said. "I really enjoyed the duel." She finished with a 70 and Lee with 68–274 to finish second, a stroke ahead of Ryu.

Nichirei Ladies
Chiba
Winner: Jiyai Shin

Jiyai Shin continued to flourish in the downsized role she chose in 2014 when she opted to return full-time to Japan, despite the stardom she had achieved on the U.S. LPGA Tour the previous six seasons, explaining that "I was losing my passion" and that she wanted to be closer to her South Korean family.

Shin, who had posted 42 victories in South Korea, Japan and on the U.S. LPGA Tour during her 10-year career, picked up her second 2015 win in Japan with a successful title defense in the Nichirei Ladies tournament in Chiba. Unlike her earlier 2015 win in the CyberAgent Ladies, a wire-to-wire victory, the 27-year-old came from three shots back in the final round at Sodegaura Country Club to score a one-stroke victory.

Four behind leader Ah-Reum Hwang with her opening 71, Shin gained a stroke Saturday with 67–138 as Ji-Hee Lee, the Yokohama Tire winner in March, went in front with 67–135. Shin produced a bogey-free 67 Sunday, the winning fifth birdie at the 17th hole breaking her tie with Lee. "I thought I'd lose if I missed that putt," she noted after attesting her winning, 11-under-par 205. Lee shot 71 for her 206, edging Ai Suzuki (68), Sun-Ju Ahn (70) and Hwang (69).

Earth Mondahmin Cup
Sodegaura, Chiba
Winner: Bo-Mee Lee

Bo-Mee won a classic battle of the Lees at the Earth Mondahmin Cup tournament and expanded her lead in her bid for her first Japan LPGA Tour money title. She and Ji-Hee Lee, two of the premier players among the South Koreans on the Japan circuit, went to extra holes to decide the victor after dueling to a deadlock with matching, 14-under-par 274s in regulation time.

Both shot final-round 68s to force the overtime work. They both made pars at the par-five 18th, then, peculiarly, the pin was moved from back left to right front for the next go-around. Bo-Mee stiffed her third shot and knocked in the winning birdie putt after Ji-Hee, who had won her 18th Japan LPGA title earlier in the season, missed hers from long range.

Large leadership ties cropped up twice during the week at Camellia Hills Country Club in Chiba Prefecture. While the two Lees were shooting routine 70s the first day, the top spot was crowded with 67 shooters — Momoko Ueda, Hiromi Mogi, Misuzu Narita and Asako Fujimoto. With 68-67 rounds, Yasuko Satoh inched a shot in front Friday, then shared first place on 206 with the two Lees, Kaori Ohe and Da-Ye Na after the third round. Ohe shot 71 and Na 73, while Satoh plummeted to 48th place with a 79 on Sunday as Bo-Mee and Ji-Hee put on their show.

Bo-Mee, in picking up her 10th win in her four years in Japan, widened her gap appreciably in the money race over Taiwan's Teresa Lu. She finished second, seventh and third in her three previous full seasons on the tour. The winner's check put her into nine digits with ¥103,180,066.

Samantha Thavasa Girls Collection Ladies
Ami, Ibaraki
Winner: Yoko Maeda

Yoko Maeda's second victory on the Japan LPGA Tour didn't come much easier than her first one at the end of the 2014 season. No playoff this time, but she had to survive the late challenges of three players before claiming victory in the Samantha Thavasa Girls Collection Ladies Tournament in mid-July.

The 30-year-old Maeda, starting the final round at Eagle Point Golf Club in Ibaraki Prefecture three shots behind leader Ji-Hee Lee, shot a four-under-par 68. With her eight-under 208, she finished a stroke ahead of Erina

Hara, who had closed with a 65, and Bo-Mee Lee, the tour's leading money winner, who birdied three of the last four holes for 67, both for 209s.

Bo-Mee had two chances to force a playoff at the end, but barely missed birdie putts at the 17th and 18th holes and finished in a three-way tie for second with her 72–209.

Jiyai Shin, the first-round leader with 67 and two-time 2015 winner, wound up in a four-way tie for fourth place at 210 with Akane Iijima, Erika Kikuchi and Onnarin Sattaya. The runner-up finish enabled Bo-Mee Lee to fatten her money lead to more than ¥40 million.

Century 21 Ladies
Shizuoka
Winner: Sun-Ju Ahn

It was about time to hear from Sun-Ju Ahn. Until the circuit reached Shizuoka and the Century 21 tournament, the three-times leading money winner had little to show for her 2015 campaign after winning five times in 2014 and adding the third season title to her fine record.

Ahn was sitting 19th on the money list with only four top-10s on her 2015 record when she teed it up in the opening round at IzuOhito Country Club in late July and vented her frustration with a fiery, eight-under-par 64 en route to a wire-to-wire victory.

The 64 gave the 27-year-old just a one-shot margin on Erika Kikuchi, but Ahn broke the race open when she followed with 67–131 Saturday. Kikuchi fell back with 72 and Hiroko Azuma assumed the runner-up spot three back with 66-68–134. Hee-Kyung Bae was next with 69-66–135, and four ladies, including Kikuchi, stood at 137.

The win, Ahn's 19th in Japan, did not come easily on Sunday. She managed only a two-under-par 70 for her concluding 201 total, while Kikuchi rebounded with another 65 and Bae shot 67 to finish just a stroke behind with their 202s.

Daito Kentaku Eheyanet Ladies
Yamanashi
Winner: Erina Hara

All signs pointed to a bright future for Erina Hara when she shot 195 and ran away with her first Japan LPGA Tour victory in 2008 in the NEC Karuizawa 72 tournament. The then-20-year-old Hara posted top-10 finishes in six of her previous seven starts and placed 10th on the season's final money list.

Alas, the promise went unfulfilled over the next five seasons. Things looked up in 2014 when Erina climbed to ninth on the money list, but the victory drought didn't end until early August of 2015, when she led from start to finish, survived Sunday challenges from two of the tour's top stars and scored a one-stroke victory in the new Daito Kentaku Eheyanet tournament.

Hara shared the first-round lead with Serena Aoki as they shot 67s at Narusawa Golf Club in Yamanashi, a stroke in front of Momoko Ueda and

Young Kim and two ahead of seven others, including Sun-Ju Ahn, coming off her victory the previous Sunday in the Century 21 tournament. Scoring went higher overall in the second round and Hara eased two strokes into the lead with 69–136. Ahn also shot 69 for 138, finishing a stroke better than Hiromi Mogi (69-70), Ueda (68-71) and amateur Hina Arakaki, whose 66 was the low round of the tournament.

Hara's final 71–207 was just enough to hold off Ahn, the 19-time winner, who shot 70, and money leader Bo-Mee Lee, who rallied from 22nd place with a closing 65 for her 208.

Meiji Cup
Kitahiroshima, Hokkaido
Winner: Yukari Nishiyama

Yukari Nishiyama faced quite a challenge on the final day of the Meiji Cup tournament. She had endured a rather undistinguished career since joining the tour in 2008, her career-high 43rd position on the 2014 money list finally indicating some promise. Yet, on the closing Sunday at Sapporo International Golf Club with a chance to get her first win, the 33-year-old Nishiyama had to go off in a first-place tie with no less than Chinese star Shanshan Feng and with leading money winner Bo-Mee Lee just a stroke back.

Nishiyama responded with a three-under-par 69 to outplay those two talented opponents, but wound up in a playoff nonetheless, as Ai Suzuki, the 2014 Japan LPGA champion, closed with a 67 for her eight-under 208. Again, Nishiyama handled the pressure. After both players parred the par-five 18th to start the playoff, Nishiyama birdied it the second time around to capture her first victory. She was just the third first-time winner of the season and the first in nearly three months.

Lee shot 69 and Feng 70 Sunday to tie for third at 209 as Lee continued to widen her money lead to nearly double that of runner-up Teresa Lu. The first-day leaders disappeared from contention quickly. Kotone Hori, who opened with 67, shot 79 Saturday and eventually tied for 25th, while Junko Omote followed her starting 68 with 76 and deadlocked at 30th place.

NEC Karuizawa 72
Karuizawa, Nagano
Winner: Teresa Lu

Sitting in second place, Teresa Lu obviously wasn't going to concede the year's money title to Bo-Mee Lee, particularly after her third victory of the season in the NEC Karuizawa tournament enabled her to take a sizeable cut out of the huge margin Lee had on the winnings list.

The 27-year-old Lu rode a bogey-free opening 64 to a two-stroke victory with her 14-under-par 202 as Lee, with three decent rounds, tied for 10th on the North course at Karuizawa 72 Golf Club in mid-August. Lu's seventh triumph in Japan followed earlier 2015 wins in the season-opening Daikin Orchid and Resort Trust tournaments.

The first-round 64 gave her a one-stroke margin over Ai Suzuki, who was coming off a playoff loss to Yukari Nishiyama the previous Sunday, and at least three over the rest of the field. Neither played well Saturday. Lu's 71 dropped her two strokes behind Mayu Hattori (67-66–133), and Suzuki fell well back with 76 on her way to a 48th-place finish.

Brushing off memories of her unsuccessful finish as a 54-hole co-leader in the Women's British Open, Lu forged ahead early on Sunday with birdies on the first, third and fifth holes and picked up two more on the back side on her way to 67 and the two-stroke win. Both Miki Sakai and Ayaka Watanabe came up with 65s Sunday to share the runner-up position.

Even with the addition of the ¥14.4 million purse, though, the Taiwanese star still trailed Lee by more than ¥40 million.

CAT Ladies
Hakone, Kanagawa
Winner: Mayu Hattori

Mayu Hattori bucked the normal practice when her game was off kilter during the early months of the season. Usually players turn to their instructor for help when things are going badly. In Hattori's case, she turned away from her teacher, legendary Ayako Okamoto, after a run of missed cuts, deciding "I was getting soft and not thinking for myself."

The move didn't pay off immediately, but two consecutive top-10 finishes in early August led to her first victory in three years in the CAT Ladies tournament and left the 27-year-old, a tour regular since 2007, wanting more.

"This is a start. My next goal is to win multiple titles in one season."

A strong 69 on the par-73 Daihakone Country Club course carried Hattori to a 205 and a four-stroke victory over four other players, including Hee-Kyung Bae, who led her by a stroke going into the final round. Bae had turned the tables on Hattori Saturday with her 69-66–135 after Hattori opened the tournament in a four-way tie at seven-under-par 66 with Ai Suzuki, Nobuko Kizawa and Yuko Mitsuka.

Hattori shot 70 in the second round, then raced away from the field Sunday. She birdied the first hole and added four more against a lone bogey for the 69 as Bae stumbled with 74 to finish in the runner-up cluster at 209 with Momoko Ueda, Teresa Lu and Kumiko Kaneda. Lu, strengthening her hold on the No. 2 spot on the money list, and Ueda closed with 69s and Kaneda with 70.

The win, the first for Hattori since 2012, was her fifth on tour.

Nitori Ladies
Otaru, Hokkaido
Winner: Bo-Mee Lee

Bo-Mee Lee refused to let Teresa Lu either close the big gap she had in the money race or one-up her in the wins department. Three times during the first six months of the season, Lu posted victories only to have Lee respond with matching wins and restoration of her huge prize margin over the Taiwanese star.

Lee's third win of the year came at the end of August in the Nitori Ladies tournament in Hokkaido, where she was never out of first place but never comfortably in front either. She was one of six 69 shooters in Friday's opening round at Otaru Country Club, sharing the lead with Ayaka Watanabe, Misuzu Narita, Mi-Jeong Jeon, Erina Hara and Ayaka Matsumori.

Another 69 moved Lee ahead to stay Saturday. Her 138 was a stroke better than the scores of Watanabe and Jeon, with 69-70s, and Lala Anai, with 67-72. On a Sunday when the best score was a lone 70 by Mayu Hattori, the previous week's winner, Lee's one-under-par 71 was good enough to give her a two-stroke victory at 209 over Watanabe, the Yamaha titlist early in the season who had another second-place finish two weeks earlier in the NEC Karuizawa 72 tournament.

Lu did not play in the Nitori tournament.

Golf 5 Ladies
Gifu
Winner: Bo-Mee Lee

Misuzu Narita made a game effort to slow down the Bo-Mee Lee express, but Lee was unstoppable for the fourth time in the season and second week in a row.

The 27-year-old South Korean led Maiko Wakabayashi by a stroke, then two the first two days with rounds of 67-68, and was within a birdie putt on the 54th hole of going wire-to-wire in the Golf 5 Ladies tournament for her fourth win. Narita had come from five strokes behind to tie her with a closing, seven-under-par 65–205. Lee missed that putt on Mizunami Country Club's 18th green, sending the two into the season's sixth playoff.

It went five holes. Lee stayed alive with a 15-foot par putt the second time they played the 18th in the overtime. Both players bogeyed it the fourth time, then Narita drove into the woods and failed to match Lee's par to end it.

Teresa Lu, Lee's pursuer in the money race, just missed joining the playoff. Like Narita five back after 36 holes, Lu shot 66 Sunday and came up one shot short. The win was Lee's 12th in Japan and seventh in the last two seasons.

Japan LPGA Championship Konica Minolta Cup
Nagasaki
Winner: Teresa Lu

Teresa Lu embellished her Japan LPGA Tour record with her third major title while continuing her pursuit of Bo-Mee Lee in the race for the season's No. 1 ranking when she captured the Japan LPGA Championship in mid-September.

Lu broke from a third-round tie with third-place Momoko Ueda to score a two-stroke victory and add the LPGA Championship to the Women's Open and Tour Championships she landed in 2014.

The win, the 27-year-old Taiwanese star's fourth of the season and eighth in less than two years, chipped away at Lee's money lead and matched her four-victory record for the season. Lee finished fourth at the Passage Kinkai Island Golf Club.

The lead changed hands each of the first three days. Mayu Hattori, the CAT Ladies winner in August, led the first day with 68, Yumiko Yoshida after Friday's round with a pair of 69s. Lu and Miki Sakai were one back at 139. As Yoshida sky-rocketed to 81 Saturday, Lu shot 70 and Ueda roared into contention with by far the week's best round — a 64 — to share first place after 54 holes at 210.

With an inconsistent finish, Lu shot 71, one of only four sub-par rounds Sunday, to close out two ahead of Sakai (71) and Ueda (73). Lu offset bogeys at the 14th and 17th holes with birdies at the 16th and 18th for her final, seven-under-par 281.

Munsingwear Ladies Tokai Classic
Minami, Aichi
Winner: Ha-Neul Kim

Yet another winner on the Korea LPGA Tour made her mark in Japan when Ha-Neul Kim squeezed out a one-stroke victory in the Munsingwear Ladies Tokai Classic in mid-September.

Kim had won eight times in her native land before joining the 2015 Japan LPGA Tour, but had not made any significant showings until she tied for fifth place the previous week in the major Japan LPGA Championship. At Shin Minami Aichi Country Club, she pieced together three rounds in the 60s to score her maiden victory.

She took the lead away from lightly regarded Ayaka Matsumori in the second round after trailing the Japanese pro's opening 66 by three strokes. Kim's Saturday 67–136 moved her into a tie for the lead with Miki Sakai and a shot ahead of veteran standouts Jiyai Shin and Sun-Ju Ahn as Matsumori posted a par 72 for 138.

Kim's four-under 68–204 was just good enough to edge Matsumori, who bounced back with a 67, and Shin, who matched the 68 for her 205. With a 70, Sakai slipped into a tie for fourth with Sakura Yokomine, the 23-time winner on the Japan LPGA Tour still without a 2015 victory.

Miyagi TV Cup Dunlop Ladies Open
Rifu, Miyagi
Winner: Junko Omote

It had been a long, almost fruitless span of golf on the Japan LPGA Tour for Junko Omote since her impressive seasons in the early 2000s when she finished in the top 10 on the money list three successive seasons and won her first two tournaments in 2005. Omote had added only one victory — the 2013 Yonex — since then, but that victory perked up her game.

It peaked at the Miyagi TV Cup Dunlop Ladies Open in late September when she broke from a 36-hole tie and rolled to a three-stroke triumph over Shiho Oyama, who ironically won 2015's Yonex Open.

The 41-year-old Omote took a three-stroke lead the first day with a five-under-par 67, the only round in the 60s. Seven players shot 70s. Omote followed with 68, but Oyama, 38 and a 16-tournament winner, overtook her with a brilliant 63 that Saturday after starting with a par round. Grouped with the two veterans for the final 18 holes was Minami Katsu, the second-year high school student who was just 14 when she won the 2014 Vantelin Ladies Open. She was in third place alone, three shots back at 138.

Neither Oyama nor Katsu challenged Omote on another tough-scoring day Sunday at Rifu Golf Club in Miyagi. Omote shot 70 for 205, three ahead of Oyama (73) and four in front of Lala Anai (70). Katsu's 74 dropped her into a four-way tie for sixth place.

Neither Bo-Mee Lee nor Teresa Lu played at Rifu.

Japan Women's Open Championship
Ishikawa
Winner: In-Gee Chun

What a trifecta! The 2013 Korean Women's Open Championship ... the 2015 U.S. Women's Open Championship ... finally in early October, the 2015 Japan Women's Open Championship. All victories achieved by 21-year-old In-Gee Chun, the latest golf sensation to come out of South Korea. And that's not all she won during the first nine-plus months of 2015. Add the major World Ladies Championship Salonpas Cup in Japan in May and four tournaments on her home circuit.

The second win in Japan was the most difficult. Chun never led over the first 71 holes at Katayamazu Golf Club, wound up in a three-way tie at two-under-par 286 and went four extra holes before prevailing in the ensuing playoff.

Chun shot 71 the first day, tied for fourth place, three strokes behind leader So Yeon Ryu. On Friday, she shot 73 and was tied for ninth, four back of Ryu (68-72–140). Another 71 in the third round pulled her back to a fourth-place tie, three behind Erika Kikuchi, who took over first place with her 67–212.

On a Sunday when 69 was the best score posted, Mi Hyang Lee, who started the day four off the lead, finished with 70 for her 286. Chun was the next of the three playoff contenders to reach the tough 18th, which she had bogeyed each of the previous three rounds. Not his time. Her par there for 71 matched Lee's 286. Kikuchi, an eight-season veteran who won her first title earlier in the year in the Vantelin Open, came to the last hole leading by a stroke, but bogeyed to send the tournament into overtime.

The three players matched pars the first two times they replayed the 18th. Lee went out with a bogey the third time around and Chun claimed the title with a bogey the final time they played the hole.

Money leader Bo-Mee Lee fattened her advantage over Teresa Lu with a tie-for-sixth finish while Lu was missing the cut.

288 / WOMEN'S TOURS

Stanley Ladies
Susano, Shizuoka
Winner: Bo-Mee Lee

The finish was different and unexpected, but Bo-Mee Lee continued her drive toward the 2015 money title on the Japan LPGA Tour with the fifth victory of her brilliant season in the Stanley Ladies tournament.

Dense fog blanketing the Tomei Country Club lasted so long the morning of the final round that officials were forced to reduce play to nine holes and Lee jumped on the opportunity. Just one shot out of the lead after 36 holes, Lee produced a four-under-par 32 that gave her a three-stroke victory with the odd score of 168, 12 under for the unusual distance.

It was pretty much a three-way race all week, as Asako Fujimoto and Maiko Wakabayashi each led for a day before tying for second place behind Lee Sunday. Fujimoto opened with 66 Friday, taking a one-stroke lead over Wakabayashi and Lee. Wakabayashi followed with a 68–135 Saturday. Lee remained a shot back, along with Megumi Kido (68-68), as Fujimoto dropped three behind with a 72–138.

Wakabayashi shot 36 and Fujimoto 33 Sunday as they tied for second at 171, a shot ahead of Kido (36–172). No. 2 Teresa Lu tied for 33rd place and dropped ¥65 million behind Lee in the money race. The win was Lee's 13th in Japan.

Fujitsu Ladies
Chiba
Winner: Teresa Lu

It became almost like a sophisticated, powderpuff prize fight. Punch! Counterpunch! Bo-Mee Lee won her fourth of the Japan LPGA season. Teresa Lu won her fourth of the year the following Sunday. Lee won her fifth four weeks later. Lu won her fifth seven days after that in the Fujitsu Ladies tournament … and it was decisive.

The 27-year-old Taiwanese star, the only player with a realistic chance of overtaking Lee in the money race, bolted in front with an opening-round 67, one of only two scores below the par 72 of the Tokyu Seven Hundred Club's West course all day. Ayaka Watanabe, the eventual runner-up, shot 70.

Lu widened her lead over Watanabe to four strokes Saturday, racking up eight birdies and a bogey for 65–132 as Watanabe, with 66, held second place by four shots herself, interestingly over Bo-Mee Lee (73-67–140). Lu wasn't as sharp Sunday. She absorbed five bogeys, but four birdies and an eagle at the 16th hole added up to 71 and the winning, 13-under-par 203. It was her career ninth victory, all since November 2013. Watanabe matched the 71 for 207, finishing second, two in front of Serena Aoki and Jiyai Shin.

Lee slipped to a 12th-place tie with a closing 74, but still maintained a ¥50 million lead on the money list.

Nobuta Group Masters Golf Club Ladies
Miki, Hyogo
Winner: Ji-Hee Lee

Ji-Hee Lee emerged from a peculiar final round with the 19th victory of her fine career in Japan, her second of the season. What were the odds that her closing, even-par 72 would hold up after she took just a one-stroke lead into the last 18 holes over runaway money leader Bo-Mee Lee and a three-stroke margin over No. 2 Teresa Lu? Who would have expected those two players to shoot 75s Sunday? Which they did.

Only four players were in the 60s in the final round, one of them three-time money champion Sun-Ju Ahn, who was the only serious challenger to Ji-Hee Lee. She shot 69 on the Masters Golf Club course, falling one stroke short of Lee's seven-under-par 279.

Erina Hara, who eventually tied for 25th, led the first day with 67, the low score of the week. She had a shot on Bo-Mee Lee, Aoi Ohnishi and Rui Kitada, but fell from contention with a 76 Friday as seven players — eventual winner Lee, Lu, Ohnishi, Rikako Morita, Misuzu Narita, Kotone Hori and Ah-Reum Hwang — swarmed the top spot with 138s. Ji-Hee Lee moved ahead of the others to stay with her third-round 69, also a tough-playing day with just four rounds in the 60s. At 207 she led Bo-Mee Lee (69) and Ohnishi (70) by a shot, Narita (71) by two, and Morita (72) and Lu (72) by three.

The win moved Ji-Hee Lee into third place on the money list, just ahead of Jiyai Shin but more than ¥100 million behind Bo-Mee Lee.

Hisako Higuchi Ponta Ladies
Hanno, Saitama
Winner: Ayaka Watanabe

Although youth prevailed once more on the Japan LPGA Tour, that storyline could have been taken to an extreme at the Hisako Higuchi Ponta tournament.

Twenty-two-year-old Ayaka Watanabe rolled to a decisive, four-stroke victory at Musashigaoka Golf Club, but only after breaking from a first-place, 36-hole tie with Hiromi Mogi and Nasa Hataoka. Mogi is a veteran with six victories on her record, but Hataoka, a second-year, 16-year-old high school student, was playing in her first professional tournament.

On a day of high scoring, Hataoka shot an opening, four-under-par 68, one stroke better than the score of Saki Takeo, the only other player in the 60s that Friday. Hataoka followed with a 71 the next day, dropping into the three-way deadlock with Mogi (70-69) and Watanabe, who advanced from her starting 72 with a 67. Asaka Fujimoto (70-70) and Takeo (69-71) trailed by a stroke.

Watanabe, notching her second win of the season and third of her career on the circuit, blew away the opposition Sunday with a seven-birdie 66, although Hataoka remained a factor until taking four consecutive bogeys in the middle of the back nine. She shot 73 and tied for seventh place. Mogi's 72 settled her in a fourth-place tie, and Fujimoto, who lost to Watanabe in the Yamaha Ladies in April after leading for three rounds, took second place with 69–209.

Watanabe moved into third place on the money list, but was ¥100 million behind leader Bo-Mee Lee and ¥50 million behind No. 2 Teresa Lu, neither of whom played the Hisako Higuchi.

Toto Japan Classic
Shima, Mie
Winner: Sun-Ju Ahn

Sun-Ju Ahn professed surprise when she won the Toto Japan Classic, outplaying a mixed field of strong golfers from the U.S. and Japan LPGA Tours in the event, formerly known as the Mizuno Classic, that highlights the late season in Japan.

But it was far from a startling development. After all, the 28-year-old South Korean had posted 19 earlier victories on the Japan LPGA Tour, 27 overall in her career and was the circuit's leading money winner three times, most recently in 2014. She had won the Century 21 Ladies earlier in the year.

"I didn't think that I'd be able to win the tournament, but I'm very happy," expressed Ahn, who landed the title with a birdie on the first hole of a playoff against American Angela Stanford and compatriot Ji-Hee Lee after the three had tied in regulation with 16-under-par 200s at Kintetsu Kashikojima Country Club.

Stanford had been the first-round leader with 65, then dropped back into a three-way tie for third the second day when Jenny Shin, winless in five seasons on the LPGA Tour, came up with a 65 of her own for 131. Ha-Neul Kim (66-66) was one back, and Ahn (68-65) and Thailand's Pornanong Phatlum (67-66) sat with Stanford at 133.

With a 70 Sunday, Shin fell a stroke short of the playoff as Lee shot 66 and Ahn and Stanford 67s for their 200s. Ahn struck her approach five feet from the cup on the playoff hole to set up the winning birdie after Lee and Stanford missed from long range.

Itoen Ladies
Chonan, Chiba
Winner: Bo-Mee Lee

Bo-Mee Lee climaxed her remarkable season on the Japan LPGA Tour with a record-setting sixth victory in the Itoen Ladies tournament that was as impressive as it was one for the books.

With her wire-to-wire triumph at the Great Island Club in Chiba, Lee became the first player in circuit history to top the ¥200 million mark in a single season — ¥207,817,057 — and she did it with two more events still on the schedule. The victory purse of ¥18 million also clinched Lee's first money title. Closest pursuer Teresa Lu, who herself was having an outstanding season with five wins, tied for third in the Itoen, but her season's earnings had her ¥65 million behind the 27-year-old South Korean whiz.

Lee, who didn't win the first of her six 2015 victories until May, took the first-round lead with a seven-under-par 65 and never looked back. The 65 gave her a one-stroke lead over Lu and Kotone Hori, and her follow-up 68 Saturday extended the gap to two shots over Serena Aoki, Erika Kikuchi and Maiko Wakabayashi, all with 68-67 rounds.

Lee's closing 69 maintained the two-stroke edge and a final 14-under-par 202. It was her 14th career win in Japan. Aoki also shot 69 to take second place, two ahead of Hori (69) and Lu (70).

Daio Paper Elleair Ladies Open
Fukushima
Winner: Bo-Mee Lee

Bo-Mee Lee's remarkable season rolled on at the Daio Paper Elleair Open as, for the second time in 2015, she posted back-to-back victories and racked up her seventh title of the Japan LPGA season. She also padded her record tournament bank account past the ¥225 million mark, more money than Toshimitsu Izawa won when he set the still-standing record total on Japan's men's circuit in 2001.

Lee seized control of the Elleair tournament with a third-round 65 at Itsuura Teien Country Club in Fukushima Prefecture and went on to a five-stroke victory, her 15th in Japan. She closed with a 69 for a final 16-under-par 272, five in front of Ai Suzuki and Ayaka Watanabe.

Suzuki, the 2014 LPGA champion, shared the first-round lead with Misuzu Narita with 68s, then, with a 66–134, moved two shots ahead of Watanabe (71-65), Junko Omote (69-67) and Narita, who repeated her 68 Friday. Lee was four behind at that point with rounds of 70-68 before charging to the fore Saturday with the 65 that gave her a three-stroke lead over Watanabe (70) and four over Momoko Ueda.

Suzuki shot 69 and Watanabe 71 Sunday in securing the joint runners-up position.

Japan LPGA Tour Championship Ricoh Cup
Miyazaki
Winner: Jiyai Shin

It was a case of domination by a few in the final two months of the Japan LPGA Tour season. Beginning with In-Gee Chun's victory in the Women's Open the first week of October, all of the titles the rest of the season went to players who had already won earlier in the year. Jiyai Shin topped it off at the end of November with a victory in the Japan LPGA Tour Championship Ricoh Cup, her third of the season and 12th in Japan.

Scoring was high all week at Miyazaki Country Club in Miyazaki Prefecture. Only four rounds in the 60s were posted, one a 68 that wrapped up 27-year-old Shin's six-stroke victory over Shiho Oyama and the rest of the elite field made up of the top 28 money winners of the season.

The first of those rounds — 69 — gave Yoko Maeda the first-round lead by one over Shin, two over Sun-Ju Ahn. The second one — 66 — vaulted Yumiko Yoshida from 18th place (75) into a first-place tie with Shin, who followed her opening 70 with a 71. Oyama, who won the Tour Championship in 2005 and 2013, pushed a stroke ahead of Shin the third day with 70–212 to Shin's 72–213, but stumbled in her bid for a third Tour Championship title with a 75 Sunday as Shin breezed to victory with the 68 and the seven-under-par 281 total.

The win, her first major in Japan, went on a record that also includes a pair of majors on the LPGA Tour (the Women's British Open in 2008 and 2012) and five on the Korean LPGA circuit.

Bo-Mee Lee, the runaway money champion of 2015, tied for sixth and added ¥4,680,000 to her tour income for the season, setting the record at ¥230,497,057.

The Queens
Miyoshi, Aichi
Winner: Japan

The Japan LPGA hosted the inaugural international match play tournament — The Queens — and were not very hospitable on the golf course at Miyoshi Country Club. The nine-player team reigned over the three groups of visitors from start to finish and accumulated 41 points to win by three over the golfers of the Korean LPGA. Far behind in the three-day event were the Ladies European Tour with 12 points and the Australian Ladies Tour with seven.

Japan got off to a flying start, winning all four of its fourball matches the first day for 12 points, five better than Korea and eight ahead of Europe. Australia was shut out. Japan widened the gap to eight over Korea with three wins and a halve in Saturday's foursomes competition, but the team from continental Asia took a run at the leaders in Sunday's singles.

Korea lost only one of its nine matches, picking up 24 points, but with each win worth three points, that lone loss of Yoon Ji Cho to Japan's Ayaka Watanabe made the difference. The Japanese team, with six wins and a halve for 19 points, emerged with the overall victory on the final cold and blustery December day.

Watanabe, Ritsuko Ryu, Erika Kikuchi, Miki Sakai and Akane Iijima won all of their matches for Japan, but Jung Min Lee was the only all-victor for the Koreans.

Korea LPGA Tour

In-Gee Chun did not only dominate in her home country in 2015, she could not stop winning major championships wherever she went. The highlight, of course, was her victory at the U.S. Women's Open when the then 20-year-old became only the fourth player to win the biggest trophy in the women's game on her debut. Chun's final round of 66 at Lancaster Country Club gave her a one-stroke victory over Amy Yang, with Inbee Park and Stacy Lewis two shots further back.

It was a stunning victory for the former maths prodigy who was nicknamed "Dumbo" by her coach due to her "superhuman hearing," not because it leads to distraction but more indicating curiosity in finding out about lots of different interests.

Chun will take up her LPGA card in America in 2016 but could also have joined the JLPGA after winning two majors in Japan. She claimed the Salonpas Cup and the Japan Woman's Open on her only two starts on that circuit.

In her third season on the LPGA Tour of Korea, Chun won five times, bringing her career KLPGA total to nine, including two more majors. She won the Hite Jinro Championship and the KB Financial Group Star Championship, where she beat world No. 1 Park by one stroke. These were her second and third Korean major wins after she won the national title in 2013. Chun also won the Samchunli Together Open, retained her title at the S-Oil Champions Invitational and claimed the Doosan Match Play Championship after winning through six rounds of often tense finishes, including the final in which she beat Han-Sol Ji by one hole.

Although Chun claimed the money list, the Grand Prize points list and the stroke average titles, she did not have everything her own way, finishing runner-up to Min Sun Kim at the KG-Edaily Ladies Open after a closing 72 to the winner's 64.

Sung Hyun Park won the Kia Motors Korea Women's Open Championship following in the footsteps of Hyo Joo Kim (2014) and Chun (2013). She beat Jung Min Lee by two strokes despite a final round of 77. Victory in her national championship was her maiden title on the KLPGA circuit, but she won twice more before finishing runner-up to Lexi Thompson at the LPGA KEB HanaBank Championship.

Jung Min Lee and Jin Young Ko also won three times, the latter leading for much of the final day of the Ricoh Women's British Open before finishing runner-up to Inbee Park at Turnberry. There were two wins apiece for 2014 Evian champion Hyo Joo Kim and Ha Na Jang.

There were a record 31 events in 2015, worth in the region of $18 million, including The Queens presented by Kowa, a team event in Japan won by the home tour, with the KLPGA contingent taking second place ahead of the LET and the ALPG. That total also included the Hyundai China Ladies Open in December which counted on the 2016 KLPGA schedule and was won by Sung Hyun Park to give her a fourth win for the calendar year.

Australian Ladies Tour

Oates Victorian Open
Barwon Heads, Victoria
Winner: Marianne Skarpnold

Seven days after moving into a new home at the 13th Beach Golf Links, Norway's Marianne Skarpnold became a winner at the venue when she claimed the Oates Victorian Open by three strokes. Extraordinarily, her fiancé Richard Green won the concurrent men's tournament. While Green needed extra holes to win and was on the practice range preparing for a playoff, Skarpnold maintained her overnight three-stroke advantage to finish clear of England's Holly Clyburn and Australia's Su-Hyun Oh, in her first event as a professional.

After an opening 70, it was two middle rounds of 68 that put the 28-year-old Norwegian, a three-time winner on the Ladies European Tour, in front, and she closed with a 73 for a 13-under-par total of 279. Clyburn also closed with a 73, while Oh had a 72. Rachel Hetherington, in her first 72-hole tournament for over four years, shared fourth place with Rebecca Artis.

"It is like a dream coming true, a fairy tale," Skarpnold said. "This week has been unreal, first we got engaged last week, moved into the house on Monday, he had an albatross on Wednesday, and here we are today winners, so don't think I can ask for anything more."

Green said: "I've seen what Marianne has been through in the last few months with her game and her wrist injury. I've seen an immense amount of work put in by her and I'm very proud of her."

RACV Ladies Masters
Benowa, Queensland
Winner: Su-Hyun Oh

After finishing second in her first tournament as a professional at the Victorian Open, Su-Hyun Oh was first on her second appearance a week later at the RACV Ladies Masters at Royal Pines. The 18-year-old Victorian produced a brilliant finish with four birdies in the last four holes to win by three strokes over compatriot Katherine Kirk and the English duo of Charley Hull and Florentyna Parker. Oh was the fourth home winner of the prestigious title, following 2009 champion Kirk, Jane Crafter and eight-time winner Karrie Webb. Oh said she was helped by an exchange of texts with Webb before the final round. "I asked her: 'What do I need to do, you've won this eight times?' Karrie said: 'Just don't think, just do it kind of. Just let it go, just keep doing what you're doing.'"

In 2013, when she won the Australian Amateur and was the world No. 1 amateur, Oh finished runner-up to Webb at Royal Pines. In her fourth appearance in the event, Oh shared the lead with an opening 69 and was one behind Hull, Holly Clyburn and Eun-Woo Choi after further scores of 75 and 72. While Hull's challenge faded after a triple bogey at the sixth, Kirk and Parker closed with 69s to post the clubhouse target.

Oh fell one behind with a bogey at the 14th before a stunning finish. She pitched close at the par-five 15th, hit her tee shot at the short 16th to six feet, hit the flagstick with her approach to the 17th, and two-putted at the last before shedding a tear of delight while embracing her father and caddie. Her closing 69 left Oh on a seven-under total of 285.

Kirk said: "She looked pretty composed out there, she's got the goods."

ISPS Handa Women's Australian Open
Black Rock, Victoria
Winner: Lydia Ko

In her second appearance as the No. 1 on the Rolex Rankings, Lydia Ko lived up to her billing with victory at the ISPS Handa Women's Australian Open. Although she became the youngest-ever world No. 1 at the Coates Championship, Ko let a win slip through her hands there, but the 17-year-old made no mistake in sweltering conditions on the famous Royal Melbourne composite tournament course.

Ko recorded scores of 70, 70, 72 and 71 for a nine-under-par total of 283 and won by two strokes over Amy Yang and by five over Ariya Jutanugarn. It was a sixth LPGA title for Ko, a ninth career title — her first came as an amateur at the 2012 NSW Open — and she added to her "youngest to" list by becoming the youngest to lift the Patricia Bridges Bowl.

Ko shared the lead with Jutanugarn, the 19-year-old Thai, at the start of the final round but began nervily, three-putting the first two greens for a bogey and a par. But at the short par-four third, Ko drove in front of the green and then chipped in from 50 yards for an eagle-two. Yang became Ko's main challenger, twice taking the lead after going out in 34 and birdieing the 10th and 14th holes. Ko made a brave bogey putt at the eighth to stay in touch and then birdied the 10th and 12th holes, making a 12-footer at the latter. As Ko parred the last six holes, Yang missed crucial putts to bogey the 15th and 17th and finish with a 72. Jutanugarn closed with a 76 to finish third.

"Whenever I saw the leaderboard, Amy had made another birdie and another one, so I was like, 'ok, you need to get your stuff together and you need to make birdies,'" Ko said. "She's such a consistent player and she's been putting so well on these fast greens, so I knew she was tough to get rid of."

Ko added: "To win on such an amazing golf course here at Royal Melbourne, I think that's another bonus. And I didn't really know how I would play and how I would react to becoming world No. 1, and I always wondered that. Sometimes I got close and I was still world No. 2, 3 or 4, and then at Ocala I couldn't pull off the win but then I became world No. 1. It's good to know that just from my confidence that I can still play good and not really think about the world rankings."

ISPS Handa New Zealand Women's Open
Christchurch, New Zealand
Winner: Lydia Ko

A week after winning the Australian Open, Lydia Ko returned home to complete the double and win the ISPS Handa New Zealand Women's Open at Clearwater. It was the second time in three years the 17-year-old world No. 1 had won her national championship, having won as an amateur in 2013. Ko finished on a record score of 202, 14 under par, and four strokes ahead of Australian amateur Hannah Green.

After an opening 70 that left her four shots off the lead, Ko lived up to her billing as the pre-tournament favorite by breaking the course record with an 11-under-par 61. Having not slept well and after a poor warm-up on the practice range, Ko bogeyed the first hole but then eagled the second and posted nine birdies in the holes from the fourth. A 10th birdie at the final hole gave her a three-shot lead over Charley Hull.

Ko birdied the first two holes on the last day but found the water at the eighth for a double bogey and bogeyed the ninth as both Ko and Hull went out in even par. Hull then got within two with an eagle at the 10th to Ko's birdie, but the Englishwoman dropped five shots in the last seven holes to fall to a tie for sixth place. Ko closed with a 71, while Green's 68 put her one ahead of Denmark's Nanna Koerstz Madsen.

"It's just great to have won the two Opens back to back," Ko said. New Zealand Prime Minister John Key played a part in Ko recovering from her blip at the end of the front nine. "I saw the PM and he kind of patted my back and that gave me a little power and I made a couple of birdies after that."

Bing Lee Fujitsu NSW Women's Open
Sydney, New South Wales
Winner: Holly Clyburn

Six days of resting and having physiotherapy on a hip injury that caused her to withdraw from the New Zealand Open after one round helped Holly Clyburn to victory in the Bing Lee Fujitsu NSW Women's Open at Oatlands in Sydney. Clyburn broke out of a large group sharing the lead at 10 under par by holing from nine feet for her fifth birdie of the day at the 14th hole. The 24-year-old Englishwoman, who won the 2013 Deloitte Ladies Open as a rookie on the Ladies European Tour, parred her way to the clubhouse, holing from three feet at the last for a one-stroke victory ahead of Rebecca Artis, Christine Wolf, Vikki Laing and Fabienne In-Albon.

Clyburn, who tied for second at the Victoria Open the previous month, opened with 69 before posting a second-round 66 that included five birdies in a row on the front. Her closing 70 left her on an 11-under-par total of 205 and ahead of the chasing pack, including Wolf's impressive closing 64.

"It means a lot," Clyburn said. "I've have been knocking on the door for a few months now. I have been working hard and did not have any expectations after last week, so yeah, it has just been great and a weight has been lifted off my shoulders." She added of her physio: "I wouldn't have gotten through this week without him."

Australia Classic
Luddenham, New South Wales
Winner: Yanhong Pan

An exciting finish to the Australia Classic at Twin Creeks, in Sydney, saw China's Yanhong Pan pip Australia's Rebecca Artis after a two-shot swing at the final hole. Artis took a one-shot lead after birdies at the 15th and 17th holes but then struggled off the tee and bogeyed the 18th. Pan hit her approach to 12 feet and holed the putt to avoid a playoff.

Artis led with an opening 65, but Pan took a one-shot lead with her own 65 on the second day, a round that included eight birdies and an eagle at the 11th. The 31-year-old, who has won four times on the China LPGA circuit, dropped a shot at the third in the final round but added birdies at the fifth, sixth and 12th holes before striking the winning blow at the last. Her closing 69 matched Artis and gave her a total of 14-under-par 202.

"It's awesome to win," said Pan. "It was a tense competition for both of us. Artis is a good player and kept chasing closely. At the last, I feel I got the chance to win. I closed my eyes to putt, I made it. Finally, I won. I'm so happy."

13. Senior Tours

The 2015 season was the Champions Tour's 36th and was set for 26 events. But two had to be removed during the season. That's one way to keep Bernhard Langer from winning.

It was another Bernhard Langer year. Jeff Maggert, in his second season on the tour, won four tournaments, two of them majors. Langer won twice, the Constellation Senior Players Championship (his fifth senior major) and the San Antonio Championship, but also piled up five seconds and two thirds, and took the season-long Charles Schwab Cup points race and its $1 million annuity bonus. He topped the money list with $2,340,288, ahead of Jeff Maggert's $2,240,836, and was the scoring leader, averaging 68.69, nipping Colin Montgomerie, at 69.20.

So Langer was voted Player of the Year for a record fifth time, and was the leading money winner for the seventh since joining the tour in 2007.

Langer turned the Senior Players into a lark. He led by eight strokes going into the final round and won by six. "It was a magical week," he said. He worked some more magic in the San Antonio Championship three months later. He came from behind with a 65 and scored his 25th tour victory by three strokes.

He almost swept everything in the season-closing Charles Schwab Cup. He passed Colin Montgomerie and Jeff Maggert to win the points race, and was about to take the tournament, too, until Billy Andrade caught up and tied him.

Heading for the playoff, Andrade, noting that Langer had already won the Schwab Cup, cracked "He doesn't need to win this tournament as well." Andrade posted his third tour win, and third of the year, with a birdie on the first extra hole. Earlier, Andrade teamed with Joe Durant to win the Bass Pro Shops Legends of Golf, and made his first solo win in the Boeing Classic.

Until Langer's closing heroics, it was Jeff Maggert's year. Maggert, a three-time winner on the PGA Tour, announced himself immediately on the Champions Tour early in 2014 by winning in his debut, the Mississippi Golf Resort Classic. He followed up with four wins in 2015.

He won his first senior major and the first major of his career, the Regions Tradition, beating Kevin Sutherland in a playoff after a four-round tug-of-war. Then Maggert won his second senior major, the U.S. Senior Open, outlasting Langer, a rejuvenated Tom Watson, now 65, and Colin Montgomerie. "The guys out here on the Champions Tour," Maggert noted, with relish, "are the same guys I was trying to beat 20 years ago." Maggert added the Shaw Charity Classic by four strokes, and then the Dick's Sporting Goods Open, where he birdied six of the first 10 holes in the last round and won by two.

Among other notable accomplishments:

Marco Dawson, winless on the PGA Tour, finally succeeded on his 44th Champions Tour start in the Tucson Conquistadores Classic. On receiving the trophy, a copy of an old Spanish helmet, he noted: "I'm going to flip it upside down, see how much wine will fit in there." Then he added the Senior Open Championship at Sunningdale, beating Langer and Montgomerie down the stretch.

Tom Lehman put on a stunning birdie-birdie-eagle-birdie finish for a 65, making the SAS Championship his ninth tour win.

Jerry Smith, in his first full season, was named the Rookie of the Year. Smith won the Encompass Championship, had two other top-five finishes, and finished 28th on the money list with $652,365 in 21 starts.

Other notable first-time winners: Duffy Waldorf, in the Toshiba Classic, on his 73rd tour start; Ian Woosnam, Insperity Invitational, 36th start, and Lee Janzen, ACE Group Classic, in his eighth Champions start, but 413 starts and 16 years since the 1998 U.S. Open.

The European Senior Tour had a meager 12-tournament schedule in 2015 and two of the events were the U.S. Senior Open and PGA Championship. Colin Montgomerie played in just five of the dozen, but did so well that he captured the Order of Merit in a breeze. Besides his win in the PGA, Montgomerie scored two other victories — the Travis Perkins Masters and the MCB Tour Championship — and finished third behind Marco Dawson in the Senior Open Championship at Sunningdale.

As a result, Monty accumulated €679,147, more than three times the earnings of Australian Peter Fowler, the runner-up and only other man with more than a single victory during the season. Fowler bagged back-to-back wins in June in the Acorn Jersey Open and ISPS Handa PGA Seniors.

Kiyoshi Murota was nearly as dominant as Montgomerie on the Japan Senior Tour. The 59-year-old Murota became the circuit's most prolific winner when he scored his first of three 2015 victories in the Starts Senior. Those wins, including his fourth Senior PGA title, and two second-place finishes, landed Murota the season's Order of Merit title for a fourth time.

With earnings of ¥61,346,999, he finished well ahead of Takeshi Sakiyama, even though Sakiyama put up four victories during the 13-tournament season. Masahiro Kuramoto, the 2014 No. 1, picked up his fifth senior win, and Taiwan's reputable Tze-Chung Chen won the season finale.

There were these other developments in senior golf:

Two tournaments were scratched from the Champions Tour's original 26 — the Quebec Championship for logistical reasons and the Pacific Links China Championship after a container explosion at the Port of Tianjin less than a month before the event.

Duffy Waldorf, on his final-round strategy in the Toshiba Classic: "I'd better keep making birdies, because if I don't, I'm going to make a bogey."

Billy Andrade, on chopping up a par-four in his Boeing Classic victory: "It was the best seven I've ever made in my life."

Paul Goydos, asked about his costly stray drive late in the Dick's Sporting Goods Open: "I think it was the eight putts I missed on the other holes that was the problem."

Esteban Toledo, on the opening of his orphanage in Mexico: "Sometimes it's not about me or you — it's about helping others in this world."

Bernhard Langer, on starting 65-65 in running away with the Constellation Senior Players: "Somebody said, 'That's pretty boring stuff, 65-65.' I don't think it is. I'd like to do it every day."

Champions Tour

Mitsubishi Electric Championship
Ka'upulehu-Kona, Hawaii
Winner: Miguel Angel Jimenez

Spain's Miguel Angel Jimenez, "the most interesting man in golf," got even more interesting in the Mitsubishi Electric Championship, the Champions Tour season-opener. Jimenez certainly isn't the biggest winner on the tour but he's got to be the most efficient.

Jimenez took the Mitsubishi for his second victory in three tour starts and, of course, he did it with the flair of a man who likes a good cigar and a fine wine. Jimenez trailed in the first round, was tied for the lead in the second, and in the third he went on a rampage, birdieing six of his last nine holes to squeak through for a one-stroke victory in the 40-player field of champions.

Lift a sympathy toast to Mark O'Meara. He was shooting an eight-under-par 64 and on the verge of scoring his third win when Jimenez's outburst knocked him back to runner-up for the 15th time.

Jimenez was a birdie machine at Hualalai Golf Club, making a tournament-high 21 of them in posting his 69-64-66–199, 17 under. "I gave myself a chance on just about every hole," he said.

But he had his odd moments. In the first round, he eagled the par-five No. 4, then double-bogeyed the par-three No. 5. He birdied four of eight holes, then bogeyed the 17th. In the second, he birdied nine of the first 16, including four straight, then bogeyed the 18th. In the final round, he double-bogeyed the fifth again, then birdied six of the last nine. The clincher was on a 20-foot putt at the par-three 17th.

"It was uphill, against the grain and into the wind," said Jimenez. "I knew I had to hit it hard."

O'Meara trailed by three through the first two rounds and made his move with a six-under 30 to start his final round. He took the lead with four holes to play, but closed with four pars while Jimenez birdied Nos. 14, 15 and 17.

"People remember the winner, not second place," O'Meara said. "I'm disappointed, but Miguel played well when he had to."

Allianz Championship
Boca Raton, Florida
Winner: Paul Goydos

If time doesn't heal all things, at least it healed enough to allow Paul Goydos to squeak through in the Allianz Championship, the Champions Tour's first full-field tournament for 2015.

"If I played today like I did 10 years ago," Goydos said, "I don't think there's any way I would have won this tournament." The big difference?

"Part of it is experience and maturity," said Goydos, who shared the lead through the first two rounds and then came out of a jam-packed field and birdied the final hole to pluck off the win by a shot. It was his second win in 12 starts. If it looked familiar, that's because in his first, the Pacific Links Championship the previous September, he had to scramble after over-hitting the final green.

With the racehorse finish at the par-72 Broken Sound, Goydos posted a card of 66-69-69–204, 12 under, to nip fast-closing Gene Sauers (67) by a stroke and hold off Michael Allen (67), Fred Funk (66) and John Huston (66) by two. They all got a big boost when Canada's Rod Spittle, leading by two, made a 10 on the par-five sixth.

Goydos was in a three-way tie for the first-round lead, then a four-way tie through the second. In the third, nine players either led or shared the lead until Goydos chipped in for birdie at the ninth to inch ahead. He went up by two with another birdie at the 12th. Then he was in trouble. Sauers, seeking his first tour win, finished his bogey-free 67 with birdies at the last two holes, and Goydos fired his second over the green at the par-five 18th, 30 feet from the flag. But he chipped down to inches and tapped in for the birdie and the win.

It was frustrating for Sauers, winless on the tour and now with four second-place finishes. "But I'm ecstatic with the way I played," he said.

Goydos was also proud of winning, he said, "...with spit and vinegar rather than be on top of my game."

ACE Group Classic
Naples, Florida
Winner: Lee Janzen

Golfers sometimes get into "the zone," a mysterious frame of mind where all shots are possible. Two-time U.S. Open champion Lee Janzen slipped into a different kind at the ACE Group Classic in February. He was in it just on the final green. He needed an eight-foot birdie putt to tie Bart Bryant, who had tied the course record with a 62 for the clubhouse lead.

"I was [thinking] I have to make birdie here to get in a playoff, or I don't, and I just go back to the drawing board," said Janzen. "But there was a peace that, to me, it didn't matter whether I won or not." He calmly made the eight-footer, completing a card of 68-65-67–200, 16 under at TwinEagles. The playoff, at No. 18, was short. Bryant watered his approach and Janzen played carefully for a par. It was his second start of the year, his eighth on the Champions Tour, and not only his first tour win but his first in 413 starts and more than 16 years, since the 1998 U.S. Open.

About winning, wherever: "I don't know if everybody has to go through the same torment, but I know I do," Janzen said.

The first two rounds belonged to Colin Montgomerie on a pair of 66s to lead by one. Montgomerie was rarin' to go after dropping a 40-footer for birdie at the first hole, then he grew testy, grinding for pars. His caddie tried to calm him. Monty agreed — a caddie's job is to keep his player patient. "Then you almost hit them over the head," Monty said, "because ... patience never won a bloody thing, not in a three-round event." He finished fifth.

Bryant was semi-satisfied. "I didn't put myself in good enough position on the back nine," he said. "But 10 under — you can't sneeze at that, for sure."

Said Janzen, on finally winning again: "Winning the U.S. Open, you're on top of the world. Then playing really poorly, you wonder how the heck you even did it."

Tucson Conquistadores Classic
Tucson, Arizona
Winner: Marco Dawson

Marco Dawson had gone 413 starts without winning on the PGA Tour, won once in 161 starts on the Web.com Tour, then was winless in 20 starts on the Champions Tour. And now at age 51, he was on the final green of the Tucson Conquistadores Classic, one short putt from a liberating victory. What was going through his mind, some in the media corps wondered.

"You know, it's funny," Dawson said, "because you get into such a routine when you play ... that it was just a routine shot. And then once that ball, I saw it go in the hole, I just thought, wow! — you just won this tournament!"

Not without a fight, though. Dawson started the last round shakily, with a bogey at No. 1. "I might have gotten a little anxious or whatever you want to call it," he said. He calmed down and birdied Nos. 2, 5, 6 and 10. Then came a test at the 15th. "Nothing but bad, bad breaks," he said. He held the damage to a bogey and slipped into a tie with Bart Bryant at 12 under. Next came the turning point, the par-four 16th, where Dawson pretty much ended a chase in which as many as four players were tied for the lead. He dropped an 18-foot putt for birdie, and his closest challenger, Bryant, bogeyed out of a fairway bunker to slip two behind. It stayed that way when both parred the last two holes.

Dawson shot 67-67-69–203, 13 under, to beat Bryant by two, Mark O'Meara by three, and Tom Pernice Jr. and Wes Short Jr., by four.

Thus ended a long, painful journey. Over his first full season on the Champions Tour in 2014 and the previous two events opening 2015, he'd had nine top-10 finishes. Now, beaming, Dawson hoisted the Tucson trophy, a helmet inspired by those of the old Spanish conquistadores. What would he do with it?

"Well," Dawson said, "I'm going to probably flip it upside down, see how much wine will fit in there."

Mississippi Gulf Resort Classic
Biloxi, Mississippi
Winner: David Frost

Who could blame David Frost if he began thinking the Mississippi Gulf Resort Classic was jinxed?

"I thought, 'You've got to be kidding me — last year disqualified and this year a one-shot penalty,'" Frost was saying. He had just survived an odd scare and posted his sixth Champions Tour win. This one came down to the last two holes, where he went from a comfortable two-stroke lead to a skin-of-his-teeth victory. When Tom Lehman missed that short birdie putt on the 18th, Frost's card held up for the one-stroke win — 68-70-68–206, 10 under at Fallen Oak.

Frost was disqualified from the 2014 Mississippi in an incorrect scorecard episode after calling a penalty on himself for moving a stone in a bunker. This time, he was two ahead with two holes to play when trouble struck on the par-three 17th green in a rare incident.

"I marked my ball, and as I picked it up, the ball … slipped out of my hand, hit the coin, and moved it," Frost said. "I knew where it was, and I just moved it back, and didn't think there was a penalty at all because I knew exactly where it was."

His penalty was for moving the marker, the same as it would have been had he moved his ball. Penalty: One stroke. Fortunately, Frost replaced his marker to its original position. If he hadn't, he would have incurred another penalty stroke.

At all events, the resulting bogey cut his lead to one. At the 18th then, Frost holed a five-foot putt for his par, then took a deep breath as Lehman missed a tying four-footer just on the right.

Frost started the final round trailing by three and played the front in one under with two birdies and a bogey. Birdies at the 11th, 12th and 13th got him the lead, and another at the 15th made it two. Then came the bizarre 17th.

"Luckily for me, in the end it didn't make any difference," Frost said. "And I'm happy Lehman didn't beat me in a playoff."

Greater Gwinnett Championship
Duluth, Georgia
Winner: Olin Browne

At age 55 and with 22 years as a pro tour golfer, Olin Browne was not about to apologize for happening to be the name atop the leaderboard when weather wiped out the final round and left him the winner.

"I was on the other side of [a cancellation] and I was hot about that," Browne said, on taking the Greater Gwinnett Championship. "Maybe it evened out my way this time."

This was in April but those weren't the April showers of song that hit the TPC Sugarloaf. Heavy rain forced the first round into a Friday-Saturday carryover. Only one group was able to finish on Friday. Tommy Armour, finishing on Saturday, held the lead with a five-under-par 67, and Browne, also finishing on Saturday, was in a crowd at 68.

As things developed, Browne won on Saturday with a tournament-record, eight-under 64 for another course record, a 12-under 132 for 36 holes, that edged Bernhard Langer by a shot. Langer finished birdie-eagle, matching Browne's 64. This was Browne's second tour win, after the 2011 U.S. Senior Open.

A light rain fell Saturday, but there were no delays. Then a downpour Saturday night added another inch of rain. "There was nothing we could do," said tour official Brian Claar. "We lost the golf course."

Browne had only one bogey for the two rounds, that at his 13th (No. 4) in the first round. He went the rest of the way, 23 holes, flawlessly.

In classical lore, golfers regret it when they win a rain-shortened tournament, but realistically, it's hard to imagine any player resenting a gift. As Browne put it: "But you know, all you can do is show up and take what the course gives you and what the conditions give you and play away."

Browne, who would have been paired with Langer for the last round, put it all in perspective. "I was really going to enjoy playing with him," he said. "Having said that, I don't mind having that big sugar jar sitting with my name on it."

Bass Pro Shops Legends of Golf
Ridgedale, Missouri
Winners: Billy Andrade and Joe Durant

In golf, it's called ham-and-egging, meaning two golfers complementing each other as neatly as the famous breakfast pairing. Which is precisely what Billy Andrade meant when he said, "We ham-and-egged it very, very nicely," after he and Joe Durant wrapped up a three-stroke victory in the Bass Pro Shops Legends of Golf at the Top of the Rock resort. They combined for the unusual scorecard of 63-51-45–159, 19 under par, frustrating the old European Ryder Cup pals, Sandy Lyle and Ian Woosnam.

In a scorekeeper's carnival, the tournament was played in better-ball and modified alternate shot — both partners hitting tee shots — with nine holes of each, except for one full round at better-ball. It was played on the resort's regulation Buffalo Ridge course and the par-three Top of the Rock course. The Legends is the only PGA Tour-sanctioned tournament ever on a par-three course.

John Cook and Joey Sindelar birdied the final four holes at Buffalo Ridge for a 10-under-par 60 in better-ball Friday. Andrade and Durant were at 63. Lyle and Woosnam shot a seven-under 47 for nine holes of modified alternate shot and nine of better-ball at the Top of the Rock. Lyle and Woosnam then took a two-shot lead Saturday with a better-ball 64 at Buffalo Ridge.

Then Andrade and Durant charged to the finish line on the par-three course in the final round. Durant underlined their bid with a hole-in-one at the 167-yard third on the second nine, using a seven iron. "I was just trying to hit it right of the flag, and it just happened to go in the hole," Durant said. They closed with a nine-under 45 for the three-stroke win, the first Champions Tour victory for both of them.

Larry Nelson and Bruce Fleisher birdied the final hole for a one-under 26 for nine holes of better-ball on the par-three course to win the Legends Division (65 and older). Jack Nicklaus and Gary Player finished second, two behind.

Insperity Invitational
The Woodlands, Texas
Winner: Ian Woosnam

Wee Woosie was thinking he was getting a bit old for all this, at 57. But then he figured, well, give it a try. Good thing.

Ian Woosnam, the little Welshman, European star and 1991 Masters champion, came from behind for his first win in 36 starts on the Champions Tour, beating Tom Lehman and Kenny Perry in a playoff.

"Great feeling," said Woosnam, knowing there's nothing like a win to soothe an aching back. "I'm getting a bit too old to go through the pain, but it paid off and I felt a lot better today."

Woosnam attracted little attention with his opening 71, which was five behind co-leaders Michael Allen and Marco Dawson. But he caught some eyes with his second-round 66, when he went on a six-birdie tear on the back nine, hurt only by a bogey at the last that put him three behind Allen.

The tournament took a sharp turn in the third round. Allen, aiming at his eighth tour win, struggled through a three-birdie, three-bogey par 72. "I played so well all week," Allen said. "To give it away like that is upsetting."

The final round was a chase. Lehman birdied four holes in a five-hole stretch for a 69, and Perry birdied five of the last 10 for a 66, tying at 11-under 205 with Woosnam, who shot a flawless four-birdie 68.

Lehman was caught in an equipment dilemma in the playoff at the par-four 18th. He'd left his three iron out of his bag, but needed it for his approach shot. "So I tried to hit a really hard four iron," he said. He sliced it into the water.

Perry fought a sore back. "I can swing a golf club but I can hardly stand and bend," he said. He left a long birdie try eight feet short. Then Woosnam rolled in a 30-footer for a birdie and the win. But he'd come to the playoff curiously ambivalent.

Said Woosnam: "I said, 'I've got a flight to catch! Please, someone birdie, whoever it is. Birdie the first hole. And it happened to be me. Great."

Regions Tradition
Shoal Creek, Alabama
Winner: Jeff Maggert

There really were other players in the field — 81 starters, in fact. It only seemed like the Jeff Maggert-Kevin Sutherland Grudge Match, the way the two locked on to the Regions Tradition from the start.

The Tradition, the first of the Champions Tour's five majors, had drawn the usual powerful field, but nobody could crack the top of the leaderboard for four days running. This one had playoff written all over it, with Sutherland, 50, going for his first tour win, and Maggert, 51, for his second and his first major. The decision went to Maggert, with a par on a three-foot putt at the first playoff hole.

"This was a tournament I was looking forward to," said Maggert, whose first win came in the 2014 Mississippi Gulf Resort Classic. "I pointed it out early in my schedule and wanted to get my game in shape to come here and play."

Said Sutherland: "The first three days I played fantastic golf and today I kind of scruffed it around, but still posted a decent score ... Unfortunately, wasn't one stroke better."

They were hooked together all the way.

First Round: Maggert birdied five of the first nine holes but stumbled coming in and shot 67. Sutherland birdied five of 10 from No. 3, shot 68.

Second Round: Both eagled the par-five 11th on outstanding hybrid approaches. Maggert shot 67, Sutherland 66, and they were tied at 10 under and leading by three.

Third Round: Maggert birdied three of the last four for a no-bogey 68, while Sutherland had five birdies, but two bogeys for a 69. Maggert led Sutherland by one at 14-under 202.

Fourth Round: Maggert shot a two-birdie, two-bogey 72 for a 14-under 274. Sutherland tied him with a 71 that included an eagle and two birdies.

Playoff: Maggert won with a three-footer for par after Sutherland bunkered his tee shot near the lip.

"The putts didn't go in like I had the first three days," Maggert said, "but fortunately I had pretty good luck coming in and was able to win the playoff."

Senior PGA Championship
French Lick, Indiana
Winner: Colin Montgomerie

It was only the first round of the Senior PGA Championship, and defending champion Colin Montgomerie — who would make it his third senior major victory — already had to get something off his chest.

"I'm very rarely happy with a round of golf — ever," Monty proclaimed. "I've shot level par today and I'm very happy leaving here."

The championship opened in bone-chilling 40-degree temperatures, and architect Pete Dye's demanding French Lick course, on a windswept hilltop, added to the miseries. At 72, Monty was only one off Masahiro Kuramoto's lead.

And Kuramoto was already writing himself off. He hadn't played much, he said. "So I don't think that I'm going to be able to keep the lead," he said. He was right.

Tom Lehman, a three-time senior major winner, took the lead in the second round on a 67–140 and a one-stroke lead over Montgomerie (69) and Brian Henninger (67), then three-putted his way to a 79 in the third round, and Bernhard Langer, winner of five senior majors, had a hole-out eagle at the par-four eighth, then finished birdie-birdie for a 69. But that merely got him to within three of Monty, who is famed for having fallen short in the regular majors.

"I've done that five times," he said. "I'm more relaxed now."

But not in the final round. Starting the day three shots ahead was a tough position, he said. "Nowhere to go but down," he said. "I could never relax. I could never relax at all." He bogeyed No. 1, but birdied Nos. 5, 7, 9, 10 and 12, going five up on Esteban Toledo. He birdied the 16th, and bogeys at 15 and 18 didn't bother him. He closed with a 69 for an eight-under 280 and won by four.

"That's what it takes — he knows how to win," said Toledo, the runner-up with a bogey-free 69.

It was Montgomerie's third senior major victory in the past six. He was making up for lost time. Said a pleased Monty: "This felt like me playing in a major championship of 20 years ago."

Principal Charity Classic
Des Moines, Iowa
Winner: Mark Calcavecchia

Mark Calcavecchia would never be mistaken for a fashion statement like, for example, John Daly and his pyrotechnic wardrobe. So who was that golfer sporting "bacon-themed" pants — pants stacked with likenesses of bacon against a black background, in recognition of Iowa, an agricultural powerhouse. Well, it was none other than Calcavecchia, appropriately attired for winning the tournament.

Calc had worn them for the first round, as a salute to Iowans, and again in the third, for their good-luck power after he'd moved ahead in the second. "All of a sudden, I grabbed the lead," he said, "and I'm like, 'I've got to wear them. I'll give them one more shot.'"

Bacon power worked. Calcavecchia, shooting the par-72 Wakonda Club in 67-68-69, took the lead in the second round and never trailed in the third on his way to a 12-under 204, a stroke better than Brian Henninger and Joe Durant. They dogged him all the way, but Davis Love was his main threat. Love, four behind to start the last round, went on a tear, getting six birdies over 11 holes from No. 5. But he bogeyed the 16th off a weak chip and double-bogeyed the par-three 17th off a tee shot into the rocks.

"Missing the green at 16 and 17 just killed me," Love said.

Calcavecchia started his move in the second round with five birdies over the last eight holes. He was rock-steady in the last, with birdies at Nos. 2, 8, 10 and 15, and a bogey at the 14th. He made only four birdies for the tournament, despite hitting only a weak 52 percent of his fairways. That lack of sharpness could be attributed to a painful right hand. He'd suffered a slashed tendon on top of the hand when he tripped and fell through a glass door at Thanksgiving. Miraculous surgery saved his career. He missed the first three events. The Principal was his eighth tournament since returning. But he was still hurting. "I kind of get over the pain and forget about it," Calc said.

Constellation Senior Players Championship
Belmont, Massachusetts
Winner: Bernhard Langer

By Bernhard Langer's standards, 2015 was looking like a bust. Coming to the Constellation Senior Players Championship in mid-July, he hadn't won yet. About a year earlier, he'd already won twice and he made the Players his third. But in any discussion of quality, it should be noted that he had to go to a playoff to win in 2014. This time, even a closing 64 by Kirk Triplett couldn't make the tournament look like a competition. Langer was leading by eight strokes heading into the final round. He won, absurdly, by six.

"It was a magical week," said Langer, after his wire-to-wire cakewalk. "To do something that Arnie did is amazing."

Langer is the first since Arnold Palmer, in 1984 and 1985, to win back-to-back Senior Players.

Langer was leading by eight going into the final round, but was 10 ahead of Triplett, who was soon birdieing six of seven holes around the turn. Never one to pass up a chuckle, Triplett offered: "I thought, 'If I make six more birdies, Bernhard's going to be nervous.'"

This was the picture: Shooting the par-71 Belmont Country Club in 65-65-67-68, Langer led by two, by four, by eight and then won by six over Triplett with a 19-under 265 total.

"I enjoy playing with a big lead," said Langer, who posted his 24th Champions Tour victory and his fifth major. "But you've still got to pay attention."

Someone noted that Langer was almost in trouble early in the final round. He three-putted No. 3 for his first bogey in 48 holes. That dropped his eight-shot lead down to six. Then at the par-five No. 4, Langer fired his second to six feet and made the eagle. He went on to birdie the sixth and eighth, take his fourth and last bogey of the tournament at the 13th, and birdied the 17th to formalize his romp.

Back in the second round, Langer could have been speaking for the entire tournament. "Somebody said, 'That's pretty boring stuff: 65-65,'" Langer said. "I don't think it is. I'd like to do it every day."

U.S. Senior Open Championship
Sacramento, California
Winner: Jeff Maggert

Jeff Maggert settled an old score and a wild scramble at the U.S. Senior Open Championship.

"I had a lot of good runs in the U.S. Open over the years and probably lacked a little maturity to pull it off," Maggert said. "But now that I'm an old guy, I've learned a lot and was able to just steady myself and play well."

Maggert, 51, in his second year on the Champions Tour, ended a wide-open race with a closing 65 to take the U.S. Senior Open at Del Paso Country Club. It was his third tour victory and his second major, after the Tradition some weeks earlier. In his pre-senior days, Maggert had 13 top-10 finishes in majors, including two solo thirds in the U.S. Open.

"Even though I have the confidence in my ball-striking to pull it off, it just seems like it's very difficult to have everything come together," Maggert said.

Maggert, who tied for 55th in his first U.S. Senior Open in 2014, got it all together this time at the par-70 Del Paso. He shot 70-65-70-65 for a 10-under 270 and a two-stroke win over defending champion Colin Montgomerie.

It was Maggert's victory but it was Hall-of-Famer Tom Watson's gallery. Win the Senior Open at 65? He sure tried. Shooting 66-69-71-69, he led the first round and shared the halfway lead, but finally faded slightly and tied for seventh.

Maggert, tied with Bernhard Langer through the third round, pulled away with three straight birdies to start the fourth. Then the course set-up played to his strength — driving. The tees were moved up on two holes. He drove the green at the 282-yard, par-four ninth and two-putted for a birdie, then got the last of his six birdies at the par-five 15th on a drive, a three iron and two putts. He bogeyed the 16th and parred in for a 65 and, at last, a U.S. Open.

And another score settled: "The guys out here on the Champions Tour," he said, "are the same guys I was trying to beat 20 years ago."

Encompass Championship
Glenview, Illinois
Winner: Jerry Smith

Winning was the last thing on Jerry Smith's mind. In fact, he was so accustomed to not winning, winning wasn't on his mind at all at the Encompass Championship.

"Well," he explained, after winning it, "in your career you don't really think about winning and so forth. At least a guy like myself who's been a so-called journeyman player all these years."

That meant many years of seeming resignation. In 28 years as a professional, the 1998 Guam Open, on the Asian Tour, was his only victory until the Encompass. Smith, 51, turned pro in 1987, played the Asian, Nationwide and PGA tours. He reached the Champions Tour through qualifying school. So, little was expected of him, or by him, at North Shore Country Club. Then he beat David Frost by three, shooting 66-64-70–200, 16 under par.

For an Encompass memento, apart from the trophy and the $285,000 check, Smith might like North Shore's 579-yard, par-five 16th. He played it sensationally — birdie-eagle-eagle — five under in a three-stroke victory.

Smith broke out of a logjam start and took command in the second round with some decidedly un-journeyman golf. Starting on the back nine, Smith went six under through his first seven holes, including his first eagle at the 16th. He reached in two and dropped an 11-foot putt. A bogey and three birdies coming in gave him a tournament record-tying 64 and a three-shot lead over Mike Goodes.

Smith lurched out of the gate in the final round, bogeying the first two holes. Then he righted himself, but apparently didn't notice that Frost, who had started five shots behind, was gaining on him. Smith said he still hadn't looked at a scoreboard when he reached the 16th. No matter. He bunkered his attempt to reach the green in two, then holed out the bunker shot for another eagle, and closed with two pars for the comfortable win.

Said Smith: "Maybe had I looked at the leaderboard on 16, who knows? Maybe I don't go for it in two. Maybe I don't make eagle."

And maybe he doesn't win.

The Senior Open Championship presented by Rolex
Winner: Marco Dawson

See European Senior Tour section.

3M Championship
Blaine, Minnesota
Winner: Kenny Perry

Shooting an 11-under-par 61 would be breathtaking by most standards. Kenny Perry shot one in the second round of the 3M Championship, and it gave him a four-stroke lead, but he wasn't altogether pleased, even though the other 80 starters would love to trade places with him.

"I like being the chaser," Perry explained. "You're relaxed, you're free, you're going, you're charging, you're going after everything. When you got a four- or five-shot lead, you're playing safe, you're playing not to mess up, and that's a hard way to play golf."

It was, finally, merely an academic point. Perry survived his fears and ran away with the tournament, becoming the first to repeat in its 23-year history and posting his eighth Champions Tour victory. Trailing only in the first round, Perry shot 69-61-68–198, 18 under at TPC Twin Cities, winning by four over Bernhard Langer, Scott Dunlap and Kevin Sutherland.

Perry served notice of his second-round 61 at the end of the first, when he bounced back from a double bogey at the par-three 17th with an eagle at the 18th. Then he started the second round with three straight birdies and a hole-in-one at the par-three fourth. After four more birdies, he eagled the par-five 18th again. Counting the eagle at 18 in the first round, Perry played a 19-hole stretch in 13 under.

Perry had an uneasy moment in the final round, though. His four-shot lead was cut to two when he bogeyed No. 1 and Sutherland birdied. But he restored order with five birdies across nine holes from No. 2.

Langer shot 67 and lamented his putting. "If I putt well it could have been nine or 10 under," he said.

Sutherland had an amazing 14-under 202. For the tournament, he was a cumulative 13 under over the first five holes, but one under for the rest. "I got off to a really good start," the winless Sutherland said, "but unfortunately, I wasn't able to extend it."

As for Perry and the plump lead: "The tournament's never really over till it's over," he said.

Shaw Charity Classic
Calgary, Alberta, Canada
Winner: Jeff Maggert

Jeff Maggert, it seemed, was just along for the ride. This would be a marquee shootout in the Shaw Charity Classic between two crafty and colorful veterans — Colin Montgomerie, the curmudgeonly Scot, and Miguel Angel Jimenez, the romantic Spaniard. Monty had breezed to the first-round lead, shooting Canyon Valley in eight-under-par 62, and Jimenez tied the course record with a 61 in the second, and they were tied at 12-under 128 going into the final round. This would be a fitting golf counterpart of the Calgary Stampede in that historic Canadian city. Sparks would be flying.

"It's going to be a very tight finish tomorrow, that's for sure," Jimenez said. "Anyone can win."

"Whether it be one of us or whoever's in contention there, it should be an interesting day," Montgomerie noted.

Said Maggert, two behind with his 67-63–130 and paired with them: "I feel I've got to shoot seven or eight under again to stay in this thing."

Actually, all it took was six under — a 64 — for a 16-under 194 and a four-stroke win over Montgomerie. It was Maggert's third win of the season, his fourth on the Champions Tour. Monty could only manage a par 70, and Jimenez slipped to a 74.

"I feel fortunate," Maggert said. "I really thought Colin and Miguel would play some solid rounds. The golf course — we had a little wind today, so it didn't play as easy."

Maggert warmed up with three pars to start, then birdied five of the last six holes on the front nine.

"Colin had a little hiccup on the ninth green," Maggert said, meaning a double bogey, "and all of a sudden I'm walking off the ninth hole with a nice, big lead, which was unexpected."

Maggert protected it through some winds coming in, making birdie at the 11th and 14th and taking a bogey at the 15th that only dented his lead. So he suddenly had in one season as many wins — three — as he'd had in 25 years on the PGA Tour. How to explain it?

"A late bloomer, maybe," Maggert said.

Boeing Classic
Snoqualmie, Washington
Winner: Billy Andrade

Billy Andrade, personable Rhode Islander, hadn't won a stroke-play tournament since 2000, so he will long cherish the shot that effectively won the 2015 Boeing Classic for him. It was a chip shot at the par-four No. 4 in in the final round that went in — for a triple bogey.

"Tried to play a little cut ... and I hit a hook," Andrade said, "and ... it was out of bounds. Then I hit a provisional left. We were lucky to find the ball. So now my mind's racing and this all of a sudden, where did this come from? Now we've got ourselves a golf tournament, letting everybody in. I hit a hell of a shot to get it to the fairway. I missed the green to the left, and I chipped in. ... It was the greatest seven I've ever made in my life."

Then there was the par-five No. 8, which Andrade favored even more. "The key to the tournament, probably," he said. He drove into a bunker and "chunked" a wedge out, then hit a wedge from 142 yards that he feared couldn't clear the fronting water. "That ball goes in the water, I'm probably done," Andrade said. But it ended up 15 feet from the cup. He made the birdie and went on to fill out a card of 69-65-73–207, nine under at TPC Snoqualmie Ridge, and a one-stroke win over Bernhard Langer.

Andrade, scoring his first individual win since the 2000 Invensys Classic in Las Vegas, surfaced in the second round on a dazzling burst. He made eight birdies — three straight from the 13th — for a 65 and a three-stroke lead over Langer and Jeff Freeman. His final round-73, with a triple bogey, a single and three birdies, definitely wasn't a lark.

"Today was a grind," Andrade said. "Today was not a day where it was fun ... you had to watch out. You didn't want to make any mistakes, and I knew on the back nine I couldn't make any, and I got lucky."

Dick's Sporting Goods Open
Endicott, New York
Winner: Jeff Maggert

Jeff Maggert said these were the guys he'd been trying to beat back on the PGA Tour. Now, on the Champions Tour, he was making up for lost time.

Chalk up the Dick's Sporting Goods Open late in August — win No. 4 in 16 starts for 2015, and two of them majors, the Regions Tradition and the U.S. Senior Open.

Maggert trailed by two strokes in the first two rounds with a pair of 68s, then closed with a 66 to beat Paul Goydos by two on a 14-under-par 202 at En-Joie Golf Club.

"Not making any bogeys today was a big key," Maggert said, displaying a gift for understatement. "And also the five birdies on the front nine was another big key."

Actually, that was six birdies through 10 holes — three straight from No. 1, and three straight from No. 8, and he went bogey-free from the eighth in the second round — 29 straight holes without one, and he made only three bogeys for the entire tournament.

When it comes to post-mortems of a round, Goydos, a two-time winner with a dry wit, doesn't spare himself. Someone wondered about his tee shot on the 15th, where he made his second and last bogey of the round, and fourth of the tournament. Said Goydos: "My response, was — I think it was the eight putts I missed on the other holes that was the problem. The reality is, I just didn't make enough putts this week to be competitive with Jeff."

The tournament was a scramble from the start. Gene Sauers and Goydos tied for the first-round lead at six-under 66, and Maggert was two behind. Rod Spittle took a one-shot lead with a 66–134 in the second round, and Maggert was four behind, facing a real chore in the third.

Then three quick birdies made it look easy. Maggert got No. 1 from four feet, No. 2 on a 30-footer, and then two-putted from 20 feet at the par-five third.

"That was the start I was looking for," Maggert said.

And the finish.

Nature Valley First Tee Open
Monterey Peninsula, California
Winner: Esteban Toledo

The drama in the Nature Valley First Tee Open came down to Pebble Beach's famed par-three 17th. It treated Esteban Toledo and Tom Watson with equal contempt. Both played it par-bogey over the last two rounds. But under the circumstances, it treated Watson worse. His bogey in the final round kept him one shot behind Toledo, and when both parred the 18th, Toledo had his third Champions Tour victory.

The 17th was "Watson's hole." It's where he chipped in for a birdie en route to beating Jack Nicklaus in the 1982 U.S. Open. But this time he bunkered his tee shot and bogeyed.

Toledo was hardly confident when he arrived at the 17th tee. "I got a little bit nervous," he said. "I had no idea where I was in the tournament and I just hit a bad shot."

Toledo ended up beating Watson by a stroke. Toledo opened the tournament with a par-71 at Poppy Hills and finished 66-69 at Pebble Beach for a nine-under-par 206. Watson was a surprise contender after his opening no-birdie 75 at Poppy Hills. Then he bounced back with a seven-under 65 at Pebble Beach and closed with a 67–207, falling short of a tie by that bogey at the 17th.

It was a wide-open tournament till those closing holes. It heated up in the second round when Colin Montgomerie, with his three victories all in majors, jumped into a one-shot lead on a 67, with Olin Browne (65) right behind. Toledo was three back with his 66–137, and Watson, on his 10-shot rocket, was five behind at 140.

Toledo wrapped it up in the final round with birdies at Nos. 2, 5 and 7 going out, and another at the 14th before the drama-producing bogey at the 17th. It was his sweetest victory. The following week, the Esteban Toledo Family Foundation Home, an orphanage in his hometown of Mexicali, Mexico, would be completed.

"It's one of the greatest accomplishments I've ever had and dreamed in my life," Toledo said. "Sometimes it's not about me or you. It's about helping others in this world."

SAS Championship
Cary, North Carolina
Winner: Tom Lehman

Golf is a marathon, not a sprint, the saying goes. But in the final round of the SAS Championship, they were sprinting.

The winner: Tom Lehman, trailing through the first two rounds, then out-legging Joe Durant, Bernhard Langer and Kenny Perry. It was his ninth Champions Tour victory but his first since June 2014.

"I've had a couple seconds and I've had some other good top finishes, but no wins," Lehman said. "So it's just nice to get back in the winner's circle. It's nice to see the putts drop when you need them most."

Early on, they weren't dropping nearly enough. Lehman trailed in each of the first two rounds.

But they were dropping for Langer in the first round — seven birdies and no bogeys for a seven-under-par 65, even though brisk winds hit Prestonwood Country Club. "I never really struggled for par," Langer said. He led a trio by two and was three ahead of Lehman, who bogeyed No. 5, then rushed to five birdies in 10 holes from No. 9 for a 68. In the second round, Lehman posted a two-birdie 71 in an early October rain and again trailed by three. Kenny Perry persevered for a 68 and a one-shot lead. "I didn't have a lot of feel in my hands coming down the stretch," he said.

The chase was on in the final round. Perry had a mixed round. He made four bogeys, all on the front nine, eagled at No. 7, then birdied 13, 17 and 18 for a 70, tying for third with Langer, who birdied four of the last six for a 68. Joe Durant, four behind at the start, put the pressure on with a flawless 68 to finish second by one.

It was Lehman's day, and bogey-free. After two birdies on the front, he closed with a fury from the 15th, going birdie-birdie-eagle-par for a 65, a 12-under 204 and a one-stroke win.

"I knew there were a lot of guys really bunched up, and nobody was making any big move," Lehman said, "so the game was still on."

San Antonio Championship
San Antonio, Texas
Winner: Bernhard Langer

"It was just a matter of who was going to close the best," Bernhard Langer was saying. Guess who was the last man standing at the San Antonio Championship?

Langer made it Champions Tour victory No. 25 and his second of the season, giving him his seventh multiple-win season in his eight seasons. Langer hung around for two rounds then came from behind and closed fast to win by three. He left three frustrated golfers in his wake with his 71-68-65, 12-under-par 204 performance at TPC San Antonio.

Scott Dunlap, looking for his second win, also rallied, but not quite enough. "I know I was doing well," said Dunlap, who finished second on a closing four-under 68. "It's a really tough, proper golf course where a lot of pars and the odd birdie here and there are going to hold you in good stead."

Michael Allen, looking for his eighth victory, and rookie Scott McCarron, seeking his first in his seventh start, were tied for the lead going into the final round. They finished tied for third, and McCarron did it with a 25-foot birdie putt at the final hole. Langer trailed them by one going into the final round, and he was driven by more than the desire to win. There were the stinging memories. He was beaten twice in playoffs in the San Antonio, by David Frost in 2012 and Kenny Perry in 2013.

"Losing both playoffs was tough," Langer said. "But I feel I can play this course well. I like fast greens, and they're usually faster here than most places."

Langer plunged into the chase with a three-under front nine — four birdies and a bogey. He hit his approach to seven feet and birdied the 12th, then added the 15th. Next came the 17th, and then he finished with a flourish, a birdie at the 18th that he didn't need, on a 25-footer.

"It's always special to play well, especially on Sunday when it really matters, when you're in contention," Langer said. He would know. He's done it 25 times in eight years.

Toshiba Classic
Newport Beach, California
Winner: Duffy Waldorf

Which round was the key to Duffy Waldorf's win in the Toshiba Classic? The dazzling, flawless 11-under-par 60 in the second round (with no bogeys) or the hang-on five-under 66 in the final round, with only three pars.

No matter. To Waldorf, 53, it was all merely academic. The real point was, this was his 73rd Champions Tour start and he'd finally won. Great timing. The Toshiba was the final full-field event of 2015. But this wasn't the classical monkey-off-the-back win.

"I never felt it was a monkey, per se," Waldorf said. "But gosh, I've been out here three years … there's part of me that's wondering if I was [ever] going to win."

Waldorf opened with a 67, four off Scott McCarron and Steve Pate's tie at eight-under 63 at Newport Beach Country Club. Then he wrapped it up with 60-66 for a tournament-record, 20-under 193 and a two-stroke win over Joe Durant, who went to bed hoping for a 10-under finish and got to nine-under 62.

Waldorf was almost clinical on the second-round 60 that put him three ahead of Fred Couples. "It seemed like everyone else was making birdies," Waldorf said. "Once I made three, I'm not even in the lead and I'm five or six under par. So, I guess it's going to be one of those low days. Better just go as low as you can."

Waldorf, starting four behind, birdied the first three holes, Nos. 5 and 6, then three straight from the ninth, and three more from the 14th, ending the rampage with a 60-foot putt at the 16th. The pressing question? What kept him from a 59?

"Only the putt at 18," Waldorf said. It was a bending 10-footer. But no regrets. "I made almost every putt inside 15, 20 feet," he said.

Waldorf had no intention of nursing his three-shot lead down the final round with conservative golf and was off on a wild ride — a 10-birdie, five-bogey 66. His strategy: "I'd better keep making birdies, because if I don't, I'm going to make a bogey."

Charles Schwab Cup Championship
Scottsdale, Arizona
Winner: Billy Andrade

Bernhard Langer outran everybody at Desert Mountain Cochise course — well, everybody except one of his biggest admirers, Billy Andrade. And so the Champions Tour's grand finale, the Charles Schwab Cup Championship, came down to a split decision. Andrade won the rainbow and Langer won the pot of gold.

Andrade, in his second season, came from behind in the fourth round to tie Langer, then beat him on the first playoff hole to win the Schwab Cup Championship — his second tour individual title — and the $440,000 first prize. Langer came from behind Colin Montgomerie and Jeff Maggert and won the season-long Schwab Cup points race and its $1 million annuity. It was Langer's second straight points victory and a record third overall. And with a $2,340,288 total, he won the money title for the fourth straight year, and for the seventh time in eight, both records.

"I just look up to him," Andrade said. "I'm just honored to be in his company."

Langer led the first round, and Andrade — who had a hole-in-one at the par-three No. 2 — and Michael Allen were two behind. Allen led through the middle rounds, then slipped. Andrade shot 65-67-70-64 and Langer 63-68-68-67 and tied at 14-under 266. Langer's chance to win in regulation died when his 18-foot eagle putt at the 18th lipped out.

Andrade tempered his admiration of Langer with an unabashed personal view, noting that maybe it should be his turn to win the tournament.

It would, but after some scares. He bogeyed the par-five 15th, missing the green from only 89 yards. ("I just nerved out," he said.) He escaped with a two-putt par at the par-three 17th after his tee shot bounced back off a rock. In the playoff, Langer missed the green and parred, and Andrade two-putted from the back fringe for his winning birdie. And, someone wondered, it's taken years of work to get to this point?

"Yeah," Andrade said. "And you've got to do it under the gun. You've got to do it under competition, when your heart's beating and all that, not when you're just hitting balls."

European Senior Tour

U.S. Senior PGA Championship
Winner: Colin Montgomerie

See Champions Tour section.

SSE Enterprise Wales Senior Open
City of Newport, Wales
Winner: Paul Wesselingh

Ian Woosnam was on the verge of winning his first tournament in his native Wales in 32 years, and his 36-hole co-leader was surprised when he instead captured the SSE Enterprise Wales Senior Open title, the opening domestic event of the European Senior Tour season.

Said Paul Wesselingh, 53, who scored his eighth victory in his three seasons on the circuit: "I honestly thought Ian would win. I played with him in the third round of the Senior PGA Championship (in America) last week and he played so well that I felt I would have to hang on to his coattails to stay with him today."

Starting the new season as he had ended 2014 — with a victory — Englishman Wesselingh, the 2013 Order of Merit winner, shot a final-round, three-under-par 67 Sunday on Celtic Manor's Roman Road course, his 203 defeating Woosnam (69) and Australian Peter Fowler (66) by two strokes.

"As it turned out, I had a perfect game plan," Wesselingh explained. "I knew with the windy conditions I had to keep the ball under control and not go for any tricky pins. I had been putting so well all week (with a putter he hadn't used for 18 months), I had confidence in my short game."

The turning point in the final round came on a two-shot swing as Woosnam bogeyed the 11th hole and Wesselingh birdied the 12th, then carried the lead to the barn. Woosnam, who had won his first senior title in the United States three weeks earlier, conceded afterward that "Paul played really well and I just didn't play good enough golf today. I hit too many wrong clubs."

Miguel Angel Martin, who shared the first-round lead with 67-year-old Denis O'Sullivan, finished fourth at 209, the only other player to break par over the distance.

Acorn Jersey Open
St. Brelade, Jersey
Winner: Peter Fowler

Peter Fowler put a positive accent on his checkered history at Jersey's La Moye Golf Club when he posted his fourth victory on the European Senior Tour there in early June.

Three years after making his debut at La Moye on the European Tour in 1983, the Australian lost a playoff to John Morgan. Twenty-six years later, Fowler was sidelined for almost a year after surgery when he injured his back on the eve of his intended Senior Tour debut at the Channel Island course in 2009.

The eventual victory, the first since 2013 for the 2011 Order of Merit champion, came at the end of a hard-fought final round against Sweden's Anders Forsbrand, with whom he shared the second-round lead after both players put up rounds of 70 and 68.

They reached the turn all even Sunday before Fowler moved in front to stay with birdies at the 11th and 13th holes. Another birdie and two bogeys, the second at the 17th, left him with a one-stroke lead, which held up when he parred the last hole for 71–209 as Forsbrand managed only his ninth back-nine par for 72–210.

In retrospect, the now-56-year-old Australian believes the back surgery may have given him additional mental strength after his recovery. "I've played some of my best golf since the surgery. Once you go through the hard work, it strengthens your resolve."

ISPS Handa PGA Seniors Championship
Newcastle-upon-Tyne, England
Winner: Peter Fowler

Peter Fowler never slowed down as the European Senior Tour moved from the Channel Islands to northern England for the ISPS Handa PGA Seniors Championship. Fresh off his victory in the Acorn Jersey Open, Fowler broke from a four-way, first-day tie atop the standings and made it two in a row, hanging up a three-stroke win in the circuit's domestic major championship.

It wasn't all gravy in the final round at roundly praised Close House at Newcastle-upon-Tyne, though. Lightly regarded Austrian Gordon Manson actually caught Fowler when the Australian, who turned 56 earlier in the week, double-bogeyed the ninth hole.

But Fowler, who exclaimed "it's the best I have played in a few years," pulled away with three back-nine birdies to shoot a one-under-par 70 for 272, three in front of Manson (68) and four ahead of a resurgent Carl Mason (70), the holder of three PGA Seniors Championships. It was Fowler's fifth tour triumph.

Of the tougher conditions the field faced in the final round, the Aussie said: "It was colder, so the ball wasn't going nearly as far and I came up short with a few iron shots, but it was great to get the job done."

He had set up the final 18 with a pair of 67s in the middle rounds, the first one putting him a stroke in front of Mason (68-68) and the second giving him a four-stroke lead over Philip Golding (66) and Mason (70). The 62-year-old Englishman was making one of his best showings since 2011, when he scored his last of his record 25 victories on the senior circuit.

U.S. Senior Open Championship
Winner: Jeff Maggert

See Champions Tour section.

Swiss Seniors Open
Bad Ragaz, Switzerland
Winner: Gordon Manson

Gordon Manson, who took a shot at the title in the PGA Seniors three weeks earlier before settling for second place, validated his ability with his first victory on the European Senior Tour in the Swiss Seniors Open.

"I feel 10 feet tall," said the 55-year-old Austrian. "This is such a special moment. I knew I'd been playing well of late, but to get the win is just fantastic."

Manson, who had carried a two-stroke lead into the final round at Golf Club Bad Ragaz, faced challenges from several players Sunday after his outgoing 35. But he holed "the putt of my life" from 60 feet for an eagle on the 16th hole following birdies at the 13th and 14th, parred in and won by two strokes with his 14-under-par 66 for 196 total.

Manson had taken the lead away from Carl Mason with his second-round 64–130 after Mason, 62, four years away from his record 25th victory on the circuit and a three-time winner at Bad Ragaz, opened with a 63. Manson's closest pursuers after 36 holes were Scotland's Ross Drummond (65-67), England's Philip Golding (67-65) and Mason, who shot 69 Saturday.

Frenchman Francois Lamare made a run Sunday with seven birdies on the first 16 holes but settled for 64 and a tie for third with Drummond (67) when he three-putted the last hole. Golding picked off second place when he birdied the last hole for 66–198.

WINSTONgolf Senior Open
Vorbeck, Germany
Winner: Pedro Linhart

When is a lead not a lead? When a player far behind shoots a lights-out front nine before the leader has even put his tee in the ground on the first hole. Pedro Linhart faced that challenge in the final round of the WINSTONgolf Senior Open and overcame it nicely to score his first victory on the European Senior Tour in mid-July.

Englishman Barry Lane, who started the last 18 holes at the classy golf venue at Vorbeck in northern Germany seven strokes behind Linhart, had already shot 29 on the outgoing nine, wiping out the two-stroke lead the 52-year-old Spaniard had established with his Saturday round of 64 before he hit a shot Sunday. Linhart proved unflappable, though, particularly when and after he holed out for an eagle-two at the second hole. Two front-nine birdies followed, but at the turn Linhart was still only a shot clear of Lane, who continued his assault on par and a remote shot at a record 59 before parring the last two holes for 62–203.

Even though struggling off the tee over the final 12 holes, Linhart "hit some great iron shots on the back nine and that did it for me." Three birdies led him to his winning, six-under-par 66 and 200 total. Lane finished second and defending champion Paul Wesselingh third at 205.

Cadiz native Linhart, who didn't qualify for the regular European Tour until he was in his 30s and scored his only win at age 36 in the Madeira Islands Open, looked optimistically to the future. "I certainly hope this is the start of bigger and better things," he opined. "I feel like I'm becoming a better player now after 50 than I was when I was younger."

The Senior Open Championship presented by Rolex
Birkshire, England
Winner: Marco Dawson

It was like David toppling a pair of Goliaths when Marco Dawson made off with the title and glory of the Senior Open Championship presented by Rolex. Here was a 51-year-old American, who went through 413 starts on the U.S. PGA Tour amid two back surgeries without a victory, battling and prevailing over two European Hall of Famers who had been dominating senior golf on both sides of the Atlantic Ocean.

Bolstered by two eagles, Dawson nudged in front in the stretch run at prestigious Sunningdale Golf Club and rolled in an 18-foot birdie putt on the final green to snuff out Bernhard Langer's bid for a repeat victory in the major championship, the crown jewel of the European Senior Tour season. Colin Montgomerie was in the thick of things in Sunday's dogfight until bogeys on two holes early on the back nine derailed his chances and dropped him into a third-place finish.

Dawson, who hinted at things to come in March when he finally won an event on the Champions Tour, was impressive throughout the rain-plagued week, sub-par rounds of 65, 67 and 68 preceding the clutch 64 that brought him the prized title. Langer, who entered the closing 18 a stroke behind co-leaders Dawson and Montgomerie, also shot 64 Sunday.

Dawson and Langer were among a record eight players who finished the first round at the top of the leaderboard with 65s. Heavy rains flooded Sunningdale Friday, forcing an afternoon suspension. When the round was completed Saturday morning, the American, at 132, had a one-stroke lead on the German great and two over Montgomerie, Americans Fred Couples and Jeff Sluman, Spaniard Miguel Angel Jimenez and Australia's Peter Fowler, already a two-time winner on the 2015 circuit.

Rain returned Saturday as Montgomerie (66) overtook Dawson (68) and Langer (68) remained a shot off the lead, setting up the exciting back-and-forth Sunday. The Scot built a three-shot lead through 10 holes with an outgoing 31 as Dawson followed his first eagle at the ninth with a bogey at the 10th. A four-shot swing followed when Dawson birdied and Monty bogeyed the next two holes. Langer, with five birdies on the first 12 holes, held the lead briefly before Dawson eagled again at the 14th hole and was in front the rest of the way.

Langer still had a shot at a tie and playoff until Dawson holed the dramatic

18-footer at the 18th to put it out of reach even when Langer matched the birdie from 10 feet.

"This is unbelievable," expressed the winner. "I can't tell you how many hours I put in on the range and I've had two back surgeries to prove it. It's a little later than most of the guys, but it came true."

Prostate Cancer UK Scottish Senior Open
North Berwick, Scotland
Winner: Paul Broadhurst

Paul Broadhurst wasted little time getting into the winner's circle on the European Senior Tour. Just 15 days after turning 50, he became the 10th player in circuit history to land a title in his first start and he had to do it the hard way. First, he had to hole a breaking downhill putt of 25 feet on the 54th hole just to force the season's first playoff and then had to birdie two overtime holes to beat Gordon Manson in the Prostate Cancer UK Scottish Senior Open.

Broadhurst had frittered away a four-shot lead in Saturday's second round at the Archerfield Links Golf Club and entered the final day deadlocked with Manson at 141. "Yesterday, when I finished the way I did, I let 15 guys back in the tournament, but today I played pretty solid," said the Englishman after matching 68s with Manson, the Scottish-born Austrian who already had a win and a runner-up finish on his 2015 record.

As for the playoff, Broadhurst remarked: "I'll have to admit I'm a bit surprised because I've got a dreadful playoff record. Absolutely dire. I was two for 12 before today."

The tournament opened with a unique twist as David J. Russell, who designed the Archerfield Links, used his knowledge of the layout to seize a share of the lead with Australian Peter O'Malley and fellow Englishman Gary Marks with wind-blown 70s, only to crash Saturday with 84.

Broadhurst, who hadn't won since his last of six victories on the European Tour in the 2005 Algarve Open, was the fourth straight first-time winner on the senior tour.

Travis Perkins Masters
Woburn, England
Winner: Colin Montgomerie

The outcome of the Travis Perkins Masters reflected another bright spot in the brilliant career of Colin Montgomerie and another dark moment in that of fellow Scot Ross Drummond.

When Montgomerie holed an 18-foot birdie putt on the second playoff hole at Woburn Golf Club to win the Travis Perkins for the third year in a row, he dashed the hopes Drummond had of finally getting a victory after 28 years of futility on the European and European Senior Tours.

While relishing his second victory of the season and seventh on the senior circuit, Montgomerie had sympathetic words for Drummond, who provided his own undoing when he three-putted the final hole of regulation. "How can you not feel sorry for someone who played the difficult (15th, 16th and 17th) holes so well?" said Monty, who birdied the last hole to force the playoff.

The 52-year-old had overcome a shaky, opening-round 73 that left him four off the leading pace of Tim Thelen, his old American college teammate at Houston Baptist University, and Bill Longmuir with a second-day 67, the low round of the week on Woburn's tough Duke's course. With his 140, Montgomerie led Spain's Santiago Luna by a stroke, Drummond, Longmuir, Phil Golding and Cesar Monasterio by two, but he fell behind solid-playing Drummond in the stretch Sunday as he three-putted the 10th and 17th greens and missed an easy birdie at the 15th. The putter became reliable, though, with the tying birdie at the 54th and the winner two holes later.

"It's very hard to take," said Ross after his sixth runner-up finish on the senior tour and two earlier on the regular circuit. "I really ought to have wrapped it up in regulation play."

The rare back-to-back-to-back triple was just the second in tour history, Carl Mason having won three consecutive English Opens in the early 2000s. It was the 47th victory in Montgomerie's pro career.

French Riviera Masters
Provence, France
Winner: Simon P. Brown

Simon P. Brown should be rooting for wet weather every time he tees it up. The 52-year-old Englishman nailed his first title on a rain-drenched course in the 2013 Russian Open and his second that same season when so much rain fell on the Dutch Senior Open that, as the 36-hole leader, he was declared the winner when the course was deemed unplayable that Sunday.

Up came the French Riviera Masters on the 2015 fall schedule of the European Senior Tour and what happens? Heavy clouds unloaded overnight and into Friday at Terre Blanche Hotel, Spa and Golf Resort, flooding the course and forcing a decision to shorten the tournament to 36 holes. That was right up Brown's alley. With rounds of 66 and 68, he scored a two-stroke victory over Angel Franco of Paraguay and fellow Englishman Barry Lane with his 10-under-par 134.

With seven birdies and a bogey, Brown "played very well from start to finish" Saturday and staked out a one-stroke lead over Franco and two over England's Gary Emerson. Lane, who opened softly with 72, exploded with a 64 Sunday, a round highlighted by a run of four birdies and an eagle on the back. Scoreboard-watching, Brown then set a goal.

"I just thought that if I could get to 10 under, I would have a chance, and here I am holding the trophy," he related afterward. His last two of four birdies on the back nine made the difference. Franco shot 69 for his 138 to tie Lane.

Pleased with the win and the course, Brown asserted: "I'm already looking forward to coming back and defending my title next year." He will, if the tournament doesn't suffer the same fate as the first two he won. Neither the Russian nor Dutch Senior Opens were played this year.

MCB Tour Championship
Poste de Flacq, Mauritius
Winner: Colin Montgomerie

It took appearances in just five of the tournaments on the 2015 schedule of
the European Senior Tour for Colin Montgomerie to wrap up his second
straight Order of Merit title. With the symbolic John Jacobs Trophy already
clinched, Montgomerie capped his season by outdueling David Frost on the
final day of the MCB Tour Championship.

His three-stroke victory in that fifth start in the December season finale
at Constance Belle Mare Plage in Mauritius followed his victories in the
U.S. Senior PGA and Travis Perkins Masters, his second-place finish in the
U.S. Senior Open and third spot in the Senior British Open. With those
outstanding showings, the 52-year-old Scotchman piled up €679,147, more
than triple the winnings of runner-up Peter Fowler, who played in a dozen
events.

Frost, a two-time winner of the Tour Championship in Mauritius, got the
jump on the field with an opening 65, then Montgomerie, who started with
68, did him one better the second day with a sparkling 64 that included a
hole-in-one at the par-three 17th. With the 132, Montgomerie sprang four
shots in front of South Africans Chris Williams (68-68) and Frost, who shot
71 Saturday.

Montgomerie got off to a shaky start Sunday and actually fell behind Frost
before Frost suffered bogeys at the 12th and 14th holes. Montgomerie then
birdied the final three holes for 69 and his 15-under-par 201. Frost finished
with 68–204.

"This win is right up there," evaluated the ebullient winner. "The 64 really
set me up, but David really pushed me all the way today."

Japan PGA Senior Tour

Kanehide Senior Okinawa Open
Okinawa
Winner: Katsumi Kubo

The Japan Senior Tour launched its 2015 season as usual in Okinawa with the 36-hole Kanehide Senior Okinawa Open and the title went to a first-time winner.

Katsumi Kubo shot a pair of 68s and his eight-under-par 136 gave him a one-stroke victory over Mitsuo Harada, another player without a senior tour victory. Tatsuya Shiraishi, yet another non-winner, opened with 65, two ahead of Harada and three in front of Kubo, but dropped to third place with a final-round 73–138. Harada held onto second place with his Saturday 70–137.

Kyoraku More Surprise Cup
Mie
Winner: Takeshi Sakiyama

Takeshi Sakiyama proved his initial victory on the Japan Senior Tour in the 2013 season's opener in Okinawa was not to be a "one and done" consequence when he scored a decisive win in the Kyoraku More Surprise Cup tournament in late May. The third-year senior breezed to a four-shot victory at Ryosen Golf Club in Mie Prefecture with his eight-under-par 208.

Sakiyama began the week with a six-under-par 66, two strokes in front of Yoshimitsu Fukuzawa and Frankie Minoza of the Philippines, a three-time winner on the circuit. He widened the gap on Minoza to three strokes with his second-round 70 as Minoza shot 71, and finished four ahead with 72 on a day when 71 was the low round. Runner-up Minoza posted a 73 Sunday, finishing two ahead of Kohki Idoki (74) and four in front of Yutaka Hagawa (73) and Naoyuki Tamura (76).

Starts Senior
Ibaraki
Winner: Kiyoshi Murota

Kiyoshi Murota became the top all-time winner on the Japan Senior Tour in June when he ran away with the title in the Starts Senior tournament in Ibaraki. Murota's four-stroke victory was his 13th on the circuit, breaking the 12-win mark he shared with Katsunari Takahashi when he won the 2014 Fuji Film Senior.

The 59-year-old standout put a stranglehold on the lead at Starts Kasama

Golf Club the second day when he fired a nine-under-par 63 and raced four strokes in front of the field. He had opened with 66, tied with Naomichi (Joe) Ozaki a stroke behind Satoshi Higashi. The 129 gave him the four-shot lead over Naoyuki Tamura (69-64) and Katsumi Kubo, the Kanehide Okinawa winner (67-66). Ozaki slipped to 69–135 and Higashi to 71–136.

Murota easily protected that lead Sunday with his two-under-par 68 for 197, even though 28 other players shot in the 60s, too. Ozaki, one of Japan's all-time stars, had 66 and climbed into a second-place tie with Tamura, who shot 68.

Maruhan Cup Taiheiyo Club Senior
Hyogo
Winner: Takeshi Sakiyama

The only two rounds of 64 posted in the Maruhan Cup Taiheiyo Club Senior tournament factored into the one-two finish at the Taiheiyo Club's Rokko course.

Naoyuki Tamura shot the first eight-under-par round the first day to take a two-stroke lead over Yoshinori Mizumaki and Katsunari Takahashi, a 12-time winner on the Japan Senior Tour. The other 64 came in the second round from Takeshi Sakiyama and it brought him his second win of the season on the circuit and his third in senior golf.

Following his opening 67, Sakiyama won by three strokes with his 13-under-par 131 when Tamura could manage only a 70 in the second round. His 134 gave him the runner-up slot, a stroke better than Kiyoshi Maita (69-66) and Mizumaki (66-69). It was his second straight second-place finish.

Fancl Classic
Susono, Shizuoka
Winner: Kiyoshi Murota

Kiyoshi Murota padded his lead as the career wins leader on the Japan Senior Tour when he won the Fancl Classic for a third time in late August. With a closing 69, the 59-year-old Murota posted a 14-under-par 202 and a five-stroke victory. He won back-to-back Fancl Classics in 2006 and 2007.

Masahiro Kuramoto shot 65 and led Murota by a stroke, Hideki Kase by two after the first round, but it was all Murota after that at Susono Country Club in Shizuoka. Murota followed his opening 66 with a 67 to go four strokes ahead of Tsukasa Watanabe (69-68), who took over second place when Kuramoto fell away with a 75. Tsuyoshi Yoneyama and Australia's Gregory Meyer had matching 68-70s to share third place.

Murota coasted to his second win of the season and 14th of his senior career with an easy 69 Sunday. Tatsuo Takasaki shot 68 to grab a share of second place with Watanabe, who had a closing 70.

Kyoshinkai Hiroshima Senior Championship
Hiroshima
Winner: Masahiro Kuramoto

It didn't take Masahiro Kuramoto long to shake off a blown lead.

A week before teeing it up in the Kyoshinkai Hiroshima Senior Championship, Kuramoto threw away his first-round lead in the Fancl Classic with a fatal second 18 of 75. He came right back at Hiroshima Country Club with a victory, his fifth on the Japan Senior Tour to go with the 34 he rang up during his prime years on the Japan Tour.

Kuramoto shot a seven-under-par 64 in the opening round of the 36-hole event, but was only in second place as Naoyuki Tamura, twice a runner-up earlier in the season, fired a sizzling 62. Tamura had to settle for another second place when managed just a par 71 the second day and Kuramoto zipped past him with 67 for a winning 131. Nobumitsu Yuhara, with 67-66, tied Tamura in the runner-up slot.

Alpha Club Cup Senior Open
Tochigi
Winner: Takeshi Sakiyama

Takeshi Sakiyama's splendid season raged on as he scored his third 2015 victory in the Alpha Club Cup Senior Open.

As he did in his earlier win in the Starts Senior, the 52-year-old Sakiyama sped away to a strong first-round lead and finished a comfortable three strokes ahead of the field.

Sakiyama, a player who came to the Senior Tour without impressive credentials from earlier years, seized the lead with his nine-under-par 63 at Yaita Country Club. He stood two strokes ahead of Nobuo Serizawa and three in front of Hideki Kase, Katsumi Kubo and Kiyoshi Murota, all four previous winners on the circuit, Kubo and Murota earlier in 2015.

Sakiyama put it away the second day with a back-nine 32 for 66–129. Nobumitsu Yuhara, who started the round four off the pace, shot 65 for 132 and second place, a stroke better than the totals of Serizawa and Kubo, who won the season opener in Okinawa.

Komatsu Open
Komatsu, Ishikawa
Winner: Takeshi Sakiyama

Less than a week after posting his third victory of the season, Takeshi Sakiyama added No. 4, coming from behind to win the Komatsu Open by two strokes. It marked the first time a player had won four times in a season since Fujio Kobayashi did it in 2000.

Sakiyama started slowly with a two-under-par 70, but trailed leaders Tsukasa Watanabe and Atsushi Takamatsu by just three strokes. He was tied for sixth with Yutaka Hagawa, Hideki Kase, Boonchu Ruangkit and Shinichi Akiba, with Naoyuki Tamura, Takeshi Nakashima and Shinji Ikeuchi in between at 69.

Watanabe took over first place Saturday with another 67 as Sakiyama surged into the runner-up slot with 65–135. Hagawa was next at 70-67–137. His 68 in the final round gave Sakiyama the victory with his 13-under-par 203, two ahead of Watanabe, who finished with a 71. Yuhara jumped into third place with 66–206.

Japan PGA Senior Championship
Ibaraki
Winner: Kiyoshi Murota

One wonders what Kiyoshi Murota would do if he went out on the international senior scene. The question came up after Murota, already the winningest player in Japan Senior Tour history, won the Japan Senior PGA Championship for a remarkable fourth time.

The Senior PGA, along with the Japan Open Championship, are the circuit's two 72-hole majors, and the 59-year-old Murota's record sports six of them — the PGAs in 2005, 2009, 2012 and the three-stroke victory in the current season at Summit Golf Club in Ibaraki to go with Senior Open Championships in 2011 and 2013.

Murota never trailed as he rolled to his 15th victory on the circuit. He opened with 68, tied for the lead with Thailand's Boonchu Ruangkit and Takeshi Sakiyama, who had already won four times on the 2015 tour. Murota went in front alone to stay the second day with 69-137, leading Ikuo Shirahama and Takeshi Oyama by two strokes. Both had 69-70 rounds.

Murota widened the gap to three with his 67 in Saturday's round. At 204, he led Seiki Okuda (71-70-66) and Naomichi (Joe) Ozaki (70-70-67) by three strokes, and he eased home with a 68–272, 16 under par, for the win. Shirahama revved up with a 66 to grab second place with his 66–275, a shot better than Toshikazu Sugihara (67–276).

Japan Senior Open Championship
Mie
Winner: Takenori Hiraishi

Victories have been few and far between for Takenori Hiraishi in his long golf career. He went 18 years and was 41 years old before winning his first and only title on the Japan Tour — the 2001 KBC Augusta — in a three-man, four-hole playoff no less. Fourteen years later, Hiraishi, then 55, won a second tournament, this time the Japan Senior Open, the richest and most prestigious event on the Japan Senior Tour.

Hiraishi put together four solid, unspectacular rounds in scoring a one-stroke victory with his nine-under-par 279.

His opening 70 on the Hakusan Village Golf Club course at the Cocopa Resort Club stationed him in an eight-way tie for fourth place, but five strokes behind leader Hideki Kase's stunning 65. In between were Daisuke

Serizawa and Spain's Miguel Angel Martin at 69. Kase came back to the field with a 73 the second day. He still led, but only by a shot over Hiraishi and four-time senior winner Tsukasa Watanabe. Both had 70-69 rounds.

Hiraishi repeated his 69 Saturday and assumed a three-stroke lead with his 208. Watanabe shot 72 for his 211 and was joined there by Tsuyoshi Yoneyama (75-70-66) and Englishman Paul Wesselingh (70-73-68). Yoneyama made the strongest run at the winner Sunday. He caught him with an outgoing 33, but Hiraishi, with an incoming 35 for 71, bagged the victory as Yoneyama closed with 36–69 for 280. Watanabe finished third with 70–281, and Kiyoshi Murota, the tour's No. 1 star, took fourth place another stroke back.

Fuji Film Senior Championship
Chiba
Winner: Tsukasa Watanabe

Tsukasa Watanabe and Kiyoshi Murota, who came up just short in the Senior Open, maintained their competitive edge days later and battled it out for the Fuji Film Senior Championship. Watanabe prevailed by two strokes over Murota, notching his first victory since capturing the Japan Senior PGA Championship in 2013 and his fifth on the Japan Senior Tour.

Murota, seeking his fourth win of the season and record 16th on the circuit, struck first with an opening-round, five-under-par 67, but the 58-year-old Watanabe was just a stroke back at 68 with Yoichi Shimuzu. Also contending at 69 were Australian Gregory Meyer, Yasuaki Takashima and Katsunari Takahashi, the enduring standout from earlier senior years.

Watanabe joined Murota at the top the second day, shooting 68 to Murota's 69. At 136, they led Meyer (68) by a shot and the rest of the field by at least four. Murota edged a stroke in front with a 35 on the outgoing nine Sunday, but Watanabe caught fire with a back-nine 32 to Murota's 35 for another 68 and a two-stroke victory with his 12-under-par 204. Murota shot 35–70–206, four strokes better than Meyer (73), Naoyuki Tamura (67) and Frankie Minoza (68), the long-time standout from the Philippines.

ISPS Handa Cup Philanthropy Senior
Chiba
Winner: Shinichi Akiba

A third first-time winner on the tour emerged at the ISPS Handa Cup Philanthropy tournament in the person of Shinichi Akiba.

Akiba survived a strong challenge from tour leader Kiyoshi Murota to put up a one-stroke victory with his 11-under-par 205 at Narita Hills Country Club in the mid-November tournament.

Akiba opened with a 67, tied with Ter-Chang Wang and one behind leader Takao Komizo, then moved into a first-place deadlock with Kunihiko Masuda the second day. He shot 67, Masuda 68 for their 135s. Komizo slipped two back with 70–137, and Murota was another shot behind after 68-70 rounds.

Murota made up the three-stroke deficit on the front nine Sunday with a 33 effort against Akiba's 36, but Akiba's 34 coming in for 70 was just enough to edge Murota's 68 and prevent him from scoring his fourth win of the season.

Iwasaki Shiratsuyu Senior
Kagoshima
Winner: Tze-Chung Chen

A blistering finish brought Taiwan veteran Tze-Chung (T.C.) Chen his first title on the Japan Senior Tour in the season-ending Iwasaki Shiratsuyu Senior tournament.

The 57-year-old Chen, a dominant figure in Asian golf for many years who drew international attention when he nearly won the U.S. Open Championship in 1985, fired a five-under-par 31 on the final nine to snare a three-stroke victory with his 15-under 201 on the Kaimon course of Ibusuki Golf Club in Kagoshima.

Chen, who had five victories on the Japan Tour and a win at Los Angeles during the decade he played in America, took the lead the second day at Ibusuki after opening with a 68, two behind leader Seiki Okuda. He shot 67 Saturday for 135, one stroke better than the 70-66–136 of Masahiro Kuramoto, the defending champion and 2014 Order of Merit leader. Chen slipped back into a tie for the lead with Okuda and Tsuyoshi Yoneyama on the front nine Sunday, shooting 35 to Okuda's 34 and Yoneyama's 33, before spurting away from them over the final nine holes.

Kiyoshi Murota, a three-time winner during the season, wrapped up the Order of Merit money-winning title for the second time in three years. He finished with ¥59,725,999, nearly ¥9 million ahead of Takeshi Sakiyama, who won four times in 2015 but did not play in the season finale.

APPENDIXES

American Tours

Hyundai Tournament of Champions

Kapalua Resort, Plantation Course, Maui, Hawaii
Par 36-37–73; 7,452 yards

January 9-12
purse, $5,700,000

	SCORES				TOTAL	MONEY
Patrick Reed	67	69	68	67	271	$1,140,000
Jimmy Walker	67	68	67	69	271	665,000
(Reed defeated Walker on first playoff hole.)						
Jason Day	70	69	71	62	272	332,666.67
Russell Henley	65	70	70	67	272	332,666.67
Hideki Matsuyama	70	66	66	70	272	332,666.66
Sangmoon Bae	66	69	69	70	274	213,000
Zach Johnson	68	67	73	67	275	190,000
Robert Streb	67	69	71	69	276	175,000
Brendon Todd	69	67	69	71	276	175,000
Bubba Watson	70	69	68	70	277	160,000
Matt Jones	69	72	68	69	278	140,000
Ben Martin	67	72	70	69	278	140,000
Seung-Yul Noh	71	70	69	68	278	140,000
Charley Hoffman	70	66	73	70	279	110,000
Chris Kirk	68	76	73	62	279	110,000
Scott Stallings	67	70	70	72	279	110,000
Brian Harman	70	70	75	65	280	90,333.34
Matt Kuchar	68	70	74	68	280	90,333.33
Hunter Mahan	71	71	69	69	280	90,333.33
Chesson Hadley	70	73	68	70	281	80,000
Ryan Moore	71	70	69	71	281	80,000
Steven Bowditch	69	73	71	69	282	70,666.67
Billy Horschel	72	70	70	70	282	70,666.67
Kevin Streelman	69	73	67	73	282	70,666.66
Tim Clark	70	75	67	71	283	65,000
John Senden	68	71	73	71	283	65,000
Matt Every	73	71	70	70	284	61,000
Geoff Ogilvy	72	69	74	69	284	61,000
Angel Cabrera	71	73	72	70	286	58,000
Ben Crane	74	67	73	72	286	58,000
Nick Taylor	69	73	72	72	286	58,000
Camilo Villegas	71	70	71	75	287	56,000
J.B. Holmes	69	71	73	76	289	55,000

Sony Open in Hawaii

Waialae Country Club, Honolulu, Hawaii
Par 35-35–70; 7,044 yards

January 15-18
purse, $5,600,000

	SCORES				TOTAL	MONEY
Jimmy Walker	66	66	62	63	257	$1,008,000
Scott Piercy	67	67	66	66	266	604,800
Harris English	66	69	65	67	267	291,200
Matt Kuchar	65	63	68	71	267	291,200
Gary Woodland	70	65	65	67	267	291,200
Zac Blair	71	66	64	67	268	163,600
Brian Davis	66	70	65	67	268	163,600

	SCORES				TOTAL	MONEY
Max Homa	69	67	63	69	268	163,600
Jerry Kelly	73	62	67	66	268	163,600
Rory Sabbatini	64	67	74	63	268	163,600
Shawn Stefani	69	66	65	68	268	163,600
Justin Thomas	67	61	70	70	268	163,600
Daniel Berger	68	66	68	67	269	105,000
Brian Harman	66	67	64	72	269	105,000
Russell Knox	66	65	69	69	269	105,000
Webb Simpson	62	66	72	69	269	105,000
Stuart Appleby	68	69	67	66	270	68,444.45
Jason Day	65	69	68	68	270	68,444.45
Russell Henley	72	64	67	67	270	68,444.45
Colt Knost	70	68	66	66	270	68,444.45
Jason Kokrak	67	69	64	70	270	68,444.44
Ryan Palmer	69	63	69	69	270	68,444.44
Pat Perez	67	68	70	65	270	68,444.44
Robert Streb	63	69	69	69	270	68,444.44
Daniel Summerhays	66	67	67	70	270	68,444.44
James Hahn	69	64	69	69	271	42,280
Charles Howell	69	66	67	69	271	42,280
Chris Kirk	66	67	74	64	271	42,280
Chez Reavie	67	67	68	69	271	42,280
Paul Casey	62	70	69	71	272	33,280
Tim Clark	65	65	68	74	272	33,280
Chad Collins	69	65	69	69	272	33,280
J.J. Henry	65	67	70	70	272	33,280
Hyung-Sung Kim	69	69	62	72	272	33,280
Scott Langley	70	68	67	67	272	33,280
Troy Merritt	66	64	67	75	272	33,280
Steven Bowditch	70	64	71	68	273	24,080
Stewart Cink	69	69	65	70	273	24,080
Marc Leishman	70	62	71	70	273	24,080
Francesco Molinari	67	68	69	69	273	24,080
Jeff Overton	67	68	69	69	273	24,080
Kenny Perry	68	69	67	69	273	24,080
John Peterson	65	70	66	72	273	24,080
K.J. Choi	68	67	65	74	274	16,528
Justin Leonard	70	65	72	67	274	16,528
Nicholas Thompson	69	67	66	72	274	16,528
Brendon Todd	69	69	69	67	274	16,528
Jhonattan Vegas	68	68	68	70	274	16,528
Camilo Villegas	63	70	67	74	274	16,528
Boo Weekley	69	65	72	68	274	16,528
Andrew Svoboda	70	66	67	72	275	12,967.12
Sangmoon Bae	67	70	70	68	275	12,967.11
Luke Donald	68	69	67	71	275	12,967.11
David Hearn	67	71	69	68	275	12,967.11
Morgan Hoffmann	70	67	68	70	275	12,967.11
Tom Johnson	70	66	67	72	275	12,967.11
Spencer Levin	69	69	67	70	275	12,967.11
Ben Martin	71	67	68	69	275	12,967.11
Kevin Streelman	72	66	69	68	275	12,967.11
Blayne Barber	66	69	71	71	277	12,152
Mark Hubbard	68	66	70	73	277	12,152
Scott Pinckney	71	63	69	74	277	12,152
Michael Putnam	66	71	70	70	277	12,152
Zach Johnson	68	69	68	73	278	11,760
Wen-Chong Liang	68	68	71	71	278	11,760
Kevin Na	66	67	71	74	278	11,760
Roger Sloan	70	67	69	73	279	11,536
Derek Fathauer	68	66	73	73	280	11,368
Nick Taylor	70	68	68	74	280	11,368
Matt Jones	68	67	72	75	282	11,200

	SCORES			TOTAL	MONEY
Fabian Gomez	71	66	71	208	10,864
Tom Hoge	71	64	73	208	10,864
William McGirt	68	68	72	208	10,864
George McNeill	71	67	70	208	10,864
Mark Wilson	69	68	71	208	10,864
Lucas Glover	70	66	73	209	10,528
*Kyle Suppa	69	69	71	209	
Martin Flores	70	68	72	210	10,192
Jim Herman	70	66	74	210	10,192
John Huh	69	68	73	210	10,192
Hideki Matsuyama	72	66	72	210	10,192
Jonathan Randolph	65	73	72	210	10,192
John Senden	70	68	73	211	9,856
Kevin Kisner	70	67	75	212	9,744
Luke Guthrie	68	70	75	213	9,632

Humana Challenge

PGA West, Palmer Course: Par 36-36–72; 6,930 yards
La Quinta CC: Par 36-36–72; 7,060 yards
PGA West, Nicklaus Course: Par 36-36–72; 6,951 yards
La Quinta, California

January 22-25
purse, $5,700,000

	SCORES				TOTAL	MONEY
Bill Haas	67	63	69	67	266	$1,026,000
Charley Hoffman	71	63	69	64	267	342,000
Matt Kuchar	65	64	71	67	267	342,000
S.J. Park	68	67	67	65	267	342,000
Brendan Steele	67	68	68	64	267	342,000
Steve Wheatcroft	65	67	68	67	267	342,000
Webb Simpson	70	66	68	64	268	177,650
Justin Thomas	68	63	68	69	268	177,650
Boo Weekley	70	66	67	65	268	177,650
Erik Compton	66	66	67	70	269	136,800
Colt Knost	71	67	68	63	269	136,800
Francesco Molinari	64	71	67	67	269	136,800
Ryan Palmer	71	61	68	69	269	136,800
Nick Watney	67	64	71	68	270	108,300
Alex Cejka	68	64	70	69	271	91,200
Lucas Glover	68	69	66	68	271	91,200
Martin Laird	68	66	68	69	271	91,200
Michael Putnam	63	67	69	72	271	91,200
Shawn Stefani	75	66	63	67	271	91,200
James Hahn	67	67	73	65	272	66,405
Mark Hubbard	69	69	67	67	272	66,405
John Peterson	64	70	69	69	272	66,405
Scott Pinckney	64	67	69	72	272	66,405
Brian Davis	67	69	68	69	273	46,170
David Lingmerth	68	72	65	68	273	46,170
Phil Mickelson	71	66	68	68	273	46,170
Patrick Reed	65	70	67	71	273	46,170
Rory Sabbatini	71	68	63	71	273	46,170
David Toms	68	71	65	69	273	46,170
Jason Bohn	67	72	66	69	274	31,090.91
Graham DeLaet	68	70	66	70	274	31,090.91
Harris English	67	68	69	70	274	31,090.91
John Huh	69	68	70	67	274	31,090.91
George McNeill	68	68	68	70	274	31,090.91
Jeff Overton	68	73	66	67	274	31,090.91
Pat Perez	66	68	70	70	274	31,090.91

	SCORES				TOTAL	MONEY
Scott Piercy	69	70	67	68	274	31,090.91
Cameron Tringale	69	70	68	67	274	31,090.91
Mark Wilson	64	73	69	68	274	31,090.91
Fabian Gomez	69	68	71	66	274	31,090.90
Chad Collins	68	72	67	68	275	19,950
Brendon de Jonge	69	65	71	70	275	19,950
Billy Horschel	71	67	65	72	275	19,950
Matt Jones	76	67	64	68	275	19,950
Bill Lunde	72	69	67	67	275	19,950
Sean O'Hair	68	67	73	67	275	19,950
Kevin Streelman	71	69	66	69	275	19,950
Blayne Barber	69	72	67	68	276	14,036.25
Keegan Bradley	68	70	69	69	276	14,036.25
Adam Hadwin	72	70	66	68	276	14,036.25
J.J. Henry	67	67	72	70	276	14,036.25
Billy Hurley	68	69	68	71	276	14,036.25
Jason Kokrak	65	68	70	73	276	14,036.25
Troy Merritt	71	69	68	68	276	14,036.25
Kevin Na	69	68	69	70	276	14,036.25
Charles Howell	67	68	72	70	277	12,882
Chris Kirk	70	68	69	70	277	12,882
Patrick Rodgers	70	67	69	71	277	12,882
Steven Alker	68	66	69	75	278	12,426
Gonzalo Fernandez-Castano	69	72	66	71	278	12,426
Tony Finau	71	65	68	74	278	12,426
Martin Flores	68	65	71	74	278	12,426
Retief Goosen	68	70	69	71	278	12,426
Brice Garnett	69	69	70	71	279	11,856
Danny Lee	68	69	70	72	279	11,856
Alex Prugh	70	70	67	72	279	11,856
Scott Stallings	68	67	71	73	279	11,856
D.J. Trahan	68	71	69	71	279	11,856
Heath Slocum	66	72	68	74	280	11,400
Nicholas Thompson	72	67	69	72	280	11,400
Scott Verplank	70	65	72	73	280	11,400
Robert Garrigus	71	69	68	74	282	11,172

Waste Management Phoenix Open

TPC Scottsdale, Scottsdale, Arizona
Par 35-36–71; 7,266 yards

January 29-February 1
purse, $6,300,000

	SCORES				TOTAL	MONEY
Brooks Koepka	71	68	64	66	269	$1,134,000
Hideki Matsuyama	69	71	63	67	270	470,400
Ryan Palmer	64	72	68	66	270	470,400
Bubba Watson	65	71	69	65	270	470,400
Martin Laird	66	66	68	72	272	252,000
*Jon Rahm	70	68	66	68	272	
Graham DeLaet	67	70	69	67	273	211,050
Freddie Jacobson	68	73	68	64	273	211,050
Jordan Spieth	70	68	70	65	273	211,050
Daniel Berger	65	69	71	69	274	157,500
Zach Johnson	66	70	67	71	274	157,500
Brandt Snedeker	70	68	70	66	274	157,500
Robert Streb	66	70	69	69	274	157,500
Brian Stuard	72	68	67	67	274	157,500
Angel Cabrera	67	69	69	70	275	116,550
Russell Knox	69	71	65	70	275	116,550
Aaron Baddeley	68	71	71	66	276	94,500

	SCORES				TOTAL	MONEY
Keegan Bradley	65	73	71	67	276	94,500
Ryan Moore	69	67	69	71	276	94,500
Andrew Svoboda	70	70	68	68	276	94,500
Justin Thomas	67	68	69	72	276	94,500
K.J. Choi	68	69	72	68	277	68,040
Tony Finau	72	68	70	67	277	68,040
Francesco Molinari	70	71	64	72	277	68,040
Rory Sabbatini	68	71	67	71	277	68,040
Brendon de Jonge	67	71	72	68	278	50,242.50
Kevin Na	73	69	66	70	278	50,242.50
Pat Perez	70	69	68	71	278	50,242.50
Brendan Steele	71	67	71	69	278	50,242.50
Kevin Chappell	75	65	65	74	279	36,729
Billy Horschel	69	70	71	69	279	36,729
Matt Kuchar	70	70	68	71	279	36,729
Hunter Mahan	69	71	71	68	279	36,729
William McGirt	67	71	74	67	279	36,729
S.J. Park	71	69	69	70	279	36,729
Michael Putnam	71	70	67	71	279	36,729
Shawn Stefani	67	74	69	69	279	36,729
Kevin Streelman	70	72	73	64	279	36,729
Boo Weekley	69	71	70	69	279	36,729
Chad Campbell	70	70	69	71	280	25,200
Harris English	72	70	71	67	280	25,200
Jason Kokrak	72	71	70	67	280	25,200
Ben Martin	66	73	75	66	280	25,200
Patrick Reed	71	69	71	69	280	25,200
Mark Wilson	70	70	71	69	280	25,200
Jamie Donaldson	68	73	68	72	281	17,658
Martin Flores	69	72	71	69	281	17,658
Rickie Fowler	70	72	72	67	281	17,658
George McNeill	70	72	67	72	281	17,658
Seung-Yul Noh	68	75	67	71	281	17,658
Geoff Ogilvy	68	69	70	74	281	17,658
Jhonattan Vegas	71	72	67	71	281	17,658
Lucas Glover	70	70	72	70	282	14,616
Charley Hoffman	69	73	71	69	282	14,616
Morgan Hoffmann	72	67	73	70	282	14,616
Justin Leonard	67	73	72	70	282	14,616
Troy Merritt	71	72	71	68	282	14,616
Carlos Ortiz	69	73	69	71	282	14,616
Stewart Cink	70	71	67	75	283	13,734
Luke Guthrie	70	72	70	71	283	13,734
James Hahn	67	73	66	77	283	13,734
Russell Henley	69	71	65	78	283	13,734
Matt Jones	70	71	70	72	283	13,734
Cory Renfrew	70	73	74	66	283	13,734
Nick Taylor	71	71	71	70	283	13,734
Charlie Beljan	69	74	70	71	284	13,041
Jason Bohn	71	70	73	70	284	13,041
Brian Harman	68	75	70	71	284	13,041
J.B. Holmes	68	73	70	73	284	13,041
Bryce Molder	72	70	71	72	285	12,726
Charles Howell	70	71	72	73	286	12,537
Michael Thompson	67	75	71	73	286	12,537
Ricky Barnes	71	71	71	75	288	12,348
Retief Goosen	70	71	71	77	289	12,222
Brian Davis	74	68	77	71	290	12,096
Bill Haas	71	72	72	77	292	11,970

Farmers Insurance Open

Torrey Pines, San Diego, California
South Course: Par 36-36–72; 7,568 yards
North Course: Par 36-36–72; 6,874 yards

February 5-8
purse, $6,300,000

	SCORES				TOTAL	MONEY
Jason Day	73	65	71	70	279	$1,134,000
J.B. Holmes	69	70	68	72	279	470,400
Harris English	68	66	73	72	279	470,400
Scott Stallings	70	72	68	69	279	470,400
(Day defeated Stallings and English on first and Holmes on second playoff hole.)						
Charles Howell	72	70	70	68	280	239,400
Alex Prugh	70	70	69	71	280	239,400
Martin Laird	68	68	76	69	281	189,787.50
Shane Lowry	74	67	72	68	281	189,787.50
Jimmy Walker	72	66	70	73	281	189,787.50
Nick Watney	71	65	72	73	281	189,787.50
Zac Blair	72	70	71	69	282	129,150
J.J. Henry	68	71	73	70	282	129,150
Spencer Levin	68	70	70	74	282	129,150
Carlos Ortiz	73	70	68	71	282	129,150
Michael Thompson	65	73	74	70	282	129,150
Jhonattan Vegas	67	69	73	73	282	129,150
Chad Collins	75	66	75	67	283	97,650
Colt Knost	69	72	71	71	283	97,650
Chad Campbell	67	71	70	76	284	76,356
Jamie Donaldson	72	71	69	72	284	76,356
Bill Haas	72	67	70	75	284	76,356
Ian Poulter	67	71	72	74	284	76,356
Brandt Snedeker	70	71	71	72	284	76,356
Daniel Berger	70	68	77	70	285	55,440
Tony Finau	73	68	70	74	285	55,440
Lucas Glover	70	68	70	77	285	55,440
Brendon de Jonge	67	72	73	74	286	44,730
Andres Gonzales	69	69	71	77	286	44,730
Marc Leishman	72	66	72	76	286	44,730
John Peterson	68	72	70	76	286	44,730
Camilo Villegas	70	70	75	71	286	44,730
Sangmoon Bae	73	69	69	76	287	32,690
Adam Hadwin	72	69	71	75	287	32,690
Brian Harman	71	69	71	76	287	32,690
Jim Herman	69	72	74	72	287	32,690
Freddie Jacobson	67	73	72	75	287	32,690
Chris Kirk	67	74	72	74	287	32,690
Danny Lee	71	70	73	73	287	32,690
Greg Owen	70	70	72	75	287	32,690
Andrew Svoboda	75	67	71	74	287	32,690
Keegan Bradley	71	70	74	73	288	23,940
James Hahn	72	70	71	75	288	23,940
Brooks Koepka	66	74	74	74	288	23,940
David Toms	70	69	76	73	288	23,940
John Huh	74	66	76	73	289	18,963
Scott Pinckney	70	72	71	76	289	18,963
Brendan Steele	69	72	74	74	289	18,963
Gary Woodland	68	72	75	74	289	18,963
Whee Kim	70	72	73	75	290	15,718.50
Carl Pettersson	72	69	72	77	290	15,718.50
Scott Piercy	69	74	71	76	290	15,718.50
John Senden	72	71	73	74	290	15,718.50
Jonas Blixt	68	75	73	75	291	14,316.75
Angel Cabrera	71	70	75	75	291	14,316.75
K.J. Choi	71	70	76	74	291	14,316.75

	SCORES				TOTAL	MONEY
Martin Flores	71	72	73	75	291	14,316.75
Retief Goosen	74	69	75	73	291	14,316.75
Cameron Percy	71	69	73	78	291	14,316.75
Brian Stuard	70	72	76	73	291	14,316.75
Nicholas Thompson	64	73	76	78	291	14,316.75
Rickie Fowler	69	72	72	79	292	13,608
Luke Guthrie	70	73	71	78	292	13,608
Mark Hubbard	70	73	74	75	292	13,608
Robert Garrigus	73	70	77	73	293	13,230
Roger Sloan	73	68	76	76	293	13,230
Steve Wheatcroft	73	67	76	77	293	13,230
Andres Romero	73	69	75	77	294	12,915
Kyle Stanley	76	67	76	75	294	12,915
Matt Every	72	71	77	75	295	12,600
Sean O'Hair	72	71	74	78	295	12,600
Cameron Tringale	66	76	75	78	295	12,600
Daniel Miernicki	76	65	74	81	296	12,348
Zack Sucher	78	65	79	76	298	12,222
Pat Perez	75	65	77	83	300	12,096

AT&T Pebble Beach National Pro-Am

Pebble Beach GL: Par 36-36–72; 6,816 yards
Spyglass Hill GC: Par 36-36–72; 6,953 yards
Monterey Peninsula CC: Par 34-37–71; 6,867 yards
Pebble Beach, California

February 12-15
purse, $6,800,000

	SCORES				TOTAL	MONEY
Brandt Snedeker	64	67	67	67	265	$1,224,000
Nick Watney	65	69	65	69	268	734,400
Charlie Beljan	70	63	70	66	269	462,400
Jason Day	72	62	69	67	270	281,066.67
Dustin Johnson	69	67	68	66	270	281,066.67
Pat Perez	66	68	68	68	270	281,066.66
Jordan Spieth	68	67	68	68	271	211,933.34
Jim Furyk	64	70	63	74	271	211,933.33
Matt Jones	65	66	67	73	271	211,933.33
Daniel Berger	67	66	69	70	272	141,100
Jon Curran	69	64	69	70	272	141,100
Andres Gonzales	68	70	64	70	272	141,100
Chesson Hadley	64	69	71	68	272	141,100
J.B. Holmes	64	73	70	65	272	141,100
Alex Prugh	66	68	69	69	272	141,100
Vaughn Taylor	70	67	67	68	272	141,100
Brendon Todd	68	71	68	65	272	141,100
Kevin Chappell	66	69	66	72	273	95,200
Marcel Siem	67	73	63	70	273	95,200
Will Wilcox	66	67	73	67	273	95,200
David Hearn	67	66	71	70	274	63,835
Whee Kim	67	70	67	70	274	63,835
Shane Lowry	69	67	67	71	274	63,835
William McGirt	68	72	66	68	274	63,835
Michael Putnam	69	64	72	69	274	63,835
Kyle Reifers	70	68	67	69	274	63,835
Brian Stuard	67	70	66	71	274	63,835
Jimmy Walker	72	67	66	69	274	63,835
Ryan Armour	68	73	67	67	275	44,200
James Hahn	73	65	70	67	275	44,200
Max Homa	66	71	71	67	275	44,200
Sean O'Hair	70	70	66	69	275	44,200

	SCORES				TOTAL	MONEY
Patrick Reed	70	67	71	67	275	44,200
Alex Cejka	68	67	70	71	276	33,611.43
Chad Collins	68	67	71	70	276	33,611.43
Brandon Hagy	74	66	66	70	276	33,611.43
Justin Hicks	64	68	72	72	276	33,611.43
Bryce Molder	69	68	70	69	276	33,611.43
Hudson Swafford	69	70	68	69	276	33,611.43
Vijay Singh	67	70	70	69	276	33,611.42
Derek Fathauer	68	68	71	70	277	25,840
Colt Knost	73	65	68	71	277	25,840
Spencer Levin	68	69	68	72	277	25,840
David Lingmerth	71	67	69	70	277	25,840
Glen Day	66	69	71	72	278	19,448
J.J. Henry	65	70	69	74	278	19,448
Billy Horschel	68	65	73	72	278	19,448
Billy Hurley	70	68	70	70	278	19,448
Chris Stroud	71	66	69	72	278	19,448
Daniel Summerhays	67	67	72	72	278	19,448
Dudley Hart	65	70	73	71	279	16,365.34
Greg Chalmers	71	65	72	71	279	16,365.33
Steve Wheatcroft	71	70	67	71	279	16,365.33
Aaron Baddeley	68	71	69	72	280	15,640
Ken Duke	73	65	70	72	280	15,640
Hunter Mahan	68	71	69	72	280	15,640
Graham DeLaet	76	65	64	76	281	15,232
Fabian Gomez	72	67	69	73	281	15,232
Cameron Percy	72	70	66	73	281	15,232
Eric Axley	68	72	67	75	282	14,892
Andrew Loupe	71	66	70	75	282	14,892
Scott Brown	75	70	62	76	283	14,688
Matt Bettencourt	66	71	70	77	284	14,552
Dicky Pride	68	72	68	78	286	14,416
Jason Bohn	70	70	69		209	13,532
Jonathan Byrd	72	70	67		209	13,532
Jim Herman	68	72	69		209	13,532
Scott Langley	73	69	67		209	13,532
Alexander Levy	72	70	67		209	13,532
Davis Love	69	71	69		209	13,532
Bill Lunde	70	68	71		209	13,532
Seung-Yul Noh	72	71	66		209	13,532
Rod Pampling	65	71	73		209	13,532
D.A. Points	68	72	69		209	13,532
Bo Van Pelt	70	69	70		209	13,532
Johnson Wagner	69	71	69		209	13,532

Northern Trust Open

Riviera Country Club, Pacific Palisades, California
Par 35-36–71; 7,349 yards

February 19-22
purse, $6,700,000

	SCORES				TOTAL	MONEY
James Hahn	66	74	69	69	278	$1,206,000
Paul Casey	70	69	71	68	278	589,600
Dustin Johnson	70	72	67	69	278	589,600
(Hahn defeated Casey on second and Johnson on third playoff hole.)						
Keegan Bradley	73	68	70	68	279	263,812.50
Sergio Garcia	71	69	68	71	279	263,812.50
Hideki Matsuyama	70	72	70	67	279	263,812.50
Jordan Spieth	69	70	70	70	279	263,812.50
Sangmoon Bae	71	71	66	72	280	187,600

		SCORES			TOTAL	MONEY
Graham DeLaet	70	67	70	73	280	187,600
Retief Goosen	66	70	69	75	280	187,600
Kyle Reifers	72	70	71	67	280	187,600
Blayne Barber	74	71	71	65	281	147,400
Vijay Singh	66	74	69	72	281	147,400
Jim Furyk	71	70	68	73	282	110,550
Matt Jones	70	72	72	68	282	110,550
William McGirt	68	74	73	67	282	110,550
Brendan Steele	74	70	69	69	282	110,550
Brendon Todd	69	72	71	70	282	110,550
Bubba Watson	70	69	70	73	282	110,550
Hunter Mahan	75	67	71	70	283	83,750
Carlos Ortiz	67	73	68	75	283	83,750
Adam Hadwin	73	71	71	69	284	58,792.50
Morgan Hoffmann	69	75	66	74	284	58,792.50
J.B. Holmes	70	69	69	76	284	58,792.50
Scott Langley	73	71	71	69	284	58,792.50
Ryan Moore	69	68	72	75	284	58,792.50
Seung-Yul Noh	71	69	73	71	284	58,792.50
Vaughn Taylor	74	68	68	74	284	58,792.50
Nick Watney	66	74	74	70	284	58,792.50
Charley Hoffman	76	68	71	70	285	38,115.56
D.A. Points	71	73	70	71	285	38,115.56
Alex Prugh	70	73	70	72	285	38,115.56
Daniel Summerhays	66	74	73	72	285	38,115.56
Camilo Villegas	73	69	71	72	285	38,115.56
Angel Cabrera	70	68	71	76	285	38,115.55
K.J. Choi	70	74	73	68	285	38,115.55
Harris English	72	69	71	73	285	38,115.55
Chris Stroud	73	71	72	69	285	38,115.55
Tom Hoge	74	70	72	70	286	29,480
Brian Stuard	71	71	71	73	286	29,480
Jason Kokrak	71	72	74	70	287	24,120
Bryce Molder	71	70	76	70	287	24,120
Pat Perez	69	73	70	75	287	24,120
Charl Schwartzel	71	70	75	71	287	24,120
Justin Thomas	68	69	75	75	287	24,120
Jimmy Walker	73	71	71	72	287	24,120
Ken Duke	72	70	70	76	288	18,894
Cameron Tringale	71	74	71	72	288	18,894
Jason Gore	73	70	73	73	289	16,233.15
Jonathan Randolph	72	73	68	76	289	16,233.15
Ricky Barnes	71	74	72	72	289	16,233.14
Chad Campbell	74	71	71	73	289	16,233.14
Matt Every	70	72	74	73	289	16,233.14
Geoff Ogilvy	68	76	75	70	289	16,233.14
Andrew Putnam	73	69	74	73	289	16,233.14
Tony Finau	70	70	77	73	290	15,008
Padraig Harrington	70	73	76	71	290	15,008
Justin Leonard	75	70	70	75	290	15,008
Spencer Levin	73	72	71	74	290	15,008
Shawn Stefani	74	71	74	71	290	15,008
Derek Fathauer	66	73	77	75	291	14,338
Russell Henley	74	71	69	77	291	14,338
Charles Howell	71	70	75	75	291	14,338
Kevin Na	72	72	72	75	291	14,338
Michael Putnam	70	72	70	79	291	14,338
Scott Stallings	70	75	73	75	293	13,936
Alex Cejka	68	77	71	78	294	13,735
Carl Pettersson	71	72	75	76	294	13,735
Charlie Beljan	72	72	74	78	296	13,400
Danny Lee	70	73	77	76	296	13,400
George McNeill	71	74	74	77	296	13,400

	SCORES				TOTAL	MONEY
Gonzalo Fernandez-Castano	71	74	74	78	297	13,132
Andrew Svoboda	72	73	72	81	298	12,998
Brandt Snedeker	73	72	79	75	299	12,864
Jhonattan Vegas	71	72	81	76	300	12,730

Honda Classic

PGA National, Champion Course, Palm Beach Gardens, Florida
Par 35-35–70; 7,140 yards

February 26-March 1
purse, $6,100,000

	SCORES				TOTAL	MONEY
Padraig Harrington	67	66	71	70	274	$1,098,000
Daniel Berger	68	71	71	64	274	658,800
(Harrington defeated Berger on second playoff hole.)						
Paul Casey	69	70	68	68	275	317,200
Russell Knox	69	68	70	68	275	317,200
Ian Poulter	71	64	66	74	275	317,200
Jamie Donaldson	68	71	71	66	276	219,600
Luke Donald	69	67	74	67	277	183,762.50
Jim Herman	65	72	71	69	277	183,762.50
Jeff Overton	71	68	69	69	277	183,762.50
Patrick Reed	67	67	70	73	277	183,762.50
Brian Harman	70	74	70	64	278	129,320
Joost Luiten	71	71	67	69	278	129,320
George McNeill	72	70	68	68	278	129,320
Rory Sabbatini	68	75	69	66	278	129,320
Brendan Steele	66	69	71	72	278	129,320
Camilo Villegas	73	71	67	68	279	103,700
Jason Dufner	71	69	70	70	280	85,400
Martin Flores	67	71	74	68	280	85,400
John Huh	70	73	68	69	280	85,400
Phil Mickelson	71	67	69	73	280	85,400
Daniel Summerhays	71	68	70	71	280	85,400
Zac Blair	71	71	69	70	281	63,440
William McGirt	71	71	69	70	281	63,440
Steve Wheatcroft	74	70	69	68	281	63,440
Sean O'Hair	70	71	71	70	282	46,563.34
Ryan Palmer	71	72	71	68	282	46,563.34
Brendon de Jonge	69	71	71	71	282	46,563.33
Ryo Ishikawa	74	65	72	71	282	46,563.33
David Lingmerth	68	75	70	69	282	46,563.33
Lee Westwood	71	73	72	66	282	46,563.33
Jonas Blixt	71	71	70	71	283	32,452
Stewart Cink	73	71	69	70	283	32,452
Sergio Garcia	72	70	70	71	283	32,452
Robert Garrigus	70	69	74	70	283	32,452
Adam Hadwin	72	71	68	72	283	32,452
Jamie Lovemark	72	70	69	72	283	32,452
Ben Martin	70	72	76	65	283	32,452
S.J. Park	68	71	72	72	283	32,452
John Peterson	74	68	71	70	283	32,452
Scott Piercy	68	73	69	73	283	32,452
Rickie Fowler	70	73	70	71	284	23,790
Stephen Gallacher	73	71	68	72	284	23,790
Nick Watney	73	71	71	69	284	23,790
Charles Howell	70	71	72	72	285	18,003.72
Michael Thompson	69	73	69	74	285	18,003.72
Cameron Tringale	71	70	72	72	285	18,003.72
Russell Henley	73	70	72	70	285	18,003.71
Martin Kaymer	68	75	72	70	285	18,003.71

	SCORES				TOTAL	MONEY
Patrick Rodgers	75	69	74	67	285	18,003.71
Y.E. Yang	71	72	72	70	285	18,003.71
Robert Allenby	72	69	76	69	286	14,274
Kevin Kisner	74	68	74	70	286	14,274
Brooks Koepka	78	64	70	74	286	14,274
Scott Langley	72	71	72	71	286	14,274
Marc Leishman	73	69	75	69	286	14,274
Carl Pettersson	72	69	71	74	286	14,274
Tim Wilkinson	73	71	68	74	286	14,274
Blayne Barber	75	69	72	71	287	13,664
Chad Campbell	71	72	71	74	288	13,359
Brian Davis	71	71	71	75	288	13,359
Derek Fathauer	74	69	71	74	288	13,359
Robert Streb	73	71	74	70	288	13,359
Ricky Barnes	74	69	70	76	289	12,871
Matt Every	70	73	76	70	289	12,871
Andres Gonzales	73	70	74	72	289	12,871
Scott Stallings	71	70	78	70	289	12,871
Derek Ernst	74	70	75	71	290	12,566
Ben Crane	69	74	73	75	291	12,383
Scott Pinckney	73	71	73	74	291	12,383
Fabian Gomez	73	69	75	75	292	12,200
Jon Curran	71	72	74	76	293	12,078

WGC - Cadillac Championship

Trump National at Doral, Miami, Florida
Par 36-36–72; 7,528 yards

March 5-8
purse, $9,250,000

	SCORES				TOTAL	MONEY
Dustin Johnson	68	73	69	69	279	$1,570,000
J.B. Holmes	62	73	70	75	280	930,000
Bubba Watson	71	69	70	71	281	540,000
Adam Scott	70	68	75	71	284	365,000
Henrik Stenson	69	71	72	72	284	365,000
Louis Oosthuizen	71	74	67	73	285	270,000
Bill Haas	74	73	65	74	286	215,000
Webb Simpson	74	69	70	73	286	215,000
Kevin Na	74	71	71	71	287	163,333.34
Rory McIlroy	73	70	72	72	287	163,333.33
Ryan Moore	66	71	74	76	287	163,333.33
Rickie Fowler	68	77	71	72	288	123,000
Jim Furyk	70	73	76	69	288	123,000
Ryan Palmer	71	70	74	73	288	123,000
Lee Westwood	71	72	70	75	288	123,000
Danny Willett	73	76	71	68	288	123,000
Morgan Hoffmann	73	71	71	74	289	97,500
Brooks Koepka	69	74	73	73	289	97,500
Shane Lowry	71	74	70	74	289	97,500
Brandt Snedeker	74	73	70	72	289	97,500
Jordan Spieth	75	69	73	72	289	97,500
Marc Warren	73	75	69	72	289	97,500
Thomas Aiken	78	69	72	71	290	83,000
Ross Fisher	78	71	69	72	290	83,000
Mikko Ilonen	78	72	67	73	290	83,000
Matt Kuchar	73	75	70	72	290	83,000
Hideki Matsuyama	76	72	72	70	290	83,000
Patrick Reed	71	73	71	75	290	83,000
Brendon Todd	72	73	72	73	290	83,000
Gary Woodland	70	74	76	70	290	83,000

	SCORES				TOTAL	MONEY
Jason Day	76	74	70	71	291	72,000
Sergio Garcia	73	69	71	78	291	72,000
Martin Kaymer	71	76	71	73	291	72,000
Phil Mickelson	74	74	71	72	291	72,000
John Senden	73	70	74	74	291	72,000
Jimmy Walker	71	76	70	74	291	72,000
Bernd Wiesberger	74	74	71	72	291	72,000
Keegan Bradley	73	74	75	70	292	65,500
Paul Casey	75	73	72	72	292	65,500
Charley Hoffman	70	74	72	76	292	65,500
Alexander Levy	68	73	79	72	292	65,500
Marcel Siem	78	72	75	67	292	65,500
Cameron Tringale	73	74	72	73	292	65,500
Jamie Donaldson	70	72	76	75	293	61,500
Charl Schwartzel	71	72	75	75	293	61,500
Sangmoon Bae	75	71	73	75	294	59,000
Billy Horschel	72	75	75	72	294	59,000
Joost Luiten	79	69	73	73	294	59,000
Greg Chalmers	77	72	73	73	295	55,000
Luke Donald	72	76	74	73	295	55,000
Jason Dufner	79	71	71	74	295	55,000
Zach Johnson	76	73	73	73	295	55,000
Ian Poulter	74	78	71	72	295	55,000
Branden Grace	75	74	72	75	296	52,000
Justin Rose	73	74	73	77	297	51,000
Russell Henley	74	74	72	78	298	48,000
Chris Kirk	76	77	73	72	298	48,000
Graeme McDowell	73	73	75	77	298	48,000
Alex Noren	73	77	74	74	298	48,000
Robert Streb	72	80	72	74	298	48,000
Geoff Ogilvy	74	76	74	75	299	45,500
Victor Dubuisson	72	73	70	85	300	44,750
Steven Jeffress	75	74	78	73	300	44,750
David Lipsky	74	73	76	77	300	44,750
Hunter Mahan	75	79	74	74	302	44,250
Stephen Gallacher	84	72	78	69	303	43,875
Danie van Tonder	74	74	75	80	303	43,875
Koumei Oda	74	78	73	79	304	43,500
Thongchai Jaidee	80	73	76	76	305	43,250
Gary Stal	75	79	77	75	306	43,000
Tommy Fleetwood	77	77	73	80	307	42,625
Anirban Lahiri	80	76	74	77	307	42,625
Hiroyuki Fujita	75	83	78	79	315	42,250

Puerto Rico Open

Trump International Golf Club, Rio Grande, Puerto Rico
Par 36-36–72; 7,506 yards

March 5-8
purse, $3,000,000

	SCORES				TOTAL	MONEY
Alex Cejka	70	67	75	69	281	$540,000
Jon Curran	70	71	70	70	281	198,000
Emiliano Grillo	69	70	72	70	281	198,000
Tim Petrovic	75	71	68	67	281	198,000
Sam Saunders	72	72	69	68	281	198,000
(Cejka won on first playoff hole.)						
Will MacKenzie	75	69	70	68	282	97,125
Scott Pinckney	70	71	71	70	282	97,125
Boo Weekley	74	71	68	69	282	97,125
Will Wilcox	77	69	69	67	282	97,125

	SCORES				TOTAL	MONEY
Scott Brown	73	70	67	73	283	66,500
Rafa Cabrera-Bello	70	75	68	70	283	66,500
John Daly	72	70	72	69	283	66,500
Brendon de Jonge	71	70	71	71	283	66,500
Rod Pampling	70	71	73	69	283	66,500
Chris Smith	69	73	68	73	283	66,500
Jonathan Byrd	70	71	72	71	284	43,500
Chad Collins	70	72	71	71	284	43,500
Martin Flores	72	73	68	71	284	43,500
Chesson Hadley	71	70	76	67	284	43,500
Brandon Hagy	71	67	78	68	284	43,500
Lee Janzen	72	71	72	69	284	43,500
Benjamin Alvarado	74	70	72	69	285	28,800
Eric Axley	71	72	76	66	285	28,800
Jerry Kelly	71	74	73	67	285	28,800
Troy Matteson	73	73	69	70	285	28,800
John Merrick	75	70	72	68	285	28,800
Arjun Atwal	73	71	72	70	286	18,736.37
Roberto Castro	74	72	71	69	286	18,736.37
Jeff Overton	73	71	71	71	286	18,736.37
Jonathan Randolph	73	72	73	68	286	18,736.37
Michael Bradley	71	72	70	73	286	18,736.36
Gonzalo Fernandez-Castano	73	69	71	73	286	18,736.36
Adam Hadwin	72	72	68	74	286	18,736.36
Mark Hubbard	68	74	71	73	286	18,736.36
Dicky Pride	70	74	70	72	286	18,736.36
Chris Stroud	72	73	70	71	286	18,736.36
Fabrizio Zanotti	72	71	69	74	286	18,736.36
Ryan Armour	73	69	74	71	287	11,700
Matt Bettencourt	75	70	73	69	287	11,700
Zac Blair	75	70	73	69	287	11,700
Daniel Chopra	74	69	73	71	287	11,700
Oscar Fraustro	72	71	75	69	287	11,700
Brice Garnett	72	74	72	69	287	11,700
Greg Owen	74	70	70	73	287	11,700
Josh Teater	71	75	72	69	287	11,700
D.J. Trahan	72	70	73	72	287	11,700
Stephen Ames	72	72	74	70	288	7,612.50
Glen Day	73	68	75	72	288	7,612.50
David Duval	70	74	72	72	288	7,612.50
Fabian Gomez	74	72	72	70	288	7,612.50
Alex Kang	76	70	74	68	288	7,612.50
Whee Kim	72	74	74	68	288	7,612.50
Shaun Micheel	71	72	72	73	288	7,612.50
Bo Van Pelt	73	72	73	70	288	7,612.50
Cameron Beckman	72	74	74	69	289	6,690
Robert Karlsson	73	73	73	70	289	6,690
Scott Langley	76	69	72	72	289	6,690
Bill Lunde	76	69	73	71	289	6,690
Billy Mayfair	69	73	74	73	289	6,690
Byron Smith	73	73	70	73	289	6,690
Tyrone van Aswegen	75	71	71	72	289	6,690
Johnson Wagner	75	71	67	76	289	6,690
*Erick Morales	75	71	74	69	289	
Guy Boros	73	69	73	75	290	6,270
Jason Gore	71	75	72	72	290	6,270
J.J. Henry	70	73	77	70	290	6,270
Andres Romero	72	73	69	76	290	6,270
Vaughn Taylor	74	71	72	73	290	6,270
Y.E. Yang	74	72	68	76	290	6,270
Brandt Jobe	76	68	72	75	291	6,000
Alvaro Quiros	73	73	75	70	291	6,000
Bobby Wyatt	74	68	73	76	291	6,000

	SCORES			TOTAL	MONEY
James Driscoll	70	76	77	69	292	5,820
Tim Herron	74	71	75	72	292	5,820
Ryo Ishikawa	74	72	75	71	292	5,820
Andrew Svoboda	71	72	73	77	293	5,700

Valspar Championship

Innisbrook Resort, Copperhead Course, Palm Harbor, Florida
Par 36-35–71; 7,340 yards

March 12-15
purse, $5,900,000

	SCORES				TOTAL	MONEY
Jordan Spieth	70	67	68	69	274	$1,062,000
Sean O'Hair	66	72	69	67	274	519,200
Patrick Reed	72	68	68	66	274	519,200
(Spieth defeated O'Hair and Reed on third playoff hole.)						
Henrik Stenson	67	70	71	67	275	283,200
Ryan Moore	69	68	67	72	276	236,000
Troy Merritt	72	69	71	66	278	212,400
Danny Lee	72	69	71	67	279	183,883.34
Luke Guthrie	68	73	70	68	279	183,883.33
Jason Kokrak	68	73	70	68	279	183,883.33
Harris English	69	72	74	65	280	126,428.58
Brian Davis	65	76	70	69	280	126,428.57
Charles Howell	70	70	72	68	280	126,428.57
Kevin Na	71	70	73	66	280	126,428.57
Vijay Singh	69	70	70	71	280	126,428.57
Daniel Summerhays	70	72	67	71	280	126,428.57
Justin Thomas	67	72	73	68	280	126,428.57
Nicholas Thompson	67	74	73	67	281	77,205.72
Cameron Tringale	71	69	73	68	281	77,205.72
Lee Westwood	71	70	71	69	281	77,205.72
Jason Bohn	70	69	72	70	281	77,205.71
Derek Ernst	67	70	69	75	281	77,205.71
Billy Hurley	69	71	70	71	281	77,205.71
Shawn Stefani	68	72	71	70	281	77,205.71
Ian Poulter	68	70	75	69	282	44,643.34
Andres Romero	74	69	71	68	282	44,643.34
Mark Wilson	70	73	72	67	282	44,643.34
Chad Campbell	70	72	69	71	282	44,643.33
Jason Dufner	70	71	71	70	282	44,643.33
Lucas Glover	69	69	72	72	282	44,643.33
Sam Saunders	70	72	69	71	282	44,643.33
Nick Taylor	70	70	70	72	282	44,643.33
Brendon Todd	70	70	73	69	282	44,643.33
Brendon de Jonge	67	69	75	72	283	30,511.43
John Huh	71	70	72	70	283	30,511.43
Russell Knox	69	71	70	73	283	30,511.43
Martin Laird	69	72	74	68	283	30,511.43
S.J. Park	71	71	72	69	283	30,511.43
Will Wilcox	68	73	72	70	283	30,511.43
Matt Kuchar	70	70	68	75	283	30,511.42
Jon Curran	72	71	72	69	284	23,600
Jim Furyk	69	73	71	71	284	23,600
Francesco Molinari	70	72	70	72	284	23,600
Kevin Streelman	68	69	74	73	284	23,600
Rafa Cabrera-Bello	74	69	70	72	285	19,470
Chesson Hadley	73	69	70	73	285	19,470
Will MacKenzie	69	72	73	71	285	19,470
Greg Chalmers	69	72	73	72	286	15,359.67
Robert Garrigus	71	71	76	68	286	15,359.67

	SCORES				TOTAL	MONEY
Freddie Jacobson	72	71	74	69	286	15,359.67
D.A. Points	73	69	74	70	286	15,359.67
Kenny Perry	69	72	71	74	286	15,359.66
Michael Putnam	70	69	74	73	286	15,359.66
Alex Cejka	67	73	73	74	287	13,468.86
Luke Donald	72	68	73	74	287	13,468.86
David Hearn	70	73	71	73	287	13,468.86
Carl Pettersson	71	72	75	69	287	13,468.86
Brandt Snedeker	70	73	71	73	287	13,468.86
Ricky Barnes	66	72	74	75	287	13,468.85
Nick Watney	72	69	71	75	287	13,468.85
Stewart Cink	69	73	75	71	288	12,862
Kevin Kisner	71	72	73	72	288	12,862
Spencer Levin	71	71	73	73	288	12,862
Ken Duke	73	67	75	74	289	12,449
Scott Langley	71	72	75	71	289	12,449
Jeff Overton	69	74	75	71	289	12,449
John Peterson	68	73	73	75	289	12,449
Sangmoon Bae	71	72	76	71	290	12,154
Carlos Ortiz	69	73	76	73	291	12,036
Andres Gonzales	70	73	77	73	293	11,859
Retief Goosen	73	70	79	71	293	11,859
Adam Hadwin	68	75	75	76	294	11,682

Arnold Palmer Invitational

Bay Hill Club & Lodge, Orlando, Florida
Par 36-36–72; 7,419 yards

March 19-22
purse, $6,300,000

	SCORES				TOTAL	MONEY
Matt Every	68	66	69	66	269	$1,134,000
Henrik Stenson	68	66	66	70	270	680,400
Matt Jones	71	65	67	68	271	428,400
Morgan Hoffmann	66	65	71	71	273	302,400
Ben Martin	68	67	68	71	274	252,000
Kevin Na	67	70	69	69	275	211,050
Kiradech Aphibarnrat	70	71	65	69	275	211,050
Jason Kokrak	67	71	65	72	275	211,050
Zach Johnson	71	71	68	66	276	176,400
Louis Oosthuizen	69	68	70	69	276	176,400
Hudson Swafford	75	66	68	68	277	151,200
Rory McIlroy	70	66	71	70	277	151,200
Ernie Els	71	67	72	68	278	118,125
David Lingmerth	69	67	73	69	278	118,125
Daniel Berger	73	68	68	69	278	118,125
Brandt Snedeker	68	74	66	70	278	118,125
Jason Day	69	71	71	68	279	91,350
Francesco Molinari	70	71	69	69	279	91,350
Danny Lee	72	64	71	72	279	91,350
D.A. Points	70	70	67	72	279	91,350
Hideki Matsuyama	70	72	70	68	280	59,141
Gary Woodland	71	69	71	69	280	59,141
Zac Blair	73	67	71	69	280	59,141
Shawn Stefani	70	71	69	70	280	59,141
Carlos Ortiz	71	70	69	70	280	59,141
Charles Howell	71	68	70	71	280	59,141
Ian Poulter	67	70	71	72	280	59,141
Camilo Villegas	69	72	67	72	280	59,141
Rickie Fowler	71	71	70	69	281	40,058
Danny Willett	71	70	70	70	281	40,058

	SCORES				TOTAL	MONEY
Russell Knox	74	68	67	72	281	40,058
Sam Saunders	70	71	67	73	281	40,058
Harris English	68	66	72	75	281	40,058
Sean O'Hair	69	68	68	76	281	40,058
Ken Duke	67	74	73	68	282	29,098
George McNeill	69	69	73	71	282	29,098
Nick Taylor	76	65	70	71	282	29,098
Nicholas Thompson	70	71	69	72	282	29,098
Adam Scott	68	73	69	72	282	29,098
Carl Pettersson	71	71	68	72	282	29,098
John Peterson	67	71	70	74	282	29,098
Brendan Steele	71	67	68	76	282	29,098
Erik Compton	70	69	72	72	283	20,202
Billy Horschel	68	71	72	72	283	20,202
Martin Laird	68	72	71	72	283	20,202
David Hearn	69	73	69	72	283	20,202
Webb Simpson	69	69	72	73	283	20,202
Ryo Ishikawa	70	69	69	75	283	20,202
Justin Thomas	69	71	73	71	284	15,393
Blayne Barber	72	65	74	73	284	15,393
Russell Henley	69	71	71	73	284	15,393
Padraig Harrington	68	71	71	74	284	15,393
Kevin Kisner	69	71	69	75	284	15,393
Keegan Bradley	68	70	69	77	284	15,393
John Huh	73	69	72	71	285	14,427
Daniel Summerhays	73	69	71	72	285	14,427
Vijay Singh	71	70	76	69	286	14,175
Hunter Mahan	68	74	69	75	286	14,175
William McGirt	70	72	75	70	287	13,860
Steve Wheatcroft	70	69	75	73	287	13,860
Jason Bohn	71	70	73	73	287	13,860
Alex Prugh	71	71	73	73	288	13,482
Branden Grace	70	72	72	74	288	13,482
Steven Bowditch	72	70	71	75	288	13,482
Davis Love	69	71	77	72	289	13,167
Spencer Levin	70	70	75	74	289	13,167
Kevin Streelman	75	67	74	74	290	12,915
Chesson Hadley	72	68	73	77	290	12,915
Freddie Jacobson	71	71	74	75	291	12,726

Valero Texas Open

JW Marriott, TPC San Antonio, San Antonio, Texas
Par 36-36–72; 7,435 yards

March 26-29
purse, $6,200,000

	SCORES				TOTAL	MONEY
Jimmy Walker	71	67	69	70	277	$1,116,000
Jordan Spieth	71	69	71	70	281	669,600
Billy Horschel	72	70	71	71	284	421,600
Chesson Hadley	71	72	71	71	285	272,800
Daniel Summerhays	71	73	72	69	285	272,800
Dustin Johnson	78	72	68	68	286	215,450
Ryan Palmer	70	75	73	68	286	215,450
Chris Kirk	71	71	73	72	287	179,800
Scott Pinckney	73	72	69	73	287	179,800
Brendan Steele	74	68	72	73	287	179,800
Charley Hoffman	67	72	79	70	288	136,400
Jason Kokrak	72	71	71	74	288	136,400
John Peterson	74	72	74	68	288	136,400
Kyle Reifers	77	68	75	68	288	136,400

	SCORES				TOTAL	MONEY
K.J. Choi	75	70	73	71	289	99,200
Matt Kuchar	72	74	74	69	289	99,200
John Merrick	72	72	72	73	289	99,200
Carlos Ortiz	79	67	70	73	289	99,200
Cameron Percy	72	74	74	69	289	99,200
George McNeill	74	70	75	71	290	67,166.67
Bryce Molder	73	74	71	72	290	67,166.67
Kevin Na	72	68	75	75	290	67,166.67
Pat Perez	78	71	69	72	290	67,166.67
Aaron Baddeley	68	71	76	75	290	67,166.66
Zach Johnson	71	71	72	76	290	67,166.66
Matt Jones	77	71	68	75	291	46,810
Kevin Kisner	76	70	76	69	291	46,810
Shawn Stefani	79	70	72	70	291	46,810
Gary Woodland	75	75	68	73	291	46,810
Harris English	75	72	73	72	292	38,502
Brice Garnett	76	72	74	70	292	38,502
Branden Grace	75	71	75	71	292	38,502
Phil Mickelson	70	72	74	76	292	38,502
Brendon Todd	73	70	75	74	292	38,502
Matt Every	78	71	71	73	293	30,566
John Huh	73	72	74	74	293	30,566
Billy Hurley	74	74	73	72	293	30,566
Hudson Swafford	79	71	70	73	293	30,566
Marc Warren	74	74	75	70	293	30,566
Chad Campbell	78	72	76	68	294	24,800
William McGirt	72	77	74	71	294	24,800
Scott Piercy	72	76	70	76	294	24,800
Cameron Tringale	75	74	74	71	294	24,800
Jon Curran	77	73	71	74	295	18,744.67
David Lingmerth	74	71	76	74	295	18,744.67
Davis Love	76	74	71	74	295	18,744.67
Michael Thompson	73	73	73	76	295	18,744.67
Cameron Beckman	71	72	79	73	295	18,744.66
Fabian Gomez	72	74	71	78	295	18,744.66
Brian Davis	73	73	75	75	296	14,838.67
Luke Guthrie	76	73	70	77	296	14,838.67
Martin Laird	76	71	73	76	296	14,838.67
Jeff Overton	75	70	74	77	296	14,838.67
Freddie Jacobson	77	73	74	72	296	14,838.66
Seung-Yul Noh	74	72	76	74	296	14,838.66
Scott Brown	75	72	73	77	297	14,074
Max Homa	69	81	77	70	297	14,074
Blake Adams	76	73	75	74	298	13,578
Jim Furyk	76	74	76	72	298	13,578
Robert Garrigus	75	70	81	72	298	13,578
Retief Goosen	74	75	74	75	298	13,578
Scott Langley	78	70	78	72	298	13,578
Shane Lowry	74	74	75	75	298	13,578
Derek Fathauer	78	71	76	74	299	13,082
Brian Stuard	74	75	78	72	299	13,082
Kevin Chappell	73	73	73	81	300	12,834
Andres Romero	75	71	76	78	300	12,834
Tony Finau	79	69	76	77	301	12,524
S.J. Park	72	74	77	78	301	12,524
Jhonattan Vegas	76	71	77	77	301	12,524
Troy Merritt	74	76	75	77	302	12,276
Thomas Birdsey	73	74	78	79	304	12,090
Andrew Putnam	76	71	78	79	304	12,090
Will MacKenzie	77	72	80	76	305	11,904
Michael Putnam	76	71	76	83	306	11,780

Shell Houston Open

Golf Club of Houston, Humble, Texas
Par 36-36-72; 7,441 yards

April 2-5
purse, $6,600,000

	SCORES				TOTAL	MONEY
J.B. Holmes	65	70	73	64	272	$1,188,000
Jordan Spieth	69	66	67	70	272	580,800
Johnson Wagner	69	68	66	69	272	580,800
(Holmes defeated Spieth on first and Wagner on second playoff hole.)						
Russell Henley	69	68	68	69	274	316,800
Keegan Bradley	70	66	70	69	275	231,825
Brendon de Jonge	73	67	68	67	275	231,825
Charles Howell	66	70	69	70	275	231,825
Cameron Tringale	68	70	69	68	275	231,825
Paul Casey	68	69	68	71	276	191,400
Scott Piercy	63	74	66	74	277	178,200
Alex Cejka	65	72	70	71	278	135,300
Chad Collins	69	69	70	70	278	135,300
Austin Cook	68	65	70	75	278	135,300
Charley Hoffman	69	68	74	67	278	135,300
Pat Perez	71	68	72	67	278	135,300
Kyle Reifers	71	69	70	68	278	135,300
Charlie Beljan	71	69	70	69	279	83,490
Jason Bohn	71	67	72	69	279	83,490
Victor Dubuisson	67	68	78	66	279	83,490
Luke Guthrie	66	68	73	72	279	83,490
John Huh	68	70	73	68	279	83,490
Phil Mickelson	66	67	75	71	279	83,490
Patrick Reed	68	71	67	73	279	83,490
Chris Stroud	68	68	74	69	279	83,490
Daniel Berger	70	70	68	72	280	44,330
Jonas Blixt	68	68	74	70	280	44,330
Adam Hadwin	70	70	71	69	280	44,330
David Hearn	69	70	73	68	280	44,330
Whee Kim	70	70	70	70	280	44,330
Hunter Mahan	67	68	72	73	280	44,330
Andrew Putnam	67	65	76	72	280	44,330
Michael Putnam	68	68	71	73	280	44,330
Brendan Steele	71	67	73	69	280	44,330
Shawn Stefani	66	69	69	76	280	44,330
Nick Watney	69	68	73	70	280	44,330
Mark Wilson	69	66	76	69	280	44,330
Scott Brown	68	72	70	71	281	29,700
Ben Crane	69	71	72	69	281	29,700
Sergio Garcia	67	71	69	74	281	29,700
Chez Reavie	68	72	72	69	281	29,700
Justin Rose	69	68	72	72	281	29,700
Kelvin Day	68	69	68	77	282	21,235.50
Graham DeLaet	67	67	75	73	282	21,235.50
Gonzalo Fernandez-Castano	70	68	71	73	282	21,235.50
Tony Finau	69	68	77	68	282	21,235.50
Cody Gribble	69	69	71	73	282	21,235.50
Alex Prugh	67	69	75	71	282	21,235.50
Charl Schwartzel	70	68	72	72	282	21,235.50
Kevin Streelman	70	69	69	74	282	21,235.50
K.J. Choi	71	69	68	75	283	15,919.20
Stewart Cink	72	68	72	71	283	15,919.20
Chesson Hadley	72	66	75	70	283	15,919.20
S.J. Park	68	72	72	71	283	15,919.20
Justin Thomas	71	68	73	71	283	15,919.20
Erik Compton	73	66	72	73	284	15,114
Jhonattan Vegas	69	69	71	75	284	15,114

	SCORES				TOTAL	MONEY
Blayne Barber	71	69	75	70	285	14,454
Ernie Els	70	70	72	73	285	14,454
Derek Ernst	71	69	74	71	285	14,454
J.J. Henry	70	70	69	76	285	14,454
Jim Herman	71	68	70	76	285	14,454
Francesco Molinari	70	70	74	71	285	14,454
Ryan Moore	69	69	76	71	285	14,454
Bo Van Pelt	74	66	70	75	285	14,454
Tom Hoge	69	70	76	71	286	13,794
Sam Saunders	69	71	73	73	286	13,794
Oscar Fraustro	71	69	75	72	287	13,464
Padraig Harrington	71	68	74	74	287	13,464
Michael Thompson	68	71	76	72	287	13,464
Matt Kuchar	67	72	71	78	288	13,200
Rickie Fowler	69	69	77	76	291	13,068

Masters Tournament

Augusta National Golf Club, Augusta, Georgia
Par 36-36–72; 7,435 yards

April 9-12
purse, $10,000,000

	SCORES				TOTAL	MONEY
Jordan Spieth	64	66	70	70	270	$1,800,000
Phil Mickelson	70	68	67	69	274	880,000
Justin Rose	67	70	67	70	274	880,000
Rory McIlroy	71	71	68	66	276	480,000
Hideki Matsuyama	71	70	70	66	277	400,000
Paul Casey	69	68	74	68	279	335,000
Dustin Johnson	70	67	73	69	279	335,000
Ian Poulter	73	72	67	67	279	335,000
Charley Hoffman	67	68	71	74	280	270,000
Zach Johnson	72	72	68	68	280	270,000
Hunter Mahan	75	70	68	67	280	270,000
Rickie Fowler	73	72	70	67	282	196,000
Bill Haas	69	71	72	70	282	196,000
Ryan Moore	74	66	73	69	282	196,000
Kevin Na	74	66	70	72	282	196,000
Kevin Streelman	70	70	70	72	282	196,000
Sergio Garcia	68	74	71	70	283	155,000
Tiger Woods	73	69	68	73	283	155,000
Louis Oosthuizen	72	69	71	72	284	135,000
Henrik Stenson	73	73	70	68	284	135,000
Russell Henley	68	74	72	71	285	120,000
Keegan Bradley	71	72	75	68	286	92,833
Angel Cabrera	72	69	73	72	286	92,833
Ernie Els	67	72	75	72	286	92,833
Mark O'Meara	73	68	77	68	286	92,833
Patrick Reed	70	72	74	70	286	92,833
Bernd Wiesberger	75	70	70	71	286	92,833
Jonas Blixt	72	70	70	75	287	68,000
Jason Day	67	74	71	75	287	68,000
Morgan Hoffmann	73	72	72	70	287	68,000
Webb Simpson	69	75	72	71	287	68,000
Steve Stricker	73	73	73	68	287	68,000
Sangmoon Bae	74	71	72	71	288	54,000
Jamie Donaldson	74	71	76	67	288	54,000
Chris Kirk	72	73	72	71	288	54,000
Brooks Koepka	74	71	71	72	288	54,000
Ryan Palmer	69	74	74	71	288	54,000
Seung-Yul Noh	70	74	72	73	289	40,000

	SCORES				TOTAL	MONEY
Charl Schwartzel	71	70	73	75	289	40,000
Adam Scott	72	69	74	74	289	40,000
John Senden	71	74	72	72	289	40,000
Cameron Tringale	71	75	69	74	289	40,000
Jimmy Walker	73	72	74	70	289	40,000
Bubba Watson	71	71	73	74	289	40,000
Danny Willett	71	71	76	71	289	40,000
Matt Kuchar	72	74	72	72	290	30,000
Lee Westwood	73	73	70	74	290	30,000
Geoff Ogilvy	74	70	73	74	291	27,400
Jason Dufner	74	71	74	73	292	25,600
Anirban Lahiri	71	75	74	72	292	25,600
Erik Compton	73	72	74	74	293	24,600
Darren Clarke	74	71	77	72	294	23,800
Graeme McDowell	71	74	76	73	294	23,800
Vijay Singh	75	70	79	71	295	23,200
Thongchai Jaidee	75	70	80	72	297	23,000

Out of Final 36 Holes

Luke Donald	75	72	147	Matt Every	73	74	147
Jim Furyk	74	73	147	Stephen Gallacher	71	76	147
James Hahn	73	74	147	J.B. Holmes	76	71	147
Mikko Ilonen	74	73	147	Bernhard Langer	73	74	147
Shane Lowry	75	72	147	Brandt Snedeker	74	73	147
Gary Woodland	71	76	147	Branden Grace	75	73	148
Brian Harman	76	72	148	Billy Horschel	70	78	148
Joost Luiten	76	72	148	Ben Martin	74	74	148
Camilo Villegas	72	76	148	Corey Conners	80	69	149
Victor Dubuisson	74	75	149	Padraig Harrington	72	77	149
Ian Woosnam	75	74	149	Sandy Lyle	74	76	150
Byron Meth	74	76	150	Jose Maria Olazabal	79	71	150
Thomas Bjorn	72	79	151	Miguel Angel Jimenez	78	73	151
Martin Kaymer	76	75	151	Larry Mize	78	73	151
Anthony Murdaca	78	73	151	Kevin Stadler	77	74	151
Brendon Todd	80	71	151	Matias Dominguez	76	76	152
Tom Watson	71	81	152	Fred Couples	79	74	153
Trevor Immelman	76	77	153	Robert Streb	80	76	156
Ben Crane	79	78	157	Scott Harvey	76	81	157
Bradley Neil	78	79	157	Gunn Yang	85	74	159
Mike Weir	82	81	163	Ben Crenshaw	91	85	176

(Professionals who did not complete 72 holes received $5,000.)

RBC Heritage

Harbour Town Golf Links, Hilton Head Island, South Carolina
Par 36-35–71; 7,101 yards

April 16-19
purse, $5,900,000

	SCORES				TOTAL	MONEY
Jim Furyk	71	64	68	63	266	$1,062,000
Kevin Kisner	68	67	67	64	266	637,200
(Furyk defeated Kisner on second playoff hole.)						
Troy Merritt	69	61	69	69	268	401,200
Brendon Todd	73	66	63	67	269	283,200
Matt Kuchar	68	66	68	68	270	236,000
Sean O'Hair	70	67	70	64	271	212,400
Branden Grace	70	67	66	69	272	190,275
Louis Oosthuizen	69	67	69	67	272	190,275
Morgan Hoffmann	68	68	69	68	273	165,200

	SCORES				TOTAL	MONEY
Bo Van Pelt	69	68	67	69	273	165,200
Blake Adams	72	65	71	66	274	129,800
Brice Garnett	72	66	65	71	274	129,800
Jordan Spieth	74	62	68	70	274	129,800
Justin Thomas	70	67	68	69	274	129,800
Luke Donald	73	66	66	70	275	100,300
Bryce Molder	74	64	70	67	275	100,300
Cameron Smith	68	73	67	67	275	100,300
Brendon de Jonge	70	68	67	71	276	69,325
Matt Every	66	70	70	70	276	69,325
Lucas Glover	70	67	70	69	276	69,325
Jerry Kelly	71	66	70	69	276	69,325
Russell Knox	75	64	67	70	276	69,325
Jason Kokrak	72	70	65	69	276	69,325
John Peterson	72	65	71	68	276	69,325
Ian Poulter	69	70	67	70	276	69,325
Graeme McDowell	66	69	70	72	277	43,660
John Merrick	69	65	71	72	277	43,660
Pat Perez	69	71	67	70	277	43,660
Carl Pettersson	72	69	69	67	277	43,660
Brandt Snedeker	77	64	67	69	277	43,660
Alex Cejka	70	71	69	68	278	34,220
Stewart Cink	70	67	71	70	278	34,220
Martin Flores	73	67	69	69	278	34,220
Bill Haas	71	70	68	69	278	34,220
Joost Luiten	69	71	70	68	278	34,220
William McGirt	71	70	68	69	278	34,220
Sangmoon Bae	67	73	70	69	279	25,370
Ricky Barnes	69	72	70	68	279	25,370
Scott Brown	74	67	71	67	279	25,370
Ben Crane	72	67	72	68	279	25,370
Jason Dufner	74	67	66	72	279	25,370
Freddie Jacobson	71	68	70	70	279	25,370
Ben Martin	69	69	70	71	279	25,370
Zac Blair	70	69	71	70	280	17,413.43
Steven Bowditch	74	68	68	70	280	17,413.43
Brian Harman	75	65	69	71	280	17,413.43
Anirban Lahiri	73	69	66	72	280	17,413.43
Robert Streb	74	68	68	70	280	17,413.43
Hudson Swafford	70	69	71	70	280	17,413.43
George McNeill	72	67	72	69	280	17,413.42
Billy Horschel	72	69	69	71	281	14,071.50
Martin Laird	72	70	70	69	281	14,071.50
Webb Simpson	71	70	69	71	281	14,071.50
Vijay Singh	71	67	70	73	281	14,071.50
Robert Allenby	71	71	67	73	282	13,334
Jason Bohn	73	68	74	67	282	13,334
Charl Schwartzel	72	70	71	69	282	13,334
Kevin Streelman	71	65	71	75	282	13,334
Brian Stuard	73	68	69	72	282	13,334
Andres Gonzales	70	72	70	71	283	12,803
James Hahn	70	69	72	72	283	12,803
Danny Lee	71	71	69	72	283	12,803
Daniel Summerhays	70	70	73	70	283	12,803
Charley Hoffman	71	70	71	72	284	12,508
*Scott Vincent	70	70	71	73	284	
Aaron Baddeley	70	67	76	72	285	12,272
Scott Langley	68	70	76	71	285	12,272
Jim Renner	69	69	74	73	285	12,272
Charlie Beljan	69	72	74	71	286	11,918
Chris Kirk	71	70	73	72	286	11,918
Chris Stroud	72	67	69	78	286	11,918
Daniel Berger	72	68	75	72	287	11,623

	SCORES				TOTAL	MONEY
Tom Watson	72	70	69	76	287	11,623
Nick Taylor	72	69	77	70	288	11,446
Ryo Ishikawa	71	70	75	75	291	11,269
Boo Weekley	74	67	77	73	291	11,269

Zurich Classic of New Orleans

TPC Louisiana, Avondale, Louisiana
Par 36-36–72; 7,341 yards

April 23-26
purse, $6,900,000

	SCORES				TOTAL	MONEY
Justin Rose	69	66	65	66	266	$1,242,000
Cameron Tringale	69	65	68	65	267	745,200
Boo Weekley	64	70	69	65	268	469,200
Jason Day	67	65	68	69	269	303,600
Jim Herman	69	68	67	65	269	303,600
Daniel Berger	66	67	68	69	270	239,775
David Hearn	65	70	67	68	270	239,775
Blayne Barber	67	70	64	70	271	193,200
Chad Campbell	67	68	68	68	271	193,200
Chesson Hadley	67	72	66	66	271	193,200
Whee Kim	68	71	68	64	271	193,200
Steven Bowditch	68	67	71	66	272	115,920
Erik Compton	66	69	68	69	272	115,920
Jason Gore	70	68	66	68	272	115,920
George McNeill	74	64	66	68	272	115,920
Sean O'Hair	65	71	68	68	272	115,920
Scott Pinckney	69	70	65	68	272	115,920
D.A. Points	70	69	68	65	272	115,920
Hudson Swafford	67	66	70	69	272	115,920
Justin Thomas	68	66	72	66	272	115,920
Steve Wheatcroft	72	66	69	65	272	115,920
Keegan Bradley	69	70	66	68	273	64,055
Brendon de Jonge	64	70	68	71	273	64,055
Jerry Kelly	70	64	70	69	273	64,055
Danny Lee	70	64	68	71	273	64,055
Scott Stallings	74	65	69	65	273	64,055
Chris Stroud	67	66	73	67	273	64,055
Retief Goosen	70	66	71	67	274	46,920
Freddie Jacobson	68	71	69	66	274	46,920
Kevin Kisner	69	68	70	67	274	46,920
Marc Leishman	74	63	70	67	274	46,920
Spencer Levin	70	69	69	66	274	46,920
D.H. Lee	70	67	71	67	275	38,985
Bryce Molder	69	67	70	69	275	38,985
Bernd Wiesberger	69	68	69	69	275	38,985
Scott Brown	70	68	72	66	276	31,099.29
Brian Davis	66	71	70	69	276	31,099.29
Carl Pettersson	72	66	69	69	276	31,099.29
Jhonattan Vegas	67	71	69	69	276	31,099.29
K.J. Choi	67	70	69	70	276	31,099.29
Morgan Hoffmann	68	66	69	73	276	31,099.28
Michael Smith	70	68	67	71	276	31,099.28
Chad Collins	70	69	68	70	277	22,770
Dustin Johnson	67	70	68	72	277	22,770
Russell Knox	69	70	68	70	277	22,770
Greg Owen	66	70	70	71	277	22,770
Cameron Smith	69	70	69	69	277	22,770
Tommy Gainey	73	66	68	71	278	16,991.25
Billy Horschel	71	68	70	69	278	16,991.25

	SCORES				TOTAL	MONEY
John Huh	69	70	66	73	278	16,991.25
John Peterson	70	68	71	69	278	16,991.25
Nick Taylor	70	69	68	71	278	16,991.25
Michael Thompson	70	68	70	70	278	16,991.25
Johnson Wagner	68	69	73	68	278	16,991.25
Tim Wilkinson	69	69	70	70	278	16,991.25
Woody Austin	70	66	70	73	279	15,594
Ben Crane	67	71	72	69	279	15,594
Mark Hubbard	66	73	72	68	279	15,594
Fabian Gomez	69	70	71	70	280	15,180
Carlos Ortiz	67	67	73	73	280	15,180
Mark Wilson	69	68	73	70	280	15,180
Jonathan Byrd	69	70	68	74	281	14,766
Lucas Glover	71	68	76	66	281	14,766
Ryo Ishikawa	70	67	72	72	281	14,766
Alex Cejka	68	69	75	71	283	14,283
Max Homa	70	68	69	76	283	14,283
Colt Knost	71	68	74	70	283	14,283
Brian Stuard	69	69	74	71	283	14,283
David Toms	72	67	73	73	285	13,938
Andres Gonzales	71	68	72	77	288	13,731
Roger Sloan	71	68	71	78	288	13,731

WGC - Cadillac Match Play

TPC Harding Park, San Francisco, California
Par 36-35–71; 7,115 yards

April 29-May 3
purse, $9,250,000

FIRST ROUND

Rory McIlroy defeated Jason Dufner, 5 and 4.
Billy Horschel defeated Brandt Snedeker, 5 and 4.
Jordan Spieth defeated Mikko Ilonen, 4 and 2.
Lee Westwood defeated Matt Every, 1 up.
John Senden defeated Henrik Stenson, 19 holes.
Bill Haas defeated Brendon Todd, 3 and 2.
Bubba Watson defeated Miguel Angel Jimenez, 5 and 4.
Louis Oosthuizen defeated Keegan Bradley, 6 and 5.
Jim Furyk defeated George Coetzee, 3 and 2.
Martin Kaymer defeated Thongchai Jaidee, 3 and 1.
Marc Leishman defeated Justin Rose, 3 and 2.
Anirban Lahiri defeated Ryan Palmer, 4 and 2.
Charley Hoffman defeated Jason Day, 4 and 3.
Zach Johnson defeated Branden Grace, 2 up.
Dustin Johnson defeated Matt Jones, 3 and 1.
Charl Schwartzel defeated Victor Dubuisson, 5 and 4.
Francesco Molinari defeated Adam Scott, 5 and 4.
Paul Casey defeated Chris Kirk, 22 holes.
Sergio Garcia defeated Tommy Fleetwood, 2 up.
Jamie Donaldson defeated Bernd Wiesberger, 1 up.
Gary Woodland defeated Jimmy Walker, 19 holes.
Webb Simpson defeated Ian Poulter, 3 and 2.
Marc Warren defeated J.B. Holmes, 2 and 1.
Brooks Koepka defeated Russell Henley, 1 up.
Rickie Fowler defeated Harris English, 1 up.
Shane Lowry defeated Graeme McDowell, 1 up.
Ben Martin defeated Matt Kuchar, 1 up.
Hunter Mahan defeated Stephen Gallacher, 7 and 6.
Patrick Reed defeated Andy Sullivan, 2 and 1.
Danny Willett defeated Ryan Moore, 3 and 2.
Hideki Matsuyama defeated Alexander Levy, 5 and 4.
Joost Luiten defeated Kevin Na, 19 holes.

SECOND ROUND

McIlroy defeated Snedeker, 2 up.
Horschel defeated Dufner, 3 and 2.
Spieth defeated Every, 4 and 3.
Westwood defeated Ilonen, 1 up.
Stenson defeated Todd, 3 and 2.
Senden defeated Haas, 4 and 3.
Watson defeated Bradley, 4 and 2.
Oosthuizen defeated Jimenez, 2 up.
Jaidee defeated Furyk, 3 and 1.
Coetzee defeated Kaymer, 19 holes.
Rose defeated Lahiri, 19 holes.
Leishman defeated Palmer, 4 and 3.
Grace defeated Day, 4 and 3.
Hoffman defeated Zach Johnson, 2 and 1.
Schwartzel defeated Dustin Johnson, 20 holes.
Jones defeated Dubuisson, 2 up.
Casey defeated Scott, 1 up.
Kirk defeated Molinari, 2 and 1.
Wiesberger defeated Garcia, 2 and 1.
Fleetwood defeated Donaldson, 21 holes.
Simpson defeated Walker, 19 holes.
Woodland defeated Poulter, 3 and 2.
Holmes defeated Henley, 19 holes.
Koepka defeated Warren, 20 holes.
Fowler defeated Lowry, 1 up.
English defeated McDowell, 2 and 1.
Kuchar defeated Gallacher, 3 and 2.
Mahan defeated Martin, 5 and 3.
Willett defeated Reed, 2 and 1.
Sullivan defeated Moore, 3 and 2.
Matsuyama defeated Luiten, 2 up.
Na defeated Levy, 3 and 1.

THIRD ROUND

McIlroy (3-0) defeated Horschel (2-1), 20 holes.
Dufner (1-2) defeated Snedeker (0-3), 1 up.
Westwood (3-0) defeated Spieth (2-1), 2 up.
Ilonen (1-2) defeated Every (0-3), 8 and 6.
Haas (2-1) defeated Stenson (1-2), 3 and 1.
Senden (3-0) defeated Todd (0-3), 1 up.
Oosthuizen (3-0) defeated Watson (2-1), 19 holes.
Jimenez (1-2) defeated Bradley (0-3), 2 up.
Furyk (2-1) defeated Kaymer (1-2), 20 holes.
Coetzee (2-1) defeated Jaidee (1-2), 21 holes.
Rose (2-1) defeated Palmer (0-3), 2 and 1.
Leishman (3-0) defeated Lahiri (1-2), 1 up.
Zach Johnson (2-1) defeated Day (0-3), 3 and 2.
Grace (2-1) defeated Hoffman (2-1), 2 and 1.
Grace defeated Hoffman and Zach Johnson in a playoff to advance.
Dustin Johnson (2-1) defeated Dubuisson (0-3), 2 and 1.
Schwartzel (3-0) defeated Jones (1-2), 20 holes.
Kirk (2-1) defeated Scott (0-3), 1 up.
Casey (3-0) defeated Molinari (1-2), 1 up.
Donaldson (2-1) defeated Garcia (1-2), 2 and 1.
Fleetwood (2-1) defeated Wiesberger (1-2), 19 holes.
Poulter (1-2) defeated Walker (0-3), 4 and 2.
Woodland (3-0) defeated Simpson (2-1), 1 up.
Holmes (2-1) defeated Koepka (2-1), 2 and 1.
Henley (1-2) defeated Warren (1-2), 1 up.
Fowler (3-0) defeated McDowell (0-3), 5 and 4.
English (2-1) defeated Lowry (1-2), 1 up.
Mahan (3-0) defeated Kuchar (1-2), 5 and 4.

Martin (2-1) defeated Gallacher (0-3), 20 holes.
Reed (2-1) defeated Moore (0-3), 1 up.
Willett (3-0) defeated Sullivan (1-2), 1 up.
Matsuyama (3-0) defeated Na (1-2), 5 and 4.
Luiten (2-1) defeated Levy (0-3), 1 up.

(Players finishing 2-1 received $85,823.53; players finishing 1-2 received $63,500; players finishing 0-3 received $49,384.61.)

ROUND OF 16

McIlroy defeated Matsuyama, 6 and 5.
Casey defeated Schwartzel, 3 and 1.
Furyk defeated Holmes, 5 and 3.
Oosthuizen defeated Fowler, 1 up.
Senden defeated Mahan, 2 and 1.
Woodland defeated Leishman, 2 and 1.
Willett defeated Westwood, 3 and 2.
Fleetwood defeated Grace, 2 and 1.

(Losing players received $150,000.)

QUARTER-FINALS

McIlroy defeated Casey, 22 holes.
Furyk defeated Oosthuizen, 4 and 2.
Woodland defeated Senden, 5 and 3.
Willett defeated Fleetwood, 4 and 3.

(Losing players received $285,000.)

SEMI-FINALS

McIlroy defeated Furyk, 1 up.
Woodland defeated Willett, 3 and 2.

PLAYOFF FOR THIRD-FOURTH PLACE

Willett defeated Furyk, 3 and 2.

(Willett received $646,000; Furyk received $520,000.)

FINAL

McIlroy defeated Woodland, 4 and 2.

(McIlroy received $1,570,000; Woodland received $930,000.)

The Players Championship

TPC Sawgrass, Ponte Vedra Beach, Florida   May 7-10
Par 36-36—72; 7,215 yards   purse, $10,000,000

	SCORES				TOTAL	MONEY
Rickie Fowler	69	69	71	67	276	$1,800,000
Kevin Kisner	73	67	67	69	276	880,000
Sergio Garcia	69	72	67	68	276	880,000
(Fowler defeated Garcia in aggregate three-hole playoff and Kisner on first sudden-death playoff hole.)						
Bill Haas	72	67	68	70	277	440,000
Ben Martin	68	71	68	70	277	440,000
Kevin Na	67	69	72	71	279	347,500

	SCORES				TOTAL	MONEY
Rory Sabbatini	70	71	69	69	279	347,500
Jamie Donaldson	70	72	71	67	280	270,000
Brian Harman	71	69	70	70	280	270,000
Ryo Ishikawa	71	69	69	71	280	270,000
Rory McIlroy	69	71	70	70	280	270,000
John Senden	73	70	67	70	280	270,000
Billy Horschel	68	72	69	72	281	187,500
Zach Johnson	71	68	71	71	281	187,500
Chris Kirk	70	68	68	75	281	187,500
David Toms	73	71	68	69	281	187,500
Russell Knox	72	70	72	68	282	130,857.15
Henrik Stenson	72	69	73	68	282	130,857.15
Derek Fathauer	68	72	69	73	282	130,857.14
Jerry Kelly	71	65	72	74	282	130,857.14
Hideki Matsuyama	67	74	72	69	282	130,857.14
George McNeill	73	70	69	70	282	130,857.14
Pat Perez	71	70	68	73	282	130,857.14
Chesson Hadley	71	72	66	74	283	81,000
Russell Henley	70	70	72	71	283	81,000
Marc Leishman	69	71	74	69	283	81,000
Geoff Ogilvy	72	72	69	70	283	81,000
Patrick Reed	72	70	69	72	283	81,000
Justin Thomas	73	70	65	75	283	81,000
Sangmoon Bae	72	68	73	71	284	58,125
Scott Brown	72	67	69	76	284	58,125
Erik Compton	74	70	72	68	284	58,125
James Hahn	70	73	72	69	284	58,125
Charley Hoffman	67	74	71	72	284	58,125
Ian Poulter	71	69	70	74	284	58,125
Robert Streb	70	73	72	69	284	58,125
Bo Van Pelt	70	72	69	73	284	58,125
Martin Flores	73	71	67	74	285	44,000
Stephen Gallacher	72	70	70	73	285	44,000
Adam Scott	72	69	69	75	285	44,000
Steve Stricker	69	75	69	72	285	44,000
K.J. Choi	70	74	70	72	286	31,400
Matt Every	74	70	70	72	286	31,400
Branden Grace	71	67	73	75	286	31,400
Padraig Harrington	71	73	75	67	286	31,400
David Hearn	67	71	70	78	286	31,400
Freddie Jacobson	70	74	70	72	286	31,400
Chris Stroud	70	69	76	71	286	31,400
Jhonattan Vegas	75	69	66	76	286	31,400
Bubba Watson	71	70	69	76	286	31,400
Luke Guthrie	74	69	69	75	287	23,680
J.B. Holmes	70	71	73	73	287	23,680
Joost Luiten	71	70	71	75	287	23,680
Charl Schwartzel	71	72	72	72	287	23,680
Brendon Todd	68	72	75	72	287	23,680
Robert Allenby	70	72	73	73	288	22,200
Graham DeLaet	75	69	70	74	288	22,200
Jim Furyk	70	70	73	75	288	22,200
Charles Howell	68	72	71	77	288	22,200
Martin Kaymer	69	72	71	76	288	22,200
Graeme McDowell	73	70	74	71	288	22,200
Cameron Tringale	69	71	72	76	288	22,200
Brendon de Jonge	73	71	71	74	289	21,200
Bryce Molder	72	71	75	71	289	21,200
Vijay Singh	71	72	76	70	289	21,200
Ernie Els	73	70	76	71	290	20,600
Scott Langley	72	72	71	75	290	20,600
Webb Simpson	69	74	78	69	290	20,600
Dustin Johnson	72	72	75	72	291	20,000

	SCORES				TOTAL	MONEY
Louis Oosthuizen	70	73	75	73	291	20,000
Tiger Woods	73	71	75	72	291	20,000
Troy Merritt	68	71	76	77	292	19,600
Nick Taylor	72	70	72	79	293	19,400
Alex Cejka	69	73	79	78	299	19,200
Scott Stallings	71	72	82	76	301	19,000

Wells Fargo Championship

Quail Hollow Club, Charlotte, North Carolina
Par 36-36–72; 7,562 yards

May 14-17
purse, $7,100,000

	SCORES				TOTAL	MONEY
Rory McIlroy	70	67	61	69	267	$1,278,000
Patrick Rodgers	68	68	70	68	274	624,800
Webb Simpson	67	67	68	72	274	624,800
Phil Mickelson	71	66	71	68	276	293,466.67
Gary Woodland	70	71	68	67	276	293,466.67
Robert Streb	65	69	71	71	276	293,466.66
Geoff Ogilvy	69	69	71	68	277	228,975
Justin Thomas	69	73	65	70	277	228,975
Jason Bohn	72	68	69	69	278	184,600
Brendan Steele	69	69	68	72	278	184,600
Shawn Stefani	69	70	70	69	278	184,600
Kevin Streelman	69	71	70	68	278	184,600
Scott Brown	71	68	69	71	279	137,266.67
Danny Lee	71	69	69	70	279	137,266.67
Jim Herman	71	69	68	71	279	137,266.66
Kevin Chappell	66	73	74	67	280	113,600
Tony Finau	73	67	70	70	280	113,600
Boo Weekley	71	70	67	72	280	113,600
Carlos Ortiz	70	71	66	74	281	99,400
Stewart Cink	67	76	68	71	282	71,621.25
Chesson Hadley	67	77	70	68	282	71,621.25
Will MacKenzie	69	68	70	75	282	71,621.25
Hideki Matsuyama	69	71	70	72	282	71,621.25
Sean O'Hair	74	69	67	72	282	71,621.25
Pat Perez	73	71	68	70	282	71,621.25
John Peterson	71	70	70	71	282	71,621.25
Jonathan Randolph	70	71	71	70	282	71,621.25
Steven Alker	69	72	72	70	283	43,310
Ricky Barnes	67	73	72	71	283	43,310
Daniel Berger	71	68	70	74	283	43,310
K.J. Choi	68	72	69	74	283	43,310
Lucas Glover	71	72	68	72	283	43,310
Morgan Hoffmann	72	70	72	69	283	43,310
Matt Jones	69	70	70	74	283	43,310
William McGirt	72	70	74	67	283	43,310
George McNeill	69	69	75	70	283	43,310
Michael Thompson	67	71	73	72	283	43,310
Retief Goosen	72	70	67	75	284	27,690
Charles Howell	75	69	71	69	284	27,690
Billy Hurley	67	75	73	69	284	27,690
Kevin Kisner	69	73	71	71	284	27,690
Ben Martin	74	69	70	71	284	27,690
John Merrick	71	70	71	72	284	27,690
Brian Stuard	70	70	73	71	284	27,690
Steve Wheatcroft	74	66	74	70	284	27,690
Mark Wilson	71	71	71	71	284	27,690
Steven Bowditch	73	71	72	69	285	18,016.25

	SCORES				TOTAL	MONEY
Martin Flores	69	67	76	73	285	18,016.25
Hunter Mahan	70	73	72	70	285	18,016.25
Ryan Moore	71	71	73	70	285	18,016.25
Carl Pettersson	68	72	72	73	285	18,016.25
Scott Pinckney	76	68	66	75	285	18,016.25
Sam Saunders	75	68	70	72	285	18,016.25
Bo Van Pelt	70	71	72	72	285	18,016.25
Aaron Baddeley	74	70	70	72	286	16,188
Jason Gore	70	71	72	73	286	16,188
Martin Laird	72	70	73	71	286	16,188
Sangmoon Bae	70	72	73	72	287	15,407
Alex Cejka	71	70	74	72	287	15,407
Andres Gonzales	72	71	73	71	287	15,407
Russell Knox	69	69	77	72	287	15,407
Michael Putnam	70	73	72	72	287	15,407
Patrick Reed	66	74	72	75	287	15,407
Carlos Sainz, Jr.	74	69	72	72	287	15,407
Henrik Stenson	72	71	73	71	287	15,407
Scott Gutschewski	69	70	75	74	288	14,697
Colt Knost	75	68	73	72	288	14,697
Chad Campbell	71	69	68	81	289	14,342
Chad Collins	72	70	73	74	289	14,342
Bill Haas	72	70	71	76	289	14,342
Andres Romero	70	73	73	75	291	14,058
David Toms	72	70	73	77	292	13,916
James Hahn	73	71	72	77	293	13,774
Blake Adams	73	71	73		217	13,561
Jim Renner	72	71	74		217	13,561
Max Homa	72	71	75		218	13,206
John Huh	70	74	74		218	13,206
Jhonattan Vegas	72	72	74		218	13,206
Angel Cabrera	69	74	76		219	12,851
Freddie Jacobson	70	74	75		219	12,851
Jon Curran	73	71	76		220	12,638

Crowne Plaza Invitational

Colonial Country Club, Fort Worth, Texas
Par 35-35–70; 7,204 yards

May 21-24
purse, $6,500,000

	SCORES				TOTAL	MONEY
Chris Kirk	68	69	65	66	268	$1,170,000
Jason Bohn	69	69	68	63	269	485,333.34
Brandt Snedeker	67	69	66	67	269	485,333.33
Jordan Spieth	64	73	67	65	269	485,333.33
Adam Hadwin	69	66	69	66	270	220,350
Kevin Kisner	67	69	67	67	270	220,350
George McNeill	65	69	69	67	270	220,350
Pat Perez	69	69	68	64	270	220,350
Ian Poulter	65	67	68	70	270	220,350
Brian Harman	68	66	69	68	271	134,875
Charley Hoffman	66	69	66	70	271	134,875
Jerry Kelly	67	70	67	67	271	134,875
Colt Knost	66	73	66	66	271	134,875
Danny Lee	66	69	70	66	271	134,875
Ben Martin	66	71	68	66	271	134,875
Kevin Na	64	66	69	72	271	134,875
Rory Sabbatini	67	70	66	68	271	134,875
John Huh	70	68	70	64	272	97,500
Kevin Chappell	71	68	68	66	273	78,780

	SCORES				TOTAL	MONEY
Tony Finau	67	72	66	68	273	78,780
Zach Johnson	70	69	67	67	273	78,780
Shawn Stefani	67	69	69	68	273	78,780
Robert Streb	71	68	68	66	273	78,780
Chesson Hadley	70	71	67	66	274	57,200
Russell Knox	71	67	69	67	274	57,200
Adam Scott	72	66	66	70	274	57,200
Fabian Gomez	70	69	67	69	275	45,175
Luke Guthrie	66	74	68	67	275	45,175
Scott Langley	68	72	68	67	275	45,175
Marc Leishman	66	69	70	70	275	45,175
Steve Stricker	67	70	71	67	275	45,175
Nick Taylor	68	68	68	71	275	45,175
Scott Brown	70	71	67	68	276	31,525
Erik Compton	73	65	69	69	276	31,525
Jon Curran	68	72	68	68	276	31,525
David Hearn	66	75	69	66	276	31,525
Jim Herman	71	68	70	67	276	31,525
David Lingmerth	71	70	70	65	276	31,525
William McGirt	73	66	67	70	276	31,525
Jeff Overton	67	73	70	66	276	31,525
Patrick Reed	70	69	68	69	276	31,525
Boo Weekley	64	69	71	72	276	31,525
Paul Casey	69	71	69	69	278	18,993
Jason Dufner	68	72	67	71	278	18,993
Lucas Glover	70	71	69	68	278	18,993
Ryo Ishikawa	64	74	69	71	278	18,993
Martin Laird	69	68	72	69	278	18,993
Geoff Ogilvy	69	70	70	69	278	18,993
Scott Piercy	70	69	68	71	278	18,993
Vijay Singh	69	66	69	74	278	18,993
Brendon Todd	70	67	71	70	278	18,993
Cameron Tringale	68	70	71	69	278	18,993
Graham DeLaet	70	68	67	74	279	14,976
Martin Flores	72	69	68	70	279	14,976
Billy Hurley	70	70	69	70	279	14,976
Hunter Mahan	67	71	71	70	279	14,976
Jhonattan Vegas	68	73	68	70	279	14,976
Bryce Molder	72	68	68	72	280	14,365
Carlos Ortiz	70	70	69	71	280	14,365
Kevin Streelman	71	69	66	74	280	14,365
Daniel Summerhays	68	71	68	73	280	14,365
Zac Blair	66	71	70	74	281	13,910
Steve Flesch	71	69	68	73	281	13,910
Brian Stuard	71	69	70	71	281	13,910
Angel Cabrera	70	71	70	71	282	13,390
Whee Kim	72	68	71	71	282	13,390
Scott Pinckney	70	70	67	75	282	13,390
Alex Prugh	72	69	70	71	282	13,390
Jimmy Walker	72	66	72	72	282	13,390
*Gunn Yang	67	70	71	74	282	
Ben Crane	66	73	72	72	283	12,935
Andres Gonzales	68	73	70	72	283	12,935
Chad Collins	73	68	71		212	12,350
Harrison Frazar	68	73	71		212	12,350
Jarrod Lyle	69	69	74		212	12,350
Patrick Rodgers	72	69	71		212	12,350
Steve Wheatcroft	70	71	71		212	12,350
John Peterson	69	71	73		213	11,960
Kyle Reifers	72	69	75		216	11,830

AT&T Byron Nelson

TPC Four Seasons Resort, Irving, Texas
Par 35-35–70; 7,166 yards

May 28-31
purse, $7,100,000

	SCORES				TOTAL	MONEY
Steven Bowditch	62	68	65	64	259	$1,278,000
Charley Hoffman	69	65	64	65	263	530,133.34
Scott Pinckney	69	64	64	66	263	530,133.33
Jimmy Walker	64	66	67	66	263	530,133.33
Zach Johnson	69	64	68	63	264	284,000
Jon Curran	67	63	67	68	265	246,725
Brandt Snedeker	71	66	64	64	265	246,725
Jason Dufner	71	65	64	66	266	213,000
Dustin Johnson	67	68	62	69	266	213,000
Daniel Berger	72	65	64	66	267	157,383.34
Nick Watney	67	65	70	65	267	157,383.34
Tony Finau	67	64	68	68	267	157,383.33
Colt Knost	68	65	66	68	267	157,383.33
Ryan Palmer	65	66	67	69	267	157,383.33
Cameron Percy	67	64	68	68	267	157,383.33
Zac Blair	69	64	66	69	268	102,950
Gonzalo Fernandez-Castano	70	68	67	63	268	102,950
Brooks Koepka	69	68	64	67	268	102,950
John Merrick	66	67	69	66	268	102,950
Kenny Perry	69	68	64	67	268	102,950
Nicholas Thompson	70	67	66	65	268	102,950
Keegan Bradley	66	70	67	66	269	62,302.50
Brendon de Jonge	70	66	63	70	269	62,302.50
Graham DeLaet	69	66	67	67	269	62,302.50
Russell Henley	70	65	69	65	269	62,302.50
Spencer Levin	71	67	65	66	269	62,302.50
Bryce Molder	69	67	65	68	269	62,302.50
Rod Pampling	69	66	69	65	269	62,302.50
Will Wilcox	68	67	67	67	269	62,302.50
Jonas Blixt	67	69	67	67	270	45,085
Jerry Kelly	68	64	68	70	270	45,085
Rory Sabbatini	69	64	69	68	270	45,085
Jordan Spieth	69	64	68	69	270	45,085
Scott Brown	70	66	70	65	271	36,636
Ken Duke	67	68	70	66	271	36,636
Danny Lee	67	69	66	69	271	36,636
Jonathan Randolph	69	63	65	74	271	36,636
Kyle Reifers	70	68	67	66	271	36,636
Martin Flores	67	69	64	72	272	27,690
Brian Harman	70	68	66	68	272	27,690
Matt Kuchar	71	67	64	70	272	27,690
Hunter Mahan	68	64	70	70	272	27,690
S.J. Park	68	68	65	71	272	27,690
Vijay Singh	70	67	66	69	272	27,690
Richard Sterne	71	65	70	66	272	27,690
Joe Affrunti	68	63	67	75	273	18,460
Greg Chalmers	69	69	68	67	273	18,460
Erik Compton	68	67	67	71	273	18,460
Derek Ernst	67	67	67	72	273	18,460
Andrew Loupe	69	65	69	70	273	18,460
Greg Owen	71	67	68	67	273	18,460
John Senden	67	67	68	71	273	18,460
Cameron Smith	70	67	68	68	273	18,460
Michael Thompson	68	66	69	70	273	18,460
Chad Collins	70	67	67	70	274	16,046
James Hahn	65	70	70	69	274	16,046
Mark Hubbard	71	66	67	70	274	16,046

	SCORES				TOTAL	MONEY
Carl Pettersson	69	69	68	68	274	16,046
Justin Thomas	70	67	68	69	274	16,046
Jonathan Byrd	67	71	68	69	275	15,407
Harris English	69	66	67	73	275	15,407
Luke Guthrie	69	65	67	74	275	15,407
Gary Woodland	72	63	71	69	275	15,407
Matt Jones	72	63	66	75	276	14,981
Jeff Overton	69	65	70	72	276	14,981
Ben Curtis	72	63	70	72	277	14,626
John Huh	69	69	67	72	277	14,626
Hudson Swafford	73	65	67	72	277	14,626
Mark Anderson	68	68	68	74	278	14,271
Jhonattan Vegas	70	68	68	72	278	14,271
Adam Hadwin	69	67	69	75	280	13,987
Sam Saunders	69	68	68	75	280	13,987
*Austin Connelly	69	66	72		207	
Jim Herman	69	68	70		207	13,561
Carlos Ortiz	71	67	69		207	13,561
Michael Putnam	72	66	69		207	13,561
Steve Wheatcroft	67	70	70		207	13,561
Robert Garrigus	70	67	71		208	12,993
Cody Gribble	72	66	70		208	12,993
Charl Schwartzel	71	67	70		208	12,993
Bo Van Pelt	71	67	70		208	12,993
Roberto Castro	69	69	71		209	12,496
Trevor Immelman	71	67	71		209	12,496
Whee Kim	72	66	71		209	12,496
Billy Hurley	73	65	72		210	12,141
Boo Weekley	68	67	75		210	12,141
Tom Gillis	66	71	74		211	11,928

Memorial Tournament

Muirfield Village Golf Club, Dublin, Ohio
Par 36-36–72; 7,392 yards

June 4-7
purse, $6,200,000

	SCORES				TOTAL	MONEY
David Lingmerth	67	65	72	69	273	1,116,000
Justin Rose	68	67	66	72	273	669,600
(Lingmerth defeated Rose on third playoff hole.)						
Francesco Molinari	68	67	69	71	275	359,600
Jordan Spieth	68	70	72	65	275	359,600
Jim Furyk	69	66	70	71	276	226,300
Marc Leishman	69	67	71	69	276	226,300
Hideki Matsuyama	64	71	71	70	276	226,300
Keegan Bradley	68	74	65	70	277	179,800
Tony Finau	71	66	73	67	277	179,800
Kevin Kisner	67	71	69	70	277	179,800
Billy Horschel	70	68	71	69	278	148,800
Vijay Singh	71	67	71	69	278	148,800
Dustin Johnson	72	71	65	71	279	116,250
George McNeill	72	71	67	69	279	116,250
Kevin Na	71	71	66	71	279	116,250
Andy Sullivan	70	64	72	73	279	116,250
Brendon Todd	67	68	71	74	280	99,200
Harris English	67	71	72	71	281	78,120
Bill Haas	70	71	71	69	281	78,120
Russell Knox	66	74	73	68	281	78,120
Ryan Moore	67	67	75	72	281	78,120
Robert Streb	73	67	71	70	281	78,120

	SCORES				TOTAL	MONEY
Kevin Streelman	71	70	65	75	281	78,120
Jason Dufner	66	67	74	75	282	57,040
Rory Sabbatini	72	67	71	72	282	57,040
Thomas Aiken	69	68	70	76	283	45,880
Graham DeLaet	69	69	72	73	283	45,880
Matt Kuchar	70	69	70	74	283	45,880
Jeff Overton	71	71	67	74	283	45,880
Patrick Reed	72	68	68	75	283	45,880
Greg Chalmers	69	73	70	72	284	36,766
Stewart Cink	72	71	71	70	284	36,766
Retief Goosen	70	71	71	72	284	36,766
Charles Howell	75	66	70	73	284	36,766
Chris Stroud	70	68	72	74	284	36,766
Erik Compton	68	69	71	77	285	29,837.50
John Huh	72	66	73	74	285	29,837.50
Chris Kirk	69	71	76	69	285	29,837.50
Carl Pettersson	72	67	72	74	285	29,837.50
Matt Jones	71	68	74	73	286	21,727.56
Patrick Rodgers	69	66	78	73	286	21,727.56
Shawn Stefani	70	72	71	73	286	21,727.56
Steve Stricker	69	73	76	68	286	21,727.56
Bo Van Pelt	64	72	78	72	286	21,727.56
Jonathan Byrd	68	71	71	76	286	21,727.55
Jim Herman	70	72	68	76	286	21,727.55
William McGirt	70	70	70	76	286	21,727.55
Camilo Villegas	73	68	72	73	286	21,727.55
Sangmoon Bae	74	66	78	69	287	15,665.34
Kevin Chappell	71	72	71	73	287	15,665.33
Chesson Hadley	74	66	73	74	287	15,665.33
Jason Bohn	75	67	74	72	288	14,458.40
Steven Bowditch	69	71	68	80	288	14,458.40
James Hahn	71	70	73	74	288	14,458.40
Brooks Koepka	71	70	69	78	288	14,458.40
Troy Merritt	70	69	72	77	288	14,458.40
Adam Hadwin	72	68	71	78	289	13,826
Pat Perez	68	70	75	76	289	13,826
John Senden	71	71	74	73	289	13,826
Andrew Svoboda	70	70	77	72	289	13,826
Zac Blair	75	68	70	77	290	13,454
Brian Stuard	68	75	74	73	290	13,454
Brendan Steele	71	67	73	80	291	13,206
Hudson Swafford	71	70	79	71	291	13,206
Ken Duke	67	75	77	74	293	12,896
Phil Mickelson	72	68	78	75	293	12,896
Nick Watney	71	72	77	73	293	12,896
Lucas Glover	68	72	82	72	294	12,524
Scott Langley	70	72	77	75	294	12,524
Andrew Putnam	72	66	74	82	294	12,524
Tiger Woods	73	70	85	74	302	12,276

FedEx St. Jude Classic

TPC Southwind, Memphis, Tennessee
Par 35-35–70; 7,239 yards

June 11-14
purse, $6,000,000

	SCORES				TOTAL	MONEY
Fabian Gomez	66	68	67	66	267	$1,080,000
Greg Owen	64	70	67	70	271	648,000
Matt Jones	69	67	68	68	272	270,600
Brooks Koepka	64	67	71	70	272	270,600

	SCORES				TOTAL	MONEY
Phil Mickelson	68	69	70	65	272	270,600
Seung-Yul Noh	69	72	66	65	272	270,600
Michael Thompson	69	69	68	66	272	270,600
Chad Campbell	69	66	70	68	273	168,000
Billy Horschel	71	67	70	65	273	168,000
Russell Knox	70	64	73	66	273	168,000
Boo Weekley	67	70	71	65	273	168,000
Scott Brown	65	69	68	72	274	114,000
Tom Hoge	69	65	71	69	274	114,000
Colt Knost	72	64	72	66	274	114,000
Chez Reavie	70	70	66	68	274	114,000
Chris Smith	67	67	71	69	274	114,000
Will Wilcox	68	72	69	65	274	114,000
Billy Hurley	72	66	70	67	275	81,000
Cameron Percy	69	69	71	66	275	81,000
Vaughn Taylor	67	74	68	66	275	81,000
Camilo Villegas	71	68	66	70	275	81,000
Steven Alker	65	68	74	69	276	54,085.72
Steven Bowditch	69	71	70	66	276	54,085.72
Alex Cejka	71	68	69	68	276	54,085.72
Kevin Chappell	71	64	71	70	276	54,085.71
Austin Cook	68	64	72	72	276	54,085.71
Spencer Levin	67	68	72	69	276	54,085.71
Ryan Palmer	64	71	70	71	276	54,085.71
Jason Bohn	70	71	69	67	277	36,525
Luke Donald	69	68	72	68	277	36,525
Ken Duke	68	71	72	66	277	36,525
Jason Gore	71	65	71	70	277	36,525
George McNeill	71	67	70	69	277	36,525
Patrick Rodgers	70	69	69	69	277	36,525
Hudson Swafford	71	68	68	70	277	36,525
Tyrone van Aswegen	69	69	70	69	277	36,525
Stewart Cink	68	70	69	71	278	28,200
Ben Crane	66	70	74	68	278	28,200
Brendon de Jonge	71	70	66	71	278	28,200
Arjun Atwal	72	65	68	74	279	23,400
Roberto Castro	69	70	74	66	279	23,400
John Merrick	69	68	70	72	279	23,400
Carl Pettersson	72	69	68	70	279	23,400
Alex Prugh	66	74	70	69	279	23,400
Chad Collins	71	66	75	68	280	16,817.15
Harris English	69	67	75	69	280	16,817.15
Eric Axley	70	69	72	69	280	16,817.14
David Hearn	71	68	71	70	280	16,817.14
Mark Hubbard	72	68	70	70	280	16,817.14
Whee Kim	73	68	70	69	280	16,817.14
Tim Wilkinson	70	70	65	75	280	16,817.14
*Bryson DeChambeau	69	71	68	72	280	
Jon Curran	70	71	72	68	281	13,992
Tom Gillis	66	68	73	74	281	13,992
Lucas Glover	67	72	70	72	281	13,992
Zack Sucher	68	72	70	71	281	13,992
Nick Watney	69	71	68	73	281	13,992
Zac Blair	69	70	72	71	282	13,380
Brian Davis	65	72	76	69	282	13,380
Martin Laird	68	71	73	70	282	13,380
John Rollins	67	70	75	70	282	13,380
Kyle Stanley	69	71	75	68	283	13,020
David Toms	70	66	69	78	283	13,020
Robert Allenby	71	70	68	75	284	12,780
Jason Kokrak	69	71	72	72	284	12,780
Max Homa	68	70	68	79	285	12,600
Harrison Frazar	70	69	81	66	286	12,480

	SCORES				TOTAL	MONEY
Charlie Beljan	74	66	73	74	287	12,360
Tommy Gainey	66	74	74	74	288	12,060
Jim Renner	69	70	76	73	288	12,060
Heath Slocum	68	72	72	76	288	12,060
Mark Wilson	67	69	74	78	288	12,060
Oscar Fraustro	69	72	71	78	290	11,760
Brian Stuard	68	70	76	77	291	11,640
Aaron Baddeley	71	70	77	76	294	11,520

U.S. Open Championship

Chambers Bay Golf Club, University Place, Washington   June 18-21
Par 35-35–70; 7,526 yards   purse, $10,000,000

	SCORES				TOTAL	MONEY
Jordan Spieth	68	67	71	69	275	$1,800,000
Louis Oosthuizen	77	66	66	67	276	877,144
Dustin Johnson	65	71	70	70	276	877,144
Adam Scott	70	71	72	64	277	407,037
Cameron Smith	70	70	69	68	277	407,037
Branden Grace	69	67	70	71	277	407,037
Charl Schwartzel	73	70	69	66	278	311,835
Brandt Snedeker	69	72	70	68	279	280,482
Rory McIlroy	72	72	70	66	280	235,316
Shane Lowry	69	70	70	71	280	235,316
Jason Day	68	70	68	74	280	235,316
Kevin Kisner	71	68	73	69	281	192,925
Matt Kuchar	67	73	72	69	281	192,925
John Senden	72	72	70	68	282	156,935
Patrick Reed	66	69	76	71	282	156,935
Tony Finau	69	68	74	71	282	156,935
Andres Romero	71	69	71	71	282	156,935
Geoff Ogilvy	69	72	75	67	283	113,686
Sergio Garcia	70	75	70	68	283	113,686
Brooks Koepka	72	72	70	69	283	113,686
Jason Dufner	68	72	73	70	283	113,686
Jamie Lovemark	70	68	75	70	283	113,686
Hideki Matsuyama	70	71	72	70	283	113,686
Charlie Beljan	69	75	69	70	283	113,686
Thomas Aiken	74	71	73	66	284	85,622
Billy Horschel	72	72	73	67	284	85,622
Morgan Hoffmann	71	74	74	66	285	64,126
Tommy Fleetwood	74	69	73	69	285	64,126
Keegan Bradley	73	71	72	69	285	64,126
Daniel Summerhays	70	67	78	70	285	64,126
Jimmy Gunn	72	73	70	70	285	64,126
Justin Rose	72	70	72	71	285	64,126
Marc Warren	68	74	72	71	285	64,126
Francesco Molinari	68	73	72	72	285	64,126
Alexander Levy	70	69	73	73	285	64,126
Henrik Stenson	65	74	72	74	285	64,126
J.B. Holmes	72	66	71	76	285	64,126
*Brian Campbell	67	72	78	68	285	
Troy Kelly	72	73	72	69	286	47,854
Paul Casey	72	69	73	72	286	47,854
Joost Luiten	68	69	74	75	286	47,854
Robert Streb	74	70	73	70	287	42,946
Jim Furyk	71	73	73	70	287	42,946
*Denny McCarthy	71	73	71	72	287	
*Ollie Schniederjans	69	73	72	73	287	

	SCORES				TOTAL	MONEY
Kevin Chappell	69	75	73	71	288	37,090
Brad Fritsch	70	74	72	72	288	37,090
Webb Simpson	72	73	71	72	288	37,090
Kevin Na	70	72	72	74	288	37,090
Lee Westwood	73	69	77	70	289	31,633
Sam Saunders	72	72	76	69	289	31,633
Ryan Palmer	74	70	73	73	290	29,384
*Nick Hardy	70	75	77	68	290	
Ernie Els	72	70	76	73	291	27,272
Mark Silvers	72	71	75	73	291	27,272
Cameron Tringale	75	68	74	74	291	27,272
Ian Poulter	72	73	69	77	291	27,272
D.A. Points	74	71	77	70	292	25,358
Brad Elder	76	68	76	72	292	25,358
Luke Donald	73	71	73	75	292	25,358
Jimmy Walker	72	73	72	75	292	25,358
*Beau Hossler	71	72	73	76	292	
*Jack Maguire	73	68	73	78	292	
Ben Martin	67	70	86	70	293	23,822
Phil Mickelson	69	74	77	73	293	23,822
Marcus Fraser	71	71	77	74	293	23,822
Cheng Tsung Pan	71	72	76	74	293	23,822
Angel Cabrera	70	75	74	74	293	23,822
Colin Montgomerie	69	76	72	76	293	23,822
Andy Pope	74	71	77	72	294	22,652
George Coetzee	72	73	72	77	294	22,652
Zach Johnson	72	72	78	73	295	22,067
John Parry	72	73	71	79	295	22,067
Camilo Villegas	72	73	80	75	300	21,628
Chris Kirk	70	73	80	78	301	21,332

Out of Final 36 Holes

Roberto Castro	74	72	146	Kevin Lucas	74	74	148
Bill Haas	73	73	146	Jason Palmer	76	73	149
Charley Hoffman	76	70	146	Shiv Kapur	72	77	149
Garth Mulroy	74	72	146	Ryo Ishikawa	74	75	149
Cody Gribble	68	78	146	*Bryson DeChambeau	74	75	149
Andy Sullivan	72	74	146	*Bradley Neil	76	73	149
Hiroyuki Fujita	72	74	146	Danny Willett	72	77	149
Marcel Siem	73	73	146	Bo Van Pelt	73	76	149
Martin Kaymer	72	74	146	Lee Janzen	73	76	149
Tom Hoge	73	74	147	Ryan Moore	75	74	149
Hunter Mahan	73	74	147	George McNeill	75	74	149
Anirban Lahiri	75	72	147	Byeong-Hun An	73	76	149
Michael Putnam	70	77	147	*Matthew Nesmith	76	73	149
Timothy O'Neal	74	73	147	Tjaart van der Walt	77	73	150
Jason Allred	74	73	147	Marc Leishman	73	77	150
Victor Dubuisson	74	73	147	Stephen Gallacher	78	72	150
Bubba Watson	70	77	147	Erik Compton	76	74	150
Bernd Wiesberger	72	75	147	*Jake Knapp	74	76	150
Wen-Chong Liang	73	74	147	Tyler Duncan	78	72	150
David Hearn	72	75	147	Jared Becher	78	72	150
Masahiro Kawamura	70	77	147	Steve Marino	75	75	150
Retief Goosen	77	71	148	Lucas Bjerregaard	73	77	150
Alex Noren	73	75	148	*Kyle Jones	78	72	150
Thongchai Jaidee	71	77	148	*Gunn Yang	74	76	150
Matt Mabrey	74	74	148	Oliver Farr	73	77	150
Brian Harman	69	79	148	Blayne Barber	78	73	151
*Lee McCoy	74	74	148	Gary Woodland	74	77	151
Graeme McDowell	74	74	148	Jamie Donaldson	74	77	151
Miguel Angel Jimenez	69	79	148	*Sam Horsfield	75	76	151
Russell Henley	71	77	148	Shunsuke Sonoda	78	73	151

Brandon Hagy	74	77	151	Sebastian Cappelen	70	85	155
Billy Hurley	80	72	152	Pat Wilson	79	76	155
Danny Lee	78	74	152	Rich Berberian, Jr.	83	72	155
Michael Davan	77	75	152	Lucas Glover	73	83	156
Brendon Todd	78	75	153	Tiger Woods	80	76	156
*Davis Riley	73	80	153	Seuk-Hyun Baek	74	82	156
Kurt Barnes	72	81	153	Darren Clarke	77	80	157
Rickie Fowler	81	73	154	*Cole Hammer	77	84	161
Josh Persons	79	75	154	Alex Kim	80	86	166
Richard Lee	74	80	154	Matt Every	78		WD
Stephan Jaeger	74	80	154				

(Professionals who did not complete 72 holes received $4,000.)

Travelers Championship

TPC River Highlands, Cromwell, Connecticut   June 25-28
Par 35-35–70; 6,841 yards   purse, $6,400,000

	SCORES				TOTAL	MONEY
Bubba Watson	62	67	68	67	264	$1,152,000
Paul Casey	67	68	64	65	264	691,200
(Watson defeated Casey on second playoff hole.)						
Brian Harman	66	65	65	69	265	435,200
Graham DeLaet	67	66	64	69	266	307,200
Carl Pettersson	65	66	70	66	267	256,000
Zach Johnson	65	70	64	69	268	230,400
Luke Donald	68	68	67	66	269	199,466.67
Bo Van Pelt	70	68	65	66	269	199,466.67
Mark Wilson	66	68	67	68	269	199,466.66
Jon Curran	67	67	67	69	270	147,200
Ken Duke	69	68	67	66	270	147,200
Jason Gore	64	68	69	69	270	147,200
Brandt Snedeker	68	68	63	71	270	147,200
Chris Stroud	65	67	68	70	270	147,200
Mark Anderson	67	71	65	68	271	102,400
Steven Bowditch	68	68	69	66	271	102,400
Martin Laird	70	67	67	67	271	102,400
Nicholas Thompson	66	67	70	68	271	102,400
Brendon Todd	67	70	67	67	271	102,400
Brice Garnett	66	69	66	71	272	71,936
Seung-Yul Noh	64	69	71	68	272	71,936
Kyle Stanley	67	68	68	69	272	71,936
David Toms	69	67	66	70	272	71,936
Gary Woodland	66	69	68	69	272	71,936
Harris English	64	71	67	71	273	41,234.29
Tony Finau	68	69	66	70	273	41,234.29
Danny Lee	66	67	69	71	273	41,234.29
William McGirt	67	69	66	71	273	41,234.29
Francesco Molinari	67	66	69	71	273	41,234.29
Scott Pinckney	67	71	67	68	273	41,234.29
Brendan Steele	67	71	68	67	273	41,234.29
Brian Stuard	64	67	71	71	273	41,234.29
Chad Campbell	68	70	69	66	273	41,234.28
Sergio Garcia	67	68	66	72	273	41,234.28
Billy Horschel	67	69	66	71	273	41,234.28
Scott Langley	65	68	73	67	273	41,234.28
Cheng Tsung Pan	67	68	71	67	273	41,234.28
Chez Reavie	70	65	71	67	273	41,234.28
Keegan Bradley	64	69	71	70	274	23,680
Chad Collins	70	67	69	68	274	23,680
Robert Garrigus	65	72	70	67	274	23,680

	SCORES				TOTAL	MONEY
Morgan Hoffmann	67	71	67	69	274	23,680
Colt Knost	67	70	69	68	274	23,680
Marc Leishman	70	67	68	69	274	23,680
Patrick Rodgers	68	70	63	73	274	23,680
Cameron Smith	73	65	68	68	274	23,680
Nick Watney	69	64	70	71	274	23,680
Jason Kokrak	69	66	69	71	275	16,085.34
Spencer Levin	68	68	67	72	275	16,085.34
Aaron Baddeley	68	66	68	73	275	16,085.33
Jeff Overton	69	69	71	66	275	16,085.33
John Peterson	70	66	69	70	275	16,085.33
Jim Renner	67	68	70	70	275	16,085.33
Scott Brown	65	67	73	71	276	14,528
Derek Ernst	68	67	67	74	276	14,528
Cameron Percy	69	69	68	70	276	14,528
Alexandre Rocha	66	70	69	71	276	14,528
Byron Smith	69	67	69	71	276	14,528
Jhonattan Vegas	66	69	67	74	276	14,528
Steven Alker	70	68	68	71	277	13,888
J.J. Henry	68	67	72	70	277	13,888
Jonathan Randolph	67	69	71	70	277	13,888
Tyrone van Aswegen	68	69	69	71	277	13,888
Tom Hoge	68	70	73	67	278	13,440
David Lingmerth	68	68	72	70	278	13,440
Bryce Molder	66	71	70	71	278	13,440
*Jon Rahm	68	69	69	72	278	
Tom Gillis	65	71	74	70	280	13,056
Jim Herman	67	71	70	72	280	13,056
Will MacKenzie	65	69	72	74	280	13,056
Eric Axley	68	70	70	73	281	12,736
Mark Hubbard	68	68	70	75	281	12,736

Greenbrier Classic

The Old White TPC, White Sulphur Springs, West Virginia
Par 34-36–70; 7,287 yards

July 2-5
purse, $6,700,000

	SCORES				TOTAL	MONEY
Danny Lee	63	69	68	67	267	$1,206,000
David Hearn	68	64	68	67	267	500,266.67
Robert Streb	68	67	67	65	267	500,266.67
Kevin Kisner	67	69	67	64	267	500,266.66
(Lee defeated Streb and Kisner on first and Hearn on second playoff hole.)						
Russell Henley	70	66	69	63	268	268,000
James Hahn	66	67	70	66	269	195,735.72
Greg Owen	65	67	70	67	269	195,735.72
Andres Romero	67	67	68	67	269	195,735.72
Chad Collins	65	67	68	69	269	195,735.71
David Lingmerth	67	70	64	68	269	195,735.71
Bryce Molder	68	64	67	70	269	195,735.71
Brendon Todd	65	69	67	68	269	195,735.71
Tony Finau	68	67	68	67	270	107,944.45
J.J. Henry	68	66	69	67	270	107,944.45
Morgan Hoffmann	68	67	69	66	270	107,944.45
Scott Langley	62	69	74	65	270	107,944.45
Jason Bohn	69	69	61	71	270	107,944.44
Steven Bowditch	68	68	67	67	270	107,944.44
Sean O'Hair	66	67	66	71	270	107,944.44
Shawn Stefani	69	67	67	67	270	107,944.44
Bubba Watson	67	68	68	67	270	107,944.44

	SCORES				TOTAL	MONEY
Ryan Armour	69	69	68	65	271	60,395.72
Derek Ernst	67	71	68	65	271	60,395.72
Chez Reavie	68	70	67	66	271	60,395.72
Jonathan Byrd	63	69	69	70	271	60,395.71
J.B. Holmes	67	69	69	66	271	60,395.71
George McNeill	67	68	68	68	271	60,395.71
Pat Perez	67	68	68	68	271	60,395.71
Keegan Bradley	68	69	71	64	272	45,560
Scott Piercy	67	66	71	68	272	45,560
Patrick Reed	68	68	67	69	272	45,560
Eric Axley	68	67	70	68	273	37,922
Brice Garnett	69	68	67	69	273	37,922
Kevin Na	65	70	71	67	273	37,922
Johnson Wagner	69	68	67	69	273	37,922
Tiger Woods	66	69	71	67	273	37,922
Paul Casey	66	71	71	66	274	22,850.95
Brian Davis	64	70	73	67	274	22,850.95
Scott Brown	67	69	67	71	274	22,850.94
Chad Campbell	66	72	68	68	274	22,850.94
Kevin Chappell	65	67	72	70	274	22,850.94
Graham DeLaet	68	70	67	69	274	22,850.94
Gonzalo Fernandez-Castano	67	70	66	71	274	22,850.94
Robert Garrigus	66	67	71	70	274	22,850.94
Andres Gonzales	68	66	72	68	274	22,850.94
Luke Guthrie	67	70	67	70	274	22,850.94
Tom Hoge	68	66	69	71	274	22,850.94
Billy Hurley	67	71	69	67	274	22,850.94
Justin Leonard	66	68	70	70	274	22,850.94
Seung-Yul Noh	69	65	68	72	274	22,850.94
S.J. Park	68	65	66	75	274	22,850.94
Chris Stroud	66	69	70	69	274	22,850.94
Jhonattan Vegas	66	65	76	67	274	22,850.94
Sangmoon Bae	68	67	71	69	275	15,209
Mark Hubbard	70	65	71	69	275	15,209
John Huh	66	71	72	66	275	15,209
Jason Kokrak	69	69	68	69	275	15,209
Davis Love	68	69	69	69	275	15,209
Justin Thomas	67	67	66	75	275	15,209
Alex Cejka	68	70	71	67	276	14,405
Brendon de Jonge	70	66	70	70	276	14,405
Cameron Percy	68	66	69	73	276	14,405
Michael Putnam	73	65	69	69	276	14,405
Patrick Rodgers	68	65	69	74	276	14,405
Byron Smith	66	71	69	70	276	14,405
*Maverick McNealy	67	68	68	73	276	
Ricky Barnes	72	66	71	68	277	13,601
Martin Flores	67	69	74	67	277	13,601
Whee Kim	69	69	68	71	277	13,601
Kyle Reifers	69	69	68	71	277	13,601
Scott Stallings	69	68	69	71	277	13,601
Hudson Swafford	70	68	69	70	277	13,601
Bill Lunde	70	66	73	69	278	13,065
Louis Oosthuizen	70	68	73	67	278	13,065
Derek Fathauer	68	70	70	71	279	12,864
Ryo Ishikawa	64	71	75	70	280	12,730
Kevin Streelman	67	70	71	73	281	12,596

John Deere Classic

TPC Deere Run, Silvis, Illinois
Par 35-36–71; 7,268 yards

July 9-12
purse, $4,700,000

	SCORES				TOTAL	MONEY
Jordan Spieth	71	64	61	68	264	$846,000
Tom Gillis	66	65	69	64	264	507,600
(Spieth defeated Gillis on second playoff hole.)						
Zach Johnson	66	68	66	65	265	272,600
Danny Lee	68	68	62	67	265	272,600
Chris Stroud	68	68	67	63	266	171,550
Justin Thomas	63	67	69	67	266	171,550
Johnson Wagner	68	63	68	67	266	171,550
Kevin Chappell	68	69	64	67	268	131,600
Daniel Summerhays	65	67	68	68	268	131,600
Steve Wheatcroft	67	66	70	65	268	131,600
Will Wilcox	66	66	69	67	268	131,600
Jason Bohn	68	68	69	64	269	103,400
Carl Pettersson	66	71	66	66	269	103,400
Luke Guthrie	64	70	67	69	270	84,600
Scott Piercy	67	69	67	67	270	84,600
Robert Streb	66	70	68	66	270	84,600
Jerry Kelly	70	66	67	68	271	75,200
Adam Hadwin	68	70	69	65	272	59,220
Scott Pinckney	66	66	71	69	272	59,220
Vijay Singh	67	68	70	67	272	59,220
Roger Sloan	70	68	67	67	272	59,220
Kyle Stanley	67	71	67	67	272	59,220
Brian Stuard	66	68	68	70	272	59,220
Robert Garrigus	65	68	70	70	273	40,067.50
Brian Harman	67	68	71	67	273	40,067.50
Mark Hubbard	69	67	70	67	273	40,067.50
Ryan Moore	70	65	69	69	273	40,067.50
Chad Campbell	72	64	72	66	274	30,583.58
Steven Alker	65	69	70	70	274	30,583.57
Gonzalo Fernandez-Castano	68	68	71	67	274	30,583.57
Bryce Molder	68	65	73	68	274	30,583.57
Alex Prugh	68	69	70	67	274	30,583.57
Michael Putnam	69	67	70	68	274	30,583.57
Josh Teater	69	68	67	70	274	30,583.57
Max Homa	70	66	70	69	275	22,677.50
Kevin Kisner	69	67	70	69	275	22,677.50
Scott Langley	68	70	71	66	275	22,677.50
Shawn Stefani	65	70	64	76	275	22,677.50
Steve Stricker	65	69	71	70	275	22,677.50
Hudson Swafford	71	66	70	68	275	22,677.50
William McGirt	69	69	69	69	276	18,330
Rod Pampling	72	66	71	67	276	18,330
Jim Renner	67	69	74	66	276	18,330
Sam Saunders	67	69	70	71	277	14,209.67
Zack Sucher	71	67	71	68	277	14,209.67
Vaughn Taylor	69	69	71	68	277	14,209.67
Jhonattan Vegas	67	70	71	69	277	14,209.67
Roberto Castro	69	68	67	73	277	14,209.66
Nicholas Thompson	63	72	70	72	277	14,209.66
John Huh	69	68	73	68	278	11,336.40
Spencer Levin	66	67	71	74	278	11,336.40
Chris Naegel	71	67	72	68	278	11,336.40
Seung-Yul Noh	69	69	70	70	278	11,336.40
Tim Wilkinson	68	69	71	70	278	11,336.40
Alex Cejka	67	71	72	69	279	10,622
Derek Fathauer	71	65	70	73	279	10,622

	SCORES				TOTAL	MONEY
Pat Perez	69	68	73	69	279	10,622
Michael Thompson	66	72	71	70	279	10,622
Tyrone van Aswegen	66	70	72	71	279	10,622
Ryan Armour	69	69	76	66	280	10,293
Charles Howell	64	72	74	70	280	10,293
Jonas Blixt	67	69	72	73	281	10,058
S.J. Park	68	70	74	69	281	10,058
Cameron Percy	68	68	75	70	281	10,058
Glen Day	67	70	72	73	282	9,823
Chez Reavie	69	68	77	68	282	9,823
Ken Duke	71	67	75	70	283	9,635
David Hearn	68	70	75	70	283	9,635
Greg Chalmers	68	70	75	73	286	9,447
Boo Weekley	66	70	72	78	286	9,447
*Lee McCoy	67	71	78	70	286	
Harris English	69	69	77	72	287	9,259
Ryo Ishikawa	69	68	77	73	287	9,259

The Open Championship

See European Tours chapter.

Barbasol Championship

RTJ Golf Trail, Grand National Course, Auburn, Alabama

Par 35-36–71; 7,302 yards

July 16-19

purse, $3,500,000

	SCORES				TOTAL	MONEY
Scott Piercy	69	66	65	65	265	$630,000
Will Wilcox	66	70	65	67	268	378,000
Ricky Barnes	67	68	65	70	270	203,000
Whee Kim	67	66	68	69	270	203,000
*Robby Shelton	68	69	66	67	270	
Austin Cook	69	70	65	67	271	122,937.50
Mark Hensby	69	64	68	70	271	122,937.50
Andrew Loupe	68	70	68	65	271	122,937.50
Boo Weekley	67	69	68	67	271	122,937.50
Aaron Baddeley	69	72	64	67	272	84,000
Blayne Barber	69	67	68	68	272	84,000
Emiliano Grillo	68	66	67	71	272	84,000
Andres Romero	71	64	69	68	272	84,000
Vaughn Taylor	71	69	63	69	272	84,000
Johnson Wagner	69	68	66	69	272	84,000
Jason Gore	65	73	63	72	273	59,500
Tom Hoge	68	71	69	65	273	59,500
Scott Langley	72	67	69	65	273	59,500
Jonathan Byrd	68	69	69	68	274	47,250
Martin Flores	66	74	68	66	274	47,250
Martin Piller	69	66	70	69	274	47,250
David Toms	69	66	72	67	274	47,250
Roberto Castro	69	70	69	67	275	29,944.45
J.J. Henry	68	67	71	69	275	29,944.45
Ryo Ishikawa	68	69	69	69	275	29,944.45
Duffy Waldorf	72	69	67	67	275	29,944.45
Steven Alker	69	72	65	69	275	29,944.44
Alex Cejka	69	66	69	71	275	29,944.44
Ken Duke	68	68	69	70	275	29,944.44
Alex Prugh	72	68	66	69	275	29,944.44
Kyle Stanley	70	67	67	71	275	29,944.44

	SCORES				TOTAL	MONEY
Zac Blair	72	66	69	69	276	21,218.75
Trevor Immelman	70	69	67	70	276	21,218.75
Sam Saunders	64	70	69	73	276	21,218.75
Chris Stroud	70	70	70	66	276	21,218.75
Charlie Beljan	70	64	74	69	277	18,025
Glen Day	72	63	70	72	277	18,025
Wes Homan	71	70	70	66	277	18,025
Matt Bettencourt	69	69	72	68	278	13,650
Erik Compton	67	73	70	68	278	13,650
Chesson Hadley	69	72	68	69	278	13,650
Charles Howell	72	68	72	66	278	13,650
Doug LaBelle	69	71	68	70	278	13,650
Spencer Levin	68	69	70	71	278	13,650
Troy Matteson	70	71	69	68	278	13,650
Jonathan Randolph	71	69	67	71	278	13,650
Michael Thompson	67	70	71	70	278	13,650
Arjun Atwal	69	68	72	70	279	8,708
Chad Campbell	70	69	72	68	279	8,708
Andres Gonzales	69	71	67	72	279	8,708
John Merrick	76	65	66	72	279	8,708
Shaun Micheel	73	68	68	70	279	8,708
Carlos Sainz, Jr.	66	71	75	67	279	8,708
Roger Sloan	71	69	68	71	279	8,708
Andrew Svoboda	71	66	69	73	279	8,708
Garrett Willis	71	70	69	69	279	8,708
Mark Wilson	69	70	68	72	279	8,708
Ryan Armour	69	72	72	67	280	7,840
Carlos Ortiz	66	69	71	74	280	7,840
Kyle Reifers	68	70	71	71	280	7,840
Cameron Beckman	70	71	74	66	281	7,560
Gonzalo Fernandez-Castano	70	68	72	71	281	7,560
Bill Lunde	69	69	68	75	281	7,560
Parker McLachlin	69	72	69	71	281	7,560
Tyrone van Aswegen	70	70	69	72	281	7,560
Smylie Kaufman	69	68	73	72	282	7,210
John Peterson	70	70	69	73	282	7,210
Chris Riley	72	68	70	72	282	7,210
Byron Smith	70	70	73	69	282	7,210
Chris Smith	70	71	69	72	282	7,210
Michael Block	72	67	73	71	283	7,000
Billy Hurley	72	68	73	71	284	6,825
Brandt Jobe	68	72	74	70	284	6,825
D.A. Points	71	70	69	74	284	6,825
Richy Werenski	73	68	72	71	284	6,825
Steve Lowery	71	68	73	73	285	6,650
Josh Teater	69	67	74	76	286	6,580
D.J. Trahan	71	70	80	69	290	6,510
*Maverick McNealy	66	75	82	67	290	
Zack Sucher	71	70	78	72	291	6,440

RBC Canadian Open

Glen Abbey Golf Club, Oakville, Ontario, Canada
Par 35-37–72; 7,253 yards

July 23-26
purse, $5,800,000

	SCORES				TOTAL	MONEY
Jason Day	68	66	69	68	271	$1,044,000
Bubba Watson	68	67	68	69	272	626,400
David Hearn	69	64	68	72	273	394,400
Jim Furyk	68	69	68	69	274	278,400

	SCORES				TOTAL	MONEY
Stewart Cink	68	73	68	66	275	220,400
Tom Hoge	70	70	69	66	275	220,400
Austin Cook	68	70	69	69	276	174,725
Adam Hadwin	74	67	67	68	276	174,725
Charley Hoffman	71	66	69	70	276	174,725
Matt Kuchar	69	69	69	69	276	174,725
Ricky Barnes	68	70	68	71	277	115,171.43
Chad Campbell	67	63	75	72	277	115,171.43
Erik Compton	66	69	71	71	277	115,171.43
James Hahn	71	68	69	69	277	115,171.43
Rory Sabbatini	72	69	69	67	277	115,171.43
Daniel Summerhays	73	69	68	67	277	115,171.43
Michael Putnam	71	65	68	73	277	115,171.42
Brooks Koepka	68	68	68	74	278	78,300
Cameron Percy	72	67	69	70	278	78,300
Pat Perez	69	69	69	71	278	78,300
Johnson Wagner	67	66	72	73	278	78,300
Tony Finau	71	70	73	65	279	46,206.67
Andres Gonzales	70	67	74	68	279	46,206.67
Jim Herman	67	75	69	68	279	46,206.67
Scott Langley	69	71	69	70	279	46,206.67
Sam Saunders	70	69	71	69	279	46,206.67
Brian Stuard	69	72	70	68	279	46,206.67
Tim Wilkinson	72	70	69	68	279	46,206.67
Mark Wilson	70	68	72	69	279	46,206.67
Jonas Blixt	69	69	69	72	279	46,206.66
Emiliano Grillo	64	72	69	74	279	46,206.66
Ollie Schniederjans	71	69	66	73	279	46,206.66
Camilo Villegas	69	69	67	74	279	46,206.66
William McGirt	67	69	75	69	280	28,668.58
Brian Harman	65	67	76	72	280	28,668.57
Justin Leonard	72	66	73	69	280	28,668.57
Andres Romero	68	73	70	69	280	28,668.57
Adam Svensson	69	73	67	71	280	28,668.57
Tyrone van Aswegen	66	75	68	71	280	28,668.57
Nick Watney	73	66	70	71	280	28,668.57
Alex Cejka	72	70	70	69	281	20,300
Chad Collins	70	70	69	72	281	20,300
J.J. Henry	72	67	71	71	281	20,300
Ryan Palmer	71	71	72	67	281	20,300
Chez Reavie	69	67	76	69	281	20,300
J.J. Spaun	67	72	73	69	281	20,300
Vaughn Taylor	65	71	74	71	281	20,300
Roberto Castro	69	72	67	74	282	14,282.50
Ben Crane	73	67	70	72	282	14,282.50
Derek Fathauer	72	70	67	73	282	14,282.50
Colt Knost	68	69	75	70	282	14,282.50
Jeff Overton	72	68	69	73	282	14,282.50
Alex Prugh	67	70	69	76	282	14,282.50
Jhonattan Vegas	71	70	68	73	282	14,282.50
Scott Verplank	72	70	72	68	282	14,282.50
D.A. Points	69	72	71	71	283	13,166
Nick Taylor	70	72	71	70	283	13,166
Eric Axley	67	68	75	74	284	12,760
Brian Davis	69	73	67	75	284	12,760
Scott Pinckney	68	68	73	75	284	12,760
Andrew Svoboda	72	70	69	73	284	12,760
Steve Wheatcroft	66	72	75	71	284	12,760
Angel Cabrera	73	69	72	71	285	12,064
Tim Clark	72	67	72	74	285	12,064
Martin Flores	68	74	70	73	285	12,064
Hunter Mahan	68	72	70	75	285	12,064
Carlos Ortiz	71	69	72	73	285	12,064

	SCORES				TOTAL	MONEY
Andrew Putnam	69	71	73	72	285	12,064
Steve Stricker	69	72	71	73	285	12,064
Zac Blair	69	70	71	76	286	11,542
Tom Gillis	73	68	73	72	286	11,542
Chesson Hadley	67	74	73	73	287	11,310
Hudson Swafford	71	68	69	79	287	11,310
Luke Donald	72	70	72	74	288	11,078
Heath Slocum	68	74	70	76	288	11,078
K.J. Choi	69	72	73	75	289	10,788
Brendon de Jonge	71	66	76	76	289	10,788
Retief Goosen	69	71	74	75	289	10,788
*Austin Connelly	73	65	77		215	
Jon Curran	70	70	75		215	10,382
Lucas Glover	70	68	77		215	10,382
*Blair Hamilton	71	68	76		215	
J.B. Holmes	69	70	76		215	10,382
Scott Piercy	70	72	73		215	10,382
Ryo Ishikawa	70	72	74		216	10,034
Seung-Yul Noh	68	74	74		216	10,034
Steven Alker	71	69	77		217	9,802
Jonathan Randolph	71	70	76		217	9,802
*Ryan Ruffels	66	75	76		217	
Marcelo Rozo	76	66	76		218	9,628
Blayne Barber	68	74	79		221	9,512

Quicken Loans National

Robert Trent Jones Golf Club, Gainesville, Virginia
Par 36-35–71; 7,385 yards

July 30-August 2
purse, $6,700,000

	SCORES				TOTAL	MONEY
Troy Merritt	70	68	61	67	266	$1,206,000
Rickie Fowler	67	65	68	69	269	723,600
David Lingmerth	68	65	68	69	270	455,600
Jason Bohn	67	67	67	71	272	242,875
Bill Haas	67	71	64	70	272	242,875
Danny Lee	67	67	69	69	272	242,875
Carl Pettersson	70	68	64	70	272	242,875
Justin Rose	66	71	65	70	272	242,875
Justin Thomas	66	71	68	67	272	242,875
Ryo Ishikawa	63	68	71	71	273	180,900
Chad Campbell	68	70	69	67	274	147,400
Charles Howell	67	67	67	73	274	147,400
Whee Kim	68	66	67	73	274	147,400
Steve Wheatcroft	65	73	68	68	274	147,400
Brian Davis	70	70	66	69	275	113,900
Greg Owen	66	68	73	68	275	113,900
Ollie Schniederjans	66	69	68	72	275	113,900
Kevin Chappell	64	68	67	77	276	93,800
Jason Kokrak	71	68	67	70	276	93,800
Tiger Woods	68	66	74	68	276	93,800
Hudson Swafford	68	72	67	70	277	61,193.34
Jimmy Walker	71	63	73	70	277	61,193.34
Will Wilcox	68	71	70	68	277	61,193.34
Brice Garnett	69	65	72	71	277	61,193.33
Adam Hadwin	67	70	69	71	277	61,193.33
Pat Perez	67	67	72	71	277	61,193.33
John Peterson	67	70	68	72	277	61,193.33
Andres Romero	69	69	67	72	277	61,193.33
Cameron Tringale	68	69	67	73	277	61,193.33

	SCORES				TOTAL	MONEY
Jonas Blixt	66	74	69	69	278	38,115.56
Ken Duke	73	67	70	68	278	38,115.56
Jim Herman	68	71	71	68	278	38,115.56
John Huh	70	67	71	70	278	38,115.56
Carlos Ortiz	71	69	72	66	278	38,115.56
K.J. Choi	69	68	71	70	278	38,115.55
George McNeill	71	68	69	70	278	38,115.55
Brendan Steele	70	68	66	74	278	38,115.55
Vaughn Taylor	70	70	64	74	278	38,115.55
Tony Finau	71	67	69	72	279	26,130
James Hahn	71	67	70	71	279	26,130
Tom Hoge	69	70	70	70	279	26,130
Colt Knost	71	67	68	73	279	26,130
Russell Knox	69	67	71	72	279	26,130
Bryce Molder	69	69	72	69	279	26,130
Mark Wilson	68	69	71	71	279	26,130
Aaron Baddeley	69	68	72	71	280	18,224
Ernie Els	64	74	68	74	280	18,224
Harris English	70	67	72	71	280	18,224
Retief Goosen	63	73	71	73	280	18,224
Billy Hurley	70	70	72	68	280	18,224
Kyle Reifers	71	67	70	72	280	18,224
Gonzalo Fernandez-Castano	66	71	69	75	281	15,467.43
Justin Leonard	64	72	70	75	281	15,467.43
S.J. Park	68	72	72	69	281	15,467.43
Jonathan Randolph	69	68	70	74	281	15,467.43
Vijay Singh	69	70	70	72	281	15,467.43
Nick Taylor	68	69	72	72	281	15,467.43
Shawn Stefani	71	67	68	75	281	15,467.42
Brendon de Jonge	69	70	73	70	282	14,807
Michael Putnam	71	66	75	70	282	14,807
Jonathan Byrd	68	72	72	71	283	14,539
John Merrick	72	68	69	74	283	14,539
Ricky Barnes	69	68	69	78	284	14,137
J.J. Henry	70	69	68	77	284	14,137
William McGirt	69	69	75	71	284	14,137
Jeff Overton	65	73	74	72	284	14,137
Steven Bowditch	68	68	67	83	286	13,668
Mark Hubbard	65	74	71	76	286	13,668
Patrick Rodgers	66	72	73	75	286	13,668
Chesson Hadley	69	71	74	73	287	13,400
Erik Compton	70	69	72	77	288	13,266
Arjun Atwal	66	71	76	76	289	13,065
Max Homa	72	68	72	77	289	13,065
Nicholas Thompson	70	69	79	74	292	12,864
Seung-Yul Noh	68	72	76	77	293	12,730

WGC - Bridgestone Invitational

Firestone Country Club, South Course, Akron, Ohio
Par 35-35–70; 7,400 yards

August 6-9
purse, $9,250,000

	SCORES				TOTAL	MONEY
Shane Lowry	70	66	67	66	269	$1,570,000
Bubba Watson	70	66	69	66	271	930,000
Jim Furyk	66	66	69	72	273	470,000
Justin Rose	67	71	63	72	273	470,000
Robert Streb	68	70	68	68	274	330,000
Brooks Koepka	69	69	68	69	275	219,000
Danny Lee	65	72	70	68	275	219,000

	SCORES				TOTAL	MONEY
David Lingmerth	70	71	66	68	275	219,000
Henrik Stenson	68	69	68	70	275	219,000
Rickie Fowler	67	72	70	67	276	149,500
Jordan Spieth	70	68	72	66	276	149,500
Steven Bowditch	73	69	63	72	277	126,000
Jason Day	69	69	70	69	277	126,000
Soren Kjeldsen	69	73	69	66	277	126,000
Kevin Na	69	70	71	68	278	109,000
Patrick Reed	71	67	72	68	278	109,000
Keegan Bradley	69	70	69	71	279	88,500
Paul Casey	68	73	71	67	279	88,500
Branden Grace	73	69	67	70	279	88,500
Russell Henley	70	70	70	69	279	88,500
Graeme McDowell	66	71	69	73	279	88,500
Ian Poulter	68	72	65	74	279	88,500
Lee Westwood	68	70	73	68	279	88,500
Danny Willett	70	71	69	69	279	88,500
Matt Kuchar	72	68	72	68	280	74,666.67
Webb Simpson	68	70	72	70	280	74,666.67
Camilo Villegas	75	69	71	65	280	74,666.67
Bernd Wiesberger	71	74	66	69	280	74,666.67
Bill Haas	74	69	67	70	280	74,666.66
Marc Warren	71	70	69	70	280	74,666.66
Charley Hoffman	75	66	71	69	281	70,500
Charl Schwartzel	70	72	70	69	281	70,500
Billy Horschel	71	73	70	68	282	67,500
Zach Johnson	70	70	71	71	282	67,500
Marc Leishman	72	70	70	70	282	67,500
Brandt Snedeker	70	70	72	70	282	67,500
Sergio Garcia	71	67	72	73	283	63,000
J.B. Holmes	74	68	70	71	283	63,000
Kevin Kisner	73	69	73	68	283	63,000
Hideki Matsuyama	69	75	73	66	283	63,000
Marcel Siem	70	73	69	71	283	63,000
James Hahn	70	70	74	70	284	59,000
Ryan Moore	71	71	69	73	284	59,000
Louis Oosthuizen	72	70	72	70	284	59,000
Mikko Ilonen	74	73	70	68	285	55,000
Martin Kaymer	70	71	71	73	285	55,000
Joost Luiten	70	72	70	73	285	55,000
Koumei Oda	68	77	69	71	285	55,000
Adam Scott	72	69	71	73	285	55,000
Jamie Donaldson	70	71	71	74	286	51,000
Victor Dubuisson	68	74	73	71	286	51,000
Pablo Larrazabal	72	70	69	75	286	51,000
Anirban Lahiri	77	72	67	71	287	48,166.67
Jimmy Walker	73	73	70	71	287	48,166.67
Dustin Johnson	69	67	75	76	287	48,166.66
Stephen Gallacher	77	67	71	73	288	47,000
Byeong-Hun An	77	68	70	74	289	45,750
Thongchai Jaidee	73	71	73	72	289	45,750
Ben Martin	75	71	72	71	289	45,750
Gary Woodland	75	69	72	73	289	45,750
Francesco Molinari	69	74	74	73	290	44,625
Brendon Todd	74	72	68	76	290	44,625
Sangmoon Bae	71	75	73	72	291	43,875
Andrew Dodt	77	71	72	71	291	43,875
Phil Mickelson	76	70	71	74	291	43,875
Gary Stal	72	73	73	73	291	43,875
Fabian Gomez	75	72	73	72	292	43,125
Oliver Wilson	74	72	75	71	292	43,125
Thomas Bjorn	70	75	73	75	293	42,750
Padraig Harrington	72	72	74	76	294	42,375

	SCORES				TOTAL	MONEY
Ryan Palmer	74	75	73	72	294	42,375
Hunter Mahan	74	79	72	70	295	42,000
David Lipsky	72	74	72	78	296	41,750
Matt Every	72	77	76	73	298	41,500
Nick Cullen	77	74	75	75	301	41,125
Wen-Chong Liang	72	73	75	81	301	41,125
Troy Merritt	82	75	70	75	302	40,750

Barracuda Championship

Montreux Golf & Country Club, Reno, Nevada
Par 36-36–72; 7,472 yards

August 6-9
purse, $3,100,000

	POINTS				TOTAL	MONEY
J.J. Henry	13	11	17	6	47	$558,000
Kyle Reifers	9	14	2	22	47	334,800
(Henry defeated Reifers on second playoff hole.)						
Patrick Rodgers	15	6	14	11	46	210,800
Andres Gonzales	5	21	7	10	43	148,800
David Toms	13	9	18	2	42	124,000
Retief Goosen	6	11	16	8	41	111,600
Derek Fathauer	11	7	11	11	40	96,616.67
Steve Flesch	11	8	15	6	40	96,616.66
Brendan Steele	8	18	6	8	40	96,616.67
Tom Hoge	12	9	10	7	38	77,500
Colt Knost	5	10	12	11	38	77,500
Will Wilcox	9	12	5	12	38	77,500
Jonas Blixt	12	12	16	-3	37	62,000
Brian Davis	5	11	6	15	37	62,000
Robert Garrigus	12	9	16	-1	36	52,700
Jason Gore	11	1	8	16	36	52,700
Tyrone van Aswegen	8	11	9	8	36	52,700
Ricky Barnes	14	6	11	2	33	44,950
Carlos Ortiz	5	7	8	13	33	44,950
Ken Duke	10	8	11	3	32	38,750
Zack Sucher	18	3	7	4	32	38,750
Austin Cook	3	8	8	12	31	32,240
Oscar Fraustro	8	4	11	8	31	32,240
Brian Stuard	8	6	8	9	31	32,240
Jason Allred	11	10	2	7	30	24,722.50
Billy Hurley	12	3	13	2	30	24,722.50
Bill Lunde	5	5	11	9	30	24,722.50
Vaughn Taylor	8	10	2	10	30	24,722.50
Roberto Castro	8	12	7	2	29	20,150
Derek Ernst	1	9	6	13	29	20,150
Gonzalo Fernandez-Castano	7	9	8	5	29	20,150
Rod Pampling	7	6	7	9	29	20,150
Mark Wilson	1	9	12	7	29	20,150
Jonathan Byrd	3	9	15	1	28	16,740
K.J. Choi	0	10	11	7	28	16,740
Martin Flores	2	16	0	10	28	16,740
Joe Affrunti	5	9	4	9	27	13,020
Zac Blair	8	4	8	7	27	13,020
Jon Curran	7	5	7	8	27	13,020
Billy Mayfair	7	9	5	6	27	13,020
Alex Prugh	2	10	6	9	27	13,020
Roger Sloan	7	4	13	3	27	13,020
Chris Smith	11	10	8	-2	27	13,020
Josh Teater	8	1	10	8	27	13,020
Max Homa	8	7	7	4	26	9,920

	POINTS				TOTAL	MONEY
John Rollins	8	1	4	13	26	9,920
Troy Kelly	6	5	11	3	25	8,514.66
Jhonattan Vegas	7	5	10	3	25	8,514.67
Steve Wheatcroft	2	7	5	11	25	8,514.67
Charlie Beljan	4	6	6	8	24	7,626
Kent Jones	5	14	2	3	24	7,626
John Merrick	8	4	10	2	24	7,626
Greg Chalmers	3	8	-1	13	23	7,212.67
Trevor Immelman	10	0	1	12	23	7,212.67
Bryce Molder	6	5	4	8	23	7,212.66
Chris Riley	9	3	6	4	22	7,006
Kyle Stanley	4	9	9	0	22	7,006
Nicholas Thompson	5	13	0	4	22	7,006
Robert Allenby	5	6	7	3	21	6,789
Ben Crane	11	8	4	-2	21	6,789
Byron Smith	4	7	11	-1	21	6,789
D.J. Trahan	10	1	-1	11	21	6,789
Matt Bettencourt	2	10	6	1	19	6,603
Tom Gillis	7	2	2	8	19	6,603
Len Mattiace	5	6	7	-1	17	6,479
Andrew Putnam	9	7	-1	2	17	6,479
Ted Purdy	-1	10	2	5	16	6,386
John Chin	4	5	6	0	15	6,262
Dicky Pride	11	2	-3	5	15	6,262
Heath Slocum	8	4	6	-3	15	6,262
Kevin Streelman	2	7	3	2	14	6,138
Tim Petrovic	11	1	-2	0	10	6,076
Michael McCabe	4	5	-9	-1	-1	6,014

PGA Championship

Whistling Straits, Sheboygan, Wisconsin
Par 36-36-72; 7,501 yards

August 13-16
purse, $10,000,000

	SCORES				TOTAL	MONEY
Jason Day	68	67	66	67	268	$1,800,000
Jordan Spieth	71	67	65	68	271	1,080,000
Branden Grace	71	69	64	69	273	680,000
Justin Rose	69	67	68	70	274	480,000
Brooks Koepka	73	69	67	66	275	367,500
Anirban Lahiri	70	67	70	68	275	367,500
George Coetzee	74	65	70	67	276	293,000
Dustin Johnson	66	73	68	69	276	293,000
Matt Kuchar	68	72	68	68	276	293,000
Tony Finau	71	66	69	71	277	243,000
Robert Streb	70	73	67	67	277	243,000
Russell Henley	68	71	70	69	278	185,400
Martin Kaymer	70	70	65	73	278	185,400
David Lingmerth	67	70	75	66	278	185,400
Brandt Snedeker	71	70	68	69	278	185,400
Brendan Steele	69	69	73	67	278	185,400
Rory McIlroy	71	71	68	69	279	148,000
Victor Dubuisson	76	70	67	67	280	126,000
Phil Mickelson	72	73	66	69	280	126,000
Justin Thomas	72	70	68	70	280	126,000
Hiroshi Iwata	77	63	70	71	281	97,666.66
Matt Jones	68	65	73	75	281	97,666.66
Bubba Watson	72	71	70	68	281	97,666.66
J.B. Holmes	68	71	69	74	282	86,000
Ernie Els	71	71	69	72	283	74,600

	SCORES				TOTAL	MONEY
Tyrrell Hatton	73	72	68	70	283	74,600
Billy Horschel	72	68	68	75	283	74,600
Cameron Smith	74	68	70	71	283	74,600
Henrik Stenson	76	66	70	71	283	74,600
Paul Casey	70	70	70	74	284	56,057.14
Rickie Fowler	73	70	70	71	284	56,057.14
Jim Furyk	73	70	69	72	284	56,057.14
Louis Oosthuizen	72	71	72	69	284	56,057.14
Patrick Reed	75	69	67	73	284	56,057.14
Steve Stricker	71	72	71	70	284	56,057.14
Nick Watney	78	68	68	70	284	56,057.14
Jason Bohn	74	71	66	74	285	39,200
Hideki Matsuyama	70	70	71	74	285	39,200
Ryan Moore	73	70	75	67	285	39,200
Charl Schwartzel	73	69	68	75	285	39,200
Vijay Singh	73	71	71	70	285	39,200
Boo Weekley	75	70	65	75	285	39,200
Kevin Chappell	73	68	78	67	286	30,000
Luke Donald	72	70	70	74	286	30,000
Danny Lee	68	77	69	72	286	30,000
Hunter Mahan	72	68	73	73	286	30,000
Lee Westwood	72	72	70	72	286	30,000
Thomas Bjorn	69	75	69	74	287	25,750
Harris English	68	71	76	72	287	25,750
Scott Piercy	68	70	74	75	287	25,750
Marcel Siem	70	70	73	74	287	25,750
Marc Warren	72	73	69	73	287	25,750
Y.E. Yang	70	72	72	73	287	25,750
Sergio Garcia	72	71	75	70	288	22,500
Mikko Ilonen	72	73	71	72	288	22,500
Troy Merritt	74	70	75	69	288	22,500
Francesco Molinari	71	73	69	75	288	22,500
Webb Simpson	71	71	72	74	288	22,500
Kevin Streelman	73	71	74	70	288	22,500
Danny Willett	74	70	71	73	288	22,500
Keegan Bradley	76	70	72	71	289	20,200
Emiliano Grillo	70	73	72	74	289	20,200
Chesson Hadley	73	71	70	75	289	20,200
Sangmoon Bae	71	72	72	75	290	19,400
Brendon de Jonge	72	71	75	73	291	18,800
Bill Haas	73	72	71	75	291	18,800
Charles Howell	70	70	77	74	291	18,800
Kiradech Aphibarnrat	72	72	73	75	292	18,200
Jason Dufner	71	75	69	77	292	18,200
Nick Taylor	73	73	75	71	292	18,200
Brian Gaffney	71	73	78	71	293	17,900
J.J. Henry	75	70	74	75	294	17,700
Sean O'Hair	75	68	73	78	294	17,700
Koumei Oda	79	67	72	76	294	17,700
Morgan Hoffmann	72	74	72	78	296	17,450
Carl Pettersson	76	70	75	75	296	17,450
James Morrison	69	74	76	78	297	17,300

Out of Final 36 Holes

Padraig Harrington	76	71	147	Ryan Palmer	75	72	147
David Hearn	76	71	147	Rory Sabbatini	71	76	147
Zach Johnson	75	72	147	John Senden	71	76	147
Kevin Kisner	75	72	147	Bernd Wiesberger	72	75	147
Martin Laird	76	71	147	Daniel Berger	74	74	148
Marc Leishman	79	68	147	Rafa Cabrera-Bello	73	75	148
Shane Lowry	78	69	147	Tim Clark	75	73	148
Shaun Micheel	74	73	147	Ryan Helminen	76	72	148

Russell Knox	77	71	148	Thongchai Jaidee	74	78	152
George McNeill	71	77	148	Davis Love	79	73	152
Kevin Na	74	74	148	Joost Luiten	80	72	152
Richie Ramsay	81	67	148	Benjamin Polland	76	76	152
Jimmy Walker	75	73	148	David Toms	77	75	152
Tiger Woods	75	73	148	Cameron Tringale	78	74	152
Byeong-Hun An	75	74	149	Brett Jones	75	78	153
Steven Bowditch	74	75	149	Alexander Levy	77	76	153
Matt Dobyns	76	73	149	Ben Martin	76	77	153
Tommy Fleetwood	77	72	149	Eddie Pepperell	78	75	153
James Hahn	75	74	149	Rich Beem	76	78	154
Graeme McDowell	73	76	149	Matt Every	74	80	154
Geoff Ogilvy	74	75	149	Johan Kok	77	77	154
Pat Perez	74	75	149	John Daly	73	82	155
Shawn Stefani	74	75	149	Brent Snyder	76	79	155
Brendon Todd	76	73	149	Fabian Gomez	79	78	157
Ross Fisher	76	74	150	Charley Hoffman	79	78	157
Miguel Angel Jimenez	76	74	150	Steven Young	77	81	158
Soren Kjeldsen	72	78	150	Darren Clarke	78	81	159
Colin Montgomerie	78	72	150	Charles Frost	76	83	159
Ian Poulter	75	75	150	Omar Uresti	77	82	159
Grant Sturgeon	77	73	150	Sean Dougherty	79	81	160
Andy Sullivan	78	72	150	Jeff Olson	79	82	161
Camilo Villegas	75	75	150	Mark Brooks	84	78	162
David Howell	73	78	151	Austin Peters	82	81	163
Pablo Larrazabal	79	72	151	Brian Cairns	83	81	164
Adam Rainaud	74	77	151	Daniel Venezio	89	76	165
Adam Scott	76	75	151	Ryan Kennedy	79	90	169
Bob Sowards	75	76	151	Alan Morin	87	82	169
Chris Wood	76	75	151	Alex Cejka	76		WD
Stephen Gallacher	76	76	152	Jamie Donaldson	79		WD
Brian Harman	78	74	152				

Wyndham Championship

Sedgefield Country Club, Greensboro, North Carolina
Par 35-35–70; 7,127 yards

August 20-23
purse, $5,400,000

	SCORES				TOTAL	MONEY
Davis Love	64	66	69	64	263	$972,000
Jason Gore	66	67	62	69	264	583,200
Scott Brown	66	65	66	68	265	280,800
Paul Casey	66	66	66	67	265	280,800
Charl Schwartzel	67	66	66	66	265	280,800
Bill Haas	65	66	68	67	266	174,825
Brooks Koepka	67	67	67	65	266	174,825
Carl Pettersson	64	67	68	67	266	174,825
Webb Simpson	67	67	64	68	266	174,825
Jonas Blixt	65	70	62	70	267	129,600
Ben Martin	67	67	67	66	267	129,600
Ryan Moore	66	69	65	67	267	129,600
Tiger Woods	64	65	68	70	267	129,600
Martin Kaymer	64	68	70	66	268	94,500
Justin Leonard	68	66	65	69	268	94,500
William McGirt	62	70	68	68	268	94,500
Sam Saunders	65	69	69	65	268	94,500
Byeong-Hun An	67	69	67	66	269	63,450
Jonathan Byrd	67	70	67	65	269	63,450
Derek Ernst	63	69	69	68	269	63,450
Lucas Glover	66	70	67	66	269	63,450
Jim Herman	63	69	66	71	269	63,450
Jerry Kelly	67	69	67	66	269	63,450

	SCORES				TOTAL	MONEY
Spencer Levin	66	71	69	63	269	63,450
Cameron Smith	67	68	69	65	269	63,450
Luke Donald	68	67	67	68	270	39,960
Oscar Fraustro	65	68	69	68	270	39,960
Morgan Hoffmann	63	71	67	69	270	39,960
Camilo Villegas	66	69	67	68	270	39,960
Will Wilcox	70	67	67	66	270	39,960
Charles Howell	67	68	69	67	271	30,625.72
Ryo Ishikawa	71	66	68	66	271	30,625.72
Vijay Singh	66	70	69	66	271	30,625.72
Chad Campbell	65	65	70	71	271	30,625.71
Harris English	68	65	67	71	271	30,625.71
George McNeill	67	68	67	69	271	30,625.71
Nick Watney	66	65	68	72	271	30,625.71
George Coetzee	65	69	69	69	272	23,220
Gonzalo Fernandez-Castano	66	69	67	70	272	23,220
Tom Hoge	62	67	72	71	272	23,220
Cameron Percy	65	66	67	74	272	23,220
Patrick Rodgers	67	66	67	72	272	23,220
Tim Clark	66	71	67	69	273	18,360
Austin Cook	70	67	69	67	273	18,360
Brandt Snedeker	70	61	67	75	273	18,360
Daniel Summerhays	67	70	69	67	273	18,360
Branden Grace	67	70	68	69	274	14,526
Kyle Reifers	68	69	69	68	274	14,526
Vaughn Taylor	67	70	67	70	274	14,526
Michael Thompson	66	68	72	68	274	14,526
Greg Chalmers	67	70	70	68	275	12,787.20
Jason Dufner	67	70	65	73	275	12,787.20
Adam Hadwin	68	68	66	73	275	12,787.20
Alex Prugh	70	67	72	66	275	12,787.20
Kyle Stanley	68	69	71	67	275	12,787.20
Martin Flores	66	68	68	74	276	12,204
Luke Guthrie	69	67	70	70	276	12,204
Justin Thomas	67	68	66	75	276	12,204
John Huh	70	65	73	69	277	11,826
Martin Laird	68	66	74	69	277	11,826
Scott Langley	71	66	68	72	277	11,826
Bryce Molder	66	67	73	71	277	11,826
K.J. Choi	68	69	72	69	278	11,502
Adam Scott	67	69	71	71	278	11,502
Bo Van Pelt	69	67	73	70	279	11,340
Roberto Castro	67	70	71	72	280	11,178
Troy Kelly	68	68	69	75	280	11,178
Ernie Els	67	70	75	73	285	11,016
Byron Smith	67	70	78	73	288	10,908

PGA Tour Playoffs for the FedExCup

The Barclays

Plainfield Country Club, Edison, New Jersey
Par 34-36–70; 7,012 yards

August 27-30
purse, $8,250,000

	SCORES				TOTAL	MONEY
Jason Day	68	68	63	62	261	$1,485,000
Henrik Stenson	68	66	67	66	267	891,000
Bubba Watson	65	68	67	69	269	561,000
Zac Blair	69	68	67	66	270	363,000
Zach Johnson	69	65	67	69	270	363,000
Sangmoon Bae	69	67	63	72	271	276,375
Ryan Palmer	69	67	65	70	271	276,375
Daniel Summerhays	67	70	68	66	271	276,375
Jason Bohn	71	64	72	65	272	231,000
Dustin Johnson	70	70	67	65	272	231,000
Jim Furyk	68	69	69	67	273	198,000
Bryce Molder	66	71	67	69	273	198,000
Steven Bowditch	71	67	72	64	274	159,500
Jim Herman	69	69	69	67	274	159,500
Hideki Matsuyama	69	69	67	69	274	159,500
Tony Finau	65	69	71	70	275	127,875
Spencer Levin	65	71	67	72	275	127,875
Justin Rose	77	65	63	70	275	127,875
Justin Thomas	71	69	68	67	275	127,875
Kevin Kisner	67	71	65	73	276	96,112.50
Russell Knox	66	71	67	72	276	96,112.50
Kevin Na	69	69	67	71	276	96,112.50
Pat Perez	68	69	70	69	276	96,112.50
Kevin Chappell	72	68	70	67	277	66,825
Luke Donald	73	68	65	71	277	66,825
Carlos Ortiz	73	68	62	74	277	66,825
Rory Sabbatini	71	70	67	69	277	66,825
Brendon Todd	70	70	66	71	277	66,825
Mark Wilson	72	68	69	68	277	66,825
Jason Gore	71	69	70	68	278	46,933.34
Brian Harman	71	68	71	68	278	46,933.34
Webb Simpson	71	68	73	66	278	46,933.34
Jason Dufner	66	68	69	75	278	46,933.33
Harris English	74	68	66	70	278	46,933.33
Danny Lee	66	71	71	70	278	46,933.33
George McNeill	71	70	68	69	278	46,933.33
Cameron Tringale	66	71	69	72	278	46,933.33
Camilo Villegas	65	70	70	73	278	46,933.33
Paul Casey	66	76	69	68	279	33,000
Stewart Cink	67	73	67	72	279	33,000
Morgan Hoffmann	70	68	70	71	279	33,000
Matt Kuchar	71	70	66	72	279	33,000
Shawn Stefani	71	67	70	71	279	33,000
Robert Streb	68	68	70	73	279	33,000
David Hearn	70	69	73	68	280	24,156
J.J. Henry	70	72	69	69	280	24,156
Sean O'Hair	68	68	70	74	280	24,156
John Senden	69	70	74	67	280	24,156
Johnson Wagner	67	71	73	69	280	24,156
Phil Mickelson	68	71	69	73	281	20,295
Scott Pinckney	70	71	69	71	281	20,295
Hudson Swafford	68	68	71	74	281	20,295
Bill Haas	71	70	67	74	282	19,008

	SCORES				TOTAL	MONEY
Matt Jones	67	72	72	71	282	19,008
Troy Merritt	71	71	69	71	282	19,008
Kevin Streelman	70	71	70	71	282	19,008
Nick Taylor	67	73	69	73	282	19,008
James Hahn	69	72	68	74	283	18,232.50
J.B. Holmes	70	71	73	69	283	18,232.50
Charles Howell	70	69	71	73	283	18,232.50
Lee Westwood	68	73	73	69	283	18,232.50
Ken Duke	71	70	68	75	284	17,572.50
Charley Hoffman	69	71	72	72	284	17,572.50
Scott Piercy	73	69	68	74	284	17,572.50
Patrick Reed	68	69	75	72	284	17,572.50
Ryo Ishikawa	68	74	68	75	285	17,077.50
Vijay Singh	70	70	72	73	285	17,077.50
Ben Martin	69	70	72	75	286	16,830
Jeff Overton	69	72	71	75	287	16,582.50
Jimmy Walker	72	69	71	75	287	16,582.50
Fabian Gomez	71	71	69	78	289	16,335
Russell Henley	73	69	76	72	290	16,170

Deutsche Bank Championship

TPC Boston, Norton, Massachusetts
Par 36-35–71; 7,242 yards

September 4-7
purse, $8,250,000

	SCORES				TOTAL	MONEY
Rickie Fowler	67	67	67	68	269	$1,485,000
Henrik Stenson	67	68	65	70	270	891,000
Charley Hoffman	67	63	76	67	273	561,000
Jim Furyk	71	65	70	70	276	311,025
Matt Jones	67	67	68	74	276	311,025
Hunter Mahan	69	73	64	70	276	311,025
Sean O'Hair	68	67	67	74	276	311,025
Patrick Reed	72	67	67	70	276	311,025
Jerry Kelly	71	66	68	72	277	222,750
Matt Kuchar	69	72	65	71	277	222,750
Daniel Summerhays	71	68	70	68	277	222,750
Daniel Berger	68	69	68	73	278	138,600
Kevin Chappell	67	67	71	73	278	138,600
Jason Day	68	68	73	69	278	138,600
Harris English	67	74	68	69	278	138,600
Brian Harman	70	70	71	67	278	138,600
Kevin Kisner	71	71	66	70	278	138,600
Russell Knox	70	65	68	75	278	138,600
William McGirt	73	70	66	69	278	138,600
Louis Oosthuizen	73	67	67	71	278	138,600
Gary Woodland	68	70	69	71	278	138,600
Brendon de Jonge	65	68	73	73	279	85,800
Zach Johnson	69	65	74	71	279	85,800
Rory Sabbatini	69	74	66	70	279	85,800
Keegan Bradley	71	66	74	69	280	65,793.75
Ben Martin	73	68	70	69	280	65,793.75
Hideki Matsuyama	71	65	69	75	280	65,793.75
Kyle Reifers	71	73	69	67	280	65,793.75
Chris Kirk	74	69	67	71	281	54,862.50
Rory McIlroy	70	74	71	66	281	54,862.50
Pat Perez	71	71	70	69	281	54,862.50
Bubba Watson	73	69	71	68	281	54,862.50
Fabian Gomez	76	69	73	64	282	43,587.50
Danny Lee	70	66	69	77	282	43,587.50

	SCORES				TOTAL	MONEY
Ian Poulter	67	72	69	74	282	43,587.50
John Senden	76	69	67	70	282	43,587.50
Hudson Swafford	69	69	68	76	282	43,587.50
Camilo Villegas	72	72	69	69	282	43,587.50
Sangmoon Bae	69	70	69	75	283	33,825
Alex Cejka	70	70	72	71	283	33,825
Luke Donald	67	71	72	73	283	33,825
Troy Merritt	74	67	68	74	283	33,825
Robert Streb	69	72	72	70	283	33,825
J.B. Holmes	74	68	69	73	284	22,343.75
Dustin Johnson	70	70	68	76	284	22,343.75
Colt Knost	67	73	75	69	284	22,343.75
Davis Love	69	75	67	73	284	22,343.75
Carl Pettersson	72	70	69	73	284	22,343.75
Webb Simpson	74	69	70	71	284	22,343.75
Brandt Snedeker	71	73	68	72	284	22,343.75
Brendan Steele	70	67	72	75	284	22,343.75
Brendon Todd	70	74	70	70	284	22,343.75
Cameron Tringale	75	66	69	74	284	22,343.75
Johnson Wagner	72	73	72	67	284	22,343.75
Nick Watney	72	70	69	73	284	22,343.75
Charles Howell	70	70	70	75	285	18,562.50
Spencer Levin	73	71	69	72	285	18,562.50
Justin Thomas	72	70	69	74	285	18,562.50
Boo Weekley	74	71	72	68	285	18,562.50
Zac Blair	70	69	71	76	286	17,820
Jason Dufner	69	70	74	73	286	17,820
Bill Haas	73	71	70	72	286	17,820
Kevin Na	72	68	72	74	286	17,820
Scott Pinckney	75	70	66	75	286	17,820
Phil Mickelson	70	73	70	74	287	17,077.50
Carlos Ortiz	74	67	70	76	287	17,077.50
Ryan Palmer	68	77	71	71	287	17,077.50
Shawn Stefani	70	74	71	72	287	17,077.50
Scott Brown	70	72	74	73	289	16,500
Kevin Streelman	73	70	69	77	289	16,500
Mark Wilson	71	74	74	70	289	16,500
Billy Horschel	73	68	77	72	290	16,170
Morgan Hoffmann	69	74	76	72	291	16,005
Chesson Hadley	73	71	70	80	294	15,840

BMW Championship

Conway Farms Golf Club, Lake Forest, Illinois
Par 35-36–71; 7,198 yards

September 17-20
purse, $8,250,000

	SCORES				TOTAL	MONEY
Jason Day	61	63	69	69	262	$1,485,000
Daniel Berger	65	64	70	69	268	891,000
Scott Piercy	67	65	67	70	269	561,000
Rickie Fowler	69	66	66	69	270	341,000
J.B. Holmes	70	65	67	68	270	341,000
Rory McIlroy	68	65	67	70	270	341,000
Dustin Johnson	71	62	68	70	271	257,125
Hideki Matsuyama	72	63	70	66	271	257,125
Cameron Tringale	72	64	69	66	271	257,125
Kevin Na	65	66	70	71	272	206,250
Henrik Stenson	71	63	71	67	272	206,250
Bubba Watson	65	70	72	65	272	206,250
Zach Johnson	68	69	72	64	273	145,750

	SCORES				TOTAL	MONEY
George McNeill	67	65	72	69	273	145,750
Justin Rose	70	64	70	69	273	145,750
Jordan Spieth	65	66	72	70	273	145,750
Brendan Steele	68	67	68	70	273	145,750
Justin Thomas	65	67	70	71	273	145,750
Harris English	65	68	69	72	274	103,537.50
Bill Haas	68	67	73	66	274	103,537.50
Louis Oosthuizen	71	66	68	69	274	103,537.50
Nick Watney	68	66	71	69	274	103,537.50
Paul Casey	67	69	71	68	275	73,425
Kevin Chappell	66	69	68	72	275	73,425
Ryan Palmer	67	67	73	68	275	73,425
Robert Streb	71	67	70	67	275	73,425
Brendon Todd	66	63	76	70	275	73,425
Keegan Bradley	68	66	72	70	276	57,337.50
David Hearn	74	69	69	64	276	57,337.50
Ryan Moore	68	67	73	68	276	57,337.50
Patrick Reed	68	69	69	70	276	57,337.50
James Hahn	74	65	70	68	277	44,667.86
Billy Horschel	71	69	70	67	277	44,667.86
Matt Jones	72	66	72	67	277	44,667.86
Phil Mickelson	68	70	72	67	277	44,667.86
Jimmy Walker	69	69	71	68	277	44,667.86
Brendon de Jonge	67	67	69	74	277	44,667.85
Hunter Mahan	68	68	69	72	277	44,667.85
Sergio Garcia	70	65	72	71	278	36,300
Fabian Gomez	70	68	71	69	278	36,300
Steven Bowditch	70	66	75	68	279	31,350
Kevin Kisner	72	70	71	66	279	31,350
Matt Kuchar	67	67	70	75	279	31,350
Daniel Summerhays	70	72	66	71	279	31,350
Russell Knox	74	68	68	70	280	26,400
Pat Perez	72	71	71	66	280	26,400
Tony Finau	72	64	77	68	281	23,265
Danny Lee	67	70	73	71	281	23,265
Russell Henley	74	67	72	69	282	20,583.75
Brooks Koepka	75	65	70	72	282	20,583.75
David Lingmerth	73	65	70	74	282	20,583.75
William McGirt	71	72	69	70	282	20,583.75
Sangmoon Bae	74	70	67	72	283	18,920
Zac Blair	70	70	74	69	283	18,920
Brian Harman	66	69	72	76	283	18,920
Charley Hoffman	72	71	70	70	283	18,920
Sean O'Hair	68	72	71	72	283	18,920
Ian Poulter	70	68	74	71	283	18,920
Shawn Stefani	72	71	71	70	284	18,315
Chris Kirk	72	72	71	70	285	18,067.50
Gary Woodland	69	71	70	75	285	18,067.50
Jerry Kelly	71	73	71	71	286	17,737.50
Troy Merritt	73	70	71	72	286	17,737.50
Jason Bohn	71	71	71	74	287	17,407.50
Webb Simpson	71	76	71	69	287	17,407.50
Brandt Snedeker	71	77	69	72	289	17,160
Rory Sabbatini	72	73	73	72	290	16,995
Ben Martin	73	71	80	71	295	16,747.50
Bryce Molder	77	71	69	78	295	16,747.50
Jim Furyk					WD	

Tour Championship

East Lake Golf Club, Atlanta, Georgia
Par 35-35–70; 7,307 yards

September 24-27
purse, $8,250,000

	SCORES				TOTAL	MONEY
Jordan Spieth	68	66	68	69	271	$1,485,000
Danny Lee	69	72	69	65	275	618,750
Justin Rose	70	68	71	66	275	618,750
Henrik Stenson	63	68	72	72	275	618,750
Paul Casey	65	70	71	70	276	302,500
Dustin Johnson	69	72	71	64	276	302,500
Bubba Watson	70	71	68	67	276	302,500
J.B. Holmes	68	72	68	69	277	255,750
Zach Johnson	66	70	71	70	277	255,750
Jason Day	69	71	70	68	278	228,525
Matt Kuchar	71	70	69	68	278	228,525
Daniel Berger	69	73	68	70	280	196,350
Steven Bowditch	68	69	73	70	280	196,350
Rickie Fowler	69	70	67	74	280	196,350
Hideki Matsuyama	69	72	69	70	280	196,350
Rory McIlroy	66	71	70	74	281	171,600
Kevin Na	68	73	70	70	281	171,600
Sangmoon Bae	73	70	72	69	284	160,050
Brooks Koepka	68	74	72	70	284	160,050
Robert Streb	75	75	69	65	284	160,050
Jimmy Walker	73	71	74	66	284	160,050
Harris English	71	76	71	67	285	148,500
Charley Hoffman	73	72	70	70	285	148,500
Brandt Snedeker	68	72	75	70	285	148,500
Scott Piercy	74	73	73	70	290	141,900
Bill Haas	72	73	72	76	293	138,600
Patrick Reed	72	74	77	71	294	136,950
Kevin Kisner	76	77	72	73	298	135,300
Louis Oosthuizen					WD	

Final Standings – PGA Tour Playoffs for the FedExCup

RANK	NAME	FEDEXCUP POINTS	BONUS MONEY
1	Jordan Spieth	3,800	$10,000,000
2	Henrik Stenson	2,307	3,000,000
3	Jason Day	2,290	2,000,000
4	Rickie Fowler	1,838	1,500,000
5	Bubba Watson	1,680	1,000,000
6	Zach Johnson	1,450	800,000
7	Dustin Johnson	1,360	700,000
8	Justin Rose	1,235	600,000
9	Danny Lee	1,123	550,000
10	Charley Hoffman	992	500,000
11	Daniel Berger	878	300,000
12	Patrick Reed	656	290,000
13	Paul Casey	632	280,000
14	J.B. Holmes	618	270,000
15	Rory McIlroy	602	250,000
16	Hideki Matsuyama	558	245,000
16	Jimmy Walker	558	240,000
18	Robert Streb	542	235,000
19	Matt Kuchar	530	230,000
20	Steven Bowditch	454	225,000
21	Kevin Kisner	444	220,000
22	Scott Piercy	432	215,000

RANK	NAME	FEDEXCUP POINTS	BONUS MONEY
23	Brandt Snedeker	416	210,000
24	Brooks Koepka	414	205,000
25	Kevin Na	410	200,000
26	Sangmoon Bae	390	195,000
27	Bill Haas	380	190,000
28	Harris English	360	185,000
29	Jim Furyk	304	180,000
30	Louis Oosthuizen	176	175,000

The Presidents Cup

See Special Events section.

Start of 2016 Season

Frys.com Open

Silverado Country Club, North Course, Napa, California
Par 36-36–72; 7,203 yards

October 15-18
purse, $6,000,000

NAME		SCORES			TOTAL	MONEY
Emiliano Grillo	68	71	65	69	273	$1,080,000
Kevin Na	68	71	64	70	273	648,000
(Grillo defeated Na on second playoff hole.)						
Jason Bohn	72	68	64	70	274	312,000
Justin Thomas	66	70	69	69	274	312,000
Tyrone van Aswegen	69	68	69	68	274	312,000
Kyle Reifers	68	71	65	72	276	194,250
Patrick Rodgers	68	69	69	70	276	194,250
Justin Rose	67	69	68	72	276	194,250
Charl Schwartzel	71	68	69	68	276	194,250
Luke Guthrie	71	70	66	70	277	128,571.43
Smylie Kaufman	68	72	69	68	277	128,571.43
Ryan Moore	72	70	67	68	277	128,571.43
Chris Stroud	69	69	71	68	277	128,571.43
Jhonattan Vegas	64	71	69	73	277	128,571.43
Will Wilcox	68	67	69	73	277	128,571.43
Andrew Loupe	68	72	63	74	277	128,571.42
Fabian Gomez	70	72	70	66	278	73,333.34
Chez Reavie	70	71	71	66	278	73,333.34
Brandt Snedeker	73	69	69	67	278	73,333.34
Daniel Berger	70	69	70	69	278	73,333.33
Lucas Glover	69	73	66	70	278	73,333.33
Charles Howell	69	69	68	72	278	73,333.33
Hideki Matsuyama	70	70	69	69	278	73,333.33
Brendan Steele	63	70	69	76	278	73,333.33
Hudson Swafford	69	72	67	70	278	73,333.33
Erik Compton	69	72	70	68	279	45,300
Rory McIlroy	68	71	71	69	279	45,300
Sean O'Hair	68	71	68	72	279	45,300
Brendon Todd	69	73	68	69	279	45,300
Mark Hubbard	68	72	70	70	280	39,900
William McGirt	72	69	70	69	280	39,900
Carlos Ortiz	71	71	69	70	281	31,133.34
Daniel Summerhays	67	74	70	70	281	31,133.34

	SCORES				TOTAL	MONEY
David Toms	71	71	69	70	281	31,133.34
Miguel Angel Carballo	72	69	67	73	281	31,133.33
Ben Crane	69	71	68	73	281	31,133.33
Graham DeLaet	67	68	69	77	281	31,133.33
Tony Finau	70	69	70	72	281	31,133.33
Freddie Jacobson	69	73	67	72	281	31,133.33
Hunter Mahan	69	73	67	72	281	31,133.33
Adam Hadwin	72	67	71	72	282	21,000
James Hahn	74	66	68	74	282	21,000
Russell Henley	67	69	72	74	282	21,000
Jerry Kelly	72	69	71	70	282	21,000
Colt Knost	71	66	72	73	282	21,000
Brooks Koepka	69	72	66	75	282	21,000
Kevin Streelman	69	73	69	71	282	21,000
Jonas Blixt	70	68	74	71	283	14,914.29
Spencer Levin	72	70	72	69	283	14,914.29
Carl Pettersson	70	72	71	70	283	14,914.29
Johnson Wagner	71	71	71	70	283	14,914.29
Jamie Lovemark	70	71	65	77	283	14,914.28
Ollie Schniederjans	70	71	70	72	283	14,914.28
Harold Varner	65	70	69	79	283	14,914.28
Tyler Aldridge	71	71	71	71	284	13,500
Aaron Baddeley	71	71	71	71	284	13,500
Angel Cabrera	70	72	72	70	284	13,500
Scott Langley	67	74	68	75	284	13,500
D.H. Lee	66	74	72	72	284	13,500
Steve Wheatcroft	71	69	72	72	284	13,500
J.J. Henry	68	69	74	74	285	12,960
Michael Kim	71	67	71	76	285	12,960
Will MacKenzie	72	70	71	72	285	12,960
Chad Collins	73	69	72	72	286	12,480
Martin Laird	65	71	74	76	286	12,480
Henrik Norlander	72	69	70	75	286	12,480
Cameron Tringale	70	72	72	72	286	12,480
Nick Watney	68	73	68	77	286	12,480
Stuart Appleby	70	72	72	74	288	12,060
Roberto Castro	71	71	70	76	288	12,060
Boo Weekley	69	69	75	76	289	11,880
Jim Herman	72	69	72	77	290	11,760
Jason Gore	67	73	73	78	291	11,640
Charlie Beljan	73	68	74		215	11,160
Shane Bertsch	71	71	73		215	11,160
Justin Leonard	72	70	73		215	11,160
Greg Owen	69	72	74		215	11,160
Scott Pinckney	70	72	73		215	11,160
Brett Stegmaier	68	71	76		215	11,160
Michael Thompson	68	74	73		215	11,160
Chris Kirk	72	70	74		216	10,620
Martin Piller	72	70	74		216	10,620

Shriners Hospitals for Children Open

TPC Summerlin, Las Vegas, Nevada
Par 35-36–71; 7,255 yards

October 22-25
purse, $6,400,000

	SCORES				TOTAL	MONEY
Smylie Kaufman	67	72	68	61	268	$1,152,000
Patton Kizzire	65	69	72	63	269	355,733.34
Cameron Tringale	68	65	70	66	269	355,733.34
Jason Bohn	68	66	69	66	269	355,733.33

	SCORES				TOTAL	MONEY
Alex Cejka	67	70	66	66	269	355,733.33
Kevin Na	68	66	68	67	269	355,733.33
Brett Stegmaier	66	66	68	69	269	355,733.33
Chad Campbell	65	67	70	68	270	192,000
William McGirt	66	73	69	62	270	192,000
Russell Henley	68	69	68	66	271	172,800
Morgan Hoffmann	66	66	69	71	272	153,600
Nick Watney	67	66	72	67	272	153,600
Patrick Rodgers	65	71	71	66	273	123,733.34
Brendon de Jonge	67	66	73	67	273	123,733.33
Jamie Lovemark	70	69	66	68	273	123,733.33
Tony Finau	69	71	66	68	274	84,053.34
Fabian Gomez	69	68	70	67	274	84,053.34
John Senden	70	65	72	67	274	84,053.34
Michael Kim	70	67	69	68	274	84,053.33
Ryan Palmer	65	69	72	68	274	84,053.33
Scott Stallings	68	71	67	68	274	84,053.33
Kevin Streelman	68	67	71	68	274	84,053.33
Daniel Summerhays	68	65	72	69	274	84,053.33
Camilo Villegas	67	69	70	68	274	84,053.33
Ricky Barnes	65	71	72	67	275	44,832
Rickie Fowler	72	65	70	68	275	44,832
David Hearn	64	70	72	69	275	44,832
Si Woo Kim	69	66	71	69	275	44,832
Kevin Kisner	68	71	67	69	275	44,832
Spencer Levin	71	65	74	65	275	44,832
Ben Martin	70	68	67	70	275	44,832
Scott Piercy	72	67	68	68	275	44,832
Rory Sabbatini	66	72	71	66	275	44,832
Nick Taylor	66	70	67	72	275	44,832
Mark Hubbard	64	70	72	70	276	32,960
D.H. Lee	65	75	68	68	276	32,960
Steve Marino	66	71	71	68	276	32,960
Russell Knox	69	70	72	66	277	28,160
Jason Kokrak	69	70	70	68	277	28,160
Ollie Schniederjans	68	67	74	68	277	28,160
Chris Stroud	66	71	72	68	277	28,160
J.J. Henry	67	72	68	71	278	24,960
Tyler Aldridge	64	68	72	75	279	19,968
Roberto Castro	67	71	69	72	279	19,968
Martin Laird	71	68	70	70	279	19,968
Ryan Moore	69	71	68	71	279	19,968
Greg Owen	65	74	71	69	279	19,968
Kyle Stanley	67	70	73	69	279	19,968
Jhonattan Vegas	70	70	70	69	279	19,968
Wes Roach	66	72	72	70	280	15,317.34
Michael Thompson	64	73	73	70	280	15,317.34
Shane Bertsch	65	70	72	73	280	15,317.33
Angel Cabrera	68	71	70	71	280	15,317.33
Ryo Ishikawa	65	72	72	71	280	15,317.33
Jimmy Walker	66	67	69	78	280	15,317.33
Stewart Cink	71	68	72	70	281	14,272
Brian Harman	68	67	75	71	281	14,272
Peter Malnati	70	67	71	73	281	14,272
Scott Pinckney	70	68	70	73	281	14,272
Webb Simpson	71	69	71	70	281	14,272
Tyrone van Aswegen	68	70	72	71	281	14,272
Kevin Chappell	69	71	70	72	282	13,568
Chad Collins	70	69	72	71	282	13,568
Chesson Hadley	68	71	72	71	282	13,568
Martin Piller	70	70	69	73	282	13,568
Shawn Stefani	69	70	71	72	282	13,568
Tom Hoge	69	71	71	72	283	13,056

	SCORES				TOTAL	MONEY
Chez Reavie	69	68	74	72	283	13,056
Steve Wheatcroft	67	70	71	75	283	13,056
Charles Howell	70	68	69	77	284	12,800
Freddie Jacobson	70	69	72	74	285	12,672
Hunter Stewart	72	68	72		212	12,544
Scott Brown	68	71	74		213	12,288
Hiroshi Iwata	67	73	73		213	12,288
Davis Love	68	69	76		213	12,288
Whee Kim	71	68	75		214	11,968
Jin Park	68	72	74		214	11,968
Alex Prugh	72	67	77		216	11,776
Colt Knost	71	69	77		217	11,648
Steven Bowditch	68	71	83		222	11,520

CIMB Classic

See Asia/Japan Tours chapter.

WGC - HSBC Champions

See Asia/Japan Tours chapter.

Sanderson Farms Championship

Country Club of Jackson, Jackson, Mississippi
Par 36-36–72; 7,364 yards
(Tournament completed on Monday—rain.)

November 5-9
purse, $4,100,000

	SCORES				TOTAL	MONEY
Peter Malnati	69	66	68	67	270	$738,000
William McGirt	71	66	66	68	271	360,800
David Toms	67	69	66	69	271	360,800
Aaron Baddeley	64	73	67	68	272	154,570
Roberto Castro	62	67	75	68	272	154,570
Patton Kizzire	67	69	66	70	272	154,570
Bryce Molder	64	69	70	69	272	154,570
Jhonattan Vegas	66	67	70	69	272	154,570
Brice Garnett	68	68	68	69	273	118,900
Andrew Loupe	66	71	70	67	274	106,600
D.J. Trahan	67	67	69	71	274	106,600
Tyler Aldridge	71	67	68	69	275	86,100
Martin Flores	67	72	67	69	275	86,100
Jason Kokrak	69	71	71	64	275	86,100
Gonzalo Fernandez-Castano	69	72	67	68	276	65,600
Cameron Percy	68	70	68	70	276	65,600
Michael Putnam	69	70	70	67	276	65,600
Brett Stegmaier	68	69	70	69	276	65,600
Johnson Wagner	69	69	69	69	276	65,600
Bronson Burgoon	68	70	68	71	277	41,358.75
Derek Ernst	69	69	69	70	277	41,358.75
Seung-Yul Noh	70	69	69	69	277	41,358.75
Patrick Rodgers	70	64	70	73	277	41,358.75
Andres Romero	66	72	72	67	277	41,358.75
Nick Taylor	69	66	71	71	277	41,358.75
Vaughn Taylor	68	71	68	70	277	41,358.75
Michael Thompson	67	67	71	72	277	41,358.75
Brian Davis	65	69	71	73	278	27,880
Adam Hadwin	65	71	73	69	278	27,880
Luke List	70	68	72	68	278	27,880

	SCORES				TOTAL	MONEY
Scott Stallings	67	73	67	71	278	27,880
Marc Turnesa	68	73	67	70	278	27,880
Ricky Barnes	68	67	74	70	279	21,661.67
Graham DeLaet	66	72	69	72	279	21,661.67
Dawie van der Walt	67	73	68	71	279	21,661.67
Tim Wilkinson	68	71	70	70	279	21,661.67
Luke Guthrie	71	70	71	67	279	21,661.66
Kelly Kraft	71	70	71	67	279	21,661.66
Jonathan Byrd	69	70	73	68	280	14,402.19
Henrik Norlander	69	69	70	72	280	14,402.19
Blayne Barber	69	72	71	68	280	14,402.18
Jason Bohn	67	70	70	73	280	14,402.18
Lucas Glover	69	68	74	69	280	14,402.18
John Huh	70	70	68	72	280	14,402.18
Sung-Hoon Kang	68	72	69	71	280	14,402.18
Carl Pettersson	67	69	73	71	280	14,402.18
Brian Stuard	70	70	75	65	280	14,402.18
Harold Varner	71	70	68	71	280	14,402.18
Boo Weekley	68	67	74	71	280	14,402.18
Michael Bradley	69	70	69	73	281	9,983.50
K.J. Choi	69	71	70	71	281	9,983.50
Derek Fathauer	70	71	70	70	281	9,983.50
Ollie Schniederjans	70	70	69	72	281	9,983.50
Mark Hubbard	69	70	73	70	282	9,307
Smylie Kaufman	71	67	73	71	282	9,307
Will MacKenzie	71	68	73	70	282	9,307
Rob Oppenheim	71	69	68	74	282	9,307
Jeff Overton	74	64	72	72	282	9,307
Tyrone van Aswegen	67	71	76	68	282	9,307
Andres Gonzales	68	70	69	76	283	9,020
Scott Langley	68	70	73	73	284	8,897
Ted Purdy	68	69	73	74	284	8,897
Billy Hurley	70	70	74	71	285	8,569
Michael Kim	66	74	72	73	285	8,569
Frank Lickliter	70	70	72	73	285	8,569
Jarrod Lyle	71	68	72	74	285	8,569
Billy Mayfair	70	70	72	73	285	8,569
Darron Stiles	69	70	71	75	285	8,569
Steve Flesch	68	71	75	72	286	8,282
Robert Garrigus	67	69	78	73	287	8,118
Tim Herron	70	70	74	73	287	8,118
Tom Hoge	71	68	72	76	287	8,118
Trey Mullinax	68	70	74	77	289	7,954
Tommy Gainey	70	71	74	75	290	7,872

OHL Classic at Mayakoba

El Camaleon Golf Club, Playa del Carmen, Mexico
Par 36-35–71; 6,987 yards
(Tournament completed on Monday—rain.)

November 12-16
purse, $6,200,000

	SCORES				TOTAL	MONEY
Graeme McDowell	67	63	70	66	266	$1,116,000
Jason Bohn	70	63	65	68	266	545,600
Russell Knox	70	65	65	66	266	545,600
(McDowell defeated Bohn and Knox on first playoff hole.)						
Derek Fathauer	65	66	66	71	268	297,600
Scott Brown	67	67	68	68	270	235,600
Harold Varner	70	62	68	70	270	235,600
Brice Garnett	67	66	69	69	271	207,700

	SCORES				TOTAL	MONEY
Keegan Bradley	67	71	68	66	272	186,000
Johnson Wagner	67	67	67	71	272	186,000
Peter Malnati	68	71	67	67	273	137,433.34
Boo Weekley	67	70	69	67	273	137,433.34
Zac Blair	68	67	68	70	273	137,433.33
Spencer Levin	68	66	68	71	273	137,433.33
Patrick Rodgers	67	66	69	71	273	137,433.33
Hunter Stewart	68	69	68	68	273	137,433.33
*Jon Rahm	69	68	66	70	273	
Jim Herman	69	67	70	68	274	84,165
Charles Howell	66	71	70	67	274	84,165
Freddie Jacobson	70	69	63	72	274	84,165
Si Woo Kim	68	64	72	70	274	84,165
Jason Kokrak	68	67	68	71	274	84,165
D.J. Trahan	66	71	67	70	274	84,165
Dawie van der Walt	66	74	64	70	274	84,165
Will Wilcox	69	66	68	71	274	84,165
Cameron Beckman	67	71	68	69	275	52,855
Bronson Burgoon	71	68	67	69	275	52,855
Roberto Castro	70	68	68	69	275	52,855
Shawn Stefani	65	68	69	73	275	52,855
Ryan Blaum	73	65	69	69	276	42,160
Jon Curran	68	71	67	70	276	42,160
Justin Leonard	65	68	67	76	276	42,160
Sam Saunders	68	71	68	69	276	42,160
Camilo Villegas	67	68	70	71	276	42,160
Tim Clark	69	69	67	72	277	32,756.67
Smylie Kaufman	68	72	66	71	277	32,756.67
Jerry Kelly	68	69	71	69	277	32,756.67
Kevin Streelman	69	67	70	71	277	32,756.67
Michael Thompson	66	68	70	73	277	32,756.66
Tim Wilkinson	69	70	69	69	277	32,756.66
James Driscoll	70	68	68	72	278	24,800
Jason Dufner	71	66	70	71	278	24,800
Brian Harman	70	68	69	71	278	24,800
Martin Laird	70	70	68	70	278	24,800
Seung-Yul Noh	70	70	67	71	278	24,800
Rory Sabbatini	70	68	67	73	278	24,800
Aaron Baddeley	65	73	70	71	279	18,153.60
Erik Compton	67	71	71	70	279	18,153.60
Henrik Norlander	68	68	69	74	279	18,153.60
Hudson Swafford	68	72	69	70	279	18,153.60
Tyrone van Aswegen	70	69	65	75	279	18,153.60
Ricky Barnes	70	69	69	72	280	14,738.29
Michael Kim	70	68	70	72	280	14,738.29
Colt Knost	67	68	69	76	280	14,738.29
D.H. Lee	69	68	70	73	280	14,738.29
Jason Gore	68	71	72	69	280	14,738.28
Sung-Hoon Kang	71	69	69	71	280	14,738.28
Jeff Overton	69	69	72	70	280	14,738.28
Blake Adams	68	69	70	74	281	13,764
Brendon de Jonge	69	69	70	73	281	13,764
Patton Kizzire	66	71	70	74	281	13,764
Will MacKenzie	67	70	72	72	281	13,764
Mark Wilson	67	72	69	73	281	13,764
Derek Ernst	68	72	68	74	282	13,144
Tom Hoge	70	70	71	71	282	13,144
Whee Kim	69	68	71	74	282	13,144
John Merrick	69	71	70	72	282	13,144
Wes Roach	70	67	70	75	282	13,144
Robert Allenby	69	71	70	73	283	12,586
Kelly Kraft	73	67	71	72	283	12,586
Matt Kuchar	72	67	68	76	283	12,586

	SCORES			TOTAL	MONEY
Brett Stegmaier	69	71	70	73	283	12,586
Shane Bertsch	69	71	67	77	284	12,214
Andres Gonzales	71	66	73	74	284	12,214
Rodolfo Cazaubon	69	71	72	73	285	11,904
David Hearn	68	70	75	72	285	11,904
Chez Reavie	71	69	70	75	285	11,904
Mark Hubbard	70	69	71	77	287	11,656
Steve Marino	72	68	72	79	291	11,532

The RSM Classic

Sea Island Resort, Sea Island, Georgia
Plantation Course: Par 36-36–72; 7,058 yards
Seaside Course: Par 35-35–70; 7,005 yards

November 19-22
purse, $5,700,000

	SCORES			TOTAL	MONEY
Kevin Kisner	65	67	64	64	260	$1,026,000
Kevin Chappell	66	65	68	67	266	615,600
Graeme McDowell	67	68	65	67	267	387,600
Jon Curran	67	70	66	66	269	273,600
Freddie Jacobson	65	67	71	67	270	228,000
Alex Cejka	67	67	67	70	271	190,950
Russell Henley	66	72	68	65	271	190,950
Jeff Overton	64	72	66	69	271	190,950
Chad Campbell	66	71	68	67	272	123,500
Jason Dufner	67	70	66	69	272	123,500
Lucas Glover	66	71	67	68	272	123,500
David Hearn	64	72	67	69	272	123,500
Tom Hoge	64	74	68	66	272	123,500
Charles Howell	67	70	67	68	272	123,500
John Huh	69	69	68	66	272	123,500
Jamie Lovemark	69	68	67	68	272	123,500
Scott Stallings	66	70	69	67	272	123,500
Mark Hubbard	68	69	69	67	273	69,377.15
Sean O'Hair	70	68	68	67	273	69,377.15
Scott Brown	67	72	65	69	273	69,377.14
Jim Herman	66	69	67	71	273	69,377.14
Si Woo Kim	66	72	67	68	273	69,377.14
Chris Kirk	68	71	69	65	273	69,377.14
Boo Weekley	72	66	71	64	273	69,377.14
Ricky Barnes	68	67	68	71	274	41,681.25
Harris English	68	71	66	69	274	41,681.25
Matt Kuchar	69	67	69	69	274	41,681.25
Trey Mullinax	65	70	70	69	274	41,681.25
Robert Streb	70	66	69	69	274	41,681.25
Brian Stuard	68	71	69	66	274	41,681.25
Jhonattan Vegas	68	72	66	68	274	41,681.25
Mark Wilson	72	67	66	69	274	41,681.25
Cameron Percy	67	69	69	70	275	27,049.10
Tyler Aldridge	70	67	67	71	275	27,049.09
Zac Blair	66	71	70	68	275	27,049.09
Brendon de Jonge	67	70	68	70	275	27,049.09
Bill Haas	67	71	71	66	275	27,049.09
Smylie Kaufman	68	70	66	71	275	27,049.09
Scott Langley	70	69	69	67	275	27,049.09
Davis Love	70	70	69	66	275	27,049.09
Chez Reavie	68	72	69	66	275	27,049.09
Kyle Stanley	66	67	71	71	275	27,049.09
Johnson Wagner	65	72	70	68	275	27,049.09
Jonathan Byrd	67	71	68	70	276	16,473

	SCORES				TOTAL	MONEY
Fabian Gomez	68	69	69	70	276	16,473
Hiroshi Iwata	67	67	72	70	276	16,473
Rob Oppenheim	65	71	69	71	276	16,473
Kyle Reifers	70	69	67	70	276	16,473
Patrick Rodgers	71	67	71	67	276	16,473
Vijay Singh	68	70	71	67	276	16,473
Tim Wilkinson	71	65	71	69	276	16,473
Stuart Appleby	69	70	67	71	277	13,224
Roberto Castro	68	70	71	68	277	13,224
K.J. Choi	68	71	69	69	277	13,224
Tim Herron	69	70	66	72	277	13,224
Michael Kim	67	67	70	73	277	13,224
Lucas Lee	71	69	69	68	277	13,224
Thomas Aiken	66	73	67	72	278	12,540
Rhein Gibson	71	69	68	70	278	12,540
D.A. Points	69	71	65	73	278	12,540
Justin Thomas	67	71	71	69	278	12,540
Dawie van der Walt	69	71	69	69	278	12,540
Matt Atkins	70	69	67	73	279	11,970
Stewart Cink	67	70	68	74	279	11,970
Jason Gore	65	69	73	72	279	11,970
David Lingmerth	66	73	69	71	279	11,970
Steve Marino	68	70	71	70	279	11,970
Andres Gonzales	68	71	68	73	280	11,571
Harold Varner	66	74	69	71	280	11,571
Derek Fathauer	67	70	71	73	281	11,286
Tim Petrovic	67	73	68	73	281	11,286
Scott Pinckney	71	69	69	72	281	11,286
Brett Stegmaier	68	70	68	76	282	11,058
Mark Hensby	68	69	71	76	284	10,944

Special Events

CVS Health Charity Classic

Rhode Island Country Club, Barrington, Rhode Island
Par 36-35–71; 6,688 yards

June 29-30
purse $1,500,000

	SCORES		TOTAL	MONEY (Team)
Keegan Bradley/Jon Curran	60	61	121	$300,000
Lexi Thompson/Harris English	60	63	123	200,000
Billy Horschel/Jimmy Walker	64	60	124	170,000
Morgan Pressel/Russell Henley	62	64	126	150,000
Steve Stricker/Bo Van Pelt	62	65	127	122,500
J.B. Holmes/Hunter Mahan	64	63	127	122,500
Billy Andrade/Brad Faxon	63	65	128	111,666
Bill Haas/Webb Simpson	61	67	128	111,666
Suzann Pettersen/Erik Compton	63	65	128	111,666
Juli Inkster/Peter Jacobsen	70	66	136	100,000

The Presidents Cup

Jack Nicklaus Golf Club Korea, Songdo IBD, Incheon, South Korea   October 8-11
Par 36-36–72; 7,380 yards

FIRST DAY
Foursomes

Bubba Watson and J.B. Holmes (US) defeated Adam Scott and Hideki Matsuyama, 3 and 2.
Louis Oosthuizen and Branden Grace (Int'l) defeated Matt Kuchar and Patrick Reed, 3 and 2.
Rickie Fowler and Jimmy Walker (US) defeated Anirban Lahiri and Thongchai Jaidee, 5 and 4.
Phil Mickelson and Zach Johnson (US) defeated Jason Day and Steven Bowditch, 2 up.
Jordan Spieth and Dustin Johnson (US) defeated Danny Lee and Marc Leishman, 4 and 3.

POINTS: United States 4, International 1

SECOND DAY
Fourball

Oosthuizen and Grace (Int'l) defeated Dustin Johnson and Spieth, 4 and 3.
Danny Lee and Sangmoon Bae (Int'l) defeated Fowler and Walker, 1 up.
Zach Johnson and Mickelson halved with Scott and Day.
Holmes and Watson (US) defeated Leishman and Bowditch, 2 up.
Charl Schwartzel and Jaidee (Int'l) defeated Bill Haas and Chris Kirk, 2 and 1.

POINTS: United States 5½, International 4½

THIRD DAY
Morning Foursomes

Oosthuizen and Grace (Int'l) defeated Reed and Fowler, 3 and 2.
Watson and Holmes (US) halved with Scott and Leishman.
Haas and Kuchar (US) halved with Bae and Matsuyama.
Spieth and Dustin Johnson (US) defeated Day and Schwartzel, 1 up.

POINTS: United States 7½, International 6½

Afternoon Fourball

Oosthuizen and Grace (Int'l) defeated Holmes and Watson, 1 up.
Mickelson and Zach Johnson (US) defeated Scott and Lahiri, 3 and 2.
Bae and Matsuyama (Int'l) defeated Jimmy Walker and Kirk, 6 and 5.
Reed and Spieth (US) defeated Day and Schwartzel, 3 and 2.

POINTS: United States 9½, International 8½

FOURTH DAY
Singles

Reed (US) halved with Oosthuizen.
Scott (Int'l) defeated Fowler, 6 and 5.
Dustin Johnson (US) defeated Lee, 2 and 1.
Matsuyama (Int'l) defeated Holmes, 1 up.
Watson (US) halved with Jaidee.
Bowditch (Int'l) defeated Walker, 2 up.
Mickelson (US) defeated Schwartzel, 5 and 4.
Kirk (US) defeated Lahiri, 1 up.
Leishman (Int'l) defeated Spieth, 1 up.
Zach Johnson (US) defeated Day, 3 and 2.
Grace (Int'l) defeated Kuchar, 2 and 1.
Haas (US) defeated Bae, 2 up.

TOTAL POINTS: United States 15½, International 14½

TaylorMade Pebble Beach Invitational

Pebble Beach GL: Par 36-36–72; 6,828 yards
Spyglass Hills GC: Par 36-36–72; 6,953 yards
Del Monte GC: Par 36-36–72; 6,365 yards
Pebble Beach, California

November 19-22
purse, $300,000

	SCORES				TOTAL	MONEY
Jeff Gove	69	69	69	66	273	$60,000
Kevin Sutherland	68	71	69	67	275	24,300
Duffy Waldorf	72	68	68	67	275	24,300
Travis Bertoni	71	69	68	69	277	10,600
Kyle Thompson	70	72	68	68	278	9,000
Joe Durant	68	70	71	70	279	7,500
Andrew Putnam	70	68	73	68	279	7,500
Ryan Armour	72	67	71	69	279	7,500
Woody Austin	75	68	72	65	280	6,250
Michael Bradley	74	67	73	67	281	5,350
Mike Goodes	69	74	71	67	281	5,350
Olin Browne	73	69	74	66	282	4,600
Marc Turnesa	68	73	71	70	282	4,600
Casey Wittenberg	71	69	70	72	282	4,600
Steve Flesch	74	69	72	68	283	3,735
Brandon Hagy	72	69	73	69	283	3,735
Tom Pernice, Jr.	72	70	68	73	283	3,735
Paul Goydos	69	72	73	70	284	3,025
Max Homa	69	73	73	69	284	3,025
Parker McLachlin	72	72	74	66	284	3,025
Arron Oberholser	69	70	75	70	284	3,025
Billy Andrade	72	75	70	68	285	2,550
Tommy Armour	73	69	73	70	285	2,550
Scott McCarron	72	73	68	72	285	2,550
Michael Schoolcraft	68	76	68	73	285	2,550
Sebastian Cappelen	74	73	70	70	287	2,275
James Driscoll	72	65	78	72	287	2,275
Natalie Gulbis	71	71	72	74	288	2,150
Gary Hallberg	73	73	71	71	288	2,150
Mark Wiebe	71	72	75	70	288	2,150
Steven Alker	75	71	71	72	289	2,070
John Mallinger	75	68	70	76	289	2,070
Billy Mayfair	70	72	74	74	290	2,020
Jeff Sluman	69	74	75	72	290	2,020
Mike Weir	74	74	71	71	290	2,020
Jennifer Johnson	74	73	72	73	292	1,970
Andy Miller	73	72	72	75	292	1,970
John Cook	73	73	72	75	293	1,920
Skip Kendall	72	73	70	78	293	1,920
Manuel Villegas	76	75	68	74	293	1,920
Brad Elder	71	71	76	77	295	1,900

Hero World Challenge

Albany, New Providence, Bahamas
Par 36-36–72; 7,267 yards

December 3-6
purse, $3,500,000

	SCORES				TOTAL	MONEY
Bubba Watson	67	67	63	66	263	$1,000,000
Patrick Reed	69	65	66	66	266	400,000
Rickie Fowler	70	68	65	64	267	250,000
Jordan Spieth	67	66	68	67	268	175,000

	SCORES				TOTAL	MONEY
Paul Casey	66	70	63	70	269	147,500
Bill Haas	67	66	68	68	269	147,500
Brooks Koepka	67	70	65	68	270	140,000
J.B. Holmes	71	68	68	64	271	130,000
Jimmy Walker	66	67	71	67	271	130,000
Chris Kirk	69	65	66	72	272	117,500
Adam Scott	67	70	66	69	272	117,500
Zach Johnson	66	70	67	70	273	110,000
Justin Rose	71	72	70	62	275	109,000
Matt Kuchar	70	66	69	71	276	108,000
Dustin Johnson	68	69	72	71	280	107,000
Billy Horschel	71	70	73	67	281	106,000
Anirban Lahiri	69	70	73	72	284	102,500
Hideki Matsuyama	75	73	70	66	284	102,500

Franklin Templeton Shootout

Tiburon Golf Course, Naples, Florida
Par 36-36–72; 7,288 yards

December 10-12
purse, $3,100,000

	SCORES			TOTAL	MONEY (Each)
Jason Dufner/Brandt Snedeker	61	64	61	186	$385,000
Harris English/Matt Kuchar	58	67	63	188	242,500
Daniel Berger/Charley Hoffman	60	64	66	190	145,000
Billy Horschel/Hunter Mahan	59	68	64	191	115,000
Cameron Tringale/Camilo Villegas	60	69	66	195	100,000
Graeme McDowell/Gary Woodland	59	70	67	196	90,000
Retief Goosen/Danny Lee	63	72	62	197	83,750
Sean O'Hair/Mike Weir	65	67	65	197	83,750
Kenny Perry/Steve Stricker	65	67	66	198	80,000
Charles Howell /Rory Sabbatini	62	68	69	199	76,250
Zach Johnson/Patrick Rodgers	64	67	68	199	76,250
J.B. Holmes/Patrick Reed	61	69	70	200	72,500

PNC Father/Son Challenge

Ritz-Carlton Golf Club, Orlando, Florida
Par 36-36–72; 7,023 yards

December 12-13
purse, $1,085,000

	SCORES		TOTAL	MONEY (Won by professional)
Lanny/Tucker Wadkins	61	63	124	$100,000
Fred/Taylor Funk	62	62	124	31,208.34
Larry/Drew Nelson	62	62	124	31,208.34
Davis/Dru Love	61	63	124	31,208.33
(Lanny and Tucker Wadkins won on first playoff hole.)				
Lee/Connor Janzen	62	63	125	24,250
Vijay/Qass Singh	59	66	125	24,250
Bernhard/Jason Langer	63	63	126	23,250
Tom/Thomas Lehman	63	63	126	23,250
Stewart/Connor Cink	63	64	127	22,375
Mark/Shaun O'Meara	63	64	127	22,375
Steve/Sam Elkington	61	67	128	21,750
Sir Nick/Matthew Faldo	62	66	128	21,750
Hale/Steve Irwin	64	64	128	21,750
Raymond/Ray Floyd, Jr.	63	66	129	21,000
Jack/Gary Nicklaus	64	65	129	21,000
Lee/Daniel Trevino	66	63	129	21,000

	SCORES		TOTAL	MONEY
				(Won by professional)
Dave/Dave Stockton, Jr.	64	66	130	20,375
Fuzzy/Gretchen Zoeller	66	64	130	20,375
Curtis/Thomas Strange	64	67	131	20,125
Nick/Greg Price	69	64	133	20,000

Web.com Tour

Panama Claro Championship

Panama Golf Club, Panama City, Panama
Par 35-35–70; 7,102 yards

January 29-February 1
purse, $625,000

	SCORES				TOTAL	MONEY
Mathew Goggin	67	65	70	67	269	$112,500
Harold Varner	67	64	71	71	273	67,500
Shane Bertsch	68	70	66	70	274	36,250
Dicky Pride	71	69	69	65	274	36,250
Henrik Norlander	68	67	68	72	275	25,000
Rick Cochran	71	69	65	71	276	19,562.50
Glen Day	72	70	69	65	276	19,562.50
Rhein Gibson	75	64	71	66	276	19,562.50
Curtis Thompson	68	69	70	69	276	19,562.50
Aaron Watkins	68	68	73	67	276	19,562.50
Hao-Tong Li	67	69	65	76	277	15,625
Oliver Goss	68	69	67	74	278	13,125
Tim Herron	71	70	69	68	278	13,125
Darron Stiles	71	71	68	68	278	13,125
Abraham Ancer	72	68	69	70	279	9,687.50
Cody Gribble	72	70	69	68	279	9,687.50
Ashley Hall	71	69	66	73	279	9,687.50
Timothy Madigan	68	71	68	72	279	9,687.50
Vaughn Taylor	72	71	68	68	279	9,687.50
Peter Tomasulo	67	73	73	66	279	9,687.50
Matt Fast	72	68	70	70	280	6,091.97
Jamie Lovemark	70	70	70	70	280	6,091.97
Brett Stegmaier	73	70	73	64	280	6,091.97
Troy Matteson	69	71	70	70	280	6,091.96
Trey Mullinax	70	69	69	72	280	6,091.96
Martin Piller	70	69	64	77	280	6,091.96
Patrick Rodgers	69	72	69	70	280	6,091.96

Colombia Championship

Bogota Country Club, Bogota, Colombia
Par 35-36–71; 7,237 yards

February 5-8
purse, $800,000

	SCORES				TOTAL	MONEY
Patrick Rodgers	69	67	66	65	267	$144,000
Steve Marino	67	67	64	69	267	86,400
(Rodgers defeated Marino on second playoff hole.)						
Chase Wright	67	67	66	69	269	46,400
Andrew Yun	71	67	66	65	269	46,400
Tyler McCumber	66	68	68	69	271	32,000
Roberto Diaz	62	71	71	68	272	27,800
Greg Eason	70	70	67	65	272	27,800
Joel Dahmen	70	68	68	67	273	22,400
Rod Pampling	72	66	66	69	273	22,400
Martin Piller	68	69	68	68	273	22,400
Brady Schnell	72	70	65	66	273	22,400
Julian Etulain	71	69	68	66	274	15,680
Michael Kim	68	71	67	68	274	15,680
Vaughn Taylor	69	71	64	70	274	15,680
Harold Varner	70	68	66	70	274	15,680
Aaron Watkins	67	68	70	69	274	15,680
Kelvin Day	68	68	70	70	276	11,600
Zack Fischer	67	68	67	74	276	11,600
Brett Stegmaier	69	68	71	68	276	11,600
Peter Tomasulo	70	70	63	73	276	11,600
Abraham Ancer	73	66	68	70	277	7,186.40
Alex Aragon	70	70	67	70	277	7,186.40
Erik Barnes	69	68	68	72	277	7,186.40
Dustin Bray	70	72	68	67	277	7,186.40
Bronson Burgoon	69	72	68	68	277	7,186.40
Miguel Angel Carballo	69	69	68	71	277	7,186.40
Patton Kizzire	66	70	74	67	277	7,186.40
Drew Scott	71	70	66	70	277	7,186.40
D.J. Trahan	68	70	71	68	277	7,186.40
Kevin Tway	68	70	68	71	277	7,186.40

Cartagena de Indias at Karibana Championship

TPC Cartagena, Cartagena, Colombia
Par 36-36–71; 7,135 yards

March 5-8
purse, $700,000

	SCORES				TOTAL	MONEY
Andrew Landry	67	74	67	69	277	$126,000
Steve Allan	68	71	72	71	282	61,600
Miguel Angel Carballo	66	69	73	74	282	61,600
Luke List	74	67	67	76	284	27,562
Kevin Tway	67	73	71	73	284	27,562
Patton Kizzire	67	72	70	75	284	27,562
John Mallinger	70	67	74	73	284	27,562
Jason Allred	69	75	69	72	285	21,000
Drew Scott	67	71	72	75	285	21,000
Alex Aragon	74	71	71	70	286	17,500
Todd Baek	68	72	72	74	286	17,500
Oliver Goss	64	74	73	75	286	17,500
Curtis Thompson	70	73	73	71	287	14,000
Jamie Lovemark	68	69	72	78	287	14,000
Roberto Diaz	75	68	75	70	288	11,550
Sung-Hoon Kang	73	69	75	71	288	11,550

	SCORES				TOTAL	MONEY
Jhared Hack	66	74	69	79	288	11,550
Nicholas Lindheim	71	68	73	76	288	11,550
Frank Lickliter	68	75	75	71	289	9,100
Roland Thatcher	69	74	74	72	289	9,100
Joel Dahmen	66	74	75	74	289	9,100
Abraham Ancer	72	71	72	75	290	7,000
Edward Loar	73	71	74	72	290	7,000
Brett Drewitt	68	74	74	74	290	7,000
Aron Price	72	70	77	71	290	7,000

Brasil Champions

Sao Paulo Golf Club, Sao Paulo, Brazil
Par 35-36–71; 6,574 yards

March 12-15
purse, $850,000

	SCORES				TOTAL	MONEY
Peter Malnati	66	62	68	66	262	$153,000
Julian Etulain	68	67	67	64	266	44,260.72
John Mallinger	67	66	67	66	266	44,260.72
Henrik Norlander	70	65	67	64	266	44,260.72
Abraham Ancer	66	66	65	69	266	44,260.71
Matt Davidson	67	64	67	68	266	44,260.71
Tyler Duncan	68	64	64	70	266	44,260.71
Timothy Madigan	66	70	64	66	266	44,260.71
Todd Baek	67	68	67	65	267	22,100
Matt Fast	70	67	66	64	267	22,100
Tommy Gainey	66	64	70	67	267	22,100
Patton Kizzire	65	64	70	68	267	22,100
Jorge Fernandez-Valdes	69	67	66	66	268	15,016.67
Adam Long	68	66	67	67	268	15,016.67
Ted Purdy	68	69	67	64	268	15,016.67
Darron Stiles	65	69	68	66	268	15,016.67
Jason Allred	65	70	66	67	268	15,016.66
Ryan Spears	67	64	69	68	268	15,016.66
Tyler Aldridge	71	64	68	66	269	10,302
Travis Bertoni	68	65	69	67	269	10,302
Jeff Corr	68	69	68	64	269	10,302
Brandon Hagy	68	67	68	66	269	10,302
Rob Oppenheim	68	69	63	69	269	10,302
Jeff Curl	66	68	68	68	270	7,358.88
James Nitties	74	63	65	68	270	7,358.88
Bronson La'Cassie	68	69	64	69	270	7,358.87
Aaron Watkins	70	64	67	69	270	7,358.87

Chile Classic

Club de Golf Mapocho, Santiago, Chile
Par 35-36–71; 7.424 yards

March 19-22
purse, $600,000

	SCORES				TOTAL	MONEY
Dawie van der Walt	64	66	68	65	263	$108,000
Erik Barnes	67	67	65	66	265	64,800
Wes Roach	66	64	68	68	266	34,800
Craig Barlow	67	64	66	69	266	34,800
Greg Eason	68	67	67	65	267	22,800
Brett Drewitt	66	64	69	68	267	22,800
Jamie Lovemark	68	64	68	68	268	20,100

	SCORES				TOTAL	MONEY
Brad Elder	69	65	68	67	269	17,400
Nicholas Lindheim	69	68	65	67	269	17,400
Alex Aragon	65	67	67	70	269	17,400
Brock Mackenzie	65	67	70	68	270	12,720
Charlie Wi	69	67	66	68	270	12,720
Kelly Kraft	68	69	65	68	270	12,720
Oliver Goss	65	67	69	69	270	12,720
Brad Hopfinger	66	71	64	69	270	12,720
Tag Ridings	70	68	68	65	271	8,145
Chase Wright	69	69	67	66	271	8,145
Luke List	70	65	69	67	271	8,145
Michael Kim	67	71	66	67	271	8,145
Andrew Landry	69	67	67	68	271	8,145
Zack Fischer	65	70	67	69	271	8,145
Kevin Tway	68	68	66	69	271	8,145
Hao-Tong Li	66	68	66	71	271	8,145
Andy Winings	69	69	68	66	272	5,520
Harold Varner	65	67	71	69	272	5,520

Chitimacha Louisiana Open

Le Triomphe Golf & Country Club, Broussard, Louisiana
Par 36-35–71; 7,006 yards

March 26-29
purse, $550,000

	SCORES				TOTAL	MONEY
Kelly Kraft	67	70	68	65	270	$99,000
Rhein Gibson	62	68	70	71	271	48,400
D.H. Lee	66	69	73	63	271	48,400
Ryan Blaum	65	68	74	65	272	20,735
Rick Cochran	66	68	65	73	272	20,735
Smylie Kaufman	71	69	66	66	272	20,735
Darron Stiles	68	71	68	65	272	20,735
Cameron Wilson	64	68	71	69	272	20,735
Bronson Burgoon	65	68	71	69	273	15,400
Dawie van der Walt	70	71	65	67	273	15,400
Tyler Aldridge	67	73	66	68	274	11,660
Michael Bradley	68	69	70	67	274	11,660
Cody Gribble	70	70	64	70	274	11,660
Hao-Tong Li	66	67	67	74	274	11,660
Roger Sloan	70	67	70	67	274	11,660
Peter Malnati	72	69	70	64	275	7,715.72
Greg Owen	66	72	70	67	275	7,715.72
Dicky Pride	69	69	71	66	275	7,715.72
Steve Allan	67	68	67	73	275	7,715.71
Erik Barnes	67	73	66	69	275	7,715.71
Si Woo Kim	68	67	72	68	275	7,715.71
Kevin Tway	72	69	67	67	275	7,715.71
Michael Hebert	69	67	71	69	276	4,475.17
Whee Kim	65	76	68	67	276	4,475.17
Andrew Landry	72	69	69	66	276	4,475.17
Jin Park	66	70	71	69	276	4,475.17
Vaughn Taylor	73	68	72	63	276	4,475.17
Brent Witcher	70	70	67	69	276	4,475.17
Jorge Fernandez-Valdes	68	69	68	71	276	4,475.16
Seamus Power	67	71	66	72	276	4,475.16
Aron Price	69	67	67	73	276	4,475.16

El Bosque Mexico Championship

El Bosque Golf Club, Leon, Guanajuato, Mexico
Par 36-36–72; 7,701 yards

April 16-19
purse, $700,000

	SCORES				TOTAL	MONEY
Wes Roach	67	71	65	68	271	$126,000
Patton Kizzire	67	70	71	67	275	61,600
Kevin Tway	67	67	70	71	275	61,600
Stephan Jaeger	68	71	68	69	276	30,800
Smylie Kaufman	68	69	70	69	276	30,800
Sung-Hoon Kang	71	69	68	69	277	24,325
Luke List	67	69	75	66	277	24,325
Jamie Lovemark	73	66	69	70	278	19,600
Peter Malnati	65	68	75	70	278	19,600
Charlie Wi	70	72	67	69	278	19,600
Andrew Yun	70	74	69	65	278	19,600
Craig Barlow	71	71	67	70	279	13,300
Matt Fast	69	69	70	71	279	13,300
Timothy Madigan	71	70	68	70	279	13,300
Will Wilcox	69	71	73	66	279	13,300
Casey Wittenberg	65	68	76	70	279	13,300
Yoshio Yamamoto	70	70	70	69	279	13,300
Miguel Angel Carballo	73	67	66	74	280	9,128
D.H. Lee	71	71	71	67	280	9,128
Jin Park	73	70	69	68	280	9,128
Darron Stiles	70	68	71	71	280	9,128
Richy Werenski	72	70	69	69	280	9,128
Jeff Corr	70	73	67	71	281	6,497.75
Kelly Kraft	74	68	69	70	281	6,497.75
Andrew Landry	69	72	72	68	281	6,497.75
Aaron Watkins	73	68	71	69	281	6,497.75

United Leasing Championship

Victoria National Golf Club, Newburgh, Indiana
Par 36-36–72; 7,242 yards

April 30-May 3
purse, $600,000

	SCORES				TOTAL	MONEY
Smylie Kaufman	72	69	64	73	278	$108,000
Adam Long	74	71	65	73	283	44,800
Jonathan Randolph	72	70	72	69	283	44,800
Ryan Spears	72	67	70	74	283	44,800
Michael Hebert	68	72	70	74	284	21,900
Tim Herron	72	71	69	72	284	21,900
Patton Kizzire	71	74	69	70	284	21,900
Steven Alker	73	70	71	71	285	18,600
Travis Bertoni	70	77	67	72	286	15,000
Tommy Gainey	71	71	71	73	286	15,000
Cody Gribble	70	68	76	72	286	15,000
Sam Love	72	71	75	68	286	15,000
Tag Ridings	67	71	75	73	286	15,000
Julian Etulain	71	68	72	76	287	10,500
Peter Malnati	70	71	72	74	287	10,500
Steve Marino	74	68	75	70	287	10,500
Aaron Watkins	74	71	73	69	287	10,500
Bronson Burgoon	75	72	68	73	288	8,700
Michael Kim	72	73	72	71	288	8,700
Dustin Bray	76	69	73	71	289	6,500
Andrew Loupe	70	74	70	75	289	6,500

	SCORES				TOTAL	MONEY
Curtis Thompson	74	71	77	67	289	6,500
Marc Turnesa	76	69	72	72	289	6,500
Matt Weibring	74	68	73	74	289	6,500
Casey Wittenberg	74	70	71	74	289	6,500

BMW Charity Pro-Am

Thornblade Club: Par 35-36–71; 7,024 yards
Green Valley Country Club: Par 36-36–72; 7,030 yards
Reserve at Lake Keowee: Par 36-36–72; 7,112 yards
Greer, South Carolina

May 14-17
purse, $675,000

	SCORES				TOTAL	MONEY
Rod Pampling	63	63	69	66	261	$121,500
Kelly Kraft	68	63	66	66	263	72,900
Roland Thatcher	71	67	67	60	265	45,900
Miguel Angel Carballo	65	68	66	67	266	29,700
Bronson LaCassie	66	66	67	67	266	29,700
Tyler Aldridge	66	70	65	66	267	22,612.50
Shane Bertsch	73	66	64	64	267	22,612.50
D.H. Lee	67	69	67	64	267	22,612.50
Ryan Blaum	68	66	67	67	268	19,575
Rick Cochran	70	68	68	63	269	16,200
Patton Kizzire	67	65	68	69	269	16,200
Seamus Power	67	65	69	68	269	16,200
Aaron Watkins	71	68	66	64	269	16,200
Andrew Loupe	68	66	67	69	270	12,487.50
Alistair Presnell	66	71	63	70	270	12,487.50
Lucas Lee	70	65	66	70	271	9,469.29
Timothy Madigan	71	63	71	66	271	9,469.29
Steve Marino	69	69	66	67	271	9,469.29
Garth Mulroy	74	64	66	67	271	9,469.29
Jason Allred	65	65	70	71	271	9,469.28
Rob Oppenheim	69	64	69	69	271	9,469.28
Will Wilcox	70	67	64	70	271	9,469.28
Brandt Jobe	67	69	71	65	272	6,480
Nicholas Lindheim	70	66	66	70	272	6,480
Trey Mullinax	67	67	72	66	272	6,480

Rex Hospital Open

TPC Wakefield Plantation, Raleigh, North Carolina
Par 36-35–71; 7,257 yards

May 28-31
purse, $625,000

	SCORES				TOTAL	MONEY
Kyle Thompson	63	68	69	67	267	$112,500
Miguel Angel Carballo	70	68	65	64	267	55,000
Patton Kizzire	69	64	68	66	267	55,000
(Thompson defeated Carballo and Kizzire on second playoff hole.)						
Scott Parel	70	68	65	65	268	27,500
Drew Scott	67	65	68	68	268	27,500
Harold Varner	70	66	62	71	269	21,718.75
Chase Wright	68	67	65	69	269	21,718.75
Todd Baek	69	66	66	69	270	18,125
Brad Fritsch	69	68	65	68	270	18,125
Brad Schneider	66	68	67	69	270	18,125
Kyle Stanley	70	68	66	67	271	14,375

	SCORES				TOTAL	MONEY
Darron Stiles	66	66	71	68	271	14,375
Richy Werenski	67	65	69	70	271	14,375
Tyler Aldridge	68	69	68	67	272	10,625
Travis Bertoni	65	71	68	68	272	10,625
Steve Marino	67	67	66	72	272	10,625
Garth Mulroy	65	68	68	71	272	10,625
Brian Richey	66	67	70	69	272	10,625
Brad Hopfinger	69	66	71	67	273	7,053.58
Scott Harrington	69	66	69	69	273	7,053.57
Michael Hebert	69	68	68	68	273	7,053.57
Brock Mackenzie	66	68	71	68	273	7,053.57
Alistair Presnell	68	71	67	67	273	7,053.57
Wes Roach	70	69	67	67	273	7,053.57
Marc Turnesa	68	69	67	69	273	7,053.57

Greater Dallas Open

The Lakes at Castle Hills, Lewisville, Texas   June 4-7
Par 36-36–72; 7,356 yards   purse, $500,000

	SCORES				TOTAL	MONEY
Tyler Aldridge	67	65	65	68	265	$90,000
Lucas Lee	68	67	67	65	267	44,000
Gregory Yates	65	69	67	66	267	44,000
Adam Long	67	64	74	63	268	24,000
Rick Cochran	69	64	69	67	269	18,250
Steve Marino	70	63	66	70	269	18,250
Troy Matteson	69	67	65	68	269	18,250
Tommy Gainey	63	69	73	65	270	14,500
Michael Kim	67	64	69	70	270	14,500
Matt Weibring	65	69	66	70	270	14,500
Travis Bertoni	68	67	66	70	271	12,500
Peter Malnati	68	68	68	68	272	11,000
Brent Witcher	69	67	67	69	272	11,000
Joel Dahmen	68	66	67	72	273	8,250
Julian Etulain	65	66	70	72	273	8,250
Jamie Lovemark	66	71	69	67	273	8,250
Tim Petrovic	67	67	70	69	273	8,250
Seamus Power	69	69	67	68	273	8,250
Mark Silvers	67	63	72	71	273	8,250
Adam Crawford	68	64	71	71	274	5,237.86
Kelvin Day	68	70	67	69	274	5,237.86
Ashley Hall	64	74	69	67	274	5,237.86
Edward Loar	69	68	70	67	274	5,237.86
John Mallinger	69	69	67	69	274	5,237.86
Bronson La'Cassie	65	68	70	71	274	5,237.85
Kyle Thompson	69	67	66	72	274	5,237.85

Rust-Oleum Championship

Lakewood Country Club, Westlake, Ohio   June 11-14
Par 36-35–71; 7,104 yards   purse, $600,000

	SCORES				TOTAL	MONEY
Shane Bertsch	67	65	68	66	266	$108,000
Lucas Lee	71	68	63	65	267	64,800
Michael Kim	68	66	66	68	268	34,800

	SCORES				TOTAL	MONEY
Patton Kizzire	70	63	68	67	268	34,800
Peter Malnati	64	67	67	72	270	22,800
Brian Richey	64	69	68	69	270	22,800
Si Woo Kim	67	71	62	71	271	20,100
Tyler Aldridge	70	64	69	69	272	17,400
Jamie Lovemark	67	72	66	67	272	17,400
James Nitties	67	70	69	66	272	17,400
Hao-Tong Li	66	70	69	68	273	14,400
Adam Svensson	68	71	69	65	273	14,400
Bronson Burgoon	72	67	68	67	274	10,920
Taylor Pendrith	68	66	70	70	274	10,920
Brett Stegmaier	67	71	67	69	274	10,920
Roland Thatcher	68	68	70	68	274	10,920
Nathan Tyler	69	67	70	68	274	10,920
Michael Arnaud	65	70	74	66	275	7,560
Dustin Bray	66	66	70	73	275	7,560
Sebastian Cappelen	70	69	69	67	275	7,560
Greg Eason	68	67	72	68	275	7,560
Luke List	69	69	70	67	275	7,560
Dawie van der Walt	62	70	72	71	275	7,560
Cody Gribble	67	71	67	71	276	4,712.25
Vince India	67	69	71	69	276	4,712.25
Smylie Kaufman	68	68	70	70	276	4,712.25
Kelly Kraft	69	69	69	69	276	4,712.25
Seamus Power	67	70	71	68	276	4,712.25
Kevin Tway	67	70	70	69	276	4,712.25
David Vanegas	67	67	73	69	276	4,712.25
Chase Wright	72	66	70	68	276	4,712.25

Air Capital Classic

Crestview Country Club, Wichita, Kansas
Par 35-35–70; 6,926 yards

June 25-28
purse, $600,000

	SCORES				TOTAL	MONEY
Rob Oppenheim	67	67	69	64	267	$108,000
Andy Winings	66	65	66	71	268	64,800
Rhein Gibson	69	68	67	65	269	34,800
Nicholas Lindheim	68	66	65	70	269	34,800
Darron Stiles	67	71	67	65	270	24,000
Bronson Burgoon	67	69	67	68	271	20,100
Rod Pampling	70	66	66	69	271	20,100
Dawie van der Walt	64	67	70	70	271	20,100
Michael Arnaud	71	68	66	67	272	15,000
Sebastian Cappelen	70	66	66	70	272	15,000
Scott Gutschewski	67	66	67	72	272	15,000
Martin Piller	66	68	70	68	272	15,000
Brett Stegmaier	67	66	67	72	272	15,000
Shane Bertsch	69	67	69	68	273	10,200
Mark Silvers	70	65	73	65	273	10,200
Ryan Spears	67	68	67	71	273	10,200
Mark Walker	69	67	68	69	273	10,200
Matt Weibring	65	70	69	69	273	10,200
Tim Herron	70	69	68	67	274	5,996.19
Edward Loar	71	68	69	66	274	5,996.19
Miguel Angel Carballo	67	65	70	72	274	5,996.18
Kevin Foley	71	68	66	69	274	5,996.18
Scott Harrington	69	67	69	69	274	5,996.18
Brad Hopfinger	70	69	66	69	274	5,996.18
Ryan Nelson	66	72	65	71	274	5,996.18

	SCORES				TOTAL	MONEY
Taylor Pendrith	71	67	68	68	274	5,996.18
Seamus Power	63	70	70	71	274	5,996.18
Tag Ridings	66	72	69	67	274	5,996.18
Andrew Yun	66	68	69	71	274	5,996.18

Nova Scotia Open

Ashburn Golf Club, New Course, Halifax, Canada   July 2-5
Par 35-36–71; 6,906 yards   purse, $650,000

	SCORES				TOTAL	MONEY
Abraham Ancer	69	70	64	68	271	$117,000
Bronson Burgoon	70	70	63	68	271	70,200
(Ancer defeated Burgoon on first playoff hole.)						
Jason Allred	69	67	72	64	272	33,800
Travis Bertoni	68	69	67	68	272	33,800
D.H. Lee	66	66	71	69	272	33,800
Oliver Goss	69	67	68	69	273	21,043.75
Andy Pope	69	69	69	66	273	21,043.75
Harold Varner	69	67	67	70	273	21,043.75
Mark Walker	70	65	69	69	273	21,043.75
Bubba Dickerson	71	67	70	66	274	14,408.34
Brady Schnell	68	70	68	68	274	14,408.34
Brian Campbell	70	66	69	69	274	14,408.33
Zack Fischer	71	70	65	68	274	14,408.33
Hunter Hamrick	70	66	68	70	274	14,408.33
Jamie Lovemark	69	64	70	71	274	14,408.33
Dominic Bozzelli	68	68	73	66	275	8,536.67
Peter Malnati	65	70	72	68	275	8,536.67
Henrik Norlander	70	67	71	67	275	8,536.67
Seamus Power	70	71	67	67	275	8,536.67
Tag Ridings	68	70	70	67	275	8,536.67
Chris Wilson	74	66	67	68	275	8,536.67
Andrew Landry	64	67	72	72	275	8,536.66
Hao-Tong Li	69	71	67	68	275	8,536.66
Ryan Yip	71	65	68	71	275	8,536.66
Tyler McCumber	67	69	73	67	276	5,164.90
Nick Rousey	69	68	73	66	276	5,164.90
Adam Svensson	70	69	66	71	276	5,164.90
Peter Tomasulo	68	73	69	66	276	5,164.90
Marc Turnesa	68	72	69	67	276	5,164.90

Albertsons Boise Open

Hillcrest Country Club, Boise, Idaho   July 9-12
Par 36-35–71; 6,807 yards   purse, $800,000

	SCORES				TOTAL	MONEY
Martin Piller	61	63	65	67	256	$144,000
Jorge Fernandez-Valdes	65	63	66	68	262	86,400
Cody Gribble	67	66	68	62	263	46,400
Jin Park	69	63	64	67	263	46,400
Michael Arnaud	66	66	66	67	265	30,400
Michael Kim	69	67	66	63	265	30,400
Sung-Hoon Kang	68	67	67	64	266	25,800
Peter Malnati	66	62	71	67	266	25,800
Bronson Burgoon	65	69	67	66	267	20,000

	SCORES				TOTAL	MONEY
Rick Cochran	66	64	67	70	267	20,000
Zack Fischer	65	66	68	68	267	20,000
Patton Kizzire	66	68	69	64	267	20,000
Peter Tomasulo	69	63	69	66	267	20,000
Jim Knous	69	66	66	67	268	12,017.78
D.H. Lee	69	67	65	67	268	12,017.78
Trey Mullinax	65	66	69	68	268	12,017.78
Henrik Norlander	66	67	67	68	268	12,017.78
Seamus Power	67	66	71	64	268	12,017.78
Dicky Pride	67	65	71	65	268	12,017.78
Tag Ridings	65	65	69	69	268	12,017.78
Steve Allan	66	66	67	69	268	12,017.77
Ben Kohles	65	64	69	70	268	12,017.77
Mark Anguiano	68	67	68	66	269	6,826.29
Jamie Lovemark	69	65	71	64	269	6,826.29
Brady Schnell	64	67	71	67	269	6,826.29
Kevin Tway	68	64	70	67	269	6,826.29
Travis Bertoni	70	65	67	67	269	6,826.28
Joel Dahmen	69	63	65	72	269	6,826.28
Andy Winings	65	69	68	67	269	6,826.28

Stonebrae Classic

TPC Stonebrae, Hayward, California
Par 35-35–70; 7,140 yards

July 16-19
purse, $600,000

	SCORES				TOTAL	MONEY
Si Woo Kim	66	65	69	68	268	$108,000
Jamie Lovemark	65	66	69	68	268	52,800
Wes Roach	66	65	69	68	268	52,800
(Kim defeated Lovemark and Roach on first playoff hole.)						
Matt Davidson	65	70	66	68	269	26,400
Trey Mullinax	68	68	67	66	269	26,400
Tyler Duncan	65	68	70	67	270	19,425
Brad Fritsch	72	66	65	67	270	19,425
Rhein Gibson	67	68	67	68	270	19,425
Cody Gribble	69	67	68	66	270	19,425
Joel Dahmen	67	71	67	66	271	13,300
Julian Etulain	69	66	66	70	271	13,300
Ben Kohles	67	66	68	70	271	13,300
Nicholas Lindheim	66	64	73	68	271	13,300
Scott Parel	73	65	67	66	271	13,300
Kyle Thompson	68	69	70	64	271	13,300
Lucas Lee	66	68	69	69	272	9,900
Timothy Madigan	69	68	68	67	272	9,900
Travis Bertoni	66	67	68	72	273	6,822
John Chin	67	66	69	71	273	6,822
Kevin Foley	70	68	68	67	273	6,822
Rick Lamb	69	65	73	66	273	6,822
Frank Lickliter	68	67	68	70	273	6,822
Brock Mackenzie	68	67	71	67	273	6,822
Ryan Spears	70	69	65	69	273	6,822
T.J. Vogel	68	71	68	66	273	6,822
Andrew Yun	69	69	68	67	273	6,822

Utah Championship

Golf Club at Thanksgiving Point, Lehi, Utah
Par 36-36–72; 7,677 yards

July 30-August 2
purse, $650,000

	SCORES				TOTAL	MONEY
Patton Kizzire	67	62	71	69	269	$117,000
Sung-Hoon Kang	68	66	68	67	269	70,200
(Kizzire defeated Kang on second playoff hole.)						
Alex Aragon	68	68	68	70	274	29,315
Zack Fischer	76	64	68	66	274	29,315
Scott Harrington	69	69	65	71	274	29,315
Garth Mulroy	71	69	66	68	274	29,315
Tag Ridings	73	65	67	69	274	29,315
Ryan Blaum	67	71	68	69	275	18,850
Stephan Jaeger	68	66	72	69	275	18,850
Lucas Lee	72	67	72	64	275	18,850
Tyler Aldridge	70	66	71	69	276	13,780
Steve Allan	69	69	68	70	276	13,780
James Driscoll	70	67	71	68	276	13,780
Trey Mullinax	72	62	71	71	276	13,780
Nathan Tyler	71	69	67	69	276	13,780
Paul Imondi	68	75	69	65	277	10,725
Kelly Kraft	63	70	73	71	277	10,725
Smylie Kaufman	74	66	71	67	278	6,956.78
Bryden Macpherson	72	70	70	66	278	6,956.78
Manuel Villegas	68	71	71	68	278	6,956.78
Kelvin Day	70	72	68	68	278	6,956.77
Cody Gribble	70	73	67	68	278	6,956.77
Si Woo Kim	73	67	67	71	278	6,956.77
Adam Long	71	72	65	70	278	6,956.77
Jamie Lovemark	73	67	69	69	278	6,956.77
Steve Marino	74	63	67	74	278	6,956.77
Corey Nagy	70	72	65	71	278	6,956.77
Scott Parel	73	70	66	69	278	6,956.77

Digital Ally Open

Nicklaus Golf Club at LionsGate, Overland Park, Kansas
Par 35-36–71; 7,247 yards

August 6-9
purse, $600,000

	SCORES				TOTAL	MONEY
Martin Piller	65	62	66	65	258	$108,000
Darron Stiles	65	67	63	67	262	64,800
Chris Baker	69	64	64	67	264	25,650
Tyler Duncan	64	64	69	67	264	25,650
Sung-Hoon Kang	67	67	65	65	264	25,650
Michael Kim	66	64	67	67	264	25,650
Sebastian Vazquez	65	68	68	63	264	25,650
Ryan Yip	64	70	65	65	264	25,650
Shane Bertsch	65	62	68	70	265	16,800
Seamus Power	67	67	65	66	265	16,800
Jorge Fernandez-Valdes	66	67	65	68	266	14,400
Jamie Lovemark	66	66	67	67	266	14,400
Ashley Hall	64	70	70	63	267	12,000
D.H. Lee	67	66	67	67	267	12,000
Steve Allan	68	66	67	67	268	8,715
Travis Bertoni	68	65	66	69	268	8,715
Sebastian Cappelen	66	68	67	67	268	8,715
Trey Mullinax	69	65	67	67	268	8,715

	SCORES				TOTAL	MONEY
Jin Park	67	68	65	68	268	8,715
Aron Price	67	66	66	69	268	8,715
Mark Silvers	70	65	67	66	268	8,715
Kevin Tway	71	64	64	69	268	8,715
Abraham Ancer	68	64	69	68	269	4,997.25
Miguel Angel Carballo	65	68	68	68	269	4,997.25
Adam Crawford	66	64	71	68	269	4,997.25
Cody Gribble	69	65	66	69	269	4,997.25
Vince India	65	67	67	70	269	4,997.25
Hao-Tong Li	65	64	71	69	269	4,997.25
Corey Nagy	65	68	70	66	269	4,997.25
Peter Tomasulo	67	64	68	70	269	4,997.25

Price Cutter Charity Championship

Highland Springs Country Club, Springfield, Missouri
Par 36-36–72; 7,115 yards

August 13-16
purse, $675,000

	SCORES				TOTAL	MONEY
Dawie van der Walt	63	65	65	72	265	$121,500
Smylie Kaufman	65	67	65	70	267	72,900
Brad Elder	66	68	66	68	268	35,100
Martin Piller	67	64	66	71	268	35,100
Dicky Pride	67	70	66	65	268	35,100
Jason Allred	69	69	65	66	269	21,853.13
Hao-Tong Li	68	66	69	66	269	21,853.13
Patton Kizzire	64	70	67	68	269	21,853.12
Steve Marino	67	69	66	67	269	21,853.12
Craig Barlow	69	69	66	66	270	14,962.50
Joel Dahmen	68	70	63	69	270	14,962.50
Glen Day	67	68	67	68	270	14,962.50
Cody Gribble	68	65	69	68	270	14,962.50
Curtis Thompson	71	63	70	66	270	14,962.50
Cameron Wilson	68	66	70	66	270	14,962.50
Edward Loar	67	68	68	68	271	9,469.29
Peter Malnati	64	68	70	69	271	9,469.29
Billy Mayfair	69	62	72	68	271	9,469.29
Andy Winings	69	67	67	68	271	9,469.29
Kelly Kraft	67	66	67	71	271	9,469.29
Sebastian Vazquez	68	67	64	72	271	9,469.28
Chase Wright	62	70	68	71	271	9,469.28
Corey Conners	68	67	71	66	272	6,079.05
Si Woo Kim	65	71	67	69	272	6,079.05
Andrew Loupe	66	70	66	70	272	6,079.05
Ryan Spears	67	67	69	69	272	6,079.05
Matt Weibring	68	68	66	70	272	6,079.05

News Sentinel Open

Fox Den Country Club, Knoxville, Tennessee
Par 35-36–71; 7,071 yards

August 20-23
purse, $550,000

	SCORES				TOTAL	MONEY
Patton Kizzire	68	68	64	64	264	$99,000
Brad Fritsch	69	68	64	67	268	48,400
Si Woo Kim	66	68	68	66	268	48,400
Steve Allan	67	69	63	70	269	20,735

	SCORES				TOTAL	MONEY
Jeff Curl	66	67	68	68	269	20,735
Matt Fast	64	66	68	71	269	20,735
Scott Harrington	68	66	67	68	269	20,735
D.H. Lee	64	67	69	69	269	20,735
Bronson Burgoon	68	70	67	65	270	14,300
Julian Etulain	70	67	69	64	270	14,300
Michael Hebert	69	67	68	66	270	14,300
Tag Ridings	64	68	69	69	270	14,300
Dominic Bozzelli	71	67	70	63	271	10,010
Corey Conners	69	66	67	69	271	10,010
Rob Oppenheim	68	67	67	69	271	10,010
Curtis Thompson	71	67	67	66	271	10,010
Richy Werenski	67	71	63	70	271	10,010
Todd Baek	70	67	66	70	273	7,700
Dicky Pride	64	71	67	71	273	7,700
Harold Varner	69	62	72	70	273	7,700
Greg Eason	67	64	71	72	274	5,720
Justin Hicks	69	69	68	68	274	5,720
Brad Hopfinger	67	71	67	69	274	5,720
Nathan Tyler	72	65	65	72	274	5,720
Dawie van der Walt	64	67	74	69	274	5,720

WinCo Foods Portland Open

Pumpkin Ridge Golf Club, Witch Hollow Course, August 27-30
North Plains, Oregon purse, $800,000
Par 36-35–71; 7,109 yards

	SCORES				TOTAL	MONEY
Dicky Pride	65	66	66	67	264	$144,000
Tim Herron	68	65	68	66	267	86,400
Tommy Gainey	69	65	70	65	269	54,400
Ryan Blaum	65	70	71	65	271	33,066.67
Curtis Thompson	62	70	71	68	271	33,066.67
Shane Bertsch	69	66	67	69	271	33,066.66
Brett Stegmaier	68	66	71	67	272	26,800
Michael Kim	65	68	71	69	273	24,800
Matt Fast	71	66	66	71	274	20,800
Cody Gribble	67	69	73	65	274	20,800
Kelly Kraft	66	68	75	65	274	20,800
Kyle Stanley	66	72	67	69	274	20,800
Rod Pampling	69	65	71	70	275	15,000
Adam Svensson	64	66	74	71	275	15,000
Sebastian Vazquez	70	69	73	63	275	15,000
T.J. Vogel	68	66	74	67	275	15,000
Sebastian Cappelen	72	66	69	69	276	12,400
D.H. Lee	69	68	68	71	276	12,400
Craig Barlow	68	71	72	66	277	10,800
Aaron Watkins	69	67	67	74	277	10,800
Rick Cochran	67	71	68	72	278	8,320
Brandon Hagy	70	67	70	71	278	8,320
Brian Richey	67	68	70	73	278	8,320
Marc Turnesa	71	69	68	70	278	8,320
Richy Werenski	67	70	71	70	278	8,320

Web.com Tour Finals

Hotel Fitness Championship

Sycamore Hills Golf Club, Fort Wayne, Indiana
Par 36-36–72; 7,319 yards

September 10-13
purse, $1,000,000

	SCORES				TOTAL	MONEY
Henrik Norlander	69	69	69	62	269	$180,000
D.H. Lee	67	68	66	71	272	88,000
Michael Thompson	69	69	69	65	272	88,000
Hiroshi Iwata	73	64	71	66	274	44,000
Sam Saunders	68	72	65	69	274	44,000
Anirban Lahiri	69	65	70	71	275	34,750
Jamie Lovemark	67	66	73	69	275	34,750
Brett Stegmaier	67	70	69	70	276	31,000
Emiliano Grillo	66	72	69	70	277	29,000
Derek Fathauer	74	66	70	68	278	23,000
Smylie Kaufman	71	71	65	71	278	23,000
Scott Langley	69	68	72	69	278	23,000
Peter Malnati	72	69	68	69	278	23,000
Chez Reavie	70	72	70	66	278	23,000
Brad Fritsch	71	64	75	69	279	18,000
Ricky Barnes	67	73	73	67	280	14,500
Jonathan Byrd	73	66	67	74	280	14,500
Brian Davis	69	72	70	69	280	14,500
Patton Kizzire	72	65	72	71	280	14,500
John Merrick	70	70	68	72	280	14,500
Kyle Stanley	70	72	67	71	280	14,500
Steve Allan	71	70	71	69	281	7,902.31
Greg Eason	68	70	71	72	281	7,902.31
Jorge Fernandez-Valdes	74	67	69	71	281	7,902.31
Lucas Glover	69	71	70	71	281	7,902.31
Oliver Goss	72	71	69	69	281	7,902.31
Tom Hoge	69	69	71	72	281	7,902.31
Adam Long	67	71	72	71	281	7,902.31
Andrew Svoboda	72	69	71	69	281	7,902.31
Harold Varner	71	68	72	70	281	7,902.31
Tim Wilkinson	69	73	67	72	281	7,902.31
Scott Harrington	68	72	66	75	281	7,902.30
Andrew Loupe	69	68	71	73	281	7,902.30
Tyrone van Aswegen	69	70	68	74	281	7,902.30

Small Business Connection Championship

River Run Country Club, Davidson, North Carolina
Par 36-36–72; 7,317 yards

September 17-20
purse, $1,000,000

	SCORES				TOTAL	MONEY
Chez Reavie	69	69	69	66	273	$180,000
Jamie Lovemark	67	68	72	67	274	74,666.67
Steve Marino	67	69	70	68	274	74,666.67
Emiliano Grillo	66	68	68	72	274	74,666.66
Brett Stegmaier	63	68	73	71	275	40,000
Ricky Barnes	73	68	67	68	276	36,000
Kyle Stanley	71	68	65	73	277	32,250
Dawie van der Walt	69	68	70	70	277	32,250

	SCORES				TOTAL	MONEY
Eric Axley	67	65	70	76	278	27,000
Roberto Castro	72	70	70	66	278	27,000
Andrew Yun	67	67	73	71	278	27,000
Ryan Armour	67	70	69	73	279	20,250
Tom Gillis	71	71	65	72	279	20,250
Justin Hicks	70	72	67	70	279	20,250
Jhonattan Vegas	70	70	70	69	279	20,250
Tyler Aldridge	75	67	68	70	280	15,000
Steve Allan	72	71	67	70	280	15,000
Anirban Lahiri	72	70	67	71	280	15,000
Bill Lunde	69	68	71	72	280	15,000
Harold Varner	67	70	70	73	280	15,000
Austin Cook	70	70	71	70	281	10,800
Gonzalo Fernandez-Castano	69	69	73	70	281	10,800
Rhein Gibson	66	72	68	75	281	10,800
Cody Gribble	70	73	68	70	281	10,800
Julian Etulain	68	73	72	69	282	7,946
Lucas Glover	69	74	71	68	282	7,946
Nicholas Lindheim	69	69	73	71	282	7,946
Rob Oppenheim	70	70	70	72	282	7,946
Vaughn Taylor	74	63	69	76	282	7,946

Nationwide Children's Hospital Championship

The OSU Golf Club, Scarlet Course, Columbus, Ohio
Par 36-35–71; 7,455 yards

September 24-27
purse, $1,000,000

	SCORES				TOTAL	MONEY
Andrew Loupe	71	70	68	70	279	$180,000
Bronson Burgoon	71	72	68	70	281	74,666.67
Tom Hoge	70	72	70	69	281	74,666.67
Roberto Castro	70	68	68	75	281	74,666.66
Derek Ernst	68	71	71	72	282	35,125
Mark Hubbard	70	69	76	67	282	35,125
Luke List	71	67	73	71	282	35,125
Dawie van der Walt	73	70	71	68	282	35,125
Lucas Glover	72	72	71	68	283	23,142.86
Billy Hurley	74	71	69	69	283	23,142.86
Henrik Norlander	69	71	73	70	283	23,142.86
Ryan Spears	70	73	68	72	283	23,142.86
Tim Wilkinson	71	70	71	71	283	23,142.86
Robert Garrigus	69	72	67	75	283	23,142.85
Rhein Gibson	70	68	72	73	283	23,142.85
Steven Alker	69	71	73	71	284	15,500
Si Woo Kim	72	71	71	70	284	15,500
Chris Smith	75	69	72	68	284	15,500
Harold Varner	70	72	66	76	284	15,500
Brian Davis	74	68	72	71	285	12,066.67
Chez Reavie	69	72	71	73	285	12,066.67
Martin Flores	67	70	73	75	285	12,066.66
Ricky Barnes	71	70	74	71	286	8,755
Travis Bertoni	72	74	69	71	286	8,755
Zack Fischer	72	67	69	78	286	8,755
Bill Lunde	70	71	73	72	286	8,755
Steve Marino	68	71	75	72	286	8,755
Michael Putnam	72	73	70	71	286	8,755

Web.com Tour Championship

TPC Sawgrass, Dye's Valley, Ponte Vedra Beach, Florida
Par 35-35–70; 6,847 yards

October 1-4
purse, $1,000,000

	SCORES				TOTAL	MONEY
Emiliano Grillo	66	64	67	69	266	$180,000
Chez Reavie	67	65	67	68	267	108,000
Sam Saunders	64	69	68	67	268	68,000
Rhein Gibson	63	76	65	65	269	48,000
Thomas Aiken	69	67	69	65	270	35,125
Patton Kizzire	70	67	66	67	270	35,125
Kyle Stanley	66	69	67	68	270	35,125
Tyrone van Aswegen	67	69	66	68	270	35,125
Derek Fathauer	69	69	67	66	271	29,000
Roberto Castro	70	70	70	62	272	26,000
Luke Guthrie	71	67	65	69	272	26,000
Oscar Fraustro	64	71	69	69	273	19,000
Robert Garrigus	69	69	67	68	273	19,000
Lucas Glover	64	67	69	73	273	19,000
Nicholas Lindheim	67	68	70	68	273	19,000
Rob Oppenheim	68	71	67	67	273	19,000
Kevin Tway	71	65	67	70	273	19,000
Greg Eason	67	67	70	70	274	12,600
Hiroshi Iwata	66	67	74	67	274	12,600
Si Woo Kim	65	71	69	69	274	12,600
Henrik Norlander	68	71	66	69	274	12,600
Andrew Putnam	67	69	68	70	274	12,600
Brett Stegmaier	67	66	71	70	274	12,600
Martin Flores	69	68	70	68	275	8,221.67
Rod Pampling	70	66	72	67	275	8,221.67
Vaughn Taylor	71	69	68	67	275	8,221.67
Tim Wilkinson	71	66	70	68	275	8,221.67
Andres Romero	68	69	66	72	275	8,221.66
Nicholas Thompson	67	69	70	69	275	8,221.66

Mackenzie Tour–PGA Tour Canada

PC Financial Open

Point Grey Golf & Country Club, Vancouver, British Columbia
Par 36-36–72; 6,801 yards

May 28-31
purse, C$175,000

	SCORES				TOTAL	MONEY
Drew Weaver	71	70	66	69	276	C$31,500
Ross Beal	70	68	71	67	276	11,550
Taylor Pendrith	72	70	70	64	276	11,550
Adam Svensson	71	68	68	69	276	11,550
Riley Wheeldon	74	68	66	68	276	11,550
(Weaver won on third playoff hole.)						
Vince Covello	69	73	69	66	277	6,300
Cody Martin	71	69	69	69	278	5,454.17
Ryan Williams	70	71	70	67	278	5,454.17
Seann Harlingten	69	70	70	69	278	5,454.16
Albin Choi	69	67	73	70	279	4,375
James Erkenbeck	73	66	72	68	279	4,375
J.R. Myers	67	71	68	73	279	4,375
Phillip Mollica	71	71	72	66	280	3,383.34
Charlie Bull	72	69	71	68	280	3,383.33
Michael Gligic	70	69	73	68	280	3,383.33
Bo Hoag	68	70	73	70	281	2,537.50
Logan McCracken	71	66	71	73	281	2,537.50
Bryn Parry	67	65	75	74	281	2,537.50
Christopher Ross	75	68	69	69	281	2,537.50
J.J. Spaun	70	71	68	72	281	2,537.50
Joshua Stone	73	70	72	66	281	2,537.50

Bayview Place Island Savings Open

Uplands Golf Club, Victoria, British Columbia
Par 35-35–70; 6,420 yards

June 4-7
purse, C$175,000

	SCORES				TOTAL	MONEY
Albin Choi	64	65	70	66	265	C$31,500
Jason Millard	71	65	65	67	268	13,066.67
Eugene Wong	65	67	70	66	268	13,066.67
Adam Svensson	68	69	62	69	268	13,066.66
John Ellis	66	68	66	69	269	6,650
Cory Renfrew	67	67	67	68	269	6,650
Sam Ryder	69	70	66	65	270	5,643.75
Ethan Tracy	68	66	70	66	270	5,643.75
Kevin Spooner	70	66	67	68	271	5,075
Vince Covello	68	67	69	68	272	4,025
Brien Davis	68	70	70	64	272	4,025
Paul McConnell	69	69	68	66	272	4,025
J.J. Spaun	65	70	66	71	272	4,025
Drew Weaver	67	68	68	69	272	4,025
Charlie Bull	69	67	69	68	273	2,800
Brad Clapp	68	70	67	68	273	2,800
Riley Fleming	68	69	69	67	273	2,800

	SCORES				TOTAL	MONEY
Dillon Rust	69	70	68	66	273	2,800
Ryan Williams	71	67	66	69	273	2,800
Mike Van Sickle	67	72	71	64	274	2,111.67
Chris Worrell	67	72	68	67	274	2,111.67
Adam Cornelson	66	68	70	70	274	2,111.66

Syncrude Boreal Open

Fort McMurray Golf Club, Ft. McMurray, Alberta
Par 36-36–72; 6,857 yards

June 25-28
purse, C$175,000

	SCORES				TOTAL	MONEY
Kevin Spooner	69	71	69	63	272	C$31,500
Talor Gooch	66	70	67	69	272	15,400
Benjamin Silverman	64	67	69	72	272	15,400
(Spooner defeated Silverman on third and Gooch on fifth playoff hole.)						
John Ellis	69	73	64	69	275	6,890.63
Christopher Trunzer	68	65	70	72	275	6,890.63
Riley Fleming	66	67	69	73	275	6,890.62
Sam Ryder	66	70	65	74	275	6,890.62
Daniel Bowden	68	71	68	69	276	4,900
Mike Miller	66	71	67	72	276	4,900
Clayton Rask	67	71	67	71	276	4,900
J.J. Spaun	69	68	67	72	276	4,900
Corey Conners	72	69	68	68	277	3,430
James Erkenbeck	69	71	68	69	277	3,430
Michael Gligic	68	71	68	70	277	3,430
Chase Marinell	64	71	70	72	277	3,430
Curtis Reed	69	71	66	71	277	3,430
Doug Letson	71	68	67	72	278	2,537.50
Nyasha Mauchaza	68	74	67	69	278	2,537.50
Richard McDonald	68	71	68	71	278	2,537.50
Dillon Rust	67	73	70	68	278	2,537.50

SIGA Dakota Dunes Open

Dakota Dunes Golf Links, Saskatoon, Saskatchewan
Par 36-36–72; 7,301 yards

July 2-5
purse, C$175,000

	SCORES				TOTAL	MONEY
Michael Letzig	67	66	70	69	272	C$31,500
Clark Klaasen	69	68	66	69	272	15,400
J.J. Spaun	69	69	67	67	272	15,400
(Letzig defeated Klaasen and Spaun on second playoff hole.)						
Charlie Bull	69	69	68	67	273	6,890.63
John Catlin	69	67	67	70	273	6,890.63
Eric Onesi	64	66	67	76	273	6,890.62
Benjamin Silverman	71	65	66	71	273	6,890.62
Zack Byrd	69	68	68	69	274	5,075
Philip Pettitt, Jr.	68	69	68	69	274	5,075
Drew Weaver	72	65	66	71	274	5,075
Ben Briscoe	66	69	70	70	275	3,368.75
Julien Brun	68	68	68	71	275	3,368.75
Vaita Guillaume	66	65	73	71	275	3,368.75
Mackenzie Hughes	69	67	68	71	275	3,368.75
Doug Letson	64	69	72	70	275	3,368.75
Sam Ryder	68	68	67	72	275	3,368.75

	SCORES				TOTAL	MONEY
David Skinns	64	71	69	71	275	3,368.75
Jack Wilson	68	67	71	69	275	3,368.75
Wade Binfield	67	66	76	67	276	1,975
Ryan Brehm	68	66	68	74	276	1,975
Yi Cao	69	66	70	71	276	1,975
Max Gilbert	70	68	69	69	276	1,975
Logan McCracken	71	67	67	71	276	1,975
Justin Snelling	65	72	71	68	276	1,975
Mike Van Sickle	66	68	69	73	276	1,975

The Players Cup

Pine Ridge Golf Club, Winnipeg, Manitoba
Par 36-35–71; 6,601 yards

July 9-12
purse, C$175,000

	SCORES				TOTAL	MONEY
Cheng Tsung Pan	71	67	65	66	269	C$31,500
Robert Karlsson	70	65	67	69	271	18,900
J.J. Spaun	69	64	67	72	272	11,900
Mackenzie Hughes	68	65	72	69	274	8,400
Krister Eriksson	72	65	68	70	275	7,000
Justin Shin	68	68	71	69	276	6,081.25
Riley Wheeldon	72	68	67	69	276	6,081.25
Daniel Balin	70	65	68	74	277	4,550
Ben Briscoe	68	71	70	68	277	4,550
Julien Brun	70	70	69	68	277	4,550
Chase Marinell	69	71	71	66	277	4,550
Christopher Ross	68	73	68	68	277	4,550
Sam Ryder	70	67	72	68	277	4,550
Vince Covello	75	67	70	66	278	3,150
Drew Weaver	66	69	71	72	278	3,150
Jared Wolfe	70	71	69	68	278	3,150
Tommy Cocha	70	70	69	70	279	2,537.50
Vaita Guillaume	68	69	75	67	279	2,537.50
Jamie Sindelar	73	65	71	70	279	2,537.50
Eugene Wong	70	72	62	75	279	2,537.50

Staal Foundation Open

Whitewater Golf Club, Thunder Bay, Ontario
Par 36-36–72; 7,293 yards

July 16-19
purse, C$175,000

	SCORES				TOTAL	MONEY
J.J. Spaun	67	67	69	67	270	C$31,500
Nicholas Reach	71	64	71	65	271	18,900
Corey Conners	67	65	70	70	272	11,900
Logan McCracken	68	69	67	69	273	7,233.34
David McKenzie	66	69	67	71	273	7,233.33
Clayton Rask	65	67	70	71	273	7,233.33
Steve Carney	68	66	71	69	274	5,862.50
Vince Covello	68	69	68	70	275	5,425
Robert Karlsson	67	69	68	72	276	4,375
Chase Marinell	66	68	68	74	276	4,375
David Pastore	66	72	68	70	276	4,375
Cameron Peck	69	69	66	72	276	4,375
Dillon Rust	71	65	71	69	276	4,375
Julien Brun	68	68	70	71	277	3,237.50

	SCORES			TOTAL	MONEY
Mike Van Sickle	68	65	70 74	277	3,237.50
Wade Binfield	66	70	68 74	278	2,222.50
Albin Choi	68	67	70 73	278	2,222.50
Krister Eriksson	73	62	72 71	278	2,222.50
Riley Fleming	69	66	72 71	278	2,222.50
Seann Harlingten	68	66	72 72	278	2,222.50
Bo Hoag	70	70	68 70	278	2,222.50
Jason Millard	66	68	73 71	278	2,222.50
Curtis Reed	72	66	68 72	278	2,222.50
Ted Smith	70	67	68 73	278	2,222.50
Brady Watt	70	71	69 68	278	2,222.50

ATB Financial Classic

Links of Glen Eagles, Calgary, Alberta
Par 35-35–70; 7,019 yards

July 30-August 2
purse, C$175,000

	SCORES			TOTAL	MONEY
Daniel Miernicki	64	66	69 64	263	C$31,500
Danny Sahl	64	70	64 66	264	18,900
Julien Brun	63	67	67 68	265	7,892.50
Mackenzie Hughes	66	67	68 64	265	7,892.50
Jonathan Khan	68	62	66 69	265	7,892.50
Adam Svensson	69	64	67 65	265	7,892.50
Chris Williams	69	65	61 70	265	7,892.50
Nate McCoy	69	68	64 65	266	5,250
Ethan Tracy	65	67	67 67	266	5,250
David Pastore	66	66	67 68	267	4,375
Taylor Pendrith	69	66	66 66	267	4,375
Mike Van Sickle	65	68	66 68	267	4,375
Matt Hansen	66	67	68 67	268	3,500
Kevin Spooner	69	68	65 66	268	3,500
Mike Ballo, Jr.	68	66	68 67	269	2,975
Maxwell Buckley	68	67	67 67	269	2,975
Wes Heffernan	67	67	66 69	269	2,975
Mookie DeMoss	69	64	64 73	270	2,282
Linus Gillgren	69	66	68 67	270	2,282
Michael Gligic	64	67	68 71	270	2,282
Michael Letzig	67	64	70 69	270	2,282

National Capital Open to Support Our Troops

Hylands Golf Club, Ottawa, Ontario
Par 35-36–71; 6,735 yards

August 20-23
purse, C$175,000

	SCORES			TOTAL	MONEY
Sam Ryder	69	65	64 66	264	C$31,500
Taylor Pendrith	69	64	65 66	264	18,900
(Ryder defeated Pendrith on first playoff hole.)					
Clayton Rask	68	67	64 67	266	11,900
Ross Beal	65	66	68 68	267	8,400
Wade Binfield	69	70	65 65	269	6,146.88
Riley Wheeldon	68	69	66 66	269	6,146.88
Seann Harlingten	69	69	65 66	269	6,146.87
J.J. Spaun	67	67	67 68	269	6,146.87
Nyasha Mauchaza	68	66	67 69	270	5,075
Mackenzie Hughes	70	67	69 65	271	4,200

	SCORES				TOTAL	MONEY
Doug Letson	67	71	67	66	271	4,200
David Pastore	68	68	69	66	271	4,200
Curtis Reed	74	65	67	65	271	4,200
Charlie Bull	66	67	69	70	272	3,237.50
Dillon Rust	70	70	66	66	272	3,237.50
Mike Ballo, Jr.	70	68	68	67	273	2,712.50
Michael Letzig	71	68	67	67	273	2,712.50
Eric Onesi	71	65	69	68	273	2,712.50
Ted Smith	71	67	67	68	273	2,712.50
Matt Hill	67	71	68	68	274	1,967
Tyler Light	69	69	65	71	274	1,967
Paul McConnell	73	66	68	67	274	1,967
J.R. Myers	70	67	66	71	274	1,967
David Skinns	70	65	69	70	274	1,967

Great Waterway Classic

Loyalist Golf & Country Club, Kingston, Ontario
Par 35-37–72; 6,584 yards

August 27-30
purse, C$175,000

	SCORES				TOTAL	MONEY
Brad Clapp	67	63	68	67	265	C$31,500
Ryan Brehm	72	66	66	65	269	9,727.09
Seath Lauer	66	70	70	63	269	9,727.09
Charlie Bull	67	70	66	66	269	9,727.08
Albin Choi	69	69	64	67	269	9,727.08
Ben Geyer	67	67	68	67	269	9,727.08
Chase Marinell	68	69	65	67	269	9,727.08
Matt Harmon	66	70	68	66	270	5,075
Tom Moore	65	69	66	70	270	5,075
Cory Renfrew	68	66	68	68	270	5,075
Max Gilbert	68	69	66	68	271	3,368.75
Talor Gooch	69	69	64	69	271	3,368.75
Seann Harlingten	67	70	69	65	271	3,368.75
Dan McCarthy	71	66	68	66	271	3,368.75
David Mills	66	68	71	66	271	3,368.75
Cheng Tsung Pan	64	68	71	68	271	3,368.75
Kyle Stough	65	70	66	70	271	3,368.75
Ethan Tracy	70	66	68	67	271	3,368.75
Olin Browne, Jr.	66	69	68	69	272	1,975
Joey Garber	64	70	69	69	272	1,975
Michael Gligic	70	69	69	64	272	1,975
Mackenzie Hughes	67	66	71	68	272	1,975
Nyasha Mauchaza	69	67	72	64	272	1,975
J.J. Spaun	70	68	69	65	272	1,975
Jared Wolfe	68	65	72	67	272	1,975

Wildfire Invitational

Wildfire Golf Club, Peterborough, Ontario
Par 36-36–72; 6,803 yards

September 3-6
purse, C$175,000

	SCORES				TOTAL	MONEY
Christopher Ross	69	66	64	64	263	C$31,500
David Skinns	66	65	67	69	267	18,900
J.J. Spaun	67	68	67	66	268	10,150
Cheng Tsung Pan	64	68	68	68	268	10,150

	SCORES				TOTAL	MONEY
Michael Miller	65	68	66	70	269	7,000
Talor Gooch	70	65	68	67	270	5,665.63
Matt Hill	67	70	65	68	270	5,665.63
Michael Letzig	64	70	67	69	270	5,665.63
Ted Brown	65	68	67	70	270	5,665.63
Corey Conners	67	68	71	65	271	3,879.17
David Pastore	68	69	69	65	271	3,879.17
John Catlin	68	69	68	66	271	3,879.17
Ethan Tracy	64	74	67	66	271	3,879.17
Kyle Wilshire	68	66	70	67	271	3,879.17
Chase Marinell	64	68	66	73	271	3,879.17
Chris Hemmerich	70	69	67	66	272	2,887.50
Daniel Bowden	66	68	70	68	272	2,887.50
Adam Svensson	64	73	70	66	273	2,450
Curtis Reed	64	73	70	66	273	2,450
Paul McConnell	67	69	70	67	273	2,450

Cape Breton Celtic Classic

Lakes Golf Club, Ben Eoin, Nova Scotia
Par 36-36–72; 6,904 yards

September 10-13
purse, C$175,000

	SCORES				TOTAL	MONEY
Cheng Tsung Pan	67	68	68	66	269	C$31,500
Taylor Pendrith	67	67	67	68	269	18,900
(Pan defeated Pendrith on second playoff hole.)						
Mike Van Sickle	70	64	71	65	270	11,900
Ryan Brehm	66	69	69	67	271	6,890.63
Adam Svensson	67	72	68	64	271	6,890.63
Talor Gooch	67	68	68	68	271	6,890.62
Dan McCarthy	68	67	67	69	271	6,890.62
Michael Letzig	68	68	68	68	272	5,250
Mike Miller	68	72	66	66	272	5,250
Ted Brown	70	67	68	68	273	3,750
Max Gilbert	70	66	66	71	273	3,750
Ryan McCormick	70	65	69	69	273	3,750
Kyle Stough	72	67	68	66	273	3,750
Ethan Tracy	68	69	68	68	273	3,750
Kyle Wilshire	68	69	65	71	273	3,750
Jack Wilson	69	68	68	68	273	3,750
Robert Karlsson	71	66	68	70	275	2,537.50
David Pastore	70	71	66	68	275	2,537.50
Nathan Stamey	69	71	66	69	275	2,537.50
Richy Werenski	68	71	69	67	275	2,537.50

Freedom 55 Financial Championship

Highland Country Club, London, Ontario
Par 34-36–70; 6,754 yards

September 17-20
purse, C$200,000

	SCORES				TOTAL	MONEY
Jason Millard	67	63	67	68	265	C$36,000
Ryan Williams	68	65	65	67	265	21,600
(Millard defeated Williams on second playoff hole.)						
Matt Hill	69	67	66	64	266	13,600
John Catlin	63	70	70	64	267	9,600
Ben Geyer	66	67	69	66	268	7,600

	SCORES				TOTAL	MONEY
Curtis Reed	71	70	67	60	268	7,600
Mike Miller	66	68	71	64	269	6,700
Ryan Brehm	68	69	70	63	270	5,800
Max Gilbert	66	68	65	71	270	5,800
Taylor Pendrith	67	67	63	73	270	5,800
Mackenzie Hughes	74	62	71	64	271	4,800
Adam Svensson	71	65	67	68	271	4,800
Albin Choi	67	67	69	69	272	3,750
Robert Karlsson	67	69	70	66	272	3,750
Logan McCracken	66	71	65	70	272	3,750
Cory Renfrew	69	69	65	69	272	3,750
Seann Harlingten	69	65	70	69	273	3,000
Doug Letson	68	68	69	68	273	3,000
Chase Marinell	69	71	67	66	273	3,000
Michael Gligic	68	69	72	65	274	2,097.15
Clayton Rask	69	72	68	65	274	2,097.15
Vince Covello	68	69	67	70	274	2,097.14
Krister Eriksson	68	68	69	69	274	2,097.14
Riley Fleming	67	68	71	68	274	2,097.14
Seath Lauer	68	66	71	69	274	2,097.14
Kyle Wilshire	68	66	74	66	274	2,097.14

PGA Tour Latinoamerica

Avianca Colombia Open

Club los Lagartos, Bogota, Colombia
Par 35-36–71; 7,394 yards

March 19-22
purse, US$175,000

	SCORES				TOTAL	MONEY
Diego Velasquez	65	69	67	65	266	US$31,500
Alex Moon	68	65	70	69	272	18,900
Nate Lashley	69	69	65	74	277	9,100
Juan Pablo Luna	70	72	70	65	277	9,100
Daniel Mazziotta	70	67	68	72	277	9,100
Rodolfo Cazaubon	66	67	71	74	278	6,300
Ian Davis	68	71	71	70	280	5,643.75
Jose Toledo	67	70	71	72	280	5,643.75
Kent Bulle	71	72	70	68	281	4,550
Grant Norton	66	73	74	68	281	4,550
Alexandre Rocha	69	70	72	70	281	4,550
Martin Trainer	73	70	71	67	281	4,550
Mark Anguiano	73	69	70	70	282	3,500
David Vanegas	71	72	69	70	282	3,500
Anthony Paolucci	75	67	72	69	283	3,062.50
Santiago Rivas	71	69	71	72	283	3,062.50
Steven Fox	69	71	70	74	284	2,625
Sergio Franky	68	72	68	76	284	2,625
Sebastian Vazquez	71	71	71	71	284	2,625
Oscar Alvarez	78	67	73	67	285	2,047.50

	SCORES				TOTAL	MONEY
Tom Berry	73	72	69	71	285	2,047.50
Augusto Nunez	71	69	71	74	285	2,047.50
Brady Watt	77	67	70	71	285	2,047.50

Mazatlan Open

Estrella del Mar Golf & Beach Resort, Mazatlan, Mexico   March 26-29
Par 36-36–72; 7,015 yards   purse, US$175,000

	SCORES				TOTAL	MONEY
Tommy Cocha	67	68	67	69	271	US$31,500
Oscar Alvarez	70	64	71	68	273	15,400
Andres Echavarria	70	69	65	69	273	15,400
Kent Bulle	72	66	69	67	274	8,400
Evan Harmeling	67	72	69	67	275	6,146.88
Julio Zapata	66	71	70	68	275	6,146.88
Wilson Bateman	70	70	65	70	275	6,146.87
Chip Lynn	72	67	66	70	275	6,146.87
Rodolfo Cazaubon	72	68	66	70	276	5,075
Steve Carney	71	67	72	67	277	4,375
Sebastian Vazquez	70	66	72	69	277	4,375
Armando Villarreal	70	68	72	67	277	4,375
Wil Collins	70	70	68	70	278	3,281.25
Brad Gehl	70	67	72	69	278	3,281.25
Leandro Marelli	68	72	68	70	278	3,281.25
Martin Trainer	70	68	71	69	278	3,281.25
Alfredo Adrian	70	68	72	69	279	2,295
Mark Anguiano	69	71	70	69	279	2,295
David Bradshaw	71	70	67	71	279	2,295
Rafael Echenique	73	69	66	71	279	2,295
Jose de Jesus Rodriguez	69	69	69	72	279	2,295
David Rose	69	71	69	70	279	2,295
Adam Schenk	66	71	72	70	279	2,295

Abierto OSDE del Centro

Cordoba Golf Club, Cordoba, Argentina   April 16-19
Par 35-36–71; 6,794 yards   purse, US$175,000

	SCORES				TOTAL	MONEY
Tommy Cocha	70	67	68	70	275	US$31,500
Angel Cabrera	68	71	68	72	279	15,400
Steven Fox	68	70	71	70	279	15,400
Nate Lashley	71	68	69	72	280	8,400
Leandro Marelli	70	68	75	69	282	7,000
Ariel Canete	73	71	67	73	284	6,300
Puma Dominguez	68	73	70	74	285	5,643.75
Matias O'Curry	74	66	72	73	285	5,643.75
Daniel Mazziotta	74	72	71	70	287	4,375
Cesar Monasterio	69	71	76	71	287	4,375
Augusto Nunez	72	72	73	70	287	4,375
Ethan Tracy	78	67	69	73	287	4,375
Diego Velasquez	68	70	72	77	287	4,375
Francisco Bide	68	73	74	73	288	2,800
Kristian Caparros	75	68	72	73	288	2,800
Vince India	68	75	72	73	288	2,800
Ryan McCarthy	74	72	70	72	288	2,800

	SCORES				TOTAL	MONEY
Francisco Ojeda	79	64	70	75	288	2,800
Anthony Paolucci	70	76	72	70	288	2,800
Paulo Pinto	70	69	71	78	288	2,800

Lexus Panama Classic

Buenaventura Golf Club, Rio Hato, Panama
Par 36-36–72; 6,545 yards

April 30-May 3
purse, US$175,000

	SCORES				TOTAL	MONEY
Rodolfo Cazaubon	67	66	74	69	276	US$31,500
Samuel Del Val	67	70	69	72	278	15,400
Ethan Tracy	66	72	70	70	278	15,400
Steve Carney	68	71	70	71	280	6,343.75
Ian Davis	70	67	73	70	280	6,343.75
Linus Gillgren	65	69	68	78	280	6,343.75
Nate Lashley	70	70	67	73	280	6,343.75
Hans Reimers	66	73	69	72	280	6,343.75
Sebastian Vazquez	69	69	73	69	280	6,343.75
Juan Pablo Luna	69	67	72	73	281	4,550
Anthony Paolucci	67	72	72	70	281	4,550
Rafael Campos	69	67	73	73	282	3,325
Andres Echavarria	71	71	70	70	282	3,325
Michael McGowan	68	70	73	71	282	3,325
Willy Pumarol	71	65	72	74	282	3,325
Daniel Stapff	68	74	68	72	282	3,325
Diego Velasquez	71	69	72	70	282	3,325
Ken Looper	70	70	73	70	283	2,080.32
Brady Watt	73	68	73	69	283	2,080.32
Kent Bulle	69	71	74	69	283	2,080.31
Ricardo Celia	70	69	73	71	283	2,080.31
Bubba Dickerson	73	70	69	71	283	2,080.31
Sebastian MacLean	72	71	71	69	283	2,080.31
Augusto Nunez	70	69	74	70	283	2,080.31
Alexandre Rocha	74	70	69	70	283	2,080.31

Abierto Mexicano de Golf

Club Campestre, Aguascalientes, Mexico
Par 35-37–72

May 14-17
purse, US$175,000

	SCORES				TOTAL	MONEY
Justin Hueber	65	68	65	67	265	US$31,500
Brad Gehl	68	68	65	65	266	15,400
Maximiliano Godoy	69	65	64	68	266	15,400
Adam Schenk	64	68	67	69	268	8,400
Jose Garrido	67	67	63	72	269	5,932.50
Daniel Mazziotta	68	64	68	69	269	5,932.50
Keith Mitchell	67	70	65	67	269	5,932.50
Derek Tolan	67	68	68	66	269	5,932.50
Gunner Wiebe	67	68	65	69	269	5,932.50
Kent Bulle	71	67	64	68	270	4,550
Bryan Martin	71	68	64	67	270	4,550
Peter Campbell	69	70	65	68	272	3,543.75
Eric Dugas	66	64	72	70	272	3,543.75
Ken Looper	63	75	68	66	272	3,543.75
Sebastian Vazquez	64	70	73	65	272	3,543.75

	SCORES			TOTAL	MONEY
Ian Davis	69	69	65	70	273	2,456.25
Christian Espinoza	66	70	65	72	273	2,456.25
Armando Favela	68	69	67	69	273	2,456.25
Matt Hill	71	65	70	67	273	2,456.25
Michael McGowan	69	67	68	69	273	2,456.25
Juan Pablo Solis	71	67	67	68	273	2,456.25
Jose Toledo	66	72	69	66	273	2,456.25

Guatemala Stella Artois Open

La Reunion Golf Resort, Fuego Maya Course, Antigua, Guatemala   May 21-24
Par 36-36–72; 7,275 yards   purse, US$175,000
(Final round cancelled—rain.)

	SCORES			TOTAL	MONEY
Danny Balin	70	65	66	201	US$31,500
Eric Dugas	69	69	67	205	18,900
Martin Trainer	71	67	68	206	9,100
Anthony Paolucci	68	68	70	206	9,100
Linus Gillgren	66	70	70	206	9,100
Marcelo Rozo	72	71	64	207	5,477.50
Puma Dominguez	71	68	68	207	5,477.50
Adam Schenk	67	70	70	207	5,477.50
Armando Favela	69	67	71	207	5,477.50
James Ross	70	65	72	207	5,477.50
Derek Tolan	68	72	68	208	4,200
Jose Toledo	69	67	72	208	4,200
Samuel Del Val	72	67	70	209	3,383.33
Santiago Rivas	68	71	70	209	3,383.33
Bryan Bigley	68	71	70	209	3,383.33
Rodolfo Cazaubon	72	71	67	210	2,887.50
Gerardo Ruiz	72	72	66	210	2,887.50
Vince India	69	74	68	211	2,537.50
Nelson Ledesma	68	71	72	211	2,537.50
Rafael Campos	70	73	69	212	2,114.58
Juan Pablo Luna	71	70	71	212	2,114.58
Matt Hill	71	74	67	212	2,114.58

Honduras Open

Indura Golf Resort, Tela, Honduras   May 28-31
Par 36-36–72; 7,250 yards   purse, US$175,000

	SCORES			TOTAL	MONEY
Felipe Velazquez	69	63	66	69	267	US$31,500
Brady Watt	70	65	64	70	269	18,900
Bryan Bigley	67	67	65	71	270	11,900
Augusto Nunez	69	71	66	65	271	7,233.34
Rafael Campos	67	70	65	69	271	7,233.33
Adam Schenk	69	64	68	70	271	7,233.33
Ian Davis	68	64	70	70	272	5,643.75
Michael McGowan	63	72	67	70	272	5,643.75
Steven Fox	68	65	69	71	273	4,900
Sebastian Vazquez	67	68	67	71	273	4,900
Tyler Weworski	67	70	69	68	274	4,375
Ricardo Celia	68	69	69	69	275	3,675
Samuel Del Val	63	75	70	67	275	3,675

	SCORES				TOTAL	MONEY
Santiago Rivas	69	70	66	70	275	3,675
Armando Favela	71	69	68	68	276	3,062.50
Jose Toledo	68	72	67	69	276	3,062.50
Eric Steger	71	69	70	67	277	2,369.80
Mark Anguiano	69	70	68	70	277	2,369.79
Puma Dominguez	67	68	73	69	277	2,369.79
Maximiliano Godoy	65	69	68	75	277	2,369.79
Justin Hueber	70	68	69	70	277	2,369.79
Sebastian Saavedra	69	70	69	69	277	2,369.79

Dominican Republic Open

Teeth of the Dog, Casa de Campo, La Romana,
Dominican Republic
Par 36-36–72; 7,471 yards

June 4-7
purse, US$175,000

	SCORES				TOTAL	MONEY
Rodolfo Cazaubon	70	69	67	72	278	US$31,500
Santiago Rivas	73	68	71	69	281	15,400
Alexandre Rocha	69	72	69	71	281	15,400
Willy Pumarol	66	74	75	67	282	7,233.34
Justin Hueber	69	72	68	73	282	7,233.33
Vince India	71	70	69	72	282	7,233.33
Rafael Becker	75	67	75	66	283	5,454.17
Keith Mitchell	71	67	76	69	283	5,454.17
Christopher Wolfe	70	72	71	70	283	5,454.16
Bryan Bigley	65	77	69	73	284	4,025
Christian Espinoza	71	69	70	74	284	4,025
Armando Favela	76	68	71	69	284	4,025
Sebastian Saavedra	68	73	73	70	284	4,025
James Vargas	75	65	73	71	284	4,025
Maximiliano Godoy	71	75	68	71	285	2,712.50
Nelson Ledesma	72	69	72	72	285	2,712.50
Jordan Russell	71	71	69	74	285	2,712.50
Julio Santos	68	72	72	73	285	2,712.50
Jose Toledo	67	71	76	71	285	2,712.50
Martin Trainer	68	75	74	68	285	2,712.50

All You Need is Ecuador Open

Quito Golf & Tennis Club, Quito, Ecuador
Par 35-36–71; 7,380 yards

September 10-13
purse, US$175,000

	SCORES				TOTAL	MONEY
Ricardo Celia	70	66	70	69	275	US$31,500
Ian Davis	69	72	68	69	278	15,400
Timothy O'Neal	68	67	72	71	278	15,400
Armando Favela	67	72	70	70	279	8,400
Juan Pablo Luna	70	74	65	71	280	6,387.50
Anthony Paolucci	70	68	73	69	280	6,387.50
Willy Pumarol	68	69	74	69	280	6,387.50
Santiago Rivas	69	69	71	72	281	5,425
Sebastian MacLean	70	68	73	71	282	4,725
Jose Toledo	73	68	70	71	282	4,725
Sebastian Vazquez	70	72	67	73	282	4,725
Mark Anguiano	72	69	72	70	283	3,543.75
Rafael Campos	68	70	70	75	283	3,543.75

	SCORES				TOTAL	MONEY
Bryan Martin	72	71	73	67	283	3,543.75
Omar Tejeira	76	65	73	69	283	3,543.75
Wil Bateman	69	73	74	68	284	2,712.50
Nate Lashley	66	73	74	71	284	2,712.50
Nelson Ledesma	73	72	70	69	284	2,712.50
Jordan Russell	69	73	70	72	284	2,712.50
Ariel Canete	69	72	77	67	285	2,187.50
Adam Schenk	71	71	72	71	285	2,187.50

Volvo Colombian Classic

Club Campestre El Rancho, Bogota, Colombia
Par 34-36–70

September 17-20
purse, US$175,000

	SCORES				TOTAL	MONEY
Mitch Krywulycz	68	69	67	66	270	US$31,500
Jaime Clavijo	67	64	72	68	271	15,400
Sebastian Vazquez	70	68	66	67	271	15,400
Jesus Amaya	72	69	67	65	273	8,400
Juan Sebastian Munoz	67	72	67	69	275	7,000
Santiago Rivas	66	70	70	70	276	6,300
Jhared Hack	69	71	69	69	278	5,454.17
Marcelo Rozo	70	68	68	72	278	5,454.17
Ken Looper	72	64	68	74	278	5,454.16
Manuel Merizalde	68	71	72	68	279	4,550
Keith Mitchell	68	71	72	68	279	4,550
Ariel Canete	69	70	69	72	280	3,850
Julio Zapata	73	65	69	73	280	3,850
Sebastian Saavedra	68	72	73	68	281	2,629.87
Mark Anguiano	70	69	69	73	281	2,629.86
Samuel Del Val	69	72	69	71	281	2,629.86
Rafael Echenique	68	72	71	70	281	2,629.86
Harry Higgs	66	73	69	73	281	2,629.86
Augusto Nunez	68	72	69	72	281	2,629.86
Eric Steger	69	68	74	70	281	2,629.86
Martin Trainer	67	70	71	73	281	2,629.86
James Vargas	73	68	72	68	281	2,629.86

Abierto do Brasil

Itanhanga Golf Club, Itanhanga, Rio de Janeiro, Brazil
Par 35-36–71

September 24-27
purse, US$175,000

	SCORES				TOTAL	MONEY
Alexandre Rocha	68	65	67	67	267	US$31,500
Kent Bulle	65	68	67	67	267	15,400
Keith Mitchell	68	68	64	67	267	15,400
(Rocha defeated Bulle on second and Mitchell on seventh playoff hole.)						
Chris Baker	67	66	70	65	268	8,400
Leandro Marelli	69	69	64	68	270	7,000
Mark Anguiano	73	65	67	66	271	6,081.25
Bryan Bigley	71	67	68	65	271	6,081.25
Adilson da Silva	70	70	66	66	272	4,725
Puma Dominguez	74	66	68	64	272	4,725
Ryan McCarthy	72	66	64	70	272	4,725
Daniel Stapff	68	67	69	68	272	4,725
Michael Weaver	72	69	67	64	272	4,725

	SCORES				TOTAL	MONEY
Felipe Navarro	70	67	64	72	273	3,675
Anthony Paolucci	67	73	64	70	274	3,237.50
Adam Schenk	71	64	69	70	274	3,237.50
Oscar Alvarez	73	66	67	69	275	2,309.03
Ariel Canete	72	68	69	66	275	2,309.03
Christian Espinoza	67	71	71	66	275	2,309.03
Vince India	69	70	67	69	275	2,309.03
Daniel Mazziotta	71	69	69	66	275	2,309.03
Jose Toledo	71	71	66	67	275	2,309.03
Sebastian Vazquez	69	72	67	67	275	2,309.03
Will Collins	68	72	66	69	275	2,309.02
Gerardo Ruiz	70	68	66	71	275	2,309.02

Hyundai-BBVA Abierto de Chile

Los Leones Golf Club, Santiago, Chile
Par 35-35–70

October 1-4
purse, US$175,000

	SCORES				TOTAL	MONEY
Wil Bateman	66	68	63	67	264	US$31,500
Rafael Campos	67	66	66	66	265	18,900
Bryan Martin	67	63	67	69	266	11,900
Jonathan Page	70	68	68	64	270	7,233.34
Rafael Echenique	68	68	66	68	270	7,233.33
Guillermo Pereira	71	67	63	69	270	7,233.33
Juan Pablo Luna	68	67	67	69	271	5,643.75
Ryan McCarthy	73	64	66	68	271	5,643.75
Evan Harmeling	68	68	65	71	272	4,725
Santiago Rivas	67	69	69	67	272	4,725
Diego Velasquez	71	69	65	67	272	4,725
Jaime Clavijo	68	68	69	68	273	3,430
Jose Garrido	70	68	67	68	273	3,430
Maximiliano Godoy	66	67	68	72	273	3,430
Nelson Ledesma	67	68	68	70	273	3,430
David Vanegas	74	68	68	63	273	3,430
Daniel Balin	69	65	72	68	274	2,537.50
Ariel Canete	69	69	68	68	274	2,537.50
Steve Carney	70	68	71	65	274	2,537.50
Franco Romero	72	66	65	71	274	2,537.50

Mundo Maya Open

Yucatan Country Club, Meridia, Mexico
Par 36-36–72; 7,282 yards

October 15-18
purse, US$175,000

	SCORES				TOTAL	MONEY
Nicholas Lindheim	71	68	66	65	270	US$31,500
Daniel Stapff	66	67	67	72	272	18,900
Nate Lashley	71	70	66	66	273	11,900
Oscar Fraustro	68	72	70	64	274	7,700
Keith Mitchell	72	66	69	67	274	7,700
Rafael Campos	70	70	69	66	275	6,300
Eric Dugas	67	75	66	68	276	5,643.75
Evan Harmeling	71	74	65	66	276	5,643.75
Wil Bateman	70	71	66	70	277	4,200
Kent Bulle	65	73	68	71	277	4,200
Rodolfo Cazaubon	73	67	66	71	277	4,200
Puma Dominguez	67	71	68	71	277	4,200

	SCORES				TOTAL	MONEY
Rafael Echenique	67	69	69	72	277	4,200
Guillermo Pereira	75	68	69	65	277	4,200
Adam Schenk	67	71	72	68	278	3,150
Brad Hopfinger	70	70	72	67	279	2,800
Alexandre Rocha	65	75	67	72	279	2,800
Robert Rohanna	66	71	71	71	279	2,800
Samuel Del Val	74	70	68	68	280	2,362.50
Steven Fox	71	69	70	70	280	2,362.50

Bridgestone America's Golf Cup

Ciudad de Mexico Country Club, Coyoacan, Mexico
Par 36-35–71; 6,777 yards

October 22-25
purse, US$300,000

	SCORES				TOTAL	MONEY (Team)
Justin Hueber/Matt Kuchar	67	60	63	60	250	US$60,000
Rafael Campos/Edward Figueroa	64	65	64	61	254	30,990
Corey Conners/Taylor Pendrith	65	65	62	63	255	18,330
Manuel Merizalde/Marcelo Rozo	68	64	63	60	255	18,330
Kent Bulle/Keith Mitchell	67	64	65	62	258	13,900
Mitch Krywulycz/Ryan McCarthy	64	66	64	64	258	13,900
Marco Ruiz/Fabrizio Zanotti	60	68	62	68	258	13,900
Nate Lashley/ Adam Schenk	66	63	62	68	259	11,550
Leandro Marelli/ Augusto Nunez	65	65	67	62	259	11,550
Alfredo Adrian/Felipe Velazquez	68	65	64	63	260	9,900
Juan Pablo Solis/Sebastian Vazquez	63	66	63	68	260	9,900
Brady Watt/Jake Younan	65	66	62	67	260	9,900

Roberto de Vicenzo Punta del Este Open Copa NEC

Club del Lago Golf, Maldonado, Uruguay
Par 35-35–70

October 29-November 1
purse, US$175,000

	SCORES				TOTAL	MONEY
Lanto Griffin	67	68	68	68	271	US$31,500
Rafael Campos	72	64	67	70	273	18,900
Rodolfo Cazaubon	70	66	70	68	274	10,150
Cesar Costilla	67	69	72	66	274	10,150
Steven Fox	65	66	73	71	275	7,000
Bryan Bigley	64	68	71	73	276	6,300
Rafael Echenique	71	67	71	68	277	5,092.50
Evan Harmeling	68	67	69	73	277	5,092.50
James Vargas	69	69	70	69	277	5,092.50
Diego Velasquez	67	64	77	69	277	5,092.50
Brady Watt	71	71	69	66	277	5,092.50
*Juan Alvarez	73	68	69	67	277	
Ariel Canete	69	72	66	71	278	3,325
Brad Gehl	67	75	71	65	278	3,325
Ryan Heisey	70	69	71	68	278	3,325
Marcelo Rozo	69	67	73	69	278	3,325
Sebastian Saavedra	71	71	66	70	278	3,325
Adam Schenk	70	70	69	69	278	3,325
Clodomiro Carranza	68	67	70	74	279	2,283.75
Linus Gillgren	68	75	70	66	279	2,283.75
Augusto Nunez	72	66	74	67	279	2,283.75
Alan Wagner	66	69	73	71	279	2,283.75
Christopher Wolfe	68	69	71	71	279	2,283.75

VISA Open de Argentina

Jockey Club, Buenos Aires, Argentina
Par 36-36–70; 6,577 yards

November 5-8
purse, US$175,000

	SCORES				TOTAL	MONEY
Kent Bulle	66	67	67	69	269	US$31,500
*Juan Alvarez	67	71	67	65	270	
Angel Cabrera	70	70	69	64	273	11,550
Clodomiro Carranza	72	67	71	63	273	11,550
Kelvin Day	65	67	70	71	273	11,550
Steven Fox	67	66	70	70	273	11,550
Daniel Balin	64	70	66	74	274	6,300
Rafael Echenique	70	65	70	70	275	5,092.50
Ricardo Gonzalez	71	67	73	64	275	5,092.50
Anthony Paolucci	70	68	65	72	275	5,092.50
Alexandre Rocha	69	67	72	67	275	5,092.50
Felipe Velazquez	69	66	72	68	275	5,092.50
Lanto Griffin	72	67	68	69	276	3,675
Santiago Rivas	68	70	67	71	276	3,675
Sebastian Saavedra	69	69	68	70	276	3,675
Nate Lashley	69	72	69	68	278	3,150
*Matias Simasky	67	72	74	65	278	
Wil Bateman	66	66	75	72	279	2,887.50
Rodrigo Lee	66	73	69	71	279	2,887.50
Corey Conners	69	72	69	70	280	2,362.50
Maximiliano Godoy	71	71	72	66	280	2,362.50
Juan Pablo Luna	69	72	70	69	280	2,362.50
Willy Pumarol	73	67	74	66	280	2,362.50

Personal Classic

Las Praderas Club, Lugan, Buenos Aires, Argentina
Par 36-36–72; 6,858 yards

November 12-15
purse, US$175,000

	SCORES				TOTAL	MONEY
Fabian Gomez	73	61	69	69	272	US$31,500
Kent Bulle	70	65	70	70	275	18,900
James Vargas	69	68	70	69	276	11,900
Puma Dominguez	69	68	69	72	278	7,700
Ryan McCarthy	74	69	69	66	278	7,700
Rafael Becker	66	73	68	72	279	5,862.50
Nelson Ledesma	71	71	68	69	279	5,862.50
Sebastian Saavedra	70	68	71	70	279	5,862.50
Eric Dugas	69	70	71	70	280	4,900
Alexandre Rocha	71	69	71	69	280	4,900
Julian Etulain	69	69	72	71	281	3,710
Ryan Heisey	68	72	70	71	281	3,710
Augusto Nunez	68	73	67	73	281	3,710
Robert Rohanna	69	69	70	73	281	3,710
Brady Watt	69	70	69	73	281	3,710
Gustavo Acosta	69	71	71	71	282	2,887.50
Evan Harmeling	68	72	70	72	282	2,887.50
*Louis Cohen	69	70	72	71	282	
Rafael Campos	68	71	71	73	283	2,362.50
Clodomiro Carranza	72	72	68	71	283	2,362.50
Jorge Fernandez-Valdes	69	68	79	67	283	2,362.50
Jorge Monroy	72	72	70	69	283	2,362.50

Lexus Peru Open

Los Inkas Golf Club, Lima, Peru
Par 36-36–72; 6,914 yards

November 19-22
purse, US$175,000

		SCORES			TOTAL	MONEY
Rodolfo Cazaubon	64	67	67	70	268	US$31,500
Kent Bulle	67	70	67	64	268	18,900
(Cazaubon defeated Bulle on first playoff hole.)						
Augusto Nunez	69	64	64	73	270	10,150
Sebastian Vazquez	68	67	66	69	270	10,150
Ken Looper	73	67	68	65	273	6,650
Adam Schenk	69	69	71	64	273	6,650
Julian Etulain	69	70	67	68	274	5,454.17
Nate Lashley	64	71	70	69	274	5,454.17
Ethan Tracy	68	68	69	69	274	5,454.16
William Kropp	70	66	70	69	275	4,375
Jose Toledo	65	67	73	70	275	4,375
Michael Weaver	66	69	68	72	275	4,375
Oscar Alvarez	68	68	70	70	276	3,500
Ryan Heisey	69	70	70	67	276	3,500
Christian Espinoza	68	69	73	67	277	3,062.50
Rafael Gomez	76	66	66	69	277	3,062.50
Robert Rohanna	67	70	73	68	278	2,537.50
Brady Schnell	68	72	65	73	278	2,537.50
Juan Pablo Solis	75	68	67	68	278	2,537.50
Derek Tolan	69	69	76	64	278	2,537.50

Latinoamerica Tour Championship

TPC Dorado Beach Resort, Dorado, Puerto Rico
Par 35-36–71; 7,192 yards

December 3-6
purse, US$200,000

		SCORES			TOTAL	MONEY
Daniel Mazziotta	68	68	69	68	273	US$36,000
Ken Looper	68	68	71	70	277	17,600
Jose Toledo	64	69	71	73	277	17,600
Augusto Nunez	69	72	70	68	279	8,266.67
Brady Watt	67	70	74	68	279	8,266.67
Puma Dominguez	71	70	67	71	279	8,266.66
Rafael Campos	69	69	72	70	280	6,450
Adam Schenk	68	72	69	71	280	6,450
Daniel Balin	73	70	66	72	281	5,400
Justin Hueber	71	66	73	71	281	5,400
Ethan Tracy	67	70	70	74	281	5,400
Lanto Griffin	73	67	74	68	282	4,050
Nate Lashley	67	74	70	71	282	4,050
Willy Pumarol	68	77	69	68	282	4,050
Martin Trainer	68	74	72	68	282	4,050
Evan Harmeling	71	73	71	69	284	3,100
Nicholas Lindheim	74	67	71	72	284	3,100
Ryan McCarthy	69	69	71	75	284	3,100
Alexandre Rocha	69	70	70	75	284	3,100
Tommy Cocha	69	70	76	70	285	2,082.50
Rafael Echenique	74	72	71	68	285	2,082.50
Armando Favela	73	70	69	73	285	2,082.50
Brad Gehl	71	74	71	69	285	2,082.50
Juan Pablo Luna	73	71	68	73	285	2,082.50
Bryan Martin	71	70	75	69	285	2,082.50
Santiago Rivas	73	69	72	71	285	2,082.50
Marcelo Rozo	77	67	76	65	285	2,082.50

European Tours

South African Open Championship

See African Sunshine Tour chapter.

Abu Dhabi HSBC Golf Championship

Abu Dhabi Golf Club, Abu Dhabi, United Arab Emirates
Par 36-36–72; 7,600 yards

January 15-18
purse, $2,700,000

	SCORES				TOTAL	MONEY
Gary Stal	68	69	67	65	269	€379,798
Rory McIlroy	67	66	71	66	270	253,199
Martin Kaymer	64	67	65	75	271	142,652
Victor Dubuisson	69	72	64	67	272	105,280
Thomas Pieters	65	67	70	70	272	105,280
Tyrrell Hatton	66	71	70	67	274	68,364
James Morrison	68	67	72	67	274	68,364
Bernd Wiesberger	72	65	66	71	274	68,364
Jamie Donaldson	73	67	65	70	275	46,183
Ross Fisher	71	69	69	66	275	46,183
Charl Schwartzel	71	68	65	71	275	46,183
Byeong-Hun An	67	75	65	69	276	33,099
Alejandro Canizares	69	70	71	66	276	33,099
Ernie Els	70	72	69	65	276	33,099
Oliver Fisher	69	70	70	67	276	33,099
Morten Orum Madsen	68	69	69	70	276	33,099
Justin Rose	73	69	69	65	276	33,099
Anthony Wall	70	71	66	69	276	33,099
Steve Webster	73	67	67	69	276	33,099
Niclas Fasth	69	70	68	70	277	25,446
Branden Grace	66	74	67	70	277	25,446
Miguel Angel Jimenez	72	67	67	71	277	25,446
Paul Lawrie	68	73	67	69	277	25,446
Alexander Levy	66	70	67	74	277	25,446
Dawie van der Walt	70	70	65	72	277	25,446
Nicolas Colsaerts	68	71	72	67	278	21,648
Richard Green	68	68	71	71	278	21,648
Anders Hansen	68	73	68	69	278	21,648
Maximilian Kieffer	70	71	68	69	278	21,648
Eddie Pepperell	70	68	68	72	278	21,648
Marcus Fraser	72	68	67	72	279	18,002
Scott Hend	70	70	70	69	279	18,002
Raphael Jacquelin	69	71	69	70	279	18,002
Mike Lorenzo-Vera	69	69	71	70	279	18,002
Peter Uihlein	67	68	70	74	279	18,002
Y.E. Yang	70	70	69	70	279	18,002
Gregory Bourdy	66	74	66	74	280	14,584
George Coetzee	68	73	68	71	280	14,584
Jordi Garcia Pinto	70	71	70	69	280	14,584
Emiliano Grillo	70	70	68	72	280	14,584
Alex Noren	67	75	68	70	280	14,584
Robert Rock	69	73	70	68	280	14,584
Richard Sterne	71	70	70	69	280	14,584
Oliver Wilson	71	71	66	72	280	14,584
Kiradech Aphibarnrat	72	67	72	70	281	11,622

	SCORES				TOTAL	MONEY
Kristoffer Broberg	69	71	70	71	281	11,622
Soren Hansen	69	69	70	73	281	11,622
Andrew Johnston	73	68	70	70	281	11,622
Robert Karlsson	67	71	69	74	281	11,622
Seve Benson	69	73	67	73	282	9,343
Bradley Dredge	72	70	70	70	282	9,343
Mikko Ilonen	66	75	68	73	282	9,343
Anirban Lahiri	72	68	72	70	282	9,343
Thorbjorn Olesen	72	69	73	68	282	9,343
Richard Bland	69	73	72	69	283	7,748
Damien McGrane	71	69	71	72	283	7,748
Oliver Farr	73	69	72	70	284	6,495
Craig Lee	73	68	70	73	284	6,495
Matthew Nixon	68	71	74	71	284	6,495
Renato Paratore	70	69	73	72	284	6,495
Andy Sullivan	71	71	67	75	284	6,495
Danny Willett	70	71	71	72	284	6,495
Jorge Campillo	72	70	77	66	285	5,469
Johan Carlsson	70	72	71	72	285	5,469
Jeev Milkha Singh	68	73	71	73	285	5,469
David Drysdale	70	71	74	71	286	4,785
Rickie Fowler	67	75	73	71	286	4,785
Simon Khan	73	67	72	74	286	4,785
Jbe Kruger	74	68	72	74	288	4,330
Darren Fichardt	69	73	77	70	289	4,152
*Tian-Lang Guan	70	69	78	72	289	
Jason Palmer	71	71	76	72	290	3,418

Commercial Bank Qatar Masters

Doha Golf Club, Doha, Qatar
Par 36-36–72; 7,400 yards

January 21-24
purse, $2,500,000

	SCORES				TOTAL	MONEY
Branden Grace	67	68	68	66	269	€353,257
Marc Warren	71	65	67	67	270	235,502
Bernd Wiesberger	69	66	68	68	271	132,685
Eddie Pepperell	69	71	65	67	272	105,978
Byeong-Hun An	67	69	72	65	273	75,880
Gregory Bourdy	70	68	70	65	273	75,880
Emiliano Grillo	67	69	67	70	273	75,880
Alejandro Canizares	67	70	68	69	274	52,989
Alex Noren	67	71	72	65	275	47,478
Oliver Fisher	65	73	69	69	276	40,695
Benjamin Hebert	72	68	69	67	276	40,695
George Coetzee	68	67	70	72	277	36,456
Johan Carlsson	74	65	69	70	278	30,592
Magnus A. Carlsson	71	69	70	68	278	30,592
Nicolas Colsaerts	70	73	67	68	278	30,592
Soren Kjeldsen	73	70	67	68	278	30,592
Justin Rose	68	73	69	68	278	30,592
Henrik Stenson	70	71	71	66	278	30,592
Seve Benson	70	71	69	69	279	25,064
Anders Hansen	71	69	70	69	279	25,064
Julien Quesne	70	72	69	68	279	25,064
Andy Sullivan	71	68	70	70	279	25,064
Felipe Aguilar	71	68	72	69	280	21,407
Matthew Baldwin	70	68	70	72	280	21,407
Ernie Els	67	72	70	71	280	21,407
Darren Fichardt	67	70	71	72	280	21,407

	SCORES				TOTAL	MONEY
Tommy Fleetwood	73	65	74	68	280	21,407
Thongchai Jaidee	69	73	69	69	280	21,407
Alvaro Quiros	70	70	72	68	280	21,407
Ross Fisher	70	70	73	68	281	18,228
Ricardo Gonzalez	69	70	73	69	281	18,228
Mike Lorenzo-Vera	70	70	69	72	281	18,228
Kristoffer Broberg	67	71	72	72	282	15,939
Rafa Cabrera-Bello	66	73	70	73	282	15,939
Stephen Gallacher	68	75	72	67	282	15,939
Pablo Larrazabal	71	71	67	73	282	15,939
Edoardo Molinari	71	70	70	71	282	15,939
Thomas Aiken	69	73	72	69	283	13,141
Kiradech Aphibarnrat	68	71	75	69	283	13,141
Richard Green	70	67	76	70	283	13,141
Shiv Kapur	70	68	72	73	283	13,141
Renato Paratore	69	69	70	75	283	13,141
Thomas Pieters	73	68	68	74	283	13,141
Brett Rumford	69	72	73	69	283	13,141
Jeev Milkha Singh	70	70	73	70	283	13,141
Sergio Garcia	69	69	77	69	284	10,173
Maximilian Kieffer	71	68	73	72	284	10,173
Paul Lawrie	67	73	73	71	284	10,173
Peter Lawrie	70	68	73	73	284	10,173
James Morrison	68	70	75	71	284	10,173
Dawie van der Walt	72	69	70	73	284	10,173
Jason Barnes	72	70	72	71	285	7,630
Edouard Espana	70	73	70	72	285	7,630
Mark Foster	67	73	70	75	285	7,630
Michael Hoey	71	69	74	71	285	7,630
Andrew Johnston	69	73	72	71	285	7,630
Tom Lewis	72	71	69	73	285	7,630
Eduardo de la Riva	70	69	72	75	286	6,040
Gregory Havret	70	69	75	72	286	6,040
Damien McGrane	68	72	74	72	286	6,040
Peter Uihlein	69	73	71	73	286	6,040
Jorge Campillo	72	70	73	72	287	5,298
Robert Karlsson	70	73	73	71	287	5,298
Mark Tullo	69	74	73	71	287	5,298
Scott Jamieson	68	73	72	75	288	4,663
Moritz Lampert	67	74	77	70	288	4,663
Jake Roos	75	68	72	73	288	4,663
Matthew Nixon	72	71	74	72	289	4,133
Adrian Otaegui	73	70	73	73	289	4,133
Richard Finch	71	72	75	72	290	3,526
Paul Waring	70	72	76	72	290	3,526
Matthew Fitzpatrick	68	71	77	77	293	3,174
Wade Ormsby	74	69	71	79	293	3,174
Mikko Korhonen	73	70	77	74	294	3,170

Omega Dubai Desert Classic

Emirates Golf Club, Dubai, United Arab Emirates
Par 35-37–72; 7,327 yards

January 29-February 1
purse, $2,650,000

	SCORES				TOTAL	MONEY
Rory McIlroy	66	64	66	70	266	€378,779
Alex Noren	68	67	69	65	269	252,519
Stephen Gallacher	66	67	70	69	272	142,272
Martin Kaymer	67	69	73	64	273	82,908
Morten Orum Madsen	71	63	66	73	273	82,908

Women's Tours

Lydia Ko, 18, became the youngest women's major winner at the Evian Championship.

Sam Greenwood/Getty Images

David Cannon/Getty Images

In-Gee Chun, U.S. Open champion.

Inbee Park, Ricoh British Open champion.

Chung Sung-Jun/Getty Images

Lexi Thompson's two wins included the KEB HanaBank Championship in South Korea.

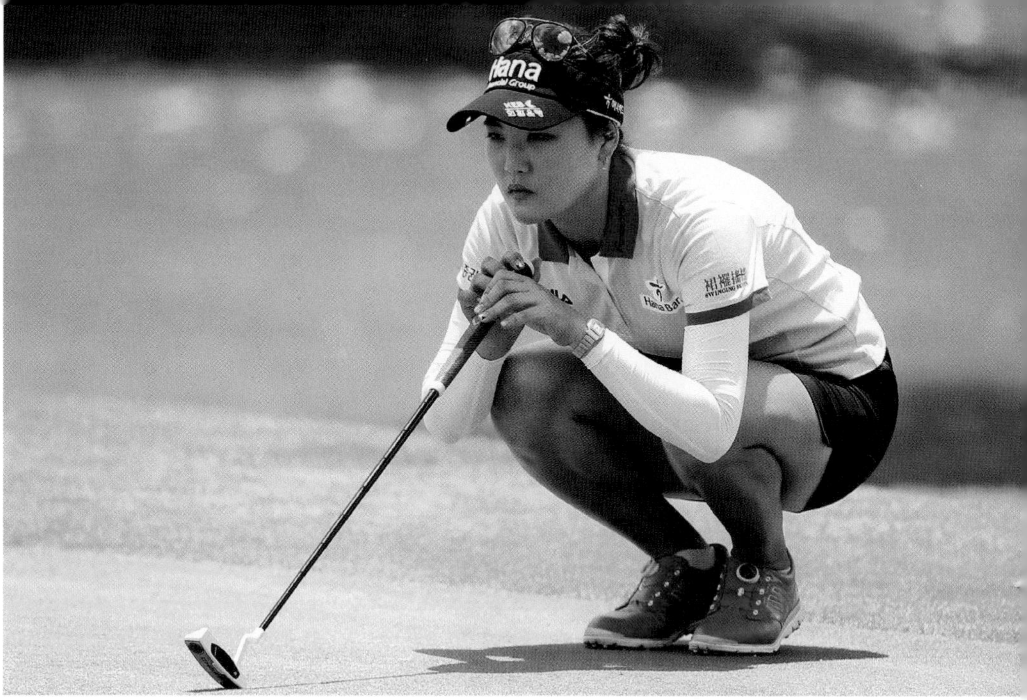

Christian Petersen/Getty Images

So Yeon Ryu won the World Ladies Championship in China and another title in South Korea.

Kent Horner/Getty Images

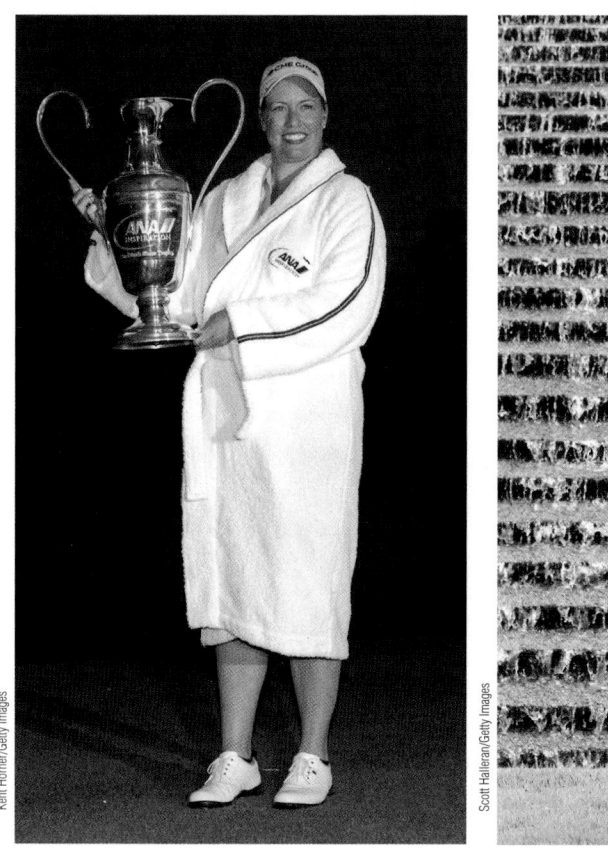

ANA Inspiration champion Brittany Lincicome.

Scott Halleran/Getty Images

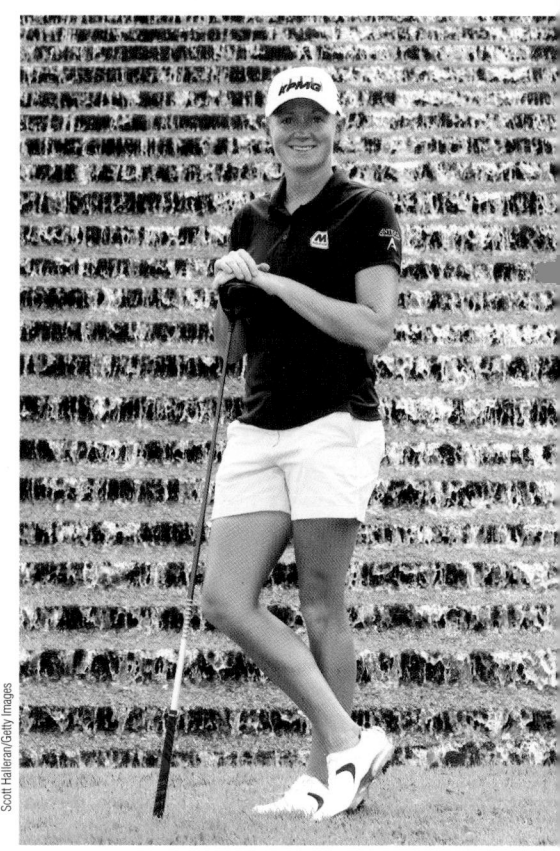

Five runner-up finishes for Stacy Lewis.

Kevin Lee/Getty Images

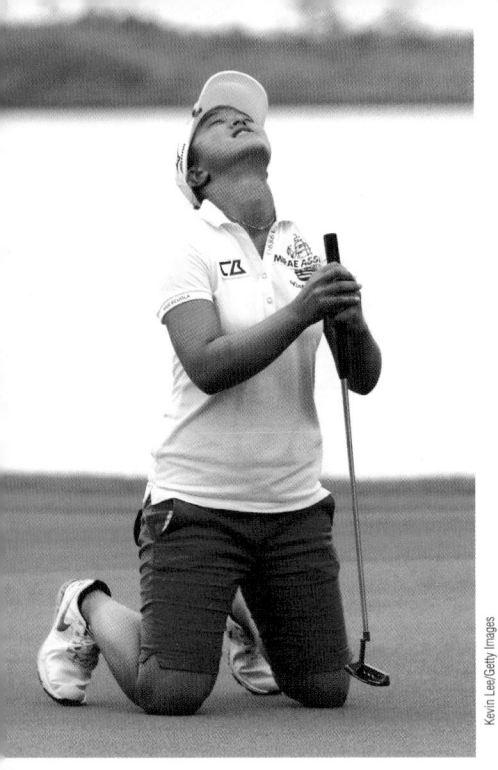

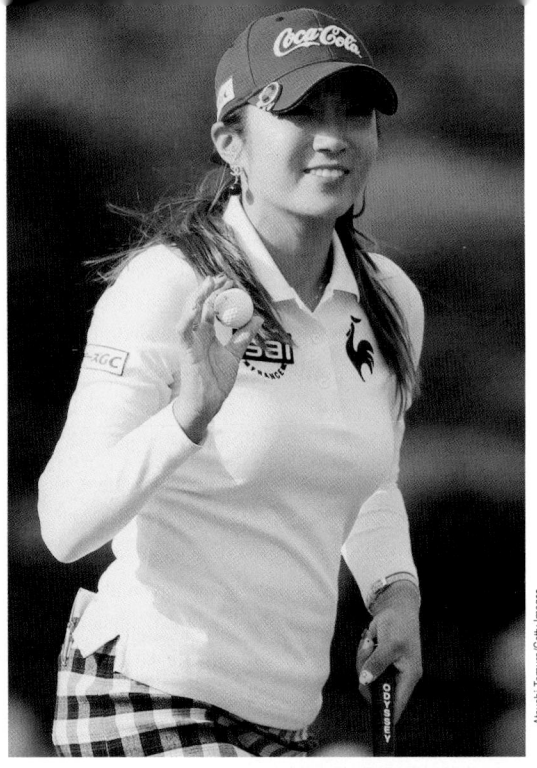

LPGA rookie of the year Sei Young Kim.

Atsushi Tomura/Getty Images

Bo-Mee Lee won seven times in Japan.

Getty Images

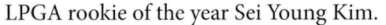

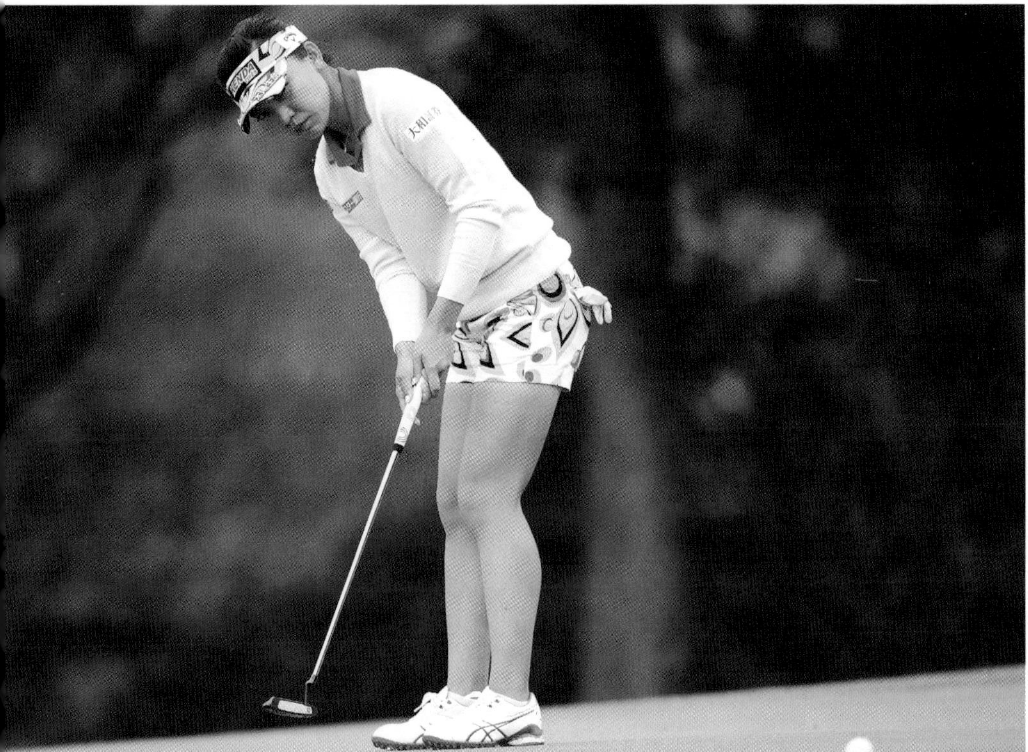

Teresa Lu won the Japan LPGA Championship, one of five wins on the circuit.

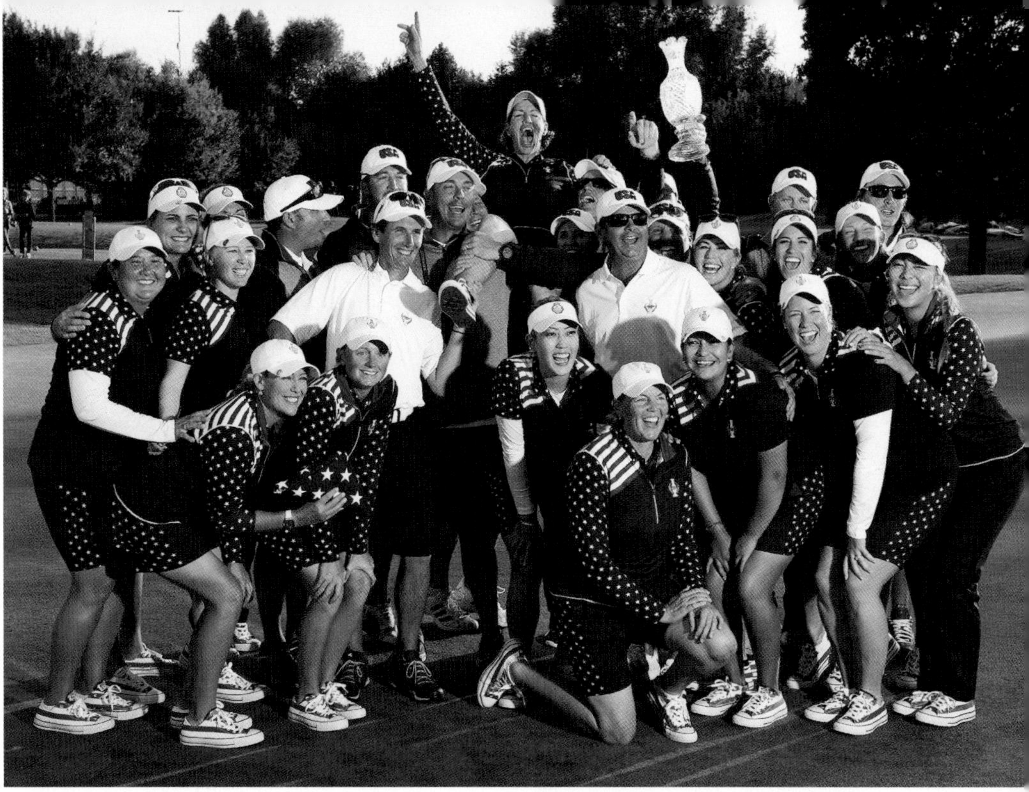

Stuart Franklin/Getty Images

America gained their first Solheim Cup win since 2009 with a record comeback in the singles.

Stuart Franklin/Getty Images

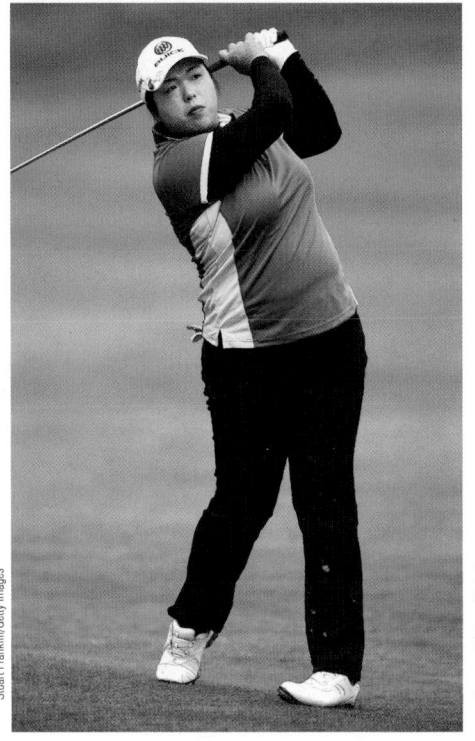

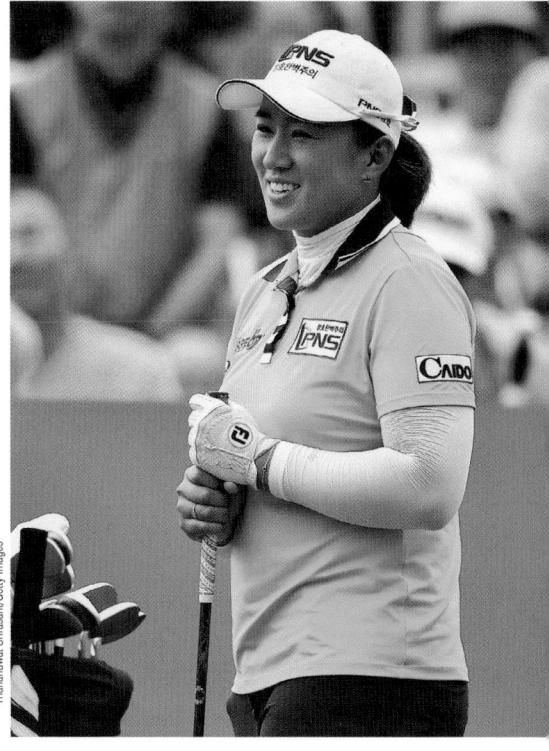

Shanshan Feng retained the Dubai Masters title.

Thananuwat Srirasant/Getty Images

Amy Yang won the Honda Thailand event.

Senior Tours

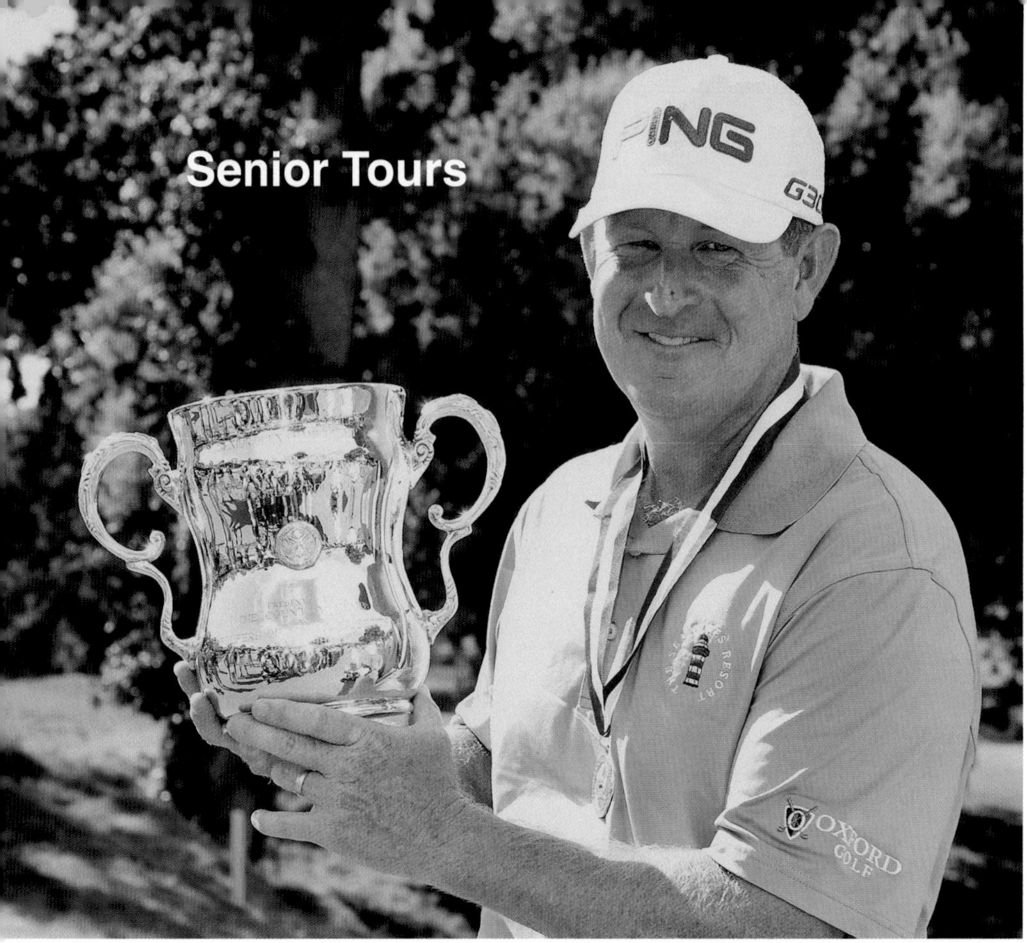

Harry How/Getty Images

Jeff Maggert won four times in 2015 with the highlight his victory in the U.S. Senior Open.

Andy Lyons/Getty Images

Christian Petersen/Getty Images

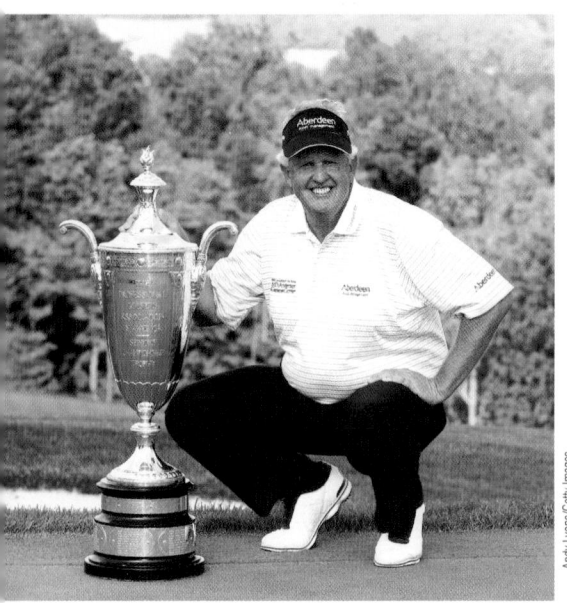

Colin Montgomerie retained his Senior PGA title.

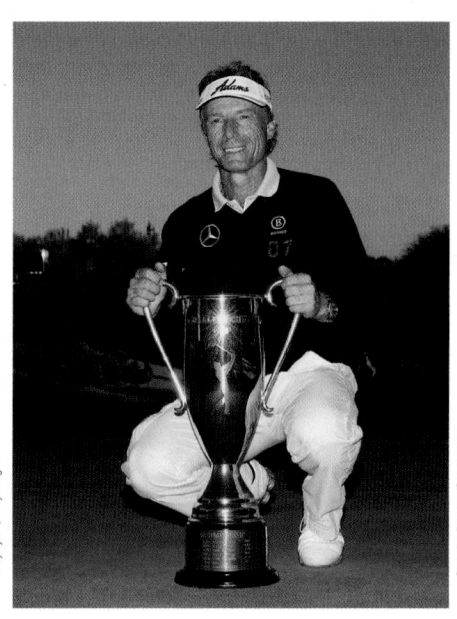

Bernhard Langer won the Charles Schwab Cup.

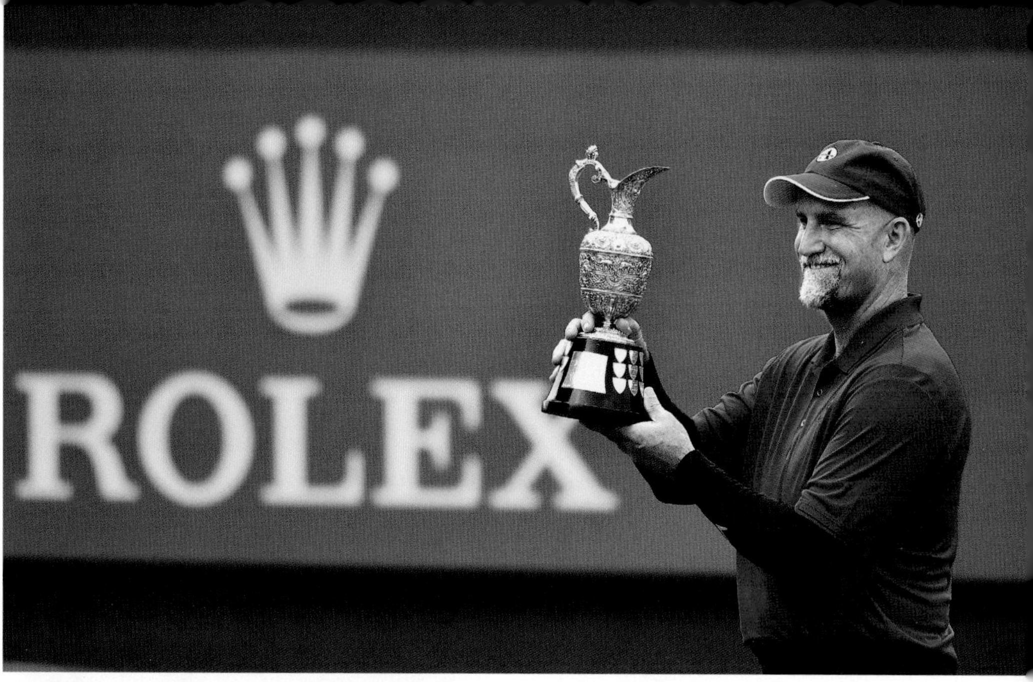

Warren Little/Getty Images

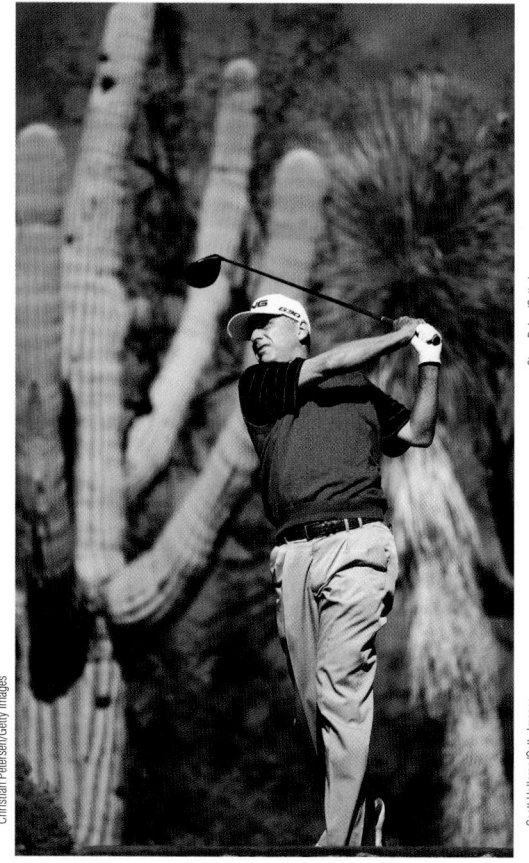

Marco Dawson birdied Sunningdale's 18th hole to win the Senior Open Championship.

Christian Petersen/Getty Images

Kevin Sutherland was a runner-up three times.

Steve Dykes/Getty Images

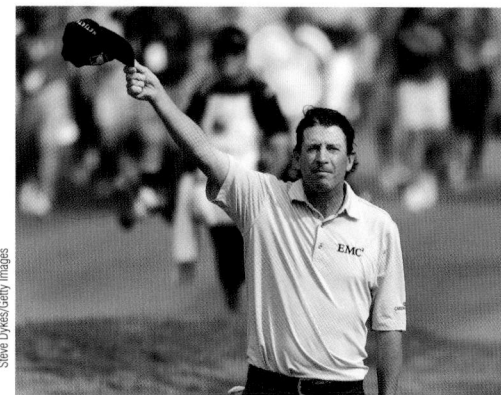

Three-time winner Billy Andrade.

Scott Halleran/Getty Images

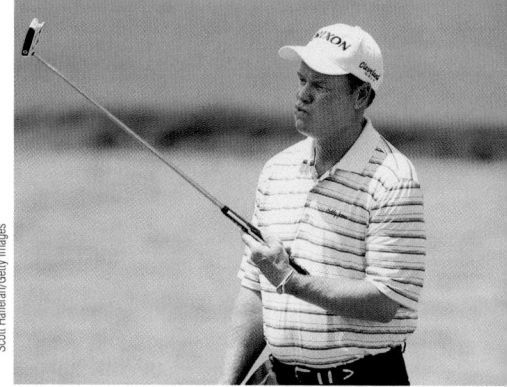

Joe Durant won the Legends with Andrade.

Peter Fowler, British Senior PGA winner.

Tom Lehman won the SAS Championship.

Michael Allen had nine top-10 finishes.

Esteban Toledo won the Nature Valley Open.

Scott Dunlap, twice a runner-up.

	SCORES				TOTAL	MONEY
Gary Stal	69	69	67	68	273	82,908
Andy Sullivan	65	68	70	70	273	82,908
Bernd Wiesberger	64	69	70	70	273	82,908
Thomas Aiken	68	71	66	69	274	44,318
Graeme McDowell	67	65	72	70	274	44,318
Robert Rock	68	67	69	70	274	44,318
Lee Westwood	65	68	69	72	274	44,318
Byeong-Hun An	70	70	66	69	275	32,143
Gregory Bourdy	69	71	69	66	275	32,143
Renato Paratore	68	66	70	71	275	32,143
Henrik Stenson	70	66	70	69	275	32,143
Peter Uihlein	65	69	70	71	275	32,143
Marc Warren	66	65	73	71	275	32,143
Danny Willett	67	66	70	72	275	32,143
Ross Fisher	71	68	71	66	276	25,727
Emiliano Grillo	67	68	69	72	276	25,727
Gregory Havret	68	71	70	67	276	25,727
Pablo Larrazabal	69	66	69	72	276	25,727
Alvaro Quiros	73	69	70	64	276	25,727
Richard Green	70	68	70	69	277	23,295
David Howell	71	69	69	68	277	23,295
Raphael Jacquelin	71	71	67	69	278	21,932
David Lipsky	68	71	68	71	278	21,932
Paul Lawrie	69	71	66	73	279	20,227
Alexander Levy	72	68	70	69	279	20,227
Dawie van der Walt	69	73	66	71	279	20,227
Nicolas Colsaerts	65	74	67	74	280	18,182
Anders Hansen	66	72	71	71	280	18,182
Maximilian Kieffer	66	68	73	73	280	18,182
Seve Benson	66	66	73	76	281	15,682
Edouard Espana	70	70	70	71	281	15,682
Jordi Garcia Pinto	70	66	72	73	281	15,682
Thongchai Jaidee	71	68	69	73	281	15,682
Andrew Johnston	68	72	71	70	281	15,682
Garth Mulroy	69	70	72	70	281	15,682
Anthony Wall	69	70	72	70	281	15,682
Felipe Aguilar	70	71	70	71	282	12,954
Kristoffer Broberg	69	69	70	74	282	12,954
Mark Foster	73	69	67	73	282	12,954
Mike Lorenzo-Vera	70	70	71	71	282	12,954
Thomas Pieters	69	69	75	69	282	12,954
Daniel Brooks	69	73	71	70	283	10,454
Jorge Campillo	67	70	75	71	283	10,454
Alejandro Canizares	72	69	69	73	283	10,454
Tommy Fleetwood	72	70	71	70	283	10,454
Joost Luiten	68	70	70	75	283	10,454
Y.E. Yang	67	73	71	72	283	10,454
Magnus A. Carlsson	71	71	65	77	284	8,636
Michael Hoey	72	70	71	71	284	8,636
Richard Bland	71	69	72	73	285	6,790
Ernie Els	72	70	72	71	285	6,790
Oliver Farr	73	68	72	72	285	6,790
Branden Grace	73	69	71	72	285	6,790
Tyrrell Hatton	71	69	72	73	285	6,790
Mikko Ilonen	67	71	74	73	285	6,790
Moritz Lampert	71	67	75	72	285	6,790
Peter Lawrie	73	69	73	70	285	6,790
Chris Doak	72	70	73	71	286	5,341
Tom Lewis	68	73	70	75	286	5,341
Edoardo Molinari	70	72	73	71	286	5,341
Hennie Otto	66	73	70	77	286	5,341
Bradley Dredge	71	71	68	77	287	4,447
Wade Ormsby	69	69	70	79	287	4,447

	SCORES				TOTAL	MONEY
Jason Palmer	74	68	72	73	287	4,447
Paul Waring	69	67	72	79	287	4,447
Matthew Baldwin	71	71	73	74	289	3,409
Dominic Foos	71	71	72	76	290	3,406
Damien McGrane	71	70	74	76	291	3,403
Scott Jamieson	74	68	70	83	295	3,400

Maybank Malaysian Open

See Asia/Japan Tours chapter.

True Thailand Classic

See Asia/Japan Tours chapter.

Hero Indian Hero Open

See Asia/Japan Tours chapter.

Joburg Open

See African Sunshine Tour chapter.

Africa Open

See African Sunshine Tour chapter.

Tshwane Open

See African Sunshine Tour chapter.

Trophee Hassan II

Golf du Palais Royal, Agadir, Morocco
Par 36-36-72; 6,951 yards

March 26-29
purse, €1,500,000

	SCORES				TOTAL	MONEY
Richie Ramsay	72	66	71	69	278	€250,000
Romain Wattel	68	74	67	70	279	166,660
George Coetzee	67	72	71	70	280	61,250
Pablo Larrazabal	70	69	73	68	280	61,250
Mikael Lundberg	70	75	66	69	280	61,250
Kevin Phelan	70	70	70	70	280	61,250
Jaco Van Zyl	69	71	70	70	280	61,250
Chris Wood	67	72	74	67	280	61,250
Richard Bland	69	70	71	71	281	28,230
Ben Evans	69	70	74	68	281	28,230
Jose Maria Olazabal	69	76	70	66	281	28,230
Wade Ormsby	71	72	68	70	281	28,230
Marcel Schneider	73	69	72	67	281	28,230
Mark Foster	73	72	71	66	282	22,050
Soren Kjeldsen	68	73	69	72	282	22,050
Anthony Wall	68	72	72	70	282	22,050
Seve Benson	73	68	72	70	283	18,150
Pelle Edberg	71	71	71	70	283	18,150
Tommy Fleetwood	70	71	73	69	283	18,150
David Horsey	70	71	69	73	283	18,150
Andrew Marshall	71	73	69	70	283	18,150

	SCORES			TOTAL	MONEY
Eddie Pepperell	71	74	69	69	283	18,150
Bernd Ritthammer	71	70	71	71	283	18,150
Scott Jamieson	74	69	71	70	284	15,600
Maximilian Kieffer	73	73	68	70	284	15,600
Julien Quesne	70	75	72	67	284	15,600
Gregory Bourdy	75	71	68	71	285	13,350
Richard Green	68	70	76	71	285	13,350
Emiliano Grillo	74	69	67	75	285	13,350
Benjamin Hebert	75	71	69	70	285	13,350
David Howell	70	70	77	68	285	13,350
Tom Lewis	69	77	71	68	285	13,350
Mike Lorenzo-Vera	74	72	70	69	285	13,350
Byeong-Hun An	72	71	71	72	286	9,900
Rafa Cabrera-Bello	69	69	74	74	286	9,900
Jorge Campillo	71	69	73	73	286	9,900
Eduardo de la Riva	68	75	71	72	286	9,900
Michael Hoey	70	73	76	67	286	9,900
Robert Karlsson	72	74	68	72	286	9,900
Joakim Lagergren	72	68	75	71	286	9,900
Moritz Lampert	68	75	73	70	286	9,900
Andrew McArthur	71	71	67	77	286	9,900
Robert Rock	74	72	72	68	286	9,900
Adrien Saddier	65	77	71	73	286	9,900
Oliver Wilson	68	73	73	72	286	9,900
Magnus A. Carlsson	73	70	70	74	287	7,500
Raphael Jacquelin	70	76	70	71	287	7,500
Shiv Kapur	72	73	67	75	287	7,500
Mikko Korhonen	68	74	71	74	287	7,500
Andrew Johnston	72	71	77	68	288	6,300
Max Orrin	70	70	72	76	288	6,300
Chris Paisley	71	70	72	75	288	6,300
Justin Walters	71	73	71	73	288	6,300
Pedro Oriol	71	75	69	74	289	5,550
David Drysdale	67	73	76	74	290	4,837
Niclas Fasth	71	73	74	72	290	4,837
Lee Slattery	77	69	76	68	290	4,837
Paul Waring	70	74	72	74	290	4,837
Oliver Farr	70	68	74	79	291	4,200
Florian Fritsch	70	72	76	73	291	4,200
Matteo Manassero	72	71	72	76	291	4,200
Nacho Elvira	73	72	73	74	292	3,900
Chris Lloyd	76	69	75	73	293	3,750
Richard Finch	75	71	77	71	294	3,525
Michio Matsumura	72	74	74	74	294	3,525
Edouard Espana	73	70	76	77	296	3,300
Kristoffer Broberg	73	70	74	80	297	3,000
Oliver Fisher	74	71	76	76	297	3,000
Ricardo Santos	69	72	73	83	297	3,000
James Morrison	72	73	72	81	298	2,495
Pontus Widegren	73	73	69	83	298	2,495
Scott Hend	71	73	84	72	300	2,247

Shenzhen International

Genzon Golf Club, Shenzhen, China
Par 36-36–72; 7,145 yards

April 16-19
purse, US$2,500,000

	SCORES				TOTAL	MONEY
Kiradech Aphibarnrat	67	69	68	72	276	€386,168
Hao-Tong Li	71	73	65	67	276	257,442
(Aphibarnrat defeated Li on first playoff hole.)						
Tommy Fleetwood	70	69	69	69	277	145,047
Marco Crespi	69	70	72	67	278	74,410
David Howell	71	70	69	68	278	74,410
Wen-Yi Huang	66	74	70	68	278	74,410
Tom Lewis	72	71	66	69	278	74,410
Julien Quesne	71	69	73	65	278	74,410
Peter Uihlein	67	68	71	72	278	74,410
Y.E. Yang	72	71	66	69	278	74,410
Emiliano Grillo	71	67	70	71	279	38,810
Wade Ormsby	73	73	67	66	279	38,810
Richie Ramsay	72	73	66	68	279	38,810
Anthony Wall	69	72	69	69	279	38,810
Lucas Bjerregaard	72	67	74	67	280	30,187
Gregory Bourdy	72	72	70	66	280	30,187
Ross Fisher	69	74	68	69	280	30,187
Tyrrell Hatton	72	70	69	69	280	30,187
Gregory Havret	70	68	73	69	280	30,187
Scott Hend	70	70	68	72	280	30,187
Alvaro Quiros	72	71	74	63	280	30,187
Kristoffer Broberg	73	69	67	72	281	25,487
Darren Fichardt	68	70	71	72	281	25,487
Pablo Larrazabal	73	69	65	74	281	25,487
Jorge Campillo	72	71	69	70	282	23,054
Marcus Fraser	72	71	68	71	282	23,054
Michael Hoey	74	71	68	69	282	23,054
Alexander Levy	71	70	69	72	282	23,054
Zhi-Peng Fan	70	72	70	71	283	19,926
Maximilian Kieffer	72	70	72	69	283	19,926
Matteo Manassero	69	70	74	70	283	19,926
Bubba Watson	70	74	74	65	283	19,926
Chris Wood	75	70	69	69	283	19,926
Richard Bland	71	71	70	72	284	16,914
Niclas Fasth	73	69	71	71	284	16,914
Matt Ford	69	69	70	76	284	16,914
Jbe' Kruger	71	74	67	72	284	16,914
Romain Wattel	69	74	69	72	284	16,914
Felipe Aguilar	67	75	74	69	285	14,597
Ben Evans	75	71	71	68	285	14,597
David Horsey	70	71	74	70	285	14,597
Mikko Korhonen	71	72	72	70	285	14,597
Adrian Otaegui	76	69	73	67	285	14,597
Alex Noren	73	71	71	71	286	12,743
Renato Paratore	72	71	72	71	286	12,743
Gary Stal	70	74	69	73	286	12,743
Rafa Cabrera-Bello	69	75	70	73	287	11,121
Magnus A. Carlsson	73	73	69	72	287	11,121
Trevor Fisher, Jr.	71	70	76	70	287	11,121
Ze-Yu He	73	73	68	73	287	11,121
Garth Mulroy	69	74	71	74	288	9,963
Shiv Kapur	69	74	70	76	289	9,268
Yan-Wei Liu	73	73	69	74	289	9,268
Andy Sullivan	69	75	72	74	290	8,573
*Yechun Yuan	71	75	76	69	291	
Johan Carlsson	72	74	76	70	292	7,877

	SCORES				TOTAL	MONEY
Morten Orum Madsen	71	71	74	76	292	7,877
Matthew Nixon	73	73	70	77	293	7,066
Wei-Huang Wu	70	73	71	79	293	7,066
Craig Lee	75	71	78	70	294	6,603
Xin-Jun Zhang	72	74	71	77	294	6,603
Jerome Lando Casanova	72	73	74	76	295	6,024
Gui-Ming Liao	74	71	72	78	295	6,024
Eddie Pepperell	73	72	74	76	295	6,024
Raphael Jacquelin	71	74	74	77	296	5,560
*Yi-Nong Yang	70	73	78	75	296	
David Lipsky	73	68	79	81	301	5,329

Volvo China Open

See Asia/Japan Tours chapter.

AfrAsia Bank Mauritius Open

See African Sunshine Tour chapter.

Open de Espana

Real Club de Golf El Prat, Terrassa, Barcelona, Spain
Par 36-36–72; 7,326 yards

May 14-17
purse, €1,500,000

	SCORES				TOTAL	MONEY
James Morrison	70	71	68	69	278	€250,000
Edouard Espana	68	69	76	69	282	99,790
David Howell	71	69	69	73	282	99,790
Miguel Angel Jimenez	72	71	72	67	282	99,790
Francesco Molinari	72	69	70	71	282	99,790
Emiliano Grillo	70	70	72	71	283	52,500
Jorge Campillo	74	70	70	70	284	41,250
Jose Manuel Lara	70	76	72	66	284	41,250
Eduardo de la Riva	66	77	74	68	285	27,350
Pelle Edberg	70	73	75	67	285	27,350
Darren Fichardt	66	73	73	73	285	27,350
Maximilian Kieffer	73	70	76	66	285	27,350
Soren Kjeldsen	70	76	70	69	285	27,350
Wade Ormsby	77	71	72	65	285	27,350
Byeong-Hun An	72	70	72	72	286	19,543
Gregory Bourdy	69	73	75	69	286	19,543
Johan Carlsson	70	76	72	68	286	19,543
Ben Evans	73	73	71	69	286	19,543
David Horsey	69	77	71	69	286	19,543
Mikko Korhonen	71	73	73	69	286	19,543
Richie Ramsay	74	73	72	67	286	19,543
Thomas Aiken	74	71	72	70	287	15,825
Trevor Fisher, Jr.	65	78	73	71	287	15,825
Matthew Fitzpatrick	72	71	73	71	287	15,825
Sergio Garcia	75	72	67	73	287	15,825
Ricardo Gonzalez	69	69	76	73	287	15,825
Gregory Havret	71	71	74	71	287	15,825
Matt Ford	67	76	72	73	288	13,800
Robert Rock	70	76	73	69	288	13,800
Y.E. Yang	73	71	72	72	288	13,800
Michael Hoey	71	68	75	75	289	12,675
Scott Jamieson	72	75	78	64	289	12,675
Kristoffer Broberg	75	70	74	71	290	10,819

	SCORES				TOTAL	MONEY
Johan Edfors	71	75	74	70	290	10,819
Ross Fisher	73	74	75	68	290	10,819
Tommy Fleetwood	66	77	77	70	290	10,819
Paul Maddy	70	70	77	73	290	10,819
Thomas Pieters	70	75	76	69	290	10,819
Jeev Milkha Singh	74	70	74	72	290	10,819
Graeme Storm	75	73	74	68	290	10,819
Alejandro Canizares	73	74	72	72	291	8,400
Carlos Del Moral	72	73	77	69	291	8,400
Benjamin Hebert	71	70	73	77	291	8,400
Mike Lorenzo-Vera	71	76	73	71	291	8,400
Mikael Lundberg	72	76	72	71	291	8,400
Matthew Nixon	72	74	72	73	291	8,400
Eddie Pepperell	75	73	75	68	291	8,400
Borja Virto Astudillo	73	72	75	71	291	8,400
Felipe Aguilar	72	74	74	72	292	6,150
Ignacio Garrido	71	76	76	69	292	6,150
Pablo Larrazabal	71	73	73	75	292	6,150
Paul Lawrie	70	73	79	70	292	6,150
Chris Paisley	75	73	73	71	292	6,150
Romain Wattel	70	73	79	70	292	6,150
Chris Wood	76	72	71	73	292	6,150
Magnus A. Carlsson	73	73	74	73	293	4,530
Andrew Dodt	71	77	71	74	293	4,530
Soren Hansen	68	75	76	74	293	4,530
Alex Noren	75	71	76	71	293	4,530
John Parry	68	73	74	78	293	4,530
Richard Finch	72	72	75	75	294	3,675
Marcus Fraser	73	73	72	76	294	3,675
Richard Green	72	75	77	70	294	3,675
Matteo Manassero	73	72	77	72	294	3,675
Alessandro Tadini	70	76	75	73	294	3,675
Alvaro Velasco	73	75	73	73	294	3,675
Marco Crespi	77	70	75	73	295	3,150
Adrian Otaegui	68	75	81	72	296	3,000
Peter Uihlein	72	73	78	74	297	2,850
Jason Palmer	71	70	77	81	299	2,740
Carlos Pigem	77	70	78	75	300	2,250
Tom Murray	74	74	80	75	303	2,247

BMW PGA Championship

Wentworth Club, Virginia Water, Surrey, England
Par 35-37–72; 7,302 yards

May 21-24
purse, €5,000,000

	SCORES				TOTAL	MONEY
Byeong-Hun An	71	64	67	65	267	€833,330
Thongchai Jaidee	70	66	68	69	273	434,275
Miguel Angel Jimenez	68	70	68	67	273	434,275
Chris Wood	68	73	68	66	275	250,000
Francesco Molinari	65	69	68	74	276	212,000
Tommy Fleetwood	69	71	65	72	277	162,500
Shane Lowry	74	67	67	69	277	162,500
Alex Noren	72	67	68	71	278	118,500
Julien Quesne	72	70	68	68	278	118,500
Alejandro Canizares	72	71	68	68	279	100,000
Felipe Aguilar	70	73	67	70	280	79,833
Thomas Bjorn	69	71	71	69	280	79,833
Branden Grace	73	68	70	69	280	79,833
Gregory Havret	70	71	69	70	280	79,833

	SCORES				TOTAL	MONEY
Joost Luiten	72	67	74	67	280	79,833
James Morrison	71	66	75	68	280	79,833
Andy Sullivan	71	72	72	66	281	67,500
Jamie Donaldson	70	73	67	72	282	61,125
Martin Kaymer	72	71	69	70	282	61,125
Soren Kjeldsen	71	69	73	69	282	61,125
Marc Warren	68	74	71	69	282	61,125
Magnus A. Carlsson	72	70	69	72	283	53,500
Nicolas Colsaerts	69	73	70	71	283	53,500
Richard Green	72	71	68	72	283	53,500
Graeme Storm	78	64	70	71	283	53,500
Y.E. Yang	68	74	69	72	283	53,500
Kiradech Aphibarnrat	72	69	74	69	284	43,750
Oliver Farr	72	69	72	71	284	43,750
Marcus Fraser	73	70	73	68	284	43,750
Peter Hanson	72	73	70	69	284	43,750
Scott Jamieson	74	68	72	70	284	43,750
Robert Karlsson	67	71	72	74	284	43,750
Maximilian Kieffer	73	71	69	71	284	43,750
Peter Uihlein	76	68	66	74	284	43,750
Thomas Aiken	74	70	69	72	285	36,500
David Lipsky	75	66	69	75	285	36,500
Prom Meesawat	71	74	71	69	285	36,500
Darren Clarke	74	71	75	66	286	31,000
Luke Donald	70	70	77	69	286	31,000
Ignacio Garrido	71	68	74	73	286	31,000
Emiliano Grillo	71	65	78	72	286	31,000
Anders Hansen	74	69	73	70	286	31,000
Justin Rose	71	72	71	72	286	31,000
Lee Westwood	72	73	72	69	286	31,000
Danny Willett	71	71	74	70	286	31,000
Tyrrell Hatton	73	71	73	70	287	24,500
Matteo Manassero	75	70	69	73	287	24,500
Jason Palmer	71	72	73	71	287	24,500
Alvaro Quiros	74	68	71	74	287	24,500
Gary Stal	74	70	70	73	287	24,500
Alexander Levy	70	71	75	72	288	20,000
Hennie Otto	74	69	70	75	288	20,000
Jeev Milkha Singh	72	72	70	74	288	20,000
Jaco Van Zyl	74	71	71	72	288	20,000
Gregory Bourdy	72	73	69	75	289	16,125
Anirban Lahiri	72	72	72	73	289	16,125
Tom Lewis	72	73	72	72	289	16,125
Mikael Lundberg	75	68	73	73	289	16,125
Jorge Campillo	68	77	70	75	290	13,750
Ernie Els	72	73	72	73	290	13,750
Peter Lawrie	69	75	72	74	290	13,750
Graeme McDowell	74	71	72	73	290	13,750
Chris Doak	72	71	73	75	291	11,500
Victor Dubuisson	71	69	75	76	291	11,500
Trevor Fisher, Jr.	73	70	75	73	291	11,500
Mike Lorenzo-Vera	74	66	74	77	291	11,500
Dawie van der Walt	73	72	70	76	291	11,500
Niclas Fasth	76	69	74	73	292	9,750
Romain Wattel	74	71	75	72	292	9,750
Bradley Dredge	71	71	77	75	294	8,310
Damien McGrane	70	74	77	73	294	8,310
Brooks Koepka	75	68	73	79	295	7,496
Eddie Pepperell	72	72	74	77	295	7,496
George Coetzee	72	70	75	79	296	7,490
Richard Finch	73	70	75	78	296	7,490
Ian Ellis	70	75	77	75	297	7,485

Dubai Duty Free Irish Open

Royal County Down Golf Club, Newcastle,
Co. Down, Northern Ireland
Par 35-36–71; 6,570 yards

May 28-31
purse, €2,500,000

	SCORES				TOTAL	MONEY
Soren Kjeldsen	69	70	67	76	282	€416,660
Eddie Pepperell	74	72	67	69	282	217,135
Bernd Wiesberger	72	67	70	73	282	217,135
(Kjeldsen defeated Pepperell and Wiesberger on first playoff hole.)						
Rafa Cabrera-Bello	71	68	69	75	283	115,500
Tyrrell Hatton	73	66	70	74	283	115,500
Andy Sullivan	74	70	69	71	284	81,250
Danny Willett	69	76	71	68	284	81,250
Matthew Fitzpatrick	71	72	70	72	285	59,250
Maximilian Kieffer	67	76	65	77	285	59,250
Bradley Dredge	72	70	71	73	286	42,375
Niclas Fasth	71	73	67	75	286	42,375
Richard Green	72	72	70	72	286	42,375
Thongchai Jaidee	72	74	70	70	286	42,375
Richie Ramsay	72	67	70	77	286	42,375
Anthony Wall	72	71	69	74	286	42,375
Jaco Van Zyl	73	74	68	72	287	34,500
Chris Wood	70	69	75	73	287	34,500
Lucas Bjerregaard	73	73	66	76	288	31,083
Luke Donald	70	70	72	76	288	31,083
Jbe' Kruger	73	73	71	71	288	31,083
Byeong-Hun An	75	71	67	76	289	26,750
Darren Fichardt	76	71	67	75	289	26,750
Tommy Fleetwood	71	75	69	74	289	26,750
Rikard Karlberg	70	76	74	69	289	26,750
Alex Noren	73	74	67	75	289	26,750
John Parry	72	70	72	75	289	26,750
Jake Roos	75	69	68	77	289	26,750
Jason Barnes	75	72	70	73	290	23,375
Darren Clarke	75	72	72	71	290	23,375
Rickie Fowler	71	71	76	73	291	20,750
Emiliano Grillo	69	75	73	74	291	20,750
Scott Jamieson	73	72	73	73	291	20,750
Graeme McDowell	72	75	69	75	291	20,750
Mark Tullo	74	72	74	71	291	20,750
Magnus A. Carlsson	72	72	73	75	292	17,750
Ross Fisher	74	71	74	73	292	17,750
Matt Ford	70	71	77	74	292	17,750
Tom Lewis	74	71	73	74	292	17,750
Matthew Nixon	77	70	71	74	292	17,750
Mark Foster	77	70	73	73	293	15,750
Anders Hansen	70	73	76	74	293	15,750
Fabrizio Zanotti	72	74	73	74	293	15,750
Thomas Aiken	73	72	72	77	294	13,000
Ernie Els	71	73	78	72	294	13,000
Marcus Fraser	73	73	74	74	294	13,000
Ricardo Gonzalez	76	67	75	76	294	13,000
Padraig Harrington	67	73	78	76	294	13,000
Miguel Angel Jimenez	72	72	74	76	294	13,000
Shane Lowry	72	74	71	77	294	13,000
Lee Slattery	72	73	73	76	294	13,000
Seve Benson	74	71	72	78	295	10,500
Francesco Molinari	71	73	79	72	295	10,500
Felipe Aguilar	74	71	73	78	296	8,542
Richard Bland	75	72	75	74	296	8,542
Trevor Fisher, Jr.	70	74	75	77	296	8,542

	SCORES			TOTAL	MONEY
Richard McEvoy	71	72	79	74	296	8,542
Romain Wattel	74	72	73	77	296	8,542
Lee Westwood	74	72	74	76	296	8,542
Moritz Lampert	76	71	70	80	297	7,250
Simon Thornton	71	76	71	80	298	6,750
Peter Uihlein	72	74	74	78	298	6,750
Steve Webster	72	74	78	74	298	6,750
Gregory Bourdy	73	74	76	76	299	6,125
Benjamin Hebert	75	72	78	74	299	6,125
Andrew Dodt	73	73	72	82	300	5,500
Soren Hansen	68	76	79	77	300	5,500
Scott Hend	73	74	71	82	300	5,500

Nordea Masters

PGA Sweden National, Malmo, Sweden
Par 36-36–72; 7,390 yards

June 4-7
purse, €1,500,000

	SCORES			TOTAL	MONEY
Alex Noren	70	68	67	71	276	€250,000
Soren Kjeldsen	72	69	68	71	280	166,660
Jens Dantorp	67	68	73	74	282	71,250
Maximilian Kieffer	68	69	70	75	282	71,250
Alexander Levy	69	70	72	71	282	71,250
Sebastian Soderberg	68	69	71	74	282	71,250
Jonas Blixt	74	68	71	70	283	33,250
Nicolas Colsaerts	73	71	68	71	283	33,250
Tom Murray	74	68	70	71	283	33,250
Bernd Ritthammer	69	75	69	70	283	33,250
Lee Slattery	68	73	72	70	283	33,250
Fabrizio Zanotti	70	74	73	66	283	33,250
Kristoffer Broberg	70	70	70	74	284	20,812
Rafa Cabrera-Bello	72	69	70	73	284	20,812
Alejandro Canizares	70	71	71	72	284	20,812
Darren Fichardt	70	70	73	71	284	20,812
Peter Hanson	71	71	70	72	284	20,812
Chris Paisley	67	73	71	73	284	20,812
Callum Shinkwin	69	73	69	73	284	20,812
Henrik Stenson	70	72	68	74	284	20,812
Thomas Bjorn	71	72	74	68	285	16,950
Bradley Dredge	72	72	72	69	285	16,950
Emiliano Grillo	72	70	71	72	285	16,950
Stephen Gallacher	71	71	71	73	286	14,250
Daniel Gaunt	74	69	72	71	286	14,250
John Hahn	69	73	71	73	286	14,250
Gregory Havret	72	71	69	74	286	14,250
Benjamin Hebert	68	72	73	73	286	14,250
James Morrison	71	71	72	72	286	14,250
Matthew Nixon	73	70	70	73	286	14,250
Thomas Pieters	68	74	72	72	286	14,250
Alvaro Quiros	75	66	72	73	286	14,250
Seve Benson	73	71	71	72	287	10,667
Lucas Bjerregaard	71	70	72	74	287	10,667
Jorge Campillo	74	70	70	73	287	10,667
Magnus A. Carlsson	68	71	75	73	287	10,667
Simon Forsstrom	70	72	70	75	287	10,667
Ricardo Gonzalez	74	68	74	71	287	10,667
Scott Hend	74	69	71	73	287	10,667
*Marcus Kinhult	67	68	77	75	287	
Tom Lewis	68	70	75	74	287	10,667

	SCORES				TOTAL	MONEY
Hennie Otto	69	70	76	72	287	10,667
Oliver Farr	70	70	75	73	288	8,250
Soren Hansen	71	72	72	73	288	8,250
Rikard Karlberg	71	73	72	72	288	8,250
Pablo Larrazabal	71	72	72	73	288	8,250
Andrew McArthur	71	69	73	75	288	8,250
Eddie Pepperell	70	68	75	75	288	8,250
Jocke Rask	74	69	75	70	288	8,250
Oliver Fisher	69	75	70	75	289	6,450
Bjorn Hellgren	70	70	77	72	289	6,450
Scott Henry	69	71	71	78	289	6,450
Steven Jeppesen	72	68	70	79	289	6,450
John Parry	71	72	69	77	289	6,450
Johan Edfors	71	73	72	74	290	4,980
Niclas Fasth	72	71	73	74	290	4,980
Florian Fritsch	70	74	71	75	290	4,980
Adrian Otaegui	68	72	72	78	290	4,980
Alessandro Tadini	69	72	73	76	290	4,980
*Oscar Bergqvist	74	69	75	73	291	
Roope Kakko	72	70	72	77	291	4,050
Peter Lawrie	69	71	76	75	291	4,050
Pedro Oriol	68	73	78	72	291	4,050
Simon Wakefield	69	75	71	76	291	4,050
Daniel Woltman	70	69	75	77	291	4,050
Trevor Fisher, Jr.	73	69	74	76	292	3,375
Niklas Lemke	74	68	76	74	292	3,375
Mikael Lundberg	73	71	74	74	292	3,375
Jake Roos	71	70	74	77	292	3,375
Robert Dinwiddie	73	69	74	77	293	2,617
Michael Hoey	74	68	76	75	293	2,617
Gareth Maybin	72	71	77	73	293	2,617
Tjaart van der Walt	72	69	78	74	293	2,617
Álvaro Velasco	70	69	80	74	293	2,617
Jason Barnes	75	69	77	73	294	2,244
Linus Gillgren	72	72	72	79	295	2,238
Jeev Milkha Singh	71	73	74	77	295	2,238
Borja Virto Astudillo	71	72	77	75	295	2,238
Mike Lorenzo-Vera	73	69	77	78	297	2,232

Lyoness Open

Diamond Country Club, Atzenbrugg, Austria
Par 36-36–72; 7,417 yards

June 11-14
purse, €1,500,000

	SCORES				TOTAL	MONEY
Chris Wood	67	69	70	67	273	€250,000
Rafa Cabrera-Bello	69	68	66	72	275	166,660
Robert Dinwiddie	67	73	70	68	278	77,500
Matthew Fitzpatrick	69	69	69	71	278	77,500
Robert Rock	71	70	71	66	278	77,500
Gregory Bourdy	65	67	69	78	279	45,000
Kristoffer Broberg	70	72	69	68	279	45,000
John Hahn	71	69	68	71	279	45,000
Mikko Korhonen	69	69	70	72	280	31,800
Gary Stal	68	68	73	71	280	31,800
Dave Coupland	71	70	73	67	281	24,510
Scott Jamieson	72	70	65	74	281	24,510
Mike Lorenzo-Vera	70	72	69	70	281	24,510
Pedro Oriol	70	70	73	68	281	24,510
Richie Ramsay	74	69	68	70	281	24,510

	SCORES				TOTAL	MONEY
Carlos Del Moral	67	76	73	66	282	19,838
Edouard Espana	75	69	68	70	282	19,838
Simon Griffiths	73	71	66	72	282	19,838
Roope Kakko	73	70	71	68	282	19,838
Michael Hoey	73	69	72	69	283	17,700
Peter Lawrie	68	71	74	70	283	17,700
Merrick Bremner	69	74	67	74	284	14,925
Simon Khan	73	70	72	69	284	14,925
Maximilian Kieffer	67	73	71	73	284	14,925
Jason Knutzon	70	74	72	68	284	14,925
Mikael Lundberg	72	70	74	68	284	14,925
Matthew Nixon	74	66	72	72	284	14,925
Florian Praegant	71	73	71	69	284	14,925
Julien Quesne	69	71	75	69	284	14,925
Jeev Milkha Singh	69	73	72	70	284	14,925
Daniel Woltman	71	73	69	71	284	14,925
Johan Carlsson	70	73	71	71	285	11,475
Ryan Evans	68	73	74	70	285	11,475
Daniel Gaunt	71	71	70	73	285	11,475
Lasse Jensen	71	70	69	75	285	11,475
Renato Paratore	72	70	71	72	285	11,475
Lee Slattery	69	71	72	73	285	11,475
David Drysdale	68	73	71	74	286	9,450
Benjamin Hebert	73	69	71	73	286	9,450
David Horsey	71	68	76	71	286	9,450
Jose Manuel Lara	72	69	73	72	286	9,450
Richard McEvoy	72	72	72	70	286	9,450
Adrian Otaegui	69	71	73	73	286	9,450
Marcel Schneider	72	72	69	73	286	9,450
Florian Fritsch	70	70	71	76	287	7,350
Jordi Garcia Pinto	73	71	68	75	287	7,350
Jeppe Pape Huldahl	74	70	72	71	287	7,350
Joakim Lagergren	73	67	76	71	287	7,350
Andrew McArthur	71	70	73	73	287	7,350
Jake Roos	74	68	72	73	287	7,350
Justin Walters	70	73	74	70	287	7,350
Antti Ahokas	71	72	79	66	288	5,271
Richard Bland	71	69	75	73	288	5,271
Kenneth Ferrie	73	69	77	69	288	5,271
Chris Paisley	71	72	74	71	288	5,271
Carlos Pigem	72	65	73	78	288	5,271
Ricardo Santos	72	72	76	68	288	5,271
Jason Scrivener	70	73	74	71	288	5,271
Scott Henry	70	74	72	73	289	3,900
Moritz Lampert	73	70	73	73	289	3,900
Martin Ovesen	72	69	75	73	289	3,900
Callum Shinkwin	69	72	75	73	289	3,900
Simon Thornton	70	74	70	75	289	3,900
Simon Wakefield	74	69	76	70	289	3,900
Anthony Wall	71	72	73	73	289	3,900
Cyril Bouniol	68	72	80	70	290	3,075
Nicolas Colsaerts	70	72	73	75	290	3,075
Sam Hutsby	74	70	75	71	290	3,075
Victor Riu	71	73	70	76	290	3,075
Pelle Edberg	71	72	77	71	291	2,495
Daniel Im	74	70	72	75	291	2,495
Soren Hansen	71	72	77	72	292	2,247
Lukas Nemecz	73	71	73	80	297	2,244

BMW International Open

Golfclub Munchen Eichenried, Munich, Germany
Par 36-36–72; 7,181 yards

June 26-29
purse, €2,000,000

	SCORES				TOTAL	MONEY
Pablo Larrazabal	70	66	69	66	271	€333,330
Henrik Stenson	67	71	69	65	272	222,220
Chris Paisley	69	67	66	71	273	125,200
Kiradech Aphibarnrat	67	71	68	68	274	84,933
Carlos Del Moral	69	71	65	69	274	84,933
Retief Goosen	68	70	69	67	274	84,933
Peter Hanson	69	68	67	71	275	55,000
Michael Hoey	69	65	71	70	275	55,000
Daniel Gaunt	65	73	70	68	276	42,400
David Howell	69	70	72	65	276	42,400
Rafa Cabrera-Bello	65	67	74	71	277	31,933
Ross Fisher	71	69	67	70	277	31,933
Tommy Fleetwood	67	74	69	67	277	31,933
David Horsey	70	68	69	70	277	31,933
Thongchai Jaidee	68	67	68	74	277	31,933
James Morrison	67	66	67	77	277	31,933
Bradley Dredge	69	68	70	71	278	25,867
Morten Orum Madsen	71	69	71	67	278	25,867
Simon Wakefield	71	70	69	68	278	25,867
Magnus A. Carlsson	70	68	72	69	279	22,029
Darren Clarke	70	71	69	69	279	22,029
Victor Dubuisson	72	67	67	73	279	22,029
Pedro Oriol	70	71	68	70	279	22,029
Hennie Otto	71	69	71	68	279	22,029
Julien Quesne	68	71	72	68	279	22,029
Marcel Schneider	68	70	71	70	279	22,029
Kristoffer Broberg	71	69	68	72	280	19,300
Bernd Wiesberger	71	68	72	69	280	19,300
Lucas Bjerregaard	71	67	71	72	281	15,673
Johan Carlsson	69	69	75	68	281	15,673
Chris Doak	71	70	69	71	281	15,673
Lasse Jensen	65	69	73	74	281	15,673
Maximilian Kieffer	72	69	69	71	281	15,673
Paul Lawrie	68	71	69	73	281	15,673
Shane Lowry	72	67	69	73	281	15,673
Thorbjorn Olesen	71	68	69	73	281	15,673
Victor Riu	67	73	70	71	281	15,673
Gary Stal	70	70	67	74	281	15,673
Jaco Van Zyl	70	68	70	73	281	15,673
Edouard Espana	69	69	72	72	282	11,800
Florian Fritsch	68	72	74	68	282	11,800
Anders Hansen	69	69	71	73	282	11,800
Andrew Johnston	66	72	72	72	282	11,800
Damien McGrane	69	72	69	72	282	11,800
Garth Mulroy	69	71	69	73	282	11,800
Anthony Wall	70	69	70	73	282	11,800
Thomas Bjorn	71	68	72	72	283	9,200
Gregory Bourdy	75	66	73	69	283	9,200
Oliver Farr	69	71	72	71	283	9,200
Tyrrell Hatton	71	70	66	76	283	9,200
Soren Kjeldsen	73	68	73	69	283	9,200
Marcel Siem	71	70	70	72	283	9,200
Alejandro Canizares	70	66	72	76	284	7,600
Peter Lawrie	70	67	77	70	284	7,600
Jorge Campillo	69	71	75	70	285	6,600
Mark Foster	76	65	69	75	285	6,600
Anton Kirstein	70	71	69	75	285	6,600

	SCORES				TOTAL	MONEY
Joakim Lagergren	68	69	75	74	286	5,900
Eddie Pepperell	69	70	78	69	286	5,900
Tjaart van der Walt	68	72	77	70	287	5,600
Joost Luiten	72	68	77	71	288	5,300
Jake Roos	71	70	74	73	288	5,300
Alvaro Velasco	71	69	72	77	289	5,000
Kevin Phelan	68	71	76	75	290	4,800
Matt Ford	70	69	76	76	291	4,600

Alstom Open de France

Le Golf National, Paris, France
Par 36-35–71; 7,331 yards

July 2-5
purse, €3,000,000

	SCORES				TOTAL	MONEY
Bernd Wiesberger	68	72	66	65	271	€500,000
James Morrison	71	68	68	67	274	333,330
Jaco Van Zyl	68	71	64	73	276	187,800
Martin Kaymer	69	69	69	70	277	150,000
Rafa Cabrera-Bello	68	70	72	69	279	127,200
Mike Lorenzo-Vera	75	70	67	68	280	84,300
Francesco Molinari	70	69	70	71	280	84,300
Brendan Steele	72	69	67	72	280	84,300
Andy Sullivan	71	70	69	70	280	84,300
Thongchai Jaidee	70	74	65	72	281	57,600
Maximilian Kieffer	70	70	65	76	281	57,600
Kristoffer Broberg	72	69	68	73	282	48,600
Victor Dubuisson	68	70	69	75	282	48,600
Tyrrell Hatton	71	68	69	74	282	48,600
Richard Bland	76	70	66	71	283	40,560
Jorge Campillo	70	73	71	69	283	40,560
Marcus Fraser	73	69	70	71	283	40,560
Soren Kjeldsen	71	73	69	70	283	40,560
Jake Roos	73	71	66	73	283	40,560
Byeong-Hun An	71	73	69	71	284	34,425
Daniel Brooks	73	66	70	75	284	34,425
Jamie Donaldson	71	74	69	70	284	34,425
Fabrizio Zanotti	73	70	73	68	284	34,425
Gregory Bourdy	69	72	74	70	285	31,200
Raphael Jacquelin	73	71	73	68	285	31,200
Marcel Siem	69	73	74	69	285	31,200
Mark Foster	70	71	68	77	286	28,500
Jerome Lando Casanova	74	70	68	74	286	28,500
Julien Quesne	73	73	73	67	286	28,500
Peter Hanson	72	71	68	76	287	25,800
Andrew Johnston	73	71	68	75	287	25,800
Anirban Lahiri	69	77	70	71	287	25,800
Thomas Bjorn	74	68	73	73	288	21,638
Magnus A. Carlsson	72	73	70	73	288	21,638
Mikko Korhonen	70	71	70	77	288	21,638
Jason Scrivener	75	69	68	76	288	21,638
Gary Stal	73	69	69	77	288	21,638
Graeme Storm	73	72	69	74	288	21,638
Alessandro Tadini	73	71	71	73	288	21,638
Daniel Woltman	71	75	69	73	288	21,638
Trevor Fisher, Jr.	74	71	65	79	289	18,000
David Lipsky	71	71	72	75	289	18,000
Chris Lloyd	71	72	71	75	289	18,000
Anthony Wall	70	74	69	76	289	18,000
Eduardo de la Riva	71	73	70	76	290	15,600

	SCORES				TOTAL	MONEY
Michael Hoey	72	73	70	75	290	15,600
Mikko Ilonen	70	76	76	68	290	15,600
Lionel Weber	74	72	72	72	290	15,600
Seve Benson	76	70	71	74	291	12,900
David Howell	71	74	71	75	291	12,900
Mikael Lundberg	75	71	75	70	291	12,900
Fabien Marty	73	73	69	76	291	12,900
Joel Stalter	72	73	72	74	291	12,900
Daniel Gaunt	69	76	70	77	292	10,500
Damien McGrane	73	70	76	73	292	10,500
Oliver Wilson	74	72	70	76	292	10,500
Cyril Bouniol	75	71	73	74	293	8,250
Robert Dinwiddie	73	73	72	75	293	8,250
Scott Hend	70	72	71	80	293	8,250
Lasse Jensen	72	71	72	78	293	8,250
Edoardo Molinari	72	73	71	77	293	8,250
Pedro Oriol	74	72	74	73	293	8,250
Richie Ramsay	71	72	78	72	293	8,250
Robert Rock	72	73	70	78	293	8,250
Felipe Aguilar	71	69	73	83	296	6,600
Carlos Del Moral	72	71	75	78	296	6,600
Andrew Dodt	69	74	72	81	296	6,600
Victor Riu	71	73	73	85	302	6,000
Adrien Saddier	70	75	79	79	303	5,700

Aberdeen Asset Management Scottish Open

Gullane Golf Club, Gullane, East Lothian, Scotland   July 9-12
Par 35-35-70; 7,133 yards   purse, £3,250,000

	SCORES				TOTAL	MONEY
Rickie Fowler	66	68	66	68	268	€760,545
Raphael Jacquelin	68	67	64	70	269	396,349
Matt Kuchar	66	68	67	68	269	396,349
Joost Luiten	71	63	66	70	270	193,789
Eddie Pepperell	70	66	65	69	270	193,789
Marc Warren	70	67	69	64	270	193,789
Daniel Brooks	64	65	69	73	271	117,734
Luke Donald	69	67	69	66	271	117,734
Ross Fisher	70	65	68	68	271	117,734
Victor Dubuisson	70	66	68	68	272	75,490
Tommy Fleetwood	67	66	67	72	272	75,490
David Howell	68	70	66	68	272	75,490
Miguel Angel Jimenez	69	65	68	70	272	75,490
Rikard Karlberg	67	71	70	64	272	75,490
Russell Knox	67	68	66	71	272	75,490
Y.E. Yang	68	67	70	67	272	75,490
Richard Finch	65	68	72	68	273	56,950
Branden Grace	69	66	68	70	273	56,950
Andrew Johnston	67	67	71	68	273	56,950
Paul Lawrie	67	67	69	70	273	56,950
Ben Martin	69	66	68	70	273	56,950
Felipe Aguilar	73	64	67	70	274	46,090
Tyrrell Hatton	68	69	71	66	274	46,090
Brooks Koepka	70	68	66	70	274	46,090
Moritz Lampert	71	66	70	67	274	46,090
Alexander Levy	68	70	68	68	274	46,090
Matthew Nixon	65	67	74	68	274	46,090
Renato Paratore	70	68	66	70	274	46,090
John Senden	68	68	71	67	274	46,090

	SCORES				TOTAL	MONEY
Fabrizio Zanotti	69	67	67	71	274	46,090
Jamie Donaldson	70	67	69	69	275	34,042
Thongchai Jaidee	67	69	69	70	275	34,042
Mike Lorenzo-Vera	67	70	69	69	275	34,042
Shane Lowry	66	66	72	71	275	34,042
Graeme McDowell	66	66	72	71	275	34,042
Phil Mickelson	69	68	70	68	275	34,042
Pedro Oriol	67	69	67	72	275	34,042
Ryan Palmer	67	65	70	73	275	34,042
Gary Stal	66	68	74	67	275	34,042
Chris Wood	69	69	67	70	275	34,042
Thomas Aiken	69	68	70	69	276	23,729
Seve Benson	65	69	71	71	276	23,729
Daniel Berger	73	65	67	71	276	23,729
Rafa Cabrera-Bello	67	66	72	71	276	23,729
Marco Crespi	69	68	68	71	276	23,729
Eduardo de la Riva	72	66	69	69	276	23,729
Emiliano Grillo	66	67	71	72	276	23,729
Gregory Havret	66	68	69	73	276	23,729
Shiv Kapur	68	70	66	72	276	23,729
Maximilian Kieffer	69	65	70	72	276	23,729
Soren Kjeldsen	72	66	68	70	276	23,729
Richard McEvoy	66	67	72	71	276	23,729
Johan Carlsson	65	67	72	73	277	14,653
Benjamin Hebert	68	70	71	68	277	14,653
Mikko Ilonen	70	68	69	70	277	14,653
Morten Orum Madsen	68	68	70	71	277	14,653
Adrian Otaegui	65	72	68	72	277	14,653
Robert Rock	69	67	70	71	277	14,653
Marcel Siem	69	67	73	68	277	14,653
Cameron Tringale	68	67	71	71	277	14,653
Jaco Van Zyl	69	66	74	68	277	14,653
Nicolas Colsaerts	73	65	71	69	278	10,267
Robert Dinwiddie	69	69	70	70	278	10,267
Mark Foster	67	70	70	71	278	10,267
Padraig Harrington	68	68	70	72	278	10,267
Jerome Lando Casanova	71	66	73	68	278	10,267
Pablo Larrazabal	71	66	69	72	278	10,267
Craig Lee	72	66	68	72	278	10,267
Andy Sullivan	68	68	73	69	278	10,267
Byeong-Hun An	70	68	69	72	279	7,213
Richard Bland	70	68	72	69	279	7,213
Greig Hutcheon	70	68	69	72	279	7,213
Romain Wattel	70	68	67	74	279	7,213
Justin Rose	66	66	72	76	280	6,836
David Drysdale	71	65	71	74	281	6,832
Sebastian Soderberg	68	69	72	72	281	6,832
Lucas Bjerregaard	69	68	68	77	282	6,822
Jorge Campillo	69	69	71	73	282	6,822
Matthew Fitzpatrick	67	67	78	70	282	6,822
Michael Hoey	70	65	70	77	282	6,822
*Ollie Schniederjans	70	67	75	70	282	
Jimmy Walker	65	70	78	70	283	6,815
Jordi Garcia Pinto	67	69	73	76	285	6,812

The Open Championship

St. Andrews, Old Course, Fife, Scotland   July 16-20
Par 36-36—72; 7,305 yards   purse, £6,300,000
(Tournament completed on Monday—rain and high winds.)

	SCORES				TOTAL	MONEY
Zach Johnson	66	71	70	66	273	€1,591,255
Marc Leishman	70	73	64	66	273	742,355
Louis Oosthuizen	67	70	67	69	273	742,355
(Johnson (15) defeated Leishman (18) and Oosthuizen (16) in four-hole aggregate playoff.)						
Jason Day	66	71	67	70	274	408,192
Jordan Spieth	67	72	66	69	274	408,192
Sergio Garcia	70	69	68	70	277	271,205
*Jordan Niebrugge	67	73	67	70	277	
Justin Rose	71	68	68	70	277	271,205
Danny Willett	66	69	72	70	277	271,205
Brooks Koepka	71	70	69	68	278	191,642
Adam Scott	70	67	70	71	278	191,642
*Ashley Chesters	71	72	67	69	279	
Luke Donald	68	70	73	68	279	143,732
Martin Kaymer	71	70	70	68	279	143,732
*Ollie Schniederjans	70	72	70	67	279	
Brendon Todd	71	73	69	66	279	143,732
Anthony Wall	70	71	68	70	279	143,732
Hideki Matsuyama	72	66	71	71	280	114,501
Robert Streb	66	71	70	73	280	114,501
Stewart Cink	70	71	68	72	281	85,063
Marcus Fraser	74	69	68	70	281	85,063
Retief Goosen	66	72	69	74	281	85,063
Branden Grace	69	72	73	67	281	85,063
Padraig Harrington	72	69	65	75	281	85,063
Russell Henley	74	66	72	69	281	85,063
Phil Mickelson	70	72	70	69	281	85,063
James Morrison	71	71	70	69	281	85,063
Greg Owen	68	73	71	69	281	85,063
Patrick Reed	72	70	67	72	281	85,063
Steven Bowditch	70	69	69	74	282	55,925
*Paul Dunne	69	69	66	78	282	
Rickie Fowler	72	71	66	73	282	55,925
Jim Furyk	73	71	66	72	282	55,925
Billy Horschel	73	71	71	67	282	55,925
Matt Jones	68	73	69	72	282	55,925
Anirban Lahiri	69	70	71	72	282	55,925
Ryan Palmer	71	71	67	73	282	55,925
Andy Sullivan	72	71	68	71	282	55,925
Jimmy Walker	72	68	71	71	282	55,925
Scott Arnold	71	73	73	66	283	38,551
Rafa Cabrera-Bello	71	73	68	71	283	38,551
Paul Lawrie	66	70	74	73	283	38,551
Francesco Molinari	72	71	73	67	283	38,551
Geoff Ogilvy	71	68	72	72	283	38,551
John Senden	72	72	68	71	283	38,551
Webb Simpson	70	70	71	72	283	38,551
Henrik Stenson	73	70	71	69	283	38,551
Marc Warren	68	69	72	74	283	38,551
Jamie Donaldson	72	71	71	70	284	25,914
David Duval	72	72	67	73	284	25,914
Ryan Fox	72	69	76	67	284	25,914
David Howell	68	73	73	70	284	25,914
Dustin Johnson	65	69	75	75	284	25,914
Hunter Mahan	72	72	67	73	284	25,914
Graeme McDowell	72	72	70	70	284	25,914

	SCORES				TOTAL	MONEY
Eddie Pepperell	72	70	66	76	284	25,914
Lee Westwood	71	73	69	71	284	25,914
Greg Chalmers	70	71	69	75	285	22,011
Jason Dufner	73	71	67	74	285	22,011
Matt Kuchar	71	73	70	71	285	22,011
David Lipsky	73	69	70	73	285	22,011
Kevin Na	67	75	70	73	285	22,011
Cameron Tringale	71	71	73	70	285	22,011
Gary Woodland	72	70	71	72	285	22,011
Ernie Els	71	73	69	73	286	21,240
Thongchai Jaidee	72	71	70	73	286	21,240
*Romain Langasque	69	72	71	74	286	
Graham DeLaet	71	73	68	75	287	20,686
Harris English	71	72	69	75	287	20,686
Ross Fisher	71	73	72	71	287	20,686
Richie Ramsay	72	71	70	74	287	20,686
Charl Schwartzel	67	72	69	79	287	20,686
Bernd Wiesberger	72	72	71	72	287	20,686
Paul Casey	70	71	75	72	288	19,994
David Lingmerth	69	72	70	77	288	19,994
Ben Martin	74	70	67	77	288	19,994
Brett Rumford	71	71	71	75	288	19,994
Bernhard Langer	74	70	73	72	289	19,579
Mark O'Meara	72	72	71	74	289	19,579
Thomas Aiken	75	69	72	74	290	19,372

Out of Final 36 Holes

John Daly	71	74	145	6,227
Victor Dubuisson	74	71	145	6,227
Tommy Fleetwood	69	76	145	6,227
Brian Harman	73	72	145	6,227
Mikko Ilonen	75	70	145	6,227
Rikard Karlberg	70	75	145	6,227
Kevin Kisner	71	74	145	6,227
Pablo Larrazabal	76	69	145	6,227
Alexander Levy	70	75	145	6,227
Shane Lowry	73	72	145	6,227
Carl Pettersson	72	73	145	6,227
Marcel Siem	70	75	145	6,227
Byeong-Hun An	74	72	146	4,981
Jonas Blixt	75	71	146	4,981
Darren Clarke	73	73	146	4,981
Pelle Edberg	72	74	146	4,981
Hiroyuki Fujita	71	75	146	4,981
Stephen Gallacher	73	73	146	4,981
Tyrrell Hatton	70	76	146	4,981
Scott Hend	74	72	146	4,981
Raphael Jacquelin	76	70	146	4,981
*Paul Kinnear	70	76	146	
Russell Knox	72	74	146	4,981
Joost Luiten	74	72	146	4,981
Matteo Manassero	73	73	146	4,981
Brandt Snedeker	73	73	146	4,981
Keegan Bradley	75	72	147	4,981
George Coetzee	74	73	147	4,981
David Hearn	74	73	147	4,981
J.B. Holmes	73	74	147	4,981
Danny Lee	73	74	147	4,981
Sandy Lyle	71	76	147	4,981
Ryan Moore	74	73	147	4,981
Ian Poulter	73	74	147	4,981
Tadahiro Takayama	75	72	147	4,981

	SCORES				TOTAL	MONEY
Shinji Tomimura	73	74			147	4,981
Bubba Watson	71	76			147	4,981
Kiradech Aphibarnrat	73	75			148	4,151
James Hahn	75	73			148	4,151
Yuta Ikeda	74	74			148	4,151
Miguel Angel Jimenez	75	73			148	4,151
Soren Kjeldsen	75	73			148	4,151
Tom Lehman	75	73			148	4,151
Jaco Van Zyl	79	69			148	4,151
Romain Wattel	75	73			148	4,151
Mark Young	74	74			148	4,151
Daniel Berger	73	76			149	4,151
Thomas Bjorn	70	79			149	4,151
Adam Bland	75	74			149	4,151
Daniel Brooks	76	73			149	4,151
Ben Curtis	74	75			149	4,151
Bill Haas	75	74			149	4,151
Morgan Hoffmann	73	76			149	4,151
Hiroshi Iwata	79	70			149	4,151
Edoardo Molinari	74	75			149	4,151
Koumei Oda	73	76			149	4,151
Taichi Teshima	76	73			149	4,151
*Alister Balcombe	74	76			150	
Robert Dinwiddie	73	77			150	4,151
Tom Gillis	76	74			150	4,151
Charley Hoffman	72	78			150	4,151
Justin Leonard	78	72			150	4,151
Wen-Chong Liang	80	70			150	4,151
Scott Strange	77	73			150	4,151
Kevin Streelman	78	72			150	4,151
*Gunn Yang	73	77			150	
Matt Every	73	78			151	4,151
Todd Hamilton	74	77			151	4,151
Tiger Woods	76	75			151	4,151
Jonathan Moore	74	78			152	4,981
Rodney Pampling	77	75			152	4,151
Sir Nick Faldo	83	71			154	4,151
Mark Calcavecchia	80	75			155	4,151
*Ben Taylor	82	73			155	
Tom Watson	76	80			156	4,151
Gary Boyd	77	80			157	4,151

Omega European Masters

Crans-sur-Sierre Golf Club, Crans Montana, Switzerland
Par 35-35–70; 6,848 yards

July 23-26
purse, €2,700,000

	SCORES				TOTAL	MONEY
Danny Willett	65	62	71	65	263	€450,000
Matthew Fitzpatrick	69	65	64	66	264	300,000
Tyrrell Hatton	65	68	70	62	265	169,020
Pelle Edberg	65	72	66	63	266	135,000
Anirban Lahiri	67	67	70	64	268	114,480
Sergio Garcia	69	70	66	64	269	94,500
Florian Fritsch	70	66	70	64	270	74,250
Raphael Jacquelin	68	64	68	70	270	74,250
Rikard Karlberg	65	67	74	65	271	60,480
Kristoffer Broberg	68	69	70	65	272	48,398
Robert Dinwiddie	70	68	71	63	272	48,398
Richard Green	65	67	71	69	272	48,398

	SCORES				TOTAL	MONEY
*Marcus Kinhult	65	66	73	68	272	
Richie Ramsay	70	66	68	68	272	48,398
Richard McEvoy	70	66	68	69	273	41,310
Alejandro Canizares	67	68	70	69	274	34,594
Johan Carlsson	66	68	70	70	274	34,594
David Howell	70	68	73	63	274	34,594
Peter Lawrie	67	68	74	65	274	34,594
David Lipsky	66	66	69	73	274	34,594
John Parry	67	70	70	67	274	34,594
Patrick Reed	67	69	69	69	274	34,594
Y.E. Yang	65	63	74	72	274	34,594
S.S.P. Chawrasia	70	66	70	69	275	27,270
Marco Crespi	68	65	72	70	275	27,270
Jamie Donaldson	67	70	71	67	275	27,270
Shiv Kapur	68	71	69	67	275	27,270
Mikko Korhonen	70	65	71	69	275	27,270
Renato Paratore	71	67	67	70	275	27,270
Julien Quesne	67	70	69	69	275	27,270
Seuk-Hyun Baek	65	63	74	74	276	22,050
Seve Benson	65	69	76	66	276	22,050
Gregory Havret	63	69	71	73	276	22,050
Scott Jamieson	71	68	70	67	276	22,050
Lasse Jensen	64	70	73	69	276	22,050
Bernd Wiesberger	67	68	73	68	276	22,050
Richard Finch	70	68	69	70	277	18,090
Nathan Holman	67	71	70	69	277	18,090
Jazz Janewattananond	65	70	70	72	277	18,090
Jyoti Randhawa	68	70	68	71	277	18,090
Graeme Storm	69	70	68	70	277	18,090
Peter Uihlein	68	66	74	69	277	18,090
Lee Westwood	68	69	68	72	277	18,090
Chris Doak	71	66	71	70	278	15,120
Maximilian Kieffer	71	67	67	73	278	15,120
Chris Paisley	69	69	72	68	278	15,120
Alessandro Tadini	66	70	72	70	278	15,120
David Drysdale	68	68	71	72	279	13,500
Marcel Siem	68	70	74	67	279	13,500
Bradley Dredge	66	67	77	70	280	12,420
Thongchai Jaidee	71	68	68	73	280	12,420
*Matthias Schwab	71	66	70	73	280	
Richard Bland	65	68	78	70	281	9,990
Magnus A. Carlsson	66	73	72	70	281	9,990
Andrew Dodt	68	71	70	72	281	9,990
Jerome Lando Casanova	68	69	72	72	281	9,990
Edoardo Molinari	67	68	71	75	281	9,990
Matthew Nixon	70	65	72	74	281	9,990
Adrian Otaegui	67	70	72	72	281	9,990
Marcus Fraser	67	65	78	72	282	7,965
Thomas Pieters	70	69	70	73	282	7,965
Anders Hansen	67	69	71	76	283	7,560
Mark Foster	70	69	71	74	284	7,020
Michael Hoey	65	73	72	74	284	7,020
Masahiro Kawamura	68	68	71	77	284	7,020
David Horsey	71	67	75	72	285	6,480
Adilson Da Silva	68	71	77	70	286	6,210
Rashid Khan	67	72	74	74	287	5,805
Jason Knutzon	68	70	78	71	287	5,805
Angelo Que	66	71	74	77	288	5,400
Jbe Kruger	71	68	73	79	291	5,130

Madeira Islands Open - Portugal - BPI

Clube de Golf do Santo da Serra, Madeira, Portugal
Par 36-36–72; 6,826 yards

July 30-August 2
purse, €600,000

	SCORES				TOTAL	MONEY
Roope Kakko	66	71	64	63	264	€100,000
Scott Henry	66	70	65	66	267	66,660
Andrew McArthur	68	70	69	63	270	37,560
Sebastian Soderberg	67	74	66	65	272	27,720
Pontus Widegren	67	66	67	72	272	27,720
Tom Murray	70	68	68	67	273	21,000
Bjorn Akesson	71	65	68	70	274	15,480
Callum Shinkwin	68	70	70	66	274	15,480
Brandon Stone	68	68	66	72	274	15,480
Fredrik Andersson Hed	72	69	68	66	275	11,120
Tiago Cruz	73	69	65	68	275	11,120
Ryan Fox	65	73	72	65	275	11,120
Jose-Filipe Lima	70	68	69	69	276	9,220
Pierre Relecom	68	68	70	70	276	9,220
Ricardo Santos	66	76	69	65	276	9,220
Rhys Davies	67	71	67	72	277	8,280
Christopher Mivis	70	69	69	69	277	8,280
Carlos Del Moral	69	70	68	71	278	7,020
Nacho Elvira	64	74	72	68	278	7,020
Andreas Harto	66	74	67	71	278	7,020
George Murray	69	71	69	69	278	7,020
Adrian Otaegui	70	71	68	69	278	7,020
Chris Paisley	66	72	70	70	278	7,020
Alessandro Tadini	68	71	70	69	278	7,020
Nico Geyger	69	72	69	69	279	5,880
Jean-Baptiste Gonnet	69	69	72	69	279	5,880
Ricardo Gouveia	68	72	71	68	279	5,880
Antonio Hortal	63	71	72	73	279	5,880
Pedro Oriol	66	71	74	68	279	5,880
Tjaart van der Walt	70	72	70	68	280	5,250
Sam Walker	67	66	73	74	280	5,250
James Heath	70	69	68	74	281	4,890
Andrea Pavan	70	70	72	69	281	4,890
Elias Bertheussen	72	69	70	71	282	4,200
Sean Einhaus	69	72	69	72	282	4,200
Adam Gee	71	70	73	68	282	4,200
Jeppe Pape Huldahl	71	69	74	68	282	4,200
Sam Hutsby	68	73	72	69	282	4,200
Jason Scrivener	72	70	69	71	282	4,200
Mads Sogaard	71	69	71	71	282	4,200
Steven Tiley	68	73	71	70	282	4,200
Marcus Armitage	71	70	73	69	283	3,480
Daan Huizing	68	71	71	73	283	3,480
Paul Maddy	68	71	73	71	283	3,480
Jamie McLeary	72	69	70	72	283	3,480
Emilio Cuartero Blanco	70	70	74	70	284	2,880
Chris Hanson	69	72	74	69	284	2,880
Steven Jeppesen	67	75	72	70	284	2,880
Stuart Manley	66	75	73	70	284	2,880
Ruaidhri McGee	69	73	72	70	284	2,880
Kevin Phelan	69	69	69	77	284	2,880
Pedro Figueiredo	73	69	71	72	285	2,340
Sebastien Gros	65	75	72	73	285	2,340
Daniel Vancsik	68	72	72	73	285	2,340
William Harrold	70	70	72	74	286	1,980
Daniel Im	67	73	69	77	286	1,980
Justin Walters	67	73	72	74	286	1,980

	SCORES				TOTAL	MONEY
Connor Arendell	69	73	71	74	287	1,770
Simon Wakefield	69	73	74	71	287	1,770
Jack Doherty	71	71	75	71	288	1,650
Scott Fallon	68	69	72	79	288	1,650
Marcel Schneider	66	72	76	75	289	1,560
Joachim B. Hansen	67	71	72	80	290	1,470
Niccolo Quintarelli	71	70	75	74	290	1,470
Francois Calmels	69	73	73	76	291	1,380

Saltire Energy Paul Lawrie Match Play

Murcar Links Golf Club, Aberdeen, Scotland
Par 36-34–70; 6,409 yards

July 30-August 2
purse, €1,000,000

FIRST ROUND

Julien Quesne defeated Tom Lewis, 1 up.
Jeev Milkha Singh defeated Scott Hend, 1 up.
Michael Hoey defeated Maximilian Kieffer, 2 and 1.
Kristoffer Broberg defeated Richard Finch, 2 and 1.
Richie Ramsay defeated Shiv Kapur, 1 up.
Edoardo Molinari defeated Magnus A. Carlsson, 5 and 4.
Matthew Fitzpatrick defeated Bradley Dredge, 6 and 4.
Peter Uihlein defeated Oliver Wilson, 2 up.
Chris Wood defeated Jbe' Kruger, 5 and 4.
Jorge Campillo defeated John Daly, 2 up.
Seve Benson defeated Rapahel Jacquelin, 2 and 1.
Gregory Havret defeated David Horsey, 5 and 4.
Alexander Levy defeated Mark Foster, 2 up.
Morten Orum Madsen defeated Alvaro Quiros, 3 and 2.
Tyrrell Hatton defeated Darren Fichardt, 4 and 3.
Mikael Lundberg defeated Robert Rock, 3 and 1.
Chris Doak defeated Anthony Wall, 1 up.
Paul Lawrie defeated Romain Wattel, 5 and 4.
Thomas Aiken defeated Scott Jamieson, 3 and 2.
Andrew Dodt defeated Oliver Fisher, 19 holes.
Alejandro Canizares defeated Lucas Bjerregaard, 7 and 6.
Robert Karlsson defeated Marcus Fraser, 3 and 2.
Nicolas Colsaerts defeated Gregory Bourdy, 2 and 1.
Trevor Fisher, Jr. defeated Thorbjorn Olesen, 2 up.
David Howell defeated Daniel Brooks, 19 holes.
David Drysdale defeated Thomas Pieters, 19 holes.
Kiradech Aphibarnrat defeated Wade Ormsby, 19 holes.
Graeme Storm defeated Andrew Johnston, 1 up.
James Morrison defeated Pelle Edberg, 2 and 1.
Johan Carlsson defeated Marco Crespi, 2 and 1.
Marc Warren defeated Richard Bland, 1 up.
Fabrizio Zanotti defeated Felipe Aguilar, 1 up.

SECOND ROUND

Wood defeated Campillo, 5 and 4.
Quesne defeated Singh, 4 and 3.
Havret defeated Benson, 2 and 1.
Hoey defeated Broberg, 5 and 4.
Madsen defeated Levy, 4 and 3.
Ramsay defeated Molinari, 4 and 3
Hatton defeated Lundberg, 4 and 2.
Uihlein defeated Fitzpatrick, 19 holes.
Howell defeated Drysdale, 6 and 4.
Doak defeated Lawrie, 1 up.
Aphibarnrat defeated Storm, 3 and 2.
Aiken defeated Dodt, 2 up.

Carlsson defeated Morrison, 2 and 1.
Karlsson defeated Canizares, 4 and 3.
Warren defeated Zanotti, 3 and 2.
Colsaerts defeated Fisher, 4 and 3.

(Losing players received €16,000.)

THIRD ROUND

Howell defeated Doak, 2 and 1.
Wood defeated Quesne, 2 up.
Aphibarnrat defeated Aiken, 4 and 3.
Hoey defeated Havret, 7 and 6.
Karlsson defeated Carlsson, 4 and 3.
Ramsay defeated Madsen, 1 up.
Warren defeated Colsaerts, 3 and 1.
Hatton defeated Uihlein, 5 and 4.

(Losing players received €22,500.)

QUARTER-FINALS

Karlsson defeated Ramsay, 1up.
Howell defeated Wood, 5 and 4.
Warren defeated Hatton, 19 holes.
Aphibarnrat defeated Hoey, 2 and 1.

(Losing players received €38,400.)

SEMI-FINALS

Karlsson defeated Howell, 20 holes.
Aphibarnrat defeated Warren, 3 and 2.

PLAYOFF FOR THIRD-FOURTH PLACE

Howell defeated Warren, 1 up.

(Howell received €67,500; Warren received €55,000.)

FINAL

Aphibarnrat defeated Karlsson, 1 up.

(Aphibarnrat received €171,000; Karlsson received €116,500.)

Made in Denmark

Himmerland Golf & Spa Resort, Farso, Denmark
Par 35-36–71; 6,809 yards

August 20-23
purse, €1,500,000

	SCORES				TOTAL	MONEY
David Horsey	63	67	68	73	271	€250,000
Kristoffer Broberg	72	69	70	62	273	99,790
Daniel Gaunt	69	67	71	66	273	99,790
Soren Kjeldsen	66	71	68	68	273	99,790
Terry Pilkadaris	66	68	65	74	273	99,790
Bradley Dredge	66	68	70	70	274	42,150
Richard Green	68	65	70	71	274	42,150
Paul Lawrie	65	72	68	69	274	42,150
Mads Sogaard	68	68	69	69	274	42,150
John Parry	66	67	69	73	275	30,000
Robert Dinwiddie	70	70	67	69	276	25,850
Michael Jonzon	70	68	70	68	276	25,850
Victor Riu	70	72	67	67	276	25,850
Julien Guerrier	71	70	66	70	277	20,725
Benjamin Hebert	69	72	67	69	277	20,725

	SCORES			TOTAL	MONEY
Rikard Karlberg	69	68	69	71	277	20,725
Peter Lawrie	66	69	70	72	277	20,725
David Lipsky	71	71	66	69	277	20,725
Jason Scrivener	69	69	71	68	277	20,725
Connor Arendell	69	72	68	69	278	16,521
Florian Fritsch	68	70	69	71	278	16,521
Jean-Baptiste Gonnet	67	72	74	65	278	16,521
Tom Lewis	68	70	69	71	278	16,521
Morten Orum Madsen	68	71	69	70	278	16,521
Paul Peterson	71	67	69	71	278	16,521
Graeme Storm	66	72	72	68	278	16,521
Thomas Bjorn	69	69	70	71	279	13,125
Richard Bland	70	72	66	71	279	13,125
Chris Doak	68	70	71	70	279	13,125
Anders Hansen	69	72	67	71	279	13,125
Michael Hoey	71	71	69	68	279	13,125
Adrian Otaegui	71	68	70	70	279	13,125
Andrea Pavan	73	69	66	71	279	13,125
Daniel Woltman	68	72	67	72	279	13,125
Ben Evans	71	69	72	68	280	10,050
Oliver Fisher	70	69	68	73	280	10,050
Lasse Jensen	67	71	71	71	280	10,050
Stuart Manley	72	69	73	66	280	10,050
Richard McEvoy	69	71	69	71	280	10,050
Pedro Oriol	71	69	72	68	280	10,050
Chris Paisley	68	68	66	78	280	10,050
Kevin Phelan	71	69	70	70	280	10,050
Thomas Pieters	70	72	71	67	280	10,050
Daniel Brooks	72	70	66	73	281	7,350
Darren Clarke	69	70	68	74	281	7,350
David Drysdale	69	71	70	71	281	7,350
Oliver Farr	64	71	73	73	281	7,350
Matthew Fitzpatrick	69	70	73	69	281	7,350
Scott Jamieson	71	69	70	71	281	7,350
Joakim Lagergren	72	70	69	70	281	7,350
Alvaro Velasco	74	68	69	70	281	7,350
Marc Warren	71	67	71	72	281	7,350
Seve Benson	68	73	70	71	282	5,250
Eduardo de la Riva	68	68	72	74	282	5,250
Shiv Kapur	69	70	70	73	282	5,250
Robert Rock	71	69	71	71	282	5,250
Jeev Milkha Singh	71	71	69	71	282	5,250
Phillip Archer	70	72	70	71	283	3,900
Magnus A. Carlsson	70	68	70	75	283	3,900
Robert Karlsson	69	70	69	75	283	3,900
Matthew Nixon	75	65	69	74	283	3,900
Martin Ovesen	68	70	75	70	283	3,900
Tapio Pulkkanen	70	72	70	71	283	3,900
Lee Slattery	67	74	70	72	283	3,900
Mark Tullo	74	68	69	72	283	3,900
Justin Walters	71	68	70	74	283	3,900
Merrick Bremner	71	71	66	76	284	2,935
Matteo Delpodio	70	72	73	69	284	2,935
Alexander Knappe	71	71	69	73	284	2,935
Joel Stalter	71	71	69	73	284	2,935
Matt Ford	71	70	72	72	285	2,244
Jocke Rask	74	67	71	73	285	2,244
Ben Stow	71	71	73	70	285	2,244
Simon Thornton	69	70	75	71	285	2,244
Peter Whiteford	72	70	69	74	285	2,244
Jason Barnes	74	68	71	73	286	2,235
Stephen Dodd	69	72	71	75	287	2,228
Johan Edfors	71	71	74	71	287	2,228

	SCORES				TOTAL	MONEY
Jaakko Makitalo	72	70	72	73	287	2,228
Peter Uihlein	71	71	68	77	287	2,228
Pelle Edberg	69	73	68	78	288	2,217
Edoardo Molinari	73	69	70	76	288	2,217
Martin Simonsen	71	71	74	72	288	2,217
Carlos Del Moral	66	75	70	78	289	2,210
Sam Hutsby	74	68	72	75	289	2,210
Darren Fichardt	68	74	77	73	292	2,205
Nicolai Kristensen	73	68	77	79	297	2,202

D+D Real Czech Masters

Albatross Golf Resort, Prague, Czech Republic
Par 36-36–72; 6,872 yards

August 27-30
purse, €1,000,000

	SCORES				TOTAL	MONEY
Thomas Pieters	66	68	65	69	268	€166,660
Pelle Edberg	66	67	67	71	271	111,110
Matthew Fitzpatrick	66	67	71	68	272	62,600
Robert Dinwiddie	69	67	68	70	274	50,000
Roope Kakko	67	72	68	70	277	35,800
Thorbjorn Olesen	67	69	67	74	277	35,800
Renato Paratore	65	73	70	69	277	35,800
Gregory Bourdy	70	70	71	67	278	20,600
Kristoffer Broberg	67	73	69	69	278	20,600
Eduardo de la Riva	65	76	69	68	278	20,600
Craig Lee	68	71	69	70	278	20,600
Damien McGrane	69	70	71	68	278	20,600
Connor Arendell	72	67	71	69	279	15,050
Gary Boyd	69	72	69	69	279	15,050
Sam Hutsby	66	70	71	72	279	15,050
Rikard Karlberg	70	68	71	70	279	15,050
Mikael Lundberg	72	71	64	73	280	12,480
Jaakko Makitalo	71	70	68	71	280	12,480
Graeme Storm	70	73	71	66	280	12,480
Peter Uihlein	70	71	66	73	280	12,480
Anthony Wall	72	70	67	71	280	12,480
Michael Hoey	67	70	71	73	281	10,700
Joakim Lagergren	69	73	69	70	281	10,700
David Lipsky	71	69	68	73	281	10,700
Eddie Pepperell	69	68	71	73	281	10,700
Marcel Schneider	72	67	71	71	281	10,700
Mathieu Decottignies-Lafon	71	69	72	70	282	8,900
David Drysdale	69	73	71	69	282	8,900
Victor Dubuisson	72	68	70	72	282	8,900
Ryan Fox	73	67	69	73	282	8,900
Florian Fritsch	69	70	69	74	282	8,900
Daniel Im	68	73	73	68	282	8,900
Jamie McLeary	69	71	72	70	282	8,900
David Dixon	69	70	74	70	283	7,200
Lasse Jensen	71	72	66	74	283	7,200
Pedro Oriol	67	73	69	74	283	7,200
Bernd Ritthammer	68	72	75	68	283	7,200
Lee Slattery	68	72	75	68	283	7,200
Mark Tullo	71	70	73	69	283	7,200
Nicolas Colsaerts	73	70	68	73	284	5,900
Bradley Dredge	74	69	72	69	284	5,900
Oliver Fisher	71	70	73	70	284	5,900
Jason Knutzon	71	72	72	69	284	5,900
Matthew Nixon	74	68	71	71	284	5,900
Chris Paisley	69	72	71	72	284	5,900

	SCORES				TOTAL	MONEY
Peter Whiteford	70	73	69	72	284	5,900
Jason Barnes	69	71	73	72	285	4,600
Mark Foster	67	72	71	75	285	4,600
Shiv Kapur	71	72	70	72	285	4,600
Jose Manuel Lara	71	68	69	77	285	4,600
Kevin Phelan	70	71	71	73	285	4,600
Alessandro Tadini	71	70	73	71	285	4,600
Daniel Brooks	69	72	75	70	286	3,600
Edouard Espana	71	72	72	71	286	3,600
John Hahn	72	71	72	71	286	3,600
Terry Pilkadaris	73	69	71	73	286	3,600
Ben Evans	71	71	73	72	287	3,050
Florian Praegant	69	74	71	73	287	3,050
Ryan Evans	73	68	71	76	288	2,750
Paul Maddy	73	69	71	75	288	2,750
Garrick Porteous	72	69	71	76	288	2,750
Adrien Saddier	71	70	75	72	288	2,750
Scott Henry	69	72	75	73	289	2,450
Prom Meesawat	70	73	72	74	289	2,450
*Vitek Novak	73	68	76	72	289	
John Parry	70	71	75	74	290	2,250
Ben Stow	72	66	76	76	290	2,250
Cyril Bouniol	70	73	73	75	291	1,866
Jordi Garcia Pinto	67	72	76	76	291	1,866
Simon Griffiths	71	68	74	78	291	1,866
Filip Mruzek	69	74	71	77	291	1,866
Hennie Otto	71	72	73	75	291	1,866
Matt Ford	71	68	73	80	292	1,494
Scott Jamieson	67	72	78	75	292	1,494
Joel Sjoholm	70	72	75	75	292	1,494
Soren Hansen	71	72	72	79	294	1,486
Pierre Relecom	68	75	75	76	294	1,486

M2M Russian Open

Skolkovo Golf Club, Moscow, Russia
Par 35-36–71; 7,025 yards

September 3-6
purse, €1,000,000

	SCORES				TOTAL	MONEY
Lee Slattery	66	67	67	69	269	€166,660
Estanislao Goya	68	67	67	68	270	111,110
David Horsey	67	70	66	68	271	62,600
James Heath	70	66	71	65	272	39,350
Oskar Henningsson	69	68	67	68	272	39,350
Michael Hoey	71	66	71	64	272	39,350
Pablo Martin Benavides	68	67	70	67	272	39,350
Ben Evans	67	68	71	67	273	22,467
Craig Lee	67	69	66	71	273	22,467
Jake Roos	68	74	68	63	273	22,467
Bradley Dredge	66	66	72	70	274	17,233
Maximilian Kieffer	68	69	71	66	274	17,233
Daniel Vancsik	69	68	70	67	274	17,233
David Drysdale	68	69	69	69	275	14,700
Ricardo Santos	74	67	69	65	275	14,700
Jason Scrivener	70	66	70	69	275	14,700
Chris Doak	71	67	70	68	276	12,480
Johan Edfors	71	68	70	67	276	12,480
Scott Jamieson	65	71	71	69	276	12,480
Lasse Jensen	70	69	68	69	276	12,480
Dodge Kemmer	71	69	68	68	276	12,480
Andrea Pavan	70	69	68	70	277	11,300

	SCORES				TOTAL	MONEY
Keith Horne	67	70	70	71	278	10,400
Jerome Lando Casanova	69	68	71	70	278	10,400
Matthew Southgate	68	69	69	72	278	10,400
Danie van Tonder	69	69	68	72	278	10,400
Simon Wakefield	69	68	75	66	278	10,400
Jacques Blaauw	71	66	73	69	279	8,750
Robert Dinwiddie	73	69	68	69	279	8,750
Daniel Gaunt	65	69	74	71	279	8,750
Tom Murray	67	74	68	70	279	8,750
Jordan L. Smith	69	68	74	68	279	8,750
Mark Tullo	69	72	68	70	279	8,750
Adilson Da Silva	72	69	69	70	280	7,600
Oliver Farr	71	67	72	70	280	7,600
Cyril Bouniol	68	69	72	72	281	7,000
Thitiphun Chuayprakong	67	71	70	73	281	7,000
Jazz Janewattananond	73	69	74	65	281	7,000
Kalem Richardson	74	68	69	70	281	7,000
Niall Kearney	70	71	72	69	282	6,400
Ryan Lynch	69	70	74	69	282	6,400
Merrick Bremner	69	71	70	73	283	5,500
Brian Casey	72	68	73	70	283	5,500
Dylan Frittelli	71	70	73	69	283	5,500
Simon Griffiths	68	71	69	75	283	5,500
Niclas Johansson	70	70	70	73	283	5,500
Matthew Nixon	68	70	73	72	283	5,500
Jyoti Randhawa	68	73	68	74	283	5,500
Mark Brown	72	70	73	69	284	4,200
Javier Colomo	69	68	72	75	284	4,200
Pariya Junhasavasdikul	69	72	73	70	284	4,200
Ross McGowan	71	69	72	72	284	4,200
Shaun Norris	70	72	73	69	284	4,200
Ben Stow	69	71	74	70	284	4,200
Jaco Ahlers	72	70	74	69	285	3,225
Jason Knutzon	73	69	71	72	285	3,225
Damien McGrane	70	72	73	70	285	3,225
Prom Meesawat	68	71	73	73	285	3,225
Rahil Gangjee	68	73	74	71	286	2,850
Chris Lloyd	69	68	76	73	286	2,850
Edouard Espana	68	72	75	72	287	2,700
Peter Erofejeff	73	66	77	72	288	2,450
Soren Hansen	69	73	72	74	288	2,450
Panuphol Pittayarat	67	71	79	71	288	2,450
Anthony Summers	68	74	75	71	288	2,450
Andrew Curlewis	72	70	75	72	289	2,100
Sebastian Garcia Rodriguez	70	67	72	80	289	2,100
Thaworn Wiratchant	69	71	78	71	289	2,100
Mardan Mamat	70	72	77	73	292	1,900
Peter Karmis	73	69	78	76	296	1,830
Andrey Pavlov	73	69	77	78	297	1,500

KLM Open

Kennemer Golf & Country Club, Zandvoort, The Netherlands   September 10-13
Par 36-34–70; 6,626 yards   purse, €1,800,000

	SCORES				TOTAL	MONEY
Thomas Pieters	68	66	62	65	261	€300,000
Eduardo de la Riva	66	66	67	63	262	156,340
Lee Slattery	66	65	63	68	262	156,340
Fabrizio Zanotti	67	66	67	63	263	90,000

	SCORES				TOTAL	MONEY
Morten Orum Madsen	64	67	66	67	264	69,660
Eddie Pepperell	67	66	67	64	264	69,660
Rafa Cabrera-Bello	65	66	63	71	265	46,440
Magnus A. Carlsson	65	66	70	64	265	46,440
Mikko Korhonen	67	70	65	63	265	46,440
Paul Lawrie	61	71	63	71	266	34,560
Wade Ormsby	61	68	68	69	266	34,560
Alejandro Canizares	68	66	68	65	267	27,270
Ben Evans	68	67	65	67	267	27,270
David Howell	68	69	63	67	267	27,270
Maximilian Kieffer	67	67	64	69	267	27,270
Soren Kjeldsen	64	64	71	68	267	27,270
Mike Lorenzo-Vera	68	67	67	65	267	27,270
Mikko Ilonen	64	71	62	71	268	21,672
Tom Lewis	69	65	65	69	268	21,672
Matthew Nixon	70	64	68	66	268	21,672
Jason Scrivener	68	67	65	68	268	21,672
Andy Sullivan	65	69	68	66	268	21,672
Gregory Bourdy	68	66	67	68	269	18,180
Robert Dinwiddie	67	70	70	62	269	18,180
Andrew Johnston	66	68	65	70	269	18,180
David Lipsky	66	71	69	63	269	18,180
Joost Luiten	63	71	68	67	269	18,180
Robert Rock	63	69	71	66	269	18,180
Simon Thornton	67	68	66	68	269	18,180
Richard Bland	62	70	70	68	270	14,700
Matthew Fitzpatrick	71	60	71	68	270	14,700
Ricardo Gonzalez	69	68	67	66	270	14,700
Scott Hend	65	72	65	68	270	14,700
David Horsey	63	66	71	70	270	14,700
Peter Uihlein	69	66	69	66	270	14,700
Oliver Fisher	68	68	69	66	271	12,420
Matt Ford	66	69	69	67	271	12,420
Stephen Gallacher	65	72	67	67	271	12,420
Rikard Karlberg	69	66	68	68	271	12,420
James Morrison	63	67	70	71	271	12,420
Richard Green	67	64	68	73	272	10,440
Simon Griffiths	67	67	70	68	272	10,440
Anders Hansen	70	67	67	68	272	10,440
Benjamin Hebert	68	67	70	67	272	10,440
Paul Peterson	68	69	68	67	272	10,440
Daniel Vancsik	66	70	69	67	272	10,440
Jason Barnes	67	64	68	74	273	7,920
Wil Besseling	69	66	69	69	273	7,920
Daniel Brooks	67	68	68	70	273	7,920
Richard Finch	69	66	69	69	273	7,920
Trevor Fisher, Jr.	68	66	70	69	273	7,920
Richard McEvoy	71	63	70	69	273	7,920
Andrea Pavan	67	70	69	67	273	7,920
Tom Watson	69	68	68	68	273	7,920
Padraig Harrington	71	65	67	71	274	6,300
Nicolas Colsaerts	69	65	72	69	275	5,940
David Drysdale	68	67	73	68	276	5,220
Edouard Espana	70	67	70	69	276	5,220
Estanislao Goya	63	71	70	72	276	5,220
Martin Kaymer	67	67	68	74	276	5,220
Espen Kofstad	69	66	69	72	276	5,220
Peter Lawrie	68	69	71	69	277	4,680
Raphael Jacquelin	67	70	71	70	278	4,410
Lasse Jensen	65	71	71	71	278	4,410
John Parry	67	70	70	73	280	4,140
Lucas Bjerregaard	66	68	77	70	281	3,780
Daniel Gaunt	70	67	70	74	281	3,780
Alvaro Quiros	67	65	77	72	281	3,780

Open D'Italia

Golf Club Milano, Parco Reale di Monza, Italy
Par 36-36–72; 7,159 yards

September 17-20
purse, €1,500,000

	SCORES				TOTAL	MONEY
Rikard Karlberg	67	67	68	67	269	€250,000
Martin Kaymer	68	66	65	70	269	166,660
(Karlberg defeated Kaymer on second playoff hole.)						
Lucas Bjerregaard	66	65	70	69	270	57,300
Jens Fahrbring	67	64	68	71	270	57,300
Matthew Fitzpatrick	70	68	67	65	270	57,300
Joakim Lagergren	72	66	69	63	270	57,300
David Lipsky	67	67	68	68	270	57,300
Danny Willett	68	67	69	66	270	57,300
Fabrizio Zanotti	66	67	68	69	270	57,300
Romain Wattel	67	66	66	72	271	30,000
Miguel Angel Jimenez	69	66	72	65	272	26,700
Roope Kakko	67	72	67	66	272	26,700
*Lorenzo Scalise	71	66	69	66	272	
Jason Barnes	69	68	69	67	273	21,650
Merrick Bremner	71	68	70	64	273	21,650
Peter Lawrie	68	67	70	68	273	21,650
Jason Scrivener	68	68	67	70	273	21,650
Jaco Van Zyl	71	65	66	71	273	21,650
Bernd Wiesberger	66	68	67	72	273	21,650
Nicolas Colsaerts	63	70	70	71	274	17,490
Darren Fichardt	69	70	69	66	274	17,490
Tom Lewis	72	67	67	68	274	17,490
Francesco Molinari	65	72	68	69	274	17,490
Ricardo Santos	69	68	68	69	274	17,490
Kristoffer Broberg	65	72	67	71	275	14,475
Alejandro Canizares	68	69	69	69	275	14,475
Florian Fritsch	68	72	70	65	275	14,475
Benjamin Hebert	69	69	69	68	275	14,475
David Howell	70	69	70	66	275	14,475
Mikko Korhonen	66	70	70	69	275	14,475
Mikael Lundberg	68	68	67	72	275	14,475
Y.E. Yang	68	71	69	67	275	14,475
Daniel Brooks	71	65	67	73	276	11,156
Tommy Fleetwood	70	67	71	68	276	11,156
Padraig Harrington	70	70	69	67	276	11,156
Shiv Kapur	65	72	70	69	276	11,156
Paul Maddy	68	69	70	69	276	11,156
Wade Ormsby	69	67	74	66	276	11,156
Andrea Perrino	67	67	74	68	276	11,156
Jeev Milkha Singh	68	69	68	71	276	11,156
Stewart Cink	69	68	70	70	277	9,450
Ricardo Gonzalez	68	72	67	70	277	9,450
Pedro Oriol	68	65	74	70	277	9,450
S.S.P. Chawrasia	69	69	71	69	278	7,800
Marco Crespi	70	70	67	71	278	7,800
Eduardo de la Riva	69	70	70	69	278	7,800
Scott Fallon	67	70	72	69	278	7,800
Matt Ford	69	68	70	71	278	7,800
Robert Karlsson	69	71	70	68	278	7,800
Jerome Lando Casanova	71	67	67	73	278	7,800
Graeme Storm	71	66	70	71	278	7,800
*Scott Fernandez	69	67	69	74	279	
Wes Homan	73	66	68	72	279	6,150
Jose Manuel Lara	68	72	70	69	279	6,150
Victor Riu	71	68	70	70	279	6,150
Oliver Fisher	70	68	71	71	280	4,779

	SCORES				TOTAL	MONEY
Mark Foster	66	71	72	71	280	4,779
Estanislao Goya	71	68	69	72	280	4,779
Craig Lee	67	67	75	71	280	4,779
Stuart Manley	72	68	70	70	280	4,779
Hennie Otto	69	71	71	69	280	4,779
John Parry	71	69	70	70	280	4,779
Paul McGinley	68	72	68	73	281	3,975
Matthew Nixon	67	69	72	73	281	3,975
*Stefano Mazzoli	66	70	74	72	282	
Edoardo Molinari	72	67	71	72	282	3,750
Trevor Fisher, Jr.	71	69	72	71	283	3,375
Thorbjorn Olesen	72	68	72	71	283	3,375
Jake Roos	70	70	73	70	283	3,375
Mark Tullo	69	71	70	73	283	3,375
Lorenzo Gagli	67	70	73	74	284	3,000
Alexander Levy	70	70	70	75	285	2,795
Garth Mulroy	72	67	73	73	285	2,795
Rafa Cabrera-Bello	70	69	72	76	287	2,248
Robert Rock	72	67	69	79	287	2,248

Porsche European Open

Golf Resort Bad Griesbach, Bad Griesbach, Germany
Par 35-36–71; 7,188 yards

September 24-27
purse, €2,000,000

	SCORES				TOTAL	MONEY
Thongchai Jaidee	68	68	64	67	267	€333,330
Graeme Storm	65	67	69	67	268	222,220
Pelle Edberg	67	71	63	69	270	125,200
Scott Hend	69	69	68	65	271	100,000
Lucas Bjerregaard	68	68	68	68	272	66,200
Jamie Donaldson	67	68	67	70	272	66,200
Ross Fisher	67	65	69	71	272	66,200
Rikard Karlberg	68	71	66	67	272	66,200
Richard Bland	65	70	71	67	273	40,533
Soren Kjeldsen	66	70	67	70	273	40,533
John Parry	66	70	70	67	273	40,533
Magnus A. Carlsson	67	68	67	72	274	29,657
Darren Fichardt	65	69	70	70	274	29,657
Richard Green	65	72	70	67	274	29,657
Benjamin Hebert	64	72	68	70	274	29,657
Mikko Korhonen	70	67	68	69	274	29,657
James Morrison	67	69	70	68	274	29,657
Peter Uihlein	68	68	67	71	274	29,657
Byeong-Hun An	68	65	73	69	275	23,320
Seve Benson	68	70	69	68	275	23,320
Peter Hanson	68	70	66	71	275	23,320
Charl Schwartzel	66	66	75	68	275	23,320
Simon Wakefield	69	70	68	68	275	23,320
Alejandro Canizares	70	67	70	69	276	19,900
Edouard Espana	69	69	70	68	276	19,900
Gregory Havret	69	70	67	70	276	19,900
Raphael Jacquelin	70	67	69	70	276	19,900
Bernhard Langer	66	71	70	69	276	19,900
Hennie Otto	67	70	68	71	276	19,900
Johan Edfors	66	68	70	73	277	16,333
Florian Fritsch	66	69	73	69	277	16,333
Joost Luiten	69	69	70	69	277	16,333
Lee Slattery	68	71	71	67	277	16,333
Alessandro Tadini	68	69	67	73	277	16,333

	SCORES				TOTAL	MONEY
Justin Walters	67	68	71	71	277	16,333
Andrew Dodt	70	68	71	69	278	13,200
Bradley Dredge	68	70	68	72	278	13,200
Lasse Jensen	68	70	67	73	278	13,200
Miguel Angel Jimenez	67	69	70	72	278	13,200
Robert Karlsson	66	72	71	69	278	13,200
Mike Lorenzo-Vera	69	70	68	71	278	13,200
Graeme McDowell	68	70	70	70	278	13,200
Philipp Mejow	68	71	73	66	278	13,200
Marcus Fraser	69	69	71	70	279	10,800
Anders Hansen	69	68	72	70	279	10,800
Mikko Ilonen	69	66	67	77	279	10,800
Mikael Lundberg	70	68	70	71	279	10,800
Oliver Fisher	66	69	72	73	280	9,400
Maximilian Kieffer	68	68	71	73	280	9,400
Fabrizio Zanotti	70	68	69	73	280	9,400
Cyril Bouniol	69	70	68	74	281	8,000
Nicolas Colsaerts	72	66	73	70	281	8,000
Richard McEvoy	66	67	73	75	281	8,000
Chris Paisley	67	72	74	68	281	8,000
Ben Evans	68	70	77	67	282	6,450
Sebastian Heisele	70	67	73	72	282	6,450
Scott Jamieson	68	70	71	73	282	6,450
Alexander Levy	72	67	73	70	282	6,450
Jordi Garcia Pinto	68	71	72	72	283	5,800
Kenneth Ferrie	70	67	72	75	284	5,300
Damien McGrane	71	67	71	75	284	5,300
Matthew Nixon	71	68	72	73	284	5,300
Peter Whiteford	67	72	70	75	284	5,300
Wade Ormsby	72	67	78	69	286	4,800
Albin Choi	70	69	71	78	288	4,600
Richard Finch	66	72	75	77	290	4,400

Alfred Dunhill Links Championship

St. Andrews Old Course: Par 36-36–72; 7,307 yards
Carnoustie Championship Course: Par 36-36–72; 7,345 yards
Kingsbarns Golf Links: Par 36-36–72; 7,227 yards
St. Andrews & Fife, Scotland

October 1-4
purse, US$5,000,000

	SCORES				TOTAL	MONEY
Thorbjorn Olesen	68	66	65	71	270	€708,171
Brooks Koepka	72	69	64	67	272	369,050
Chris Stroud	68	66	70	68	272	369,050
Kiradech Aphibarnrat	75	63	66	69	273	155,005
Benjamin Hebert	69	67	67	70	273	155,005
Joakim Lagergren	71	71	62	69	273	155,005
Bernd Wiesberger	70	68	69	66	273	155,005
Chris Wood	71	72	65	65	273	155,005
Stewart Cink	73	65	69	67	274	82,856
David Drysdale	68	72	66	68	274	82,856
David Horsey	72	70	64	68	274	82,856
Soren Kjeldsen	65	72	69	68	274	82,856
Felipe Aguilar	67	73	67	68	275	61,328
Jamie Donaldson	69	65	71	70	275	61,328
Bradley Dredge	73	63	68	71	275	61,328
Tommy Fleetwood	70	71	67	67	275	61,328
Peter Hanson	70	72	66	67	275	61,328
James Morrison	67	70	70	68	275	61,328
Paul Dunne	64	70	72	70	276	47,536

	SCORES				TOTAL	MONEY
Ben Evans	70	72	65	69	276	47,536
Florian Fritsch	68	70	64	74	276	47,536
Stephen Gallacher	67	72	68	69	276	47,536
Nathan Holman	68	68	72	68	276	47,536
Shane Lowry	74	69	66	67	276	47,536
Graeme McDowell	68	69	69	70	276	47,536
Anthony Wall	65	68	73	70	276	47,536
Nick Dougherty	72	67	70	68	277	40,366
Ernie Els	72	67	66	72	277	40,366
Scott Piercy	69	69	68	71	277	40,366
Branden Grace	73	64	68	73	278	36,542
Jimmy Mullen	64	69	74	71	278	36,542
Justin Walters	72	69	68	69	278	36,542
Christiaan Bezuidenhout	72	65	71	71	279	31,953
Oliver Fisher	70	72	66	71	279	31,953
Scott Jamieson	72	68	69	70	279	31,953
Graeme Storm	69	68	68	74	279	31,953
Romain Wattel	70	70	69	70	279	31,953
Kristoffer Broberg	64	74	70	72	280	27,619
Magnus A. Carlsson	70	72	67	71	280	27,619
Soren Hansen	71	69	70	70	280	27,619
Matthew Nixon	72	72	63	73	280	27,619
Marc Warren	68	69	71	72	280	27,619
Alejandro Canizares	69	67	70	75	281	23,370
Victor Dubuisson	74	68	67	72	281	23,370
Mikko Ilonen	71	67	69	74	281	23,370
Jyoti Randhawa	70	69	71	71	281	23,370
Y.E. Yang	72	68	70	71	281	23,370
Gregory Bourdy	71	70	69	72	282	19,546
Edouard Espana	73	68	68	73	282	19,546
Jbe' Kruger	73	68	69	72	282	19,546
Adrian Otaegui	68	70	70	74	282	19,546
Richard Finch	69	73	67	74	283	16,146
David Lingmerth	71	66	73	73	283	16,146
Danny Willett	74	68	68	73	283	16,146
Fabrizio Zanotti	67	75	66	75	283	16,146
Martin Kaymer	68	68	74	74	284	14,022
Nicolas Colsaerts	73	70	67	75	285	12,960
Robert Dinwiddie	71	69	68	77	285	12,960
Nick Cullen	70	73	67	77	287	12,110
Gary Stal	69	73	68	77	287	12,110
Danie van Tonder	69	70	71	78	288	11,472
Richard Bland	65	73	73		211	9,060
Merrick Bremner	70	71	70		211	9,060
Darren Clarke	71	68	72		211	9,060
Mark Foster	68	72	71		211	9,060
Richard Green	69	73	69		211	9,060
Moritz Lampert	67	71	73		211	9,060
Alexander Levy	67	71	73		211	9,060
Wade Ormsby	73	72	66		211	9,060
Tjaart van der Walt	75	66	70		211	9,060
Oliver Wilson	74	74	63		211	9,060

British Masters

Woburn Golf Club, Woburn, England
Par 35-36–71; 7,150 yards

October 8-11
purse, £3,000,000

	SCORES				TOTAL	MONEY
Matthew Fitzpatrick	64	69	68	68	269	€671,550
Soren Kjeldsen	65	68	69	69	271	300,465
Shane Lowry	66	69	69	67	271	300,465
Fabrizio Zanotti	68	68	66	69	271	300,465
Kiradech Aphibarnrat	67	67	67	72	273	133,370
Luke Donald	67	72	65	69	273	133,370
Marcus Fraser	66	73	67	67	273	133,370
Mike Lorenzo-Vera	70	67	69	67	273	133,370
Oliver Fisher	68	70	71	65	274	78,571
Julien Quesne	70	67	69	68	274	78,571
Anthony Wall	68	71	66	69	274	78,571
Chris Wood	69	69	69	67	274	78,571
Richard Bland	67	67	70	71	275	60,641
Tommy Fleetwood	72	70	68	65	275	60,641
Tyrrell Hatton	71	68	69	67	275	60,641
Robert Karlsson	65	70	70	70	275	60,641
Kristoffer Broberg	71	67	69	69	276	50,286
Darren Fichardt	73	68	66	69	276	50,286
Peter Hanson	70	70	68	68	276	50,286
Alexander Levy	67	71	69	69	276	50,286
Lee Westwood	69	70	67	70	276	50,286
Edouard Espana	71	69	69	68	277	44,322
Lee Slattery	65	71	69	72	277	44,322
Romain Wattel	66	71	67	73	277	44,322
Daniel Brooks	69	69	67	73	278	39,487
Paul Dunne	71	69	70	68	278	39,487
Andrew Johnston	70	69	70	69	278	39,487
Niall Kearney	69	69	69	71	278	39,487
Jaco Van Zyl	68	69	70	71	278	39,487
David Howell	71	66	71	71	279	34,652
Graeme McDowell	70	67	70	72	279	34,652
Graeme Storm	72	70	72	65	279	34,652
Michael Hoey	69	73	67	71	280	30,300
Joost Luiten	68	69	71	72	280	30,300
Eddie Pepperell	72	68	69	71	280	30,300
Ian Poulter	68	70	70	72	280	30,300
Marc Warren	65	71	74	70	280	30,300
Gregory Bourdy	71	69	75	66	281	24,982
Johan Edfors	70	70	72	69	281	24,982
Padraig Harrington	66	72	73	70	281	24,982
Rikard Karlberg	68	70	70	73	281	24,982
Francesco Molinari	71	69	70	71	281	24,982
Wade Ormsby	68	69	71	73	281	24,982
Robert Rock	72	65	71	73	281	24,982
Y.E. Yang	71	68	70	72	281	24,982
Jorge Campillo	71	71	71	69	282	18,535
Ashley Chesters	69	69	73	71	282	18,535
Benjamin Hebert	73	69	72	68	282	18,535
David Horsey	69	72	67	74	282	18,535
Sam Hutsby	69	68	76	69	282	18,535
Craig Lee	72	70	69	71	282	18,535
Andy Sullivan	67	69	72	74	282	18,535
Danny Willett	69	72	70	71	282	18,535
Niclas Fasth	70	70	73	70	283	13,095
Richard Finch	69	73	75	66	283	13,095
Anders Hansen	70	70	71	72	283	13,095
Scott Hend	71	71	72	69	283	13,095

	SCORES				TOTAL	MONEY
Miguel Angel Jimenez	72	70	73	68	283	13,095
Jeev Milkha Singh	67	73	71	72	283	13,095
Alejandro Canizares	69	72	75	68	284	10,678
Marco Crespi	69	72	68	75	284	10,678
Jamie Donaldson	69	72	71	72	284	10,678
Garth Mulroy	70	72	72	70	284	10,678
David Drysdale	72	69	74	71	286	9,267
Thomas Pieters	72	70	76	68	286	9,267
Gary Stal	72	70	73	71	286	9,267
Magnus A. Carlsson	69	72	72	74	287	8,260
Mikael Lundberg	66	70	71	80	287	8,260
Nicolas Colsaerts	69	70	71	78	288	7,015
Gregory Havret	70	71	69	78	288	7,015
Pablo Larrazabal	71	68	75	74	288	7,015
Jordi Garcia Pinto	72	69	76	80	297	6,041

Portugal Masters

Oceanico Victoria Golf Course, Vilamoura, Portugal
Par 35-36–71; 7,209 yards

October 15-18
purse, €2,000,000

	SCORES				TOTAL	MONEY
Andy Sullivan	64	64	67	66	261	€333,330
Chris Wood	68	69	65	68	270	222,220
Eduardo de la Riva	65	67	68	71	271	103,333
Trevor Fisher, Jr.	66	68	70	67	271	103,333
Anthony Wall	69	64	72	66	271	103,333
Jorge Campillo	66	69	67	70	272	60,000
Craig Lee	67	71	69	65	272	60,000
Thomas Pieters	65	66	72	69	272	60,000
Lucas Bjerregaard	72	69	66	66	273	35,457
Edouard Espana	70	67	69	67	273	35,457
Stephen Gallacher	67	71	68	67	273	35,457
Mikko Korhonen	69	69	69	66	273	35,457
Garth Mulroy	69	67	70	67	273	35,457
Bernd Ritthammer	69	66	73	65	273	35,457
Robert Rock	70	67	70	66	273	35,457
David Drysdale	65	71	69	69	274	27,600
Bernd Wiesberger	68	64	72	70	274	27,600
Nicolas Colsaerts	64	71	68	72	275	24,450
Richard Green	68	70	73	64	275	24,450
Hennie Otto	70	65	69	71	275	24,450
Alvaro Quiros	67	68	71	69	275	24,450
Tommy Fleetwood	69	64	72	71	276	22,000
Anders Hansen	68	67	72	69	276	22,000
Romain Wattel	67	71	73	65	276	22,000
Thomas Aiken	65	70	72	70	277	19,900
Thomas Bjorn	67	67	70	73	277	19,900
Richard Bland	71	70	72	64	277	19,900
Paul Maddy	66	69	74	68	277	19,900
Jbe' Kruger	72	69	69	68	278	18,100
Damien McGrane	67	72	73	66	278	18,100
Darren Fichardt	68	70	74	67	279	15,800
Ricardo Gouveia	71	68	72	68	279	15,800
Padraig Harrington	70	70	70	69	279	15,800
Benjamin Hebert	75	64	69	71	279	15,800
Jeev Milkha Singh	69	66	73	71	279	15,800
Jaco Van Zyl	71	67	70	71	279	15,800
Chris Doak	69	69	70	72	280	13,000
Lasse Jensen	73	67	71	69	280	13,000

	SCORES				TOTAL	MONEY
Soren Kjeldsen	68	66	74	72	280	13,000
Adrian Otaegui	67	67	74	72	280	13,000
Chris Paisley	67	67	76	70	280	13,000
Justin Walters	71	68	72	69	280	13,000
Marc Warren	71	68	75	66	280	13,000
Gregory Bourdy	70	69	74	68	281	10,400
Steven Brown	73	68	71	69	281	10,400
Alejandro Canizares	70	69	76	66	281	10,400
Andrew Johnston	70	69	70	72	281	10,400
Maximilian Kieffer	71	70	72	68	281	10,400
Graeme Storm	68	70	73	70	281	10,400
Oliver Fisher	69	69	72	72	282	8,600
Martin Kaymer	70	70	74	68	282	8,600
Thorbjorn Olesen	71	70	71	70	282	8,600
Rafa Cabrera-Bello	68	68	75	72	283	7,200
Johan Carlsson	66	73	75	69	283	7,200
Ben Evans	73	68	75	67	283	7,200
Scott Jamieson	67	68	75	73	283	7,200
Daniel Brooks	68	69	74	73	284	5,600
Marco Crespi	68	73	77	66	284	5,600
Ricardo Gonzalez	70	70	75	69	284	5,600
Sam Hutsby	72	68	71	73	284	5,600
Renato Paratore	70	71	75	68	284	5,600
Jason Scrivener	70	69	78	67	284	5,600
Ben Stow	69	69	72	74	284	5,600
Kristoffer Broberg	66	70	76	73	285	4,500
Daniel Gaunt	72	69	72	72	285	4,500
Gregory Havret	71	70	75	69	285	4,500
Paul Lawrie	71	70	74	70	285	4,500
Paul Dunne	68	72	77	70	287	4,000
*Tomas Silva	71	68	73	75	287	
Mikael Lundberg	70	69	78	71	288	3,800
Kevin Phelan	70	71	76	72	289	3,650
Julien Quesne	70	68	79	78	295	3,000

UBS Hong Kong Open

See Asia/Japan Tours chapter.

The Final Series

Turkish Airlines Open

Montgomerie Maxx Royal, Antalya, Turkey
Par 35-37–72; 7,132 yards

October 29-November 1
purse, US$7,000,000

	SCORES				TOTAL	MONEY
Victor Dubuisson	69	64	67	66	266	€1,027,669
Jaco Van Zyl	61	69	70	67	267	687,109
Kiradech Aphibarnrat	67	68	66	67	268	387,600
Byeong-Hun An	70	68	65	66	269	308,406
Chris Wood	66	66	71	68	271	261,806
Rory McIlroy	67	67	67	71	272	201,331
Peter Uihlein	68	69	67	68	272	201,331

	SCORES			TOTAL	MONEY
Shane Lowry	68	70	69	66	273	156,449
Lee Slattery	68	68	72	66	274	140,064
Andrew Johnston	70	66	72	67	275	123,855
Rafa Cabrera-Bello	67	69	70	70	276	100,864
Jamie Donaldson	71	68	69	68	276	100,864
Soren Kjeldsen	72	68	70	66	276	100,864
Lee Westwood	64	71	69	72	276	100,864
Danny Willett	69	70	68	69	276	100,864
Richard Bland	67	65	72	73	277	84,831
Ian Poulter	69	70	71	67	277	84,831
Benjamin Hebert	70	70	68	70	278	79,766
Alexander Levy	69	65	74	70	278	79,766
Jorge Campillo	69	70	72	68	279	72,058
Maximilian Kieffer	71	69	71	68	279	72,058
David Lipsky	70	69	70	70	279	72,058
Julien Quesne	67	70	69	73	279	72,058
Graeme Storm	71	74	71	63	279	72,058
Anthony Wall	73	69	69	69	280	65,451
Lucas Bjerregaard	68	69	75	69	281	57,208
Matthew Fitzpatrick	73	63	73	72	281	57,208
Stephen Gallacher	71	68	70	72	281	57,208
Tyrrell Hatton	69	70	72	70	281	57,208
Thongchai Jaidee	69	69	69	74	281	57,208
Hao-Tong Li	72	68	70	71	281	57,208
Thomas Pieters	72	66	72	71	281	57,208
Alejandro Canizares	69	71	71	71	282	47,040
Gregory Havret	73	72	69	68	282	47,040
Rikard Karlberg	70	73	72	67	282	47,040
Joakim Lagergren	70	68	75	69	282	47,040
Richard Green	71	70	72	70	283	41,138
David Howell	70	69	73	71	283	41,138
Graeme McDowell	70	65	73	75	283	41,138
Romain Wattel	70	71	67	75	283	41,138
Thomas Aiken	68	72	74	70	284	34,267
Gregory Bourdy	69	70	72	73	284	34,267
David Drysdale	69	72	69	74	284	34,267
Thorbjorn Olesen	71	71	69	73	284	34,267
Marcel Siem	74	73	68	69	284	34,267
Gary Stal	74	68	73	69	284	34,267
Thomas Bjorn	72	69	75	69	285	28,629
Marcus Fraser	69	73	74	69	285	28,629
Raphael Jacquelin	68	69	72	76	285	28,629
Kristoffer Broberg	71	69	74	72	286	23,094
John Daly	77	71	69	69	286	23,094
Pelle Edberg	73	71	71	71	286	23,094
Charl Schwartzel	71	71	72	72	286	23,094
Bernd Wiesberger	67	74	75	70	286	23,094
Fabrizio Zanotti	67	66	74	79	286	23,094
Trevor Fisher, Jr.	70	72	72	73	287	17,221
Morten Orum Madsen	70	70	73	74	287	17,221
Richie Ramsay	73	72	74	68	287	17,221
Robert Rock	72	73	69	73	287	17,221
Tommy Fleetwood	71	70	73	74	288	12,614
Pablo Larrazabal	71	71	72	74	288	12,614
Joost Luiten	72	71	72	73	288	12,614
James Morrison	70	68	78	72	288	12,614
Andy Sullivan	76	67	73	72	288	12,614
Mikko Ilonen	72	69	76	72	289	10,659
Magnus A. Carlsson	70	74	79	67	290	9,954
Alex Noren	70	71	74	75	290	9,954
Ross Fisher	76	69	69	77	291	9,073
Michael Hoey	72	75	72	72	291	9,073
Miguel Angel Jimenez	78	71	68	74	291	9,073

	SCORES				TOTAL	MONEY
Eduardo de la Riva	72	73	75	72	292	8,368
*Ali Altuntas	73	74	67	79	293	
Marc Warren	79	69	71	76	295	8,016
David Horsey	73	73	76	74	296	7,663
Darren Clarke	75	71	75	80	301	7,311
Mike Lorenzo-Vera	71	81	75	75	302	7,135
*Serkan Akarsu	74	78	77	81	310	
*Ediz Kemaloglu	77	80	84	85	326	

WGC - HSBC Champions

See Asia/Japan Tours chapter.

BMW Masters

Lake Malaren Golf Club, Shanghai, China
Par 36-36–72; 7,594 yards

November 12-15
purse, US$7,000,000

	SCORES				TOTAL	MONEY
Kristoffer Broberg	69	70	64	68	271	€1,070,334
Patrick Reed	71	69	64	67	271	715,635
(Broberg defeated Reed on first playoff hole.)						
Byeong-Hun An	65	71	66	70	272	305,750
Lucas Bjerregaard	66	66	70	70	272	305,750
Thongchai Jaidee	67	68	66	71	272	305,750
Henrik Stenson	68	71	65	68	272	305,750
Paul Casey	67	69	68	69	273	177,807
Justin Rose	67	72	67	67	273	177,807
Soren Kjeldsen	72	67	71	64	274	137,071
Julien Quesne	70	69	69	66	274	137,071
Sergio Garcia	64	71	67	73	275	115,235
Ian Poulter	68	68	68	71	275	115,235
Ross Fisher	66	71	67	72	276	95,853
Matthew Fitzpatrick	68	71	67	70	276	95,853
Marcus Fraser	70	70	65	71	276	95,853
Thomas Pieters	71	71	63	71	276	95,853
Victor Dubuisson	65	73	68	71	277	81,839
Scott Hend	69	73	66	69	277	81,839
David Howell	69	71	69	68	277	81,839
Francesco Molinari	68	70	69	70	277	81,839
Andy Sullivan	74	71	67	65	277	81,839
Branden Grace	71	71	69	68	279	73,719
Chris Wood	70	69	70	70	279	73,719
Trevor Fisher, Jr.	71	71	69	69	280	66,884
Emiliano Grillo	71	70	74	65	280	66,884
Graeme Storm	72	72	69	67	280	66,884
Bernd Wiesberger	71	69	70	70	280	66,884
Alexander Levy	73	76	63	69	281	59,361
Peter Uihlein	71	66	72	72	281	59,361
Danny Willett	72	69	70	70	281	59,361
Kiradech Aphibarnrat	72	74	67	69	282	50,614
Benjamin Hebert	69	72	71	70	282	50,614
Maximilian Kieffer	72	68	71	71	282	50,614
Danny Lee	70	71	71	70	282	50,614
James Morrison	70	69	71	72	282	50,614
Gary Stal	69	73	69	71	282	50,614
Ze-Cheng Dou	68	72	72	71	283	42,662
Thorbjorn Olesen	75	71	68	69	283	42,662
Louis Oosthuizen	70	71	68	74	283	42,662

	SCORES			TOTAL	MONEY
Marc Warren	72	70	75	66	283	42,662
Gregory Bourdy	70	70	71	73	284	36,167
Tommy Fleetwood	72	68	71	73	284	36,167
Martin Kaymer	69	69	70	76	284	36,167
Hao-Tong Li	71	74	68	71	284	36,167
Anthony Wall	73	70	70	71	284	36,167
Rafa Cabrera-Bello	72	73	69	71	285	28,350
John Daly	72	75	68	70	285	28,350
Stephen Gallacher	72	73	72	68	285	28,350
Joost Luiten	70	74	72	69	285	28,350
Alex Noren	70	77	70	68	285	28,350
Jaco Van Zyl	68	74	70	73	285	28,350
Ashun Wu	74	73	69	69	285	28,350
Paul McGinley	71	71	73	71	286	21,958
Eddie Pepperell	68	74	72	72	286	21,958
Richie Ramsay	68	75	74	69	286	21,958
Tyrrell Hatton	74	73	73	67	287	18,349
Rikard Karlberg	70	73	72	72	287	18,349
Shane Lowry	70	75	74	68	287	18,349
Ze-Yu He	74	74	71	69	288	15,964
Pablo Larrazabal	74	71	76	68	289	13,731
Marcel Siem	72	80	68	69	289	13,731
Lee Slattery	72	71	71	75	289	13,731
Alejandro Canizares	73	71	71	75	290	10,973
Yi Cao	73	72	71	74	290	10,973
Wen-Chong Liang	70	71	78	71	290	10,973
Kyong-Jun Moon	72	74	70	74	290	10,973
Fabrizio Zanotti	70	75	76	69	290	10,973
Jamie Donaldson	76	71	75	70	292	9,450
David Horsey	70	75	76	71	292	9,450
Zi-Hao Chen	72	71	79	72	294	8,716
Raphael Jacquelin	78	74	71	71	294	8,716
Huilin Zhang	71	70	80	75	296	7,982
Xin-Jun Zhang	68	80	72	76	296	7,982
Miguel Angel Jimenez	78	75	72	73	298	7,431
Mu Hu	77	79	66	79	301	7,156
Zheng Ouyang	77	71	81	72	301	7,156
Xiongyi Zhao	78	75	75	77	305	6,881
*Zhou Huan Yuan	80	75	76	77	308	

DP World Tour Championship

Jumeirah Golf Estates, Dubai, United Arab Emirates
Par 36-36–72; 7,675 yards

November 19-22
purse, US$8,000,000

	SCORES			TOTAL	MONEY
Rory McIlroy	68	68	65	66	267	€1,230,792
Andy Sullivan	66	66	68	68	268	820,522
Branden Grace	68	69	69	67	273	462,286
Byeong-Hun An	70	68	66	71	275	256,620
Matthew Fitzpatrick	68	69	68	70	275	256,620
Emiliano Grillo	69	64	71	71	275	256,620
Francesco Molinari	67	71	69	68	275	256,620
Charl Schwartzel	71	65	70	69	275	256,620
Danny Willett	68	70	67	70	275	256,620
Martin Kaymer	66	71	71	68	276	142,246
Soren Kjeldsen	71	70	67	68	276	142,246
Patrick Reed	70	65	68	73	276	142,246
Luke Donald	69	72	68	70	279	115,733
Victor Dubuisson	72	67	69	71	279	115,733

	SCORES				TOTAL	MONEY
Tyrrell Hatton	69	69	72	69	279	115,733
Chris Wood	68	70	69	72	279	115,733
Kristoffer Broberg	70	73	67	70	280	96,002
Thorbjorn Olesen	70	74	68	68	280	96,002
Richie Ramsay	71	70	68	71	280	96,002
Lee Slattery	76	71	68	65	280	96,002
Bernd Wiesberger	72	65	72	71	280	96,002
Kiradech Aphibarnrat	73	65	73	70	281	77,632
Rafa Cabrera-Bello	76	70	69	66	281	77,632
Alejandro Canizares	68	71	70	72	281	77,632
Pablo Larrazabal	69	72	72	68	281	77,632
Thomas Pieters	69	69	73	70	281	77,632
Justin Rose	71	66	78	66	281	77,632
Gary Stal	71	70	68	72	281	77,632
Peter Uihlein	71	69	69	72	281	77,632
Anthony Wall	71	70	70	70	281	77,632
Lucas Bjerregaard	69	71	71	71	282	63,785
Thongchai Jaidee	69	67	69	77	282	63,785
Joost Luiten	69	72	68	73	282	63,785
Jamie Donaldson	70	71	71	71	283	57,555
Marcus Fraser	66	72	74	71	283	57,555
Anirban Lahiri	73	67	72	71	283	57,555
Marc Warren	72	68	70	73	283	57,555
Gregory Bourdy	73	68	69	74	284	51,278
Stephen Gallacher	73	72	69	70	284	51,278
Alex Noren	71	66	71	76	284	51,278
Louis Oosthuizen	73	68	70	73	284	51,278
David Howell	72	76	69	68	285	45,000
Ian Poulter	66	74	71	74	285	45,000
Jaco Van Zyl	72	70	70	73	285	45,000
Lee Westwood	71	70	74	70	285	45,000
Ross Fisher	69	73	71	73	286	40,293
Alexander Levy	74	71	73	68	286	40,293
Raphael Jacquelin	76	69	74	68	287	34,800
Miguel Angel Jimenez	68	74	72	73	287	34,800
Maximilian Kieffer	71	71	71	74	287	34,800
Shane Lowry	75	70	69	73	287	34,800
Graeme Storm	73	72	71	71	287	34,800
Tommy Fleetwood	77	72	69	70	288	28,523
Rikard Karlberg	72	72	70	74	288	28,523
Julien Quesne	73	71	67	77	288	28,523
Scott Hend	77	69	74	69	289	24,600
Fabrizio Zanotti	68	73	73	75	289	24,600
Eddie Pepperell	71	72	73	74	290	23,077
James Morrison	71	73	71	76	291	21,969
Henrik Stenson	77	69	72	73	291	21,969

Race to Dubai Final Rankings

RANK	NAME	RACE TO DUBAI POINTS	BONUS MONEY
1	Rory McIlroy	4,727,253	US$1,250,000
2	Danny Willett	3,670,310	800,000
3	Branden Grace	3,056,948	530,000
4	Justin Rose	2,827,024	400,000
5	Shane Lowry	2,729,144	350,000
6	Louis Oosthuizen	2,711,457	300,000
7	Byeong-Hun An	2,417,356	250,000
8	Andy Sullivan	2,263,573	200,000
9	Bernd Wiesberger	2,163,180	170,000
10	Thongchai Jaidee	2,150,076	150,000
11	Victor Dubuisson	2,132,753	140,000
12	Matthew Fitzpatrick	2,094,933	130,000
13	Kiradech Aphibarnrat	2,055,618	120,000
14	Kristoffer Broberg	2,003,321	110,000
15	Soren Kjeldsen	1,996,684	100,000

Alfred Dunhill Championship
See African Sunshine Tour chapter.

Australian PGA Championship
See Australasian Tour chapter.

Nedbank Golf Challenge
See African Sunshine Tour chapter.

Challenge Tour

Barclays Kenya Open

Karen Country Club, Nairobi, Kenya
Par 35-35–71; 6,953 yards

April 9-12
purse, €200,000

	SCORES				TOTAL	MONEY
Haydn Porteous	66	65	72	68	271	€32,000
Brandon Stone	69	66	67	69	271	22,000
(Porteous defeated Stone on first playoff hole.)						
George Woolgar	70	66	69	67	272	14,000
Sam Walker	69	68	67	69	273	12,000
Daan Huizing	67	68	69	71	275	10,000
Jens Fahrbring	68	73	68	67	276	6,667
Jaakko Makitalo	68	68	72	68	276	6,667
Victor Riu	69	67	72	68	276	6,667

	SCORES				TOTAL	MONEY
Emilio Cuartero Blanco	66	72	72	67	277	4,400
Jose-Filipe Lima	64	69	72	72	277	4,400
Andrew Marshall	69	71	68	69	277	4,400
Ricardo Gouveia	70	68	68	72	278	3,800
Cyril Bouniol	68	67	75	69	279	3,400
Mads Sogaard	70	71	67	71	279	3,400
Jeff Winther	69	71	69	70	279	3,400
Jacob Glennemo	72	70	70	68	280	2,800
Max Orrin	71	68	71	70	280	2,800
Damian Ulrich	67	69	71	73	280	2,800
Louis de Jager	69	67	75	70	281	2,077
Joachim B. Hansen	70	72	67	72	281	2,077
Sebastian Heisele	66	74	69	72	281	2,077
Ross Kellett	69	69	68	75	281	2,077
Stuart Manley	70	69	70	72	281	2,077
Ruaidhri McGee	69	69	74	69	281	2,077
Andreas Harto	68	70	71	73	282	1,800
David Law	70	68	71	73	282	1,800
Nicolo Ravano	71	70	71	70	282	1,800

Challenge de Madrid

El Encin Golf Hotel, Alcala de Henares, Madrid, Spain
Par 36-36–72; 7,539 yards

April 22-25
purse, €160,000

	SCORES				TOTAL	MONEY
Nacho Elvira	66	68	66	67	267	€25,600
Ricardo Gouveia	66	68	68	69	271	14,400
Ruaidhri McGee	65	67	68	71	271	14,400
Chris Hanson	68	70	69	65	272	9,600
Stuart Manley	70	68	69	66	273	7,200
Sam Walker	70	68	70	65	273	7,200
Paul Maddy	68	71	67	69	275	4,800
Pedro Oriol	69	69	67	70	275	4,800
Alfredo Garcia-Heredia	64	73	68	71	276	3,400
Ross Kellett	67	70	71	68	276	3,400
Sebastian Soderberg	67	66	70	73	276	3,400
Borja Virto Astudillo	71	65	71	69	276	3,400
Ben Evans	73	67	68	69	277	2,400
Nicolo Ravano	66	75	69	67	277	2,400
Adrien Saddier	70	69	71	67	277	2,400
Elliot Saltman	70	66	72	69	277	2,400
Brandon Stone	69	67	70	71	277	2,400
Alessandro Tadini	70	68	66	73	277	2,400
Justin Walters	72	70	66	69	277	2,400
Sebastien Gros	65	70	69	74	278	1,566
Jose Manuel Lara	68	73	68	69	278	1,566
Pablo Martin Benavides	69	71	69	69	278	1,566
Andrew McArthur	67	72	68	71	278	1,566
Jamie McLeary	70	71	70	67	278	1,566
Victor Riu	71	70	67	70	278	1,566
Manuel Trappel	68	69	72	69	278	1,566

Turkish Airlines Challenge

Gloria Golf Club, Belek, Antalya, Turkey
Par 37-35–72; 7,141 yards

May 7-10
purse, €175,000

	SCORES				TOTAL	MONEY
Rhys Davies	69	70	65	70	274	€28,000
Lorenzo Gagli	72	69	69	68	278	19,250
Bjorn Akesson	70	66	72	71	279	8,820
Phillip Archer	70	69	71	69	279	8,820
William Harrold	71	66	70	72	279	8,820
Sihwan Kim	76	63	69	71	279	8,820
Callum Shinkwin	71	68	70	70	279	8,820
Adrien Bernadet	70	70	70	70	280	3,588
Jens Dantorp	72	66	70	72	280	3,588
Edouard Dubois	66	67	73	74	280	3,588
Sean Einhaus	72	72	66	70	280	3,588
Ricardo Gouveia	70	73	68	69	280	3,588
Andreas Harto	74	69	67	70	280	3,588
Ruaidhri McGee	73	71	65	71	280	3,588
Garrick Porteous	70	70	71	69	280	3,588
Joel Girrbach	74	67	72	68	281	2,625
Charlie Ford	73	67	76	66	282	2,118
Jacob Glennemo	69	71	68	74	282	2,118
Julien Guerrier	68	71	68	75	282	2,118
Joachim B. Hansen	71	69	73	69	282	2,118
Daniel Im	73	71	66	72	282	2,118
Emilio Cuartero Blanco	72	71	70	70	283	1,610
Rhys Enoch	71	69	74	69	283	1,610
Nico Geyger	71	72	72	68	283	1,610
Jose-Filipe Lima	74	70	68	71	283	1,610
Jocke Rask	71	69	72	71	283	1,610
Pierre Relecom	71	73	71	68	283	1,610
Joel Stalter	71	72	70	70	283	1,610

Made in Denmark Challenge

Royal Golf Club, Copenhagen, Denmark
Par 35-36–71; 7,187 yards

May 14-17
purse, €170,000

	SCORES				TOTAL	MONEY
Max Orrin	74	68	72	71	285	€27,200
Andrew McArthur	70	70	72	74	286	18,700
Edouard Dubois	70	72	70	75	287	11,900
Jack Senior	68	70	74	77	289	9,350
Peter Whiteford	73	70	71	75	289	9,350
Chris Hanson	76	70	74	70	290	5,667
Andreas Harto	76	72	70	72	290	5,667
Ruaidhri McGee	67	72	76	75	290	5,667
Adrien Bernadet	76	68	67	80	291	3,740
Ben Parker	72	74	70	75	291	3,740
James Robinson	72	72	71	76	291	3,740
Maarten Lafeber	71	74	73	74	292	3,145
Mads Sogaard	71	71	71	79	292	3,145
Nino Bertasio	69	73	69	82	293	2,380
Jens Dantorp	77	71	73	72	293	2,380
Sebastien Gros	73	70	71	79	293	2,380
John Hahn	72	73	73	75	293	2,380
Paul Howard	73	75	74	71	293	2,380
Jeppe Pape Huldahl	71	71	72	79	293	2,380

	SCORES				TOTAL	MONEY
Niclas Johansson	70	73	73	77	293	2,380
Charlie Ford	75	70	73	76	294	1,670
Christian Gloet	76	72	72	74	294	1,670
Jose-Filipe Lima	69	74	75	76	294	1,670
Bernd Ritthammer	74	75	70	75	294	1,670
Alexander Bjork	73	72	76	74	295	1,547
Ryan Evans	72	74	75	74	295	1,547

Karnten Golf Open

Golfclub Schloss Finkenstein, Godersdorf, Austria
Par 36-35–71; 6,932 yards

May 21-24
purse, €180,000

	SCORES				TOTAL	MONEY
Nacho Elvira	64	67	67	65	263	€28,800
Jens Dantorp	63	65	72	64	264	19,800
Ryan Evans	66	71	66	62	265	11,700
Sebastien Gros	65	71	64	65	265	11,700
Alexander Bjork	66	65	67	68	266	9,000
Ricardo Gouveia	67	68	66	66	267	6,000
Paul Maddy	68	65	66	68	267	6,000
Borja Virto Astudillo	67	65	69	66	267	6,000
Daan Huizing	67	68	65	68	268	4,140
Hugues Joannes	68	68	67	65	268	4,140
Daniel Im	62	72	68	67	269	3,240
Garrick Porteous	66	67	71	65	269	3,240
Nicolo Ravano	66	71	67	65	269	3,240
Maximilian Rohrig	69	67	66	67	269	3,240
Damian Ulrich	66	69	66	68	269	3,240
Scott Arnold	67	65	71	67	270	2,265
Ruaidhri McGee	68	70	70	62	270	2,265
Andrea Rota	65	73	66	66	270	2,265
Benjamin Rusch	65	69	69	67	270	2,265
Simon Thornton	68	70	68	64	270	2,265
Manuel Trappel	70	66	67	67	270	2,265
Gary Boyd	67	67	67	70	271	1,656
Matteo Delpodio	69	69	69	64	271	1,656
Sebastian Heisele	68	68	66	69	271	1,656
Gareth Shaw	67	69	68	67	271	1,656
Joel Stalter	66	66	73	66	271	1,656
Steven Tiley	69	68	68	66	271	1,656
George Woolgar	71	67	66	67	271	1,656

D+D Real Czech Challenge

Golf & Spa Kuneticka Hora, Dritec, Czech Republic
Par 36-36–72; 7,337 yards

May 28-31
purse, €170,000

	SCORES				TOTAL	MONEY
Jens Fahrbring	66	70	67	68	271	€27,200
Ross McGowan	65	70	71	66	272	18,700
Andrew McArthur	68	69	69	67	273	11,900
Nico Geyger	68	66	67	74	275	8,500
Sebastien Gros	69	68	68	70	275	8,500
John Hahn	71	66	68	70	275	8,500
Jaakko Makitalo	69	66	72	69	276	5,100
Joel Sjoholm	69	69	70	68	276	5,100

	SCORES			TOTAL	MONEY
Carlos Del Moral	68	68	72	69	277	3,612
Ricardo Gouveia	69	69	69	70	277	3,612
Jamie McLeary	65	74	68	70	277	3,612
Garrick Porteous	67	69	72	69	277	3,612
Nino Bertasio	68	69	76	65	278	2,805
Steven Brown	65	69	72	72	278	2,805
Scott Fallon	70	69	70	69	278	2,805
James Robinson	66	69	74	69	278	2,805
Jacob Glennemo	67	69	72	71	279	2,057
Terry Pilkadaris	68	69	72	70	279	2,057
Chris Selfridge	70	67	70	72	279	2,057
Alessandro Tadini	69	70	70	70	279	2,057
Alvaro Velasco	68	67	71	73	279	2,057
Sebastian Heisele	70	71	67	72	280	1,649
Daniel Im	71	68	70	71	280	1,649
Scott Arnold	69	69	74	69	281	1,513
Matteo Delpodio	70	70	71	70	281	1,513
Edouard Dubois	70	68	74	69	281	1,513
Nacho Elvira	74	65	73	69	281	1,513
Pierre Relecom	68	72	72	69	281	1,513
Pontus Widegren	70	69	73	69	281	1,513

Swiss Challenge

Golf Sempachersee, Lucerne, Switzerland
Par 36-35–71; 7,147 yards

June 4-7
purse, €170,000

	SCORES			TOTAL	MONEY
Daniel Im	74	66	68	65	273	€27,200
Gary Boyd	66	70	69	68	273	18,700
(Im defeated Boyd on first playoff hole.)						
Dominic Foos	70	71	67	66	274	11,900
Sebastian Garcia Rodriguez	72	69	70	64	275	7,735
James Heath	69	70	67	69	275	7,735
Oscar Stark	67	70	70	68	275	7,735
Steven Tiley	69	68	70	68	275	7,735
Antti Ahokas	67	71	69	69	276	4,420
Rhys Enoch	71	67	68	70	276	4,420
Oliver Bekker	67	66	70	74	277	3,457
Dylan Frittelli	74	67	67	69	277	3,457
Ricardo Gouveia	68	70	70	69	277	3,457
Jack Doherty	67	67	72	72	278	2,720
Nico Geyger	71	68	70	69	278	2,720
Jack Harrison	71	71	69	67	278	2,720
David Palm	68	71	68	71	278	2,720
Chris Selfridge	71	70	65	72	278	2,720
Alessio Bruschi	69	69	72	69	279	1,867
Joachim B. Hansen	72	67	67	73	279	1,867
Stiggy Hodgson	69	71	71	68	279	1,867
Haydn Porteous	67	69	71	72	279	1,867
Niccolo Quintarelli	68	73	71	67	279	1,867
Toby Tree	71	67	75	66	279	1,867
Scott Arnold	71	68	72	69	280	1,496
Geoffrey Drakeford	70	72	69	69	280	1,496
Joel Girrbach	69	69	73	69	280	1,496
Sebastian Heisele	72	71	70	67	280	1,496
Jamie McLeary	71	72	69	68	280	1,496
Taco Remkes	72	69	68	71	280	1,496
Benjamin Rusch	75	68	69	68	280	1,496

KPMG Trophy

Golf de Pierpont, Les Bons Villers, Belgium
Par 36-36–72; 6,848 yards

June 11-14
purse, €160,000

	SCORES				TOTAL	MONEY
Jamie McLeary	71	67	70	67	275	€25,600
Taco Remkes	67	67	75	67	276	17,600
Stiggy Hodgson	72	69	70	67	278	10,400
Ruaidhri McGee	69	70	71	68	278	10,400
Gary Boyd	67	69	75	68	279	6,507
Garrick Porteous	72	68	71	68	279	6,507
Gareth Shaw	68	73	68	70	279	6,507
Francois Calmels	75	68	71	66	280	3,760
Birgir Hafthorsson	71	74	69	66	280	3,760
Zane Scotland	71	69	71	69	280	3,760
Toby Tree	72	72	67	69	280	3,760
Oliver Bekker	70	71	69	71	281	2,480
Jacob Glennemo	67	78	73	63	281	2,480
Tim Gornik	72	67	72	70	281	2,480
James Heath	71	66	76	68	281	2,480
Billy Hemstock	72	68	73	68	281	2,480
Steven Jeppesen	71	74	69	67	281	2,480
Jordan L. Smith	72	69	72	68	281	2,480
Ben Stow	74	69	71	67	281	2,480
Wil Besseling	71	74	70	67	282	1,610
Rhys Davies	73	70	69	70	282	1,610
Dylan Frittelli	71	69	72	70	282	1,610
Andreas Harto	74	67	71	70	282	1,610
Charles-Edouard Russo	71	64	73	74	282	1,610
Lee Corfield	69	69	73	72	283	1,392
Sebastian Garcia Rodriguez	71	68	70	74	283	1,392
Sebastian Heisele	69	69	73	72	283	1,392
Maarten Lafeber	71	67	73	72	283	1,392
Thomas Linard	74	70	71	68	283	1,392
Peter Whiteford	68	72	75	68	283	1,392

Najeti Open

Aa St. Omer Golf Club, Lumbres, France
Par 36-35–71; 6,537 yards

June 18-21
purse, €200,000

	SCORES				TOTAL	MONEY
Sebastien Gros	68	66	67	69	270	€32,000
Thomas Linard	69	69	72	66	276	22,000
Roope Kakko	67	71	71	68	277	14,000
Terry Pilkadaris	66	72	70	71	279	12,000
Ryan Fox	67	73	68	72	280	9,000
Justin Walters	71	70	68	71	280	9,000
Oliver Bekker	71	73	67	70	281	6,400
Merrick Bremner	72	70	69	71	282	4,933
Joachim B. Hansen	70	71	72	69	282	4,933
Brandon Stone	71	70	69	72	282	4,933
Ricardo Santos	73	69	70	71	283	4,000
Francois Calmels	74	67	72	71	284	3,300
Robert Coles	71	74	70	69	284	3,300
Daniel Gaunt	73	69	71	71	284	3,300
Stiggy Hodgson	69	67	73	75	284	3,300
Hugues Joannes	66	73	71	74	284	3,300
Prom Meesawat	70	72	72	70	284	3,300

	SCORES				TOTAL	MONEY
Javier Ballesteros	74	68	69	74	285	2,197
Sean Einhaus	71	71	71	72	285	2,197
Julien Guerrier	74	71	70	70	285	2,197
James Heath	76	68	70	71	285	2,197
George Murray	72	72	71	70	285	2,197
Sam Walker	71	72	73	69	285	2,197
Carlos Aguilar	72	71	68	75	286	1,760
Fredrik Andersson Hed	68	73	74	71	286	1,760
Jens Dantorp	71	68	74	73	286	1,760
Jack Doherty	69	74	69	74	286	1,760
Lorenzo Gagli	73	70	70	73	286	1,760
Stuart Manley	72	72	67	75	286	1,760
Duncan Stewart	73	72	70	71	286	1,760

SSE Scottish Hydro Challenge

Macdonald Spey Valley Golf Club, Aviemore, Scotland
Par 35-36–71; 7,108 yards

June 25-28
purse, €250,000

	SCORES				TOTAL	MONEY
Jack Senior	66	69	66	67	268	€40,000
Robert Coles	66	66	66	70	268	22,500
Prom Meesawat	65	69	66	68	268	22,500
(Senior defeated Coles and Meesawat on fourth playoff hole.)						
Gary Boyd	64	64	70	72	270	15,000
Joachim B. Hansen	68	68	69	66	271	12,500
James Heath	68	70	68	67	273	7,750
Maarten Lafeber	65	71	68	69	273	7,750
Ross McGowan	66	71	67	69	273	7,750
Max Orrin	68	65	72	68	273	7,750
Ryan Fox	68	69	70	68	275	5,083
Simon Griffiths	72	67	67	69	275	5,083
Chris Selfridge	69	65	71	70	275	5,083
Ryan Evans	68	68	68	72	276	4,125
Steven Jeppesen	68	70	67	71	276	4,125
Ross Kellett	68	67	70	71	276	4,125
Joel Stalter	67	67	72	70	276	4,125
Jose-Filipe Lima	65	73	68	71	277	3,250
Haydn Porteous	67	71	67	72	277	3,250
Taco Remkes	69	67	68	73	277	3,250
Phillip Archer	72	67	70	69	278	2,688
Ricardo Gouveia	70	70	70	68	278	2,688
Oliver Bekker	70	69	68	72	279	2,275
Dean Burmester	66	70	70	73	279	2,275
Charlie Ford	70	66	73	70	279	2,275
Sebastian Heisele	68	69	70	72	279	2,275
Andrew McArthur	70	67	68	74	279	2,275
Terry Pilkadaris	68	71	73	67	279	2,275
Elliot Saltman	66	74	69	70	279	2,275
Mads Sogaard	72	68	68	71	279	2,275

Aegean Airlines Challenge

Hartl Resort, Bad Griesbach, Germany
Par 35-36–71; 7,188 yards

July 2-5
purse, €170,000

	SCORES				TOTAL	MONEY
Ricardo Gouveia	63	70	69	67	269	€27,200
Dean Burmester	67	63	70	73	273	18,700
Sebastien Gros	70	68	63	73	274	11,050
Jeff Winther	71	66	68	69	274	11,050
Christian Gloet	69	71	72	63	275	6,375
Steven Jeppesen	72	67	69	67	275	6,375
Marcel Schneider	65	73	68	69	275	6,375
Matthew Southgate	69	65	73	68	275	6,375
Carlos Aguilar	71	67	67	71	276	3,740
Bjorn Akesson	66	68	72	70	276	3,740
Florian Praegant	71	69	69	67	276	3,740
Alexander Bjork	70	66	70	71	277	2,890
Jens Fahrbring	69	69	70	69	277	2,890
Mathieu Fenasse	70	67	69	71	277	2,890
Pablo Herreria	72	69	70	66	277	2,890
David Palm	72	70	69	66	277	2,890
Hugues Joannes	67	67	67	77	278	2,295
Justin Walters	68	72	68	70	278	2,295
Robert Coles	69	69	71	70	279	1,799
Daniel Im	70	71	68	70	279	1,799
Haydn Porteous	72	69	66	72	279	1,799
Jocke Rask	69	67	72	71	279	1,799
Pierre Relecom	71	70	66	72	279	1,799
Scott Arnold	71	71	67	71	280	1,547
Tim Gornik	73	64	70	73	280	1,547
Max Orrin	72	70	68	70	280	1,547
Chris Selfridge	71	70	72	67	280	1,547

D+D Real Slovakia Challenge

Penati Golf Resort, Senica, Slovakia
Par 36-36–72; 7,115 yards

July 9-12
purse, €165,000

	SCORES				TOTAL	MONEY
Borja Virto Astudillo	69	67	69	66	271	€26,400
Ricardo Gouveia	69	66	69	68	272	18,150
Jeff Winther	66	71	66	70	273	11,550
Jack Doherty	65	71	68	71	275	8,250
Scott Henry	73	70	66	66	275	8,250
Jamie McLeary	68	70	68	69	275	8,250
Simon Wakefield	68	74	68	66	276	5,280
Alexander Bjork	70	68	70	69	277	4,620
Luis Claverie	71	65	72	70	278	3,399
Joachim B. Hansen	70	70	69	69	278	3,399
Niall Kearney	68	71	69	70	278	3,399
James Robinson	73	68	69	68	278	3,399
Tim Sluiter	69	69	73	67	278	3,399
Connor Arendell	74	68	71	66	279	2,640
Daan Huizing	71	70	68	70	279	2,640
Michael McGeady	70	68	72	69	279	2,640
Jacob Glennemo	74	70	71	65	280	2,228
Nathan Kimsey	75	69	69	67	280	2,228
James Heath	70	71	70	70	281	1,898
Jose-Filipe Lima	69	71	73	68	281	1,898

	SCORES				TOTAL	MONEY
Rhys Davies	71	73	73	65	282	1,563
Jens Fahrbring	70	74	71	67	282	1,563
Joel Girrbach	68	74	71	69	282	1,563
Steven Jeppesen	70	65	73	74	282	1,563
George Murray	71	71	73	67	282	1,563
Duncan Stewart	69	72	72	69	282	1,563
Steven Tiley	70	71	67	74	282	1,563

Fred Olsen Challenge de Espana

Tecina Golf, La Gomera, Canary Islands, Spain
Par 36-35–71; 6,937 yards

July 16-19
purse, €160,000

	SCORES				TOTAL	MONEY
Rhys Davies	60	67	67	68	262	€25,600
Geoffrey Drakeford	67	71	62	64	264	17,600
Charles-Edouard Russo	68	64	66	68	266	10,400
Juan Sarasti	69	65	69	63	266	10,400
Alexander Bjork	69	66	67	67	269	5,568
Dave Coupland	67	67	69	66	269	5,568
Birgir Hafthorsson	68	66	68	67	269	5,568
Brinson Paolini	65	70	64	70	269	5,568
Jeff Winther	70	68	70	61	269	5,568
Ben Parker	71	67	67	65	270	3,520
Ryan Evans	67	70	69	65	271	2,880
Antonio Hortal	64	69	67	71	271	2,880
Bradley Neil	66	68	72	65	271	2,880
James Ross	71	67	65	68	271	2,880
Borja Virto Astudillo	70	66	66	69	271	2,880
Scott Henry	66	67	69	70	272	2,080
Stuart Manley	68	70	64	70	272	2,080
Ross McGowan	66	68	69	69	272	2,080
Chris Selfridge	72	66	71	63	272	2,080
Joshua White	70	65	70	67	272	2,080
Clement Berardo	69	68	66	70	273	1,552
Alfredo Garcia-Heredia	66	69	68	70	273	1,552
Garry Houston	72	65	68	68	273	1,552
Jack Senior	66	65	74	68	273	1,552
Toby Tree	67	69	70	67	273	1,552

Le Vaudreuil Golf Challenge

Golf PGA France du Vaudreuil, Le Vaudreuil, France
Par 35-36–71; 6,764 yards

July 23-26
purse, €200,000

	SCORES				TOTAL	MONEY
Ryan Fox	62	67	68	73	270	€32,000
Thomas Linard	67	64	69	71	271	22,000
Connor Arendell	65	65	72	73	275	13,000
Steven Jeppesen	71	63	68	73	275	13,000
Mathieu Decottignies-Lafon	71	70	70	65	276	6,960
Stiggy Hodgson	70	71	69	66	276	6,960
Haydn Porteous	68	65	70	73	276	6,960
Duncan Stewart	68	70	69	69	276	6,960
Pontus Widegren	69	66	69	72	276	6,960
Hugues Joannes	67	70	76	64	277	4,200
Damien Perrier	70	69	67	71	277	4,200

	SCORES				TOTAL	MONEY
Jens Fahrbring	67	67	72	72	278	3,700
Sam Walker	72	69	72	65	278	3,700
Ben Evans	69	69	74	67	279	3,200
Jose-Filipe Lima	69	69	72	69	279	3,200
Jamie McLeary	67	67	76	69	279	3,200
Merrick Bremner	70	69	73	68	280	2,283
Jack Doherty	70	71	73	66	280	2,283
Ryan Evans	67	68	72	73	280	2,283
Brinson Paolini	72	68	73	67	280	2,283
Anthony Snobeck	70	69	71	70	280	2,283
Peter Whiteford	69	69	70	72	280	2,283
Daniel Woltman	71	70	72	67	280	2,283
Robert Coles	63	71	73	74	281	1,720
Christian Gloet	67	70	73	71	281	1,720
Joachim B. Hansen	71	69	71	70	281	1,720
James Heath	69	67	77	68	281	1,720
Daan Huizing	68	68	73	72	281	1,720
Roope Kakko	71	67	72	71	281	1,720
Alexander Knappe	67	67	71	76	281	1,720
Andrea Pavan	67	73	73	68	281	1,720
Borja Virto Astudillo	69	69	72	71	281	1,720

Madeira Islands Open

See European Tour section.

Northern Ireland Open

Galgorm Castle, Ballymena, Northern Ireland
Par 35-36–71; 6,933 yards

August 6-9
purse, €170,000

	SCORES				TOTAL	MONEY
Clement Sordet	67	66	68	66	267	€27,200
John Hahn	65	66	71	66	268	18,700
Ricardo Gouveia	70	67	66	66	269	11,050
Daan Huizing	65	68	70	66	269	11,050
Jamie McLeary	67	65	69	69	270	6,913
Haydn Porteous	65	69	69	67	270	6,913
Peter Whiteford	68	69	65	68	270	6,913
Dave Coupland	69	69	66	67	271	3,995
Emilio Cuartero Blanco	65	65	69	72	271	3,995
David Law	67	67	69	68	271	3,995
Simon Wakefield	66	69	68	68	271	3,995
Niall Turner	65	66	68	73	272	3,230
Jose Manuel Lara	70	66	70	67	273	2,975
George Murray	70	67	70	66	273	2,975
Marcus Armitage	72	65	66	71	274	2,720
Sebastien Gros	66	66	71	72	275	1,970
Daniel Im	68	67	71	69	275	1,970
Stuart Manley	66	70	70	69	275	1,970
Andrew McArthur	68	67	69	71	275	1,970
Terry Pilkadaris	69	65	71	70	275	1,970
Chris Selfridge	68	66	71	70	275	1,970
Simon Thornton	66	69	71	69	275	1,970
Borja Virto Astudillo	73	64	69	69	275	1,970
Jeff Winther	67	68	67	73	275	1,970
Ryan Evans	66	70	72	68	276	1,462
Christian Gloet	73	65	67	71	276	1,462
Hugues Joannes	69	68	71	68	276	1,462

	SCORES				TOTAL	MONEY
Ross Kellett	66	69	72	69	276	1,462
Peter Lawrie	68	70	71	67	276	1,462
Thomas Linard	68	70	69	69	276	1,462
Victor Riu	67	69	70	70	276	1,462

GANT Open

Aura Golf Club, Turku, Finland
Par 36-35–71; 6,396 yards

August 13-16
purse, €170,000

	SCORES				TOTAL	MONEY
Dominic Foos	65	69	69	67	270	€27,200
Jose Manuel Lara	73	69	67	64	273	12,325
Jamie McLeary	67	68	70	68	273	12,325
Marcel Schneider	68	67	72	66	273	12,325
Brandon Stone	67	68	71	67	273	12,325
Jesper Billing	70	67	70	67	274	5,667
Alexander Knappe	69	70	71	64	274	5,667
David Law	70	67	67	70	274	5,667
Mikael Salminen	71	69	70	65	275	4,080
Alexander Bjork	71	68	71	66	276	3,570
Francois Calmels	68	67	73	68	276	3,570
Scott Arnold	71	67	72	67	277	2,890
Oliver Bekker	73	68	69	67	277	2,890
Nicolai Kristensen	70	69	70	68	277	2,890
Ross McGowan	69	68	69	71	277	2,890
Terry Pilkadaris	70	67	71	69	277	2,890
Bjorn Akesson	67	70	71	70	278	1,992
Dave Coupland	68	71	67	72	278	1,992
Steven Jeppesen	71	71	70	66	278	1,992
Niklas Lemke	67	73	71	67	278	1,992
Thomas Linard	73	69	70	66	278	1,992
Steven Tiley	67	71	70	70	278	1,992
Nino Bertasio	70	72	69	68	279	1,547
Joachim B. Hansen	70	69	71	69	279	1,547
Niclas Hellberg	73	67	71	68	279	1,547
Sihwan Kim	71	70	70	68	279	1,547
*Kristian Kulokorpi	67	69	73	70	279	
James Robinson	69	68	74	68	279	1,547
Daniel Vancsik	70	68	71	70	279	1,547

Rolex Trophy

Golf Club de Geneve, Geneva, Switzerland
Par 36-36–72; 6,727 yards

August 19-22
purse, €230,000

	SCORES				TOTAL	MONEY
Nacho Elvira	63	65	69	67	264	€30,000
Ricardo Gouveia	68	65	67	66	266	22,000
Ryan Fox	62	70	67	70	269	15,000
Gary Boyd	70	70	64	67	271	11,000
Ryan Evans	66	67	67	71	271	11,000
Jens Dantorp	65	68	70	70	273	8,500
Haydn Porteous	66	67	69	71	273	8,500
Steven Jeppesen	69	69	66	70	274	7,000
Ruaidhri McGee	65	68	72	70	275	6,250
Brandon Stone	69	67	72	67	275	6,250

	SCORES				TOTAL	MONEY
Sam Walker	67	69	72	68	276	5,500
Bjorn Akesson	71	66	71	70	278	4,750
Jens Fahrbring	71	67	73	67	278	4,750
Joachim B. Hansen	72	69	69	68	278	4,750
Jeff Winther	72	66	68	72	278	4,750
Robert Coles	72	67	72	68	279	3,700
Daan Huizing	75	66	68	70	279	3,700
Thomas Linard	64	74	69	72	279	3,700
Andrew McArthur	71	71	69	68	279	3,700
Borja Virto Astudillo	69	74	71	65	279	3,700
Dominic Foos	65	71	74	70	280	3,200
John Hahn	69	67	71	74	281	3,100
Alexander Bjork	68	72	71	71	282	2,980
Scott Henry	69	68	68	77	282	2,980
Rhys Davies	70	69	71	73	283	2,880
Sebastien Gros	68	72	73	70	283	2,880

Cordon Golf Open

Golf Blue Green de Pleneuf Val Andre, Pleneuf, France
Par 35-35–70; 6,447 yards

September 3-6
purse, €200,000

	SCORES				TOTAL	MONEY
Scott Arnold	71	65	67	68	271	€32,000
Daan Huizing	68	68	66	71	273	18,000
James Robinson	69	69	69	66	273	18,000
Clement Berardo	73	67	65	69	274	8,400
John Hahn	71	70	64	69	274	8,400
Gareth Shaw	70	69	68	67	274	8,400
Borja Virto Astudillo	67	68	70	69	274	8,400
Sam Walker	67	73	68	66	274	8,400
Jack Doherty	66	70	72	67	275	4,120
Hugues Joannes	68	70	69	68	275	4,120
David Law	64	69	70	72	275	4,120
Chris Selfridge	69	67	67	72	275	4,120
Peter Whiteford	68	71	67	69	275	4,120
Fredrik Andersson Hed	70	68	71	67	276	3,000
Jens Dantorp	67	73	67	69	276	3,000
Rhys Enoch	70	69	66	71	276	3,000
Joel Sjoholm	74	67	64	71	276	3,000
Niall Turner	68	69	73	66	276	3,000
Ryan Fox	72	68	64	73	277	2,233
Stiggy Hodgson	71	71	66	69	277	2,233
Taco Remkes	68	69	70	70	277	2,233
Nino Bertasio	70	71	66	71	278	1,920
Jens Fahrbring	70	67	69	72	278	1,920
Sebastian Heisele	71	70	70	67	278	1,920
Duncan Stewart	71	70	69	69	279	1,820
Jeff Winther	70	71	68	70	279	1,820

Kazakhstan Open

Nurtau Golf Club, Almaty, Kazakhstan
Par 36-36–72; 7,336 yards

September 10-13
purse, €450,000

	SCORES				TOTAL	MONEY
Sebastien Gros	68	67	70	69	274	€72,000
Mads Sogaard	64	72	69	70	275	49,500
Jens Fahrbring	68	69	73	67	277	24,750
Daniel Im	72	69	70	66	277	24,750
George Murray	72	69	67	69	277	24,750
Callum Shinkwin	69	69	70	69	277	24,750
Bjorn Akesson	74	69	66	69	278	14,400
Emilio Cuartero Blanco	71	71	71	66	279	10,170
Rhys Davies	70	69	70	70	279	10,170
Sihwan Kim	64	69	72	74	279	10,170
Thomas Linard	73	69	68	69	279	10,170
Joel Sjoholm	75	68	68	68	279	10,170
Shaun Norris	68	67	76	69	280	7,875
Clement Sordet	69	71	66	74	280	7,875
Lorenzo Gagli	72	72	69	68	281	6,975
Jeff Winther	66	72	72	71	281	6,975
Sebastian Heisele	74	70	70	68	282	5,625
Jaakko Makitalo	69	71	70	72	282	5,625
Jamie McLeary	68	69	73	72	282	5,625
James Robinson	71	68	74	69	282	5,625
Scott Fallon	72	70	71	70	283	4,262
Jacob Glennemo	74	70	69	70	283	4,262
Ricardo Gouveia	74	67	73	69	283	4,262
Julien Guerrier	69	71	71	72	283	4,262
Joachim B. Hansen	63	73	73	74	283	4,262
Adrien Saddier	71	69	72	71	283	4,262
Marcel Schneider	75	67	72	69	283	4,262

EMC Challenge Open

Olgiata Golf Club, Rome, Italy
Par 35-36–71; 7,566 yards

October 1-4
purse, €180,000

	SCORES				TOTAL	MONEY
Matteo Delpodio	69	68	71	71	279	€28,800
Gary Boyd	72	73	69	68	282	19,800
Edouard Dubois	72	71	70	71	284	10,800
Thomas Linard	72	73	71	68	284	10,800
Sebastian Soderberg	72	69	71	72	284	10,800
Filippo Bergamaschi	73	71	72	69	285	5,580
Ricardo Gouveia	72	69	71	73	285	5,580
Simon Griffiths	71	71	72	71	285	5,580
Borja Virto Astudillo	70	70	69	76	285	5,580
Michael Jonzon	73	71	72	70	286	3,780
Max Orrin	74	72	71	69	286	3,780
Steven Brown	72	73	74	68	287	3,330
Chris Hanson	75	70	72	70	287	3,330
Alexander Bjork	71	72	75	70	288	2,790
Andrew McArthur	73	69	75	71	288	2,790
Tim Sluiter	74	73	68	73	288	2,790
Simon Wakefield	71	71	75	71	288	2,790
Jens Dantorp	73	71	71	74	289	2,092
Stuart Manley	73	68	75	73	289	2,092
Joel Sjoholm	75	73	74	67	289	2,092

	SCORES				TOTAL	MONEY
Toby Tree	75	70	72	72	289	2,092
Antti Ahokas	70	76	74	70	290	1,656
Jaakko Makitalo	76	72	73	69	290	1,656
Stefano Pitoni	74	73	73	70	290	1,656
Florian Praegant	76	70	76	68	290	1,656
Jocke Rask	72	71	72	75	290	1,656
Victor Riu	76	70	72	72	290	1,656
Sam Walker	75	70	74	71	290	1,656

Volopa Irish Challenge

Mount Wolseley Hotel Spa & Golf Resort, Carlow, Ireland
Par 36-36—72; 7,084 yards

October 8-11
purse, €180,000

	SCORES				TOTAL	MONEY
Tom Murray	69	67	69	67	272	€28,800
Nino Bertasio	68	66	68	70	272	19,800
(Murray defeated Bertasio on second playoff hole.)						
Gary Boyd	71	69	66	68	274	12,600
Robert Coles	65	69	69	72	275	9,900
Garrick Porteous	70	69	69	67	275	9,900
Ryan Evans	68	72	68	68	276	6,480
Max Orrin	70	70	70	66	276	6,480
Simon Griffiths	70	71	71	65	277	4,440
Steven Tiley	69	70	70	68	277	4,440
Simon Wakefield	69	69	70	69	277	4,440
John Hahn	71	69	68	71	279	3,330
Stuart Manley	67	76	67	69	279	3,330
Joel Stalter	70	69	72	68	279	3,330
Sam Walker	69	71	74	65	279	3,330
Jens Dantorp	69	71	70	70	280	2,700
Haydn Porteous	70	73	68	69	280	2,700
Sebastian Soderberg	72	69	69	70	280	2,700
Scott Fallon	75	67	69	70	281	2,092
Joachim B. Hansen	70	69	73	69	281	2,092
Daniel Im	67	70	72	72	281	2,092
*Romain Langasque	67	73	71	70	281	
Marcel Schneider	68	72	70	71	281	2,092
Antti Ahokas	70	69	72	71	282	1,656
Phillip Archer	69	69	71	73	282	1,656
Daan Huizing	72	66	73	71	282	1,656
Steven Jeppesen	72	70	72	68	282	1,656
Thomas Linard	68	73	72	69	282	1,656
Duncan Stewart	69	74	68	71	282	1,656
Brandon Stone	72	66	67	77	282	1,656

Foshan Open

Foshan Golf Club, Shishan, Nanhai, China
Par 36-36—72; 7,148 yards

October 22-25
purse, US$500,000

	SCORES				TOTAL	MONEY
Borja Virto Astudillo	64	67	72	70	273	€69,588
Bjorn Akesson	67	71	68	69	275	47,842
Ricardo Gouveia	70	66	72	68	276	26,096
John Hahn	71	69	68	68	276	26,096
Joachim B. Hansen	70	65	71	70	276	26,096

	SCORES				TOTAL	MONEY
Jun-Seok Lee	69	72	67	69	277	17,397
Jeff Winther	72	67	71	68	278	13,918
Hugues Joannes	72	71	67	69	279	10,221
Tom Murray	71	69	71	68	279	10,221
Callum Shinkwin	71	71	70	67	279	10,221
Sam Walker	71	70	70	68	279	10,221
Matteo Delpodio	69	72	69	70	280	7,394
Chris Hanson	69	69	71	71	280	7,394
Max Orrin	67	75	67	71	280	7,394
Steven Tiley	71	68	70	71	280	7,394
Martin Wiegele	70	71	69	70	280	7,394
Gunn Charoenkul	70	70	71	70	281	4,964
Sebastien Gros	72	67	69	73	281	4,964
Thomas Linard	72	67	73	69	281	4,964
Andrew McArthur	74	67	68	72	281	4,964
Haydn Porteous	65	68	73	75	281	4,964
Chris Selfridge	69	70	68	74	281	4,964
Mads Sogaard	72	69	68	72	281	4,964
Gary Boyd	72	72	65	73	282	3,914
William Harrold	70	72	72	68	282	3,914
Steven Jeppesen	72	72	69	69	282	3,914
Peter Whiteford	73	71	68	70	282	3,914
Hui-Lin Zhang	72	71	71	68	282	3,914

NBO Golf Classic Grand Final

Almouj Golf, The Wave, Muscat, Oman
Par 36-36–72; 7,310 yards

November 4-7
purse, €375,000

	SCORES				TOTAL	MONEY
Ricardo Gouveia	67	67	76	65	275	€64,000
Joachim B. Hansen	66	67	76	67	276	42,000
Nacho Elvira	70	69	70	68	277	20,333
Callum Shinkwin	69	72	68	68	277	20,333
Jeff Winther	70	68	73	66	277	20,333
Brandon Stone	71	71	68	68	278	15,000
Jens Dantorp	69	70	70	70	279	11,840
Rhys Davies	73	68	70	68	279	11,840
Scott Henry	69	71	72	67	279	11,840
Max Orrin	70	66	76	67	279	11,840
James Robinson	68	70	71	70	279	11,840
Ryan Evans	68	71	71	70	280	8,300
Thomas Linard	70	70	72	68	280	8,300
Ruaidhri McGee	73	69	70	68	280	8,300
Jens Fahrbring	73	72	69	68	282	6,375
Ross McGowan	72	68	72	70	282	6,375
Sebastien Gros	69	74	69	71	283	5,033
John Hahn	70	71	70	72	283	5,033
Borja Virto Astudillo	71	71	69	72	283	5,033
Dominic Foos	72	67	72	73	284	4,293
Daan Huizing	70	69	76	69	284	4,293
Sebastian Soderberg	74	70	72	68	284	4,293
Daniel Im	71	67	77	70	285	4,000
Alexander Bjork	73	73	71	70	287	3,815
George Murray	70	71	77	69	287	3,815

Asian Tour

Maybank Malaysian Open

Kuala Lumpur Golf & Country Club, Kuala Lumpur, Malaysia

Par 36-36–72; 6,967 yards

February 5-8

purse, US$3,000,000

	SCORES				TOTAL	MONEY
Anirban Lahiri	70	72	62	68	272	US$500,000
Bernd Wiesberger	70	66	63	74	273	333,330
Paul Waring	69	68	65	73	275	168,900
Alejandro Canizares	68	65	68	74	275	168,900
Gregory Bourdy	70	70	68	69	277	99,300
Richard T. Lee	69	69	68	71	277	99,300
Paul Peterson	72	69	64	72	277	99,300
Lee Westwood	66	67	69	75	277	99,300
Marc Warren	70	71	69	68	278	67,200
S.S.P. Chawrasia	76	67	68	68	279	60,000
Wade Ormsby	73	69	71	67	280	51,700
Nathan Holman	72	71	71	66	280	51,700
Richard Bland	68	70	73	69	280	51,700
Scott Hend	73	72	66	70	281	45,000
Jeung-Hun Wang	77	66	67	71	281	45,000
Robert Rock	70	70	74	68	282	39,675
Peter Lawrie	71	66	75	70	282	39,675
Thomas Pieters	73	73	70	66	282	39,675
Peter Uihlein	72	72	65	73	282	39,675
Thanyakon Khrongpha	74	69	70	70	283	33,960
Thongchai Jaidee	72	73	67	71	283	33,960
Pablo Larrazabal	73	69	67	74	283	33,960
Alvaro Quiros	70	70	67	76	283	33,960
Jake Higginbottom	69	71	67	76	283	33,960
Marcus Fraser	72	69	72	71	284	28,950
Juvic Pagunsan	71	69	74	70	284	28,950
Raphael Jacquelin	71	72	70	71	284	28,950
*Gavin Kyle Green	74	68	73	69	284	
Morten Orum Madsen	72	70	70	72	284	28,950
Prom Meesawat	68	72	70	74	284	28,950
Danny Chia	67	74	69	74	284	28,950
Wen-Chong Liang	74	72	67	72	285	24,450
Gregory Havret	72	72	69	72	285	24,450
Anders Hansen	68	76	69	72	285	24,450
Julien Quesne	71	72	71	71	285	24,450
Emilliano Grillo	70	73	71	72	286	21,000
Terry Pilkadaris	71	72	70	73	286	21,000
Andrew Dodt	69	73	73	71	286	21,000
Graeme McDowell	66	73	72	75	286	21,000
Johan Carlsson	74	69	68	75	286	21,000
Rashid Khan	73	73	73	67	286	21,000
Miguel Angel Jimenez	72	71	71	73	287	18,000
Carlos Pigem	73	71	69	74	287	18,000
David Lipsky	72	73	70	72	287	18,000
Sung-Hoon Kang	67	74	69	77	287	18,000
Shiv Kapur	72	71	74	71	288	16,500
Jazz Janewattananond	77	69	69	74	289	14,700
Andy Sullivan	70	70	72	77	289	14,700
Nicolas Colsaerts	70	74	67	78	289	14,700
Robert Karlsson	70	76	72	71	289	14,700
Edoardo Molinari	72	73	73	71	289	14,700

	SCORES				TOTAL	MONEY
Michael Hoey	75	70	68	77	290	11,400
Sukree Othman	73	71	70	76	290	11,400
Felipe Aguilar	70	74	70	76	290	11,400
Chawalit Plaphol	76	68	72	74	290	11,400
Chien-Yao Hung	75	70	73	72	290	11,400
Mark Foster	71	73	74	72	290	11,400
Scott Jamieson	73	72	72	74	291	9,150
Angelo Que	72	72	74	73	291	9,150
Romain Wattel	70	73	71	78	292	8,250
Stephen Gallacher	69	77	71	75	292	8,250
Antonio Lascuna	74	72	73	73	292	8,250
Oliver Fisher	73	73	73	73	292	8,250
Hennie Otto	73	69	76	75	293	7,050
Wei-Chih Lu	77	67	74	75	293	7,050
Miguel Tabuena	74	72	76	71	293	7,050
Sam Brazel	73	71	78	71	293	7,050
Richard Finch	73	73	75	73	294	6,300
Mikael Lundberg	71	74	72	78	295	5,723.33
Simon Dyson	72	73	72	78	295	5,723.33
Nicholas Fung	71	71	76	77	295	5,723.33
R. Nachimuthu	73	72	75	77	297	4,499.81
Tommy Fleetwood	67	79	73	80	299	4,494.70
Paul McGinley	69	76	77	77	299	4,494.70

True Thailand Classic

Black Mountain Golf Club, Hua Hin, Thailand
Par 36-36–72; 7,346 yards

February 12-15
purse, US$2,000,000

	SCORES				TOTAL	MONEY
Andrew Dodt	71	67	67	67	272	US$333,330
Thongchai Jaidee	69	66	67	71	273	173,710
Scott Hend	67	68	66	72	273	173,710
Richard T. Lee	68	67	73	66	274	84,933.33
Jason Knutzon	72	66	69	67	274	84,933.33
Kiradech Aphibarnrat	67	67	70	70	274	84,933.33
Carlos Pigem	65	72	72	66	275	48,700
Johan Carlsson	69	67	70	69	275	48,700
Wade Ormsby	72	65	68	70	275	48,700
Miguel Angel Jimenez	67	66	69	73	275	48,700
John Parry	71	69	70	66	276	33,500
Sam Brazel	69	69	71	67	276	33,500
Shiv Kapur	66	73	69	68	276	33,500
Alex Noren	67	70	68	71	276	33,500
Anthony Wall	72	68	70	67	277	26,533.33
Jeung-Hun Wang	68	69	71	69	277	26,533.33
Jorge Campillo	73	68	66	70	277	26,533.33
Jyoti Randhawa	71	70	65	71	277	26,533.33
Javi Colomo	74	67	65	71	277	26,533.33
Richard Green	71	67	67	72	277	26,533.33
Anirban Lahiri	69	72	70	67	278	22,300
Pariya Junhasavasdikul	67	73	70	68	278	22,300
Nathan Holman	71	67	71	69	278	22,300
Berry Henson	70	69	69	70	278	22,300
Marc Warren	69	71	72	67	279	19,300
Mikko Korhonen	73	69	70	67	279	19,300
Adrian Otaegui	69	69	71	70	279	19,300
Prayad Marksaeng	67	72	68	72	279	19,300
Thomas Bjorn	69	72	66	72	279	19,300
Tom Lewis	69	67	70	73	279	19,300

	SCORES				TOTAL	MONEY
Arjun Atwal	73	67	74	66	280	15,571.43
Prom Meesawat	73	65	73	69	280	15,571.43
Chris Lloyd	69	71	71	69	280	15,571.43
Marcus Fraser	69	71	70	70	280	15,571.43
Michael Hoey	64	72	73	71	280	15,571.43
Magnus A. Carlsson	71	71	67	71	280	15,571.43
Romain Wattel	70	68	70	72	280	15,571.43
Terry Pilkadaris	69	73	73	66	281	12,400
Johan Edfors	69	72	72	68	281	12,400
Kristoffer Broberg	70	71	72	68	281	12,400
Danny Chia	71	71	71	68	281	12,400
Emilliano Grillo	70	69	71	71	281	12,400
Thanyakon Khrongpha	68	72	69	72	281	12,400
Rikard Karlberg	72	65	70	74	281	12,400
Rafa Cabrera-Bello	72	66	69	74	281	12,400
Sung-Hoon Kang	74	68	72	68	282	10,000
Anders Hansen	71	71	69	71	282	10,000
Chawalit Plaphol	71	71	69	71	282	10,000
Mardan Mamat	70	68	70	74	282	10,000
Simon Dyson	73	69	72	69	283	7,260
Rattanon Wannasrichan	68	71	74	70	283	7,260
Piya Swangarunporn	75	67	71	70	283	7,260
Sattaya Supupramai	72	68	72	71	283	7,260
Jason Barnes	72	70	70	71	283	7,260
Felipe Aguilar	70	70	71	72	283	7,260
Maximilian Kieffer	73	68	70	72	283	7,260
Julien Quesne	70	71	70	72	283	7,260
Jbe Kruger	69	69	70	75	283	7,260
David Lipsky	65	73	69	76	283	7,260
Pavit Tangkamolprasert	71	71	73	69	284	5,100
Juvic Pagunsan	72	70	71	71	284	5,100
Paul Peterson	68	72	72	72	284	5,100
Chien-Yao Hung	65	73	72	74	284	5,100
Matthew Baldwin	69	67	73	75	284	5,100
Gregory Havret	69	68	72	75	284	5,100
Damien McGrane	74	67	74	70	285	4,200
Kalem Richardson	73	68	73	71	285	4,200
Paul Maddy	70	70	73	72	285	4,200
Komei Oda	70	71	74	71	286	3,725
Masahiro Kawamura	68	72	71	75	286	3,725
Matt Ford	67	74	72	74	287	2,998.53
Brett Rumford	69	72	70	76	287	2,998.53
Steve Lewton	70	71	76	71	288	2,993.35
Scott Jamieson	70	72	72	75	289	2,989.90
Renato Paratore	67	75	73	76	291	2,984.73
Andrea Pavan	70	72	71	78	291	2,984.73
S.S.P. Chawrasia	71	71	71	79	292	2,979.55
Arnond Vongvanij	72	69	80	74	295	2,976.10

Hero Indian Open

Delhi Golf Club, New Delhi, India
Par 36-35–71; 6,923 yards

February 19-22
purse, US$1,500,000

	SCORES				TOTAL	MONEY
Anirban Lahiri	73	65	70	69	277	US$250,000
S.S.P. Chawrasia	65	67	69	76	277	166,660
(Lahiri defeated Chawrasia on first playoff hole.)						
Joakim Lagergren	65	71	73	69	278	71,250
Mithun Perera	67	72	70	69	278	71,250

	SCORES				TOTAL	MONEY
Prayad Marksaeng	68	70	69	71	278	71,250
Marcus Fraser	69	70	67	72	278	71,250
Romain Wattel	70	74	67	68	279	38,700
Richard McEvoy	70	67	72	70	279	38,700
Siddikur Rahman	65	68	70	76	279	38,700
Paul Peterson	69	68	71	72	280	30,000
Daniel Chopra	70	72	65	74	281	27,600
Chapchai Nirat	65	71	75	71	282	23,220
Pariya Junhasavasdikul	73	70	68	71	282	23,220
Adrian Otaegui	70	70	70	72	282	23,220
Ben Evans	72	70	68	72	282	23,220
Adilson Da Silva	71	70	68	73	282	23,220
Thanyakon Khrongpha	68	74	73	68	283	18,150
Shubhankar Sharma	69	72	73	69	283	18,150
Lionel Weber	68	74	72	69	283	18,150
John Parry	70	74	69	70	283	18,150
John Hahn	70	71	71	71	283	18,150
Jyoti Randhawa	74	69	69	71	283	18,150
Arnond Vongvanij	72	72	68	71	283	18,150
Alvaro Velasco	71	71	74	68	284	14,700
Carlos Pigem	70	72	72	70	284	14,700
Rashid Khan	71	72	71	70	284	14,700
Victor Riu	71	72	71	70	284	14,700
Manav Jaini	73	69	71	71	284	14,700
Mikko Korhonen	68	72	72	72	284	14,700
Jeev Milkha Singh	72	72	68	72	284	14,700
Arjun Atwal	70	70	75	70	285	12,225
Carlos Del Moral	69	71	72	73	285	12,225
Chikka S.	69	75	68	73	285	12,225
Peter Lawrie	69	70	71	75	285	12,225
Sam Walker	72	72	72	70	286	10,800
Mark Tullo	72	69	73	72	286	10,800
Mukesh Kumar	71	73	69	73	286	10,800
Anthony Wall	72	70	70	74	286	10,800
N. Thangaraja	71	73	74	69	287	9,300
Amardip Malik	75	69	71	72	287	9,300
Wade Ormsby	75	68	71	73	287	9,300
Kapil Kumar	72	72	70	73	287	9,300
Chiragh Kumar	69	74	70	74	287	9,300
Kalem Richardson	67	74	70	76	287	9,300
Jason Scrivener	72	72	72	72	288	7,650
Soren Kjeldsen	71	71	72	74	288	7,650
Adam Groom	74	69	71	74	288	7,650
Jason Knutzon	71	72	71	74	288	7,650
Miguel Angel Jimenez	70	71	71	76	288	7,650
Gareth Maybin	72	70	75	72	289	6,600
Om Prakash Chouhan	71	73	73	72	289	6,600
Jorge Campillo	71	73	72	74	290	5,400
Jazz Janewattananond	68	74	73	75	290	5,400
Panuphol Pittayarat	72	71	72	75	290	5,400
Prom Meesawat	71	71	72	76	290	5,400
Chris Lloyd	74	70	68	78	290	5,400
Jason Palmer	70	71	69	80	290	5,400
Sebastian Soderberg	72	71	74	74	291	4,200
Nathan Holman	71	73	73	74	291	4,200
Mardan Mamat	73	71	72	75	291	4,200
Max Orrin	71	72	70	78	291	4,200
Jake Roos	70	69	72	80	291	4,200
Danny Chia	68	76	71	77	292	3,525
Miguel Tabuena	72	72	71	77	292	3,525
Angad Cheema	72	70	71	79	292	3,525
Kieran Pratt	75	69	68	80	292	3,525
Chris Paisley	75	68	78	72	293	3,150
Shiv Kapur	73	69	73	79	294	3,000

CIMB Niaga Indonesian Masters

Royale Jakarta Golf Club, Jakarta, Indonesia
Par 36-36–72; 7,322 yards

April 23-26
purse, US$750,000

	SCORES				TOTAL	MONEY
Lee Westwood	69	74	65	73	281	US$135,000
Chapchai Nirat	68	74	73	66	281	82,500
(Westwood defeated Nirat on first playoff hole.)						
Kalem Richardson	75	70	70	67	282	47,250
Thomas Bjorn	66	76	71	70	283	37,500
Thitiphun Chuayprakong	71	77	67	69	284	27,862.50
Y.E. Yang	73	71	69	71	284	27,862.50
Angelo Que	72	75	72	66	285	21,375
Paul Peterson	71	73	73	69	286	16,250
Prayad Marksaeng	73	72	72	69	286	16,250
Berry Henson	75	72	69	70	286	16,250
Matthew Giles	74	73	71	69	287	11,869.25
Adilson Da Silva	73	76	69	69	287	11,869.25
Lionel Weber	73	74	69	71	287	11,869.25
Bryce Easton	73	77	65	72	287	11,869.25
Jazz Janewattananond	71	76	71	70	288	9,503
Raphael De Sousa	72	76	68	72	288	9,503
Yosuke Tsukada	71	71	73	73	288	9,503
Jeung-Hun Wang	74	71	70	73	288	9,503
Khalin Joshi	71	76	68	73	288	9,503
Shaun Norris	69	75	77	68	289	7,942.60
Keith Horne	74	73	70	72	289	7,942.60
Unho Park	67	73	76	73	289	7,942.60
Shih-Chang Chan	66	75	74	74	289	7,942.60
Namchok Tantipokhakul	69	73	71	76	289	7,942.60
Seuk-Hyun Baek	71	79	70	70	290	7,162.50
Kalle Samooja	69	76	69	76	290	7,162.50

AfrAsia Bank Mauritius Open

See African Sunshine Tour chapter.

Bashundhara Bangladesh Open

Kurmitola Golf Club, Dhaka, Bangladesh
Par 35-36–71

May 27-30
purse, US$300,000

	SCORES				TOTAL	MONEY
Mardan Mamat	66	67	68	69	270	US$54,000
Soomin Lee	70	70	65	67	272	25,950
Khalin Joshi	71	68	65	68	272	25,950
Carlos Pigem	67	67	73	66	273	15,000
Janne Kaske	68	67	71	69	275	12,300
Chinnarat Phadungsil	74	67	69	67	277	9,990
Thaworn Wiratchant	70	72	70	66	278	7,012.50
Berry Henson	71	67	71	69	278	7,012.50
Amardip Malik	67	74	68	69	278	7,012.50
Panuphol Pittayarat	69	66	72	71	278	7,012.50
Rattanon Wannasrichan	67	73	72	67	279	5,055
Sujjan Singh	68	74	70	67	279	5,055
Rahil Gangjee	74	70	67	69	280	4,440
Om Prakash Chouhan	69	73	66	72	280	4,440
Chieh-Po Lee	73	69	73	66	281	3,885

	SCORES				TOTAL	MONEY
Akinori Tani	72	71	71	67	281	3,885
Chih Bing Lam	73	72	67	69	281	3,885
Chapchai Nirat	73	68	71	69	281	3,885
Pavit Tangkamolprasert	71	74	69	68	282	3,360
Shakhawat Sohel	74	71	68	69	282	3,360
Hyung-Joon Lee	72	69	67	74	282	3,360
Chikka S.	77	68	72	66	283	3,090
Josh Younger	73	70	68	72	283	3,090
Sung Lee	72	70	67	74	283	3,090
M. Dharma	69	74	72	69	284	2,820
Sam Cyr	72	69	72	71	284	2,820
Sutijet Kooratanapisan	71	73	69	71	284	2,820

Queen's Cup

Santiburi Samui Country Club, Koh Samui, Thailand
Par 36-35–71; 6,832 yards

June 18-21
purse, US$300,000

	SCORES				TOTAL	MONEY
Prayad Marksaeng	69	65	71	65	270	US$54,000
Thanyakon Khrongpha	74	65	68	65	272	33,000
Jazz Janewattananond	69	72	67	66	274	16,950
Siddikur Rahman	69	70	67	68	274	16,950
Mithun Perera	67	72	68	69	276	12,300
Paul Peterson	69	72	68	68	277	8,077.50
Richard T. Lee	69	67	71	70	277	8,077.50
S.S.P. Chawrasia	73	67	67	70	277	8,077.50
Akinori Tani	68	70	64	75	277	8,077.50
Thaworn Wiratchant	69	68	76	66	279	5,482.50
Danny Chia	69	69	72	69	279	5,482.50
Thitiphun Chuayprakong	71	70	70	69	280	4,477.50
Wolmer Murillo	72	66	71	71	280	4,477.50
Chinnarat Phadungsil	68	71	70	71	280	4,477.50
Piya Swangarunporn	74	66	67	73	280	4,477.50
Miguel Tabuena	73	69	70	69	281	3,712.50
Chieh-Po Lee	73	69	70	69	281	3,712.50
Lindsay Renolds	74	69	69	69	281	3,712.50
Atthaphon Sriboonkaew	66	71	70	74	281	3,712.50
Antonio Lascuna	76	69	69	68	282	3,177
Niclas Johansson	68	76	70	68	282	3,177
Namchok Tantipokhakul	71	73	69	69	282	3,177
Jeung-Hun Wang	68	71	73	70	282	3,177
Pannakorn Uthaipas	68	72	70	72	282	3,177
Chawalit Plaphol	74	70	73	66	283	2,820
Sorachut Hansapiban	73	71	74	65	283	2,820
Sutijet Kooratanapisan	77	66	68	72	283	2,820

Asia-Pacific Diamond Cup

See Japan Tour section.

Mercuries Taiwan Masters

Taiwan Golf & Country Club, Chinese Taipei
Par 36-36–72; 6,923 yards

October 1-4
purse, US$650,000

	SCORES				TOTAL	MONEY
Danny Chia	67	72	73	73	285	US$130,000
Wen-Chong Liang	70	73	68	76	287	78,000
Adilson Da Silva	75	69	73	72	289	39,000
Rashid Khan	68	70	75	76	289	39,000
Unho Park	75	69	76	70	290	24,375
Chien-Yao Hung	74	72	72	72	290	24,375
Javi Colomo	75	74	73	69	291	14,300
Wen-Tang Lin	75	69	77	70	291	14,300
Miguel Tabuena	73	73	74	71	291	14,300
Siddikur Rahman	69	74	75	73	291	14,300
Mao-Chang Sung	73	77	68	73	291	14,300
Cheng Tsung Pan	71	72	76	73	292	10,075
Antonio Lascuna	72	71	72	77	292	10,075
Thaworn Wiratchant	74	76	72	71	293	8,775
Boonchu Ruangkit	71	77	71	74	293	8,775
Hao-Sheng Hsu	76	74	71	73	294	7,637.50
Wei-Chih Lu	75	70	75	74	294	7,637.50
Wei-Tze Yeh	71	73	73	77	294	7,637.50
Jazz Janewattananond	75	71	71	77	294	7,637.50
Sam Brazel	73	73	76	73	295	6,695
Wei-Hou Liu	73	73	75	74	295	6,695
Himmat Rai	73	75	73	74	295	6,695
Shih-Chang Chan	75	74	74	73	296	6,175
Jake Stirling	74	76	73	73	296	6,175
Gaganjeet Bhullar	76	72	74	74	296	6,175
Wen-Teh Lu	76	73	73	74	296	6,175

Yeangder Tournament Players Championship

Linkou International Golf & Country Club, Chinese Taipei
Par 36-36–72; 7,125 yards
(Final round cancelled—rain and wind.)

October 8-11
purse, US$500,000

	SCORES			TOTAL	MONEY
Shaun Norris	68	68	68	204	US$90,000
Miguel Tabuena	68	65	73	206	55,000
Giwhan Kim	69	71	68	208	21,580
Panuphol Pittayarat	68	71	69	208	21,580
Hao-Sheng Hsu	69	70	69	208	21,580
Keith Horne	69	68	71	208	21,580
Natipong Srithong	70	65	73	208	21,580
Antonio Lascuna	70	69	70	209	11,475
Danny Chia	71	67	71	209	11,475
Jeung-Hun Wang	72	68	70	210	8,240
Prom Meesawat	70	70	70	210	8,240
Berry Henson	70	70	70	210	8,240
Wen-Teh Lu	68	71	71	210	8,240
Chikka S.	73	65	72	210	8,240
Lindsay Renolds	71	71	69	211	6,335
Lee Sung	72	68	71	211	6,335
Jason Knutzon	73	70	68	211	6,335
Niall Turner	70	66	75	211	6,335
Wen-Tang Lin	67	68	76	211	6,335
Chien-Yao Hung	68	72	72	212	5,512.50

	SCORES			TOTAL	MONEY
Lu-Sen Lien	71	65	76	212	5,512.50
Christopher Cannon	70	71	72	213	5,000
Cheng Tsung Pan	71	71	71	213	5,000
Chun-Kang Hung	67	73	73	213	5,000
Scott Barr	69	70	74	213	5,000
Gaganjeet Bhullar	69	69	75	213	5,000

Venetian Macau Open

Macau Golf & Country Club, Macau
Par 35-36–71; 6,624 yards

October 15-18
purse, US$1,000,000

	SCORES				TOTAL	MONEY
Scott Hend	66	68	64	66	264	US$180,000
Chiragh Kumar	67	66	69	65	267	86,500
Anirban Lahiri	66	67	68	66	267	86,500
Brett Munson	66	74	65	65	270	50,000
Niall Turner	70	68	67	67	272	41,000
Jazz Janewattananond	67	72	67	67	273	30,900
Kiradech Aphibarnrat	68	71	66	68	273	30,900
Javi Colomo	66	72	69	67	274	21,666.67
Sam Brazel	68	66	69	71	274	21,666.67
Rashid Khan	70	65	68	71	274	21,666.67
Cheng Tsung Pan	71	68	68	68	275	16,850
Adilson Da Silva	68	65	72	70	275	16,850
Bongsub Kim	71	68	69	68	276	14,800
Steve Lewton	72	66	67	71	276	14,800
David Lipsky	71	67	67	72	277	13,550
Jeung-Hun Wang	65	68	71	73	277	13,550
Chien-Yao Hung	68	64	77	69	278	11,314.29
Terry Pilkadaris	69	67	72	70	278	11,314.29
Gaganjeet Bhullar	69	68	71	70	278	11,314.29
Siddikur Rahman	65	74	69	70	278	11,314.29
Lee Sung	70	65	72	71	278	11,314.29
S.S.P. Chawrasia	70	68	68	72	278	11,314.29
Andrew Dodt	71	69	66	72	278	11,314.29
Jarrod John Freeman	71	69	70	69	279	8,844.44
Jonathan Moore	68	72	70	69	279	8,844.44
Mithun Perera	70	71	69	69	279	8,844.44
Paul Peterson	70	67	72	70	279	8,844.44
Adam Groom	68	73	68	70	279	8,844.44
Ben Leong	71	66	71	71	279	8,844.44
Seuk-Hyun Baek	70	71	67	71	279	8,844.44
Akinori Tani	70	68	68	73	279	8,844.44
Nathan Holman	72	67	67	73	279	8,844.44

UBS Hong Kong Open

Hong Kong Golf Club, Fanling, Hong Kong
Par 34-36–70; 6,699 yards

October 22-25
purse, US$2,000,000

	SCORES				TOTAL	MONEY
Justin Rose	65	66	64	68	263	US$333,330
Lucas Bjerregaard	66	66	63	69	264	222,220
Soomin Lee	70	69	66	64	269	95,000
Patrick Reed	68	69	65	67	269	95,000
Jason Scrivener	68	68	65	68	269	95,000

	SCORES				TOTAL	MONEY
Matthew Fitzpatrick	67	67	66	69	269	95,000
Wen-Tang Lin	67	68	68	67	270	48,700
Matt Ford	69	65	67	69	270	48,700
Y.E. Yang	68	66	67	69	270	48,700
Anirban Lahiri	67	67	65	71	270	48,700
Masahiro Kawamura	68	69	69	65	271	35,600
Ben Evans	69	71	66	65	271	35,600
Angelo Que	72	67	67	66	272	29,480
Peter Uihlein	70	70	66	66	272	29,480
Cheng Tsung Pan	65	73	67	67	272	29,480
Gaganjeet Bhullar	69	66	67	70	272	29,480
Thongchai Jaidee	71	67	64	70	272	29,480
Richard McEvoy	67	68	73	65	273	23,733.33
David Drysdale	68	71	68	66	273	23,733.33
Andrew Dodt	71	68	68	66	273	23,733.33
Sam Brazel	69	67	68	69	273	23,733.33
Rahil Gangjee	66	70	68	69	273	23,733.33
Siddikur Rahman	67	71	66	69	273	23,733.33
Jazz Janewattananond	69	68	70	67	274	20,200
Graeme McDowell	66	69	71	68	274	20,200
Estanislao Goya	73	66	67	68	274	20,200
Oliver Fisher	66	69	68	71	274	20,200
Jeev Milkha Singh	65	70	65	74	274	20,200
Prom Meesawat	67	69	73	66	275	17,800
Ian Poulter	67	66	73	69	275	17,800
Carlos Pigem	69	71	66	69	275	17,800
Victor Dubuisson	68	70	70	68	276	16,000
Marcus Fraser	72	66	68	70	276	16,000
Peter Hanson	69	70	67	70	276	16,000
Mithun Perera	71	69	69	68	277	13,800
Robert Dinwiddie	69	68	71	69	277	13,800
Justin Walters	71	68	69	69	277	13,800
Adilson Da Silva	71	68	69	69	277	13,800
Prayad Marksaeng	70	67	70	70	277	13,800
Shih-Chang Chan	71	69	66	71	277	13,800
Nathan Holman	68	66	68	75	277	13,800
Ricardo Gonzalez	69	68	74	67	278	10,600
Roope Kakko	67	73	70	68	278	10,600
Matthew Nixon	70	67	71	70	278	10,600
Craig Lee	71	67	70	70	278	10,600
Jbe' Kruger	71	68	68	71	278	10,600
Chapchai Nirat	67	72	67	72	278	10,600
Jason Knutzon	68	68	69	73	278	10,600
Simon Yates	69	68	68	73	278	10,600
Wei-Chih Lu	64	69	71	74	278	10,600
Adam Groom	68	70	73	68	279	8,000
Lasse Jensen	70	68	71	70	279	8,000
Wade Ormsby	71	69	69	70	279	8,000
Danny Chia	71	66	70	72	279	8,000
Mikael Lundberg	71	68	71	70	280	6,450
Andrea Pavan	64	71	74	71	280	6,450
Daniel Gaunt	68	71	70	71	280	6,450
Mark Foster	69	69	69	73	280	6,450
Lionel Weber	73	66	71	71	281	5,400
Terry Pilkadaris	69	71	70	71	281	5,400
Scott Jamieson	71	67	71	72	281	5,400
Jyoti Randhawa	70	70	68	73	281	5,400
S.S.P. Chawrasia	66	70	71	74	281	5,400
David Lipsky	68	70	73	71	282	4,600
Rikard Karlberg	69	69	73	71	282	4,600
Nicholas Fung	71	67	73	71	282	4,600
Chris Paisley	70	70	70	73	283	4,100
Jeung-Hun Wang	71	69	69	74	283	4,100

	SCORES				TOTAL	MONEY
Rattanon Wannasrichan	69	67	74	74	284	3,725
Gregory Havret	72	68	69	75	284	3,725
Sattaya Supupramai	68	69	73	76	286	2,998.79
Unho Park	68	70	71	77	286	2,998.79
Paul Maddy	70	70	67	80	287	2,993.61
Panuphol Pittayarat	70	70	72	76	288	2,990.61
Pavit Tangkamolprasert	71	69	75	76	291	2,986.71
Danie van Tonder	73	67	79	75	294	2,983.26

CIMB Classic

Kuala Lumpur Golf & Country Club, Kuala Lumpur, Malaysia
Par 36-36–72; 6,985 yards

October 29-November 1
purse, US$7,000,000

	SCORES				TOTAL	MONEY
Justin Thomas	68	61	67	66	262	$1,260,000
Adam Scott	68	66	66	63	263	756,000
Kevin Na	67	66	64	67	264	406,000
Brendan Steele	67	63	66	68	264	406,000
Hideki Matsuyama	65	66	68	67	266	280,000
James Hahn	70	65	64	68	267	252,000
Brian Harman	70	63	66	70	269	225,750
Scott Piercy	62	69	69	69	269	225,750
Tony Finau	71	67	66	66	270	203,000
Jim Herman	70	66	68	67	271	168,000
Charles Howell	66	72	67	66	271	168,000
Ryan Moore	67	69	66	69	271	168,000
Patrick Reed	68	68	66	69	271	168,000
David Lingmerth	73	65	64	70	272	126,000
Daniel Summerhays	71	66	69	66	272	126,000
Cameron Tringale	70	68	65	69	272	126,000
Alex Cejka	66	71	66	70	273	101,500
Stewart Cink	68	64	70	71	273	101,500
Branden Grace	67	70	69	67	273	101,500
Spencer Levin	67	64	68	74	273	101,500
Russell Knox	70	69	67	68	274	78,400
Anirban Lahiri	70	67	67	70	274	78,400
Troy Merritt	68	66	72	68	274	78,400
Paul Casey	69	69	69	68	275	61,600
Sergio Garcia	70	67	69	69	275	61,600
Hudson Swafford	70	69	69	67	275	61,600
Brendon de Jonge	69	69	71	67	276	52,850
Scott Hend	67	70	72	67	276	52,850
Ben Crane	71	70	68	68	277	44,508.34
David Hearn	70	65	74	68	277	44,508.34
Chad Campbell	68	70	69	70	277	44,508.33
Kevin Chappell	69	69	70	69	277	44,508.33
Marc Leishman	71	70	70	66	277	44,508.33
Paul Peterson	70	67	68	72	277	44,508.33
Jason Dufner	69	75	69	65	278	36,925
Ryo Ishikawa	69	69	71	69	278	36,925
Jason Gore	66	68	70	75	279	30,800
Matt Jones	67	71	73	68	279	30,800
Kevin Kisner	71	65	70	73	279	30,800
Colt Knost	70	70	72	67	279	30,800
John Senden	70	70	72	67	279	30,800
Cameron Smith	66	72	72	69	279	30,800
Zac Blair	70	71	67	72	280	23,800
Harris English	71	71	69	69	280	23,800
Kyle Reifers	70	66	71	73	280	23,800

	SCORES				TOTAL	MONEY
Nick Watney	70	70	72	68	280	23,800
Ben Martin	70	70	68	73	281	18,223.34
Henrik Stenson	71	67	71	72	281	18,223.34
Keegan Bradley	66	70	72	73	281	18,223.33
Morgan Hoffmann	67	68	74	72	281	18,223.33
Carlos Ortiz	71	74	67	69	281	18,223.33
Nick Taylor	74	70	69	68	281	18,223.33
Jon Curran	69	70	67	76	282	16,286.67
Robert Streb	69	69	72	72	282	16,286.67
Rory Sabbatini	69	69	77	67	282	16,286.66
Scott Brown	68	72	72	71	283	15,540
Andrew Dodt	72	70	74	67	283	15,540
Padraig Harrington	68	72	73	70	283	15,540
Prayad Marksaeng	72	76	68	67	283	15,540
Greg Owen	70	72	69	72	283	15,540
Scott Pinckney	69	73	68	73	283	15,540
Gary Woodland	75	68	69	71	283	15,540
Pat Perez	71	69	72	72	284	14,980
Daniel Berger	76	66	67	76	285	14,630
Luke Donald	74	73	70	68	285	14,630
Ernie Els	72	69	72	72	285	14,630
Ben Leong	71	72	76	66	285	14,630
Danny Chia	71	71	71	73	286	14,140
Chesson Hadley	71	71	73	71	286	14,140
Jerry Kelly	73	72	71	70	286	14,140
Steven Bowditch	73	73	73	69	288	13,860
Matt Every	72	72	72	73	289	13,720
S.S.P. Chawrasia	72	74	74	71	291	13,580
Mardan Mamat	74	73	74	72	293	13,440
Arie Ahmad Irawan	75	74	72	74	295	13,230
Richard Lee	71	77	70	77	295	13,230
John Peterson	80	74	78	66	298	13,020
Danny Lee	73	68			WD	

WGC - HSBC Champions

Sheshan International Golf Club, Shanghai, China
Par 36-36–72; 7,261 yards

November 5-8
purse, US$8,500,000

	SCORES				TOTAL	MONEY
Russell Knox	67	65	68	68	268	$1,400,000
Kevin Kisner	64	66	70	70	270	850,000
Ross Fisher	69	69	65	68	271	422,500
Danny Willett	65	74	70	62	271	422,500
Branden Grace	63	71	70	68	272	276,500
Dustin Johnson	65	71	65	71	272	276,500
Matthew Fitzpatrick	68	69	69	67	273	173,750
Hao-Tong Li	66	69	66	72	273	173,750
Patrick Reed	65	70	68	70	273	173,750
Jordan Spieth	68	72	63	70	273	173,750
Daniel Berger	68	71	69	66	274	106,166.67
Sergio Garcia	68	70	68	68	274	106,166.67
Rory McIlroy	68	72	68	66	274	106,166.67
Henrik Stenson	69	72	66	67	274	106,166.67
Thongchai Jaidee	72	68	66	68	274	106,166.66
Marc Leishman	69	72	65	68	274	106,166.66
Rickie Fowler	68	72	68	67	275	89,000
Bernd Wiesberger	70	66	69	70	275	89,000
Byeong-Hun An	69	68	68	72	277	83,000
Scott Hend	68	69	67	73	277	83,000

	SCORES				TOTAL	MONEY
Hunter Mahan	68	68	71	70	277	83,000
Thorbjorn Olesen	64	74	66	73	277	83,000
Paul Casey	67	72	71	68	278	75,750
Harris English	67	71	70	70	278	75,750
Thomas Pieters	67	71	71	69	278	75,750
Gary Woodland	69	71	73	65	278	75,750
Kyung-Tae Kim	74	71	68	66	279	72,000
James Morrison	69	70	68	72	279	72,000
Justin Thomas	72	69	70	68	279	72,000
Kiradech Aphibarnrat	69	70	70	71	280	68,000
Tommy Fleetwood	67	71	72	70	280	68,000
David Howell	73	68	69	70	280	68,000
Martin Kaymer	69	71	73	67	280	68,000
Ian Poulter	72	71	70	67	280	68,000
Emiliano Grillo	69	71	69	72	281	63,000
Scott Piercy	70	73	66	72	281	63,000
Charl Schwartzel	68	72	69	72	281	63,000
Robert Streb	73	69	68	71	281	63,000
Bubba Watson	68	73	68	72	281	63,000
Steven Bowditch	64	75	68	75	282	58,500
Luke Donald	71	69	70	72	282	58,500
Matt Jones	74	70	68	70	282	58,500
Anirban Lahiri	70	75	66	71	282	58,500
Louis Oosthuizen	68	69	73	73	283	55,500
Daniel Summerhays	68	74	67	74	283	55,500
S.S.P. Chawrasia	69	72	71	72	284	52,000
Miguel Angel Jimenez	73	72	70	69	284	52,000
Soren Kjeldsen	68	71	70	75	284	52,000
Richard Lee	68	72	73	71	284	52,000
Xin-Jun Zhang	67	72	73	72	284	52,000
Ze-Cheng Dou	70	71	73	71	285	49,000
Lee Westwood	72	69	71	73	285	49,000
Chris Wood	68	76	69	72	285	49,000
Thomas Aiken	70	71	73	72	286	47,500
Tyrrell Hatton	70	76	70	70	286	47,500
Alexander Noren	70	76	66	74	286	47,500
Kevin Na	72	72	72	71	287	46,500
Greg Chalmers	73	73	69	73	288	44,791.67
Nick Cullen	74	71	70	73	288	44,791.67
Trevor Fisher, Jr.	67	74	70	77	288	44,791.67
Danny Lee	71	73	71	73	288	44,791.67
Ashun Wu	69	74	72	73	288	44,791.66
Wen-Chong Liang	71	73	73	71	288	44,791.66
Hiroshi Iwata	70	77	69	73	289	43,250
Cameron Smith	71	73	70	75	289	43,250
Andy Sullivan	70	74	70	75	289	43,250
Danny Chia	72	73	74	71	290	42,750
Andrew Dodt	70	80	76	66	292	42,375
Shane Lowry	74	75	72	71	292	42,375
Adam Scott	75	76	72	70	293	42,000
Satoshi Kodaira	74	76	76	68	294	41,750
David Lingmerth	70	72	76	77	295	41,375
Danie van Tonder	77	73	71	74	295	41,375
Yi Cao	70	78	71	78	297	41,000
Steven Jeffress	76	78	73	74	301	40,750
Chris Kirk	71	79	74	79	303	40,375
Marc Warren	75	74	81	73	303	40,375
Hideki Matsuyama	71	73			WD	

Panasonic Open India

Delhi Golf Club, New Delhi, India
Par 36-36–72; 6,963 yards

November 5-8
purse, US$400,000

	SCORES				TOTAL	MONEY
Chiragh Kumar	67	66	72	70	275	US$72,000
Thaworn Wiratchant	68	72	69	69	278	34,600
Siddikur Rahman	68	70	68	72	278	34,600
Namchok Tantipokhakul	71	71	71	66	279	15,280
Jyoti Randhawa	69	72	71	67	279	15,280
Shubhankar Sharma	70	73	67	69	279	15,280
Mithun Perera	66	70	73	70	279	15,280
Manav Jaini	72	71	69	68	280	8,666.67
Shankar Das	69	71	71	69	280	8,666.67
Vikrant Chopra	71	68	71	70	280	8,666.67
Rashid Khan	71	71	69	70	281	6,980
Pariya Junhasavasdikul	74	72	68	68	282	5,970
Rahil Gangjee	70	74	69	69	282	5,970
Sujjan Singh	71	70	70	71	282	5,970
Chikka S.	69	71	68	74	282	5,970
Sanjay Kumar	70	71	74	68	283	4,950
Khalin Joshi	69	73	72	69	283	4,950
Mukesh Kumar	70	71	72	70	283	4,950
Panuphol Pittayarat	72	71	70	70	283	4,950
Niall Kearney	71	71	74	68	284	4,353.33
Gaganjeet Bhullar	71	73	71	69	284	4,353.33
Pawin Ingkhapradit	70	68	75	71	284	4,353.33
Poom Saksansin	73	72	71	69	285	3,940
Lionel Weber	73	70	73	69	285	3,940
Abhishek Jha	71	73	71	70	285	3,940
Zamal Hossain	71	67	70	77	285	3,940

World Classic Championship

Laguna National Golf & Country Club, Singapore
Par 35-36–71; 7,207 yards

November 12-15
purse, US$750,000

	SCORES				TOTAL	MONEY
Danthai Boonma	72	69	72	69	282	US$135,000
Nicholas Fung	74	67	70	72	283	82,500
Jeung-Hun Wang	69	75	71	69	284	47,250
Sam Brazel	69	74	72	70	285	37,500
Jazz Janewattananond	71	71	77	67	286	25,700
Prom Meesawat	73	73	70	70	286	25,700
Chapchai Nirat	76	69	69	72	286	25,700
Scott Barr	69	71	76	71	287	17,212.50
Danny Chia	73	72	70	72	287	17,212.50
Jyoti Randhawa	79	68	68	73	288	14,325
Gaganjeet Bhullar	74	69	74	73	290	11,300.50
Josh Younger	73	71	72	74	290	11,300.50
Akinori Tani	74	74	67	75	290	11,300.50
Chinnarat Phadungsil	71	69	74	76	290	11,300.50
Paul Peterson	71	73	70	76	290	11,300.50
Berry Henson	70	70	73	77	290	11,300.50
Daniel Chopra	75	73	72	71	291	9,063
Soomin Lee	75	71	72	73	291	9,063
Panuphol Pittayarat	72	73	70	76	291	9,063
Antonio Lascuna	75	73	71	73	292	7,383.80
Rashid Khan	75	69	75	73	292	7,383.80

	SCORES				TOTAL	MONEY
Steve Lewton	75	74	69	74	292	7,383.80
Wei-Chih Lu	74	73	73	72	292	7,383.80
Niall Turner	73	72	73	74	292	7,383.80
Casey O'Toole	76	73	71	72	292	7,383.80
Namchok Tantipokhakul	71	71	74	76	292	7,383.80
S.S.P. Chawrasia	73	75	73	71	292	7,383.80
Choo Tze Huang	74	75	72	71	292	7,383.80
Jbe' Kruger	72	74	70	76	292	7,383.80

Resorts World Manila Masters

Manila Southwoods Golf & Country Club, Manila, Philippines
Par 36-36–72; 6,535 yards

November 19-22
purse, US$1,000,000

	SCORES				TOTAL	MONEY
Natipong Srithong	71	69	66	67	273	US$180,000
Jbe' Kruger	69	65	69	71	274	110,000
Chieh-Po Lee	68	66	71	70	275	56,500
Chien-Yao Hung	67	67	68	73	275	56,500
Rahil Gangjee	72	66	70	68	276	31,825
Chan Kim	69	71	68	68	276	31,825
Prom Meesawat	72	68	67	69	276	31,825
Carlos Pigem	68	71	67	70	276	31,825
Paul Peterson	70	67	74	66	277	19,316.67
Lionel Weber	72	67	70	68	277	19,316.67
Sam Brazel	68	72	67	70	277	19,316.67
Jeung-Hun Wang	69	69	69	71	278	15,700
Sukree Othman	71	68	68	71	278	15,700
Tirawat Kaewsiribandit	69	67	73	70	279	13,550
Panuphol Pittayarat	73	66	70	70	279	13,550
Adam Groom	69	67	71	72	279	13,550
S.S.P. Chawrasia	70	70	67	72	279	13,550
Berry Henson	71	70	74	65	280	10,935.71
Poom Saksansin	67	76	70	67	280	10,935.71
Miguel Tabuena	70	68	72	70	280	10,935.71
Arnond Vongvanij	72	66	72	70	280	10,935.71
Mithun Perera	70	70	70	70	280	10,935.71
Pariya Junhasavasdikul	71	68	70	71	280	10,935.71
Angelo Que	71	71	66	72	280	10,935.71
Jyoti Randhawa	68	74	74	65	281	8,828.57
Antonio Lascuna	70	69	73	69	281	8,828.57
Sutijet Kooratanapisan	72	71	69	69	281	8,828.57
Jonathan Moore	69	74	68	70	281	8,828.57
Javi Colomo	71	73	67	70	281	8,828.57
Terry Pilkadaris	70	72	68	71	281	8,828.57
Wei-Chih Lu	72	71	67	71	281	8,828.57

Ho Tram Open

The Bluffs, Ho Tram Strip, Vietnam
Par 35-36–71

December 3-6
purse, US$1,500,000

	SCORES				TOTAL	MONEY
Sergio Garcia	66	68	68	68	270	US$270,000
Himmat Rai	66	69	68	67	270	111,500
Thaworn Wiratchant	64	71	68	67	270	111,500
Wen-Tang Lin	65	67	68	70	270	111,500
(Garcia defeated Wiratchant and Lin on first and Rai on second playoff hole.)						
Thomas Bjorn	69	70	68	64	271	61,500
Sam Cyr	69	69	70	65	273	46,350
Shaun Norris	66	71	65	71	273	46,350
Sung-Hoon Kang	72	68	67	67	274	36,750
Chawalit Plaphol	68	67	72	68	275	28,975
Terry Pilkadaris	71	67	69	68	275	28,975
Paul Peterson	66	70	68	71	275	28,975
Nicholas Fung	65	70	72	69	276	23,550
Charlie Wi	62	72	72	70	276	23,550
Jeung-Hun Wang	75	67	70	65	277	20,775
Prom Meesawat	69	71	68	69	277	20,775
Geoff Ogilvy	69	70	67	71	277	20,775
David Lipsky	65	70	73	70	278	18,525
Jason Knutzon	66	72	70	70	278	18,525
Thanyakon Khrongpha	69	73	70	67	279	17,025
Kalle Samooja	68	72	68	71	279	17,025
Oliver Wilson	70	71	73	66	280	15,450
Phachara Khongwatmai	72	69	73	66	280	15,450
Rahil Gangjee	66	76	71	67	280	15,450
Siddikur Rahman	69	67	74	70	280	15,450
Masahiro Kawamura	72	68	68	72	280	15,450

Thailand Golf Championship

Amata Spring Country Club, Chonburi, Thailand
Par 36-36–72; 7,453 yards

December 10-13
purse, US$1,000,000

	SCORES				TOTAL	MONEY
Jamie Donaldson	63	68	71	65	267	US$180,000
Lee Westwood	71	68	64	67	270	86,500
Clement Sordet	71	66	63	70	270	86,500
Sergio Garcia	66	69	70	69	274	45,500
Byeong-Hun An	69	67	68	70	274	45,500
Phachara Khongwatmai	68	71	70	66	275	33,300
S.S.P. Chawrasia	72	69	68	67	276	24,800
Kiradech Aphibarnrat	69	72	67	68	276	24,800
Martin Kaymer	68	65	72	71	276	24,800
Sung-Hoon Kang	70	68	70	69	277	19,100
*Cheng Jin	73	67	69	69	278	
Matthew Fitzpatrick	68	67	72	71	278	17,450
Nicolas Colsaerts	70	70	71	68	279	15,700
Shingo Katayama	71	70	70	68	279	15,700
Bubba Watson	71	70	72	67	280	14,150
Jeung-Hun Wang	73	71	69	67	280	14,150
Shaun Norris	70	74	70	67	281	12,650
Chieh-Po Lee	72	70	71	68	281	12,650
Jbe' Kruger	68	76	64	73	281	12,650
Jason Knutzon	72	68	72	70	282	11,050
Berry Henson	70	70	71	71	282	11,050

	SCORES				TOTAL	MONEY
Brett Munson	67	72	71	72	282	11,050
Yusaku Miyazato	68	74	66	74	282	11,050
Terry Pilkadaris	71	71	70	71	283	9,550
Juvic Pagunsan	72	70	69	72	283	9,550
Shiv Kapur	71	71	69	72	283	9,550
Arjun Atwal	73	69	69	72	283	9,550
Joost Luiten	69	70	71	73	283	9,550
Sam Brazel	70	68	68	77	283	9,550

Philippine Open

Luisita Golf & Country Club, Tarlac, Philippines
Par 36-36–72
(Final round cancelled—rain.)

December 17-20
purse, US$300,000

	SCORES			TOTAL	MONEY
Miguel Tabuena	67	69	66	202	US$54,000
Scott Barr	69	66	68	203	33,000
Himmat Rai	71	70	63	204	16,950
Chinnarat Phadungsil	67	70	67	204	16,950
Seuk-Hyun Baek	69	71	66	206	8,922
Simon Griffiths	70	68	68	206	8,922
Jeung-Hun Wang	67	70	69	206	8,922
Niall Turner	69	68	69	206	8,922
Keith Horne	69	68	69	206	8,922
Wei-Chih Lu	70	70	67	207	4,812.50
Charlie Wi	70	69	68	207	4,812.50
Khalin Joshi	70	67	70	207	4,812.50
Gaganjeet Bhullar	67	69	71	207	4,812.50
Kalle Samooja	69	67	71	207	4,812.50
Lindsay Renolds	66	68	73	207	4,812.50
Charles Hong	71	68	69	208	3,885
Mardan Mamat	68	71	69	208	3,885
Brett Munson	70	69	70	209	3,375
Adam Groom	70	69	70	209	3,375
Janne Kaske	71	68	70	209	3,375
Tirawat Kaewsiribandit	68	70	71	209	3,375
Antonio Lascuna	72	72	65	209	3,375
Wolmer Murillo	71	70	69	210	2,955
Taewoo Kim	70	71	69	210	2,955
Namchok Tantipokhakul	72	68	70	210	2,955
Juvic Pagunsan	68	71	71	210	2,955

OneAsia Tour

Volvo China Open

Tomson Shanghai Pudong Golf Club, Shanghai, China

April 23-26

Par 36-36–72; 7,315 yards

purse, RMB20,000,000

	SCORES				TOTAL	MONEY
Ashun Wu	73	66	69	71	279	US$544,591.47
David Howell	68	72	68	72	280	363,060.98
Emiliano Grillo	73	70	69	69	281	168,823.52
Prom Meesawat	72	70	68	71	281	168,823.52
Alexander Levy	69	68	71	73	281	168,823.52
Hao-Tong Li	71	68	69	74	282	114,364.32
Richie Ramsay	72	68	70	73	283	98,026.56
Byeong-Hun An	72	68	76	68	284	64,860.91
Peter Uihlein	70	67	76	71	284	64,860.91
Romain Wattel	72	67	74	71	284	64,860.91
Tyrrell Hatton	75	69	69	71	284	64,860.91
Julien Quesne	69	67	76	72	284	64,860.91
Magnus A. Carlsson	73	72	65	74	284	64,860.91
Mark Foster	72	71	74	68	285	47,052.75
Lucas Bjerregaard	75	70	70	70	285	47,052.75
Bradley Dredge	68	74	72	71	285	47,052.75
Seve Benson	75	69	66	75	285	47,052.75
Renato Paratore	74	71	71	70	286	37,699.38
Ilhwan Park	70	74	71	71	286	37,699.38
Mikko Ilonen	73	71	70	72	286	37,699.38
James Morrison	73	70	70	73	286	37,699.38
Richard Green	73	71	69	73	286	37,699.38
Benjamin Hebert	70	76	67	73	286	37,699.38
Matteo Manassero	71	68	73	74	286	37,699.38
Thomas Pieters	70	71	70	75	286	37,699.38
Robert Rock	73	73	72	69	287	31,041.74
Taehee Lee	74	71	71	71	287	31,041.74
Kiradech Aphibarnrat	71	68	76	72	287	31,041.74
Alex Noren	73	70	72	72	287	31,041.74
Robert Karlsson	75	70	70	72	287	31,041.74
Chris Wood	73	70	75	70	288	24,031.36
Shiv Kapur	70	72	75	71	288	24,031.36
Rafa Cabrera-Bello	73	69	74	72	288	24,031.36
Gregory Havret	76	68	72	72	288	24,031.36
Gregory Bourdy	74	72	70	72	288	24,031.36
Matthew Griffin	75	68	72	73	288	24,031.36
Soren Kjeldsen	75	71	69	73	288	24,031.36
Johan Edfors	74	72	69	73	288	24,031.36
Michael Hendry	68	73	73	74	288	24,031.36
Raphael Jacquelin	74	68	72	74	288	24,031.36
Ross Fisher	76	69	68	75	288	24,031.36
Craig Lee	70	75	72	72	289	18,625.05
Trevor Fisher, Jr.	75	71	71	72	289	18,625.05
Rhein Gibson	71	71	74	73	289	18,625.05
David Horsey	72	73	71	73	289	18,625.05
Scott Strange	71	72	69	77	289	18,625.05
Ryan Carter	71	73	77	69	290	15,684.25
Mikko Korhonen	71	72	75	72	290	15,684.25
Marcus Fraser	69	76	73	72	290	15,684.25

	SCORES				TOTAL	MONEY
Terry Pilkadaris	72	73	70	75	290	15,684.25
Xin-Jun Zhang	75	71	79	66	291	12,743.45
Johan Carlsson	70	75	75	71	291	12,743.45
Oliver Wilson	70	76	72	73	291	12,743.45
Jun Seok Lee	72	74	72	73	291	12,743.45
Matthew Nixon	73	70	72	76	291	12,743.45
David Drysdale	75	69	76	72	292	10,047.72
Maximilian Kieffer	73	72	73	74	292	10,047.72
Felipe Aguilar	80	65	70	77	292	10,047.72
Nick Cullen	72	73	70	77	292	10,047.72
Tian Yuan	75	69	77	73	294	8,822.39
Scott Hend	71	73	76	74	294	8,822.39
Andrew Johnston	72	70	74	78	294	8,822.39
Edouard Espana	74	72	77	72	295	8,168.88
Jin Zhang	72	70	78	76	296	7,842.12
Jerome Lando Casanova	71	68	77	81	297	7,515.37
Soren Hansen	75	70	78	76	299	7,188.61
Steve Jeffress	72	74	77	78	301	6,861.86

GS Caltex Maekyung Open

Namseoul Country Club, Seoul, South Korea
Par 36-36–72; 6,947 yards

May 14-17
purse, KRW1,000,000,000

	SCORES				TOTAL	MONEY
Kyong-Jun Moon	71	66	74	73	284	US$180,995.48
Do-Hoon Kim	76	67	75	68	286	64,253.40
Ryan Fox	73	73	68	72	286	64,253.40
Jason Norris	68	69	72	77	286	64,253.40
Gareth Paddison	69	73	70	74	286	64,253.40
Taehee Lee	71	72	72	72	287	29,864.25
Taehoon Kim	71	73	73	71	288	27,149.32
Sung-Hoon Kang	72	74	73	70	289	18,950.23
Steve Jeffress	70	74	74	71	289	18,950.23
Woochan Kim	70	74	73	72	289	18,950.23
Jeonghyup Hyun	73	73	71	72	289	18,950.23
Junwon Park	69	75	69	76	289	18,950.23
Nathan Holman	72	71	77	70	290	11,085.97
Thaworn Wiratchant	74	74	72	70	290	11,085.97
Soomin Lee	74	73	72	71	290	11,085.97
Sang-Hyun Park	73	72	73	72	290	11,085.97
Rattanon Wannasrichan	73	76	71	71	291	9,411.77
Hosung Choi	74	72	77	68	291	9,411.77
*Jaekyeoung Lee	73	70	74	74	291	
Jaehyun An	71	71	79	71	292	8,733.04
Jinho Choi	72	70	73	77	292	8,733.04
*Youngwoong Kim	67	74	75	76	292	
Hyung-Joon Lee	79	68	75	71	293	8,030.16
Daesub Kim	72	73	75	73	293	8,030.16
Ryan Dillon	75	71	73	74	293	8,030.16

SK Telecom Open

Sky 72 Ocean Course, Incheon, South Korea
Par 36-36–72; 7,241 yards

May 21-24
purse, KRW1,000,000,000

	SCORES				TOTAL	MONEY
Jinho Choi	68	68	70	72	278	US$183,385.29
Soomin Lee	73	72	63	71	279	91,692.65
Dimitrios Papadatos	74	69	69	68	280	39,097.74
Gareth Paddison	70	73	68	69	280	39,097.74
J.B. Park	72	69	69	70	280	39,097.74
Kyung-Tae Kim	73	69	68	70	280	39,097.74
Jeung-Hun Wang	70	74	63	73	280	39,097.74
Sang-Hyun Park	68	75	70	68	281	22,495.26
Seung-Hyuk Kim	74	68	67	72	281	22,495.26
Sung-Hoon Kang	69	69	69	74	281	22,495.26
Taehee Lee	78	67	66	71	282	18,338.53
Mingyu Cho	70	71	67	74	282	18,338.53
Anthony Summers	74	69	69	71	283	14,915.34
Ryan Fox	68	71	72	72	283	14,915.34
David McKenzie	69	72	69	73	283	14,915.34
Changwoo Lee	70	71	70	73	284	12,836.97
Sengyong Kim	69	72	69	74	284	12,836.97
Daesub Kim	71	72	73	69	285	11,369.89
Inchoon Hwang	71	70	71	73	285	11,369.89
*Jiho Yang	72	76	70	67	285	
Giwhan Kim	68	74	73	71	286	9,169.26
Michael Wright	72	69	73	72	286	9,169.26
Seungtaek Lee	70	73	74	69	286	9,169.26
Jordan Zunic	73	74	67	72	286	9,169.26
Gyoungyoon Yu	76	70	72	68	286	9,169.26
Taehoon Kim	72	72	69	73	286	9,169.26
K.J. Choi	73	71	68	74	286	9,169.26

Singha Corporation Thailand Open

Siam Country Club, Plantation Course, Pattaya, Thailand
Par 36-36–72; 7,295 yards

June 11-14
purse, US$1,000,000

	SCORES				TOTAL	MONEY
Kyung-Tae Kim	71	64	67	65	267	US$180,000
Jeung-Hun Wang	69	70	64	67	270	105,000
Joshua Younger	67	70	64	73	274	70,000
Yusaku Miyazato	72	68	67	68	275	46,000
Jazz Janewattananond	69	66	68	72	275	46,000
Hiroshi Iwata	74	62	72	68	276	32,550
Daehyun Kim	71	69	68	68	276	32,550
Chapchai Nirat	69	69	69	69	276	32,550
Prom Meesawat	69	68	67	72	276	32,550
Kiradech Aphibarnrat	70	68	69	70	277	24,600
Namchok Tantipokhakul	70	66	68	73	277	24,600
Jakraphan Premsirigorn	72	68	72	66	278	16,571.43
Sutijet Kooratanapisan	76	67	67	68	278	16,571.43
Rattanon Wannasrichan	73	66	71	68	278	16,571.43
Hyung-Sung Kim	65	72	71	70	278	16,571.43
Soonsang Hong	71	68	68	71	278	16,571.43
Mingyu Cho	72	68	67	71	278	16,571.43
Xin-Jun Zhang	69	67	68	74	278	16,571.43
Kodai Ichihara	72	69	68	70	279	11,200
Tadahiro Takayama	72	67	69	71	279	11,200

	SCORES				TOTAL	MONEY
Kyong-Jun Moon	69	67	71	72	279	11,200
Katsumasa Miyamoto	71	68	65	75	279	11,200
Sungyeol Kwon	70	70	69	71	280	9,560
Younghan Song	70	67	71	72	280	9,560
Yoshinobu Tsukada	69	72	67	72	280	9,560
Bio Kim	68	70	69	73	280	9,560
Antonio Lascuna	73	67	66	74	280	9,560

Kolon Korea Open

Woo Jeong Hills Country Club, Cheonan, South Korea
Par 36-35–71; 7,215 yards

September 10-13
purse, KRW1,200,000,000

	SCORES				TOTAL	MONEY
Kyoung-Hoon Lee	68	69	68	66	271	US$248,642
Meenwhee Kim	70	71	68	66	275	99,457
Jeung-Hun Wang	70	71	67	70	278	52,214.50
Dongmin Lee	73	68	66	71	278	52,214.50
Kyong-Jun Moon	70	73	68	69	280	32,758
Steve Jeffress	65	70	73	72	280	32,758
Jihoon Lee	69	71	73	68	281	25,319.67
Sengyong Kim	73	68	68	72	281	25,319.67
Jaebum Park	69	67	73	72	281	25,319.67
Sang-Hyun Park	70	74	70	68	282	17,998.33
David Oh	71	69	73	69	282	17,998.33
Younghan Song	68	67	72	75	282	17,998.33
*Inhoi Hur	69	67	71	75	282	
Kyung-Tae Kim	72	70	70	71	283	12,556
Dong-Kyu Jang	70	70	71	72	283	12,556
Hyun-Woo Ryu	70	68	73	72	283	12,556
Sungmin Hong	70	73	71	70	284	9,966
Nick Cullen	73	67	73	71	284	9,966
Giwhan Kim	70	71	71	72	284	9,966
Bongsub Kim	68	73	71	72	284	9,966
Sangyeop Lee	74	70	69	72	285	8,992
Heungchol Joo	69	76	70	71	286	8,018.13
Hyung-Tae Kim	71	73	71	71	286	8,018.13
Geonha Kim	70	68	76	72	286	8,018.13
*Seungtaek Oh	68	69	76	73	286	
Ilhwan Park	73	68	70	75	286	8,018.13
Stephen Dartnall	72	69	69	76	286	8,018.13
Ryan Dillon	72	69	76	69	286	8,018.13
Hosung Choi	72	72	73	69	286	8,018.13
Jinjae Byun	72	70	73	71	286	8,018.13

Fiji International

Natadola Bay Championship Golf Course, Sigatoka, Fiji
Par 36-36–72; 7,068 yards

October 15-18
purse, A$1,125,000

	SCORES				TOTAL	MONEY
Matt Kuchar	74	72	69	69	284	US$147,186.11
Aron Price	78	70	69	71	288	83,405.46
Vijay Singh	78	75	71	65	289	42,384.15
Ryan Fox	76	73	73	67	289	42,384.15
Nick Cullen	74	76	71	68	289	42,384.15
Daniel Valente	80	74	72	68	294	27,801.82

	SCORES				TOTAL	MONEY
Brad Shilton	77	76	70	71	294	27,801.82
Matthew Guyatt	78	75	74	68	295	22,895.62
Peter Wilson	76	76	72	71	295	22,895.62
Maxwell McCardle	76	81	73	67	297	16,681.09
Michael Sim	80	74	73	70	297	16,681.09
Anthony Summers	80	74	72	71	297	16,681.09
Daniel Nisbet	74	82	69	72	297	16,681.09
Scott Laycock	75	75	74	73	297	16,681.09
Josh Geary	72	82	74	70	298	11,829.40
Garrett Sapp	78	77	73	70	298	11,829.40
Jamie Hook	77	78	73	70	298	11,829.40
Adam Blyth	82	75	73	69	299	9,280.90
Steve Jeffress	76	78	73	72	299	9,280.90
Daniel Fox	78	75	72	74	299	9,280.90
Peter Cooke	75	79	75	71	300	8,046.18
David Klein	76	81	71	72	300	8,046.18
David McKenzie	79	70	77	74	300	8,046.18
Matthew Millar	78	80	68	74	300	8,046.18
Ryan Haller	79	75	70	76	300	8,046.18

Emirates Australian Open

See Australasian Tour chapter.

PGA Tour China

Buick Open

Mission Hills, Sandbelt Trails Golf, Haikou, Hainan
Par 36-36–72; 7,228 yards

April 2-5
purse, CN¥1,200,000

	SCORES				TOTAL	MONEY
Josh Geary	73	70	69	68	280	CN¥216,000
Jeung-Hun Wang	71	71	69	70	281	129,600
Gunn Charoenkul	74	69	69	71	283	81,600
Jamie Arnold	70	73	69	72	284	47,250
John Young Kim	68	72	68	76	284	47,250
Yi Cao	68	69	71	76	284	47,250
Ze-Cheng Dou	72	73	67	72	284	47,250
Shih-Chang Chan	72	73	68	72	285	33,600
Anthony Brown	75	73	72	65	285	33,600
Eugene Wong	70	73	71	71	285	33,600
Niall Platt	74	75	67	69	285	33,600
T.K. Kim	72	71	70	73	286	22,800
Michael Choi	71	73	71	71	286	22,800
David Lutterus	75	68	74	69	286	22,800
Alex Hawley	71	72	72	71	286	22,800

	SCORES				TOTAL	MONEY
Justin Shin	75	70	71	70	286	22,800
Jon McLean	72	68	76	70	286	22,800
Rohan Blizard	70	71	72	74	287	16,200
Wen-Yi Huang	74	70	73	70	287	16,200
Chien-Yao Hung	70	74	73	70	287	16,200
Anthony Kang	70	75	69	73	287	16,200

Eternal Courtyard Open

St. Andrews Zhengzhou Golf Club, Zhengzhou, Henan
Par 36-36–72; 7,261 yards

May 14-17
purse, CN¥1,200,000

	SCORES				TOTAL	MONEY
Shih-Chang Chan	71	77	67	64	279	CN¥216,000
Xin-Jun Zhang	71	75	72	64	282	129,600
Yi Cao	76	72	70	67	285	62,400
Peter Cooke	78	72	69	66	285	62,400
David Lutterus	69	75	74	67	285	62,400
Paul Imondi	75	74	72	66	287	38,850
Ze-Cheng Dou	73	70	72	72	287	38,850
John Delprete	74	71	69	73	287	38,850
Jazz Janewattananond	73	72	70	72	287	38,850
Sejun Yoon	76	70	75	68	289	27,600
Benjamin John Campbell	71	75	72	71	289	27,600
Matt Jager	72	74	70	73	289	27,600
Jongheon Park	73	77	70	69	289	27,600
Alex Hawley	76	73	69	71	289	27,600
Scott Laycock	74	72	72	72	290	20,400
Rak Hyun Cho	75	74	69	72	290	20,400
Maxwell McCardle	73	74	72	71	290	20,400
Shota Fukuhara	77	73	71	70	291	16,200
Benjamin Lein	77	72	68	74	291	16,200
John Young Kim	70	77	73	71	291	16,200
Christopher Brown	76	73	70	72	291	16,200

United Investment Real Estate Wuhan Open

Yishan Golf Club, Wuhan, Hubei
Par 36-36–72; 7,236 yards

May 21-24
purse, CN¥1,200,000

	SCORES				TOTAL	MONEY
Justin Shin	71	64	72	69	276	CN¥216,000
Eugene Wong	69	70	73	67	279	129,600
Rohan Blizard	72	70	66	72	280	81,600
Peter Cooke	71	74	66	71	282	57,600
Alex Hawley	73	70	69	72	284	43,800
*Zihan She	72	74	68	70	284	
Daniel Pearce	73	71	70	70	284	43,800
T.K. Kim	71	72	67	74	284	43,800
Josh Geary	71	72	71	71	285	34,800
Gavin Flint	73	71	71	70	285	34,800
Mathew Perry	70	73	68	74	285	34,800
Wei-Huang Wu	71	76	68	71	286	26,400
Maxwell McCardle	75	74	67	70	286	26,400
Teemu Putkonen	74	71	68	73	286	26,400
*Cheng Jin	77	71	69	69	286	
Guowu Zhou	74	73	71	68	286	26,400

	SCORES				TOTAL	MONEY
Kyle Souza	73	70	72	72	287	20,400
Yi Keun Chang	73	71	71	72	287	20,400
Aaron Townsend	72	72	72	71	287	20,400
Sejun Yoon	71	75	74	68	288	14,100
Christopher Brown	71	74	70	73	288	14,100
Jarin Todd	72	74	71	71	288	14,100
Hanmil Jung	69	74	73	72	288	14,100
Chien-Yao Hung	71	72	73	72	288	14,100
Mu Hu	72	76	66	74	288	14,100
Yi Cao	75	73	72	68	288	14,100
Jia Zhang	73	71	75	69	288	14,100

Lanhai Open

Lan Hai International Golf Club, Shanghai   May 28-31
Par 36-36–72; 7,272 yards   purse, CN¥1,200,000

	SCORES				TOTAL	MONEY
Josh Geary	67	72	68	69	276	CN¥216,000
Jeung-Hun Wang	67	71	68	71	277	129,600
David McKenzie	71	69	70	69	279	81,600
Maxwell McCardle	75	70	70	69	284	57,600
Peter Cooke	78	71	70	66	285	45,600
Eugene Wong	71	74	69	71	285	45,600
*Cheng Jin	75	70	70	72	287	
Thomas Petersson	71	69	75	72	287	40,200
Ze-Yu He	72	69	71	76	288	33,600
Daniel Pearce	75	65	71	77	288	33,600
Christopher Brown	73	76	69	70	288	33,600
Shaocai He	73	72	72	71	288	33,600
Jongheon Park	72	74	72	71	289	22,800
Kyle Souza	73	72	75	69	289	22,800
Wen-Yi Huang	75	72	70	72	289	22,800
Sejun Yoon	68	71	76	74	289	22,800
Jinoh Song	72	71	72	74	289	22,800
Scott Laycock	72	73	73	71	289	22,800
Chien-Yao Hung	71	71	70	78	290	16,200
Raymond Beaufils	77	70	72	71	290	16,200
Tommy Mou	71	72	74	73	290	16,200
Matt Jager	77	70	70	73	290	16,200

Pingan Bank Open

Qinghe Bay Golf Club, Beijing   September 10-13
Par 37-35–72   purse, CN¥1,200,000

	SCORES				TOTAL	MONEY
Eugene Wong	70	67	63	72	272	CN¥216,000
Zihao Chen	71	69	70	67	277	105,600
Rak Hyun Cho	70	68	74	65	277	105,600
Huilin Zhang	72	69	67	72	280	49,600
Niall Platt	73	66	70	71	280	49,600
Seungyun Lee	73	69	69	69	280	49,600
Scott Barr	72	68	71	70	281	40,200
T.K. Kim	74	68	72	68	282	32,400
Jarin Todd	69	72	71	70	282	32,400
Sejun Yoon	70	67	72	73	282	32,400

	SCORES				TOTAL	MONEY
Byungmin Cho	71	70	71	70	282	32,400
Chien-Yao Hung	71	70	70	71	282	32,400
*Cheng Jin	67	71	73	72	283	
Rohan Blizard	69	69	71	74	283	22,500
Justin Shin	72	70	70	71	283	22,500
Josh Geary	75	72	68	68	283	22,500
Bryden Macpherson	71	72	70	70	283	22,500
Tian Yuan	69	72	71	72	284	16,800
Mu Hu	71	67	72	74	284	16,800
Yi Cao	71	68	72	73	284	16,800
Masamichi Ito	69	72	73	70	284	16,800
Shih-Chang Chan	76	68	71	69	284	16,800

Cadillac Championship

Topwin Golf & Country Club, North County, Huairou, Beijing
Par 36-36–72

September 24-27
purse, CN¥1,200,000

	SCORES				TOTAL	MONEY
Bryden Macpherson	72	63	69	68	272	CN¥216,000
Byungmin Cho	67	69	66	73	275	129,600
Junghwan Lee	70	65	69	72	276	69,600
Zihao Chen	70	69	67	70	276	69,600
Ze-Cheng Dou	68	71	67	71	277	48,000
John Young Kim	70	69	69	70	278	43,200
Yi Keun Chang	70	71	68	70	279	38,700
*Cheng Jin	68	67	75	69	279	
Justin Shin	69	68	71	71	279	38,700
Daniel Pearce	71	74	66	69	280	31,200
Xin-Jun Zhang	65	70	71	74	280	31,200
Sejun Yoon	74	70	66	70	280	31,200
Jin Zhang	72	70	67	71	280	31,200
Seungyun Lee	66	72	72	71	281	24,000
Paul Imondi	69	69	68	75	281	24,000
Xu Wang	71	70	71	70	282	20,400
Jinho Choi	69	75	67	71	282	20,400
Masamichi Ito	74	72	71	65	282	20,400
Jack Munro	73	68	66	76	283	18,000
Wen-Yi Huang	68	68	73	75	284	12,698
Sam Chien	72	70	70	72	284	12,698
Jamie Arnold	75	72	66	71	284	12,698
Yeong Su Kim	70	73	70	71	284	12,698
Niall Platt	70	70	71	73	284	12,698
Ze-Yu He	75	71	69	69	284	12,698
Garrett Daniel Sapp	68	72	75	69	284	12,698
Aaron Townsend	71	68	70	75	284	12,698
Huilin Zhang	68	71	73	72	284	12,698

Yulongwan Yunnan Open

Yulongwan Golf Club, Kunming, Yunnan
Par 36-36–72; 7,453 yards

October 1-4
purse, CN¥1,200,000

	SCORES				TOTAL	MONEY
Josh Geary	66	65	64	71	266	CN¥216,000
Gunn Charoenkul	64	65	67	71	267	129,600
Daniel Pearce	70	65	68	69	272	69,600

	SCORES				TOTAL	MONEY
Bryden Macpherson	67	66	72	67	272	69,600
Shirakura Shohei	69	71	65	68	273	48,000
Sam Chien	68	65	70	71	274	38,850
David McKenzie	71	66	71	66	274	38,850
Yi Cao	63	70	73	68	274	38,850
Masamichi Ito	73	71	65	65	274	38,850
Rohan Blizard	73	68	67	67	275	31,200
Huilin Zhang	69	72	65	69	275	31,200
Guangming Yang	71	70	68	67	276	27,600
Jarin Todd	68	72	69	68	277	24,000
Yi Keun Chang	70	67	69	71	277	24,000
Bin Yan	70	72	70	66	278	21,000
Sungi Yu	73	69	69	67	278	21,000
Ze-Cheng Dou	70	68	72	69	279	18,600
Justin Shin	72	66	70	71	279	18,600
Shaocai He	74	67	67	72	280	16,800
Jongheon Park	76	67	71	67	281	12,571
John Young Kim	67	67	73	74	281	12,571
Xinyang Li	69	71	70	71	281	12,571
Seungyun Lee	73	68	72	68	281	12,571
Xiaoma Chen	70	72	67	72	281	12,571
Anthony Houston	69	68	75	69	281	12,571
Zihao Chen	74	70	70	67	281	12,571

Lushan Open

Lushan International Golf Club, Jiujiang City, Jiangxi

October 8-11

Par 35-35–70

purse, CN¥1,200,000

	SCORES				TOTAL	MONEY
Bryden Macpherson	68	68	68	68	272	CN¥216,000
T.K. Kim	69	69	69	67	274	105,600
Sejun Yoon	68	68	67	71	274	105,600
Rohan Blizard	67	70	70	68	275	52,800
Yi Keun Chang	70	67	67	71	275	52,800
Rak Hyun Cho	71	69	69	67	276	43,200
Ze-Cheng Dou	67	70	72	68	277	40,200
Sam Chien	67	69	70	72	278	37,200
Zheng Ouyang	70	72	68	69	279	32,400
Byungmin Cho	69	69	70	71	279	32,400
Huilin Zhang	72	69	68	70	279	32,400
John Young Kim	72	70	68	70	280	24,300
Alexander Kang	69	68	73	70	280	24,300
Justin Shin	70	73	70	67	280	24,300
Xin-Jun Zhang	69	70	65	76	280	24,300
Maxwell McCardle	72	69	70	70	281	19,800
Thomas Petersson	72	71	70	68	281	19,800
Alex Hawley	70	75	73	64	282	15,648
Jarin Todd	70	75	69	68	282	15,648
Raymond Beaufils	70	71	71	70	282	15,648
Peter Cooke	71	74	70	67	282	15,648
Sungi Yu	68	73	69	72	282	15,648

Chongqing Open

King Run Nanshan Golf Club, Chongqing
Par 36-36–72

October 15-18
purse, CN¥1,200,000

	SCORES				TOTAL	MONEY
Xin-Jun Zhang	69	74	65	65	273	CN¥216,000
Bryden Macpherson	71	70	68	68	277	129,600
Daniel Pearce	71	74	67	66	278	81,600
Rory Hie	72	71	70	68	281	49,600
Yi Cao	71	68	75	67	281	49,600
Justin Shin	72	73	65	71	281	49,600
Jack Munro	68	72	71	71	282	40,200
Byungmin Cho	74	72	68	69	283	36,000
Raymond Beaufils	71	71	67	74	283	36,000
Rohan Blizard	68	74	70	72	284	25,715
Junghwan Lee	74	72	67	71	284	25,715
John Young Kim	71	73	68	72	284	25,715
Yi Keun Chang	72	72	70	70	284	25,715
Benjamin Lein	76	71	69	68	284	25,715
Teemu Putkonen	72	70	73	69	284	25,715
Tian Yuan	71	70	72	71	284	25,715
Rak Hyun Cho	71	77	71	66	285	18,000
Jarin Todd	77	73	70	65	285	18,000
Thomas Petersson	67	71	76	71	285	18,000
Dinggen Chen	76	68	70	72	286	14,480
Seungyun Lee	72	70	68	76	286	14,480
Dong Su	74	72	71	69	286	14,480

Nine Dragons Open

Nine Dragons Golf Club, Jiaxing, Zhejiang
Par 36-36–72

November 19-22
purse, CN¥1,200,000

	SCORES				TOTAL	MONEY
Haimeng Chao	74	71	68	66	279	CN¥216,000
Ze-Cheng Dou	70	69	71	69	279	129,600
(Chao defeated Dou on first playoff hole.)						
James Gibellini	68	70	69	73	280	81,600
Jarin Todd	71	69	69	72	281	57,600
Bryden Macpherson	70	72	70	71	283	40,680
Wen-Yi Huang	68	69	72	74	283	40,680
Guangming Yang	70	71	73	69	283	40,680
Bin Yan	70	75	68	70	283	40,680
Yi Keun Chang	70	69	74	70	283	40,680
*Cheng Jin	70	74	72	69	285	
Tian Yuan	66	73	74	73	286	28,800
Justin Shin	72	72	68	74	286	28,800
Chao Li	68	76	72	70	286	28,800
Dinggen Chen	76	73	68	69	286	28,800
Alex Ching	75	77	70	65	287	21,000
Josh Geary	67	72	74	74	287	21,000
Wei-Tze Yeh	72	70	75	70	287	21,000
Jihoon Lee	68	72	72	75	287	21,000
Benjamin Lein	71	78	70	69	288	18,000
David Lutterus	72	75	72	70	289	16,800

Hainan Open

Dragon Valley Golf Course, Sanya, Hainan
Par 36-36–72; 7,131 yards

November 26-29
purse, CN¥1,200,000

	SCORES				TOTAL	MONEY
Huilin Zhang	75	73	71	67	286	CN¥216,000
Tian Yuan	73	76	69	69	287	129,600
Ze-Cheng Dou	69	76	70	73	288	69,600
Bryden Macpherson	72	75	72	69	288	69,600
Xin-Jun Zhang	72	71	73	73	289	45,600
Yi-Keun Chang	71	75	72	71	289	45,600
Jooneob Son	65	74	78	73	290	38,700
Jack Munro	73	76	72	69	290	38,700
Quincy Quek	73	75	70	73	291	32,400
Zheng Ouyang	70	72	74	75	291	32,400
Alex Ching	76	71	71	73	291	32,400
Shaocai He	72	75	72	73	292	23,520
Mu Hu	74	70	71	77	292	23,520
Hidetomo Sato	71	76	72	73	292	23,520
Christopher Brown	69	76	74	73	292	23,520
Gavin Flint	71	72	73	76	292	23,520
Benjamin Lein	75	74	69	75	293	18,000
Paul Imondi	74	78	70	71	293	18,000
Fei-Hao Yang	70	76	74	73	293	18,000
Peter Martin	77	75	71	71	294	14,480
Gunn Charoenkul	74	74	74	72	294	14,480
Rak-Hyun Cho	76	75	71	72	294	14,480

Capital Airline - HNA Real Estate Championship

Hillview Golf Club, Dongguan
Par 36-36–72; 6,890 yards

December 3-6
purse, CN¥1,200,000

	SCORES				TOTAL	MONEY
Ze-Yu He	67	65	68	70	270	CN¥216,000
Rohan Blizard	68	70	69	65	272	129,600
Ze-Cheng Dou	70	68	69	66	273	81,600
Xin-Jun Zhang	71	68	68	67	274	52,800
Yi Keun Chang	71	67	65	71	274	52,800
David Lutterus	75	67	68	65	275	43,200
Tsung Chieh Wang	73	69	66	68	276	38,700
Rak Hyun Cho	73	69	65	69	276	38,700
Chao Li	70	70	70	67	277	31,200
Teemu Putkonen	72	70	65	70	277	31,200
Paul Imondi	74	69	65	69	277	31,200
Scott Laycock	73	67	69	68	277	31,200
James Gibellini	68	71	70	69	278	23,200
Jack Munro	72	70	70	66	278	23,200
Jongheon Park	72	66	67	73	278	23,200
Mathew Perry	68	70	71	70	279	18,000
Tian Yuan	68	68	71	72	279	18,000
Benjamin Lein	71	72	68	68	279	18,000
Gavin Flint	67	69	71	72	279	18,000
Alexander Kang	69	72	70	68	279	18,000

Japan Tour

Token Homemate Cup

Token Tado Country Club, Nagoya, Mie
Par 35-36–71; 7,081 yards

April 16-19
purse, ¥130,000,000

	SCORES				TOTAL	MONEY
Michael Hendry	67	69	69	64	269	¥26,000,000
Kazuhiro Yamashita	68	70	66	66	270	13,000,000
Hyun-Woo Ryu	67	70	65	69	271	8,840,000
Daisuke Kataoka	67	69	68	68	272	6,240,000
Katsumasa Miyamoto	67	77	65	64	273	4,940,000
Toru Taniguchi	67	73	65	68	273	4,940,000
S.K. Ho	71	67	69	67	274	4,290,000
Tadahiro Takayama	69	72	70	64	275	3,545,750
Yoshinori Fujimoto	69	70	71	65	275	3,545,750
Atomu Shigenaga	69	70	68	68	275	3,545,750
Prayad Marksaeng	66	71	68	70	275	3,545,750
Kiyoshi Murota	69	71	70	66	276	2,626,000
Sang-Hyun Park	69	71	69	67	276	2,626,000
I.J. Jang	66	69	70	71	276	2,626,000
Mamo Osanai	71	69	70	67	277	2,041,000
Kyung-Tae Kim	70	72	68	67	277	2,041,000
Akio Sadakata	69	72	67	69	277	2,041,000
Seuk-Hyun Baek	67	74	67	69	277	2,041,000
Do-Hoon Kim	66	73	71	68	278	1,586,000
Jinichiro Kozuma	70	74	68	66	278	1,586,000
Ryutaro Nagano	69	71	70	68	278	1,586,000
Brad Kennedy	68	71	69	70	278	1,586,000
Tomohiro Kondo	66	74	71	68	279	1,071,777
K.T. Kwon	69	70	71	69	279	1,071,777
Kunihiro Kamii	69	70	71	69	279	1,071,777
Nobuhiro Masuda	71	70	69	69	279	1,071,777
Hyung-Sung Kim	72	72	70	65	279	1,071,777
Dong-Kyu Jang	75	69	65	70	279	1,071,777
Hiroo Kawai	66	72	70	71	279	1,071,777
Hiroyuki Fujita	71	70	68	70	279	1,071,777
Katsunori Kuwabara	70	71	66	72	279	1,071,777

The Crowns

Nagoya Golf Club, Wago Course, Togo, Aichi
Par 36-36–72; 6,545 yards

April 30-May 3
purse, ¥120,000,000

	SCORES				TOTAL	MONEY
I.J. Jang	66	69	68	67	270	¥24,000,000
Hideto Tanihara	71	70	65	68	274	8,640,000
Kazuhiro Yamashita	67	68	70	69	274	8,640,000
Tomohiro Kondo	72	66	67	69	274	8,640,000
Kurt Barnes	71	70	68	66	275	4,560,000
Taichi Teshima	68	66	71	70	275	4,560,000
Ashun Wu	70	69	67	70	276	3,960,000
Satoshi Kodaira	71	70	66	70	277	3,522,000

	SCORES				TOTAL	MONEY
Yoshitaka Takeya	70	68	68	71	277	3,522,000
Yuki Inamori	68	70	72	68	278	2,564,000
Kyung-Tae Kim	68	73	69	68	278	2,564,000
Kenichi Kuboya	73	68	68	69	278	2,564,000
Tadahiro Takayama	71	69	68	70	278	2,564,000
Kyoung-Hoon Lee	65	67	73	73	278	2,564,000
Shingo Katayama	72	65	66	75	278	2,564,000
Daisuke Kataoka	73	71	68	67	279	1,718,400
Prayad Marksaeng	70	74	68	67	279	1,718,400
Daisuke Maruyama	71	69	71	68	279	1,718,400
Brad Kennedy	74	69	68	68	279	1,718,400
J.B. Park	71	69	66	73	279	1,718,400
Tsuneyuki Nakajima	72	71	70	67	280	1,233,600
Hiroyuki Fujita	67	70	74	69	280	1,233,600
Brendan Jones	66	70	74	70	280	1,233,600
Hidemasa Hoshino	73	69	68	70	280	1,233,600
Wen-Chong Liang	68	68	71	73	280	1,233,600

Japan PGA Championship

Taiheiyo Club, Kohnan Course, Saitama
Par 36-35–71; 7,053 yards

May 14-17
purse, ¥150,000,000

	SCORES				TOTAL	MONEY
Adam Bland	64	68	64	72	268	¥30,000,000
Sang-Hee Lee	66	70	67	68	271	15,000,000
Yoshinori Fujimoto	66	69	69	68	272	10,200,000
Satoshi Tomiyama	67	68	70	68	273	5,625,000
Hyung-Sung Kim	68	71	66	68	273	5,625,000
Scott Strange	68	70	67	68	273	5,625,000
Shintaro Kobayashi	71	70	64	68	273	5,625,000
Masahiro Kawamura	69	66	67	71	273	5,625,000
Yuki Kono	70	67	69	68	274	4,080,000
Tatsunori Nukaga	68	71	67	68	274	4,080,000
Atomu Shigenaga	68	71	70	66	275	2,604,000
Ryuji Masaoka	70	70	67	68	275	2,604,000
Jay Choi	68	67	70	70	275	2,604,000
Min-Gyu Cho	67	69	69	70	275	2,604,000
Yoshinobu Tsukada	68	69	68	70	275	2,604,000
Juvic Pagunsan	68	69	68	70	275	2,604,000
Yusaku Miyazato	70	66	68	71	275	2,604,000
K.T. Kwon	63	71	69	72	275	2,604,000
Michael Hendry	69	67	67	72	275	2,604,000
Hiroshi Iwata	71	67	64	73	275	2,604,000
David Oh	72	68	68	68	276	1,710,000
Wen-Chong Liang	70	68	69	69	276	1,710,000
Hidemasa Hoshino	69	68	71	69	277	1,267,500
Hideto Tanihara	68	71	69	69	277	1,267,500
Ryuichi Oda	73	67	67	70	277	1,267,500
Tadahiro Takayama	68	71	68	70	277	1,267,500
Yuki Inamori	69	67	70	71	277	1,267,500
Hiroo Kawai	67	68	70	72	277	1,267,500
Satoshi Kodaira	72	68	65	72	277	1,267,500
Shigeru Nonaka	68	67	68	74	277	1,267,500

Kansai Open

Meishin Yokaichi Country Club, Shiga
Par 36-35–71; 6,900 yards

May 21-24
purse, ¥70,000,000

	SCORES				TOTAL	MONEY
Daisuke Kataoka	66	67	67	67	267	¥14,000,000
Brad Kennedy	70	66	67	67	270	7,000,000
Yosuke Tsukada	69	67	72	63	271	4,060,000
Won-Joon Lee	68	65	68	70	271	4,060,000
Akio Sadakata	73	68	67	64	272	2,441,250
Tomohiro Kondo	69	69	68	66	272	2,441,250
Juvic Pagunsan	69	66	71	66	272	2,441,250
Hiroyuki Fujita	68	67	69	68	272	2,441,250
Yoshinori Fujimoto	68	66	69	70	273	1,834,000
Toshinori Muto	71	66	66	70	273	1,834,000
Kazuhiro Yamashita	70	64	65	74	273	1,834,000
Yoshinobu Tsukada	76	66	66	66	274	1,361,500
Yusaku Miyazato	70	68	70	66	274	1,361,500
Young-Han Song	72	67	64	71	274	1,361,500
Hiroshi Iwata	69	66	65	74	274	1,361,500
I.J. Jang	71	71	65	68	275	1,099,000
Koumei Oda	70	71	64	70	275	1,099,000
Angelo Que	70	70	70	66	276	910,000
*Shohei Hasegawa	71	70	69	66	276	
Adam Bland	74	67	69	66	276	910,000
Mikumu Horikawa	73	69	66	68	276	910,000
Wen-Chong Liang	68	66	68	74	276	910,000
Futoshi Fujita	68	70	69	70	277	770,000
Kodai Ichihara	71	71	67	69	278	606,000
Scott Strange	68	73	68	69	278	606,000
Hidemasa Hoshino	72	67	70	69	278	606,000
Ryutaro Nagano	70	70	70	68	278	606,000
Prayad Marksaeng	69	70	69	70	278	606,000
Masaki Nakanishi	76	65	67	70	278	606,000
Atomu Shigenaga	71	68	67	72	278	606,000

Gateway to the Open Mizuno Open

JFE Setonaikai Golf Club, Kasaoka, Okayama
Par 36-36–72; 7,415 yards

May 28-31
purse, ¥100,000,000

	SCORES				TOTAL	MONEY
Taichi Teshima	69	69	66	69	273	¥20,000,000
Scott Strange	69	67	68	71	275	10,000,000
Shinji Tomimura	72	71	67	67	277	5,800,000
Tadahiro Takayama	69	71	67	70	277	5,800,000
Shugo Imahira	67	69	73	69	278	4,000,000
Won-Joon Lee	68	72	69	70	279	3,450,000
Prayad Marksaeng	70	70	67	72	279	3,450,000
Kyung-Tae Kim	68	69	72	71	280	3,050,000
Wen-Chong Liang	70	70	73	68	281	2,620,000
Brendan Jones	71	67	71	72	281	2,620,000
Sang-Hyun Park	68	70	70	73	281	2,620,000
Ryutaro Nagano	70	70	74	68	282	2,120,000
Hideto Tanihara	70	70	70	72	282	2,120,000
Toru Taniguchi	66	76	72	69	283	1,442,222
Koumei Oda	72	70	72	69	283	1,442,222
Michael Hendry	63	73	77	70	283	1,442,222
Shinichi Yokota	70	66	75	72	283	1,442,222

	SCORES				TOTAL	MONEY
Chan Kim	71	72	68	72	283	1,442,222
Masaya Tomida	69	72	70	72	283	1,442,222
Kyong-Jun Moon	72	70	69	72	283	1,442,222
Ryuichi Oda	71	67	72	73	283	1,442,222
Seung-Hyuk Kim	70	72	67	74	283	1,442,222
Ryuji Masaoka	70	69	74	71	284	824,444
Yoshitaka Takeya	71	71	71	71	284	824,444
Kyoung-Hoon Lee	70	72	70	72	284	824,444
Dong-Kyu Jang	73	70	69	72	284	824,444
Hyung-Sung Kim	66	74	71	73	284	824,444
Shih-Chang Chan	71	73	71	69	284	824,444
Yui Ueda	70	74	72	68	284	824,444
Kiyoshi Miyazato	66	71	73	74	284	824,444
Mikumu Horikawa	72	68	70	74	284	824,444

Japan Golf Tour Championship

Shishido Hills Country Club, West Course, Kasama, Ibaraki
Par 36-35–71; 7,326 yards

June 4-7
purse, ¥150,000,000

	SCORES				TOTAL	MONEY
Wen-Chong Liang	67	68	65	70	270	¥30,000,000
Young-Han Song	68	68	70	69	275	10,800,000
Brad Kennedy	70	67	68	70	275	10,800,000
Ryutaro Nagano	68	71	67	69	275	10,800,000
Koumei Oda	72	68	69	70	279	5,700,000
Satoshi Kodaira	69	70	70	70	279	5,700,000
Mikumu Horikawa	69	73	70	69	281	4,950,000
Ryuichi Oda	76	67	74	65	282	4,245,000
Yosuke Tsukada	79	66	70	67	282	4,245,000
Nobuhiro Masuda	71	74	69	68	282	4,245,000
Shunsuke Sonoda	73	70	71	69	283	3,330,000
Yusaku Miyazato	75	70	69	69	283	3,330,000
Katsumasa Miyamoto	72	69	69	73	283	3,330,000
I.J. Jang	68	70	75	71	284	2,655,000
Hyun-Woo Ryu	71	69	70	74	284	2,655,000
Shingo Katayama	74	71	72	68	285	1,961,250
Hidemasa Hoshino	74	71	72	68	285	1,961,250
Sang-Hyun Park	70	71	75	69	285	1,961,250
Shinichi Yokota	74	70	72	69	285	1,961,250
Shugo Imahira	70	74	72	69	285	1,961,250
K.T. Kwon	71	71	72	71	285	1,961,250
J.B. Park	72	73	69	71	285	1,961,250
Kurt Barnes	68	72	70	75	285	1,961,250
Y.E. Yang	69	71	76	70	286	1,350,000
Azuma Yano	70	73	73	70	286	1,350,000
Katsufumi Okino	72	69	72	73	286	1,350,000

Singha Corporation Thailand Open

See OneAsia Tour section.

ISPS Handa Global Cup

Vintage Golf Club, Hokuto, Yamanashi
Par 35-36–71; 6,774 yards

June 25-28
purse, ¥100,000,000

	SCORES				TOTAL	MONEY
Toshinori Muto	68	68	66	68	270	¥20,000,000
Angelo Que	70	68	68	64	270	10,000,000
(Muto defeated Que on second playoff hole.)						
Hyung-Sung Kim	66	71	67	67	271	6,800,000
David Smail	70	69	68	65	272	3,925,000
Ippei Koike	68	68	67	69	272	3,925,000
Ian Poulter	67	68	68	69	272	3,925,000
Hyun-Woo Ryu	69	67	66	70	272	3,925,000
Min-Gyu Cho	68	70	70	65	273	2,935,000
John Senden	69	71	66	67	273	2,935,000
Ho-Sung Choi	70	67	71	66	274	2,136,666
Yoshinori Fujimoto	68	68	70	68	274	2,136,666
Katsumasa Miyamoto	70	69	67	68	274	2,136,666
Charl Schwartzel	70	68	67	69	274	2,136,666
Dong-Kyu Jang	69	69	67	69	274	2,136,666
Toru Taniguchi	71	70	64	69	274	2,136,666
Ryutaro Nagano	69	68	72	66	275	1,475,000
Namchok Tantipokhakul	71	69	68	67	275	1,475,000
Sang-Hyun Park	71	69	68	67	275	1,475,000
Azuma Yano	66	66	70	73	275	1,475,000
Soon-Sang Hong	70	69	71	66	276	960,000
Ashun Wu	67	71	70	68	276	960,000
Taichi Teshima	66	72	70	68	276	960,000
Hidemasa Hoshino	70	69	69	68	276	960,000
Shugo Imahira	67	69	71	69	276	960,000
K.T. Kwon	70	72	65	69	276	960,000
Yoshitaka Takeya	70	69	68	69	276	960,000
Ryuji Masaoka	68	70	68	70	276	960,000
Kyung-Tae Kim	66	73	67	70	276	960,000
Atomu Shigenaga	70	70	66	70	276	960,000

Shigeo Nagashima Invitational

North Country Golf Club, Chitose, Hokkaido
Par 36-36–72; 7,167 yards

July 2-5
purse, ¥150,000,000

	SCORES				TOTAL	MONEY
Hiroshi Iwata	70	69	67	66	272	¥30,000,000
Shugo Imahira	69	67	70	67	273	15,000,000
Hyung-Sung Kim	66	71	67	71	275	8,700,000
J.B. Park	65	68	71	71	275	8,700,000
Yusaku Miyazato	69	71	66	70	276	6,000,000
Shingo Katayama	70	71	68	68	277	4,788,750
Kyung-Tae Kim	66	71	71	69	277	4,788,750
Yoshinori Fujimoto	71	68	69	69	277	4,788,750
Koumei Oda	68	67	72	70	277	4,788,750
Yuki Inamori	70	71	70	67	278	3,630,000
Ryutaro Nagano	70	68	72	68	278	3,630,000
Min-Gyu Cho	68	71	68	71	278	3,630,000
I.J. Jang	71	69	71	68	279	2,692,500
Hiroyuki Fujita	70	68	71	70	279	2,692,500
Satoshi Kodaira	67	70	70	72	279	2,692,500
Daisuke Kataoka	73	66	68	72	279	2,692,500
Shintaro Kai	72	70	69	69	280	2,077,500

	SCORES				TOTAL	MONEY
Adam Bland	69	68	74	69	280	2,077,500
Shinichi Yokota	69	68	71	72	280	2,077,500
Yuta Ikeda	69	69	68	74	280	2,077,500
Kazuhiro Yamashita	71	69	72	69	281	1,425,000
Kurt Barnes	69	72	71	69	281	1,425,000
Kyoung-Hoon Lee	70	72	67	72	281	1,425,000
Hyun-Woo Ryu	68	71	70	72	281	1,425,000
Brad Kennedy	71	71	71	68	281	1,425,000
Hideto Tanihara	68	73	72	68	281	1,425,000
Young-Han Song	71	69	68	73	281	1,425,000
Sang-Hyun Park	67	72	68	74	281	1,425,000

Musee Platinum Open

Japan Memorial Golf Club, Miki, Hyogo
Par 35-36–71; 7,012 yards

July 9-12
purse, ¥100,000,000

	SCORES				TOTAL	MONEY
Kyung-Tae Kim	68	67	63	66	264	¥20,000,000
Min-Gyu Cho	69	60	72	64	265	7,200,000
Brad Kennedy	66	65	65	69	265	7,200,000
J.B. Park	63	66	65	71	265	7,200,000
Yuta Ikeda	65	66	67	68	266	4,000,000
Koumei Oda	72	65	63	67	267	3,450,000
Sang-Hyun Park	70	63	66	68	267	3,450,000
Matthew Griffin	69	64	68	68	269	2,935,000
Young-Han Song	68	67	66	68	269	2,935,000
Yoshikazu Haku	69	68	67	66	270	2,520,000
Michael Hendry	68	65	64	73	270	2,520,000
Toshinori Muto	70	69	67	65	271	1,820,000
Hyun-Woo Ryu	67	68	69	67	271	1,820,000
Kyoung-Hoon Lee	67	69	67	68	271	1,820,000
Prayad Marksaeng	66	67	69	69	271	1,820,000
Azuma Yano	69	64	69	69	271	1,820,000
Ippei Koike	64	68	69	70	271	1,820,000
Toru Taniguchi	69	67	66	70	272	1,300,000
Yusaku Miyazato	66	71	65	70	272	1,300,000
Akio Sadakata	66	67	68	71	272	1,300,000
Shunsuke Sonoda	67	66	66	73	272	1,300,000
Masamichi Uehira	70	69	65	69	273	1,020,000
Jay Choi	64	69	71	69	273	1,020,000
Kyong-Jun Moon	67	72	65	69	273	1,020,000
Shingo Katayama	72	67	66	69	274	840,000
Daisuke Kataoka	68	68	69	69	274	840,000
Won-Joon Lee	69	68	68	69	274	840,000
Ryuji Masaoka	67	68	67	72	274	840,000

Dunlop Srixon Fukushima Open

Grandee Nasushirakawa Golf Club, Nishigo, Fukushima
Par 36-36–72; 6,954 yards

July 23-26
purse, ¥50,000,000

	SCORES				TOTAL	MONEY
Prayad Marksaeng	69	65	67	63	264	¥10,000,000
Young-Han Song	68	65	66	66	265	5,000,000
Yusaku Miyazato	72	64	66	66	268	2,900,000
Dong-Kyu Jang	70	66	65	67	268	2,900,000

	SCORES				TOTAL	MONEY
Akio Sadakata	67	67	69	66	269	1,743,750
Satoshi Kodaira	67	66	69	67	269	1,743,750
Hiroyuki Fujita	70	67	64	68	269	1,743,750
S.K. Ho	66	67	67	69	269	1,743,750
Hideki Matsuyama	70	67	69	64	270	1,360,000
Kyung-Tae Kim	70	64	67	69	270	1,360,000
Satoshi Tomiyama	69	69	66	67	271	1,160,000
Ippei Koike	68	69	66	68	271	1,160,000
David Oh	70	68	68	66	272	897,500
Matthew Griffin	70	67	69	66	272	897,500
Sung-Youl Kwon	68	67	70	67	272	897,500
Ryuko Tokimatsu	67	71	66	68	272	897,500
Jin-Jae Byun	69	68	68	68	273	713,333
Yosuke Asaji	70	66	67	70	273	713,333
Kiyoshi Murota	66	69	68	70	273	713,333
Kazuhiro Yamashita	67	69	70	68	274	550,000
Shugo Imahira	67	69	68	70	274	550,000
Koumei Oda	67	67	70	70	274	550,000
Hyung-Sung Kim	71	68	65	70	274	550,000
Hidemasa Hoshino	66	71	66	71	274	550,000
Hiroyuki Nagamatsu	70	69	68	68	275	390,000
Masamichi Uehira	69	71	66	69	275	390,000
Atomu Shigenaga	69	71	67	68	275	390,000
Kazuki Ishiwata	69	69	67	70	275	390,000
David Smail	67	69	72	67	275	390,000
Katsumasa Miyamoto	72	65	67	71	275	390,000
J.B. Park	72	68	70	65	275	390,000

RIZAP KBC Augusta

Keya Golf Club, Shima, Fukuoka
Par 36-36–72; 7,151 yards

August 27-30
purse, ¥110,000,000

	SCORES				TOTAL	MONEY
Yuta Ikeda	66	65	71	66	268	¥22,000,000
Koumei Oda	68	66	70	69	273	11,000,000
Brad Kennedy	67	67	72	68	274	6,380,000
Atomu Shigenaga	70	70	66	68	274	6,380,000
Yosuke Tsukada	72	71	68	64	275	3,836,250
Daisuke Kataoka	67	68	71	69	275	3,836,250
K.T. Kwon	66	72	67	70	275	3,836,250
Keiichiro Fukabori	68	67	68	72	275	3,836,250
Thanyakon Khrongpha	68	73	69	66	276	2,772,000
Yoshitaka Takeya	70	69	70	67	276	2,772,000
Hiroyuki Fujita	71	68	67	70	276	2,772,000
Kaname Yokoo	70	68	67	71	276	2,772,000
Toru Taniguchi	70	67	72	68	277	1,914,000
Satoshi Kodaira	68	70	71	68	277	1,914,000
Ippei Koike	71	67	70	69	277	1,914,000
I.J. Jang	69	68	69	71	277	1,914,000
Tomoyo Ikemura	68	67	68	74	277	1,914,000
Shugo Imahira	69	72	70	67	278	1,342,000
Tadahiro Takayama	68	74	70	66	278	1,342,000
Taichi Teshima	69	67	74	68	278	1,342,000
Kyoung-Hoon Lee	69	69	70	70	278	1,342,000
Ashun Wu	68	69	71	70	278	1,342,000
Hiroshi Iwata	72	69	66	71	278	1,342,000
Akio Sadakata	72	67	72	68	279	902,000
Prayad Marksaeng	74	66	69	70	279	902,000
Jung-Gon Hwang	71	66	71	71	279	902,000

	SCORES				TOTAL	MONEY
Young-Han Song	69	70	68	72	279	902,000
Yuki Inamori	68	69	69	73	279	902,000
Scott Strange	68	72	66	73	279	902,000
Yasuki Hiramoto	69	70	66	74	279	902,000

Fujisankei Classic

Fujizakura Country Club, Fujikawaguchiko, Yamanashi
Par 35-36–71; 7,471 yards

September 3-6
purse, ¥110,000,000

	SCORES				TOTAL	MONEY
Kyung-Tae Kim	70	64	68	73	275	¥22,000,000
Kyoung-Hoon Lee	64	74	70	68	276	11,000,000
Masahiro Kawamura	70	67	70	70	277	7,480,000
Hiroshi Iwata	70	74	69	65	278	4,840,000
Shunsuke Sonoda	71	70	71	66	278	4,840,000
Yasuki Hiramoto	70	69	72	68	279	3,648,333
Matthew Griffin	71	68	70	70	279	3,648,333
Brad Kennedy	69	70	67	73	279	3,648,333
Ippei Koike	74	68	68	70	280	2,992,000
S.K. Ho	71	69	69	71	280	2,992,000
I.J. Jang	69	75	70	67	281	2,244,000
Tatsunori Nukaga	68	73	71	69	281	2,244,000
Young-Han Song	69	72	71	69	281	2,244,000
Min-Gyu Cho	72	70	69	70	281	2,244,000
Kodai Ichihara	70	68	71	72	281	2,244,000
Dong-Kyu Jang	73	69	70	70	282	1,727,000
Sang-Hyun Park	73	69	70	70	282	1,727,000
Shingo Katayama	73	72	70	68	283	1,474,000
Shugo Imahira	74	70	70	69	283	1,474,000
Brendan Jones	69	75	68	71	283	1,474,000
Adam Bland	76	68	70	70	284	1,130,800
Katsumasa Miyamoto	75	69	72	68	284	1,130,800
Seuk-Hyun Baek	69	73	71	71	284	1,130,800
Ryutaro Nagano	72	68	71	73	284	1,130,800
Keiichiro Fukabori	69	71	71	73	284	1,130,800

ANA Open

Sapporo Golf Club, Wattsu Course, Kitahiroshima, Hokkaido
Par 36-36–72; 7,063 yards

September 17-20
purse, ¥110,000,000

	SCORES				TOTAL	MONEY
Ryo Ishikawa	68	68	67	69	272	¥22,000,000
Yusaku Miyazato	71	67	69	67	274	11,000,000
Kyoung-Hoon Lee	69	69	69	68	275	7,480,000
Katsumasa Miyamoto	69	70	67	70	276	5,280,000
Michio Matsumura	68	72	71	66	277	4,400,000
Taichi Teshima	73	71	67	67	278	3,385,800
Yuta Ikeda	67	70	73	68	278	3,385,800
Toru Taniguchi	68	68	71	71	278	3,385,800
Koumei Oda	71	71	61	75	278	3,385,800
Daisuke Kataoka	70	70	66	72	278	3,385,800
I.J. Jang	70	73	70	66	279	2,332,000
Shingo Katayama	72	68	68	71	279	2,332,000
Prayad Marksaeng	66	66	75	72	279	2,332,000
Kyong-Jun Moon	71	66	70	72	279	2,332,000

	SCORES				TOTAL	MONEY
Hyun-Woo Ryu	69	71	68	72	280	1,892,000
Satoshi Kodaira	74	70	69	68	281	1,483,428
Hidemasa Hoshino	73	68	71	69	281	1,483,428
Kiyoshi Miyazato	70	72	70	69	281	1,483,428
Jay Choi	70	73	71	67	281	1,483,428
Yuki Inamori	70	72	69	70	281	1,483,428
Tetsuji Hiratsuka	69	68	73	71	281	1,483,428
Hiroo Kawai	71	71	68	71	281	1,483,428
Kurt Barnes	71	73	69	69	282	885,500
Katsufumi Okino	71	72	70	69	282	885,500
Yuki Kono	69	74	69	70	282	885,500
Seuk-Hyun Baek	72	71	69	70	282	885,500
Ryuichi Oda	70	69	72	71	282	885,500
Yasuki Hiramoto	72	67	72	71	282	885,500
Toshinori Muto	67	77	70	68	282	885,500
Shintaro Kai	71	69	70	72	282	885,500
Yoshinori Fujimoto	72	69	69	72	282	885,500
Satoshi Tomiyama	70	68	68	76	282	885,500

Asia-Pacific Diamond Cup

Otone Country Club, West Course, Ibaraki
Par 35-35–70; 7,101 yards

September 24-27
purse, ¥150,000,000

	SCORES				TOTAL	MONEY
Kyung-Tae Kim	67	69	67	68	271	¥30,000,000
Toshinori Muto	69	68	70	67	274	14,025,000
Yuta Ikeda	68	70	67	69	274	14,025,000
Michio Matsumura	70	71	69	65	275	7,500,000
Tadahiro Takayama	72	71	66	67	276	5,775,000
Yuki Inamori	73	65	69	69	276	5,775,000
Shingo Katayama	71	68	72	66	277	3,637,500
Hideto Tanihara	69	68	73	67	277	3,637,500
Daisuke Kataoka	69	70	70	68	277	3,637,500
Satoshi Kodaira	71	68	66	72	277	3,637,500
Shugo Imahira	70	68	70	70	278	2,350,000
Yusaku Miyazato	70	70	68	70	278	2,350,000
Prayad Marksaeng	67	68	72	71	278	2,350,000
Javi Colomo	71	71	69	68	279	1,770,000
Atomu Shigenaga	70	70	70	69	279	1,770,000
Tomohiro Kondo	68	72	69	70	279	1,770,000
Brendan Jones	72	69	72	67	280	1,315,500
Kyoung-Hoon Lee	70	73	70	67	280	1,315,500
I.J. Jang	71	69	71	69	280	1,315,500
Toru Taniguchi	69	74	68	69	280	1,315,500
Paul Petterson	70	72	69	69	280	1,315,500
Shunsuke Sonoda	70	67	73	70	280	1,315,500
Lionel Weber	69	71	69	71	280	1,315,500
Keiichiro Fukabori	68	72	69	71	280	1,315,500
Scott Barr	70	71	68	71	280	1,315,500
Scott Strange	64	74	68	74	280	1,315,500

Top Cup Tokai Classic

Miyoshi Country Club, West Course, Miyoshi, Aichi
Par 36-36–72; 7,315 yards

October 1-4
purse, ¥110,000,000

	SCORES				TOTAL	MONEY
Hyung-Sung Kim	69	72	69	66	276	¥22,000,000
Shingo Katayama	65	74	70	67	276	11,000,000
(Kim defeated Katayama on second playoff hole.)						
Sang-Hyun Park	67	69	73	69	278	6,380,000
Yuta Ikeda	70	70	68	70	278	6,380,000
Ryuichi Oda	68	73	69	69	279	4,400,000
Masahiro Kawamura	71	69	74	66	280	3,648,333
Ryo Ishikawa	68	70	71	71	280	3,648,333
Seuk-Hyun Baek	69	69	70	72	280	3,648,333
Tadahiro Takayama	74	68	68	71	281	3,102,000
Yusaku Miyazato	72	73	70	67	282	2,772,000
Kyung-Tae Kim	70	73	71	68	282	2,772,000
Prayad Marksaeng	69	70	72	72	283	2,442,000
Toshinori Muto	73	73	69	69	284	2,112,000
Tomohiro Kondo	72	73	69	70	284	2,112,000
Brendan Jones	72	73	70	70	285	1,676,400
Yoshinori Fujimoto	71	74	70	70	285	1,676,400
Shugo Imahira	74	71	69	71	285	1,676,400
Daisuke Kataoka	71	69	72	73	285	1,676,400
Keiichiro Fukabori	68	74	71	72	285	1,676,400
Won-Joon Lee	70	74	73	69	286	1,342,000
Hideto Tanihara	72	72	71	71	286	1,342,000
Hiroyuki Fujita	72	73	73	69	287	1,122,000
Adam Bland	74	71	71	71	287	1,122,000
Atomu Shigenaga	68	73	71	75	287	1,122,000
Yuki Inamori	75	73	72	68	288	946,000
Akio Sadakata	71	74	70	73	288	946,000
David Oh	73	73	69	73	288	946,000

Honma TourWorld Cup at Trophia Golf

Ishioka Golf Club, Ibaraki
Par 36-35–71; 7,071 yards

October 8-11
purse, ¥100,000,000

	SCORES				TOTAL	MONEY
Kyoung-Hoon Lee	71	65	65	67	268	¥20,000,000
Ryuichi Oda	71	70	65	63	269	6,400,000
Ashun Wu	69	67	68	65	269	6,400,000
Taichi Teshima	69	69	64	67	269	6,400,000
Tomohiro Kondo	70	62	67	70	269	6,400,000
Wen-Chong Liang	69	69	65	67	270	3,450,000
Yusaku Miyazato	69	68	64	69	270	3,450,000
Yuta Ikeda	69	68	69	65	271	2,830,000
Jung-Gon Hwang	70	64	71	66	271	2,830,000
Tadahiro Takayama	69	66	68	68	271	2,830,000
Katsufumi Okino	71	70	67	64	272	2,120,000
Ryutaro Nagano	68	67	69	68	272	2,120,000
Keiichiro Fukabori	69	68	68	67	272	2,120,000
Yuki Inamori	71	66	67	68	272	2,120,000
Hiroyuki Fujita	71	72	64	66	273	1,670,000
Yoshinori Fujimoto	72	71	64	66	273	1,670,000
Azuma Yano	70	74	63	67	274	1,520,000
Koki Shiomi	68	70	70	67	275	1,380,000
Ippei Koike	70	72	65	68	275	1,380,000

	SCORES				TOTAL	MONEY
Michio Matsumura	72	71	66	67	276	1,140,000
I.J. Jang	68	67	72	69	276	1,140,000
Satoshi Tomiyama	69	72	67	68	276	1,140,000
Yoshitaka Takeya	72	65	67	72	276	1,140,000
Shintaro Kobayashi	73	68	70	66	277	820,000
Atomu Shigenaga	75	68	68	66	277	820,000
Hideto Tanihara	72	72	66	67	277	820,000
Mikumu Horikawa	70	68	72	67	277	820,000
Kunihiro Kamii	71	72	66	68	277	820,000
Scott Strange	70	69	68	70	277	820,000
Yasuki Hiramoto	67	73	66	71	277	820,000

Japan Open Championship

Rokko Kokusai Golf Club, East Course, Kobe, Hyogo
Par 36-36–72; 7,394 yards

October 15-18
purse, ¥200,000,000

	SCORES				TOTAL	MONEY
Satoshi Kodaira	71	62	70	72	275	¥40,000,000
Yuta Ikeda	68	68	69	71	276	22,000,000
Young-Han Song	69	69	69	71	278	15,400,000
Jung-Gon Hwang	68	68	72	72	280	10,000,000
Prayad Marksaeng	70	70	72	69	281	8,400,000
Shingo Katayama	69	71	73	69	282	7,000,000
Adam Scott	70	70	74	69	283	5,200,000
Hideto Tanihara	69	71	70	73	283	5,200,000
Kyung-Tae Kim	70	72	69	72	283	5,200,000
Kyoung-Hoon Lee	69	73	70	72	284	3,800,000
*Takumi Kanaya	69	66	74	76	285	
Adam Bland	69	73	74	70	286	3,133,333
Kodai Ichihara	70	74	69	73	286	3,133,333
Ryutaro Nagano	67	70	72	77	286	3,133,333
David Oh	72	72	75	68	287	2,295,000
J.B. Park	70	71	75	71	287	2,295,000
Angelo Que	68	74	74	71	287	2,295,000
Won-Joon Lee	74	68	73	72	287	2,295,000
Hiroyuki Fujita	70	72	76	70	288	1,824,000
Sang-Hyun Park	69	72	76	71	288	1,824,000
Taichi Nabetani	74	68	73	73	288	1,824,000
*Junya Kameshiro	72	71	72	73	288	
Ryuichi Oda	73	71	71	73	288	1,824,000
Azuma Yano	70	74	70	74	288	1,824,000
Yoshinori Fujimoto	70	76	76	67	289	1,540,000
Toru Suzuki	72	72	73	72	289	1,540,000
I.J. Jang	70	75	72	72	289	1,540,000
Koumei Oda	68	74	72	75	289	1,540,000
Juvic Pagunsan	66	74	73	76	289	1,540,000
Hyun-Woo Ryu	72	68	72	77	289	1,540,000

Bridgestone Open

Sodegaura Country Club, Chiba
Par 35-36–71; 7,119 yards

October 22-25
purse, ¥150,000,000

	SCORES				TOTAL	MONEY
Michio Matsumura	69	68	71	67	275	¥30,000,000
Kyung-Tae Kim	72	68	71	66	277	9,600,000

	SCORES				TOTAL	MONEY
Adam Bland	72	69	67	69	277	9,600,000
Yuki Inamori	68	66	71	72	277	9,600,000
Mikumu Horikawa	64	71	69	73	277	9,600,000
Shintaro Kobayashi	70	66	71	72	279	5,175,000
Hideto Tanihara	70	67	69	73	279	5,175,000
Yusaku Miyazato	72	71	67	71	281	4,245,000
David Oh	68	68	73	72	281	4,245,000
Katsumasa Miyamoto	71	69	69	72	281	4,245,000
I.J. Jang	72	68	74	68	282	3,330,000
Hyun-Woo Ryu	72	69	70	71	282	3,330,000
Jung-Gon Hwang	67	71	72	72	282	3,330,000
Ryuichi Oda	68	74	70	71	283	2,360,000
Koumei Oda	70	70	72	71	283	2,360,000
Kunihiro Kamii	68	72	69	74	283	2,360,000
Yoshinori Fujimoto	71	66	72	74	283	2,360,000
Yoshitaka Takeya	67	69	72	75	283	2,360,000
Shingo Katayama	70	67	69	77	283	2,360,000
Yosuke Tsukada	71	68	72	73	284	1,710,000
Hiroyuki Fujita	70	68	72	74	284	1,710,000
Min-Gyu Cho	70	70	70	74	284	1,710,000
Won-Joon Lee	67	68	74	75	284	1,710,000
Yoshinobu Tsukada	68	71	73	73	285	1,290,000
Kyong-Jun Moon	69	74	68	74	285	1,290,000
Sang-Hee Lee	70	69	71	75	285	1,290,000
Do-Hoon Kim	70	69	71	75	285	1,290,000
Tomohiro Kondo	65	69	74	77	285	1,290,000

Mynavi ABC Championship

ABC Golf Club, Kato, Hyogo
Par 35-36–71; 7,130 yards

October 29-November 1
purse, ¥150,000,000

	SCORES				TOTAL	MONEY
Kyung-Tae Kim	66	69	68	69	272	¥30,000,000
Katsumasa Miyamoto	69	71	69	65	274	10,800,000
Daisuke Kataoka	70	67	71	66	274	10,800,000
Won-Joon Lee	70	69	66	69	274	10,800,000
Dong-Kyu Jang	67	71	67	70	275	5,700,000
Hyun-Woo Ryu	67	70	66	72	275	5,700,000
Kyoung-Hoon Lee	69	70	66	71	276	4,950,000
Brendan Jones	70	73	68	66	277	4,402,500
Yoshinori Fujimoto	70	67	71	69	277	4,402,500
Jung-Gon Hwang	67	71	71	69	278	3,930,000
I.J. Jang	75	67	71	66	279	3,180,000
Ashun Wu	68	72	71	68	279	3,180,000
Toshinori Muto	69	70	71	69	279	3,180,000
Hyung-Sung Kim	72	70	67	70	279	3,180,000
Taichi Teshima	69	69	74	68	280	2,430,000
Akio Sadakata	70	70	70	70	280	2,430,000
Toru Taniguchi	69	70	69	72	280	2,430,000
Shintaro Kobayashi	71	71	72	67	281	1,950,000
Kurt Barnes	69	71	71	70	281	1,950,000
David Smail	72	69	69	71	281	1,950,000
Hiroyuki Fujita	73	70	67	71	281	1,950,000
Kodai Ichihara	73	73	68	68	282	1,650,000
Koumei Oda	73	72	69	69	283	1,430,000
Hidemasa Hoshino	72	70	72	69	283	1,430,000
Ho-Sung Choi	72	67	70	74	283	1,430,000

Heiwa PGM Championship

Sohbu Country Club, Sohbu, Chiba
Par 35-35–70; 7,123 yards

November 5-8
purse, ¥200,000,000

	SCORES				TOTAL	MONEY
Hideto Tanihara	67	67	66	69	269	¥40,000,000
Yoshinori Fujimoto	68	68	66	69	271	20,000,000
Michio Matsumura	69	66	68	70	273	13,600,000
Ho-Sung Choi	63	70	69	72	274	8,800,000
Kodai Ichihara	66	69	67	72	274	8,800,000
Ryutaro Nagano	64	70	74	67	275	6,156,000
Yuta Ikeda	68	68	72	67	275	6,156,000
Young-Han Song	67	70	69	69	275	6,156,000
Hiroyuki Fujita	67	69	70	69	275	6,156,000
Shingo Katayama	70	66	69	70	275	6,156,000
David Oh	66	72	70	68	276	3,811,428
Akio Sadakata	70	68	69	69	276	3,811,428
Dong-Kyu Jang	67	69	70	70	276	3,811,428
Yusaku Miyazato	70	66	70	70	276	3,811,428
Koumei Oda	66	72	68	70	276	3,811,428
Yoshitaka Takeya	66	71	69	70	276	3,811,428
Satoshi Tomiyama	68	66	70	72	276	3,811,428
Daisuke Kataoka	71	68	70	68	277	2,760,000
Tomohiro Kondo	73	66	68	70	277	2,760,000
Tadahiro Takayama	69	70	72	67	278	2,440,000
Hyun-Woo Ryu	71	68	70	69	278	2,440,000
Atomu Shigenaga	68	70	73	68	279	1,928,000
Mikumu Horikawa	67	72	71	69	279	1,928,000
Thanyakon Khrongpha	67	70	72	70	279	1,928,000
Brad Kennedy	73	69	66	71	279	1,928,000
Prayad Marksaeng	70	69	69	71	279	1,928,000

Mitsui Sumitomo VISA Taiheiyo Masters

Taiheiyo Club, Gotemba Course, Gotemba, Shizuoka
Par 36-36–72; 7,246 yards
(Final round cancelled—fog.)

November 12-15
purse, ¥150,000,000

	SCORES			TOTAL	MONEY
Shingo Katayama	64	68	70	202	¥22,500,000
Thanyakon Khrongpha	65	67	71	203	11,250,000
Bubba Watson	63	69	72	204	7,650,000
Yuki Inamori	68	70	67	205	4,415,625
I.J. Jang	70	67	68	205	4,415,625
Toshinori Muto	67	66	72	205	4,415,625
Yusaku Miyazato	66	67	72	205	4,415,625
Yoshinori Fujimoto	69	70	67	206	3,068,437
Jung-Gon Hwang	73	66	67	206	3,068,437
Koumei Oda	68	70	68	206	3,068,437
Sang-Hyun Park	69	66	71	206	3,068,437
Kurt Barnes	69	71	67	207	2,385,000
Prayad Marksaeng	67	69	71	207	2,385,000
Young-Han Song	71	68	69	208	1,935,000
Tomohiro Kondo	68	73	67	208	1,935,000
Hiroyuki Fujita	71	70	67	208	1,935,000
Michio Matsumura	70	70	69	209	1,420,714
Shigeru Nonaka	71	69	69	209	1,420,714
Kodai Ichihara	72	68	69	209	1,420,714
Dong-Kyu Jang	71	68	70	209	1,420,714

	SCORES			TOTAL	MONEY
Yoshitaka Takeya	67	72	70	209	1,420,714
Hideto Tanihara	70	67	72	209	1,420,714
Juvic Pagunsan	69	67	73	209	1,420,714
Seung-Hyuk Kim	72	68	70	210	967,500
Ryo Ishikawa	68	72	70	210	967,500
Shugo Imahira	72	69	69	210	967,500
Daisuke Maruyama	69	67	74	210	967,500
Ryutaro Nagano	70	66	74	210	967,500

Dunlop Phoenix

Phoenix Country Club, Miyazaki
Par 36-35–71; 7,027 yards

November 19-22
purse, ¥200,000,000

	SCORES				TOTAL	MONEY
Yusaku Miyazato	67	70	64	69	270	¥40,000,000
Hideki Matsuyama	70	68	67	67	272	16,800,000
Yoshinori Fujimoto	69	66	68	69	272	16,800,000
Jung-Gon Hwang	70	68	69	66	273	8,266,666
Shugo Imahira	72	67	66	68	273	8,266,666
Tomohiro Kondo	72	68	65	68	273	8,266,666
Will Wilcox	72	68	68	66	274	6,350,000
Thanyakon Khrongpha	69	66	71	68	274	6,350,000
Danny Lee	70	69	68	68	275	5,440,000
Kyung-Tae Kim	72	65	68	70	275	5,440,000
Hiroyuki Fujita	71	68	70	67	276	4,240,000
Shingo Katayama	70	71	66	69	276	4,240,000
I.J. Jang	71	70	65	70	276	4,240,000
Dong-Kyu Jang	69	68	68	71	276	4,240,000
Hideto Tanihara	73	68	67	69	277	3,340,000
Tatsunori Nukaga	68	69	67	73	277	3,340,000
Young-Han Song	69	69	70	70	278	2,853,333
Yoshitaka Takeya	65	71	71	71	278	2,853,333
Shunsuke Sonoda	71	68	68	71	278	2,853,333
Ricardo Gouveia	69	70	73	67	279	2,360,000
Katsumasa Miyamoto	71	66	70	72	279	2,360,000
Satoshi Tomiyama	69	71	67	72	279	2,360,000
Koumei Oda	69	72	70	69	280	1,860,000
Prayad Marksaeng	70	70	68	72	280	1,860,000
Masanori Kobayashi	69	70	68	73	280	1,860,000
Ho-Sung Choi	72	68	66	74	280	1,860,000

Casio World Open

Kochi Kuroshio Country Club, Geisei, Kochi
Par 36-36–72; 7,315 yards

November 26-29
purse, ¥200,000,000

	SCORES				TOTAL	MONEY
Jung-Gon Hwang	70	67	70	66	273	¥40,000,000
Ryo Ishikawa	68	65	73	68	274	20,000,000
Shingo Katayama	72	68	69	68	277	13,600,000
Ryutaro Nagano	73	70	70	65	278	8,800,000
Yoshinori Fujimoto	71	72	68	67	278	8,800,000
Hideto Tanihara	69	71	70	69	279	6,900,000
Brendan Jones	72	67	68	72	279	6,900,000
Ho-Sung Choi	72	67	72	69	280	6,100,000
Taichi Teshima	71	74	70	66	281	5,240,000

	SCORES				TOTAL	MONEY
Ashun Wu	71	70	72	68	281	5,240,000
Tatsunori Nukaga	71	73	70	67	281	5,240,000
Won-Joon Lee	73	70	72	67	282	3,320,000
Ryuichi Oda	72	73	71	66	282	3,320,000
Yuta Ikeda	73	69	72	68	282	3,320,000
Tomoyo Ikemura	73	71	70	68	282	3,320,000
Masahiro Kawamura	71	72	71	68	282	3,320,000
Prayad Marksaeng	74	70	70	68	282	3,320,000
Yosuke Asaji	70	71	72	69	282	3,320,000
Azuma Yano	70	73	70	69	282	3,320,000
Masanori Kobayashi	69	73	70	70	282	3,320,000
Brad Kennedy	71	72	72	68	283	2,000,000
Mikumu Horikawa	74	68	74	67	283	2,000,000
Daisuke Kataoka	72	70	72	69	283	2,000,000
Shunsuke Sonoda	71	72	71	69	283	2,000,000
Adam Bland	72	67	73	71	283	2,000,000
Young-Han Song	71	70	70	72	283	2,000,000

Golf Nippon Series JT Cup

Tokyo Yomiuri Country Club, Inagi, Tokyo
Par 35-35–70; 7,023 yards

December 3-6
purse, ¥130,000,000

	SCORES				TOTAL	MONEY
Ryo Ishikawa	68	68	63	67	266	¥40,000,000
Yoshinori Fujimoto	66	71	69	65	271	12,500,000
Koumei Oda	66	70	66	69	271	12,500,000
Yuta Ikeda	67	70	69	68	274	6,211,593
Shingo Katayama	64	74	68	69	275	5,171,593
Katsumasa Miyamoto	72	70	66	68	276	4,456,593
Jung-Gon Hwang	66	70	69	71	276	4,456,593
Toshinori Muto	71	74	68	64	277	3,517,343
Hyung-Sung Kim	71	73	65	68	277	3,517,343
Yusaku Miyazato	69	71	68	69	277	3,517,343
Hideto Tanihara	70	70	66	71	277	3,517,343
Hiroshi Iwata	67	77	68	67	279	2,597,593
Adam Bland	72	70	68	69	279	2,597,593
Hyun-Woo Ryu	69	70	67	73	279	2,597,593
Michael Hendry	67	75	70	68	280	2,142,593
Satoshi Kodaira	68	73	68	71	280	2,142,593
Kyung-Tae Kim	68	73	69	71	281	1,772,092
Shugo Imahira	69	73	68	71	281	1,772,092
Daisuke Kataoka	73	67	69	72	281	1,772,092
Young-Han Song	71	70	68	72	281	1,772,092
Ashun Wu	67	72	73	70	282	1,401,592
Brad Kennedy	72	72	67	71	282	1,401,592
Yuki Inamori	71	72	67	72	282	1,401,592
Ryutaro Nagano	70	77	69	68	284	1,167,592
I.J. Jang	69	72	69	74	284	1,167,592

Australasian Tour

Oates Victorian Open

13th Beach Golf Links, Barwon Heads, Victoria
Par 36-36–72; 7,036 yards

February 5-8
purse, A$250,000

		SCORES			TOTAL	MONEY
Richard Green	66	72	67	67	272	A$37,500
Nick Cullen	70	66	67	69	272	23,750
(Green defeated Cullen on second playoff hole.)						
Scott Arnold	71	67	67	69	274	17,500
*Ryan Ruffels	70	68	66	70	274	
*Ben Eccles	70	65	68	71	274	
Adam Bland	68	69	70	68	275	9,812.50
Gareth Paddison	68	69	69	69	275	9,812.50
Dimitrios Papadatos	70	69	66	70	275	9,812.50
Matthew Millar	72	64	69	70	275	9,812.50
Nick Gillespie	70	70	70	66	276	7,000
Anthony Brown	69	68	72	68	277	5,812.50
Andrew Schonewille	69	64	72	72	277	
Jason Scrivener	70	64	68	75	277	5,812.50
Aaron Townsend	71	64	74	69	278	4,312.50
Stephen Dartnall	71	66	71	70	278	4,312.50
Daniel Nisbet	66	71	70	71	278	4,312.50
Mitchell A. Brown	71	63	71	73	278	4,312.50
Max McCardle	70	67	72	70	279	3,375
Callan O'Reilly	70	66	71	72	279	3,375
Matthew Giles	73	69	71	67	280	2,865
Daniel Pearce	70	68	71	71	280	2,865
Todd Sinnott	68	69	72	71	280	2,865
Jason Norris	69	71	71	69	280	2,865
Ryan Fox	71	69	71	69	280	2,865
Matthew Griffin	69	72	72	68	281	2,575
Josh Geary	71	69	69	72	281	2,575
Daniel Valente	74	68	68	71	281	2,575
Steven Jeffress	71	69	70	71	281	2,575

Mercedes-Benz Truck & Bus Victorian PGA Championship

Huntingdale Golf Club, Oakleigh South, Victoria
Par 36-36-72

February 10-13
purse, A$100,000

		SCORES			TOTAL	MONEY
Aaron Townsend	67	73	69	66	275	A$15,000
Scott Strange	69	70	70	67	276	9,500
Kristopher Mueck	73	67	70	67	277	6,000
Ryan Haller	67	71	70	69	277	6,000
David Bransdon	64	75	72	67	278	3,800
Ryan Fox	68	67	70	73	278	3,800
Matthew Millar	66	72	69	73	280	3,100
Josh Geary	75	69	71	67	282	2,625
Adam Bland	70	67	73	72	282	2,625
Marcus Cain	70	72	72	69	283	2,100
Jason Norris	73	70	69	71	283	2,100
Bradley Lamb	72	73	72	67	284	1,633.33

	SCORES				TOTAL	MONEY
Anthony Brown	74	70	71	69	284	1,633.33
Michael Hendry	69	71	72	72	284	1,633.33
Daniel Valente	70	74	72	69	285	1,400
Scott Laycock	72	71	74	69	286	1,190
Scott Arnold	73	72	71	70	286	1,190
Won-Joon Lee	68	74	72	72	286	1,190
Peter Cooke	71	72	71	72	286	1,190
Jamie Hook	70	72	67	77	286	1,190
Daniel Nisbet	70	71	75	71	287	1,060
Kurt Barnes	70	71	74	72	287	1,060
Ben Wharton	71	74	68	74	287	1,060
Ryan Lynch	72	70	78	68	288	970
Leigh McKechnie	72	71	76	69	288	970
Paul Spargo	76	67	73	72	288	970
Peter Wilson	72	71	71	74	288	970
Josh Younger	74	67	72	75	288	970
Matt Jager	72	67	73	76	288	970

Coca-Cola Queensland PGA Championship

City Golf Club, Toowoomba, Queensland
Par 33-37-70; 6,332 yards

February 19-22
purse, A$120,000

	SCORES				TOTAL	MONEY
Ryan Fox	72	64	65	62	263	A$18,000
Cameron Smith	69	66	66	63	264	9,900
Matthew Millar	65	69	65	65	264	9,900
Brad Kennedy	65	66	69	67	267	5,460
Tim Hart	68	67	64	68	267	5,460
Edward Stedman	72	66	68	63	269	4,200
Brad Shilton	69	64	71	66	270	3,165
David Bransdon	68	69	67	66	270	3,165
Alex Hawley	69	70	65	66	270	3,165
Aaron Pike	69	67	66	68	270	3,165
Steven Jeffress	73	69	65	64	271	2,160
*Troy Moses	71	69	65	66	271	
Scott Arnold	68	67	67	69	271	2,160
Anthony Brown	68	68	65	70	271	2,160
*Cory Crawford	68	72	62	70	272	
Neven Basic	69	68	68	68	273	1,680
Daniel Pearce	73	66	64	70	273	1,680
Michael Sim	69	66	67	71	273	1,680
Adam Blyth	64	74	70	66	274	1,395
Scott Strange	69	65	72	68	274	1,395
Aaron Townsend	64	67	73	70	274	1,395
Adam Stephens	66	71	66	71	274	1,395
Jason Norris	68	69	68	70	275	1,284
Michael Wright	69	68	68	70	275	1,284
Geoff Drakeford	72	70	65	69	276	1,236
Matt Jager	65	70	71	70	276	1,236

Holden New Zealand PGA Championship

Remuera Golf Club, Auckland, New Zealand
Par 35-37–72; 6,792 yards

March 5-8
purse, NZ$125,000

	SCORES				TOTAL	MONEY
Matthew Millar	68	67	64	71	270	A$17,648.73
Kristopher Mueck	64	68	70	71	273	8,432.17
Geoff Drakeford	70	65	67	71	273	8,432.17
Josh Geary	66	66	69	72	273	8,432.17
Jared Pender	71	70	67	68	276	4,196.47
Azuma Yano	72	70	65	69	276	4,196.47
Ryan Fox	69	68	66	73	276	4,196.47
Anthony Brown	70	67	70	70	277	2,921.85
Scott Arnold	70	70	66	71	277	2,921.85
Jordan Zunic	67	66	69	75	277	2,921.85
Peter Lonard	70	69	69	70	278	2,235.51
Harry Bateman	68	70	69	71	278	2,235.51
Ryan Lynch	70	69	70	70	279	1,823.70
Nick Gillespie	67	70	71	71	279	1,823.70
Jake Stirling	69	73	69	69	280	1,537.40
Rory Bourke	69	72	70	69	280	1,537.40
Thomas Campbell	68	72	69	71	280	1,537.40
Samuel Eaves	74	68	68	71	281	1,364.84
Peter Fowler	67	71	68	75	281	1,364.84
Anthony Summers	70	73	69	70	282	1,274.63
Daniel Popovic	70	72	70	70	282	1,274.63
Aaron Townsend	70	69	69	74	282	1,274.63
Michael Freake	70	71	70	72	283	1,200.11
Douglas Holloway	72	68	68	75	283	1,200.11
Daniel Valente	71	70	67	75	283	1,200.11

BMW New Zealand Open

The Hills, Arrowtown, New Zealand
Par 36-36–72; 7,116 yards

March 12-15
purse, NZ$1,000,000

	SCORES				TOTAL	MONEY
Jordan Zunic	68	66	66	66	266	A$160,563.38
David Bransdon	63	69	71	64	267	90,985.92
Kristopher Mueck	70	65	65	69	269	60,211.27
Cameron Smith	68	72	64	66	270	39,248.83
Brad Kennedy	66	70	66	68	270	39,248.83
Daniel Fox	69	69	69	64	271	32,112.68
Peter Fowler	68	69	69	66	272	26,165.88
Scott Arnold	68	70	67	67	272	26,165.88
Aaron Pike	66	67	68	71	272	26,165.88
Harry Bateman	71	68	67	67	273	20,962.44
Marcus Fraser	67	68	69	69	273	20,962.44
Hiroshi Iwata	69	70	69	66	274	16,353.68
David Oh	68	69	69	68	274	16,353.68
Kieran Pratt	67	68	70	69	274	16,353.68
Akio Sadakata	69	69	67	70	275	12,354.46
Geoff Drakeford	71	68	66	70	275	12,354.46
Josh Geary	69	69	66	71	275	12,354.46
Matt Jager	70	63	68	74	275	12,354.46
Michael Hendry	67	73	69	67	276	9,511.15
Nathan Holman	71	68	69	68	276	9,511.15
Stephen Dartnall	70	70	68	68	276	9,511.15
Won-Joon Lee	63	71	70	72	276	9,511.15

	SCORES				TOTAL	MONEY
Matthew Griffin	70	69	70	68	277	7,569.42
Yoshitaka Takeya	69	70	70	68	277	7,569.42
Toshinori Muto	68	68	71	70	277	7,569.42
Mark Brown	69	70	68	70	277	7,569.42
*Joshua Munn	73	67	67	70	277	
Matthew Guyatt	65	70	71	71	277	7,569.42
Jamie Hook	71	64	71	71	277	7,569.42
Samuel Eaves	68	67	69	73	277	7,569.42

Isuzu Queensland Open

Brookwater Golf & Country Club, Brisbane, Queensland
Par 36-36-72; 7,114 yards

August 20-23
purse, A$110,000

	SCORES				TOTAL	MONEY
David Bransdon	69	71	67	69	276	A$16,500
Rohan Blizard	75	67	67	67	276	10,450
(Bransdon defeated Blizard on third playoff hole.)						
Mark Brown	74	67	70	69	280	7,700
Adam Blyth	73	70	70	68	281	5,005
*Jake McLeod	74	72	67	68	281	
Aaron Townsend	72	69	71	69	281	5,005
Edward Stedman	70	71	72	69	282	3,850
Michael Wright	69	73	73	68	283	3,245
Michael Sim	69	71	70	73	283	3,245
Matthew Millar	69	71	77	67	284	2,323.75
Josh Younger	75	69	70	70	284	2,323.75
Matthew Guyatt	71	71	71	71	284	2,323.75
Rory Bourke	68	71	73	72	284	2,323.75
Taylor Macdonald	70	75	71	69	285	1,705
Michael Choi	70	71	69	75	285	1,705
Jamie Hook	72	72	72	70	286	1,402.50
Daniel Nisbet	76	71	69	70	286	1,402.50
Marcus Cain	70	74	71	71	286	1,402.50
Steven Jeffress	72	70	72	72	286	1,402.50
Kalem Richardson	72	74	72	69	287	1,194.60
Damien Jordan	73	71	74	69	287	1,194.60
Paul Spargo	75	73	71	68	287	1,194.60
*Blake Proverbs	75	73	71	68	287	
Max McCardle	71	73	72	71	287	1,194.60
Michael Long	75	74	71	67	287	1,194.60

South Pacific Open Championship

Tina Golf Club, Noumea, New Caledonia
Par 36-35-71; 6,442 yards

September 30-October 3
purse, A$150,000

	SCORES				TOTAL	MONEY
James Nitties	65	67	67	69	268	A$22,500
Matthew Millar	65	68	68	73	274	14,250
Christopher Wood	71	73	69	64	277	10,500
Matthew Guyatt	66	73	71	68	278	5,887.50
Brad Shilton	71	72	67	68	278	5,887.50
Jason Norris	67	71	67	73	278	5,887.50
Michael Wright	66	72	66	74	278	5,887.50
Alex Edge	67	69	71	72	279	4,200
Damien Jordan	73	67	69	71	280	3,675

	SCORES				TOTAL	MONEY
Nick Gillespie	67	73	76	65	281	3,000
Andrew Martin	71	68	72	70	281	3,000
Michael Long	71	67	71	72	281	3,000
Daniel Hoeve	71	73	71	67	282	2,106
Callan O'Reilly	70	69	72	71	282	2,106
Daniel Valente	64	71	75	72	282	2,106
Andrew Campbell	67	71	72	72	282	2,106
Brett Rankin	68	72	68	74	282	2,106
*Cory Crawford	67	72	73	71	283	
Daniel Popovic	66	69	71	77	283	1,700
Jason Chellew	78	68	72	66	284	1,665
Daniel Fox	67	69	78	70	284	1,665
Neven Basic	67	74	71	72	284	1,665
Jamie Hook	70	70	75	70	285	1,575
Tim Hart	73	68	72	72	285	1,575
*Jake McLeod	73	71	66	75	285	

Fiji International

See Asia/Japan Tours chapter.

TX Civil & Logistics WA PGA Championship

Kalgoorlie Golf Club, Kalgoorlie, Western Australia
Par 36-36–72; 7,399 yards

October 29-November 1
purse, A$120,000

	SCORES				TOTAL	MONEY
Brett Rumford	67	67	67	71	272	A$18,000
Daniel Fox	69	71	68	66	274	11,400
Edward Stedman	68	71	71	65	275	7,200
Daniel Nisbet	65	69	71	70	275	7,200
Aaron Pike	69	68	70	69	276	4,920
Jason Norris	65	69	71	72	277	4,200
Max McCardle	69	71	69	69	278	3,540
Michael Long	68	74	66	70	278	3,540
Chris Gaunt	73	66	71	69	279	2,940
R.J. Caracella	65	71	78	67	281	2,022.86
Antonio Murdaca	66	72	77	66	281	2,022.86
Ashley Hall	70	71	70	70	281	2,022.86
Anthony Houston	70	71	70	70	281	2,022.86
Ben Wharton	69	71	70	71	281	2,022.86
Samuel Eaves	73	71	66	71	281	2,022.86
Jarryd Felton	69	71	69	72	281	2,022.86
Josh Younger	76	68	70	68	282	1,416
Troy Cox	69	72	72	69	282	1,416
Michael Wright	69	72	70	71	282	1,416
David Bransdon	72	73	68	70	283	1,300
Brody Ninyette	66	73	74	70	283	1,300
Andrew Evans	67	69	74	73	283	1,300
Andrew Martin	71	72	72	69	284	1,212
Jake McLeod	72	71	70	71	284	1,212
Peter Lonard	69	70	73	72	284	1,212
Darren Beck	68	72	72	72	284	1,212

Nexus Risk TSA Group WA Open

Royal Fremantle Golf Club, Fremantle, Western Australia
Par 36-36–72

November 5-8
purse, A$100,000

	SCORES				TOTAL	MONEY
Daniel Fox	70	68	69	70	277	A$15,000
*Curtis Luck	66	72	72	70	280	
Mitchell A. Brown	69	71	72	71	283	6,400
Aaron Pike	70	73	69	71	283	6,400
Daniel Valente	69	69	72	73	283	6,400
Jason Scrivener	68	70	70	75	283	6,400
Michael Sim	66	70	72	76	284	3,500
Matthew Giles	71	72	72	70	285	2,950
Matthew Millar	73	68	70	74	285	2,950
Ben Wharton	69	75	72	70	286	2,112.50
Michael Wright	72	71	72	71	286	2,112.50
Stephen Dartnall	70	70	72	74	286	2,112.50
Anthony Houston	69	71	72	74	286	2,112.50
*Min Woo Lee	70	71	69	76	286	
*Ben Eccles	70	71	73	73	287	
Gavin Reed	67	74	73	73	287	1,550
Josh Younger	71	72	70	74	287	1,550
Andrew Martin	70	71	75	72	288	1,306.67
Brett Rumford	74	71	73	70	288	1,306.67
David McKenzie	67	74	72	75	288	1,306.67
Daniel McGraw	74	68	74	73	289	1,114
Jason Norris	68	77	71	73	289	1,114
Max McCardle	74	71	73	71	289	1,114
Jordan Zunic	70	70	75	74	289	1,114
*Shae Wools-Cobb	72	71	72	74	289	
Jarryd Felton	72	72	70	75	289	1,114

New South Wales Open

Stonecutters Ridge Golf Club, Sydney, New South Wales
Par 36-36–72

November 12-15
purse, A$110,000

	SCORES				TOTAL	MONEY
*Ben Eccles	64	67	66	72	269	
Rohan Blizard	69	62	73	68	272	A$13,475
Matthew Millar	67	67	68	70	272	13,475
Tim Hart	65	68	72	68	273	4,994
Jared Pender	72	65	68	68	273	4,994
Tom Bond	67	71	67	68	273	4,994
Daniel Fox	66	67	71	69	273	4,994
Peter Lonard	68	67	66	72	273	4,994
Troy Cox	66	71	69	68	274	2,731.67
Mitchell A. Brown	68	68	68	70	274	2,731.67
Aaron Wilkin	69	62	71	72	274	2,731.67
David Klein	69	69	68	69	275	2,090
Clayton Bridges	66	68	67	74	275	2,090
Aaron Townsend	71	69	68	68	276	1,705
Deyen Lawson	69	70	69	68	276	1,705
Ryan Haller	70	68	69	70	277	1,485
Jordan Zunic	69	69	69	70	277	1,485
Alex Hawley	67	67	75	69	278	1,260.60
Matt Jager	68	70	70	70	278	1,260.60
*Dale Brandt-Richards	72	69	66	71	278	
Darren Beck	64	69	74	71	278	1,260.60

	SCORES				TOTAL	MONEY
Brett Rankin	71	65	71	71	278	1,260.60
Jarryd Felton	67	70	70	71	278	1,260.60
*Daniel Gale	65	70	71	72	278	
*Isaac Noh	67	71	73	68	279	
Michael Choi	70	69	70	70	279	1,144
Scott Laycock	66	72	70	71	279	1,144
Daniel Nisbet	70	68	66	75	279	1,144

UNIQLO Masters

Huntingdale Golf Club, South Oakleigh, Victoria
Par 35-36–71; 6,958 yards

November 19-22
purse, A$750,000

	SCORES				TOTAL	MONEY
Peter Senior	70	70	68	68	276	A$135,000
*Bryson DeChambeau	69	70	72	67	278	
John Senden	69	68	71	70	278	63,562.50
Andrew Evans	68	69	70	71	278	63,562.50
Adam Scott	64	70	77	69	280	36,000
Richard Green	72	70	71	68	281	23,625
Brett Rumford	72	64	74	71	281	23,625
Alistair Presnell	68	71	71	71	281	23,625
Matthew Guyatt	69	66	73	73	281	23,625
Michael Sim	71	69	68	73	281	23,625
Matthew Millar	71	67	68	75	281	23,625
Wade Ormsby	71	72	73	66	282	14,437.50
Michael Long	74	67	74	67	282	14,437.50
Mathew Goggin	67	70	74	71	282	14,437.50
Daniel Fox	65	74	71	72	282	14,437.50
George McNeill	70	66	73	74	283	12,000
Nathan Holman	71	66	78	69	284	10,800
Aaron Townsend	72	73	75	65	285	7,856.25
Geoff Drakeford	72	73	72	68	285	7,856.25
Peter Wilson	67	67	80	71	285	7,856.25
Stephen Allan	70	69	74	72	285	7,856.25
Stephen Leaney	69	70	74	72	285	7,856.25
Scott Laycock	72	71	70	72	285	7,856.25
Ashley Hall	71	67	74	73	285	7,856.25
Peter Fowler	69	72	71	73	285	7,856.25
Nick O'Hern	70	70	71	74	285	7,856.25
Daniel Pearce	73	69	69	74	285	7,856.25

Emirates Australian Open

The Australian Golf Club, Sydney, New South Wales
Par 35-36–71; 7,230 yards

November 26-29
purse, A$1,250,000

	SCORES				TOTAL	MONEY
Matt Jones	67	68	68	73	276	A$225,000
Adam Scott	71	73	68	65	277	105,937.50
Jordan Spieth	71	68	67	71	277	105,937.50
Rod Pampling	71	72	74	61	278	60,000
Nick Cullen	70	73	70	68	281	47,500
Lincoln Tighe	66	73	70	72	281	47,500
Terry Pilkadaris	71	71	73	67	282	40,000
Todd Sinnott	68	70	74	71	283	30,750
Brett Rumford	69	74	69	71	283	30,750

	SCORES				TOTAL	MONEY
Geoff Ogilvy	68	71	71	73	283	30,750
Aron Price	71	68	70	74	283	30,750
Rhein Gibson	72	68	68	75	283	30,750
Cameron Smith	74	71	73	66	284	20,437.50
John Senden	69	72	76	67	284	20,437.50
David Klein	72	71	73	68	284	20,437.50
Brett Rankin	73	68	74	69	284	20,437.50
Rohan Blizard	73	71	71	70	285	16,250
Lee Westwood	70	72	75	69	286	14,187.50
Nicolas Colsaerts	73	66	76	71	286	14,187.50
Jin-Ho Choi	75	68	71	72	286	14,187.50
*Ryan Ruffels	70	74	75	68	287	
Nathan Holman	74	69	75	69	287	11,390.63
Stephen Allan	72	74	72	69	287	11,390.63
Stephen Dartnall	70	71	76	70	287	11,390.63
Richard Green	72	69	75	71	287	11,390.63
Alistair Presnell	69	73	74	71	287	11,390.63
Cheng Tsung Pan	73	70	73	71	287	11,390.63
David Bransdon	73	73	70	71	287	11,390.63
Daniel Valente	72	74	70	71	287	11,390.63

Australian PGA Championship

RACV Royal Pines Resort, Gold Coast, Queensland
Par 36-36-72; 6,734 yards

December 3-6
purse, A$1,750,000

	SCORES				TOTAL	MONEY
Nathan Holman	77	68	70	73	288	A$315,000
Dylan Frittelli	70	72	71	75	288	148,312.50
Harold Varner	74	73	66	75	288	148,312.50
(Holman defeated Frittelli and Varner at first playoff hole.)						
Zander Lombard	67	75	71	76	289	84,000
Cameron Smith	78	69	70	73	290	70,000
Dimitrios Papadatos	75	71	71	74	291	56,583.33
Richard Green	73	74	70	74	291	56,583.33
Matthew Millar	72	70	74	75	291	56,583.33
Adam Stephens	71	76	75	70	292	33,522.22
Peter Lonard	76	72	73	71	292	33,522.22
Mathew Goggin	76	73	72	71	292	33,522.22
Jordan Zunic	73	72	75	72	292	33,522.22
Anthony Brown	73	71	75	73	292	33,522.22
Nino Bertasio	75	72	72	73	292	33,522.22
Matthew Griffin	76	72	71	73	292	33,522.22
Rory Bourke	74	76	68	74	292	33,522.22
David Lingmerth	73	68	75	76	292	33,522.22
Stuart Manley	77	69	76	71	293	19,862.50
Michael Wright	76	70	71	76	293	19,862.50
Daniel Nisbet	75	75	67	76	293	19,862.50
Colin Nel	78	71	75	70	294	16,375
Jarrod Lyle	77	73	72	72	294	16,375
Aaron Pike	72	73	76	73	294	16,375
Borja Virto Astudillo	72	77	72	73	294	16,375
Aron Price	75	74	72	73	294	16,375
Josh Geary	77	73	70	74	294	16,375
Mark Foster	69	73	77	75	294	16,375
Jason Scrivener	72	71	79	73	295	11,450
Ryan Fox	74	70	78	73	295	11,450
Ashley Hall	70	73	77	75	295	11,450
Tom Lewis	72	71	77	75	295	11,450
Max McCardle	74	74	72	75	295	11,450

	SCORES				TOTAL	MONEY
Pablo Martin Benavides	75	67	77	76	295	11,450
Todd Sinnott	71	72	75	77	295	11,450
David Klein	77	71	76	72	296	9,450
Nathan Green	76	74	73	73	296	9,450
Anthony Summers	80	70	73	73	296	9,450
Scott Fernandez	74	72	79	72	297	7,875
Ben Eccles	74	72	78	73	297	7,875
Craig Parry	77	71	76	73	297	7,875
Erik van Rooyen	76	71	75	75	297	7,875
Peter Uihlein	75	67	79	76	297	7,875
Nick Cullen	72	74	73	78	297	7,875
Jamie Hook	76	74	77	71	298	6,125
Rhein Gibson	79	64	79	76	298	6,125
Paul Dunne	72	75	75	76	298	6,125
Josh Younger	75	73	74	76	298	6,125
David McKenzie	74	76	77	72	299	4,620
John Senden	73	77	76	73	299	4,620
Peter Cooke	79	71	75	74	299	4,620
Rourke van der Spuy	76	73	75	75	299	4,620
Marcus Fraser	76	73	74	76	299	4,620
James Nitties	76	72	78	74	300	3,806.25
Brett Rankin	76	73	77	74	300	3,806.25
Tyrone Mordt	79	71	76	74	300	3,806.25
Ben Wharton	76	70	78	76	300	3,806.25
Neven Basic	74	73	77	76	300	3,806.25
Laurie Canter	79	70	73	78	300	3,806.25
Daniel Fox	75	74	76	76	301	3,657.50
Darryn Lloyd	78	72	75	76	301	3,657.50
Hyo-Won Park	80	67	79	76	302	3,605
Bjorn Akesson	74	74	75	80	303	3,540.83
Brett Rumford	74	72	75	82	303	3,540.83
Jack Wilson	73	73	71	86	303	3,540.83
Nicolo Ravano	73	76	82	73	304	3,416.88
J.C. Ritchie	76	72	80	76	304	3,416.88
Harry Bateman	76	74	75	79	304	3,416.88
Deyen Lawson	75	70	79	80	304	3,416.88
Andrew Curlewis	76	72	77	80	305	3,325
Divan van den Heever	76	74	80	76	306	3,290
Corey Hale	78	72	82	77	309	3,255

NSW PGA Championship

Riverside Oaks Golf Resort, Cattai, New South Wales
Par 35-37–72; 6,767 yards

December 10-13
purse, A$110,000

	SCORES				TOTAL	MONEY
Jarryd Felton	65	74	68	68	275	A$16,500
James Nitties	70	69	69	69	277	6,402
Anthony Summers	68	72	68	69	277	6,402
Matthew Millar	68	73	67	69	277	6,402
Geoff Drakeford	67	72	68	70	277	6,402
Rhein Gibson	66	68	71	72	277	6,402
Max McCardle	69	74	64	71	278	3,410
David McKenzie	68	71	72	68	279	2,731.67
Peter Cooke	70	71	69	69	279	2,731.67
Christopher Wood	68	68	70	73	279	2,731.67
Chris Gaunt	69	73	68	70	280	2,090
Ewan Porter	70	68	71	71	280	2,090
*Kieran Muir	68	72	73	68	281	
*Mitchell A. Brown	72	71	69	69	281	

	SCORES				TOTAL	MONEY
Todd Sinnott	69	70	71	71	281	1,595
Lucas Herbert	68	67	70	76	281	1,595
Damien Jordan	70	74	69	69	282	1,244.83
Daniel Fox	71	72	69	70	282	1,244.83
Ben Wharton	69	71	71	71	282	1,244.83
Deyen Lawson	66	71	73	72	282	1,244.83
Tom Bond	73	69	67	73	282	1,244.83
Ashley Hall	70	71	67	74	282	1,244.83
Marcus Cain	65	74	74	71	284	1,122
Daniel Valente	68	75	70	71	284	1,122
Brett Rankin	67	71	73	73	284	1,122

African Sunshine Tour

South African Open Championship

Glendower Golf Club, Gauteng, Johannesburg, South Africa

January 8-11

Par 36-36–72; 7,564 yards

purse, €1,000,000

	SCORES				TOTAL	MONEY
Andy Sullivan	66	70	74	67	277	€158,500
Charl Schwartzel	68	69	66	74	277	115,000
(Sullivan defeated Schwartzel on first playoff hole.)						
Lee Slattery	70	74	65	69	278	69,200
Pablo Martin Benavides	71	68	71	69	279	49,100
Thomas Aiken	70	71	70	70	281	28,667
Matthew Fitzpatrick	73	68	67	73	281	28,667
Jared Harvey	71	69	70	71	281	28,667
Paul Maddy	71	71	68	71	281	28,667
Gary Stal	75	66	69	71	281	28,667
Alessandro Tadini	71	68	73	69	281	28,667
David Drysdale	68	72	68	74	282	17,300
Jason Scrivener	73	72	66	71	282	17,300
Raphael Jacquelin	69	76	72	66	283	15,200
Hennie Otto	72	71	70	70	283	15,200
Trevor Fisher, Jr.	72	73	71	68	284	13,200
Branden Grace	71	71	69	73	284	13,200
Rikard Karlberg	70	70	71	73	284	13,200
James Morrison	71	69	72	72	284	13,200
Neil Schietekat	74	72	68	70	284	13,200
Carlos Del Moral	72	72	69	72	285	11,120
Ernie Els	67	77	69	72	285	11,120
Lasse Jensen	67	71	72	75	285	11,120
Matthew Nixon	72	69	72	72	285	11,120
Richard Sterne	67	74	69	75	285	11,120
Jorge Campillo	73	71	69	73	286	9,188
Adilson Da Silva	72	73	68	73	286	9,188
Niclas Fasth	69	73	73	71	286	9,188
Matt Ford	70	71	72	73	286	9,188
Alex Haindl	73	72	71	70	286	9,188
Colin Nel	68	70	72	76	286	9,188
Andrea Pavan	74	71	71	70	286	9,188
Rhys West	75	71	71	69	286	9,188
Estanislao Goya	74	69	71	73	287	7,700
Jean Hugo	73	72	70	72	287	7,700
Jerome Lando Casanova	70	74	70	73	287	7,700
John Parry	70	69	76	72	287	7,700
Erik van Rooyen	69	75	75	68	287	7,700
Gareth Maybin	71	73	69	75	288	6,900
Pedro Oriol	71	73	71	73	288	6,900
J.J. Senekal	71	67	74	76	288	6,900
Keith Horne	71	74	72	72	289	6,100
Morten Orum Madsen	73	71	71	74	289	6,100
Edoardo Molinari	69	76	69	75	289	6,100
Shaun Norris	70	76	72	71	289	6,100
Chris Paisley	74	69	74	72	289	6,100
Nacho Elvira	70	71	75	74	290	5,000
Anders Hansen	73	70	72	75	290	5,000
Soren Hansen	74	69	74	73	290	5,000
Tyrone Mordt	72	72	71	75	290	5,000
Ricardo Santos	72	71	72	75	290	5,000

	SCORES				TOTAL	MONEY
Tjaart van der Walt	70	73	70	77	290	5,000
Daniel Brooks	73	73	70	75	291	4,100
Doug McGuigan	73	70	71	77	291	4,100
Chris Swanepoel	70	71	73	77	291	4,100
Paul Lawrie	71	75	73	73	292	3,500
Danie van Tonder	78	68	71	75	292	3,500
Jaco Van Zyl	72	73	75	72	292	3,500
Louis de Jager	70	75	69	79	293	3,150
John Hahn	75	71	75	72	293	3,150
Jake Roos	73	70	77	74	294	3,000
Jbe' Kruger	66	80	72	79	297	2,900
Keenan Davidse	74	71	77	77	299	2,650
Justin Harding	70	75	74	80	299	2,650
Tom Murray	69	76	76	78	299	2,650
Renato Paratore	72	71	74	82	299	2,650
Dean Burmester	74	72	79	77	302	2,400

Dimension Data Pro-Am

Montagu Golf Course, Fancourt, George, South Africa
Par 36-36–72; 7,342 yards

February 19-22
purse, R4,500,000

	SCORES				TOTAL	MONEY
Branden Grace	71	68	69	70	278	R673,625
Keith Horne	71	72	68	69	280	488,750
Jaco Van Zyl	70	71	69	71	281	176,445.83
Hennie Otto	68	70	73	70	281	176,445.83
Callum Mowat	73	71	69	68	281	176,445.83
Danie van Tonder	66	72	74	69	281	176,445.83
Tjaart van der Walt	68	68	71	74	281	176,445.83
Darren Fichardt	69	65	72	75	281	176,445.83
Jordan Smith	71	68	76	67	282	83,725
Jean Hugo	74	69	71	68	282	83,725
Justin Walters	72	66	71	73	282	83,725
Dean Burmester	75	72	69	67	283	68,850
Jacques Blaauw	72	69	68	74	283	68,850
Merrick Bremner	70	75	67	72	284	62,475
Andrew Georgiou	71	67	73	74	285	60,350
Jaco Ahlers	68	70	79	69	286	53,125
Andrew Marshall	73	72	72	69	286	53,125
Garth Mulroy	70	73	77	66	286	53,125
Oliver Bekker	68	70	75	73	286	53,125
George Coetzee	66	73	77	70	286	53,125
Lyle Rowe	70	71	70	75	286	53,125
Peter Karmis	74	66	76	71	287	46,537.50
Estanislao Goya	69	71	74	73	287	46,537.50
Heinrich Bruiners	74	72	72	70	288	40,800
Martin Rominger	72	72	71	73	288	40,800
Pablo Martin Benavides	74	70	72	72	288	40,800
Wallie Coetsee	69	74	70	75	288	40,800
Ruan de Smidt	68	76	72	72	288	40,800
Tyrone Mordt	72	68	75	73	288	40,800
Dawie van der Walt	68	74	72	74	288	40,800

Joburg Open

Royal Johannesburg & Kensington Golf Club,
Johannesburg, South Africa
Par 36-35–71; 7,590 yards

February 26-March 1
purse, €1,300,000

	SCORES				TOTAL	MONEY
Andy Sullivan	71	65	68	66	270	R2,678,650
Kevin Phelan	67	68	71	66	272	1,047,800
Jaco Van Zyl	69	67	70	66	272	1,047,800
Anthony Wall	67	66	71	68	272	1,047,800
David Howell	66	69	68	69	272	1,047,800
Wallie Coetsee	66	65	70	71	272	1,047,800
Byeong-Hun An	65	72	70	66	273	426,443.33
Chris Swanepoel	70	67	67	69	273	426,443.33
Jacques Blaauw	67	69	67	70	273	426,443.33
Adrian Otaegui	71	68	69	66	274	305,326.67
Kristoffer Broberg	67	67	72	68	274	305,326.67
Thomas Aiken	67	67	70	70	274	305,326.67
Dean Burmester	64	73	73	65	275	241,670
Callum Mowat	71	65	71	68	275	241,670
Garth Mulroy	64	68	72	71	275	241,670
Anthony Michael	68	67	69	71	275	241,670
Paul Waring	68	69	67	71	275	241,670
Andrew McArthur	69	69	71	67	276	197,166.67
Oliver Bekker	73	66	70	67	276	197,166.67
Richard Bland	68	67	72	69	276	197,166.67
Jaco Ahlers	70	68	69	69	276	197,166.67
Darren Fichardt	68	71	67	70	276	197,166.67
Steve Webster	72	66	65	73	276	197,166.67
Jordi Garcia Pinto	68	68	73	68	277	159,916.25
Matthew Baldwin	70	65	72	70	277	159,916.25
Haydn Porteous	71	65	71	70	277	159,916.25
Victor Riu	66	70	71	70	277	159,916.25
Tom Lewis	68	70	69	70	277	159,916.25
Justin Walters	71	66	69	71	277	159,916.25
George Coetzee	66	69	69	73	277	159,916.25
Tjaart van der Walt	63	69	71	74	277	159,916.25
Trevor Fisher, Jr.	71	68	72	67	278	133,510
David Horsey	68	70	72	68	278	133,510
Jorge Campillo	65	72	72	69	278	133,510
Ricardo Santos	71	68	68	71	278	133,510
Maximilian Kieffer	70	67	68	73	278	133,510
Titch Moore	63	76	73	67	279	114,920
Joachim B. Hansen	65	70	76	68	279	114,920
Sam Hutsby	66	69	74	70	279	114,920
Matthew Nixon	69	68	71	71	279	114,920
Scott Henry	65	71	71	72	279	114,920
Simon Dyson	65	67	72	75	279	114,920
Matt Ford	68	70	72	70	280	99,710
Alex Noren	71	63	74	72	280	99,710
Keith Horne	68	69	71	72	280	99,710
Tyrrell Hatton	69	70	75	67	281	79,430
Johan Carlsson	70	68	74	69	281	79,430
Alessandro Tadini	70	67	74	70	281	79,430
Johan Edfors	67	71	73	70	281	79,430
Pedro Oriol	69	68	73	71	281	79,430
Richard Sterne	69	68	72	72	281	79,430
Jared Harvey	70	67	72	72	281	79,430
Renato Paratore	66	71	71	73	281	79,430
Ryan Tipping	67	70	70	74	281	79,430
Madalitso Muthiya	68	71	73	70	282	56,784
Neil Schietekat	72	64	75	71	282	56,784

	SCORES				TOTAL	MONEY
Ben Evans	67	68	75	72	282	56,784
Erik van Rooyen	73	66	71	72	282	56,784
Thomas Pieters	63	72	73	74	282	56,784
Niclas Fasth	66	67	77	73	283	47,320
Charl Coetzee	72	64	74	73	283	47,320
Mike Lorenzo-Vera	69	68	73	73	283	47,320
Ryan Evans	69	68	72	74	283	47,320
Stuart Manley	67	67	74	75	283	47,320
Graeme Storm	72	66	72	74	284	42,250
Sean Jacklin	68	69	77	71	285	38,870
Andrew Curlewis	65	74	75	71	285	38,870
Seve Benson	72	67	73	73	285	38,870
Le Roux Ferreira	66	72	76	72	286	35,490
Francois Coetzee	73	65	75	74	287	29,575
Bernd Ritthammer	72	66	73	76	287	29,575
Ockie Strydom	69	69	76	77	291	25,291.50
Thriston Lawrence	67	71	75	78	291	25,291.50
Allan Versfeld	72	67	81	75	295	25,233

Africa Open

East London Golf Club, East London, Eastern Cape, South Africa   March 5-8
Par 37-35–72; 6,679 yards   purse, €1,000,000

	SCORES				TOTAL	MONEY
Trevor Fisher, Jr.	69	68	63	64	264	R2,193,640
Matt Ford	67	66	69	67	269	1,591,600
Eduardo de la Riva	68	66	72	66	272	736,288
Jorge Campillo	71	68	67	66	272	736,288
Morten Orum Madsen	71	71	64	66	272	736,288
John Parry	68	69	69	68	274	449,108
Jaco Van Zyl	70	66	68	70	274	449,108
Maximilian Kieffer	74	63	71	67	275	319,704
Julien Quesne	70	72	66	67	275	319,704
Moritz Lampert	74	66	69	67	276	250,042.67
Keith Horne	72	68	68	68	276	250,042.67
Mark Tullo	70	67	70	69	276	250,042.67
Magnus A. Carlsson	74	67	71	65	277	197,912
Paul Maddy	72	67	72	66	277	197,912
Erik van Rooyen	70	66	74	67	277	197,912
Mikko Korhonen	73	69	66	69	277	197,912
Joakim Lagergren	72	67	68	70	277	197,912
Scott Jamieson	71	69	72	66	278	161,466.67
Oliver Bekker	69	71	71	67	278	161,466.67
Lucas Bjerregaard	72	69	70	67	278	161,466.67
Gregory Havret	69	67	72	70	278	161,466.67
Dean Burmester	72	66	70	70	278	161,466.67
Jean Hugo	72	67	69	70	278	161,466.67
Jbe' Kruger	74	69	69	67	279	137,016
Chris Lloyd	69	70	72	68	279	137,016
Adilson Da Silva	71	70	69	69	279	137,016
David Drysdale	70	71	68	70	279	137,016
Justin Walters	70	70	68	71	279	137,016
Damien McGrane	72	70	70	68	280	117,916.80
Rhys West	73	68	70	69	280	117,916.80
Dylan Frittelli	71	72	68	69	280	117,916.80
Neil Schietekat	68	69	73	70	280	117,916.80
Garth Mulroy	74	66	70	70	280	117,916.80
Andrew Johnston	71	70	72	68	281	105,184
Mikael Lundberg	70	72	71	68	281	105,184

	SCORES				TOTAL	MONEY
Jordi Garcia Pinto	72	68	72	69	281	105,184
David Howell	68	69	71	73	281	105,184
Ruan de Smidt	71	72	72	67	282	89,960
Brett Rumford	74	69	69	70	282	89,960
Matthew Baldwin	71	72	69	70	282	89,960
Lee Slattery	71	71	69	71	282	89,960
Richard Bland	68	72	70	72	282	89,960
Simon Dyson	75	66	69	72	282	89,960
Peter Karmis	74	67	68	73	282	89,960
Craig Lee	75	64	77	67	283	67,816
Steve Webster	73	70	73	67	283	67,816
Justin Harding	74	67	72	70	283	67,816
Jared Harvey	72	70	70	71	283	67,816
Wallie Coetsee	74	68	70	71	283	67,816
James Morrison	72	71	69	71	283	67,816
Byeong-Hun An	73	65	72	73	283	67,816
Oliver Farr	72	68	69	74	283	67,816
Seve Benson	70	73	66	74	283	67,816
Todd Sinnott	75	68	73	68	284	47,748
Shaun Norris	70	73	73	68	284	47,748
Mark Foster	73	69	73	69	284	47,748
Felipe Aguilar	70	71	71	72	284	47,748
Pablo Martin Benavides	71	69	71	73	284	47,748
Jacques Blaauw	72	69	69	74	284	47,748
Sam Hutsby	72	70	76	67	285	38,752
Edoardo Molinari	72	71	71	71	285	38,752
Bryce Easton	72	71	71	71	285	38,752
Kevin Phelan	67	72	74	72	285	38,752
Matthew Fitzpatrick	69	72	70	74	285	38,752
Brandon Stone	73	70	72	71	286	33,908
Lyle Rowe	72	67	74	73	286	33,908
Marco Crespi	76	67	73	72	288	30,448
Chris Doak	71	71	73	73	288	30,448
Darren Clarke	72	68	72	76	288	30,448
Darren Fichardt	75	66	73	75	289	27,680
Merrick Bremner	73	70	78	69	290	20,739.24
Jaco Ahlers	71	70	73	76	290	20,739.24
Tom Lewis	69	70	78	76	293	20,676.96
Titch Moore	73	68	76	77	294	20,635.44
Louis de Jager	71	68	78	79	296	20,593.92

Tshwane Open

Pretoria Country Club, Waterkloof, South Africa
Par 35-35–70; 7,063 yards

March 12-15
purse, €1,500,000

	SCORES				TOTAL	MONEY
George Coetzee	67	66	68	65	266	R2,932,250
Jacques Blaauw	72	65	69	61	267	2,127,500
Dean Burmester	65	68	71	67	271	984,200
Tjaart van der Walt	69	69	66	67	271	984,200
Craig Lee	67	68	66	70	271	984,200
Jaco Ahlers	69	67	70	66	272	600,325
Adrian Otaegui	67	62	72	71	272	600,325
Gregory Bourdy	70	67	70	66	273	427,350
Robert Rock	69	70	66	68	273	427,350
Rhys West	70	68	69	67	274	313,020
Dylan Frittelli	68	69	69	68	274	313,020
Mikael Lundberg	70	68	66	70	274	313,020
Erik van Rooyen	66	69	67	72	274	313,020

	SCORES				TOTAL	MONEY
David Horsey	63	69	69	73	274	313,020
Dawie van der Walt	67	69	72	67	275	231,943.75
Matthew Fitzpatrick	71	67	70	67	275	231,943.75
Jaco Van Zyl	74	65	69	67	275	231,943.75
Merrick Bremner	65	66	76	68	275	231,943.75
Darren Clarke	71	67	68	69	275	231,943.75
Adilson Da Silva	70	69	67	69	275	231,943.75
Edoardo Molinari	66	66	71	72	275	231,943.75
Morten Orum Madsen	63	72	68	72	275	231,943.75
Ulrich van den Berg	68	70	70	68	276	183,150
David Howell	72	68	68	68	276	183,150
Jared Harvey	68	69	70	69	276	183,150
Keith Horne	65	67	73	71	276	183,150
Justin Walters	66	71	67	72	276	183,150
Ockie Strydom	66	69	67	74	276	183,150
Trevor Fisher, Jr.	66	66	69	75	276	183,150
Ross Fisher	69	67	74	67	277	153,550
Maximilian Kieffer	71	68	71	67	277	153,550
Jean Hugo	71	67	71	68	277	153,550
Chris Swanepoel	66	72	69	70	277	153,550
Wallie Coetsee	64	69	68	76	277	153,550
Anthony Michael	68	68	73	69	278	131,350
Scott Jamieson	70	69	70	69	278	131,350
Ricardo Santos	66	68	74	70	278	131,350
Mike Lorenzo-Vera	67	71	70	70	278	131,350
Richard McEvoy	70	66	69	73	278	131,350
Felipe Aguilar	68	69	68	73	278	131,350
Raphael Jacquelin	65	70	68	75	278	131,350
Doug McGuigan	70	70	71	68	279	111,000
Oliver Bekker	66	70	73	70	279	111,000
Ricardo Gonzalez	69	68	70	72	279	111,000
Moritz Lampert	68	70	67	74	279	111,000
Jason Palmer	70	70	71	69	280	90,650
Steve Webster	66	71	73	70	280	90,650
Joakim Lagergren	72	67	71	70	280	90,650
Lucas Bjerregaard	71	68	71	70	280	90,650
Shaun Norris	71	69	70	70	280	90,650
Todd Sinnott	71	69	69	71	280	90,650
Eduardo de la Riva	71	68	66	75	280	90,650
Toby Tree	71	63	79	68	281	66,908.33
Andrew Curlewis	70	70	71	70	281	66,908.33
Pablo Martin Benavides	74	64	72	71	281	66,908.33
Oliver Fisher	67	72	71	71	281	66,908.33
John Parry	71	67	70	73	281	66,908.33
Oliver Farr	69	70	68	74	281	66,908.33
Byeong-Hun An	70	70	70	72	282	56,425
Michael Hoey	70	69	69	74	282	56,425
Rhys Enoch	66	74	73	70	283	53,650
Vaughn Groenewald	67	73	73	71	284	51,800
Marco Crespi	67	70	74	74	285	49,950
Jake Redman	68	69	74	75	286	45,325
Benjamin Hebert	70	68	73	75	286	45,325
Seve Benson	69	71	71	75	286	45,325
Mark Williams	70	70	70	76	286	45,325

Investec Cup

Millvale & Lost City Golf Clubs, Sun City, South Africa
Par 36-36–72; 7,401 yards

March 19-22
purse, R1,000,000

	SCORES				TOTAL	MONEY
Jaco Ahlers	72	73	68	66	279	R163,400
Jaco Van Zyl	73	67	73	66	279	117,700
(Ahlers defeated Van Zyl on third playoff hole.)						
Justin Harding	71	71	73	65	280	59,950
George Coetzee	68	70	71	71	280	59,950
Chris Swanepoel	73	71	69	68	281	37,833.33
Charl Schwartzel	68	74	70	69	281	37,833.33
Jbe' Kruger	75	71	65	70	281	37,833.33
Dean Burmester	72	71	74	66	283	30,500
Shaun Norris	71	73	70	69	283	30,500
Tjaart van der Walt	73	71	69	70	283	30,500
Danie van Tonder	75	71	72	67	285	26,700
Keith Horne	72	73	70	70	285	26,700
Trevor Fisher, Jr.	78	73	70	66	287	24,700
Rhys West	75	75	72	66	288	22,366.67
Ulrich van den Berg	73	71	76	68	288	22,366.67
Jacques Blaauw	79	70	67	72	288	22,366.67
Oliver Bekker	76	78	65	72	291	20,600
Morten Orum Madsen	74	79	71	68	292	19,175
Darren Fichardt	74	69	78	71	292	19,175
Wallie Coetsee	75	73	73	71	292	19,175
Christiaan Basson	75	71	70	76	292	19,175
Adilson Da Silva	80	76	67	71	294	17,900
Jean Hugo	72	71	72	79	294	17,900
Louis de Jager	78	72	73	72	295	17,300
Haydn Porteous	73	77	76	70	296	16,900

Golden Pilsener Zimbabwe Open

Royal Harare Golf Club, Harare, Zimbabwe
Par 36-36–72; 7,337 yards

April 9-12
purse, R1,800,000

	SCORES				TOTAL	MONEY
Dean Burmester	67	66	72	67	272	R285,300
Adilson Da Silva	66	68	68	71	273	207,000
Erik van Rooyen	71	69	67	70	277	106,470
J.C. Ritchie	67	70	69	71	277	106,470
Jacques Blaauw	69	69	68	72	278	74,340
Ulrich van den Berg	70	73	68	68	279	58,410
Andrew Curlewis	72	72	66	69	279	58,410
Neil Schietekat	74	68	69	69	280	41,580
Christiaan Basson	67	70	72	71	280	41,580
Jbe' Kruger	64	68	73	76	281	35,280
Anthony Michael	74	70	68	70	282	32,220
Tyrone Mordt	73	69	72	69	283	29,160
Mark Murless	73	69	69	72	283	29,160
Rhys West	70	70	74	70	284	25,110
Jacques Kruyswijk	70	71	72	71	284	25,110
Ryan Cairns	71	72	70	71	284	25,110
Justin Harding	72	67	72	73	284	25,110
Coert Groenewald	75	72	70	68	285	22,020
Chris Swanepoel	70	69	74	72	285	22,020
Jeff Inglis	72	70	71	72	285	22,020
Andrew Georgiou	70	77	69	70	286	19,980

	SCORES				TOTAL	MONEY
Divan van den Heever	71	71	71	73	286	19,980
Merrick Bremner	72	73	65	76	286	19,980
Mark Williams	68	75	75	69	287	18,090
Danie van Tonder	72	71	72	72	287	18,090
Wallie Coetsee	78	68	69	72	287	18,090
Grant Doverspike	72	71	70	74	287	18,090

Mopani/Redpath Zambia Open

Nkana Golf Club, Kitwe, Zambia
Par 36-36–72; 7,011 yards

April 23-26
purse, R3,200,000

	SCORES				TOTAL	MONEY
Ross McGowan	68	69	71	67	275	R507,200
Danie van Tonder	74	68	69	66	277	368,000
Rhys West	71	70	65	72	278	221,440
Colin Nel	68	68	73	70	279	157,120
Chris Swanepoel	68	72	74	66	280	122,720
Erik van Rooyen	68	70	71	71	280	122,720
Jacques Blaauw	72	69	72	69	282	94,400
Zander Lombard	72	66	74	71	283	78,720
Dean Burmester	71	74	73	66	284	69,120
Vaughn Groenewald	75	68	74	68	285	55,920
Merrick Bremner	76	70	68	71	285	55,920
Etienne Bond	72	73	67	73	285	55,920
Theunis Spangenberg	66	72	72	75	285	55,920
Andre Cruse	73	76	68	69	286	44,640
Lyle Rowe	71	69	76	70	286	44,640
Justin Harding	71	73	70	72	286	44,640
Breyten Meyer	71	73	70	72	286	44,640
Ryan Cairns	71	71	74	71	287	38,480
Oliver Bekker	71	73	68	75	287	38,480
Christiaan Basson	72	69	69	77	287	38,480
Morne Buys	68	66	73	80	287	38,480
JeanPaul Strydom	76	70	74	68	288	33,600
Madalitso Muthiya	73	76	71	68	288	33,600
Steve Surry	73	72	73	70	288	33,600
Jacques Kruyswijk	76	71	68	73	288	33,600
Ulrich van den Berg	71	69	72	76	288	33,600

Zambia Sugar Open

Lusaka Golf Club, Lusaka, Zambia
Par 35-38–73; 7,225 yards

April 30-May 3
purse, R1,500,000

	SCORES				TOTAL	MONEY
Vaughn Groenewald	68	65	71	68	272	R237,750
Jean Hugo	68	72	68	68	276	172,500
Dean Burmester	69	69	68	71	277	103,800
Daniel Greene	67	72	71	68	278	62,900
Justin Harding	70	69	70	69	278	62,900
Haydn Porteous	67	72	67	72	278	62,900
Danie van Tonder	70	70	67	72	279	40,575
Rhys Enoch	67	66	72	74	279	40,575
Divan van den Heever	73	68	69	70	280	30,900
Andrew Georgiou	71	62	71	76	280	30,900
Peter Karmis	71	67	71	72	281	25,950

	SCORES				TOTAL	MONEY
Francesco Laporta	71	69	69	72	281	25,950
Titch Moore	68	66	77	71	282	22,800
Jacques Kruyswijk	72	62	76	72	282	22,800
Tyrone Mordt	70	72	72	69	283	21,300
Colin Nel	71	68	73	72	284	19,800
Allan Versfeld	70	65	73	76	284	19,800
Mark Williams	69	70	69	76	284	19,800
Jake Redman	74	67	71	73	285	18,300
Tyrone Ryan	69	73	74	70	286	17,400
Madalitso Muthiya	71	71	74	70	286	17,400
Charl Coetzee	71	73	73	70	287	15,750
Grant Veenstra	74	69	74	70	287	15,750
Patrick Newcomb	70	75	73	69	287	15,750
Hennie du Plessis	73	70	72	72	287	15,750
Tyrone Ferreira	69	72	72	74	287	15,750

Investec Royal Swazi Open

Royal Swazi Sun Country Club, Mbabane, Swaziland May 6-9
Par 36-36–72; 6,715 yards purse, R1,200,000

	POINTS				TOTAL	MONEY
P.H. McIntyre	11	7	15	12	45	R158,500
Morne Buys	8	3	15	17	43	115,000
Grant Veenstra	11	5	11	15	42	71,400
James Kamte	10	8	12	11	41	43,066.67
Ockie Strydom	8	12	13	8	41	43,066.67
Tyrone Mordt	9	14	11	7	41	43,066.67
Francesco Laporta	5	13	6	16	40	27,650
Rhys West	14	7	7	12	40	27,650
Chris Swanepoel	2	7	10	17	36	20,168.67
Steven Ferreira	5	11	9	11	36	20,168.67
Heinrich Bruiners	11	3	9	13	36	20,168.67
Ryan Tipping	6	9	12	8	35	16,806
Drikus van der Walt	16	14	-1	6	35	16,806
Daniel Greene	6	13	2	13	34	14,306
Ruan de Smidt	-1	12	13	10	34	14,306
Mark Williams	10	9	8	7	34	14,306
Allan Versfeld	10	10	2	12	34	14,306
Jacques Kruyswijk	11	8	11	4	34	14,306
Andrew McLardy	9	13	3	8	33	12,331
Bryce Bibby	9	9	10	5	33	12,331
J.C. Ritchie	13	2	7	11	33	12,331
Peter Karmis	5	16	11	1	33	12,331
Doug McGuigan	17	10	-4	9	32	11,356
Zander Lombard	5	10	13	4	32	11,356
Charl Coetzee	13	13	4	1	31	10,906

AfrAsia Bank Mauritius Open

Heritage Golf Club, Domaine de Bel Ombre, Mauritius May 7-10
Par 35-36–71; 7,036 yards purse, €1,000,000

	SCORES				TOTAL	MONEY
George Coetzee	70	67	65	69	271	€166,660
Thorbjorn Olesen	65	68	70	68	271	111,110

(Coetzee defeated Olesen on second playoff hole.)

	SCORES				TOTAL	MONEY
Mardan Mamat	69	69	67	67	272	62,600
Thomas Aiken	69	66	68	70	273	50,000
Masahiro Kawamura	68	69	71	66	274	35,800
John Parry	67	70	71	66	274	35,800
Scott Hend	72	66	70	66	274	35,800
Bernd Ritthammer	71	70	68	67	276	22,466.67
Oliver Bekker	66	71	71	68	276	22,466.67
Merrick Bremner	71	70	66	69	276	22,466.67
Rahil Gangjee	67	70	74	66	277	17,800
Tjaart van der Walt	73	66	69	69	277	17,800
Richard T. Lee	72	68	72	66	278	14,142.86
Keith Horne	70	69	71	68	278	14,142.86
Justin Walters	67	73	69	69	278	14,142.86
Pelle Edberg	68	66	74	70	278	14,142.86
Jake Roos	70	71	67	70	278	14,142.86
Jazz Janewattananond	69	70	68	71	278	14,142.86
Andrew McArthur	68	70	68	72	278	14,142.86
Chris Lloyd	73	70	69	67	279	10,711.11
Mikael Lundberg	68	71	72	68	279	10,711.11
Andrew Dodt	72	69	70	68	279	10,711.11
Andrea Pavan	73	69	68	69	279	10,711.11
Sam Brazel	69	70	70	70	279	10,711.11
Matthew Fitzpatrick	68	67	73	71	279	10,711.11
Dean Burmester	67	68	71	73	279	10,711.11
Carlos Pigem	65	72	69	73	279	10,711.11
Nathan Holman	67	73	66	73	279	10,711.11
Scott Barr	69	73	71	67	280	8,187.50
Jordi Garcia Pinto	71	69	72	68	280	8,187.50
Jean Hugo	73	69	69	69	280	8,187.50
Carlos Del Moral	68	74	69	69	280	8,187.50
Unho Park	72	70	69	69	280	8,187.50
Ben Evans	70	70	70	70	280	8,187.50
Victor Riu	71	70	68	71	280	8,187.50
Chris Paisley	72	69	68	71	280	8,187.50
Terry Pilkadaris	66	71	74	70	281	6,500
Borja Virto Astudillo	68	72	71	70	281	6,500
Alessandro Tadini	71	69	70	71	281	6,500
Adam Groom	71	71	68	71	281	6,500
Jason Palmer	71	69	69	72	281	6,500
Thanyakon Khrongpha	69	72	68	72	281	6,500
Madalitso Muthiya	67	74	67	73	281	6,500
Adilson Da Silva	72	69	73	68	282	5,200
Gaganjeet Bhullar	72	71	71	68	282	5,200
Colin Nel	69	69	75	69	282	5,200
Kevin Phelan	68	73	72	69	282	5,200
Chien Yao Hung	70	71	69	72	282	5,200
John Hahn	70	72	68	72	282	5,200
Steve Lewton	70	69	70	74	283	4,500
Javier Colomo	72	69	72	71	284	4,000
Eduardo de la Riva	71	71	71	71	284	4,000
Chinnarat Phadungsil	72	71	70	71	284	4,000
Pablo Martin Benavides	72	66	73	73	284	4,000
Cyril Bouniol	71	70	76	68	285	3,042.86
Joakim Lagergren	70	71	73	71	285	3,042.86
Divan van den Heever	73	70	71	71	285	3,042.86
Kalem Richardson	73	66	73	73	285	3,042.86
Paul Peterson	69	70	72	74	285	3,042.86
Mithun Perera	72	71	68	74	285	3,042.86
Danie van Tonder	73	70	66	76	285	3,042.86
Rikard Karlberg	68	75	72	71	286	2,500
Estanislao Goya	70	71	72	73	286	2,500
Thaworn Wiratchant	71	71	70	74	286	2,500
Panuphol Pittayarat	67	74	75	71	287	2,250

	SCORES				TOTAL	MONEY
Daniel Chopra	70	68	77	72	287	2,250
Daniel Woltman	67	74	75	72	288	1,866
Sattaya Supupramai	70	73	73	72	288	1,866
Jason Scrivener	71	72	72	73	288	1,866
Jeung-Hun Wang	65	72	76	75	288	1,866
Ross McGowan	70	72	70	76	288	1,866
Pedro Oriol	70	73	72	74	289	1,495.50
Rattanon Wannasrichan	74	69	71	75	289	1,495.50
Ryan Cairns	69	74	72	75	290	1,491

Lombard Insurance Classic

Royal Swazi Sun Country Club, Mbabane, Swaziland
Par 36-36–72; 6,715 yards

May 22-24
purse, R1,000,000

	SCORES			TOTAL	MONEY
Dean Burmester	63	65	65	193	R158,500
Keith Horne	72	64	62	198	93,200
Peter Karmis	67	65	66	198	93,200
Thanda Mavundla	63	70	66	199	50,500
Rourke van der Spuy	67	68	65	200	39,350
Jared Harvey	62	67	71	200	39,350
James Kamte	66	68	67	201	30,200
Neil Schietekat	71	66	65	202	25,100
Ruan de Smidt	71	66	66	203	19,453
Madalitso Muthiya	66	69	68	203	19,453
Andrew Curlewis	66	68	69	203	19,453
Ockie Strydom	67	65	71	203	19,453
Jean Hugo	67	67	70	204	16,306
Shaun Norris	70	69	66	205	14,806
Keenan Davidse	69	69	67	205	14,806
Drikus Bruyns	66	70	69	205	14,806
Ryan Tipping	69	72	65	206	13,131
Werner van Niekerk	72	68	66	206	13,131
Francesco Laporta	73	67	66	206	13,131
Mark Murless	71	64	71	206	13,131
Jaco Prinsloo	71	71	65	207	10,906
Michael Hollick	70	71	66	207	10,906
Jaco Ahlers	71	67	69	207	10,906
Michiel Bothma	71	67	69	207	10,906
Jake Redman	71	67	69	207	10,906
Bradford Vaughan	71	67	69	207	10,906
Heinrich Bruiners	67	71	69	207	10,906
Ulrich van den Berg	65	71	71	207	10,906
Wallie Coetsee	67	67	73	207	10,906

Vodacom Origins of Golf - Langebaan

Langebaan Country Estate, Western Cape, South Africa
Par 36-36–72; 6,952 yards

June 4-6
purse, R650,000

	SCORES			TOTAL	MONEY
Justin Harding	72	68	68	208	R103,025
Vaughn Groenewald	73	69	66	208	74,750
(Harding defeated Groenewald on first playoff hole.)					
Andrew Georgiou	69	72	68	209	46,475
Henry Featherstone	73	66	70	209	46,475

	SCORES			TOTAL	MONEY
Madalitso Muthiya	70	71	69	210	30,550
Rhys West	73	70	68	211	24,700
Christiaan Basson	74	69	69	212	16,510
Ruan de Smidt	76	66	70	212	16,510
Lyle Rowe	71	71	70	212	16,510
Titch Moore	74	67	71	212	16,510
Andrew Curlewis	73	66	73	212	16,510
Neil Schietekat	76	67	70	213	12,350
Ulrich van den Berg	72	69	72	213	12,350
Le Roux Ferreira	69	71	73	213	12,350
JeanPaul Strydom	74	71	69	214	9,999.17
Jake Redman	76	68	70	214	9,999.17
C.J. du Plessis	74	70	70	214	9,999.17
Mark Williams	73	70	71	214	9,999.17
Jacques Kruyswijk	73	69	72	214	9,999.17
Tyrone Ryan	70	72	72	214	9,999.17
Hennie du Plessis	73	72	70	215	7,930
Allister de Kock	75	70	70	215	7,930
Maritz Wessels	76	68	71	215	7,930
Chris Swanepoel	72	72	71	215	7,930
Jaco Prinsloo	73	68	74	215	7,930
Derik Ferreira	70	70	75	215	7,930
Allan Versfeld	75	70	71	216	6,370

Sun City Challenge

Lost City Golf Course, Sun City, South Africa August 5-7
Par 36-36–72; 7,343 yards purse, R700,000

	SCORES			TOTAL	MONEY
Keith Horne	68	71	64	203	R110,950
Andrew Curlewis	67	70	71	208	80,500
Breyten Meyer	71	70	69	210	56,000
Dean Burmester	71	74	66	211	28,980
Adilson Da Silva	75	68	68	211	28,980
Danie van Tonder	71	71	69	211	28,980
Neil Schietekat	68	73	70	211	28,980
Wallie Coetsee	70	70	71	211	28,980
Etienne Bond	70	67	75	212	17,150
Charl Coetzee	71	73	69	213	15,225
Christiaan Basson	74	68	71	213	15,225
Jared Harvey	72	75	67	214	12,656
Doug McGuigan	75	70	69	214	12,656
Ryan Cairns	72	72	70	214	12,656
Ruan de Smidt	71	70	73	214	12,656
Bryce Bibby	70	70	74	214	12,656
Mark Williams	74	70	71	215	10,920
Toto Thimba	72	73	71	216	10,290
Ulrich van den Berg	64	78	74	216	10,290
Erik van Rooyen	72	75	70	217	8,866.67
Jacques Blaauw	76	70	71	217	8,866.67
Bradford Vaughan	77	69	71	217	8,866.67
Trevor Fisher, Jr.	79	66	72	217	8,866.67
Tyrone Ferreira	69	73	75	217	8,866.67
Thabang Simon	69	72	76	217	8,866.67

Vodacom Origins of Golf - San Lameer

San Lameer Country Club, Southbroom, South Africa
Par 36-36–72; 6,678 yards

August 20-22
purse, R650,000

	SCORES			TOTAL	MONEY
Jean Hugo	67	69	74	210	R103,025
Derick Petersen	74	69	68	211	63,375
Peter Karmis	70	72	69	211	63,375
Jacques Blaauw	70	72	70	212	40,950
J.C. Ritchie	71	71	71	213	30,550
Justin Turner	75	70	69	214	21,016.67
Shaun Smith	68	75	71	214	21,016.67
Adilson Da Silva	73	67	74	214	21,016.67
Jared Harvey	70	74	71	215	14,733.33
Ruan de Smidt	71	71	73	215	14,733.33
Christiaan Basson	70	71	74	215	14,733.33
Michael Hollick	71	73	72	216	11,752
Neil Schietekat	69	75	72	216	11,752
Shaun Norris	71	72	73	216	11,752
Ulrich van den Berg	75	68	73	216	11,752
Chris Swanepoel	72	70	74	216	11,752
Tyrone Ferreira	70	76	72	218	8,738.89
Mark Williams	74	72	72	218	8,738.89
Gert Myburgh	75	71	72	218	8,738.89
Tyrone Mordt	72	73	73	218	8,738.89
Mark Murless	73	72	73	218	8,738.89
Keith Horne	71	73	74	218	8,738.89
Desvonde Botes	69	74	75	218	8,738.89
Allan Versfeld	70	73	75	218	8,738.89
Keenan Davidse	73	69	76	218	8,738.89

Sun Wild Coast Sun Challenge

Wild Coast Sun Country Club, KwaZulu-Natal, South Africa
Par 35-35–70; 6,367 yards

August 26-28
purse, R700,000

	SCORES			TOTAL	MONEY
Vaughn Groenewald	64	67	67	198	R110,950
Mark Williams	68	69	62	199	80,500
Jaco Van Zyl	66	68	66	200	56,000
Jake Redman	66	70	65	201	31,412.50
Keith Horne	70	66	65	201	31,412.50
Shaun Norris	67	69	65	201	31,412.50
Jacques Blaauw	67	67	67	201	31,412.50
Jean Hugo	71	67	64	202	18,200
Andrew Georgiou	64	72	66	202	18,200
Chris Swanepoel	69	68	66	203	14,070
Callum Mowat	68	68	67	203	14,070
Adilson Da Silva	68	67	68	203	14,070
Jared Harvey	66	68	69	203	14,070
Justin Harding	68	66	69	203	14,070
Heinrich Bruiners	68	68	68	204	11,433.33
Erik van Rooyen	65	67	72	204	11,433.33
Ulrich van den Berg	66	64	74	204	11,433.33
Hennie du Plessis	68	69	68	205	10,290
Desvonde Botes	64	70	71	205	10,290
Jacquin Hess	68	70	68	206	8,710
Stuart Smith	71	65	70	206	8,710
Peter Karmis	70	66	70	206	8,710

	SCORES			TOTAL	MONEY
Anthony Michael	70	66	70	206	8,710
Andrew Curlewis	70	65	71	206	8,710
Steven Ferreira	72	63	71	206	8,710
Theunis Spangenberg	67	68	71	206	8,710

Sun Sibaya Challenge

Mount Edgecombe Country Club, Mount Edgecombe, South Africa
Par 35-36–712; 6,612 yards

September 2-4
purse, R700,000

	SCORES			TOTAL	MONEY
Michael Hollick	67	70	67	204	R110,950
Madalitso Muthiya	69	71	65	205	68,250
Jean Hugo	64	71	70	205	68,250
Mark Murless	67	73	66	206	38,500
Erik van Rooyen	66	72	68	206	38,500
Justin Harding	71	69	67	207	20,160
Brandon Stone	69	71	67	207	20,160
Mark Williams	69	70	68	207	20,160
Bryce Easton	69	70	68	207	20,160
Andrew Georgiou	69	67	71	207	20,160
J.C. Ritchie	69	73	66	208	14,700
Allan Versfeld	69	71	69	209	12,967.50
Drikus Bruyns	69	70	70	209	12,967.50
Heinrich Bruiners	70	69	70	209	12,967.50
Maritz Wessels	70	69	70	209	12,967.50
Daniel Greene	71	70	69	210	11,165
Wallie Coetsee	69	72	69	210	11,165
Zander Lombard	72	71	68	211	9,744
Lean Boezaart	67	75	69	211	9,744
Rourke van der Spuy	69	71	71	211	9,744
Jean-Paul Strydom	72	68	71	211	9,744
Titch Moore	66	73	72	211	9,744
Keenan Davidse	73	71	68	212	8,064
Ulrich van den Berg	68	76	68	212	8,064
Divan van den Heever	69	74	69	212	8,064
Doug McGuigan	68	74	70	212	8,064
Charl Coetzee	69	72	71	212	8,064

Vodacom Origins of Golf - Vaal de Grace

Vaal de Grace Golf Estate, Parys, South Africa
Par 36-36–72; 7,341 yards

September 10-12
purse, R650,000

	SCORES			TOTAL	MONEY
Jean Hugo	65	66	64	195	R103,025
Jacques Kruyswijk	66	63	67	196	74,750
Zander Lombard	66	67	65	198	52,000
Michael Hollick	69	67	63	199	40,950
Jaco Ahlers	67	66	69	202	30,550
Drikus van der Walt	64	73	66	203	22,587.50
Tyrone Ryan	70	65	68	203	22,587.50
Ockie Strydom	75	65	65	205	15,518.75
Justin Harding	71	66	68	205	15,518.75
J.J. Senekal	69	67	69	205	15,518.75
Jacquin Hess	64	70	71	205	15,518.75
C.J. du Plessis	68	70	68	206	12,041.25

	SCORES			TOTAL	MONEY
Brandon Stone	70	67	69	206	12,041.25
Dean Burmester	67	68	71	206	12,041.25
Ulrich van den Berg	66	67	73	206	12,041.25
Jared Harvey	72	67	68	207	9,598.33
Ruan de Smidt	68	71	68	207	9,598.33
Glen de Waal	69	70	68	207	9,598.33
Dayne Moore	71	68	68	207	9,598.33
Tyrone Ferreira	70	69	68	207	9,598.33
Jeff Inglis	67	68	72	207	9,598.33
Teboho Sefatsa	71	69	68	208	7,774
M.J. Viljoen	75	63	70	208	7,774
Rhys West	71	66	71	208	7,774
Stuart Smith	74	63	71	208	7,774
Andrew Curlewis	69	67	72	208	7,774

Sun Windmill Challenge

Bloemfontein Golf Club, Bloemfontein, South Africa   September 16-18
Par 36-36–72; 7,302 yards   purse, R700,000

	SCORES			TOTAL	MONEY
Dean Burmester	69	64	65	198	R110,950
Callum Mowat	62	71	69	202	80,500
Makhetha Mazibuko	67	70	67	204	56,000
Rourke van der Spuy	67	65	73	205	44,100
Jared Harvey	68	67	71	206	32,900
Le Roux Ferreira	72	69	66	207	24,325
Danie van Tonder	71	70	66	207	24,325
Christiaan Basson	69	67	72	208	18,200
Michael Hollick	69	66	73	208	18,200
Jean-Paul Strydom	66	73	70	209	15,225
Colin Nel	67	70	72	209	15,225
Jaco Prinsloo	75	65	70	210	13,300
Vaughn Groenewald	69	69	72	210	13,300
Theunis Spangenberg	67	69	74	210	13,300
Ryan Cairns	74	69	68	211	10,768.33
Justin Turner	70	71	70	211	10,768.33
Zander Lombard	68	73	70	211	10,768.33
Allan Versfeld	70	71	70	211	10,768.33
Etienne Bond	71	69	71	211	10,768.33
Anthony Michael	66	71	74	211	10,768.33
C.J. du Plessis	72	71	69	212	8,694
Heinrich Bruiners	73	68	71	212	8,694
Oliver Bekker	72	69	71	212	8,694
Roux Jeffery	71	69	72	212	8,694
Jean Hugo	71	67	74	212	8,694

Vodacom Origins of Golf - St. Francis

St. Francis Links, Eastern Cape, South Africa   October 1-3
Par 36-36–72; 7,283 yards   purse, R650,000

	SCORES			TOTAL	MONEY
Christiaan Basson	70	66	69	205	R103,025
Mark Williams	70	67	69	206	74,750
Zander Lombard	69	71	67	207	46,475
Bryce Bibby	69	64	74	207	46,475

	SCORES			TOTAL	MONEY
Madalitso Muthiya	70	70	68	208	30,550
Jean Hugo	67	72	70	209	24,700
J.J. Senekal	75	67	68	210	18,091.67
Andrew Curlewis	68	71	71	210	18,091.67
Ulrich van den Berg	67	71	72	210	18,091.67
Ruan de Smidt	71	69	71	211	13,758.33
Trevor Mahoney	69	71	71	211	13,758.33
J.C. Ritchie	71	68	72	211	13,758.33
Le Roux Ferreira	70	72	70	212	11,440
Heinrich Bruiners	71	71	70	212	11,440
Allan Versfeld	70	71	71	212	11,440
Lyle Rowe	73	70	69	212	11,440
Tyrone Ferreira	69	73	71	213	9,945
Gert Myburgh	77	68	68	213	9,945
Divan Gerber	70	72	73	215	9,360
Tyron Roelofsz	70	72	74	216	8,872.50
Mark Murless	73	70	73	216	8,872.50
Eddie Taylor	70	72	75	217	7,502.86
Ryan Tipping	70	73	74	217	7,502.86
Werner van Niekerk	73	69	75	217	7,502.86
Louis de Jager	73	71	73	217	7,502.86
Tyrone Ryan	70	74	73	217	7,502.86
Rhys Enoch	75	69	73	217	7,502.86
Jean-Paul Strydom	67	78	72	217	7,502.86

Sun Boardwalk Challenge

Humewood Golf Club, Port Elizabeth, South Africa
Par 35-37–72; 6,967 yards

October 7-9
purse, R700,000

	SCORES			TOTAL	MONEY
Chris Swanepoel	67	69	72	208	R110,950
Ulrich van den Berg	70	67	71	208	80,500
(Swanepoel defeated van den Berg on first playoff hole.)					
Andrew Georgiou	74	72	65	211	44,333.33
Lindani Ndwandwe	70	73	68	211	44,333.33
Mark Fensham	74	69	68	211	44,333.33
Michael Hollick	76	68	68	212	21,262.50
J.J. Senekal	71	72	69	212	21,262.50
Jean Hugo	73	69	70	212	21,262.50
Neil Schietekat	69	72	71	212	21,262.50
Doug McGuigan	71	73	69	213	14,070
Andrew Curlewis	70	73	70	213	14,070
Tyrone Mordt	69	73	71	213	14,070
Drikus Bruyns	70	69	74	213	14,070
Jake Redman	66	72	75	213	14,070
J.C. Ritchie	66	80	68	214	11,433.33
Derik Ferreira	70	74	70	214	11,433.33
Rourke van der Spuy	71	72	71	214	11,433.33
Alan Michell	72	75	68	215	9,922.50
Steven Ferreira	65	79	71	215	9,922.50
Christiaan Bezuidenhout	73	69	73	215	9,922.50
Ruan de Smidt	66	75	74	215	9,922.50
Pieter Moolman	71	76	69	216	8,080
Desvonde Botes	72	72	72	216	8,080
Wallie Coetsee	72	72	72	216	8,080
Christiaan Basson	69	74	73	216	8,080
Mark Murless	72	71	73	216	8,080
Rhys Enoch	71	71	74	216	8,080
Rhys West	69	72	75	216	8,080

Sun Fish River Sun Challenge

Fish River Sun Country Club, Port Alfred, South Africa   October 14-16
Par 36-36–72; 6,908 yards   purse, R700,000
(Tournament reduced to 36 holes—wind.)

	SCORES		TOTAL	MONEY
Rourke van der Spuy	65	67	132	R110,950
Merrick Bremner	68	65	133	80,500
Callum Mowat	67	68	135	56,000
Derick Petersen	70	66	136	38,500
Christiaan Basson	69	67	136	38,500
Rhys Enoch	68	69	137	24,325
Lyle Rowe	70	67	137	24,325
M.J. Viljoen	67	71	138	16,170
Otto van Greunen	66	72	138	16,170
Doug McGuigan	70	68	138	16,170
Ulrich van den Berg	68	70	138	16,170
Andrew Curlewis	69	69	138	16,170
J.J. Senekal	71	68	139	13,300
Henry Featherstone	68	72	140	10,056.67
Pieter Moolman	69	71	140	10,056.67
Antonio Rosado	71	69	140	10,056.67
Grant Veenstra	69	71	140	10,056.67
Colin Nel	67	73	140	10,056.67
Neil Schietekat	68	72	140	10,056.67
Desvonde Botes	70	70	140	10,056.67
Vaughn Groenewald	70	70	140	10,056.67
Oliver Bekker	69	71	140	10,056.67
Tyrone Ferreira	70	70	140	10,056.67
Steve Surry	68	72	140	10,056.67
Ruan de Smidt	69	71	140	10,056.67

Vodacom Origins of Golf - Koro Creek

Koro Creek Bushveld Golf Estate, Modimolle, South Africa   October 22-24
Par 36-36–72; 7,432 yards   purse, R650,000

	SCORES			TOTAL	MONEY
Dean Burmester	64	66	67	197	R103,025
Vaughn Groenewald	66	66	70	202	74,750
Toto Thimba	68	67	68	203	52,000
Anthony Michael	70	71	64	205	40,950
Neil Schietekat	71	71	64	206	25,241.67
Jean Hugo	73	67	66	206	25,241.67
Christiaan Basson	68	67	71	206	25,241.67
Andrew Georgiou	71	68	68	207	16,900
Theunis Spangenberg	71	67	69	207	16,900
Callie Swart	73	67	68	208	14,137.50
Drikus Bruyns	71	65	72	208	14,137.50
Rhys West	68	73	68	209	11,752
Gert Myburgh	70	71	68	209	11,752
Jaco Ahlers	72	67	70	209	11,752
Louis de Jager	66	73	70	209	11,752
Jacques Blaauw	70	68	71	209	11,752
Roberto Lupini	73	67	70	210	10,140
Ulrich van den Berg	69	73	69	211	9,048
M.J. Viljoen	73	68	70	211	9,048
Rourke van der Spuy	72	69	70	211	9,048
Andre Cruse	69	72	70	211	9,048

	SCORES			TOTAL	MONEY
Jacques Kruyswijk	69	69	73	211	9,048
Chris Swanepoel	73	69	70	212	6,760
Russel Franz	75	67	70	212	6,760
Ruan de Smidt	75	67	70	212	6,760
Andrew Curlewis	70	72	70	212	6,760
Tyrone Ryan	72	69	71	212	6,760
Dylan Frittelli	72	69	71	212	6,760
Charl Coetzee	70	71	71	212	6,760
Tyrone Ferreira	71	69	72	212	6,760
Dayne Moore	72	67	73	212	6,760
Zander Lombard	71	68	73	212	6,760
Coert Groenewald	66	70	76	212	6,760

Nedbank Affinity Cup

Lost City Golf Club, Sun City, South Africa
Par 36-36–72; 7,385 yards

November 3-5
purse, R800,000

	SCORES			TOTAL	MONEY
Ruan de Smidt	70	70	67	207	R126,800
Andrew Curlewis	66	72	69	207	78,000
Jean Hugo	66	70	71	207	78,000
(De Smidt defeated Curlewis and Hugo on first playoff hole.)					
Wallie Coetsee	70	72	66	208	44,000
Theunis Spangenberg	70	69	69	208	44,000
Adilson Da Silva	72	72	65	209	25,866.67
Keith Horne	68	71	70	209	25,866.67
Anthony Michael	69	67	73	209	25,866.67
Madalitso Muthiya	71	72	67	210	18,133.33
Breyten Meyer	70	70	70	210	18,133.33
Keenan Davidse	69	71	70	210	18,133.33
Callum Mowat	71	73	67	211	14,464
Ockie Strydom	72	72	67	211	14,464
Desvonde Botes	71	71	69	211	14,464
Divan van den Heever	68	70	73	211	14,464
Justin Harding	68	69	74	211	14,464
Drikus Bruyns	70	73	69	212	11,360
Chris Swanepoel	69	74	69	212	11,360
Rhys West	68	74	70	212	11,360
Tjaart van der Walt	70	70	72	212	11,360
Rourke van der Spuy	66	74	72	212	11,360
Andrew Georgiou	69	70	73	212	11,360
Jared Harvey	71	71	71	213	9,216
J.C. Ritchie	72	70	71	213	9,216
Darren Fichardt	71	70	72	213	9,216
Jbe' Kruger	71	69	73	213	9,216
Lindani Ndwandwe	71	68	74	213	9,216

Vodacom Origins of Golf Final

Zebula Country Club, Limpopo, South Africa
Par 36-36–72; 7,469 yards

November 11-13
purse, R650,000

	SCORES			TOTAL	MONEY
Darren Fichardt	61	71	70	202	R103,025
Callum Mowat	65	70	68	203	55,900
Tyrone Mordt	68	67	68	203	55,900

	SCORES			TOTAL	MONEY
Jake Redman	65	67	71	203	55,900
J.J. Senekal	66	70	68	204	27,625
Neil Schietekat	67	67	70	204	27,625
Grant Veenstra	66	71	68	205	17,225
Zander Lombard	73	64	68	205	17,225
Toby Tree	70	65	70	205	17,225
Anthony Michael	65	70	70	205	17,225
Jacques Kruyswijk	69	68	69	206	13,650
Chris Swanepoel	65	71	71	207	13,000
Andrew Curlewis	70	68	70	208	12,025
Vaughn Groenewald	69	67	72	208	12,025
Ryan Cairns	67	72	70	209	10,855
J.C. Ritchie	66	71	72	209	10,855
Tyrone Ferreira	68	74	68	210	9,945
Ockie Strydom	69	71	70	210	9,945
Christiaan Basson	71	70	70	211	9,035
P.H. McIntyre	68	71	72	211	9,035
Louis de Jager	70	68	73	211	9,035
Thanda Mavundla	71	70	71	212	7,637.50
M.J. Viljoen	72	70	70	212	7,637.50
Stephen Ferreira	71	71	70	212	7,637.50
Daniel Greene	71	72	69	212	7,637.50
Divan van den Heever	70	73	69	212	7,637.50
Madalitso Muthiya	70	69	73	212	7,637.50

Lion of Africa Cape Town Open

Royal Cape Golf Club, Cape Town, South Africa
Par 36-36–72; 6,843 yards

November 19-22
purse, R1,200,000

	SCORES				TOTAL	MONEY
Brandon Stone	73	66	63	70	272	R190,200
Ockie Strydom	67	70	73	67	277	111,840
Steve Surry	71	71	68	67	277	111,840
Scott Vincent	68	73	70	68	279	60,600
Jean-Paul Strydom	71	71	69	69	280	43,560
Peter Karmis	74	66	69	71	280	43,560
Erik van Rooyen	64	71	70	75	280	43,560
Garth Mulroy	73	69	72	67	281	24,698.80
Jaco Ahlers	74	66	73	68	281	24,698.80
Tjaart van der Walt	71	70	71	69	281	24,698.80
Chris Swanepoel	72	70	70	69	281	24,698.80
Christiaan Basson	64	76	71	70	281	24,698.80
Andrew Georgiou	62	73	76	71	282	17,887
Michael Hollick	67	71	72	72	282	17,887
Hennie Otto	68	70	72	72	282	17,887
Adrian Ford	70	71	69	72	282	17,887
Shaun Norris	72	71	67	72	282	17,887
Justin Harding	66	69	76	72	283	15,727
Theunis Spangenberg	70	70	71	72	283	15,727
Jacques Blaauw	68	75	72	69	284	14,007
Christiaan Bezuidenhout	71	69	73	71	284	14,007
Bradford Vaughan	71	70	72	71	284	14,007
J.J. Senekal	70	69	72	73	284	14,007
Toby Tree	68	71	71	74	284	14,007
Richard Sterne	72	67	70	75	284	14,007

Alfred Dunhill Championship

Leopard Creek Golf Club, Malelane, South Africa
Par 35-37–72; 7,287 yards

November 26-29
purse, €1,500,000

	SCORES				TOTAL	MONEY
Charl Schwartzel	66	67	70	70	273	R3,209,625
Gregory Bourdy	70	72	67	68	277	2,328,750
Benjamin Hebert	68	70	68	72	278	1,401,300
Sebastien Gros	71	72	63	73	279	994,275
Matt Ford	67	74	69	70	280	716,850
Thomas Linard	72	71	67	70	280	716,850
Joost Luiten	68	70	71	71	280	716,850
Jaco Van Zyl	71	72	74	64	281	444,150
Eddie Pepperell	74	65	74	68	281	444,150
Branden Grace	71	73	66	71	281	444,150
Mikael Lundberg	71	71	72	68	282	306,932.14
Pablo Martin Benavides	69	69	75	69	282	306,932.14
Shaun Norris	70	70	71	71	282	306,932.14
Dean Burmester	71	70	70	71	282	306,932.14
Tom Murray	71	71	69	71	282	306,932.14
Lasse Jensen	70	72	67	73	282	306,932.14
Dylan Frittelli	69	73	66	74	282	306,932.14
Brandon Stone	69	75	72	67	283	226,350
Romain Wattel	73	71	72	67	283	226,350
Ricardo Gouveia	72	72	71	68	283	226,350
Justin Walters	73	70	71	69	283	226,350
Rhys West	71	73	69	70	283	226,350
Thomas Aiken	72	68	72	71	283	226,350
Vaughn Groenewald	68	73	70	72	283	226,350
Keith Horne	70	72	69	72	283	226,350
David Drysdale	71	69	69	74	283	226,350
Andrew Georgiou	73	70	72	69	284	185,287.50
Darren Fichardt	70	72	71	71	284	185,287.50
Jbe' Kruger	73	70	70	71	284	185,287.50
Jason Scrivener	69	70	72	73	284	185,287.50
Erik van Rooyen	72	70	73	70	285	168,075
Doug McGuigan	69	72	72	72	285	168,075
Ryan Evans	71	70	71	73	285	168,075
Alex Haindl	71	72	74	69	286	149,850
Richard Sterne	68	70	77	71	286	149,850
Daniel Im	70	74	71	71	286	149,850
Laurie Canter	71	73	71	71	286	149,850
Jean-Paul Strydom	68	75	69	74	286	149,850
Andrew Curlewis	70	72	69	75	286	149,850
Renato Paratore	73	69	74	71	287	135,675
Jorge Campillo	75	69	75	69	288	127,575
Scott Jamieson	70	74	71	73	288	127,575
Ben Evans	71	69	73	75	288	127,575
Richard Bland	71	71	76	71	289	107,325
Jacques Blaauw	73	70	74	72	289	107,325
Chris Hanson	70	71	75	73	289	107,325
Felipe Aguilar	70	73	73	73	289	107,325
Andrew Johnston	75	67	73	74	289	107,325
Callum Shinkwin	74	69	69	77	289	107,325
Niclas Fasth	68	74	69	78	289	107,325
Colin Nel	69	75	75	71	290	87,075
Linus Gillgren	70	74	73	73	290	87,075
Jens Fahrbring	71	72	72	75	290	87,075
Rourke van der Spuy	73	70	77	71	291	74,925
Lyle Rowe	69	73	72	77	291	74,925
Clement Berardo	73	69	72	77	291	74,925
Tyrone Mordt	73	71	73	75	292	65,812.50

	SCORES				TOTAL	MONEY
Christiaan Basson	64	76	72	80	292	65,812.50
Johan Carlsson	71	70	76	76	293	60,750
Mark Williams	67	72	76	78	293	60,750
Louis de Jager	72	70	73	78	293	60,750
Lindani Ndwandwe	69	75	74	76	294	56,700
Tyrone Ferreira	71	73	76	75	295	53,662.50
Jaco Ahlers	72	70	71	82	295	53,662.50
Lee Slattery	72	70	75	80	297	50,625

Nedbank Golf Challenge

Gary Player Country Club, Sun City, South Africa
Par 36-36–72; 7,831 yards

December 3-6
purse, US$6,500,000

	SCORES				TOTAL	MONEY
Marc Leishman	68	68	66	67	269	$1,250,000
Henrik Stenson	66	67	70	72	275	775,000
Chris Wood	70	71	70	68	279	433,000
Danny Willett	67	75	70	68	280	270,750
Victor Dubuisson	71	73	68	68	280	270,750
Branden Grace	68	74	67	71	280	270,750
Robert Streb	69	66	72	73	280	270,750
Byeong-Hun An	72	70	71	68	281	175,000
Charl Schwartzel	71	74	67	70	282	160,000
Thongchai Jaidee	70	72	69	71	282	160,000
Emiliano Grillo	72	69	73	69	283	152,000
Louis Oosthuizen	70	72	68	73	283	152,000
Thomas Aiken	73	69	72	70	284	144,000
Jaco Van Zyl	66	68	72	78	284	144,000
Ross Fisher	69	71	73	72	285	138,000
Keegan Bradley	72	69	73	72	286	130,500
Matthew Fitzpatrick	69	77	68	72	286	130,500
Andy Sullivan	71	71	70	74	286	130,500
Kiradech Aphibarnrat	70	68	73	75	286	130,500
Scott Piercy	73	68	72	74	287	123,000
Webb Simpson	75	72	72	69	288	117,166
Miguel Angel Jimenez	70	72	75	71	288	117,166
Tommy Fleetwood	71	72	73	72	288	117,166
Russell Knox	69	76	68	76	289	112,000
Martin Kaymer	75	71	72	72	290	107,000
Shane Lowry	74	71	70	75	290	107,000
Bernd Wiesberger	70	71	68	81	290	107,000
Lee Westwood	72	81	72	75	300	103,000
Soren Kjeldsen	74	81	77	73	305	101,500
Steven Bowditch	77	78	77	75	307	100,000

Women's Tours

Coates Golf Championship

Golden Ocala Golf & Equestrian Club, Ocala, Florida
Par 36-36–72; 6,541 yards

January 28-31
purse, $1,500,000

	SCORES				TOTAL	MONEY
Na Yeon Choi	68	70	66	68	272	$225,000
Ha Na Jang	67	65	71	70	273	104,587
Lydia Ko	68	69	65	71	273	104,587
Jessica Korda	66	72	69	66	273	104,587
Amy Yang	74	68	65	71	278	61,979
Alison Walshe	74	71	68	66	279	50,710
Brittany Lang	74	69	67	70	280	42,446
Sun Young Yoo	70	72	70	69	281	33,681
So Yeon Ryu	72	67	70	72	281	33,681
Stacy Lewis	66	70	70	75	281	33,681
Ariya Jutanugarn	74	70	70	68	282	28,171
Minjee Lee	70	73	70	70	283	26,293
Alison Lee	71	72	69	72	284	20,434
Azahara Munoz	66	71	72	75	284	20,434
Inbee Park	71	75	67	71	284	20,434
Mo Martin	73	73	68	70	284	20,434
Austin Ernst	67	70	70	77	284	20,434
Mirim Lee	72	68	69	75	284	20,434
Sydnee Michaels	70	76	70	68	284	20,434
Mariajo Uribe	72	73	68	71	284	20,434
Yueer Cindy Feng	71	77	66	71	285	16,077
Cristie Kerr	71	69	71	74	285	16,077
Sandra Gal	77	71	68	69	285	16,077
Mina Harigae	74	71	70	71	286	13,560
Michelle Wie	72	70	73	71	286	13,560
Anna Nordqvist	74	69	70	73	286	13,560
Angela Stanford	71	65	74	76	286	13,560
Pernilla Lindberg	70	70	71	75	286	13,560
Pornanong Phatlum	77	69	68	72	286	13,560
Jennifer Johnson	75	73	71	68	287	10,893
Meena Lee	77	70	70	70	287	10,893
Wei Ling Hsu	70	71	72	74	287	10,893

Pure Silk Bahamas LPGA Classic

Ocean Club Golf Course, Paradise Island, Nassau, Bahamas
Par 36-37–73; 6,644 yards

February 5-8
purse, $1,300,000

	SCORES				TOTAL	MONEY
Sei Young Kim	70	68	72	68	278	$195,000
Sun Young Yoo	70	69	69	70	278	103,323
Ariya Jutanugarn	69	70	70	69	278	103,323
(Kim defeated Yoo and Jutanugarn on first playoff hole.)						
Brittany Lincicome	68	73	68	70	279	67,210
Inbee Park	68	70	70	72	280	49,178
Danielle Kang	70	72	69	69	280	49,178
Gerina Piller	69	70	72	70	281	31,310
Azahara Munoz	69	72	70	70	281	31,310

	SCORES				TOTAL	MONEY
Lydia Ko	72	71	70	68	281	31,310
Lexi Thompson	71	73	66	71	281	31,310
Sandra Gal	70	69	71	72	282	21,651
Hee Young Park	70	71	68	73	282	21,651
Stacy Lewis	71	73	67	71	282	21,651
Kelly Shon	69	71	71	71	282	21,651
Jaye Marie Green	72	70	70	70	282	21,651
Mina Harigae	72	70	72	69	283	17,092
Caroline Masson	72	71	69	71	283	17,092
Perrine Delacour	71	70	70	72	283	17,092
Amy Yang	72	69	72	71	284	14,557
Mika Miyazato	71	70	72	71	284	14,557
Anna Nordqvist	72	70	70	72	284	14,557
Jenny Shin	69	71	73	71	284	14,557
Line Vedel	73	68	72	71	284	14,557
Ai Miyazato	73	71	69	72	285	12,524
Min Lee	72	70	72	71	285	12,524
Moriya Jutanugarn	75	66	70	74	285	12,524
Karine Icher	73	73	71	69	286	10,524
Christina Kim	71	73	71	71	286	10,524
Suzann Pettersen	73	73	70	70	286	10,524
Amelia Lewis	73	71	69	73	286	10,524
Xi Yu Lin	72	75	69	70	286	10,524
Minjee Lee	74	70	69	73	286	10,524

ISPS Handa Women's Australian Open

See Australian Ladies Tour section.

Honda LPGA Thailand

Siam Country Club, Old Course Golf Club, Chonburi, Thailand
Par 36-36–72; 6,548 yards

February 26-March 1
purse, $1,500,000

	SCORES				TOTAL	MONEY
Amy Yang	67	66	71	69	273	$225,000
Yani Tseng	66	72	70	67	275	106,941
Stacy Lewis	66	64	73	72	275	106,941
Mirim Lee	67	69	70	69	275	106,941
Beatriz Recari	72	71	70	63	276	57,612
Sei Young Kim	70	73	68	65	276	57,612
Suzann Pettersen	67	75	68	67	277	38,536
Inbee Park	70	74	68	65	277	38,536
Sandra Gal	71	66	68	72	277	38,536
Shanshan Feng	70	69	71	68	278	31,111
Karrie Webb	72	69	71	67	279	27,845
Azahara Munoz	69	70	71	69	279	27,845
Karine Icher	71	72	70	67	280	20,064
Ilhee Lee	72	71	69	68	280	20,064
Julieta Granada	70	74	71	65	280	20,064
Brittany Lang	66	73	72	69	280	20,064
Sun Young Yoo	75	67	71	67	280	20,064
Lee-Anne Pace	71	67	71	71	280	20,064
Mo Martin	68	71	70	71	280	20,064
Anna Nordqvist	72	70	69	69	280	20,064
Ariya Jutanugarn	67	69	77	67	280	20,064
Haru Nomura	73	72	71	64	280	20,064
Mika Miyazato	69	72	73	67	281	14,687
Jenny Shin	70	66	70	75	281	14,687

	SCORES				TOTAL	MONEY
Lexi Thompson	68	71	71	71	281	14,687
Hyo Joo Kim	72	70	69	70	281	14,687
Kim Kaufman	72	69	70	70	281	14,687
Caroline Masson	70	66	74	72	282	13,059
Catriona Matthew	71	66	76	70	283	12,060
Chella Choi	71	69	69	74	283	12,060
Carlota Ciganda	76	70	71	66	283	12,060

HSBC Women's Champions

Sentosa Golf Club, Serapong Course, Singapore
Par 36-36–72; 6,600 yards

March 5-8
purse, $1,400,000

	SCORES				TOTAL	MONEY
Inbee Park	66	69	68	70	273	$210,000
Lydia Ko	68	70	67	70	275	133,258
Stacy Lewis	69	69	67	72	277	96,669
Shanshan Feng	70	71	68	69	278	61,406
Azahara Munoz	70	67	70	71	278	61,406
So Yeon Ryu	70	69	69	70	278	61,406
Caroline Masson	71	68	72	68	279	41,221
Ilhee Lee	72	72	71	65	280	31,372
Anna Nordqvist	69	70	68	73	280	31,372
Carlota Ciganda	69	66	74	71	280	31,372
Hyo Joo Kim	70	74	69	67	280	31,372
Suzann Pettersen	71	68	68	74	281	23,273
Na Yeon Choi	71	74	67	69	281	23,273
Lizette Salas	70	72	69	70	281	23,273
Lexi Thompson	69	75	70	67	281	23,273
Mo Martin	68	72	73	70	283	19,480
Sei Young Kim	73	73	70	67	283	19,480
Brittany Lincicome	74	71	67	72	284	17,413
Jenny Shin	68	70	73	73	284	17,413
Jessica Korda	72	67	70	75	284	17,413
Catriona Matthew	72	72	71	70	285	15,321
Karrie Webb	68	70	74	73	285	15,321
Yani Tseng	66	75	71	73	285	15,321
Danielle Kang	70	70	72	73	285	15,321
Beatriz Recari	72	74	70	70	286	13,680
Haru Nomura	70	70	75	71	286	13,680
Karine Icher	74	71	70	72	287	12,403
Chella Choi	73	70	73	71	287	12,403
Mina Harigae	73	73	69	72	287	12,403
Jane Park	73	71	72	72	288	10,798
Pornanong Phatlum	75	71	69	73	288	10,798
Jodi Ewart Shadoff	70	69	75	74	288	10,798
Minjee Lee	70	73	75	70	288	10,798

JTBC Founders Cup

Wildfire Golf Club at JW Marriott Phoenix Desert Ridge
Resort & Spa, Phoenix, Arizona
Par 36-36–72; 6,583 yards

March 19-22
purse, $1,500,000

	SCORES				TOTAL	MONEY
Hyo Joo Kim	65	69	66	67	267	$225,000
Stacy Lewis	64	71	67	68	270	135,414

	SCORES				TOTAL	MONEY
Ilhee Lee	69	67	70	66	272	78,463
Pornanong Phatlum	68	71	66	67	272	78,463
Mi Hyang Lee	70	66	68	68	272	78,463
Na Yeon Choi	70	66	71	66	273	38,330
Anna Nordqvist	72	67	70	64	273	38,330
Lydia Ko	66	69	69	69	273	38,330
Austin Ernst	68	67	73	65	273	38,330
Sei Young Kim	69	66	73	65	273	38,330
Sandra Gal	68	70	67	69	274	26,875
Lizette Salas	73	65	67	69	274	26,875
Jane Park	67	72	67	69	275	22,241
Amy Yang	68	69	68	70	275	22,241
Ha Na Jang	68	68	68	71	275	22,241
Kim Kaufman	66	67	70	72	275	22,241
Angela Stanford	67	70	71	68	276	17,137
Ai Miyazato	70	69	71	66	276	17,137
Jessica Korda	72	66	71	67	276	17,137
Ariya Jutanugarn	69	66	70	71	276	17,137
Moriya Jutanugarn	67	69	70	70	276	17,137
Xi Yu Lin	71	66	68	71	276	17,137
Q. Baek	69	69	71	67	276	17,137
Yueer Cindy Feng	73	66	69	69	277	13,641
Haru Nomura	69	70	70	68	277	13,641
Jaye Marie Green	69	70	69	69	277	13,641
Alison Lee	70	70	63	74	277	13,641
Cheyenne Woods	70	70	67	70	277	13,641
Paula Creamer	69	68	71	70	278	11,195
Brittany Lincicome	70	67	71	70	278	11,195
Alena Sharp	68	72	69	69	278	11,195
Jenny Shin	72	70	70	66	278	11,195
Carlota Ciganda	70	69	68	71	278	11,195

Kia Classic

Aviara Golf Club, Carlsbad, California
Par 36-36–72; 6,593 yards

March 26-29
purse, $1,700,000

	SCORES				TOTAL	MONEY
Cristie Kerr	67	68	68	65	268	$255,000
Mirim Lee	65	69	66	70	270	156,242
Lydia Ko	67	70	67	67	271	113,342
Alison Lee	69	66	66	71	272	87,679
Inbee Park	68	70	68	67	273	70,572
Hyo Joo Kim	68	68	72	66	274	53,036
Ha Na Jang	70	69	67	68	274	53,036
Moriya Jutanugarn	69	69	69	68	275	40,205
Sakura Yokomine	69	67	67	72	275	40,205
Ilhee Lee	71	71	70	64	276	30,213
Anna Nordqvist	72	69	68	67	276	30,213
Lexi Thompson	68	72	65	71	276	30,213
Se Ri Pak	69	71	64	72	276	30,213
Paula Creamer	69	69	66	72	276	30,213
Jessica Korda	74	68	68	67	277	22,925
Stacy Lewis	68	69	70	70	277	22,925
Morgan Pressel	70	64	72	71	277	22,925
Jennifer Song	70	68	66	73	277	22,925
I.K. Kim	73	68	71	68	280	17,365
Caroline Masson	71	70	71	68	280	17,365
Austin Ernst	68	73	70	69	280	17,365
Shanshan Feng	70	69	72	69	280	17,365

	SCORES				TOTAL	MONEY
Beatriz Recari	69	71	70	70	280	17,365
Carlota Ciganda	70	72	67	71	280	17,365
Lee-Anne Pace	71	67	71	71	280	17,365
Julieta Granada	71	69	67	73	280	17,365
Maria Hernandez	70	66	71	73	280	17,365
Katie Burnett	71	67	68	74	280	17,365
Karine Icher	68	74	72	67	281	12,660
Sandra Gal	72	71	70	68	281	12,660
Michelle Wie	69	74	70	68	281	12,660
Eun-Hee Ji	71	70	72	68	281	12,660
Sei Young Kim	71	71	70	69	281	12,660
Amy Yang	70	72	70	69	281	12,660

ANA Inspiration

Mission Hills Country Club, Dinah Shore Course,
Rancho Mirage, California
Par 36-36–72; 6,769 yards

April 2-5
purse, $2,500,000

	SCORES				TOTAL	MONEY
Brittany Lincicome	72	68	70	69	279	$375,000
Stacy Lewis	72	69	68	70	279	231,449
(Lincicome defeated Lewis on third playoff hole.)						
Morgan Pressel	67	72	71	70	280	167,900
Carlota Ciganda	74	71	68	68	281	106,653
Anna Nordqvist	71	72	69	69	281	106,653
Sei Young Kim	72	65	69	75	281	106,653
Lexi Thompson	72	69	71	70	282	71,595
Suzann Pettersen	76	68	72	67	283	56,812
Mi Hyang Lee	74	68	70	71	283	56,812
Shanshan Feng	71	70	70	72	283	56,812
Angela Stanford	72	69	76	67	284	37,606
Karine Icher	74	72	70	68	284	37,606
Hyo Joo Kim	71	74	70	69	284	37,606
Christina Kim	73	70	72	69	284	37,606
Catriona Matthew	71	69	74	70	284	37,606
Inbee Park	74	69	70	71	284	37,606
Mirim Lee	71	70	72	71	284	37,606
Moriya Jutanugarn	71	70	70	73	284	37,606
Jenny Shin	71	69	71	73	284	37,606
Gerina Piller	75	72	73	65	285	26,632
Austin Ernst	70	75	74	66	285	26,632
Pernilla Lindberg	71	71	75	68	285	26,632
Stephanie Meadow	76	68	70	71	285	26,632
So Yeon Ryu	69	72	71	73	285	26,632
Ariya Jutanugarn	71	73	66	75	285	26,632
Danielle Kang	75	67	77	67	286	22,429
Paula Reto	74	73	70	69	286	22,429
Charley Hull	70	72	73	71	286	22,429
Mika Miyazato	74	73	73	67	287	18,754
Eun-Hee Ji	73	70	74	70	287	18,754
Amy Yang	71	72	73	71	287	18,754
Na Yeon Choi	70	72	74	71	287	18,754
Ilhee Lee	76	68	70	73	287	18,754
Karrie Webb	74	72	67	74	287	18,754
Paula Creamer	76	69	73	70	288	14,657
Ayako Uehara	72	73	72	71	288	14,657
Q. Baek	76	70	70	72	288	14,657
Brittany Lang	73	72	70	73	288	14,657
Alison Lee	71	71	73	73	288	14,657

	SCORES				TOTAL	MONEY
Teresa Lu	76	69	69	74	288	14,657
Cristie Kerr	75	70	75	69	289	11,683
Ai Miyazato	68	74	78	69	289	11,683
Sakura Yokomine	73	72	74	70	289	11,683
In-Gee Chun	71	74	72	72	289	11,683
Ha Na Jang	72	72	71	74	289	11,683
Jennifer Song	73	74	75	68	290	9,630
Caroline Hedwall	75	67	76	72	290	9,630
Katherine Kirk	76	70	71	73	290	9,630
Sandra Gal	75	68	74	73	290	9,630
Pat Hurst	71	71	70	78	290	9,630
Mina Harigae	76	71	75	69	291	7,983
Mo Martin	74	72	73	72	291	7,983
Lydia Ko	71	73	74	73	291	7,983
Haeji Kang	71	74	72	74	291	7,983
I.K. Kim	75	70	71	75	291	7,983
Marina Alex	73	71	69	78	291	7,983
Jodi Ewart Shadoff	74	73	73	72	292	6,445
Michelle Wie	73	73	74	72	292	6,445
Meena Lee	71	73	74	74	292	6,445
Maria Hernandez	74	70	73	75	292	6,445
Wei Ling Hsu	73	70	74	75	292	6,445
Katie Burnett	72	71	74	75	292	6,445
Caroline Masson	72	73	71	76	292	6,445
Juli Inkster	69	75	77	72	293	5,702
Mariajo Uribe	74	73	73	73	293	5,702
Pornanong Phatlum	72	72	75	74	293	5,702
Amy Anderson	74	70	77	73	294	5,450
*Haley Moore	73	74	73	74	294	
Lee-Anne Pace	77	69	76	73	295	5,195
Candie Kung	72	75	73	75	295	5,195
Kris Tamulis	74	72	72	77	295	5,195
Mi Jung Hur	75	72	78	71	296	5,006
Thidapa Suwannapura	74	73	74	76	297	4,941

Lotte Championship

Ko Olina Golf Club, Kapolei, Oahu, Hawaii
Par 36-36–72; 6,383 yards

April 15-18
purse, $1,800,000

	SCORES				TOTAL	MONEY
Sei Young Kim	67	67	70	73	277	$270,000
Inbee Park	67	70	69	71	277	167,061
(Kim defeated Park on first playoff hole.)						
I.K. Kim	65	69	71	74	279	121,191
Hyo Joo Kim	69	73	70	69	281	84,605
Chella Choi	70	68	71	72	281	84,605
Sandra Gal	70	72	71	69	282	61,739
Shanshan Feng	70	73	72	69	284	43,675
Mika Miyazato	71	71	71	71	284	43,675
Cristie Kerr	69	76	67	72	284	43,675
Jenny Shin	68	70	70	76	284	43,675
Pornanong Phatlum	71	69	74	71	285	33,155
Michelle Wie	70	69	73	73	285	33,155
Minjee Lee	72	72	71	71	286	28,232
So Yeon Ryu	70	74	71	71	286	28,232
Alison Walshe	74	73	67	72	286	28,232
Belen Mozo	73	74	69	71	287	25,061
*So Young Lee	71	69	73	74	287	
Tiffany Joh	70	74	72	72	288	21,142

	SCORES				TOTAL	MONEY
Brittany Lang	73	70	73	72	288	21,142
Xi Yu Lin	69	72	72	75	288	21,142
Brittany Lincicome	73	67	73	75	288	21,142
Morgan Pressel	69	72	71	76	288	21,142
Ai Miyazato	70	69	71	78	288	21,142
Paula Creamer	69	69	72	78	288	21,142
Ji Young Oh	76	70	72	71	289	16,509
Wei-Ling Hsu	74	71	71	73	289	16,509
Danielle Kang	71	71	73	74	289	16,509
Lee-Anne Pace	72	71	71	75	289	16,509
Haru Nomura	69	70	74	76	289	16,509
Beatriz Recari	69	71	72	77	289	16,509

Swinging Skirts LPGA Classic

Lake Merced Golf Club, Daly City, California
Par 36-36–72; 6,507 yards

April 23-26
purse, $2,000,000

	SCORES				TOTAL	MONEY
Lydia Ko	67	72	71	70	280	$300,000
Morgan Pressel	69	72	67	72	280	182,956
(Ko defeated Pressel on second playoff hole.)						
Brooke M. Henderson	70	65	72	74	281	132,721
Min Seo Kwak	72	67	69	74	282	102,670
Shanshan Feng	70	70	71	72	283	82,638
Ha Na Jang	68	71	77	68	284	57,930
Amy Yang	72	68	75	69	284	57,930
Stacy Lewis	69	71	71	73	284	57,930
Mirim Lee	74	68	73	70	285	42,571
Sei Young Kim	74	69	70	72	285	42,571
Sakura Yokomine	71	67	77	71	286	36,310
Na Yeon Choi	69	68	78	71	286	36,310
P.K. Kongkraphan	68	76	71	72	287	31,853
Sandra Gal	74	67	72	74	287	31,853
Gerina Piller	72	73	73	70	288	27,512
Juli Inkster	68	74	75	71	288	27,512
Moriya Jutanugarn	70	72	72	74	288	27,512
Cristie Kerr	71	74	75	69	289	21,874
Q. Baek	73	72	74	70	289	21,874
Hyo Joo Kim	71	73	74	71	289	21,874
Inbee Park	73	71	73	72	289	21,874
Minjee Lee	71	72	74	72	289	21,874
Tiffany Joh	70	70	74	75	289	21,874
Julieta Granada	70	69	75	75	289	21,874
Yueer Cindy Feng	70	68	76	75	289	21,874
Michelle Wie	75	74	72	69	290	16,413
Ai Miyazato	73	70	77	70	290	16,413
Caroline Hedwall	69	72	77	72	290	16,413
Kelly Tan	72	70	74	74	290	16,413
Jenny Shin	72	69	75	74	290	16,413
Anna Nordqvist	70	74	70	76	290	16,413
So Yeon Ryu	73	68	71	78	290	16,413

Volunteers of America North Texas Shootout

Las Colinas Country Club, Irving, Texas
Par 36-35–71; 6,462 yards

April 30-May 3
purse, $1,300,000

	SCORES				TOTAL	MONEY
Inbee Park	69	66	69	65	269	$195,000
Cristie Kerr	66	71	69	66	272	104,626
Hee Young Park	69	67	70	66	272	104,626
Maria McBride	69	69	70	65	273	61,418
Lexi Thompson	67	69	68	69	273	61,418
Angela Stanford	67	71	67	69	274	44,818
Stacy Lewis	69	73	66	67	275	33,310
Juli Inkster	66	69	73	67	275	33,310
Karrie Webb	73	68	64	70	275	33,310
Ilhee Lee	73	69	68	66	276	26,891
Danielle Kang	70	72	67	68	277	24,068
Hyo Joo Kim	69	69	70	69	277	24,068
Morgan Pressel	70	71	69	68	278	19,919
Ha Na Jang	68	69	71	70	278	19,919
Sandra Gal	67	70	71	70	278	19,919
Brooke M. Henderson	69	65	71	73	278	19,919
Amy Yang	68	69	74	68	279	16,511
Alena Sharp	67	71	71	70	279	16,511
Karine Icher	67	69	73	70	279	16,511
Q. Baek	71	70	72	67	280	14,209
Mirim Lee	68	73	72	67	280	14,209
Lizette Salas	71	70	71	68	280	14,209
Pornanong Phatlum	71	69	71	69	280	14,209
Mi Hyang Lee	70	66	72	72	280	14,209
Sun Young Yoo	73	69	71	68	281	11,752
Julieta Granada	71	70	72	68	281	11,752
Christina Kim	68	73	71	69	281	11,752
Mi Jung Hur	71	69	72	69	281	11,752
Natalie Gulbis	67	71	70	73	281	11,752
Azahara Munoz	69	70	74	69	282	9,080
Na Yeon Choi	72	70	70	70	282	9,080
Jacqui Concolino	71	70	71	70	282	9,080
Mina Harigae	70	71	71	70	282	9,080
Ayako Uehara	71	68	73	70	282	9,080
Michelle Wie	68	70	74	70	282	9,080
Candie Kung	71	69	71	71	282	9,080
Brittany Lang	69	69	71	73	282	9,080

Kingsmill Championship

Kingsmill Resort, River Course, Williamsburg, Virginia
Par 36-35–71; 6,379 yards
(Tournament completed on Monday—rain.)

May 14-18
purse, $1,300,000

	SCORES				TOTAL	MONEY
Minjee Lee	68	67	69	65	269	$195,000
So Yeon Ryu	67	69	68	67	271	118,120
Alison Lee	66	67	70	69	272	85,688
Perrine Delacour	67	68	67	71	273	66,286
Hyo Joo Kim	70	69	67	68	274	44,515
Suzann Pettersen	72	65	69	68	274	44,515
Paula Creamer	67	71	66	70	274	44,515
Candie Kung	72	70	68	66	276	28,994
Catriona Matthew	70	67	73	66	276	28,994

	SCORES				TOTAL	MONEY
Lexi Thompson	72	66	67	71	276	28,994
Anna Nordqvist	70	69	71	67	277	22,699
Mi Jung Hur	68	73	67	69	277	22,699
Jing Yan	70	67	69	71	277	22,699
Julieta Granada	72	66	70	70	278	19,336
Angela Stanford	68	70	68	72	278	19,336
Paula Reto	69	70	73	67	279	16,491
Eun-Hee Ji	70	72	68	69	279	16,491
Lydia Ko	71	69	70	69	279	16,491
Inbee Park	72	67	70	70	279	16,491
Jacqui Concolino	67	72	72	69	280	13,839
Ai Miyazato	73	71	66	70	280	13,839
Maria McBride	71	69	69	71	280	13,839
Mariajo Uribe	68	71	70	71	280	13,839
Kris Tamulis	70	70	68	72	280	13,839
Brooke M. Henderson	71	69	74	67	281	10,218
Sakura Yokomine	74	70	69	68	281	10,218
P.K. Kongkraphan	69	75	69	68	281	10,218
Stacy Lewis	69	74	70	68	281	10,218
Jee Young Lee	71	72	68	70	281	10,218
Amy Yang	71	72	68	70	281	10,218
Soo-Bin Kim	73	68	70	70	281	10,218
Haru Nomura	70	71	70	70	281	10,218
Pornanong Phatlum	70	69	72	70	281	10,218
Sarah Kemp	73	69	68	71	281	10,218
Kelly Tan	74	69	64	74	281	10,218

ShopRite LPGA Classic

Stockton Seaview Hotel & Golf Club, Galloway, New Jersey
Par 37-34–71; 6,177 yards

May 29-31
purse, $1,500,000

	SCORES			TOTAL	MONEY
Anna Nordqvist	67	69	69	205	$225,000
Christel Boeljon	68	70	68	206	135,995
Kelly Shon	70	68	70	208	87,486
Morgan Pressel	66	69	73	208	87,486
Austin Ernst	72	73	64	209	44,748
Karrie Webb	70	73	66	209	44,748
Inbee Park	71	70	68	209	44,748
Mirim Lee	70	70	69	209	44,748
Gerina Piller	68	70	71	209	44,748
Mo Martin	69	75	66	210	25,513
Maria McBride	70	73	67	210	25,513
Hee Young Park	68	74	68	210	25,513
Shanshan Feng	70	70	70	210	25,513
Moriya Jutanugarn	69	71	70	210	25,513
Kim Kaufman	69	70	71	210	25,513
Meena Lee	73	72	66	211	17,933
Pornanong Phatlum	71	74	66	211	17,933
Sarah Kemp	72	72	67	211	17,933
Mariajo Uribe	70	71	70	211	17,933
Paula Creamer	72	68	71	211	17,933
Sun Young Yoo	69	70	72	211	17,933
Catriona Matthew	68	70	73	211	17,933
Brooke M. Henderson	68	77	67	212	12,970
Angela Stanford	72	72	68	212	12,970
Ha Na Jang	73	70	69	212	12,970
Hyo Joo Kim	71	72	69	212	12,970
Jane Park	71	72	69	212	12,970

	SCORES			TOTAL	MONEY
Soo-Bin Kim	70	73	69	212	12,970
Jenny Shin	68	75	69	212	12,970
Wei-Ling Hsu	72	70	70	212	12,970
Suzann Pettersen	72	70	70	212	12,970
Ryann O'Toole	67	73	72	212	12,970

Manulife LPGA Classic

Whistle Bear Golf Club, Cambridge, Ontario, Canada — June 4-7
Par 36-36–72; 6,613 yards — purse, $1,500,000

	SCORES				TOTAL	MONEY
Suzann Pettersen	66	65	66	69	266	$225,000
Brittany Lang	65	68	69	65	267	139,572
Mariajo Uribe	65	66	67	72	270	101,250
Minjee Lee	69	66	70	67	272	59,030
So Yeon Ryu	68	69	66	69	272	59,030
Jacqui Concolino	71	64	68	69	272	59,030
Cristie Kerr	63	69	67	73	272	59,030
Shanshan Feng	67	67	72	67	273	37,826
Hyo Joo Kim	66	67	72	69	274	32,477
Ilhee Lee	66	72	66	70	274	32,477
Inbee Park	69	68	70	68	275	26,000
Jenny Shin	67	70	70	68	275	26,000
Charley Hull	68	68	70	69	275	26,000
Julieta Granada	65	69	69	72	275	26,000
Anna Nordqvist	65	74	68	69	276	20,479
Alison Lee	69	68	70	69	276	20,479
Sarah Jane Smith	70	70	66	70	276	20,479
Catriona Matthew	69	66	71	70	276	20,479
Caroline Masson	72	66	69	70	277	16,076
Sandra Gal	64	71	72	70	277	16,076
Mi Hyang Lee	71	67	68	71	277	16,076
Thidapa Suwannapura	68	70	67	72	277	16,076
Sei Young Kim	65	73	67	72	277	16,076
Laetitia Beck	64	69	70	74	277	16,076
Katie Burnett	67	68	67	75	277	16,076
Pernilla Lindberg	66	67	68	76	277	16,076
Jane Park	69	70	70	69	278	10,934
P.K. Kongkraphan	63	75	71	69	278	10,934
Mo Martin	66	71	71	70	278	10,934
Lydia Ko	71	68	68	71	278	10,934
Lizette Salas	68	69	70	71	278	10,934
Pornanong Phatlum	71	67	68	72	278	10,934
Karlin Beck	68	69	69	72	278	10,934
Na Yeon Choi	66	71	69	72	278	10,934
Alena Sharp	67	70	68	73	278	10,934
Victoria Elizabeth	67	66	71	74	278	10,934
Kelly Tan	70	67	66	75	278	10,934
Yani Tseng	68	65	69	76	278	10,934

KPMG Women's PGA Championship

Westchester Country Club, Harrison, New York
Par 36-37–73; 6,670 yards

June 11-14
purse, $3,500,000

	SCORES				TOTAL	MONEY
Inbee Park	71	68	66	68	273	$525,000
Sei Young Kim	70	68	69	71	278	323,230
Lexi Thompson	70	72	72	66	280	234,480
Brittany Lincicome	70	74	69	68	281	181,389
Morgan Pressel	73	70	69	70	282	132,725
Brooke M. Henderson	67	73	71	71	282	132,725
Suzann Pettersen	74	66	71	72	283	93,793
Karrie Webb	68	71	72	72	283	93,793
Gerina Piller	72	70	73	69	284	72,261
Anna Nordqvist	71	73	70	70	284	72,261
Hyo Joo Kim	70	74	69	71	284	72,261
Sandra Gal	70	74	75	66	285	61,937
Minjee Lee	72	74	73	67	286	50,376
Karine Icher	69	75	72	70	286	50,376
So Yeon Ryu	72	72	71	71	286	50,376
Sakura Yokomine	74	71	69	72	286	50,376
Stacy Lewis	70	71	73	72	286	50,376
Shanshan Feng	73	72	68	73	286	50,376
Lizette Salas	74	71	73	69	287	41,410
Cristie Kerr	70	72	73	72	287	41,410
Wei-Ling Hsu	74	71	72	71	288	39,288
Sadena Parks	74	73	75	67	289	35,792
Catriona Matthew	73	72	72	72	289	35,792
Jenny Shin	66	75	76	72	289	35,792
Julieta Granada	72	71	71	75	289	35,792
Amy Yang	73	73	75	69	290	29,553
Sydnee Michaels	71	74	75	70	290	29,553
Mo Martin	72	71	75	72	290	29,553
Mirim Lee	72	72	73	73	290	29,553
Charley Hull	68	74	75	73	290	29,553
Chella Choi	70	74	72	74	290	29,553
Mi Jung Hur	71	74	74	72	291	25,128
Q. Baek	74	71	71	75	291	25,128
Felicity Johnson	73	74	75	70	292	20,907
Moriya Jutanugarn	68	78	74	72	292	20,907
Paula Creamer	71	76	72	73	292	20,907
Na Yeon Choi	76	70	73	73	292	20,907
Dori Carter	72	72	75	73	292	20,907
Jennifer Song	70	73	75	74	292	20,907
Candie Kung	70	72	74	76	292	20,907
Becky Morgan	72	73	78	70	293	15,440
Michelle Wie	75	72	75	71	293	15,440
Thidapa Suwannapura	72	75	74	72	293	15,440
Angela Stanford	73	72	76	72	293	15,440
Hee Kyung Seo	74	73	73	73	293	15,440
Ha Na Jang	72	73	73	75	293	15,440
Mika Miyazato	74	71	72	76	293	15,440
Jane Rah	70	74	73	76	293	15,440
Perrine Delacour	71	76	77	70	294	12,255
Brittany Lang	71	75	75	73	294	12,255
Jee Young Lee	75	70	76	73	294	12,255
Jane Park	72	74	74	74	294	12,255
Juli Inkster	73	73	79	70	295	9,930
Marina Alex	72	72	80	71	295	9,930
Meena Lee	72	75	76	72	295	9,930
Kelly Tan	74	73	75	73	295	9,930
Min Lee	70	77	75	73	295	9,930

	SCORES				TOTAL	MONEY
Haru Nomura	73	73	74	75	295	9,930
Laura Davies	72	74	74	75	295	9,930
Mi Hyang Lee	73	72	75	75	295	9,930
Azahara Munoz	70	73	75	77	295	9,930
Alison Lee	72	74	80	70	296	8,318
Lee-Anne Pace	73	72	81	70	296	8,318
Joanna Klatten	70	74	78	74	296	8,318
Mina Harigae	71	75	77	74	297	7,609
Kris Tamulis	71	72	80	74	297	7,609
Kelly Shon	71	76	75	75	297	7,609
Jenny Suh	73	73	75	76	297	7,609
Alena Sharp	72	74	75	76	297	7,609
Amy Anderson	74	73	77	75	299	7,080
Caroline Hedwall	71	71	82	76	300	6,992
Gwladys Nocera	71	75	78	77	301	6,900
P.K. Kongkraphan	74	73	79	76	302	6,812

Walmart NW Arkansas Championship

Pinnacle Country Club, Rogers, Arkansas
Par 36-35–71; 6,374 yards

June 26-28
purse, $2,000,000

	SCORES			TOTAL	MONEY
Na Yeon Choi	66	63	69	198	$300,000
Mika Miyazato	66	67	67	200	184,703
Azahara Munoz	65	70	66	201	107,022
Stacy Lewis	68	65	68	201	107,022
Anna Nordqvist	65	66	70	201	107,022
Lydia Ko	70	69	63	202	58,483
Paula Creamer	67	69	66	202	58,483
Minjee Lee	68	66	68	202	58,483
Cristie Kerr	69	68	66	203	39,817
Marina Alex	66	69	68	203	39,817
Mariajo Uribe	66	69	68	203	39,817
Amy Yang	65	68	70	203	39,817
Min Seo Kwak	68	70	66	204	31,213
Paula Reto	71	64	69	204	31,213
Austin Ernst	69	65	70	204	31,213
Sei Young Kim	72	68	65	205	24,809
Pernilla Lindberg	69	71	65	205	24,809
Sandra Gal	67	72	66	205	24,809
Lizette Salas	65	74	66	205	24,809
Brittany Lincicome	65	68	72	205	24,809
Mi Jung Hur	63	68	74	205	24,809
Lexi Thompson	71	68	67	206	19,358
Meena Lee	71	67	68	206	19,358
Eun-Hee Ji	69	69	68	206	19,358
Suzann Pettersen	69	68	69	206	19,358
Q. Baek	71	64	71	206	19,358
Alison Lee	70	65	71	206	19,358
Angela Stanford	68	66	72	206	19,358
Haeji Kang	71	69	67	207	14,677
Amelia Lewis	70	70	67	207	14,677
Xi Yu Lin	70	69	68	207	14,677
*Gaby Lopez	73	65	69	207	
So Yeon Ryu	73	65	69	207	14,677
Jenny Shin	68	68	71	207	14,677
Jee Young Lee	68	67	72	207	14,677

U.S. Women's Open Championship

Lancaster Country Club, Lancaster, Pennsylvania

July 9-12

Par 35-35–70; 6,406 yards

purse, $4,500,000

	SCORES				TOTAL	MONEY
In-Gee Chun	68	70	68	66	272	$810,000
Amy Yang	67	66	69	71	273	486,000
Inbee Park	68	70	70	67	275	267,072
Stacy Lewis	69	67	69	70	275	267,072
Brooke M. Henderson	70	73	68	66	277	141,396
So Yeon Ryu	72	68	70	67	277	141,396
Pernilla Lindberg	70	70	70	67	277	141,396
Morgan Pressel	68	70	71	68	277	141,396
Jane Park	66	72	71	68	277	141,396
Shiho Oyama	70	66	71	70	277	141,396
Michelle Wie	72	68	68	70	278	100,542
Lydia Ko	70	72	69	68	279	89,589
Min Lee	71	68	70	70	279	89,589
Lizette Salas	71	69	72	68	280	70,838
Brittany Lang	70	70	72	68	280	70,838
Karrie Webb	66	72	73	69	280	70,838
Rumi Yoshiba	70	68	72	70	280	70,838
Mi Hyang Lee	68	72	68	72	280	70,838
Jenny Shin	74	68	69	70	281	59,245
Ayako Uehara	71	70	73	68	282	48,082
Lee Lopez	71	70	72	69	282	48,082
Sydnee Michaels	68	74	69	71	282	48,082
Marina Alex	66	71	74	71	282	48,082
Ryann O'Toole	71	70	69	72	282	48,082
Chella Choi	71	73	64	74	282	48,082
Alison Lee	70	73	74	66	283	34,363
Jaye Marie Green	71	73	72	67	283	34,363
Ha Na Jang	72	72	71	68	283	34,363
Angela Stanford	71	69	72	71	283	34,363
Na Yeon Choi	67	74	70	72	283	34,363
Kris Tamulis	72	69	69	73	283	34,363
Q. Baek	70	71	71	72	284	28,199
Azahara Munoz	69	72	71	72	284	28,199
Ai Suzuki	70	71	69	74	284	28,199
Kim Kaufman	72	72	71	70	285	23,683
I.K. Kim	74	69	72	70	285	23,683
Mo Martin	71	72	72	70	285	23,683
Erika Kikuchi	71	71	72	71	285	23,683
*Megan Khang	71	70	73	71	285	
Teresa Lu	71	71	70	73	285	23,683
Jung-Min Lee	70	71	70	74	285	23,683
*Mariel Galdiano	70	74	71	71	286	
Paula Creamer	69	73	73	71	286	19,030
Sei Young Kim	73	67	75	71	286	19,030
Charley Hull	71	72	71	72	286	19,030
Lexi Thompson	71	72	68	75	286	19,030
Mirim Lee	71	73	72	71	287	14,796
Maria Balikoeva	74	69	73	71	287	14,796
Danielle Kang	71	73	71	72	287	14,796
Austin Ernst	68	74	72	73	287	14,796
Laura Davies	70	72	70	75	287	14,796
Sakura Yokomine	71	73	67	76	287	14,796
*Hannah O'Sullivan	72	71	74	71	288	
Gerina Piller	71	72	72	73	288	12,795
*Muni He	68	74	73	73	288	
Lee-Anne Pace	73	69	77	70	289	12,268
Karine Icher	73	71	71	74	289	12,268

	SCORES				TOTAL	MONEY
Candie Kung	71	70	72	76	289	12,268
Lala Anai	71	70	75	74	290	11,843
Haruka Morita-Wanyao Lu	71	73	75	72	291	11,690
*Emma Talley	70	72	74	75	291	
Mi Jung Hur	73	69	76	76	294	11,537
Elizabeth Nagel	68	75	83	70	296	11,402

Marathon Classic

Highland Meadows Golf Club, Sylvania, Ohio
Par 34-37–71; 6,571 yards

July 16-19
purse, $1,500,000

	SCORES				TOTAL	MONEY
Chella Choi	73	66	65	66	270	$225,000
Ha Na Jang	66	67	69	68	270	139,217
(Choi defeated Jang on first playoff hole.)						
Lydia Ko	71	66	67	67	271	89,559
Shanshan Feng	69	67	68	67	271	89,559
Hyo Joo Kim	71	68	67	67	273	52,465
Brittany Lang	68	71	66	68	273	52,465
Q. Baek	68	67	68	70	273	52,465
Azahara Munoz	73	68	68	65	274	34,173
Angela Stanford	68	68	69	69	274	34,173
Inbee Park	70	67	67	70	274	34,173
Cristie Kerr	69	72	69	65	275	26,753
Haru Nomura	71	69	67	68	275	26,753
Austin Ernst	70	68	66	71	275	26,753
Kim Kaufman	71	68	71	66	276	21,570
So Yeon Ryu	72	69	67	68	276	21,570
Stacy Lewis	71	68	69	68	276	21,570
Sei Young Kim	68	70	69	69	276	21,570
Lexi Thompson	72	67	71	67	277	17,874
Jenny Shin	68	73	66	70	277	17,874
Mi Hyang Lee	71	68	68	70	277	17,874
Jaye Marie Green	69	70	68	70	277	17,874
Amy Anderson	68	74	71	65	278	13,804
Sakura Yokomine	72	68	71	67	278	13,804
Danielle Kang	72	71	67	68	278	13,804
Minjee Lee	69	72	69	68	278	13,804
Mo Martin	72	68	70	68	278	13,804
Yani Tseng	71	65	71	71	278	13,804
Moriya Jutanugarn	71	66	69	72	278	13,804
Lee-Anne Pace	67	70	69	72	278	13,804
Alena Sharp	68	70	67	73	278	13,804
Dewi Claire Schreefel	68	68	69	73	278	13,804

Meijer LPGA Classic

Blythefield Country Club, Grand Rapids, Michigan
Par 36-35–71; 6,414 yards

July 23-26
purse, $2,000,000

	SCORES				TOTAL	MONEY
Lexi Thompson	69	64	68	65	266	$300,000
Gerina Piller	69	65	69	64	267	156,096
Lizette Salas	64	69	64	70	267	156,096
So Yeon Ryu	70	68	65	66	269	91,631
Kris Tamulis	66	68	67	68	269	91,631

	SCORES				TOTAL	MONEY
Brittany Lang	69	69	66	66	270	66,866
Brittany Lincicome	70	68	65	69	272	55,970
Xi Yu Lin	71	70	66	66	273	42,596
Amy Anderson	68	70	69	66	273	42,596
Hee Young Park	70	69	65	69	273	42,596
Alison Lee	67	66	70	70	273	42,596
Ilhee Lee	66	71	70	67	274	32,557
Jaye Marie Green	65	69	73	67	274	32,557
Q. Baek	66	68	70	70	274	32,557
Juli Inkster	69	71	70	65	275	28,727
Sarah Jane Smith	68	70	71	67	276	24,303
Sun Young Yoo	73	66	69	68	276	24,303
Cristie Kerr	73	65	70	68	276	24,303
Julieta Granada	71	68	68	69	276	24,303
Wei-Ling Hsu	65	69	71	71	276	24,303
Caroline Masson	69	69	65	73	276	24,303
Chella Choi	71	69	70	67	277	19,674
Eun-Hee Ji	70	69	68	70	277	19,674
Morgan Pressel	71	66	69	71	277	19,674
Dori Carter	64	73	69	71	277	19,674
Pernilla Lindberg	70	66	69	72	277	19,674
Haru Nomura	72	70	69	67	278	15,899
Alena Sharp	68	70	72	68	278	15,899
Lee-Anne Pace	71	69	69	69	278	15,899
Azahara Munoz	70	69	69	70	278	15,899
Jane Rah	66	72	69	71	278	15,899
Katie Burnett	69	68	66	75	278	15,899

Ricoh Women's British Open

See Ladies European Tour section.

Cambia Portland Classic

Columbia Edgewater Country Club, Portland, Oregon
Par 36-36–72; 6,476 yards

August 13-16
purse, $1,300,000

	SCORES				TOTAL	MONEY
Brooke M. Henderson	66	67	65	69	267	$195,000
Pornanong Phatlum	69	69	69	68	275	89,641
Ha Na Jang	68	70	67	70	275	89,641
Candie Kung	69	66	70	70	275	89,641
Austin Ernst	72	66	70	68	276	44,322
Azahara Munoz	68	70	69	69	276	44,322
Mo Martin	67	69	71	69	276	44,322
Jaye Marie Green	76	68	63	70	277	30,264
Alison Lee	66	71	69	71	277	30,264
Cristie Kerr	67	71	69	71	278	24,253
Alena Sharp	67	70	70	71	278	24,253
Morgan Pressel	71	67	65	75	278	24,253
Sakura Yokomine	73	69	72	65	279	18,802
Joanna Klatten	72	72	67	68	279	18,802
Soo-Bin Kim	69	72	67	71	279	18,802
So Yeon Ryu	68	71	69	71	279	18,802
Amy Anderson	65	72	71	71	279	18,802
Brittany Lang	70	71	73	66	280	13,815
Carlota Ciganda	70	74	69	67	280	13,815
Jennifer Song	70	71	70	69	280	13,815
Minjee Lee	68	72	70	70	280	13,815

	SCORES				TOTAL	MONEY
Yani Tseng	70	69	71	70	280	13,815
Sun Young Yoo	72	69	68	71	280	13,815
Lisa Ferrero	71	67	70	72	280	13,815
Min Lee	72	67	68	73	280	13,815
Jenny Shin	67	68	71	74	280	13,815
Giulia Sergas	69	72	73	67	281	9,940
Ju Young Park	71	68	72	70	281	9,940
Karine Icher	69	73	68	71	281	9,940
Stacy Lewis	71	69	70	71	281	9,940
P.K. Kongkraphan	71	68	70	72	281	9,940
Julieta Granada	66	69	72	74	281	9,940
Sandra Gal	67	72	65	77	281	9,940
Caroline Masson	70	64	70	77	281	9,940

Canadian Pacific Women's Open

Vancouver Golf Club, Vancouver, British Columbia, Canada
Par 35-37–72; 6,656 yards

August 20-23
purse, $2,250,000

	SCORES				TOTAL	MONEY
Lydia Ko	67	68	69	72	276	$337,500
Stacy Lewis	68	70	71	67	276	206,304
(Ko defeated Lewis on first playoff hole.)						
So Yeon Ryu	71	72	70	64	277	132,716
Sei Young Kim	69	71	69	68	277	132,716
Alison Lee	70	70	66	72	278	84,713
Candie Kung	69	64	71	74	278	84,713
Shanshan Feng	70	72	67	70	279	59,864
Charley Hull	69	73	67	70	279	59,864
Lexi Thompson	72	72	66	70	280	46,121
Inbee Park	71	69	70	70	280	46,121
Karine Icher	65	70	72	73	280	46,121
Lee-Anne Pace	71	71	72	67	281	38,289
Mi Jung Hur	70	73	69	69	281	38,289
Mi Hyang Lee	72	70	74	66	282	29,819
Hyo Joo Kim	71	68	74	69	282	29,819
Ilhee Lee	71	74	67	70	282	29,819
Eun-Hee Ji	71	69	72	70	282	29,819
Ariya Jutanugarn	75	68	68	71	282	29,819
Jaye Marie Green	73	68	69	72	282	29,819
Xi Yu Lin	70	66	73	73	282	29,819
Lizette Salas	71	72	69	71	283	24,623
Azahara Munoz	71	67	70	75	283	24,623
Brooke M. Henderson	70	75	72	67	284	22,816
Minjee Lee	74	68	71	71	284	22,816
Paula Reto	74	71	72	68	285	19,250
Ha Na Jang	69	72	75	69	285	19,250
Sun Young Yoo	73	72	70	70	285	19,250
Cristie Kerr	71	71	73	70	285	19,250
Mo Martin	73	68	74	70	285	19,250
Wei-Ling Hsu	71	72	71	71	285	19,250
Jennifer Song	71	71	71	72	285	19,250

Yokohama Tire LPGA Classic

RTJ Golf Trail, Capitol Hill-Senator Course, Prattville, Alabama
Par 36-36–72; 6,955 yards

August 27-30
purse, $1,300,000

	SCORES				TOTAL	MONEY
Kris Tamulis	71	68	67	65	271	$195,000
Yani Tseng	70	64	71	67	272	103,575
Austin Ernst	70	65	68	69	272	103,575
Sydnee Michaels	67	70	70	67	274	60,800
Lexi Thompson	69	67	69	69	274	60,800
Stacy Lewis	70	68	72	66	276	40,753
Jaye Marie Green	71	67	71	67	276	40,753
Wei-Ling Hsu	69	70	74	64	277	32,537
Nannette Hill	71	70	69	68	278	26,840
Julieta Granada	68	68	71	71	278	26,840
Sei Young Kim	69	70	67	72	278	26,840
Alena Sharp	71	72	69	67	279	23,005
Shanshan Feng	72	70	70	68	280	18,273
Hyo Joo Kim	68	72	72	68	280	18,273
Hee Young Park	73	69	69	69	280	18,273
Brooke M. Henderson	71	70	70	69	280	18,273
Xi Yu Lin	70	71	68	71	280	18,273
Tiffany Joh	67	70	71	72	280	18,273
Brittany Lang	65	73	69	73	280	18,273
Ariya Jutanugarn	68	73	73	67	281	14,592
Angela Stanford	72	71	69	69	281	14,592
Jing Yan	72	70	68	71	281	14,592
Brittany Lincicome	74	69	73	66	282	12,335
Jodi Ewart Shadoff	73	68	73	68	282	12,335
Sarah Jane Smith	73	73	66	70	282	12,335
Cydney Clanton	72	67	73	70	282	12,335
Minjee Lee	72	70	69	71	282	12,335
Anna Nordqvist	72	70	69	71	282	12,335
Min Lee	74	72	69	68	283	9,728
Kim Kaufman	71	75	69	68	283	9,728
Candie Kung	69	73	71	70	283	9,728
Christina Kim	72	69	71	71	283	9,728
Ryann O'Toole	67	71	73	72	283	9,728
Sadena Parks	71	69	69	74	283	9,728

Evian Championship

See Ladies European Tour section.

The Solheim Cup

See Ladies European Tour section.

Sime Darby LPGA Malaysia

Kuala Lumpur Golf & Country Club, Kuala Lumpur, Malaysia
Par 35-36–71; 6,260 yards

October 8-11
purse, $2,000,000

	SCORES				TOTAL	MONEY
Jessica Korda	69	67	65	65	266	$300,000
Lydia Ko	71	65	68	66	270	141,128
Shanshan Feng	66	69	69	66	270	141,128
Stacy Lewis	72	66	65	67	270	141,128

	SCORES				TOTAL	MONEY
Yani Tseng	66	68	71	66	271	83,633
Ha Na Jang	67	65	71	69	272	68,427
Anna Nordqvist	71	67	70	65	273	50,856
Mika Miyazato	68	69	68	68	273	50,856
Xi Yu Lin	65	68	71	69	273	50,856
Haru Nomura	71	65	70	68	274	39,535
I.K. Kim	68	68	69	69	274	39,535
Ryann O'Toole	72	66	68	69	275	34,365
Amy Yang	67	68	70	70	275	34,365
Caroline Masson	71	69	67	69	276	31,223
Eun-Hee Ji	70	68	71	68	277	27,844
Alison Lee	65	69	73	70	277	27,844
Inbee Park	68	66	71	72	277	27,844
Q. Baek	68	72	73	65	278	22,534
Sakura Yokomine	67	70	76	65	278	22,534
Azahara Munoz	71	67	73	67	278	22,534
Mirim Lee	73	71	65	69	278	22,534
Jaye Marie Green	69	71	67	71	278	22,534
Ariya Jutanugarn	71	67	69	71	278	22,534
Chella Choi	66	69	72	71	278	22,534
Lexi Thompson	71	69	72	67	279	17,943
Karine Icher	70	72	69	68	279	17,943
Charley Hull	74	66	71	68	279	17,943
Gerina Piller	73	69	67	70	279	17,943
Morgan Pressel	71	73	63	72	279	17,943
Sandra Gal	68	71	73	68	280	15,611
Mi Hyang Lee	69	71	70	70	280	15,611

LPGA KEB HanaBank Championship

See Korea LPGA Tour section.

Fubon LPGA Taiwan Championship

Miramar Golf Country Club, Chinese Taipei
Par 36-36–72

October 22-25
purse, $2,000,000

	SCORES				TOTAL	MONEY
Lydia Ko	69	67	67	65	268	$300,000
So Yeon Ryu	70	69	70	68	277	157,123
Eun-Hee Ji	66	69	72	70	277	157,123
Charley Hull	68	69	71	70	278	102,205
Suzann Pettersen	74	66	71	68	279	82,264
Paula Creamer	71	73	70	67	281	61,822
Xi Yu Lin	67	70	74	70	281	61,822
Amy Yang	69	73	72	69	283	49,359
Brittany Lang	77	71	66	70	284	44,373
Lizette Salas	69	71	77	68	285	36,345
Minjee Lee	72	73	70	70	285	36,345
Anna Nordqvist	70	70	71	74	285	36,345
Catriona Matthew	72	70	68	75	285	36,345
Michelle Wie	73	73	70	70	286	25,801
Hyo Joo Kim	74	70	72	70	286	25,801
Mika Miyazato	69	74	73	70	286	25,801
Jessica Korda	73	73	69	71	286	25,801
Mirim Lee	71	72	71	72	286	25,801
Shanshan Feng	70	76	67	73	286	25,801
Karine Icher	69	73	71	73	286	25,801
Jenny Shin	69	72	72	73	286	25,801

	SCORES				TOTAL	MONEY
Hee Young Park	71	72	70	74	287	21,338
Azahara Munoz	74	72	73	69	288	18,713
Sei Young Kim	78	69	71	70	288	18,713
Christina Kim	73	71	72	72	288	18,713
I.K. Kim	74	69	73	72	288	18,713
Haru Nomura	69	73	74	72	288	18,713
Lee-Anne Pace	75	70	70	73	288	18,713
Sakura Yokomine	70	74	73	72	289	15,057
Morgan Pressel	68	75	74	72	289	15,057
Wei-Ling Hsu	74	73	69	73	289	15,057
Ariya Jutanugarn	72	71	72	74	289	15,057
Carlota Ciganda	70	74	70	75	289	15,057

Blue Bay LPGA

Jian Lake Blue Bay Golf Course, Hainan Island, China
Par 36-367–72; 6,778 yards

October 29-November 1
purse, $2,000,000

	SCORES				TOTAL	MONEY
Sei Young Kim	70	72	74	70	286	$300,000
Kim Kaufman	72	72	74	69	287	140,103
Stacy Lewis	71	73	73	70	287	140,103
Candie Kung	71	72	73	71	287	140,103
Sandra Gal	73	73	74	71	291	69,272
Xi Yu Lin	67	77	75	72	291	69,272
Alena Sharp	74	70	74	73	291	69,272
Lydia Ko	77	75	70	70	292	41,664
Ariya Jutanugarn	74	73	75	70	292	41,664
Ilhee Lee	72	75	74	71	292	41,664
Jane Park	70	74	77	71	292	41,664
Suzann Pettersen	74	69	75	74	292	41,664
Jennifer Song	75	73	74	71	293	33,008
Pernilla Lindberg	77	72	75	70	294	26,040
Michelle Wie	76	72	76	70	294	26,040
Jenny Shin	70	78	75	71	294	26,040
Shanshan Feng	73	75	74	72	294	26,040
Jing Yan	74	77	69	74	294	26,040
Minjee Lee	74	70	76	74	294	26,040
Wei-Ling Hsu	76	75	68	75	294	26,040
Ryann O'Toole	70	73	76	75	294	26,040
Mirim Lee	72	77	74	72	295	21,536
Danielle Kang	72	73	81	70	296	18,532
Yani Tseng	74	78	73	71	296	18,532
Caroline Masson	71	76	76	73	296	18,532
Sakura Yokomine	76	71	75	74	296	18,532
Brittany Lang	71	75	75	75	296	18,532
Austin Ernst	68	75	78	75	296	18,532
Haru Nomura	73	73	72	78	296	18,532
Sun Young Yoo	73	77	76	71	297	15,196
Pornanong Phatlum	74	75	75	73	297	15,196
Carlota Ciganda	74	74	75	74	297	15,196

Toto Japan Classic

See Japan LPGA Tour section.

Lorena Ochoa Invitational

Club de Golf Mexico, Mexico City, Mexico
Par 36-36–72; 6,804 yards

November 12-15
purse, $1,000,000

	SCORES				TOTAL	MONEY
Inbee Park	68	71	67	64	270	$200,000
Carlota Ciganda	72	69	69	63	273	103,449
Sei Young Kim	73	66	70	66	275	75,045
So Yeon Ryu	71	70	69	67	277	58,053
Sakura Yokomine	72	70	69	68	279	46,726
Mariajo Uribe	71	73	71	65	280	35,115
Caroline Masson	73	71	70	66	280	35,115
Jaye Marie Green	71	70	72	69	282	24,354
Suzann Pettersen	69	71	73	69	282	24,354
Cristie Kerr	74	69	69	70	282	24,354
Christina Kim	73	66	73	70	282	24,354
Jennifer Song	72	73	69	69	283	18,615
Minjee Lee	69	69	75	70	283	18,615
Pernilla Lindberg	71	70	71	71	283	18,615
Chella Choi	73	71	71	70	285	16,425
Sydnee Michaels	71	77	70	69	287	14,764
Karine Icher	75	70	72	70	287	14,764
Angela Stanford	69	70	76	72	287	14,764
Gerina Piller	73	70	74	71	288	13,253
Lizette Salas	73	70	72	73	288	13,253
Austin Ernst	73	76	71	69	289	12,347
Pornanong Phatlum	72	71	72	74	289	12,347
Brittany Lang	74	72	73	71	290	11,233
Brittany Lincicome	72	73	74	71	290	11,233
Hee Young Park	73	71	74	72	290	11,233
Julieta Granada	75	74	73	71	293	10,422
*Gaby Lopez	71	74	73	75	293	
Lexi Thompson	73	74	73	74	294	10,024
Na Yeon Choi	78	70	74	73	295	9,430
Alena Sharp	76	73	72	74	295	9,430

CME Group Tour Championship

Tiburon Golf Club, Naples, Florida
Par 36-36–72; 6,540 yards

November 19-22
purse, $2,000,000

	SCORES				TOTAL	MONEY
Cristie Kerr	68	69	66	68	271	$500,000
Gerina Piller	68	70	67	67	272	139,869
Ha Na Jang	69	65	69	69	272	139,869
Lexi Thompson	70	69	67	68	274	90,982
Karine Icher	71	67	68	69	275	73,230
Inbee Park	71	69	67	69	276	59,915
Sydnee Michaels	72	71	69	65	277	42,385
Minjee Lee	75	66	67	69	277	42,385
Amy Yang	72	69	67	69	277	42,385
Lydia Ko	69	67	69	72	277	42,385
Jennifer Song	68	69	72	69	278	32,176
Brittany Lincicome	68	70	68	72	278	32,176
Brooke M. Henderson	72	70	71	66	279	29,114
Xi Yu Lin	74	69	69	68	280	23,936
Suzann Pettersen	71	70	69	70	280	23,936
Hee Young Park	71	69	70	70	280	23,936
Austin Ernst	66	73	71	70	280	23,936

	SCORES				TOTAL	MONEY
Stacy Lewis	72	70	67	71	280	23,936
Ai Miyazato	72	67	68	73	280	23,936
Ryann O'Toole	72	69	73	67	281	19,351
Eun-Hee Ji	72	69	71	69	281	19,351
I.K. Kim	69	71	70	71	281	19,351
Jenny Shin	71	69	69	72	281	19,351
Sei Young Kim	68	71	71	72	282	17,575
Anna Nordqvist	71	75	68	69	283	15,711
Paula Creamer	70	73	71	69	283	15,711
Catriona Matthew	70	69	74	70	283	15,711
Karrie Webb	70	72	70	71	283	15,711
Jessica Korda	70	71	69	73	283	15,711
Ariya Jutanugarn	70	76	67	71	284	13,669
Mo Martin	73	68	72	71	284	13,669

Ladies European Tour

RACV Ladies Masters

See Australian Ladies Tour section.

ISPS Handa Women's Australian Open

See Australian Ladies Tour section.

ISPS Handa New Zealand Women's Open

See Australian Ladies Tour section.

World Ladies Championship

Mission Hills, Blackstone Course, Haikou, Hainan, China
Par 36-37–73; 6,440 yards

March 12-15
purse, US$500,000

	SCORES				TOTAL	MONEY
So Yeon Ryu	72	73	65	69	279	€70,881.15
Inbee Park	69	69	71	71	280	47,962.91
Suzann Pettersen	73	72	67	70	282	29,297.54
Xi Yu Lin	71	68	73	70	282	29,297.54
Ursula Wikstrom	74	72	68	69	283	20,035.74
Pamela Pretswell	73	72	69	71	285	16,538.94
Shin-Ae Ahn	71	74	71	70	286	14,176.23
Rebecca Artis	72	72	69	74	287	11,813.53
Holly Clyburn	74	65	74	75	288	10,584.92
Yu-Ling Hsieh	75	74	71	71	291	9,545.33
Marianne Skarpnord	77	73	72	70	292	8,379.73
Becky Morgan	69	74	73	76	292	8,379.73

	SCORES				TOTAL	MONEY
Pei-Yun Chien	74	72	70	76	292	8,379.73
Nontaya Srisawang	71	73	73	76	293	7,324.39
Melissa Reid	73	74	71	75	293	7,324.39
Marion Ricordeau	76	73	72	72	293	7,324.39
Nicole Broch Larsen	74	70	77	73	294	6,454.91
Valentine Derrey	75	72	72	75	294	6,454.91
Vikki Laing	75	72	75	72	294	6,454.91
Caroline Martens	75	74	71	74	294	6,454.91
Ssu-Chia Cheng	73	73	72	76	294	6,454.91

Lalla Meryem Cup

Golf de l'Ocean, Agadir, Morocco
Par 36-35–71; 6,210 yards

March 26-29
purse, €450,000

	SCORES				TOTAL	MONEY
Gwladys Nocera	68	65	68	70	271	€67,500
Nicole Garcia	69	65	69	70	273	29,250
Melissa Reid	69	68	70	66	273	29,250
Felicity Johnson	68	68	70	67	273	29,250
Nanna Koerstz Madsen	69	68	70	68	275	16,200
Celine Herbin	68	69	70	69	276	13,950
Melanie Maetzler	71	69	68	69	277	12,600
Anais Maggetti	73	71	70	64	278	10,350
Pamela Pretswell	70	68	71	69	278	10,350
Isabelle Boineau	72	69	68	69	278	10,350
Charley Hull	74	71	67	66	278	10,350
Anne-Lise Caudal	68	68	72	70	278	10,350
Amy Boulden	71	70	70	68	279	8,145
Tonje Daffinrud	67	72	71	69	279	8,145
Eleanor Givens	68	69	68	74	279	8,145
Rebecca Hudson	70	71	70	68	279	8,145
Florentyna Parker	68	70	69	72	279	8,145
Camilla Lennarth	73	69	71	67	280	7,087.50
Malene Jorgensen	72	68	69	71	280	7,087.50
Ursula Wikstrom	67	68	70	76	281	6,300
Rebecca Artis	70	72	69	70	281	6,300
Emily Kristine Pedersen	71	69	69	72	281	6,300
Chloe Leurquin	72	68	70	71	281	6,300
Liz Young	73	71	69	68	281	6,300

Buick Championship

Qizhong Garden Golf Club, Shanghai, China
Par 36-36–72; 6,430 yards

May 8-10
purse, €557,000

	SCORES				TOTAL	MONEY
Shanshan Feng	65	67	69	70	271	€72,880.50
Hyeon Seo Kang	72	67	69	69	277	49,315.81
Nicole Broch Larsen	71	74	65	70	280	34,010.90
Amy Boulden	74	70	67	70	281	18,113.23
Marianne Skarpnord	69	70	69	73	281	18,113.23
Margherita Rigon	69	74	68	70	281	18,113.23
Stacey Keating	63	75	75	68	281	18,113.23
Wichanee Meechai	69	72	73	67	281	18,113.23
Ursula Wikstrom	75	69	70	68	282	10,349.03
Ai-Chen Kuo	68	73	70	71	282	10,349.03

	SCORES				TOTAL	MONEY
Rebecca Artis	71	69	71	72	283	8,616.09
Pamela Pretswell	71	71	70	71	283	8,616.09
Tzu-Chi Lin	70	71	71	71	283	8,616.09
Liz Young	73	72	68	71	284	7,652.45
Ziqi Ye	70	72	71	71	284	7,652.45
Florentyna Parker	71	74	68	72	285	7,190.88
Xi Yu Lin	66	72	75	72	285	7,190.88
Nanna Koerstz Madsen	71	74	67	74	286	6,057.18
Anne-Lise Caudal	72	73	72	69	286	6,057.18
Ssu-Chia Cheng	69	76	71	70	286	6,057.18
Beth Allen	69	75	69	73	286	6,057.18
Charley Hull	72	72	67	75	286	6,057.18
So-Young Jang	68	74	73	71	286	6,057.18
Pavarisa Yoktuan	69	74	70	73	286	6,057.18
Pei-Yun Chien	69	71	74	72	286	6,057.18
Bo Bea Kim	72	69	70	75	286	6,057.18

Turkish Airlines Ladies Open

Carya Golf Club, Belek, Antalya, Turkey
Par 36-37–73

May 17-20
purse, €500,000

	SCORES				TOTAL	MONEY
Melissa Reid	65	69	74	73	281	€75,000
Gwladys Nocera	68	70	76	71	285	45,000
Laura Davies	66	77	71	72	286	23,500
Sally Watson	72	71	68	75	286	23,500
Kylie Walker	72	74	68	72	286	23,500
Pamela Pretswell	72	65	72	78	287	15,500
Lucie Andre	71	70	71	76	288	12,833.33
Emily Kristine Pedersen	75	73	70	70	288	12,833.33
Titiya Plucksataporn	71	73	72	72	288	12,833.33
Lynn Carlsson	72	71	72	75	290	10,500
Rebecca Artis	69	71	72	78	290	10,500
Carly Booth	70	70	75	75	290	10,500
Nanna Koerstz Madsen	72	75	67	76	290	10,500
Beth Allen	72	71	73	74	290	10,500
Marianne Skarpnord	72	74	74	71	291	8,300
Lina Boqvist	73	73	70	75	291	8,300
Louise Stahle	76	73	69	73	291	8,300
Patricia Sanz Barrio	74	74	72	71	291	8,300
Isabelle Boineau	70	73	73	75	291	8,300
Lauren Taylor	71	76	72	73	292	6,750
Tonje Daffinrud	75	68	72	77	292	6,750
Camilla Lennarth	71	71	76	74	292	6,750
Chloe Leurquin	70	73	73	76	292	6,750
Bree Arthur	76	72	68	76	292	6,750
Malene Jorgensen	70	75	75	72	292	6,750
Georgia Hall	72	71	77	72	292	6,750

Deloitte Ladies Open

International Golf Club, Amsterdam, The Netherlands
Par 36-36–72; 6,404 yards

June 19-21
purse, €250,000

	SCORES			TOTAL	MONEY
Christel Boeljon	69	69	71	209	€37,500
Ursula Wikstrom	74	69	70	213	18,750
Emily Kristine Pedersen	72	71	70	213	18,750
Christine Wolf	72	71	71	214	9,333.33
Lucie Andre	73	73	68	214	9,333.33
Stacy Lee Bregman	72	69	73	214	9,333.33
Lynn Carlsson	72	71	72	215	6,416.67
Holly Clyburn	72	70	73	215	6,416.67
Rebecca Hudson	70	73	72	215	6,416.67
Melissa Reid	73	73	70	216	5,750
Camilla Lennarth	73	73	71	217	5,250
Nina Holleder	75	72	70	217	5,250
Anne-Lise Caudal	73	72	72	217	5,250
Sally Watson	76	70	72	218	4,325
Caroline Martens	76	72	70	218	4,325
Beth Allen	76	69	73	218	4,325
Carly Booth	74	70	74	218	4,325
Laura Murray	71	74	73	218	4,325
Minea Blomqvist	75	75	69	219	3,750
Malene Jorgensen	76	72	71	219	3,750
Noora Tamminen	75	73	71	219	3,750

ISPS Handa Ladies European Masters

Buckinghamshire Golf Club, Denham, England
Par 36-36–72; 6,498 yards

July 2-5
purse, €500,000

	SCORES				TOTAL	MONEY
Beth Allen	71	70	68	67	276	€75,000
Leona Maguire	69	70	69	69	277	
Nontaya Srisawang	67	70	69	72	278	45,000
Rebecca Artis	70	72	66	71	279	23,500
Nicole Broch Larsen	69	69	71	70	279	23,500
Caroline Masson	70	67	67	75	279	23,500
Laura Davies	71	70	72	67	280	13,500
Trish Johnson	68	71	75	66	280	13,500
Anne-Lise Caudal	72	69	69	70	280	13,500
Noora Tamminen	73	71	67	69	280	13,500
Pamela Pretswell	69	70	74	68	281	11,250
Ssu-Chia Cheng	68	70	70	73	281	11,250
Melissa Reid	71	70	71	70	282	9,375
Gwladys Nocera	69	72	74	67	282	9,375
Diana Luna	68	73	70	71	282	9,375
Louise Friberg	71	69	70	72	282	9,375
Becky Morgan	69	71	70	72	282	9,375
Ashleigh Simon	67	72	72	71	282	9,375
Alex Peters	70	63	77	73	283	8,000
Holly Clyburn	70	71	70	72	283	8,000
Georgia Hall	74	70	71	68	283	8,000

Aberdeen Asset Management Ladies Scottish Open

Dundonald Links, Troon, Scotland
Par 36-36–72; 7,100 yards

July 24-26
purse, €500,000

	SCORES			TOTAL	MONEY
Rebecca Artis	75	69	66	210	€75,000
Suzann Pettersen	68	70	74	212	50,750
Holly Clyburn	73	67	74	214	35,000
Klara Spilkova	74	69	72	215	24,100
Lydia Ko	68	73	74	215	24,100
Hannah Burke	72	73	72	217	17,500
Beth Allen	75	70	73	218	15,000
Amy Boulden	71	74	74	219	10,066.67
Emily Kristine Pedersen	74	74	71	219	10,066.67
Pamela Pretswell	79	71	69	219	10,066.67
Gwladys Nocera	73	74	72	219	10,066.67
Stacey Keating	74	72	73	219	10,066.67
Charley Hull	76	68	75	219	10,066.67
Christine Wolf	70	73	77	220	7,750
Jade Schaeffer	73	76	71	220	7,750
Catriona Matthew	74	72	74	220	7,750
Sally Watson	74	72	75	221	6,340
Leigh Whittaker	74	74	73	221	6,340
Sophie Giquel-Bettan	74	72	75	221	6,340
Becky Brewerton	76	74	71	221	6,340
Noora Tamminen	76	73	72	221	6,340
Ssu-Chia Cheng	75	72	74	221	6,340
Liz Young	74	72	75	221	6,340
Nanna Koerstz Madsen	77	74	70	221	6,340
Carin Koch	72	77	72	221	6,340
Cathryn Bristow	75	72	74	221	6,340

Ricoh Women's British Open

Trump Turnberry Resort, Turnberry, Scotland
Par 36-36–72; 6,410 yards

July 30-August 2
purse, US$3,000,000

	SCORES				TOTAL	MONEY
Inbee Park	69	73	69	65	276	€425,256
Jin Young Ko	68	71	69	71	279	276,421
Lydia Ko	66	73	72	69	280	177,822
So Yeon Ryu	67	72	73	68	280	177,822
Suzann Pettersen	68	69	72	72	281	124,854
Teresa Lu	68	71	69	74	282	102,154
Anna Nordqvist	69	72	73	69	283	80,209.70
Mika Miyazato	68	72	70	73	283	80,209.70
Minjee Lee	69	72	70	73	284	61,796.40
Melissa Reid	73	70	69	72	284	61,796.40
Amy Boulden	71	74	68	71	284	61,796.40
Maria McBride	79	66	69	72	286	52,966.50
Hyo Joo Kim	65	78	73	71	287	46,712.10
Cristie Kerr	66	77	73	71	287	46,712.10
Yani Tseng	72	72	72	71	287	46,712.10
*Luna Sobron	70	77	71	69	287	
Stacy Lewis	70	75	72	71	288	38,591.30
Lexi Thompson	71	75	70	72	288	38,591.30
Mi Hyang Lee	70	75	74	69	288	38,591.30
Hannah Burke	74	72	71	71	288	38,591.30
Angela Stanford	69	78	73	69	289	33,596.90

	SCORES				TOTAL	MONEY
Nanna Koerstz Madsen	70	78	76	65	289	33,596.90
Jung Min Lee	70	75	76	68	289	33,596.90
Shanshan Feng	71	74	76	69	290	29,473.60
Lee-Anne Pace	75	73	74	68	290	29,473.60
Nicole Broch Larsen	69	74	70	77	290	29,473.60
Sun Young Yoo	71	73	74	72	290	29,473.60
Caroline Hedwall	73	74	75	69	291	25,727.10
Jenny Shin	71	74	76	70	291	25,727.10
Maria Balikoeva	73	73	75	70	291	25,727.10
Charley Hull	73	73	77	69	292	21,943.60
Ha Na Jang	71	75	77	69	292	21,943.60
Jane Park	72	74	72	74	292	21,943.60
Christina Kim	71	72	75	74	292	21,943.60
In-Gee Chun	72	76	71	73	292	21,943.60
Marina Alex	73	74	76	70	293	17,165.80
Sandra Gal	74	74	76	69	293	17,165.80
Amy Yang	69	76	74	74	293	17,165.80
Gerina Piller	70	79	76	68	293	17,165.80
Marianne Skarpnord	71	74	73	75	293	17,165.80
Sakura Yokomine	72	77	73	71	293	17,165.80
Candie Kung	72	75	70	76	293	17,165.80
Lizette Salas	72	76	77	69	294	14,529.70
Julieta Granada	70	74	71	80	295	13,367.80
Gwladys Nocera	70	75	74	76	295	13,367.80
Florentyna Parker	68	77	74	76	295	13,367.80
Q. Baek	67	82	75	72	296	11,955.70
Jennifer Song	71	74	76	75	296	11,955.70
Katie Burnett	68	81	71	76	296	11,955.70
Azahara Munoz	68	78	79	72	297	10,164.60
Catriona Matthew	71	77	77	72	297	10,164.60
Brittany Lincicome	75	74	77	71	297	10,164.60
Chella Choi	72	77	75	73	297	10,164.60
Holly Clyburn	76	73	75	73	297	10,164.60
Misuzu Narita	69	75	76	77	297	10,164.60
Stacey Keating	71	76	73	78	298	8,474.81
Austin Ernst	75	74	77	72	298	8,474.81
Danielle Kang	70	79	73	76	298	8,474.81
Alison Walshe	70	74	72	82	298	8,474.81
Jaye Marie Green	72	74	78	74	298	8,474.81
Na Yeon Choi	72	75	76	76	299	7,264.57
Xi Yu Lin	72	76	74	77	299	7,264.57
Kelly Shon	70	76	74	79	299	7,264.57
Tiffany Joh	72	75	77	75	299	7,264.57
Brooke M. Henderson	73	75	79	72	299	7,264.57
Ssu-Chia Cheng	72	77	71	80	300	6,658.98
Alena Sharp	72	77	77	74	300	6,658.98
Ashleigh Simon	72	77	76	75	300	6,658.98
Wei Ling Hsu	74	74	77	76	301	6,279.83
Mina Harigae	72	76	80	73	301	6,279.83
Su Oh	77	72	79	74	302	5,978.08
Nina Holleder	72	77	76	77	302	5,978.08
Carly Booth	72	77	79	74	302	5,978.08

Tipsport Golf Masters

Golf Park Pilsen, Czech Republic
Par 36-35–71

August 7-9
purse, €250,000

	SCORES			TOTAL	MONEY
Hannah Burke	68	68	64	200	€37,500
Nicole Broch Larsen	64	68	70	202	25,375
Lina Boqvist	66	70	67	203	15,500
Becky Morgan	62	70	71	203	15,500
Florentyna Parker	69	68	67	204	7,291.67
Noora Tamminen	71	67	66	204	7,291.67
Nanna Koerstz Madsen	67	68	69	204	7,291.67
Gwladys Nocera	65	70	69	204	7,291.67
Melissa Reid	68	67	69	204	7,291.67
Georgia Hall	71	69	64	204	7,291.67
Rebecca Artis	67	70	68	205	4,433.33
Jade Schaeffer	69	68	68	205	4,433.33
Marta Sanz Barrio	67	69	69	205	4,433.33
Eleanor Givens	69	68	69	206	3,875
Maria Balikoeva	68	70	68	206	3,875
Miriam Nagl	67	71	68	206	3,875
Marianne Skarpnord	71	69	67	207	3,650
Isabelle Boineau	72	67	69	208	3,203.57
Sophie Giquel-Bettan	72	70	66	208	3,203.57
Stefania Croce	71	67	70	208	3,203.57
Alex Peters	70	68	70	208	3,203.57
Chloe Leurquin	74	63	71	208	3,203.57
Whitney Hillier	69	71	68	208	3,203.57
Celine Herbin	69	67	72	208	3,203.57

Helsingborg Open

Vasatorps Golf Club, Helsingborg, Skane, Sweden
Par 36-37–73; 6,215 yards

September 3-6
purse, €250,000

	SCORES				TOTAL	MONEY
Nicole Broch Larsen	68	69	68	75	280	€37,500
Ashleigh Simon	73	65	71	72	281	22,500
Malene Jorgensen	74	68	69	71	282	15,000
Nanna Koerstz Madsen	69	72	73	73	287	10,125
Joanna Klatten	71	70	72	74	287	10,125
Camilla Lennarth	72	74	68	74	288	6,750
Pernilla Lindberg	70	74	72	72	288	6,750
Maria McBride	73	72	69	74	288	6,750
Felicity Johnson	72	70	70	76	288	6,750
Lynn Carlsson	75	70	71	73	289	5,625
Marianne Skarpnord	74	67	73	75	289	5,625
Ursula Wikstrom	73	71	72	74	290	4,645.83
Charlotte Ellis	71	71	74	74	290	4,645.83
Olivia Cowan	72	69	73	76	290	4,645.83
Anne Van Dam	75	72	68	75	290	4,645.83
Klara Spilkova	73	72	73	72	290	4,645.83
Giulia Sergas	73	70	74	73	290	4,645.83
Hannah Burke	74	68	72	77	291	3,875
Katie Burnett	71	69	75	76	291	3,875
Rebecca Artis	73	73	68	77	291	3,875

Evian Championship

Evian Golf Club, Evians-les-Bains, France
Par 35-36–71; 6,470 yards

September 10-13
purse, US$3,250,000

	SCORES				TOTAL	MONEY
Lydia Ko	69	69	67	63	268	€434,260.13
Lexi Thompson	66	72	66	70	274	266,077.19
Shanshan Feng	68	68	70	70	276	193,019.94
Ilhee Lee	71	67	69	70	277	134,749.80
Mi Hyang Lee	66	67	70	74	277	134,749.80
Alison Lee	70	70	72	66	278	90,318.98
Lee-Anne Pace	71	72	65	70	278	90,318.98
Eun-Hee Ji	67	73	67	72	279	65,311.83
Inbee Park	72	69	70	68	279	65,311.83
Amy Yang	72	66	68	73	279	65,311.83
Nicole Broch Larsen	68	67	71	74	280	48,100.88
Sei Young Kim	68	71	73	68	280	48,100.88
Candie Kung	71	71	71	67	280	48,100.88
Minjee Lee	68	72	68	72	280	48,100.88
Morgan Pressel	69	65	71	75	280	48,100.88
I.K. Kim	71	67	74	69	281	37,147.72
Stacy Lewis	73	70	70	68	281	37,147.72
Jennifer Song	70	72	69	70	281	37,147.72
Michelle Wie	75	66	70	70	281	37,147.72
Karine Icher	71	68	71	72	282	31,174.98
Hyo Joo Kim	73	69	71	69	282	31,174.98
Mirim Lee	71	71	69	71	282	31,174.98
Pornanong Phatlum	67	71	72	72	282	31,174.98
Thidapa Suwannapura	75	70	67	70	282	31,174.98
Chella Choi	72	72	69	70	283	26,804.76
Brooke M. Henderson	70	74	72	67	283	26,804.76
Emily Kristine Pedersen	73	71	68	71	283	26,804.76
Jin Young Ko	69	73	70	72	284	24,764.85
Kim Kaufman	73	74	68	70	285	21,997.17
Min Lee	68	74	72	71	285	21,997.17
Xi Yu Lin	71	68	73	73	285	21,997.17
Gerina Piller	67	75	68	75	285	21,997.17
Sun Young Yoo	76	70	69	70	285	21,997.17
*Leona Maguire	72	73	73	68	286	
Mika Miyazato	74	72	72	68	286	18,646.02
Haru Nomura	70	69	74	73	286	18,646.02
Suzann Pettersen	75	72	72	67	286	18,646.02
Marina Alex	73	72	70	72	287	14,913.61
Carlota Ciganda	73	72	73	69	287	14,913.61
Charley Hull	70	70	70	77	287	14,913.61
Juli Inkster	76	68	68	75	287	14,913.61
Ai Miyazato	75	71	70	71	287	14,913.61
Ryann O'Toole	72	73	71	71	287	14,913.61
Mariajo Uribe	70	70	75	72	287	14,913.61
Karrie Webb	71	74	70	72	287	14,913.61
Ariya Jutanugarn	73	74	70	71	288	11,726.36
Pernilla Lindberg	70	73	68	77	288	11,726.36
So Yeon Ryu	72	73	72	71	288	11,726.36
Ayako Uehara	74	70	70	74	288	11,726.36
Sandra Gal	71	71	74	73	289	10,415.12
Anna Nordqvist	72	72	74	71	289	10,415.12
*Hannah O'Sullivan	76	68	74	71	289	
Cristie Kerr	75	71	72	72	290	9,760.39
Catriona Matthew	72	73	75	70	290	9,760.39
Ssu-Chia Cheng	73	73	71	74	291	8,885.63
Laura Davies	73	74	70	74	291	8,885.63
Jenny Shin	69	76	73	73	291	8,885.63

	SCORES				TOTAL	MONEY
Klara Spilkova	75	70	73	73	291	8,885.63
Kyeong Bae	74	72	70	76	292	7,721.37
Hannah Burke	74	73	72	73	292	7,721.37
Jacqui Concolino	71	75	74	72	292	7,721.37
Danielle Kang	76	67	78	71	292	7,721.37
Amy Anderson	72	74	72	75	293	7,139.68
Beth Allen	68	73	77	76	294	6,700.52
Julieta Granada	72	73	77	72	294	6,700.52
Mina Harigae	71	74	75	74	294	6,700.52
Christina Kim	73	73	76	72	294	6,700.52
Gwladys Nocera	72	70	75	77	294	6,700.52
Sarah Kemp	77	69	74	75	295	6,264.93
Austin Ernst	72	75	71	78	296	5,784.79
Jodi Ewart Shadoff	70	77	73	76	296	5,784.79
Wei-Ling Hsu	74	73	74	75	296	5,784.79
Lizette Salas	73	73	74	76	296	5,784.79
Alena Sharp	75	68	75	78	296	5,784.79
Kelly Shon	75	72	76	73	296	5,784.79
Kelly Tan	73	71	80	72	296	5,784.79
Moriya Jutanugarn	77	70	79	74	300	5,468.56

The Solheim Cup

St. Leon Golf Club, St. Leon-Rot, Germany   September 18-20
Par 36-36–72; 6,535 yards

FIRST DAY
Morning Foursomes

Morgan Pressel and Paula Creamer (US) defeated Anna Nordqvist and Suzann Pettersen,
3 and 2.
Charley Hull and Melissa Reid (Europe) defeated Michelle Wie and Brittany Lincicome,
2 and 1.
Cristie Kerr and Lexi Thompson (US) defeated Karine Icher and Azahara Munoz, 2 and 1.
Sandra Gal and Catriona Matthew (Europe) defeated Stacy Lewis and Lizette Salas, 3 and 2.

POINTS: United States 2, Europe 2

Afternoon Fourball

Nordqvist and Caroline Hedwall (Europe) defeated Pressel and Creamer, 4 and 2.
Hull and Gwladys Nocera (Europe) defeated Alison Lee and Angela Stanford, 3 and 2.
Kerr and Thompson (US) halved with Reid and Carlota Ciganda.
Gerina Piller and Brittany Lang (US) halved with Caroline Masson and Gal.

POINTS: United States 3, Europe 5

SECOND DAY
Morning Foursomes

Reid and Ciganda (Europe) defeated Lee and Wie, 4 and 3.
Hull and Pettersen (Europe) defeated Creamer and Pressel, 1 up.
Gal and Matthew (Europe) defeated Stanford and Lincicome, 1 up.
Lewis and Piller (US) defeated Nordqvist and Hedwall, 5 and 4.

POINTS: United States 4, Europe 8

Afternoon Fourball

Thompson and Kerr (US) defeated Munoz and Ciganda, 3 and 2.
Salas and Lang (Europe) defeated Icher and Matthew, 2 and 1.
Pettersen and Hull (Europe) defeated Lee and Lincicome, 2 up.
Lewis and Piller (US) defeated Mason and Hedwall, 1 up.

POINTS: United States 6, Europe 10

THIRD DAY
Singles

Thompson (US) halved with Ciganda.
Pressel (US) defeated Matthew, 2 up.
Icher (Europe) defeated Lincicome, 3 and 2.
Reid (Europe) defeated Lang, 2 and 1.
Lee (US) defeated Nocera, 3 and 1.
Piller (US) defeated Masson, 1 up.
Nordqvist (Europe) defeated Lewis, 2 and 1.
Salas (US) defeated Munoz, 3 and 1.
Stanford (US) defeated Pettersen, 2 and 1.
Kerr (US) defeated Hull, 3 and 2.
Wie (US) defeated Hedwall, 6 and 4.
Creamer (US) defeated Gal, 4 and 3.

TOTAL POINTS: United States 14½, Europe 13½

Lacoste Ladies Open de France

Golf de Chantaco, Saint-Jean-de-Luz, Aquitaine, France
Par 35-35–70; 6,006 yards

September 24-27
purse, €250,000

	SCORES				TOTAL	MONEY
Celine Herbin	66	68	65	70	269	€37,500
Emily Kristine Pedersen	67	64	68	70	269	25,375
(Herbin defeated Pedersen on third playoff hole.)						
Malene Jorgensen	69	67	68	67	271	17,500
Charley Hull	68	69	68	67	272	13,500
Joanna Klatten	68	71	67	67	273	10,600
Anne-Lise Caudal	72	66	69	67	274	8,750
Azahara Munoz	68	69	66	72	275	6,100
Pamela Pretswell	69	68	66	72	275	6,100
Klara Spilkova	70	70	69	66	275	6,100
Cristie Kerr	74	67	65	69	275	6,100
Marianne Skarpnord	67	72	66	71	276	4,235
Holly Clyburn	71	73	67	65	276	4,235
Eleanor Givens	72	69	69	66	276	4,235
Georgia Hall	76	64	68	68	276	4,235
Dewi Claire Schreefel	68	70	71	67	276	4,235
Stacy Lee Bregman	70	70	68	69	277	3,650
Trish Johnson	68	70	69	70	277	3,650
Amy Boulden	69	74	66	68	277	3,650
Gwladys Nocera	65	71	68	74	278	3,450
Sally Watson	71	71	70	67	279	3,085
Jade Schaeffer	70	72	69	68	279	3,085
Beth Allen	75	65	68	71	279	3,085
Camilla Lennarth	71	71	66	71	279	3,085
Katie Burnett	70	70	71	68	279	3,085

Xiamen International Ladies Open

Orient Golf & Country Club, Xiamen, China
Par 37-35–72; 6,305 yards

October 8-11
purse, €300,000

		SCORES			TOTAL	MONEY
Hye In Yeom	71	68	65	68	272	€45,000
Ssu-Chia Cheng	72	73	64	68	277	22,500
Kusuma Meechai	68	69	67	73	277	22,500
Gwladys Nocera	67	68	71	73	279	11,200
Nanna Koerstz Madsen	71	72	66	70	279	11,200
Tzu-Chi Lin	72	69	68	70	279	11,200
Ashleigh Simon	75	70	69	66	280	7,700
Nontaya Srisawang	73	69	70	68	280	7,700
Beth Allen	71	69	69	71	280	7,700
Liz Young	70	68	72	71	281	6,450
Wei-Wei Zhang	72	67	72	70	281	6,450
Nicole Broch Larsen	70	72	70	69	281	6,450
Pei-Yun Chien	71	67	72	71	281	6,450
Alexandra Vilatte	70	73	68	72	283	5,287.50
Stacey Keating	70	68	69	76	283	5,287.50
Thidapa Suwannapura	70	73	70	70	283	5,287.50
Yanhong Pan	71	72	69	71	283	5,287.50
Szu-Han Chen	71	72	68	73	284	4,800
Hannah Burke	69	69	72	75	285	4,500
Sarah Kemp	75	69	70	71	285	4,500
Punpaka Phuntumabamrung	70	71	74	70	285	4,500
*Man Jin	70	71	74	70	285	
*Xiang Sui	69	74	70	72	285	

Hero Women's Indian Open

DLF Golf & Country Club, Gurgaon, India
Par 36-36–72; 7,204 yards

October 23-25
purse, US$400,000

		SCORES		TOTAL	MONEY
Emily Kristine Pedersen	70	73	73	216	€53,256.15
Becky Morgan	73	71	73	217	23,077.67
Malene Jorgensen	73	72	72	217	23,077.67
Cheyenne Woods	77	69	71	217	23,077.67
Liz Young	73	73	72	218	12,781.48
Giulia Sergas	71	76	73	220	11,006.27
Tanaporn Kongkiatkrai	77	71	73	221	9,941.15
Ursula Wikstrom	73	73	76	222	8,698.50
Kanphanitnan Muangkhumsakul	75	73	74	222	8,698.50
Sarah Kemp	76	76	71	223	7,988.42
Punpaka Phuntumabamrung	78	70	75	223	7,988.42
Gwladys Nocera	75	78	71	224	7,455.86
Sophia Popov	72	76	77	225	6,745.78
Nontaya Srisawang	73	73	79	225	6,745.78
Klara Spilkova	74	75	76	225	6,745.78
*Aditi Ashok	75	73	77	225	
Eleanor Givens	78	75	73	226	5,858.18
Valentine Derrey	80	73	73	226	5,858.18
Georgia Hall	79	72	75	226	5,858.18
Christine Wolf	75	77	75	227	4,661.69
Ann-Kathrin Lindner	80	74	73	227	4,661.69
Minea Blomqvist	72	74	81	227	4,661.69
Alexandra Vilatte	76	76	75	227	4,661.69
Florentyna Parker	76	75	76	227	4,661.69

	SCORES			TOTAL	MONEY
Camilla Lennarth	77	73	77	227	4,661.69
Noora Tamminen	76	78	73	227	4,661.69
Saraporn Chamchoi	71	76	80	227	4,661.69
Vani Kapoor	79	73	75	227	4,661.69
Hyeon Seo Kang	74	78	75	227	4,661.69

Sanya Ladies Open

Yalong Bay Golf Club, Sanya, China
Par 36-36–72; 6,461 yards

November 6-8
purse, €300,000

	SCORES			TOTAL	MONEY
Xi Yu Lin	70	68	65	203	€45,000
Jing Yan	69	68	68	205	27,000
Shanshan Feng	70	66	70	206	18,000
Beth Allen	71	68	68	207	12,150
Ssu-Chia Cheng	73	66	68	207	12,150
Marianne Skarpnord	70	68	70	208	8,850
Ashleigh Simon	71	68	69	208	8,850
Amelia Lewis	67	70	72	209	7,050
Sarah-Jane Smith	71	70	68	209	7,050
Patcharajutar Kongkraphan	70	72	67	209	7,050
Kusuma Meechai	68	66	75	209	7,050
Yan-Hong Pan	68	72	70	210	6,150
Yu Liu	70	69	71	210	6,150
Christine Wolf	71	71	69	211	5,100
Ainil Bakar	68	68	75	211	5,100
Isabella Ramsay	68	71	72	211	5,100
Holly Clyburn	69	70	72	211	5,100
Kanphanitnan Muangkhumsakul	73	67	71	211	5,100
Wanchana Poruangrong	70	69	72	211	5,100
Ursula Wikstrom	69	72	71	212	3,860
Anne Van Dam	71	73	68	212	3,860
Nicole Broch Larsen	72	69	71	212	3,860
Rebecca Artis	72	71	69	212	3,860
Thidapa Suwannapura	67	73	72	212	3,860
Budsabakorn Sukapan	71	69	72	212	3,860
Yuting Shi	71	70	71	212	3,860
Pavarisa Yoktuan	67	75	70	212	3,860
Jiayi Zhou	75	69	68	212	3,860

Omega Dubai Ladies Masters

Emirates Golf Club, Dubai, United Arab Emirates
Par 35-37–72; 6,426 yards

December 9-12
purse, €500,000

	SCORES				TOTAL	MONEY
Shanshan Feng	67	67	67	66	267	€75,000
Thidapa Suwannapura	69	72	65	73	279	45,000
Melissa Reid	75	66	70	69	280	30,000
Pornanong Phatlum	71	68	73	69	281	18,666.67
Jade Schaeffer	69	71	70	71	281	18,666.67
Caroline Masson	69	75	67	70	281	18,666.67
Nontaya Srisawang	75	70	69	68	282	14,000
Lucie Andre	71	73	72	68	284	11,750
O. Sattaya	73	70	69	72	284	11,750
Malene Jorgensen	70	72	73	69	284	11,750

	SCORES			TOTAL	MONEY
Caroline Hedwall	71	68	78	67	284	11,750
Emma Cabrera-Bello	71	71	72	71	285	9,500
Diana Luna	69	75	70	71	285	9,500
Rebecca Hudson	73	72	69	71	285	9,500
Isabella Ramsay	71	72	69	73	285	9,500
Georgia Hall	69	75	68	73	285	9,500
Emily Kristine Pedersen	69	78	70	69	286	7,625
Laura Davies	68	68	77	73	286	7,625
Alexandra Vilatte	73	70	71	72	286	7,625
Gwladys Nocera	71	71	74	70	286	7,625
Stacey Keating	74	70	71	71	286	7,625
Joanna Klatten	76	70	68	72	286	7,625

Japan LPGA Tour

Daikin Orchid Ladies

Ryukyu Golf Club, Nanjo, Okinawa
Par 36-36–72; 6,529 yards

March 6-8
purse, ¥100,000,000

	SCORES			TOTAL	MONEY
Teresa Lu	69	68	65	202	¥18,000,000
Rikako Morita	69	71	66	206	8,800,000
Lala Anai	69	67	71	207	7,000,000
Hikari Kawamitsu	71	67	70	208	6,000,000
Mika Miyazato	69	73	67	209	4,166,666
Asako Fujimoto	74	68	67	209	4,166,666
Bo-Mee Lee	71	70	68	209	4,166,666
Jiyai Shin	71	69	70	210	2,750,000
Momoko Ueda	72	68	70	210	2,750,000
Nachiyo Ohtani	73	70	68	211	1,842,500
Shinobu Moromizato	71	71	69	211	1,842,500
Misuzu Narita	72	70	69	211	1,842,500
Shiho Oyama	72	68	71	211	1,842,500
Sun-Ju Ahn	68	74	70	212	1,540,000
Megumi Kido	73	69	70	212	1,540,000
O. Sattaya	73	71	69	213	1,240,000
Ji-Hee Lee	70	72	71	213	1,240,000
Sakura Yokomine	70	72	71	213	1,240,000
Nobuko Kizawa	73	67	73	213	1,240,000
Miki Sakai	69	74	71	214	960,000
Yukari Baba	71	72	71	214	960,000
Shiho Toyonaga	73	69	72	214	960,000
Satsuki Oshiro	70	70	74	214	960,000

Yokohama Tire PRGR Ladies Cup

Tosa Country Club, Kanan, Kochi
Par 36-36–72; 6,217 yards

March 13-15
purse, ¥80,000,000

	SCORES			TOTAL	MONEY
Ji-Hee Lee	67	69	71	207	¥14,400,000
Ai Suzuki	70	69	68	207	7,040,000
(Lee defeated Suzuki on first playoff hole.)					
Erika Kikuchi	67	74	67	208	5,200,000
Rui Kitada	71	68	69	208	5,200,000
Yuri Fudoh	71	69	69	209	3,600,000
Mi-Jeong Jeon	64	74	71	209	3,600,000
Teresa Lu	73	70	67	210	2,800,000
Momoko Ueda	67	74	70	211	1,868,000
Ritsuko Ryu	70	71	70	211	1,868,000
Saiki Fujita	68	72	71	211	1,868,000
Junko Omote	70	69	72	211	1,868,000
Asako Fujimoto	71	71	70	212	1,272,000
Shiho Oyama	70	70	72	212	1,272,000
Ha-Neul Kim	69	70	73	212	1,272,000
Hee-Kyung Bae	70	69	73	212	1,272,000
Shanshan Feng	70	72	71	213	1,032,000
Akane Iijima	71	69	73	213	1,032,000
Bo-Mee Lee	73	71	70	214	790,400
Megumi Kido	68	75	71	214	790,400
Hiroko Fukushima	71	71	72	214	790,400
Hikari Fujita	72	74	68	214	790,400
Soo-Yun Kang	69	69	76	214	790,400

T-Point Ladies

Wakagi Golf Club, Takeo, Saga
Par 36-36–72; 6,304 yards

March 20-22
purse, ¥70,000,000

	SCORES			TOTAL	MONEY
Akane Iijima	71	70	72	213	¥12,600,000
Mi-Jeong Jeon	74	72	67	213	6,160,000
(Iijima defeated Jeon on sixth playoff hole.)					
Asako Fujimoto	71	74	69	214	4,200,000
Momoko Ueda	74	69	71	214	4,200,000
Yuki Ichinose	71	70	73	214	4,200,000
Erika Kikuchi	72	72	71	215	2,800,000
Yasuko Satoh	75	73	68	216	2,275,000
Shinobu Moromizato	75	70	71	216	2,275,000
Saiki Fujita	70	74	73	217	1,493,333
Soo-Yun Kang	71	72	74	217	1,493,333
Ritsuko Ryu	69	72	76	217	1,493,333
Ji-Hee Lee	70	76	72	218	1,120,000
Teresa Lu	71	75	72	218	1,120,000
Bo-Mee Lee	72	74	72	218	1,120,000
*Kana Nagai	71	73	74	218	
Yukari Baba	73	71	74	218	1,120,000
Yuko Saitoh	74	69	75	218	1,120,000
Jae-Eun Chung	72	75	72	219	748,000
Jiyai Shin	73	74	72	219	748,000
Hiromi Mogi	73	75	71	219	748,000
Ha-Neul Kim	75	74	70	219	748,000
Hikari Fujita	75	71	73	219	748,000
Natsuka Hori	66	77	76	219	748,000
O. Sattaya	67	71	81	219	748,000

AXA Ladies

UMK Country Club, Miyazaki
Par 36-36–72; 6,494 yards

March 27-29
purse, ¥80,000,000

	SCORES			TOTAL	MONEY
Ritsuko Ryu	70	70	69	209	¥14,400,000
Bo-Mee Lee	67	73	69	209	7,040,000
(Ryu defeated Lee on third playoff hole.)					
Hiromi Mogi	69	71	70	210	5,200,000
Yun-Jye Wei	71	69	70	210	5,200,000
Jae-Eun Chung	72	69	70	211	3,600,000
Erina Hara	73	68	70	211	3,600,000
Esther Lee	69	74	69	212	2,400,000
Erika Kikuchi	69	74	69	212	2,400,000
Jiyai Shin	69	73	70	212	2,400,000
Ayaka Watanabe	68	75	70	213	1,382,400
Misuzu Narita	70	73	70	213	1,382,400
Akane Iijima	71	72	70	213	1,382,400
Ji-Hee Lee	72	71	70	213	1,382,400
Mina Nakayama	72	70	71	213	1,382,400
Yumiko Yoshida	72	73	69	214	928,000
Yeon-Ju Jung	70	74	70	214	928,000
Na-Ri Lee	71	73	70	214	928,000
Akane Saeki	70	73	71	214	928,000
Mi-Jeong Jeon	71	71	72	214	928,000
Megumi Kido	75	67	72	214	928,000

Yamaha Ladies Open

Katsuragi Golf Club, Yamana Course, Fukuroi, Shizuoka
Par 36-36–72; 6,568 yards

April 2-5
purse, ¥100,000,000

	SCORES				TOTAL	MONEY
Ayaka Watanabe	72	70	72	67	281	¥18,000,000
Yoko Maeda	75	69	70	69	283	7,900,000
Bo-Mee Lee	73	72	68	70	283	7,900,000
Asako Fujimoto	67	68	74	76	285	6,000,000
Kaori Yamamoto	69	75	76	68	288	3,333,333
Mihoko Iseri	72	73	73	70	288	3,333,333
Sun-Ju Ahn	74	68	75	71	288	3,333,333
Shiho Toyonaga	70	73	73	72	288	3,333,333
Mi-Jeong Jeon	70	73	73	72	288	3,333,333
Yuko Mitsuka	69	74	70	75	288	3,333,333
Megumi Kido	72	73	72	72	289	1,700,000
Ritsuko Ryu	69	73	73	74	289	1,700,000
Jia-Yun Li	75	74	73	68	290	1,350,000
Airi Saitoh	73	69	77	71	290	1,350,000
Soo-Yun Kang	71	76	72	71	290	1,350,000
Lala Anai	72	73	73	72	290	1,350,000
Akane Iijima	70	74	73	73	290	1,350,000
Mami Fukuda	74	72	75	70	291	880,000
Hiroko Azuma	72	76	71	72	291	880,000
Yeon-Ju Jung	72	72	74	73	291	880,000
Yumiko Yoshida	72	73	73	73	291	880,000
Momoko Ueda	75	72	71	73	291	880,000
Da-Ye Na	75	73	69	74	291	880,000

Studio Alice Ladies Open

Hanayashiki Golf Club, Yokawa Course, Miki, Hyogo
Par 36-36–72; 6,376 yards

April 10-12
purse, ¥60,000,000

	SCORES			TOTAL	MONEY
Misuzu Narita	73	70	64	207	¥10,800,000
Hikari Fujita	70	70	69	209	5,280,000
Erika Kikuchi	72	71	69	212	4,200,000
Teresa Lu	74	72	67	213	3,600,000
Rikako Morita	76	69	69	214	3,000,000
Akane Iijima	73	72	70	215	2,250,000
Hibiki Kitamura	74	71	70	215	2,250,000
Soo-Yun Kang	72	73	71	216	1,800,000
Na-Ri Lee	73	75	69	217	1,150,000
Megumi Kido	80	68	69	217	1,150,000
Hiroko Azuma	76	72	69	217	1,150,000
Ritsuko Ryu	70	75	72	217	1,150,000
Mami Fukuda	71	74	72	217	1,150,000
Momoko Ueda	73	72	72	217	1,150,000
Megumi Shimokawa	73	74	71	218	726,857
Ai Suzuki	73	74	71	218	726,857
*Tomoko Nishi	77	72	69	218	
Eri Fukuyama	73	76	69	218	726,857
Mihoko Iseri	73	73	72	218	726,857
Kurumi Dohi	76	70	72	218	726,857
Ayaka Watanabe	73	70	75	218	726,857
Saki Okamura	76	67	75	218	726,857

Vantelin Ladies Open KKT Cup

Kumamoto Kuko Country Club, Kikuyo, Kumamoto
Par 36-36–72; 6,452 yards

April 17-19
purse, ¥100,000,000

	SCORES			TOTAL	MONEY
Erika Kikuchi	68	70	69	207	¥18,000,000
Bo-Mee Lee	73	72	67	212	8,000,000
Maiko Wakabayashi	69	71	72	212	8,000,000
Hikari Fujita	73	71	69	213	5,066,666
Momoko Ueda	73	69	71	213	5,066,666
Ayaka Watanabe	69	72	72	213	5,066,666
Jiyai Shin	70	75	69	214	3,250,000
Da-Ye Na	71	72	71	214	3,250,000
Chie Arimura	77	71	67	215	2,250,000
Sun-Ju Ahn	72	71	72	215	2,250,000
Yuki Ichinose	71	76	69	216	1,820,000
Kana Taneda	75	73	68	216	1,820,000
Saiki Fujita	74	71	71	216	1,820,000
Ritsuko Ryu	71	76	70	217	1,370,000
Miki Sakai	72	74	71	217	1,370,000
Hee-Kyung Bae	72	74	71	217	1,370,000
Yukari Baba	75	74	68	217	1,370,000
*Kana Nagai	70	74	73	217	
Misuzu Narita	74	70	73	217	1,370,000
Hikari Kawamitsu	69	74	74	217	1,370,000

Fujisankei Ladies Classic

Kawana Hotel Golf Club, Fuji Course, Ito, Shizuoka
Par 36-36–72; 6,367 yards

April 24-26
purse, ¥80,000,000

	SCORES			TOTAL	MONEY
Hikari Fujita	71	69	69	209	¥14,400,000
Bo-Mee Lee	74	68	68	210	4,928,000
Ayaka Matsumori	67	73	70	210	4,928,000
Junko Omote	69	71	70	210	4,928,000
Na-Ri Kim	73	66	71	210	4,928,000
Yuki Ichinose	70	67	73	210	4,928,000
Misuzu Narita	75	70	66	211	2,056,000
Miki Sakai	71	72	68	211	2,056,000
Soo-Yun Kang	71	71	69	211	2,056,000
Erina Hara	69	71	71	211	2,056,000
Tomoko Kanai	71	69	71	211	2,056,000
Yukari Nishiyama	69	76	67	212	1,320,000
Shiho Oyama	76	68	68	212	1,320,000
Teresa Lu	71	71	70	212	1,320,000
Hee-Kyung Bae	74	70	69	213	1,080,000
Ji-Hee Lee	72	70	71	213	1,080,000
Yuko Mitsuka	70	71	72	213	1,080,000
Ah-Reum Hwang	72	72	70	214	840,000
Yumiko Yoshida	75	68	71	214	840,000
Ritsuko Ryu	75	68	71	214	840,000

CyberAgent Ladies

Tsurumai Country Club, West Course, Ichihara, Chiba
Par 36-36–72; 6,515 yards

May 1-3
purse, ¥70,000,000

	SCORES			TOTAL	MONEY
Jiyai Shin	68	71	69	208	¥12,600,000
Erika Kikuchi	72	71	66	209	6,160,000
Megumi Kido	71	69	70	210	4,900,000
Sun-Ju Ahn	71	71	69	211	4,200,000
Yumiko Yoshida	73	71	69	213	3,500,000
Hikari Fujita	73	71	70	214	2,625,000
Bo-Mee Lee	71	72	71	214	2,625,000
Asako Fujimoto	74	74	67	215	1,643,250
Maiko Wakabayashi	73	73	69	215	1,643,250
Hiroko Azuma	71	74	70	215	1,643,250
Ritsuko Ryu	69	74	72	215	1,643,250
Ah-Reum Hwang	76	71	69	216	1,113,000
Ji-Woo Lee	74	73	69	216	1,113,000
Haruka Kudo	74	72	70	216	1,113,000
Miki Sakai	73	75	68	216	1,113,000
Rumi Yoshiba	74	71	71	216	1,113,000
Kumiko Kaneda	72	74	71	217	728,000
Akane Iijima	73	73	71	217	728,000
Hee-Kyung Bae	69	76	72	217	728,000
Mami Fukuda	72	73	72	217	728,000
Kotone Hori	72	73	72	217	728,000
Teresa Lu	76	69	72	217	728,000
Yukari Nishiyama	70	73	74	217	728,000
Phoebe Yao	70	71	76	217	728,000

World Ladies Championship Salonpas Cup

Ibaraki Golf Club, East Course, Tsukubamirai, Ibaraki
Par 36-36–72; 6,550 yards

May 7-10
purse, ¥120,000,000

	SCORES				TOTAL	MONEY
In-Gee Chun	66	70	67	73	276	¥24,000,000
Momoko Ueda	69	69	70	72	280	12,000,000
Bo-Mee Lee	65	72	72	75	284	9,000,000
Akane Iijima	72	74	71	68	285	5,460,000
Yuko Mitsuka	71	72	72	70	285	5,460,000
Serena Aoki	69	74	71	71	285	5,460,000
Jessica Korda	72	67	72	74	285	5,460,000
Lala Anai	73	68	74	71	286	2,640,000
Jae-Eun Chung	66	73	74	73	286	2,640,000
Ai Suzuki	73	66	72	75	286	2,640,000
Erika Kikuchi	69	71	75	72	287	2,100,000
Na-Ri Lee	69	72	74	73	288	1,668,000
Ritsuko Ryu	67	75	73	73	288	1,668,000
Kotone Hori	70	75	70	73	288	1,668,000
Yuri Fudoh	69	72	73	74	288	1,668,000
I.K. Kim	70	73	69	76	288	1,668,000
Teresa Lu	69	74	69	76	288	1,668,000
Ji-Hee Lee	69	73	75	72	289	1,164,000
Jiyai Shin	71	74	69	75	289	1,164,000
Hikari Kawamitsu	73	72	74	71	290	936,000
Yeon-Ju Jung	72	70	73	75	290	936,000
Misuzu Narita	72	74	69	75	290	936,000
Asako Fujimoto	71	74	69	76	290	936,000
Rikako Morita	74	72	67	77	290	936,000

Hoken no Madoguchi Ladies

Fukuoka Country Club, Wajiro Course, Asakura, Fukuoka
Par 36-36–72; 6,375 yards

May 15-17
purse, ¥120,000,000

	SCORES			TOTAL	MONEY
Bo-Mee Lee	68	72	66	206	¥21,600,000
Shiho Oyama	72	70	68	210	10,560,000
Teresa Lu	67	74	70	211	8,400,000
Momoko Ueda	72	72	68	212	7,200,000
Jae-Eun Chung	67	72	74	213	6,000,000
Miki Sakai	72	73	69	214	4,200,000
Jiyai Shin	72	73	69	214	4,200,000
Asuka Kashiwabara	70	74	70	214	4,200,000
Rumi Yoshiba	78	69	68	215	2,536,000
Mi-Jeong Jeon	73	72	70	215	2,536,000
Phoebe Yao	70	74	71	215	2,536,000
Erina Hara	74	73	69	216	2,088,000
Ritsuko Ryu	72	76	69	217	1,908,000
Kaori Ohe	72	72	73	217	1,908,000
Saiki Fujita	75	73	70	218	1,668,000
Yeon-Ju Jung	71	73	74	218	1,668,000
Asako Fujimoto	73	76	70	219	1,267,200
Na-Ri Lee	73	76	70	219	1,267,200
Kaori Aoyama	72	77	70	219	1,267,200
Shanshan Feng	71	78	70	219	1,267,200
Lala Anai	69	77	73	219	1,267,200

Chukyo TV Bridgestone Ladies Open

Chukyo Golf Club, Ishino Course, Toyota, Aichi
Par 36-36–72; 6,459 yards

May 22-24
purse, ¥70,000,000

	SCORES			TOTAL	MONEY
Yumiko Yoshida	68	65	68	201	¥12,600,000
Jae-Eun Chung	68	67	67	202	6,160,000
Momoko Ueda	70	68	69	207	4,550,000
Lala Anai	67	69	71	207	4,550,000
Kotone Hori	69	72	68	209	3,150,000
Akane Iijima	69	70	70	209	3,150,000
Yuko Fukuda	71	70	69	210	2,100,000
Misuzu Narita	71	68	71	210	2,100,000
Saki Nagamine	69	69	72	210	2,100,000
Ayaka Watanabe	74	71	67	212	1,295,000
Yuko Mitsuka	71	70	71	212	1,295,000
Mayu Hattori	67	73	72	212	1,295,000
Bo-Mee Lee	68	70	74	212	1,295,000
*Mone Inami	69	68	75	212	
Na-Ri Lee	74	70	69	213	1,015,000
Saki Takeo	71	72	70	213	1,015,000
Ah-Reum Hwang	73	73	67	213	1,015,000
Soo-Yun Kang	71	70	72	213	1,015,000
Kotono Kozuma	71	73	70	214	749,000
P. Chutichai	71	73	70	214	749,000
Ritsuko Ryu	73	72	69	214	749,000
Haruka Kudo	74	68	72	214	749,000

Resort Trust Ladies

Maple Point Golf Club, Yamanashi
Par 36-36–72; 6,532 yards

May 29-31
purse, ¥80,000,000

	SCORES			TOTAL	MONEY
Teresa Lu	68	67	67	202	¥14,400,000
Jiyai Shin	68	68	67	203	7,200,000
Yumiko Yoshida	68	71	65	204	5,600,000
Soo-Yun Kang	68	68	70	206	4,000,000
Yuko Mitsuka	71	65	70	206	4,000,000
Kaori Ohe	69	65	72	206	4,000,000
Ai Suzuki	71	71	66	208	2,200,000
Ayaka Matsumori	71	71	66	208	2,200,000
Rumi Yoshiba	70	68	70	208	2,200,000
Hikari Kawamitsu	71	67	70	208	2,200,000
Kumiko Kaneda	71	69	69	209	1,408,000
Na-Ri Lee	71	69	69	209	1,408,000
*Minami Katsu	68	74	67	209	
Na-Ri Kim	69	68	72	209	1,408,000
Erina Hara	68	68	73	209	1,408,000
Kotono Kozuma	68	72	70	210	1,168,000
Shiho Toyonaga	71	68	71	210	1,168,000
Nana Yamashiro	69	72	70	211	880,000
Da-Ye Na	72	68	71	211	880,000
Saiki Fujita	70	69	72	211	880,000
Miki Sakai	68	70	73	211	880,000
Jae-Eun Chung	67	69	75	211	880,000
Yukari Nishiyama	71	65	75	211	880,000

Yonex Ladies

Yonex Country Club, Nagaoka, Niigata
Par 36-36–72; 6,352 yards

June 5-7
purse, ¥60,000,000

	SCORES			TOTAL	MONEY
Shiho Oyama	68	67	71	206	¥10,800,000
Teresa Lu	66	71	70	207	5,280,000
Junko Omote	67	68	73	208	4,200,000
Kyoko Furuya	71	69	69	209	3,600,000
Erika Kikuchi	69	69	73	211	3,000,000
Nana Yamashiro	73	72	67	212	1,950,000
Ayaka Watanabe	70	72	70	212	1,950,000
Saki Nagamine	69	70	73	212	1,950,000
O. Sattaya	68	70	74	212	1,950,000
Saki Takeo	71	73	69	213	1,078,500
Kaori Nakamura	71	72	70	213	1,078,500
Kumiko Kaneda	72	70	71	213	1,078,500
Sun-Ju Ahn	69	72	72	213	1,078,500
Kana Taneda	71	73	70	214	888,000
Aiko Ueno	69	71	74	214	888,000
Rikako Morita	72	73	70	215	708,000
Hiroko Azuma	74	69	72	215	708,000
Akane Saeki	77	70	68	215	708,000
Kotone Hori	69	73	73	215	708,000
*Rio Ishii	75	67	73	215	

Suntory Ladies Open

Rokko Kokusai Golf Club, Kobe, Hyogo
Par 36-36–72; 6,511 yards

June 11-14
purse, ¥100,000,000

	SCORES				TOTAL	MONEY
Misuzu Narita	63	71	68	70	272	¥18,000,000
Bo-Mee Lee	68	68	70	68	274	8,800,000
Ritsuko Ryu	69	67	70	69	275	7,000,000
Akane Iijima	70	70	70	67	277	6,000,000
Soo-Yun Kang	69	69	71	70	279	4,500,000
Momoko Ueda	70	71	68	70	279	4,500,000
Yumiko Yoshida	71	73	68	68	280	2,750,000
Jiyai Shin	71	67	73	69	280	2,750,000
Teresa Lu	74	65	70	71	280	2,750,000
Kotone Hori	68	69	71	72	280	2,750,000
*So-Young Lee	68	71	72	70	281	
Da-Ye Na	67	70	70	74	281	1,820,000
Hikari Fujita	68	66	76	72	282	1,670,000
Mayu Hattori	69	71	70	72	282	1,670,000
Nachiyo Ohtani	71	71	69	72	283	1,520,000
Mi-Jeong Jeon	71	75	70	68	284	1,370,000
Esther Lee	73	68	73	70	284	1,370,000
Erika Kikuchi	75	71	71	68	285	1,070,000
Ji-Hee Lee	72	70	71	72	285	1,070,000
Sun-Ju Ahn	66	77	69	73	285	1,070,000
Ayaka Watanabe	74	68	69	74	285	1,070,000

Nichirei Ladies

Sodegaura Country Club, Shinsode Course, Chiba
Par 36-36–72; 6,584 yards

June 19-21
purse, ¥80,000,000

	SCORES			TOTAL	MONEY
Jiyai Shin	71	67	67	205	¥14,400,000
Ji-Hee Lee	68	67	71	206	7,040,000
Ai Suzuki	73	66	68	207	4,800,000
Ah-Reum Hwang	67	71	69	207	4,800,000
Sun-Ju Ahn	70	67	70	207	4,800,000
Teresa Lu	72	72	65	209	3,200,000
Na-Ri Lee	68	73	70	211	2,600,000
Ayaka Matsumori	70	68	73	211	2,600,000
Rumi Yoshiba	71	72	69	212	1,628,000
Eun-Bi Jang	71	70	71	212	1,628,000
Maiko Wakabayashi	73	68	71	212	1,628,000
Ritsuko Ryu	69	71	72	212	1,628,000
Yuko Saitoh	74	70	69	213	1,176,000
Aiko Ueno	74	71	68	213	1,176,000
Phoebe Yao	69	73	71	213	1,176,000
Misae Yanagisawa	73	69	71	213	1,176,000
Kumiko Kaneda	74	68	71	213	1,176,000
Hikari Kawamitsu	72	72	70	214	787,428
Erina Yamato	71	73	70	214	787,428
Na-Ri Kim	69	74	71	214	787,428
Shiho Oyama	70	73	71	214	787,428
Rui Kitada	74	69	71	214	787,428
Akane Iijima	70	71	73	214	787,428
Hiromi Mogi	69	71	74	214	787,428

Earth Mondahmin Cup

Camellia Hills Country Club, Sodegaura, Chiba
Par 36-36–72; 6,541 yards

June 25-28
purse, ¥140,000,000

	SCORES				TOTAL	MONEY
Bo-Mee Lee	70	69	67	68	274	¥25,200,000
Ji-Hee Lee	70	67	69	68	274	12,320,000
(Bo-Mee Lee defeated Ji-Hee Lee on second playoff hole.)						
Rikako Morita	73	69	65	68	275	9,800,000
Momoko Ueda	67	71	73	66	277	7,000,000
Hiromi Mogi	67	70	71	69	277	7,000,000
Kaori Ohe	69	69	68	71	277	7,000,000
Ayaka Watanabe	69	71	70	68	278	4,900,000
Saki Nagamine	69	71	72	67	279	2,905,000
Kyoko Furuya	73	68	69	69	279	2,905,000
Yukari Baba	70	67	72	70	279	2,905,000
Miki Sakai	72	68	69	70	279	2,905,000
Kumiko Kaneda	70	68	69	72	279	2,905,000
Da-Ye Na	68	68	70	73	279	2,905,000
Nana Yamashiro	68	72	74	66	280	1,467,200
Shanshan Feng	71	72	70	67	280	1,467,200
Teresa Lu	71	71	70	68	280	1,467,200
Kaori Nakamura	71	71	70	68	280	1,467,200
Mi-Jeong Jeon	72	70	69	69	280	1,467,200
Young Kim	70	69	71	70	280	1,467,200
Shiho Oyama	70	69	70	71	280	1,467,200
Hikari Fujita	69	70	70	71	280	1,467,200
Yukari Nishiyama	71	70	67	72	280	1,467,200
Serena Aoki	68	69	70	73	280	1,467,200

Samantha Thavasa Girls Collection Ladies

Eagle Point Golf Club, Ami, Ibaraki
Par 36-36–72; 6,554 yards

July 17-19
purse, ¥60,000,000

	SCORES			TOTAL	MONEY
Yoko Maeda	71	69	68	208	¥10,800,000
Erina Hara	74	70	65	209	4,360,000
Bo-Mee Lee	75	67	67	209	4,360,000
Ji-Hee Lee	68	69	72	209	4,360,000
Akane Iijima	71	72	67	210	2,325,000
Erika Kikuchi	70	72	68	210	2,325,000
Jiyai Shin	67	74	69	210	2,325,000
O. Sattaya	69	72	69	210	2,325,000
*Hina Arakaki	74	71	68	213	
Saki Nagamine	72	72	69	213	1,227,000
Sun-Ju Ahn	69	74	70	213	1,227,000
Kaori Yamamoto	70	72	71	213	1,227,000
Rumi Yoshiba	72	66	75	213	1,227,000
Hiroko Fukushima	75	70	69	214	834,000
Ikue Asama	78	68	68	214	834,000
Yuko Fukuda	73	72	69	214	834,000
Yukari Baba	74	71	69	214	834,000
Ji-Woo Lee	70	73	71	214	834,000
Hiroko Azuma	73	69	72	214	834,000
Kaori Nakamura	70	71	73	214	834,000

Century 21 Ladies

IzuOhito Country Club, Shizuoka
Par 36-36–72; 6,531 yards

July 24-26
purse, ¥60,000,000

	SCORES			TOTAL	MONEY
Sun-Ju Ahn	64	67	70	201	¥10,800,000
Erika Kikuchi	65	72	65	202	4,740,000
Hee-Kyung Bae	69	66	67	202	4,740,000
Maiko Wakabayashi	67	70	67	204	3,300,000
Hiroko Azuma	66	68	70	204	3,300,000
*Hina Arakaki	68	70	68	206	
Akane Iijima	72	65	69	206	2,400,000
*Minami Katsu	68	71	68	207	
Erina Hara	69	69	69	207	1,950,000
Ai Suzuki	72	66	69	207	1,950,000
*Minami Hiruta	67	74	67	208	
Rumi Yoshiba	69	70	69	208	1,230,000
Hikari Fujita	67	71	70	208	1,230,000
Kumiko Kaneda	69	69	70	208	1,230,000
Bo-Mee Lee	69	68	71	208	1,230,000
Momoko Ueda	70	70	69	209	990,000
Mami Fukuda	72	66	71	209	990,000
Nachiyo Ohtani	72	69	69	210	900,000
Jiyai Shin	67	74	70	211	698,000
Kaori Yamamoto	73	68	70	211	698,000
P. Chutichai	71	70	70	211	698,000
Phoebe Yao	73	68	70	211	698,000
Miki Sakai	70	70	71	211	698,000
Asako Fujimoto	71	68	72	211	698,000

Daito Kentaku Eheyanet Ladies

Narusawa Golf Club, Yamanishi
Par 37-35–72; 6,587 yards

July 31-August 2
purse, ¥80,000,000

	SCORES			TOTAL	MONEY
Erina Hara	67	69	71	207	¥14,400,000
Bo-Mee Lee	70	73	65	208	6,320,000
Sun-Ju Ahn	69	69	70	208	6,320,000
Nana Yamashiro	70	72	68	210	4,000,000
Kumiko Kaneda	72	74	64	210	4,000,000
Phoebe Yao	71	71	68	210	4,000,000
Asako Fujimoto	74	70	67	211	2,200,000
Serena Aoki	67	73	71	211	2,200,000
Momoko Ueda	68	71	72	211	2,200,000
Hiromi Mogi	69	70	72	211	2,200,000
*Hina Arakaki	73	66	72	211	
Yuko Fukuda	71	69	72	212	1,456,000
Mi-Jeong Jeon	70	69	73	212	1,456,000
Soo-Yun Kang	74	71	68	213	1,256,000
Hiroko Azuma	74	70	69	213	1,256,000
Maiko Wakabayashi	69	70	74	213	1,256,000
Miki Sakai	70	74	70	214	1,016,000
Aya Ezawa	71	71	72	214	1,016,000
Rumi Yoshiba	72	68	74	214	1,016,000
Erika Kikuchi	72	72	71	215	797,333
Na-Ri Lee	69	73	73	215	797,333
Saki Okamura	71	70	74	215	797,333

Meiji Cup

Sapporo International Country Club, Kitahiroshima, Hokkaido
Par 36-36–72; 6,500 yards

August 7-9
purse, ¥90,000,000

	SCORES			TOTAL	MONEY
Yukari Nishiyama	69	70	69	208	¥16,200,000
Ai Suzuki	69	72	67	208	7,920,000
(Nishiyama defeated Suzuki on second playoff hole.)					
Bo-Mee Lee	69	71	69	209	5,850,000
Shanshan Feng	72	67	70	209	5,850,000
Jiyai Shin	70	70	70	210	4,500,000
Erika Kikuchi	74	70	67	211	3,375,000
Akane Iijima	70	72	69	211	3,375,000
Sun-Ju Ahn	71	70	71	212	2,700,000
Mami Fukuda	72	72	69	213	1,695,000
Saki Nagamine	72	72	69	213	1,695,000
Teresa Lu	74	70	69	213	1,695,000
Ayaka Watanabe	71	72	70	213	1,695,000
Yuko Fukuda	72	69	72	213	1,695,000
Mayu Hattori	74	66	73	213	1,695,000
Soo-Yun Kang	75	71	68	214	1,215,000
Shiho Oyama	73	70	71	214	1,215,000
Eun-Bi Jang	72	70	72	214	1,215,000
Shiho Toyonaga	74	71	70	215	867,857
Maiko Wakabayashi	78	67	70	215	867,857
Jae-Eun Chung	73	71	71	215	867,857
Mihoko Iseri	72	71	72	215	867,857
Lala Anai	70	72	73	215	867,857
Ji-Min Lee	69	72	74	215	867,857
Yuko Mitsuka	74	66	75	215	867,857

NEC Karuizawa 72

Karuizawa 72 Golf Club, Karuizawa, Nagano
Par 36-36–72; 6,583 yards

August 14-16
purse, ¥80,000,000

	SCORES			TOTAL	MONEY
Teresa Lu	64	71	67	202	¥14,400,000
Miki Sakai	71	68	65	204	6,320,000
Ayaka Watanabe	72	67	65	204	6,320,000
Erina Hara	71	67	67	205	3,700,000
Yukari Nishiyama	67	69	69	205	3,700,000
Shiho Oyama	68	66	71	205	3,700,000
Mayu Hattori	67	66	72	205	3,700,000
Hee-Kyung Bae	69	69	68	206	2,200,000
Asako Fujimoto	67	70	69	206	2,200,000
Saki Nagamine	69	69	69	207	1,536,000
Jiyai Shin	68	69	70	207	1,536,000
Saiki Fujita	74	69	65	208	1,352,000
Bo-Mee Lee	68	71	69	208	1,352,000
Airi Saitoh	72	69	68	209	1,112,000
Ah-Reum Hwang	69	70	70	209	1,112,000
Soo-Yun Kang	71	68	70	209	1,112,000
Maiko Wakabayashi	67	69	73	209	1,112,000
Megumi Shimokawa	70	71	69	210	832,000
Kotone Hori	69	71	70	210	832,000
Ritsuko Ryu	70	69	71	210	832,000

CAT Ladies

Daihakone Country Club, Hakone, Kanagawa
Par 37-36–73; 6,701 yards

August 21-23
purse, ¥60,000,000

	SCORES			TOTAL	MONEY
Mayu Hattori	66	70	69	205	¥10,800,000
Momoko Ueda	72	68	69	209	4,020,000
Teresa Lu	72	68	69	209	4,020,000
Kumiko Kaneda	71	68	70	209	4,020,000
Hee-Kyung Bae	69	66	74	209	4,020,000
Jiyai Shin	70	73	67	210	2,250,000
Lala Anai	69	73	68	210	2,250,000
Saiki Fujita	69	73	69	211	1,650,000
Nana Yamashiro	69	73	69	211	1,650,000
Hiromi Mogi	70	73	69	212	954,666
Miki Sakai	72	71	69	212	954,666
Ritsuko Ryu	68	74	70	212	954,666
Yukari Nishiyama	69	72	71	212	954,666
Saki Nagamine	68	72	72	212	954,666
Yumiko Yoshida	68	72	72	212	954,666
Ji-Hee Lee	69	70	73	212	954,666
Ai Suzuki	66	72	74	212	954,666
Ayaka Watanabe	69	68	75	212	954,666
Erina Hara	69	74	70	213	600,000
Nobuko Kizawa	66	76	71	213	600,000
Ji-Min Lee	67	73	73	213	600,000
Yuko Mitsuka	66	71	76	213	600,000

Nitori Ladies

Otaru Country Club, Otaru, Hokkaido
Par 36-36–72; 6,483 yards

August 28-30
purse, ¥80,000,000

	SCORES			TOTAL	MONEY
Bo-Mee Lee	69	69	71	209	¥14,400,000
Ayaka Watanabe	69	70	72	211	7,040,000
Lala Anai	72	67	73	212	5,600,000
Mayu Hattori	72	72	70	214	4,000,000
Mami Fukuda	73	70	71	214	4,000,000
Ji-Hee Lee	70	72	72	214	4,000,000
Misuzu Narita	69	75	71	215	2,400,000
Yuko Fukuda	74	70	71	215	2,400,000
Mi-Jeong Jeon	69	70	76	215	2,400,000
Kotono Kozuma	74	68	74	216	1,600,000
O. Sattaya	75	71	72	218	1,272,000
Aya Ezawa	74	71	73	218	1,272,000
Akane Iijima	72	71	75	218	1,272,000
Erina Hara	69	72	77	218	1,272,000
Eika Ohtake	74	70	75	219	1,032,000
Soo-Yun Kang	71	72	76	219	1,032,000
Hiroko Fukushima	71	76	73	220	744,000
Junko Omote	73	73	74	220	744,000
Phoebe Yao	73	73	74	220	744,000
Megumi Kido	74	70	76	220	744,000
Maiko Wakabayashi	70	73	77	220	744,000
Yumiko Yoshida	74	67	79	220	744,000

Golf 5 Ladies

Mizunami Country Club, Gifu
Par 36-36–72; 6,559 yards

September 4-6
purse, ¥60,000,000

	SCORES			TOTAL	MONEY
Bo-Mee Lee	67	68	70	205	¥10,800,000
Misuzu Narita	72	68	65	205	5,280,000
(Lee defeated Narita on fifth playoff hole.)					
Teresa Lu	70	70	66	206	4,200,000
Momoko Ueda	71	67	69	207	3,600,000
Sun-Ju Ahn	72	70	66	208	2,000,000
Yumiko Yoshida	72	70	66	208	2,000,000
Asuka Kashiwabara	73	68	67	208	2,000,000
Hikari Fujita	69	69	70	208	2,000,000
Yuko Mitsuka	72	66	70	208	2,000,000
Mihoko Iseri	69	68	71	208	2,000,000
Aya Ezawa	69	71	70	210	1,104,000
Serena Aoki	70	69	71	210	1,104,000
*Mone Inami	71	68	71	210	
Yukari Nishiyama	71	70	70	211	1,014,000
Miki Uehara	73	68	71	212	924,000
Maiko Wakabayashi	68	69	75	212	924,000
Yoko Maeda	69	73	71	213	774,000
Ayaka Matsumori	69	71	73	213	774,000
Erika Kikuchi	68	70	75	213	774,000
Da-Ye Na	77	66	71	214	584,000
Shiho Oyama	74	70	70	214	584,000
Shiho Toyonaga	71	70	73	214	584,000
Esther Lee	73	72	69	214	584,000
Lala Anai	70	70	74	214	584,000
Eri Okayama	71	69	74	214	584,000

Japan LPGA Championship Konica Minolta Cup

Passage Kinkai Island Golf Club, Nagasaki
Par 36-36–72; 6,735 yards

September 10-13
purse, ¥145,000,000

	SCORES				TOTAL	MONEY
Teresa Lu	73	67	70	71	281	¥25,200,000
Miki Sakai	71	69	72	71	283	11,060,000
Momoko Ueda	76	70	64	73	283	11,060,000
Bo-Mee Lee	73	71	68	72	284	8,400,000
Ha-Neul Kim	74	68	72	71	285	6,300,000
Sun-Ju Ahn	71	71	71	72	285	6,300,000
Phoebe Yao	73	72	72	70	287	4,200,000
Mayu Hattori	68	73	74	72	287	4,200,000
Erina Hara	73	67	74	73	287	4,200,000
Jiyai Shin	72	70	73	73	288	2,557,333
Ayaka Watanabe	76	67	72	73	288	2,557,333
Erika Kikuchi	71	71	71	75	288	2,557,333
Saki Nagamine	73	67	74	75	289	2,156,000
Na-Ri Lee	73	70	71	75	289	2,156,000
Akane Iijima	72	69	74	75	290	1,946,000
Asako Fujimoto	69	72	74	76	291	1,806,000
Yumiko Yoshida	69	69	81	73	292	1,596,000
Lala Anai	75	72	71	74	292	1,596,000
Young Kim	72	71	74	76	293	1,283,333
Yuko Fukuda	73	71	73	76	293	1,283,333
Shiho Oyama	73	72	69	79	293	1,283,333

Munsingwear Ladies Tokai Classic

Shin Minami Aichi Country Club, Minama, Aichi
Par 36-36–72; 6,374 yards

September 18-20
purse, ¥80,000,000

	SCORES			TOTAL	MONEY
Ha-Neul Kim	69	67	68	204	¥14,400,000
Ayaka Matsumori	66	72	67	205	6,400,000
Jiyai Shin	68	69	68	205	6,400,000
Sakura Yokomine	71	67	68	206	4,400,000
Miki Sakai	69	67	70	206	4,400,000
Shiho Oyama	70	69	68	207	3,000,000
Sun-Ju Ahn	69	68	70	207	3,000,000
Momoko Ueda	70	72	66	208	2,200,000
Hee-Kyung Bae	68	73	67	208	2,200,000
Serena Aoki	71	71	67	209	1,564,000
Airi Saitoh	71	69	69	209	1,564,000
Yoko Maeda	70	71	69	210	1,328,000
Soo-Yun Kang	70	70	70	210	1,328,000
Rikako Morita	68	71	71	210	1,328,000
*Minami Katsu	68	71	71	210	
Megumi Kido	68	69	73	210	1,328,000
Miki Uehara	75	67	69	211	1,008,000
Mayu Hattori	72	70	69	211	1,008,000
Bo-Mee Lee	72	70	69	211	1,008,000
Rui Kitada	70	69	72	211	1,008,000

Miyagi TV Cup Dunlop Ladies Open

Rifu Golf Club, Rifu, Miyagi
Par 36-36–72; 6,534 yards

September 25-27
purse, ¥70,000,000

	SCORES			TOTAL	MONEY
Junko Omote	67	68	70	205	¥12,600,000
Shiho Oyama	72	63	73	208	6,300,000
Lala Anai	71	68	70	209	4,900,000
Yeo-Jin Kang	72	70	69	211	3,850,000
Mayu Hattori	70	71	70	211	3,850,000
Ai Suzuki	72	72	68	212	2,625,000
Rui Kitada	72	69	71	212	2,625,000
*Minami Katsu	71	67	74	212	
Megumi Shimokawa	72	72	69	213	1,570,800
Erika Kikuchi	73	71	69	213	1,570,800
Na-Ri Lee	70	73	70	213	1,570,800
Ayaka Matsumori	72	71	70	213	1,570,800
Erina Hara	72	69	72	213	1,570,800
*Minami Hiruta	70	73	71	214	
Rikako Morita	72	71	71	214	1,092,000
Momoko Ueda	75	68	71	214	1,092,000
Saki Nagamine	71	71	72	214	1,092,000
O. Sattaya	70	71	73	214	1,092,000
Yuko Mitsuka	71	75	69	215	812,000
Miki Sakai	73	71	71	215	812,000
Ayaka Watanabe	72	75	68	215	812,000
Airi Saitoh	74	67	74	215	812,000

Japan Women's Open Championship

Katayamazu Golf Club, Hakusan Course, Ishikawa
Par 36-36–72; 6,613 yards

October 1-4
purse, ¥140,000,000

	SCORES				TOTAL	MONEY
In-Gee Chun	71	73	71	71	286	¥28,000,000
Mi Hyang Lee	71	72	73	70	286	13,090,000
Erika Kikuchi	72	73	67	74	286	13,090,000
(Chun defeated Lee on third and Kikuchi on fourth playoff hole.)						
Bo-Mee Lee	74	69	74	71	288	6,440,000
Asuka Kashiwabara	71	70	72	75	288	6,440,000
Ji-Hee Lee	73	71	75	71	290	3,696,000
Shanshan Feng	75	70	74	71	290	3,696,000
Mi-Jeong Jeon	76	71	72	71	290	3,696,000
Shiho Oyama	76	72	71	71	290	3,696,000
Kotono Kozuma	72	70	73	75	290	3,696,000
*Minami Katsu	75	71	73	72	291	
Ayaka Watanabe	76	71	72	72	291	2,331,000
Sun-Ju Ahn	70	73	75	73	291	2,331,000
Ha-Neul Kim	74	74	73	71	292	1,841,000
So Yeon Ryu	68	72	74	78	292	1,841,000
Hee-Kyung Bae	74	72	73	74	293	1,596,000
Maiko Wakabayashi	72	74	73	74	293	1,596,000
Kyu-Jung Baek	77	73	76	69	295	1,309,000
*Kana Nagai	74	73	76	72	295	
*Yumi Matsubara	77	73	73	72	295	
O. Sattaya	75	71	75	74	295	1,309,000
Shoko Sasaki	72	71	76	76	295	1,309,000
Hyo Joo Kim	77	70	72	76	295	1,309,000
Erina Hara	73	72	73	77	295	1,309,000
Kotone Hori	72	73	72	78	295	1,309,000

Stanley Ladies

Tomei Country Club, Susano, Shizuoka
Par 36-36–72; 6,583 yards
(Third round reduced to 9 holes—fog and rain.)

October 9-11
purse, ¥90,000,000

	SCORES			TOTAL	MONEY
Bo-Mee Lee	67	69	32	168	¥16,200,000
Asako Fujimoto	66	72	33	171	7,200,000
Maiko Wakabayashi	67	68	36	171	7,200,000
Megumi Kido	68	68	36	172	5,400,000
Jiyai Shin	73	69	31	173	3,532,500
Hee-Kyung Bae	70	70	33	173	3,532,500
Kotono Kozuma	70	69	34	173	3,532,500
Kaori Ohe	71	66	36	173	3,532,500
Ritsuko Ryu	71	70	33	174	2,250,000
Ayaka Watanabe	69	70	36	175	1,764,000
Ai Suzuki	72	66	37	175	1,764,000
Mayu Hattori	69	71	36	176	1,638,000
Hikari Fujita	71	71	35	177	1,458,000
*Kana Nagai	72	70	35	177	
Shiho Oyama	68	71	38	177	1,458,000
Misuzu Narita	69	70	38	177	1,458,000
Ji-Hee Lee	75	70	33	178	1,098,000
Yumiko Yoshida	73	71	34	178	1,098,000
O. Sattaya	74	69	35	178	1,098,000
Saki Nagamine	71	71	36	178	1,098,000
Sun-Ju Ahn	71	69	38	178	1,098,000

Fujitsu Ladies

Tokyu Seven Hundred Club, West Course, Chiba
Par 36-36–72; 6,635 yards

October 16-18
purse, ¥80,000,000

	SCORES			TOTAL	MONEY
Teresa Lu	67	65	71	203	¥14,400,000
Ayaka Watanabe	70	66	71	207	7,200,000
Serena Aoki	73	69	67	209	5,200,000
Jiyai Shin	72	69	68	209	5,200,000
Ha-Neul Kim	73	68	69	210	4,160,000
Mami Fukuda	72	70	69	211	3,360,000
Sun-Ju Ahn	73	72	67	212	2,800,000
Mayu Hattori	72	73	68	213	1,886,000
Kaori Ohe	73	70	70	213	1,886,000
Ritsuko Ryu	74	68	71	213	1,886,000
Hee-Kyung Bae	75	67	71	213	1,886,000
Hikari Fujita	73	72	69	214	1,344,000
*Hina Arakaki	74	70	70	214	
Satsuki Oshiro	73	70	71	214	1,344,000
Ji-Hee Lee	74	69	71	214	1,344,000
Bo-Mee Lee	73	67	74	214	1,344,000
Yuko Mitsuka	77	70	68	215	1,064,000
Megumi Shimokawa	73	71	71	215	1,064,000
*Nozomi Uetake	74	70	71	215	
Momoko Ueda	75	69	71	215	1,064,000

Nobuta Group Masters Golf Club Ladies

Masters Golf Club, Miki, Hyogo
Par 36-36–72; 6,543 yards

October 22-25
purse, ¥140,000,000

	SCORES				TOTAL	MONEY
Ji-Hee Lee	71	67	69	72	279	¥25,200,000
Sun-Ju Ahn	71	69	71	69	280	12,320,000
Ayaka Watanabe	72	71	71	69	283	8,400,000
Rikako Morita	70	68	72	73	283	8,400,000
Bo-Mee Lee	68	71	69	75	283	8,400,000
Shiho Oyama	72	70	73	69	284	5,600,000
Young Kim	70	70	78	67	285	4,200,000
Teresa Lu	70	68	72	75	285	4,200,000
Aoi Ohnishi	68	70	70	77	285	4,200,000
Ai Suzuki	70	71	74	71	286	2,622,666
Mi-Jeong Jeon	71	73	70	72	286	2,622,666
Misuzu Narita	69	69	71	77	286	2,622,666
Mihoko Iseri	73	70	72	72	287	2,184,000
Erika Kikuchi	70	73	71	73	287	2,184,000
Lala Anai	73	71	67	76	287	2,184,000
Rumi Yoshiba	70	70	75	73	288	1,694,000
Yukari Nishiyama	72	70	73	73	288	1,694,000
Akane Iijima	73	69	71	75	288	1,694,000
Miki Sakai	75	67	69	77	288	1,694,000
Jiyai Shin	73	70	73	73	289	1,288,000
Jae-Eun Chung	70	72	74	73	289	1,288,000
Hikari Fujita	72	70	72	75	289	1,288,000
Ritsuko Ryu	70	70	73	76	289	1,288,000
Kotone Hori	69	69	73	78	289	1,288,000

Hisako Higuchi Ponta Ladies

Musashigaoka Golf Club, Hanno, Saitama
Par 36-36–72; 6,605 yards

October 30-November 1
purse, ¥70,000,000

	SCORES			TOTAL	MONEY
Ayaka Watanabe	72	67	66	205	¥12,600,000
Asako Fujimoto	70	70	69	209	6,160,000
Rumi Yoshiba	71	70	69	210	4,900,000
Miki Sakai	70	71	70	211	3,500,000
Ai Suzuki	73	68	70	211	3,500,000
Hiromi Mogi	70	69	72	211	3,500,000
Yukari Baba	70	71	71	212	2,450,000
*Nasa Hataoka	68	71	73	212	
Shiho Oyama	71	72	70	213	1,750,000
Hikari Fujita	72	71	70	213	1,750,000
Saki Nagamine	70	71	72	213	1,750,000
Erika Kikuchi	73	73	68	214	1,225,000
Momoko Ueda	72	73	69	214	1,225,000
Serena Aoki	74	71	69	214	1,225,000
Mi-Jeong Jeon	74	71	70	215	1,085,000
*Nozomi Uetake	73	69	74	216	
Keiko Sasaki	73	69	74	216	980,000
Saki Takeo	69	71	76	216	980,000
Eri Joma	73	73	71	217	805,000
Aya Ezawa	71	74	72	217	805,000
Kotone Hori	71	72	74	217	805,000

Toto Japan Classic

Kintetsu Kashikojima Country Club, Shima, Mie
Par 36-36–72; 6,506 yards

November 6-8
purse, US$1,500,000

	SCORES			TOTAL	MONEY
Sun-Ju Ahn	68	65	67	200	US$225,000
Ji-Hee Lee	67	67	66	200	118,379
Angela Stanford	65	68	67	200	118,379
(Ahn defeated Lee and Stanford on first playoff hole.)					
Jenny Shin	66	65	70	201	77,003
Ariya Jutanugarn	70	68	64	202	61,979
Hyo Joo Kim	69	67	68	204	37,062
Stacy Lewis	67	69	68	204	37,062
Jiyai Shin	67	68	69	204	37,062
Lexi Thompson	67	68	69	204	37,062
Pornanong Phatlum	67	66	71	204	37,062
Ha-Neul Kim	66	66	72	204	37,062
Lala Anai	73	64	68	205	23,964
Yukari Nishiyama	68	67	70	205	23,964
Caroline Masson	67	68	70	205	23,964
Ai Suzuki	66	68	71	205	23,964
Teresa Lu	70	67	69	206	18,781
Danielle Kang	70	66	70	206	18,781
Mirim Lee	69	67	70	206	18,781
Mi-Jeong Jeon	66	70	70	206	18,781
Yani Tseng	67	68	71	206	18,781
Mi Hyang Lee	70	68	69	207	16,678
Wei-Ling Hsu	69	70	69	208	14,114
Ilhee Lee	66	72	70	208	14,114
Ha Na Jang	69	68	71	208	14,114
Misuzu Narita	68	69	71	208	14,114
Shiho Oyama	70	66	72	208	14,114
Erina Hara	69	67	72	208	14,114
Alena Sharp	67	69	72	208	14,114
Eun-Hee Ji	69	66	73	208	14,114
Maiko Wakabayashi	68	72	69	209	11,118
Ritsuko Ryu	70	69	70	209	11,118
Hee-Kyung Bae	70	67	72	209	11,118
Ryann O'Toole	65	70	74	209	11,118

Itoen Ladies

Great Island Club, Chonan, Chiba
Par 36-36–72; 6,639 yards

November 13-15
purse, ¥100,000,000

	SCORES			TOTAL	MONEY
Bo-Mee Lee	65	68	69	202	¥18,000,000
Serena Aoki	68	67	69	204	8,800,000
Kotone Hori	66	71	69	206	6,500,000
Teresa Lu	66	70	70	206	6,500,000
Na-Ri Lee	68	70	69	207	5,000,000
Yuri Fudoh	71	68	69	208	4,000,000
Misuzu Narita	70	71	68	209	3,000,000
Ritsuko Ryu	67	69	73	209	3,000,000
Erika Kikuchi	68	67	74	209	3,000,000
Junko Omote	71	71	68	210	1,700,000
Mayu Hattori	71	68	71	210	1,700,000
Shiho Oyama	67	71	72	210	1,700,000
Soo-Yun Kang	68	69	73	210	1,700,000

	SCORES			TOTAL	MONEY
Sun-Ju Ahn	70	67	73	210	1,700,000
Maiko Wakabayashi	68	67	75	210	1,700,000
Mi-Jeong Jeon	70	71	70	211	1,140,000
Rikako Morita	71	71	69	211	1,140,000
O. Sattaya	67	72	72	211	1,140,000
Akane Saeki	67	72	72	211	1,140,000
Ji-Hee Lee	72	67	72	211	1,140,000

Daio Paper Elleair Ladies Open

Itsuura Teien Country Club, Fukushima
Par 36-36–72; 6,460 yards

November 19-22
purse, ¥100,000,000

	SCORES				TOTAL	MONEY
Bo-Mee Lee	70	68	65	69	272	¥18,000,000
Ai Suzuki	68	66	74	69	277	7,900,000
Ayaka Watanabe	71	65	70	71	277	7,900,000
Momoko Ueda	70	67	70	71	278	6,000,000
Ritsuko Ryu	70	68	73	68	279	4,166,666
Sun-Ju Ahn	73	69	69	68	279	4,166,666
Na-Ri Lee	69	71	70	69	279	4,166,666
Junko Omote	69	67	78	66	280	3,000,000
Mi-Jeong Jeon	74	71	71	65	281	2,123,333
Yumiko Yoshida	72	70	70	69	281	2,123,333
Misuzu Narita	68	68	73	72	281	2,123,333
Erika Kikuchi	71	70	71	70	282	1,770,000
Rikako Morita	71	72	70	70	283	1,520,000
Asami Kikuchi	69	74	70	70	283	1,520,000
Kotone Hori	72	68	72	71	283	1,520,000
Mami Fukuda	73	68	71	71	283	1,520,000
Saiki Fujita	71	70	72	71	284	1,220,000
Erina Yamato	71	70	69	74	284	1,220,000
Megumi Shimokawa	70	73	71	71	285	996,666
Mihoko Iseri	71	71	71	72	285	996,666
Hiromi Mogi	73	72	67	73	285	996,666

Japan LPGA Tour Championship Ricoh Cup

Miyazaki Country Club, Miyazaki
Par 36-36–72; 6,448 yards

November 26-29
purse, ¥100,000,000

	SCORES				TOTAL	MONEY
Jiyai Shin	70	71	72	68	281	¥25,000,000
Shiho Oyama	72	70	70	75	287	14,500,000
Misuzu Narita	72	71	75	70	288	8,200,000
Yumiko Yoshida	75	66	75	72	288	8,200,000
Miki Sakai	74	72	69	73	288	8,200,000
Bo-Mee Lee	72	73	73	71	289	4,680,000
Teresa Lu	76	71	71	71	289	4,680,000
In-Gee Chun	74	71	72	72	289	4,680,000
Ayaka Watanabe	72	75	71	72	290	2,200,000
Erina Hara	72	71	73	74	290	2,200,000
Ai Suzuki	73	79	71	68	291	1,360,000
Sun-Ju Ahn	71	77	72	71	291	1,360,000
Momoko Ueda	75	72	72	72	291	1,360,000
Junko Omote	74	72	70	76	292	1,010,000
Ha-Neul Kim	73	75	74	72	294	820,000

	SCORES				TOTAL	MONEY
Yoko Maeda	69	77	77	72	295	633,333
Lala Anai	72	77	73	73	295	633,333
Ritsuko Ryu	73	73	73	76	295	633,333
Akane Iijima	73	73	77	73	296	500,000
Ji-Hee Lee	74	75	74	73	296	500,000
Rikako Morita	75	71	76	74	296	500,000
Hikari Fujita	75	75	72	75	297	480,000
Mi-Jeong Jeon	79	73	74	72	298	465,000
Erika Kikuchi	79	73	71	75	298	465,000
Mayu Hattori	76	76	74	73	299	450,000
Asako Fujimoto	78	78	73	74	303	435,000
Maiko Wakabayashi	76	76	75	76	303	435,000
Yukari Nishiyama	76	79	75	78	308	420,000

The Queens

Miyoshi Country Club, West Course, Aichi
Par 36-36–72; 6,500 yards

December 4-6
purse, ¥100,000,000

FIRST ROUND
Fourballs

Ayaka Watanabe and Erika Kikuchi (JLPGA) defeated Laura Davies and Melissa Reid (LET), 6 and 4.
In-Gee Chun and Yoon Ji Cho (KLPGA) defeated Katherine Kirk and Nikki Garrett (APLG), 4 and 3.
Hannah Burke and Emily Kristine Pedersen (LET) defeated Sarah Kemp and Sarah Jane Smith (ALPG), 4 and 3.
Shiho Oyama and Misuzu Narita (JLPGA) defeated Seon Woo Bae and Jin Young Ko (KLPGA), 2 and 1.
Ritsuko Ryu and Miki Sakai (JLPGA) defeated Rachel Hetherington and Whitney Hillier (ALPG), 4 and 3.
Jung Min Lee and Min Sun Kim (KLPGA) defeated Gwladys Nocera and Marianne Skarpnord (LET), 1 up.
Momoko Ueda and Erina Hara (JLPGA) defeated Lindsey Wright and Stephanie Na (ALPG), 6 and 5.
Catriona Matthew and Karine Icher (LET) halved with Sung Hyun Park and Bo-Mee Lee (KLPGA).

POINTS: JLPGA 12, KLPGA 7, LET 4, ALPG 0.

SECOND ROUND
Foursomes

Oyama and Narita (JLPGA) halved with Burke and Reid (LET).
Kemp and Smith (ALPG) halved with Park and Min Sun Kim (KLPGA).
Ryu and Akane Iijima (JLPGA) defeated Hetherington and Hillier (ALPG), 2 and 1.
Cho and Jung Min Lee (KLPGA) defeated Skarpnord and Pedersen (LET), 2 up.
Watanabe and Kikuchi (JLPGA) defeated Nocera and Matthew (LET), 2 and 1.
Ko and Bo-Mee Lee (KLPGA) defeated Wright and Garrett (ALPG), 3 and 2
Icher and Nanna Koertz Madson (LET) defeated Kirk and Nikki Campbell (ALPG), 4 and 3.
Ueda and Hara (JLPGA) defeated Sei Young Kim and Chun (KLPGA), 5 and 4.

POINTS: JLPGA 22, KLPGA 14, LET 8, ALPG 1.

FINAL ROUND
Singles

Narita (JLPGA) defeated Matthew (LET), 6 and 5.
Ko (KLPGA) defeated Hillier (ALPG), 1 up.
Davies (LET) defeated Kemp (ALPG), 2 and 1.
Min Sun Kim (KLPGA) defeated Oyama (JLPGA), 3 and 2.

Iijima (JLPGA) defeated Wright (ALPG), 4 and 2.
Sei Young Kim (KLPGA) defeated Reid (LET), 5 and 4.
Bae (KLPGA) defeated Na (ALPG), 5 and 4.
Kikuchi (JLPGA) defeated Nocera (LET), 4 and 3.
Smith (ALPG) defeated Pedersen (LET), 5 and 4.
Watanabe (JLPGA) defeated Cho (KLPGA), 1 up.
Bo-Mee Lee (KLPGA) defeated Burke (LET), 3 and 2.
Ryu (JLPGA) defeated Kirk (ALPG), 5 and 4.
Chun (KLPGA) defeated Madsen (LET), 6 and 4.
Sakai (JLPGA) defeated Campbell (ALPG), 7 and 6.
Icher (LET) halved with Hara (JLPGA).
Jung Min Lee (KLPGA) defeated Garrett (ALPG), 4 and 2.
Hetherington (ALPG) defeated Skarpnord (LET), 2 and 1.
Park (KLPGA) defeated Ueda (JLPGA), 5 and 4.

TOTAL POINTS: JLPGA 41, KLPGA 38, LET 12, ALPG 7.

(JLPGA players earned ¥5,000,000 each; KLPGA players earned ¥3,000,000 each; LET players earned ¥2,000,000 each; ALPG players earned ¥1,000,000 each.)

Korea LPGA Tour

Lotte Mart Women's Open

Sky Hill Jeju Country Club, Seogwipo, Jeju Island
Par 72; 6,187 yards

April 9-12
purse, KRW600,000,000

	SCORES				TOTAL	MONEY
Bo Kyung Kim	68	70	68	73	279	KRW120,000,000
Jeong Eun Lee₅	72	69	71	70	282	58,500,000
Hye Youn Kim	70	69	70	73	282	58,500,000
Jung Min Lee	74	66	74	70	284	25,000,000
Shin Young Park	74	70	70	70	284	25,000,000
*Jin Choi Hye	68	66	76	74	284	25,000,000
Seung Hyun Lee	69	69	72	74	284	15,000,000
Ji Ram Kweon	70	72	71	72	285	15,000,000
Yeun Jung Seo	69	69	75	72	285	15,000,000
Jae-Eun Chung	71	66	72	76	285	9,000,000
Yoon Ji Cho	67	75	69	75	286	7,800,000
Yea Lin Kang	69	72	73	73	287	7,800,000
Hyun Soo Kim	67	75	68	77	287	6,990,000
Hee Won Jung	71	73	74	70	288	6,990,000
Ji Hyun Kim₂	73	73	72	70	288	6,320,000
Ji Hee Kim	72	73	71	73	289	6,320,000
Eun Bin Lee	76	71	70	72	289	6,320,000
Hae Rym Kim	71	73	72	73	289	5,720,000
In-Gee Chun	73	70	74	73	290	5,720,000
Cho Hui Kim	71	72	71	76	290	5,720,000

Samchunli Together Open

Island Country Club, Ansan
Par 72; 6,612 yards

April 17-19
purse, KRW700,000,000

	SCORES		TOTAL	MONEY
In-Gee Chun	70	69	139	KRW140,000,000
Jin Young Ko	71	69	140	80,500,000
Ji Hyun Kim	70	71	141	45,500,000
Ji Young Park	71	70	141	45,500,000
Yeun Jung Seo	70	72	142	26,250,000
Hae Rym Kim	73	69	142	26,250,000
Jung Min Lee	73	70	143	21,000,000
Hye Youn Kim	73	71	144	17,500,000
*Hye Park So	71	73	144	
Jeong Eun Lee$_5$	76	69	145	11,316,667
Min Sun Kim$_5$	73	72	145	11,316,667
Jin-Joo Hong	72	73	145	11,316,667
Char Young Kim	74	72	146	8,172,500
Song Yi Ahn	76	70	146	8,172,500
Ka Ram Choi	74	72	146	8,172,500
Bo Kyung Kim	73	73	146	8,172,500
Na Rae Ko	76	71	147	6,270,833
So Yeon Nam	74	73	147	6,270,833
You Na Park	75	72	147	6,270,833
Dana Kim	75	72	147	6,270,833

Nexen-Saint Nine Masters

Gaya Country Club, Gimhae
Par 72; 6,649 yards

April 24-26
purse, KRW500,000,000

	SCORES			TOTAL	MONEY
Jin Young Ko	70	65	68	203	KRW100,000,000
Seung Hyun Lee	68	67	69	204	57,500,000
Ye Jin Kim	71	71	65	207	25,625,000
Seon Woo Bae	68	71	68	207	25,625,000
Jae-Eun Chung	72	67	68	207	25,625,000
Song Yi Ahn	67	68	72	207	25,625,000
Ji Hyun Kim	69	68	71	208	13,750,000
Bo Ah Kim	71	65	72	208	13,750,000
Gyeol Park	72	71	66	209	8,083,333
Yoon Kyung Heo	69	67	73	209	8,083,333
Hee Jeong Choo	70	70	69	209	8,083,333
Sung Hyun Park	73	66	71	210	5,837,500
Ji Na Lim	73	69	68	210	5,837,500
Seul A Yoon	70	70	70	210	5,837,500
Ji Hee Kim	68	69	73	210	5,837,500
Jung Min Lee	69	73	69	211	5,175,000
Bo Kyung Kim	67	74	70	211	5,175,000
So Yi Kim	69	71	72	212	4,700,000
Min Song Ha	70	72	70	212	4,700,000
Ji Young Park	71	71	70	212	4,700,000

KG-Edaily Ladies Open

Muju Anseong Country Club, Muju Anseong
Par 72; 6,513 yards

May 1-3
purse, KRW500,000,000

	SCORES			TOTAL	MONEY
Min Sun Kim₅	66	68	64	198	KRW100,000,000
In-Gee Chun⁵	64	68	72	204	57,500,000
Bo Kyung Kim	66	71	68	205	40,000,000
Hye Youn Kim	68	70	68	206	25,000,000
Chae Young Yoon	66	73	68	207	15,000,000
Ye Jin Kim	67	71	69	207	15,000,000
So Yi Kim	67	73	67	207	15,000,000
Ji Hyun Kim₂	68	67	72	207	15,000,000
Jung Min Lee	69	68	70	207	15,000,000
Hye In Yeom	69	72	67	208	6,450,000
So Yeon Park	71	71	66	208	6,450,000
Jin Young Ko	66	70	72	208	6,450,000
Jae-Eun Chung	66	71	71	208	6,450,000
Yoo Lim Choi	68	69	71	208	6,450,000
Hee Won Jung	71	71	67	209	5,425,000
Dana Kim	70	68	71	209	5,425,000
Cho Hui Kim	69	69	72	210	5,125,000
*Hye Park So	72	70	68	210	
Char Young Kim	67	73	70	210	5,125,000
Ji Hee Kim	67	73	71	211	4,557,143

Kyochon Honey Ladies Open

Inter-Burgo Country Club, Gyeongsan
Par 73; 6,742 yards

May 8-10
purse, KRW500,000,000

	SCORES			TOTAL	MONEY
Jin Young Ko	70	68	70	208	KRW100,000,000
Seon Woo Bae	70	69	72	211	57,500,000
Jeongmin Cho	74	71	68	213	32,500,000
Char Young Kim	72	71	70	213	32,500,000
Chae-lin Yang	73	72	69	214	20,000,000
*Rin Lee Hyo	75	70	70	215	
Jeong Eun Lee₅	70	72	73	215	17,500,000
You Na Park	76	71	69	216	9,666,667
Hyejung Lee	72	74	70	216	9,666,667
Eun Ji Lee	78	69	69	216	9,666,667
Ji Hyun Oh	72	72	72	216	9,666,667
Han Sol Ji	73	73	70	216	9,666,667
Yoon Kyung Heo	71	73	72	216	9,666,667
Na Rae Ko	74	73	70	217	4,929,167
Ji Hyun Kim	74	73	70	217	4,929,167
Ji Young Park	72	74	71	217	4,929,167
Chae Yoon Park	71	72	74	217	4,929,167
Bo Mi Park	74	73	70	217	4,929,167
So Yi Kim	72	74	71	217	4,929,167
Dana Kim	71	75	71	217	4,929,167

NH Investment & Securities Ladies Championship

Suwon Country Club, Yongin
Par 72; 6,463 yards

May 15-17
purse, KRW500,000,000

	SCORES			TOTAL	MONEY
Jung Min Lee	69	67	67	203	KRW100,000,000
Gyeol Park	70	70	66	206	48,750,000
Chae Yoon Park	68	70	68	206	48,750,000
Min Sun Kim₅	69	71	68	208	25,000,000
Han Sol Ji	69	72	68	209	20,000,000
Ji Hyun Oh	70	71	69	210	13,750,000
Cho Hui Kim	73	69	68	210	13,750,000
Sung Hyun Park	68	71	71	210	13,750,000
In-Gee Chun	69	71	70	210	13,750,000
Se Mi Jo	73	69	69	211	6,833,333
Yoon Ji Cho	73	70	68	211	6,833,333
Su Yeon Jang	71	68	72	211	6,833,333
Bo Kyung Kim	69	71	72	212	5,400,000
Min Song Ha	74	71	67	212	5,400,000
Ju Yeon In	72	67	73	212	5,400,000
Ji Hyun Kim	68	70	74	212	5,400,000
Ji Young Park	70	71	71	212	5,400,000
Jin Young Ko	73	68	71	212	5,400,000
Shi Hyun Ahn	72	72	69	213	4,372,222
Seung Hyun Lee	68	73	72	213	4,372,222

Doosan Match Play Championship

Ladena Country Club, Chuncheon
Par 72; 6,323 yards

May 21-24
purse, KRW600,000,000

QUARTER-FINALS

Han Sol Ji defeated MinYoung Lee, 2 up.
In-Gee Chun defeated Cho Hui Kim, 19 holes.
Song Yi Ahn defeated Seon Woo Bae, 2 and 1.
Char Young Kim defeated Ji Hyun Kim, 19 holes.

(Losing players received KRW 19,500,000.)

SEMI-FINALS

In-Gee Chun defeated Song Yi Ahn, 1 up.
Han Sol Ji defeated Char Young Kim, 1 up.

PLAYOFF FOR THIRD-FOURTH PLACE

Song Yi Ahn defeated Char Young Kim, 3 and 2.

(Ahn received KRW 48,000,000; Kim received KRW 30,000,000.)

FINAL

In-Gee Chun defeated Han Sol Ji, 1 up.

(Chun received KRW 120,000,000; Ji received KRW 69,000,000.)

E1 Charity Open

Phoenix Springs Country Club, Incheon
Par 72; 6,456 yards

May 29-31
purse, KRW600,000,000

	SCORES			TOTAL	MONEY
Jung Min Lee	71	68	65	204	KRW120,000,000
Ji Hyun Kim₂	68	69	68	205	69,000,000
Seon Woo Bae	68	68	70	206	34,000,000
Yoon Ji Cho	70	72	64	206	34,000,000
Hee Won Jung	68	67	71	206	34,000,000
Min Sun Kim₅	69	71	67	207	19,500,000
Ha-Neul Kim₅	68	70	69	207	19,500,000
Young Jin Chi	70	71	67	208	12,000,000
Shi Hyun Ahn	66	72	70	208	12,000,000
MinYoung Lee₂	68	73	67	208	12,000,000
Gyeol Park	70	70	69	209	8,100,000
In-Gee Chun	71	71	68	210	7,320,000
Yeun Jung Seo	71	69	70	210	7,320,000
Ka Ram Choi	73	70	68	211	6,348,000
Sung Hyun Park	71	71	69	211	6,348,000
Bo Kyung Kim	72	71	68	211	6,348,000
Ji Ram Kweon	72	69	70	211	6,348,000
Hye Jung Choi	71	68	72	211	6,348,000
Hae Rym Kim	70	67	75	212	5,760,000
Seung Hyun Lee	72	74	67	213	5,340,000

Lotte Cantata Ladies Open

Sky Hill Jeju Country Club, Seogwipo, Jeju Island
Par 72; 6,161 yards

June 5-7
purse, KRW600,000,000

	SCORES			TOTAL	MONEY
Jung Min Lee	68	69	71	208	KRW120,000,000
Sung Hyun Park	66	68	74	208	69,000,000
(Jung Min Lee defeated Sung Hyun Park in playoff.)					
Yoon Ji Cho	69	69	71	209	39,000,000
Hae Rym Kim	70	69	70	209	39,000,000
MinYoung Lee₂	74	70	67	211	19,500,000
Ji Hyun Oh	73	68	70	211	19,500,000
Soo Hwa Jang	67	74	70	211	19,500,000
Soo Jin Yang	65	73	73	211	19,500,000
Shin-Ae Ahn	71	70	71	212	9,700,000
Hyun Min Byun	72	72	68	212	9,700,000
Min Sun Kim₅	68	72	72	212	9,700,000
Ju Young Park	71	71	71	213	7,320,000
Seon Woo Bae	70	73	70	213	7,320,000
Ye Na Chung	70	72	72	214	6,450,000
Seung Hyun Lee	71	68	75	214	6,450,000
Ji Hyun Kim₂	69	69	76	214	6,450,000
Yeun Jung Seo	73	68	73	214	6,450,000
Sun Jeung Youn	75	70	70	215	5,208,000
Yoo Lim Choi	70	72	73	215	5,208,000
Ji Young Park	73	69	73	215	5,208,000

S-Oil Champions invitational

Elysian Jeju Country Club, Jeju Island
Par 72; 6,625 yards

June 12-14
purse, KRW600,000,000

	SCORES			TOTAL	MONEY
In-Gee Chun	68	71	69	208	KRW120,000,000
Bo Kyung Kim	68	71	70	209	58,500,000
Yoon Kyung Heo	66	72	71	209	58,500,000
Hae Rym Kim	72	69	71	212	25,000,000
Su Yeon Jang	69	71	72	212	25,000,000
Ji Hee Kim	70	71	71	212	25,000,000
Min Sun Kim₅	71	71	71	213	15,000,000
Dana Kim	66	74	73	213	15,000,000
Ran Hong	68	72	73	213	15,000,000
Ji Hyun Oh	74	71	69	214	9,000,000
Hyun Soo Kim	70	72	73	215	8,100,000
Su Yeon Yu	73	70	73	216	7,005,000
Yoon Ji Cho	70	75	71	216	7,005,000
Rye Jung Lee	72	74	70	216	7,005,000
Ji Young Park	68	77	71	216	7,005,000
Hye Youn Kim	73	76	68	217	6,120,000
Chae Yoon Park	68	75	74	217	6,120,000
Shi Hyun Ahn	73	74	70	217	6,120,000
Hyun Min Byun	70	77	71	218	5,540,000
Sung Hyun Park	69	75	74	218	5,540,000

Kia Motors Korea Women's Open Championship

Bears Best CheongNa, Incheon
Par 72; 6,635 yards

June 18-21
purse, KRW700,000,000

	SCORES				TOTAL	MONEY
Sung Hyun Park	73	69	70	77	289	KRW200,000,000
Jung Min Lee	76	73	68	74	291	75,000,000
Shin-Ae Ahn	70	77	71	74	292	42,000,000
Soo Jin Yang	73	70	77	72	292	42,000,000
Su Yeon Jang	73	76	73	72	294	19,333,333
*Young Lee So	71	81	70	72	294	
So Young Kim₂	75	70	75	74	294	19,333,333
Ye Jin Kim	72	70	78	74	294	19,333,333
Song Yi Ahn	72	76	78	69	295	14,000,000
Hyo Joo Kim	73	73	76	73	295	14,000,000
Min Song Ha	73	72	75	75	295	14,000,000
Seon Woo Bae	75	74	73	74	296	11,750,000
Jin Young Ko	73	72	78	73	296	11,750,000
*Jin Choi Hye	71	75	75	75	296	
Ji Young Park	71	75	78	73	297	10,800,000
*Jung Sung Eun	75	76	75	72	298	
Char Young Kim	73	73	79	73	298	10,000,000
Ji Hee Kim	72	77	74	76	299	8,766,666
Hee Won Jung	72	77	75	75	299	8,766,666
So Yeon Nam	76	72	73	78	299	8,766,666

BC Card Hankyung Ladies Open

Island Country Club, Ansan
Par 72; 6,490 yards

June 25-28
purse, KRW700,000,000

	SCORES				TOTAL	MONEY
Ha Na Jang	70	69	69	68	276	KRW140,000,000
Su Yeon Jang	71	69	70	67	277	57,166,667
Hee Won Jung	74	70	66	67	277	57,166,667
Min Song Ha	68	68	68	73	277	57,166,667
Hyun Soo Kim	68	70	70	70	278	28,000,000
Hae Rym Kim	68	70	74	67	279	19,250,000
Yoon Ji Cho	67	67	75	70	279	19,250,000
Jung Min Lee	68	69	69	73	279	19,250,000
In-Gee Chun	68	69	69	73	279	19,250,000
Jeong Eun Lee₅	70	72	72	66	280	10,500,000
*Jin Choi Hye	69	74	66	71	280	
Gyeol Park	74	69	67	71	281	9,100,000
Sung Hyun Park	74	72	66	69	281	9,100,000
Jin Young Ko	71	72	69	70	282	7,980,000
So Yeon Park	70	71	71	70	282	7,980,000
MinYoung Lee₂	72	67	68	75	282	7,980,000
Jin Eui Hong	68	72	72	71	283	7,245,000
Song Yi Ahn	73	69	69	72	283	7,245,000
Hye Youn Kim	71	69	65	79	284	6,930,000
Ji Young Park	72	72	73	68	285	6,120,000

Kumhotire Ladies Open

Weihai Point Golf Resort, Weihai
Par 72; 6,146 yards

July 3-5
purse, KRW500,000,000

	SCORES			TOTAL	MONEY
Hyo Joo Kim	68	66	72	206	KRW100,000,000
Shanshan Feng	69	73	68	210	57,500,000
Su Yeon Jang	73	67	71	211	40,000,000
Bo Ah Kim	74	71	68	213	22,500,000
Ha Na Jang	70	68	75	213	22,500,000
So Yeon Nam	73	70	71	214	15,000,000
Han Sol Ji	68	69	77	214	15,000,000
Yoo Lim Choi	70	70	74	214	15,000,000
Ji Hyun Kim	71	75	69	215	10,000,000
Bo Bea Kim	76	71	69	216	6,266,667
Jae-Eun Chung	69	76	71	216	6,266,667
Seong Weon Park	79	68	69	216	6,266,667
Jiae Hwang	70	69	77	216	6,266,667
Cho Hui Kim	69	71	76	216	6,266,667
Se Yeong Park	65	75	76	216	6,266,667
Yeun Jung Seo	72	70	75	217	5,175,000
Chae-lin Yang	70	70	77	217	5,175,000
Hye Youn Kim	73	71	74	218	4,737,500
Sung Hyun Park	72	71	75	218	4,737,500
Hui Mang Kim	69	73	76	218	4,737,500

ChoJung Sparkling Water Youngpyong Resort Open

Birch Hill Golf Club, Weihai
Par 72; 6,391 yards

July 10-12
purse, KRW500,000,000

	SCORES			TOTAL	MONEY
Jin Young Ko	67	67	69	203	KRW100,000,000
Ye Jin Kim	68	68	68	204	57,500,000
Seon Woo Bae	69	70	66	205	40,000,000
Hyejung Lee	68	68	70	206	25,000,000
Shi Hyun Ahn	70	70	69	209	18,750,000
Yena Hwang	70	66	73	209	18,750,000
Min Jeong Ko	69	72	69	210	15,000,000
Sion Lee	68	70	73	211	11,250,000
Su Yeon Jang	69	73	69	211	11,250,000
Seung Hyun Lee	70	73	69	212	6,266,667
Song Yi Ahn	73	71	68	212	6,266,667
Hae Rym Kim	70	72	70	212	6,266,667
Hee Won Jung	73	69	70	212	6,266,667
Jeong Eun Lee$_5$	68	72	72	212	6,266,667
Yoon Ji Cho	68	67	77	212	6,266,667
Ji Hyun Kim$_2$	70	72	71	213	5,150,000
Soo Jin Yang	73	69	71	213	5,150,000
gyu been Kim	70	74	69	213	5,150,000
Yeun Jung Seo	73	69	72	214	4,610,000
Hyun Min Byun	71	70	73	214	4,610,000

BMW Ladies Championship

Sky 72 Golf Club, Incheon
Par 72; 6,642 yards

July 16-19
purse, KRW1,200,000,000

	SCORES				TOTAL	MONEY
Yoon Ji Cho	70	68	69	63	270	KRW300,000,000
Min Sun Kim$_5$	72	68	66	66	272	115,200,000
Yeun Jung Seo	71	70	67	65	273	80,400,000
Min Ji Kim$_2$	70	69	70	66	275	48,000,000
Yoon Kyung Heo	70	70	67	68	275	48,000,000
Jae-Eun Chung	71	70	71	64	276	30,600,000
Hee-Kyung Bae	71	68	69	68	276	30,600,000
Seon Woo Bae	69	67	69	71	276	30,600,000
Jin-Joo Hong	70	69	69	68	276	30,600,000
Ji Hyun Kim$_2$	71	70	68	68	277	15,870,000
Sung Hyun Park	70	66	72	69	277	15,870,000
Ji Hyun Oh	73	68	69	67	277	15,870,000
MinYoung Lee$_2$	71	68	68	70	277	15,870,000
So Yi Kim	70	68	72	68	278	13,120,000
Je Youn Yang	69	69	73	67	278	13,120,000
Ju Yeon In	72	68	68	70	278	13,120,000
Song Yi Ahn	71	69	74	65	279	11,472,000
Soo Jin Yang	72	72	70	65	279	11,472,000
Jin Young Ko	70	70	71	68	279	11,472,000
You Na Park	69	72	70	68	279	11,472,000

Hite Jinro Championship

Blue Heron Golf Club, Yeoju
Par 72; 6,766 yards

July 23-26
purse, KRW800,000,000

	SCORES			TOTAL	MONEY
In-Gee Chun	69	66	73	208	KRW160,000,000
Gyeol Park	70	69	72	211	78,000,000
Yoon Ji Cho	70	70	71	211	78,000,000
Hyun Soo Kim	72	70	70	212	36,000,000
Hyo Joo Kim	70	69	73	212	36,000,000
Ka Ram Choi	72	72	69	213	22,000,000
Ji Young Park	71	70	72	213	22,000,000
MinYoung Lee$_2$	70	71	72	213	22,000,000
Song Yi Ahn	70	70	73	213	22,000,000
Ha-Neul Kim	70	72	72	214	10,933,333
Ji Hyun Kim	71	71	72	214	10,933,333
Hye Youn Kim	67	70	77	214	10,933,333
Min Sun Kim$_5$	75	71	69	215	8,784,000
Ji Hyun Kim$_2$	73	69	73	215	8,784,000
Sung Hyun Park	67	71	77	215	8,784,000
Shin Young Park	70	72	73	215	8,784,000
Ran Hong	69	73	73	215	8,784,000
Min Song Ha	75	71	70	216	7,520,000
Sun Jeung Youn	70	73	73	216	7,520,000
Jin Young Ko	72	70	74	216	7,520,000

Jeju Samdasu Masters

ORA Country Club, Jeju Island
Par 72; 6,519 yards

August 7-9
purse, KRW500,000,000

	SCORES			TOTAL	MONEY
Jeong Eun Lee$_5$	69	71	70	210	KRW100,000,000
So Yeon Park	68	72	70	210	57,500,000
(Jeong Eun Lee defeated So Yeon Park in playoff.)					
Jeong Hwa Lee	69	73	70	212	28,333,333
You Na Park	68	72	72	212	28,333,333
Ji Hee Kim	71	71	70	212	28,333,333
Eun Woo Choi	68	70	75	213	16,250,000
Ji Hyun Oh	71	72	70	213	16,250,000
Cho Hui Kim	73	69	72	214	10,000,000
In-Bee Park	67	75	72	214	10,000,000
Sung Hyun Park	73	72	69	214	10,000,000
Jin Young Ko	73	71	71	215	6,162,500
Ka Ram Choi	72	73	70	215	6,162,500
Su Yeon Jang	72	69	74	215	6,162,500
Na Rae Ko	72	69	74	215	6,162,500
Ji Hyun Lee	73	72	71	216	5,016,667
MinYoung Lee$_2$	71	74	71	216	5,016,667
Bo Kyung Kim	71	72	73	216	5,016,667
Gi Ppuem Lee	75	69	72	216	5,016,667
Ye Na Chung	72	70	74	216	5,016,667
So Yeon Nam	70	74	72	216	5,016,667

Bogner MBN Ladies Open

Star Hue Country Club, Yangpyeong
Par 72; 6,672 yards

August 20-23
purse, KRW500,000,000

	SCORES				TOTAL	MONEY
Min Song Ha	69	66	65	69	269	KRW100,000,000
Seon Woo Bae	67	70	69	69	275	48,750,000
Jin-Joo Hong	71	67	66	71	275	48,750,000
MinYoung Lee$_2$	71	69	64	72	276	22,500,000
In-Gee Chun	69	69	66	72	276	22,500,000
Bo Bae Kim$_2$	71	69	69	68	277	15,000,000
Ye Jin Kim	75	65	71	66	277	15,000,000
Ka Ram Choi	74	66	67	70	277	15,000,000
Seul A Yoon	71	69	69	69	278	7,625,000
Ji Hyun Kim$_2$	72	68	71	67	278	7,625,000
Soo Hwa Jang	71	66	70	71	278	7,625,000
Su Yeon Jang	71	69	67	71	278	7,625,000
Hyun Soo Kim	69	71	67	72	279	5,700,000
You Na Park	74	66	67	72	279	5,700,000
Jeong Eun Lee$_5$	70	68	70	71	279	5,700,000
Hye Jin Jung	73	70	67	70	280	4,858,333
Hye Jung Choi	70	70	69	71	280	4,858,333
Cho Hui Kim	72	71	67	70	280	4,858,333
Yoon Ji Cho	68	69	70	73	280	4,858,333
Ji Hyun Kim	67	70	72	71	280	4,858,333

HighOne Resort Ladies Open

HighOne Country Club, Jeongseon-gun, Gangwon-do
Par 72; 6,667 yards

August 27-30
purse, KRW800,000,000

	SCORES				TOTAL	MONEY
So Yeon Ryu	71	67	69	70	277	KRW160,000,000
Ha Na Jang	68	71	68	72	279	92,000,000
Sun Jeung Youn	71	69	69	74	283	64,000,000
Ji Young Park	72	71	73	68	284	33,333,333
MinYoung Lee$_2$	71	71	72	70	284	33,333,333
Yeun Jung Seo	72	65	71	76	284	33,333,333
Hee Won Jung	72	66	77	70	285	16,560,000
In-Gee Chun	78	68	68	71	285	16,560,000
Do Yeon Kim	71	74	68	72	285	16,560,000
Hae Rym Kim	73	72	68	72	285	16,560,000
Chae-lin Yang	76	68	72	69	285	16,560,000
Bo Ah Kim	73	70	73	70	286	9,340,000
Seung Hyun Lee	72	65	75	74	286	9,340,000
You Na Park	72	69	71	74	286	9,340,000
Shin-Ae Ahn	72	73	66	75	286	9,340,000
Shi Hyun Ahn	73	71	73	70	287	7,888,000
Eun Bin Lee	73	71	72	71	287	7,888,000
Ji Hyun Oh	73	71	70	73	287	7,888,000
Ji Hyun Kim	71	72	73	71	287	7,888,000
Ka Ram Choi	72	65	77	73	287	7,888,000

Hanhwa Finance Classic

Golden Bay Golf Club, Taean-gun, Chungcheongnam-do
Par 72; 6,631 yards

September 3-6
purse, KRW1,200,000,000

		SCORES			TOTAL	MONEY
Haru Nomura	73	65	74	75	287	KRW300,000,000
Seon Woo Bae	67	68	73	79	287	115,200,000
(Haru Nomura defeated Seon Woo Bae in playoff.)						
I.K. Kim	70	72	72	74	288	80,400,000
Han Sol Ji	73	72	72	74	291	48,000,000
Ji Hyun Kim	70	73	73	75	291	48,000,000
*Jin Choi Hye	71	72	72	77	292	
Ye Jin Kim	67	78	71	77	293	32,800,000
Ye Na Chung	74	71	75	73	293	32,800,000
Hyun Soo Kim	73	72	70	78	293	32,800,000
Jenny Shin	68	72	76	78	294	19,400,000
Ran Hong	73	72	74	75	294	19,400,000
Hae Rym Kim	69	73	74	78	294	19,400,000
Eun-Hee Ji	72	74	76	73	295	13,752,000
Su Yeon Jang	72	71	78	74	295	13,752,000
Cho Hui Kim	70	72	77	76	295	13,752,000
Yeun Jung Seo	73	75	72	75	295	13,752,000
Shin-Ae Ahn	68	76	74	77	295	13,752,000
Jae-Eun Chung	74	71	74	77	296	11,820,000
Jin-Joo Hong	71	73	76	76	296	11,820,000
Sung Hyun Park	71	73	74	78	296	11,820,000

Isugroup KLPGA Championship

Ferrum Club, Yeoju
Par 72; 6,631 yards

September 10-13
purse, KRW700,000,000

		SCORES			TOTAL	MONEY
Shin-Ae Ahn	71	73	69	67	280	KRW140,000,000
MinYoung Lee$_2$	70	64	72	74	280	57,166,667
Jung Min Lee	72	65	70	73	280	57,166,667
Yeun Jung Seo	69	71	68	72	280	57,166,667
(Ahn won in playoff.)						
Hae Rym Kim	68	70	71	72	281	28,000,000
Ye Na Chung	67	69	73	73	282	21,000,000
Shi Hyun Ahn	70	70	69	73	282	21,000,000
Min Sun Kim$_5$	68	69	70	75	282	21,000,000
Su Yeon Jang	67	69	72	76	284	10,675,000
Yoo Lim Choi	72	70	68	74	284	10,675,000
Seung Hyun Lee	68	70	73	73	284	10,675,000
Ka Ram Choi	69	69	69	77	284	10,675,000
Chae Young Yoon	73	68	72	72	285	7,560,000
Sun Hwa Lee$_2$	70	72	72	71	285	7,560,000
Jin-Joo Hong	72	70	71	72	285	7,560,000
Ji Hyun Kim	69	73	69	74	285	7,560,000
Gyeol Park	68	71	70	76	285	7,560,000
Cho Hui Kim	71	68	72	74	285	7,560,000
Ji Hyun Oh	71	71	72	72	286	6,206,667
Seon Woo Bae	72	71	71	72	286	6,206,667

KDB Daewoo Securities Classic

Elysian Gangchon Golf Club, Chuncheon
Par 72; 6,450 yards

September 18-20
purse, KRW600,000,000

	SCORES			TOTAL	MONEY
Sung Hyun Park	68	66	69	203	KRW120,000,000
*Jung Sung Eun	71	69	65	205	
Song Yi Ahn	67	67	71	205	58,500,000
Hye Youn Kim	70	66	69	205	58,500,000
Ji Hee Kim	70	71	65	206	27,000,000
Chae Young Yoon	67	69	70	206	27,000,000
Min Sun Kim₅	69	68	70	207	19,500,000
Jin Young Ko	71	69	67	207	19,500,000
Jeongmin Cho	65	71	72	208	13,500,000
Seo Young Park	66	69	73	208	13,500,000
Bo Kyung Kim	71	67	71	209	7,716,000
Hae Rym Kim	70	68	71	209	7,716,000
Hee-Young Park	72	68	69	209	7,716,000
MinYoung Lee₂	68	69	72	209	7,716,000
In-Gee Chun	68	66	75	209	7,716,000
Ji Ram Kweon	68	69	73	210	6,320,000
Sun Hwa Lee₂	71	70	69	210	6,320,000
Bo Bae Kim₂	69	69	72	210	6,320,000
Hyun Min Byun	69	73	69	211	5,332,500
Jin-Joo Hong	70	70	71	211	5,332,500

YTN-Volvik Ladies Open

Lakewood Country Club, Yangju
Par 72; 6,812 yards

September 24-26
purse, KRW500,000,000

	SCORES			TOTAL	MONEY
Ha Na Jang	65	65	70	200	KRW100,000,000
Min Song Ha	68	68	68	204	40,833,333
Jeongmin Cho	66	68	70	204	40,833,333
Min Sun Kim₅	67	65	72	204	40,833,333
Ji Young Park₅	67	71	67	205	17,500,000
Gyeol Park	68	69	68	205	17,500,000
Sung Hyun Park	69	67	69	205	17,500,000
Eun Woo Choi	65	71	70	206	9,187,500
Yeun Jung Seo	66	73	67	206	9,187,500
Hye Jin Jung	69	69	68	206	9,187,500
Chella Choi	69	68	69	206	9,187,500
Seung Hyun Lee	68	73	66	207	5,542,857
Cho Hui Kim	68	72	67	207	5,542,857
Ji Hyun Kim	67	72	68	207	5,542,857
Ha-Neul Kim	70	70	67	207	5,542,857
Bo Kyung Kim	69	69	69	207	5,542,857
Hui Mang Kim	67	70	70	207	5,542,857
Chae Young Yoon	69	68	70	207	5,542,857
Hyun Min Byun	73	66	69	208	4,558,333
Eun Ji Hyun	68	70	70	208	4,558,333

OKSavingsBank Se Ri Pak Invitational

Solmoro Country Club, Yeoju
Par 72; 6,484 yards

October 2-4
purse, KRW600,000,000

	SCORES			TOTAL	MONEY
Sung Hyun Park	71	67	68	206	KRW120,000,000
Ji Hyun Kim	72	68	67	207	58,500,000
Hae Rym Kim	70	67	70	207	58,500,000
Yoon Ji Cho	72	67	69	208	30,000,000
Hye Jung Choi	72	70	67	209	24,000,000
Jung Min Lee	71	70	69	210	21,000,000
Chae Young Yoon	70	72	69	211	18,000,000
Ji Hyun Oh	71	73	68	212	11,025,000
MinYoung Lee₂	67	72	73	212	11,025,000
Min Sun Kim₅	73	69	70	212	11,025,000
Ye Jin Kim	70	70	72	212	11,025,000
Jiae Hwang	72	71	70	213	7,160,000
Hyun Soo Kim	74	71	68	213	7,160,000
Shi Hyun Ahn	70	69	74	213	7,160,000
Hyun Min Byun	74	72	68	214	6,020,000
Hyejung Lee	74	73	67	214	6,020,000
Hee Won Jung	77	68	69	214	6,020,000
Seon Woo Bae	71	71	72	214	6,020,000
Ji Hee Kim	69	72	73	214	6,020,000
Seul A Yoon	70	69	75	214	6,020,000

LPGA KEB HanaBank Championship

Sky 72 Golf Club, Ocean Course, Incheon
Par 36-36–72; 6,364 yards

October 15-18
purse, US$2,000,000

	SCORES				TOTAL	MONEY
Lexi Thompson	68	67	69	69	273	US$300,000
Yani Tseng	70	67	69	68	274	158,579
Sung Hyun Park	62	74	67	71	274	158,579
Amy Yang	71	72	70	62	275	84,703
Gerina Piller	66	74	68	67	275	84,703
Lydia Ko	69	65	69	72	275	84,703
Suzann Pettersen	70	69	68	69	276	53,338
Shanshan Feng	67	71	69	69	276	53,338
Mika Miyazato	71	69	71	67	278	37,084
Brittany Lincicome	71	70	69	68	278	37,084
Chella Choi	67	72	71	68	278	37,084
Mi Hyang Lee	71	67	71	69	278	37,084
Yoon-Ji Cho	68	68	69	73	278	37,084
Mirim Lee	68	69	67	74	278	37,084
Lee-Anne Pace	70	68	75	67	280	25,830
Sei Young Kim	70	70	72	68	280	25,830
Inbee Park	69	72	70	69	280	25,830
Brittany Lang	68	71	72	69	280	25,830
In-Gee Chun	73	68	68	71	280	25,830
Pernilla Lindberg	68	70	70	72	280	25,830
Na Yeon Choi	68	74	71	68	281	21,134
So Yeon Ryu	73	73	66	69	281	21,134
Jin Young Ko	71	70	71	69	281	21,134
Moriya Jutanugarn	70	68	67	76	281	21,134
Hyo Joo Kim	67	73	71	71	282	18,517
Mariajo Uribe	72	67	72	71	282	18,517
Minjee Lee	69	69	72	72	282	18,517

	SCORES				TOTAL	MONEY
Xi Yu Lin	71	73	71	68	283	15,515
Anna Nordqvist	71	71	72	69	283	15,515
Yeun Jung Seo	70	69	73	71	283	15,515
Sakura Yokomine	74	69	68	72	283	15,515
Eun-Hee Ji	67	75	69	72	283	15,515
Han Sol Ji	67	72	70	74	283	15,515

KB Financial Group Star Championship

Namchon Country Club, Gwangju
Par 72; 6,571 yards

October 22-25
purse, KRW700,000,000

	SCORES				TOTAL	MONEY
In-Gee Chun	69	69	67	69	274	KRW140,000,000
Inbee Park	65	73	68	69	275	68,250,000
Hae Rym Kim	66	66	70	73	275	68,250,000
Jung Min Lee	68	67	69	73	277	35,000,000
Ka Ram Choi	71	69	69	69	278	26,250,000
Seon Woo Bae	68	69	69	72	278	26,250,000
Ji Hyun Kim₂	66	72	71	71	280	17,500,000
Min Song Ha	65	71	70	74	280	17,500,000
Sun Jeung Youn	70	68	68	74	280	17,500,000
Seung Hyun Lee	67	70	74	70	281	9,002,000
Ye Jin Kim	71	68	73	69	281	9,002,000
So Yeon Nam	72	68	74	67	281	9,002,000
Chae Yoon Park	71	70	72	68	281	9,002,000
So Yeon Park	71	68	70	72	281	9,002,000
Yoon Ji Cho	71	69	73	69	282	7,525,000
Gyeol Park	72	71	69	70	282	7,525,000
Char Young Kim	70	74	70	69	283	6,640,000
Soo-Bin Kim	71	70	71	71	283	6,640,000
Ran Hong	70	72	72	69	283	6,640,000
Hye Jung Choi	67	72	76	68	283	6,640,000

Seokyung-Moonyoung Queens Park Ladies Classic

DeBeach Golf Club, Geoje
Par 72; 6,482 yards

October 30-November 1
purse, KRW500,000,000

	SCORES			TOTAL	MONEY
Hye Youn Kim	73	73	64	210	KRW100,000,000
Yoon Ji Cho	75	69	68	212	57,500,000
So Yeon Park	74	71	71	216	28,333,333
Yoo Lim Choi	69	78	69	216	28,333,333
Hae Rym Kim	72	71	73	216	28,333,333
Ji Hyun Kim	78	74	65	217	15,000,000
Jae-Eun Chung	77	69	71	217	15,000,000
Chae Young Yoon	70	71	76	217	15,000,000
Sung Hyun Park	73	75	70	218	7,290,000
Jeongmin Cho	78	68	72	218	7,290,000
So Yeon Nam	74	72	72	218	7,290,000
Eu Ddeum Lee	71	75	72	218	7,290,000
Soo Jin Yang	72	73	73	218	7,290,000
Seo Young Park	75	72	72	219	5,375,000
Ha Kyung Seo	70	77	72	219	5,375,000
Dana Kim	73	73	73	219	5,375,000
Je Yoon Yang	71	75	73	219	5,375,000

	SCORES			TOTAL	MONEY
Min Gee Song	76	77	67	220	4,766,667
Hyun Soo Kim	76	73	71	220	4,766,667
Su Yeon Jang	74	75	71	220	4,766,667

ADT CAPS Championship

Haeundae Beach Golf & Resort, Busan
Par 72; 6,591 yards

November 6-8
purse, KRW500,000,000

	SCORES			TOTAL	MONEY
Ji Hyun Oh	70	67	65	202	KRW100,000,000
Min Song Ha	70	74	64	208	48,750,000
Bo Kyung Kim	70	72	66	208	48,750,000
Shin-Ae Ahn	70	70	70	210	20,833,333
Hye Jung Choi	73	68	69	210	20,833,333
Jin Young Ko	68	68	74	210	20,833,333
Jeong Hwa Lee	72	71	68	211	13,750,000
Seung Hyun Lee	70	71	70	211	13,750,000
Hae Rym Kim	73	68	71	212	8,083,333
Ye Jin Kim	68	71	73	212	8,083,333
Jeong Eun Lee₅	67	72	73	212	8,083,333
Sung Hyun Park	71	72	70	213	5,966,667
Char Young Kim	70	74	69	213	5,966,667
Ji Hyun Kim₂	72	71	70	213	5,966,667
Yoo Lim Choi	73	72	69	214	5,187,500
Ka Ram Choi	74	71	69	214	5,187,500
Soo Jin Yang	72	73	69	214	5,187,500
Ji Young Park	68	75	71	214	5,187,500
Han Sol Ji	73	72	70	215	4,371,429
So Yi Kim	70	76	69	215	4,371,429

Chosunilbo-Posco Championship

Lake Side Country Club, Yongin
Par 72; 6,619 yards

November 13-15
purse, KRW700,000,000

	SCORES			TOTAL	MONEY
Hye Jung Choi	67	64	68	199	KRW140,000,000
Sung Hyun Park	70	65	67	202	80,500,000
Bo Kyung Kim	71	68	64	203	39,666,667
So Yeon Park	73	64	66	203	39,666,667
Jeongmin Cho	69	63	71	203	39,666,667
MinYoung Lee₂	69	66	69	204	22,750,000
Su Yeon Jang	66	67	71	204	22,750,000
So Yeon Nam	71	66	68	205	15,750,000
Yoon Ji Cho	71	66	68	205	15,750,000
Ran Hong	69	69	68	206	10,500,000
Jeong Eun Lee₅	73	69	65	207	8,627,500
Yeun Jung Seo	70	68	69	207	8,627,500
Chae-lin Yang	70	67	70	207	8,627,500
Seon Woo Bae	69	66	72	207	8,627,500
Cho Hui Kim	70	71	67	208	7,630,000
Ji Hyun Kim	70	70	69	209	6,606,250
Gyeol Park	71	68	70	209	6,606,250
Mi Rim Lee	70	70	69	209	6,606,250
Julie Yang	69	71	69	209	6,606,250
Ka Ram Choi	72	68	69	209	6,606,250

Hyundai China Ladies Open

Mission Hills Golf Club, Haikou
Par 72; 6,342 yards

December 11-13
purse, US$550,000

	SCORES			TOTAL	MONEY
Sung Hyun Park	64	68	67	199	US$110,000
Hyo Joo Kim	66	68	67	201	63,250
Su Yeon Jang	68	68	68	204	44,000
In-Gee Chun	69	68	68	205	27,500
Ji Yeon Park	72	68	68	208	19,250
Song Yi Ahn	71	67	70	208	19,250
Gyeol Park	70	67	71	208	19,250
Min Sun Kim	71	69	69	209	12,375
Bo Bea Kim	70	69	70	209	12,375
Seon Woo Bae	70	72	68	210	7,516.70
Meng-Chu Chen	67	72	71	210	7,516.70
Hee Won Jung	72	69	69	210	7,516.70
Yuting Shi	70	71	70	211	6,270
Cho Hui Kim	70	70	71	211	6,270
Seul A. Yoon	69	70	72	211	6,270
Hye Youn Kim	69	73	70	212	5,610
Bo Kyung Kim	67	74	71	212	5,610
Saraporn Chamchoi	68	72	72	212	5,610
Jing Yan	73	74	66	213	4,809.40
MinYoung Lee₂	70	72	71	213	4,809.40
Bo Ah Kim	71	74	68	213	4,809.40
Ye Jin Kim	70	75	68	213	4,809.40
*Muni He	71	71	71	213	
Shin-Ae Ahn	71	71	71	213	4,809.40
Ran Hong	69	75	69	213	4,809.40
Wei-Wei Zhang	67	74	72	213	4,809.40
Hyun Min Byun	70	72	71	213	4,809.40
Ji Hee Kim	70	73	70	213	4,809.40

Australian Ladies Tour

Moss Vale Classic

Moss Vale Golf Club, Moss Vale, New South Wales
Par 73; 5,300 yards

January 22-23
purse, A$30,000

	SCORES		TOTAL	MONEY
Sarah Oh	70	64	134	A$4,500
Sarah Kemp	68	67	135	3,000
Whitney Hillier	66	70	136	2,250
Emma de Groot	69	68	137	1,500
Lorie Kane	70	67	137	1,500
Ellen Davies-Graham	68	69	137	1,500
Lauren Hibbert	70	68	138	1,200
Nikki Campbell	71	69	140	1,050
Jenna Hunter	71	70	141	870
Breanna Elliott	71	70	141	870
Nancy Harvey	74	68	142	630
Beth Allen	74	68	142	630
Hannah Burke	71	71	142	630
Elissa-Jayne Orr	69	73	142	630
Christine Wolf	69	73	142	630
Eleanor Givens	71	71	142	630
Rachel Hetherington	74	69	143	450
Stephanie Na	72	72	144	360
Samantha Troyanovich	71	73	144	360
Nikki Garrett	72	72	144	360
Jayde Panos	71	73	144	360
Julia Boland	71	73	144	360

Oates Victorian Open

13th Beach Golf Links, Barwon Heads, Victoria
Par 36-37–73; 6,225 yards

February 5-8
purse, A$250,000

	SCORES				TOTAL	MONEY
Marianne Skarpnord	70	68	68	73	279	A$37,500
Su-Hyun Oh	73	65	72	72	282	21,250
Holly Clyburn	72	68	69	73	282	21,250
Rebecca Artis	73	71	69	71	284	11,500
Rachel Hetherington	73	70	73	68	284	11,500
Sophie Walker	73	67	72	73	285	9,500
Jayde Panos	73	72	70	71	286	8,375
Laura Davies	78	67	70	73	288	6,750
Lorie Kane	72	71	72	73	288	6,750
Sally Watson	69	69	73	77	288	6,750
*Shelly Shin	72	67	72	78	289	
Breanna Elliott	77	74	66	72	289	4,675
Eleanor Givens	73	72	67	77	289	4,675
Nikki Garrett	73	75	68	74	290	4,000
Isabelle Boineau	74	69	74	74	291	3,625
Pennapa Pulsawath	74	68	71	78	291	3,625
*Hayley Bettencourt	76	75	69	71	291	

	SCORES				TOTAL	MONEY
Tiranan Yoopan	73	73	74	72	292	3,125
Beth Allen	70	72	74	77	293	3,075
Kristie Smith	78	71	72	737	294	2,979.17
Nikki Campbell	75	73	74	7	294	2,979.17
Liv Cheng	75	69	72	78	294	2,979.17
*Hannah Green	71	72	72	79	294	

RACV Ladies Masters

RACV Royal Pines Resort, Benowa, Queensland
Par 37-36–73; 6,527 yards

February 12-15
purse, €250,000

	SCORES				TOTAL	MONEY
Su-Hyun Oh	69	75	72	69	285	€37,500
Florentyna Parker	71	74	74	69	288	18,791.67
Charley Hull	70	70	75	73	288	18,791.67
Katherine Kirk	70	75	74	69	288	18,791.67
Eun Woo Choi	69	71	75	74	289	10,600
Sally Watson	77	70	74	69	290	6,620
Camilla Lennarth	71	75	72	72	290	6,620
Lee-Anne Pace	73	73	72	72	290	6,620
Ssu-Chia Cheng	74	69	74	73	290	6,620
Emma de Groot	72	75	73	70	290	6,620
*Rebecca Kay	74	70	73	73	290	
Melissa Reid	72	73	74	72	291	4,308.33
Laura Jansone	73	74	75	69	291	4,308.33
Michelle Koh	74	71	72	74	291	4,308.33
*Jiwon Jeon	72	73	74	72	291	
Beth Allen	76	73	75	68	292	3,668.75
Tonje Daffinrud	74	70	72	76	292	3,668.75
Holly Clyburn	70	71	74	77	292	3,668.75
Rebecca Artis	71	66	79	76	292	3,668.75
Felicity Johnson	73	73	74	73	293	3,268.75
Amy Boulden	72	73	73	75	293	3,268.75
Gwladys Nocera	72	71	76	74	293	3,268.75
Connie Chen	75	73	75	70	293	3,268.75

ISPS Handa Women's Australian Open

Royal Melbourne Golf Club, Black Rock, Victoria
Par 35-38–73; 6,741 yards

February 19-22
purse, US$1,200,000

	SCORES				TOTAL	MONEY
Lydia Ko	70	70	72	71	283	US$180,000
Amy Yang	73	70	70	72	285	110,822
Ariya Jutanugarn	69	71	72	76	288	80,393
Ilhee Lee	68	82	69	71	290	51,067
Chella Choi	72	75	71	72	290	51,067
Jenny Shin	76	71	74	69	290	51,067
Julieta Granada	73	72	70	76	291	27,728
Paz Echeverria	71	76	71	73	291	27,728
Ha Na Jang	71	69	76	75	291	27,728
Minjee Lee	76	71	72	72	291	27,728
Charley Hull	71	71	76	73	291	27,728
Mika Miyazato	73	74	74	71	292	19,355
Gwladys Nocera	71	73	74	74	292	19,355
Jessica Korda	72	71	75	74	292	19,355

	SCORES				TOTAL	MONEY
Q. Baek	77	72	71	72	292	19,355
Katherine Kirk	72	73	70	78	293	15,472
Karrie Webb	73	78	71	71	293	15,472
Beatriz Recari	75	71	72	75	293	15,472
Marianne Skarpnord	75	72	73	73	293	15,472
Pernilla Lindberg	76	74	71	73	294	13,955
Beth Allen	78	71	70	76	295	12,287
Shanshan Feng	74	74	74	73	295	12,287
Tiffany Joh	72	75	76	72	295	12,287
Sydnee Michaels	73	76	73	73	295	12,287
Melissa Reid	71	74	75	75	295	12,287
So Yeon Ryu	77	74	71	73	295	12,287
Catriona Matthew	74	74	72	76	296	10,314
Mo Martin	77	73	72	74	296	10,314
Laetitia Beck	78	71	73	74	296	10,314
Mina Harigae	75	71	73	78	297	9,162
Marina Alex	72	77	73	75	297	9,162
Marion Ricordeau	72	73	76	76	297	9,162

ISPS Handa New Zealand Women's Open

Clearwater Golf Club, Christchurch, New Zealand
Par 36-36–72; 5,658 yards

February 27-March 1
purse, €200,000

	SCORES			TOTAL	MONEY
Lydia Ko	70	61	71	202	€30,000
*Hannah Green	68	70	68	206	
Nanna Koerstz Madsen	67	69	71	207	20,300
Marianne Skarpnord	67	69	72	208	12,400
Beth Allen	68	67	73	208	12,400
Pamela Pretswell	69	67	73	209	6,620
Amelia Lewis	73	65	71	209	6,620
Marta Sanz	71	67	71	209	6,620
Charley Hull	70	64	75	209	6,620
Sarah-Jane Smith	72	68	70	210	4,080
Min Lee	75	66	69	210	4,080
Marina Alex	69	67	74	210	4,080
Giulia Sergas	68	67	76	211	3,310
Florentyna Parker	71	69	71	211	3,310
Nicole Broch Larsen	71	68	72	211	3,310
Fabienne In-Albon	72	71	68	211	3,310
Katie Burnett	69	74	69	212	2,880
Anne-Lise Caudal	66	75	71	212	2,880
Noora Tamminen	68	73	71	212	2,880
*Chantelle Cassidy	71	71	70	212	
Wei Ling Hsu	75	69	68	212	2,880

Bing Lee Fujitsu NSW Women's Open

Oatlands Golf Club, Sydney, New South Wales
Par 36-36–72; 5,954 yards

March 6-8
purse, A$125,000

	SCORES			TOTAL	MONEY
Holly Clyburn	69	66	70	205	A$18,750
Christine Wolf	72	70	64	206	8,125
Vikki Laing	71	68	67	206	8,125
Fabienne In-Albon	69	68	69	206	8,125

	SCORES			TOTAL	MONEY
Rebecca Artis	67	71	68	206	8,125
Nikki Garrett	72	65	70	207	4,500
Tamie Durdin	69	71	68	208	3,812.50
Stacey Keating	72	70	66	208	3,812.50
*Shelly Shin	70	69	69	208	
Joanna Klatten	69	68	72	209	2,958.33
Mireia Prat	68	71	70	209	2,958.33
Breanna Elliott	71	65	73	209	2,958.33
Sarah Kemp	69	69	72	210	2,425
Michele Thomson	76	67	68	211	2,062.50
Danielle Montgomery	71	69	71	211	2,062.50
*Jenny Lee	70	74	68	212	
Felicity Johnson	70	73	69	212	1,875
Valentine Derrey	71	72	70	213	1,555
Adriana Brent	71	73	69	213	1,555
Daisy Nielson	73	66	74	213	1,555
Isabelle Boineau	70	73	70	213	1,555
Rachel Hetherington	71	70	72	213	1,555

Australia Classic

Twin Creeks Golf & Country Club, Luddenham, New South Wales
Par 36-36–72; 6,291 yards

April 17-19
purse, A$150,000

	SCORES			TOTAL	MONEY
Yanhong Pan	68	65	69	202	A$22,500
Rebecca Artis	65	69	69	203	15,375
Ziqi Ye	69	67	70	206	10,650
Sarah Oh	65	74	71	210	8,250
Nikki Campbell	70	70	72	212	5,955
Michelle Koh	70	67	75	212	5,955
Alison Whitaker	70	70	73	213	4,650
Adriana Brent	75	71	68	214	3,705
Weiwei Zhang	69	69	76	214	3,705
Sha Wu	72	71	72	215	3,060
Cathryn Bristow	70	73	72	215	3,060
Wichanee Meechai	68	73	7	216	2,745
Stephanie Na	69	71	76	216	2,745
Pavarisa Yoktuan	74	71	72	217	2,550
Bree Arthur	74	72	72	218	2,267.14
Rachel Hetherington	73	73	72	218	2,267.14
Nikki Garrett	72	74	72	218	2,267.14
Tamie Durdin	72	73	73	218	2,267.14
Vicky Thomas	71	70	77	218	2,267.14
Whitney Hillier	70	71	77	218	2,267.14
Pennapa Pulsawath	74	73	71	218	2,267.14

Senior Tours

Mitsubishi Electric Championship

Hualalai Golf Course, Ka'upulehu-Kona, Hawaii
Par 36-36–72; 7,107 yards

January 23-25
purse, $1,800,000

	SCORES			TOTAL	MONEY
Miguel Angel Jimenez	69	64	66	199	$309,000
Mark O'Meara	69	67	64	200	187,000
Fred Couples	72	64	66	202	133,000
Rocco Mediate	66	67	70	203	111,500
Olin Browne	68	67	69	204	76,750
Bernhard Langer	72	65	67	204	76,750
Colin Montgomerie	70	66	68	204	76,750
Wes Short, Jr.	68	70	66	204	76,750
Bart Bryant	68	69	69	206	53,500
Corey Pavin	67	72	67	206	53,500
Loren Roberts	75	68	64	207	42,750
Kirk Triplett	73	65	69	207	42,750
Scott Dunlap	69	70	69	208	35,218.75
David Frost	71	69	68	208	35,218.75
Tom Lehman	73	65	70	208	35,218.75
Kenny Perry	69	69	70	208	35,218.75
Michael Allen	73	68	68	209	27,125
Roger Chapman	70	73	66	209	27,125
Paul Goydos	68	71	70	209	27,125
John Riegger	74	67	68	209	27,125
Russ Cochran	69	73	68	210	20,625
John Cook	68	74	68	210	20,625
Tom Pernice, Jr.	70	71	69	210	20,625
Esteban Toledo	68	69	73	210	20,625
Tom Watson	68	74	68	210	20,625
Mark Wiebe	69	69	72	210	20,625
Fred Funk	74	67	70	211	17,125
Jay Haas	69	72	71	212	15,750
Peter Jacobsen	74	71	67	212	15,750
Davis Love	70	69	74	213	14,750
Jeff Maggert	71	72	70	213	14,750

Allianz Championship

Old Course at Broken Sound, Boca Raton, Florida
Par 36-36–72; 6,807 yards

February 6-8
purse, $1,700,000

	SCORES			TOTAL	MONEY
Paul Goydos	66	69	69	204	$255,000
Gene Sauers	71	67	67	205	149,600
Fred Funk	67	73	66	206	101,433.34
Michael Allen	70	69	67	206	101,433.33
John Huston	72	68	66	206	101,433.33
Tommy Armour	73	68	66	207	61,200
Jose Coceres	74	70	63	207	61,200
Jay Haas	69	69	69	207	61,200
Bart Bryant	66	69	73	208	45,900
Rod Spittle	69	66	73	208	45,900

	SCORES			TOTAL	MONEY
Guy Boros	69	68	72	209	34,000
Olin Browne	70	67	72	209	34,000
Rocco Mediate	72	66	71	209	34,000
Tom Pernice, Jr.	66	69	74	209	34,000
Jerry Smith	70	72	67	209	34,000
Esteban Toledo	69	69	71	209	34,000
Scott Dunlap	75	65	70	210	25,500
Steve Lowery	73	66	71	210	25,500
Jeff Sluman	70	72	68	210	25,500
Billy Andrade	70	72	69	211	19,408.34
Wes Short, Jr.	72	72	67	211	19,408.34
Mark Brooks	68	69	74	211	19,408.33
Tom Lehman	73	68	70	211	19,408.33
Corey Pavin	71	70	70	211	19,408.33
Loren Roberts	68	71	72	211	19,408.33
Jay Don Blake	69	75	68	212	14,450
John Cook	71	71	70	212	14,450
Bernhard Langer	67	70	75	212	14,450
Jeff Maggert	73	72	67	212	14,450
Kevin Sutherland	72	70	70	212	14,450
Duffy Waldorf	71	73	68	212	14,450

ACE Group Classic

TwinEagles Golf Club, Talon Course, Naples, Florida
Par 36-36–72; 7,193 yards

February 13-15
purse, $1,600,000

	SCORES			TOTAL	MONEY
Lee Janzen	68	65	67	200	$240,000
Bart Bryant	70	68	62	200	140,800
(Janzen defeated Bryant on first playoff hole.)					
Esteban Toledo	69	67	66	202	115,200
Scott Dunlap	69	67	67	203	95,200
Colin Montgomerie	66	66	72	204	76,000
Kevin Sutherland	72	67	66	205	64,000
Olin Browne	71	66	70	207	54,400
Marco Dawson	69	71	67	207	54,400
Michael Allen	69	70	69	208	44,800
Tom Byrum	74	67	68	209	36,800
Paul Goydos	69	70	70	209	36,800
Jeff Maggert	72	65	72	209	36,800
Jeff Sluman	73	69	67	209	36,800
Brad Bryant	71	69	70	210	29,600
Tom Pernice, Jr.	75	67	68	210	29,600
Roger Chapman	75	66	70	211	26,400
Sandy Lyle	70	70	71	211	26,400
Stephen Ames	71	67	74	212	20,000
Tommy Armour	67	72	73	212	20,000
Jose Coceres	70	73	69	212	20,000
John Cook	72	69	71	212	20,000
Greg Kraft	71	73	68	212	20,000
Rocco Mediate	72	70	70	212	20,000
Jerry Smith	71	72	69	212	20,000
Jay Haas	73	68	72	213	14,920
Brian Henninger	70	74	69	213	14,920
Rod Spittle	71	71	71	213	14,920
Fuzzy Zoeller	71	72	70	213	14,920
Jeff Hart	71	73	70	214	11,588.58
Frank Esposito	73	70	71	214	11,588.57
Gary Koch	72	67	75	214	11,588.57

	SCORES			TOTAL	MONEY
Larry Mize	76	72	66	214	11,588.57
Gene Sauers	72	71	71	214	11,588.57
Kirk Triplett	68	72	74	214	11,588.57
Duffy Waldorf	73	68	73	214	11,588.57

Tucson Conquistadores Classic

Omni Tucson National, Tucson, Arizona
Par 36-36–72; 7,143 yards

March 20-22
purse, $1,700,000

	SCORES			TOTAL	MONEY
Marco Dawson	67	67	69	203	$255,000
Bart Bryant	68	67	70	205	149,600
Mark O'Meara	71	69	66	206	122,400
Tom Pernice, Jr.	69	70	68	207	90,950
Wes Short, Jr.	69	66	72	207	90,950
Scott Hoch	70	71	67	208	61,200
Jeff Sluman	70	71	67	208	61,200
Russ Cochran	69	71	68	208	61,200
Bernhard Langer	69	71	69	209	40,800
Gene Sauers	70	70	69	209	40,800
Jeff Maggert	70	70	69	209	40,800
Colin Montgomerie	67	72	70	209	40,800
Jerry Smith	65	71	73	209	40,800
Kirk Triplett	68	73	69	210	29,750
Kevin Sutherland	71	70	69	210	29,750
Jay Don Blake	71	69	70	210	29,750
Billy Andrade	69	70	71	210	29,750
Tom Lehman	72	72	67	211	23,857
Rocco Mediate	74	68	69	211	23,857
Corey Pavin	68	72	71	211	23,857
Mark Calcavecchia	73	71	68	212	17,971
Duffy Waldorf	70	72	70	212	17,971
Rod Spittle	72	71	69	212	17,971
Kenny Perry	74	68	70	212	17,971
Joe Durant	73	69	70	212	17,971
Mark McNulty	70	71	71	212	17,971
Greg Bruckner	69	72	71	212	17,971
John Cook	73	71	69	213	12,622
John Huston	71	72	70	213	12,622
Steve Jones	71	71	71	213	12,622
Steve Pate	67	73	73	213	12,622
Brad Bryant	70	70	73	213	12,622
Scott Dunlap	69	71	73	213	12,622
Michael Allen	71	67	75	213	12,622
David Frost	67	71	75	213	12,622

Mississippi Gulf Resort Classic

Fallen Oak Golf Club, Biloxi, Mississippi
Par 36-36–72; 7,088 yards

March 27-29
purse, $1,600,000

	SCORES			TOTAL	MONEY
David Frost	68	70	68	206	$240,000
Tom Lehman	71	66	70	207	128,000
Kevin Sutherland	68	67	72	207	128,000
Joe Durant	67	72	69	208	95,200

	SCORES			TOTAL	MONEY
Woody Austin	68	71	70	209	70,000
Colin Montgomerie	67	72	70	209	70,000
Billy Andrade	69	71	70	210	54,400
Tom Pernice, Jr.	69	69	72	210	54,400
Olin Browne	71	68	72	211	41,600
Jose Coceres	73	70	68	211	41,600
Scott Dunlap	74	65	72	211	41,600
Michael Allen	70	70	72	212	33,600
Brad Bryant	72	72	68	212	33,600
Jeff Maggert	73	70	70	213	30,400
Fred Couples	71	70	73	214	28,000
Kenny Perry	73	72	69	214	28,000
Brad Faxon	68	73	74	215	23,240
Lee Janzen	71	74	70	215	23,240
Gene Sauers	68	72	75	215	23,240
Peter Senior	71	73	71	215	23,240
Esteban Toledo	76	72	68	216	19,680
Bart Bryant	78	70	69	217	16,832
Mike Goodes	71	74	72	217	16,832
Scott Hoch	73	69	75	217	16,832
Miguel Angel Jimenez	76	70	71	217	16,832
Mark O'Meara	74	69	74	217	16,832
Stephen Ames	71	73	74	218	13,600
Guy Boros	72	75	71	218	13,600
John Huston	72	71	75	218	13,600
Kirk Triplett	70	75	73	218	13,600

Greater Gwinnett Championship

TPC Sugarloaf, Duluth, Georgia
Par 36-36–72; 7,179 yards
(Final round cancelled—rain.)

April 17-19
purse, $1,800,000

	SCORES		TOTAL	MONEY
Olin Browne	68	64	132	$270,000
Bernhard Langer	69	64	133	158,400
Rocco Mediate	68	67	135	129,600
Stephen Ames	70	67	137	82,350
Mark O'Meara	68	69	137	82,350
Jesper Parnevik	68	69	137	82,350
Tom Pernice, Jr.	69	68	137	82,350
Tommy Armour	67	71	138	54,000
Rod Spittle	72	66	138	54,000
Bart Bryant	69	70	139	39,960
Joe Durant	69	70	139	39,960
Miguel Angel Jimenez	69	70	139	39,960
Colin Montgomerie	71	68	139	39,960
Esteban Toledo	69	70	139	39,960
Tom Byrum	69	71	140	28,800
Paul Goydos	71	69	140	28,800
Gary Hallberg	69	71	140	28,800
Sandy Lyle	72	68	140	28,800
Doug Rohrbaugh	72	68	140	28,800
Jeff Coston	69	72	141	21,060
Mike Goodes	70	71	141	21,060
Kirk Triplett	70	71	141	21,060
Willie Wood	72	69	141	21,060
Ian Woosnam	68	73	141	21,060
Michael Allen	71	71	142	16,050
Mark Brooks	70	72	142	16,050

	SCORES			TOTAL	MONEY
Brad Faxon	70	72		142	16,050
Steve Jones	70	72		142	16,050
Larry Mize	72	70		142	16,050
Joey Sindelar	68	74		142	16,050

Bass Pro Shops Legends of Golf

Buffalo Ridge: Par 35-36–71; 7,026 yards
Top of the Rock: Par 27-27–54; 2,840 yards
Ridgedale, Missouri

April 24-26
purse, $2,400,000

	SCORES			TOTAL	MONEY (Each)
Billy Andrade/Joe Durant	63	51	45	159	$230,000
Sandy Lyle/Ian Woosnam	47	64	51	162	130,000
Mark Calcavecchia/Steve Lowery	51	65	47	163	91,250
Loren Roberts/Mark Wiebe	48	67	48	163	91,250
Bob Gilder/Bobby Wadkins	50	66	48	164	46,500
Roger Chapman/Russ Cochran	50	66	48	164	46,500
Tom Lehman/Jeff Sluman	65	49	50	164	46,500
Corey Pavin/Duffy Waldorf	62	51	51	164	46,500
John Cook/Joey Sindelar	60	53	51	164	46,500
Lee Janzen/Rocco Mediate	64	53	48	165	32,000
Tom Kite/Gil Morgan	53	64	48	165	32,000
Tommy Armour/Jesper Parnevik	54	63	48	165	32,000
Dan Forsman/Mike Reid	49	65	51	165	32,000
Tom Pernice, Jr./Bob Tway	62	55	49	166	27,000
Colin Montgomerie/Mark O'Meara	66	51	50	167	23,166.67
Larry Mize/Hal Sutton	48	69	50	167	23,166.67
Mark Brooks/John Huston	61	53	53	167	23,166.67
Jay Don Blake/David Frost	61	57	50	168	18,125
Tom Jenkins/Joe Daley	48	70	50	168	18,125
Andy North/Tom Watson	51	66	51	168	18,125
Paul Goydos/Kevin Sutherland	65	52	51	168	18,125
Jay Haas/Peter Jacobsen	64	54	51	169	15,500
Olin Browne/Steve Pate	67	54	50	171	14,000
Hale Irwin/Wes Short, Jr.	55	65	51	171	14,000
Ben Crenshaw/Jerry Pate	50	68	53	171	14,000
Morris Hatalsky/Don Pooley	53	68	51	172	12,500
Scott Hoch/Craig Stadler	64	56	52	172	12,500
Wayne Levi/Scott Simpson	66	52	54	172	12,500
Brad Bryant/Bart Bryant	64	55	54	173	11,500
Fred Funk/Eduardo Romero	70	56	54	180	11,000
Fuzzy Zoeller/John Jacobs	53	71	58	182	10,500

Insperity Invitational

The Woodlands Country Club, The Woodlands, Texas
Par 36-36–72; 7,002 yards

May 1-3
purse, $2,050,000

	SCORES			TOTAL	MONEY
Ian Woosnam	71	66	68	205	$307,500
Tom Lehman	70	66	69	205	164,000
Kenny Perry	70	69	66	205	164,000
(Woosnam defeated Lehman and Perry on first playoff hole.)					
Michael Allen	66	68	72	206	109,675
Joe Durant	67	68	71	206	109,675

	SCORES			TOTAL	MONEY
Mark McNulty	70	68	69	207	77,900
Duffy Waldorf	70	70	67	207	77,900
Jeff Maggert	67	70	71	208	65,600
Stephen Ames	69	71	69	209	49,200
Woody Austin	70	66	73	209	49,200
Russ Cochran	70	70	69	209	49,200
Scott Dunlap	71	65	73	209	49,200
Wes Short, Jr.	69	71	69	209	49,200
Olin Browne	69	69	72	210	35,875
Marco Dawson	66	72	72	210	35,875
Colin Montgomerie	67	72	71	210	35,875
Tom Pernice, Jr.	71	69	70	210	35,875
Esteban Toledo	69	73	69	211	28,768.34
Scott Hoch	69	69	73	211	28,768.33
Kirk Triplett	70	67	74	211	28,768.33
Corey Pavin	71	73	68	212	23,848.34
Brian Henninger	71	71	70	212	23,848.33
Bernhard Langer	71	66	75	212	23,848.33
Joe Daley	72	70	71	213	19,167.50
Gil Morgan	71	72	70	213	19,167.50
Steve Pate	68	73	72	213	19,167.50
Gene Sauers	71	72	70	213	19,167.50
Peter Senior	71	71	71	213	19,167.50
Jeff Sluman	69	69	75	213	19,167.50
Bob Tway	72	73	69	214	15,443.34
Mike Goodes	70	69	75	214	15,443.33
Larry Mize	71	70	73	214	15,443.33

Regions Tradition

Shoal Creek, Shoal Creek, Alabama
Par 36-36–72; 7,231 yards

May 14-17
purse, $2,300,000

	SCORES				TOTAL	MONEY
Jeff Maggert	67	67	68	72	274	$345,000
Kevin Sutherland	68	66	69	71	274	202,400
(Maggert defeated Sutherland on first playoff hole.)						
Jeff Hart	71	69	68	69	277	151,225
Gene Sauers	70	70	68	69	277	151,225
Michael Allen	70	67	74	68	279	89,412.50
Bernhard Langer	73	66	70	70	279	89,412.50
Tom Lehman	76	66	68	69	279	89,412.50
Kenny Perry	70	69	70	70	279	89,412.50
Fred Funk	70	69	67	74	280	62,100
Tom Pernice, Jr.	71	70	68	71	280	62,100
Jeff Sluman	75	69	67	70	281	55,200
John Huston	75	71	65	71	282	50,600
Billy Andrade	71	74	67	71	283	42,550
Joe Durant	73	75	69	66	283	42,550
Esteban Toledo	70	71	70	72	283	42,550
Tom Watson	69	72	71	71	283	42,550
Brad Bryant	72	71	74	67	284	34,500
Paul Goydos	74	73	69	68	284	34,500
Chien Soon Lu	74	71	69	70	284	34,500
Mike Goodes	75	70	72	68	285	27,600
Rod Spittle	74	69	70	72	285	27,600
Duffy Waldorf	76	70	69	70	285	27,600
Ian Woosnam	72	72	70	71	285	27,600
Scott Hoch	71	74	68	73	286	21,988
Lee Janzen	78	68	70	70	286	21,988

	SCORES				TOTAL	MONEY
Larry Mize	75	72	68	71	286	21,988
Colin Montgomerie	69	73	72	72	286	21,988
Wes Short, Jr.	69	75	70	72	286	21,988
Woody Austin	72	71	72	72	287	18,170
John Cook	71	73	73	70	287	18,170
Mark McNulty	73	68	71	75	287	18,170
Olin Browne	71	71	73	73	288	16,215
John Riegger	72	68	75	73	288	16,215
Jay Don Blake	71	75	71	72	289	14,145
Brad Faxon	73	71	73	72	289	14,145
David Frost	70	74	72	73	289	14,145
Sandy Lyle	74	74	69	72	289	14,145
Marco Dawson	75	72	72	71	290	12,190
Larry Nelson	77	68	73	72	290	12,190
Mark O'Meara	71	73	72	74	290	12,190
Bart Bryant	73	71	74	73	291	10,120
Tom Byrum	70	75	75	71	291	10,120
Mike Reid	75	72	72	72	291	10,120
Joey Sindelar	72	76	72	71	291	10,120
Kirk Triplett	71	72	72	76	291	10,120
Bob Tway	73	70	76	72	291	10,120
Guy Boros	70	75	70	77	292	7,590
Gil Morgan	70	72	74	76	292	7,590
Jesper Parnevik	80	76	70	66	292	7,590
Jerry Pate	76	73	72	71	292	7,590
Jerry Smith	75	70	75	72	292	7,590
Mark Brooks	77	77	70	69	293	5,692.50
Mark Calcavecchia	74	75	72	72	293	5,692.50
Scott Verplank	74	69	71	79	293	5,692.50
Willie Wood	77	71	73	72	293	5,692.50
Joe Daley	72	75	76	71	294	5,060
Jose Coceres	73	75	72	75	295	4,370
Russ Cochran	71	75	73	76	295	4,370
Brian Henninger	72	77	74	72	295	4,370
Steve Pate	74	73	73	75	295	4,370
Peter Senior	72	75	76	72	295	4,370
Tommy Armour	76	70	73	77	296	3,450
Morris Hatalsky	73	75	72	76	296	3,450
Doug Rohrbaugh	77	73	72	74	296	3,450
Scott Dunlap	72	79	75	72	298	2,760
Bob Gilder	74	72	73	79	298	2,760
Peter Jacobsen	78	75	72	73	298	2,760
Jeff Coston	79	73	72	75	299	2,231
Dan Forsman	79	76	69	75	299	2,231
Gary Hallberg	76	72	76	76	300	1,955
Mark Wiebe	74	76	77	73	300	1,955
Tom Kite	77	76	73	75	301	1,748
Tom Purtzer	72	75	74	82	303	1,610
Roger Chapman	75	79	73	77	304	1,518
Wayne Levi	77	80	77	74	308	1,426
Curtis Strange	80	75	75	82	312	1,334
Steve Lowery	78	77	79	79	313	1,196
Bobby Wadkins	81	78	80	74	313	1,196
Jim Gallagher, Jr.	81	82	80	78	321	1,058
Nick Price	75				WD	
Loren Roberts	75				WD	

Senior PGA Championship

Pete Dye Course at French Lick, French Lick, Indiana
Par 36-36–72; 7,147 yards

May 21-24
purse, $2,750,000

	SCORES				TOTAL	MONEY
Colin Montgomerie	72	69	70	69	280	$495,000
Esteban Toledo	74	68	73	69	284	297,000
Woody Austin	73	71	72	69	285	187,000
Brian Henninger	74	67	74	71	286	117,500
Scott Verplank	73	72	70	71	286	117,500
Bernhard Langer	73	72	69	74	288	90,000
Jeff Sluman	74	73	73	69	289	77,500
Tom Pernice, Jr.	73	73	71	72	289	77,500
Marco Dawson	77	72	73	68	290	65,000
Mark McNulty	77	74	70	69	290	65,000
Sandy Lyle	75	71	70	74	290	65,000
Steve Jones	78	70	68	74	290	65,000
Kirk Triplett	76	74	70	71	291	49,750
Roger Chapman	79	70	71	71	291	49,750
Joe Durant	75	71	73	72	291	49,750
Kevin Sutherland	75	74	70	72	291	49,750
Russ Cochran	73	77	72	71	293	37,000
Olin Browne	79	69	71	74	293	37,000
Jerry Haas	73	74	72	74	293	37,000
Peter Senior	75	74	70	74	293	37,000
Paul Goydos	75	70	72	76	293	37,000
Barry Lane	72	76	74	72	294	27,000
Kiyoshi Murota	73	74	73	74	294	27,000
Joel Edwards	76	70	73	75	294	27,000
Jeff Maggert	76	73	69	76	294	27,000
Duffy Waldorf	73	74	76	72	295	18,500
Bart Bryant	72	74	76	73	295	18,500
Grant Waite	74	76	72	73	295	18,500
Rocco Mediate	76	74	71	74	295	18,500
Michael Allen	76	72	73	74	295	18,500
Jerry Smith	73	77	70	75	295	18,500
Tom Lehman	73	67	78	77	295	18,500
Chien Soon Lu	76	72	70	77	295	18,500
Rod Spittle	77	75	75	69	296	12,000
Billy Andrade	72	78	73	73	296	12,000
Jesper Parnevik	78	71	71	76	296	12,000
Masahiro Kuramoto	71	72	76	77	296	12,000
Jean-Francois Remesy	72	72	74	78	296	12,000
Skip Kendall	74	72	71	79	296	12,000
Chip Beck	76	73	76	72	297	9,000
Anders Forsbrand	77	74	73	73	297	9,000
Lee Rinker	73	78	73	73	297	9,000
Christopher Williams	75	71	76	75	297	9,000
Willie Wood	76	74	75	72	297	9,000
Peter Fowler	77	67	80	74	298	7,000
Mark O'Meara	75	76	72	75	298	7,000
Jeff Hart	73	78	71	76	298	7,000
Eddie Kirby	74	77	71	76	298	7,000
Ian Woosnam	76	73	68	81	298	7,000
Mark Brooks	78	73	74	74	299	6,050
Scott Dunlap	78	73	74	74	299	6,050
Jay Haas	76	71	77	75	299	6,050
Sonny Skinner	77	75	76	72	300	5,600
Joey Sindelar	75	76	76	73	300	5,600
Tommy Armour	80	72	73	75	300	5,600
Greg Bruckner	78	74	72	76	300	5,600
Mike Goodes	75	75	72	78	300	5,600

	SCORES				TOTAL	MONEY
Gary Hallberg	76	76	78	71	301	5,058
Philip Golding	75	77	75	74	301	5,058
Steve Pate	77	74	74	76	301	5,058
John Riegger	76	74	74	77	301	5,058
David Frost	73	73	77	78	301	5,058
Rick Schuller	78	72	73	78	301	5,058
Marc Farry	77	75	74	76	302	4,775
Nick Faldo	76	75	71	80	302	4,775
Jay Don Blake	76	75	79	74	304	4,650
Scott Hoch	74	77	74	79	304	4,650
John Cook	79	69	75	81	304	4,650
Andre Bossert	79	72	76	79	306	4,525
Paul Wesselingh	74	75	76	81	306	4,525
Jim Estes	81	71	77	78	307	4,400
Yutaka Hagawa	75	77	77	78	307	4,400
Gene Fieger	75	75	78	79	307	4,400
Kirk Hanefeld	77	71	81	80	309	4,300
John DalCorobbo	76	76	77	84	313	4,250
Todd McCorkle	78	74	81	83	316	4,200

Principal Charity Classic

Wakonda Club, Des Moines, Iowa
Par 36-36–72; 6,831 yards

June 5-7
purse, $1,750,000

	SCORES			TOTAL	MONEY
Mark Calcavecchia	67	68	69	204	$262,500
Joe Durant	68	68	69	205	140,000
Brian Henninger	67	70	68	205	140,000
Rod Spittle	68	70	68	206	104,125
John Cook	69	70	68	207	64,225
Paul Goydos	67	70	70	207	64,225
Davis Love	70	69	68	207	64,225
Jeff Maggert	71	67	69	207	64,225
Tom Pernice, Jr.	67	74	66	207	64,225
Michael Allen	67	70	71	208	36,500
Billy Andrade	66	76	66	208	36,500
Guy Boros	69	73	66	208	36,500
David Frost	71	68	69	208	36,500
Steve Lowery	73	69	66	208	36,500
Peter Senior	70	68	70	208	36,500
Kirk Triplett	71	67	70	208	36,500
John Huston	73	67	69	209	27,125
Chien Soon Lu	70	72	67	209	27,125
Russ Cochran	72	71	67	210	22,983.34
Tommy Armour	71	70	69	210	22,983.33
Rocco Mediate	70	70	70	210	22,983.33
Dan Forsman	69	73	69	211	17,215.63
Jay Haas	74	68	69	211	17,215.63
Jeff Hart	69	73	69	211	17,215.63
P.H. Horgan	73	69	69	211	17,215.63
Jose Coceres	66	73	72	211	17,215.62
Mike Goodes	69	71	71	211	17,215.62
Jeff Sluman	68	72	71	211	17,215.62
Grant Waite	67	73	71	211	17,215.62
Olin Browne	75	70	67	212	11,136.37
Tom Byrum	71	72	69	212	11,136.37
Joel Edwards	74	70	68	212	11,136.37
Doug Rohrbaugh	73	70	69	212	11,136.37
Jay Don Blake	69	72	71	212	11,136.36

	SCORES			TOTAL	MONEY
Bart Bryant	71	67	74	212	11,136.36
Jim Carter	69	72	71	212	11,136.36
Jeff Coston	67	72	73	212	11,136.36
Jeff Freeman	71	69	72	212	11,136.36
Loren Roberts	73	68	71	212	11,136.36
Duffy Waldorf	71	70	71	212	11,136.36

Constellation Senior Players Championship

Belmont Country Club, Belmont, Massachusetts   June 11-14
Par 36-35–71; 6,812 yards   purse, $2,700,000

	SCORES				TOTAL	MONEY
Bernhard Langer	65	65	67	68	265	$405,000
Kirk Triplett	70	68	69	64	271	237,600
Russ Cochran	69	65	71	69	274	161,100
Joe Durant	70	68	69	67	274	161,100
Colin Montgomerie	68	71	67	68	274	161,100
Lee Janzen	67	69	71	68	275	108,000
Billy Andrade	70	71	66	69	276	86,400
Marco Dawson	69	69	70	68	276	86,400
Jeff Hart	70	69	67	70	276	86,400
Kevin Sutherland	71	66	71	69	277	67,500
Willie Wood	71	70	69	67	277	67,500
Olin Browne	69	70	68	71	278	51,840
Scott Dunlap	73	66	70	69	278	51,840
Paul Goydos	73	67	69	69	278	51,840
Jeff Maggert	71	68	71	68	278	51,840
Gene Sauers	68	71	69	70	278	51,840
Jesper Parnevik	70	66	72	71	279	40,500
Esteban Toledo	69	71	67	72	279	40,500
Scott Verplank	69	71	66	73	279	40,500
Bart Bryant	72	70	70	68	280	30,825
Mark Calcavecchia	69	72	68	71	280	30,825
Rick Gibson	70	70	70	70	280	30,825
Tom Lehman	72	68	70	70	280	30,825
Tom Pernice, Jr.	70	75	70	65	280	30,825
Jeff Sluman	73	69	70	68	280	30,825
Michael Allen	73	66	71	71	281	24,570
Woody Austin	71	67	72	71	281	24,570
Rocco Mediate	67	74	69	71	281	24,570
Steve Pate	73	63	71	75	282	21,870
Loren Roberts	69	69	71	73	282	21,870
Mark Brooks	72	67	68	76	283	19,440
Tom Byrum	72	75	68	68	283	19,440
Grant Waite	72	71	69	71	283	19,440
Jeff Coston	72	72	66	74	284	16,254
Steve Jones	72	74	66	72	284	16,254
Kenny Perry	70	69	70	75	284	16,254
Joey Sindelar	72	70	71	71	284	16,254
Duffy Waldorf	75	72	69	68	284	16,254
Guy Boros	67	70	69	79	285	12,420
Brad Bryant	73	70	71	71	285	12,420
Roger Chapman	72	71	72	70	285	12,420
Brad Faxon	74	64	77	70	285	12,420
Fred Funk	74	74	69	68	285	12,420
Brian Henninger	71	72	71	71	285	12,420
John Riegger	74	69	68	74	285	12,420
Wes Short, Jr.	74	69	70	72	285	12,420
John Cook	78	65	75	68	286	8,370

	SCORES				TOTAL	MONEY
Chien Soon Lu	72	72	73	69	286	8,370
Mark Mouland	71	71	70	74	286	8,370
Corey Pavin	75	72	69	70	286	8,370
Mike Reid	71	72	71	72	286	8,370
Jerry Smith	73	69	71	73	286	8,370
Rod Spittle	73	71	72	70	286	8,370
Jay Don Blake	72	71	75	69	287	6,210
Barry Lane	75	73	67	72	287	6,210
Mark McNulty	78	70	68	71	287	6,210
Hale Irwin	72	74	70	72	288	5,535
Mark Wiebe	75	72	71	70	288	5,535
Jim Carter	74	71	71	73	289	4,590
David Frost	70	73	71	75	289	4,590
Scott Hoch	70	74	71	74	289	4,590
John Inman	73	79	70	67	289	4,590
Larry Mize	76	72	70	71	289	4,590
Joe Daley	72	74	75	70	291	3,375
Mike Goodes	72	72	75	72	291	3,375
Gary Hallberg	71	70	75	75	291	3,375
Sandy Lyle	76	75	70	70	291	3,375
Jose Coceres	77	71	72	72	292	2,619
Bob Gilder	73	76	71	72	292	2,619
Hal Sutton	73	75	73	72	293	2,376
Dan Forsman	75	72	73	75	295	2,052
John Huston	73	78	72	72	295	2,052
Skip Kendall	78	72	72	73	295	2,052
Jim Rutledge	78	70	74	75	297	1,782
Steve Lowery	78	78	71	71	298	1,674
Bob Tway	77	71	78	76	302	1,566
Wayne Levi	73	76	77	82	308	1,458

U.S. Senior Open Championship

Del Paso Country Club, Sacramento, California
Par 36-34–70; 6,994 yards

June 25-28
purse, $3,500,000

	SCORES				TOTAL	MONEY
Jeff Maggert	70	65	70	65	270	$675,000
Colin Montgomerie	68	68	70	66	272	405,000
Bernhard Langer	71	66	68	68	273	214,542
Grant Waite	69	68	69	67	273	214,542
Billy Andrade	69	71	71	63	274	138,984
Lee Janzen	67	72	71	64	274	138,984
Scott Dunlap	68	70	68	69	275	105,281
Kevin Sutherland	68	69	70	68	275	105,281
Tom Watson	66	69	71	69	275	105,281
Scott Hoch	71	69	70	66	276	84,221
Duffy Waldorf	72	67	68	69	276	84,221
Bart Bryant	71	65	71	70	277	69,518
Barry Lane	68	70	69	70	277	69,518
Kenny Perry	70	72	64	71	277	69,518
Jim Carter	67	69	70	72	278	58,123
Russ Cochran	72	67	70	69	278	58,123
Peter Fowler	69	66	72	72	279	50,413
Jeff Hart	67	72	71	69	279	50,413
Miguel Angel Jimenez	72	68	67	72	279	50,413
Fred Funk	70	68	68	74	280	42,201
Kohki Idoki	70	71	73	66	280	42,201
Rocco Mediate	72	66	70	72	280	42,201
Tom Lehman	70	71	69	71	281	35,047

	SCORES				TOTAL	MONEY
Esteban Toledo	69	70	72	70	281	35,047
Paul Wesselingh	69	68	74	70	281	35,047
Michael Allen	67	71	74	70	282	27,603
Woody Austin	67	70	69	76	282	27,603
Guy Boros	72	68	72	70	282	27,603
Tom Byrum	71	72	71	68	282	27,603
Corey Pavin	70	68	74	70	282	27,603
Peter Senior	69	69	74	70	282	27,603
Michael McCoy	70	72	71	69	282	
Marco Dawson	71	69	71	72	283	21,846
David Frost	73	70	71	69	283	21,846
Neal Lancaster	74	71	71	67	283	21,846
Kiyoshi Murota	68	69	74	72	283	21,846
Ian Woosnam	70	70	70	73	283	21,846
Stephen Ames	72	71	72	69	284	16,385
Olin Browne	73	69	71	71	284	16,385
Paul Goydos	71	74	72	67	284	16,385
Jay Haas	71	69	69	75	284	16,385
Masahiro Kuramoto	71	68	75	70	284	16,385
Brad Lardon	73	69	71	71	284	16,385
Tom Pernice, Jr.	70	73	68	73	284	16,385
John Riegger	70	71	68	75	284	16,385
Willie Wood	71	72	74	67	284	16,385
Philip Golding	69	74	70	72	285	12,445
Gene Sauers	69	70	76	70	285	12,445
Tommy Armour	73	69	74	70	286	11,490
Joel Edwards	70	70	73	74	287	10,451
P.H. Horgan	67	74	74	72	287	10,451
Scott Simpson	72	73	71	71	287	10,451
Scott Verplank	71	70	71	75	287	10,451
Brad Bryant	70	70	74	74	288	9,676
Jay Delsing	74	71	72	71	288	9,676
Geoffrey Sisk	74	69	71	74	288	9,676
Chien Soon Lu	74	71	75	69	289	9,272
Kirk Triplett	69	73	75	72	289	9,272
Brian Wilson	70	75	77	67	289	9,272
Marion Dantzler	72	73	75	70	290	8,995
Steve Jones	76	69	70	75	290	8,995
Greg Bruckner	71	73	74	73	291	8,722
Steve Schneiter	69	75	76	71	291	8,722
Mark Wiebe	74	69	73	75	291	8,722
Mark Brooks	70	75	76	71	292	8,504
Mike Mitchell	71	71	74	77	293	8,341
Jerry Smith	72	73	69	79	293	8,341
Jon Levitt	72	69	74	80	295	8,123
Mark Mielke	73	72	77	73	295	8,123
Hale Irwin	70	73	76	77	296	7,951
Mike Finster	76	69	79	73	297	
Dave Ryan	73	72	74	81	300	

Encompass Championship

North Shore Country Club, Glenview, Illinois
Par 36-36–72; 7,103 yards

July 10-12
purse, $1,900,000

	SCORES			TOTAL	MONEY
Jerry Smith	66	64	70	200	$285,000
David Frost	65	70	68	203	167,200
Wes Short, Jr.	70	66	68	204	136,800
Woody Austin	67	68	70	205	101,650

	SCORES			TOTAL	MONEY
Bart Bryant	69	66	70	205	101,650
Fred Funk	65	70	71	206	64,600
Mike Goodes	66	67	73	206	64,600
Lee Janzen	65	70	71	206	64,600
Duffy Waldorf	69	67	70	206	64,600
Fred Couples	68	72	67	207	45,600
Tom Lehman	71	68	68	207	45,600
Kenny Perry	69	70	68	207	45,600
Jeff Maggert	68	69	71	208	34,200
Tom Pernice, Jr.	72	67	69	208	34,200
Peter Senior	68	72	68	208	34,200
Kevin Sutherland	70	69	69	208	34,200
Grant Waite	70	70	68	208	34,200
Jim Rutledge	74	71	64	209	26,663.34
Michael Allen	70	73	66	209	26,663.33
Rod Spittle	66	72	71	209	26,663.33
Brad Bryant	65	73	72	210	21,565
John Cook	70	70	70	210	21,565
Steve Elkington	69	71	70	210	21,565
Kirk Triplett	70	70	70	210	21,565
Scott Hoch	69	71	71	211	16,941.67
Chien Soon Lu	71	70	70	211	16,941.67
Steve Pate	69	73	69	211	16,941.67
Corey Pavin	68	72	71	211	16,941.67
Geoffrey Sisk	73	65	73	211	16,941.66
Esteban Toledo	67	69	75	211	16,941.66

The Senior Open Championship presented by Rolex

See European Senior Tour section.

3M Championship

TPC Twin Cities, Blaine, Minnesota
Par 36-36–72; 7,114 yards

July 31-August 2
purse, $1,750,000

	SCORES			TOTAL	MONEY
Kenny Perry	69	61	68	198	$262,500
Bernhard Langer	68	67	67	202	128,041.67
Kevin Sutherland	69	65	68	202	128,041.67
Scott Dunlap	67	67	68	202	128,041.66
Marco Dawson	68	67	68	203	83,125
Tom Lehman	64	71	69	204	70,000
Stephen Ames	72	65	68	205	49,000
Mike Goodes	69	68	68	205	49,000
Paul Goydos	72	65	68	205	49,000
P.H. Horgan	67	69	69	205	49,000
Greg Kraft	69	69	67	205	49,000
Kirk Triplett	68	68	69	205	49,000
Tommy Armour	71	66	69	206	32,375
Frank Esposito	71	66	69	206	32,375
Corey Pavin	70	68	68	206	32,375
Wes Short, Jr.	70	68	68	206	32,375
Billy Andrade	69	69	69	207	23,916.67
Guy Boros	74	64	69	207	23,916.67
Lee Janzen	75	66	66	207	23,916.67
Scott McCarron	72	65	70	207	23,916.67
Scott Hoch	68	68	71	207	23,916.66
Esteban Toledo	69	67	71	207	23,916.66

	SCORES			TOTAL	MONEY
Olin Browne	70	73	65	208	17,937.50
David Frost	70	70	68	208	17,937.50
John Huston	69	68	71	208	17,937.50
Jeff Sluman	68	70	70	208	17,937.50
Bart Bryant	72	69	68	209	13,606.25
Brad Bryant	70	69	70	209	13,606.25
Mark Calcavecchia	71	70	68	209	13,606.25
Fred Funk	72	69	68	209	13,606.25
Steve Pate	71	69	69	209	13,606.25
Gene Sauers	70	70	69	209	13,606.25
Hal Sutton	69	71	69	209	13,606.25
Ian Woosnam	72	68	69	209	13,606.25

Shaw Charity Classic

Canyon Meadows Golf & Country Club, Calgary, Alberta, Canada
Par 35-35–70; 7,086 yards

August 7-9
purse, $2,350,000

	SCORES			TOTAL	MONEY
Jeff Maggert	67	63	64	194	$352,500
Colin Montgomerie	62	66	70	198	206,800
Scott Dunlap	68	67	64	199	154,512.50
Mark O'Meara	66	67	66	199	154,512.50
Michael Allen	65	68	67	200	86,245
Stephen Ames	65	68	67	200	86,245
Tommy Armour	65	70	65	200	86,245
Fred Couples	67	65	68	200	86,245
Peter Senior	63	72	65	200	86,245
Woody Austin	68	64	69	201	58,750
Skip Kendall	65	71	65	201	58,750
Joe Durant	67	70	65	202	42,635.72
David Frost	69	68	65	202	42,635.72
Rod Spittle	70	67	65	202	42,635.72
Tom Byrum	67	66	69	202	42,635.71
Miguel Angel Jimenez	67	61	74	202	42,635.71
Scott McCarron	65	70	67	202	42,635.71
Kirk Triplett	68	66	68	202	42,635.71
Blaine McCallister	68	70	65	203	30,863.34
John Riegger	66	73	64	203	30,863.33
Gene Sauers	70	66	67	203	30,863.33
Guy Boros	67	67	70	204	22,113.50
Olin Browne	67	69	68	204	22,113.50
Jose Coceres	70	64	70	204	22,113.50
Mike Goodes	72	66	66	204	22,113.50
Jeff Hart	66	71	67	204	22,113.50
John Huston	67	70	67	204	22,113.50
Corey Pavin	65	69	70	204	22,113.50
Tom Pernice Jr.	67	71	66	204	22,113.50
Wes Short, Jr.	70	65	69	204	22,113.50
Duffy Waldorf	66	70	68	204	22,113.50

Boeing Classic

TPC Snoqualmie Ridge, Snoqualmie, Washington
Par 36-36–72; 7,172 yards

August 21-23
purse, $2,000,000

	SCORES			TOTAL	MONEY
Billy Andrade	69	65	73	207	$300,000
Bernhard Langer	71	66	71	208	176,000
Guy Boros	71	70	68	209	109,500
Fred Couples	69	71	69	209	109,500
Mark O'Meara	73	68	68	209	109,500
Fran Quinn	72	68	69	209	109,500
Frank Esposito	73	70	67	210	68,000
Chien Soon Lu	69	72	69	210	68,000
Stephen Ames	71	74	66	211	42,222.23
Wes Short, Jr.	77	69	65	211	42,222.23
Michael Allen	70	70	71	211	42,222.22
Woody Austin	70	70	71	211	42,222.22
Jay Don Blake	73	69	69	211	42,222.22
Scott Dunlap	74	67	70	211	42,222.22
Jeff Freeman	69	68	74	211	42,222.22
Gene Sauers	73	69	69	211	42,222.22
Jeff Sluman	72	69	70	211	42,222.22
Carlos Franco	69	72	71	212	27,200
Mike Goodes	71	71	70	212	27,200
Larry Mize	67	73	72	212	27,200
Loren Roberts	72	70	70	212	27,200
Tom Byrum	74	71	68	213	22,600
Rod Spittle	72	69	72	213	22,600
Paul Goydos	72	73	69	214	20,000
Corey Pavin	70	73	71	214	20,000
Kevin Sutherland	73	69	72	214	20,000
Fred Funk	74	70	71	215	17,400
Steve Jones	74	72	69	215	17,400
Joey Sindelar	75	73	67	215	17,400
Mark Calcavecchia	73	71	72	216	14,133.34
Gil Morgan	75	69	72	216	14,133.34
Russ Cochran	73	71	72	216	14,133.33
Marco Dawson	71	70	75	216	14,133.33
Skip Kendall	73	76	67	216	14,133.33
Willie Wood	78	71	67	216	14,133.33

Dick's Sporting Goods Open

En-Joie Golf Course, Endicott, New York
Par 37-35–72; 6,969 yards

August 28-30
purse, $1,900,000

	SCORES			TOTAL	MONEY
Jeff Maggert	68	68	66	202	$285,000
Paul Goydos	66	70	68	204	167,200
David Frost	71	71	64	206	96,900
Corey Pavin	71	66	69	206	96,900
Peter Senior	68	73	65	206	96,900
Jerry Smith	71	68	67	206	96,900
Ian Woosnam	67	69	70	206	96,900
Scott Dunlap	71	68	68	207	52,250
Bob Friend	68	70	69	207	52,250
John Huston	67	68	72	207	52,250
Larry Mize	72	67	68	207	52,250
Michael Allen	69	73	66	208	36,480

	SCORES			TOTAL	MONEY
Stephen Ames	72	64	72	208	36,480
Joe Durant	74	66	68	208	36,480
Lee Janzen	69	69	70	208	36,480
Rod Spittle	68	66	74	208	36,480
Jose Coceres	70	68	71	209	28,500
Fred Funk	72	70	67	209	28,500
Kevin Sutherland	69	71	69	209	28,500
Brad Bryant	71	68	71	210	21,691.67
Bernhard Langer	71	71	68	210	21,691.67
Lance Ten Broeck	73	69	68	210	21,691.67
Duffy Waldorf	72	68	70	210	21,691.67
Scott McCarron	71	64	75	210	21,691.66
Willie Wood	68	69	73	210	21,691.66
Bart Bryant	71	70	70	211	15,461.25
Marco Dawson	71	68	72	211	15,461.25
Bob Gilder	71	70	70	211	15,461.25
Scott Hoch	72	71	68	211	15,461.25
Steve Jones	68	71	72	211	15,461.25
Jesper Parnevik	70	74	67	211	15,461.25
Gene Sauers	66	72	73	211	15,461.25
Jeff Sluman	73	67	71	211	15,461.25

Nature Valley First Tee Open

Pebble Beach Golf Links: Par 36-36–72; 6,837 yards
Poppy Hills: Par 36-35–71; 6,879 yards
Monterey Peninsula, California

September 25-27
purse, $2,000,000

	SCORES			TOTAL	MONEY
Esteban Toledo	71	66	69	206	$300,000
Tom Watson	75	65	67	207	176,000
Vijay Singh	70	69	69	208	119,333
Woody Austin	68	70	70	208	119,333
Colin Montgomerie	68	67	73	208	119,333
Jeff Sluman	74	68	67	209	68,000
David Frost	70	70	69	209	68,000
Fred Couples	72	66	71	209	68,000
Olin Browne	71	65	73	209	68,000
Scott McCarron	72	71	67	210	52,000
Rod Spittle	73	70	68	211	46,000
Mark O'Meara	70	70	71	211	46,000
Tom Lehman	70	71	71	212	37,000
Jesper Parnevik	66	75	71	212	37,000
Wes Short, Jr.	72	68	72	212	37,000
Tom Byrum	67	73	72	212	37,000
Duffy Waldorf	76	68	69	213	28,160
Kevin Sutherland	71	72	70	213	28,160
Fred Funk	73	70	70	213	28,160
Jay Haas	71	72	70	213	28,160
John Cook	72	69	72	213	28,160
Marco Dawson	71	68	75	214	23,200
Willie Wood	73	73	69	215	16,160
Mark Brooks	73	73	69	215	16,160
Michael Allen	74	71	70	215	16,160
Scott Dunlap	72	73	70	215	16,160
Craig Stadler	73	72	70	215	16,160
Jeff Hart	74	70	71	215	16,160
Tommy Armour	73	71	71	215	16,160
Mark McNulty	68	75	72	215	16,160
Jeff Maggert	74	69	72	215	16,160

	SCORES			TOTAL	MONEY
Roger Chapman	69	74	72	215	16,160
Bobby Wadkins	70	73	72	215	16,160
Steve Pate	74	67	74	215	16,160
Sandy Lyle	68	73	74	215	16,160
Stephen Ames	70	69	76	215	16,160
Mike Goodes	70	70	75	215	16,160

SAS Championship

Prestonwood Country Club, Cary, North Carolina
Par 35-37–72; 7,240 yards

October 9-11
purse, $2,100,000

	SCORES			TOTAL	MONEY
Tom Lehman	68	71	65	204	$315,000
Joe Durant	69	68	68	205	184,800
Bernhard Langer	65	73	68	206	138,075
Kenny Perry	68	68	70	206	138,075
Lee Janzen	70	68	70	208	86,450
Colin Montgomerie	70	72	66	208	86,450
John Riegger	67	72	69	208	86,450
Kevin Sutherland	68	72	69	209	67,200
Scott Dunlap	67	73	71	211	47,100
Brad Faxon	69	73	69	211	47,100
Paul Goydos	70	71	70	211	47,100
Jeff Hart	71	71	69	211	47,100
Jeff Maggert	73	67	71	211	47,100
Loren Roberts	70	71	70	211	47,100
Wes Short, Jr.	70	73	68	211	47,100
Stephen Ames	72	71	69	212	30,590
Billy Andrade	74	67	71	212	30,590
Woody Austin	72	70	70	212	30,590
David Frost	69	72	71	212	30,590
Steve Jones	71	71	70	212	30,590
Kirk Triplett	70	76	66	212	30,590
Michael Allen	71	70	72	213	22,627.50
Olin Browne	68	74	71	213	22,627.50
Sandy Lyle	73	70	70	213	22,627.50
Peter Senior	73	71	69	213	22,627.50
Tom Pernice, Jr.	74	72	68	214	19,950
Bart Bryant	69	77	69	215	17,045
Russ Cochran	71	73	71	215	17,045
John Cook	72	69	74	215	17,045
Fred Funk	71	71	73	215	17,045
Corey Pavin	73	71	71	215	17,045
Duffy Waldorf	68	75	72	215	17,045

San Antonio Championship

TPC San Antonio, AT&T Canyons Course, San Antonio, Texas
Par 36-36–72; 6,923 yards

October 16-18
purse, $1,800,000

	SCORES			TOTAL	MONEY
Bernhard Langer	71	68	65	204	$270,000
Scott Dunlap	68	71	68	207	158,400
Michael Allen	69	69	70	208	118,350
Scott McCarron	69	69	70	208	118,350
Kenny Perry	70	73	66	209	78,750

	SCORES			TOTAL	MONEY
Wes Short, Jr.	67	72	70	209	78,750
Olin Browne	70	71	69	210	57,600
Paul Goydos	68	72	70	210	57,600
Scott Hoch	70	71	69	210	57,600
Woody Austin	69	71	71	211	45,000
Tom Pernice, Jr.	72	68	71	211	45,000
Fred Funk	73	72	67	212	36,600
Corey Pavin	72	71	69	212	36,600
Loren Roberts	72	70	70	212	36,600
Stephen Ames	68	74	71	213	27,930
Tom Byrum	69	73	71	213	27,930
Mark Calcavecchia	73	72	68	213	27,930
Fred Couples	70	69	74	213	27,930
Colin Montgomerie	71	70	72	213	27,930
Jeff Sluman	68	72	73	213	27,930
Tommy Armour	75	69	70	214	19,944
Jay Don Blake	76	70	68	214	19,944
Russ Cochran	70	75	69	214	19,944
Brandt Jobe	73	72	69	214	19,944
Jesper Parnevik	70	72	72	214	19,944
Lee Janzen	71	72	72	215	16,020
Chien Soon Lu	75	73	67	215	16,020
Joey Sindelar	72	73	70	215	16,020
Duffy Waldorf	68	76	71	215	16,020
Rod Spittle	71	74	71	216	13,275
Kevin Sutherland	69	74	73	216	13,275
Esteban Toledo	71	74	71	216	13,275
Scott Verplank	75	74	67	216	13,275

Toshiba Classic

Newport Beach Country Club, Newport Beach, California
Par 35-36–71; 6,584 yards

October 30-November 1
purse, $1,800,000

	SCORES			TOTAL	MONEY
Duffy Waldorf	67	60	66	193	$270,000
Joe Durant	67	66	62	195	158,400
Kevin Sutherland	65	66	65	196	129,600
Paul Goydos	65	67	66	198	107,100
Fred Couples	65	65	69	199	78,750
Kenny Perry	66	65	68	199	78,750
Lee Janzen	66	69	65	200	61,200
Peter Senior	65	68	67	200	61,200
Stephen Ames	68	66	67	201	41,700
Woody Austin	68	63	70	201	41,700
Tom Byrum	67	67	67	201	41,700
Doug Garwood	70	65	66	201	41,700
Scott McCarron	63	68	70	201	41,700
Rod Spittle	64	69	68	201	41,700
Michael Allen	69	64	69	202	30,600
Mark Brooks	67	67	68	202	30,600
Jeff Maggert	68	66	68	202	30,600
Billy Andrade	64	68	71	203	20,898
Olin Browne	65	70	68	203	20,898
Bart Bryant	68	65	70	203	20,898
Carlos Franco	71	67	65	203	20,898
Fred Funk	70	66	67	203	20,898
Todd Hamilton	66	68	69	203	20,898
Brian Henninger	67	69	67	203	20,898
Bernhard Langer	70	67	66	203	20,898

	SCORES			TOTAL	MONEY
Wes Short, Jr.	68	67	68	203	20,898
Scott Verplank	68	68	67	203	20,898
John Huston	69	67	68	204	14,580
Tom Lehman	68	65	71	204	14,580
Mark O'Meara	67	67	70	204	14,580
Gene Sauers	68	68	68	204	14,580

Charles Schwab Cup Championship

Desert Mountain Club, Cochise Course, Scottsdale, Arizona   November 5-8
Par 35-35–70; 7,019 yards   purse, $2,500,000

	SCORES				TOTAL	MONEY
Billy Andrade	65	67	70	64	266	$440,000
Bernhard Langer	63	68	68	67	266	254,000
(Andrade defeated Langer on first playoff hole.)						
Michael Allen	65	64	69	70	268	213,000
Mark O'Meara	68	68	66	68	270	158,000
Jeff Sluman	69	64	71	66	270	158,000
Stephen Ames	68	67	67	69	271	111,000
Kirk Triplett	70	68	66	67	271	111,000
Joe Durant	69	66	68	69	272	93,000
Olin Browne	66	67	71	69	273	76,000
Fred Couples	66	69	69	69	273	76,000
Duffy Waldorf	68	68	69	68	273	76,000
Tom Lehman	69	65	71	69	274	64,000
Jerry Smith	74	63	70	68	275	59,000
Jeff Maggert	72	67	71	66	276	52,000
Colin Montgomerie	70	68	71	67	276	52,000
Kenny Perry	66	66	74	70	276	52,000
Woody Austin	71	64	73	69	277	44,500
Kevin Sutherland	68	67	70	72	277	44,500
Bart Bryant	68	67	74	69	278	39,250
Ian Woosnam	70	72	69	67	278	39,250
Paul Goydos	68	68	78	65	279	35,000
Tom Pernice, Jr.	70	68	68	73	279	35,000
Russ Cochran	70	68	72	72	282	32,000
Scott Dunlap	71	70	74	68	283	29,500
Esteban Toledo	72	73	69	69	283	29,500
Wes Short, Jr.	68	72	69	75	284	27,000
Marco Dawson	73	66	75	71	285	25,166.67
David Frost	72	68	74	71	285	25,166.67
Lee Janzen	72	67	71	75	285	25,166.66
Gene Sauers	73	72	76	71	292	24,000

European Senior Tour

U.S. Senior PGA Championship

See Champions Tour section.

SSE Enterprise Wales Senior Open

The Celtic Manor Resort, City of Newport, Wales
Par 37-33–70; 6,556 yards

May 29-31
purse, £250,000

	SCORES			TOTAL	MONEY
Paul Wesselingh	69	67	67	203	€52,889
Peter Fowler	72	67	66	205	29,971
Ian Woosnam	70	66	69	205	29,971
Miguel Angel Martin	67	72	70	209	19,393
Andre Bossert	70	71	69	210	15,021
Mark James	72	68	70	210	15,021
Mark Davis	73	70	68	211	12,693
Carl Mason	70	74	68	212	11,283
Simon P. Brown	72	68	73	213	8,168
Luis Carbonetti	75	71	67	213	8,168
Wraith Grant	77	67	69	213	8,168
Barry Lane	74	74	65	213	8,168
Andrew Oldcorn	72	75	66	213	8,168
Gary Wolstenholme	76	67	70	213	8,168
Mauro Bianco	74	68	72	214	5,483
Gary Emerson	71	69	74	214	5,483
Anders Forsbrand	72	73	69	214	5,483
Pedro Linhart	72	68	74	214	5,483
Denis O'Sullivan	67	73	74	214	5,483
Steen Tinning	72	70	72	214	5,483

Acorn Jersey Open

La Moye Golf Club, St. Brelade, Jersey
Par 36-36–72; 6,581 yards

June 4-6
purse, £200,000

	SCORES			TOTAL	MONEY
Peter Fowler	70	68	71	209	€42,959
Anders Forsbrand	70	68	72	210	28,640
Andre Bossert	68	72	71	211	17,900
Mark Mouland	73	69	69	211	17,900
Marc Farry	70	71	72	213	10,969
Andrew Sherborne	72	68	73	213	10,969
Des Smyth	73	72	68	213	10,969
Philip Walton	73	72	68	213	10,969
Rick Gibson	69	72	73	214	6,874
Mark James	72	72	70	214	6,874
Jean-Francois Remesy	71	72	71	214	6,874
Gary Rusnak	75	73	66	214	6,874
Ken Tarling	70	72	72	214	6,874
Gordon Brand, Jr.	73	72	70	215	4,730

	SCORES			TOTAL	MONEY
Ross Drummond	75	71	69	215	4,730
Philip Golding	72	69	74	215	4,730
Barry Lane	70	76	69	215	4,730
David J. Russell	73	71	71	215	4,730
Tim Thelen	75	68	72	215	4,730
Mark Davis	69	71	76	216	3,362
Mike Harwood	74	71	71	216	3,362
Gordon Manson	74	72	70	216	3,362
Carl Mason	70	75	71	216	3,362
Paul Wesselingh	73	71	72	216	3,362

ISPS Handa PGA Seniors Championship

Close House, Newcastle-upon-Tyne, England
Par 36-35–71; 6,685 yards

June 11-14
purse, £260,000

	SCORES				TOTAL	MONEY
Peter Fowler	68	67	67	70	272	€57,217
Gordon Manson	69	73	65	68	275	40,052
Carl Mason	68	68	70	70	276	26,820
Miguel Angel Martin	69	74	67	68	278	21,814
Philip Golding	72	68	66	73	279	17,508
Tim Thelen	70	73	69	69	281	13,589
Gary Emerson	68	75	72	68	283	10,485
Jean Pierre Sallat	68	71	75	69	283	10,485
Anders Forsbrand	71	75	70	68	284	7,741
Pedro Linhart	72	72	71	69	284	7,741
Philip Walton	70	70	71	73	284	7,741
Andrew Oldcorn	74	70	69	72	285	6,299
Gary Rusnak	77	66	73	69	285	6,299
Gary Wolstenholme	73	72	69	71	285	6,299
Paul Eales	72	75	69	70	286	5,607
Angel Franco	74	73	67	73	287	5,092
Terry Price	70	76	70	71	287	5,092
Mike Harwood	70	74	71	73	288	4,563
Andre Bossert	70	72	71	78	291	3,633
Simon P. Brown	73	73	72	73	291	3,633
Jose Manuel Carriles	73	72	75	71	291	3,633
Cesar Monasterio	73	74	68	76	291	3,633
Steen Tinning	69	75	71	76	291	3,633
Christopher Williams	71	72	74	74	291	3,633

U.S. Senior Open Championship

See Champions Tour section.

Swiss Seniors Open

Golf Club Bad Ragaz, Bad Ragaz, Switzerland
Par 35-35–70; 6,157 yards

July 3-5
purse, €300,000

	SCORES			TOTAL	MONEY
Gordon Manson	66	64	66	196	€45,000
Philip Golding	67	65	66	198	30,000
Ross Drummond	65	67	67	199	17,020
Francois Lamare	66	69	64	199	17,020

	SCORES			TOTAL	MONEY
Jerry Smith	67	68	64	199	17,020
Peter Fowler	66	68	66	200	11,400
Carl Mason	63	69	68	200	11,400
Andre Bossert	67	73	61	201	8,600
Jose Manuel Carriles	66	72	63	201	8,600
Ken Tarling	66	69	66	201	8,600
Simon P. Brown	68	66	68	202	6,600
Luis Carbonetti	68	68	66	202	6,600
Peter O'Malley	67	70	65	202	6,600
Barry Lane	69	68	66	203	5,100
Pedro Linhart	69	66	68	203	5,100
Cesar Monasterio	69	67	67	203	5,100
Andrew Oldcorn	66	70	67	203	5,100
Paul Wesselingh	67	68	68	203	5,100
Jorge Berendt	73	63	68	204	3,848
Bill Longmuir	69	71	64	204	3,848
Des Smyth	70	68	66	204	3,848
Gary Wolstenholme	70	68	66	204	3,848

WINSTONgolf Senior Open

WINSTONopen Course, Vorbeck, Germany
Par 36-36–72; 6,833 yards

July 10-12
purse, €300,000

	SCORES			TOTAL	MONEY
Pedro Linhart	70	64	66	200	€45,000
Barry Lane	73	68	62	203	30,000
Paul Wesselingh	70	67	68	205	21,000
Jose Manuel Carriles	72	66	68	206	16,500
Mike Harwood	71	67	69	207	13,560
Andre Bossert	74	66	68	208	10,200
John Gould	70	69	69	208	10,200
Santiago Luna	72	68	68	208	10,200
Gary Marks	71	65	72	208	10,200
Wraith Grant	76	67	66	209	7,500
Bill Longmuir	71	69	69	209	7,500
Anders Forsbrand	72	68	70	210	5,600
Angel Franco	72	66	72	210	5,600
Philip Golding	73	67	70	210	5,600
John Harrison	72	73	65	210	5,600
Des Smyth	71	69	70	210	5,600
Christopher Williams	69	68	73	210	5,600
Jorge Berendt	72	69	70	211	3,978
Gordon Brand, Jr.	70	71	70	211	3,978
Bob Cameron	70	67	74	211	3,978
Ross Drummond	69	70	72	211	3,978
Jean-Francois Remesy	78	68	65	211	3,978

The Senior Open Championship presented by Rolex

Sunningdale Golf Club, Old Course, Berkshire, England
Par 35-35–70; 6,618 yards

July 23-26
purse, £1,300,000

	SCORES				TOTAL	MONEY
Marco Dawson	65	67	68	64	264	€295,395
Bernhard Langer	65	68	68	64	265	196,978
Colin Montgomerie	67	67	66	67	267	110,872

	SCORES				TOTAL	MONEY
Miguel Angel Jimenez	65	69	68	67	269	88,626
Woody Austin	69	67	70	66	272	68,575
Fred Couples	68	66	69	69	272	68,575
Jeff Maggert	71	67	66	69	273	48,705
Philip Walton	71	67	65	70	273	48,705
Peter Fowler	69	65	68	72	274	35,906
Jeff Sluman	65	69	70	70	274	35,906
Esteban Toledo	73	68	68	65	274	35,906
Bart Bryant	65	70	70	70	275	28,654
Barry Lane	68	70	68	69	275	28,654
Peter Senior	69	67	70	69	275	28,654
Brian Henninger	66	73	67	70	276	24,383
Duffy Waldorf	69	68	69	70	276	24,383
Tom Watson	67	72	66	71	276	24,383
Lian-Wei Zhang	65	71	72	68	276	24,383
Billy Andrade	67	73	67	70	277	21,503
Scott Dunlap	70	72	68	67	277	21,503
Kevin Sutherland	72	69	66	70	277	21,503
Stephen Ames	69	67	69	73	278	19,691
Tom Lehman	69	69	70	70	278	19,691
Miguel Angel Martin	70	70	68	70	278	19,691
Michael Allen	65	71	71	72	279	17,021
Andre Bossert	71	71	70	67	279	17,021
Mark Brooks	68	73	70	68	279	17,021
Scott McCarron	71	67	72	69	279	17,021
Steen Tinning	69	70	68	72	279	17,021
Kirk Triplett	68	69	69	73	279	17,021
Russ Cochran	70	70	67	73	280	14,601
Mark McNulty	68	73	73	66	280	14,601
Peter O'Malley	68	71	71	70	280	14,601
Joe Durant	68	72	68	73	281	12,753
Fred Funk	70	71	67	73	281	12,753
Paul Goydos	67	69	74	71	281	12,753
Masahiro Kuramoto	70	70	68	73	281	12,753
Fran Quinn	73	70	70	68	281	12,753
Jamie Spence	74	68	68	71	281	12,753
Jay Don Blake	71	72	71	68	282	10,521
Kohki Idoki	69	73	68	72	282	10,521
Lee Janzen	65	70	70	77	282	10,521
Rocco Mediate	70	73	69	70	282	10,521
Cesar Monasterio	66	72	71	73	282	10,521
Jean-Francois Remesy	69	72	70	71	282	10,521
Gary Rusnak	70	68	68	76	282	10,521
Jeff Hart	67	72	72	72	283	8,666
Steve Jones	70	69	72	72	283	8,666
Tom Pernice, Jr.	68	71	72	72	283	8,666
Wes Short, Jr.	67	76	69	71	283	8,666
Gordon Brand, Jr.	69	69	70	76	284	6,829
Mark Calcavecchia	67	68	74	75	284	6,829
Ross Drummond	71	70	68	75	284	6,829
Sandy Lyle	70	73	71	70	284	6,829
Jesper Parnevik	73	69	69	73	284	6,829
Gene Sauers	69	71	72	72	284	6,829
Lance Tenbroeck	69	72	70	73	284	6,829
Greg Bruckner	69	69	72	75	285	5,250
Jerry Pate	72	69	70	74	285	5,250
Roger Sabarros	71	68	75	71	285	5,250
Mark Wiebe	70	70	72	73	285	5,250
Bruce Davidson	72	71	73	70	286	4,305
Seiki Okuda	70	73	68	75	286	4,305
Jerry Smith	70	70	71	75	286	4,305
Gary Wolstenholme	69	73	71	73	286	4,305
Ian Woosnam	69	69	74	74	286	4,305

	SCORES				TOTAL	MONEY
David Frost	68	71	71	77	287	3,460
Dick Mast	72	69	71	75	287	3,460
Andrew Oldcorn	76	67	71	73	287	3,460
Rod Spittle	69	73	73	72	287	3,460
Tim Thelen	70	71	71	75	287	3,460
Greg Turner	70	73	69	76	288	3,117
Christopher Williams	69	73	70	76	288	3,117
Olin Browne	70	71	71	77	289	3,009
Bob Cameron	67	76	75	72	290	2,865
Mark Mouland	66	75	78	71	290	2,865
Sam Torrance	69	70	73	78	290	2,865
Jose Rivero	69	74	76	72	291	2,721
Marc Farry	70	73	76	74	293	2,649
Richard Backwell	73	69	76	76	294	2,541
Pedro Linhart	71	72	75	76	294	2,541

Prostate Cancer UK Scottish Senior Open

Archerfield Links Golf Club, North Berwick, Scotland
Par 36-36–72; 6,837 yards

August 27-29
purse, £250,000

	SCORES			TOTAL	MONEY
Paul Broadhurst	72	69	68	209	€53,778
Gordon Manson	71	70	68	209	35,852
(Broadhurst defeated Manson on second playoff hole.)					
Mark Mouland	71	73	68	212	25,096
Cesar Monasterio	73	72	68	213	16,755
Tim Thelen	71	73	69	213	16,755
Lian-Wei Zhang	74	72	67	213	16,755
Carl Mason	71	72	71	214	12,907
Barry Lane	77	69	70	216	10,278
Pedro Linhart	71	72	73	216	10,278
Bill Longmuir	72	70	74	216	10,278
Stephen McAllister	71	72	74	217	8,246
Juan Quiros	74	70	73	217	8,246
Bob Cameron	75	69	74	218	6,633
Peter Fowler	74	68	76	218	6,633
Santiago Luna	73	70	75	218	6,633
Ken Tarling	72	70	76	218	6,633
Graeme Bell	71	73	75	219	4,918
Gordon Brand, Jr.	72	71	76	219	4,918
Wraith Grant	73	72	74	219	4,918
Jean-Francois Remesy	77	68	74	219	4,918
Gary Rusnak	71	74	74	219	4,918
Gary Wolstenholme	74	73	72	219	4,918

Travis Perkins Masters

Woburn Golf Club, Woburn, England
Par 35-37–72; 6,904 yards

September 4-6
purse, £320,000

	SCORES			TOTAL	MONEY
Colin Montgomerie	73	67	71	211	€65,975
Ross Drummond	70	72	69	211	43,983
(Montgomerie defeated Drummond on second playoff hole.)					
Santiago Luna	71	70	71	212	30,788
Philip Golding	72	70	72	214	24,191

	SCORES			TOTAL	MONEY
Cesar Monasterio	72	70	73	215	17,769
Andrew Oldcorn	73	70	72	215	17,769
Tim Thelen	69	73	73	215	17,769
Jose Manuel Carriles	72	72	72	216	12,609
Rick Gibson	75	68	73	216	12,609
Christopher Williams	73	72	71	216	12,609
Peter Fowler	71	72	74	217	10,116
Miguel Angel Martin	72	73	72	217	10,116
Roger Chapman	70	78	70	218	7,917
Anders Forsbrand	73	72	73	218	7,917
Barry Lane	73	71	74	218	7,917
Bill Longmuir	69	73	76	218	7,917
Jamie Spence	72	71	75	218	7,917
Mark James	72	73	75	220	5,832
Carl Mason	72	74	74	220	5,832
Mark Mouland	76	75	69	220	5,832
Jerry Smith	74	72	74	220	5,832
Steen Tinning	72	72	76	220	5,832

French Riviera Masters

Terre Blanche Hotel, Spa & Golf Resort, Tourrettes, Provence, France
Par 36-36–72; 6,955 yards
(Tournament reduced to 36 holes—rain.)

October 2-4
purse, €400,000

	SCORES		TOTAL	MONEY
Simon P. Brown	66	68	134	€60,000
Angel Franco	67	69	136	34,000
Barry Lane	72	64	136	34,000
Paul Broadhurst	71	67	138	20,040
Gary Marks	69	69	138	20,040
Paul Eales	71	68	139	14,400
Gary Emerson	68	71	139	14,400
Jean Pierre Sallat	71	68	139	14,400
Mark Davis	72	68	140	10,000
Philip Golding	72	68	140	10,000
Gordon Manson	69	71	140	10,000
Andrew Oldcorn	71	69	140	10,000
Andre Bossert	71	71	142	6,806
Rick Gibson	71	71	142	6,806
Glenn Joyner	72	70	142	6,806
Pedro Linhart	72	70	142	6,806
Roger Sabarros	71	71	142	6,806
Tim Thelen	73	69	142	6,806
Lian-Wei Zhang	73	69	142	6,806
Peter Fowler	73	70	143	4,580
John Gould	70	73	143	4,580
Mark James	72	71	143	4,580
Francois Lamare	72	71	143	4,580
Miguel Angel Martin	71	72	143	4,580
Steen Tinning	75	68	143	4,580

MCB Tour Championship

Constance Belle Mare Plage, Poste de Flacq, Mauritius
Par 36-36–72; 6,614 yards

December 11-13
purse, €420,000

	SCORES			TOTAL	MONEY
Colin Montgomerie	68	64	69	201	€65,136
David Frost	65	71	68	204	43,424
Paul Eales	67	72	66	205	27,140
Christopher Williams	68	68	69	205	27,140
Barry Lane	71	66	73	210	18,498
Andrew Sherborne	69	70	71	210	18,498
Peter Fowler	70	71	70	211	14,764
Gary Wolstenholme	71	72	68	211	14,764
Miguel Angel Martin	69	72	71	212	12,158
Paul Broadhurst	69	72	72	213	10,856
Luis Carbonetti	68	73	72	213	10,856
Gordon Brand, Jr.	69	71	74	214	8,829
Gary Marks	74	72	68	214	8,829
Paul Wesselingh	69	76	69	214	8,829
Anders Forsbrand	71	72	72	215	7,816
Ross Drummond	70	72	74	216	6,947
Jean-Francois Remesy	72	74	70	216	6,947
Jerry Smith	70	70	76	216	6,947
Simon P. Brown	74	73	70	217	6,122
Andre Bossert	74	75	69	218	4,972
Bob Cameron	70	74	74	218	4,972
Roger Chapman	72	74	72	218	4,972
Francois Lamare	75	72	71	218	4,972
Des Smyth	72	70	76	218	4,972
Tim Thelen	72	72	74	218	4,972

Japan PGA Senior Tour

Kanehide Senior Okinawa Open

Kise Country Club, Okinawa
Par 36-36–72; 6,881 yards

April 17-18
purse, ¥22,000,000

	SCORES		TOTAL	MONEY
Katsumi Kubo	68	68	136	¥3,600,000
Mitsuo Harada	67	70	137	1,800,000
Tatsuya Shiraishi	65	73	138	1,200,000
Takeshi Sakiyama	69	70	139	940,000
Yoshinori Mizumaki	68	71	139	940,000
Hiroshi Tominaga	73	67	140	620,000
Ter-Chang Wang	71	69	140	620,000
Hideto Shigenobu	70	70	140	620,000
Tsutomu Higa	69	71	140	620,000
Masahiro Kuramoto	69	71	140	620,000
Kohki Idoki	70	71	141	380,000
Frankie Minoza	70	71	141	380,000
Seiki Okuda	68	73	141	380,000
Tsukasa Watanabe	68	74	142	320,000
Jong-Duck Kim	68	74	142	320,000
Yoichi Shimizu	68	74	142	320,000
Atsushi Takamatsu	72	71	143	260,000
Nobuo Serizawa	71	72	143	260,000
Takenori Hiraishi	68	75	143	260,000
Naoyuki Tamura	71	73	144	200,000
Hiroshi Ueda	71	73	144	200,000
Tateo Ozaki	71	73	144	200,000
Tsuyoshi Yoneyama	70	74	144	200,000

Kyoraku More Surprise Cup

Ryosen Golf Club, Mie
Par 36-36–72; 7,040 yards

May 29-31
purse, ¥75,000,000

	SCORES			TOTAL	MONEY
Takeshi Sakiyama	66	70	72	208	¥15,000,000
Frankie Minoza	68	71	73	212	7,500,000
Kohki Idoki	71	69	74	214	5,250,000
Yutaka Hagawa	70	73	73	216	2,812,500
Naoyuki Tamura	71	69	76	216	2,812,500
Shoichi Yamamoto	74	68	75	217	2,325,000
Tsuyoshi Yoneyama	73	72	73	218	1,912,500
Katsumi Kubo	72	72	74	218	1,912,500
Seiki Okuda	74	74	71	219	1,350,000
Tatsuya Shiraishi	74	73	72	219	1,350,000
Yoshinori Mizumaki	71	75	73	219	1,350,000
Tsutomu Higa	71	75	73	219	1,350,000
Masahiro Kuramoto	72	72	75	219	1,350,000
Yoshitaka Yamamoto	71	73	75	219	1,350,000
Naomichi Ozaki	72	74	74	220	967,500
Anthony Gilligan	70	76	74	220	967,500

	SCORES			TOTAL	MONEY
Tsukasa Watanabe	71	73	76	220	967,500
Yoshimitsu Fukuzawa	68	74	78	220	967,500
Hideki Kase	77	71	73	221	810,000
Yoichi Shimizu	74	73	74	221	810,000
Boonchu Ruangkit	76	70	75	221	810,000
Katsunari Takahashi	70	74	77	221	810,000
Nobuo Serizawa	70	72	79	221	810,000

Starts Senior

Starts Kasama Golf Club, Ibaraki
Par 36-36–72; 6,936 yards

June 12-14
purse, ¥60,000,000

	SCORES			TOTAL	MONEY
Kiyoshi Murota	66	63	68	197	¥14,000,000
Naomichi Ozaki	66	69	66	201	5,450,000
Naoyuki Tamura	69	64	68	201	5,450,000
Satoshi Higashi	65	71	66	202	2,130,000
Katsumi Kubo	67	66	69	202	2,130,000
Nobumitsu Yuhara	68	70	66	204	1,410,750
Tatsuya Shiraishi	67	71	66	204	1,410,750
Ter-Chang Wang	70	67	67	204	1,410,750
Richard Backwell	69	67	68	204	1,410,750
Frankie Minoza	68	68	69	205	1,106,000
Yoichi Shimizu	70	67	69	206	1,031,000
Gregory Meyer	74	70	63	207	869,000
Yutaka Hagawa	72	68	67	207	869,000
Shinji Ikeuchi	69	70	68	207	869,000
Hiroshi Makino	69	69	69	207	869,000
Kazuhiro Takami	67	71	69	207	869,000
Tsuneyuki Nakajima	70	71	67	208	593,500
Hideki Kase	71	69	68	208	593,500
Kiyoshi Maita	70	70	68	208	593,500
Yoshinori Mizumaki	68	71	69	208	593,500
Eiji Mizoguchi	72	66	70	208	593,500
Masahiro Kuramoto	67	71	70	208	593,500
Hiroya Kamide	69	68	71	208	593,500
Mitsuo Harada	71	65	72	208	593,500

Maruhan Cup Taiheiyo Club Senior

Taiheiyo Club, Rokko Course, Hyogo
Par 36-36–72; 6,830 yards

August 1-2
purse, ¥50,000,000

	SCORES		TOTAL	MONEY
Takeshi Sakiyama	67	64	131	¥10,000,000
Naoyuki Tamura	64	70	134	5,000,000
Kiyoshi Maita	69	66	135	2,625,000
Yoshinori Mizumaki	66	69	135	2,625,000
Kohki Idoki	70	66	136	1,750,000
Kiyoshi Murota	69	67	136	1,750,000
Tsukasa Watanabe	68	68	136	1,750,000
Ikuo Shirahama	70	67	137	1,256,250
Katsumi Kubo	69	68	137	1,256,250
Kazuhiro Takami	68	69	137	1,256,250
Frankie Minoza	68	69	137	1,256,250
Satoshi Oide	71	67	138	1,020,000

	SCORES			TOTAL	MONEY
Masahiro Kuramoto	67	71		138	1,020,000
Naomichi Ozaki	70	69		139	870,000
Ter-Chang Wang	69	70		139	870,000
Shinichi Akiba	69	70		139	870,000
Kazuo Seike	72	68		140	655,000
Tze-Chung Chen	72	68		140	655,000
Nobumitsu Yuhara	71	69		140	655,000
Tsuyoshi Yoneyama	70	70		140	655,000
Boonchu Ruangkit	68	72		140	655,000

Fancl Classic

Susono Country Club, Susono, Shizuoka
Par 36-36–72; 6,911 yards

August 21-23
purse, ¥60,000,000

	SCORES			TOTAL	MONEY
Kiyoshi Murota	66	67	69	202	¥15,000,000
Tatsuo Takasaki	69	70	68	207	5,100,000
Tsukasa Watanabe	69	68	70	207	5,100,000
Katsumi Kubo	70	72	68	210	2,100,000
Takashi Miyoshi	68	73	69	210	2,100,000
Gregory Meyer	68	70	72	210	2,100,000
Kiyoshi Maita	70	72	69	211	1,410,000
Tsuyoshi Yoneyama	68	70	73	211	1,410,000
Tatsuya Shiraishi	68	76	68	212	1,032,000
Ikuo Shirahama	74	69	69	212	1,032,000
Kazuhiro Takami	71	72	69	212	1,032,000
Hideki Kase	67	74	71	212	1,032,000
Masahiro Kuramoto	65	75	72	212	1,032,000
Naoyuki Tamura	70	75	68	213	840,000
Takao Komizo	75	72	67	214	732,750
Shinichi Akiba	75	70	69	214	732,750
Hirokazu Hagiwara	69	73	72	214	732,750
Ter-Chang Wang	72	68	74	214	732,750
Tsuneyuki Nakajima	72	74	69	215	596,571
Yasuaki Takashima	70	75	70	215	596,571
Akihito Yokoyama	73	71	71	215	596,571
Hiroshi Ueda	72	72	71	215	596,571
Katsunari Takahashi	70	74	71	215	596,571
Katsuyoshi Tomori	72	70	73	215	596,571
Tsutomu Higa	69	72	74	215	596,571

Kyoshinkai Hiroshima Senior Championship

Hiroshima Country Club, Saijo Course, Hiroshima
Par 36-35–71; 6,624 yards

August 27-28
purse, ¥20,000,000

	SCORES		TOTAL	MONEY
Masahiro Kuramoto	64	67	131	¥3,600,000
Nobumitsu Yuhara	67	66	133	1,500,000
Naoyuki Tamura	62	71	133	1,500,000
Takashi Miyoshi	72	63	135	770,000
Shinji Ikeuchi	69	66	135	770,000
Hideki Kase	67	68	135	770,000
Ter-Chang Wang	66	69	135	770,000
Shoichi Yamamoto	69	67	136	504,000
Yoichi Shimizu	69	67	136	504,000

	SCORES		TOTAL	MONEY
Tsuyoshi Yoneyama	68	68	136	504,000
Katsuyoshi Tomori	67	69	136	504,000
Takeshi Nakashima	66	70	136	504,000
Yoshimitsu Fukuzawa	71	66	137	300,000
Frankie Minoza	70	67	137	300,000
Anthony Gilligan	70	67	137	300,000
Seiki Okuda	69	68	137	300,000
Kiyoshi Maita	69	68	137	300,000
Takeshi Sakiyama	69	68	137	300,000
Eiji Mizoguchi	68	69	137	300,000
Tatsuya Shiraishi	65	72	137	300,000

Alpha Club Cup Senior Open

Yaita Country Club, Tochigi
Par 36-36–72; 6,742 yards

September 5-6
purse, ¥50,000,000

	SCORES		TOTAL	MONEY
Takeshi Sakiyama	63	66	129	¥10,000,000
Nobumitsu Yuhara	67	65	132	5,000,000
Katsumi Kubo	66	67	133	2,625,000
Nobuo Serizawa	65	68	133	2,625,000
Hiroshi Ueda	67	67	134	2,000,000
Yoichi Shimizu	71	64	135	1,379,166
Masahiro Kuramoto	70	65	135	1,379,166
Ikuo Shirahama	70	65	135	1,379,166
Katsunari Takahashi	68	67	135	1,379,166
Gregory Meyer	68	67	135	1,379,166
Hideki Kase	66	69	135	1,379,166
Gohei Sato	70	66	136	960,000
Frankie Minoza	69	67	136	960,000
Hajime Meshiai	68	68	136	960,000
Satoshi Higashi	68	68	136	960,000
Kiyoshi Maita	72	65	137	680,833
Hatsuo Nakane	70	67	137	680,833
Takeshi Nakashima	70	67	137	680,833
Boonchu Ruangkit	69	68	137	680,833
Kohki Idoki	67	70	137	680,833
Kiyoshi Murota	66	71	137	680,833

Komatsu Open

Komatsu Country Club, Komatsu, Ishikawa
Par 36-36–72; 6,917 yards

September 10-12
purse, ¥60,000,000

	SCORES			TOTAL	MONEY
Takeshi Sakiyama	70	65	68	203	¥12,000,000
Tsukasa Watanabe	67	67	71	205	5,700,000
Nobumitsu Yuhara	72	68	66	206	4,020,000
Naoyuki Tamura	69	70	68	207	2,535,000
Yutaka Hagawa	70	67	70	207	2,535,000
Paul Wesselingh	71	68	69	208	2,010,000
Seiki Okuda	74	68	67	209	1,623,000
Hideki Kase	70	70	69	209	1,623,000
Nobuo Serizawa	75	69	66	210	1,223,500
Tsuyoshi Yoneyama	71	72	67	210	1,223,500
Kazuhiro Takami	70	71	69	210	1,223,500

	SCORES			TOTAL	MONEY
Yoichi Shimizu	70	71	69	210	1,223,500
Tsutomu Higa	71	69	70	210	1,223,500
Boonchu Ruangkit	70	69	71	210	1,223,500
Barry Lane	72	72	67	211	838,800
Kiyoshi Maita	72	69	70	211	838,800
Takao Komizo	71	70	70	211	838,800
Takeshi Nakashima	69	72	70	211	838,800
Atsushi Takamatsu	67	72	72	211	838,800
Ter-Chang Wang	74	71	67	212	573,666
Hajime Meshiai	71	74	67	212	573,666
Kiyoshi Murota	71	72	69	212	573,666
Shinichi Akiba	70	73	69	212	573,666
Yoshimitsu Fukuzawa	68	75	69	212	573,666
Hiroya Kamide	72	70	70	212	573,666
Tatsuo Takasaki	72	70	70	212	573,666
Katsumi Kubo	71	70	71	212	573,666
Hatsuo Nakane	72	67	73	212	573,666

Japan PGA Senior Championship

Summit Golf Club, Ibaraki
Par 36-36–72; 6,935 yards

October 8-11
purse, ¥50,000,000

	SCORES				TOTAL	MONEY
Kiyoshi Murota	68	69	67	68	272	¥10,000,000
Ikuo Shirahama	69	70	70	66	275	5,000,000
Toshikazu Sugihara	70	71	68	67	276	3,500,000
Boonchu Ruangkit	68	72	70	67	277	2,250,000
Seiki Okuda	71	70	66	70	277	2,250,000
Paul Wesselingh	75	69	64	70	278	1,500,000
Hatsuo Nakane	73	68	68	70	279	1,200,000
Gregory Meyer	69	71	69	70	279	1,200,000
Takeshi Oyama	69	70	70	70	279	1,200,000
Naomichi Ozaki	70	70	67	72	279	1,200,000
Yoichi Shimizu	73	72	66	69	280	950,000
Takeshi Sakiyama	68	73	69	70	280	950,000
Taijiro Tanaka	75	70	64	71	280	950,000
Shoichi Yamamoto	72	71	69	69	281	825,000
Tsuyoshi Yoneyama	72	73	66	70	281	825,000
Katsumi Kubo	75	72	66	69	282	680,000
Shinji Ikeuchi	73	70	68	71	282	680,000
Naoyuki Tamura	71	71	69	71	282	680,000
Anthony Gilligan	74	68	68	72	282	680,000
Richard Backwell	72	72	71	68	283	547,500
Tsuneyuki Nakajima	70	74	70	69	283	547,500
Ter-Chang Wang	71	71	70	71	283	547,500
Yasuaki Takashima	75	66	70	72	283	547,500

Japan Senior Open Championship

Cocopa Resort Club, Hakusan Course, Mie
Par 36-36–72; 6,840 yards

October 29-November 1
purse, ¥80,000,000

	SCORES				TOTAL	MONEY
Takenori Hiraishi	70	69	69	71	279	¥16,000,000
Tsuyoshi Yoneyama	75	70	66	69	280	8,800,000
Tsukasa Watanabe	70	69	72	70	281	6,160,000

	SCORES				TOTAL	MONEY
Kiyoshi Murota	74	69	69	70	282	4,000,000
Barry Lane	70	72	73	69	284	3,360,000
Naomichi Ozaki	73	75	68	69	285	2,426,666
Daisuke Serizawa	69	73	73	70	285	2,426,666
Hideki Kase	65	73	77	70	285	2,426,666
Chien-Soon Lu	73	72	71	70	286	1,760,000
Masahiro Kuramoto	71	72	73	71	287	1,257,600
Takeshi Sakiyama	71	71	73	72	287	1,257,600
Miguel Angel Martin	69	71	73	74	287	1,257,600
Yoichi Shimizu	72	69	71	75	287	1,257,600
Paul Wesselingh	70	73	68	76	287	1,257,600
Hiroya Kamide	75	74	71	69	289	912,000
Nobumitsu Yuhara	73	70	73	73	289	912,000
Tatsuo Takasaki	78	68	70	74	290	820,000
Kohki Idoki	73	70	72	75	290	820,000
Gregory Meyer	73	73	71	74	291	740,000
Naoki Hattori	70	74	73	74	291	740,000

Fuji Film Senior Championship

The Country Club of Japan, Chiba
Par 36-36–72; 7,006 yards

November 5-7
purse, ¥70,000,000

	SCORES			TOTAL	MONEY
Tsukasa Watanabe	68	68	68	204	¥14,000,000
Kiyoshi Murota	67	69	70	206	6,650,000
Naoyuki Tamura	70	73	67	210	3,663,333
Frankie Minoza	72	70	68	210	3,663,333
Gregory Meyer	69	68	73	210	3,663,333
Seiki Okuda	70	73	68	211	1,925,000
Katsunari Takahashi	69	71	71	211	1,925,000
Hiroya Kamide	70	71	71	212	1,540,000
Yoichi Shimizu	68	72	72	212	1,540,000
Tsuyoshi Yoneyama	71	72	70	213	1,270,500
Satoshi Higashi	71	71	71	213	1,270,500
Barry Lane	70	72	71	213	1,270,500
Ter-Chang Wang	71	70	72	213	1,270,500
Takeshi Sakiyama	73	72	69	214	1,043,000
Boonchu Ruangkit	70	74	70	214	1,043,000
Tsuneyuki Nakajima	71	72	71	214	1,043,000
Yoshinori Mizumaki	72	70	72	214	1,043,000
Ikuo Shirahama	74	71	70	215	847,000
Anthony Gilligan	74	70	71	215	847,000
Paul Wesselingh	75	68	72	215	847,000

ISPS Handa Cup Philanthropy Senior

Narita Hills Country Club, Chiba
Par 36-36–72; 6,763 yards

November 20-22
purse, ¥50,000,000

	SCORES			TOTAL	MONEY
Shinichi Akiba	67	68	70	205	¥10,000,000
Kiyoshi Murota	68	70	68	206	5,000,000
Yoshinori Mizumaki	71	69	68	208	2,160,000
Boonchu Ruangkit	70	69	69	208	2,160,000
Kazuhiro Takami	69	70	69	208	2,160,000
Takao Komizo	66	71	71	208	2,160,000

	SCORES			TOTAL	MONEY
Kunihiko Masuda	68	67	73	208	2,160,000
Atsushi Takamatsu	69	71	69	209	1,300,000
Ter-Chang Wang	67	72	70	209	1,300,000
Ikuo Shirahama	74	68	68	210	1,000,000
Katsumi Kubo	74	68	68	210	1,000,000
Hiroya Kamide	71	70	69	210	1,000,000
Junji Kawase	70	70	70	210	1,000,000
Kiyoshi Maita	71	68	71	210	1,000,000
Yutaka Hagawa	72	72	67	211	758,333
Akihito Yokoyama	75	66	70	211	758,333
Hatsuo Nakane	70	71	70	211	758,333
Nobuo Serizawa	77	68	67	212	662,500
Hirokazu Hagiwara	71	71	70	212	662,500
Tatsuya Shiraishi	72	69	71	212	662,500
Nobumitsu Yuhara	70	71	71	212	662,500

Iwasaki Shiratsuyu Senior

Ibusuki Golf Club, Kaimon Course, Kagoshima
Par 36-36–72; 6,923 yards

November 27-29
purse, ¥60,000,000

	SCORES			TOTAL	MONEY
Tze-Chung Chen	68	67	66	201	¥12,000,000
Tsuyoshi Yoneyama	69	68	67	204	5,700,000
Boonchu Ruangkit	73	69	66	208	3,300,000
Masahiro Kuramoto	70	66	72	208	3,300,000
Katsumi Kubo	70	72	67	209	2,280,000
Kiyoshi Murota	69	73	68	210	1,620,000
Kiyoshi Maita	71	70	69	210	1,620,000
Tatsuya Shiraishi	72	68	70	210	1,620,000
Seiki Okuda	66	72	72	210	1,620,000
Frankie Minoza	70	74	67	211	1,245,000
Tatsuo Takasaki	72	68	71	211	1,245,000
Yoichi Shimizu	71	72	69	212	1,140,000
Kazuhiro Takami	71	74	68	213	1,050,000
Yutaka Hagawa	74	69	70	213	1,050,000
Hajime Meshiai	71	74	69	214	930,000
Ikuo Shirahama	69	71	74	214	930,000
Richard Backwell	72	73	70	215	780,000
Takao Komizo	71	74	70	215	780,000
Hiroshi Makino	69	74	72	215	780,000
Anthony Gilligan	74	72	70	216	558,000
Kazuo Seike	73	73	70	216	558,000
Minoru Hatsumi	74	70	72	216	558,000
Kimpachi Yoshimura	71	73	72	216	558,000
Nobumitsu Yuhara	73	70	73	216	558,000
David Ishii	71	69	76	216	558,000
Ter-Chang Wang	71	69	76	216	558,000
Paul Wesselingh	70	70	76	216	558,000